The LEGAL, ETHICAL, and REGULATORY ENVIRONMENT of BUSINESS

Seventh Edition

BRUCE D. FISHER
University of Tennessee

MICHAEL J. PHILLIPS
Indiana University

WEST WEST LEGAL STUDIES IN BUSINESS
Thomson Learning™

Australia • Canada • Mexico • Singapore • Spain • United Kingdom • United States

The Legal, Ethical, and Regulatory Environment of Business, Seventh Edition
by Bruce D. Fisher and Michael J. Phillips

Vice President/Publisher: Jack W. Calhoun
Senior Acquisitions Editor: Rob Dewey
Senior Developmental Editor: Susanna C. Smart
Marketing Manager: Michael Worls
Production Editor: Tamborah E. Moore
Media Technology Editor: Kurt Gerdenich
Media Developmental Editor: Vicky True
Media Production Editor: Peggy K. Buskey
Manufacturing Coordinator: Charlene Taylor
Cover Design: Paul Neff Design
Production House: DPS Associates
Printer: West Group
Copyeditor: Cheryl Wilms

Printed in the United States of America
3 4 5 03 02

For more information contact West Legal Studies in Business, South-Western College Publishing, 5191 Natorp Blvd, Mason, OH 45040 or find us on the Internet at http://www.westbuslaw.com

For permission to use material from this text or product, contact us by
- **telephone: 1-800-730-2214**
- **fax: 1-800-730-2215**
- **web: http://www.thomsonrights.com**

Library of Congress Cataloging-in-Publication Data

Fisher, Bruce D.
The legal, ethical and regulatory environment of business / Bruce D. Fisher, Michael Phillips.--7th ed.
p. cm.
Includes index.
ISBN 0-324-02042-2 (text and InfoTrac package)
ISBN 0-324-07267-8 (text only)
1. Trade regulation--United States. 2. Commercial law--United States. 3. Business law--United States. 4. Business ethics--United States. I. Phillips, Michael J. II. Title

KF1600.F57 2000
346.7307--dc21

00-035190

This book is printed on acid-free paper.

West's Online Research Guide--GOVERNMENT

Updates and Additions at http://www.westbuslaw.com

Federal Government (executive)

White House	http://www.whitehouse.gov
Department of Justice	http://www.usdoj.gov/
Antitrust Division	http://www.usdoj.gov/atr/
Bureau of Justice Statistics	http://www.ojp.usdoj.gov/bjs/
Computer Crime and Intellectual Property Section	http://www.usdoj.gov/criminal/cybercrime/index.html
Civil Rights Division	http://www.usdoj.gov/crt/
Department of State	http://www.state.gov/
Department of Labor	http://www.dol.gov/
Employment and Training Administration	http://www.doleta.gov/
Occupational Safety and Health Administration	http://www.osha.gov/
Department of Commerce	http://www.doc.gov/
Bureau of the Census	http://www.census.gov/
International Trade Administration	http://www.ita.doc.gov/
Patent and Trademark Office	http://www.uspto.gov/
Department of the Treasury	http://www.ustreas.gov/
Internal Revenue Service	http://www.irs.treas.gov/
Department of Health and Human Services	http://www.dhhs.gov/
Food and Drug Administration	http://www.fda.gov/

Federal Government (legislative)

House of Representatives	http://www.house.gov/
Senate	http://www.senate.gov/
Thomas: Legislative Information	http://thomas.loc.gov/

Federal Government (judicial)

Federal Court Locator	http://vls.law.vill.edu/compass/
Federal Judicial Center	http://www.fjc.gov/
Federal Judiciary	http://www.uscourts.gov/
Supreme Court (Legal Information Institute)	http://supct.law.cornell.edu/supct/

Federal Government (independent agencies)...

Consumer Product Safety Commission	http://www.cpsc.gov/
Environmental Protection Agency	http://www.epa.gov/
Equal Employment Opportunity Commission	http://www.eeoc.gov/
Federal Communications Commission	http://www.fcc.gov/
Federal Trade Commission	http://www.ftc.gov/
National Labor Relations Board	http://www.nlrb.gov/
Securities and Exchange Commission	http://www.sec.gov/
Small Business Administration	http://www.sba.gov/

state and local governments

State and Local Governments (Library of Congress)	http://lcweb.loc.gov/global/state/stategov.html
State and Local Governments (P	v.piperinfo.com/state/index.cfm

dedicated to Yves,
Patron Saint of Lawyers
(1253 circa to 1303)
the late Marvin R. Wollin
and Beatrice M. Wollin

BRIEF CONTENTS

CONTENTS

8 International Business: Public Law 210

9 Private Business Dealings in International Contexts 227

MODULE 4
Law Affecting the Business Personnel Department 353

CASES

Principal cases in this text are listed below. References are to chapter and page numbers.

PREFACE

This is the seventh edition of *The Legal, Ethical, and Regulatory Environment of Business*. Since the sixth edition, a number of political, social, and economic factors have come about that may have an impact on several broad areas of the legal environment of business. First is the transition from one administration to another and all the uncertainties that go along with such changes. This kind of shift creates indecision, which businesses and financial markets detest. Will there be more or less regulation of the largest industry—the $1.5 trillion health care sector? Will higher tariffs be imposed on imported goods made with low-cost foreign labor lacking environmental and other employee protections costs, or will the trend toward tariff reduction continue?

Second is the economic boom, which businesses and financial markets embrace. Will efforts be made to share the benefits of a generally prosperous economy in which limited strata of the economy have shared? The U.S. has the highest disparity of any western nation between top executives' compensation levels—salaries plus stock options and bonuses—and the compensation of the lowest rank-and-file workers for those companies. Employee compensation increases in the general U.S. economy have been rather small, if not flat, particularly when compared to compensation packages for top executives. Thus, while top executives enjoy the economic boom, those less fortunate continue to struggle. When needed, the legal system has made available the solution of last resort, bankruptcy, which has been running at record levels until recent times. Will a new national administration and Congress tighten bankruptcy rules to hurt further the workers who have missed out in the late 20th century stock market surge? The answers to these questions will be shaped by the political environment, which affects the legal environment of business.

The current philosophical contradiction in U.S. law and regulation continues: a reluctance toward much government regulation, and a need for rights and protections. This edition attempts to reflect this philosophical schism through coverage of the factors affecting the legal environment.

At least four factors prominently affect the legal environment of today's business. First, the *increasing polarization of the economy*, where workers are driven to produce more while reaping few benefits. Second, increased productivity due in part to increased use of *intellectual property and technology*—such as is evidenced by the widespread use of the Internet and computers. Third, *leaner organizations, the ultra-competitive atmosphere*, and contingent work that marks today's business environment. And fourth, the increased need for *practical legal knowledge*. Of course, areas that adopters have found popular—environmental law, ethical considerations, how regulations are made and enforced, constitutional powers, employment law, and other areas of the legal environment—have all been updated.

OUR PHILOSOPHY AND APPROACH

Economic polarization. Cases have been added to sensitize future business leaders and students to the fact that many workers are not sharing in the economic boom in contemporary America. Cases with this objective include a Truth-in-Lending Act suit involving non-disclosure of true interest rates on a home improvement loan, a suit involving an Equal Credit Opportunity Act claim for Medicaid, a tenants' suit to forestall rent increases at a mobile home park, and a case involving marginal Social Security disability claims (for back injuries, one of the highest frequency claims; marginal employee benefit claims are often seen as a disguised form of welfare payment).

Impact of Technology and Business. Technology has left its imprint on today's business, and the impact of computers on society in general and business in particular is well documented. In fact almost a decade ago TIME magazine's "Person of the Year" was the computer. The seventh edition of this book takes the computer into account in at least three ways. First, there are new and expanded Internet exercises in every chapter to acquaint students with legal resources germane to each chapter. For instance, in the Overview and Finding Law chapter, Internet addresses help students find judicial branch sites so they can read court opinions and have access to federal statutes and legislative histories. Second, technology is further emphasized by the expansion of Chapter 13 on intellectual property. This chapter surveys several legal protections for businesses, and includes a new case involving trademarks allegedly infringed when "cybersquatters" lodge competing claims. Additionally, a section on Internet law and new Web sites are also included.

Leaner Organizations, Ultra-Competitiveness, and Contingent Employment. By "leaner" organizations, we refer to the fact that many overhead positions in firms—personnel specialists and community outreach, marketing, legal, and engineering staff—are now recognized as being overhead. Certainly, these functions of large organizations are worthwhile, but managers now are forced to means test these and similar functions. Are benefits of such staff commensurate with their costs? If not, given the internationalization of business—in which U.S. firms must now compete with foreign competitors that frequently lack such overhead—U.S. businesses have been forced to cut personnel from such functions. Outsourcing to less costly plants, collective bargaining, and the scope of federal labor laws are dealt with in Chapter 17 on labor law, and includes a new case on who determines what a bargaining unit is in a business.

Contingent employment refers to the practice of reducing the number of permanent workers in a firm's workforce. It is common practice for corporations in the Dow Jones Industrial Average, such as General Motors and Coca Cola, to drastically cut their workforces. An almost daily feature of any business section of the newspaper reports another firm's *downsizing*, or *right-sizing*, of its workforce. Efforts to protect workers subject to dismissal, common law protections, and whistleblower protections are noted in various chapters.

Practical Legal Knowledge. Although this book has always had a practical approach, the seventh edition makes a special attempt to emphasize practicality even more. To this end, cases have been added that represent very common situations, with respect to a legal doctrine. For example, in the area of Social Security disability claims, a case dealing with very common *back injuries* claims is presented. Coverage of the Family and Medical Leave Act, which affects many workers' rights for "time off" without prejudicing their employment, has been included. *Runaway juries*—when juries realize they are using *other people's money* to award verdicts—give what some see as overly generous recoveries, and as an example a new case involving remittiturs is presented. As OSHA has become more employer friendly, a case is presented that deals with the question of OSHA's liability under the Federal Tort Claims Act for negligent inspections resulting in serious employee injuries. In the environmental area, a new NEPA case shows the interconnection of environmental assessments (EAs) and environmental impact statements (EISs). Practicality begins in the first chapter's discussion of Ethics and Positive Law through a discussion of trust—how reliable are lie-detector tests in measuring an employee's truthfulness? In the first regulatory chapter, privacy rights concerning employer use of Social Security numbers is presented in a new case about strangers' access to personal information through our Social Security numbers. In the second regulatory chapter, a case involving a *pro se* claimant for Social Security disability benefits is presented. Since one in six in the entire U.S. population—many of whom represent themselves in Social Security matters—presently receives some type of Social Security benefit, this case takes on great significance.

Perhaps the most practical feature of this new edition is the expansion of the Internet resources in each chapter. The Internet enables every student of law to realize that s/he has a "virtual" law library if s/he has a computer with a modem, as the number of sites on the Internet having legal implications is incredibly vast. This book enables students to access many of the more practical sites.

PROVOCATIVE CASES

Approximately 20 percent of the cases in the seventh edition are new. Almost every chapter in this edition has at least one new principal case in the body of the chapter or in the end-of-chapter problems. However, classic cases such as the *Erie Railroad v. Tomkins*, *Riggs v. Palmer*, and *Palsgraf v. Long Island Railroad Co.* remain, while other cases have been changed due to changes in certain areas of the law.

New cases throughout the text include *Anderson v. Conwood*, on whether courts should grant remittiturs to control jury verdicts considered by some to be excessive in light of the facts; *Brower v. Gateway 2000*, which presents the question of whether "bubble wrap" computer purchases with ADR provisions included in the preprinted packages are valid against buyers; *Gilbert v. Homar*, dealing with procedural due process, and *Truckers United for Safety v. Federal Highway Administration*, on the validity of a rule-making proceeding labeled "interpretative." *Frank v. Chater* examines the duty of the Social Security Administration to provide an attorney to a Social Security disability applicant; *Oncale v. Sundowner Offshore Services, Inc.* deals with Title VII and same-sex sexual harassment; *Sutton v. United Airlines* addresses the question of whether "disability" includes correctable physical conditions; and *Nesser v. Trans World Airlines* deals with what is a "reasonable accommodation" under the ADA. Additional new cases include *Quality King Distributors v. L'Anza Research International, Inc., East v. Bullock's, Inc., LLC, Irving v. U.S., Schmidt v. Apfel, U.S. v. Best Foods, Kendall-Jackson Winery, Ltd. v. E. & J. Gallo Winery, U.S. v. O'Hagan, Barney v. Holzer*, among many others.

RETAINED EMPHASES

We continue to place a prime emphasis on American Assembly of Collegiate Schools of Business (AACSB) suggestions on appropriate legal coverage for business students. The AACSB sets the accreditation standards for schools and colleges of business nationwide; the revised Standard C.1.1 reads: Both undergraduate and MBA curricula should provide an understanding of perspectives that form the context for business. Coverage should include: ethical and global issues; the influence of political, social, legal and regulatory, environmental, and technological issues; and the impact of demographic diversity on organizations.

Thus, environmental coverage has been expanded, not only in the environmental law chapters, but where appropriate. The continued emphasis in the business arena of international business issues have resulted in increased and updated international law coverage, as well as employment law coverage.

Issues concerning ethics continues to be an important part of business dealings globally. Clearly there is no more important ethic than the positive law—the constitution, treaties, statutes, and regulations on the books—with which the business community must contend on a daily basis. Further, it is essential that business be aware of the social, political, and demographic context that has shaped positive law, particularly positive law that regulates business. By being familiar with these forces, businesses—and citizens generally—can understand why the law is as it is today. This edition also addresses the recent developments that promise to shape our national and international legal, regulatory, and ethical environment for years to come.

TEXT FEATURES

Expanded Internet Addresses in Each Chapter

The seventh edition continues to utilize Internet addresses, but with textual marginal notations so inquisitive students can have easy access to topical areas peripheral to chapter content, or in more depth than the chapter content. Given the volatility of this rapidly changing area of technology, the Internet addresses in the text are updated periodically on the text's Web site at http://fisher.westbuslaw.com.

"Closed-Loop" Approach to Ethical Pedagogy in Every Chapter

Each chapter starts with a Positive Law Ethical Problem and concludes with a Manager's Ethical Dilemma. This forces students to take note of ethical considerations when they start each chapter and to apply their skills anew to another ethical problem at the end of each chapter. The introductory ethical problem in each chapter is answered either by chapter cases or discussion. The Manager's Ethical Dilemma, however, is open-ended.

Manager's Ethical Dilemmas

Unlike the positive law ethical problems, at least one of which starts each chapter, a Manager's Ethical Dilemma concludes each chapter. In contrast to positive law ethical problems, the Manager's Ethical Dilemma is more open-ended. This is in keeping with the managerial focus of this text, where some actual ethical problems are presented that managers either have faced or are likely to encounter in their roles. These segments—placed near the end of the chapter immediately after the discussion questions and before the suggested readings—are suitable for class discussion. Some are based on actual cases while others present hypothetical situations. The Manager's Ethical Dilemma deals with topics raised by or is an extension of the chapter's material.

Chapter Summaries

The chapter summary at the conclusion of each chapter enables the student to review briefly the material s/he has just studied. key points in the chapter are summarized. Students who are vague on key concepts can return to the full text and reread problem segments.

Supplements

- An *Instructor's Manual with Test Bank* has been prepared by Professor Hamilton Peterson of American University, and contains case briefs, answers to end-of-case questions, solutions to end-of-chapter problems, and Internet exercises, as well as an expanded test bank.
- The text Web site at http://fisher.westbuslaw.com contains Internet Updates, Case Updates by legal topics, links to the West Business Law Faculty Center and its many teaching resources, and to the Student Center with links to Black's Legal Dictionary, news, legal, and government links, InfoTrac College Edition, and much more.
- *Westlaw.* Ten complimentary hours of Westlaw are available to qualified adopters from West's premier legal research system.
- West's Video Library. Qualified adopters may choose from West's vast video library including titles from
  - CNN
  - Court TV
- A *Handbook of Basic Law Terms Black's Dictionary Series* may be shrink-wrapped with the text at a discounted price. A Handbook of Basic Law Terms is a guide to the most important and most common words and phrases used in the law today. Students can keep this comprehensive and helpful dictionary for both their professional and personal lives.

ACKNOWLEDGMENTS

The authors wish to acknowledge their editors' efforts in preparing this edition, and thanks go to Rob Dewey, Susanna Smart, Tamborah Moore and Crystal Chapin. We also wish to thank the following reviewers for their contributions to this and previous editions: David Kent, Plymouth State College; Paula S. Hearn, University of Tennessee–Martin; Robert B. Bennett, Butler University; Leo J. Stevenson, Western Michigan University; Jay Erstling, University of St. Thomas; David W. Murphy, Madisonville Community College–University of Kentucky; Kurtis P. Klumb, University of Wisconsin–Milwaukee; Vince Enslein, Clinton Community College; Michael G. Walsh, Villanova University; Roger W. Reinsch, Emporia State University; James T. Poindexter, Duquesne University; Richard D. Sambuco, West Virginia Northern Community College; Pamela Poole Weber, Seminole Community College; Ann C. Morales, University of Miami; David I. Kapelner, Merrimack College; Hamilton Peterson, American University; E. Bruce Mather, Emory University; and Paul J. Krazeise, Jr., Bellermine College.

CARTOONS OF MARSHALL RAMSEY

We also thank Marshall Ramsey, award-winning cartoonist for the *Conroe Courier* (Conroe, Texas) whose cartoons are found in several chapters. Marshall's wit, wisdom, and, at times, sardonic perspective all add an extra dimension to chapter material.

MODULE

1

LEGAL AND BUSINESS ETHICS, OVERVIEW, AND FINDING THE LAW

CHAPTER 1

THE LAW, AND LEGAL AND BUSINESS ETHICS

"JURISPRUDENCE IS THE PRINCIPAL AND . . . PERFECT BRANCH OF ETHICS."

Blackstone

"IF THERE WERE A READING PUBLIC NUMEROUS, DISCERNING, AND IMPARTIAL, THE SCIENCE OF ETHICS, AND ALL THE VARIOUS SCIENCES WHICH ARE NEARLY RELATED TO ETHICS, WOULD ADVANCE WITH UNEXAMPLED RAPIDITY."

John Austin

POSITIVE LAW ETHICAL PROBLEMS

"They don't believe me!" exclaimed Wilson Ford, after he had been dismissed by his employer, A&P grocery store.

"But why should they?" asked a friend. "You failed a lie detector test. You said that you deposited A&P's cash into the night depository slot at NCNB Bank. But the bank did not find the deposit bag the next morning when it looked, so your employer, A&P assumed that you lied about depositing the money in the bank. They fired you when you failed a lie detector test about the matter."

Should an employee's failing a lie detector test be conclusive as to a person's trustworthiness?

"Eric, I am not going to pay you the contract amount of $5107.40 for building the swimming pool for my trailer park," said Dorothy Powell to an astounded Eric Rushing.

"But, why, Ms. Powell?" asked Eric. "The pool works fine and it looks great in your trailer park."

Dorothy replied, "Well, Eric, I have learned that you don't have a swimming pool contractor's license, and the law says that your contracts to build swimming pools are invalid."

Eric thought this was legal mumbo-jumbo, "Look, Ms. Powell, people today are relying too much on the law to determine what is right or wrong. You came to me and asked me to bid on your swimming pool, which I did. I was the low bidder. I built the pool, and it works fine. The licensing law does not say you may not pay me; it only says that you *legally* do not have to pay me. Rise above the law. Do the *morally* right thing: Pay me."

Ralph had been a socially conscious person while in college. He had written letters to Congresspersons demanding strong pollution control and worker protection laws, including a higher federal minimum wage, affirmative action laws, and the rights of a worker to bargain collectively. He believed that all of these actions would contribute to a more just, socially inclusive society. Also, Ralph heeded his economics professors' teachings and tried to maximize his utility when spending his money.

The time arrived for Ralph to enter the workforce. After scoring satisfactorily on an aptitude exam, he was hired by the Chrysler automobile corporation. When, after a short time a slot opened up in a Chrysler supervisors' training program, Ralph applied and was selected. Ralph aggressively pushed Chrysler to hire women and minorities, to comply with environmental laws, and to adopt and enforce employee protections such as those envisioned by the Occupational Safety and Health Act.

Upon receiving his first paycheck, Ralph decided to purchase a new car. He considered a Chrysler product but decided on a Korean-made Hyundai because it was about $2,000 cheaper and of comparable quality to Chrysler vehicles. When he drove the Hyundai to work, several coworkers asked Ralph why he had bought a foreign car. He responded, "Quality and price. I don't have money to burn, and this car was cheaper and about equal in reliability." A coworker noted that Korea does not have minimum wage laws, environmental laws, and employee rights such as affirmative action programs as meaningful or as rigorously enforced as Ralph had urged Chrysler to follow.

Ralph replied, "So what? I have a limited income and have to make that money stretch as far as possible by buying the lowest-priced goods in the market. That doesn't only apply to cars, but to food, clothing, and all else." What legal ethics are involved in this scenario?[1]

The preceding stories trouble us because of their many conflicting ideas about proper conduct. Determining appropriate conduct in a given situation is what ethics is about. This chapter introduces the topic of ethics in the following way: first, a general discussion of the meaning, nature, and limits of ethics is presented. Second, the ethic of positive law is explained. Third, **jurisprudence**—the study of legal ethics—is discussed and defined along with a brief discussion of various recognized beliefs about ethical values associated with law. Fourth comes an examination of **business ethics**—values that the business community uses to determine proper conduct. By the time one considers the many various aspects of ethics, the very notion of what *is* ethical conduct can become confusing. To help alleviate some of that confusion, our ethical discussion concludes with a strategy for managers to follow when confronting situations presenting ethical issues.

THE MEANING, NATURE, AND LIMITS OF ETHICS

Ethics (also called **deontology**) refers to the study of conduct that is right, good, or moral in a given set of circumstances. Said another way, ethics involves the study of clashes of moral values. In other words, ethical problems exist because we have choices. For example, should a rich person offer money to a beggar who asks for it on the street? The rich person might ponder the situation and conclude that giving a small amount is "a good thing" because doing so will enable the beggar to buy food and thereby survive. On the other hand, the rich person might think that giving money to panhandlers will encourage begging rather than working, which is the socially preferable means of acquiring money. Thus, ethics assumes a person has several choices in a situation. Most situations do, in fact, offer several choices of conduct.

Consider another example. A businessperson might not want to pay income taxes. In such a situation one might say that the businessperson has no choice but to pay because the law requires it. However, the business could cease to operate; then it

[1] Bruce D. Fisher, "The Ethical Consumer: A Rejecter of Positive Law Arbitrage," 25 *Seton Hall Review* 230 (1994).

would owe no taxes. This choice may seem absurd when survival is an ethic that most recognize, but the decision to continue in business is a choice. Another choice would be to lie about one's income, claiming that no taxable income exists. Here the choice involves violating the law (or positive law, as we shall soon define it) or obeying it. The study of ethics does not necessarily assume that the positive law must in all circumstances be obeyed.

One often hears of ethical codes for accountants, lawyers, doctors, architects, engineers, and other professions. These codes attempt to establish in advance what professionals should do in situations involving clashes of values. For example, an accountant may face an ethical dilemma when a client insists on following a risky tax strategy that the accountant knows has been questioned in the past by the tax authorities. The accountant is supposed to observe the law if it is certain, but the client is paying the accountant's salary and the law might not be that definite. A professional code of ethics may help to address this matter.

NATURE (A PRIORI) AND LIMITS TO ETHICS (ETHICAL AMBIGUITY)

A Priori. Several points emerge from the study of ethics. First, ethics are by their nature ultimate values. That is, we attribute a moral value to something because we value that thing. Because ethics are ultimate values, they self-justify. Said another way, ethics are *a priori,* meaning that they are assumed valuable with no further need for justification. If one says *justice* is an ethic or ultimate value, further explanation is seldom needed because most people readily understand the desirability of justice.

Ethical Ambiguity. Ethics or ultimate values sometimes conflict, and one ethic can even justify opposite sides of the same issue. When this type of conflict occurs, we have ethical ambiguity. Each of the stories at the start of this chapter contains ethical ambiguity. For another example, consider a law allowing the death penalty. A believer in the ethic of justice might argue that capital punishment laws are unjust and invalid because society is doing the very thing it condemns (murder) by intentionally taking the life of the murderer. The supporter of the capital punishment law, on the other hand, might argue that justice demands the death penalty as a deterrent to would-be murderers, and also cite the *Bible's* "eye for an eye" proposition that if one person deprives another of her life, the murderer should give up his life. Who is right about capital punishment? Both sides have strong ethical arguments. Ethical arguments do not necessarily result in *one* correct answer. Hence, we have what is called an "ethical ambiguity," or ethical dilemma.

How do we resolve ethical dilemmas? We make a decision. We do something. Although ethical dilemmas may at times confuse us, their value lies in helping us make informed decisions. We are taking all relevant factors into account in making our decisions. Also, ethical knowledge makes us more articulate. The more articulate we are in justifying projects or positions, the more power we give to those positions and their potential acceptance by others.

In the practical world the ethic that can resolve much ambiguity for us in our daily lives is positive law. The next section of this chapter examines the ethic of positive law.

THE ETHIC OF POSITIVE LAW

Positive Law Defined

Upon exiting the trial of former aid John Poindexter, former President Ronald Reagan reportedly said, "I followed the law." In so doing, Mr. Reagan was implicitly saying that a person who follows the law is ethical.

When most people use the word *law* they are referring to **positive law**.[2] An Englishman named John Austin, writing in the nineteenth century, is credited with developing the idea of positive law as we know it today. Austin said that positive law consists of three parts:

1. a rule
2. from a political superior to a political inferior which the inferior habitually obeys
3. with sanctions imposed if the rule is broken.

Some Positive Law Characteristics

Command Element of Positive Law. One aspect of positive law is that it commands us to do certain things, such as drive no more than 25 mph or pay income taxes. In other words, positive law often imposes a duty or obligation on us.

Sometimes positive law does not command but merely permits us to do something. For example, the positive law might say that 18-year-olds may make a contract, but it does not require 18-year-olds to make contracts.

No Requirements on the Type of Ruler. Positive law supports lawful authority and does not question how the ruler got its authority. Thus, a king, a dictator, the U.S. Supreme Court, a U.S. president, the local city council, and state judges are all positive lawmakers. Note that some of these lawmakers are elected and others are not.

In the United States, with its strong democratic tradition, persons with authority to make law generally are elected and thus receive their authority from the people they rule. Being democratically elected confers legitimacy on a ruler. By legitimacy we mean people are not as likely to question something's origin. If people question the rules democratically elected rulers make, voters face the challenge, "Well, you elected them. If you do not like what the rulers have done, vote them out at the next election." However, positive law theorists generally do not require that the rulers be elected nor do they say anything about how the lawmaker is selected. Thus according to positive law theorists, tyrants such as Hitler and Stalin were rulers even if they were not democratically elected.

Classical Positive Law Expects Habitual Obedience to the Rules. Some positive law advocates say that both citizens and rulers must obey the law. (Actually John Austin, an early legal positivist, believed the ruler was above the law and did not have to obey it, but other legal positivists do not take such an extreme position.) Perhaps the

[2] The terms *positive law* and *analytical positivism* are used interchangeably here. Positive law is actually a broader term than analytical positivism. John Austin's command definition is a recognized positive law definition although Professor Hart has outlined four other definitions of legal positivism: (1) the separation of law and morality; (2) noncognitivism, the idea that law represents choices among competing values that are a priori or presumptively good, such as "family values;" (3) the "mechanical view" that law is a logically contained system and that judges therefore mechanically apply the rules to specific cases; and (4) that people should obey law even if it is unjust. Analytical positivists would fall into the "mechanical" school of legal positivism.

strongest aspect of positive law is the **rule of law**, which states that all citizens—the president, governors, members of the Supreme Court, star athletes, and average citizens—must obey the rules. However, modern positive law theory also requires that rulers obey their own system's procedures and rules for passing laws.

Although talk shows and other media highlight legal controversies such as mercy killings and same sex marriages making it seem that the U.S. legal system is in turmoil, most people agree with the vast majority of laws on the books in the United States that deal with mundane matters such as contracts, property transfers and traffic regulation.

Positive Law Generally Advances Constructive Goals. Virtually all positive law tries to promote constructive goals. For example, the rules forbidding fraud, murder, environmental degradation, and many other antisocial activities are the result of positive law.

Positive Law Can Be Moral, Amoral, or Immoral. Suppose a country tried to control population growth by limiting couples to one child and killed all children beyond the firstborn. Would positive law say that such a law is valid? If such a law is passed according to that country's legal procedures and conforms to all of its laws, then positive law theorists would say that an infanticide (baby killing) law is valid.

The preceding example leads to another point about positive law: Positive law theory does not require that the positive law be moral or fair. In fact, some legal positivists agree that questions of law and morality are separate issues in the sense that if positive law settles a matter, it settles the legal matter only but not the moral issue. That is, just because a law is immoral does not make it invalid. Also, moral conduct is not necessarily legal conduct.

Of course, positive laws that most of us encounter in our daily lives have some rational basis, and thus we consider them fair or moral. For example, most people would say that it is wrong to misrepresent facts in our business dealings with others, and so does positive law when it forbids fraud. Thus positive law and morality frequently overlap as a practical matter.

However, in Hitler's Germany, it was against the law for a Jew to have a driver's license, attend certain universities, or hold certain jobs. Should these restrictions be so simply because of one's religion or ethnic background? Even a legal positivist would say that if Hitler's laws are legally valid, they do not resolve the separate moral question, "Should I obey this law?" Thus legal positivists recognize that morality exists. Also legal positivists know that morality and positive law can overlap, and often they reach the same conclusion on an issue. For example, both moralists and legal positivists would probably agree that arson be illegal.

The following case presents the issue of whether the positive law should be followed when obeying it would arguably produce an unjust result. Ask yourself whether positive law or fairness (which we shall see later in this chapter refers to "natural law") wins out.

Rushing v. Powell

California Court of Appeal (5th Dist.)
130 Cal Rptr. 110 (1976)

Background and Facts:

Dorothy Powell hired Eric Rushing to build a swimming pool for her trailer park for $5,107.40. Eric had an individual California concrete contractor's license. However, he did not have a California swimming pool contractor's license. California law forbids persons from doing work for which they are unlicensed.

Junior Ray Anderson had a California swimming pool contractor's license. Eric used Junior to get a swimming pool contractor's license so he could build Dorothy Powell's pool. Eric and Junior got a joint swimming pool contractor's license under the name "Stardust Pools." Because Junior already had such a license, the California licensing officials waived Eric from taking and passing the licensing exam or showing fitness to be a swimming pool contractor. Eric gave Junior equipment worth $6,000 for helping him get the license. Junior never actually did any swimming pool construction with Eric.

Eric built Dorothy Powell's pool, but she refused to pay. She claimed that Eric did not follow the plans. Eric sued Dorothy for breach of contract. Dorothy defended by arguing that Eric had not complied with California's fictitious business name statute or California's contractor licensing law. The trial court awarded Eric $5,107.40 (the contract amount) plus $198.73 for extras beyond the contract. Dorothy appealed.

Issue

May a contractor recover for work if he or she does not have the proper contractor's license and has not complied with the fictitious name statute?

Decision

A contractor may not recover for work if he or she is unlicensed. The contractor's licensing law is intended to protect the public against dishonesty and incompetence and deter would-be violators. The unlicensed contractor may not collect the $5,107.40 contract amount. However, the contractor may recover $198.73 for extras that were not part of the contract.

The contractor (Eric) complied with the fictitious name statute by filing a certificate showing that he was doing business as an individual.

Questions

1. Which prevailed in the *Rushing v. Powell* case, the "rules on the books," that is, positive law, or justice?
2. Is it necessarily unjust for a person such as Ms. Powell to avail herself of a rule to excuse performance of an otherwise legally owing debt? But was the debt *legally* owing?
3. If the purpose of the licensing law—one of the rules at issue in *Rushing v. Powell*—is to protect the public against dishonesty and incompetence, how was Ms. Powell cheated or harmed by incompetence? Could it be argued that Ms. Powell, as the person whom the licensing law was attempting to protect, was the wrongdoer in this instance?

Possible Weaknesses of Positive Law. Positive law can, but does not necessarily have several other weaknesses. It can be vague, causing people to wonder what is legal or illegal. For example, the **Robinson-Patman Act** is an antitrust law making the selling of goods at unreasonably low prices a criminal act. Many businesspeople ask, "What is an unreasonably low price?" If they guess incorrectly, they could be criminally charged.

Positive law is, as a practical matter, vast and unknowable. Consider the following: A motorist from New York drives to Tennessee where it is raining and rams another car. The police officer issues the New Yorker a ticket for driving without her headlights on during a rainstorm. The New Yorker argues that she is ignorant of Tennessee's traffic laws and that because it was daylight, she had no reason to put on her headlights. Ignorance of the law is no excuse. We are held responsible for obeying (and knowing) the positive laws of every jurisdiction into which we venture. We can understand why ignorance should not be a defense, because one could literally get away with murder (the first time at least) by arguing ignorance of murder laws when charged with murdering one's spouse. Therefore ignorance is not a defense and people are expected to know the positive law even though as a practical matter complete knowledge is impossible. For an extreme example of this requirement, read the *Federal Crop Insurance v. Merrill* case in Chapter 7 in which a farmer was expected to know the requirements of crop regulations contained in the *Federal Register,* which typically has over 50,000 pages each year.

Finally, the positive law may not address specific matters of what is right or wrong. For example, as of this writing, leveraged buyouts (LBOs) are not generally illegal, according to the positive law, even though they often destroy companies, cause workers to lose their jobs, and disrupt communities where the destroyed employers used to operate. Should LBOs be made illegal? This issue is repeatedly debated by financial, economic, legal, and other experts, with positive law providing few definite answers.

Often, in areas where there previously has been no positive law, courts (one positive lawmaker) speak out on a matter followed by the legislature's (another type of positive lawmaker) actions if a general social consensus develops. If no consensus develops, the courts can either leave the matter unregulated or deal with the situation on a piecemeal basis.

Democratic, Constitutional, Empirically Based Positive Law: The Ethic of Our Time

This book follows the view that democratic, (small "d," thus covering Republicans as well as Democrats) constitutional, empirically based positive law is the ethic of our time. First, let us point out *the* major difference between traditional positive law and modern democratic, constitutional positive law. As already discussed, traditional positive law does not require that the law be moral or immoral, but democratic, constitutional positive law *does* have a moral element in several senses. First, it is moral in that the lawmaker derives its authority from the people. In a democracy the people either make the law or elect those who do. People have the right to vote and thus share to some extent in the lawmaking. Democracy gives legitimacy and hence confers morality on the law.

Second, constitutionality confers morality on positive law because a constitution limits what positive law can do according to general principles that have a moral element. For example, the U.S. Constitution's Bill of Rights contains many limits on positive law based on fairness—the right to express oneself freely, the right to due process (such as notice and hearing before one can be punished), the privilege against self-incrimination, and the protection against cruel and unusual punishment, to name but a few.

Third, positive law intrudes into the lives of individuals and businesses as never before. We are told to clean up toxic waste dumps, which can cost billions. People rightly ask to see the science behind such positive law demands. What harm do small amounts of lead cause? If the answer is "serious harm," then, of course, positive law regulations should stand. The use of data, facts, and empirical evidence as the basis for positive law commands is called **philosophical positivism**. It differs from positive law, which is the law on the books. If the regulation is based merely on a "hunch" or intuition, the "feeling" that lead harms people, a philosophical positivist would say that no positive law should regulate lead until facts establish that it is harmful.

Why Democratic, Constitutional, Empirically Based Law Is the Ethic of Our Time

Today, more than ever, democratic, constitutional, empirically based positive law is the dominant ethic in U.S. society. In other words, when people try to determine what is the proper course of conduct, they ask, "What does the law require?" For several reasons the authors of this book adopt the view that democratic, constitutional, empirically based positive law is the guide to ethical (proper) conduct.

The Lack of Trust in Society. Today, a decline in trust in U.S. society, and, perhaps, in the world generally, is evident. We need only read the newspapers to learn of stories in which high-placed government or corporate officials have lied to us. The average person thinks, "Why should I trust people who lie?"

People tend to think that the pain of perjury punishment will cause people to be more honest in their claims under oath and in their dealings. However, even U.S. presidents can lie under oath. Of course, one must raise the further judgmental question,

"Is what a person lies about important or is it a trivial matter unrelated to the larger question a person's fitness to do the job and, if so, do we overlook what he or she lies about?" For example, one might ask a presidential candidate, "Do you wear false teeth?" If the person does, in fact, wear false teeth but answers "No," we might dismiss this untruth as the result of vanity and elect that candidate anyway. To claim that small lies can lead to big lies is to overextrapolate and tends to lead to moral zealotry: "If he lies about false teeth, he'll lie about Social Security." The logic of this proposition does not always hold true.

To ascertain truth, one might subject individuals thought to be lying to polygraph (lie detector) tests. However, people can tell the truth even though lie detectors say they are lying and therefore not trustworthy. The following case illustrates illustrates the unreliability of lie detectors as a measure of trust.

Ford v. NCNB Corporation

Court of Appeals of North Carolina
104 N.C. App. 172 (1991)

Background and Facts:

On August 19, 1987, Wilson Ford sued NCNB Corporation (a bank) to recover damages that allegedly resulted from the bank's losing, for about two years, $5,000.15 that Ford placed in one of defendant bank's night depositories for his employer, A&P. The only theory of liability initially alleged was the breach of a special bailment in regard to the deposit. The complaint alleged that the bank's negligent failure to have the depository properly searched caused plaintiff to lose his job and suffer loss of earnings, emotional anguish, humiliation, scorn, and derision. The bank searched the depository for the missing bag but did not disassemble it. Prior to dismissing Ford, A&P questioned him and had him submit to a polygraph test at the store's request. After the test indicated some of his answers were deceptive, A&P terminated plaintiff's employment on October 9, 1984, and so advised the bank a few days later.

During the first few months following his dismissal in trying to obtain employment elsewhere Ford truthfully told prospective employers what had happened at A&P and was not hired. After he stopped listing A&P as a former employer he immediately obtained employment at minimum wages and within a few months thereafter earned more than what he had received at the A&P.

Before the deposit bag was lost Ford enjoyed a good reputation among A&P employees and was outgoing and sociable, helped to support his mother and three younger brothers, and was paying for a new car on the installment plan. After being discharged he became withdrawn and lost sleep and weight. When his "friends" either avoided him or teased him for refusing to share the "lost" money with them, he was embarrassed and depressed and would sit in his room for hours wondering what could have happened to the deposit bag. His new car was repossessed when he could not make payments and his good credit rating was ruined.

On June 19, 1986—about two years later—the lock on the NCNB Bank's night deposit was serviced to correct another customer's misuse of the night depository. The service technician heard a scraping sound in the depository and upon removing the head of the depository found the missing deposit bag. After learning that the "lost" deposit had been found, A&P's store manager offered Ford his job back, which Ford declined. Ford then sued NCNB for negligent failure to have the depository properly searched. A jury found NCNB's negligence damaged Ford in the amount of $100,000, and judgment was entered for that amount. NCNB appealed.

Issue

Was NCNB's negligence the "proximate" or close cause of A&P's dismissing Ford?

Decision

Yes. When the bank reported that it had not received the deposit, this caused A&P to distrust Ford. NCNB caused A&P to investigate, administer the polygraph test, and fire Ford when he failed the test. Thus NCNB's act of negligently investigating and not finding the bag that was in fact there, set in motion the events that led up to the polygraph test. Thus NCNB's negligence was the "close" or proximate cause of Ford's dismissal.

Questions

1. What evidence was there that Ford lied?
2. What could have been done to avoid the problem the *Ford* case presents?

Cultural Pluralism. A further reason for the shift of positive law to moral status is the rise of cultural pluralism. The United States has always been a nation of diversity. Consider the inscription on our money: "E pluribus unum," which means "From many, one," or from many peoples, we form one nation.

People from all parts of Europe, Africa, Asia, South America, and Australia have come to the United States in search of freedom and economic prosperity. These people have brought with them different religions, different values, and differing life styles—in short, different cultures. The positive law—our constitution and laws enacted as well as those passed by each state—have been the melding force for this diversity. One might see current diversity or dissension over issues ranging from legalized abortion, to legalization of gay marriages, to the appropriate role of women in society, to questions of "what is a family," as reflections of this diverse thought. Like it or not, the traditional U.S. approach to settling controversial issues involving cultural clashes is by "passing a law," which leads to the next manifestation of the shift of law to moral status.

The Trend Toward Legalizing All Areas of Society. Since the early 1960s an unprecedented expansion of positive law has taken place in the United States. A definite trend has been toward making laws regulating more and more areas of human endeavor, and for justifiable reasons. For example, no one wants water or air pollution, discrimination based on race, religion, or sex, or mistreatment of employees. Thus, the U.S. legal system has witnessed the civil rights revolution, the explosion of employer/employee laws, the consumer movement and its accompanying laws, and environmentalism with its lengthy statutes and regulations to name four prominent issues within the positive law explosion. Among the positive laws reaching the books since the mid?1960s are: the Civil Rights Act of 1964, the Clean Air Act Amendments of 1970, 1977, and 1990, the Federal Water Pollution Control Act of 1972 (later renamed the Clean Water Act), the National Environmental Policy Act (1970), the Occupational Safety and Health Act (1970), the Fair Credit Reporting Act (1970), the Federal Noise Control Act of 1972, the Endangered Species Act (1973), the Safe Drinking Water Act (1974), the Employee Retirement Income Security Act (1974), the Equal Credit Opportunity Act (1974), the Federal Privacy Act (1974), the Fair Credit Billing Act (1975), the Resource Conservation and Recovery Act (1976), the Toxic Substances Control Act (1976), the Electronic Fund Transfer Act (1978), the Bankruptcy Reform Act (1978), the Nuclear Waste Policy Act (1982), the Clean Water Act amendments of 1986, and the Glass Ceiling Act of 1991, and the Americans With Disabilities Act (1990) to name just a few of the federal laws falling into this category. In addition, most of these statutes have pages of implementing regulations that micromanage how businesses and each of us must act. States and municipalities also have been busy during the same period, passing economically and socially aggressive laws and regulations.

Given the onslaught of positive laws that impose many costly, burdensome (in terms of paperwork), and desirable responsibilities on businesses, public institutions, and other segments of society, people in the United States are inclined to say, "If I have done all that the law requires, I am ethical." These enacted regulations are not a limit on the responsibilities we may take. For example, one could contribute to the United Fund even though no positive law requires us to do so. However, this book takes the position that, given the extensive and expensive burdens that today's positive law places upon us, businesspeople or anyone can justifiably say that they are ethical if they follow the positive law. Further, one could argue that by extending positive law into areas formerly left for private morality (civil rights laws, for example), the positive law is merging with natural law. In other words, what *is* commanded (the positive law) is becoming what *ought* (natural law) to be done. Thus following the positive law today involves doing far more than it did a generation ago.

Massive Noncompliance with Positive Law and Resort to the Courts as the Way to Achieve Justice. The number of lawsuits—criminal and civil in one year in the early 1990s was 98 million! While this figure does include minor traffic violations, it suggests that resorting to the legal process is necessary to determine what is right. People cannot obey many laws. The United States has the highest incarceration rate of any nation in the world; approximately 1.4 million people are in jail or in prison (roughly one in every 250 people), indicating that a significant number of people do not comply with the criminal law.

Failure to Keep Our Promises. Further evidence that the "law on the books" is the most that we as individuals can do is supported by the failure of each of us to keep our promises. For example, in 1999 more than 1.3 million bankruptcies were filed in the United States, which means that people who had made contracts, or legally binding promises, were not keeping them. People were not paying their bills on time or conforming to contracts and contract law. For such people contracts and contract law are a ceiling—the most they could do—not a floor. Of course, on the positive side we should not lose sight of the fact that more people were keeping their contractual promises than breaking them. m.

A further disturbing example of not keeping one's promises is the divorce rate. The United States has the world's highest divorce rate; half the marriages end in divorce, indicating failure to observe the marital promise.

Greed. One of the overriding values of modern society appears to be greed. Just as the fictional character Gordon Gekko in the movie *Wall Street* shouts that "Greed is good," many real life persons seemingly follow the same philosophy. When federal district court judge John M. Walker, Jr., sentenced hotel entrepreneur and millionairess Leona Helmsley to a four-year prison term and fined her $7.1 million for tax fraud, the judge remarked, "Unlike many defendants who come before this court, you were not driven to this crime by financial need. Rather, your conduct was the product of naked greed." (Ms. Helmsley's conviction was upheld on appeal. She has since been released from federal prison.) Similarly, stockbroker Michael Milken's pleading guilty in 1990 to six felony counts in connection with his security dealings also illustrates greed. Because Milken was a millionaire before committing the acts for which he pleaded guilty, one can logically conclude that greed drove him to violate the positive law in pursuit of even more money.

On a broader scale, consider the refusal of wealthy retirees to allow Congress and the president to put Social Security on a needs basis. Today wealthy retirees continue to draw Social Security payments long after they have withdrawn in benefits what they have contributed to the Social Security system, even though other sectors of the population—the homeless, for example—clearly have greater financial need. What motivates such wealthy retirees? Greed.

Given the abundant evidence of greed, obedience to the positive law is realistically what society can expect of us.

Lack of Personal Responsibility. The perception today is that personal responsibility has fallen to new lows in the United States. An area that supports this notion is in credit card use coupled with the increasing use of the positive law of bankruptcy to pay off one's debts. In today's consumer society, persons purchase items using credit cards. The *U.S. Statistical Abstract* (1998) reports that there will be 157 million credit card holders in the United States by the year 2000. That same source reports that in 2000 more than 1.4 billion credit cards will be in use in the United States and projects credit card debt for that year at $677 billion. Approximately 27 percent of credit card holders seldom pay off the entire balance owed. Undoubtedly failure to pay off one's credit card debt with high interest rates for unpaid balances is a contributor to the large number of bankruptcies in the United States. Many of the more than one million people who file for bankruptcy in the United States each year are using the positive law of bankruptcy to pay off their otherwise legally owing debts. If people assert that "the law allows it," they show their agreement that positive law is setting the level for the most that one can be expected to do. Said another way, the positive law of bankruptcy has become an "ethic."

The high number of bankruptcies, while showing evidence of a decline in personal responsibility, can be attributed to other factors as well. For instance, many persons enter bankruptcy for reasons beyond their control unrelated to credit card use—unexpected job loss, overwhelming medical expenses, and death of a family breadwinner.

The Rewards for Winning Stimulate Cheating. In today's society winning is the name of the game. People idolize the honor student, the prominent and successful businessperson, the champion athlete, and anyone who has "made it." You are what you have done. Statistics show that better-educated people, prominent athletes, and professional people do make significantly higher incomes than the general population. Businesses are judged by the bottom line—how much money have they made, what is their market share. Salespeople are judged on how much they sell, not on the techniques used to make sales. The desire to succeed, unfortunately, too often causes otherwise good people to "cut corners" to succeed. The "corners" in society are the positive law. An example of the high stakes in business would be multimillion-dollar U.S. Defense Department contracts. Contracts for missiles, ships, or planes can mean millions—even billions—of dollars for a company and also help the local and state economies. With such large amounts of money at stake, it is understandable that military procurement fraud occurs. Such high stakes increase the incentive to obtain a competitive advantage, even though violating the positive law. Unfortunately, violation of the law today is occurring with alarming frequency.

The Tendency to Resolve Problems by Passing Laws. Legislators want to be reelected. And when voters take their problems to their legislators and demand solutions, legislators can show their concern with voters' problems by enacting positive laws that purport to solve voters' problems. Often well-intentioned laws are worthless. For example, low-income workers claim that they need more money to live on, so they urge Congress to increase the federal minimum wage law. The idea is to increase the pay of low-income workers. What actually may happen is that low-income jobs are lost to Third World countries or eliminated entirely because low-income workers are paid low wages for a good reason: They are only worth what they are being paid. Thus passing a law forcing employers to pay an artificially higher minimum wage to *help* low-income workers could end up *hurting* such workers if their jobs are lost. What has been gained by passing such a law?

JURISPRUDENCE: THE STUDY OF OTHER ETHICS (VALUES) INFLUENCING POSITIVE LAW

The search for proper or ethical conduct has led to many answers in addition to the view that positive law determines what is right. The next section surveys a number of these views and offers several other values that can either support or challenge the positive law for ethical supremacy.

Jurisprudence is an area of study that examines the values or ethics associated with positive law. The word *jurisprudence* is derived from the Latin words *juris* meaning "the law" and *prudens* meaning "wisdom." Thus, by studying jurisprudence we are going beyond just learning "the rules" (positive law). We are trying to learn what values the rules attempt to impart to society. The next subsections explore the ethic of justice, the ethic of power, the ethic of custom, the ethic of conduct, the ethic of civilization, the ethic of reality, and the ethic of utility.

The Ethic of Justice

Justice is a highly important legal ethic. Every legal system, no matter how good or bad, has claimed to promote justice. The **natural law** school of jurisprudence defines law in terms of justice. Natural law ideas have a long history, reaching at least from the time of the Stoics in ancient Greece. Natural law thinkers include medieval philosophers such as St. Thomas Aquinas, the eighteenth century English jurist, Sir William Blackstone, and modern egalitarian philosophers such as John Rawls. Natural law thinkers such as Blackstone say, "An unjust law is not law and should not be obeyed." The *Riggs v. Palmer* case on page 16 illustrates the concept of natural law.

Due Process. Another example of natural law (the justice ethic) is due process. Due process refers to the right to a notice and a fair hearing before the law imposes sanctions on us. Due process gives all people in the United States rights including the right to jury trials in cases where their rights are substantially affected. Thus, if businesspeople are accused of violating the Sherman Antitrust Act by price fixing, they have a jury trial right, and the crime must be proved before they can be punished.

Equity Courts. Equity courts and equitable remedies also show how the justice ethic influences positive law. The word *equity* means "fairness." Equity courts originated in England when law courts became inflexible in remedying wrongs.

Advantage of the Justice Ethic. The legal ethic of justice has broad appeal. Who can be against it as a general idea? But closer analysis reveals its major weakness.

Disadvantages of the Justice Ethic. The main weakness in the justice ethic is that one person's idea of justice is not necessarily the same as another's, which might be called the **multiple-conscience problem**. In other words, we all might agree to be fair, but we might disagree about what fairness means in a legal matter.

In many, if not most, instances, people agree on what justice is in a particular case. For example, most of us would probably agree that the law forbidding murder is fair and just. But we might disagree on the punishment for murderers: Some believe in the death penalty, and some do not.

Should the Law Be "Moral"? Natural law deals with whether the positive law is "right," which leads to the question of whether the positive law should be moral. One scholar who has tackled this question is former Harvard Law School Professor Lon Fuller. Fuller developed what he called the **internal morality of law (IML)**. According to Fuller, positive law must meet eight tests to be considered internally moral. These eight tests are as follows:

1. *There should be law; that is, rules should exist.* This point seems obvious except when one considers the alternative: Law made by a particular person. Without rules, a mayor responsible for setting speed limits could set *different* speed limits every time a different person was charged with speeding. This randomness would destroy uniformity and could lead to different rules for different people depending on whether the mayor liked or disliked the individual charged. Clearly such a

situation would deny people a cherished right guaranteed by the U.S. Constitution: *Equal* protection of the laws.

2. *The rules should be promulgated.* The idea here is that the rules should be made publicly available so they can be followed. Said another way, the rules must be knowable. When rules are promulgated, citizens are protected because they can conduct themselves knowing what is allowed and forbidden. If the rules are not publicly available, citizens could be arrested for violations of laws they never knew existed. Secret laws were once part of the Nazi legal system in Germany.
3. *The rules must be clear.* An income tax law that tells citizens to "pay their fair share" of the taxes is vague. Is a fair share 10 percent, 20 percent, or 50 percent of one's income? If this determination is left up to the Internal Revenue Service, it might be 50 percent, but to each taxpayer what is fair would likely be much lower. One reason for the clarity requirement is to have laws the citizens can reasonably obey. As we shall learn later in this text, the idea that laws should be clear is required by the U.S. Constitution's due process clause.
4. *The rules should be retroactive as seldom as possible.* Suppose you go fishing on Monday and catch a 10" bass, which is then allowed. If on Tuesday the legislature passes a statute making catching bass less than 12" in length illegal *anytime during the previous week*, you have broken the law. You cannot avoid breaking this law because you caught the 10" bass before the law was passed. Retroactive laws are thought to be unfair when they punish a person for committing an act that was legal when it was done. The U.S. Constitution forbids *ex post facto* laws, which are retroactive criminal laws that work to the disadvantage of the accused. Two other parts of the U.S. Constitution—the Fifth Amendment and the Fourteenth Amendment—generally forbid retroactive laws, whether civil or criminal. Occasionally in the United States, certain rules, such as tax laws, apply to events that have already occurred. For example, under the 1993 Federal Budget Reform Act, certain parts of that statute were applied to taxable events occurring prior to that law's passage.
5. *The rules should be noncontradictory.* If one rule says, "Dump toxic wastes in your backyard" and another law forbids such dumping, citizens scratch their heads and wonder what to do. Rules should be consistent so people can act legally.

   Reportedly, all states except Virginia have legalized auto radar detectors (devices that help drivers violate the speed limits and evade the police). One wonders why a state would pass a law setting speed limits and later enact another statute enabling people to violate that same law.
6. *The rules should not require the impossible.* The Clean Water Act declared in 1972 that by 1985 no pollutants should be discharged into U.S. waters. This result was not achieved in 1985, nor is it likely ever to be achieved. What the law demands should be "doable." A law or set of laws that seeks the impossible makes the legal system appear foolish and undercuts public respect for law.
7. *The rules should not change often.* Learning the law can be difficult. Learning the law and then seeing it change the next week and then change again the following week is confusing and frustrating. Why bother learning rules that will only change? Fortunately, many rules are stable. Property law, contract law, and many areas of commercial law seldom change. Tax law, criminal law, environmental law, and employer/employee relations law have changed frequently in recent years.
8. *There should be congruence between official conduct and the rules.* Said another way, rule-makers and those in charge should obey the rules just as much as the average citizen. If a mayor, congressperson, senator, or president makes speeches condemning illegal drug use, tax evasion, or other crimes, and then is caught committing those crimes, people correctly call the official a hypocrite. Citizens

like to see their leaders follow the rules. When the average person observes the mayor commit tax evasion, individuals might wonder why they should follow the rules the leading citizen in town does not follow.

A Natural Law Concept of John Rawls: The Original Position. A leading twentieth-century philosopher named John Rawls developed several natural law ideas including the "original position." According to this idea, if each of us did not know what position we would start from in society—that is, whether we would be rich or poor, smart or stupid, male or female, black or white, gay or straight, handicapped or not handicapped, of Asian or African or European extraction, and all of the other possible characteristics—what would we want the rules to be? Rawls called this starting point the "original position." It is helpful in justifying laws protective of classes of persons who have traditionally been discriminated against, such as women and racial minorities.

A Final Natural Law Concept: Kant's Categorical Imperative. The philosopher Immanuel Kant, who lived in the eighteenth century, suggested an ethic called the **categorical imperative**. This idea has natural law roots and says we should act in the same way we would want the law to be. In other words, if we would want the law to prohibit stealing, we as individuals should not steal. This ethic follows the same principle as the golden rule, which says, "Do unto others as you would have them do unto you."

How would the categorical imperative deal with tax fraud? Would you want others to cheat on their taxes? Most would say that taxpayers should pay all that they legally owe the government; thus, the categorical imperative tells each of us to be honest in paying our taxes.

Riggs v. Palmer

New York Court of Appeals
115 N.Y. 509 (1889)

Background and Facts:

On August 13, 1880, Francis Palmer, a wealthy farmer, made his will, which gave the bulk of his estate to his grandson, Elmer Palmer. Francis was a widower, and in March 1882 he married Mrs. Bresee, with whom he entered a prenuptial agreement in which it was agreed that instead of giving Mrs. Bresee a claim on Francis' estate if she survived him, she would be given a claim on Francis' farm for her support.

When Francis executed his will, Elmer lived with Francis as a member of his family, and at Francis' death, Elmer was 16 years old. Elmer knew of the provisions of Francis' will and that Francis had shown some intent to change the will so Elmer would take less. To prevent his grandfather from modifying his will and get speedy enjoyment and immediate possession of his will expectancy, Elmer murdered Francis by poisoning him.

Elmer was convicted of murder, but nonetheless claimed his inheritance under his grandfather's will. Mr. Francis Palmer's two daughters, Mrs. Riggs and Mrs. Preston, sued Elmer arguing that they, not Elmer, should take Francis' estate because to give it to Elmer would allow him to profit from his wrong. Elmer argued that the will gave the bulk of the estate to him and that the statute governing wills literally would require that the property go to him.

Issue

Could Elmer recover under the valid will of the grandfather even though Elmer had murdered his grandfather to accelerate his inheritance?

Decision

No, a beneficiary who murders his testator (person who makes a will) cannot take under the testator's will. Even though the statutes regulating the making, proof, and effect of wills, if literally read, would give the property to the murderer, in some cases the letter of a statute is restrained by an equitable construction. The objective is to imagine what the legislators if present meant or would do if they had seen a similar situation when they wrote the statute.

Blackstone, the great English jurisprudent, stated that if absurd consequences manifestly contradictory to common reason would arise by reading the statute literally, judges are, in decency, to conclude the legislature did not foresee such consequences. In such a case judges are free to read the statute by equity (general fairness). All laws may be controlled in their operation and effect by general, fundamental maxims of the common law. No one shall be permitted to profit by his own fraud, or to take advantage of his own wrong, or to found any claim upon his own iniquity, or to acquire property by his own crime. These maxims are dictated by public policy and have their foundation in universal law administered in all civilized countries, and have nowhere been superseded by statutes.

The New York Court of Appeals held that Elmer took no property from Francis and that the will was ineffective to pass ownership to Elmer because Elmer murdered Francis. Francis's two daughters were declared to be the owner of his estate subject to Francis's widow's claim

Questions

1. Who was arguing for natural law, Elmer or the deceased's sisters? Why?
2. If a statute literally covers a situation, and a court (judge) departs from the meaning of the statute to achieve "justice," what, if any, dangers does this situation present?

The Ethic of Power

Power is a basic ethic. Plato[3] recognized this in his book, *The Republic,* when through the character Thrasymachus he said, "Justice is the will of the stronger." Another way of expressing this idea is "Might makes right."

Power is essential for positive law, because positive law assumes that a political superior exists. Some suggest that positivists are merely power worshippers. One gets and keeps political superiority by being powerful. Furthermore, power is needed to provide positive law's sanctions.

Power can take several forms. It can be military might. It can also take the form of economic power. The ability to cut off someone's budget or benefits or job is economic power. The power of an idea is, in many ways, the most long-lasting form of power.

[3] Some will argue that Plato himself did not believe power as an ethic, given the ensuing discussion among Socrates, Thrasymachus, and others in this segment of *The Republic.*

Rent controls are a contemporary example of the power ethic's influence on positive law. Many municipalities throughout the United States have passed rent control ordinances that stop landlords from raising rent more than a specified amount each year. These controls are controversial laws that show the power ethic of tenants in the municipal population. These people use their electoral power to force city councils to pass rent control laws. Such ordinances are politically popular because there are more tenants than landlords. However, rent control laws could be unwise economically. New rental housing will not be built because landlords will not get a fair return on their investment if rent cannot be raised to reflect the property's market value. Rent controls actually are a legal attempt to repeal an economic "law," the law of supply and demand, which sets prices. The power ethic can legally control rents, but it jeopardizes the supply of future rental housing. Whatever the wisdom of rent control laws, they illustrate the power ethic.

Advantages of the Power Ethic. Order is a major advantage of the power ethic. Whoever has power can by force or threat of force bring law and order to a society. Order when based on sound economics can bring long-run stability, which encourages people to make investments and long-range commitments of resources that work to the betterment of society. Investments in plant, equipment, and people (by training and education) improve a society's quality of life, but a long time frame is needed to realize benefits from investments. People and companies are willing to invest only where long-run order and stability make gains from investments likely. Gains are not likely to be realized where the government constantly changes its rules. (Consider the economic decline of modern Italy which, at last count, has had more than forty governments since World War II.) Order and stability exist because of the power ethic.

Disadvantages of the Power Ethic. Power can be abused. For example, many years ago the railroads charged farmers and small businesses higher rates for hauling freight than they did certain large customers. This unfair rate discrimination led to regulation of common carriers by the Interstate Commerce Commission (ICC).

Another abuse of power can occur when businesses hire or promote people because of race, religion, sex, national origin, or age. A reward system should be based on productivity and not on the employer's dislike of, for example, Catholics, blacks, and women (or men).

Yancey v. State Personnel Board illustrates how knowledge about a person's personal life can be used as a control and, hence, power device.

Yancy v. State Personnel Board

California Court of Appeal (1st Dist.)
213 Cal. Rptr. 634 (1985)

Background and Facts:

Lanny Vance and Len Cimino, city of Fairfield police officers, were on special duty to make security checks in residential and school areas where there had been incidents of burglary. As they pulled into the parking lot of an elementary school at approximately 10 P.M., they saw a figure running westerly in the yard area. Officer Vance accelerated the patrol car, and the figure ran into the bushes in front of a fence separating the school grounds from the residential area. The officers apprehended Yancey, the appellant, wearing thongs, female undergarments and an unbuttoned white cotton shirt. No other persons were in the area. Yancey identified himself; his residence was adjacent to the west school fence. The officers detained Yancey for questioning, determined he had committed no crime, and released him.

Officer Vance made a report of the incident and referred a copy to CMF (California Medical Facility,

Yancey's employer). Vance felt that given "the capacity that [Yancey] was working in that it should be brought to the attention of the [sic] superiors. . . ." Vance also felt that Yancey had at all times been completely truthful and straightforward with the officers, and that he did not conceal any information. Vance testified at the subsequent hearing he "really didn't think [the report] would go this far."

As a result of this incident, Yancey was dismissed pursuant to California Government Code, which permits discipline of an employee for "failure of good behavior either during or outside of duty hours, which is of such a nature that it causes discredit to the appointing authority or the person's employment." The matter was heard before a Board hearing officer, who made the following pertinent findings: "[Appellant] was considered a good Officer and had no blemishes on his prior seven-year employment record. However, it must be found that the dismissal action was warranted. [Appellant] has attributed his wearing of female clothing to job-related stress which he now feels he can handle. But it must be recognized that this incident is widely known at the institution and would as a practical matter cause [Appellant] to have great difficulty in working with other Correctional Officers and inmates. This in itself would create a difficult if not impossible situation and in addition would place [Appellant] in an atmosphere far more stressful than the normal job circumstances which existed at the time of the . . . episode. The Department [of Corrections] just cannot be required to run the risk of employing [Appellant] in a stressful security position when his reaction to stress is so unusual."

The Board adopted the hearing officer's findings and decision. Following intradepartment proceedings the matter went to a trial court, which found that evidence supported the Board's decision and denied relief. Experts—a psychiatrist and a 14-year correctional officer—concluded that being caught wearing women's clothing would make Yancey a likely target for blackmail by the inmates and distrust by the officers, thereby creating dangerous situations for himself and other officers. On cross-examination they readily conceded that because the incident in question was known, the blackmail theory was unrealistic.

Experts testified that Yancey's problem was medical in nature and related to stress, and that he would be subject to manipulation by the inmates if the incident received notoriety within the institution because many inmates have the ability to "pick up a weakness or indiscretion to develop situations that could be—that are advantageous for them but could be dangerous to others." However, an expert did not consider Yancey to be homosexual, and he knew of nothing in Yancey's character to indicate he was the sort to be blackmailed or otherwise manipulated. He believed the "big point" in deciding whether Yancey could presently function as a corrections officer was how the other employees responded to him. If Yancey's fellow officers were willing to accept him "as he is, there would be no problem" of dangerous situations developing. Yancey had maintained social contact with 20 to 30 of his former colleagues, and Yancey testified that they all asked him when he was returning to work. Yancey said none of them expressed any concerns about his ability to function as a correctional officer. Yancey appealed the trial court decision to the California Court of Appeals.

Issue

Was there substantial evidence at the trial court level to support dismissal of Yancey as unfit for his employment and was dismissal grossly excessive discipline here?

Decision

The trial court's decision was reversed and the matter was sent back to determine whether substantial evidence indicated that Yancey was unfit for his job. The court of appeals found that the experts at the trial court level had not actually spoken to any of Yancey's coworkers and had no basis for their opinion as to their reaction to Yancey's conduct.

Questions

1. How might knowledge by a subordinate of potentially embarrassing conduct of someone in a supervisory position confer power on the subordinate? In the case of such a role reversal, does the subordinate become the dominant party?
2. Can sex or allegations of sexual practices ever be a tool to control someone or influence someone's conduct?
3. Can any sort of indiscretion or alleged misconduct by anyone—subordinate or superior—be a control device? Can you think of any recent incidents involving high-level politicians, government officials, or business leaders where alleged legal indiscretions might lead such individuals to compromise their actions as officials? Is anyone perfect?
4. Much talk is heard today about the need for diversity in society and for toleration of diverse conduct as long as such conduct does not injure others. Does the *Yancey* case give comfort to those hoping for greater toleration of diversity?

The Ethic of Custom

Custom refers to long-standing conduct. How people have acted and continue to act is an ethic influencing positive law. Savigny, a German writing in the early nineteenth century, helped develop the historical school of law. It says that positive law reflects long-standing custom.

Many examples demonstrate how custom influences positive law. Consider wills, the documents we customarily use to transfer property when we die. A will takes effect only when a person dies, but the testator (or testatrix,[4] if a woman) is no longer with us. In effect, a dead person is telling the living what to do with resources such as money and other property that are left. Transferring property by will is a long-standing custom recognized by positive law.

Owning private property—the idea that one person can own a house or car—is another long-standing custom recognized by positive law. The definition of private property occasionally changes. At one time in the United States, slaves were property that could be bought and sold. Perhaps one day planets will be considered property capable of ownership.

Contracts are a third example of how the legal ethic of custom can affect positive law. Contracts are agreements voluntarily entered between private individuals or between groups and are enforceable in court. A graduating student who agrees to work for IBM for $35,000 per year has made a contract. Contracts have long been enforceable in the United States. People can change their lives by entering a contract. Which job offer should one accept? Should one buy a house or raw land that might have oil under it?

To appreciate the control over your life that freedom of contract gives you, contrast it with feudal society, wherein a person's status was set by birth. If you were lucky enough to be born a noble, you remained a noble. If you were born a serf, you generally stayed a serf. In medieval society, contract in its modern form did not exist. Later, with the development of the merchant class, private agreements were made and enforced in merchant courts. Trade custom, recognized in settling contract disagreements, was called the **law merchant**. Contracts themselves, as well as the law merchant, came to be recognized by society's law and equity courts. Thus, the ethic of custom is deeply embedded in commercial law. An example of a long-standing custom that has found its way into positive law is that of an employer who may fire an employee any time for any reason in an at-will employment relationship.

Geary v. U.S. Steel Corporation provides an example of the custom ethic.

Geary v. U.S. Steel Corporation

Supreme Court Pennsylvania
318 A.2d 174 (1974)

Background and Facts:

George B. Geary was continuously employed by appellee, U.S. Steel Corporation (hereinafter "company"), from 1953 until July 13, 1967, when he was dismissed from his position. Geary's duties involved the sale of tubular products to the oil and gas industry. His employment was at-will. The dismissal is said to have stemmed from a disagreement concerning one of the company's new products, a tubular casing designed for use under high pressure. Geary alleges that he believed the product had not been adequately tested and constituted a serious danger to anyone who used it; that he voiced his misgivings to his superiors and was ordered

[4] Testators and testatrixes are persons who make a will.

to "follow directions," which he agreed to do; that he nevertheless continued to express his reservations, taking his case to a vice-president in charge of sale of the product; that as a result of his efforts the product was reevaluated and withdrawn from the market; that he at all times performed his duties to the best of his ability and always acted with the best interests of the company and the general public in mind; and that because of these events he was summarily discharged without notice. Geary asserts that the company's conduct in so acting was "wrongful, malicious and abusive," resulting in injury to his reputation in the industry, mental anguish, and direct financial harm, for which he seeks both punitive and compensatory damages. . . .

No court in this Commonwealth has ever recognized a nonstatutory cause of action for an employer's termination of an at-will employment relationship.

The Pennsylvania law is in accordance with the weight of authority elsewhere. Absent a statutory or contractual provision to the contrary, the law has taken for granted the power for either party to terminate an employment relationship for any or no reason. . . .

Appellant's final argument is an appeal to considerations of public policy. Geary asserts in his complaint that he was acting in the best interests of the general public, as well as of his employer, in opposing the marketing of a product which he believed to be defective.

The praiseworthiness of Geary's motives does not detract from the company's legitimate interest in preserving its normal operational procedures from disruption.

We hold only that where the complaint itself discloses a plausible and legitimate reason for terminating an at-will employment relationship and no clear mandate of public policy is violated thereby, an employee at-will has no right of action against his employer for wrongful discharge.

Issue

Did the employer have the right to dismiss Geary even though he pointed out a defect in a company product?

Decision

The Supreme Court of Pennsylvania said that the whistleblower was not wrongfully dismissed by his employer. Geary recovered nothing from his former employer.[5]

Questions

1. What evidence supported the whistleblower's claim that the company's product was defective?
2. What legal ethic supports the company's firing the whistleblower?

Advantages of Custom. Because customs are longstanding, they are known and observed by most people. People implicitly are saying that they agree with a custom when they follow it. Hence, custom provides stability to society. Also, customs help people plan because they know the custom seldom changes.

Disadvantages of Custom. Custom can be backward, oppressive, or simply wrong. Racial prejudice has been a long-standing custom in the United States. Sexism has also been a long-standing custom in the United States, especially in the job market. An effect of sexism and racism is that until recently the U.S. job market has been dominated by white males. Title VII of the Civil Rights Act of 1964 has to some extent changed the customs of white male dominance. But customs are slow to change. Passage of such positive laws as the Civil Rights Act is an attempt to change custom. Some other long-standing customs such as sexual harassment are illegal today.

The Ethic of Norms of Conduct

Norms of conduct, which refer to how most people act, are another ethic influencing positive law. Norms are like customs, except they are not as long-standing. Eugen Ehrlich's sociological school of law has conduct as its ethic, or value. Some groups'

[5] The Geary case has *not,* as of this writing, been reversed by the Pennsylvania Supreme Court. However, exceptions (loopholes) in the *Geary* result exist. See Chapter 14 under the topic "Employment At-Will" for a discussion of exceptions to the at-will rule.

norms of conduct include sexual promiscuity, drunkenness, marijuana smoking, price fixing, and bid rigging, which have a negative image. But these norms of conduct are not necessarily illegal (in the positive law sense). For example, all types of drunkenness and sexual promiscuity are not illegal, although public drunkenness, drunken driving, and certain sexual practices often are. Thus, norms that some groups in society would question on grounds of morality are not necessarily illegal. On the other hand, marijuana smoking, bid rigging, and price-fixing are generally illegal in the positive law sense even though these activities could be the norm of conduct for certain sectors of society. As we can see, norms could be above or below the positive law and still be questioned based on various other values such as public health or morality.

Advantages of Norms of Conduct. The ethic of conduct is an advantage because it is how, by definition, people act. We could solve the problem of lawbreaking simply by changing positive law so that it agrees with social conduct. If positive law and conduct were the same, law enforcement would be easier and cheaper.

Disadvantages of Norms of Conduct. Conduct can also be socially undesirable, such as murder, arson, rape, price-fixing, drug taking, and cheating on one's income tax. Positive law should help society improve. If positive law were to be relaxed to allow the worst conduct, civilization would be endangered. People would no longer be safe; they could not believe what others say; and property could be stolen without fear of punishment.

Positive law and the ethic of conduct are often at odds because positive law encourages ideal conduct. Norms of conduct attempt to lower positive law's ideal by claiming it sets unrealistically high standards.

The Ethic of Civilization

Civilization is an ethic influencing positive law. Psychoanalyst Sigmund Freud said that law shows the ethic of civilization because it frustrates (tries to stop) instincts such as the desires to lie, cheat, and steal. The more we as individuals and as a society frustrate our base instincts, the more civilized we become.

Law helps us to be civilized because it states rules telling us what we may or may not do. We may not misrepresent the mileage on our car when we sell it because this could be fraud. We may not cheat our business partner because this would violate our fiduciary duty, our duty of loyalty. We may not dump untreated chemicals into a stream because this would violate the Clean Water Act. We may not drive our car above the speed limit. We may not fail to turn over part of our income to the government as taxes. In employment, we may not discriminate based on age. These and other laws frustrate our base instincts. However, they do not totally restrict us, because many activities we enjoy doing do not arise from our base instincts—for example, working, studying, and helping others.

Advantages of the Civilization Ethic. The advantage of civilization is practical freedom from harm. Under civilization, people, business, and government are under control and are modulated, and everyone gets a taste of freedom's good life.

Disadvantages of the Civilization Ethic. The civilization ethic also has its disadvantages or costs. Civilization causes frustrations, and people must direct their hostilities and aggressions inward, which can cause ulcers, heart attacks, high blood pressure, allergies, and psychosomatic illnesses.

Regina v. Dudley and Stephens illustrates the civilization ethic.

Regina v. Dudley and Stephens

Queens Bench
L.R., Q.B. 61 (1884)

Background and Facts:

On July 25, 1884, three seamen and a young boy drifted in a small boat in the ocean. They were 1,000 miles off the African coast, had no fresh water, and had not eaten for eight days, with no signs of rescue. They had been floating for twenty days after their yacht was wrecked in a storm. The three men argued quietly among themselves about sacrificing one of them so that the others could be saved. The three knew they meant the boy would be the one killed. They said nothing to the boy. On the nineteenth day, two of the three men wanted to draw lots to decide who would die so the others could eat. One man refused to draw. On the twentieth day, one man with the other's consent (the third man disagreeing) went to the boy, told him what was going to happen, put a knife to the boy's throat, and killed him. The boy did not agree to be murdered. All three men ate the boy and survived four more days until their rescue.

The two men who agreed to sacrifice the boy were later tried in England for murder. They raised the defense of necessity.

Issue

Is the deliberate killing of an unoffending and unresisting boy murder if the killing is necessary to permit others to survive?

Decision

Yes, it was murder. The English court held that it was not a case of necessity. The court said that morality and law are not always the same but should be the same as often as possible. Separating law from morality would be a mistake, which would happen if necessity were a defense to murder in this case. Dudley and Stephens were convicted of murder. (The death sentence was commuted to six months' imprisonment.)

Questions

1. What argument did the sailors make to justify their cannibalism?
2. Did the court's decision support or undercut the civilization ethic?

The Ethic of Reality

Have you ever thought that, even though a positive law rule requires a certain result, the result would never happen because of human factors, such as a jury or a judge's liking or disliking one of the parties? Do you also think that definitions of law ignoring human factors are inadequate? If so, you think like a legal realist.

One prominent legal realist was Jerome Frank, a former federal judge and University of Chicago Law School professor who wrote in the 1930s. He thought how law was applied in court cases was as important as, if not more important than, the law in the books, and that an ethic of realism is at work when trial juries and judges decide cases. In other words, what trial judges and juries do in fact, even if the positive law rule differs, is the ethic of realism. Legal realism can also be present in legal matters outside the courtroom.

> **http://** *For examples of how courts act in fact, visit* ***http://www.courttv.com***

Why do judges and juries sometimes disregard positive law in deciding cases? They usually *do* obey positive law, but sometimes do not, and this makes a difference. In its one business case, some high-level certified public accountants were prosecuted criminally for violating the federal securities laws. The CPAs wanted another professional—the judge—to act as the jury (fact trier). The prosecutor wanted a jury made up of average people to decide fact issues. Why the concern? Who would be more sympathetic to high-level CPAs: another professional such as a judge, or a group of jurors, the majority of whom seldom are professionals but rather people from socioeconomic circumstances different from CPAs? The prosecutor won the point, and the jurors ended up convicting the CPAs. That the CPAs' wealth and status worked against them is not certain but it is possible. If it did, it supports the legal realists.

Advantage of Reality. At times, extreme circumstances may justify not following positive law. Cases have occurred in which physicians have permanently put to sleep deathly ill patients who were in great pain and beyond saving. When such physicians were criminally charged with manslaughter, juries sometimes refused to convict. Such a refusal is based on the jury's belief that the law is unfair, reflecting the legal ethic of realism in a good way.

Disadvantage of Reality. Prejudice is undesirable in legal proceedings. We have trials to hear legal arguments and prove facts so that we can make judgments. The ideal is to avoid prejudging people based on their wealth, race, color, national origin, sex, religion, or other irrelevant factors. When such prejudice occurs, the objective of jury trials is defeated.

Do you think the following case shows the advantage or disadvantage of legal realism?

Delaware Tire v. Fox

Delaware Supreme Court
411 A.2d 606 (1980)

Background and Facts:

On April 13, 1973, Earl A. Fox, Jr. suffered an injury at work and subsequently recovered workers' compensation. He continued to have pain from the injury and in 1975 attempted suicide unsuccessfully. In February 1977, Fox's doctor referred him to a psychologist to help him overcome pain and hold a job. The psychologist said the 1973 injury caused an emotional disorder (depression) due to pain. On June 8, 1977, Fox killed himself. His wife filed a claim for workers' compensation death benefits. Such claims must be job-related to allow recovery. The state workers' compensation statute (Delaware's) specifically did not allow recovery for deaths of "wilful intention."

Issue

Could Mrs. Fox recover under the workers' compensation statute for her husband's suicide?

Decision

The Delaware Supreme Court held that Mrs. Fox could recover. The court reasoned that Earl's suicide was caused by severe pain and despair, which proximately resulted from a compensable accident. Furthermore, the pain and despair were so great that they overcame normal, rational judgment. Therefore, there was no "wilful intention" to take his life.

Questions

1. What factor made the plaintiff's (Mrs. Fox's) claim sympathetic?
2. Was the law ambiguous, thereby, permitting the court to take account of Mrs. Fox's personal situation?

The Ethic of Utility

http://
For a site providing economic information, go to ***http://www.dismal.com***

English jurist and philosopher Jeremy Bentham wrote in the late 1700s and early 1800s of the need to promote the greatest good for the greatest number, also known as the **ethic of utilitarianism**. The basic idea of utilitarianism is to maximize the happiness of society. Happiness has come to mean utility (satisfaction). Modern economics is based on Bentham's ideas of utility because economics says that society's resources are limited and, therefore, we should use them to maximize their utility.

Hence, persons who use the ethic of utilitarianism as their guide to proper conduct try to maximize utility. In so doing they are constantly weighing one course of action against others, in effect, balancing alternatives to see which produces the greatest good for the greatest number.

The utility ethic is often reflected in the positive law. The lawmaker (a court or legislature) often balances competing arguments or claims to decide what is the proper rule for the conduct of society. Balancing is a form of utilitarian reasoning. For example, suppose O owns a diamond ring. T, a thief, steals the ring and sells it to G, a good-faith purchaser for value, who believes that T owns the ring. O later learns that G has the ring and sues G to get it back. (T cannot be found.) G will argue that she bought the ring in good faith for value without notice that T did not own it. G will also argue that people should be able to buy goods from persons who appear to own them, which promotes the value of freedom of contract and encourages business. O, on the other hand, will argue that she has a property right (owns) the ring, which a thief should not be able to destroy by selling it to a good-faith purchaser. The judge in this case must choose between the values of property (promoting stability of property ownership) and promoting business (by encouraging people to enter contracts). (In the United States, most judges would decide that O would win over G.)

Utilitarianism has been refined to include two different ideas: **rule utilitarianism** and **act utilitarianism**. Rule utilitarians try to maximize society's happiness within the rules (the positive law). Act utilitarians try to maximize society's utility even if it means breaking the positive law. The difference between rule and act utilitarianism can be understood by considering illegal drug use. Assume a positive law forbids the use of drugs unless one has a physician's approval. A rule utilitarian would not use such drugs without a physician's approval even if doing so would *temporarily* make her feel better. An act utilitarian, on the other hand, might use illegal drugs if they made her more relaxed. This reasoning follows because act utilitarians ignore positive law when they try to maximize utility. A rule utilitarian who wanted to relax might exercise vigorously for 20 minutes. Exercising does not violate any positive law and it generates endorphin betas, a natural type of painkiller, which naturally and legally relaxes one. Thus when you see joggers, you most likely are observing rule utilitarians!

Advantages of the Utilitarian Ethic. Weighing competing claims causes people to think and consider alternatives before they act, which is clearly desirable. When a court or legislature makes a law and uses the utilitarian ethic as a guide, the weightier value (in the eyes of the lawmaker) will prevail.

http://

Cites to historic Supreme Court cases can be found at ***http://supct.law.cornell. edu/supct/cases/historic.htm***

The earth faces a reality: scarce resources and more people all over the world wanting to improve their living standard. Utilitarians place a high value on maximizing total social utility. Thus utilitarians play an important role in setting positive law today, because the rules should be written to maximize social utility given the increasingly scarce resources.

A third advantage of the utilitarian ethic is that it emphasizes the market as the way to ration scarce resources. The market—as distinct from governments—is more efficient than most bureaucracies. The market is currently being looked at as a mechanism for health care delivery, rather than government regulators, given the need for efficiency in this important area.

The utilitarian ethic provides a fourth advantage, which in a sense, repeats something implicit in the first three strengths just noted, but which is so important that it deserves special mention: Utilitarianism provides a way to limit in a rational way the positive law. Today the law and economics (another way of saying utilitarianism) movement is an important analytical tool in devising positive law. The reason is that people demand rights, but fail to see that such demands have associated costs. The law and economics movement, by imposing the cost/benefit discipline on positive law, has the potential of making positive law (and the public) more sensitive to the fact that giving people rights imposes costs. Costs of positive laws should not exceed their benefits. If they do, the positive law fails the test of utilitarianism.

Disadvantages of the Utilitarian Ethic. Using utility as a guide to ethical conduct has several disadvantages. First, utilitarianism gives the decision maker (you, the judge, or the legislature, for instance) too much power, because competing claims always exist when any decision is made. Judges can slant their opinions to favor one competing claim over another by making the strongest arguments for the favored claim and only weak arguments for the disfavored competing claim. For example, in the O and G case involving who had the greater right to the ring, legal systems of some European countries would allow G to win. If we are intellectually honest, we must admit that when judges decide cases, sometimes—maybe often—strong arguments exist for the opposite result.

A second criticism of utilitarianism is that it is amoral if not immoral. Consider the following example: Dr. Swan is a wife beater. He also is a creative research scientist who is on the brink of discovering a cure for cancer. His work is unique and cannot be pursued by anyone else. You are the head of the laboratory that employs Dr. Swan. Dr. Swan's wife has just called you asking that you intervene on her behalf and urge that Dr. Swan see a psychiatrist. You know that Dr. Swan is temperamental and that even discussing his personal life with him would result in his ceasing his research, setting back the development of a cancer cure for years to come. You also learn that Mrs. Swan has never been beaten so severely that her life has been threatened. Because thousands are dying and suffering from cancer, if you follow utilitarian dictates you might well reason that the harm done to Mrs. Swan is not as great as the relief that will be enjoyed by the cancer victims when his cure is forthcoming. Thus, you would sympathize with Mrs. Swan but point out why it is more important that Dr. Swan continue his research, which could save many lives, rather than attend to her, which, after all, is the nonlife-threatening plight of one person.

A third criticism of utilitarianism is that it often involves a market analysis, which uses supply and demand curves. Supply and demand curves are aggregates, representing mythical "average" consumers and "average" suppliers. In effect, by concentrating on averages, everyone is reduced to a clone of everyone else. Is everyone, in fact, identical? No, but by treating everyone as identical, market analysis denies individuality.

A fourth criticism of utilitarianism is that consumers—you and I—are sovereign, the most important people in society. What could be wrong with treating consumers as important? The answer is that some consumers are undiscerning: Some may prefer hog-calling contests, for example, over symphony orchestras. An answer to this criticism is, "That is freedom. People can choose what means the most to them as individuals. Who is to say what is best way to maximize utility from our incomes?" But if people buy and eat potato chips instead of salads, their behavior affects national health care costs, so freedom is not without social costs.

A fifth criticism of utilitarianism is the assumption that all things have a dollar value. Said another way, "Can every decision be reduced to a question of dollars and cents?" Loved ones take care of aged or sick relatives without concern for the economic cost, as do parents of a sick child. The parent never looks at the child and says, "Honey, here's your breakfast. That'll be $1.95."

What claims did the court have to balance in the *Baby M* case?

In the Matter of BABY M, a pseudonym for an actual person

Supreme Court of New Jersey
109 N.J. 396, 537 A.2d 1227 (1988)

Background and Facts:

In February 1985, William Stern and Mary Beth Whitehead entered into a surrogacy contract. It recited that Stern's wife, Elizabeth, was infertile, that they wanted a child, and that Mrs. Whitehead as the mother was willing to provide that child with Mr. Stern as the father.

The contract provided that through artificial insemination using Mr. Stern's sperm, Mrs. Whitehead would become pregnant, carry the child to term, bear it, deliver it to the Sterns, and thereafter do whatever was necessary to terminate her maternal rights so that Mrs. Stern could thereafter adopt the child. Mrs. Whitehead's husband, Richard, was also a party to the contract; Mrs. Stern was not. Mr. Whitehead promised to do all acts necessary to rebut the presumption of paternity under the Parentage Act. . . . Although Mrs. Stern was not a party to the surrogacy agreement, the contract gave her sole custody of the child in the event of Mr. Stern's death. Mrs. Stern's status as a nonparty to the surrogate parenting agreement presumably was to avoid the application of the baby-selling statute to this agreement.

Mr. Stern, on his part, agreed to attempt the artificial insemination and to pay Mrs. Whitehead $10,000 after the child's birth, on its delivery to him. In a separate contract, Mr. Stern agreed to pay $7,500 to the Infertility Center of New York ("ICNY"). The Center's advertising campaigns solicit surrogate mothers and encourage infertile couples to consider surrogacy. ICNY arranged for the surrogacy contract by bringing the parties together, explaining the process to them, furnishing the contractual form, and providing legal counsel.

Mrs. Whitehead was artificially inseminated with Mr. Stern's sperm, became pregnant, had her baby, "bonded" with it, and after initially relinquishing it to the Sterns, went to them and convinced them to turn Baby M over to her for "a week." Mrs. Whitehead kept the baby for several months, however, despite the Sterns' pleas for the child's return. Mr. Stern filed a lawsuit in which he tried to enforce the surrogacy contract against Mrs. Whitehead. A lower court enforced the surrogacy contract, and the Sterns took custody of the child. Mrs. Whitehead then appealed the result to the New Jersey Supreme Court.

Issue

Is a surrogacy contract, under which a married couple unable to have children pays money to a surrogate mother who is artificially inseminated with the natural father's sperm, valid?

Decision

No, the contract here was invalid. "We invalidate the surrogacy contract because it conflicts with the law and public policy of this State. While we recognize the depth of the yearning of infertile couples to have their own children, we find the payment of money to a 'surrogate' mother illegal, perhaps criminal, and potentially degrading to women. Although in this case we grant custody to the natural father, the evidence having clearly proved such custody to be in the best interests of the infant, we void both the termination of the surrogate mother's parental rights and the adoption of the child by the wife/stepparent. We thus restore the 'surrogate' as the mother of the child. We remand the issue of the natural mother's visitation rights to the trial court, since that issue was not reached below and the record before us is not sufficient to permit us to decide it de novo.

"We find no offense to our present laws where a woman voluntarily and without payment agrees to act as a 'surrogate' mother, provided that she is not subject to a binding agreement to surrender her child. Moreover, our holding today does not preclude the Legislature from altering the current statutory scheme, within constitutional limits, so as to permit surrogacy contracts. Under current law, however, the surrogacy agreement before us is illegal and invalid."

Questions

1. Did the Sterns or Mrs. Whitehead assert the ethic or value of freedom of contract? Does the result in the "Baby M" case uphold the principle of complete freedom of contract? What was peculiar about this contract that made it an extremely unattractive case for application of the freedom of contract ethic?
2. What claim or value did Mrs. Whitehead, the natural mother, make to recover "her" child? Was Mr. Stern the natural father? Are we absolutely certain of this?
3. The "Baby M" case holds that certain surrogacy contracts are invalid. Does this result support or undercut the concept of regulation?
4. In focusing on the Sterns and Mrs. Whitehead, are we forgetting the most important party, Baby M? Who does the court focus on in deciding to void the surrogacy contract but in granting Mr. Stern custody rights subject to Mrs. Whitehead's parental rights? If a court ultimately gives custody to one natural parent (which it did, to Mr. Stern) and visitation rights to the other natural parent (which it did, to Mrs. Whitehead), what does this do to Baby M's perception of her parents when she is a child?

Summary

You should be familiar with (1) the names of the theories of law that represent the various ethics examined, (2) a philosopher representing each value, and (3) some advantages and disadvantages of each ethic. You should also be able to give an example of each ethic.

FURTHER POINTS ABOUT LEGAL ETHICS

Ethical Unity

The ethics in positive law we have examined do not represent all of the possible values influencing positive law. Recall that we discussed legal ethics by first seeing what positive law (the rules on the books) requires of us. All other legal values (norms of conduct, long-standing customs, reality, and justice may point toward the same result as the positive law rule. In this case, we have what is called **ethical unity**, which means that all ethics or ethical values are in agreement on a particular matter.

Example of Ethical Unity. An example of a positive law with probable ethical unity is the rule forbidding murder. Such a positive law is just and represents a long-standing custom. Murder is contrary to society's accepted norm of conduct. The rule forbidding murder certainly promotes civilization, because it inhibits us. Finally, juries often follow the law in murder cases so that positive law and realism do not conflict.

Which Ethic Is "Right"?

The shipwrecked seamen and fired employee stories earlier in this chapter indicate that different legal ethics can lead to opposite conclusions. The same ethic (justice or utility) can even lead to opposite conclusions about what is "right." For example, in the seamen case, society viewed the killing as murder while the seamen saw what they did as right because of the need to survive. What, then, is the value of ethics? Should people simply give up and conclude that ethics only confuse an already difficult problem? Four points can be made.

Positive Law: Society's Ethical Floor and Sometimes, Its Ethical Ceiling. First, positive law represents the basic social ethic on a matter. In other words, positive law is society's ethical floor because society (via the government) has ordered or prohibited certain conduct and will punish violators. If people do not follow positive law, they should be prepared to be punished.

Other Ethics: No Defense to Positive Law. Second, other legal ethics may lead an individual to break the positive law. although these other ethics provide no defense to the charge of violating positive law. They represent a personal defense or rejection of society's rules. If enough people agree that the positive law is wrong, society can change or eliminate the positive law; but once individuals start selectively obeying and disobeying positive law, civilization is threatened. Every time positive law is broken, a minirevolution breaks out. Also, violating positive law can work against individual interests. Many positive laws, such as the U.S. Constitution's Bill of Rights, protect individuals, and one presumes that individual lawbreakers want government officials to respect these laws. If individuals and government officials can exempt themselves from one positive law, they break the delicate social contract that holds civilization together.

Ethics That Raise Conduct Above Positive Law. Third, if positive law is an ethical floor, other legal ethics should rarely be used to justify conduct below that floor. However, other ethics could justify raising conduct above positive law requirements. For example, in the United States a swimmer usually has no positive law duty to save a drowning person even if rescue presents little or no danger to the swimmer. Justice, utility, and balancing competing claims are ethics that suggest rescue is proper even though not required.

Ethics That Lower or Limit Positive Law Demands. Today positive law places demands on all sectors of society, but especially on business, so great that ways are being sought to limit or lower such requirements. The law and economics movement—based on utilitarianism—is today an important device used to question and, perhaps, lower certain positive law requirements such as protective labor laws (minimum wage laws, plant closure laws) and environmental laws. The idea is, if benefits from such laws are less than their costs, such laws should be eliminated or modified until benefits exceed costs. .

Further, you and I as consumers economically veto U.S. positive laws when we buy cheap, but good quality, foreign-made goods, which are less costly than comparable U.S. goods because they lack the "social overhead" of U.S. positive laws related to employee and environmental protection. It is a known fact that many nations' positive laws—or, more importantly, their enforcement—are a joke. Korea, Japan, and Mexico are notorious environmental abusers. So, too, are they sexist societies, depriving women of the equal employment opportunity women have in the United States. By not having effective positive laws regarding environmental and employee protections, these nations are able to cut costs for their manufacturers thereby undercutting U.S. manufacturers' prices. When U.S. consumers purchase such foreign goods, consumers economically veto U.S. positive laws providing those same protections. Ethical consumers have a duty to support, via their purchasing patterns, businesses subject to positive laws from which the consumer receives substantial benefits from or with which the consumer philosophically agrees. To do otherwise is to act in a manner lower than the U.S. positive law. aw.

Positive Law Changes. Fourth, positive law and legal ethics are a process, not always a hard-and-fast rule. Government must be flexible and wise enough to realize that times change. For positive law to survive, it must reflect shifts in the various legal ethics.

COMMUNITARIANISM

Several philosophers, including Professor Amitai Etzioni, have recently advanced the idea of communitarianism. Communitarianism refers to the need for community values—commonly shared values—that bind us as a multicultural society. These values are often independent of the positive law, and thus could be seen as social values or norms. They hold a society together and include concern about community peace, tranquillity, and mutual respect as well as a recognition that each of us has community duties as well as rights.

Communitarianism can be shown in many ways from actions as simple as not ridiculing others because of their dress or lifestyles to efforts to not deface or destroy public parks. Communitarianism also stresses recognition of responsibilities as well as rights. Too often today, sectors of society are eager to demand rights without recognizing that every right places a burden on someone else.

Communitarianism has elements of natural law, positive law, utilitarianism, and the sociological school of jurisprudence. The natural law dimension occurs due to communitarianism's implicit ideas of fairness. Communitarianism has positive law aspects because it recognizes the legal correlatives of right and duty. The utilitarianism can be seen in the maximizing of human happiness resulting from the active practice of communitarian principles. Sociological jurisprudence is evident from the emphasis communitarianism places on conduct.

BUSINESS ETHICS

Definition of Business Ethics

Recall from our earlier discussion that ethics refer to values. Business ethics refer to values that a business follows in conducting its affairs. Businesses express values more accurately by actions than by words, which does not mean that any business necessarily lies about its ethics.

Rather, a business does not always have the time or objectivity to perceive correctly the significance of what it is doing when it is making or selling a product. Also, business, as does everyone, tries to "put the best face" on what it does by making public statements with an eye to promoting positive public relations (PR). By watching what a business does, however, one can get a clearer picture of that business's ethics than by merely reading its press releases.

Examples of Business Ethics. Some positive ethical values that a business can promote in its operations include (1) making a profit, (2) delivering the best products and services to consumers, (3) providing workers with jobs, (4) giving stockholders a good return on their investment, and (5) being a good community citizen. We shall examine each of these in greater detail.

- *Making a Profit.* Business has profit making as its prime objective. In other words, selling goods or services for more than it costs to make and distribute them is the primary ethic of business. Even though this motivation sounds selfish, at least three factors make it a positive selfishness. First, consumers voluntarily decide to buy from one particular seller; no one forces them to spend their money. Thus the consumers maximize their utility by voluntarily purchasing what they want. Second, by having fair tariffs and antitrust laws that promote an open market, competition should keep prices as low as possible. Furthermore, competitors will have the incentive of profit to enter the market, which will insure that consumers will be supplied. Third, businesses that make a profit in the face of competition are both keeping costs under control and producing what consumers want. In other words, they maximize society's utility and make efficient use of scarce resources.
- *Delivering the Best Products and Services to Consumers.* Because sellers want to make a profit, and they generally face competition, businesses have an incentive to deliver products and services that will outsell those of competitors. To win sales over competitors, businesses attempt to make products and services perceived as superior to those of competitors.

  Also, today's consumers are knowledgeable about goods and services as a result of increasing consumer education levels as well as availability of consumer buying guides on every topic from autos to can openers. Such information increases the pressure on business to produce the highest quality products and services.
- *Providing Workers with Jobs.* Businesses employ workers and so provide them with a means of financial support. It has been said that a job is the best welfare system

that people can have. This statement asserts that jobs not only contribute to workers' economic well-being but also give their lives meaning and a sense of purpose thereby contributing to workers' self-esteem.

- *Giving Owners a Good Return on Their Investment.* Closely related to earning a profit is the ethic of giving the business owners (stockholders in the case of a corporation) a good return on their investment. A difference between a business's earning a profit and giving the owners a handsome return lies in whether profit can be kept in the business for expansion and improvement of operations. On the other hand, when profits are distributed to the business's owners, such earnings are taken out of the business and can be used by the owners for whatever purpose they desire, which often has nothing to do with improving or developing the firm.
- *Being a Good Citizen.* Businesses can be good citizens by paying taxes that support community schools, hospitals, and other governmental services. Also, by following laws that promote environmental and consumer protection, equal employment, product quality, and other such concerns, the business community acts as a good citizen.

  Business efforts at good citizenship, however, extend beyond merely following the positive law. Many businesses support charities such as the United Way, contribute to community development by donating property for parks and playgrounds, make financial contributions to colleges, art museums, symphony orchestras, ballets, sporting teams, and scout troops, and make many other efforts to enhance community life. Also, employees contribute their time by serving on school boards, as members of charity drives, and as coaches of Little League ball clubs. Businesspeople engage in these civic-minded activities because they believe such contributions make their communities a more appealing place to live, which in turn provides an incentive for qualified employees to remain in the community even when job opportunities appear elsewhere.

Making Business Ethics Mutually Compatible with Each Other. Businesses can sometimes make decisions that satisfy all business ethics. For example, a decision to dump toxic wastes in a properly prepared site will promote long-term profits by preventing huge future lawsuits from not following proper dumping practices. Also, proper dumping can provide the business owners with a long-run return on their investment by insuring that they will still be in business if and when their dumping is challenged. Further, by remaining in business, the ethic of providing employees with a job will be accomplished. The ethic of providing consumers with excellent products and services also comes into play because a product or service cannot be judged excellent if it is made under conditions that ruin the human environment. Finally, following safe and proper dumping practices is good citizenship because environmental problems such as contaminated water supplies are avoided.

Dealing with Conflicting Business Ethics. If the business ethic of making a profit is viewed in the short run, it can, and too often does, conflict with other business ethics. For example, a corporation with many plants in the United States may feel great pressure to close down a marginally profitable plant that is not making profits at the level desired for the corporation as a whole. But what if the plant is the sole economic base of a small community and closure threatens the livelihood of the community? In this case, being a good citizen and providing the workers with jobs might conflict with making a profit or giving the shareholders a fair return on their investment. Also, one could ask whether the business is giving the consumer the desired product or service if a particular plant is only marginally profitable. (It is simplistic to ask such a question when many considerations of intrafirm resource allocation, such as marketing and product development, are involved in assessing the performance of one plant in a multiplant operation.) Nonetheless, the business ethics in such a case do not necessarily all point toward one "right" answer.

How Business Ethics Relate to Legal Ethics

Ethical Floor. A business decision involving ethics is generally assumed to follow the positive law. In other words, the legal ethic of positive law is an ethical floor for business. Thus, a business should not have to ask whether it should follow laws regulating occupational health and safety, dumping of toxic wastes, equal employment opportunity, insider trading, or any of the thousands of other laws regulating business. It is assumed that businesses follow the positive law ethic.

Business Ethics Above Positive Law Requirements. Even though positive law often is assumed to dictate proper ethical conduct for business, it often falls short of this expectation. Businesses often engage in desirable ethical conduct *before* positive law mandates it. For example, some businesses, in an effort to hasten the arrival of a racially integrated workforce, voluntarily instituted affirmative action plans beyond that required by positive law. On occasion, though, this policy has resulted in a business being sued for discriminating against white males. (However, in *United Steelworkers v. Weber* the white males lost their suit for reverse discrimination.)

Business Ethics Conflicting with and Falling Below Positive Law. Sometimes businesses, in their effort to make profits and provide workers with jobs, can violate the positive law. In November 1989 the former president of Beech-Nut Nutrition Corporation reportedly pleaded guilty to ten felony counts for violating the Food, Drug, and Cosmetic Act. Under a plea bargain this person was fined $100,000 and given five years probation and six consecutive months of full-time community service. Federal Judge Thomas Platt accepted the plea bargain to end the case, which had been going on for three years. The defendant stated, "I did not intend to defraud, but I do plead guilty with intent to mislead the public. I did it knowingly." After the plea agreement was approved by the judge, the U.S. Attorney remarked, "This case has probably cost Nestle, the corporate parent of Beech-Nut, in fines and legal fees, many times the few millions they saved in passing off this bogus apple juice to the public."

Beech-Nut Corp. had earlier pleaded guilty to 215 counts of violating the Food, Drug, and Cosmetic Act and was fined $2 million. The product in question was misrepresented as apple juice even though it consisted of sugar, corn syrup, and various other ingredients but little, if any, apple juice. After the company's then chief executive learned of the misrepresented product, he relied at least partially on attorneys' opinions and continued to sell the product. Had sales not continued, the company would have lost money, the prosecutor alleged. Here is a clear case in which the business ethic of making a profit (in the short run, at least) conflicted with the legal ethic of the positive law. The business ethic of keeping the company workers employed arguably might have prompted this positive law violation. With regard to the business ethic of giving the consumer the best product, the prosecution did not prove that the juice was harmful. However, few would claim that sugar water with possibly small amounts of apple juice is as healthy or healthier than pure apple juice.

MANAGER'S ETHICAL DECISION MODEL

Strategy for Managers Confronting an Ethical Problem

As we have seen throughout this chapter, businesspeople confront many situations in which they must ask, "What should I do? What is the proper, ethical conduct in this matter?" The following Ethical Manager's Strategy is suggested:[6]

1. State the problem. This statement may be modified as additional facts appear.
2. Choose your goals or objectives in dealing with the problem.
3. Determine the facts and other contextual factors in the situation, which is often difficult if some or all of the parties have an interest in concealing or misrepresenting key facts. Contextual factors include:
   a. identifying the stakeholders
   b. learning the stakeholders' demands and expectations
   c. ascertaining what resources are available to satisfy stakeholders and whether those resources are available to the decision makers
   d. noting the relevant institutional framework (Is this a matter within a company, or does it involve community matters such as positive law issues?)
   e. learning the customary practices in settling such matters
   f. identifying major social trends or movements that could affect the problem
4. Identify *all possible courses of action* you could take to deal with the problem. This involves brainstorming (creative, uninhibited thinking).
5. Project the probable outcomes for each course of action, and select the course that conforms to positive law as well as has the highest likelihood of achieving your goal with the least adverse impact on stakeholders while affording the greatest benefits.

Caveats in Applying the Manager's Ethical Decision Model

Managers should keep several warnings in mind in applying the Manager's Ethical Decision Model. First, this model is an approach to finding an ethical course of action; it does not guarantee the "correctness" of the decision itself. Second, sometimes a manager might want to change the order of the steps, for example, when a manager wants to do fact-finding *before* trying to state the problem. The model even suggests that the statement of the problem may have to be modified in light of later developed facts.

Lastly, this decision model requires that persons using it exercise *judgment.* Judgment refers to the ability to see relationships, distinguish alternatives, and make reasonable decisions in light of those relationships and alternatives.

OBJECTIVES OF LAW

Six key objectives of law are justice, speed, economy, flexibility, stability, and knowability. Law has more than six objectives, but the six chosen represent major legal goals and to some extent complement our earlier discussion of legal ethics.

[6] The authors acknowledge Professors Mayo and Jones's Basic Decision Model in devising this decision approach.

Justice, Speed, and Economy

One legal rule that expressly requires the three objectives of justice, speed, and economy is Rule 1 of the Federal Rules of Civil Procedure, which tells how to conduct civil trials. That law says the rules for running federal trials should promote the "just, speedy, and inexpensive determination of every action."

The justice, speed, and economic objectives do not always agree, however. An example is the rule concerning jury size. With a smaller jury (six instead of twelve), an agreement can generally be reached faster. Small juries have fewer jurors to be paid; however, smaller juries might not represent the community as well. For example, the smaller the jury, the less likely are minorities to be on them. On the other hand, extremely large juries are costly, slow, and perhaps unjust, because justice delayed is justice denied.

Flexibility

Laws should be flexible to take into account differences among people. For example, real estate taxes are generally higher on large houses than on small ones. But too much flexibility can unnecessarily complicate the law. The present federal income tax laws are an example. They take into account such factors as the taxpayer's age, marital status, and whether the taxpayer rents or owns a home or pays a mortgage.

Great flexibility can also make law enforcement too difficult. An extreme case might be different speed limits for motorists depending on their age, reaction time, and condition of their car. Under such a law, different speed limits would be needed for each of us, which is clearly impractical.

Stability and Knowability

Stable law is desirable because people find it easy to plan if the law does not change. Also, legal training costs are lower, because once a person knows the law, changes occur infrequently. When law is knowable, people can obey it more easily and take greater interest in it because they can learn what it is.

Special interest groups sometimes see knowability of the law as a disadvantage because they have a legal advantage that they want to hide. For example, in some states learning salaries of public officials or school budgets is difficult. Such secrecy is sometimes defended on privacy grounds. When public agencies such as schools are involved, however, the general rule should be one of disclosure (knowability).

WHY STUDY LAW?

The reasons for studying law are many, but in business three are paramount. First, law (technically, positive law) is the cutting edge of society, telling us what we must do and what we cannot do. Students in general and business students in particular should be adequately informed about the legal system's mandates.

Second, the business environment today is increasingly legalized. Rules, often with criminal *and* civil sanctions, outlaw conduct that at first may seem perfectly harmless. For example, corporate directors who buy or sell stock in their company and make a profit may be engaging in conduct that is illegal. A corporation (or anyone) dumps untreated pollutants into a stream is acting illegally. Dumping something into a stream or buying stock may seem harmless to the average person. However, laws regulate these and many other activities.

Third, future businesspeople should practice preventive law. That is, business should take steps to stop or reduce the potentially adverse impact of law on them while law is being made. For example, by knowing the steps in making administrative regulations, business can point out weaknesses in agency proposals *before* they become law. This knowledge can reduce the cost of complying with proposed regulations before millions of dollars have to be spent.

WHAT IS THE LEGAL ENVIRONMENT?

Figure 1.1 shows law covered in the legal environment of business and is a modern way of classifying law. Its focus is on problems or situations. We see a problem or situation and then look at clusters of rules that try to solve or cope with the problem or situation. For example, product liability shown in Figure 1.1 deals with products that do not work. The figure groups together legal theories that help people recover if a defective product injures them or their property.

Constitutional law appears in the figure. Such law is above all other law because it limits what other laws can do. The remainder of this book looks at all of the legal areas presented in Figure 1.1.

CHAPTER SUMMARY

Ethics refer to desirable conduct. Determining what is desirable conduct in a given situation depends on what values one follows. The value that the authors of this book recommend to guide managers and, indeed, everyone is positive law.

Jurisprudence is the study of values concerning law and legal systems. Schools of jurisprudence present different values for judging whether positive law is appropriate ethical conduct.

This chapter has examined the ethic of justice. Natural law is what each person thinks is fair, just, or right even though it might be different from positive law. In considering justice, the matter of morality was discussed. Lon Fuller's internal morality of law (IML) lays out eight characteristics of moral positive law. John Rawls's original position is a type of natural law. Kant's categorical imperative expresses a natural law concept similar to the "golden rule."

Justice (natural law) often, but not always, agrees with positive law.

Power is an ethic that shapes positive law. Unless power supports positive law, the positive law will not last.

Custom (historical jurisprudence) is a value or ethic that refers to repeated conduct over a long period of time. Many positive laws, such as contract law and those creating private property, reflect custom. A German, Savigny, espoused the ethic of custom.

Eugen Ehrlich's sociological school of jurisprudence emphasizes the ethic of norms of conduct. How the average person acts is an ethic.

The ethic of civilization refers to frustration of our base instincts, such as the desire to steal. Sigmund Freud espoused this idea.

Legal realism refers to what trial court judges and juries do in fact, regardless of what the positive law requires. This ethic of reality was developed by Jerome Frank.

Jeremy Bentham advocated the ethic of utilitarianism. This ethic says that appropriate conduct is determined by trying to promote the greatest good for the greatest number.

Business ethics focus on appropriate conduct for business to follow. Business ethics can focus on stakeholders affected by business decisions. **Stakeholders**

FIGURE 1.1 Legal Environment of Business

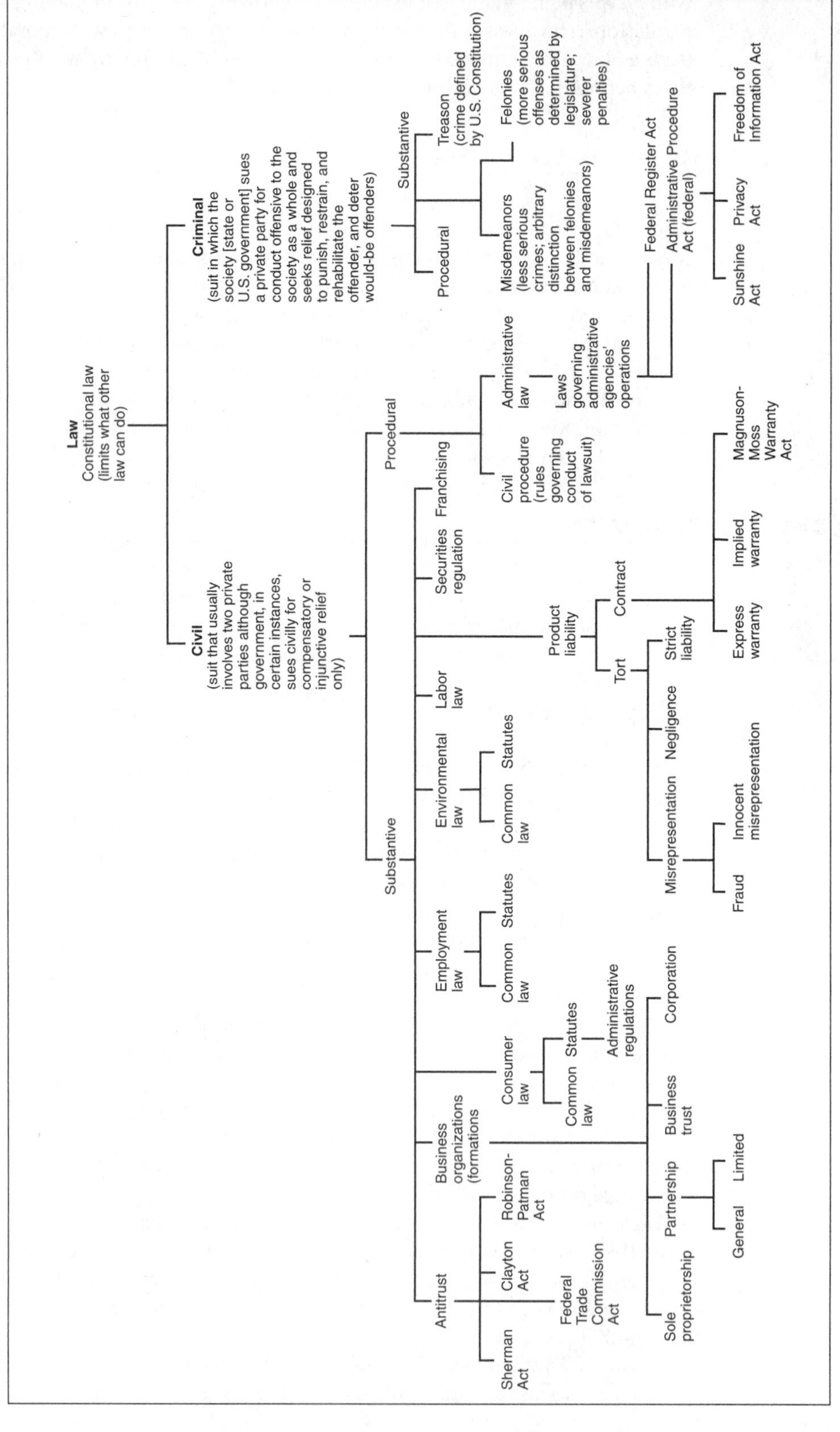

MANAGER'S ETHICAL DILEMMA

Jean was nearing retirement. She lived in a house that was too large for her, so she planned to sell it and move into a condominium that would be more manageable. She was not knowledgeable about property values, so thinking her house was worth $100,000, she listed it with a realtor for that amount. The fair market value for her property was actually closer to $140,000. Given the low price, several persons called and told her they would give her the asking price. Jean orally accepted the first buyer's offer, but put nothing in writing.

That evening she had dinner with Bob, a friend who was also a lawyer. She told Bob that she had sold her house for $100,000. Bob was shocked at how low the price was and told Jean that she should have gotten at least $140,000 to $150,000. Bob then asked Jean if she had signed any document yet. When Jean replied "No," Bob told her that a statute called the Statute of Frauds requires all contracts for the sale of an interest in realty have to be written and signed by the seller to bind the seller.

Bob: Jean, I advise you to call the buyer and tell him that you have changed your mind.

Jean: But, Bob, I gave the seller my word to sell it to him for $100,000. It wouldn't be morally right to back out now.

Bob: Jean, this is a matter of money, $40,000 or $50,000 to be specific. You are going to retire soon and you will need that money to supplement your pension.

What ethical conflicts are present in this scenario? If you were Jean, what would you do?

include stockholders, customers, employees, the community in which the business operates, and society in general.

Business ethics relate to legal ethics in several ways. The ethic of positive law sets an ethical floor. If business ethics conflict with or do less than the positive law requires, persons following business ethics should be prepared to be punished.

Some objectives of positive law are the promotion of justice, speed, and economy. Positive law should be flexible, yet stable and knowable.

The Manager's Ethical Decision Model provides a step-by-step process that can assist persons confronting ethical issues.

Discussion Questions

1. A movement on in certain sectors of the United States supports a "no consumption" day. In other words, some persons believe that excessive consumerism is "sick." That is, excessive consumption exploits the environment at unsustainable levels as well as devaluing time spent with families and friends on matters unrelated to wealth accumulation (such as having a family picnic or going fishing). What philosophies discussed in this chapter are implicit in "no consumption" days? What approach should a clothing manufacturer take when confronted with a petition circulated in the community urging citizens to participate in a "no buy" day?
2. A surrogate mother was implanted with the zygote (fertilized genetic matter) of a married man and woman (the commissioning parents), who desired to have their "own child." The commissioning parents were of different races; the mother was Filipina and the father Caucasian. They entered a contract with a surrogate mother, who was African-American, who agreed to be implanted with the commissioning couple's zygote and carry it to term. The surrogate mother was paid for this service and was also to renounce any parental claim to the child. Prior to giving birth the surrogate mother repudiated the surrogacy contract and sued for custody of "her" child. How is this case different from the *Baby M* case presented in this chapter? [*Johnson v. Calvert*, 19 Cal. Rptr. 2d 494 (1993)].
3. You are president of BMA, a company that makes computers, that it sells worldwide. The company sells to a largely upscale market with particular emphasis on business and professional clients. As part of the marketing strategy, BMA has sponsored on national TV

the Professional Golf Championship, an event that draws the best golfers worldwide. The event is scheduled to be played next year at Pleasant Hills Country Club, which has an internationally famous golf course that has hosted several world-class golf tournaments in the past. The club receives about $250,000 in net income from TV sponsors, the sale of food, tickets, and other concessions operating during the tournament. Also, the club gains enormous prestige from hosting such highly visible events. The club also does not admit women, minority, or Jewish members. This fact has come to light as you are in the final stages of confirming arrangements for next year's tournament. You fear that the national media will learn of this fact. Several contestants in the tournament are African Americans and some others are Jewish. What business ethics occur to you in deciding what course of conduct to take? Are any other values (ethics) discussed in this chapter relevant to resolving the matter?

4. Guy Burgess was the manager of Mother's Home Cooking Shops. Guy held traditional values and emphasized them when instructing his employees and conducting his business, a chain of restaurants and grocery stores catering to motorists on U.S. interstate highways in the southeastern United States. Guy determined that two waitresses and a male cook were homosexual. He immediately fired them although the sexual preference of each was not apparent to any customers or other workers. Guy sent a memo to all 9,000 company employees saying that homosexual employees would be dismissed because "Mother's Home Cooking Shops were founded on concepts of traditional American values. Employment of persons whose sexual preference fails to demonstrate normal heterosexual values which have been the foundation of families in our society is inconsistent with perceived values of our customer base."

   You are Guy Burgess's immediate superior and must review this policy that Guy has drafted. What action should you take based on business ethics? On other ethics discussed in this chapter?

5. The U.S. Secretary of Transportation announced a zero tolerance program for enforcing U.S. drug laws. Under the program ships and vehicles carrying *any* amount of illegal drugs are subject to confiscation by the U.S. Coast Guard. A boat seized under the zero tolerance program will be returned to its owners only when allegations of illegal drugs on board turn out to be false. If the allegations are true, the boat is turned over to the U.S. Customs Service to be auctioned off. Under the zero tolerance program the Coast Guard seized a $2.5 million, 133-foot yacht that contained a teaspoon of marijuana. Only the crew of six, not the owners or other passengers, were on board at the time of seizure. Discuss the legal ethics involved in the zero tolerance program that permit such a result.

6. The Railway Labor Executives Association, an unincorporated association representing all crafts of railroad workers in the United States, sued the U.S. Secretary of Transportation over regulations requiring that blood and urine samples be taken from all crew members of a train involved in various events. Among the events giving rise to the blood and urine testing are: major train accidents involving a fatality, release of hazardous material with either evacuation or injury, or $500,000 damage to railroad property; impact accidents involving a reportable injury or damage to railroad property of $50,000; and fatal accidents involving the death of an on-duty railroad employee. The blood samples are to be taken at independent medical facilities by qualified medical professionals or technicians. Refusal to provide the sample results in a nine-month period of disqualification. The regulations authorize railroads to require covered employees to submit to breath or urine tests when a supervisor has a reasonable suspicion that an employee is under the influence or impaired by alcohol or drugs. To require a urine test, two supervisors must have reasonable suspicion, and, if drug use is suspected, one of them must have been trained in spotting drug use.

   This case had no factual disputes except the extent of alcohol and drug abuse in the railroad industry and the number of accidents involving either substance. The record shows that between 1975 and 1984, 37 of 791 fatalities caused by railroad employees (or 4.7 percent) resulted from accidents or incidents involving drug use. The Federal Railroad Administration (FRA) contended that the problem was more serious than 4.7 percent would indicate because of underreporting by the railroad industry of alcohol and drug involvement, because of the increased dangers involved in railroad transport of hazardous materials, and because drug and alcohol abuse has become more pervasive in recent years. The federal district court upheld the FRA regulations.

On appeal, the U.S. Court of Appeals for the Ninth Circuit analyzed the case in the following terms: "On the one side of the balance are the railroad employees' reasonable expectations of privacy and on the other side is the governmental interest in the safe and efficient operation of the railroads for the benefit of railroad employees and the public affected by that operation." The court of appeals then proceeded to invalidate the regulations on grounds that they violated the U.S. Constitution's prohibition of unreasonable searches and seizures under the Fourth Amendment. The U.S. Supreme Court ultimately upheld the regulations. What legal ethics are present in this decision? What business ethics are involved? [*Skinner v. Railway Labor Executives' Ass'n*, 489 U.S. 602 (1989)]

7. In some countries, notably France and Italy, the reputed practice of businesspeople is to keep two sets of books: one for the tax assessor, which understates income, and the other for themselves, which accurately reflects business earnings. How would the various legal ethics view this situation? Would they all condemn this conduct?
8. Larry Wieland audited the Falconer Company's books. During the audit, Larry discovered that a company clerk was embezzling on a regular basis. He reported his findings to Falconer's president, Harvey Slater, who asked the amount of the embezzlement. Upon being told the employee was stealing $3,000 per year, Slater replied, "Don't say anything. The clerk is worth $18,000, his salary is $10,000, and he's stealing $3,000, so the company is coming out ahead." What legal ethics does Slater's remark reflect? What legal ethics does it ignore?
9. The economy was in a recession. The United Motor Manufacturing Company had to lay off 30 percent of its workforce because of low demand for its cars. Because the most recently hired employees were minorities and women, the layoffs would fall most heavily on them. Suppose no positive law requires any order for layoffs. Devise a layoff scheme that will promote the natural law ethic, the utility ethic, and the ethic of custom.
10. Diane Wentworth was a 30-year-old MBA who worked for a *Fortune* 500 company. Diane performed her job well and socialized extensively with the company president, John Dough. After Diane worked for the firm for eighteen months, Mr. Dough promoted her to a vice-president's position over several more experienced people. Are any legal ethics involved here? If so, what are they?
11. The Foreign Corrupt Practices Act of 1977 makes it a crime for a U.S. corporation or its agent to offer a bribe to an official of a foreign government to obtain business. The act does not forbid paying small amounts (called grease payments) to low-level foreign officials who do minor clerical jobs that speed up the flow of work. The act does not outlaw paying money that foreign officials extort from U.S. business. (In extortion, the demand for money comes from the other person, not the individual paying.) Discuss the act in light of the following legal ethics: positive law, natural law, and sociological jurisprudence.
12. In 1965 Adolpho Perez, an uninsured motorist, had an auto accident in Tucson, Arizona. Perez injured Miss Pinkerton in the mishap. She sued Perez and won a judgment of $2,425.98. Perez immediately went bankrupt to escape paying his debts, which included the $2,425.98 now owed to his accident victim. The state of Arizona has a statute that suspends the driver's license of anyone filing bankruptcy to escape debts resulting from auto accidents. Was this Arizona statute valid, resulting in Perez having to pay Miss Pinkerton to get his driver's license back, or did this statute violate the U.S. Constitution? What does this case tell you about positive law? If Perez escaped paying, how would natural law evaluate it? Is it possible to balance of bankruptcy laws and the right of a creditor to be paid? [*Perez v. Campbell*, 402 U.S. 637 (1971)]
13. Booker ran a migrant agricultural camp in Johnson County, North Carolina. Two of his lieutenants, Rollins and Gibson, brought Gary Walters and two others to the camp from Florida, having promised them free transportation and steady work. But Walters and the others discovered that employment was only occasional, that they would be charged both for their meals while idle and for their transportation from Florida, and that Booker withheld their wages and made

them buy everything they needed at the camp. They were also not allowed to leave the camp until they had paid Booker any debts allegedly owed to him. Booker repeatedly threatened workers at the camp with death or serious injury if they tried to leave without paying their debts. He backed up his threats with severe beatings and assaults with firearms. Prosecutors charged Booker and his lieutenants with violating the U.S. Constitution's Thirteenth Amendment and antislavery statutes. Booker argued that it was not formal slavery but merely a work camp. What was the result? What legal philosophies would find Booker guilty? Innocent? [*United States v. Booker*, 655 F.2d 562 (4th Cir. 1981)]

14. Give an example of a positive law that violates natural law principles.
15. Can a positive law ever be illegal? How?
16. Farouk Al Attar and Rima Al Attar were husband and wife and also business partners in the Apollo Paint and Body Shop. One of their employees, Janet Brunner, told Farouk that she would be volunteering her free time on Saturdays and Sundays and in the evenings with the AIDS Foundation. Brunner promised that her volunteer work would not interfere with her position at Apollo. She told Farouk that the employees at Apollo Paint & Body were not in danger of contracting AIDS because Brunner could not catch AIDS from the patients' touching, sneezing, or breathing on her. Brunner further informed Farouk that his customers did not have to know about her volunteer work.

    Farouk thought about what Brunner had said. Brunner had been a good worker, and, in a way, Farouk admired her community spiritedness and compassion for persons afflicted with AIDS. On the other hand, he did not want to place himself, his family, and the other office workers in jeopardy. He urged Brunner to resign from her volunteer work. She refused. Should Farouk fire her, retain her, or do something else? [*Brunner v. Al Attar*, 786 S.W.2d 784 (Tex. App.—Houston 1st Dist. 1990)].
17. "But he's the star quarterback. The team will lose every game if we lose him," said William Winn, head coach of Kallikak State University. Charges had been brought against Ron Guy, the star football player on Kallikak's team after Guy had been caught by police in an opened appliance store window at 2 A.M. with a television in his hands. The athletic department hired Mack E. Velli, famed criminal lawyer, to represent Guy.

    The case came to trial and Mack made the following argument to the court: "What would happen to gate receipts at Kallikak University, to say nothing of the community's restaurant, motel, and retail store receipts, if Kallikak's football team started losing games because its star was locked up?"

    Mack then put Guy on the stand and asked him this question: "What was in your mind when the police caught you?"

    Guy responded, "I realized just before the police arrived that what I was doing was wrong, and I was *entering*, not exiting, the store to *return* the TV."

    The judge looked down at Guy and said, "You are accused of larceny. The law defines larceny as taking away another's property with intent to deprive the owner of it permanently. Obviously, because you recognized the error of your ways and were in the act returning the property when the police arrived, you did not have the intent to deprive the owner of the television. Charges dismissed!"

    What legal philosophies are implicit in this case?

Suggested Readings

Articles

ADAMS, "Fuzzifying the Natural Law—Legal Positivist Debate," 43 *Buffalo Law Review* 85 (1995).

CARPENTER, "The Problem of Value Judgments as Norms of Law," 7 *Journal of Legal Education* 163 (1954).

CARRASCO, "Critical Race Theory and Development," 91 *Proceedings of the Annual Meeting—American Society of International Law* 427 (1997).

COHEN, "Transcendental Nonsense and the Functional Approach," 35 *Columbia Law Review* 809 (1935).

COLLINS, "Experience-Based Ethics Study: The Implications for Business Law Teachers," 10 *Journal of Legal Studies Education* 107 (1992).

CONRY, "Philosophical Dialogue," 28 *American Business Law Journal* 201 (1990).

DUNFEE, "The Case for Professional Norms of Business Ethics," 25 *American Business Law Journal* 385 (1987).

FARBER, "Is American Law Inherently Racist?" 15 *Thomas M. Cooley Law Review* 361 (1998).

FARBER, "Parody Lost/Pragmatism Regained: The Ironic History of the Coase Theorem," 83 *Virginia Law Review* 397 (1997).

FARBER, "The Jurisprudential Cabride: A Socratic Dialogue," 1992 *Brigham Young University Law Review* 363 (1992).

FISHER, "Positive Law as an Ethic: Illustrations of the Ascent of Positive Law to Ethical Status in the Commercial Sector," 25 *Journal of Business Ethics* 1 (2000).

FISHER, "Positive Law as the Ethic of Our Time," 33 Business Horizons 28 (1990).

FISHER, "The Ethical Consumer: A Rejecter of Positive Law Arbitrage," 25 *Seton Hall Law Review* 230 (1994).

FISHER, "A Role for Jurisprudence in the Business Law Curriculum," 15 *American Business Law Journal* 38 (1977).

GILMORE, "Legal Realism: Its Cause and Cure," 70 *Yale Law Journal* 1037 (1961).

GREEN, "Legal Realism, Lex Fori, and the Choice-of-Law Revolution," 104 *Yale Law Journal* 967 (1995).

HART, "Positivism and the Separation of Law and Morals," 71 *Harvard Law Review* 107 (1958).

HOVENKAMP, "Law and Morals in Classical Legal Thought," 82 *Iowa Law Review* 1327 (1997).

JENNINGS, "Teaching Stakeholder Theory: It's for Strategy, Not Business Ethics," 16 *Journal of Legal Studies Education* 203 (1998).

KELSEN, "On the Basic Norm," 47 *California Law Review* 107 (1959).

LANDERS, "Wittgenstein, Realism, and CLS: Undermining Rule Skepticism," 9 *Law & Philosophy* 177 (1990).

LINDER, "Eisenhower-Era Marxist-Confiscatory Taxation: Requiem for the Rhetoric of Rate Reduction for the Rich," 70 *Tulane Law Review* 905 (1996).

LINDER, "MacKinnon on Marx on Marriage and Morals an Otsogistic Odyssey," 41 *Buffalo Law Review* 451 (1993).

LINDER, "Opening Coase's Other Black Box: Why Workers Submit to Vertical Integration into Firms," 18 *Journal of Corporation Law* 371 (1993).

MAYO and JONES, "Legal-Policy Decision Process: Alternative Thinking and the Predictive Function," 33 *George Washington Law Review* 318 (1964).

McDOUGAL and LASSWELL, "Jurisprudence in Policy-Oriented Perspective," 19 *University of Florida Law Review* 530 (Winter 1966-67).

METZGER, "Law, Social Change, and the Legalization of Management Practice," 33 *Business Horizons* 6 (1990)

NATHAN, "Reflections on Pragmatic Jurisprudence: A Case Study of *Bob Jones University v. United States*," 22 *American Business Law Journal* 227 (1984).

NORTHRUP, "Contemporary Jurisprudence and International Law," 61 *Yale Law Journal* 623 (1952).

REEVES, "Bloom's Global Pedagogical Goals, Business Ethics, and the Legal Environment of Business," 9 *Journal of Legal Studies Education* (1991).

RIVKIN, "Lawyering, Power, and Reform: The Legal Campaign to Abolish the Broad Form Mineral Deed," 66 *Tennessee Law Review* 467 (1999).

SILVERSTEIN, "Managing Corporate Social Responsibility in a Changing Legal Environment," 25 *American Business Law Journal* 523 (1987).

UNGER, "The Critical Legal Studies Movement," 96 *Harvard Law Review* 561 (1983).

Books

AUSTIN, *Lectures on Jurisprudence,* 5th ed. (1885).

BECKER, *The Heavenly City of the Eighteenth-Century Philosophers* (1932).

BODENHEIMER, *Jurisprudence: The Philosophy and Method of the Law* (1962).

CARDOZO, *The Nature of the Judicial Process* (1921).

DWORKIN, *The Philosophy of Law* (1977).

FISHER, *Introduction to the Legal System* (1972).

FRANK, *Courts on Trial* (1949).

FULLER, *The Problems of Jurisprudence* (1949).

GOLDZIHER, *Introduction to Islamic Theology and Law* (1980).

HALL, *Foundations of Jurisprudence* (1930).

HARRISON, *Hume's Theory of Justice* (1981).

HART, *The Concept of Law* (1961).

HOLMES, *The Common Law* (1881).

HUME, *Enquiry Concerning Human Understanding* (1748).

KELSEN, *General Theory of Law and State* (1945).

LLEWELLYN, *The Bramble Bush* (1930).

MORRIS, *The Great Legal Philosophers* (1959).

PIRSIG, *Zen and the Art of Motorcycle Maintenance* (1974).

POUND, *An Introduction to the Philosophy of Law* (1954 ed.).

QUINT, *Jewish Jurisprudence: Its Sources and Modern Applications* (1980).

RAWLS, *A Theory of Justice* (1972).

SUTHERLAND, *An Introduction to Law* (1968).

CHAPTER

2

OVERVIEW AND FINDING THE LAW

"I WILL NOT SAY WITH LORD HALE, THAT 'THE LAW WILL ADMIT NO RIVAL' . . . BUT I WILL SAY THAT IT IS A JEALOUS MISTRESS, AND REQUIRES A LONG AND CONSTANT COURTSHIP. IT IS NOT TO BE WON BY TRIFLING FAVORS BUT BY LAVISH HOMAGE."

Joseph Story, Inaugural Address as Dane Professor of Law at Harvard University (1829)

Positive Law Ethical Problems

"It's being tried twice for the same offense," screamed Jack Rackley, former president of the First National Bank of Tipton and a former member of the board of the First National Bank of Hammon. "Jack Hudson and I were assessed civil penalties for making improper loans to Hudson, former chairman and controlling stockholder of the First National Bank of Tipton and the First National Bank of Hammon. After agreeing to pay 'civil assessments' and agreeing not to engage in banking until further approval by the Office of Controller of the Currency, we were both criminally indicted and convicted based on the same facts as the prior civil case. This is double jeopardy under the Fifth Amendment of the U.S. Constitution!" Was Rackley correct?

This chapter provides an overview of law. We examine forms law takes and then look at several legal classifications. The chapter also gives some idea of how to find the law. Because this book contains legal cases, the chapter tells how to analyze, or brief, a legal case.

FORMS OF LAW

Law comes in many forms, including constitutions, statutes, administrative regulations, and municipal ordinances (see Figure 2.1).

Constitutions

A constitution is the skeleton for a legal system. It sets out the form and basic principles by which the government will operate. It covers matters such as the number of branches of government and the powers given to each. In the Western world, constitutions, such as the U.S. Constitution's Bill of Rights, create individual protections. Constitutions generally are written, although those of some nations, notably Great Britain, are not. They tend to be vague, broad statements that leave to statutes, judges, and administrative agencies the job of making specific rules that govern society. Since constitutions are enduring statements of principle, they are designed so that changing them is difficult.

FIGURE 2.1 Diagram of the Forms of Law

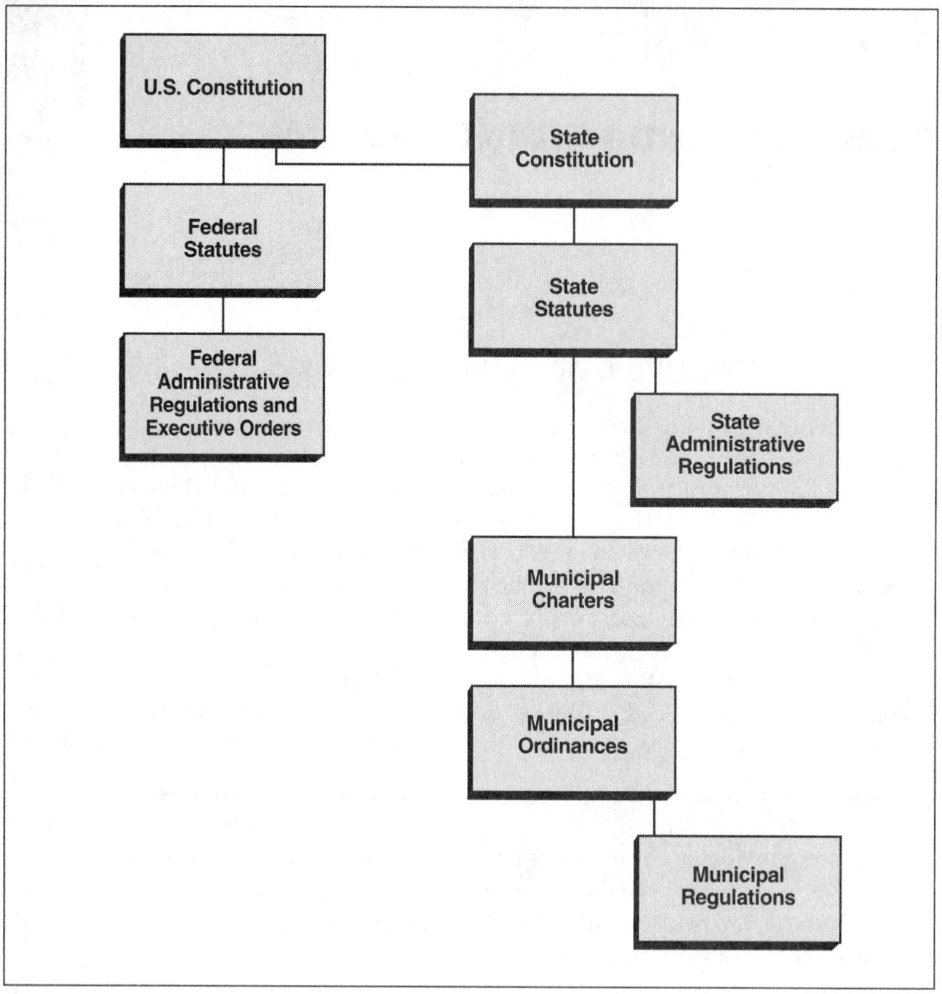
U.S. Constitution
State Constitution
Federal Statutes
State Statutes
Federal Administrative Regulations and Executive Orders
State Administrative Regulations
Municipal Charters
Municipal Ordinances
Municipal Regulations

Statutes

http://

The Library of Congress website: ***http://thomas.loc.gov***

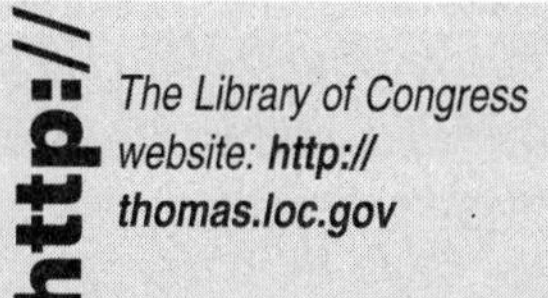

Statutes are enactments by national and state legislatures. Laws passed by city governments are referred to as **ordinances**, not statutes, even though they represent efforts by city councils, which are legislative bodies. States and the national government are separate sovereigns according to the dual sovereignty notion that is the basis for federalism. However, cities, being mere creations of the state in which they are located, are not on the same level politically with either national or state governments.

Uniform Statutes. All states pass many statutes regulating business. With fifty sovereign states, fifty different rules could regulate the same thing. For example, each state could have a different rule on when a contract exists. Wide differences in legal rules on the same matter are generally undesirable for the many firms doing business in several states. Business generally favors uniformity and simplicity in order to promote efficiency. Consider the problem of the Michigan salesperson who may think she has a million dollar-contract made in Louisiana "in the bag," only to learn that Louisiana law would not enforce the deal even though the deal would be enforceable if subject to Michigan law.

To help states make laws regulating business more uniform, a private group of legal scholars and business lawyers called the **National Conference of Commissioners on Uniform State Laws** was formed in the 1800s. It drafted **model statutes** to provide the needed regulation in the most effective, efficient way. The model statutes were actually not "laws" at all because the commissioners had no lawmaking authority. The commissioners would present their model statutes to each state's legislature and urge passage of the particular model act.

Over the years state legislatures have reacted favorably to the model statutes and have passed many into law. This practice has tended to reduce variation in many rules regulating multistate businesses. Among the more important model statutes that have been passed are the Uniform Commercial Code (UCC), the Uniform Partnership Act, and the Uniform Bills of Lading Act. The most significant of the uniform acts is the UCC. It lays down rules for contracts dealing with goods, negotiable instruments, bank deposits and collections, letters of credit, bulk transfers, investment securities, and secured transactions.

Federal Administrative Regulations and Executive Orders

Federal administrative regulations are rules made by federal administrative agencies. (See Chapter 7 for further discussion of this topic.) Executive orders refer to rules made by the president to interpret, promote, or put into operation some statute, treaty, or constitutional provision.

CLASSIFICATIONS OF LAW

Law can be classified in a number of ways. Two of the main classifications are substantive-procedural and civil-criminal.

Substantive Law and Procedural Law

Substantive law refers to rules that govern people's relations with one another in their daily lives. Some examples are a rule of contract law that an acceptance takes effect when sent, the rule of environmental law that a person must have an NPDES[1] permit to discharge into U.S. waters, and the consumer law rule that lets homeowners escape contracts with door-to-door salespeople within three days after the contract is made. Such rules determine what people can do in society.

> http://
>
> *Access to public statutes can be obtained through* ***http://ww1.access.gpo.gov/nara/nara005.html***

Contrast substantive law with **procedural law**. Procedural laws are rules of legal administration. Statutes of limitations, for instance, are usually procedural laws that tell us that a suit against someone must be filed within a specified time period. The rule setting the number of people on a jury is procedural because it deals with an administrative matter. Unlike substantive law, it does not tell people how to act in their everyday lives.

[1] The National Pollutant Discharge Elimination System is a permit system to control water pollution. It was established by the Clean Water Act.

Civil Law and Criminal Law

Law can be divided into civil law and criminal law. Figure 2.2 shows civil law and criminal law and many of their subcategories.

Civil law refers to several things. For our purposes, it refers principally to rules that determine rights and duties between and among private individuals, for example, rules involving tort, contract, and property law. Civil law also has another meaning: the law of certain European and other countries relies on codes (lengthy statutes) to a greater extent than the discretionary power of a judge (common law) to make rules. France is a civil law country because it relies on a code for the source of its rules. But the important definition of civil law for our purposes is the establishment of legal relations between private parties.

Criminal law refers to the rules designed to protect and vindicate society's interest with respect to individuals. For example, in a murder, even though only one member of society is killed, society is deemed to be harmed. Such outrageous, antisocial conduct threatens the tacit bond of restraint that distinguishes civilization from the jungle.

Differences between Civil and Criminal Law

Civil Law Objectives. Several differences distinguish civil from criminal law. First, each has a different objective. Civil law is generally **compensatory**, whereas criminal law is generally **punitive**. For example, when one person sues another for breaking a contract, the party suing (the plaintiff) hopes to recover damages sustained as a result of the other person's (the defendant's) breach of the plaintiff's rights. Even though the damage recovery (called **compensatory damages**) is taken from the defendant and turned over to the plaintiff, this action is not considered punishment of the defendant. The reasoning is that the defendant is only paying for harm that has been caused, which agrees with basic natural law concepts of fairness. It also follows historical jurisprudence, which requires wrongdoers to compensate their victims, and is a long-standing community custom.

Contrast compensatory damages with a second type of recovery sometimes awarded in civil law: **punitive damages**. As the word *punitive* suggests, punitive damages are designed to punish wrongdoers, not to compensate victims for harm sustained. Punitive damages represent an exception to the general rule that civil law does not punish. Because punitive damages do punish, they are awarded when the defendant's conduct is particularly reprehensible. Punitive damages are most commonly awarded in intentional **tort** cases—cases in which the defendant often intends to harm someone. For example, spitting in someone's face is the intentional tort of battery (unauthorized touching of another) and might not result in any compensatory damages, although punitive damages are appropriate owing to the offensive, outrageous character of the spitting. Punitive damages are not awarded in all or even most successful intentional tort suits, because not all intentional torts involve reprehensible conduct.

Sometimes civil and criminal law objectives overlap. For example, one objective of criminal law is to punish violators. Generally civil law aims only to "make the victim whole" by awarding compensatory damages. However, occasionally civil law assesses punitive damages—that is, damages designed to punish the wrongdoer—against someone who intentionally harms another.

Nominal damages are a final type of damage awarded in civil law. Nominal damages, as the name suggests, involve a nominal amount of money—one dollar or six cents, for example. This recovery is given to the plaintiff to indicate that the plaintiff's

FIGURE 2.2 Overview of Civil and Criminal Law

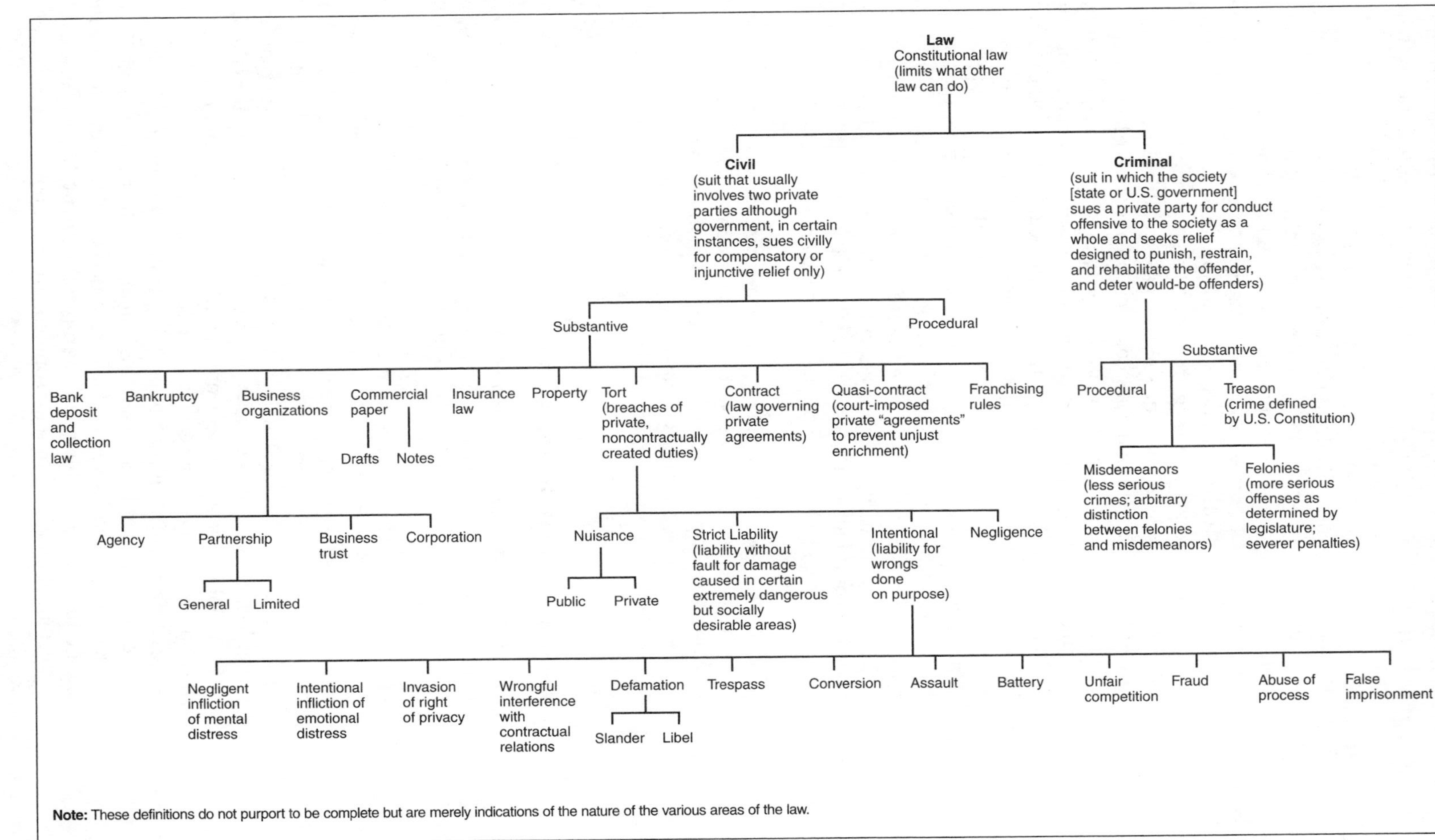

Note: These definitions do not purport to be complete but are merely indications of the nature of the various areas of the law.

rights have been broken but that no actual damages have been sustained. For example, if the defendant who agreed to buy a car from the plaintiff for $400 broke the contract, and if the plaintiff sold the car to another person for $500 and then sued the defendant for breach of contract, then clearly, the plaintiff had a right breached but sustained no actual damages.

Equitable Remedies. In addition to the three types of damages—compensatory, punitive, and nominal—civil law remedies include the equitable remedies of **an injunction** (a court order to do or not do something) and **specific performance** (a court order to do what one has by contract agreed to do). **Equitable remedies** arose in ancient England when litigants who had lost their cases in law court went to the king's minister to tell him their troubles. The king's minister was called the chancellor and was known as the king's conscience. Occasionally, the chancellor was convinced that the litigant in the law court lost because the strict common law rules were formulated without anticipation of this person's unusual situation. If he believed the loser had been ill-treated by the common law courts, the chancellor issued an injunction against the sheriff executing the law court's judgment. Other losers in law courts heard about the chancellor's injunctions against unfair common law court judgments and rushed to the chancellor to convince him of the injustice of the law courts' handling of their cases. Soon a court developed around the person of the chancellor to handle all such cases. This court became known as the **equity** (or chancery) **court**; *equity* means "fairness," which the chancellor supposedly dispensed.

The law court judges, hearing about how the chancellor in effect overruled or nullified law court judgments, took the matter to the king. The king settled the matter of which court prevailed when the law court judges and chancellor clashed by dividing the jurisdiction between law and equity courts so that the average case would be decided by a law court. Equity courts were given jurisdiction to settle cases only in which legal remedies (typically, the award of money damages) were inadequate. This situation can occur when one contracts to buy a unique item (an antique, a rare gem, or land) but the seller refuses to carry out the contract. A rare gem or any piece of the earth's surface is unique, and money is inadequate to procure it because only one person has claim to the item.

Criminal Law Objectives

Thus far, we have discussed the objectives of civil law. Now we briefly turn our attention to criminal law objectives. One most frequently mentioned objective is punishment of those who break society's criminal laws. This objective is sometimes referred to as **retribution**, which occurs by imprisonment, imposition of fines, or a combination of the two. The death penalty also effects the retribution goal.

The punitive aspect of criminal law is but one of four ends of that branch of the law. Others frequently mentioned include **restraint**, **deterrence**, and **rehabilitation**. Restraint occurs when people are convicted and imprisoned so that they cannot repeat—at least not immediately—the sort of antisocial activity that landed them in prison. Deterrence occurs when one person's punishment by the criminal law system serves to inhibit or stop other would-be criminals from committing crimes. This justification is commonly given for the death penalty. The rehabilitation objective of criminal law is usually more a hope than a reality. Too often, it is "achieved" by sending people to prison for several years where, after being counseled by various prison officials, they emerge several years later as persons skilled in effecting more sophisticated crimes. Perhaps this point is an overstatement, but the restraint, vengeance, and deterrent objectives of imprisonment are more obviously served by the criminal justice system as it now exists. Rehabilitation seems better achieved by probation so that a person can learn a skill as well as resist the social pressures to commit crimes. Probation, on the other hand, has short-run social costs, such as subjecting other members of society to the criminal's **recidivism**.

Plaintiffs. Aside from their objectives, other differences exist between civil and criminal law. The plaintiff in criminal cases is always a national, state, or municipal government. The official who represents the government as attorney is usually called the **prosecutor**, **district attorney**, or **attorney general**. In civil cases, the plaintiff is usually a private party, such as a business or an individual.

Burden of Proof. One final distinction between civil and criminal law lies in the different burdens of proof the respective plaintiffs must satisfy in each type of case. In civil cases, plaintiffs must generally prove their case by a **preponderance of the evidence**. In a criminal case, the government (the plaintiff) must prove its case **beyond a reasonable doubt**, a heavier burden than that which the civil plaintiff must satisfy. The objective of the heavier criminal burden on the government is not to promote crime in the streets but to effect the presumption of innocence long recognized in Anglo-American jurisprudence. One is not a criminal until adjudged to be such in a court of law. Anglo-American jurisprudence has followed the philosophy, "Better to let a hundred criminals go free than convict one innocent person."

Possible Overlap of Civil and Criminal Law

Legal Effect of Drunk Driving. Civil and criminal law may overlap because a fact situation could give rise to both a criminal lawsuit and a civil lawsuit. For example, if a person gets drunk, drives a car carelessly, and kills another person, the prosecutor could sue the drunk driver for manslaughter (a criminal lawsuit), and the surviving family of the person killed could sue the drunk driver for wrongful death (a civil lawsuit). In other words, two lawsuits may arise from the same basic fact pattern.

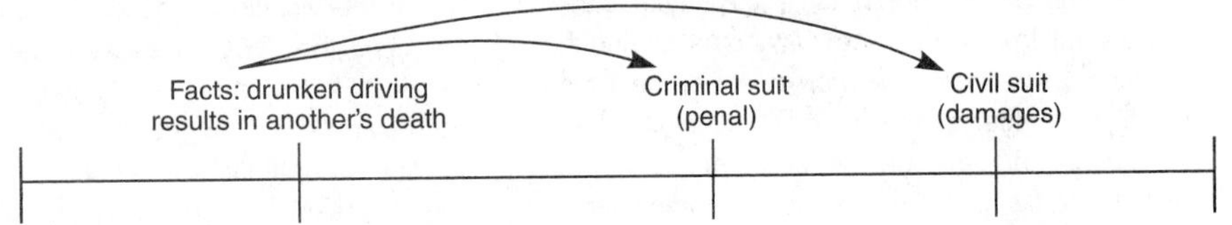

Legal Effect of Sherman Act Violation. Another example of the possible civil-criminal overlap occurs when a Sherman Act Section 1 case is brought by both the federal government suing criminally and a private party suing civilly for damages (which are tripled under the Sherman Act to encourage private parties' enforcement of this act) sustained as a result of others' violating Section 1 of the Sherman Act. Diagrammatically the resulting lawsuits would appear as follows:

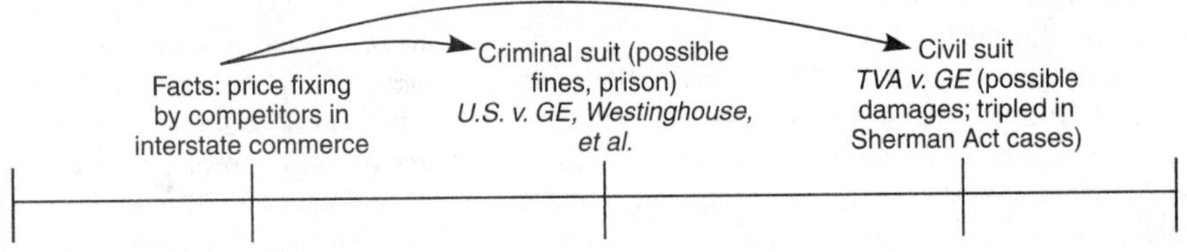

Not all wrongful acts give rise to both civil and criminal lawsuits against the same individual. The Sherman Act does allow both types of suits to be brought for having done the same act. Why is facing both civil and criminal proceedings for the same act not a violation of the constitutional principle that no person may be put in jeopardy twice for the same crime? The answer is apparent when one considers the nature of the two suits being brought against one person for the same act: That person is not being tried twice criminally but only once criminally; the other suit is civil, not criminal. The double jeopardy prohibition only prohibits being tried *criminally* more than once for the same act by the same sovereign, that is, the federal government or a particular state.

Incidentally, no law dictates a particular order in which civil or criminal suits must be brought when two such suits arise from the same general facts. However, because the government usually has more resources to develop evidence, because such evidence is a matter of public record if introduced in the criminal case, and because a criminal conviction is usually harder to get, a civil plaintiff often waits to sue until after the government has sued criminally on the matter.

If the federal government brings two cases arising out of the same facts, is it considered double jeopardy? The *Hudson* case illustrates that even federal judges can disagree about this matter; the U.S. district court held it was double jeopardy and the U.S. Court of Appeals held that it was not. The matter then was taken to the U.S. Supreme Court, whose decision follows.

Hudson v. United States
118 S.Ct. 488 (1997)

Background and Facts:

During the early and mid-1980s, John Hudson was the chairman and controlling shareholder of the First National Bank of Tipton (Tipton) and the First National Bank of Hammon (Hammon). Tipton and Hammon banks are in two small towns in western Oklahoma. During the same period, Jack Rackley was president of the Tipton bank and a member of the board of directors of the Hammon bank, and Larry Baresel was a member of the board of directors of both the Tipton and Hammon banks.

An examination of Tipton and Hammon banks led the Office of Comptroller of the Currency (OCC) to conclude that petitioners Hudson, Rackley, and Baresel had used their bank positions to arrange a series of loans to third parties, in violation of various federal banking statutes and regulations. According to the OCC, those loans, while nominally made to third parties, were in reality made to Hudson in order to enable him to redeem bank stock that he had pledged as collateral on defaulted loans.

On February 13, 1989, OCC issued a Notice of Assessment of Civil Money Penalty. "The notice alleged that petitioners had violated [banking laws] . . . by causing the banks with which they were associated to make loans to nominee borrowers in a manner that unlawfully allowed Hudson to receive the benefit of the loans." The notice also alleged that the illegal loans resulted in losses to the Tipton and Hammon banks of almost $900,000 and contributed to the failure of those banks. However, the notice contained no allegation of any harm to the government as a result of petitioners' conduct. "After taking into account the size of the financial resources and the good faith of the petitioners, the gravity of the violations and other matters as justice may require, the OCC assessed penalties of $100,000 against Hudson and $50,000 each against both Rackley and Baresel. On August 31, 1989, OCC also issued a Notice of Intention to Prohibit Further Participation against each petitioner. These notices, which were premised on the identical allegations that formed the basis for the previous notices, informed petitioners that OCC intended to bar them from further participation in the conduct of any insured depositary institution."

In October 1989, petitioners resolved the OCC proceedings against them by each entering into a Stipulation and Consent Order. These consent orders provided that Hudson, Baresel, and Rackley would pay assessments of $16,500, $15,000, and $12,500 respectively. In addition, each petitioner agreed not to "participate in any manner" in the affairs of any banking institution without the written authorization of the OCC and all other relevant regulatory agencies.

In August 1992, petitioners were indicted in the Western District of Oklahoma in a 22-count indictment on charges of conspiracy, misapplication of bank funds, and making false bank entries. The violations charged in the indictment rested on the same lending transactions that formed the basis for the prior administrative actions brought by OCC. Petitioners moved to dismiss the indictment on double jeopardy grounds, but the District Court denied the motions. The Court of Appeals affirmed the District Court's holding on the nonparticipation sanction issue, but vacated and remanded to the District Court on the money sanction issue.

The District Court on remand granted petitioners' motion to dismiss the indictments. This time the government appealed and the Court of Appeals reversed. That court held, following *Halper* (another case dealing with the double jeopardy issue) that the actual fines imposed by the government were not so grossly disproportional to the proven damages to the government as to render the sanctions "punishment" for double jeopardy purposes. The case was then taken to the U.S. Supreme Court.

Body of Opinion

Justice Rehnquist

The Double Jeopardy Clause provides that no "person [shall] be subject for the same offense to be twice put in jeopardy of life or limb." We have long recognized that the Double Jeopardy Clause does not prohibit the imposition of an additional sanction that could "in common parlance" be described as punishment.... The Clause protects only against the imposition of multiple *criminal* punishments for the same offense....

Whether a particular punishment is criminal or civil is, at least initially, a matter of statutory construction.... A court must first ask whether the legislature, "in establishing the penalizing mechanism, indicated either expressly or impliedly a preference for one label or the other."... Even in those cases where the legislature "has indicated an intention to establish a civil penalty, we have inquired further whether the statutory scheme was so punitive either in purpose or effect... as to "transform what was clearly intended as a civil remedy into a criminal penalty."...

In making this latter determination, the factors listed in *Kennedy v. Mendoza-Martinez* [a 1963 U.S. Supreme Court case]... provide useful guideposts, including (1) "whether the sanction involves an affirmative disability or restraint"; (2) "whether it has historically been regarded as a punishment"; (3) "whether it comes into play only on a finding of scienter"; (4) "whether its operation will promote the traditional aims of punishment-retribution and deterrence"; (5) "whether the behavior to which it applies is already a crime"; (6) "whether an alternative purpose to which it may rationally be connected is assignable for it"; and (7) "whether it appears excessive in relation to the alternative purpose assigned." It is important to note, however, that "those factors must be considered in relation to the statute on its face,"...and "only the clearest proof" will suffice to override legislative intent and transform what has been denominated a civil remedy into a criminal penalty....

Our opinion in *United States v. Halper* marked the first time we applied the Double Jeopardy Clause to a sanction without first determining that it was criminal in nature. In that case, Irwin Halper was convicted of... violating the criminal false claims statute... based on his submission of 65 inflated Medicare claims each of which overcharged the Government by $9.00. He was sentenced to two years' imprisonment and fined $5,000. The Government then brought an action against Halper under the civil False Claims Act.... The remedial provisions of the False Claims Act provided that a violation of the Act rendered one "liable to the United States Government for a civil penalty of $2,000, an amount equal to 2 times the amount of damages the Government sustains because of the act of that person, and costs of the civil action."... Given Halper's 65 separate violations of the Act, he appeared to be liable for a penalty of $130,000, despite the fact he actually defrauded the Government of less than $600. However, the District Court concluded that a penalty of this magnitude would violate the Double Jeopardy Clause in light of Halper's previous criminal conviction. While explicitly recognizing that the statutory damages provision of the Act "was not itself a criminal punishment," the District Court nonetheless concluded that application of the full penalty to Halper would constitute a second "punishment" in violation of the Double Jeopardy Clause....

On direct appeal, this Court affirmed. As the *Halper* court saw it, the imposition of "punishment" of any kind was subject to double jeopardy constraints, and whether a sanction constituted "punishment" depended primarily on whether it served the traditional "goals of punishment," namely "retribution and deterrence."... Any sanction that was so "overwhelmingly disproportionate" to the injury caused that it could not "fairly be said *solely* to serve [the] remedial purpose" of compensating the government for its loss, was thought to be explainable only as "serving either retributive or deterrent purposes."...

The analysis applied by the *Halper* Court deviated from our traditional double jeopardy doctrine in two key respects. First, the *Halper* Court bypassed the threshold question whether the successive punishment at issue is a "criminal" punishment. Instead, it focused on whether it was civil or criminal, was so grossly disproportionate to the harm caused as to constitute "punishment." In so doing, the Court elevated a single *Kennedy* [the *Kennedy* case] factor—whether the sanction appeared excessive in relation to its nonpunitive purpose—to dispositive status. But as we emphasized in *Kennedy* itself, no one factor should be considered controlling as they "may often point in differing directions."... The second significant departure in *Halper* was the Court's decision to "assess the character of the actual sanctions imposed,"... "rather than, as *Kennedy* demanded, evaluating the "statute on its face" to determine whether it provided for what amounted to a criminal sanction."...

We believe that *Halper*'s deviation from longstanding double jeopardy principles was ill considered. As subsequent cases have demonstrated, *Halper*'s test... has proved unworkable. We have since recognized that all civil penalties have some deterrent effect.... If a sanction must be "solely" remedial (i.e., entirely nondeterrent) to avoid implicating the Double Jeopardy Clause, then no civil penalties are beyond the scope of the Clause....

Applying the traditional double jeopardy principles to the facts of this case, it is clear that the criminal prosecution of these petitioners would not violate the Double Jeopardy Clause. It is evident that Congress intended the OCC money penalties and debarment sanctions imposed for violating [the federal statutes at issue]... which authorize the imposition of monetary penalties for violations of [federal law]... expressly provide that such penalties are "civil."...

Turning to the second stage of the *Ward* test, we find that there is little evidence, much less the clearest proof that we require, suggesting that either OCC money penalties or debarment sanctions are "so punitive in form and effect as to render them criminal despite Congress' intent to the contrary."... First, neither money penalties nor debarment have historically been viewed as punishment. We have long recognized that "revocation of a privilege voluntarily granted," such as a debarment, "is characteristically free of the punitive criminal element."... Similarly, "the payment of fixed or variable sums of money [is a] sanction which has been recognized as enforceable by civil proceedings since the original revenue law of 1789....

Second, the sanctions imposed do not involve an "affirmative disability or restraint," as that term is normally understood. While petitioners have been prohibited from further participating in the banking industry, this is "certainly nothing approaching the infamous punishment of imprisonment."... Third, neither sanction comes into play "only" on a finding of scienter. The provisions under which money penalties are imposed... allow for the assessment of a penalty against any person "who violates" any of the underlying banking statutes, without regard to the violator's state of mind. "Good faith" is considered by OCC in determining the amount of the penalty to be imposed... but a penalty can be imposed even in the absence of bad faith.... Similarly, while debarment may be imposed for a "willful" disregard "for the safety or soundness of an insured depository institution," willfulness is not a prerequisite to debarment; it is sufficient that the disregard for the safety and soundness of the institution was "continuing."...

Fourth, the conduct for which OCC sanctions are imposed may also be criminal.... This fact is insufficient to render the money penalties and debarment sanctions criminally punitive....

Finally, we recognize that the imposition of both money penalties and debarment sanctions will deter others from emulating petitioners' conduct, a traditional goal of criminal punishment. But the mere presence of this purpose is insufficient to render a sanction criminal, as deterrence "may serve civil as well as criminal goals."... To hold the mere presence of a deterrent purpose renders such sanctions "criminal" for double jeopardy purposes would severely limit the Government's ability to engage in effective regulation of institutions such as banks....

Judgment and Result

The U.S. Supreme Court held that the first civil suit by the OCC imposing debarment and money payments followed by a criminal lawsuit for essentially the same acts did not violate the Fifth Amendment's Double Jeopardy Clause.

Questions

1. Has the Supreme Court ever held that a criminal action followed by a civil action based on essentially the same facts could violate the Double Jeopardy Clause? The Court mentioned the *Halper* case in which the Court stated that a criminal suit resulting in a fine and prison term followed by a civil suit by the Government for the same offense could violate the Double Jeopardy Clause. There the Court said that "a civil penalty may be so extreme ... as to constitute punishment." Is not the precluding of someone from engaging in banking coupled with a significant monetary penalty not "extreme" punishment, as was done in *Hudson*?
2 Does the Rehnquist opinion in *Hudson* say that a criminal case followed by a civil case based on essentially the same facts can never be double jeopardy?
3. What is the reason for imposing criminal and civil sanctions on essentially the same facts?
4. The *Hudson* opinion criticizes the *Halper* decision for laying out an unworkable test for determining when criminal followed by civil proceedings for essentially the same facts violate the Double Jeopardy Clause. Yet, another concurring opinion in *Hudson*, omitted, points out that the *Halper* decision in 1989 was unanimous. Does this suggest that the line between civil and criminal is difficult to draw for double jeopardy purposes?

Diagrams of Civil and Criminal Law

Figure 2.2 is a traditional way of looking at law. The two broad categories of civil law and criminal law are broken down into substantive and procedural rules. There are civil procedural laws, such as a statute of limitations for breach of contract, and criminal procedural laws, such as a statute of limitations for the crime of federal income tax evasion. Civil substantive laws include tort law, which deals with broad classes of breaches of noncontractual duties that do not arise by contract; specific examples of torts are fraud and negligence. An example of criminal substantive laws is the law forbidding arson. Figure 2.2 looks detailed but is by no means complete. Many legal theories are not shown here.

FINDING THE LAW

Finding National and State Constitutions

U.S. Code. The national and state governments are legally separate sovereigns with lawmaking authority. The national government and each of the fifty states have a set of law books, called a code, which usually contains the constitution of the applicable government unit. The U.S. Constitution is also in the books containing the U.S. Code Annotated. Technically, the Constitution has not been codified; however, it is contained in the same books as the U.S. Code Annotated. When the code contains reference to cases interpreting it, it is called the annotated code. The **unannotated** version is legislative law without reference to case interpretations.

State Code. Each state has a constitution, and, similarly, each state has a code that contains a copy of the state constitution. Again, state constitutions are usually not part of the state code in a legal sense but are contained in the same books as the state code. Also, state codes come in **annotated** versions as well as unannotated versions. Annotated codes have footnotes referring to cases interpreting particular code words. Because of this feature, annotated codes are considered more helpful than unannotated codes. A state code could have the word *code* in its name, such as Tennessee Code Annotated or Iowa Code Annotated, but could be known by other names, such as New Mexico Statutes Annotated, Michigan Compiled Laws, or New York Consolidated Laws.

Finding Legislative Enactments

The reason this section has been called "Finding Legislative Enactments" instead of "Finding Statutes" requires a bit of explanation. When a legislator drops a proposed law into the hopper in the state or national legislature, this proposed statute is technically called a bill. If the bill is passed by the legislature and signed into law by the chief executive or becomes law over an executive veto, the bill then becomes an act (also called a statute or **session law**). If the matter ended there, the legislatures would wind up producing a series of acts or statutes unrelated in subject matter and not easily accessible, because legislatures obviously do not pass laws in alphabetical order (with Adoptions first and Zoning last, for example).

Codes Organize Statutes by Subject

The solution to the disorganized, uncompiled law problem associated with acts, statutes, or session laws is the code. A **code** is a set of law books that contain the public statutes passed by Congress or by a state legislature. It is organized by subject matter, such as by taxation, domestic law, recording laws, and criminal law. No magic determines how the topics for a code are organized. The selection of topics is to some extent arbitrary and reflects recognized legal subject matters that cover wide areas. For example, criminal law is a more likely general topic than murder. Subject indexes to the codes help identify specific topics. Although municipal (city) codes contain municipal ordinances, only national and state codes are discussed here.

Updating Codes. Copies of the U.S. Code are available in most public libraries and so, most likely, is the state code. Codes are periodically, usually annually, updated by the insertion of **pocket parts** in the back of each of the bound volumes of the code.

Meaning of Codification. A law or statute that has been put into a national or state code is said to have been codified. Codes are arranged according to subject matter called *titles* (general areas of the law such as commercial law, domestic law, and probate law). Each title contains a number of subcategories called sections, which in turn are subdivided into subsections. Thus, referring to a particular part of a code is done in the following manner. The title is given first, then the particular code, followed by the section or sections of the title. For example, Title 5 of the U.S. Code, Section 552 is how one refers to a particular part of the U.S. Code. This reference is usually shortened to 5 U.S.C. § 552, which is known as a cite to a part of the U.S. Code. The date of the code edition is usually included. A similar process takes place when one refers to part of a state code.

Finding Federal Administrative Regulations

Code of Federal Regulations. The Securities and Exchange Commission (SEC), Environmental Protection Agency (EPA), Interstate Commerce Commission (ICC), and various other agencies make law by issuing regulations. At the federal level, most agency regulations are contained in a set of law books called the ***Code of Federal Regulations***, abbreviated *C.F.R.* The *Code of Federal Regulations* is arranged according to titles and sections in much the same way as statutory codes. A customary practice in referring to a *C.F.R.* section is to use the *C.F.R.* cite. An example of a *C.F.R.* cite is 40 *C.F.R.* § 124.2 (1981), the 40 being the title, C.F.R. being the series of books containing federal regulations, and 124.2 being the section. The book's date is usually included, too.

The Federal Register. When a federal agency first promulgates regulations, the regulations are published in the ***Federal Register***, a type of official newspaper and notice giver of the federal government. The *C.F.R.* is revised annually so that those federal regulations made by the agencies since publication of the last annual *C.F.R.* can update the preceding edition of the *C.F.R.*

Between annual publications of the *C.F.R.*, the agencies will be revising their regulations and making new regulations. To find those regs (as regulations are informally but respectfully called) issued after publication of the last *C.F.R.* and before publication of the next *C.F.R.*, it is necessary to consult the *Federal Register*. This process is somewhat tedious, because the *Federal Register* is issued every federal agency business day, Monday through Friday, but *Federal Register* indexes are published periodically for affected *C.F.R.* sections.

States are increasingly developing state register systems to help people find state administrative law.

Finding Information about Federal Agencies

Occasionally a person must find the address, phone number, regional office location nearest them, or some other feature of a federal agency. The *U.S. Government Manual*, published annually, provides this, and much more information. Any public library should have a copy. Also copies can be purchased from the U.S. Government Printing Office for a nominal amount.

Finding Common Law

Only Written Opinions Count. A final source of legal authority is common law, which is law made by judges who settle disputes brought to them by litigants (people who are parties to lawsuits). A judge may announce a decision and provide no opinion or rationale as to why one party prevails over the other. One reason for giving no opinion is a lack of time brought on by the need to settle many cases. Another reason was succinctly stated by Louis Brandeis before his appointment to the U.S. Supreme Court: "I do not wish to argue the matter; therefore, I give no reasons for my decision." Most judges, however, do at least announce orally the reasons they decide a case one way or the other. Yet, such decisions amount to nothing for nonparties to the suit because they are not written down as precedent. Hence, the opinions that are of significance to future litigants in other lawsuits and which function as guideposts for society because they announce rules or the law are found in *written* opinions of judges pursuant to settling a dispute. Written judicial opinions are discussed here.

Courts That Do Not Write Opinions. Most trial court judges do not write opinions in cases they decide because they simply are not required to do so. Traffic court judges, probate court judges, juvenile court judges, small claims court judges, and judges in most state trial courts of general jurisdiction do not write opinions. All of these judges are excused from the task of writing opinions largely because of the need to speed up decision making. The value of having a written opinion is outweighed by the slow-down in decision making created by written opinions and by the need for more judges to handle the extra work that would be brought on by such a requirement.

Courts That Write Opinions. A number of courts do write opinions that are a source of legal authority. Federal district courts, federal courts of appeal, the U.S. Supreme Court, state courts of last resort (usually referred to as state supreme courts, except in New York), and state appellate courts above the trial court level all write opinions.

Reporters

Reporters Contain Common Law. An intricate set of books (called **reporters**) has been established to compile the written opinions of the courts issuing written opinions. (The reporter system is not to be confused with individuals called court reporters, who transcribe comments made in the open courtroom and at depositions.) The books known as reporters look like sets of encyclopedias. Each reporter is made up of many books. A different reporter is established for each different court system. The U.S. Supreme Court opinions are reported in three different sets of reporters: ***United States Reports*** (the official government-published reporter), the ***Supreme Court Reporter***, and ***Lawyers Edition***. U.S. courts of appeals opinions are reported in the ***Federal Reporter***, and federal district courts are reported in the ***Federal Supplement***. In the state of New York, where the highest state court is called the court of appeals, the reporter covering that court is *New York Appellate Reports*. Thus, separate sets of books called reporters cover the different states' appellate courts and all federal courts. Regional reporters (privately published by West Publishing Company) also publish state appellate opinions for states within a particular geographic region. The seven regional reporters are Pacific, North Western, South Western, North Eastern, Atlantic, South Eastern, and Southern.

Case Cites Help Find Cases. The following discussion uses the case of *Hynes v. New York Central Railroad* to explain how to locate a case in a reporter. Cases have cites, which are used to find the case in the law library. Most cases contained in law texts are shortened to remove material irrelevant to its teaching purpose and to simplify case reading considerably for students. However, if students want to read the full opinion and they have an extensive law library nearby (which usually occurs only if a law school or state or federal court law library is available), the cite enables them to do so. Assuming you have the cite to the *Hynes* case, which is 231 N.Y. 229, you can now find the case in the law library. The numbers and letters that make up the case cite mean the following. The 231 refers to the volume number in a series of books called the reporter, the N.Y. tells what reporter the case appears in—here the New York Reports—and the 229 refers to the page number in volume 231 of the New York Reports on which the *Hynes* opinion starts. Much the same system is used for the West Regional Reporters, in which most state cases are also found.

Printed in Figure 2.3 is a portion of the *Hynes* opinion. It is used to illustrate case parts.

Using Computers to Find the Law

Legal research has become computerized. The two major computerized legal research systems are Westlaw and Lexis. Westlaw was developed by the West Publishing Company of St. Paul, Minnesota, the nation's largest law publisher. Lexis was developed by Mead Data Corporation. Both are private, nongovernmental publishers.

Both Westlaw and Lexis use video monitors, computer keyboards, and phone lines to access constitutions, treaties, codes, session laws, cases, regulations, and some bar journals and law reviews that make up the databases of these respective companies. The databases of Lexis and Westlaw differ somewhat, so it is possible that a researcher might find on one what she or he cannot find on the other.

Essentially both Westlaw and Lexis use symbols, key words, and phrases as ways to access legal authority in the database. A key word or phrase is "punched into" the keyboard, sent off, and in a matter of seconds the computer "reads" literally thousands or even millions of pages of statutes and casebooks for a match to the key word or phrase the researcher plugged into his or her research request. The computer reports back the cases, statutes, or whatever was requested, or reports that nothing was found. Usually the researchers modify their requests until they find what they are looking for.

Advantages and Disadvantages of Computerized Legal Research. The advantages of computerized legal research are apparent: time is saved when a computer scans hundreds of books in seconds and reports the results immediately. Also, it permits individually tailored research formats not readily available through traditional, noncomputerized legal research. In particular, computers allow research based on fact patterns, whereas law books are organized around legal theories, not facts.

Certain disadvantages, however, limit computerized legal research. First, the years in the database may be limited. For example, if the database goes back only a certain number of years, cases and statutes and other laws passed or occurring *before* that date would be missed by the research. It is possible that a key decision helpful to the researcher might be found in those missing years. Second, the laws covered in the database may be limited. Some computer databases do not cover all regulations or

FIGURE 2.3 Case Parts Illustrated

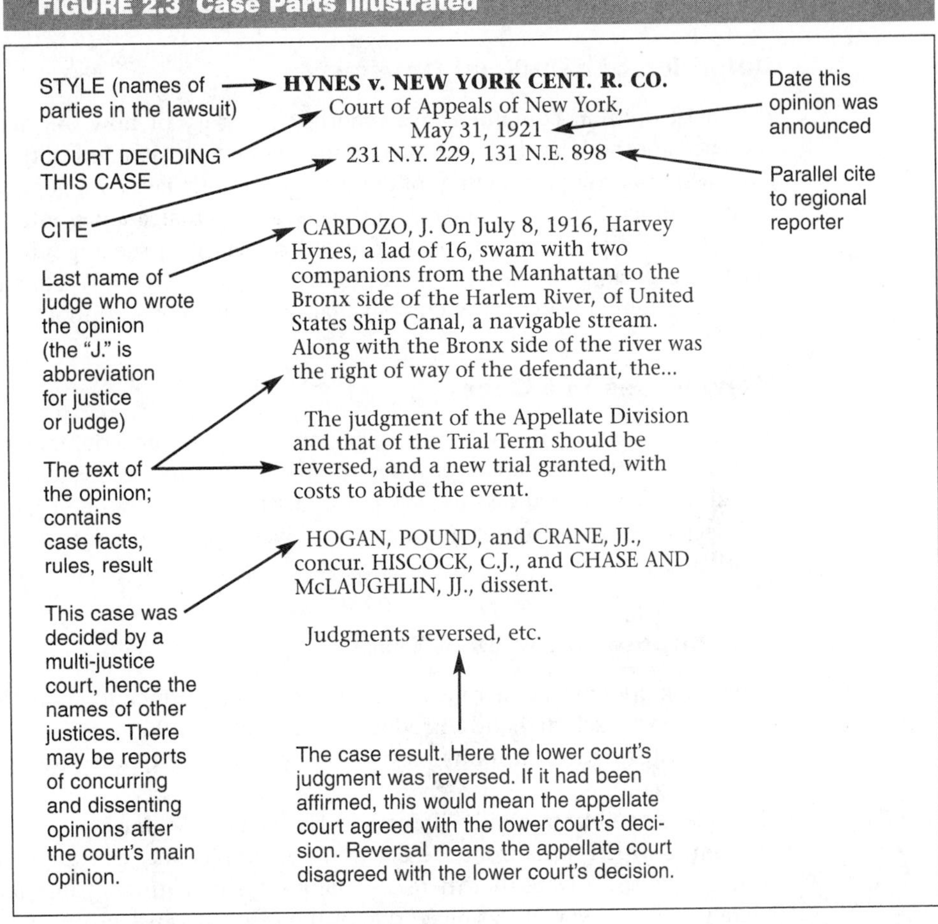

repealed regulations, or legislative reports giving background on statutes or bills pending in Congress or state legislatures. Third, some systems are not user friendly; they have rigid ways of framing research requests and, unless the researcher can come within these request protocols, the request will fail. Finally, computerized research can be costly. The cost of the computerized research systems is usually measured by a monthly rental. The cost for a private attorney to use a law school Westlaw system is often measured in terms of dollars per minute. As of this writing, the rate in one medium-sized U.S. city for Westlaw is $4 per minute with a 20-minute minimum. However, when the cost of hiring someone to conduct this research by hand is compared with an efficient computer operator, the cost of computer research may be lower. Of course, not everyone is competent to use computerized legal research efficiently; to place sophisticated research tools in the hands of the unskilled can be wasteful.

Internet Searches to Find the Law

The Internet is now available to assist in finding the law. If you have a computer with a modem, you, as a practical matter, have a law library.

You should obtain a legally based Internet address so that you can access the law that you want. One Internet address (among many) valid for locating the U.S. Constitution as well as other legal materials is http://www.access.gpo.gov/nara/nara005.html,which gives access to statutes.

HOW TO ANALYZE A CASE

Definition of a Judicial Opinion

A judicial opinion contained in a reporter is a story of how one person allegedly breached another's legal rights. The opinion contains a statement of the relevant facts, a discussion of rules competing for application to these facts, and a judicial resolution of this conflict. Issues or problems, both legal and factual, are presented in an opinion of a case. For example, in a breach of contract case a legal issue might be, "Can a breach of contract occur before the date of contract performance is due?" A factual issue would be, "Did defendant sign the document that purports to be a contract?"

Many Issues in a Case

A case could have many issues—legal and factual, procedural and substantive. Generally, by the time a case reaches an appellate court, the issues are reduced to a few, and they almost always are legal, not factual, because either a jury or trial judge will decide fact questions at the trial court level. Appellate courts do not have juries or other fact finders.

The Purpose of Cases in Texts

A textbook presents a case to teach at least one legal principle. Assuming the case is reasonably well selected and introduced in a casebook, the problem confronting the student is to reduce the puffy, cotton-candy language of the case opinion into a one-line legal rule.

A rule derived from a judicial decision is called a *ratio decidendi*, which is Latin for "reasoning which flows from the decision." A simpler way of expressing it is to say, "rule of the case." Note that there are many ways of stating a case's ratio decidendi. There is not one way of stating a "rule of the case." Because of this, studying cases is analogous to examining modern art. Just as many meanings can be found in a Picasso portrait, many interpretations can be drawn from a case. This is not to say that a given case means whatever one wants it to mean. Rather, a ratio decidendi is limited to a case's facts. A ratio decidendi beyond a case's facts is invalid as a ratio decidendi. Thus, in the *Hudson* case earlier in this chapter, one could develop a broad ratio decidendi, such as a civil suit by the federal government against a person, followed by a criminal suit by the same sovereign against the same person, where both suits are based on essentially the same facts and thus do not violate the U.S. Constitution's double jeopardy clause. A narrow ratio decidendi of *Hudson* might be a federal, civil penalty suit based on a federal banking law violation in which the defendant paid a penalty, followed by a federal, criminal case against a defendant fined in the prior civil case, does not offend the U.S. Constitution's double jeopardy clause. An invalid or overly broad ratio decidendi would be a state criminal suit followed by a federal criminal suit based on essentially the same facts that does not violate the double jeopardy clause. This last ratio decidendi is invalid for *Hudson* because no state criminal prosecution was brought in *Hudson*. Some other case will have to support the last offered ratio decidendi.

The Meaning of Briefing

We brief cases to analyze them. *Brief*, like so many words, has at least two meanings when used in a legal context. One meaning of *brief* is a set of written legal arguments an attorney draws up to support a client's legal position in a court case. That is not the sense in which the word brief is used here. **Brief**, as described here, means the result of a student's analyzing a case by dividing the case into five parts:

1. The **case style** includes the parties suing and being sued, along with the case cite and date of the case's decision.
2. The crucial case *facts* must be succinctly stated. One way to tell whether a fact is crucial is to ask if the result would have been different had the fact not been present; if so, the fact is crucial.
3. The *issue* must be stated as precisely as possible. Legal, not factual, issues are important because the legal issue states in question form a possible legal rule presented by the case (e.g., "Do all contracts have to be written to be enforceable?"). However, separating fact from law issues is often difficult because no single way is always best to state a legal issue. An issue can be stated in as many ways as there are staters of the issue. It can also be stated narrowly or broadly (e.g., "Do all contracts have to be written to be enforceable?" versus "Do all contracts for the sale of land have to be written to be enforceable?").
4. The *holding* is a yes or no answer to the question presented by the issue.
5. The *rationale* is the reason for the holding. For example, why do some contracts have to be evidenced by a signed writing to be enforceable, whereas others do not? The reasons could run the gamut from historical (it has always been the rule that has been followed) to policy considerations (to prevent fraud).

The following is a possible way of briefing the *Carroll v. Exxon* case.

Facts:

Single, working woman applied for Exxon credit card in August 1976.

- Exxon denied her credit card application on 9/14/76. No reason was given for credit denial.
- Applicant sends Exxon letter on 9/28/76 asking reason for credit denial.
- Exxon sends applicant undated response indicating credit bureau did not give adverse information about application but could not get enough information about her credit history.
- Neither letter from Exxon to applicant gave investigating credit bureau's name.
- Applicant sued Exxon on 10/26/76 claiming violation of Fair Credit Reporting Act.
- Exxon sends applicant name and address of investigating credit bureau on 11/2/76.

Issue 1:
Did Exxon's conduct violate the Fair Credit Reporting Act (FCRA)?

Holding:
Yes

Issue 2:
Was Exxon's conduct willful, entitling plaintiff to punitive damages?

Holding:
Yes

Rationale:
The court found Exxon's violations willful. Exxon did not immediately and voluntarily furnish the credit reporting agency's name and address.
The court rejected the Exxon defenses:

- That it did not deny credit based on the credit bureau's report
- That it gave plaintiff the name of the credit reporting agency
- That Exxon had reasonable procedures to assure compliance with the FCRA.

Notes: Students usually brief cases before class and reserve this half of the page for modifications, additions, and other notes from class.

Aside from providing the holding(s), which means answering a specific legal or fact question that must be answered to settle the case, judges will often include "might have been" situations in their opinions. These situations are similar to but different enough from the case at hand that the judge believes a different result would be justified. Such remarks, not essential to resolution of the case, are referred to as **dicta** or **obiter dicta**.

Students can add a number of embellishments to a brief but should not forget that the more complex and detailed the brief, the harder it is for students to remember. The purpose of the brief is to simplify complex cases and make life easy for students. The brief is just a tool to help distill a few rules from a case, enable quick review of those rules for exams, and help students when their professors ask about cases in class.

CHAPTER SUMMARY

Law (positive law) is found in the form of constitutions, statutes, administrative regulations, and executive orders.

Classifications of law include substantive and procedural as well as civil and criminal, with some overlap between civil and criminal law.

Positive law is found in several places, including session laws as well as federal and state codes. Codes organize session laws alphabetically by topic. Annotated codes contain footnote references to case interpretations of words in codes.

Federal administrative regulations are found in the *Federal Register* and in the *Code of Federal Regulations*. The *Federal Register* publishes regulations chronologically in no particular order. The *Code of Federal Regulations* organizes regulations by agency.

Computer systems such as Westlaw and Lexis can help find the law. Persons having a computer equipped with a modem have a cyberspace law library.

Briefing a case is an analytical tool that divides a case into facts, issues, holding, and rationale.

Manager's Ethical Dilemma

The Michigan police found marijuana growing adjacent to Guy Usery's house, and discovered marijuana seeds, stems, stalks, and a growlight within the house. The United States instituted civil forfeiture proceedings against the house, alleging that the property was subject to forfeiture under a federal forfeiture statute because it had been used for several years to facilitate the unlawful processing and distribution of a controlled substance. Usery ultimately paid the United States $13,250 to settle the forfeiture claim in full. Shortly before the settlement, Usery was indicted for manufacturing marijuana in violation of another section of the U.S. Code. A jury found him guilty, and he was sentenced to prison for 63 months.

The Court of Appeals for the Sixth Circuit by a divided vote reversed Usery's criminal conviction, holding that the conviction violated the Double Jeopardy Clause of the Fifth Amendment of the U.S. Constitution. The Sixth Circuit read Supreme Court decisions, *U.S. v. Halper* and *Austin v. United States*, as saying that any civil forfeiture under U.S. Code section 881 (a)(7) was punishment under the Fifth Amendment's Double Jeopardy Clause. Usery in the Sixth Circuit's view had therefore been "punished" in the forfeiture proceeding against his property, and could not later be criminally tried in violation of U.S. Code section 841 (a)(1). The Supreme Court granted the federal petition for certiorari (a way to appeal a case to a higher court). Do you believe the second trial for essentially the "same offense" is double jeopardy? Although businesspeople typically do not grow marijuana, they do engage in conduct where civil and criminal penalties are possible for the same act. As a matter of public policy, do you believe that businesses should support or condemn successive civil and criminal punishments for essentially the same act?

Discussion Questions

1. A New Yorker, Bernhard H. Goetz, was allegedly assaulted on a New York City subway and, in defending himself, Goetz shot and paralyzed one of his perceived assailants. Goetz, the original victim of the alleged assault and robbery, was then tried criminally but was acquitted for crimes based on self-defense. Then, one of his original assailants whom Goetz paralyzed by use of a gun sued goetz civilly in a New York court. A Bronx jury awarded Darrell Cabgey, one of the four young men originally trying to rob Goetz, $43 million—$18 million for past and future pain and suffering and $25 million for punitive damages. Do you think that Goetz was being "twice put in jeopardy" in violation of the Fifth Amendment's double jeopardy prohibition?
2. Guilt in criminal cases and liability in civil cases can be the result of race. Racial overtones were part of the Goetz case in the previous question—the four young men trying to rob Goetz are black and Goetz is white. This fact gives rise to the question of whose legal philosophies are used in analyzing this series of cases related to Goetz.
3. Describe the function of a cite. Which of the following have cites?
   a. cases
   b. statutes
   c. regulations
4. The Clean Water Act makes illegal the dumping of pollutants into U.S. waters without a permit. People who break this law can be subject to civil damages and can be punished criminally by fines or imprisonment or both for certain offenses. The objectives of the Clean Water Act include making the nation's waters swimmable and fishable by 1983 and having zero discharges of pollutants by 1985. Given these objectives, could they best be achieved by civil law, criminal law, or a combination of both? Does the risk presented by water pollution justify the imposition of criminal sanctions? What are some consequences of making something both a civil and criminal offense? (As we shall see throughout this book, a number of federal statutes set up regulatory schemes imposing both civil and criminal liability).
5. Why should some acts be criminal offenses, others only civil wrongs, and still others be completely legal? For example, is there anything inherently wrong with one person's talking to another? What if they are talking about dividing markets and bid rigging in violation of the Sherman Antitrust Act?
6. Do civil and criminal law have any common objectives? What are they? In what way do they differ?
7. A major distinction in law is that of rights and remedies. Rights are sometimes known as **primary rights** and remedies are called **secondary rights**. Laws telling us what we can and cannot do in society are generally primary rights. For example, agency law allows people to hire employees, while the Civil Rights Act of 1964 makes it illegal to discriminate in hiring based on race or religion. Both agency law and the Civil Rights Act create primary rights. If W discriminates illegally against B, W breaks B's primary rights. B can seek a remedy, such as damages (money) or an order directing W to hire B. Remedies are not the same for all primary rights. Secondary rights are usually proportional to the primary right to which they attach. For example, society's remedy if someone commits murder could be life imprisonment. (Because murder is a serious offense, a severe punishment such as life imprisonment seems appropriate.) The idea that the primary and secondary rights should be proportional is sometimes expressed as "Let the punishment fit the crime." This statement is true for criminal law, but civil law speaks in terms of remedies, usually not of punishment. What are some examples of secondary rights—remedies or punishments—that are not proportional to the attached primary rights? Would imposing the death penalty on someone who jaywalks be an example?
8. Sarah Romberg owned a clothing store that obtained 95 percent of its business through mail orders. A selling point for her business was her payment of all shipping costs (usually using the U.S. Postal Service). Sarah learned that the U.S. Postal Service had recently published a regulation requiring that packages be double wrapped. She wanted to read the regulation to determine its exact requirements. Where would she obtain this information? Assume she is in a town of 15,000 people.

Suggested Readings

Articles

BERRING and VANDEN HEUVEL, "Discussion of Legal Research: Should Students Learn It or Wing It?" 81 *Law Library Journal* 431 (1989).

BRYDEN, "Scholarship About Scholarship," 63 *University of Colorado Law Review* 641 (1992).

COLLINS, "Law in the Business Curriculum," 15 *American Business Law Journal* 46 (1977).

FABER, "Interpreting Statutes: A Comparative Study," 81 *Cornell Law Review* 513 (1996).

HILLER, "Business Law in the MBA Program: A Survey and Comparison," 23 *American Business Law Journal* 299 (1985).

KLAYMAN and NESSER, "Eliminating the Disparity Between the Businessperson's Needs and What Is Taught in the Basic Business Law Course," 22 *American Business Law Journal* 41 (1984).

McGUIRE, "Logic and the Law Curriculum: A Proposed Conceptual Framework for 'The Legal Environment of Business,'" 23 *American Business Law Journal* 479 (1986).

MOORE and GILLEN, "Managerial Competence in Law and the Business Law Curriculum: The Corporate Counsel Perspective," 23 *American Business Law Journal* 351 (1985).

RASNIC, "The Persistent Credibility Gap of Respectability for Legal Research," 10 *Journal of Legal Studies Education* (1992).

TRUSLOW, "Legal Education, Legal Studies, and Business Law," 15 *American Business Law Journal* 1 (1977).

WINTER, "Finding the Law—the Values, Identity, and Function of the International Law Advisor," 128 *Mil. L. Rev.* 1 (1990).

MODULE

2

BUSINESS AND LEGAL SYSTEMS: COURTS, LEGISLATURES, ADMINISTRATIVE AGENCIES, CONSTITUTIONAL AND INTERNATIONAL LAW AFFECTING REGULATION

CHAPTER

3

SOURCES OF LAW: POLITICAL AND INSTITUTIONAL

"POWER TENDS TO CORRUPT; ABSOLUTE POWER CORRUPTS ABSOLUTELY."

Lord Acton
Letter to Bishop Mandell Creighton (1887)

POSITIVE LAW ETHICAL PROBLEMS

"No judge can reduce what a jury says a plaintiff is entitled to. It violates my constitutional right to a jury trial," declared Bob Anderson. A jury had just declared that Anderson was entitled to $2 million in compensatory damages and $3.5 million in punitive damages when Conwood Co. used Anderson's private credit information in litigation in violation of the Fair Credit Reporting Act.

What bothered Anderson was the trial judge wanted to reduce his jury verdict by millions of dollars to a mere $50,000 in compensatory damages and totally nullify the jury's $3.5 million punitive damage award. Is this change legally possible?

"The statute is unfair because it is vague," shouted Mr. McBoyle, after being criminally convicted of transporting a stolen airplane interstate. The statute he was convicted under made it illegal to transport a stolen "motor vehicle" interstate. Lower courts held that the statute applied to "airplanes." Did the U.S. Supreme Court agree?

In Chapters 1 and 2 we saw what law is and examined some legal and business ethics. This chapter focuses on sources of law in the United States. A wide variety of approaches can be taken in the study of legal sources. One can consider law as the product of political, institutional, historical, economic, or anthropological sources. Chapter 3 is limited to political and institutional sources.

POLITICAL SOURCES OF LAW

The discussion of the political sources of law refers to the number of people involved in the rule-making process.

Monarchy

An efficient way to make a legal rule is to have as few people as possible involved in developing it. One person who has absolute power to govern is known as a monarch. The monarch spends no time consulting various groups to learn what laws the groups desire. **Monarchy** probably is most workable when the people ruled are uneducated, tractable, and indifferent to how their lives are managed. Because the ruler answers to no one, the monarch is not politically accountable. Such an arrangement creates considerable potential for rulers to abuse their law-making power. Individuals and businesses might have no right to criticize the monarch for excessive taxes or absurd laws. Various freedoms (speech, press, and religion) and rights (such as trial by jury) that U.S. citizens take for granted would probably not exist under a monarchy.

Oligarchy

In an **oligarchy**, a small group makes the rules. An oligarchy's characteristics are similar to those of a dictatorship. Greater continuity of rule exists in an oligarchy, however, because, unlike a dictatorship, if one member of the ruling clique should die, others in the group can continue to carry on the functions of government. Selection to membership in the oligarchy is usually thought to result from the oligarchy's decision rather than the wishes of the general population.

Democracy

In a **democracy**, the ruled make the rules. In a technical sense, democratic government includes all of the people. However, practical as well as policy considerations result in, for example, denying suffrage to a one-year-old child, a convicted criminal, people who have recently moved, and foreign exchange students.

An effective democracy requires an educated, informed **body politic**. Given the unwieldiness and impracticability of getting an entire population together every time a new law is proposed, having people represent the population has developed. Such **representative democracy** gives rise to potential distortion of the popular will and promotes popular apathy regarding public matters. Pressure groups, coupled with soaring campaign costs, further accentuate the potential for representatives to distort the popular will.

The major positive factors of a democracy are responsiveness of leaders to the desires of the governed and political stability born of political equality.

Anarchy

Anarchy exists when no one has legal authority to make rules binding others. In other words, anarchy exists when no government exists. Every person must govern himself or herself. In Chapter 1 we learned that Sigmund Freud saw civilization as the step individuals make when they join together collectively and replace individual will with group will. When anarchy exists, no civilization exists because no law restrains people. Anarchy sometimes is referred to as the **state of nature**, meaning people in a prebody politic or unorganized state without a legally recognized lawmaker (government).

The Social Compact (Government)

Two philosophers who provided theories about the organization of the body politic are Thomas Hobbes and John Locke, Englishmen who wrote in the seventeenth century. The body politic is simply society in an organized state, meaning it has a government. Because they have sufficient cultural, philosophical, and geographic factors in common, as well as common needs, people decide they should organize politically and name someone or some group to make rules.

The state of nature vanished when people joined to form the body politic, which had a government making rules binding on all. Both Hobbes and Locke then introduced another concept: the **social compact** or **social contract**, or the agreement among people who lived in a state of nature to form an organized society with a government. The government would have authority to make rules binding on all persons in the body politic. The document that comes closest to representing the social compact, or social contract, is a government's **constitution**. A constitution usually establishes the government's organizational framework and announces which rule-making power the government has or does not have, what governmental institutions have lawmaking authority, and the extent of the government's authority.

Hobbesian and Lockean Social Compacts

A main difference between the Hobbesian social compact and the Lockean compact lies in the extent to which individuals surrender their rights to the state or government when the social compact is formed. Hobbes, being a strong positive law advocate who stressed the need for stability and order in society, said that people relinquish all of their rights to the state, which he called the Leviathan, when the social compact is formed. In so doing, Hobbes provided a theoretical justification for a dictatorship or totalitarian government. Unlike many modern totalitarians, however, Hobbes wanted repressive rule because it could provide the social benefit of order and stability. One reason for his view was the civil unrest that characterized the period in which Hobbes wrote. He was disturbed by the social costs of disorder and violence. When viewed in this context, Hobbes's desire for order is understandable.

Locke, on the other hand, saw the dangers of oppressive government that could result from giving up all rights to government. According to his view of the social compact, people relinquish some but not all of their rights when they form the social compact (government). Those rights retained by individuals were so-called inalienable rights—rights that according to Locke could not be relinquished. The rights to life, liberty, and property were the basic inalienable rights recognized by Locke. Locke's notion of inalienable rights is recognized in the Fifth and Fourteenth Amendments to the U.S. Constitution. These clauses state that no person may be deprived of life, liberty, or property *without due process of law*. Chapter 6 further develops the due process concept.

The U.S. Social Compact

The United States has followed the social compact of John Locke. The U.S. Constitution is the basic social compact establishing who or what institutions have lawmaking authority and to what extent. The important Lockean idea of limited government has been followed in the U.S. legal system. It is evident in the Bill of Rights (the first ten amendments to the U.S. Constitution), which sets out areas of freedom whereby the national government may not make any law that would limit these freedoms. For example, the First Amendment right to freedom of speech limits the lawmaking authority of the federal government when it tries to control or limit free speech.

Federalism

Federalism, another example of limited government in the United States, means that lawmaking authority is divided between dual sovereigns. Given the word **sovereign**, meaning supreme lawmaker, one might wonder how dual sovereigns could be within the same country. The United States resolved this problem in its social compact, or

Constitution, by the *division of powers* concept. According to this concept, the national government has authority to make law in enumerated areas (areas listed in the Constitution), and the regional or state governments have authority to make laws in the reserved areas.

When one of the dual sovereigns of the federal system attempts to make law outside its area of lawmaking authority, such attempted exercise violates the social compact and is invalid as unconstitutional if challenged in court. The power marble diagram in Figure 3.1 illustrates federalism's division of lawmaking power.

The concept of a limited national government in domestic lawmaking was well stated in *Carter v. Carter Coal Co.*, 298 U.S. 238 (1936), where the U.S. Supreme Court noted that "the proposition often advanced and as often discredited, that the power of the federal government inherently extends to purposes affecting the nation as a whole with which the states severally cannot deal or cannot adequately deal, and the related notion that Congress, entirely apart from those powers delegated by the Constitution, may enact laws to promote the general welfare, have never been accepted but always definitely rejected by this court." As early as 1816, Mr. Justice Story laid down the cardinal rule that has since been followed—that the national government "can claim no powers which are not granted to it by the Constitution, and the powers actually granted, must be such as are expressly given, or given by necessary implication."

Interestingly, the U.S. government has no federalism principle with respect to foreign affairs. In foreign affairs, governmental power is consolidated solely in the national government. The individual states have no power in foreign affairs. The state of New York may not make a treaty with Israel, nor may South Dakota make a treaty with Saudi Arabia. Only the national government may make treaties with foreign governments. We deal with the strength of unlimited power in foreign affairs.

FIGURE 3.1 Federalism's Division of Lawmaking Power

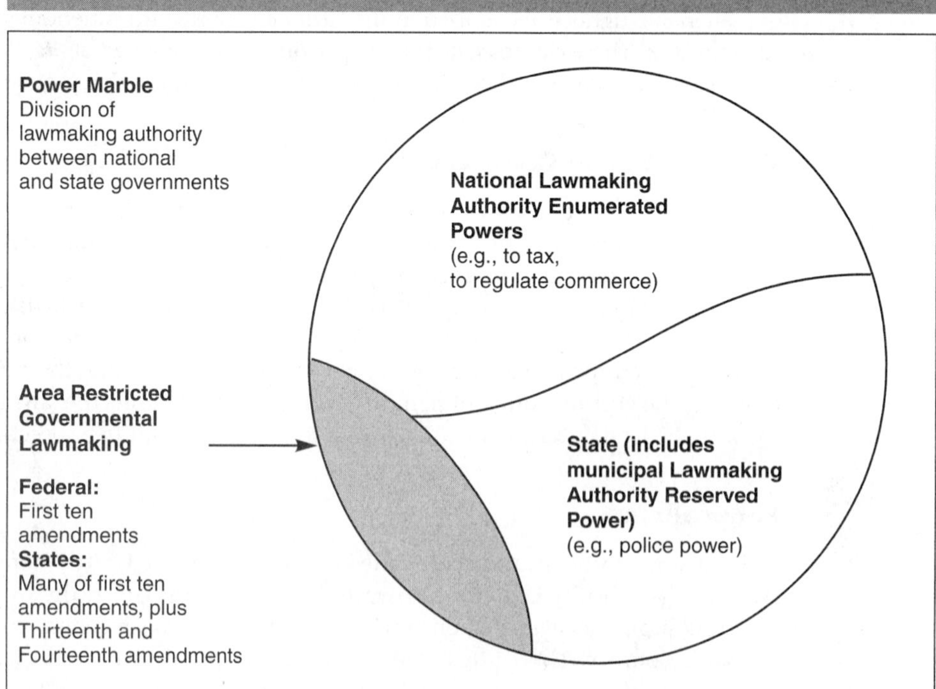

Federalism Today

Federalism at the year 2000 has some characteristics of earlier years: Federal statutes such as the Clean Water Act, the Clean Air Act, and OSHA set national standards, but these laws allow states to administer federal standards if states show they have adequate funding and legal authority.

Budget crunches for the federal government in the 1990s led the Bush administration to push more matters formerly handled by the federal government to the states. The Clinton administration's reaction to such division of federal legal mandates and state financing of such programs is, as of this writing, uncertain. As a former governor, President Clinton undoubtedly realizes the financial stress modern federalism imposes on the states. Realizing that they lack the money to pay for these matters, states are reluctant to assume federally imposed mandates. Health care, highways, welfare, and education are but four such matters that come readily to mind. Mayors also resisted the Bush "federalism" proposals because they believed that state governments shove funding responsibilities onto the municipalities. Mayors also fear that, even if federal money accompanies federal program delegations, cash-starved state governors will skim money for state coffers that was intended for local government. The direction federalism will take will no doubt be shaped by the 2000 presidential election.

INSTITUTIONAL SOURCES OF LAW: COURTS AND LEGISLATURES

Institutional sources of law refer to governmental bodies empowered to make law. Ask for institutional sources of law, and the average person will probably name courts and legislatures. However, before exploring courts and legislatures and the limits of their lawmaking authority, note the major governmental institutional source of rules in our society today: the **administrative agency**. An administrative agency is any nonlegislative, nonjudicial, governmental lawmaker. Later chapters discuss these lawmakers in detail.

Courts and Court Systems

> **http://**
> *Many cases on "Court TV" that are of current public interest can be found at* ***http://www.courttv.com***

Courts (meaning judges) are a major source of law in the United States. Judge-made law is called **common law**. The United States has two major **court systems**: the federal court system and the state court system. Several reasons exist for having two court systems when one would seem to be enough. First, we have dual sovereigns (that is, the federal and state governments), and each sovereign wants its own court system. When the U.S. Constitution was set up, many resisted a federal court system. They argued that federal courts unnecessarily duplicate state courts. Also, they feared a strong national government. Others, realizing how provincial the individual states and their citizens were, saw a need for a more neutral court when out-of-staters are sued. Federal courts, with judges appointed for life, are more neutral than elected state court judges. Many also felt that federal judges would be more knowledgeable about national laws and would interpret them more sympathetically than would state courts. Thus, Article III of the U.S. Constitution established the U.S. Supreme Court and gave Congress the power to create other federal courts.

State Courts. The Tenth Amendment to the U.S. Constitution reserves to the states powers not delegated to the national government or prohibited to the states. This amendment, among other things, lets states set up their own court systems. Each state has done so in its constitution or its statutes. In effect, the United States has 51 separate court systems (the 50 separate state court systems, plus the one federal court system, with at least one federal district court in every state).

Most lawsuits in the United States take place in state courts. Figure 3.2 diagrams the typical state court system. Keep in mind, however, that the 50 states' court structures do differ.

FIGURE 3.2 State Judicial System

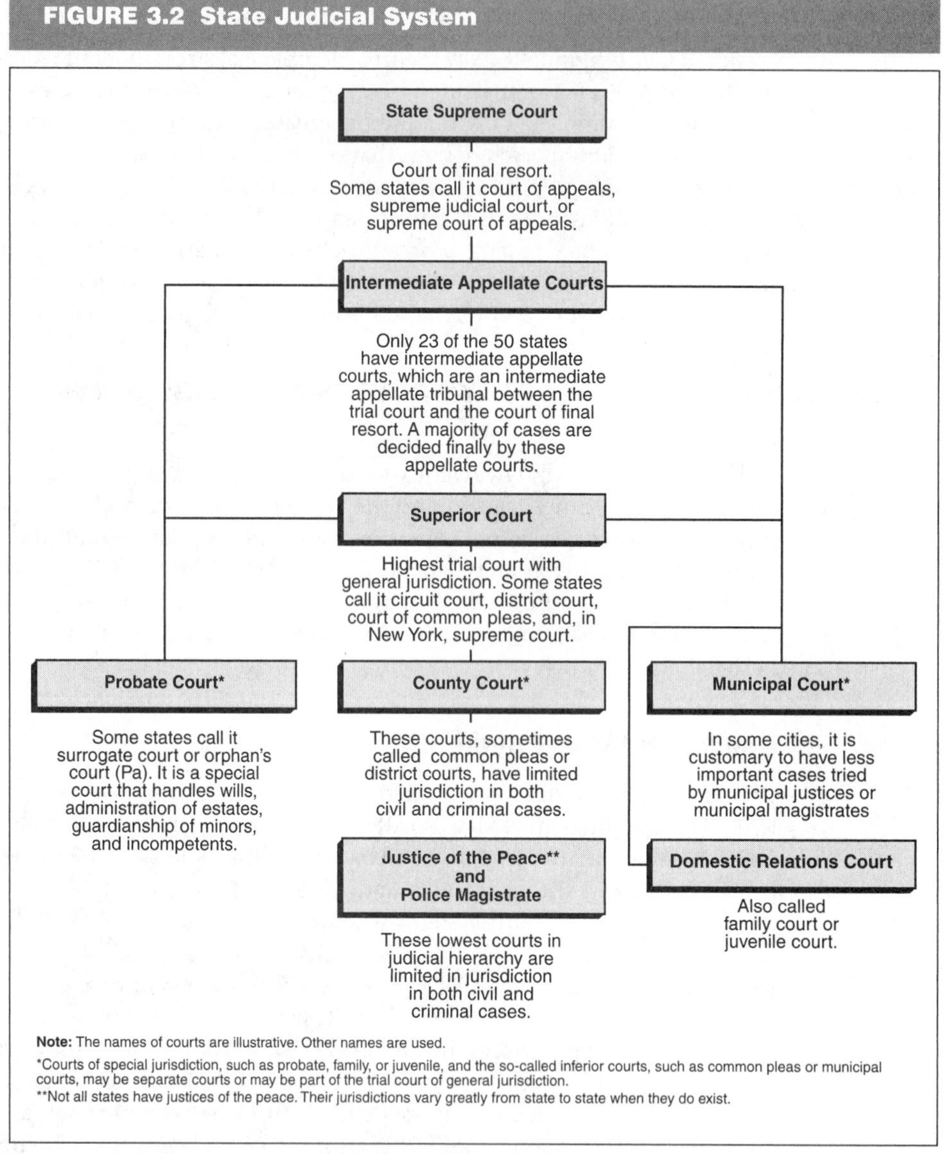

Note: The names of courts are illustrative. Other names are used.

*Courts of special jurisdiction, such as probate, family, or juvenile, and the so-called inferior courts, such as common pleas or municipal courts, may be separate courts or may be part of the trial court of general jurisdiction.

**Not all states have justices of the peace. Their jurisdictions vary greatly from state to state when they do exist.

Where Cases Start: Courts of Original Jurisdiction. Note in Figure 3.2 the eight kinds of courts. The court where a case starts is called a **court of original jurisdiction**. A case that deals with juvenile delinquency or divorce, for example, starts in a **domestic relations court**. If someone's father dies and leaves a will disposing of his property, that person (or the person's lawyer) would take the will to a **probate court** (called a surrogate court or orphan's court in some states). Probate courts deal with estate administration, which involves collecting dead people's assets, paying off their debts, and distributing any remaining assets according to the will or the **statute of descent** (a legislatively drafted will). **County courts** hear cases involving relatively small civil matters, such as a homeowner breaking a contract with a painter, or criminal matters, such as a bank teller embezzling $1,500. Such courts are also called **common pleas courts** or **district courts** in a number of states. County courts typically have jurisdiction up to a certain dollar amount, such as $3,000.

Some, but not all, states have **justice of the peace courts**, often called J.P. courts. Along with **police magistrates**, these courts deal with minor legal violations—traffic violations, for example—of both a civil and a criminal nature.

In a number of states, the **municipal courts** also deal with minor civil and criminal offenses. You may be wondering why so many types of low-level courts have overlapping, or concurrent, jurisdiction. This duplication is sometimes justified on the basis of specializing to create judicial expertise. In less populous areas, one court, such as the county court, may do the job of several different types of low-level state courts, such as domestic relations courts, J.P. courts, and municipal courts.

The courts in the diagram in Figure 3.2 that are lower than the superior court (those already described) are not courts of record, which means that no court stenographer makes a record of the proceedings. Not having a record saves society money. If a litigant in such a court wishes to appeal the result to the superior court, the case is retried from beginning to end, a so-called **de novo trial**, because no lower court record of witnesses' testimony is available for review. Economy is also promoted by not having juries in courts below the superior court level. The judge in such courts fills the jury fact-finder role as well as presides over the proceedings and rules on legal issues.

Where Jury Trials Occur. The basic trial-level courts are called **superior** or **circuit courts**. (In New York state they are called supreme courts.) Because they are courts of

record, a court stenographer makes a record of the proceedings so that, if the matter is appealed, all comments made by any witness or attorney or by the judge will be available for the appellate court to consider. The presence of the stenographer taking a record of the proceedings tends to make all persons in the courtroom—including the judge—more careful about their remarks. Juries are available, if requested, for most types of cases. Superior courts can usually hear civil or criminal cases. In larger cities, superior courts are sometimes separated into civil and criminal courts.

Law and Equity Courts. Occasionally, one hears the terms **law courts** and **equity courts**. (Recall that we discussed these terms in Chapter 1 under the legal ethic of justice.) The distinction between law and equity is historical, not logical. It is the result of the way the United States patterned its legal system after that of England. The English law court judges could give remedies only *in rem* (in a thing), which meant that if wrongs occurred and a remedy could not be given in a thing—for example, where money damages were not satisfactory—then the injured person had no remedy. This system frustrated some injured people. They went to one of the English king's advisors, the **chancellor**, and asked for an order directing the wrongdoer to do or not do something. If the chancellor thought the person had an inadequate legal remedy, an order called an *injunction* or other equitable remedy might be given. The chancellor intervened in this way often enough that a court arose about him called the **chancery** or **equity court**. Persons could get their cases into equity courts only if the legal remedies were inadequate. Legal remedies included such things as money, land, or other property. (Refer to the law-equity discussion under the justice ethic in Chapter 1 for an example of when legal remedies are inadequate.) Equity courts are civil, not criminal. No right to a jury exists in equity courts. Chancellors sometimes appoint advisory juries in equity cases. Early settlers in the United States brought the English law and equity courts with them. By the mid-twentieth century, the law and equity court functions had been combined in most states as well as in the federal courts.

Correcting Judges' Mistakes. What happens if a state judge makes a mistake in a case? The person who thinks an error has occurred may appeal to a higher court. Generally, cases decided by a lower court can be appealed to the next higher court in Figure 3.2. For example, a matter decided by a probate court can be appealed to the superior court and from there to the intermediate state appellate court. If a person is still not satisfied, the case can be appealed to the state supreme court. If it involves a federal constitutional, federal statutory, or federal treaty issue, the U.S. Supreme Court might hear the case.

State Courts of Appeal. A few points should be noted about state intermediate appellate and supreme courts. First, no juries or witnesses appear in them—only lawyers, who argue law, not usually facts. Generally, the facts in a dispute are decided by the trial court. Appellate courts accept the trial court facts unless they are clearly erroneous. Second, every state has at least one appellate court level. Many have two levels of appellate courts, such as in the state court diagram in Figure 3.2. All states have a highest level appellate court called the state supreme court (except in New York, where it is called the court of appeals). Third, appellate courts above the superior court level have several judges, called justices, at the highest level. The idea is that several heads are better than one, particularly if the legal issue is complex or politically sensitive.

Wrong Court. The state court system is complex. What happens if people take their cases to the wrong court? First, people should hire attorneys to prevent this problem from occurring. However, if a layperson insists on acting **pro se** (as one's own attorney) and starts the case in the wrong court, it will be dismissed (thrown out without a trial). One basic reason for having a case in the wrong court is lack of jurisdiction, which means that for some reason the court does not have the power to hear and try the case.

Court's Power to Hear Cases: Jurisdiction. **Jurisdiction** has several aspects: subject matter, territorial, in rem, quasi in rem, and in personam. **Subject matter jurisdiction** refers to the court's power to hear the type of lawsuit in question. Some courts, such as probate courts, have limited subject matter jurisdiction and hear only certain kinds of cases. Probate courts cannot, for example, try murder cases. Other courts, such as superior courts, have **general jurisdiction** and can try any kind of case. Subject matter jurisdiction must always be present for a court to hear a case. In a civil action, one of the other types of jurisdiction (in rem, in personam, quasi in rem) must also exist. **In rem jurisdiction** refers to power over things and is based on the physical presence of property in the state. If a case in an Indiana court involves Nevada land, the Indiana court has no in rem jurisdiction because that land is in another state.

In personam jurisdiction refers to power over a person and is commonly based on one of the following: (1) physical presence within the state, (2) state citizenship, (3) consent to the state's jurisdiction (e.g., by coming into the state to defend), (4) sufficient contacts with the state (e.g., a sales office in the state), or (5) commission of a tort (civil wrong) within the state. If, for example, the owner of the Nevada land is served with process while in Indiana, the Indiana court has in personam jurisdiction over the Nevada landowner. If a Nevadan is not served with process in Indiana but owns a vacation cottage in Indiana, Indiana courts have **quasi in rem** (literally, like in a thing) **jurisdiction** over the Nevadan to the extent of the Indiana land. In other words, the Indiana land is like (or personifies) the Nevadan in Indiana. Therefore, someone can sue the Nevadan in Indiana and collect a judgment against the Nevadan in Indiana up to the value of the Indiana land (but only if the claim giving rise to the lawsuit relates to the Indiana land, such as a trespass to the land).

The *Kopycinski v. Aserkoff* case illustrates the an increasingly common feature of the U.S. legal system: A screening tribunal of experts can make it more difficult for plaintiffs to pursue certain types of claims (here medical malpractice) before such claim can go to a jury trial. In Massachusetts if the tribunal rules that the plaintiff's claim is spurious, the plaintiff may, nonetheless pursue the claim by going to court only after posting a bond payable to the defendant for costs if plaintiff loses at a jury trial.

The idea behind such screening tribunals is to discourage ridiculous claims from going to a jury. Just the threat of a jury trial—even one based on spurious grounds—can induce some defendants to settle even if they think the claim is groundless because the attorney cost of defending such claims, the prejudice against the wealthy, and the time spent to defend weigh in the balance. Such screening tribunals are controversial. On the one hand, they can reduce claims and thus control insurance and other litigation costs. On the other hand, they can reduce access to jury trial, which is a constitutionally protected right, although it has never been an absolute right. Judges, for example, have generally had the power to reduce (called a *remittitur*) or increase (called an *additur*) jury awards.

Kopycinski v. Aserkoff shows some problems that can arise with such screening panels. The *Anderson v. Conwood* case following *Kopycinski* deals with controlling jury verdicts by use of remittiturs.

Kopycinski v. Aserkoff

Supreme Judicial Court of Massachusetts
573 N.E.2d 961 (1991)

Background and Facts:

Catherine Kopycinski's claim arises from the treatment of her late husband Joseph V. Kopycinski, while he was a patient at Massachusetts General Hospital (MGH). On December 31, 1986, Joseph went to MGH's emergency ward complaining of vomiting, inability to eat, and excessive weight loss. He was examined by defendant, Dr. Hopkins, who admitted Joseph to the hospital. Thereafter, Dr. Hopkins consulted with Dr. Aserkoff, also a defendant, as to Joseph's treatment. Dr. Aserkoff's notes concerning the decedent appear throughout the medical records. Dr. Aserkoff ordered a number of tests, including an abdominal CT-Scan, to determine the causes of Joseph's condition. Although the CT-Scan showed evidence of an inguinal hernia, the defendant physicians allegedly failed to determine that the hernia was the cause of the decedent's medical problems.

On January 6, 1987, less than 24 hours before his death, the defendant doctors obtained a surgical consultation from Dr. Carter. Dr. Carter recommended an exploratory laparotomy after the decedent's condition was stabilized. On January 7, 1987, the decedent died while an inpatient at MGH.

On November 20, 1989, the plaintiff, Catherine Kopycinski, filed a complaint for medical malpractice against the defendants. The complaint alleged that the defendants had failed to properly identify and treat the decedent's medical condition, and that the decedent suffered damages as a result of this failure. On March 26, 1990, a medical malpractice tribunal convened as required by state law to review the plaintiff's offer of proof (to show she had a meritorious, not a spurious, claim). The tribunal consisted of a physician, an attorney, and a judge of the Superior court (a trial court). The attorney and the physician found in favor of each defendant. The judge, however, overruled the majority, stating that, as a matter of law, the plaintiff's offer of proof was sufficient and her claim should go to trial. The defendants appealed to Court of Appeals and eventually the case reached the Massachusetts Supreme Judicial Court.

Body of Opinion

Justice Nolan

We are faced with the question whether the decision of a medical malpractice tribunal as to the sufficiency of a plaintiff's offer of proof must conform to the conclusion of the tribunal's judicial member, in spite of the contrary views of the medical and legal members....

General Laws... provides for the screening claims of medical malpractice by a tribunal. The statute states, in part, that "[e]very action for malpractice, error or mistake against a provider of health care shall be heard by a tribunal consisting of a single justice of the superior court, a physician licensed to practice medicine in the commonwealth... and an attorney authorized to practice law in the commonwealth, at which hearing the plaintiff shall present an offer of proof and said tribunal shall determine if the evidence presented if properly substantiated is sufficient to raise a legitimate question of liability appropriate for judicial inquiry or whether the plaintiff's case is merely an unfortunate medical result." The statute provides that, if the tribunal finds for the defendant, the plaintiff may pursue the claim through the regular judicial process, but only upon filing a bond in the amount of $6000.

The plaintiff argues that the question which the tribunal is ultimately asked to resolve is a legal one and, thus, solely within the purview of the judicial member of the tribunal. The defendants rely on our decision in *Paro v. Longwood Hospital*... arguing that the question for the tribunal is not a legal question and should be decided by the majority vote of the tribunal. We agree with defendants. The question to be decided ultimately by the tribunal is a factual one. The plain meaning of the statute, and the legislative guidelines for interpreting statutes which involve tribunals, make it clear that the Legislature intended that a majority vote of the tribunal would determine whether a plaintiff's offer of proof is sufficient.

The words of the statute themselves suggest that the tribunal's decision is a factual and not a legal determination. Words such as "legitimate" and "appropriate," which are used to describe the standard of proof, suggest determinations of fact. Moreover, the statute repeatedly refers to the "finding" of the tribunal, once again suggesting that the task of the tribunal is a fact-finding mission. Perhaps most telling is the "either," "or" language used in the framing of the tribunal's task. The tribunal determines whether the evidence is "sufficient to raise a legitimate question of liability appropriate for judicial inquiry OR whether the plaintiff's case is merely an unfortunate medical result" [emphasis supplied]. Surely the determination whether a medical result is merely "unfortunate" is not a legal determination. The plain meaning of the words used within the statute suggests that the task of the tribunal is fact-finding, for which the judicial member is no better equipped than the legal or medical member....

The plain meaning of the language "said tribunal shall determine" says that the tribunal as a whole, and not one particular member, shall make the determination.

When the legislature intended for the judicial member to have specific powers with regard to the tribunal, it said so explicitly. For instance, [the statute]... provides that the judge is to select the health service professional and the attorney who are to serve as co-members of the tribunal; the section also provides that the judicial member may increase or decrease the amount of the bond to be filed.

We note that the judicial member of the tribunal would certainly be solely responsible for deciding purely legal issues. In *Paro v. Longwood Hospital*... we rejected the ... argument that the tribunal statute violated... the Massachusetts Declaration of Rights because it allows the two lay panel members to override the judge in the decision of legal issues. The *Paro* court stated that "[t]he lawyer and the health service representative are placed on the panel because of their expertise in relevant fields. This expertise is useful in deciding *the primary question* faced by the tribunal—whether the plaintiff has presented a legally sufficient claim. As to the determination of *this issue*, the tribunal decision is a collective one, with all three panel members participating equally. The responsibility for deciding purely legal questions, however, is left solely with the judge-member of the tribunal, and thus no interference with his function occurs."

[In determining the standard the tribunal is to use to judge the plaintiff's offer of proof the Massachusetts Supreme Judicial Court held it was] comparable to a trial judge's function in ruling on a motion for a directed verdict....

Moreover, our decision in *Broadard v. Hubbard Regional Hospital*... supports our determination that the tribunal must come to a decision as a whole. In *Broadard*, the judicial member felt that it was clear that the offer of proof would be sufficient to raise a legitimate question of liability appropriate for judicial inquiry, and that he intended to find for the plaintiff. Therefore, the judge did not convene the tribunal, seeing it as a "needless exercise." We reversed the judge's decision stating that, even though the judge was certain, the statute called for an interplay among the judicial, legal, and medical members.... Here we determine that... [the statute] not only requires a convening of the tribunal, but also an interplay in which all three members play an equal role in determining the outcome.

Judgment and Result

The Massachusetts Supreme Court decided that the decision of a majority of the tribunal shall determine the finding of the tribunal. Therefore, the judge sitting as a member of the tribunal was without power to rule that the plaintiff's offer of proof was sufficient to raise a legitimate question of liability appropriate for judicial inquiry. However because the matter was fully before the state supreme court, it decided that plaintiff's offer of proof was sufficient and that the plaintiff should have been allowed to proceed without posting bond. Therefore, it affirmed.

Questions

1. Does the tribunal have the power to bar totally a plaintiff from going to a jury trial?
2. Why should there be three distinct experts on the screening tribunal? May they act alone or must they act together? Why?
3. If a clear legal question arises, who decides? Who decides if something is a legal question as opposed to a fact question? Does this procedure represent a weakness in the court's opinion?

Motions can be made prior to, during, and after a verdict and judgment have been entered. One type of motion that occurs after a jury verdict is for either an additur or a remittitur. Generally, if credible evidence supports a jury's verdict, a court (judge) will not change it. In the case of the motion for an additur, the plaintiff's attorney claims that the jury has been "too stingy" in the amount it has awarded plaintiff. The *Elena DeZavala* judgment in Chapter 4 is an example of a judge raising a jury's verdict to a higher amount. The following case of *Anderson v. Conwood* illustrates a remittitur where the court reduces the jury's verdict because it is too high.

Anderson v. Conwood Co.

U.S. District Court (W.D. Tennessee)
34 F.Supp.2d 650 (1999)

Background and Facts:

Plaintiffs filed suit against the defendants for violations of the Fair Credit Reporting Act (FCRA). The plaintiffs complained that their credit reports were improperly acquired by defendant Conwood on May 25, 1994. The credit reports provided by Equifax, were to be used by the defendants in civil litigation against the plaintiffs. Equifax's contractual agreement prohibited its subscribers from accessing the consumer credit information if the intended use was for employment or judicial/litigation purposes. Additionally, plaintiffs claimed that the subsequent sharing, dissemination, and usage of their credit reports by the defendants violated provisions of the FCRA.

Plaintiffs sought damages on the basis of pecuniary loss, emotional distress, and other related claims. After an August 1998 trial on the merits, in which the plaintiffs presented minimal evidence of damages and made no precise demand in the presence of the jury, the jury awarded each plaintiff compensatory damages in the amount of $2,000,000. The jury also awarded plaintiffs punitive damages in the amount of $3,500,000.

Body of Opinion

District Judge Donald

Judicial review of the size of punitive damages has been a safeguard against excessive verdicts for as long as punitive damages awards have been awarded.... Punitive damages are not compensation for injury.... Instead, they are private fines levied by civil juries to punish reprehensible conduct, and deter its future occurrence....

Case law from the U.S. Supreme Court, recognizes that "the Constitution imposes a substantive limit on the size of punitive damages awards.... Although the cases fail to draw a mechanical bright line between the constitutionally acceptable and the constitutionally unacceptable, "a majority of the Justices agree that the Due Process Clause imposes a limit on punitive damages awards.... The Supreme Court has repeatedly expressed its concern about punitive damages that "run wild."...

The Sixth Circuit's general rule governing the remission of compensatory damages is that the jury's verdict should not be reduced "unless it is beyond the maximum damages that the jury reasonably could find to be compensatory for a party's loss."... The *Farber* court held that a trial court is within its discretion in remitting a verdict only when "after reviewing all evidence in the light most favorable to the awardee," it is convinced that the verdict is clearly excessive, or the result of bias, prejudice, or passion.... A trial court has the authority to reduce a verdict that is so excessive or inadequate, it shocks the judicial conscience of the court.... In appropriate cases, reductions in awards may well be justified even when the amount in controversy does not necessarily "shock the conscience," but rather leaves us with "the definite and firm conviction that a mistake has been committed," resulting in a plain injustice....

If there is any credible evidence to support a verdict, it should not be set aside.... The trial court may not substitute its judgment, or credibility determinations, for those of the jury....

When a defect in a jury's award is readily identified and measured, remittitur is more appropriate than a new trial.... District courts should grant a motion for remittitur only if the award clearly exceeds "the amount which, under the evidence in the case was the maximum that a jury could reasonably find to be compensatory" for the plaintiff's loss.... Unless the award is beyond the range supportable by proof, the court must let the award stand....

Conwood avers that opposing counsel's comments regarding the financial condition of the defendants, and how they spent time "at country clubs," had a prejudicial effect on the jury.... Moreover, counsel for the plaintiffs described himself as a representative of "little people," and commented on how his clients were bearing the heat of the day while defendants spent time at their clubs.... Conwood argues that such remarks were intended to prejudice the jury, and draw attention to class distinctions and social positions....

Conwood argues that the verdict of the jury, regarding both compensatory and punitive damages, is so outrageous, enormous and shocking as to indicate passion and prejudice by this sympathetic jury.... Conwood claims that unaccountable caprice was definitely prevalent given the extremely meager evidence of damages proximately caused by the defendants.... Conwood contends that the verdict of the jury should be set aside, because it was arbitrary, capricious and the result of passion and/or prejudice.... On this point, the Court concurs. Conwood states that the information contained within the credit reports was admittedly public information.... Conwood further avers that the plaintiffs' lives did not change as a result of their credit reports being acquired.... The record supports this fact.

In the instant case the Court finds that the verdict was clearly excessive. The record is void of any proof of damages beyond plaintiffs' testimony of worry, stress, anxiety, loss of sleep and expense in bringing litigation. Indeed, plaintiffs failed to present any demand for a monetary amount of damages as evidenced by the jury's first question, "what amount of damages did the plaintiffs ask for?" Thus the jury's verdict lacks an evidentiary foundation.

Based upon the lack of evidence showing actual damage to the plaintiffs, the jury's compensatory damage awards must be remitted, as they are clearly excessive.... The inescapable conclusion is that rational thought was vacated by the jury, and replaced with their own passion and prejudices....

Notwithstanding the jury's sentiments that punitive damages were justified and warranted in the present case, the Court finds that there was no proof of any action on the part of defendants which warranted the imposition of punitive damages. Therefore the court will vacate the award of punitive damages against the defendants....

Judgment and Result

The district court granted a remittitur reducing Anderson's jury award for compensatory damages from $2,000,000 to $50,000; plaintiff's $3,500,000 punitive damages award is vacated totally. Plaintiffs are awarded reasonable attorney fees. The jury verdict was clearly excessive because it lacked an evidentiary foundation.

Questions

1. What was the amount of the remittitur in the *Anderson* case? Who makes a remittitur?
2. What might make a remittitur objectionable? Who would most likely object to a remittitur—plaintiff or defendant?
3. Given the tendency of some juries to award huge punitive damage amounts, why do you suppose the trial judges do not employ remittiturs more often?
4. Whose legal philosophies mentioned in Chapter 1 are in evidence in this case?

Federal Courts

Federal District Courts: Where Cases Start. The federal district courts are those courts where most lawsuits begin in the federal court system. The federal court system, diagrammed in Figure 3.3, has 89 federal district courts in the 50 states, one in the District of Columbia, and another in Puerto Rico, bringing the total number of federal districts to 91. With 91 federal districts, one might expect 91 federal district judges, but this is not the case. There are from 2 to 27 federal judges in each district, depending on the population and amount of litigation in the district. Where more than one federal district judge presides in a district, the district is divided into divisions. The 50 states contain 541 permanent federal district judgeships, 15 more in the

FIGURE 3.3 Federal Judicial System

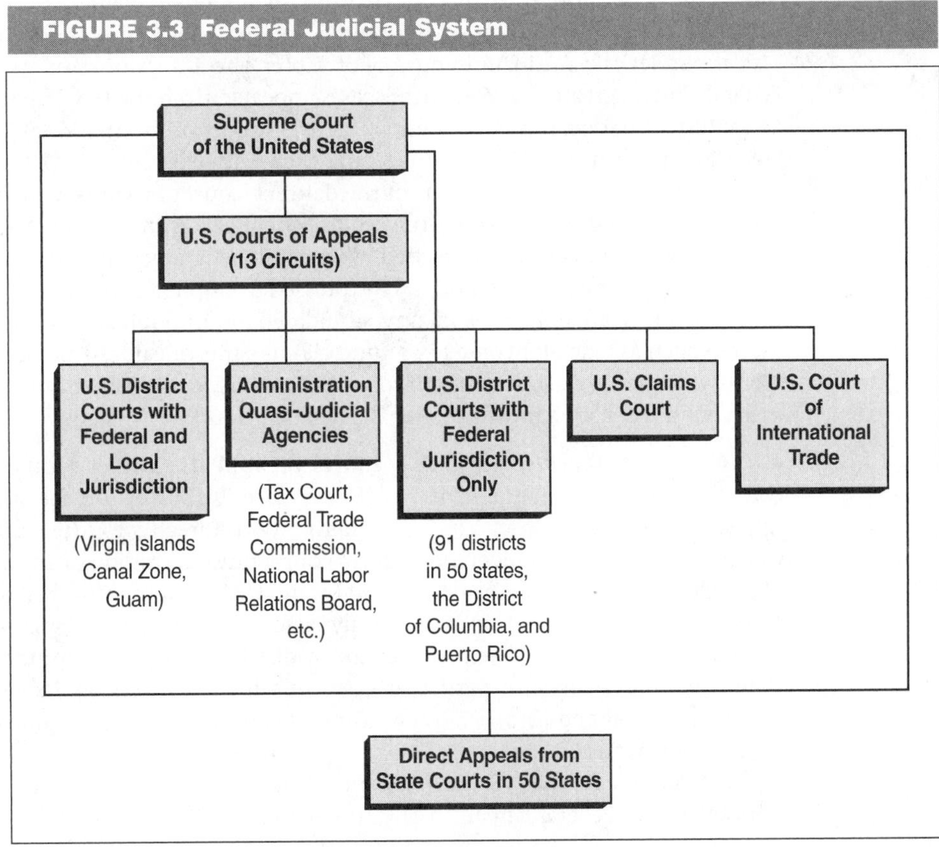

District of Columbia, and seven more in Puerto Rico. Also, temporary federal judgeships may be created by Congress to last only for the life of the person appointed to fill them.

Federal district judges perform the function of a law court judge and equity court chancellor. They also have subject matter jurisdiction to hear either civil or criminal cases. However, federal courts are courts of limited jurisdiction. That is, not all civil or criminal lawsuits may be heard there. Basically, two types of civil cases may be brought into federal district courts: **diversity of citizenship** cases, which are cases involving lawsuits brought by a person from one state against a person from a different state, and **federal question** cases in which a federal constitutional or statutory right is at issue. A $75,000 jurisdictional limit in diversity cases was also designed to keep out small disputes better handled in state courts. Such a limit no longer exists in federal question cases.

Administrative Quasi-Judicial Agencies. The **administrative quasi-judicial agencies** in Figure 3.3 refer to nonjudicial, nonlegislative government entities having rule-making authority. As such, these agencies are not even courts in a strict sense, although their rules and adjudications may often be appealed directly to the federal courts of appeal, thus bypassing the trial-level federal district courts. Two reasons for no retrial of administrative adjudications from scratch in district courts are to defer to the expertise of administrative law judges and to be expedient; it saves money not to have to redevelop in district court evidence already produced at the administrative level.

Other Federal Courts. The **U.S. Court of International Trade.** (formerly the U.S. Customs Court) is a federal court with exclusive jurisdiction over civil actions arising under the U.S. tariff laws in such matters as appraised value or classification of imported goods. It tries cases without juries and has appellate authority from customs officers under the Anti-Dumping Act of 1921. The **U.S. Court of Appeals** for the Federal Circuit, created in 1982, hears cases appealed from the U.S. Patent Office (such as validity of trademarks and patents), the U.S. Court of International Trade, and the U.S. Claims Court. The **U.S. Claims Court** came into existence on October 1, 1982. It takes over the trial court functions of the defunct Court of Claims, which are basically those of a limited jurisdictional trial court where a person may sue the federal government on a claim arising from the U.S. Constitution, any congressional statute, any executive department regulation, any expressed or implied contract to which the U.S. government is an obligor, and any liquidated or unliquidated nontort damages. Matters such as federal income tax refund claims, suits on supply or construction contracts with the federal government, back-pay claims for civilian and military government employees are handled by the U.S. Claims Court.

U.S. Courts of Appeals. Most **U.S. courts of appeals** (formerly called U.S. circuit courts of appeals) were established in 1891 to ease the burden on the Supreme Court. Appeals from U.S. district courts formerly went directly to the Supreme Court. Generally, appeals from federal trial-level courts must go to one of the 13 U.S. courts of appeals before they can be considered by the U.S. Supreme Court. Two exceptions, where the U.S. courts of appeals are bypassed and appeal is directly to the U.S. Supreme Court, are (1) when a three-judge district court issues injunctions against state court proceedings in particular cases in which congressional statutes are held unconstitutional and (2) when a few criminal cases follow a direct appellate route to the Supreme Court.

The United States has 13 courts of appeals including the recently created Court of Appeals for the Federal Circuit in D.C. (refer to Figure 3.3). Cases do not start in U.S.

courts of appeals. Cases in courts of appeals come from one of the courts or administrative agencies shown in the boxes directly below the U.S. courts of appeals. Each court of appeals hears cases in divisions made up of three judges. Currently, each U.S. court of appeals has from 4–23 judges. In important cases, U.S. courts of appeals sit **en banc**, meaning all judges hear the case.

Figure 3.4 shows the states contained in each of the 13 federal judicial circuits covering the 50 states and territories, plus the federal circuits in the District of Columbia.

U.S. Supreme Court. The U.S. Supreme Court was formed on February 2, 1790, pursuant to Article III, Section 1 of the U.S. Constitution and the Judiciary Act of 1789. The Court now consists of a Chief Justice and eight associate justices. At various times as many as ten and as few as six justices have presided. Supreme Court justices assume office after presidential nomination and U.S. Senate confirmation. No legal requirement exists stating that a Supreme Court nominee must be an attorney although, as a practical matter, Senate confirmation would probably be impossible for someone not legally trained.

The Supreme Court has the power to hear cases pursuant to Article III, Section 2, of the U.S. Constitution, which notes:

> The judicial power shall extend to all Cases, in Law and Equity, arising under this constitution, the Laws of the United States, and Treaties made, or which shall be made, under their Authority;—to all Cases affecting Ambassadors, other public Ministers and Consuls;—to all Cases of admiralty and maritime Jurisdiction;—to Controversies to which the United States shall be a Party;—to Controversies between two or more States;—between a State and Citizens of another State;—between Citizens of different States;—between Citizens of the same State claiming Lands under Grants of different States, and between a State, or the Citizens thereof, and foreign States, Citizens or Subjects.
>
> In all cases affecting Ambassadors, other public Ministers and Consuls, and those in which a State shall be Party, the Supreme Court shall have original jurisdiction. In all other cases before mentioned, the Supreme Court shall have appellate jurisdiction, both as to Law and Fact, with such Exceptions, and under such Regulations as the Congress shall make.

As the prior language illustrates, some, but not all, of the Supreme Court's authority to hear cases comes from the Constitution. Other authority to hear cases comes from congressional statutes. Such statutory jurisdiction generates many of the cases the Supreme Court decides. Congress has some power to remove the Supreme Court's jurisdiction to hear particular types of cases if the Congress originally gave the Court that jurisdiction. This power is a potent check on Supreme Court decisions, and threats of its use are frequent when decisions are handed down that are unpopular with some members of Congress. The extent of congressional power to cut federal court jurisdiction is uncertain and controversial.

In Which Court System Should I Sue?

When a federal court hears a diversity case, it sits as a state court but presumably without the local prejudice of the state court judge. But what is the limit on federal judges' lawmaking authority when they sit in a diversity case? What if the state court had ruled one way on an issue? Could the federal court in another later case involving similar facts in the same state make a contrary rule? In *Erie Railroad Co. v. Tompkins*,

FIGURE 3.4 The Thirteen Federal Judicial Circuits

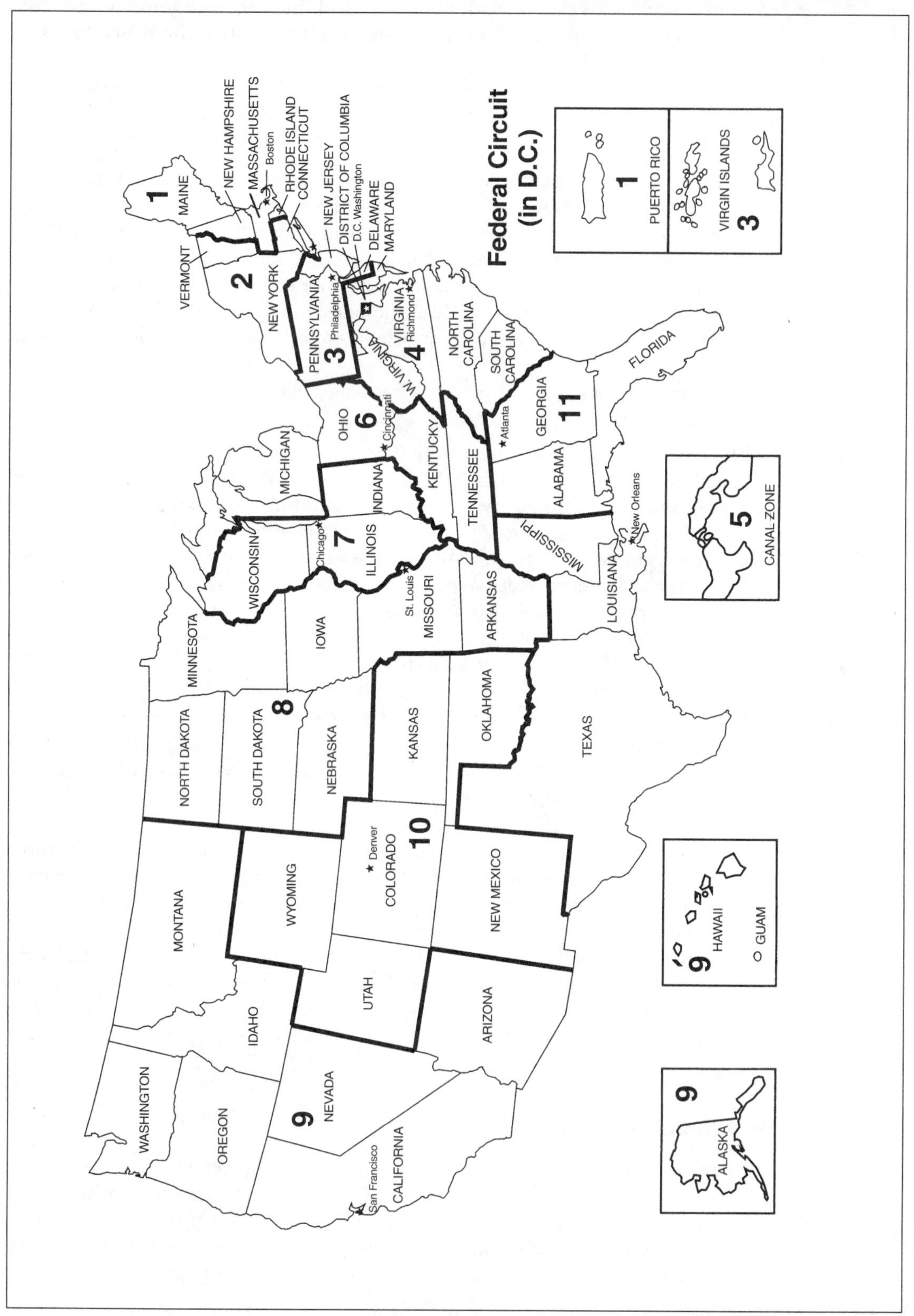

Harry Tompkins lost an arm and learned that federal judges have no power to make common law in nonenumerated areas (areas reserved to the states by the U.S. Constitution). This means federal judges must follow state law when they decide diversity cases and the case involves a reserved power matter (that is, most property, contract, and tort civil wrongs such as slander and negligence covered by state law—areas *reserved* for state lawmaking).

Erie Railroad Co. v. Tompkins

U.S. Supreme Court
304 U.S. 64 (1938)

Background and Facts:

Tompkins, a citizen of Pennsylvania, was injured on a dark night by a passing freight train of the Erie Railroad Company while walking along its right of way at Hughestown in that state. He claimed that the accident occurred through negligence in the operation, or maintenance, of the train; that he was rightfully on the premises as licensee because on a commonly used, beaten footpath which ran for a short distance alongside the tracks; and that he was struck by something which looked like a door projecting from one of the moving cars. To enforce that claim he brought an action in the federal court for southern New York, which had jurisdiction because the company is a corporation of that State. It denied liability and the case was tried by a jury.

Erie insisted that its duty to Tompkins was no greater than that owed to a trespasser. It contended, among other things, that its duty to Tompkins, and hence its liability, should be determined in accordance with the Pennsylvania law; that under the law of Pennsylvania, as declared by its highest court, persons who use pathways along the railroad right of way—that is, a longitudinal pathway as distinguished from a crossing—are to be deemed trespassers; and that the railroad is not liable for injuries to undiscovered trespassers resulting from its negligence, unless it be wanton or willful. Tompkins denied that any such rule had been established by the decision of the Pennsylvania courts and contended that, since there was no statute of the State on the subject, the railroad's duty and liability is to be determined in federal courts as a matter of general law.

The trial judge refused to rule that the applicable law precluded recovery. The jury brought in a verdict of $30,000; and the judgment entered thereon was affirmed by the Circuit Court of Appeals, which held,... that it was unnecessary to consider whether the law of Pennsylvania was as contended because the question was one not of local, but of general law and that "upon questions of general law the federal courts are free, in the absence of local statute, to exercise their independent judgment as to what the law is; and it is well settled that the question of the responsibility of a railroad for injuries caused by its servants is one of general law.... Where the public has made open and notorious use of a railroad right of way for a long period of time and without objection, the company owes to persons on such permissive pathway a duty of care in the operation of the trains.... It is likewise generally recognized law that a jury may find that negligence exists toward a pedestrian using a permissive path on the railroad right of way if he is hit by some object projecting from the side of the train."

Body of Opinion

Justice Brandeis

The Erie had contended that application of the Pennsylvania rule was required, among other things, by §34 of the Federal Judiciary Act of September 24, 1789, c. 20, 28 U.S.C. §725, which provides:

The laws of the several States, except where the Constitution, treaties, or statutes of the United States otherwise require or provide, shall be regarded as rules of decision in trials at common law, in the courts of the United States, in cases where they apply.

Because of the importance of the question whether the federal court was free to disregard the alleged rule of the Pennsylvania common law, we granted certiorari.

First, *Swift v. Tyson*... held that federal courts exercising jurisdiction on the ground of diversity of citizenship need not, in matters of general jurisprudence, apply the unwritten law of the State as declared by its highest court; that they are free to exercise an independent judgment as to what the common law of the State is—or should be....

Experience in applying the doctrine of *Swift v. Tyson* had revealed its defects, political and social; and the benefits expected to flow from the rule did not accrue....

Diversity of citizenship jurisdiction was conferred in order to prevent apprehended discrimination in state courts against those not citizens of the State. *Swift v. Tyson* introduced grave discrimination by non-citizens against citizens. It made rights enjoyed under the unwritten "general law" vary according to whether enforcement was sought in the state or in the federal court; and the privilege of selecting the court in which the right should be determined was conferred upon the non-citizen. Thus, the doctrine rendered impossible equal protection of the law. In attempting to promote uniformity of law throughout the United States, the doctrine had prevented uniformity in the administration of the law of the State. The discrimination resulting became in practice far-reaching. This resulted in part from the broad provision accorded to the so-called "general law" as to which federal courts exercised an independent judgment. In addition to questions of purely commercial law, "general law" was held to include the obligations under contracts entered into and to be performed within the State, the extent to which a carrier operating within a State may stipulate for exemption from liability for his own negligence or that of his employee; the liability for torts committed within the State upon persons resident or property located there, even where the question of liability depended upon the scope of a property right conferred by the State; and the right to exemplary or punitive damages. Furthermore, state decisions construing local deeds, mineral conveyances, and even devises of real estate were disregarded.

In part the discrimination resulted from the wide range of persons held entitled to avail themselves of the federal rule by resort to the diversity of citizenship jurisdiction. Through this jurisdiction individual citizens willing to remove from their own State and become citizens of another might avail themselves of the federal rule. And without even change of residence, a corporate citizen of the State could avail itself of the federal rule by re-incorporating under the laws of another State, as was done in the Taxicab case.

The injustice and confusion incident to the doctrine of *Swift v. Tyson* have been repeatedly urged as reasons for abolishing or limiting diversity of citizenship jurisdiction. Other legislative relief has been proposed. If only a question of statutory construction were involved, we should not be prepared to abandon a doctrine so widely applied throughout nearly a century. But the unconstitutionality of the course pursued has now been made clear and compels us to do so. The fallacy underlying the rule declared in Swift v. Tyson is made clear by Mr. Justice Holmes. The doctrine rests upon the assumption that there is a "transcendental body of law outside of any particular State but obligatory within it unless and until changed by statute," that federal courts have the power to use their judgment as to what the rules of common law are; and that in the federal courts "the parties are entitled to an independent judgment on matters of general law":

"But law in the sense in which courts speak of it today does not exist without some definite authority behind it. The common law so far as it is enforced in a State, whether called common law or not, is not the common law generally but the law of that State existing by the authority of that State without regard to what it may have been in England or anywhere else. . . .

"The authority and only authority is the State, and if that be so, the voice adopted by the State as its own (whether it be of its Legislature or of its Supreme Court) should utter the last word."

Thus the doctrine of *Swift v. Tyson* is, as Mr. Justice Holmes said, "an unconstitutional assumption of powers by courts of the United States which no lapse of time or respectable array of opinion should make us hesitate to correct." In disapproving that doctrine we do not hold unconstitutional §34 of the Federal Judiciary Act of 1789 or any other Act of Congress. We merely declare that in applying the doctrine this Court and the lower courts have invaded the rights which, in our opinion are reserved by the Constitution to the several States. . . .

Judgment and Result

The U.S. Supreme Court decided the case in favor of the railroad. Tompkins lost. The Supreme Court said federal courts deciding a diversity case must apply state substantive law where the *federal* government has *no enumerated power.* In this case, rules dealing with landowners' liability to people on their land fall into the *states' reserved* area of lawmaking, *not* the *federal enumerated area* of lawmaking. (Refer to the power marble in Figure 3.1.) Thus, in this case, the New York federal district court should have applied the Pennsylvania rule, which would have denied Tompkins recovery because he was a trespasser on the railroad property.

Legislatures and Legislative Forms

Legislatures are public bodies of elected officials who make law by passing statutes. The national legislature is called the Congress of the United States, which comprises the House and Senate. Each state also has a legislature. This section focuses on how a bill becomes a statute, some ways to influence legislation, and differences between courts and legislatures. The work of the U.S. Congress starts with a proposal taking one of the following four forms: a **bill**, a **joint resolution**, a **concurrent resolution**, or a **simple resolution**.

Bills. Most federal legislation takes the form of a bill when proposed. A bill becomes an act or **session law** when it is passed by both houses of Congress and is signed by the president, when two-thirds of each House overrides a presidential veto, or when the president fails to return it with his objections to the originating house within ten days while Congress is in session. Federal bills can start in either the House or Senate, except for revenue-raising or general appropriation bills (tax bills), which must originate in the House of Representatives. A bill originating in the House is designated H.R. (for House of Representatives), followed by a number, such as H.R. 2070, which it keeps all during its parliamentary stages. Senate bills are similarly designated S (for Senate), followed by a number, such as S.7.

http://

The website to the Library of Congress is ***http://thomas.loc.gov***

Figure 3.5 indicates some major steps by which a bill becomes a statute. A proposed statute introduced by a member of Congress is called a **bill**. If the bill survives and becomes law, it is called an act, statute, or session law. Acts can be private acts (a law passed to deal with nonrecurring, private matters, such as a law to pay a farmer when a military jet crashes into and destroys the farmer's barn) or public acts (laws having general social impact).

Joint Resolutions. A joint resolution can originate in either the House or Senate. Little practical difference exists between bills and joint resolutions. When enacted, they are just as much laws as are bills that become acts. They are slightly different in form but are used indiscriminately. Statutes that begin as bills are sometimes amended by joint resolution, and vice versa. The steps for passing joint resolutions into law are the same as for bills, except for those proposing U.S. constitutional amendments, which must be approved by two-thirds of each House and are then sent to the states for ratification, bypassing the president.

Concurrent Resolutions. The concurrent resolution is not usually a law at all. Rather, it deals with matters affecting the running of both houses of Congress. For example, concurrent resolutions are used to express *facts, principles, opinions,* and *purposes* of both houses of Congress. They are not equal to bills or joint resolutions because they cannot become laws.

FIGURE 3.5 How a Bill Becomes an Act

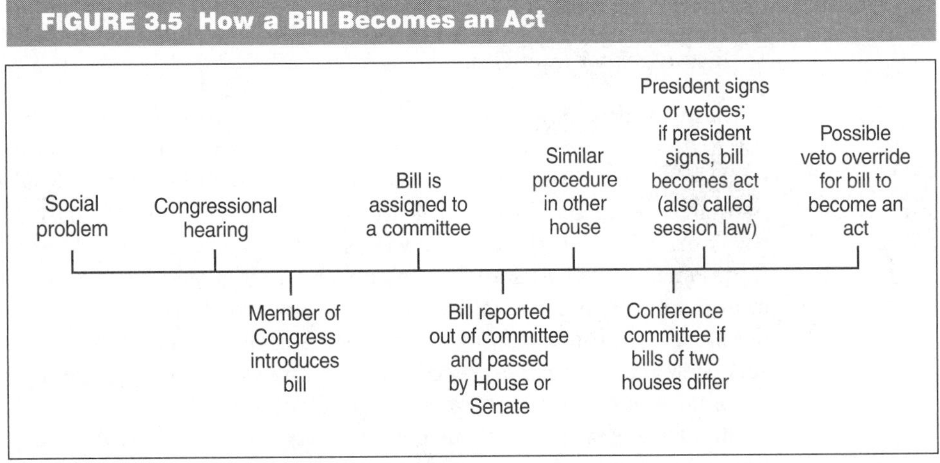

Simple Resolutions. Simple resolutions deal with matters concerning the running of only one house of Congress; they are not laws. They are designated H. Res. or S. Res., followed by a number, such as H. Res. 386, and are published in the *Congressional Record*.

Statutory Construction. One role the judiciary must play is that of gap filler. The gaps arise when legislatures pass statutes that do not address all possible situations arising under a statute and such an unanticipated situation arises in an actual lawsuit. Judicial gap filling is commonly referred to as **interstitial lawmaking** or **statutory construction**.

A number of rules and maxims of statutory construction have been developed by judges over at least two centuries of deciding reported cases in the United States. They are not binding rules because the maxims themselves are not always consistent with one another. For example, one maxim is that "a statute will be read to give it a rational rather than arbitrary meaning." Yet another maxim says that nonlegal words and phrases will be interpreted in their ordinary sense. Thus, the U.S. Supreme Court, in one of its less-publicized opinions, has held that "tomatoes are vegetables." What makes this decision notable is that it offends botany, since tomatoes are technically fruit. Arguably, then, this decision observes the ordinary sense rule but violates the rational rather than arbitrary meaning rule.

Despite such peculiarities, some of the more common maxims of statutory construction worth listing include the following:

1. Words of plain meaning will not be extended to mean something different or additional to that plain meaning.
2. The purpose of statutory interpretation (by judges) is to determine legislative intent.
3. Penal statutes are to be strictly construed in favor of the accused.
4. Statutes in derogation of the common law are to be strictly construed to reverse or modify the common law rules as little as possible.
5. Where words are omitted from a statute by inadvertence or clerical error and the legislative intent is clear, the court will insert the missing words.
6. *Expressio unius, exclusio alterius* (what is expressed implies exclusion of other matters).
7. When general words follow particular classes, the *ejusdem generis* principle is applied (limiting words to same class as were named).
8. *Reddendo singula singulis* (each word or phase in a statute will be applied to its appropriate referent).
9. Legislative history will be used only when the statute, to which the legislative history relates, is unclear.

Many other maxims and rules of statutory construction exist. Those maxims just listed are used frequently by courts. Some are obvious rules of common sense or, at least, good sense, such as the maxim that where words are omitted from a statute by inadvertence or clerical error and the rule that where legislative intent is clear, the court will insert the missing words. Other of the maxims deserve some elaboration. Penal (criminal) statutes are construed strictly in the accused's favor because criminal punishment is meted out in limited portions, particularly when prison is possible. Also, the presumption of innocence attributed by the U.S. legal system to each defendant and the procedural due process notice requirement as to what is criminal support construction of criminal statutes in the accused's favor.

Statutes in derogation of the common law, such as **survival statutes** or **statutes of limitations** are strictly construed to preserve the common law rules, thereby promoting legal stability. Such rules have been developed over many years and are relied on by many in planning their affairs.

The maxim that "when general words follow particular classes, the *ejusdem generis* principle is applied," can be best explained by example. If a statute read, "Whoever operates a restaurant, bar, . . . or other place of public accommodation shall obtain a license," would the statute require a license for a dentist's office? According to *ejusdem generis*, the answer is, "No," because this maxim limits general words to the same class as named by the preceding specific words.

Likewise, *reddendo singula singulis* is best explained by illustration. The statute commands: "Go to London by rail and by steamer." The *reddendo* maxim would not be applied so the command would be read to require one to go to London once using one mode (rail) and go to London again using another mode (steamer). Rather, one would be required to go to London once, using both modes on appropriate land and water segments to make one trip.

Legislative history is sometimes a problem for those engaging in statutory construction. Courts are supposed to follow the intent of the legislatures. Usually, intent is clear from reading the statute. Legislative history is usually used only when the statute is unclear on its face. It will not be used to read language out of the statute or to thwart legislative intent—usually. However, if statutory language is unclear or an advocate can convince a judge that statutory language is unclear, whether it in fact is unclear, legislative history will be used to clear up the uncertainty. A problem with consulting legislative history to clear up statutory ambiguities is that it too is often ambiguous, because any member of Congress may testify before the congressional committee or subcommittee responsible for drafting a bill. Members of Congress may also stand up on the floor of Congress during final deliberations on a bill and state his or her interpretation of a controversial section. Even though such a personal interpretation is probably not so persuasive of true legislative intent as the committee report, all individual remarks made at committee hearings during the drafting of a bill and floor remarks during debate are part of the legislative history of an act. Given that members of Congress are highly individualistic, one can frequently find "rebel" statements in the legislative history that are contrary to the intent of most members of Congress. Such statements are available for an effective advocate to use to induce or mislead a judge into construing a statute to a client's advantage. It is up to the good judgment of the court, aided by opposing counsel, to resist atypical interpretations and instead accurately perceive legislative intent.

The following case shows a problem of statutory construction. There, a federal statute punished whoever transported in interstate commerce a motor vehicle knowing it to have been stolen. The statute defined "motor vehicle" to include many things but it did not include "airplanes." The question then became, "Did the statute cover airplanes?" Read *McBoyle v. United States* to learn the answer.

McBoyle v. United States

U.S. Supreme Court
283 U.S. 25 (1931)

Background and Facts:

McBoyle was convicted of transporting from Ottawa, Illinois, to Guymon, Oklahoma, an airplane that he knew to have been stolen, and was sentenced to serve three years' imprisonment and to pay a fine of $2,000. The judgment was affirmed by the Circuit Court of Appeals for the Tenth Circuit. The Supreme Court granted a writ of certiorari so it could hear McBoyle's case on the question of whether the National Motor Vehicle Theft Act applies to aircraft.

Body of Opinion

Justice Holmes

The [National Motor Vehicle Theft] Act provides: "Sec. 2. That when used in this Act: (a) The term 'motor vehicle' shall include an automobile, automobile truck, automobile wagon, motor cycle, or any other self-propelled vehicle not designed for running on rails;... Sec. 3. That whoever shall transport or cause to be transported in interstate or foreign commerce a motor vehicle, knowing the same to have been stolen, shall be punished by a fine of not more than $5,000, or by imprisonment of not more than five years, or both."

Section 2 defines motor vehicles of which the transportation in interstate commerce is punished in § 3. The question is the meaning of the word "vehicle" in the phrase "any other self-propelled vehicle not designed for running on rails." No doubt etymologically it is possible to use the word to signify a conveyance working on land, water or air, and sometimes legislation extends the use in that direction, e.g., land and air, water being separately provided for, in the Tariff Act.... But in everyday speech "vehicle" calls up the picture of a thing moving on land. Thus in Rev. Stats. §4, intended, the Government suggests, rather to enlarge than to restrict the definition, vehicle includes every contrivance capable of being used "as a means of transportation on land." And this is repeated, expressly excluding aircraft, in the Tariff Act.... So here, the phrase under discussion calls up the popular picture. For after including automobile truck, automobile wagon and motor cycle, the words "any other self-propelled vehicle not designed for running on rails" still indicate that a vehicle in the popular sense, that is a vehicle running on land, is the theme. It is a vehicle that runs, not something not commonly called a vehicle, that flies. Airplanes were well known in 1919, when this statute was passed; but it is admitted that they were not mentioned in the reports or in the debates in Congress. It is impossible to read words that so carefully enumerate the different forms of motor vehicles and have no reference of any kind to aircraft, as including airplanes under a term that usage more and more precisely confines to a different class. The counsel for the petitioner have shown that the phraseology of the statute as to motor vehicles follows that of earlier statutes of Connecticut, Delaware, Ohio, Michigan, and Missouri, not to mention the late Regulations of Traffic for the District of Columbia... none of which can be supposed to leave the earth.

Although it is not likely that a criminal will carefully consider the text of the law before he murders or steals, it is reasonable that a fair warning should be given to the world in language that the common world will understand, of what the law intends to do if a certain line is passed. To make the warning fair, so far as possible the line should be clear. When a rule of conduct is laid down in words that evoke in the common mind only the picture of vehicles moving on land, the statute should not be extended to aircraft, simply because it may seems to us that a similar policy applies, or upon the speculation that, if the legislature had thought of it, very likely broader words would have been used.

Judgment and Result

Judgment of the Court of Appeals was reversed. The expression "motor vehicle" as used in the National Motor Vehicle Theft Act does not cover airplanes.

Questions

1. Were "airplanes" known to exist when Congress wrote the statute in the *McBoyle* case? If so, what does the exclusion of "airplanes" suggest? Did Justice Holmes rely on the *ejusdem generis* principle, the *expressio unius* doctrine of statutory construction, the "penal statutes are to be strictly construed in favor of the accused" doctrine, or the "plain [no pun intended] meaning" rule? Or could some or all be used implicitly if not explicitly?
2. Is it likely that the accused here, Mr. McBoyle, ever read the act in question before flying a plane interstate? How, then, could he be said to be prejudiced by the ambiguity in the statute?
3. Why are rules of statutory construction necessary? Because the legislature did its job well or poorly? How could the problem here have been corrected?

Differences between Courts and Legislatures

The following differences exist between courts and legislatures as lawmakers:

1. Courts and legislatures make law in different *form.*
2. Courts mete out *commutative* justice, whereas legislatures dispense *distributive* justice.
3. Courts are *passive* lawmakers, while legislatures are *self-animating* lawmakers.
4. The *procedural due process protections* afforded litigants when courts make law are greater than the procedural due process protection afforded people when legislatures make law.
5. Courts deal with *legal* questions, while legislatures deal with *political* questions.

Form. Judge-made law is common law. The form in which courts make law includes decisions in cases in which no opinion is rendered, decisions in cases in which an opinion is rendered, and situations in which various court orders are entered. For practical purposes and for purposes of cases other than the case in which a rule is made, the instance in which a court makes a rule and renders an opinion is most important because these rules serve as precedents for future cases.

Generally speaking, judge-made law having precedential effect is found in state appellate court opinions and all federal court decisions resulting in a majority opinion. State trial court opinions usually are not significant for other cases because they are seldom written due to time constraints and the pressure of other work. Also, state trial court opinions bind only the court that gives them, not other trial courts, so they would only be persuasive, not binding, precedent for other trial courts. One might ask why the same reasoning does not hold for federal trial-level courts (federal district courts). Federal courts are generally regarded as more powerful and prestigious than state courts; they are fewer in number than state courts; they write opinions more frequently than do state courts; and they are courts of limited jurisdiction and hence involve fewer and generally more significant legal issues, often presenting problems having nationwide interest.

Legislatures, contrary to courts, issue their laws in the form of statutes or acts. As discussed earlier, when a proposed law is introduced into the legislature, it is called a bill. Once it is signed into law by the president or governor or passes the legislature over a veto, it becomes an act, statute, or a session law.

Commutative versus Distributive Justice. Justice handed out by judges when they settle lawsuits is referred to as commutative justice. It is usually designed to correct a past wrong between specific parties. Justice meted out by legislatures is referred to as distributive justice. It is designed to address broad, societal problems and usually to take effect in the future.

Passive versus Self-Animating Lawmakers. Judges are by nature passive lawmakers. Millions of wrongs may be committed in society, but a judge will not lift an official finger to correct any situation unless someone refers the matter to court in a lawsuit. The litigation will examine the alleged breach of the alleged right to see whether a legally recognized right has been broken and, if so, the extent of the damage sustained. It is up to people claiming their rights have been broken to prove it. The judge just sits in court, listens to the assertions made, and presides over the proceedings. The judge has no duty to collect the evidence for either party.

Legislatures, on the other hand, are active, self-animating lawmakers. If they think wrongs are being committed, they can pass laws forbidding such conduct and attach criminal penalties to them. Usually, legislative hearings are held in which members of the public may point out the need for statutes in a particular area. Nonetheless, the legislature need not wait for a wrong to occur before doing something to improve a social situation. Also, an attorney does not have to be hired to generate legislation.

Greater Procedural Due Process Protections in Courts Than in Legislatures. Procedural due process refers to the constitutional requirement that a person be given notice and a fair hearing. This requirement applies in general to both courts when they make law in deciding a lawsuit and to legislatures when they pass laws. However, the degree to which procedural due process must be provided or observed is considerably greater in courts than in legislatures partly because court disputes involve particular parties, not everyone in society. Also, the matters courts are called upon to decide have occurred before the lawsuit in 99 percent of the cases. Additionally, courts are called upon to take something (usually money or property) from one party and turn it over to the other party in civil cases. In criminal cases, courts may fine, imprison, or even take a person's life. Legislatures, on the other hand, usually act upon the population as a whole. Their mandates take effect at some time in the future (generally not in the past); and legislative enactments that involve extracting money or property from someone often have broad impact (such as to increase income tax rates). In such cases of generalized extractions on the population, a general public legislative hearing or a public discussion of the proposed statute with juries, cross-examination, counsel, and many of the other trappings of procedural due process would be uneconomical.

Courts Deal with Legal Issues, and Legislatures Deal with Political Issues. One of the basic dogmas of our system is that courts decide legal questions, whereas legislatures decide political questions. But what does this mean? Is not a legislature making a law when it passes a statute imposing higher income tax rates for single people than for families with one wage earner? Here, the legislature is not applying this law to a specific case. Also, the decision to tax one group at rates higher than other groups is essentially a matter of political strength, the will of the stronger. Because married voters with one income outnumber single taxpayers, married people support laws imposing higher taxes on singles. Matters decided by *power* tend to be political, and matters determined by *logic* tend to be legal. The courts must determine the many unanticipated matters not addressed by the statute. For example, a court must determine if a wage earner who marries during the tax year is treated as single for tax purposes for the entire year, or is treated as single for that part of the year the wage earner was single and as married for the remainder of the year. Such court clarifications of statutes are known as interstitial lawmaking.

In *Baker v. Carr*, 369 U.S. 186 (1962), the U.S. Supreme Court tried to state the difference between a legal issue (suitable for courts to decide) and a political issue (suitable for legislatures):

> Prominent on the surface of any case held to involve a political question is found a textually demonstrable constitutional commitment of the issue to a coordinate political department; or a lack of judicially discoverable and manageable standards for resolving it; or the impossibility of deciding without an initial policy determination of a kind clearly for nonjudicial discretion; or the impossibility of a court's undertaking independent resolution without expressing lack of the respect due coordinate branches of government; or an unusual need for unquestioning adherence to a political decision already made; or the potentiality of embarrassment from multifarious pronouncements by various departments on one question.

The Supreme Court's statement would prompt the following kinds of questions:

1 Has the Constitution expressly said the legislature, and not the courts, is to decide the matter?
2. Is there a way for a court to settle the dispute?
3. Does settling the dispute require a policy decision that should be made by an elected official?
4. If the Supreme Court decides the matter, will its decision show disrespect for the president or Congress?
5. Has another branch of government (the president or Congress) already decided the matter, and does a need exist to stick to this decision?

The answers to these questions help the U.S. Supreme Court decide whether a matter is political or legal. Is busing to achieve racial balance in public schools legal or political? (Because courts decide this issue, it must be a legal one.) What about abortion? (Courts have decided this question, so it, too, must be a legal issue.) Yet, busing and abortion seem like political matters when using the *Baker v. Carr* factors just listed. The previous examples indicate that the modern U.S. Supreme Court is a *political* actor, which tells you that deciding whether something is political or legal is not always predictable.

Relationship between Legislative Law and Court Law. As noted previously, both courts and legislatures make law. Courts (federal and state) may make law in any area subject to constitutional limits. Court lawmaking is generally subordinate to legislatively made law. Judges may have spent years developing an elaborate rule in thousands of cases, only to see it reversed by legislative passage of one statute. For example, judges decided thousands of cases over many years that said workers injured on the job could recover from their employer only if the employer were at fault. But in the early twentieth century, state legislatures passed workers' compensation statutes. These laws eliminated fault as the basis for worker recovery from employers. In effect, legislatures repealed judge-made law simply by passing a statute, indicating that legislatively made law is usually superior to judge-made law. The exception occurs when legislatures pass statutes that courts later declare unconstitutional.

CHAPTER SUMMARY

Political sources of law include monarchy, oligarchy, and democracy. Democracy can be organized into a federal system. Federalism means dual sovereigns. Do not confuse federal government (one of the sovereigns in federalism) with federalism (government with two sovereigns).

Law also comes from institutions such as courts and legislatures. Each sovereign in a federal system has a court system; thus, along with a federal court system, each state has its own court system.

Law made by courts is called common law. Laws made by Congress are called statutes, acts, or resolutions.

Rules of statutory construction help judges clear up problems created by poorly drafted statutes.

MANAGER'S ETHICAL DILEMMA

Monica Long was the product liability manager for the Cotter Ladder Company. One of Monica's major headaches was liability exposure brought on by the product they made: Stepladders. Every year the Cotter Ladder Company was sued by individuals after falls from Cotter-built ladders that resulted in serious injury or even death.

One aspect of her legal environment that baffled Monica was that a consumer in California and a consumer in Florida could each fall off a Cotter ladder, sustain the same injuries, and yet the rules that governed whether they recovered or not were significantly different. It seemed unfair to both the injured consumers and to the Cotter Ladder Company. Why should it make a difference whether the consumer were injured in one state instead of another with respect to the consumer's ability to recover? Also, the crazy quilt of different state liability laws made it difficult for the Cotter Ladder Company to predict its liability exposure. Monica had heard that a federal product liability bill had been introduced in Congress. If passed, this bill would wipe out the different state product liability laws and replace them with uniform product liability standards in all states. Thus, consumers injured in exactly the same way in different states would stand a good chance of having the same result in their cases. This law seemed like equal justice to Monica. Should she support the federal product liability law?

Discussion Questions

1. Some private, "rebel" organizations—often "hate" groups—have established their own courts in which they kidnap people and try such individuals for violating the rebel groups' laws. These groups hand out punishment—often killing offenders. How can these groups claim to be legitimate courts? How do such courts differ from those established by alternative dispute resolution (ADR)? Should a hate group have the same rights as a bank or stockbroker to establish ADR?
2. If a manufacturing company sells its products in all 50 states, would it prefer regulation by state law or by federal law?
3. The two ideas of federalism and separation of powers are cornerstones in the U.S. government. Separation of powers refers to the idea that, at a particular level of government, lawmaking power is separated among the executive, judicial, and legislative branches. Each branch acts as a check on the other, thereby preventing any one branch from abusing its power. What is the idea behind federalism? Does a similarity exist between federalism and separation of powers? Do improved communications and mobility of the U.S. population bring into question the continued validity of federalism? Did the U.S. Supreme Court, in telling President Nixon to turn over the White House tapes to government authorities, illustrate federalism or separation of powers?
4. Several times in recent years, Congress has attempted to cut back on federal court jurisdiction, largely in response to federal court decisions that some legislators disagreed with, such as enlarging the rights of the criminally accused, desegregating schools, busing students to achieve racial balance, and prohibiting prayer in public schools. What were the original reasons federal courts were set up? To make popular decisions? Which branch of government caters to popularity: courts or legislatures?
5. Must a country have courts? The Appellate Division of the New York Supreme Court said, "It is a fundamental obligation of every civilized government to provide a system of impartial courts which can fairly adjudicate disputes involving its citizens." The case involved a suit by the country of Iran against the former Empress of Iran for alleged wrongs she committed against the people of Iran while in Iran [*Islamic Republic of Iran v. Pahlavi*, 94 A.D. 2d 374, 464 N.Y.S.2d 487 (1983)].

Suggested Readings

Articles

CLINTON, "Tribal Courts and the Federal Union," 26 *Willamette Law Review* 841 (1990).

DOUCETTE, "Court Congestion and the Right to a Speedy Trial in Massachusetts," 24 *New England Law Review* 1095 (1990).

EPSTEIN, "The PAC Phenomenon: An Overview," 22 *Arizona Law Review* 355 (1980).

GREEN, "Statutory Compliance and Tort Liability: Examining the Strongest Case," 30 *University of Michigan Journal of Law Reform* 461 (1997).

NOTE, "Justice Scalia's Use of Sources in Statutory and Constitutional Interpretation: How Congress Always Loses," 1990 *Duke Law Journal* 160 (1990).

SCHANCK, "An Essay on the Role of Legislative Histories in Statutory Interpretation," 80 *Law Library Journal* 391 (1988).

Books

BERMAN and GREINER, *The Nature and Functions of Law* (1966).

CARDOZO, *The Nature of the Judicial Process* (1921).

FISHER, *Introduction to the Legal System*, 2d ed. (1977).

CHAPTER

4

SETTLING LEGAL DISPUTES: ALTERNATIVE DISPUTE RESOLUTION AND CIVIL LAWSUITS

"LAWSUIT: A MACHINE YOU GO INTO AS A PIG AND COME OUT AS A SAUSAGE."

Ambrose Bierce, The Devil's Dictionary

POSITIVE LAW ETHICAL PROBLEMS

"My attorney settled my auto accident case by signing my name to a liability release without my knowledge, authorization, or approval. Furthermore, he deposited a settlement check received from defendant's insurer in his trust account and did not remit any of the proceeds to me or to my doctor for my medical bills associated with my accident," said Jane Smith.

Do attorneys have any legal or ethical duties to keep clients informed and not settle civil cases without the client's consent?

"I consider the unsolicited contact from you after my child's accident to be of the rankest form of ambulance chasing and in incredibly poor taste. . . . I cannot begin to express with my limited vocabulary the utter contempt in which I hold you and your kind," wrote Mary Smith to a Florida lawyer who had contacted her following her child's injury.

The lawyer wrote back to Ms. Smith: "I can understand your sensitivity, Ms. Smith, but the legal profession today is a 'dog eat dog' business—not a profession. The U.S. Supreme Court has legalized attorney advertising, in effect, ruling that law practice is a business. What I am doing is as legal as a soap suds ad on TV." Are targeted, direct mail ads to accident victims immediately following mishaps legal?

Abraham Lincoln, a lawyer at one point in his career, once said, "Avoid lawsuits." Lincoln's advice is sound for businesses and all types of people because lawsuits are often expensive, slow, and emotionally draining. They may cause long-lasting bad will and yet not end the way the parties desire. But people do have disputes about contracts, auto accidents, and many other matters that need resolution. This chapter is organized on the theme that a lawsuit should only be used as a last resort to settle disputes. Thus, the first topic is alternative dispute resolution followed by selection of a lawyer, a discussion of attorney fees, and a survey of civil lawsuits.

ALTERNATIVE DISPUTE RESOLUTION

Courts are the usual means of settling legal disputes. **Alternative dispute resolution (ADR)** refers to any means of settling legal disputes without using courts. The several types of ADR include conciliation, mediation, and arbitration.

Conciliation

Conciliation means that the two disputants get together and work things out between themselves without having anyone else present. This form of ADR generally works when the parties really want to end the dispute. Conciliation is private and minimizes publicity.

Mediation

Mediation involves using a neutral third party, called a mediator, to hear both sides of the dispute and to communicate between the disputants and reach a compromise. Mediators do not have to be lawyers (although many are) or be trained in the law, for their advice and decisions are nonbinding. *Nonbinding* means the parties do not have to follow the mediator's suggestion. Mediation can be used in most types of disputes *if* both disputants agree to it. In the international arena, for example, Pope John Paul II acted as a mediator between two South American countries. If a mediator has prestige and unquestioned goodwill, the disputants and public tend to attach great significance to the mediator's suggestions.

Arbitration

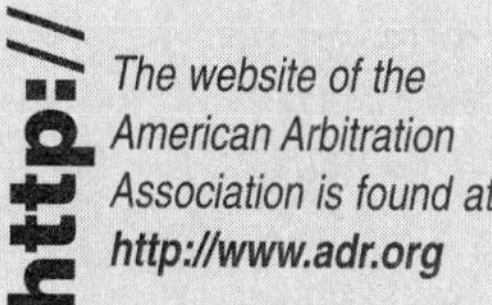

Arbitration is the formal submission of a dispute to a nonjudicial third person. Arbitration can be nonbinding or binding, although typically it is binding. *Binding* means the parties must do what the arbitrator requires.

People are usually not forced to arbitrate their disputes unless they have by contract agreed to do so or if a statute requires it. Agreements to arbitrate can be made anytime, even after the dispute occurs.

In effect, an arbitrator is a privately hired judge. Sometimes more than one arbitrator is used. Arbitrators do not have to be lawyers, although some are. They follow their own procedures and rules of evidence, which are usually more relaxed than those used in courts. Arbitrators can also make up their own rules of substantive law, within limits. Arbitrators give decisions, called **awards**, which bind the parties. Courts will enforce an arbitrator's decision just as though it were a court's judgment, even though the arbitrator did not follow the rules of law a court would have applied. Arbitrators also do not have to give reasons for their opinions, although they usually do. A period follows the filing in court of an arbitrator's award during which a party can raise an objection. However, courts give only limited review to an arbitrator's decisions and will overturn these decisions for only a few reasons: if arbitrator fraud or misconduct exists (such as the taking of a bribe); if a decision is given on an issue not submitted for arbitration; or if arbitrators go beyond their powers in fashioning an award.

Advantages of ADR

ADR is usually faster, cheaper, and less emotionally draining than a lawsuit in court because no jury is needed to settle fact issues. Although no judge who is a governmental employee presides, ADR usually involves using a neutral third party who serves as both judge and jury. Some forms of ADR, such as "Rent-a-Judge" programs (usually a form of arbitration) use neutral third parties called judges, who in actuality are not publicly employed judges, to settle the case. Such individuals usually work on an hourly rate.

Litigation costs can be lower with ADR than for conventional lawsuits, which can be a major consideration when attorney fees run more than $100 per hour. Such matters as discovery, pretrial hearings, legal research, and brief writing are part of an attorney's services and costs.

One major advantage of ADR is its privacy. The parties' "dirty laundry" is not publicly exposed. Competitors (other than the parties themselves) and others cannot, therefore, obtain information that would damage or embarrass the parties. This privacy can be particularly important in commercial matters involving trade secrets or other intellectual property.

ADR also does not establish a precedent as do published judicial decisions, which is either an advantage or disadvantage depending on whether the decision is favorable or unfavorable to one's interests.

Disadvantages of ADR

ADR has several drawbacks. First, it is an attack on the jury system. Juries are a time-honored way of determining facts: Did the doctor sew the sponge into the plaintiff's stomach? Did the stockbroker churn the client's account? Juries are asked to resolve these sorts of fact questions. None of the ADR methods covered here uses a jury. Insurance companies, physicians accused of medical malpractice, and other defendants frequently lambaste lawyers and courts in media ads complaining about million-dollar verdicts. Such ads seldom mention, though, that it is juries, not lawyers or judges, that render these verdicts. Juries, average men and women drawn from the community, hear the facts under rules of evidence, subject to the right of cross examination and rebuttal, and then award a plaintiff damages. By complaining about jury verdicts are critics really saying that plaintiffs should not be able to recover fully as judged by a jury of their peers? Also, for every horror story about runaway juries, many more stories can be told of skeptical juries that give plaintiffs little or nothing. Consider the Elena DeZavala case in this chapter to see what a Tennessee jury awarded a nine-year-old, orphaned when a driver killed her father in an auto accident. This is a more typical result than the million-dollar verdict.

A second ADR weakness is that it substitutes amateurs for professionals when it displaces lawyers and judges with mediators or arbitrators who often are not lawyers. Crucial problems in settling disputes may be ignored; questionable evidence is admitted because rules of evidence are not followed; and careless, amateurish conduct of the process is the order of the day.

Third, arbitration agreements (a form of ADR) often appear to favor one of the disputants over the other. This lack of objectivity is often due to how the arbitrator is selected. For example, in the *Shearson/American Express* case, a customer had to select arbitrators from securities industry sources (the National Association of Securities Dealers in New York or American Stock Exchange arbitrators) instead of independent arbitrators. Such arbitrators often favor brokers.

A fourth drawback to ADR settlements is that they can always be challenged in court. This means that arbitration, for instance, may not be faster and cheaper than suing in court. The parties can refuse to obey the arbitrator's award, which forces the other party to court to enforce the award. Even though court review of arbitrators' awards is not de novo (is not "from scratch" where every bit of evidence is reintroduced) but is limited, court review takes time and adds costs. In effect, arbitration merely adds another layer of dispute settlement overhead to the court system.

Fifth, arbitration "agreements" are not knowingly entered; that is, people often do not realize they are agreeing to arbitration when they sign complicated contracts for something else, such as hiring a stockbroker. The agreement to arbitrate is often buried in the fine print and is never read by the client. ADR should be permitted, but such agreements should also be knowingly entered by *both* parties with a full understanding of what they mean.

Types of Disputes for ADR Settlement

ADR can be used to settle most types of legal disputes, such as breach of contract matters, divorce, international disputes between multinational businesses, and labor disputes. Tort disputes seem less likely ADR candidates because plaintiffs prefer juries rather than arbitrators to assess their damages.

ADR under the Federal Arbitration Act of 1925[1]

ADR is not new. It was recognized in 1925 when Congress enacted the Federal Arbitration Act. This act required courts to enforce arbitration agreements just as they would any other contract. This law thus encouraged and established a federal policy promoting arbitration as a form of ADR. The Federal Arbitration Act was a legislative attempt to reverse common law (judicial) hostility to arbitrators.

Hostility to ADR in Brokerage Disputes: *Wilko v. Swan*

Stockbrokers soon recognized possible advantages of ADR. By putting arbitration provisions in customers' brokerage contracts (when the brokerage contract was opened) and controlling who were the arbitrators, brokers could, in effect, "stack the deck" against customers and thereby minimize customer claims against the brokers. However, in 1953 the Supreme Court decided in *Wilko v. Swan* that broker-customer predispute arbitration agreements were invalid because they deprived customers of their right to select a court instead of arbitration. The Supreme Court in *Wilko* was skeptical of arbitrators' ability to protect investors' rights under federal securities laws.

Supreme Court Reassessment of Arbitration

In the 1980s several U.S. Supreme Court cases upheld arbitration provisions in contracts. In *Southland v. Keating* (1983) the Court enforced a franchise agreement arbitration clause. Support for arbitration was again forthcoming in *Mitsubishi Motors v. Soler Chrysler-Plymouth*. In this 1985 decision the Supreme Court stated that it was "well past the time when judicial suspicion of the desirability of arbitration and of the competence of arbitration tribunals inhibited the development of arbitration as an alternative means of dispute resolution."

The *Mitsubishi* and *Southland* cases dealt with arbitration in areas other than brokerage contracts. The *Shearson/American Express v. McMahon* case in 1987 resulted in the Supreme Court's upholding a predispute brokerage arbitration agreement regarding customer claims under the Securities Exchange Act of 1934. This decision was made even in the presence of considerable evidence of brokers' abuse of customers' accounts and a vigorous dissent by Justice Blackmun.

Another predispute arbitration agreement—this time under the Securities Act of 1933—was at issue in *Rodriguez de Quijas v. Shearson/American Express, Inc.* In this case

---

[1] The authors acknowledge reliance on Bedell & Bosch, "The Rodriguez Decision: A New Tradition in the Arbitration of Securities Disputes," 18 *Securities Regulation Law Journal* 53 (1990).

the Supreme Court upheld such predispute arbitration agreements in 1989 and expressly overruled *Wilko v. Swan.*

In recent years employers and businesses such as retailers and banks have routinely placed arbitration clauses in employment contracts as well as contracts for the sale of goods and services. Then, if the consumer has a dispute with the employer, retailer, or bank, they must go to arbitration instead of going to court to settle the matter.

Courts generally uphold arbitration clauses in contracts when challenged on grounds of unconscionability if such clauses meet both procedural and substantive fairness tests. Although drawing the line between procedural and substantive fairness is not always easy, procedural fairness involves an examination of the setting when the contract was entered: Did the parties have a chance to think about what they were doing; were high pressure tactics used to "close" the deal; did the agreement have a lot of "fine print"; how balanced were the parties' bargaining power; and generally, did both parties have a meaningful choice? Substantive fairness involves an examination of the rules in the arbitration itself; matters such as independence of the arbitrator from the parties, convenience of the location and timing of the arbitration, even-handedness of the duty to arbitrate (some arbitration agreements require consumers or employees but not business sellers or employers to arbitrate), what remedies the arbitrator can award, and whether the arbitration requires excessive fees of the parties as a condition to arbitrate. Various consumer and employer groups are currently trying to articulate standards for fair arbitration, but as of this writing, no universal standards are in place.

A strong public policy favors arbitration. Recently, however, in California and New York, where many U.S. legal developments tend to originate, courts have invalidated some arbitration agreements and allowed the plaintiff (usually the consumer or employee) to go directly to court bypassing arbitration or have modified the arbitration to make it fairer. The grounds for invalidation or modification include adhesion contracts, unconscionability, or the lack of consent (no "meeting of the minds" of the parties on the matter). Courts examining the unconscionability of arbitration agreements focus on both procedural and substantive fairness issues. In *Brower v. Gateway 2000,* a court rewrote an arbitration agreement on grounds it was unconscionable.

Brower v. Gateway 2000, Inc.

Appellate Division of New York Supreme Court
676 N.Y.S.2d 569 (1998)

Background and Facts:

Brower and other consumers purchased consumers and software products from defendant Gateway 2000 through a direct sales system, by phone and mail order. As of July 3, 1995, it was Gateway's practice to include, along with the merchandise, a copy of its Standard Terms and Conditions Agreement and any relevant warranties for the products in the shipment. The Agreement begins with a "NOTE TO CUSTOMER," which provides, in slightly larger print than the remainder of the document, in a box that spans the width of the page: "This document contains Gateway 2000's Standard Terms and Conditions. By keeping your Gateway 2000 computer system beyond thirty (30) days after the date of delivery, you accept these Terms and Conditions." This document consists of 16 paragraphs, and, as is relevant to this appeal, paragraph 10 of the agreement entitled "DISPUTE RESOLUTION," reads as follows:

"Any dispute or controversy arising out of or relating to this Agreement or its interpretation shall be settled exclusively and finally by arbitration. The arbitration shall be conducted in accordance with the Rules of Conciliation and Arbitration of the International Chamber of Commerce. The arbitration shall be conducted in Chicago, Illinois, U.S.A. before a sole arbitrator. Any award rendered in any such arbitration proceeding shall be final and binding on each of the parties, and judgment may be entered thereon in a court of competent jurisdiction."

Plaintiffs brought this action on behalf of themselves and others similarly situated for compensatory and punitive damages, alleging deceptive sales practices in seven causes of action, including breach of warranty, breach of contract, fraud, and unfair trade practices. In particular, the allegations focused on Gateway's representations and advertising that promised "service when you need it," including around-the-clock free technical support, free software technical support, and certain on-site services. According to plaintiffs, not only were they unable to avail themselves of this offer because it was virtually impossible to get through to a technician, but also Gateway continued to advertise this claim notwithstanding numerous complaints and reports about the problem.

Insofar as is relevant to Brower and the other plaintiffs, who purchased their computers after July 3, 1995, Gateway moved to dismiss the complaint based on the arbitration clause in the Agreement. Brower and other plaintiffs argued that the arbitration clause is unconscionable under UCC 2-302 and an unenforceable contract of adhesion. Specifically, they claimed that the provision was obscure; that a customer could not reasonably be expected to appreciate or investigate its meaning and effect; that the International Chamber of Commerce (ICC) was not a forum commonly used for consumer matters; and that because ICC headquarters were in France, it was particularly difficult to locate the organization and its rules. To illustrate just how inaccessible the forum was, Brower advised the court that the ICC was not registered with the Secretary of State, that efforts to locate and contact the ICC had been unsuccessful, and that apparently the only way to attempt to contact the ICC was through the U.S. Council for International Business, with which the ICC maintained some sort of relationship.

In support of their arguments, Brower and other plaintiffs submitted a copy of the ICC's Rules of Conciliation and Arbitration and contended that the cost of ICC arbitration was prohibitive, particularly given the amount of the typical consumer claim involved. For example, a claim of less than $50,000 required advance fees of $4,000 (more than the cost of most Gateway products), of which the $2,000 registration fee was nonrefundable even if the consumer prevailed at the arbitration. Consumers would also incur travel expenses disproportionate to the damages sought, which plaintiffs' counsel estimated would not exceed $1,000 per customer in this action, as well as bear the cost of Gateway's legal fees if the consumer did not prevail at the arbitration; in this respect, the ICC rules follow the "loser pays" rule used in England. Also, although Chicago was designated as the site of the actual arbitration, all correspondence must be sent to ICC headquarters in France.

The IAS court dismissed the complaint as to plaintiff/appellants based on the arbitration clause in the Agreements delivered with their computers.

Body of Opinion

Justice Milonas

...With respect to plaintiff/appellants' claim that the arbitration claim is unenforceable as a contract of adhesion, in that it involved no choice or negotiation on the part of the consumer but was a "take it or leave it" proposition...we find that this argument, too, was properly rejected by the IAS court.

Although the parties clearly do not possess equal bargaining power, this factor alone does not invalidate the contract as one of adhesion. As the IAS court observed, with the ability to make the purchase elsewhere and the express option to return the goods, the consumer is not in a "take it or leave it" position at all; if any term of the agreement is unacceptable to the consumer, he or she can easily buy a competitor's product instead—either from a retailer or directly from the manufacturer—and reject Gateway's agreement by returning the merchandise.... The consumer has 30 days to make that decision. Within that time, the consumer can inspect the goods and examine and seek clarification of the terms of the agreement: until those 30 days have elapsed, the consumer has the unqualified right to return the merchandise, because the goods or terms are unsatisfactory or for no reason at all.

...That a consumer does not read the agreement or thereafter claims he or she failed to understand or appreciate some term therein does not invalidate the contract any more than such claim would undo a contract formed under other circumstances....

Finally, we turn to appellant/plaintiffs' argument that the IAS court should have declared the contract unenforceable, pursuant to UCC 2-302, on the ground that the arbitration clause is unconscionable due to the unduly burdensome procedure and cost for the individual consumer. The IAS court found that while a class action lawsuit such as the one herein, may be a less costly alternative to the arbitration (which is generally less costly than litigation), that does not alter the binding effect of the arbitration clause contained in the agreement....

As a general matter, under New York law, unconscionability requires a showing that a contract is "both procedurally and substantively unconscionable when made."... That is, there must be "some showing of 'an absence of meaningful choice on the part of one of the parties together with contract terms which are unreasonably favorable to the other party.'"... The Acco court (in another case) took pains to note, however, that the purpose of this doctrine is not to redress the inequality between the parties but simply to insure that the more powerful party cannot "surprise the other party with some overly oppressive term."...

As to the procedural element, a court will look to the contract formation process to determine if in fact one party lacked any meaningful choice in entering into the contract taking into consideration such factors as the setting of the transaction, the experience and education of the party claiming unconscionability, whether the contract contained "fine print," whether the seller used "high pressure tactics" and any disparity in the parties' bargaining power.... None of these factors supports plaintiff/appellants' claims here.... The Agreement itself, which is entitled in large print "STANDARD TERMS AND CONDITIONS AGREEMENT," consists of only three pages and 16 paragraphs, all of which appear in the same size print. Moreover, despite appellant/plaintiffs' claims to the contrary, the arbitration clause is in no way "hidden" or "tucked away" within a complex document of inordinate length, nor is the option of returning the merchandise, to avoid the contract, somehow a "precarious" one....

With respect to the substantive element... we do not find that the possible inconvenience of the chosen site (Chicago) alone rises to the level of unconscionability. We do find, however, that the excessive cost factor that is necessarily entailed in arbitrating before the ICC is unreasonable and surely serves to deter the individual consumer from invoking the process.... Barred from resorting to the courts by the arbitration clause in the first instance, the designation of a financially prohibitive forum effectively bars consumers from this forum as well; consumers are thus left with no forum at all in which to resolve a dispute....

Gateway's brief includes the text of a new arbitration agreement that it claims has been extended to all customers, past, present, and future.... The new arbitration agreement provides for the consumer's choice of the AAA [American Arbitration Association] or the ICC as the arbitral body and the designation of any location for the arbitration by agreement of the parties, which "shall not be unreasonably withheld." It also provides telephone numbers for information regarding the "organizations and their procedures."

As noted, however, plaintiff/appellants complain that the AAA fees are also excessive and thus in no way have they accepted defendant's offer... because they make the same claim as to the ICC, the issue of unconscionability is not rendered moot, as defendant suggests. We cannot determine on this record whether the AAA process and costs would be so "egregiously oppressive" that they, too, would be unconscionable....

Judgment and Result

The New York Supreme Court order dismissing plaintiff/appellants' complaint on the ground that a valid agreement to arbitrate had been entered was modified by the New York Supreme Court, Appellate Division. The appellate court vacated the part of the trial court order requiring arbitration before the International Chamber of Commerce and left the parties to seek appointment of a substitute arbitrator under the Federal Arbitration Act.

Questions

1. When and under what circumstances does a customer enter an arbitration agreement with the seller of a computer?
2. Why did the appellate court refuse to hold that the arbitration provision was an adhesion contract?
3. Was the arbitration contract in *Brower v. Gateway* unconscionable? Was the arbitration provision procedurally or substantively unconscionable?
4. If the arbitration provision was substantively unconscionable, why did the court end up ordering arbitration?

SEC Rules Regarding Arbitration

Concern about the fairness of predispute arbitration clauses in customer brokerage agreements following the *McMahon* case led the SEC to regulate such forms of ADR. Here are two regulated matters. Introductory language in customer agreements must explain the effect of the arbitration clause; that is, brokers' customers give up the right to sue their broker in court, accept that arbitration as final, accept that the arbitrator does not have to give reasons for its award or make fact findings, and accept that the arbitration panel usually will have some persons who have been stockbrokers. Second, these disclosures must be conspicuous in the customer's agreement, and another warning must appear above the signature line pointing out where the arbitration provision is in the brokerage contract. Also, the SEC refuses to allow arbitration agreements to deprive customers of remedies they could have gotten in court. For example, if punitive damages are possible in court, the arbitration clause may not prevent the stock buyer from obtaining them. One matter the SEC regs do not require is that customers, when they open an account, be given an option to sue brokers in court or seek arbitration.

Keep in mind that the *McMahon* and *Rodriguez* cases expressly uphold arbitration of Securities Exchange Act or Securities Act claims against brokers—not against other businesses. However, these cases, coupled with the 1925 Federal Arbitration Act and the *Southland* and *Mitsubishi* cases, clearly do signal greater Supreme Court approval of arbitration (ADR) in many contexts.

THE ATTORNEY'S ROLE IN THE LEGAL SYSTEM

Three objectives of law are justice, speed, and economy. They can be achieved by having professionals, called attorneys or lawyers, advocate others' claims.

The Reason for Attorneys

The social justification for attorneys' existence occurs when they raise appropriate, persuasive arguments on behalf of their client. These arguments expose judges to better ideas, which can lead to sound rules of law and reasonable precedent for future cases. Also, because attorneys are familiar with court procedures, speed is potentially promoted. The qualifying word *potentially* is added because attorneys may also use their skills to delay matters to benefit their clients.

Attorney Fees

A sensitive issue concerning attorneys is the manner and amount of payment for their professional services. In civil cases, attorneys can be paid by fixed or contingent fees. Under the fixed fee arrangement attorneys tell the client how much the service will cost before it is given. The fixed fee is used for much nonlitigation legal work, such as drafting contracts, wills, trusts, and organizing partnerships and corporations. Attorney ethics only allow fixed fees—not contingent fees—for criminal cases.

Contingent fees mean that one's attorney gets a fee only after winning the lawsuit or a settlement acceptable to the client. One advantage of contingent fees is that a poor person with a potentially large claim could get the best lawyer in town. A **contingent fee** option is available only in those cases in which one can win money. Thus such fees are possible for plaintiffs but not for defendants unless they bring counterclaims.

In the United States the *American rule* is that each party pays its own attorney fees no matter who wins the case unless a statute or contract provides otherwise. This rule is to be contrasted with the *English rule* under which the loser pays the winner's attorney fees. In effect, the English rule discourages litigation.

Some Aspects of Attorney Fees. The economics of the practice of law are not well understood by the general public. TV programs and movies would have you believe that all attorneys drive BMWs, live in swanky houses or condos, wear $1,000 suits, and work in fancy offices. The reality is different.

Types of law practice include corporate, tax, trial, family law, poverty law, environmental law, general practice, and many others. Income expectations can vary widely depending on what type of law one practices and where one practices it. One hears about $1 million judgments and concludes that all lawyers must be experiencing such success. However, consider that most lawsuits end with a winner and a loser. In such a case the attorneys for one party will get no fee, assuming the matter is handled on a contingency basis.

Also consider that attorneys who are in private practice have overhead expenses associated with running a law office, such as paying rent for an office, plus the costs for heating, lighting, secretarial help, a law library, bar association dues, Social Security taxes, income taxes, and health insurance for the attorney and office staff. Also, many law office personnel want child-care allowances, vacation pay, retirement plans, and flex time. All of these benefits cost money. Thus, when one hears of an attorney winning a $100,000 judgment for a client and asking the client for $33,333 (one-third of the fee), it is *not* all profit. This fee must pay for the expenses of the law firm.

Some argue that the 25 percent or 33 1/3 percent contingency fees are too high. However, consider the following: A Wall Street financial firm several years ago found that the amount paid to workers' compensation beneficiaries as a percentage of premium dollar going to insurance was 59 percent, meaning that the workers' compensation insurers had a 41 percent overhead—several percentage points higher than the contingent fees of attorneys. Also consider another fact: Most major universities in the United States impose an overhead charge of 40–60 percent on grants received by professors from the government or private foundations, a much higher overhead charge than attorneys. These examples suggest, though perhaps not conclusively, that the impression that attorneys are scalping the public is untrue. No doubt some are earning high incomes, but others make far more modest incomes.

Attorney-Client Control of the Case

Most civil lawsuits are settled out of court when the plaintiff and defendant agree on an outcome and drop the suit at some point in the proceedings, often before trial. Settlement of a case can result in the plaintiff's attorney getting a lower fee either because fewer billable hours are spent on the client's behalf or because contingent fees often give the attorney a lower percentage of the settlement when the case does not go to trial.

A related issue concerns an attorney's duty to keep a client informed about the progress of a civil case, explain matters to clients so they can make informed decisions about the course the wish to follow (for example, accept a settlement offer or "roll the dice" and go for a larger jury verdict), and follow the client's wishes as to whether to accept a settlement offer. *In Re Samai* discusses duties attorneys owe their clients.

In Re Samai

Supreme Court of Indiana
706 N.E.2d 146 (1999)

Background and Facts:

Benedict Samai was hired to represent a client in a personal injury action arising from an automobile accident in 1995. Within two weeks after the collision, Samai contacted Erie Insurance Company, the insurer of the other driver. Samai also arranged a medical evaluation of his client. Immediately thereafter, Samai lost contact with his client. His subsequent efforts to locate her were unsuccessful.

Approximately six months after the collision and without having any further contact with his client, Samai submitted to Erie a demand for $5,000 for settlement of his client's claim. Erie responded with an offer of $2,000, which Samai accepted. Samai executed a release of claim on behalf of the client by signing her name on the release. The client was not aware of the negotiations between Erie and Samai and had not authorized Samai to settle her claim.

On November 11, 1995, Samai received from Erie a check for $2,000 made payable to the client and him. Samai endorsed the settlement check by signing both his name and that of his client. He deposited the settlement check into his trust account on November 14, 1995. During the next 17 days, several checks were drawn against the trust account, but none was made payable to the client for whom the $2,000 settlement had been reached. The balance of the trust account fell below $2,000 during late November, and the balance at the end of that month was $733.16. His client never received any portion of the settlement check, and none of the settlement proceeds were used to pay the doctor who treated the client.

The client contacted Samai in March 1996 and asked that her file be forwarded to another attorney. Samai told her that he had settled her claim for $2,000 because he had not heard from her in six months. Samai contacted Erie and explained that his client might have medical bills beyond that which he originally contemplated. He sent Erie a cashier's check for $2,000 in an apparent attempt to nullify the settlement and renew negotiations. Erie returned the check and informed the respondent that it considered the client's case closed.

The client subsequently filed a grievance with the Disciplinary Commission.

Body of Opinion

Per curiam.

Samai's response to the grievance filed by his counsel represented that the proceeds from the settlement check remained in the trust account from the date of deposit on November 11, 1995, through the date of the filing of respondent's response on October 26, 1996. In fact, the funds remained in the trust account no longer than 15 days beyond the date of deposit. By July 2, 1996—three months before the filing of the response—the trust account was overdrawn by $1,266.93. . . .

The parties agree, and we hereby find, that with respect to Count I, Samai violated Ind. Professional Conduct Rule 1.2(a) when he agreed to settle his client's personal injury claim for $2,000 without informing her or obtaining her consent. Prof. Cond. R. 1.2(a) provides: "A lawyer shall abide by a client's decisions concerning the objectives of representation, subject to paragraphs (c), (d), and (e), and shall consult with the client as to the means by which they are to be pursued. A lawyer shall abide by a client's decision whether to accept an offer of settlement of a matter. . . ." He also violated Prof. Cond. R. 1.2(a) when he signed the release which waived his client's right to further recourse with Erie. Samai violated Prof. Cond. R. 1.4(b) when he failed to consult with his client before making a settlement demand. Prof. Cond. R. 1.4(b) provides: "A lawyer shall explain a matter to the extent reasonably necessary to permit the client to make informed decisions regarding the representation." He violated Prof. Cond. R. 8.4(b) when he committed criminal acts—specifically, forgery and conversion. Prof. Cond. R. 8.4(b) provides: "It is professional misconduct for a lawyer to b) commit a criminal act that reflects adversely on the lawyer's honesty, trustworthiness or fitness as a lawyer in other respects." He violated Prof. Cond. R. 8.4(c) by signing his client's name on documents and converting his client's settlement funds. He also violated Prof. Cond. R. 8.1(a) when he knowingly allowed his attorney to falsely represent to the Commission that the settlement proceeds remained in Samai's trust account. . . .

Through his actions, Samai has shown a general predilection to deceive clients as to the status of their cases and to represent them in a manner inconsistent with their best interests. Such actions suggest a lack of integrity, honesty, and diligence integral to the practice of law.

Judgment and Result

The Supreme Court of Indiana suspended Samai's license to practice law for a period of not less than 18 months, beginning March 15, 1999. At the conclusion of that period he may petition the Indiana Supreme Court for reinstatement to practice law.

Questions

1. In what ways does this case show that an attorney can be dishonest?
2. Does the *Samai* case say that attorneys may not settle a case without first getting the client's approval? If the client cannot be located, as apparently happened here, should the attorney settle?
3. Attorneys have a duty to inform clients about the status of their case. Does this case discuss clients' duties to their attorneys? For example, a civil plaintiff's attorney often takes a case on a contingent fee basis. How can the attorney be paid if during the course of the case the client hires another attorney for the same matter? Clients may dismiss their attorneys at any time subject to any contractual obligations the client may have to the attorney, such as paying the attorney for time spent in the case or reimbursing for expenses. However, if the attorney takes a case strictly on a contingency basis and the client fires the attorney, what risks does the attorney face?
4. Where did the clients go to complain about the poor service they had received from their attorney? Note that the client filed a grievance with the Disciplinary Commission several months after hiring Samai based on her inability to contact him. Does this claim undermine Samai's assertion that he could not find his client?
5. How might a client confer authority on an attorney to settle claims or sign legal documents without the client's actually knowing about such actions? What is a "power of attorney"?

Finding a Lawyer—Attorney Advertising

Until recently various rules (mainly state bar association ethical rules) outlawed attorney advertising. This rule actually discouraged many laypeople from seeking professional help from an attorney because they were unsure about the charge for an initial contact as well as other potential fees. Often people would ask a realtor, accountant, or insurance agent for legal help when they should have been asking a legal expert.

In 1977 the U.S. Supreme Court decided *Bates v. State Bar of Arizona*. This case held that states may *not* prevent truthful attorney ads concerning the availability and terms of routine legal services. Since the *Bates* case broke the ice, attorney ads in various media (TV, radio, and newspapers) are now common, and the public is better informed about fee basics. But the effect of this decision should not be exaggerated. It is highly unlikely that the president of IBM would thumb through the want ads to find a cheap lawyer to handle an antitrust case. Big users of legal services (corporations, unions, large organizations, and wealthy individuals) are largely unaffected by this decision.

In 1995 the U.S. Supreme Court took another look at attorney advertising. This time the case involved the propriety of truthful but possibly offensive contacting of accident victims or their immediate families immediately following an injury. The Florida Bar had imposed a 30-day blackout period during which attorneys were forbidden to send targeted, direct-mail attorney solicitations to such persons. *Florida Bar v. Went For It* presents the Supreme Court's view on the legality of such restrictions on attorney advertising.

Florida Bar v. Went For It, Inc.

U.S. Supreme Court
115 S.Ct. 2371 (1995)

Background and Facts:

In 1989, the Florida Bar completed a two-year study of the effects of lawyer advertising on public opinion. After conducting hearings, commissioning surveys, and reviewing extensive public commentary, the Bar determined that several changes to its advertising rules were in order. In late 1990, the Florida Supreme Court adopted the Bar's proposed amendments with some modifications.... Two of those amendments are at issue in this case. Rule 4-7.4 (b)(1) provides that "[a] lawyer shall not send, or knowingly permit to be sent, ...a written communication to a prospective client for the purpose of obtaining professional employment if: (A) the written communication concerns an action for personal injury or wrongful death or otherwise relates to an accident or disaster involving the person to whom the communication addressed or a relative of that person, unless the accident or disaster occurred more than 30 days prior to the mailing of the communication." Rule 4-7.8(a) states that "[a] lawyer shall not accept referrals from a lawyer referral service unless the service: (1) engages in no communication with the public and in no direct contact with prospective clients in a manner that would violate the Rules of Professional Conduct if the communication or contact were made by the lawyer." Together, these rules create a brief 30-day blackout period after an accident during which lawyers may not, directly or indirectly, single out accident victims or their relatives in order to solicit their business.

In March 1992, G. Stewart McHenry and his wholly owned lawyer referral service, Went For It, Inc., filed this action for declaratory and injunctive relief in the U.S. District Court challenging Rules 4-7.4(b)(1) and 4-7.8 as violative of the First and Fourteenth Amendments of the Constitution. McHenry alleged that he routinely sent targeted solicitations to accident victims or their survivors within 30 days after accidents and that he wished to continue doing so in the future. In October 1992 McHenry was disbarred for reasons unrelated to this suit and another Florida lawyer, John Blakely, was substituted.

The District Court rejected a Magistrate Judge's report and recommendations and entered judgment for plaintiffs relying on *Bates v. State Bar of Arizona*. The Eleventh Circuit affirmed on similar grounds. The Supreme Court granted certiorari.

Body of Opinion

Justice O'Connor

Constitutional protection for attorney advertising, and for commercial speech generally, is of recent vintage. Until the mid-1970s, we adhered to the broad rule laid out in *Valentine v. Chrestensen*... (1942), that, while First Amendment guards against government restriction of speech in most contexts, "the Constitution imposes no such restraint on government as respects purely commercial advertising." In 1976, the Court changed course. In *Virginia State Bd. of Pharmacy v. Virginia Citizens Consumer Council, Inc.*... we invalidated a state statute barring pharmacists from advertising prescription drug prices....

In *Virginia State Board*, the Court limited its holding to advertising by pharmacists.... One year later, however, the Court applied the Virginia State Board principles to invalidate a state rule prohibiting lawyers from advertising in newspapers and other media. In *Bates v. State Bar of Arizona*... the Court struck a ban on price advertising for what it deemed "routine" legal services....

Nearly two decades of cases have built upon the foundation laid by *Bates*. It is now well established that lawyer advertising is commercial speech and, as such, is accorded a measure of First Amendment protection.... Such First Amendment protection is, of course, not absolute.... We have always been careful to distinguish commercial speech from speech at the First Amendment's core. "'Commercial speech [enjoys] a limited measure of protection, commensurate with its subordinate position in the scale of First Amendment values', and is subject to 'modes of regulation that might be impermissible in the realm of noncommercial expression.'"...

Mindful of these concerns, we engage in "intermediate" scrutiny of restrictions on commercial speech, analyzing them in the framework set forth in *Central Hudson Gas & Electric Corp. v. Public Service Comm'n. of N.Y.* (1980). Under *Central Hudson*, the government may freely regulate commercial speech that concerns unlawful activity or is misleading.... Commercial speech that falls into neither of those categories, like the advertising at issue here, may be regulated if the government satisfies a test consisting of three related prongs: first, the government must assert a substantial interest in support of its regulation; second, the government must demonstrate that the restriction on commercial speech directly and materially advances that interest; and third, the regulation must be "narrowly drawn...."

We have little trouble crediting the Bar's interest as substantial....

Under *Central Hudson's* second prong, the State must demonstrate that the challenged regulation "advances the Government's interest 'in a direct and material way.'"... That burden, we have explained, "is not satisfied by mere speculation and conjecture; rather, a governmental body seeking to sustain a restriction on commercial speech must demonstrate that the harms it recites are real and that its restriction will in fact alleviate them to a material degree.'"...

The direct mail solicitation regulation before us does not suffer from such infirmities. The Florida Bar submitted a 106-page summary of its two-year study of lawyer advertising and solicitation to the District Court. That summary contains data—both statistical and anecdotal—supporting the Bar's contentions that the Florida public views direct-mail solicitations in the immediate wake of accidents as an intrusion on privacy that reflects poorly upon the profession. As of June 1989, lawyers mailed 700,000 direct solicitations in Florida annually, 40% of which were aimed at accident victims or their survivors.... Significantly, 27% of direct-mail recipients reported that their regard for the legal profession and for the judicial process as a whole was "lower" as a result of receiving the direct mail....

The anecdotal record mustered by the Bar is noteworthy for its breadth and detail.... The study summary also includes page upon page of excerpts from complaints of direct-mail recipients.... For example, a Florida citizen described how he was "'appalled and angered by the brazen attempt'" of a law firm to solicit him by letter shortly after he was injured and his fiance was killed in an auto accident.... Still another described as "'beyond comprehension'" a letter his nephew's family received the day of the nephew's funeral.... One citizen wrote, "'I consider the unsolicited contact from you after my child's accident to be of the rankest form of ambulance chasing and in incredibly poor taste.... I cannot begin to express with my limited vocabulary the utter contempt in which I hold you and your kind.'"

In light of this showing... we conclude that the Bar has satisfied the second prong of the *Central Hudson* test....

Passing to *Central Hudson's* third prong, we examine the relationship between the Florida Bar's interests and the means chosen to serve them.... Respondents' second point would have force if the Bar's rule were not limited to a brief period and if there were not many other ways for injured Floridians to learn about the availability of legal representation during that time... Florida permits lawyers to advertise on prime-time television and radio as well as in newspapers and other media. They may rent space on billboards. They may send untargeted letters to the general population, or to discrete segments thereof. There are, of course, pages upon pages devoted to lawyers in the Yellow Pages of Florida telephone directories.... We see no defect in Florida's regulation....

Judgment and Result

The judgment of the U.S. Court of Appeals was reversed. The Florida bar rules prohibiting lawyers from using direct mail to solicit personal injury clients within 30 days of an accident was valid.

Questions

1. U.S. Supreme Court decisions starting with *Bates* have generally supported attorneys' rights to advertise truthful, nondeceptive services. Does this case impose a limit on attorney advertising? Why?
2. Could Florida attorneys contact accident victims during the 30-day period immediately following an accident using less intrusive means such as billboards and television advertising? Are billboards and TV ads "targeted" or aimed at a "general" audience? Does their ruling suggest that the Supreme Court was bothered by the "targeted" aspect of the ads in *Went For It*?
3. Was the advertising in *Went For It* untruthful? Deceptive? Distasteful and degrading to the practice of a "great" profession?
4. What are the prongs of the *Central Hudson* test on regulation of nondeceptive, legal activity? Did the Court apply that test in *Went For It*?
5. Is the practice of law a profession or a business? What does the *Bates* decision suggest? How about the *Went For It* case?
6. Note that the *Went For It* decision was decided 5 to 4. What does this result indicate about the strength of the arguments competing for dominance in this case? How important was the empirical evidence? Does it suggest a link between positive law and philosophical positivism discussed in Chapter 1?

Attorneys and the Middle Class

Today the public and the legal profession find themselves in an awkward situation: An oversupply of well-trained, capable attorneys to serve the public where the middle class must do without legal help because it cannot afford the price of counsel. The rich can afford to hire attorneys, and the poor qualify for legal aid, but the middle class is often underserved by the legal profession. The law of supply and demand seems to work for most types of professional compensation except for the legal profession's fee schedules, which remain fixed. In part, the high fees are due to the high costs of being an attorney, such as office rent, costs of maintaining a law library and office staff, and phone bills, to say nothing of regaining a return on the high costs and opportunity costs of a legal education.

Judicare. Whether relaxing regulations on attorney advertising will resolve the dual problem of the oversupply of attorneys and the legal underrepresentation of large segments of the population remains an imponderable issue. Two avenues seem worth exploring as ways to solve this middle-class underrepresentation problem: judicare and small claims courts with pro se litigants.

Judicare is a concept similar to the Medicare concept used to provide medical care for certain members of society, but judicare could help provide *legal* services for all segments of the population.

Many ways of implementing judicare exist. For example, everyone could be given an opportunity to receive a fixed-dollar amount of legal service each year. Under judicare, the government would provide a person with a voucher entitling that person to go to any lawyer and receive legal services up to the amount of the voucher. The attorney would then turn in the vouchers and receive payment from the government for services rendered. Judicare could also be implemented by a federal tax deduction or tax credit for expenditures for legal services during the tax year. Possibly, too, the state or federal government could establish large legal aid societies to render socialized legal services for all people or for those earning less than a certain income. The principal problem is whether society is willing to allocate its scarce resources for legal services rather than for other goods or services.

One answer to the problem of providing legal services to the middle class has come from the American Express Company. For a small monthly charge, a customer qualifies for a legal services plan. Some issues concerning these plans are what services are covered and not covered; what are the provider's qualifications; and are these services really needed? (It should be noted that most liability insurance policies provide attorney services if you are sued.)

Pro se Litigants. Another possible solution to the problem of the legally underrepresented lies in expansion of small claims courts where only **pro se litigants** are allowed. *Pro se* means "through oneself," and pro se litigants are people involved in lawsuits who act as their own attorney.

Small Claims Courts. Small claims courts have been established in a number of states to allow people with small-dollar claims a forum to collect them without high court costs and attorney fees to deter the suit. Consider the plight of the newspaper carrier who has a customer with an unpaid bill of $25. This amount is hardly worth suing for in a conventional court because the fee to file a complaint is often $10 or $12, to say nothing of attorney fees necessary to get the complaint properly drafted and filed in the appropriate court. If conventional courts were to deal with such a matter, the newspaper carrier would be without remedy for all practical purposes.

Small claims courts, however, have simplified procedures. Litigants may not have attorneys, court costs are low, and the courts do provide a realistic solution to the problem of satisfying the needs of small claimants. But small claims courts are not problem free. A provision usually allows appeal of small claims court judgments to courts of record, so a recalcitrant defendant might effectively undercut many of the advantages of small claims courts simply by appealing the judgment to the higher court. This appeal could prompt the plaintiff to drop the matter.

OVERVIEW OF CIVIL LAWSUITS

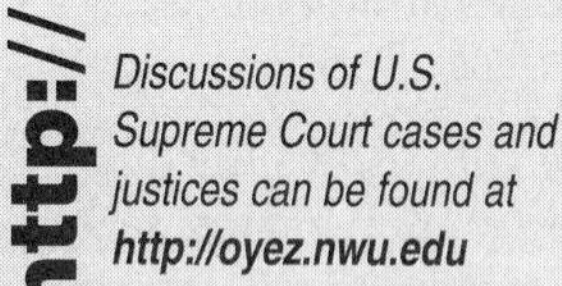

This part of the chapter deals with civil procedure or civil adjective law, which is law designed to guide a legal dispute through the civil justice system. The usual objective of civil lawsuits is compensatory, either to obtain money for wrongs done to one or to force someone to do or not do something.

Figure 4.1 shows some of the steps in a civil lawsuit. Each of these steps is discussed in the following paragraphs.

Who May Sue: The Standing Issue

Standing is a concept that limits who may sue to correct a legal wrong. In the usual civil case, the standing concept means that a person directly and tangibly injured by another may bring suit. For example, if B punches C in the nose, C is said to have standing to sue B for committing the legal wrong (here, battery) against C.

One reason for the standing rule is to control the amount of litigation arising from a wrong by letting the injured party, but no one else, sue for recovery. The legal system does not exist to facilitate or encourage endless arguments, but rather to settle them. The belief is that the injured party (or the party allegedly injured)—not a stranger—is in the best position to determine whether to seek legal rectification of the wrong. Also, in federal courts, standing provides the possibility that the party in the lawsuit has something to lose and hence will argue and present issues with an intensity and vigor not found by a disinterested litigant who has no personal stake in the case outcome.

Standing issues usually do not arise in the average suit in which one private party sues another private party for breaking a contract or a leg. Rather, standing problems

FIGURE 4.1 Steps in a Civil Lawsuit

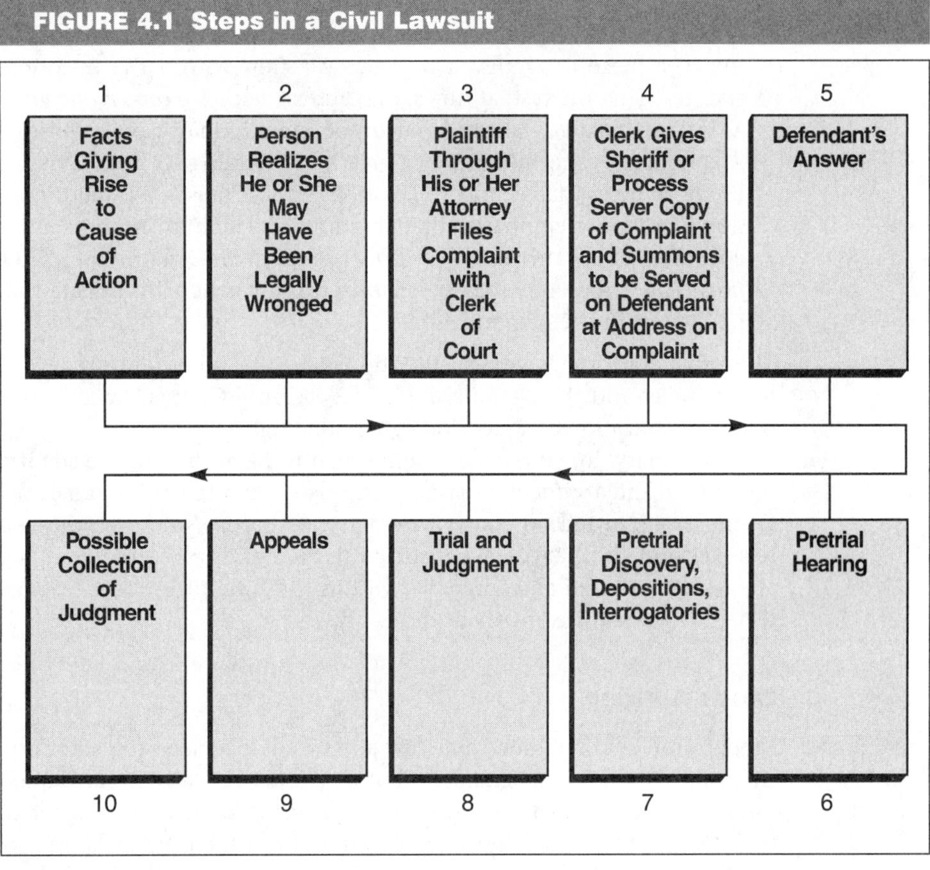

occur in lawsuits involving public law, such as where taxpayers sue the government to stop the spending of their tax dollars on programs with which the taxpayers disagree. Such suits are now usually tolerated, but at one time were barred by the standing rule.

Today, standing issues are prominent in environmental lawsuits. A case in point would arise where an environmental group such as the Wilderness Society sues an agency of the federal government or the secretary of the U.S. Department of Interior to halt construction of the trans-Alaska pipeline. In such a case, if the Wilderness Society owned no land or other interests that could possibly be harmed by construction of the pipeline, the argument could be made that the society is meddling by sticking its unwanted nose into someone else's business. Along this line, one case held that consumer advocate Ralph Nader lacked standing to sue to stop the merger of an insurance company with the International Telephone and Telegraph Company.

A basic question involved in standing is, "Does the plaintiff have some legal, potential loss that is close enough to someone else's wrong to justify holding the wrongdoer liable?" Certainly the potential loss of money would amount to sufficient interest to give a plaintiff standing to sue. Other potential losses were noted by the U.S. Supreme Court in *Association of Data Processing Service Organizations, Inc. v. Camp*, 397 U.S. 150 (1970), when it observed:

> The question of standing concerns, apart from the *case* or *controversy* test, the question whether the interest sought to be protected by the complainant is arguably

> within the zone of interests to be protected or regulated by the statute or constitutional guarantee in question. Thus the Administrative Procedure Act grants standing to a person "aggrieved by agency action within the meaning of a relevant statute." That interest, at times, may reflect *aesthetic, conservational, and recreational* as well as *economic* values. A person or a family may have a spiritual stake in First Amendment value sufficient to give him standing to raise issues concerning the Establishment Clause and the Free Exercise Clause. We mention these noneconomic values to emphasize that standing may stem from them as well as from the economic injury on which petitioner relies here. Certainly he who is "likely to be *financially*" injured may be a reliable attorney general to litigate the issues of public interest in the present case.

The private attorneys general mentioned in the quote are private parties, such as Ralph Nader and the National Resources Defense Council, who, though not official public organizations, sue to vindicate public rights.

In summary, litigants today are deemed to have standing to sue if they are tangibly injured and a sufficient connection exists between the broken duty and the harm. Furthermore, in federal courts where private parties sue to vindicate rights under a federal statute or the federal constitution, the standing requirement is satisfied if they are actually injured and "arguably within the zone of interests" designed to be protected by the statute or constitution.

Class Actions

Modern rules of civil procedural law allow people to sue others not only on behalf of themselves but also on behalf of all other people similarly situated and injured by the same defendant in what is called a *class action*. The justification for the class action becomes clear when we consider what might be called the socialized wrong, that is, a small wrong inflicted upon many people by one person. Class actions make suits against social wrongdoers economically feasible in cases in which suits brought by individual litigants would be uneconomical.

Consider an example. A consumer, X, who buys stock on the New York Stock Exchange (NYSE), might well be charged the same commission irrespective of the broker used. X might claim that the commission paid was $70 too high due to price fixing, a violation of the Sherman Act. Hiring an attorney, incurring court costs, and taking the time and trouble of going to court is not worth possibly recovering $70 in alleged commission overcharge (or $210 due to trebled damages under the Sherman Act if the case is proved). Yet, if each of the thousands of purchasers of securities through brokers is damaged about the same amount as X, the total amount of all of their injuries would be huge.

Basically, the class action works as follows. A person injured by a small amount hires an attorney, who files a complaint on behalf of the client and all the people injured by the same defendant. The attorney then estimates the number of transactions, multiplies the amount of damage each person probably sustained by the wrong (here, the price fixing), and sues the defendant (the broker or NYSE or both) on behalf of all such consumers, even though they do not actually authorize or in person join the suit. The class action can be used in environmental cases, consumer cases, corporate shareholder **derivative suits**, and cases in which small, fragmented injury exists among many. The class action device allows attorneys enough of a financial incentive to offer their services to such class action clients.

The greatest advantage of the class action is that people have a legal vehicle enabling them to recover for injuries caused by another in cases in which this recovery would not have been available through the conventional lawsuit where each plaintiff sues separately. Society benefits in at least two ways from the class action. First, the social interest is promoted in seeing that wrongdoers are held accountable for the harm they cause. Second, class actions are a substitute for the ongoing government regulation that would otherwise be needed to protect the individual's interests. In class actions, attorneys eager to collect their fee get relief for their clients quickly, something for which government regulatory agencies are not noted. Once judgments against the social wrongdoers are collected and distributed to all members of the class, the attorneys disappear until needed again.

The class action sounds like a cure-all promoting consumerism and corporate responsibility and ending bureaucratic government. However, some recent U.S. Supreme Court cases have cut back on the class action device in federal courts by requiring that each individual member of the class meet the jurisdictional amount to sue in federal courts ($75,000) and that the plaintiff starting the suit give actual notice to all people who are members of the class. As an economic matter, the costs of giving actual notice to all class members is prohibitive, and the identification of all class members, while possible, is difficult. The limits on class actions do not apply to class actions brought in state courts. Here, though, the problem is either that state rules of civil procedure do not allow class actions in the first place or that rules forbidding attorney solicitation of clients inhibit such actions. Nonetheless, federal legislation could reverse the Supreme Court rulings inhibiting class suits, and state legislatures could enact laws allowing such devices.

http://

Many landmark cases are listed at **http://www.nytimes com/library/politics/scotus/court-major-cases.html**

Probably the greatest deterrent to such legal reform is the fear that some aggressive attorney will do such an effective selling job to a jury that it will bring in a huge verdict to bankrupt large U.S. corporations. (Class action claims and recoveries can be tremendous.) The ripple effects are not to be underestimated: loss of jobs for employees, loss of the value of stock for stockholders, loss of pensions for retired individuals whose retirement income is tied to the income-generating capacity of the corporation's stock, and elimination of orders to suppliers, with resultant reduced demand for their products and further layoffs of employees.

Recognizing a Legal Wrong

In many cases, the abruptness with which one's rights are broken by another brings home that one might have a good legal case against such a person. Having one's nose punched, for example, will usually give rise to the civil action of battery. Even though laypeople do not know the legal theory that should be used to recover for damages, they intuitively know a wrong has been committed and that a visit to an attorney is in order.

But some wrongs are subtler, or the circumstances of their occurrence might lead the victim to doubt whether any wrong has been committed. For example, if a person bought stock in a company relying on financial statements audited by an accountant, and the stock later proved worthless because the statement of financial position (balance sheet) greatly overstated the inventory, the stock purchaser may just philosophically accept this loss, never realizing legal recourse was available against the accountant who did the audit. Then a few months later, the "victim" bump into a lawyer, relate the stock loss story, and ask what to do. Assuming the attorney is reasonably familiar with federal Securities Act of 1933, the lawyer would explain that a possible avenue of recovery exists against the accountant.

Note that the failure of people to realize that they have been legally wronged is not unusual. Many people are simply ignorant of their legal rights. Another factor that to some extent reduces the number of lawsuits is the set of legal and ethical rules governing attorneys.

Statute of Limitations

Assuming that people do realize they have been wronged and seek out an attorney, a next major hurdle awaits: the statute of limitations.

A statute of limitations is a law that bars a plaintiff's lawsuit because the complaint is filed too long after the wrong occurred. The objective of the statute of limitations is repose—community peace. Also, evidence is lost and witnesses move away or die as times passes. The statute of limitations implies to a potential plaintiff, "Sue promptly, or you lose." Note that a statute of limitations means that people who wait too long to sue after they were wronged lose the lawsuit even if they clearly were wronged. In effect, a statute of limitations takes away someone's right to be restored after being wronged.

Many statutes of limitations exist—not just one. They vary in length, and different statutes of limitations apply to different theories of recovery. For example, torts[2] generally have statutes of limitations of one year, whereas contract matters often have longer statute of limitations periods, such as six years. Some property matters have even longer periods ranging up to 20 years or more. The length of the time period reflects the importance of the right under challenge. For example, in the statutes of limitations periods already mentioned, one can conclude that property rights are more important than contract rights, which in turn are more crucial than rights attached to recovery for injuries to the person (torts).

Note that statutes of limitations do not require that a lawsuit be completed before the statute of limitations period expires. It is only necessary to *start* the suit (file the complaint) before the statutory period ends. Sometimes the statute of limitations is *tolled*, meaning that time is not considered to run, because of war or other extraordinary event. Finally, note that it is the defendant who seeks to raise the statute of limitations, because the statute of limitations stops lawsuits. It does not create rights.

Burden of Proof

Burden of proof is not an exciting concept, yet it is probably the single largest reason people lose lawsuits. The burden of proof in a civil case is generally said to rest on the person who wants the legal system to do something for him or her. This person is usually the plaintiff—the party suing. However, if the defendant files what is called a **counterclaim**, the burden of proof with respect to matters asserted in the counterclaim falls on the defendant. A counterclaim arises when the plaintiff sues the defendant and the defendant sues the plaintiff in return, claiming the plaintiff did something wrong to the defendant. An example is a case in which a merchant sells a toaster to a consumer on an installment plan, the toaster does not work, the consumer stops payment on the toaster, the merchant sues the consumer for the installment payments, and the consumer counterclaims against the merchant for breach of warranty because the toaster does not work.

After establishing who has the burden of proof, the next matter to determine is what one has to prove. Generally, all elements of the legal theory that the moving

[2] Torts or civil wrongs are those breaches of civil duties that do not arise by contract, such as the duty not to slander another.

party (usually the plaintiff) must establish must be proved to induce the legal system to force the defendant to pay something or do something for the plaintiff. The amount of proof a moving party must present to win a civil lawsuit is generally said to be a preponderance of the evidence.

Jurisdiction

Jurisdiction connotes power or authority over something. When used in reference to courts, it refers to the power to hear and try a case. Jurisdiction has both personal and subject matter aspects.

Subject matter jurisdiction refers to a court's power to deal with a particular type of case. A number of courts have jurisdiction over only a limited sort of case. For example, probate courts deal only with determining the validity of wills. Thus, a murder case could not be brought in a probate court because it has no subject matter jurisdiction over criminal matters. Subject matter jurisdiction is in part a result of history and in part recognition of the large case load that no single court could bear.

In personam jurisdiction refers to a court's power over people. State courts generally have *in personam* jurisdiction over people physically within their borders who are served with process, which refers to delivering a summons and complaint to the defendant personally or to the defendant's residence. **Long-arm statutes** let a state get in personam jurisdiction over out-of-staters for certain wrongs occurring within the state (usually in such incidents as auto accidents). For example, if an Oregonian injured a Californian in San Francisco and hurried back to Oregon before process could be served on him, and if California had a long-arm statute covering auto accidents, the Californian could get in personam jurisdiction over the Oregonian *in California*. Mechanically, the Californian sends the process to a state official (usually the state's secretary of state), who sends it to the Oregonian. If the Oregonian does not answer, the plaintiff wins a default judgment for the amount sued for. This judgment can then be taken to the defendant's home state and enforced against the defendant just as if the case had been tried there.

Cause of Action

The term ***cause of action*** has a special legal meaning. It refers to facts that indicate that someone has been *legally wronged* by someone else and is entitled to have a court provide relief or a remedy.

Just because someone is injured by another person does not necessarily mean the injured victim has a cause of action. The person injuring the victim might have legal defenses. Any legal defense usually completely stops a victim from getting legal relief. For example, in the following *complaint* (Figure 4.2), the injured victim (the little girl suing through her grandfather) tries to state a cause of action in the complaint. Note paragraph VI of the complaint. The plaintiff points out several laws she claims the defendants violated when Betty Hobbs killed the plaintiff's father.

The defendants in their answer (Figure 4.3, the document following the complaint) admit certain things (for instance, diversity jurisdiction in paragraph 2) and set up certain defenses (in paragraphs 5, 6, 7, and 8). Note that in paragraph 6, the defendants claim the plaintiff's father died instantly. If this claim is true, it would mean the plaintiff's father sustained no pain and suffering. (Note paragraph V of the complaint: "plaintiff's intestate [her father] was crushed and mangled in a horrible manner . . . after suffering a large amount of pain and mental anguish." Damages for pain and suffering can sometimes be recovered.)

FIGURE 4.2 Example of a Complaint

IN THE UNITED STATES DISTRICT COURT
FOR THE EASTERN DISTRICT OF TENNESSEE,
NORTHERN DIVISION

ELENA DeZAVALA a minor who sues by next friend and grandfather, LOUIS B. DeZAVALA, citizens and residents of Linn County, Iowa, and of no other place, PLAINTIFFS

vs.

BETTY J. HOBBS AND JAMES B. HOBBS, 126 South Purdue Avenue, Oak Ridge, Anderson County, Tennessee, DEFENDENTS

No. 3-75-125

COMPLAINT

The plaintiff, Elena DeZavala, is a minor, nine years of age, who sues by next friend and grandfather, Louis B. DeZavala, both of whom are citizens and residents of Linn County, Iowa, and of no other place, and further aver that said plaintiff, Elena DeZavala, is the sole surviving child and lineal descendant and next of kin of Louis Victor DeZavala who died in Sullivan County, Tennessee on May 2, 1975. Said plaintiffs complain of the defendants, Betty J. Hobbs and James B. Hobbs, of 126 South Purdue Avenue, Oak Ridge, Tennessee, who are citizens and residents of Anderson County, Tennessee, and of no other place and State.

Said plaintiff, Elena DeZavala, brings this suit by her grandfather and next friend, Louis B. DeZavala, by reason of the wrongful death of her father, Louis Victor DeZavala, who was divorced from the mother of the plaintiff, said mother having remarried.

I

Plaintiff avers that the amount in controversy exceeds the sum of Ten Thousand Dollars ($10,000)* exclusive of interest and costs, and that a complete diversity of citizenship exists between the plaintiff and the defendents, and jurisdiction of this Honorable Court is based on Title 28 U. S. Code Section 1332(a).

II

Plaintiff avers that on May 2, 1975, at approximately 11:00 a.m., that the plaintiff's intestate-father was operating his vehicle in a southwardly direction along Interstate Highway 81, approximately one mile south of the intersection of said Interstate 81 with Tennessee highway 137. Plaintiff avers that said vehicle of Louis Victor DeZavala was being operated in a southwardly direction in a proper and lawful manner upon its right hand side of said Interstate which at that point was a two lane two-way highway.

* Today the jurisdictional amount is $75,000 in diversity cases.

FIGURE 4.2 (*Continued*)

III

Plaintiff avers that said highway was plainly marked every thousand feet as a two-way highway for more than six miles in each direction from the location aforedescribed.

IV

Plaintiff avers that at said time and place as plaintiff's intestate and deceased father, Louis Victor DeZavala, was operating his said vehicle in a southwardly direction along said highway in a proper and lawful manner and upon its right hand side of the highway in broad daylight, that the defendant, Betty J. Hobbs, operating a vehicle within the purview of the Family Purpose Doctrine, which said vehicle was the property of her husband, James B. Hobbs, in a northwardly direction along said highway, meeting the automobile of the plaintiff's intestate father. That the said defendant, Betty J. Hobbs, while operating her automobile at a high, reckless, wrongful and negligent rate of speed, and without keeping her said vehicle under control, and without keeping a lookout ahead, undertook to overtake and pass a truck traveling northwardly along said highway, and drove her said vehicle from its right hand or proper side of the highway to its left hand or improper side of the highway in an effort to overtake and pass said tractor-trailer traveling in the same direction in which she was traveling and drove her said vehicle in the manner and under the conditions aforedescribed into a violent head-on collision with the vehicle operated by the plaintiff's intestate and father.

V

Plaintiff avers that as the direct and proximate result of the negligence of the defendent as aforedescribed, operating her vehicle upon the highway upon the business of the defendant, James B. Hobbs, and within the purview of the Family Purpose Doctrine, that the plaintiff's intestate was crushed and mangled in a horrible manner sustaining such comprehensive, mangling and horrible injuries that as a direct and proximate result thereof after suffering a large amount of pain and mental anguish, that said plaintiff's intestate died, as a result of said injuries and as a proximate result of the negligence of the defendants as aforedescribed.

VI

Plaintiff avers that the defendants by the negligence as aforedescribed violated the following sections of the 1956 Tennessee Code Annotated, and that such violations on their part were the proximate contributing cause to the collision heretofore described and the death of plaintiff's intestate and the destruction of the automobile belonging to him at the time and place complained of:

Section 59-815
Driving on right side of roadway.

FIGURE 4.2 (*Continued*)

Section 59-819
Limitations on overtaking on the left.

Section 59-820
Further limitations on driving to the left of center of roadway. (1)

Section 59-821
No passing zones.

Section 59-823
Driving on roadways laned for traffic (a).

Section 59-852
Speed limit (a).

Section 59-858
Reckless driving (a).

VII

Plaintiff avers that the death of plaintiff's intestate resulted solely from the negligence of the defendants as aforedescribed and that the plaintiff's intestate was a young and healthy man, 30 years of age. Plaintiff was the intestate's only child. Plaintiff has further been put to the expense of the funeral bills and medical expenses, and the destruction of the automobile being occupied by the plaintiff's intestate at the time and place complained of.

WHEREFORE, plaintiff respectfully prays judgment against the defendants and each of them in the sum of Six Hundred Thousand Dollars ($600,000) and respectfully demands a jury to try the issues joined.

KENNERLY, MONTGOMERY, HOWARD & FINLEY

By George D. Montgomery
George D. Montgomery,
Attorneys for Plaintiff
12th Floor Bank of Knoxville Building
Post Office Box 442
Knoxville, Tennessee 37901

COST BOND

We do hereby acknowledge ourselves as surely for the costs in this cause in an amount not to exceed Two Hundred Fifty Dollars (250.00).

KENNERLY, MONTGOMERY,
HOWARD & FINLEY

By George D. Montgomery

FIGURE 4.3 Example of an Answer

IN THE UNITED STATES DISTRICT COURT
FOR THE EASTERN DISTRICT OF TENNESSEE,
NORTHERN DIVISION

ELENA DeZAVALA b/n/f
LOUIS B. DeZAVALA, PLAINTIFFS
VS.
BETTY J. HOBBS
and
JAMES B. HOBBS, DEFENDENTS NO. 3-75-125

ANSWERS

The defendents, Betty J. Hobbs and James B. Hobbs, for answer to the complaint filed against them in this cause, say as follows:

1. They admit that they are citizens of Tennessee and that Louis Victor DeZavala died in Sullivan County, Tennessee, on May 2, 1975, but they have no knowledge as to the other allegations in the first and second paragraphs of the complaint so they neither admit nor deny such allegations and demand strict proof thereof.

2. They admit that this Court has jurisdiction of this action, provided there is diversity of citizenship, as alleged.

3. They admit that the defendant, Betty J. Hobbs, was driving the automobile which collided with the automobile driven by the deceased, Louis Victor DeZavala at or about the time and place alleged.

4. They admit that the defendant, James B. Hobbs, was the owner of the automobile being driven by his wife, Betty J. Hobbs, at the time of this accident, and that the family purpose doctrine is applicable.

5. They deny all allegations of negligence and statutory violations on the part of the defendant, Betty J. Hobbs.

6. They admit that the deceased, Louis Victor DeZavala, died as a result of injuries in this accident, but they aver that his death was instantaneous.

7. For lack of knowledge, they neither admit nor deny the allegations in paragraph VII of the complaint, and demand strict proof thereof.

8. They plead proximate or remote contributory negligence on the part of the deceased.

AND NOW HAVING ANSWERED, the defendants pray to be hence dismissed with their costs and demand a jury to try this cause.

Fred H. Cagle, Jr.
Fred H. Cagle, Jr.
P. O. Box 39
Knoxville, Tennessee 37901

Attorney for Defendants
FRANTZ, McCONNELL & SEYMOUR

CERTIFICATION OF SERVICE

I certify that an exact copy the the forgoing document has been served upon counsel for all parties to the litigation to which it pertains, either by hand delivery of a copy thereof to the officer of said counsel, or by mailing a copy to said counsel in a properly addressed and stamped envelope regularly deposited in the United States Mail.

This 17 day of July, 1975

Fred H. Cagle, Jr.
For FRANTZ, McCONNELL & SEYMOUR

Starting Lawsuits: The Complaint

A person does not start a lawsuit by walking into the courthouse, finding the nearest judge, and stating the problem to the judge. Procedural due process requires that all sorts of legal niceties be observed to protect defendants, who presumably do not yet know they are about to be sued. Assuming the plaintiff does *not* act pro se but instead hires an attorney to present the claim against the defendant, the plaintiff's attorney drafts a complaint (see Figure 4.2). The complaint is designed to notify the defendant of the suit and the reasons for the suit—breach of contract or slanderous remarks, for example.

The complaint and two copies are taken to the clerk of the court, who puts a stamp on the complaint, indicating the time and date the complaint is filed. (The sample complaint has a time stamp in the right-hand center of the first page.) The complaint is put in a file folder that the clerk starts for the case, a copy is given to the plaintiff, and another copy is given along with a summons to an official process server, such as a deputy sheriff or some other person employed to perform this task. The summons directs the defendant to appear in court to answer the complaint. The process server takes a copy of the complaint and the summons to the address the plaintiff put on the complaint and hands them to the defendant or leaves them at the address indicated if the defendant is not there.

Defendant's Response: The Answer

Upon receiving the complaint, the defendant will realize s/he has just been sued, possibly for more money than s/he has or ever expects to have. Once the defendant recovers from the shock of having been sued, s/he will probably hire an attorney to draft an **answer**. The answer is a piece of paper the defendant must file with the clerk of court where the plaintiff sued. The answer must be filed within a short time after the defendant has received a copy of the complaint—usually 30 days. The answer will explain the defendant's version of the incident the plaintiff mentioned in the complaint. It may also state defenses the defendant relies on to escape liability. If the defendant does not file an answer, the plaintiff wins without even having to go to trial, barring unusual circumstances, through a **default judgment**. Figure 4.3 is the answer filed in response to the sample complaint. The complaint and answer together are referred to as the **pleadings**.

Pretrial Discovery and Pretrial Conferences

Pretrial discovery permits a party to find out what sort of evidence the other party has that relates to the suit at hand, although certain privileged matters are not subject to discovery. Both parties also attempt to gather evidence in support of their contentions. To gather certain evidence, procedural rules permit the taking of **depositions**, sworn statements by someone on a matter relating to the suit at hand. Depositions are solicited by one of the parties to buttress his or her case; they add to the cost of a lawsuit; and they are usually made to preserve testimony of witnesses who will be unavailable for trial or to preserve witnesses' reactions to evidence while it is still fresh in their minds.

Pretrial conferences are simply meetings at which the opposing attorneys get together with the judge before the actual trial to state the heart of their case and how they intend to prove it. This meeting, coupled with pretrial discovery, reduces trial time and the gamesmanship element that formerly existed when opposing lawyers would delay trials with spurious arguments or conceal their evidence and theories until the last moments of the trial to surprise their opponent and win the case. Movies often have courtroom scenes of an attorney producing a key witness who, in the final moments wins the case with the disclosure of some devastating fact. Such histrionics are unlikely in a modern procedural system with effective pretrial discovery and conferences.

Motions

During the various stages of a suit, the parties may make several types of motions. After the pleadings are completed, for example, the defendant may decide that the plaintiff's claim can easily be defeated. The device the defendant uses to achieve this end is called the **motion to dismiss**. A motion to dismiss can be based on a wide variety of grounds. For instance, the defendant may claim that the court has no jurisdiction over the case.

The most important type of motion to dismiss, though, is the motion to dismiss for failure to state a claim upon which relief can be granted, often called the *demurrer*. This motion hypothetically assumes the truth of all the facts stated in the plaintiff's complaint—just for purposes of the motion. It asserts that even if all these facts are true, the plaintiff cannot win because no legal theory will support a recovery on those facts. In effect the demurrer says "So what?" to the factual allegations in the complaint. Suppose, to take an extreme example, that A sues B on a theory of aesthetic pollution because B's ugliness constitutes an affront to civilized people. Such a claim, even if amply bolstered by descriptions of B's ugliness, will fail because no legal rules exist that impose civil liability simply for being ugly.

The Trial, Verdict, and Judgment

The function of the trial is to settle disputes without resorting to violence. A trial is a civilized substitute for jungle law, where the stronger prevails. It gives litigants an opportunity to have their day in court to publicly present their evidence and legal theories of recovery. Aside from the litigants and their attorneys, the judge and jury are the principal actors in a trial. The judge's function is to ensure that only proper evidence and legal arguments are presented for the fact trier's consideration. When a case reaches the trial stage, some conflict inevitably arises in what the parties claim are the facts. The jury's function is to resolve fact disputes, unless a jury trial is waived, in which case the judge assumes the jury's function. Jury selection involves questioning prospective jurors to reveal competence, bias, prejudice, or conflicts of interest. Such questioning is the *voir dire*.

Once each party's case has been presented, the fact trier decides who is telling the truth by announcing its verdict (Latin derivation, *vera dicta*, meaning "say what is true"). The court usually then pronounces judgment in accordance with the jury's verdict. The judgment is a court declaration that the plaintiff recovers or that his or her action be dismissed. A court's judgment does not have to follow what the jury has decreed as its verdict. If, for example, the jury has returned a verdict completely at odds with the evidence (motivated, for instance, by sympathy for one of the parties), the other party can ask the court for **judgment notwithstanding the verdict**. This motion is a jury control device. Much the same is true of the **directed verdict**, which is a motion a party's counsel makes during the actual trial, asking, in effect, that the judge stop the trial and direct or order what the verdict should be. This motion is made on the premise that the evidence presented up to that point is fatal to the other party's case so that nothing subsequently introduced could reverse the inevitable result. Figure 4.4 contains an example of a judgment.

FIGURE 4.4 Example of a Judgment

United States District Court

FOR THE

EASTERN DISTRICT OF TENNESSEE, NORTHERN DIVISION

ELENA DeZAVALA, b/n/f/
and grandfather
LOUIS B. DeZavala

vs.

BETTY J. HOBBS &
JAMES HOBBS

CIVIL ACTION FILE NO. 3-75-125

JUDGMENT

This action came on trial before the Court and a jury, Honorable Robert L. Taylor , United States District Judge, presiding, and the issues having been duly tried and the jury having duly rendered its verdict;

It is Ordered and Adjudged that the Plaintiffs, Elena DeZavala, b/n/f and grandfather, Louis B. DeZavala, recover of the defendents Betty J. Hobbs and James Hobbs, the sum of Twenty-Five Thousand ($25,000)* Dollars, plus property damage in the amount of Three Hundred ($300) Dollars, with interest thereon at the rate of six percent as provided by law, and their costs of action.

Dated at Knoxville, Tennessee, this 25th day of August, 1975.

Filed 25 day of Aug 19 75
Ent'd ____ Order Book 71, p. 326
KARL D. SAULPAW, JR., CLERK
by Jean Medlock Dep.Clerk

KARL D. SAULPAW, JR.
Clerk of Court

By Jean Medlock

* Later raised to $50,000 by an additur.

Motions can be made prior to, during, and after a verdict and judgment have been entered. One type of motion that occurs after a jury verdict is for either an additur or a remittitur. Generally, if credible evidence supports a jury's verdict, a court judge will not change it. In the case of the motion for an additur, the plaintiff's attorney claims that the jury has been "too stingy" in the amount it has awarded plaintiff. The Elena DeZavala judgment illustrates a judge's raising a jury's verdict to a higher amount, whereas *Anderson v. Conwood,* presented in Chapter 3, illustrates a remittitur where the court reduces the jury's verdict because it is too high.

Res Judicata

Parties to a dispute do have a right to have their case tried, but only once, given normal circumstances, under the **res judicata** principle. If this rule were not available, disputes would never be settled. The losing party would return to court asking for a retrial of the case until a more sympathetic judge or jury granted the relief requested. At that point, the other party would follow the same procedure until receiving a favorable judgment—again. The legal process would thus be interminable, and the legal system's objective of settling disputes would be lost.

Appeals

The finality objective of the res judicata rule has one escape valve: the appeal. A party dissatisfied with the trial court's disposition of the case may appeal to a higher court on the theory that the trial court made a mistake at some point. An appeal is usually pursued after a motion for a new trial has been made in the trial court, wherein the loser asks the trial judge to correct mistakes that resulted in the unfavorable judgment. A new trial not surprisingly, seldom happens.

Because most trial courts are **courts of record** (meaning that a clerk keeps a transcript of the courtroom proceedings), the evidence and witnesses are not reintroduced at the appellate level. Instead, the justices consult the record, accepting the conclusions of the fact trier at the lower level unless a blatant error appears to have been made. The appellate court's main function is to ensure that the proper legal rules were recognized and correctly applied in disposing of the case in the lower court. If an error of law or if an outrageous determination affecting the outcome was made, the appellate court returns the case to the lower court and directs a retrial to apply the correct principles.

Collecting Judgment

Suppose a civil lawsuit and all appeals have ended in the defendant's favor. Assuming no counterclaim was filed by defendant in the case, the matter would end with no order of payment of money from the defendant to the plaintiff.

If, on the other hand, the plaintiff has won the lawsuit, prevailed on any appeals, and been awarded a money judgment, the plaintiff becomes a **judgment creditor**. The losing defendant becomes a **judgment debtor** in such a case. If the world were perfect from the judgment creditor's standpoint, the judgment debtor would pull out his wallet, peel off cash in the amount of the judgment, and turn it over to the judgment creditor. The dispute would then end.

Successful plaintiffs in civil lawsuits seldom see this happen, of course. Often, defendant's liability insurance pays the judgment fully, which ends the matter. Other times, the defendant proves **judgment proof**, meaning that the defendant is so poor that any attempt to collect would be futile. However, judgments last for a number of years and can be renewed. Therefore, a judgment creditor may have a number of years to collect from a judgment debtor. Thus, one should not quickly give up hope of collecting the judgment. Also, a judgment that has not been paid by the defendant can be sold by the judgment creditor (for a fraction of the judgment's face value) to a third party who was not involved in the original suit.

Judgment Debtor's Property. Assume the judgment creditor tries to collect the judgment from the judgment debtor's assets. The first question that arises concerns what property of the debtor is available to pay the creditor's claims. The general rule is that all of the debtor's property presently owned or possibly acquired at some future date may be seized by the judgment creditor unless it is exempt.[3] For example, the debtor's car, house, personal belongings, club memberships (to the extent they have commercial value), stocks, bonds, notes receivable from third parties, money market accounts, and proprietary interests in a sole proprietorship or partnership business may all be seized and sold to pay amounts owed to a judgment creditor unless they are exempt.

Exempt Property. Exempt property results from state and federal laws designed to protect the debtor's ability to survive by allowing the retention of bare necessities required to survive. The theory of state exemption laws is that, while a debtor should pay legal debts, the debtor should not be cast naked and penniless on welfare with no place to live or without clothes or basic household goods. Nor should that punitive relic from Charles Dickens's era—the debtor's prison—be revived.

Having examined the theory of exemption laws, what specific items fall into the category of exempt property that may not be seized to pay his or her debts? The answer is complex because exemption laws are both state and federal, and a variance exists among the states as to items exempted. Most states give a debtor a **homestead exemption** which, as the name suggests, refers to the house in which the debtor lives, although the exemption is often limited to a low dollar figure (which may or may not be enough to protect debtor's home equity). All states exempt life insurance policies to some extent. The earnings or wages of the debtor are generally not exempt under exemption laws, but state and federal garnishment limitations, discussed later, do limit a creditor's ability to take a debtor's wages. It would seem incredible to allow a judgment creditor to seize a debtor's welfare payments, given the live-and-let-live philosophy of exemption laws, yet about half of the states do not exempt welfare payments. Generally, amounts of money debtors receive from retirement programs—both public and private—are exempt from creditor's claims, although some private plans are exempt only up to a specific dollar amount. Usually alimony and child support payments are not exempt—another peculiar anomaly, given the philosophy of exemption laws. Certain household and personal items, such as furniture, stoves, refrigerators, beds, and televisions, are exempt, again on the theory that they are essential for the debtor's survival. Professor Vukowich has assembled a picturesque list of miscellaneous exempted property that includes wedding rings, Bibles, family pictures, books, guns, historical and scientific collections, and cemetery lots.

Exemption Waivers. Two final points about exemptions warrant discussion: they may be waived, and certain debts may be collected even from property that would otherwise be exempt. The **waiver** idea is easily understood when one considers someone who buys a house and finances it by borrowing the bulk of the purchase price from a local savings and loan association. If the homeowner does not repay the loan

[3] The authors wish to acknowledge the article by William T. Vukowich, "Debtors' Exemption Rights," 62 *Georgetown Law Journal* 779 (1974), from which many ideas and much information for this chapter were obtained.

and the lending institution sues for the money loaned, winning a judgment against the defaulting house buyer, it would be ludicrous to let the homeowner assert that the homestead exemption prevented the lender from selling the house to recover the amount loaned to buy it. Sellers of exempt property would require cash and would not risk selling on credit to avoid the risk of default and noncollection due to the exemption.

A need exists for credit transactions in many property items receiving exemptions under state law, particularly high-priced items such as houses, where people seldom have the entire purchase price at the time of purchase. The problem of extending credit to buy exempt property is handled by getting borrowers to waive their exemption. Thus, if a savings and loan association loans money to a person to purchase a house, the lending institution will not make the loan unless the homeowner-borrower waives (usually in the borrowing contract) the homestead exemption.

The second concluding point about exemptions is that they do not apply to situations in which the judgment debtor owes certain types of debts. For example, exemptions may not be asserted against claims for child support and alimony.

Writs of Execution and Garnishment. As the prior discussion illustrates, much potential property of the judgment debtor is available to pay off a judgment obtained by the successful plaintiff. The next inquiry is, "What legal devices are available to enable the judgment creditor to obtain such property?" Generally speaking, a judgment creditor may not simply walk onto a judgment debtor's property and take whatever property can be found that appears valuable enough to pay off the judgment debt. Rather, the judgment creditor must again return to the legal system and bring what, in many states, are ancillary actions (in effect, sue again, though technically it is part of the same suit) to collect the judgment. After-judgment legal devices the judgment creditor may use to obtain the judgment debtor's property include writs of execution and garnishment, which are state law remedies and thus vary in detail from state to state.

A **writ of execution** is a form the judgment creditor gets from the court clerk that tells a court official, such as the sheriff, to go to the judgment debtor's property and take nonexempt assets. After the official seizes the property, he conducts a public auction to sell it and turns over the money received to the judgment creditor. Any amount greater than the judgment debt is returned to the judgment debtor. If the amount received is insufficient to pay the judgment, more nonexempt property of the judgment debtor may be seized and sold in like manner.

If the writ of execution results in the seizure and sale of all the debtor's nonexempt property and it is still not enough to pay off the judgment debt, **garnishment** is another legal method available to the judgment creditor to obtain payment of the judgment. One could well ask what value garnishment has if the writ of execution has already resulted in the sale of all of the debtor's nonexempt property. The answer is that writs of execution are used only to take property directly from the judgment debtor. However, many times other people (called garnishees if a creditor goes after the debtor's property in their hands) owe the judgment debtor money. An employer, for example, could owe the judgment debtor salary or wages. Also, debtors may own property that is not in their possession. A writ of execution cannot reach such property. The garnishment order may be obtained from the clerk of court to reach assets of the sorts described. However, it usually may not be obtained until after a writ of execution fails to produce enough property to satisfy the judgment.

Prejudgment Attachment and Garnishment. The execution process just described sometimes proves unsatisfactory from the judgment creditor's standpoint because the creditor is forced to wait until the case has slowly dragged through the courts before collecting the claim. How nice it would be if the plaintiff could seize the defendant's property *before* the suit even reached the trial stage of the proceedings to prevent such unethical defendant practices as running away, plundering the property, or giving the property to friends or relatives so that the plaintiff cannot have any debtor property to satisfy the judgment the plaintiff *might* get in the lawsuit.

For hundreds of years, in some instances, the legal system provided at least two ways in which the plaintiff in a lawsuit could obtain a defendant's property *before* winning a full-blown lawsuit. Neither of these devices observed the defendant's due process protections of notice and full and fair hearing on the matter sued over. The devices are known as prejudgment attachment and garnishment.

Prejudgment attachment lets a plaintiff seize a defendant's property at the start of the lawsuit before it is even determined that the plaintiff has won the suit. The violation of procedural due process created by such a process is obvious: The defendant has had property taken from him or her without a trial. The *protection* given to defendant in such case flows from the requirement that the plaintiff is required to post a bond (similar to an insurance policy) that supposedly covers the defendant's opportunity cost of being deprived of her own property until the matter can be fully litigated in court. Certain limits on availability of the attachment devices vary somewhat from state to state. Some of the limits on attachment are found in circumstances that must exist before attachment's issuance: the defendant's absconding, or absenting himself or herself; the defendant's nonresidence in the state; the defendant's fraudulent transfer or disposition of property; the defendant's removing or concealing property; and various other miscellaneous grounds, such as impairment of security (the defendant's tearing up or abusing property in which the plaintiff has a security interest).

Prejudgment garnishment is a serious violation of a person's procedural due process rights. It allows the taking of a person's wages directly from his employer *before* trial is held to determine if any debt is owed. A defendant could be put on welfare if this were allowed. Postjudgment garnishment is a recognized, legitimate creditor remedy not violative of a defendant's procedural due process rights since it is not forthcoming until *after* notice and trial have been held on the validity of a plaintiff's claim and a determination has been made that the plaintiff has a valid claim against the defendant.

Constitutionality of Prejudgment Creditor Remedies. The constitutionality of prejudgment creditor remedies is open to question today. This conclusion follows from the apparently conflicting U.S. Supreme Court decisions on the subject in the past several years, plus the fact that each state's prejudgment garnishment and attachment vary as to the extent of their applicability. In 1969 the Supreme Court held that prejudgment wage garnishment without notice and a hearing before such garnishment violates procedural due process.[4] In a similar vein, the Supreme Court held in 1972 that prejudgment seizure of goods that the seller sold and retained a security interest without a hearing or notice to the defendant debtor, by **ex parte** proceeding (only plaintiff is at and knows about the proceeding) violates the due process clause of the Fourteenth Amendment.[5] Only two years later, however, the Supreme Court said that Louisiana's prejudgment remedy, allowing the creditor-plaintiff to take the defendant-debtor's property that had an unpaid balance and on which the plaintiff-creditor had a lien, satisfied due process requirements if the plaintiff filed a bond.[6] Due process was satisfied even though the seizure was authorized ex parte without notice

[4] *Sniadach v. Family Finance Corp.*, 395 U.S. 337 (1969).
[5] *Fuentes v. Shevin*, 407 U.S. 67 (1972).
[6] *Mitchell v. W.T. Grant Co.*, 416 U.S. 600 (1974).

to or hearing before the taking of the defendant's property. However, ex parte prejudgment garnishments, as opposed to attachments where no notice or hearing is provided to the defendant, do still appear to be unconstitutional.

Consumer Credit Protection Act. In 1968 the Consumer Credit Protection Act became federal law. One of its many accomplishments was to set limits on the amount of a person's earnings that could be garnished by a creditor to pay amounts owed to the creditor. These limits are 25 percent of the debtor's weekly disposable income (take-home pay, after income taxes and Social Security have been deducted) or the amount by which the person's weekly take-home pay exceeds 30 times the existing federal minimum hourly wage. Which alternative is taken depends on which amount is the smaller, the smaller figure being the one that is required to be taken. In other words, an objective of this federal law is to limit the amount that can be taken from a person's earnings by garnishment so that the debtor will not have to go on welfare.

The Federal Consumer Credit Protection Act applies to all states. Because employers do not enjoy having employees' earnings garnished because of the added bookkeeping expense and harassment that results, they frequently would fire employees whose earnings were garnished. The federal law now allows states to prohibit firing employees for this reason. Also, states *may* totally eliminate the garnishment process now available to creditors in most states. As the title of this act indicates, it is a *Consumer* Credit Protection Act, designed to enlarge debtors' rights and reduce creditor's rights.

Uniform Consumer Credit Code. Another model or suggested law, the Uniform Consumer Credit Code (UCCC) enacted in some states, exempts more of a debtor's earned income from garnishment than does the federal law, which the federal law allows individual states to do. It makes the alternatives available for garnishment the lesser of 25 percent of weekly take-home pay or the amount by which disposable income is greater than 40 times the federal minimum hourly wage per week (instead of 30). Thus, the UCCC provides a greater protection from garnishment to defaulting consumer judgment debtors than does federal law.

Bankruptcy. Two final devices are available to judgment debtors to escape paying judgments obtained against them: voluntary bankruptcy and transferring ownership of their property to noncreditor relatives or friends to hold for the debtor's benefit. The power to allow a person, business, or other entity to go bankrupt is exclusively a federal—not a state—power. Basically, any natural person, partnership, or corporation may go bankrupt. The objective of the Bankruptcy Code is to allow people or business organizations hopelessly in debt to turn over all their nonexempt assets to a court-appointed official or trustee, who distributes them among the creditors. Secured creditors (lenders with claims against specific assets such as a house or a car) may generally have their claims paid before those of unsecured creditors, primarily because mortgaged property or property subject to a timely **perfected security interest** is not considered part of the bankrupt's estate.

Assuming that here we are examining bankruptcy as a device to escape paying judgment debts, attention must turn to the limits on a person's ability to go bankrupt. The two ways of going bankrupt are voluntarily and involuntarily. In the first case, because debtors *want* to go bankrupt to rid themselves of overwhelming debts, they voluntarily start bankruptcy proceedings. In the second case—involuntary bankruptcy—at least three creditors from among at least 12 or more creditors in all with claims totaling $5,000 or more against the debtor must petition the federal district court (the *only* court where bankruptcy proceedings start) for such action. If the debtor has fewer than 12 creditors, only one creditor having $5,000 or more in claims may put the debtor into bankruptcy.

Limits have been placed on who may petition a federal bankruptcy court to go through voluntary bankruptcy. The debtor alone is petitioning in a voluntary bankruptcy, but the nature of the debtor is first determined. Any natural person, partnership, or corporation may go bankrupt voluntarily with a few exceptions: Banks, railroads, municipalities, savings and loan associations, and insurance companies may not go bankrupt voluntarily; however, municipalities may now "adjust their debts." Most of these same institutions that affect the public interest may *not* go bankrupt *in*voluntarily, either. Second, it is not essential that a voluntary bankrupt be insolvent (not paying debts as they come due in the ordinary course of business or being unable to do so); but it is necessary that a voluntary bankrupt owe debts. Also, the limit on receiving a straight bankruptcy discharge is *once every six years*, and certain obligations may not be escaped (so-called nondischargeable debts) by going bankrupt. These include judgments for the commission of intentional torts, alimony, and child support. **Negligence** judgments, however, are dischargeable in bankruptcy.

Fraudulent Transfers. A property transfer is another possible way to escape judgment debts. The debtor transfers title to a friend or relative who will hold the property voluntarily with the understanding that it will remain the debtor's property although on paper title and possession will reside with the friend. Then, when the judgment creditor seeks a writ of attachment against the judgment debtor's property, the judgment debtor will be execution-proof with no property to seize.

The law that deals with this problem is called the Uniform Fraudulent Conveyance Act. This act does not allow creditors to go to *all* third parties and reclaim property that their debtor has ever transferred to them, but it does permit reclamation where a fraudulent conveyance has occurred. The term ***fraudulent conveyance*** refers to a transfer of property by a debtor to third parties with the purpose of depriving creditors of the debtor's property that they could otherwise seize to repay amounts the debtor owes them. A transfer by a debtor is presumed fraudulent when the debtor is insolvent. Insolvency in this context means debtors are unable to pay their debts as they come due. The debtor may challenge this presumption in court, but if a transfer of property by a debtor is determined to be a fraudulent transfer under the Uniform Fraudulent Conveyance Act, the transfer may be set aside. In such a case the property held by the debtor's friend may be reclaimed, again put in the debtor's estate, and be available so that creditors may seize it.

Conclusion

As you can see from this look at the anatomy of a civil lawsuit, lawsuits have a to-and-fro motion, a battle of forms filed with court officials by the respective litigants. The complexity of this process, which was only alluded to here, is, at least in part, the result of forces designed to refine justice by spelling out specific rules for the many different situations that can arise in a lawsuit. This increased complexity of the legal process creates two problems: The average person will not understand the process, and the process will become too lengthy and expensive.

CHAPTER SUMMARY

Alternative dispute resolution (ADR) refers to settling disputes without resort to lawsuits. Conciliation, mediation, and arbitration are forms of ADR. The U.S. Supreme Court has approved the use of ADR to settle investor complaints against stockbrokers.

MANAGER'S ETHICAL DILEMMA

Petitioners are individuals who invested about $400,000 in securities. They signed a standard customer agreement with the broker, which included a clause stating that the parties agreed to settle any controversies "relating to [the] accounts" through binding arbitration that complies with specified procedures. The agreement to arbitrate these controversies is unqualified, unless it is found to be unenforceable under federal or state law. . . . The investments turned sour, and petitioners eventually sued respondent and its broker-agent in charge of the accounts, alleging that their money was lost in unauthorized and fraudulent transactions. In their complaint they pleaded various violations of federal and state law, including claims under §12(2) of the Securities Act of 1933 . . . and claims under three sections of the Securities Exchange Act of 1934.

The District Court ordered all the claims to be submitted to arbitration except for those raised under §12(2) of the Securities Act. It held that the latter claims must proceed in the court action under our clear holding on the point in *Wilko v. Swan*. . . (1953). The District Court reaffirmed its ruling upon reconsideration, and also entered a default judgment against the broker, who is no longer in the case. The Court of Appeals reversed, concluding that the arbitration agreement is enforceable because this Court's subsequent decisions have reduced Wilko to "obsolescence." . . . The U.S. Supreme Court granted certiorari.

What arguments can a securities firm make before the U.S. Supreme Court in favor of upholding its arbitration agreement with its customers? Do you think that public policy reasons justify striking down or upholding this arbitration agreement?

Attorneys represent persons involved in legal disputes. Attorneys can be paid on a fixed or contingency basis. Provisions in attorney-client contracts requiring clients to give up control of the right to settle their suits are generally void. Attorneys may advertise their fees and services in routine legal matters provided the ads are truthful and not misleading. Companies such as American Express, unions, and some law firms have legal plans that entitle consumers to certain legal services for a year at a set fee. Also, many liability insurance policies provide free legal assistance as part of the policy's coverage.

It is legal for a person who is not an attorney to plead his or her own case. Such a person is called a pro se litigant. The steps in civil lawsuits may include the facts giving rise to the cause of action, the realization that one has a cause of action, filing of the complaint, serving of the complaint and process on the defendant, the defendant's filing an answer, the pretrial hearing, pretrial discovery, depositions, and interrogatories, the trial and judgment, appeals, and collection of the judgment.

Discussion Questions

1. Recently states have reached multi-billion dollar settlement of lawsuits brought against tobacco companies for contributions to Medicare and other government programs that have paid out benefits to cigarette smokers for various ailments. Several states—notably Texas and Florida—were represented by private attorneys against the tobacco companies. These attorneys were successful on the states' behalf, winning several billion dollars in settlement (a reported $15.3 billion for the state of Texas alone). The attorney fees for Texas were reportedly $2.3 billion. Governor George Bush of Texas stated that such attorney fees were "outrageous." What public policy arguments can you adduce both to support and to challenge such high attorney fees?
2. What are some public policy considerations behind the following legal subjects?
   a. standing
   b. class actions
   c. statutes of limitations
3. In the past, attorney advertising was legally prohibited. What arguments can be made supporting such a ban? Does advertising

promote consumer knowledge or mislead consumers? Is a little knowledge always a dangerous thing? Sometimes? Do we ever know everything about a subject?

4. Rule 4 of the Missouri Supreme Court regulates lawyer advertising. The rule says a lawyer may include 10 categories of information in a published ad: name, address, and phone number; areas of practice; date and place of birth; schools attended; foreign language ability; office hours; fee for initial consultation; availability of a fee schedule; credit arrangements; and the fixed fee to be charged for certain routine legal services. The Missouri Supreme Court interpreted Rule 4 as allowing release of *only* these 10 categories of information. The Missouri Advisory Committee charged R. M. J., an unidentified lawyer practicing in St. Louis, with violating Rule 4. R. M. J. allegedly published ads listing areas of practice in words other than what Rule 4 allowed. R. M. J. also listed courts where R. M. J. was admitted to practice, although this information was not included among the 10 categories of information that Rule 4 authorized. Also, R. M. J. allegedly mailed announcements of R. M. J.'s law practice to people other than what Rule 4 allowed. R. M. J. argued that Rule 4 violated the First and Fourteenth Amendments. The Missouri Supreme Court said Rule 4 was constitutional and reprimanded R. M. J.who then appealed the judgment to the U.S. Supreme Court. What result? [*Matter of R. M. J.*, 455 U.S. 191 (1982)]
5. Why should an attorney not have the exclusive power to settle a client's civil case? What policy arguments favor giving the client the right to settle?

Suggested Readings

Articles

ADAMS, "Tracing Proceeds to Attorneys' Pockets (and the Dilemma of Paying for Bankruptcy)," 78 *Minnesota Law Review* 1079 (1994).

CARPER and BUNTZ, "Alternative Dispute Resolution and the Business Law/Legal Environment Curriculum," 9 *Journal of Legal Studies Education* 53 (1990).

COUND, "A Very New Lawyer's First Case," 15 *Constitutional Commentary* 57 (1998).

DRISCOLL, "The Decline of the English Jury," 17 *American Business Law Journal* 99 (1979).

FOX and HUFFMIRE, "The Use of Court Reports and Other Writing Assignments in the Business Law Curriculum," 9 *Journal of Legal Studies Education* 117 (1990).

FRETZ and VOLANCEK, "Codes of Judicial Ethics: Do They Affect Judges' Views of Proper Off-the-Bench Behavior?" 17 *American Business Law Journal* 493 (1979).

HENKEL, "The Civil Jury—Modification or Abolition?" 14 *American Business Law Journal* 97 (1976).

HUFFMIRE, "Repossession Without Judicial Process: What Lies Ahead?" 15 *American Business Law Journal* 319 (1978).

KATZ, "Enforcing an ADR Clause—Are Good Intentions All You Have?" 27 *American Business Law Journal* 575 (1988).

MARINELLI, "Automobile Searches and the Fourth Amendment," 12 *American Business Law Journal* 327 (1975).

NOONAN, "Are There Disadvantages to ADR," 63 *Wisconsin Lawyer* 14 (1990).

ROBINSON, "ADR in the Insurance Industry: One Company's Perspective," 45 *Arbitration Journal* 24 (1990).

SHAW, "Due Process Constraints on Class Actions: Federal Rule of Civil Procedure 23," 14 *American Business Law Journal* 111 (1976).

ZOLLARS, "Alternative Dispute Resolution and Product Liability Reform," 27 *American Business Law Journal* 479 (1989).

CHAPTER

5

BUSINESS AND THE CONSTITUTION

POSITIVE LAW ETHICAL PROBLEMS

New York's Professional Midwifery Practice Act (PMPA) says that, in order to be licensed to practice midwifery, one basically must complete the educational requirements for both midwifery and nursing. The act also says the midwifery can only be practiced pursuant to a written practice agreement between a midwife and an appropriate physician or hospital. Because she was a "direct-entry" midwife who trained through apprenticeship, this first requirement prevented Julia Lange-Kessler from practicing midwifery in New York. For this reason, and due also to the PMPA's practice-agreement requirement, three of Lange-Kessler's former patients, Nancy Quaglia, Susan Snyder, and Nancy LaChance, could not have Lange-Kessler assist them with future pregnancies.

The four women challenged the PMPA's constitutionality in federal court. Lange-Kessler claimed that the act denied her due process by unjustifiably restricting her right to earn a living her in chosen profession. The other three women made a different due process claim. Their argument was that the PMPA violated due process because it unjustifiably restricted their right to decide how to give birth to a child. Like the rights to marry, to use contraceptives, and to have an abortion, they claimed, this right is fundamental. As a result, laws restricting it should get the toughest judicial scrutiny, and the PMPA could not survive such scrutiny.

Was either of these claims successful? In any event, should either have succeeded? Is the right to give birth as one wishes as important or "fundamental" as the rights to marry, use contraceptives, or have an abortion? If not, what differentiates it from these rights? For that matter, is the right to practice the profession of one's choice less important or fundamental than these three rights? If not, why not?

"[W]E MUST NEVER FORGET THAT IT IS A **CONSTITUTION** WE ARE EXPOUNDING. . . A CONSTITUTION INTENDED TO ENDURE FOR AGES TO COME, AND, CONSEQUENTLY, TO BE ADAPTED TO THE VARIOUS CRISES OF HUMAN AFFAIRS."

Chief Justice John Marshall in McCulloch v. Maryland, *4 Wheat. 316 (1819)*

A constitution is the fundamental law of the society it governs. In the Western world, constitutions serve two broad purposes. First, they set up the basic structure of government, which includes establishing the various branches of the central government and the powers granted and denied to each, as well as defining the power relations between the central government and subordinate units of government. The U.S. Constitution states what the federal government can do, what the states can do, and what happens when state and federal laws conflict. Second, Western constitutions generally limit the power of government. In part, they do so by the way they state the powers given to, and withheld from, the various branches and subunits. In addition, constitutions specifically block certain government actions. For example, constitutions routinely forbid government behavior that deprives people of certain rights. The most important example is the Bill of Rights in the U.S. Constitution. Finally, to promote these two general purposes, constitutions must be supreme—the last word—on legal questions. All these generalizations are true of the U.S. Constitution.

THE U.S. CONSTITUTION: AN OVERVIEW

This chapter does not discuss all areas of American constitutional law. Instead, it only examines the most important constitutional doctrines affecting government regulation of business. To see how those doctrines fit within the Constitution's larger scheme, and to learn something about that scheme, we begin with a brief overview of the Constitution as a whole.

Article I of the Constitution gives Congress the sole power to *legislate* at the federal level. It also sets out rules for the passage of legislation, including the presidential veto and Congress's ability to override a veto by a two-thirds vote of each House. Section 8 of Article I states a long list of federal legislative powers: the specific ways in which Congress is allowed to legislate. Most important here are the commerce, taxing, and spending powers discussed later in the chapter. Article I, section 9 states a brief list of specific powers that Congress is not allowed to exercise. Article I, section 10 declares that the states are not allowed certain powers. One example, discussed later in the chapter, is the states' inability to impair the obligations of contracts.

Article II begins by placing the *executive power* (the power to execute the laws passed by Congress) in the president. Article II also lists the president's powers, which include the role of commander-in-chief of the armed forces and the ability to make treaties, which must be approved by two-thirds of the Senate. But Article II's list of presidential powers understates the practical importance of the presidency in our scheme of government today.

Article III of the Constitution deals with the *judicial power* of the federal government. It establishes the U.S. Supreme Court and gives Congress the power to create other federal courts, a power Congress has exercised. Article III also describes the types of cases the federal courts can hear.

Article IV of the Constitution sets out a number of rules governing relationships among the states. It provides, for instance, that each state must give "Full Faith and Credit" to the laws and legal proceedings of other states.

Article V sets out the procedures for amending the Constitution.

Article VI contains the supremacy clause, which makes federal law supreme over state law in case of a clash between them. This clause is the basis for the doctrine of *federal preemption* discussed toward the end of the chapter.

The U.S. Constitution has 26 amendments. The first 10 comprise the Bill of Rights. This chapter discusses three important Bill of Rights provisions: the Fifth Amendment's due process and "takings" clauses and the First Amendment's guarantee of free speech. Originally, the Bill of Rights applied only to the activities of the federal government. But due to the *incorporation* doctrine examined later in this chapter, most of these constitutional protections now limit the states as well. This chapter also examines two provisions of the Constitution's Fourteenth Amendment: its due process and equal protection clauses. The former is worded like the Fifth Amendment's due process clause, but applies to the states. The latter, which now applies both to the states and the federal government, forbids many kinds of discriminatory lawmaking.

THE NATURE OF CONSTITUTIONAL DECISION MAKING

People often make confident statements about what the U.S. Constitution means. These people apparently assume that the Constitution's provisions are clear and unchanging. They also seem to think that courts deciding constitutional cases simply follow the Constitution's literal language and the historical materials accompanying its enactment.

Like it or not, the beliefs just described generally are incorrect. Some constitutional provisions are anything but clear. Moreover, often courts do not passively interpret constitutional language. Instead, they frequently *create* constitutional law. As a result, many constitutional provisions now mean something different from what they once meant, and the Constitution as a whole evolves rather than remains stable.

Why the Constitution's Meaning Changes

Why does the meaning of constitutional provisions change over time? For one thing, many of those provisions lacked a clear meaning in the first place. Often their language is obscure. For example, such imprecise terms as "due process of law" and "equal protection of the laws" can be—and have been—interpreted in many ways. In addition, the debates and other history surrounding the enactment of constitutional provisions often do not cure their ambiguity. Thus, courts must fill in the blanks where the language and history of a constitutional provision are unclear.

Probably the most important reason for constitutional change, however, is social change. For better or worse, new social conditions and values sometimes lead judges to alter constitutional doctrine to reflect such changes. As the old saying goes, the Supreme Court's decisions tend to follow the election returns. The Constitution's adaptability also might reflect the wishes of the Founders, who may have used broad and flexible language to make future change possible. In addition, it probably reflects the wishes of most Americans, who may like the idea of a fixed and certain constitution in the abstract, but would be unhappy if they had to live under one.

The Supreme Court's Power and Its Limits

For the reasons just discussed, the Supreme Court and other courts play a major role in determining the Constitution's practical meaning. To quote another old saying, the Constitution often is what the Court's justices say it is. Theoretically, constitutional change can be achieved through the Constitution's formal amendment process, but this process is difficult to use. For better or worse, therefore, the Supreme Court has been the Constitution's principal amender.

From the points just made, it follows that the Supreme Court exercises political power. Under the doctrine of **judicial review**, the Court (and courts in general) can declare the actions of other government bodies unconstitutional. If the Court exercised judicial review under clear constitutional provisions whose meaning it passively followed, no one would regard it as especially powerful. In fact, however, the Court often invalidates federal and state laws under ambiguous provisions whose meaning it largely determines. These discretionary exercises of power resemble legislative or administrative policy making. Because of this discretionary power, the values, judicial philosophies, and political beliefs of judges are important factors in determining how the United States is governed. That is why the nomination of Supreme Court justices often involves so much political controversy.

The Supreme Court's political power creates a problem. In theory, such power is supposed to be exercised only by democratically elected bodies such as legislatures. The Supreme Court and other courts are not democratically elected bodies. Thus, when courts declare a statute unconstitutional, they basically are telling the people's elected representatives that they cannot govern the country as they like. This might be permissible if, when doing so, the Court was passively following a Constitution to which the people theoretically have consented. But as we have seen, this is not the case. Thus, there is a clash between majority rule and the power exercised by the modern judiciary.

Due to the clash just described, the Supreme Court and other courts do not have a completely free hand when they decide constitutional cases. In other words, they do not push their power as far as they can by interpreting the Constitution as loosely as they might. One reason is that many judges genuinely believe in majority rule. Another is the courts' potential political vulnerability. Courts are dependent on the executive branch of government to enforce their decisions. Moreover, legislatures usually have the power to impeach judges, and also may determine their compensation. Thus, courts often are reluctant to engage in direct power struggles with the other branches of government. If courts do engage in such a struggle, their ability to prevail may depend on how much their decisions reflect, if not general public sentiment, at least the wishes of important groups. It may also depend on their ability to convince the public that they are being faithful to "the Constitution" and are not merely enacting their own political views.

Another restraint on the courts concerns the Constitution's language. Although constitutional language often is indefinite, it almost always has some meaning. In fact, certain constitutional provisions—for example, those governing the ages of senators and representatives—are perfectly clear on their face. Even the constitution's indefinite provisions express general values whose moral authority has continued over time. A broad phrase like "equal protection of the laws," for example, at least suggests that the government cannot make completely arbitrary and irrational distinctions in its lawmaking. And the term "due process of law" at least implies that government should use fair procedures before depriving someone of life, liberty, or property.

ENUMERATED POWERS AND INDEPENDENT CONSTITUTIONAL CHECKS

This chapter discusses constitutional doctrines that determine government's ability to regulate the economy. The constitutionality of government regulation requires courts to answer two general questions. First, did the government act pursuant to a *constitutionally granted* power when it enacted the law in question? Second, even if it did act pursuant to such a power, did its exercise of this power collide with an *independent constitutional check* contained elsewhere in the Constitution? If the first question is answered in the negative, the law in question is unconstitutional. And regardless of how the first question is answered, a positive answer to the second question also means that the law is unconstitutional. Figure 5.1 summarizes these points as they apply at the federal level.

FIGURE 5.1 Enumerated Powers and Independent Constitutional Checks at the Federal Level

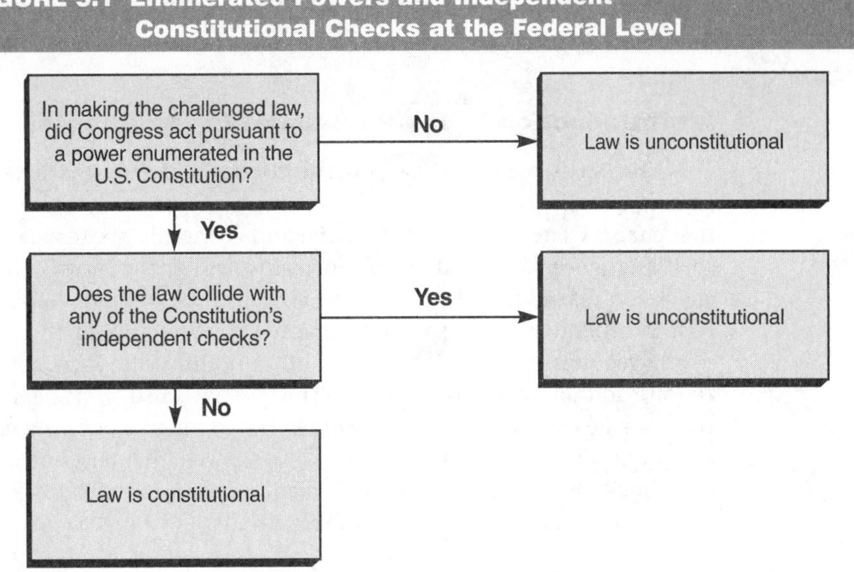

Enumerated Powers

One of the U.S. Constitution's main aims is to limit government power, and the two questions already mentioned represent two distinct ways of doing so. First, the Constitution limits congressional power by specifically listing or enumerating the areas in which Congress can make law, and by tacitly saying that it can exercise those powers and no others. Article I, section 8 of the Constitution and a few other constitutional provisions give Congress a lengthy, but not unlimited, collection of powers. Under the long-settled doctrine of **enumerated powers**, Congress only can do those things listed or enumerated in the Constitution, and cannot exercise any powers other than those specifically granted it by the Constitution.

In reality, however, congressional regulatory power now greatly exceeds anything one might expect after reading the specific powers enumerated in the Constitution. Extensive federal regulation of the economy has been a fact of life for most of the twentieth century. Since the late 1930s, the enumerated powers doctrine has not been a major obstacle to such regulation, because the Supreme Court has interpreted many of Congress's enumerated powers broadly. The following discussion of the commerce, tax, and spending powers provides examples. But as that discussion also reveals, the enumerated powers doctrine has shown signs of renewed life in recent years.

Independent Constitutional Checks

Due to the way Congress's enumerated powers have been interpreted in the twentieth century, the main constitutional restrictions on federal regulation of the economy now lie outside the enumerated power on which a regulation is based. We call these external restrictions **independent constitutional checks**. Independent constitutional checks create protected zones into which government regulation cannot reach. A regulation intruding into one of these zones is unconstitutional even if it is based on an enumerated power. As you will see shortly, for example, Congress has the power to regulate commerce between the states. By itself, this power might enable Congress to pass a statute prohibiting women from conducting business in interstate commerce. But such a law would be unconstitutional under one of the Constitution's independent checks—the equal protection clause.

An Introduction to the Remainder of the Chapter

This chapter is organized around the concepts already discussed. After briefly discussing state legislative authority, it examines three important enumerated powers that enable Congress to regulate social and economic matters: its commerce, tax, and spending powers. Then attention turns to three of the most significant independent checks on federal and state power to regulate: due process, equal protection, and the First Amendment's free speech guarantee. Understanding these three independent checks requires that we discuss three other notions: the incorporation doctrine, state action, and means-ends scrutiny. The chapter also considers three independent checks—the contract clause, the burden-on-commerce doctrine, and federal preemption—that only limit state regulatory power. The chapter concludes by examining a provision—the Fifth Amendment's takings clause—that both recognizes a governmental power and limits that power's exercise.

STATE POWER TO REGULATE THE ECONOMY

Strictly speaking, the enumerated powers doctrine only applies to Congress. In other words, the U.S. Constitution does not list or enumerate specific powers that the states may exercise.[1] However, state constitutions may do so. The most important state regulatory power is the **police power**. This is a broad state power to regulate to advance the public health, safety, morals, and welfare. Of course, exercises of the police power and other powers granted by state constitutions are subject to the independent checks discussed later. In particular, state laws may be unconstitutional because they are *preempted* by federal regulation of the same subject.

THREE ENUMERATED CONGRESSIONAL POWERS

The Commerce Power

Article I, section 8 of the Constitution says that Congress has the power "[t]o regulate Commerce . . . among the several States." This **commerce clause** has two main thrusts: one represents its purpose, and one reflects its language. The Framers put the commerce clause in the Constitution to promote national commercial activity by preventing the states from engaging in the economic protectionism that was common after the Revolution. In line with this purpose, the clause is an independent check on state lawmaking that hinders or burdens interstate commerce. We discuss this use of the commerce clause later in the chapter. Here, our concern is the scope of Congress's enumerated power to regulate interstate commerce.

The language of the commerce clause seems to limit it to business or commercial matters. Perhaps more importantly, it only appears to reach *interstate* commerce (commerce between or among the states) and not *intrastate* matters (things happening within a state). By the mid-twentieth century, however, the commerce clause had

[1] However, the U.S. Constitution does say that certain powers—for example, creating currency and taxing imports—may only be exercised by Congress. In most other areas, Congress and the state legislatures have *concurrent powers*; in these areas, both can make law.

become an all-purpose federal police power with great intrastate reach. That is, the clause enabled Congress to legislate on a wide range of subjects and to reach deep within the states while doing so. This happened because it came to be accepted Congress could regulate intrastate matters if they had a sufficient effect on interstate commerce. In 1914, for example, the Court let Congress regulate railroad rates within Texas (an intrastate matter) because of the economic impact those rates had on an interstate subject Congress obviously could regulate: rail traffic between Texas and Louisiana.

In that 1914 case, Congress was regulating for broadly commercial reasons, and not for "police power" purposes such as the public health, safety, morals, and welfare. Eventually, though, the "affecting commerce" doctrine was used to justify federal regulation of noneconomic matters within the states. In 1964, for instance, the Court considered whether the 1964 Civil Rights Act's ban on racial discrimination by restaurants applied to Ollie's Barbecue, a 220-seat family-owned establishment in Birmingham, Alabama whose business was almost totally local. In fact, there was no claim that interstate travelers ever visited Ollie's. Nonetheless, the Court found that Ollie's racial discrimination was within the commerce power because it affected interstate commerce. For one thing, such discrimination restricted interstate travel by black people. Furthermore, Ollie's discrimination meant that it did less business and therefore reduced its interstate meat purchases. The Court conceded that, due to Ollie's relatively small size, each of these effects on interstate commerce was insignificant taken by itself. But the aggregate effect of racial discrimination by all similarly situated restaurants was significant, which was enough to justify federal regulation of Ollie's.

Due to such decisions, it used to be widely believed that there were few, if any, limits on Congress's regulatory power under the commerce clause. To be sure, an effect on interstate commerce had to be shown if Congress was to regulate intrastate activities. But in the complex, interconnected social and economic life of modern America, some such effect usually could be found if a court wanted to find it. In addition, courts often would defer to congressional statements that the necessary effect on interstate commerce exists.

In 1995, however, the *Lopez* case breathed new life into the enumerated powers doctrine. It did so by saying and holding that there are some inherent limits to Congress's power under the commerce clause. Now, intrastate activities must have a *substantial* effect on interstate commerce to be within Congress's commerce power.

United States v. Lopez

U.S. Supreme Court
514 U.S. 549 (1995)

Background and Facts:

Alfonso Lopez, Jr., a 12th-grade student, carried a concealed .38 caliber handgun and five bullets into the Edison High School in San Antonio, Texas. For this reason, he was arrested and charged with violating section 922(q) of the federal Gun-Free School Zones Act of 1990, which forbids the knowing possession of a firearm within a school zone. After being found guilty in a federal district court trial, Lopez appealed his conviction. He argued that section 922(q) exceeded Congress's legislative power under the commerce clause. The Fifth Circuit Court of Appeals agreed, reversing Lopez's conviction. The government then appealed to the U.S. Supreme Court.

Body of Opinion

Chief Justice Rehnquist

We start with first principles. The Constitution creates a Federal Government of enumerated powers. As James Madison wrote, "[t]he powers delegated by the proposed Constitution to the federal government are few and defined. Those which are to remain in the State governments are numerous and indefinite." This constitutionally mandated division of authority was adopted by the

Framers to ensure protection of our fundamental liberties. Just as the separation and independence of the coordinate branches of the federal government serve to prevent the accumulation of excessive power in any one branch, a healthy balance of power between the States and the Federal Government will reduce the risk of tyranny and abuse from either front.

The Constitution delegates to Congress the power "[t]o regulate commerce with foreign Nations, and among the several States, and with the Indian Tribes."... Congress's commerce authority includes the power to regulate those activities having a substantial relation to interstate commerce, i.e., those activities that substantially affect interstate commerce.... [I]f section 922(q) is to be sustained, it must be... as a regulation of an activity that substantially affects interstate commerce....

The government's essential contention... is that we may determine here that section 922(q) is valid because possession of a firearm in a local school zone indeed does substantially affect interstate commerce. The Government argues that possession of a firearm in a school zone may result in violent crime and that violent crime can be expected to affect the functioning of the national economy in two ways. First, the costs of violent crime are substantial, and through the mechanism of insurance, those costs are spread throughout the population. Second, violent crime reduces the willingness of individuals to travel to areas of the country that are perceived to be unsafe. The Government also argues that the presence of guns in schools poses a substantial threat to the educational process by threatening the learning environment. A handicapped educational process, in turn, will result in a less productive citizenry. That, in turn, would have an adverse effect on the Nation's economic well-being. As a result, the Government argues that Congress could rationally have concluded that section 922(q) substantially affects interstate commerce.

We pause to consider the implications of the Government's arguments. The Government admits, under its "costs of crime" reasoning, that Congress could regulate not only all violent crime, but all activities that might lead to violent crime, regardless of how tenuously they relate to interstate commerce. Similarly, under the Government's "national productivity" reasoning, Congress could regulate any activity that it found was related to the economic productivity of individual citizens: family law (including marriage, divorce, and child custody), for example. Under the theories that the Government presents in support of section 922(q), it is difficult to perceive any limitation on federal power, even in areas such as criminal law enforcement or education where States historically have been sovereign. Thus, if we were to accept the Government's arguments, we are hard-pressed to posit any activity by an individual that Congress is without power to regulate....

To uphold the Government's contentions here, we would have to pile inference upon inference in a manner that would bid fair to convert congressional authority under the Commerce Clause to a general police power of the sort retained by the States. Admittedly, some of our prior cases have taken long steps down that road, giving great deference to congressional action. The broad language in these opinions has suggested the possibility of additional expansion, but we decline here to proceed any further. To do so would require us to conclude that the Constitution's enumeration of powers does not presuppose something not enumerated, and that there will never be a distinction between what is truly national and what is truly local. This we are unwilling to do.

Judgment and Result

Court of Appeals decision affirmed; Lopez wins.

Questions

1. Does the Court's decision in *Lopez* mean that from now on, people will be free to carry guns in school zones?
2. The government made three arguments that the possession of firearms in a school zone affects interstate commerce. What exactly are they? State them by drawing diagrams with arrows indicating how one thing causes another.
3. Did Chief Justice Rehnquist's opinion show that the possession of guns in school zones has no effect on interstate commerce? If not, how did he argue?

The Taxing Power

Article I, section 8 gives Congress "Power To lay and collect Taxes, Duties, Imposts and Excises." The purpose behind this language is to let Congress raise revenue for the operations of government.[2] But our concern here is with the use of this **taxing power** to regulate. Taxation can regulate because it tends to discourage the activity taxed. The power to tax, it is said, is the power to destroy.

[2] The Constitution places certain restrictions on the use of taxation to raise revenue, but these restrictions are beyond the scope of this text.

Since the 1930s, the courts usually have upheld Congress's use of the taxing power for regulatory purposes unrelated to the raising of revenue. In recent years, few cases have explored the limits of Congress's regulatory authority under the taxing power. To some extent, this reflects the broad reach of the commerce power and the inefficiencies involved with using taxation to regulate, both of which make the commerce power the preferred basis for federal regulation of the economy. But even though its outer limits are uncertain, the taxing power is still a sweeping source of congressional regulatory authority.

The Spending Power

Immediately after stating the taxing power, Article I, section 8 goes on to give Congress the power "to pay the Debts and provide for the common Defence and general Welfare of the United States." This language has been read as giving Congress broad authority to spend for the public welfare. The **spending power** is an important source of federal authority to regulate. This is accomplished by conditioning federal appropriations on compliance with a specified course of behavior. Just as the taxing power is a stick compelling chosen conduct through fear of financial loss, the spending power is a carrot inducing favored behavior through the promise of economic reward.

Although the spending power can be employed for a wide range of purposes, there are some limits on its use. The constitutional language previously quoted above limits federal spending to the promotion of *general* purposes, and this requirement could block conditional grant programs that serve special interests. Also, the Supreme Court has declared that if Congress wishes to put a condition on the receipt of federal money, it must do so *clearly*. Moreover, the Court has said that the condition must be *reasonably related to the purpose* behind the federal expenditure. For example, Congress might run into constitutional problems if it tries to condition the receipt of federal health care money on a state's elimination of highway billboards. Finally, note that in theory the would-be recipient of a conditional federal grant always can avoid the condition by doing without federal money.

INDEPENDENT CONSTITUTIONAL CHECKS APPLYING TO BOTH CONGRESS AND THE STATES

This portion of the chapter examines certain constitutional limitations that apply to both the federal government and the states. The provisions we discuss are the due process guarantees contained in the Fifth and Fourteenth Amendments, the First Amendment's guarantee of free speech, and the Fourteenth Amendment's equal protection clause. Each has its business applications, and our discussion is largely limited to those applications. Before examining them, however, we must consider some preliminary matters.

Incorporation

The Fifth Amendment applies only to the federal government and the Fourteenth Amendment only to the states. Because each amendment contains a due process clause, due process applies at both the federal and state levels. The First Amendment, however, only restricts the federal government. Its application to the states, which first occurred early in this century, happened because of its incorporation within the liberty protected by the Fourteenth Amendment's due process clause. By now, most other Bill of Rights provisions also have been incorporated within Fourteenth Amendment due process liberty and thus apply to the states. This process was reversed in the case of the Fourteenth Amendment's equal protection clause. The Fourteenth Amendment applies only to the states, but its equal protection guarantee has been incorporated within the Fifth Amendment's due process clause and thus applies to the federal government. Figure 5.2 summarizes the points made in this and the preceding paragraph.

Means-Ends Tests

Means-ends tests are used when laws are challenged under the constitution's individual rights provisions. They exist because no constitutional right is absolute in the sense that it can never be restricted by the government. Thus, such tests try to strike a balance between individual rights and the needs of society. They do so by (1) stating how important a challenged law's *ends* must be in order for that law to be constitutional, and (2) stating *how effectively* the challenged law must advance that end in order for the law to be constitutional.

Because courts regard some rights as more important than others and therefore require more justification for favored rights to be restricted, means-ends tests come in many forms. Here, we oversimplify by identifying three different kinds of means-ends scrutiny:

1. *Full Strict Scrutiny* This tough test of constitutionality is reserved for rights of special importance. A court employing full strict scrutiny might say that, to be constitutional, a challenged law must be *necessary* to the achievement of a *compelling* government purpose.
2. *Intermediate Scrutiny* This fairly tough test of constitutionality comes in many different forms. One example discussed later in the chapter is the test applied to laws that discriminate on the basis of gender. This test says that such laws must be *substantially* related to the promotion of an *important* government purpose.
3. *The Rational Basis Test* A typical formulation of this lenient test of constitutionality says that a challenged law must be *rationally* related to a *legitimate* government purpose in order to be constitutional. The rational basis test is the basic constitutional standard under the equal protection clause.

State Action

Most of the Constitution's individual rights protections only protect people against government activity. Such activity typically is described as **government action** or

FIGURE 5.2 The Application of Independent Checks to the Federal Government and the States

	Federal Government	States
Due Process	Fifth Amendment	Fourteenth Amendment
Free Speech	First Amendment	Incorporation within Fourteenth Amendment
Equal Protection	Incorporation within Fifth Amendment	Fourteenth Amendment

state action. Thus, the Constitution's individual rights provisions usually do not protect people when their rights are infringed by private actors.[3] However, state and federal statutes often provide such protection.

The Supreme Court's attempts to draw the line between government activity and private activity have created great confusion, in part because the Court has drawn the line differently at different times. Before World War II, state action was limited to the activities of formally governmental bodies such as legislatures, administrative agencies, courts, municipalities, and state universities. Beginning in the late 1940s, however, the definition of state action expanded considerably, with all sorts of formally private activities being subjected to constitutional restrictions. In a 1948 case, the Supreme Court found that a private agreement among white property owners forbidding the transfer of their land to nonwhites was unconstitutional state action because the state of Missouri enforced it in court. Two years earlier, the Court applied the First Amendment to a company town owned by a private corporation, because the town performed all the functions of a regular municipality. This **public function doctrine** reached its high point in 1968, when it was extended to cover a private shopping center. During the 1960s and early 1970s, courts considered various other factors when making government action determinations. Among the considerations leading courts to find state action were extensive government *regulation* of a private activity, substantial government *funding* of such activity, and *public-private cooperation* (or "symbiosis") of the sort found in the defense industry.

Why did state action expand so dramatically in the 25 years following World War II? One reason is that for much of that time, the Supreme Court was dominated by Justices who were anxious to protect certain individual rights and concerned about the way private bodies might infringe those rights. "Constitutionalizing" private bodies through an expansion of state action was a way to prevent them from discriminating and from threatening personal liberty.

Beginning in the early 1970s, however, the Court's composition began to change. The result was a contraction in the reach of government action. To be sure, state action has not yet returned to its narrow pre-World War II definition, and the cases expanding the doctrine have not been overruled. Nonetheless, constitutional challenges to formally private activity are less likely to succeed today than they were 20 or 30 years ago. The public function doctrine, for instance, is now limited to situations in which a private entity exercises powers, such as police protection, that have *traditionally* been *exclusively* reserved to government. Even private activity that is extensively regulated and/or publicly funded is not necessarily state action. Recent state action cases have stated that, for a state action to be present, the government must be *responsible* for the activity challenged as unconstitutional by directly compelling or encouraging it.

In 1987, for example, the Court held that a lawsuit by the United States Olympic Committee (USOC) was not government action. The most important reason was that the federal government, which created the USOC by statute, did not coerce or encourage the USOC to enter the suit in question. In addition, Congress's giving the USOC a corporate charter, its extensive regulation of the USOC, and its intent to help the USOC get funding were not enough to make the USOC a government actor. Finally, the public function doctrine did not apply because the USOC's activities, while serving the public interest, traditionally had been performed by private entities.

---

[3] One exception is the Thirteenth Amendment, which flatly says that neither slavery nor involuntary servitude shall exist within the United States, except as punishment for crimes. Also, some state constitutions do not have a government action requirement.

Business and the First Amendment

Under the First Amendment's free speech guarantee, many kinds of expression receive a high degree of constitutional protection. Laws restricting such expression receive something like the full strict scrutiny described earlier. The most common justification for this protection is the social interest in the free competition of ideas. "[T]he best test of truth," Justice Oliver Wendell Holmes once wrote, "is the power of the thought to get itself accepted in the competition of the market." If government can exclude speech from the market, many believe, our ability to separate truth from falsehood would suffer.

Most of the issues raised by the First Amendment's free speech guarantee are beyond the scope of this text, as are the special problems of the communications media and of corporate political financing. Here, we limit ourselves to two First Amendment doctrines affecting government's ability to regulate speech by corporations and other business entities. In each case, the "marketplace" argument for free speech is the basis for the First Amendment protection business receives.

Corporate Political Speech. In *First National Bank of Boston v. Bellotti* (1978), the Supreme Court struck down a state law forbidding corporate expenditures to influence a public vote on a matter not involving the property or business of the affected corporation. In the process, *Bellotti* established a corporation's First Amendment right to express itself on public issues unrelated to its direct economic interests. In 1980, the Court used this right to strike down a state public service commission's refusal to allow a utility to include inserts promoting nuclear power in the bills it sent to its customers. And in 1986 it invalidated a state utility commission order compelling a regulated private utility to periodically include the comments of a rate reform group in its billing envelopes.

The policy behind *Bellotti's* protection of corporate political speech is the social interest in the free competition of ideas—an interest that would be frustrated by arbitrarily removing corporations from the political marketplace of ideas. Therefore, laws restricting the right of corporate political speech receive strict scrutiny. Critics of business, however, have attacked *Bellotti* as an unjustified boost to corporate power. The assets and communications skills possessed by large corporations, these critics argue, enable corporations to distort the free market of ideas in favor of their own interests.

Commercial Speech. Commercial speech might be defined as expression proposing a commercial transaction. The main example is commercial advertising. Drawing the line between commercial speech and other forms of protected First Amendment speech can be difficult. In a 1983 case, for example, a corporation's marketing campaign for condoms included the mass mailing of "informational pamphlets" discussing the usefulness of condoms (especially the corporation's own brand) for preventing venereal disease and aiding family planning. Individually, the fact that the pamphlets were advertisements, their reference to a specific product, and the corporation's economic motivation for mailing them were not enough to convince the Supreme Court that they should be regarded as commercial speech. The combination of all these characteristics, however, made the pamphlets commercial speech.

In 1942, the Supreme Court held that commercial speech is not entitled to First Amendment protection. During the 1970s, however, the Court concluded that commercial speech is covered by the First Amendment, but that it receives an intermediate level of constitutional protection. The test, which comes from *Central Hudson Gas & Electric Corporation v. Public Service Commission* (1980), says that state restrictions on commercial speech must (1) advance a substantial government interest, (2) do so directly, and (3) be no more extensive than is necessary to advance the interest. The *44 Liquormart* case applies this test.

The main reason for protecting commercial speech is to increase the flow of consumer information, and thus to promote free competition and economic efficiency. This purpose probably was achieved in some Supreme Court decisions striking down state restrictions on advertising by professionals such as lawyers and pharmacists. These restrictions most likely limited competition for such professionals' products and services and allowed them to charge inflated prices. The same may be true of the statutes at issue in *44 Liquormart.* As the Court recognizes in that case, however, some restrictions on commercial advertising are consistent with the purposes underlying the constitutional protection of commercial speech. Thus, laws that regulate deceptive, misleading, or overaggressive advertising, or that require firms to disclose information useful to consumers, get light scrutiny.

44 Liquormart, Inc. v. Rhode Island

U.S. Supreme Court
517 U.S. 484 (1996)

Background and Facts:

44 Liquormart, a licensed Rhode Island retailer of alcoholic beverages, ran a newspaper advertisement containing an implied reference to the bargain prices at which its liquor could be purchased. As a result, the Rhode Island Liquor Control Administrator assessed a $400 fine against the store. The Administrator did so under Rhode Island statutes forbidding price advertising for alcoholic beverages (with an exception for in-store price tags or signs not visible from the street).

44 Liquormart challenged its fine in federal district court, arguing that the statutes violated the First Amendment. After the district court held for 44 Liquormart, the court of appeals reversed, finding the statutes constitutional. 44 Liquormart then appealed to the U.S. Supreme Court.

Body of Opinion

Justice Stevens

In *Central Hudson Gas & Electric Corporation v. Public Service Commission* (1980), . . . we considered a regulation completely banning all promotional advertising by electric utilities. . . . Five members of the Court recognized that the state interest in the conservation of energy was substantial, and that there was an immediate connection between advertising and demand for electricity. Nevertheless, they concluded that the regulation was invalid because the Commission had failed to make a showing that a more limited speech regulation would not have adequately served the state's interest. In reaching its conclusion, the majority explained that although the special nature of commercial speech may require less than strict review of its regulation, special concerns arise from regulations that entirely suppress commercial speech in order to pursue a nonspeech-related policy. . . . As a result, the Court concluded that special care should attend the review of such blanket bans. . . .

Rhode Island errs in concluding that all commercial speech regulations are subject to a similar form of constitutional review simply because they target a similar category of expression. . . . When a state regulates commercial messages to protect consumers from misleading, deceptive, or aggressive sales practices, or requires the disclosure of beneficial consumer information, the purpose of its regulation is consistent with the reasons for according constitutional protection to commercial speech and therefore justifies less than strict review. However, when a state entirely prohibits the dissemination of truthful, nonmisleading commercial messages for reasons unrelated to the preservation of a fair bargaining process, there is far less reason to depart from the rigorous review that the First Amendment generally demands. . . .

There is no question that Rhode Island's price advertising ban constitutes a blanket prohibition against truthful, nonmisleading speech about a lawful product. There is also no question than the ban serves an end unrelated to consumer protection. Accordingly, we must review the price advertising ban with special care, mindful that speech prohibitions of this type rarely survive constitutional review.

The state argues that the price advertising prohibition should be upheld because it directly advances the state's substantial interest in promoting temperance, and because it is no more extensive than necessary. . . . However, without any findings of fact, or indeed any evidentiary support whatsoever, we cannot agree. . . . Although the record suggests that the price advertising ban may have some impact on the purchasing patterns of temperate drinkers of modest means, the state has presented no evidence to suggest that its speech prohibition will significantly reduce marketwide consumption. . . . Moreover, the evidence suggests that the abusive drinker will probably not be deterred by a marginal price increase, and that the true alcoholic may simply reduce his purchases of other necessities. . . . Any conclusion that elimination of the ban would significantly increase alcohol consumption would require us to engage in the sort of speculation or conjecture that is an unacceptable means of demonstrating that a restriction on commercial speech directly advances the state's asserted interest. Such speculation certainly does not suffice when the state takes aim at accurate commercial information for paternalistic ends.

The state also cannot satisfy the requirement that its restriction on speech be no more [extensive] than necessary.... Higher prices can be maintained either by direct regulation or by increased taxation. Per capita purchases could be limited as is the case with prescription drugs. Even educational campaigns focused on the problems of excessive, or even moderate, drinking might prove to be more effective.

Judgment and Result

The court of appeals judgment upholding the statute was reversed; 44 Liquormart wins.

Questions

1. The Court said that two levels of scrutiny now may apply in commercial speech cases. Which level was applied here, and why?
2. Which two elements of the *Central Hudson* test were not satisfied in this case?
3. The statutes at issue in this case were passed in 1956. Over the years, do you think that most Rhode Island liquor dealers were happy or unhappy with these laws? Why?

Due Process

The Fifth and Fourteenth Amendments prevent the federal government and the states from depriving any person of life, liberty, or property without due process of law. A violation of these provisions occurs, when a person is (1) deprived of life, liberty, or property; (2) by government (the state action requirement discussed earlier); (3) without due process of law. The due process guarantee has both *procedural* and *substantive* dimensions. Rules of substantive law establish rights, duties, and standards of behavior governing individuals as they act in society. Procedural rules concern the legal machinery through which substantive rules are enforced. For example, the law of contract is substantive. But the legal rules detailing the steps through which a court must proceed in a suit for breach of contract are procedural. When due process is substantive, it involves a constitutional attack on the fairness of substantive rules. When it is procedural, it involves a constitutional attack on the fairness of procedural rules. In each case, the relevant notions of fairness are quite different.

http:// *Check out the actual text of the Fifth and Fourteenth Amendments' due process clauses at* ***http://www.law.cornell.edu/*** *under "Constitutions and Codes."*

Procedural Due Process. The traditional definition of due process is procedural. The central theme of this **procedural due process** is that people are entitled to reasonable notice of the charges brought against them and a fair trial or hearing before government can deprive them of life, liberty, or property. Historically, procedural due process probably has been most important in criminal cases. But it can apply any time that either a state or the federal government deprives a person of life, liberty, or property.

In order to suffer a violation of due process, the claimant must have been deprived of either liberty or property. Procedural due process liberty is broadly defined, and it is difficult to specify its scope with any precision. Procedural due process property interests, on the other hand, usually are created by state law. For individuals to have such an interest, moreover, they must have an actual, legitimate claim of entitlement to it, rather than some abstract need or desire for it. The range of protected property interests is broad. Examples include a horse trainer's license, utility service, disability benefits, welfare benefits, government employment, and a driver's license.

The typical procedural due process claim arises when the government deprives a person of life, liberty, or property, and the person claims that the deprivation occurred without constitutionally adequate procedural safeguards. What procedural standards is government required to meet in such cases? As we saw earlier, the central requirements are reasonable notice and some fair trial or hearing. But the actual standards courts apply inevitably vary from situation to situation. Someone who loses welfare benefits, for instance, is not entitled to the same procedural due process as a defendant in a murder case. *Gilbert v. Homar* discusses some factors that courts examine when determining what process is due.

Gilbert v. Homar

United States Supreme Court
520 U.S. 924 (1997)

Background and Facts:

On August 26, 1992, while employed as a policeman at East Stroudsburg University (ESU), a state institution, Richard Homar was arrested by the state police and charged with a drug felony. ESU officials then suspended Homar without pay pending their own investigation. Although the criminal charges were dismissed on September 1, Homar's suspension remained in effect. On September 18, he finally was provided the opportunity to tell his side of the story to ESU officials. Subsequently, he was demoted to groundskeeper. He then filed suit under a federal civil rights statute, claiming that university officials' failure to provide him with notice and a hearing before suspending him without pay violated due process. The federal district court granted ESU summary judgment, but the court of appeals reversed. ESU appealed to the U.S. Supreme Court.

Body of Opinion

Justice Scalia

The protections of the due process clause apply to government deprivation of those perquisites of government employment in which the employee has a constitutionally protected property interest. Although we have previously held that public employees who can be discharged only for cause have a constitutionally protected property interest in their tenure and cannot be fired without due process, we have not had occasion to decide whether the protections of the due process clause extend to discipline of tenured public employees short of termination. ESU, however, does not contest this preliminary point, and so without deciding it we will, like the district court, assume that the suspension infringed a protected property interest, and turn at once to ESU's contention that Homar received all the process he was due.

In *Cleveland Board of Education v. Loudermill* (1985), we concluded that a public employee dismissible only for cause was entitled to a very limited hearing prior to his termination, to be followed by a more comprehensive post-termination hearing. Stressing that the pre-termination hearing should be an initial check against mistaken decisions—essentially, a determination of whether there are reasonable grounds to believe that the charges against the employee are true and support the proposed action—we held that pre-termination process need only include oral or written notice of the charges, an explanation of the employer's evidence, and an opportunity for the employee to tell his side of the story....

It is by now well established that due process, unlike some legal rules, is not a technical conception with a fixed content unrelated to time, place and circumstances. Due process is flexible and calls for such procedural protections as the particular situation demands. This Court has recognized, on many occasions, that where a state must act quickly, or where it would be impractical to provide pre-deprivation process, post-deprivation process satisfies the requirements of the due process clause....

To determine what process is constitutionally due, we have generally balanced three distinct factors: first, the private interest that will be affected by the official action; second, the risk of an erroneous deprivation of such interest through the procedures used, and the probable value, if any, of additional or substitute procedural safeguards; and finally, the government's interest. Homar contends that he has a significant private interest in the uninterrupted receipt of his paycheck. But while our opinions have recognized the severity of depriving someone of the means of his livelihood, they have also emphasized that in determining what process is due, account must be taken of the length and finality of the deprivation. Unlike the employee in *Loudermill*, who faced termination, Homar faced only a temporary suspension without pay. So long as the suspended employee receives a sufficiently prompt post-suspension hearing, the lost income is relatively insubstantial (compared with termination), and fringe benefits such as health and life insurance are often not affected at all.

On the other side of the balance, the state has a significant interest in immediately suspending, when felony charges are filed against them, employees who occupy positions of great public trust and high public visibility, such as police officers. Homar contends that this interest in maintaining public confidence could have been accommodated by suspending him with pay until he had a hearing. We think, however, that the government does not have to give an employee charged with a felony a paid leave at taxpayer expense. If his services to the government are no longer useful once the felony charge has been filed, the Constitution does not require the government to bear the added expense of hiring a replacement while still paying him....

The last factor in the balancing, and the factor most important to resolution of this case, is the risk of erroneous deprivation and the likely value of any additional procedures.... We noted in *Loudermill* that the purpose of a pre-termination hearing is to determine whether there are reasonable grounds to believe the charges against the employee are true and support the proposed action. By parity of reasoning, the purpose of any pre-*suspension* hearing would be to assure that there are reasonable grounds to support the suspension without pay. But here that has already been assured by the arrest and the filing of charges.... They serve to assure that the state employer's decision to suspend the employee is not baseless or unwarranted, in that an independent third party has determined that there is probable cause to believe the employee committed a serious crime....

Whether Homar was provided an adequately prompt post-suspension hearing in the present case is a separate question. Although the charges against Homar were dropped on September 1..., he did not receive any sort of hearing until September 18. Once the charges were dropped, the risk of erroneous deprivation increased substantially, and, as petitioners conceded at oral argument, there was likely value in holding a prompt hearing. Because neither the Court of Appeals nor the District Court addressed whether, under the particular facts of this case, ESU violated due process by failing to provide a sufficiently prompt post-suspension hearing, we will not consider this issue in the first instance, but remand for consideration by the Court of Appeals.

Judgment and Result

The Court held that ESU's failure to give Homar notice and a hearing before suspending him without pay did not violate due process. The failure to give Homar a prompt *post*-suspension hearing, however, might have violated due process. The court of appeals' decision was reversed and the case was returned to the court of appeals for it to consider whether Homar should have received a post-deprivation hearing.

Questions

1. Did ESU deprive Homar of a property interest? How did the Court deal with this question?
2. Of the three factors the Court considered, which favored ESU and which favored Homar?

Substantive Due Process. On occasion, the Supreme Court has given due process a substantive meaning by deciding whether a deprivation of liberty or property is justified as a matter of sound public policy. Here, the Court is looking at the reasonableness of a rule for the governance of social life, and not at the procedural machinery through which such a substantive rule is enforced. In its various forms, this **substantive due process** usually involves two steps: (1) choosing certain preferred rights and including them within the liberty or property protected by the Fifth and Fourteenth amendments, and (2) giving such liberty or property interests substantive protection by applying some kind of means-ends scrutiny to laws that deprive people of those interests.

In the late nineteenth and early twentieth centuries, the Supreme Court created the doctrine known as economic substantive due process. It did so by including various economic freedoms among the liberty and property rights protected by the Fifth and Fourteenth Amendments, and by requiring that laws restricting these freedoms meet some fairly rigorous means-ends test or other test of constitutionality. In *Lochner v. New York* (1905), for example, it required that for freedom of contract to be restricted by government, there had to be a real and substantial relationship between the restriction and a valid governmental purpose. Then it used this test to strike down a New York statute setting maximum hours of work for bakery employees. It concluded that this law, which obviously restricted freedom of contract, did not have a sufficiently close relationship to valid public purposes such as protecting worker health.

As the previous example indicates, the old economic form of substantive due process sometimes was a threat to laws regulating working conditions and to other kinds of government regulations. Still, most social and economic regulations challenged on substantive due process grounds in the first part of this century survived the attack. After 1937, moreover, the doctrine ceased to be a serious check on government regulation of social and economic matters. Since then, such regulations have usually been tested under a weak rational basis test when they are challenged on substantive due process grounds. Thus, they have virtually always survived the challenge.

But substantive due process lives on in noneconomic areas of life. The main example consists of several fundamental privacy rights that receive an extremely high degree of constitutional protection. Recently the Supreme Court has said that these include the rights to marry, have children, direct their education and upbringing, enjoy marital privacy, use contraception, and have an abortion. Laws restricting these rights, it continued, must be narrowly tailored to meet a compelling government purpose. Laws that restrict nonfundamental rights, however, receive some sort of rational basis review.

The following case presents two distinct substantive due process claims. The first is an economic substantive due process argument based on the right to pursue the trade, profession, or occupation of one's choice. The second is a privacy claim based on a woman's right to choose how she shall give birth to a child.

Lange-Kessler v. Department of Education

U.S. Courts of Appeals for the Second Circuit
109 F.3d 137

Background and Facts:

New York's Professional Midwifery Practice Act (PMPA) limits the practice of midwifery. One provision of the act requires that midwifery must be practiced in accordance with a written practice agreement between the midwife and: (1) a board-certified obstetrician-gynecologist; (2) a licensed physician who practices obstetrics; or (3) a hospital that provides obstetric services. Another PMPA provision basically requires that all applicants for a professional midwifery license meet educational requirements for both the practice of nursing and the practice of midwifery.

Julia Lange-Kessler was a direct-entry midwife. A direct-entry midwife trains through apprenticeship with other midwives rather than through formal education. Because Lange-Kessler could not be licensed under the PMPA, she sued in federal district court, claiming that the act deprived her of the ability to earn a living in her chosen profession, in violation of the Fourteenth Amendment's due process clause. Joining Lange-Kessler's lawsuit were three women of child-bearing age who had previously used Lange-Kessler's home-birthing services and who wished to do so again. These women claimed that, by restricting their right to choose a birthing style and a qualified attendant of their choice, the PMPA violated their right to privacy under Fourteenth Amendment due process.

The state then moved for summary judgment. In support of its motion, the state submitted an affidavit from Mary Applegate, who was Medical Director for Reproductive and Perinatal Health at the New York State Department of Health, and was responsible for reviewing the credentials and practice arrangements of nurse-midwives applying for practice in New York State. Dr. Applegate asserted that direct-entry midwives are not qualified to handle the physical complications that may arise during pregnancy and childbirth. In response, the plaintiffs filed approximately 28 affidavits from consumers of direct-entry midwives' services, various midwives, and physicians. Collectively, those affidavits contended that home births supervised by direct-entry midwives are just as safe as births performed by doctors or nurse-midwives. In addition, the affidavits of the licensed nurse-midwives claimed that licensed obstetricians refused to enter into practice agreements with them, thus preventing the midwives from performing home births. The district court granted the state's motion for summary judgment, and the plaintiffs appealed.

Body of Opinion

Judge Parker

This action presents a substantive due process challenge to the Professional Midwifery Practice Act. There are principally two issues on appeal: (1) whether the district court erred when it determined that the PMPA is rationally related to a legitimate state interest; and (2) whether the district court erred when it determined that the right to privacy does not encompass the right to choose a direct-entry midwife to assist with childbirth. We affirm the district court on both issues. . . .

The right to follow a chosen profession is a property interest protected by the Fifth and Fourteenth Amendments. State-imposed restrictions on this right must be rationally related to a legitimate state interest. A statute regulating a profession is presumed to have a rational basis unless the plaintiff shows that the legislative facts upon which the statute is apparently based could not reasonably be conceived to be true by the governmental decisionmaker. To defeat this challenge, the state is not required to come forth with empirical evidence tending to show that the facts underlying the restrictions are true. Rather, a statute withstands a substantive due process challenge if it might be thought that enacting the statute was a rational way to further a legitimate interest.

In the instant case, the state has identified an interest in protecting the health and welfare of mothers and infants. In *Roe v. Wade*, the Supreme Court specifically categorized those same interests as "important and legitimate" ones. Therefore, as long as the restrictions that the PMPA places on the practice of midwifery are rationally related to protecting the health and welfare of mothers and infants, those restrictions must be upheld. Put another way, the relevant question is whether the legislature might have thought that an applicant with (1) a formal education and (2) a written practice agreement with a licensed physician or hospital is more fit to practice midwifery than is an applicant without these qualifications. This question must be answered in the affirmative.

The affidavit of Dr. Applegate describes two conditions that may arise during pregnancy: pregnancy-induced hypertension and gestational diabetes mellitus. According to Dr. Applegate, if left untreated, these conditions may result in the death of mother and fetus. In addition, Dr. Applegate describes several potentially fatal complications that may arise during the birthing process, including fetal distress, failure to progress, postpartum hemorrhaging, and ruptured uterus. . . . In light of these risks, the legislature could reasonably have believed that midwives who have completed a nursing program, and who are affiliated with a medical professional, are more fit than direct-entry midwives to practice midwifery. Moreover, insuring the fitness of midwives is rationally related to the state's legitimate interest in protecting the health and welfare of mothers and infants. Plaintiffs argue, however, that genuine issues of material fact exist as to whether direct-entry midwives are less capable than other professionals of diagnosing and treating the various complications associated with pregnancy and childbirth. For example, they argue that because their own experts contested Dr. Applegate's assertions that direct-entry midwives exhibit poor judgment while attending home births, summary judgment was improper as the district court could not conclude, as a matter of law, that the state legislature could reasonably rely on the facts asserted in her affidavit. Plaintiffs' argument, in and of itself, demonstrates the futility of their constitutional challenge: If reasonable minds could differ on the issue of a direct-entry midwife's competence, then it is wholly conceivable that the legislature took the view that direct-entry midwives are not likely to be sufficiently competent. Accordingly, we affirm the district court on this issue.

In *Griswold v. Connecticut* (1965), the Supreme Court established that the Constitution guarantees the fundamental right to privacy. Since that time, the right to privacy has been interpreted to protect freedom of choice in certain matters related to childbearing [such as the purchase and use of contraceptives, as well as abortion]. Whenever it is determined that legislation significantly interferes with the exercise of a fundamental right, a court must review the legislation with strict judicial scrutiny. Under this heightened standard of review, the state must demonstrate that the statute serves a compelling state interest and that the state's objectives could not be achieved by any less restrictive measures. We are unable to conclude, however, that the PMPA significantly interferes with the exercise of a fundamental right. In the abortion context, the Supreme Court has not interpreted the right to privacy so broadly that it encompasses the right to choose a particular healthcare provider. . . . [Thus,] we hold that the right to privacy does not encompass the right to choose a direct-entry midwife to assist with childbirth. Therefore, the appropriate standard of review is whether the challenged provisions bear a rational relationship to a legitimate state purpose. As we concluded in the previous section, insuring the fitness of midwives is rationally related to the state's legitimate interest in protecting the health and welfare of mothers and infants. Therefore, we affirm the district court on this issue.

Judgment and Result

The decision of the district court granting the state's motion for summary judgment was affirmed.

Questions

1. In your opinion, how convincing are Dr. Applegate's justifications of the PMPA? In any event, do you think that arguments such as these motivated the legislature when it passed the act? Who benefits from the PMPA? Who loses out? Which of these groups probably has the most political power?
2. The rights to purchase and use contraceptives and to have an abortion are fundamental, and laws restricting these rights get full strict scrutiny. Why is the right to choose a midwife to assist with childbirth not fundamental too? What makes it less important than these other rights?
3. Lange-Kessler's claim involves a right that occasionally got considerable substantive protection during the first third of this century: the right to pursue the trade, calling, or profession of one's choice. Based on this case, how much protection does it get today? Why is *this* right not fundamental? That is, what makes occupational freedom less important than, say, the rights to buy and use contraceptives, or to have an abortion?

Equal Protection

The Fourteenth Amendment's equal protection guarantee says that the states cannot deny people the "equal protection of the laws." As we have seen, equal protection standards now apply to the federal government as well. The equal protection clause was added to the Constitution shortly after the Civil War. Some historians argue that it originally was intended to apply only to discrimination against blacks. By the beginning of the twentieth century, however, the equal protection guarantee had become a general check against arbitrary and unjustified governmental distinctions of all sorts.

For another discussion of equal protection doctrine, see ***http://www.law.cornell.edu/*** *under "law about."*

http://

Law making inevitably requires that government discriminate by creating distinctions and classifications. Some individuals, groups, or activities are subjected to burdens or given advantages, and some are not. Equal protection sets the standards for the constitutionality of such distinctions and classifications. For example, if State X legislates in such a way as to subject A to a disadvantage or give A a benefit, but does not do the same for B, equal protection requires that there be a reason for the distinction. The reasons that might justify governmental classifications vary from situation to situation. In other words, the tests imposed by the equal protection clause vary depending on the type of discrimination at issue.

The Rational Basis Test. The basic equal protection standard—and the equal protection standard applied to social and economic regulation—is the **rational basis test** described earlier in the chapter. As the *Stanglin* case suggests, the rational basis test usually is not a significant obstacle to government regulation of social and economic matters. Under this standard, courts typically defer to the government's judgment. Usually, only the most arbitrary classifications are endangered by rational basis review.

City of Dallas v. Stanglin

U.S. Supreme Court
490 U.S. 19 (1989)

Background and Facts:

In 1985, the city of Dallas passed an ordinance stating that only those age 14 through 18 could be admitted to so-called "Class E" dance halls. However, the ordinance did not apply to other places where teenagers might congregate, such as roller skating rinks. Charles Stanglin operated the Twilight Skating Rink, a combined roller skating rink and Class E dance hall. To achieve this combination, Stanglin divided the floor of his rink into two sections by using movable plastic cones or pylons. On one side, those between the ages of 14 and 18 would dance, while on the other side people of all ages would skate to the same music.

Apparently becoming fed up with this arrangement, Stanglin challenged the ordinance's constitutionality in the Texas courts. After a Texas appellate court struck down the ordinance's time limitation, the city appealed to the U.S. Supreme Court.

Body of Opinion

Chief Justice Rehnquist

The Dallas ordinance . . . implicates no suspect class and impinges upon no constitutionally protected right. The question remaining is whether the classification engaged in by the city survives rational basis scrutiny under the equal protection clause. The city has chosen to impose a rule that separates 14- to 18-year-olds from what may be the corrupting influences of older teenagers and young adults. Ray Couch, an urban planner for the city, testified:

> [O]lder kids [whom the ordinance prohibits from entering Class E dance halls] can access drugs and alcohol, and they have more mature sexual attitudes, more liberal sexual attitudes in general. . . . And we're concerned about mixing up these [older] individuals with youngsters that [sic] have not fully matured. . . .

Stanglin claims that this restriction has no real connection with the city's stated interests and objectives. Except for saloons and teenage dance halls, he argues, teenagers and adults in Dallas may associate with each other, including at the skating area of the Twilight Skating rink. . . .

We think Stanglin's arguments misapprehend the nature of rational basis scrutiny, which is the most relaxed and tolerant form of judicial scrutiny under the equal protection clause. . . . [I]n the local economic sphere, it is only the invidious discrimination, the wholly arbitrary act, which cannot stand consistently with the Fourteenth Amendment. The city could reasonably conclude, as Couch stated, that teenagers might be susceptible to corrupting influences if permitted to frequent a dance hall with older persons. . . . The city could properly conclude that limiting dance-hall contacts between juveniles and adults would make less likely illicit or undesirable juvenile involvement with alcohol, illegal drugs, and promiscuous sex. It is true that the city allows teenagers and adults to roller-skate together, but skating involves less physical contact than dancing. The differences between the two activities may not be striking, but differentiation need not be striking in order to survive rational basis scrutiny.

Judgment and Result

Texas appellate court decision reversed; the ordinance is constitutional and Stanglin loses.

Questions

1. In equal protection cases, the claimant is challenging a governmental classification. What precisely was the challenged classification in this case? How did the Supreme Court justify the classification under the rational basis test?
2. Would the Dallas ordinance have survived full strict scrutiny?

Stricter Scrutiny. As a result of changes in approach that mainly occurred during the 1960s and 1970s, the courts now use more rigorous equal protection standards when examining two general types of classifications: (1) those creating unequal enjoyment of certain **fundamental rights**, and (2) those discriminating on the basis of a **suspect classification**. Figure 5.3 summarizes the degree of equal protection scrutiny received by the various kinds of governmental classifications.

In equal protection cases involving fundamental rights, the challenged law discriminates by, in effect, giving one class of people less of a fundamental right than other classes of people. The rights deemed fundamental for equal protection purposes

FIGURE 5.3 Equal Protection Scrutiny

	Very Strict	Fairly Strict	Rational Basis
Social and economic regulation that does not implicate fundamental rights or suspect classifications			X
Discrimination regarding fundamental rights	X		
Racial discrimination	X		
Most discrimination against aliens		X	
Sex discrimination		X	
Discrimination against illegitimates		X	

are not completely clear and are not the same as the rights deemed fundamental for due process purposes. Included, however, are the rights to vote, to travel interstate, and to enjoy certain procedural protections in criminal cases. Laws creating unequal enjoyment of such rights generally receive quite strict scrutiny. For example, a state statute restricting voting in school district elections to parents of schoolchildren and to property owners within the district was held unconstitutional in a 1969 case.

Suspect classification cases involve a claim that the challenged law unconstitutionally discriminates on the basis of personal traits that rarely, if ever, afford legitimate grounds for differentiating people. The traits in question—the "suspect" bases of classification—are race (including national origin), alienage (status as an alien), sex (or gender), and illegitimacy. The degree of scrutiny applied to laws distinguishing people on these grounds varies from suspect classification to suspect classification.

1. Racial classifications that expressly disadvantage African Americans and other racial or national minorities receive full strict scrutiny. The same is true for discrimination that favors such groups and disadvantages whites. This full strict scrutiny applies regardless of whether a state or the federal government has enacted the challenged the classification. In the past, however, racial preferences favoring minorities have received less strict scrutiny, especially when enacted by Congress. In this contentious area, such reverse discrimination may again receive more favorable constitutional treatment in the future.
2. The Supreme Court has said that laws discriminating against aliens should receive strict scrutiny, but this scrutiny is not likely to be as rigorous as the scrutiny applied in race discrimination cases. Nonetheless, laws expressly disadvantaging aliens often are found unconstitutional. For example, the Court struck down state laws denying aliens welfare benefits and the right to practice law.

   Not all laws disadvantaging aliens, however, get strict scrutiny. Under the "political function" exception, measures blocking aliens from employment in positions that are intimately related to democratic self-government are tested under rational basis standards and usually are upheld. This exception has been read broadly to allow the Supreme Court to uphold laws preventing aliens from being state troopers, public school teachers, and probation officers.
3. As the Court declared in a 1996 case, gender-based discrimination requires an "exceedingly persuasive" justification. The usual test is that laws discriminating on the basis of sex must be substantially related to the furtherance of an important government purpose. This is a fairly strict form of intermediate scrutiny. Although this test is less strict than the test used for laws that disadvantage racial minorities, it is tough enough to strike down almost all government action disadvantaging women. The Supreme Court has said that the same test applies to discrimination against men. In 1981, however, the Supreme Court found the draft registration system constitutional even though it did not include women, and also upheld a California law making statutory rape a crime for men but not for women.
4. Discrimination on the basis of illegitimacy receives a degree of scrutiny that is fairly strict but does not approach the full strict scrutiny applied to laws discriminating against racial minorities. For example, the Supreme Court struck down laws denying illegitimate children wrongful death benefits and workers' compensation recoveries for the death of a parent.

INDEPENDENT CONSTITUTIONAL CHECKS APPLYING ONLY TO THE STATES

The Contract Clause

Article I, section 10 of the Constitution says that "No State shall . . . pass any . . . Law impairing the Obligation of Contracts." This **contract clause** was included in the Constitution to protect contract creditors against the many debtor relief statutes passed by the states after the Revolution. These laws erased contract-based debts and thus impaired the obligations of contracts. In the famous cases of *Fletcher v. Peck* (1810) and *Dartmouth College v. Woodward* (1819), the Supreme Court extended the contract clause to governmental contracts, grants, and charters, and not just to private contractual obligations. In 1827, moreover, the Court made it clear that the clause is retroactive or retrospective in operation. That is, it only poses a constitutional obstacle to state laws impairing contracts formed before these laws were passed, and not to prospective state regulation of contracts. Thus, for example, the contract clause would prevent a state debtor relief law from canceling debts created before the law's enactment, but would not prevent it from can canceling debts arising after its passage.

The contract clause probably was the most important constitutional check on state regulation of the economy during the nineteenth century. By the mid-twentieth century, however, it was fashionable to regard the contract clause as a constitutional dead letter. The reason is that, throughout most of this century, the courts have subordinated contract clause claims to the states' exercise of their police powers. For example, a state prohibition law was held constitutional even though it impaired contracts for the sale of beer; a law forbidding lotteries was upheld even though it invalidated existing lottery tickets; and a workers' compensation law was valid even though it changed the terms of contracts between employers and employees.

However, in *United States Trust Company v. New Jersey* (1977) the Supreme Court breathed new life into the contract clause. In this case, the Court announced a tough new test for state laws impairing the obligations of their own contracts: that laws restricting such *governmental* contracts must be "reasonable and necessary to serve an important public purpose." This test seems to significantly restrict the states' ability to impair their own contract obligations. For the most part, however, the Court has continued to defer to the states when regulation impairing *private* contracts is at issue. For example, in *Exxon Corporation v. Eagerton* (1983), it upheld an Alabama law preventing oil and gas producers from passing on a severance tax increase to their customers. This law impaired Exxon's contracts with its customers—contracts that required the customers to reimburse Exxon for the severance taxes Exxon paid on the gas and oil it sold them. The Court's justification for upholding the Alabama statute was that, like prohibition laws, laws banning lotteries, and workers' compensation, it was a generally applicable measure designed to advance a broad social interest: protecting consumers from excessive gas and oil prices. In particular, the Alabama statute applied to all oil and gas producers, regardless of whether they had made any contracts permitting them to pass increased severance taxes on to their customers. A law aimed only at parties with existing contracts, the Court suggested, might be unconstitutional under the contract clause.

State Regulation of Interstate Commerce

Recall from earlier in the chapter that the original purpose behind the commerce clause was to nationalize trade by restricting state economic favoritism and protectionism. Article I, section 8, however, merely gives Congress the power to regulate interstate commerce. It says nothing about the states' ability or inability to do so. If Congress chooses to regulate commerce among the states, inconsistent state laws are invalid under the Constitution's supremacy clause. But what about the constitutionality of state laws that affect interstate commerce but do not conflict with federal law? Here, Congress and the state legislatures have concurrent lawmaking powers, with the state law subject to commerce clause checks. In such cases, courts examine the state law in light of the purposes behind the commerce clause. That is, they inquire whether the state regulation unduly hinders, burdens, or discriminates against interstate commerce, which involves use of the commerce clause as an implicit check on state lawmaking. As has been said, this is a matter of "negative implication" arising from one of the "great silences" of the Constitution.

The tests employed by the Supreme Court in cases involving state restrictions on interstate commerce have varied over time. In a 1994 case, the Court said that state laws that discriminate against interstate commerce must satisfy the strictest scrutiny in order to be constitutional and rarely survive this test. By *discrimination*, the Court meant any different treatment of in-state and out-of-state economic interests that significantly benefits the former and burdens the latter. The following *Wyoming* case involves a state law that expressly discriminates against interstate commerce. But state laws that have a discriminatory effect may be unconstitutional even though they are neutral on their face. For example, state pure food laws setting standards for the sale of certain food products will face constitutional problems if (1) they favor local food producers while disadvantaging out-of-state producers, and (2) do not clearly advance important state interests.

On the other hand, nondiscriminatory regulations that have only incidental effects on interstate commerce are constitutional unless the burden they impose on interstate commerce clearly exceeds their local benefits. In such cases, the courts must balance the state law's bad effects on interstate commerce against its local benefits. In a 1981 case, the Supreme Court struck down an Iowa statute imposing complicated limitations on the length of the trucks that could pass through the state. It did so mainly because the law's burden on interstate commerce exceeded its local benefits. Because other states had different standards, Iowa's unusual truck-length limits imposed significant additional costs on trucking firms. Because the trucks that Iowa allowed were scarcely safer than those it banned, moreover, the measure did little to serve legitimate state interests.

In the past, the Court also has said laws that directly regulate interstate commerce usually are unconstitutional. In a 1986 case, for instance, the New York State Liquor Authority attempted to revoke a liquor seller's license under a state law allowing revocation if the prices the licensee charged in other states were lower than those it charged in New York. The Supreme Court found the law unconstitutional because its practical effect was to control the prices at which liquor could be sold in other states.

Wyoming v. Oklahoma

U.S. Supreme Court
502 U.S. 437 (1992)

Background and Facts:

From 1981 to 1986, Wyoming mines provided virtually all the coal purchased by four Oklahoma electric utilities. In 1986, the Oklahoma legislature enacted a statute requiring Oklahoma coal-fired electric generating plants producing power for sale in Oklahoma to burn at least 10% Oklahoma-mined coal. This regulation caused the state of Wyoming to lose severance tax revenues it otherwise would have received. Thus, Wyoming sued Oklahoma under the Supreme Court's original jurisdiction, seeking a declaratory judgment that the Oklahoma statute violated the commerce clause and a permanent injunction against its enforcement.

Body of Opinion

Justice White

While a literal reading [of the commerce clause] evinces a grant of power to Congress, the commerce clause also directly limits the power of the states to discriminate against interstate commerce. This "negative" aspect of the commerce clause prohibits economic protectionism—that is, regulatory measures designed to benefit in-state economic interests by burdening out-of-state competitors. When a state statute clearly discriminates against interstate commerce, it will be struck down unless the discrimination is demonstrably justified by a valid factor unrelated to economic protectionism. Indeed, when the state statute amounts to simple economic protectionism, a virtual per se rule of invalidity has applied....

[T]he act...discriminates against interstate commerce. Section 939 of the act expressly reserves a segment of the Oklahoma coal market for Oklahoma-mined coal, to the exclusion of coal mined in other states. Such a preference for coal from domestic sources cannot be characterized as anything other than protectionist and discriminatory....

Oklahoma...emphasize[s] that the act sets aside only a small portion of the Oklahoma coal market, without placing an overall burden on out-of-state coal producers doing business in Oklahoma. [But] the volume of commerce affected measures only the *extent* of the discrimination; it is of no relevance to the determination whether a state has discriminated against interstate commerce....

Because the act discriminates, ... the burden falls on Oklahoma to justify it....At a minimum such facial discrimination invokes the strictest scrutiny of any purported legitimate local purpose.... Oklahoma has not met its burden in this respect. In this Court, Oklahoma argues quite briefly that the act's discrimination against out-of-state coal is justified because sustaining the Oklahoma coal-mining industry lessens the state's reliance on a single source of coal delivered over a single rail line. This justification...is foreclosed by the Court's reasoning in [two previous cases], cases that the state's brief ignores.... The state embellishes this argument somewhat when suggesting that, by requiring the utilities to supply 10% of their needs for fuel from Oklahoma coal, which because of its higher sulfur content cannot be the primary source of supply, the state thereby conserves Wyoming's cleaner coal for future use. We have no reason to doubt Wyoming's unrebutted factual response to this argument: reserves of low-sulfur, clean-burning sub-bituminous coal from the Powder River Basin are estimated to be in excess of 110 billion tons, thus providing Wyoming coal for several hundred years at current rates of extraction.

Judgment and Result

Judgment for Wyoming; permanent injunction against enforcement of the Oklahoma statute issued.

Questions

1. Who benefits economically from the Oklahoma statute?
2. As a matter of general policy, what's bad about protectionist statutes such as this one?

FEDERAL PREEMPTION

Article VI of the Constitution provides that the Constitution, laws, and treaties of the United States "shall be the Supreme Law of the Land, ... any Thing in the Constitution or Laws of any State to the Contrary notwithstanding." This provision is called the **supremacy clause**, and it establishes the principle of **federal supremacy**. According to this principle, the U.S. Constitution, treaties, and other federal laws defeat inconsistent state law. Where a state law is declared unconstitutional under the supremacy clause because it conflicts with a federal statute, it is said to be *preempted* by federal law. Preemption questions are decided on a case-by-case basis. As the following *Mortier* case indicates, however, a few general preemption principles have emerged over time. A state law normally is preempted (and therefore is unconstitutional) when any one of the following occurs:

1. The state law conflicts on its face with a valid federal measure, allowing no way to follow both rules simultaneously.
2. The federal statute explicitly declares that state law is to be preempted in certain areas, and the challenged state law falls within one of those areas.

3. The federal regulation is so pervasive or comprehensive that it is reasonable to conclude that Congress did not want the states to regulate the area. This conclusion may result from the fact that Congress has regulated some subject in great breadth and/or considerable detail, or has given an administrative agency broad powers to deal with the subject.
4. The challenged state law conflicts with the goals or purposes of the federal law. In defining these goals or purposes, courts generally look to the federal statute's legislative history.

Wisconsin Public Intervenor v. Mortier

U.S. Supreme Court
501 U.S. 597 (1991)

Background and Facts:

The small town of Casey in rural Wisconsin adopted an ordinance regulating the use of pesticides. The ordinance required that one applying pesticides to public lands, to private lands subject to public use, or to private lands by air obtain a permit. Ralph Mortier applied for a permit to spray part of his land from the air. The town granted him a permit, but refused to let him spray by air, and also restricted the areas in which Mortier could spray.

Mortier sued for a declaratory judgment against the ordinance in a state trial court. He argued that the ordinance was preempted by the Federal Insecticide, Fungicide, and Rodenticide Act (FIFRA). The Wisconsin Public Intervenor, an assistant attorney general for the protection of environmental rights, was admitted as a defendant in Mortier's suit. The trial court decided in Mortier's favor, and the Wisconsin Supreme Court affirmed. The state intervenor appealed to the U.S. Supreme Court.

Body of Opinion

Justice White

Under the supremacy clause, state laws that interfere with, or are contrary to, the laws of Congress, made in pursuance of the Constitution, are invalid. The ways in which federal law may preempt state law are well established, and...turn on Congressional intent. Congress's intent to supplant state authority in a particular field may be express in the terms of the statute. Absent explicit preemptive language, Congress's intent to supersede state law may nonetheless be implicit if a scheme of federal regulation is so pervasive as to make reasonable the inference that Congress left no room for the states to supplement it.... Even when Congress has not chosen to occupy a particular field, preemption may occur to the extent that state and federal law actually conflict. Such a conflict arises when compliance with both federal and state regulations is a physical impossibility, or when a state law stands as an obstacle to the accomplishment and execution of the full purposes and objectives of Congress....

Applying these principles, we conclude that FIFRA does not preempt the town's ordinance either explicitly, implicitly, or by virtue of an actual conflict.... FIFRA nowhere expressly supersedes local regulation of pesticide use.... Likewise, FIFRA fails to provide any clear and manifest indication that Congress sought to supplant local authority over pesticide regulation impliedly.... While [its] 1972 amendments turned FIFRA into a comprehensive regulatory statute, the resulting scheme was not so pervasive as to make reasonable the inference that Congress left no room for the states to supplement it.... FIFRA addresses numerous aspects of pesticide control in considerable detail, in particular: registration and classification, applicator certification, inspection of pesticide production facilities, and the possible ban and seizure of pesticides that are misbranded or that otherwise fail to meet federal requirements.... FIFRA nonetheless leaves substantial portions of the field vacant, including the area at issue in this case. FIFRA nowhere seeks to establish an affirmative permit scheme for the actual use of pesticides. It certainly does not equate registration and labeling requirements with a general approval to apply pesticides throughout the nation without regard to regional and local factors like climate, population, geography, and water supply. Whatever else FIFRA may supplant, it does not occupy the field of pesticide regulation in general or the area of local use permitting in particular....

Finally,...we discern no actual conflict either between FIFRA and the ordinance before us or between FIFRA and local regulation generally. Mortier does not rely, nor could he, on the theory that compliance with the ordinance and FIFRA is a physical impossibility. Instead, he urges that the town's ordinance stands as an obstacle to the statute's goals of promoting pesticide regulation that is coordinated solely on the federal and state levels, that rests upon some degree of technical expertise, and that does not unduly burden interstate commerce. Each one of these assertions rests on little more than snippets of legislative history and policy speculations. None of them is convincing.

Judgment and Result

Judgment reversed in favor of the Wisconsin intervenor.

Questions

1. What would have been the result in this case if FIFRA had explicitly stated that it preempts local regulation of pesticide use?
2. What would have been the result if plenty of legislative history supported the assertion that FIFRA's aim was to nationalize pesticide regulation so that the impediments to business and to interstate commerce posed by a mass of conflicting local regulations would be eliminated?

THE TAKINGS CLAUSE

The Fifth Amendment states that "[p]rivate property [shall not] be taken for public use, without just compensation." Although the Fifth Amendment applies only to the federal government, this **takings clause** has been incorporated within Fourteenth Amendment due process and thus applies to the states as well. The takings clause recognizes government's power to condemn or otherwise appropriate private property, but also limits government's exercise of that power. That is, a governmental *taking* of *property* is unconstitutional unless it is for a *public use* and the property owner receives *just compensation*. Figure 5.4 outlines how takings clause cases should be analyzed.

Taking

The takings clause obviously applies when the government takes property by formally condemning it through the power of eminent domain. As *Lucas* makes clear, a taking also occurs where government *physically occupies* private property or authorizes a private party to do so.

FIGURE 5.4 Analyzing Takings Clause Cases

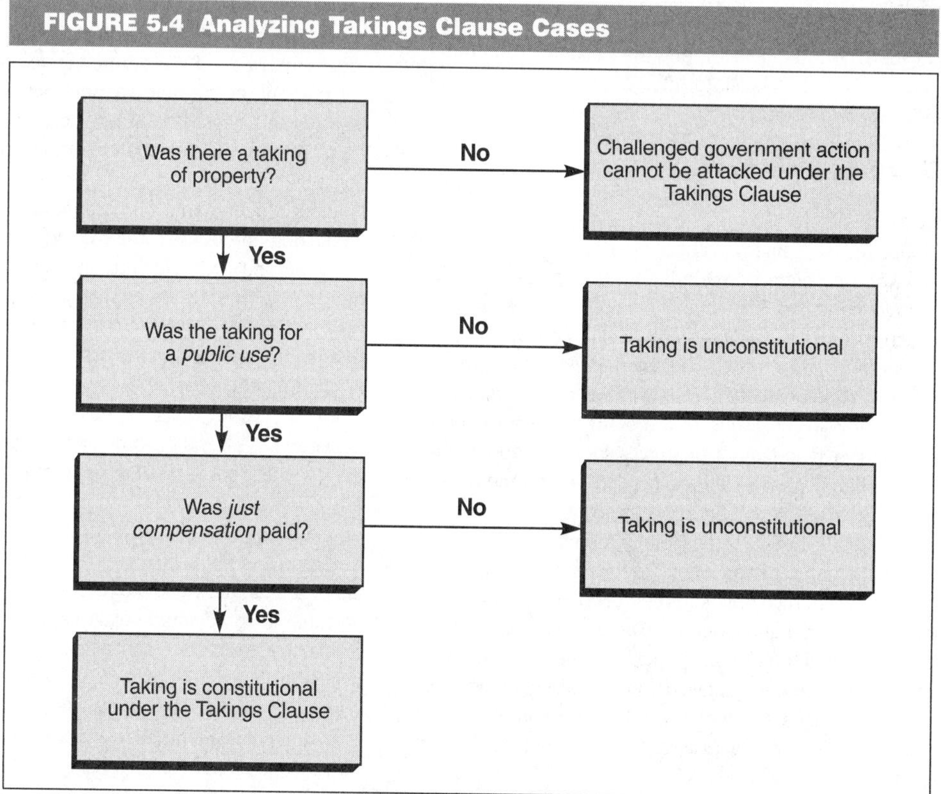

In addition, government regulation may create a so-called regulatory taking if it adversely affects the value or usefulness of private property. However, not every such regulation can qualify as a taking, or the government's power to regulate would be severely crippled by the need to compensate property owners. Traditionally, general police measures that apply to a wide range of properties generally have not been takings. For example, although zoning laws often limit the uses to which private property may be put and thus have definite economic consequences, they usually are not takings.

No exact formula determines when regulation constitutes a taking, and courts examine a number of factors when considering the question. One of those factors involves a means-ends test. In a 1987 case, for example, the Supreme Court said that land use regulation does not effect a taking if it substantially advances legitimate state interests. Another factor is the economic impact of the regulation on the owner; the greater this impact, the more likely the regulation will be deemed a taking, especially when the regulation interferes with the owner's definite expectations regarding the future use of his property, and the owner has made investments to advance these expectations. As *Lucas* makes clear, moreover, a regulation definitely will be a taking if it deprives owners of *all* economically viable uses of their land.

Property

The takings clause potentially has a wide reach; it could apply to all kinds of government regulation. Another reason for the clause's broad potential scope is the range of property interests it covers. Obviously, land and interests in land are property for takings clause purposes, as is tangible personal property. In a 1984 case, moreover, the Supreme Court stated that valid contracts, various kinds of liens, and trade secrets also qualify as property. Many other kinds of personal property probably enjoy protection as well.

Public Use

Once a taking of property has occurred, that taking is unconstitutional if it is not for a public use. Today the public use test is easy to meet. For example, courts have said that the challenged taking need only be rationally related to a conceivable public purpose to meet the test.

Just Compensation

Even if a taking of property is for a public use, it still is unconstitutional unless the owner receives just compensation. Usually, just compensation is the fair market value of the property that has been taken. Where the effect of the taking is merely to diminish property values, the standard for compensation often is the difference between the fair market value of the property before the taking and its fair market value after the taking.

Lucas v. South Carolina Coastal Council

U.S. Supreme Court
505 U.S. 1003 (1992)

Background and Facts:

In 1986, David Lucas paid $975,000 for two residential lots on the Isle of Palms in Charleston County, South Carolina. He intended to build single-family homes on the lots. In 1988, however, the South Carolina legislature enacted the Beachfront Management Act, which effectively barred Lucas from erecting any permanent habitable structures on the two lots. Lucas then sued in a South Carolina trial court, arguing that the state had taken his property without just compensation. The trial court held in his favor, but the South Carolina Supreme Court reversed the trial court's decision. Lucas appealed to the U.S. Supreme Court.

Body of Opinion

Justice Scalia

Prior to Justice Holmes's exposition in *Pennsylvania Coal Co. v. Mahon* (1922), it was generally thought that the takings clause reached only a direct appropriation of property, or the functional equivalent of a practical ouster of the owner's possession.... [T]hat case [gave birth to] the oft-cited maxim that while property may be regulated to a certain extent, if regulation goes too far it will be recognized as a taking. Nevertheless, our decision in *Mahon* offered little insight into when, and under what circumstances, a given regulation would be seen as going "too far" for purposes of the Fifth Amendment. In 70-odd years of succeeding "regulatory takings" jurisprudence, we have generally eschewed any set formula for determining how far is too far, preferring to engage in essentially ad hoc factual inquiries. We have, however, described at least two discrete categories of regulatory action as compensable without case-specific inquiry into the public interest advanced in support of the restraint. The first encompasses regulations that compel the property owner to suffer a physical "invasion" of his property. In general (at least with regard to permanent invasions), no matter how minute the intrusion, and no matter how weighty the public purpose behind it, we have required compensation. For example in *Loretto v. Teleprompter Manhattan CATV Corp.* (1982), we determined that New York's law requiring landlords to allow television cable companies to place cable facilities in their apartment buildings constituted a taking, even though the facilities occupied at most only 1 ½ cubic feet of the landlords' property.

The second situation in which we have found categorical treatment appropriate is where the regulation denies all economically beneficial or productive use of land.... [W]hen the owner of real property has been called upon to sacrifice *all* economically beneficial uses in the name of the common good, that is, to leave his property economically idle, he has suffered a taking. The trial court found Lucas's two beachfront lots to have been rendered valueless by [the state's] enforcement of the coastal-zone construction ban. Under Lucas's theory of the case, which rested upon our "no economically viable use" statements, that finding entitled him to compensation....

Where the state seeks to sustain regulation that deprives land of all economically beneficial use, we think it may resist compensation only if the logically antecedent inquiry into the nature of the owner's estate shows that the proscribed use interests were not part of his title to begin with.... Any limitation so severe [as a regulation that prohibits all economically viable uses of land] cannot be newly legislated or decreed (without compensation), but must inhere in the title itself, in the restrictions that background principles of the state's law of property and nuisance already place upon land ownership. A law or decree with such an effect must, in other words, do no more than duplicate the result that could have been achieved in the courts—by adjacent landowners (or other uniquely affected persons) under the state's law of private nuisance, or by the state under its complementary power to abate nuisances that affect the public generally, or otherwise. On this analysis, the owner of a lake bed, for example, would not be entitled to compensation when he is denied the requisite permit to engage in a landfilling operation that would have the effect of flooding others' land.... Such regulatory action may well have the effect of eliminating the land's only economically productive use, but it does not proscribe a productive use that was previously permissible under relevant property and nuisance principles.... When, however, a regulation that declares off-limits all economically productive or beneficial uses of land goes beyond what the relevant background principles would dictate, compensation must be paid to sustain it....

It seems unlikely that common-law principles would have prevented the erection of any habitable or productive improvements on [Lucas's] land. The question, however, is one of state law to be dealt with on remand. We emphasize that to win its case South Carolina must... identify background principles of nuisance and property law that prohibit the uses [Lucas] now intends in the circumstances in which the property is presently found. Only on this showing can the state fairly claim that, in proscribing all such beneficial uses, the Beachfront Management Act is taking nothing.

Judgment and Result

The South Carolina Supreme Court's judgment against Lucas was reversed, and the case was returned to the South Carolina courts for proceedings not inconsistent with the Supreme Court's opinion.

Questions

1. Why did the Supreme Court not have to consider the purposes underlying the Beachfront Management Act, and to balance those purposes against the harm done to Lucas?
2. To win in the South Carolina courts, precisely what must the state now show?
3. Suppose that the state loses after the case is returned to the South Carolina courts. How can it still stop Lucas from building his structures?

CHAPTER SUMMARY

Constitutions generally try to limit government power, and the U.S. Constitution does so in two general ways. First, the Constitution limits Congress to those powers it specifically enumerates. Second, it imposes various independent constitutional checks on both Congress and the state legislatures.

The Constitution gives Congress the power to regulate interstate commerce. Although it has recently been limited by the Supreme Court, this commerce power basically remains a wide-ranging federal police power that can reach almost all intrastate matters. In addition, Congress can regulate by using its enumerated taxing power to discourage disfavored activities by taxing them. Congressional spending power regulation works in the opposite fashion. Here Congress regulates by telling its would-be recipient that it will not receive the money unless it follows a certain course of conduct. Both the taxing and the spending powers have few inherent limits.

Even though Congress's enumerated powers and the states' police powers have few innate limits, they are subject to certain independent constitutional checks. These checks fall into two broad classes. Some apply both to the federal government and to the states, while others apply to the states alone. For these checks to apply, there must be government action. In determining whether a particular regulation really violates a particular independent check, courts often use means-ends tests of constitutionality.

The most important business-related independent checks that apply to both the federal government and the states are the First Amendment's free speech guarantee, the due process clauses of the Fifth and Fourteenth Amendments, and the Fourteenth Amendment's equal protection clause. The First Amendment applies to the states because it has been incorporated within Fourteenth Amendment due process, and the equal protection clause applies to the federal government because it has been incorporated within Fifth Amendment due process. The First Amendment's most important business-related application is the obstacle it poses to government regulation of commercial speech such as commercial advertising. An intermediate test of constitutionality applies to such regulations.

Due process comes in two forms—procedural and substantive. In each case, a person must have been deprived of life, liberty, or property before due process standards apply. Substantive due process concerns the actual policy merits of government action, while procedural due process concerns the fairness of the machinery through which substantive laws are enforced. The central elements of procedural due process are fair notice of the action to be taken, and some sort of fair trial or hearing before that action can occur. Over time, substantive due process has assumed many forms. Once it was an important check on government regulation of the economy, but today it most often is significant when personal rights are at issue.

Equal protection law determines the constitutionality of governmental distinctions or classifications. Most such classifications—including those created when government regulates business—are tested under the lenient rational basis test. However, governmental distinctions that involve certain fundamental rights or suspect classifications are subjected to stricter scrutiny by the courts. The "suspect" bases of classification are race or national origin, gender, alienage, and illegitimacy.

At least three important constitutional provisions limit state regulation of business. The contract clause puts some restrictions on laws that impair the obligations of existing contracts, both private and governmental. In addition to giving Congress the power to regulate interstate commerce, the commerce clause restricts state laws that unduly

Manager's Ethical Dilemma

You are the owner and operator of a teenage dance hall in a major American urban area. Your business has been terrific for some time. The reason that business has been so great, however, is that your dance hall has become a major center for the distribution of illegal drugs to teenagers. Right now, the drug trade at your establishment is limited to marijuana and hashish, but that may change.

Of course, you most likely can stop the distribution of drugs at your dance hall by notifying the police, but doing so probably would ruin your business. Unfortunately, many of your patrons want to do drugs, and if they can't get them at your establishment, they'll get them somewhere else. Also, if the police action becomes public knowledge, the straight kids may well stay away, too. Because the users and their suppliers simply will move elsewhere, you are also beginning to wonder whether tipping the police really would accomplish anything. Why should you suffer to achieve little or nothing? Also, it's not as if *you* are dealing the drugs—isn't there a moral difference between actively causing harm and merely permitting it to happen? (By the way, your lawyer thinks that if you keep your mouth shut and play dumb, you probably won't have any *legal* problems either.) Finally, just how much harm is being caused anyhow?

Despite all this, the drug trade at your dance hall is still bothering you. What should you do? Why?

burden such commerce. Finally, federal regulation may preempt state law in certain cases. Whether preemption occurs essentially is a matter of statutory interpretation.

The U.S. Constitution's takings clause both recognizes a government power possessed by Congress and the state legislatures, and puts some restrictions on its use. The power in question is the power to "take" private property. The main restrictions on its use are the requirements that the taking be for a public use, and that government pay just compensation for property taken. Today the public use requirement is easily met. Before these requirements come into play, however, a taking must first have occurred, and the law on this subject is complex.

Discussion Questions

1. This chapter's discussion of the commerce, tax, and spending powers paid little attention to the principle of *federalism*, under which the federal government is supposed to respect state sovereignty in certain spheres. Yet the U.S. Constitution's Tenth Amendment plainly says that "[t]he powers not delegated to the United States by the Constitution, nor prohibited by it to the States, are reserved to the States respectively, or to the people." How have courts managed to get around Tenth Amendment arguments when considering Congress's authority under the commerce, tax, and spending powers? *Hint:* Pay close attention to the first eleven words of the preceding quote.
2. Review the quotation from Justice Black that opened this chapter. Based on the materials in this chapter, how accurate is it? In which areas discussed in the chapter does it seem to be true? In which areas does it seem to be false?

3. As Justice Black's words suggest, one valid generalization about the 1937 Supreme Court is that it abandoned its earlier role as a protector of economic rights in favor of a new role as promoter of personal liberties. Based on the materials in this chapter, what is the most important example of the Court's earlier role? Although this chapter does not focus on personal rights, what examples of the Court's later role does it provide? Over the past 15–20 years, the Court has given somewhat greater constitutional protection to economic rights. Based on this chapter, provide as many examples as you can.
4. The Supreme Court has had a hard time articulating reasons why some due process rights are fundamental and others are not. The dominant test asks whether the right in question is "deeply rooted in this nation's history and tradition" and "implicit in the concept of ordered liberty." But traditions are living things, and this raises the question whether the Court should be looking at our tradition's past manifestations, or its more recent manifestations. Why does this question matter in determining whether economic rights ought to be fundamental?

   The other approach for determining which rights are fundamental asks questions such as whether the right in question is central to one's life, one's self-definition, and one's personal development. How do economic rights fare under this test?

   How do the two substantive due process rights asserted in the *Lange-Kessler* case fare under each our tests? What does this whole exercise suggest to you about the Supreme Court's choice of fundamental rights?
5. Review the discussion of constitutional means-ends tests. From the materials in this chapter, identify as many of these constitutional tests as you can. Then try to classify them according to their "strictness." (*Hint:* You might use categories such as "very strict," "somewhat strict," and "lenient.") Do you think that laws restricting the various rights to which these tests apply really should get the degree of scrutiny that they actually receive? Should they receive stricter or less strict review by the courts?
6. Why is it so difficult for the Supreme Court to come up with precise standards in areas such as the burden-on-commerce doctrine and federal preemption?
7. Prior to the 1970s, few cases challenged laws that discriminated against women, and in these cases the challenged law was usually upheld. Today, of course, laws discriminating against women almost always are unconstitutional. The change began early in the 1970s and was completed by the end of that decade. What do you think best explains the change? What does this shift tell you about constitutional interpretation and about the way the Supreme Court sometimes decides cases? What does it do to the idea that we live under a fixed, unchanging Constitution?
8. In *Romer v. Evans* (1996), the Supreme Court struck down a Colorado constitutional amendment, passed in a statewide referendum, that forbade all action by any level of state or local government to protect against discrimination on the basis of sexual orientation or give homosexuals any "quota preferences." The amendment apparently was a response to Aspen, Boulder, and Denver ordinances forbidding various kinds of discrimination on the basis of sexual orientation. The amendment, the Court concluded, violated equal protection because it lacked a rational basis. One strand in the Court's reasoning was that the amendment made it more difficult for one group of citizens (in this case, gay people) to seek protection from the government. Another was that the amendment originated in animosity toward gays, and that such motives could never serve as a rational basis for law making. For its part, the state of Colorado argued that the amendment was rationally related to a legitimate state objective: protecting the freedom of association of landlords or employers who object to homosexuality. As far as the rational basis test is concerned, who has the better argument? Is the Court really engaging in something other than rational basis review?

   Interestingly *Romer v. Evans* did not consider another possible argument for its result—the idea that sexual orientation should be a suspect basis of classification under the equal protection clause. This approach would mean that laws classifying people on the basis of their sexual orientation would receive some kind of stricter scrutiny. Perhaps it would mean that laws classifying people on the basis of their sexual behavior also would receive stricter scrutiny. Over time, courts and commentators have suggested criteria for determining whether particular personal traits should be "suspect." They include (1) a history of discrimination and disapproval that makes those possessing the trait a "discrete and insular minority"; (2) the fact that the trait is not voluntarily acquired and cannot be voluntarily eliminated; and (3) the fact that the trait bears no relation to the individual's ability to contribute fully to society. Based on these criteria, should sexual orientation join race, national origin, gender, alienage, and illegitimacy as a suspect classification?

9. Suppose that a local government passes an ordinance regulating trailer parks. The ordinance says that the owner must give his tenants a permanent lease and that he can terminate the lease only for good cause; in addition, it establishes a system of rent control. Two stereotypes sometimes are used to describe laws of this kind. On the one hand, such laws may be regarded as enlightened, compassionate efforts to protect society's victims against those who would oppress them through superior economic power. On the other hand, such laws can be depicted as abuses of the democratic process in which politicians attract the votes of society's unproductive losers by passing laws enabling them to take wealth from society's achievers. As applied to our ordinance, which of these two stereotypes generally seems more accurate to you?

Suggested Readings

Articles

BECK-DUDLEY and MACDONALD, "*Lucas v. South Carolina Coastal Council*, Takings, and the Search for the Common Good," 33 *American Business Law Journal* 153 (1995).

LANGVARDT and RICHARDS, "The Death of *Posadas* and the Birth of Change in Commercial Speech Doctrine: Implications of *44 Liquormart*," 34 *American Business Law Journal* 483 (1997).

MCCLOSKEY, "Economic Due Process and the Supreme Court: An Exhumation and Reburial," 1962 *Supreme Court Review* 34.

PHILLIPS, "The Life and Times of the Contract Clause," 20 *American Business Law Journal* 139 (1982).

REED, "Is Commercial Speech Really Less Valuable than Political Speech? On Replacing Values and Categories in First Amendment Jurisprudence," 34 *American Business Law Journal* 1 (1996).

REED, "Should the First Amendment Protect Joe Camel? Toward an Understanding of Constitutional `Expression,'" 32 *American Business Law Journal* 311 (1995).

Books

CONANT, *The Constitution and Capitalism*, chs. 4–7 (1974).

CURRIE, *The Constitution in The Supreme Court: The Second Century*, 1888–1986 (1990).

ELY, *The Guardian of Every Other Right: A Constitutional History of Property Rights* (1992).

ENGDAHL, *Constitutional Power: Federal and State in a Nutshell* (1974).

NOWAK, ROTUNDA, and YOUNG, *Constitutional Law* chs. 8–14, 16, 3d ed. (1986).

SIEGAN, *Economic Liberties and the Constitution* (1980).

TRIBE, *American Constitutional Law*, chs. 6–12, 16, 18, 2d ed. (1988).

CHAPTER 6

GOVERNMENT REGULATION: OVERVIEW

"THE RISE OF ADMINISTRATIVE BODIES PROBABLY HAS BEEN THE MOST SIGNIFICANT LEGAL TREND OF THE LAST CENTURY."

Justice Jackson, dissenting in FTC v. Ruberoid Co., 343 U.S. 470 (1952)

POSITIVE LAW ETHICAL PROBLEMS

"Our daughter has dangerously high lead levels in her blood," Mrs. Jones said to her husband.

"I'll bet it comes from the lead plumbing in our house," said Mr. Jones.

"No way," replied Mrs. Jones. "The Farmers Home Administration inspector examined our house before we moved in in May 1991, and pronounced the house 'fit for human occupancy,' and loaned us money to buy it."

If a federal government agency inspects property it finances and declares the property "fit for human occupancy," is it liable under the Federal Tort Claims Act for harm later sustained by the purchasers?

"They're trying to make our Social Security numbers public," said John Lincoln, a municipal employee of Pleasantville, Ohio. Smith was one of 2,500 city employees on a computerized tape that the local newspaper sought for an investigative story. Pleasantville provided the newspaper with the tape but deleted the Social Security numbers on grounds that it violated the employees' rights under the Federal Privacy Act. Was the city correct?

This chapter presents a survey of administrative law that consists of several parts. First we present some basic definitions of administrative law and administrative agencies. We then examine the purposes of administrative agencies. Finally, we discuss controls on administrative agencies.

Administrative law, also known as generic regulation making and enforcement, takes place in the United States in an environment that could fairly be characterized as schizophrenic: Americans are philosophically conservative, and hence, are against "big government" usually associated with government regulation; at the same time they are functionally "liberal," demanding public protections against unsafe airlines, uncooked hamburgers, and blood tainted with HIV virus. It is in such a philosophically splintered environment that regulators in the United States must operate.

ADMINISTRATIVE LAW AND ADMINISTRATIVE AGENCIES

Broadly defined, **administrative law** is all law concerning administrative agencies, including statutes, rules, and regulations, and court and agency interpretations. Narrowly defined, administrative law means court review of what administrative agencies have done. This chapter follows the broad definition.

An **administrative agency** is any nonlegislative, nonjudicial governmental lawmaker. This definition excludes rules made by private business corporations. An administrative agency could be a person or an institution clothed with governmental authority. It has no single official label and need not have the word *agency* in its name. It could be called the Environmental Protection Agency, the Federal Trade Commission, the Police Department of Portland, Maine, or the Department of Public Health of the State of Tennessee. As these names suggest, administrative agencies exist at the federal, state, and municipal levels of government.

Agencies are usually created by a statute called the agency's organic act. In an agency's organic act, the legislature recognizes that a problem exists, creates an agency to deal with the problem, and delegates legislative authority to the agency to make appropriate regulations to cope with the problem. The **organic act** also gives judicial authority for the agency to hear cases dealing with the agency's subject matter. Finally, the organic act confers executive authority, which allows the agency to investigate and administer its subject matter.

The number of administrative agencies at the federal level runs into the hundreds. The SEC, ICC, FDA, EPA, OMB, and many more acronyms identify different federal agencies. Figure 6.1 dramatizes the nature and extent of federal agencies and distinguishes between executive departments and independent agencies. This difference is based on executive agency inclusion within the executive branch of the government; independent agencies are not. Because of this difference, the president's control over executive agencies is greater than that over independent agencies.

Origin and Purpose of Administrative Agencies

Executive orders create a few administrative agencies, but most federal agencies are created by federal statutes. As such, Congress can legally dissolve these agencies. For instance, Congress could eliminate all statutorily created federal administrative agencies merely by passing another law. Although Congress will probably never take this action, the example shows the extent of congressional power over federal agencies.

Expertise. Administrative agencies have arisen for several reasons. First, legislatures and courts do not have the technical expertise to deal with the many complicated problems the United States currently faces. For example, the technical problems associated with toxic waste disposal require the skills of specialists, not courts or legislatures.

Oversight of Socialized Harm. Second, a need exists for ongoing supervision in areas in which the potential for harm is small on an individual level but great on a collective level. For example, the harm from air pollution on a single person is small, but over time such pollution could cause skin cancer, destroy crops, and cause other damage.

Protect the Weak. Third, administrative agencies are designed to help the weak and poor fight corporate giants. For example, farmers in the Midwest in the late 1800s were victims of discriminatory railroad rates. They took their case against the railroads to Congress, and the Interstate Commerce Commission was created to regulate railroad rates, among other things. Ironically, the ICC has since been captured by the powerful organized interests it was originally designed to regulate.

FIGURE 6.1 Number of Federal Agency Employees

Organization	Employees in the United States	Personnel Outside United States	Total Paid Employees Jan. 1 1997	Jan. 1 1990	Jan. 1 1980	Jan. 1 1970
Executive Office of the President	1,576	....	1,576	1,663	1,897	4,044
Executive Departments	1,614,860	[1]101,650	1,716,510	2,088,260	1,937,476	2,005,150
1. Department of Agriculture	96,183	558	96,741	124,171	122,259	106,484
2. Department of Commerce	33,854	713	34,567	41,139	42,142	30,823
3. Department of Defense	715,879	79,313	795,192	1,076,777	960,063	1,272,800
Organizations and Agencies	*109,172*	*16,043*	*147,098*	*95,197*	*76,891*	*69,546*
Department of the Air Force	*166,981*	*14,486*	*181,467*	*260,575*	*233,471*	*321,849*
Department of the Army	*233,366*	*26,712*	*260,078*	*377,858*	*343,773*	*469,297*
Department of the Navy	*206,360*	*21,256*	*227,616*	*343,147*	*305,928*	*402,108*
4. Department of Education	4,716	....	4,716	4,915	....	....
5. Department of Energy	17,624	....	17,624	17,135	20,988	....
6. Department of Health and Human Services	58,632	....	58,632	121,682	[2]163,883	[2]106,280
7. Department of Housing and Urban Development	11,282	....	11,282	13,447	16,862	14,777
8. Department of the Interior	68,010	....	68,010	73,298	79,905	67,880
9. Department of Justice	110,512	873	111,385	80,074	55,737	36,505
10. Department of Labor	15,263	....	15,263	18,793	24,220	10,479
11. Department of State	9,376	15,649	25,025	26,028	23,738	41,547
12. Department of Transportation	62,904	509	63,413	66,136	73,364	62,189
13. Department of the Treasury	163,841	1,150	164,991	179,293	123,777	88,884
14. Department of Veterans Affairs	246,811	2,885	249,696	245,372	[3]230,538	[3]166,502
Independent Agencies	**950,862**	**[4]14,996**	**965,860**	**924,055**	**881,159**	**890,909**
1. Advisory Commission on Intergovernmental Relations	2	....	2	39	52	43
2. Advisory Council on Historic Preservation	32	....	32	....	....	....
3. African Development Foundation	30	....	30	....	....	....
4. American Battle Monuments Commission	14	355	369	404	398	411
5. Appalachian Regional Commission	10	....	10	10	9	9
6. Commission of Fine Arts	7	....	7	7	7	4
7. Commission on Immigration Reform	21	....	21	....	....	....
8. Commodity Futures Trading Commission	563	....	563	569	447	....
9. Corporation for National and Community Service	522	....	522	....	....	....
10. Defense Nuclear Facilities Safety Board	105	....	105	....	....	....
11. Environmental Protection Agency	17,221	....	17,221	16,513	12,891	....
12. Equal Employment Opportunity Commission	2,634	....	2,634	2,957	3,622	645
13. Export-import Bank of the United States	427	....	427	329	412	333
14. Farm Credit Administration	334	....	334	569	280	224
15. Federal Communications Commission	2,057	....	2,057	1,770	2,233	1,487
16. Federal Deposit Insurance Corporation	9,157	....	9,157	11,707	3,598	2,242
17. Federal Election Commission	291	....	291	242	270	....
18. Federal Emergency Management Agency	2,358	....	2,358	2,594	2,300	....
19. Federal Housing Finance Board	120	....	120	....	....	....
20. Federal Labor Relations Authority	220	....	220	246	319	....
21. Federal Maritime Commission	148	....	148	230	342	219
22. Federal Mediation and Conciliation Service	287	....	287	320	527	450
23. Federal Mine Safety and Health Review Commission	52	....	52	47	88	....
24. Federal Reserve System (Board of Governors)	1,746	....	1,746	1,498	1,456	....
25. Federal Retirement Thrift Investment Board	116	....	116	....	....	....
26. Federal Trade Commission	970	....	970	999	2,032	1,268
27. General Services Administration	15,516	81	15,597	20,097	37,936	37,894
28. Inter-American Foundation	73	....	73	66	62	....
29. Legal Services	77	....	77	....	....	....
30. National Aeronautics and Space Administration	20,408	24	20,432	23,694	23,179	32,882
31. National Archives and Records Administration	2,844	....	2,844	3,088	....	....
32. National Capital Planning Commission	55	....	55	50	58	66
33. National Commission on Libraries and Information Science	9	....	9	....	....	....
34. National Council on Disability	24	....	24	....	....	....
35. National Credit Union Administration	940	....	940	910	675	....
36. National Foundation on the Arts and the Humanities	593	....	593	618	664	444

FIGURE 6.1 Number of Federal Agency Employees, continued

Organization	Employees in the United States	Personnel Outside United States	Total Paid Employees Jan. 1 1997	Jan. 1 1990	Jan. 1 1980	Jan. 1 1970
37. National Labor Relations Board	1,948	...	1,948	2,238	3,032	2,239
38. National Mediation Board	47	...	47	57	67	130
39. National Science Foundation	1,306	4	1,310	1,329	2,477	1,735
40. National Transportation Safety Board	367	...	367	306	372	...
41. Neighborhood Reinvestment Corporation	195	...	195	...	...	...
42. Occupational Safety and Health Review Commission	70	...	70	88	183	...
43. Office of Government Ethics	76	...	76	39	...	...
44. Office of Personnel Management	3,751	19	3,770	6,689	8,069	...
45. Overseas Private Investment Corporation	200	...	200	145	141	...
46. Panama Canal Commission	22	9,390	9,412	8,219	8,578	16,212
47. Peace Corps	667	475	1,142	1,178	...	...
48. Pension Benefit Guaranty Corporation	766	...	766	589	...	...
49. Postal Rate Commission	47	...	47	56	74	...
50. Railroad Retirement Board	1,406	...	1,406	1,698	1,912	1,698
51. Securities and Exchange Commission	2,729	...	2,729	2,073	2,155	1,390
52. Selective Service System	229	...	229	303	98	9,437
53. Small Business Administration	4,442	...	4,442	5,966	6,225	4,202
54. Smithsonian Institution	4,170	175	4,345	...	...	...
55. Social Security Administrations	64,581	...	64,581	...	...	...
56. Surface Transportation Board[5]	127	...	127	676	2.092	1,813
57, Susquehanna River Basin Commission	1	...	1	2	2	...
58. Tennessee Valley Authority	15,620	...	15,620	26,404	49,930	20,677
59. Thrift Depositor Protection Oversight Board	1	...	1	...	...	...
60. U.S. Architectural and Transp. Barriers Compl. Board	32	...	32	...	...	...
61. U.S. Arms Control and Disarmament Agency	357	...	357	296	286	286
62. U.S. Commission on Civil Rights	90	...	90	72	312	245
63. U.S. Enrichment Corporation	164	...	164	...	...	...
64. U.S. Holocaust Council	211	...	211	29	4	...
65. U.S. Information Agency	3,425	3,274	6,699	8,718	8,235	10,518
66. U.S. International Development Cooperation Agency	1,741	1,201	2,942	4,741	6,004	...
67. U.S. International Trade Commission	359	...	359	464	371	245
68. U.S. Merit Systems Protection Board	254	...	254	308	338	...
69. U.S. Nuclear Regulatory Commission	3,080	...	3,080	3,237	3,078	...
70. U.S. Office of Special Counsel	89	...	89	86	...	...
71. U.S. Postal Service	758,271	...	758,271	758,501	683,242	[6]741,461
72. U.S. Trade and Development Agency	38	...	38	...	...	...
Total, Executive Branch	**2,567,298**	**116,648**	**2,683,946**	**3,014,003**	**2,820,507**	**2,900,103**
Total, Legislative Branch	**30,657**	**11**	**[7]30,668**	**[8]37,365**	**[9]39,334**	**[10]28,349**
Total, Judiciary Branch	**29,095**	**333**	**29,428**	**21,917**	**14,117**	**6,713**
Total	**2,627,050**	**116,992**	**2,744,042**	**3,073,285**	**2,873,958**	**2,935,165**

[1] Total American citizens, 47,809; nationals of other countries, 53,839.

[2] Listed as Department of Health, Education, and Welfare on 1970 and 1980 charts.

[3] Listed as the Veterans Administration on 1970 and 1980 charts.

[4] Total American citizens, 3,034; nationals of other countries, 11,674.

[5] Renamed from Interstate Commerce Commission.

[6] Listed as Post Office Department on 1970 chart.

[7] Does not include the Central Intelligence Agency, National Security Agency, Defense Intelligence Agency, and National Imagery and Mapping Agency.

[8] Includes the Congress, Architect of the Capitol, U.S. Botanic Garden, Congressional Budget Office, Copyright Royalty Tribunal, General Accounting Office, Government Printing Office, Library of Congress, National Bankruptcy Review Commission, National Commission Restructuring IRS Office of Compliance, Office of Technology Assessment, United States. Tax Court, Commission for the Study of International Migration and Cooperative Economic Development, National Commission to Prevent Infant Mortality, Physicians Payment Review Commission, and the Prospective Payment Assessment Commission.

[9] Includes the Congress, General Accounting Office, Library of Congress, Government Printing Office, Architect of the Capitol, United States Tax Court, Cost Accounting Standards Board, Botanic Garden, Congressional Budget Office, and the Copyright Royalty Tribunal.

[10] Includes the Congress, General Accounting Office, Government Printing Office, Architect of the Capitol, and the Library of Congress.

Source: U.S. Senate

Speed and Economy. Fourth, the growth of administrative agencies also occurred because of the need for speed and economy in running the government. For example, having court proceedings to license a barber is wasteful.

Class Struggle. Finally, some people see the administrative agency as a way to solve social roadblocks put up by judges. In the late nineteenth century, workers who tried to form labor unions were brought before courts and tried for criminal conspiracy. Judges at that time often saw unions as threats to the individual right to manage one's own business. Labor leaders, on the other hand, viewed labor as part of the production process. They tried to get the judges to legalize unions. In the short run, they failed. Later, a combination of events legalized the labor union: the removal of much federal court jurisdiction to stop union activity and the establishment of a federal administrative agency—the National Labor Relations Board (NLRB)—to deal with labor matters such as union recognition. The NLRB is probably the most prominent example of an administrative agency created to get around the judiciary. The creation of the NLRB strengthened the political power of organized labor compared with business.

Legislative Delegations to Agencies: Enabling Acts

A statute is a law passed by a federal or state legislature. Statutes are important in administrative law because agencies have the power to make legally binding regulations, or rules[1] only if the legislature gives them the power. Legislatures give agencies power through what is called legislative delegation. Statutes delegating legislative power to make regulations are called **enabling statutes**.

Administrative agencies have the power to make laws, which are called **regulations** (regs) or **rules**. The two general types of regulations are interpretative and substantive, sometimes called legislative. Substantive regulations are given the force and effect of law by courts; they are legally binding. They must be made in what is called rulemaking, or regulation making, as set forth by the federal Administrative Procedure Act (APA).

Interpretative rules, general agency policy statements, or rules of agency procedure, practice, or organization are not given the effect of law by courts. Interpretative rules are generally effective as soon as the federal agency announces their existence.

SOME IMPORTANT FEDERAL ADMINISTRATIVE STATUTES

The Federal Register Act

A little known but important federal law is the Federal Register Act, passed in 1935. The act provides a way to get up-to-date information about an agency and its regulations. This function is done by the **Federal Register system**, created by the Federal Register Act.

The Federal Register System. The Federal Register system has three parts: the federal *Government Manual* (formerly called the *Government Organization Manual*), the *Federal Register*, and the *Code of Federal Regulations*.

- *Government Manual*. The *Government Manual* lists the names and addresses of all U.S. government agencies and provides additional information about each agency. A new edition of this book is published each year and can be purchased from the U.S. Government Printing Office.

http:// *To access the Government Manual go to* ***http://ww1.access.gpo.gov/nara/nara001.html***

[1] The words *rules* and *regulations* (regs) are used interchangeably here. Professor Kenneth Culp Davis considers them synonymous, though some authorities do not.

- *Federal Register.* The *Federal Register* resembles a small newspaper and is published by the federal government every business day, Monday through Friday. Among the more important items it contains are presidential proclamations, notices of federal agency public meetings, proposed federal regulations, and promulgated federal regulations. A federal agency's substantive regulation is usually not the law unless it is promulgated in the *Federal Register*. The function of the *Federal Register* is to give public notice of federal agencies' official acts. The *Federal Register* is available in most large libraries. Also, thanks to the Internet, anyone with access to a computer and modem has the *Federal Register* at his or her fingertips. An Internet address to the *Federal Register* is provided in the Internet exercises at the end of this chapter.

http:// *To research items within the Federal Register, go to* ***http://www.gpo.gov/su_docs/aces/aces140.html***

- *Code of Federal Regulations.* The *Code of Federal Regulations* (*C.F.R.*) is the third part of the Federal Register system. It arranges all currently effective federal agency regulations by agency. (Regulations promulgated in the *Federal Register* are not arranged in this way.) A regulation appears when the agency delivers a regulation to the *Federal Register* office. The *C.F.R.* is a multivolume set of paperbound books, and each book usually contains all current regulations of federal agencies.

http:// *The website for Code of Federal Regulations can be found at* ***http://ww1.access.gpo.gov/nara/cfr/index.html***

***Need to Read the* Federal Register.** Is the average citizen bound by what appears in the *Federal Register* daily editions and the *C.F.R.*? In *Federal Crop Ins. Corp. v. Merrill*, an Idaho farmer learned the hard way about his duty to read the *Federal Register*.

Federal Crop Insurance Corp. v. Merrill

U.S. Supreme Court
332 U.S. 380 (1947)

Background and Facts:

Merrill applied for crop insurance with the Federal Crop Insurance Corporation to insure a wheat crop in Idaho. Because part of the crop was reseeded, Merrill asked the government employee if his crop was insurable. The government official said it was, so Merrill bought crop insurance. When his crops were later destroyed by drought, Merrill filed a claim under his crop insurance. The government agency refused to pay because a regulation said that reseeded crops were not insurable. Merrill said he did not know of the regulation and claimed that the agency official had said his crop was insurable.

The trial jury and judge said Merrill could recover. The Idaho Supreme Court agreed. The Federal Crop Insurance Corporation appealed to the U.S. Supreme Court.

Body of Opinion

Justice Frankfurter

The case no doubt presents phases of hardship. We take for granted that, on the basis of what they were told by the Corporation's local agent, the respondents reasonably believed that their entire crop was covered by petitioner's insurance. And so we assume that recovery could be had against a private insurance company. But the Corporation is not a private insurance company.... Whatever the form in which the Government functions, anyone entering into an arrangement with the Government takes the risk of having accurately ascertained that he who purports to act for the Government stays within the bounds of his authority. The scope of this authority may be explicitly defined by Congress or be limited by delegated legislation, properly exercised through the rule-making power. And this is so even though, as here, the agent himself may have been unaware of the limitations upon his authority....

If the Federal Crop Insurance Act had by explicit language prohibited the insurance of spring wheat which is reseeded on winter wheat acreage, the ignorance of such a restriction, either by the respondents or the Corporation's agent, would be immaterial and recovery could not be had against the Corporation for loss of such reseeded wheat. Congress could hardly define the multitudinous details appropriate for the business of crop insurance when the Government entered it.

Inevitably, the "terms and conditions" upon which valid governmental insurance can be had must be defined by the agency acting for the Government. And so Congress has legislated in this instance, as in modern regulatory enactments it so often does, by conferring the rule-making power upon the agency created for carrying out its policy. Just as everyone is charged with knowledge of the United States Statutes at Large, Congress has provided that the appearance of rules and regulations in the *Federal Register* gives legal notice of their contents.

Accordingly, the Wheat Crop Insurance Regulations were binding on all who sought to come within the Federal Crop Insurance Act, regardless of actual knowledge of what is in the Regulations or of the hardship resulting from innocent ignorance. The oft-quoted observation in *Rock Island, Arkansas & Louisiana Railroad Co. v. United States*, 254 U.S. 141, that "Men must turn square corners when they deal with the Government," does not reflect a callous outlook. It merely expresses the duty of all courts to observe the conditions defined by Congress for charging the public treasury. The "terms and conditions" defined by the Corporation, under authority of Congress, for creating liability on the part of the Government preclude recovery for the loss of the reseeded wheat no matter with what good reason the respondents thought they had obtained from the Government. Indeed, not only do the Wheat Regulations limit the liability of the Government as if they had been enacted by Congress directly, but they were in fact incorporated by reference in the application, as specifically required by the Regulations.

We have thus far assumed, as did the parties here and the courts below, that the controlling regulation in fact precluded insurance coverage for spring wheat reseeded on winter wheat acreage. It explicitly states that the term "wheat crop shall not include . . . winter wheat in the 1945 crop year, and spring wheat which has been reseeded on winter wheat acreage in the 1945 crop year." . . . The circumstances of this case tempt one to read the regulation, since it is for us to read it, with charitable laxity. But not even the temptations of a hard case can elude the clear meaning of the regulation. It precludes recovery for "spring wheat which has been reseeded on winter wheat acreage in the 1945 crop year." Concerning the validity of the regulation, as "not inconsistent with the provisions" of the Federal Crop Insurance Act, no question has been raised.

The judgment is reversed and the cause remanded for further proceedings not inconsistent with this opinion.

Judgment and Result

The farmer lost.

Mr. Justice Black and Mr. Justice Rutledge dissent. [Dissents do not count, since they represent a minority of the justices. However, sometimes they make more sense than the majority opinion.]

Mr. Justice Jackson, dissenting.

I would affirm the decision of the court below. If crop insurance contracts made by agencies of the United States Government are to be judged by the law of the State in which they are written, I find no error in the court below. If, however, we are to hold them subject only to federal law and to declare what that law is, I can see no reason why we should not adopt a rule which recognizes the practicalities of the business.

It was early discovered that fair dealing in the insurance business required that the entire contract between the policyholder and the insurance company be embodied in the writings which passed between the parties, namely, the written application, if any, and the policy issued. It may be well enough to make some types of contracts with the Government subject to long and involved regulations published in the *Federal Register*. To my mind, it is an absurdity to hold that every farmer who insures his crop knows what the *Federal Register* contains or even knows that there is such a publication. If he were to peruse this voluminous and dull publication as it is issued from time to time in order to make sure whether anything has been promulgated that affects his rights, he would never need crop insurance, for he would never get time to plant any crops. Nor am I convinced that a reading of technically-worded regulations would enlighten him much in any event. . . .

It is very well to say that those who deal with the government should turn square corners. But there is no reason why the square corners should constitute a one-way street. . . .

Mr. Justice Douglas joins in this opinion.

Questions

1. The dissenting opinion does not count in the preceding case. A dissent is a way for a Supreme Court justice to blow off steam by telling why he or she thinks the majority opinion is wrong. Which opinion is more persuasive to you: Frankfurter's majority or Jackson's dissent? Why?
2. Which opinion represents positive law? Natural law?
3. Does the majority opinion encourage or discourage reading the *Federal Register*?
4. Does the majority opinion encourage or discourage relying on government employees' interpretations of federal regulations?

Administrative Procedure Act (APA)

Even though the 1930s saw the creation of many new administrative agencies at the federal level, the APA was not passed until 1946. It was enacted because of widespread concern with the lack of regularized procedures for agency actions. For example, before the APA was created some federal agencies decided cases after hearing only the government's evidence.

Administrative agencies make rules. They decide cases by applying agency rules. The APA sets the requirements (structure) for conducting rulemakings and adjudications.

The APA has been amended several times since its original passage in 1946. Among the more important APA amendments are the Freedom of Information Act, the Federal Privacy Act of 1974, and the Government in the Sunshine Act.

Freedom of Information Act

The Freedom of Information Act (FOIA) was passed in 1966. Its main purpose is to disclose information that federal agencies have in their possession. The information might include pictures, studies, files, letters, and many other tangible bits of information.

A brief letter directed to the particular agency's FOIA office is usually sufficient to make an **FOIA request**. An FOIA request must have a reasonable description of the records one wants, which helps the agency locate the material. For example, a request for all information the Federal Trade Commission has about price discrimination is too broad, but a request for the FTC study of the life insurance industry in the late 1970s would probably be specific enough. The request must be made in accordance with an agency's rules about the time, place, fees, and procedures to be followed. An agency must make records promptly available after an FOIA request has been made. An agency usually has 10 business days to decide whether to honor an FOIA request.

Exemptions. The federal FOIA has nine exemptions, meaning that certain types of information falling within any one of the nine exemptions do not have to be disclosed, even if the public requests this information. However, the **FOIA exemptions** do not allow agencies to withhold information from Congress. The nine FOIA exemptions cover the following:

1. National defense or foreign policy matters
2. Internal personnel rules and practices of an agency
3. Other statutes specifically allowing nondisclosure
4. Trade secrets and commercial or financial information obtained from a person and privileged or confidential
5. Interagency or intra-agency memoranda or letters
6. Personnel, medical, and similar files, the disclosure of which would clearly be an unwarranted invasion of personal privacy
7. Investigatory records compiled for law enforcement purposes
8. Material in reports of agencies responsible for regulating or supervising financial institutions (such as bank examiners' reports)
9. Geological or geophysical information and data (including maps) concerning wells

Federal Privacy Act of 1974

Congress passed the Federal Privacy Act (FPA) of 1974 to protect against violation of individual privacy resulting from misuse of federal agency information. The alleged misuse of information took many forms and involved both government and private sources. For example, Social Security cards were used for identification purposes, such as check cashing, even though the card states that it is not to be used for identification.

Conflict. Federal agency use and assembly of information involves an inherent conflict of values. Agencies need accurate, complete information to perform efficiently. However, the United States was established to promote individual freedom, which includes the right of privacy and to have a limited government. The FPA tries to strike a proper compromise between efficient government management and individual privacy.

Main Provision. The main provision of the FPA stops an agency from disclosing any record in a system of records by any means of communication to any person or agency without the prior written consent of the individual. This provision has several key points and many qualifications. The FPA is generally limited to federal agencies, although it also applies to federal contractors, including states or businesses receiving federal contracts, unless otherwise exempt. One other point about the FPA: An individual's name and address may not be sold or rented by a federal agency unless specifically authorized by another law.

Because many state governments and private company employers are federal contractors, they are covered by the Federal Privacy Act. Consequently, many employers are reluctant to give out information about employees or former employees (such as job references) to third parties such as other employers who might want to know how a worker performed for them. If former employers have information about former employees in a "system of records," the former employers may be reluctant to say anything without first getting prior written consent of the employees. Because getting written permission in advance from former employees is cumbersome, former employers may be unwilling to say anything to third persons about former employees. Much information employers have about former employees is contained in employee records and is based also on first-hand observation by supervisors. If the former employer discloses such information without first getting the former employee's written permission, one case has held that the former employer does not violate the Federal Privacy Act if the former employer consults personal memory but not any system of records in doing so.

Another Federal Privacy Act problem involves the disclosure of Social Security numbers by an employer to third parties. In the following case, an employer (a city) was asked by a local investigative newspaper reporter to disclose computer tapes with salary and other information including employees' Social Security numbers. Read the case to see whether the city was correct in refusing to disclose its employees' Social Security numbers because of the Privacy Act.

State Ex Rel. Beacon Journal Pub. v. Akron

Supreme Court of Ohio
640 N.E.2d 164 (1994)

Background and Facts:

Appellee Beacon Journal Publishing Company ("ABJ") publishes the newspaper known as The Akron Beacon Journal. Appellee Robert Paynter is a project editor and employee of ABJ. Appellant Linda Sowa was the finance director of the appellant city of Akron. Akron, therefore, is appealing the lower court's disposition of this case to the Ohio Supreme Court.

ABJ and Paynter asked the city and Sowa to provide them with computer tape records of the city's year-end employee master files for the years 1990 and 1991 pursuant to Ohio's public records statute. These payroll files contain various information including employees' names, addresses, telephone numbers, Social Security numbers (SSNs), birth dates, education, employment status and positions, pay rates, service ratings, annual and sick leave information, overtime hours and pay, and year-to-date employee earnings. The city has approximately 2,500 employees. Thirteen employees have access to the computerized employee master payroll file.

Sowa and the city provided copies of these records with the SSNs deleted. ABJ and Paynter then requested a copy of the same records complete with SSNs. Sowa and the city refused to disclose the employees' SSNs.

In August 1992, ABJ and Paynter filed a complaint in mandamus (a court order to someone directing that they do something) in the Court of Appeals for Summit County against Sowa and Akron, alleging that under the Ohio Records Act they were entitled to obtain payroll records complete with SSNs. Sowa and the city denied the existence of this obligation, alleging that disclosure of employees' SSNs would violate the employees' right to privacy.

The court of appeals granted the petition for mandamus. The appellate court found that SSNs were public records and their disclosure would not violate the right of privacy.

Body of Opinion

Justice Pfeifer

We are asked to determine whether the city is obligated to provide the ABJ with the SSNs of approximately two thousand five hundred city employees pursuant to Ohio's public records statute. For the following reasons, we find that disclosure of this information is not required. [The Ohio Supreme Court first decided that SSNs were "records" but not "public records" within the Ohio Records Statute.]

. . . Due to the federal legislative scheme involving the use of SSNs, city employees have a legitimate expectation of privacy in their SSNs. Uncodified Section 7 of the Privacy Act of 1974 provides the following:

> "(a)(1) It shall be unlawful for any Federal, State, or local government agency to deny to any individual any right, benefit, or privilege provided by law because of such individual's refusal to disclose his social security account number. . . .
>
> "(b) Any Federal, State, or local government agency which requests an individual to disclose his social security account number shall inform that individual whether that disclosure is mandatory or voluntary, by what statutory or other authority such number is solicited, and what uses will be made of it." . . .

The purpose of the Privacy Act of 1974 was "to curtail the expanding use of social security numbers by federal and local agencies and, by so doing, to eliminate the threat to individual privacy and confidentiality of information posed by common numerical identifiers." . . .

Congress when enacting the Privacy Act of 1974 was codifying the societal perception that SSNs should not to (sic) be available to all. This legislative scheme is sufficient to create an expectation of privacy in the minds of city employees concerning the use and disclosure of their SSNs. . . .

Having held that employees of the city have a reasonable expectation of privacy regarding the disclosure of their social security numbers, we must weigh these privacy interests against those favoring disclosure. . . .

It is a fundamental tenet of democracy that the people, the press, and the media be fully informed about the processes of their government. As John Adams noted, "[l]iberty cannot be preserved without a general knowledge among the people, who have a right...and a desire to know; but besides this, they have a right, an indisputable, unalienable, indefeasible, divine right to that most dreaded and envied kind of knowledge, I mean of the characters and conduct of their rulers." John Adams, A Dissertation on the Canon and Feudal Law (1765). However, this right is by no means boundless or unconditional.

The city's refusal to release its employees' SSNs does not significantly interfere with the public's right to monitor governmental conduct. . . .

While the release of all city employees' SSNs would provide inquirers with little useful information about the organization of their government, the release of the numbers could allow an inquirer to discover the intimate, personal details of each city employee's life, which are completely irrelevant to the operations of government. . . . A person's SSN is a device which can quickly be used by the unscrupulous to acquire a tremendous amount of information about a person.

During recent Congressional hearings, journalist Jeffrey Rothfeder testified before the House Subcommittee on Social Security that, during a journalistic investigation, he was able to obtain highly confidential information about then Vice-President Dan Quayle with the use of Quayle's SSN. Rothfeder obtained Quayle's private Virginia address and the Vice-President's unlisted phone number. Through this exercise, Rothfeder "wanted to show that with privacy at a premium and data banks proliferating, even the Vice President of the United States is easy pickings for somebody with prying eyes." . . .

Thanks to the abundance of data bases in the private sector that include the SSNs of persons listed in their files, an intruder using a SSN can quietly discover the intimate details of a victim's personal life without the victim ever knowing of the intrusion.

We find today that the high potential for fraud and victimization caused by the unchecked release of city employee SSNs outweighs the minimal information about governmental processes gained through the release of the SSNs. Our holding is not intended to interfere with meritorious investigations by the press, but instead is intended to preserve one of the fundamental principles of American constitutional law—ours is a government of limited power.

Judgment and Result

The Ohio Supreme Court concluded that the Privacy Act of 1974 precluded the city's disclosure of city employees' SSNs.

Questions

1. Does the *State Ex Rel. Beacon Journal Pub.* say that employee SSNs can never be disclosed to third parties? Might disclosure of SSNs depend on who is requesting such numbers? What if the Internal Revenue Service were making such a request for confidential use involving matters of taxpayer compliance?
2. Does the *State Ex Rel. Beacon Journal Pub.* case strengthen or weaken the Federal Privacy Act?
3. Could a private employer (note the employer in the preceding case was a governmental body) provide SSNs of its employees to third parties without violating the Privacy Act?

Government in the Sunshine Act

The Government in the Sunshine Act became federal law in 1976. It is sometimes called an **open meeting law**. Its main objective is to open up the official decision-making process of the federal government. The Sunshine Act requires that an agency headed by a collegial body must not conduct or dispose of agency business unless every portion of the business meeting is open to the public. A collegial body is two or more individuals heading an agency, a majority of whom are presidential appointees confirmed by the U.S. Senate. Thus, the Sunshine Act would apply to the Federal Trade Commission because it is headed by five presidentially appointed, Senate-confirmed commissioners. The Sunshine Act would not apply to the U.S. Environmental Protection Agency, because only one person—the administrator—heads it.

Protection for Federal Whistleblowers

Whistleblowers are people who expose waste, fraud, and abuse in an organization. Generally speaking, people praise whistleblowers because who can be in favor of the wrongdoings that whistleblowers expose? Yet when people do blow the whistle, those in the organization who are engaged in the allegedly improper conduct frequently retaliate against the whistleblowers, often by demoting, reassigning, or firing them. This occurs because frequently the person on whom the whistle is blown is the whistleblower's own boss or agency. Bosses and coworkers do not like criticism, and they retaliate by finding some shortcoming in the whistleblower's job performance as a pretext for punishing him or her for the whistleblowing. In other words, the boss finds the whistleblower is "stealing paper clips" (which, of course, is wrong) and uses it as the basis for punishment, even though the real reason is to "even the score."

Many statute-specific whistleblower protections have been in place for years. For example, the Clean Water Act and OSHA contain protections for employees who blow the whistle on violations. These protections apply to both private- and public-sector employees.

The Civil Service Reform Act. In 1978 Congress passed the Civil Service Reform Act (CSRA) which protects many, but not all, civilian federal employees. The CSRA established the Merit Systems Protection Board (MSPB) to hear whistleblower complaints of federal employees and also created the Office of Special Counsel (OSC) to investigate and champion federal employee whistleblowers. The CSRA's whistleblower protections failed miserably. (In fact, one occupant of the Special Counsel's office gave seminars to federal agencies on how to fire whistleblowers!)

In 1989 President Bush signed into law the Whistleblower Protection Act of 1989 to amend and strengthen the CSRA's whistleblower protections. It does several things to help federal employees who blow the whistle in federal agencies, including the following:

1. Giving whistleblowers a cause of action to pursue their own case if the OSC does not do so after a certain time. (The CSRA allowed only the OSC to pursue whistleblower complaints.)
2. Lessening the burden of proof the whistleblower must meet to prove a connection between the whistleblowing and the whistleblower's punishment.
3. Restating the OSC's primary mission as being protection of federal employees who whistleblow rather than protecting the Civil Service System by punishing the supervisor who punishes whistleblowers.

Problems in Dealing with Whistleblowers. Significant problems remain with both the Whistleblower Protection Act of 1989 and whistleblowing generally. First, the 1989 Act exempts many federal agencies from its protections including any federal corporation, including TVA, the Federal Deposit Insurance Corporation, the Resolution Trust Corporation (charged with the S&L "cleanup"), the CIA, and the FBI.

A major dilemma left unsolved after the 1989 Act is dual causation (also referred to as the "nexus" problem) whistleblowing, which happens when a whistleblower does something wrong at work that is either preceded or followed by an act of whistleblowing. Then, after both events have occurred, the supervisor disciplines the whistleblower in some way, such as not giving a salary increase. The question is, was the failure to give a salary increase the result of the whistleblowing or because the employee genuinely deserved no pay increase? If the employee complains that the boss was punishing him or her for whistleblowing, and the boss points out the whistleblower's faults, who prevails? This dual causation problem is present with all whistleblower protection statutes, not just the 1989 Act.

CONTROLLING ADMINISTRATIVE AGENCIES

The growth of administrative agencies over the past 60 years has been tremendous. Consult Figure 6.1 earlier in this chapter to see the large number of federal employees. Even though some functions the agencies perform are essential and many more are desirable, society has limited resources and wants limited intrusion into its members' lives. Thus, ways have been developed to legally and economically control administrative agencies at all levels of government. The following sections discuss such controls.

The Courts

Administrative agency actions are reviewable by courts, the major legal control over administrative agencies. Generally, state courts review state administrative agency actions, and federal courts review federal agency actions. This rule has exceptions. Judicial review of agency action is established by the Administrative Procedure Act (APA) at the federal level and by state APAs and common law at the state level. Courts can overturn agency actions for the following reasons:

1. The agency violated the U.S. Constitution.
2. The agency acted *ultra vires* (beyond its statutory authority).

3. The agency action was arbitrary, capricious, or an abuse of discretion, or it broke some other law.
4. The agency did not follow legal procedures.
5. The agency adjudication was unsupported by substantial evidence.

Evidence to Support Agency Action. The concept of limited judicial review of administrative action permits courts to review questions of law and lets agencies decide the facts. Agency fact decisions must be supported by evidence. Courts use two separate tests to judge whether the evidence is sufficient to support administrative agency actions: (1) the substantial evidence test, and (2) the arbitrary, capricious, and unreasonable test. The **substantial evidence test** is used to review adjudications (agency orders resulting from hearings) and formal and hybrid rulemaking.[2]

The **arbitrary, capricious, and unreasonable test** is usually used to judge informal rulemaking unless a statute requires the stricter substantial evidence rule. This test comes from the federal Administrative Procedure Act and is not as strict as the substantial evidence test. In other words, the federal agency does not have to produce as much evidence to justify what it does under the arbitrary, capricious, and unreasonable rule as it does under the substantial evidence test.

Sunset Laws

So-called **sunset laws** have been enacted at different levels of government. They terminate administrative agencies in one of several ways: cutting off the agency's budget, revoking the law that creates the agency, or requiring periodic renewal of the law creating the agency. For example, every time an agency's budget is up for renewal, the sun could set on all or part of that agency's operations. Other laws have the same objective but are called by other names. Budgets (via appropriations bills) could be sunset laws for an agency or its programs.

Ombudspersons

Agency employees who check to see that the agency is operating properly are called **ombudspersons**. In other words, an agency polices itself when it uses ombudspersons. Universities, cities, states, and various federal departments have such employees who are sometimes known by other names, such as inspectors general. The jurisdiction of ombudspersons may be broad or narrow. For example, some university ombudspersons may investigate student complaints but not those of the faculty.

Federal Civil Rights Suits

Federal civil rights suits refer to lawsuits based on sections 1981, 1982, and 1983 of Title 42 of the U.S. Code. These sections allow people whose federal civil rights are denied by private individuals or by state or municipal officials to sue the wrongdoer in federal court. These laws can be used to hold state or municipal agency employees liable for abusing their power and violating people's civil rights. Possible remedies available for federal civil rights violations include injunctions, actual damages, and punitive damages.

---

[2] The term *hybrid rulemaking* refers to a process an agency uses to make regulations that add to the notice and comment (*Federal Register* notice of the rule and comments—often critical—filed by the public in response to agency proposals) procedures agencies follow in informal rulemaking. Added procedures could include public hearings.

Examples of federal civil rights violations that subject state or municipal officials to liability include the following:

1. A refusal of a municipality to license a public coffeehouse run by hippies, solely because the officials do not like hippies
2. Denying a radical (right- or left-wing) student group access to a state-owned auditorium when such access is routinely granted to other public groups (assuming no other basis for the denial exists)
3. Refusal of state welfare administrators to conform to federal welfare standards that require a hearing before ending welfare payments.

Legislative Vetoes

A legislative veto is the U.S. House or Senate or both saying to a regulator, "We invalidate your regulation." Because Congress created most administrative agencies, some argue that it should have the power to veto particular agency regulations it does not like.

The **legislative veto** is controversial for several reasons. First, it interferes with the orderly rulemaking process (described in Chapter 7). Second, Congress arguably takes an inconsistent position when it vetoes a regulation after it gave the agency the power to make the regulation by passing an enabling statute. Supporters of the legislative veto first point to it as a way to get government off the people's backs, thereby helping to increase productivity.

In 1983 the U.S. Supreme Court decided in *I.N.S. v. Chadha*, that federal legislative vetoes are unconstitutional unless they involve both houses of Congress and the president as well. In other words, if the Congress wants to legislatively veto an administrative regulation, it must do so by passing a statute. Therefore, the legislative veto will be less frequently used than if only one house of Congress, acting alone, could veto a regulation.

Federal Tort Claims Act

Sovereign Immunity. The federal government and its agencies are protected from lawsuits by the sovereign immunity doctrine. As a result, the Defense Department is not liable to soldiers injured when poor battle plans cause high casualties. Also, federal employees as individuals are protected from suit based on their official acts. For example, if a mail carrier puts a Social Security check in the wrong mailbox, causing a retiree to miss a car payment and resulting in the repossession of the retiree's car, neither the federal government nor the carrier is liable, with some exceptions.

Waiver. The federal government is liable for damages, injuries, property loss, or death if it has waived its sovereign immunity and the claimant otherwise establishes a theory of recovery. One important instance in which the federal government has waived its sovereign immunity is in the Federal Tort Claims Act. By virtue of this act, the federal government allows suit against itself, its agencies, and employees for torts[3] they commit. If, for example, an Internal Revenue Service (IRS) agent trespasses into a person's business to obtain evidence, the federal government and the employee as an individual would be liable, assuming no valid defense is available.

[3] The Federal Tort Claims Act (FTCA) does not waive sovereign immunity for certain intentional torts (assault, battery, false imprisonment, false arrest, malicious prosecution, abuse of process, libel, slander, misrepresentation, deceit, or interference with contract rights). However, the FTCA waives intentional tort immunity when the tort is committed by investigative or law enforcement officers.

Limits. Several important limits have been placed on the liability of federal agencies and their employees. First, the law of the state where the alleged wrong occurred defines whether the behavior causing the suit is a legal wrong. For example, if the alleged wrong were an invasion of privacy and had occurred in Alabama, but Alabama did not recognize invasion of privacy as a civil wrong, no basis would exist for suit under the Federal Tort Claims Act. Second, the alleged wrong must be within the scope of the federal employee's official duties. Third, recoveries under this act include damages and injunctions; punitive damages are not available. Also, the Federal Tort Claims Act does not waive sovereign immunity for discretionary, policy conduct or for misrepresentations, whether negligent or intentional. Thus, when a federal regulator has the option to do or not do certain things and the outcome damages a member of the public, the federal agency is not liable. On the other hand, when the regulator undertakes mandatory functions affecting regulated parties, the regulator is liable for negligence under the Federal Tort Claims Act if those decisions cause damage. Finally, the Federal Tort Claims Act does not waive sovereign immunity when the federal official negligently or intentionally misrepresents something. *Lemke* discusses this exception further.

Lemke by Lemke v. City of Port Jervis

U.S. Dist. Court (S.D.N.Y.)
991 F. Supp. 261 (1998)

Background and Facts:

This suit arises from the government financed purchase and occupancy by Edward Lemke and his wife, Gina Lemke, of a house at 48 Hudson Street in Port Jervis, New York. Subsequent to the Lemkes' purchase of the home in 1991, the house was found to have high levels of lead, which allegedly caused personal injury to the Lemke's daughter, Christina, who was born in 1993.

Plaintiffs filed suit against the U.S. Department of Agriculture and its agency, the U.S. Rural Economic Development Agency (collectively, the "government defendants") under the Federal Tort Claims Act. The government defendants seek to have the suit dismissed.

Body of Opinion

District Judge Parker

The Lemkes purchased the home at 48 Hudson Street in August 1991 with the aid and assistance of the United States Rural Economic Development Agency (then known as the Farmers Home Administration), which financed the purchase by extending a Rural Housing Program loan authorized by...the Housing Act of 1949.

The Farmers Home Administration (the "Administration") advised the Lemkes that any house they selected would be subject to inspection by and approval of the Administration in order to insure that the house was adequate for the family and met applicable Administration standards, including suitability requirements. After the Lemkes located a house, a representative of the Administration visually inspected the entire house in May 1991 and approved it for the Section 502 loan program. According to the Administration representative who inspected the house, if a premises contained extensive lead plumbing, it was clearly unsuitable for the Section 502 loan program. The house was approximately 90 years old and was constructed during a period in which many homes contained lead plumbing and lead-based paint. The property's lead plumbing was clearly visible to a person with a basic knowledge of plumbing.

In April 1992, the Administration representative who had inspected the property was informed that the house contained lead plumbing. After being advised repeatedly that Christina Lemke had dangerously high levels of lead in her blood and, as a result, had suffered substantial developmental difficulties, the Administration conducted tests for lead contamination. In April 1995, after receiving the results of these tests, the Administration determined that the home was unfit for occupancy and advised the Lemke family to vacate immediately.

In December 1995, the Lemkes filed a Notice of Claim against the government defendants under the Federal Tort Claims Act....

In this case, the government defendants contend that plaintiffs' claims are barred by the misrepresentation and discretionary function exceptions to the Federal Tort Claims Act....

The misrepresentation exception to the Federal Tort Claims Act precludes any claim against the government "arising out of... misrepresentation, deceit, or interference with contract rights."... This exception encompasses "claims arising out of negligent, as well as willful, misrepresentation." . . . The misrepresentation exception also bars claims based on the conduct underlying the misrepresentation. . . . Thus, a claim based on negligent conduct that results in a misrepresentation is not actionable under the FTCA. . . .

The misrepresentation exception, however, "does not bar negligence actions which focus not on the Government's failure to use due care in communicating information, but rather on the Government's breach of a different duty." . . . A claim that is "distinct from any duty to use due care in communicating information" is not barred by the misrepresentation exception. . . .

In this case, the government defendants contend that the essence of plaintiffs' claim is that the government did not use due care in obtaining and communicating information about the lead paint in the house the Lemkes purchased. If this were the gravamen of plaintiffs' claim, then indeed it would be barred by the misrepresentation exception. . . . But the essence of plaintiffs' claim is that not the government provided misinformation or failed to provide information. Rather, the core of plaintiffs' claim is that the government, having voluntarily assumed the responsibility to inspect the house, conducted an inspection in a manner that failed to identify unconcealed characteristics of the property that made it, according to government's own inspector, unsafe for occupancy and unsuitable for the Section 502 loan program. If the lead plumbing had been recognized, the proper course, according to the government's own inspector, would have been to declare the house unsuitable for the Section 502 loan program because it was unsafe for occupancy. The claim that the government breached this duty is distinct from any misrepresentation claim that the plaintiffs might also have sought to assert. Indeed, if the government had a duty, in these circumstances, to declare the house unsuitable for the Section 502 loan program, that duty could have existed separate and apart from any duty to use due care in obtaining and communicating information.

The government defendants also assert that plaintiffs' claim is barred by the discretionary function exception to the Federal Tort Claims Act. The discretionary function exception bars "any claim based upon an act or omission of an employee of the Government, exercising due care, in the execution of a statute or regulation, whether or not such statute or regulation be valid, or based upon the exercise or performance or failure to exercise or perform a discretionary function or duty on the part of a federal agency or an employee of the Government, whether or not the discretion involved be abused." . . .

In order for the government to be insulated from liability under the discretionary function exception, the challenged acts must involve "an element of judgment or choice." . . . Additionally, the challenged conduct must be "based on considerations of public policy." . . . In order for a claim not to be precluded by the discretionary function exception, it must involve "facts which support a finding that the challenged actions are not the kind of conduct that can be said to be grounded in the policy of the regulatory regime." . . .

In this case, the government contends that the process and standards utilized in evaluating a property for participation in the Section 502 loan program involve the exercise of discretion and are based on policy considerations. The government is certainly correct that the policy decision not to inspect for lead every house considered for the Section 502 loan program is within the ambit of the discretionary function exception. The government may establish or not establish an inspection policy as it sees fit. Having established a policy that mandates the inspection of houses considered for the Section 502 loan program, the government is also free to set standards for safety and suitability. . . . The conduct of administration representatives in inspecting homes also comes within the discretionary function exception insofar as the conduct is "grounded in the policy of the regulatory regime." . . . The conduct must be "based on considerations of public policy." . . .

The plaintiffs' claim, however, does not challenge any policy determination or any inspection decision made in furtherance of any governmental policy. Rather, the plaintiffs' claim is that, having determined to inspect homes in order to assess their suitability for the Section 502 loan program, and having defined safety as one element of suitability, the government's failure to detect clearly apparent conditions that made the home unsafe, and therefore unsuitable for the Section 502 loan program, is not clearly "susceptible to policy analysis." . . . The inspector's decision not to obtain information that would have revealed the presence of lead plumbing does not implicate any policy consideration and, thus, does not warrant protection under the discretionary function exception. . . . The government's failure to identify harmful conditions present in the property cannot be understood as in furtherance of any governmental policy or as the exercise of discretion pursuant to any governmental policy. . . .

Judgment and Result

Plaintiffs' claim may go forward. The court refused to recognize the applicability of misrepresentation exception or the discretionary function exception to the Federal Tort Claims Act.

Questions

1. If, as a part of a federal loan program, a federal agency decides to inspect homes for the presence of lead, and the government official negligently fails to detect the presence of lead, does this failure fall within the "negligent misrepresentation" exemption to the Federal Tort Claims Act? Or was this a "negligent failure to communicate" the presence of lead?

2. If a federal official in the line of duty misrepresents either negligently or intentionally, is this misrepresentation actionable under the Federal Tort Claims Act? Why? Do we want government officials to "lie" to the public? Then why not hold them liable under the Federal Tort Claims Act rather than exempting such misrepresentations from suit as is now the case? Would the liabilities simply be too overwhelming? Recall that a recent survey of Internal Revenue Service advice to taxpayers in filling out their 1040 income tax returns revealed that one in three "answers" to questions was incorrect. Would this not be "negligent" representation subjecting the federal government to liability unless the misrepresentation exemption existed?
3. If a federal regulator undertakes a discretionary function that negligently damages a member of the public, may the member of the public recover damages from the regulator?

   Is a federal agency's decision to conduct a housing inspection to detect lead discretionary? If an agency makes a policy decision to inspect houses for lead, once having made this decision is the manner of conducting the inspection "grounded in the policy of the regulatory regime" according to the Lemke decision? Once having made a policy decision to inspect for lead for safety reasons is the failure to detect clearly apparent conditions a "policy decision"?
4. Does the fact that a statute or regulation forces a regulator to do something make it more or less likely that a member of the public can successfully sue the regulator for negligent performance of this function? What if the federal official is told to do something and commits no tort in doing so, is the federal government liable under the Federal Tort Claims Act?
5. If the president's chauffeur has the choice of whether to take one street instead of another in getting the President to the airport, and while in route negligently drives over a pedestrian, should the federal government be immune from liability because the chauffeur had a choice of what route to take? Is the chauffeur's choice grounded in social, economic, or political goals of a statute?
6. Is a tort lawsuit against the federal government a desirable place to test the propriety of federal policy, such as discretionary decisions? Does this option explain why the discretionary function exception from liability under the FTCA is desirable, that is, no waiver of federal tort liability for discretionary acts under the FTCA?

CHAPTER SUMMARY

Administrative law deals with laws and regulations affecting administrative agencies. Administrative agencies are nonlegislative, nonjudicial governmental lawmakers. Such agencies exist at the federal, state, and local levels of government.

Administrative agencies exist to provide expertise, to oversee socialized harm, to protect the weak, to provide economy in government regulation, and to correct wrongs resulting from class struggle.

Legislatures give administrative agencies the legal authority to regulate by passing enabling acts.

Agencies have the authority to promulgate regulations. Regulations can be either interpretative or substantive. Substantive regulations are also known as legislative regulations.

The federal Administrative Procedure Act (APA) sets out the rules by which federal administrative agencies make regulations, adjudicate, and carry out their executive function.

The Federal Register Act created the *Federal Register* system.

In 1966 Congress enacted the Freedom of Information Act, which allows persons to obtain information from federal administrative agencies.

The Federal Privacy Act of 1974 restricts what information persons may obtain from a federal agency in a system of records under certain circumstances.

To open up federal agency management, Congress passed the Government in the Sunshine Act, also known as the open meeting law.

MANAGER'S ETHICAL DILEMMA

Thomas Gaubert was the major shareholder of IASA, the Independent American Savings Association, a Texas-chartered and federally insured savings and loan association (S&L). Gaubert was IASA's chairman of the board and largest shareholder. In 1984, officials at the Federal Home Loan Bank Board (FHLBB) sought an IASA merger with Investex Savings, a failing Texas S&L. Because FHLBB was concerned about Gaubert's other financial dealings, they requested that he sign a "neutralization agreement" that effectively removed him from IASA's management. They also asked him to post a $25 million interest in real property as security for his personal guarantee that IASA's net worth would exceed regulatory minimums. Gaubert agreed to both conditions. Federal officials then provided regulatory and financial advice to enable IASA to consummate the merger with Investex. Throughout this period, the regulators instituted no formal action against IASA. Instead, they relied on the likelihood that IASA and Gaubert would follow their suggestions and advice.

In 1986, the regulators threatened to close IASA unless its management and board of directors were replaced; all of the directors agreed to resign. The new officers and directors were recommended by the FHLBB (the regulators). After the new management took over, FHLBB officials became more involved in IASA's day-to-day business. The regulators recommended the hiring of a certain consultant to advise IASA on operational and financial matters. Regulators advised IASA concerning whether, when, and how its subsidiaries should be placed into bankruptcy. Regulators mediated salary disputes and urged IASA to convert from state to federal charter.

Although IASA was thought to be financially sound while Gaubert managed it, the new directors soon announced that IASA had a substantial negative net worth. You are Gaubert. You decided to sue the FHLBB for negligent regulation causing your stock in IASA to decline in value. What legal arguments is Gaubert likely to face under the Federal Tort Claims Act?

Federal agency employees—called whistleblowers—who expose waste, fraud, and abuse in government are protected by a number of federal statutes. One such law is the Whistleblower Protection Act of 1989.

Ways of controlling federal administrative agencies include the courts (that is, by suing the agency), sunset laws, ombudspersons, and the Federal Tort Claims Act.

Discussion Questions

1. Is the often heard allegation that "regulators are liberals" true? Would the extensive regulations in consumer matters, environmental affairs, equal employment opportunity, antitrust, and handgun control lend credence to this idea? How about regulations restricting access to pornography, regulating the use of marijuana and other drugs, restricting abortions, limiting the use of bankruptcy, imposing tough vagrancy laws, and imposing strict dress codes (no public nudity)?

   Consider further regulations that impose food labeling requirements, require driver's licenses, restrict entry into various occupations by imposing occupational licenses, regulate clothing labels, disclose terms of auto leases. What part of the political spectrum favors these regulations? Everyone?
2. This chapter tells us that the federal Sunshine Act requires open meetings by agencies headed by a collegial body composed of two or more individual members. Does the Sunshine Act apply to the U.S. Department of Justice? Who heads this department? [*Nichols v. Reno*, 931 F. Supp. 748 (D. Colo., 1996)]
3. Former U.S. government employees and political employees brought a common law right of privacy claim against the First Lady and former White House staff, which alleged the First Lady and the staff requested Federal Bureau of Investigation (FBI) files of plaintiffs for the improper purpose of obtaining embarrassing or damaging information for partisan political purposes. Does the federal privacy act preempt (that is, "knock out" or invalidate) the common law tort of invasion of the right of privacy

or merely add to common law privacy rights? [*Alexander v. F.B.I.*, 971 F. Supp. 608 (1997)].

4. What are some of the reasons for the growth of administrative agencies? Which reasons are the most persuasive today?
5. What are the controls on administrative agencies?
6. The Federal Tort Claims Act lets people sue and recover damages from the U.S. government for torts (noncontractual civil wrongs) that federal employees commit. The act does not, however, let a person recover punitive damages against the U.S. government. In one case, a government employee negligently drove a federal car and permanently brain damaged an innocent victim. The victim's relatives sued and recovered $1,300,000 for the victim, who was in a permanent coma. Was this jury award punitive and therefore not allowed by the Federal Tort Claims Act? [*Flannery v. U.S.*, 718 F.2d 108 (4th Cir. 1983)]
7. Is the Texas Parole Board an agency covered by the federal Administrative Procedure Act? [*Johnson v. Wells*, 566 F.2d 1016 (5th Cir. 1978)]
8. Congress and congressional committees have much valuable information about the Central Intelligence Agency. Can the public get this information by bringing a freedom of information suit against Congress? [*Paisley v. C.I.A.*, 724 F.2d 201 (D.C. Cir. 1984)]
9. The FBI was investigating Tom Miller. It went to the Fort Worth National Bank to get records on Miller's bank account and use of money orders. The bank turned such information over to the FBI without Miller's consent. Miller claimed this action violated the Federal Privacy Act. In doing so, he argued that a national bank is an agent of the federal government and is thus covered by the Federal Privacy Act. Is Miller correct? [*Ausherman v. Stump*, 643 F.2d 715 (10th Cir. 1981)]

Suggested Readings

Articles

ABBOTT, "Case Studies on the Costs of Federal Statutory and Judicial Deadlines," 39 *Administrative Law Review* 467 (1987).

BAGBY AND GITTINGS, "The Elusive Discretionary Function Exception from Government Tort Liability: The Narrowing Scope of Federal Liability," 30 *American Business Law Journal* 223 (1992).

CALABRESI, "A Government of Limited and Enumerated Powers: In Defense of *United States v. Lopez*," 94 *Michigan Law Review* 752 (1995).

COASE, "The Problem of Social Cost," 3 *Journal of Law and Economics* 1 (1960).

COMMENT, "Legislative Ethics: Improper Influence by a Lawmaker on an Administrative Agency," 42 *Maine Law Review* 423 (1990).

COOPER, "The Need for an Ombudsman in State Government," 1 *Prospectus* 27 (1968).

DELONG, "Informal Rulemaking and the Integration of Law and Policy," 65 *Virginia Law Review* 257 (1979).

FISHER, "Controlling Government Regulation: Cost-Benefit Analysis Before and After the 'Cotton-Dust' Case," 36 *Administrative Law Review* 179 (1984).

FISHER, "The Federal Register: Capitalist Tool," *The Wall Street Journal* June 3, 1985.

FISHER, "The Whistleblower Protection Act of 1989: A False Hope for Whistleblowers," 43 *Rutgers Law Review* 355 (1991).

GIFFORD, "Federal Administrative Law Judges: The Relevance of Past Choices to Future Decisions," 49 *Administrative Law Review* 1 (1997).

GREEN, "Safety as an Element of Pharmaceutical Quality: The Respective Roles of Regulation and Tort Law," 42 *Saint Louis University Law Journal* 163 (1998).

HOVENKAMP, "The Limits of Preference-Based Legal Policy," 89 *Northwestern University Law Review* 4 (1994).

McGARITY, "Regulatory Analysis and Regulatory Reform," 65 *Texas Law Review* 1243 (1987).

NOTE, "The Need for an Additional Notice and Comment Period When Final Rules Differ Substantially from Interim Rules," 1981 *Duke Law Journal* 377 (1981).

PEDERSON, "Formal Records and Informal Rulemaking," 85 *Yale Law Journal* 38 (1975).

REVESZ, "Rehabilitating Interstate Competition: Rethinking the 'Race-to-the-Bottom' Rationale for Federal Environmental Regulation," 67 *New York University Law Review* 1210 (1992).

SCHWARTZ, "Cost-Benefit Analysis in Administrative Law: Does It Make Priceless Procedural Rights Worthless?" 37 *Administrative Law Review* 1 (1985).

CHAPTER

7

GOVERNMENT REGULATION: ANATOMY AND ENFORCEMENT OF A REGULATION

"OF EVEN GREATER IMPORTANCE, THOUGH, IS THE PURPOSE BEHIND THE REQUIREMENT THAT THE PARTIES BE ABLE TO COMMENT ON THE RULE WHILE IT IS STILL IN THE FORMATIVE OR PROPOSED STAGE. THE PURPOSE IS BOTH (1) TO ALLOW THE AGENCY TO BENEFIT FROM THE EXPERTISE AND INPUT OF THE PARTIES WHO FILE COMMENTS WITH REGARD TO THE PROPOSED RULE, AND (2) TO SEE TO IT THAT THE AGENCY MAINTAINS A FLEXIBLE AND OPEN-MINDED ATTITUDE TOWARDS ITS OWN RULES."

Judge Wilkey in National Tour Brokers Ass'n. v. United States (1978)

POSITIVE LAW ETHICAL PROBLEMS

"They haven't given us notice of this rule in the *Federal Register*; therefore the rule is invalid," said Marvin Wollin. Wollin was a truck driver who belonged to an organization promoting trucker safety. The Federal Highway Administration issued an "interpretative rule" imposing liability on trucking companies for infractions such as exceeding maximum driving time and failure to complete a record of duty activities. However, the trucking industry and individual drivers and their representatives had no opportunity to comment on the regulation. Marvin thought this violated the rulemaking procedures set out in the Administrative Procedure Act. Was Marvin correct?

"The no-lead regulation is arbitrary and capricious because studies indicate that the lead in gasoline is just one contributor to the lead in people's blood. Furthermore, no one knows exactly how much lead in the air will endanger people's health. Therefore, EPA's no-lead regulation for gasoline is invalid, and we should challenge it in court," concluded an executive at the Ethyl Corporation. Was he successful?

This chapter discusses the legislative, judicial, and executive functions of administrative agencies: making regulations, adjudicating (deciding cases), and enforcing agency statutes and regulations.

THE FUNCTIONS OF ADMINISTRATIVE AGENCIES

Figure 7.1 sets out the major steps that could be involved in the life of a federal regulation and shows the adjudicatory, legislative, and executive jobs of the typical agency.

Executive

The *executive* functions involve law enforcement and administration. These functions consist of investigating and enforcing regulations and doing the scores of mundane tasks that make any organization run, such as hiring, firing, and issuing licenses.

FIGURE 7.1 Major Steps in the Life of a Federal Regulation (Reg) Informal Rulemaking

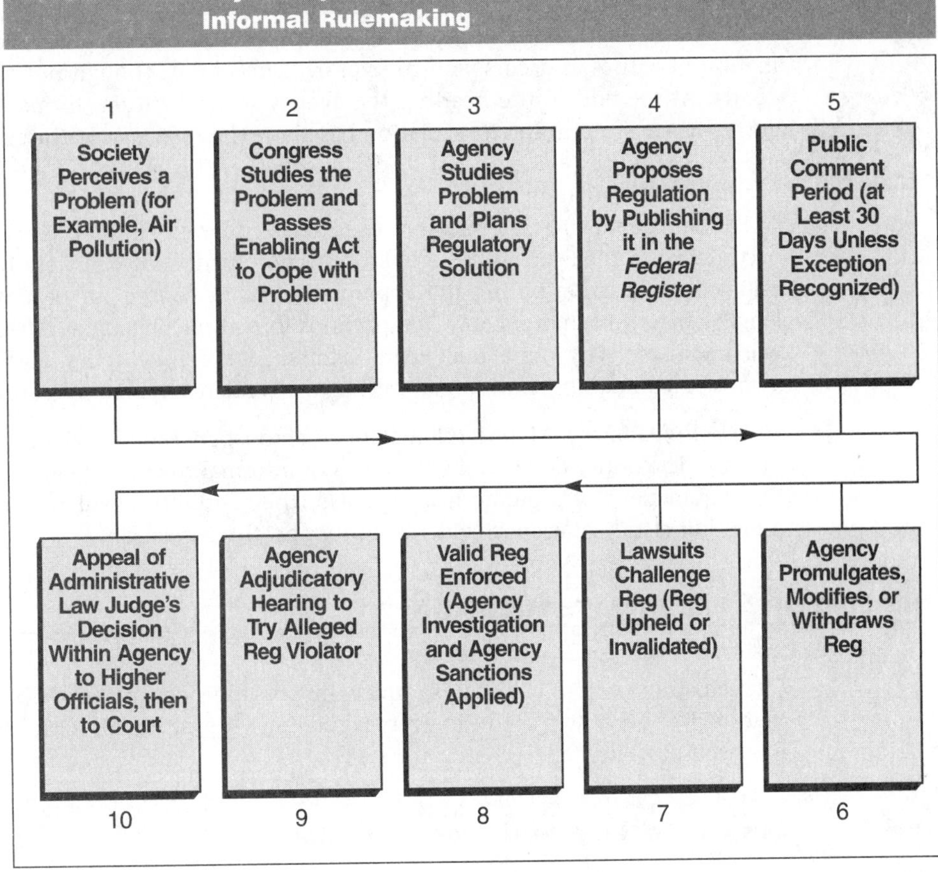

Adjudicative

Agency *adjudication* refers to hearings before administrative law judges (ALJs), who are legally independent of agency prosecutors, investigators, and rulemakers. ALJs make rulings on admissibility of evidence (the rules of evidence are usually more lenient here than in courts) and control the conduct of the hearing.

Legislative

The *legislative* function of an administrative agency refers to rulemaking. The three kinds of rulemaking are informal, formal, and hybrid.

Informal Rulemaking. Informal rulemaking uses the notice and comment process discussed later in this chapter. Agencies usually make regulations in this way. Essentially, in the process, a federal agency places a notice of **proposed rulemaking** in the *Federal Register*, receives comments from interested people on the proposed regulation, makes any changes, and promulgates the regulation. No trials or hearings are held. No face-to-face contact is made between the regulator and the public. Regulation making done this way takes place on paper. If a court challenge is offered to an informal rule, the arbitrary, capricious, and unreasonable evidentiary standard is used to review it.

Formal Rulemaking. Formal rulemaking occurs when a statute requires rulemaking on the record. A notice of the proposed rulemaking takes place, and a hearing follows: Witnesses give testimony under oath, transcripts of testimony are made, cross-examination of witnesses occurs, and rules of evidence apply, though not as strictly as in courts. At the end of the hearing, the agency makes written, formal findings. The agency then promulgates a regulation based on the evidence at the hearing. Courts use the substantial evidence test to decide whether the agency has enough evidence to justify the regulation's existence.

Formal rulemaking is extremely expensive and can be slow. A classic example occurred when the Food and Drug Administration spent approximately 10 years to promulgate a regulation setting the appropriate peanut content of peanut butter.[1] The lengthy transcript (more than 7,700 pages) is formal rulemaking and free speech gone wild and shows why formal rulemaking is impractical despite its desirable qualities such as cross-examination. Thus, formal rulemaking is rarely required by statutes today.

Hybrid Rulemaking. Hybrid rulemaking is a cross between formal and informal rulemaking. The notice and comment aspects of informal rulemaking are combined with the requirement of a public hearing. Also, the substantial evidence test is used to judge sufficiency of agency evidence to support the regulation.

THE LIFE OF A FEDERAL REGULATION

The remainder of this chapter examines the possible steps in the life of a federal regulation. Not every step occurs in every regulation's life, although some regulations follow each possible step.

Step 1. Society Perceives a Problem

Society often perceives problems before legislatures do. Individuals may bring problems to the attention of the legislature by writing letters, forming citizens' groups, hiring lobbyists, and making campaign contributions. Congress must then study the problem to understand its exact nature. Members of Congress do not personally study all problems brought to their attention; no one has that much time. Instead, each member of Congress has a sizable staff, often exceeding 100 people. In addition, the congressional committees (and often subcommittees) have large staffs who do the work of studying problems.

Step 2. Congress Passes an Enabling Act

People sometimes blame administrative agencies for causing the oversupply of regulations. This action is analogous to a patient blaming an optometrist for the patient's bad eyesight when told to get glasses. The doctor is doing only what the patient asks. Similarly, the legislature tells agencies what to do when it passes an enabling act.

Statutes that empower administrative agencies to make regulations are enabling acts. Agency regulations are valid only if the legislature gives the agency the necessary power. Agencies have no inherent power to make legally binding regulations. They may do only what the legislature lets them do in enabling acts. (Under discussion here are legislative regulations only, not interpretative regulations.)

[1] The content was set at 90 percent peanuts. The case is *Corn Prod. Co. v. FDA*, 427 F.2d 511 (3d Cir., 1970), *cert. denied sub. nom. Derby Foods, Inc. v. FDS*, 400 U.S. 957 (1970).

Example of an Enabling Act. The following is an enabling act. It is a section of a federal statute (the Magnuson-Moss Warranty—Federal Trade Commission Improvement Act) that gives a federal agency the power to make regulations.

The enabling statute (the exact words Congress used to tell the Federal Trade Commission to make a rule) is as follows:

> (b) The Commission shall initiate within one year after January 4, 1975, a rule-making proceeding dealing with warranties and warranty practices in connection with the sale of used motor vehicles; and, to the extent necessary to supplement the protections offered the consumer by this chapter, shall prescribe rules dealing with such warranties and practices. In prescribing rules under this subsection, the Commission may exercise any authority it may have under this chapter, or other law, and in addition it may require disclosure that a used motor vehicle is sold without any warranty and specify the form and content of such disclosure. Publ. L. 93?637, Title I, §109, Jan. 4, 1975, 88 Stat, 2183.

Step 3. An Agency Studies the Problem

When the legislature passes an enabling statute, it has implicitly said that society has a problem. The enabling statute tells an agency to do something about the problem and gives it some guidelines to make regulations to solve the problem. Before an agency can propose or promulgate a regulation, it must conduct a study. The study can be done in-house or contracted out to a consulting firm or to university professors. The study is the key to the regulation because it is the scientific or factual justification for the regulation. For example, if the FTC promulgates a regulation forcing used car dealers to put window stickers on cars telling consumers about the car's condition, used car dealers will ask why. In response, the FTC will refer to the Magnuson-Moss—FTC Improvement Act, the law that tells the FTC to make the used car industry fairer to consumers.

> **http://** *For more information about the Federal Trade Commission, see* ***http://www.ftc.gov***

Consider the cost of such a regulation to the used car industry: Hundreds of millions, perhaps billions, of dollars might be needed for this one industry group to comply with the regulation. Nevertheless, defective used cars present a serious consumer problem, causing great damage to people. The study on which the regulation is based must be excellent in purpose, design, and execution, and must be logical in its conclusions.

Step 4. The Agency Proposes a Regulation

After the agency concludes its study, it drafts a regulation based on the study's conclusions. Different agency offices or personnel examine the draft regulation, such as the Office of General Counsel, the agency's lawyers, economists, and scientists, to try to find problems with it.

Once the agency's draft regulation has been reviewed within the agency, the heads of the agency sign it and send it to the *Federal Register* Office in the National Archives and Records Service, where the draft regulation is published in a daily edition of the *Federal Register*.

> **http://** *The website for the Federal Register can be found at* ***http://www.gpo.gov/su_docs/aces/aces140.html***

The Law Governing Federal Agencies' Regulation Making. The federal law governing regulation making comes from the Administrative Procedure Act (APA), which governs most federal agencies. The APA's regulation-making rules do not apply to U.S. military or foreign affairs functions, to matters relating to agency management and personnel, or to public property, loans, grants, benefits, or contracts. Also, state and municipal regulation making is not covered by the federal APA. Many states have state APAs that govern state administrative agencies. In addition to the APA, special statutes, such as the Occupational Safety and Health Act, sometimes put other requirements on agency rulemaking.

***The Notice in the* Federal Register**. When an agency proposes a regulation, general notice of the proposed regulation must be published in the *Federal Register*, with two exceptions: when people subject to the regulation are named and either (1) are personally served or (2) otherwise have actual notice.

***Contents of Notice*.** The following items must be in the notice of the proposed rulemaking published in the *Federal Register*:

1. The time, place, and nature of public regulation making in general
2. The laws the agency says give it the authority to make the proposed rule
3. The provisions of the proposed rule or a description of the subjects and issues involved (in other words, the rule itself does not have to be published when it is proposed).

http:// To access the Government Manual, go to **http://ww1.access.gpo.gov/nara/nara001.html**

http:// The Department of Transportation provides a variety of information at **http://www.dot.gov**

***Regulations That Need Not Be Published*.** Interpretative regulations, general policy statements, or rules of agency organization, procedure, or practice do not have to be published in the *Federal Register* because they are too general or trivial and because courts do not treat such items as law. One other instance excuses an agency from giving notice of a proposed substantive regulation. When an agency for good cause finds that notice and public procedure thereon are impracticable, unnecessary, or contrary to the public interest, *Federal Register* notice is not required of even a substantive regulation.

In the following case, *Truckers United For Safety v. Fed. Highway Administration*, which reason did the court give for excusing *Federal Register* notice?

Truckers United For Safety v. Fed. Highway Administration

U.S. Court of Appeals (D.C. Cir.)
139 F.3d 934 (1998)

Background and Facts:

Truckers United For Safety (TUFS), a nonprofit trade association of motor carriers, petitioned the court for review of a portion of the regulatory guidance issued by the Federal Highway Administration for private parties seeking to comply with motor carrier safety regulations.

TUFS contends that the Administration should have afforded interested parties notice and and an opportunity to comment under the Administrative Procedure Act (APA).

Body of Opinion

Judge Rogers

Under the Motor Carrier Act of 1935 and the Motor Carrier Safety Act of 1984, the Federal Highway Administration has the authority to issue regulations pertaining to commercial motor vehicle safety and to enforce those regulations.... Pursuant to that authority, the Administration promulgated the Federal Motor Carrier Safety Regulations, including the following regulations:

§ 390.11 Motor carrier to require observance of driver regulations.

Whenever... a duty is prescribed for a driver or a prohibition is imposed upon the driver, it shall be the duty of the motor carrier to require observance of such duty or prohibition. If the motorcarrier is a driver, the driver shall likewise be bound.

§395.3 Maximum driving time.

(a) Except as provided (elsewhere)... no motor carrier shall permit or require any driver used by it to drive nor shall any such driver drive:

(1) More than 10 hours following 8 consecutive hours off duty; or

(2) For any period after having been on duty 15 hours following 8 consecutive hours off duty.

(b) No motor carrier shall permit or require a driver of a commercial motor vehicle to drive, nor shall any driver drive, regardless of the number of motor carriers using the driver's services, for any period after—

(1) Having been on duty 60 hours in any 7 consecutive days if the employing motor carrier does not operate commercial motor vehicles every day of the week; or

(2) Having been on duty 70 hours in any period of 8 consecutive days if the employing motor carrier operates commercial motor vehicles every day of the week.

§ 395.8 Driver's record of duty status.

(a) Except for a private motor carrier of passengers (nonbusiness), every motor carrier shall require every driver used by the motor carrier to record his/her duty status for each 24-hour period using the methods prescribed (herein)....

(b) Failure to complete the record of duty activities of this section or §395.15, failure to preserve a record of such duty activities, or making of false reports in connection with such duty activities shall make the driver and/or the carrier liable to prosecution....

The administration has developed and periodically updated regulatory guidance in question-and-answer format to assist parties bound by these regulations.... In the most recent edition of this regulatory guidance, published in the *Federal Register* on April 4, 1997, the Administration "consolidated previously issued interpretations and regulatory guidance materials and developed concise interpretative guidance in question-and-answer form."... Three particular questions and answers within the guidance are of concern here. First and second, in interpretation of 49 C.F.R. §395.3:

Question 7: What is the liability of a motor carrier for hours of service violations?

Guidance: The carrier is liable for violations of the hours of service regulations if it had or should have had the means by which to detect the violations. Liability under the Federal Motor Vehicle Safety regulations does not depend upon actual knowledge of the violations.

Question 8: Are carriers liable for the actions of their employees even though the carrier contends that it did not require or permit the violations to occur?

Guidance: Yes. Carriers are liable for the actions of their employees. Neither intent to commit, nor actual knowledge of, a violation is a necessary element of the liability. Carriers "permit" violations of the hours of service if they fail to have in place management systems that effectively prevent such violations....

Third, in interpretation of 49 C.F.R. §395.8:

Question 21: What is the carrier's liability when its drivers falsify records of duty status?

Guidance: A carrier is liable both for the actions of its drivers in submitting false documents and for its own actions in accepting false documents. Motor carriers have a duty to require drivers to observe the Federal Motor Carrier Safety Regulations.

...TUFS' further contention, that the set of three questions and answers in the regulatory guidance is invalid because the Administration did not provide interested parties with notice and an opportunity to comment in accordance with the APA is similarly unpersuasive.... Under the APA, legislative rules are subject to notice-and-comment requirements, whereas interpretative rules are not.... To distinguish between the two, the court asks

> "whether the purported interpretative rule has 'legal effect,' which in turn is best ascertained by asking (1) whether in the absence of the rule there would not be an adequate legislative basis for enforcement action or other agency action to confer benefits or ensure the performance of duties, (2) whether the agency has published the rule in the Code of Federal Regulations, (3) whether the agency has explicitly invoked its general legislative authority, or (4) whether the rule effectively amends a prior legislative rule."...

Although this inquiry may be "fuzzy" in some cases... in the instant case, each of these criteria points toward the same conclusion: the three questions and answers represent interpretative rules not subject to the APA's notice and comment requirements.

First, as discussed, the three questions and answers do not appear to impose a new strict liability standard on motor carriers, and thus the Administration has no apparent need to rely upon them for authority to take any enforcement action. The regulations in force both before and after the Administration issued the regulatory guidance provided that motor carriers have a duty to require their drivers' compliance with the regulations... and in particular, with the maximum hours of duty and record keeping regulations with which the regulatory guidance in question is concerned.... The regulatory guidance appears only to elaborate upon that duty, and then only in a manner consistent with earlier applications of the regulations.... Even if the regulatory guidance did not exist, the Administration could rely upon earlier authority to apply the rules embodied in the three challenged questions and answers.

Second, the regulatory guidance is not published in the Code of Federal Regulations. It was published only in the *Federal Register*, and the Administration gave no indication there that it would publish the Regulatory Guidance again elsewhere....

Third, the Administration did not invoke its legislative authority in publishing the regulatory guidance. To the contrary, the Administration explained that this was "interpretative guidance" meant to "provide the motor carrier industry with a clearer understanding of the applicability of many of the requirements contained in the Federal Motor Carrier Safety Regulations in particular situations."... Although the label an agency places on a rule is not dispositive,... the label, as indicative of intent, does carry some weight in our consideration whether the underlying rule is legislative or interpretative.

Finally the three questions and answers do not amend a prior legislative rule. As noted, they appear consistent with prior law....

All four factors indicate that the Administration was not required to afford interested parties notice and an opportunity to comment before promulgating the three questions and answers....

Judgment and Result

The Federal Highway Administration won. The Court of Appeals held the FHA's rules were interpretative. Therefore the FHA did not have to provide the public with notice and an opportunity to comment on the rules under the Administrative Procedure Act.

Questions

1. Did the Federal Highway Administration give the public 30 days to comment on the proposed regulation?
2. Does the APA give a clear definition of "interpretative regulation" excusing compliance with the 30-day comment period? Who makes the initial determination that the regulation is "interpretative" justifying no commenting period? If no one such as TUFS here, challenges the agency determination that a regulation is interpretative, is not the agency's determination always right?
3. What is the purpose of the 30-day comment period between the proposal and promulgation of a federal rule?
4. How could the Internet facilitate the commenting process? Take a look at the Internet cites throughout this chapter. A number of federal agencies now allows the public to comment on proposed regulations over the Internet. Does this type of access make it easier for members of the public located in remote communities to comment on proposed regulations?

Problems in Finding the Notice. In the majority of cases, publication in the *Federal Register* is the only official notice the public gets before a regulation takes effect. The average person has never seen the *Federal Register*, let alone read a proposed regulation.

Figure 7.2 is a proposed regulation limiting used-car dealers.[2] These proposed regulations are published to implement the enabling statute quoted earlier in the chapter. Several points should be noted:

1. The proposed regs were published on pages 1089 and 1090 on January 6, 1976. The numbering starts at page 1 on each calendar year. From the page count, one can get some idea of the many things published each year: proclamations, notices of federal agency meetings, proposed regulations, and promulgated regulations. Figure 7.2 shows that six days after the new year began the *Federal Register* already had more than one thousand pages.
2. Remarks are often made before or after the proposed regulation. The remarks in Figure 7.2 are not the proposed regulation; they primarily explain what the proposed regulation is about. The remarks identify the proposing agency, tell what the enabling statutes are, and indicate where in the *Code of Federal Regulations* the agency plans to put the proposed regulations once they are promulgated.
3. The proposed regulations *do not* go into the *Code of Federal Regulations*.
4. When the regulations are later promulgated, the introductory remarks explain that the regulations when promulgated will go into 16 *C.F.R.* Part 455. The 16 indicates that the promulgated regulations will go into book 16, specifically in Part 455 of that book.

[2] This chapter focuses on informal (notice and comment) rulemaking. Technically, the FTC used-car warranty rule set out in Figure 7.2 is a product of hybrid rulemaking because it contains the basic notice and comment format of informal rulemaking but adds other procedures such as public hearings to the notice and comment format. Also, several rounds of notices and comments took place between 1976, the time of the first notice, and 1984 when the rule was ultimately promulgated. The authors use this rulemaking as an example because of its interesting subject matter.

FIGURE 7.2 A Proposed Regulation

FEDERAL TRADE COMMISSION

116 CFR Part 451

SALE OF USED MOTOR VEHICLES

Disclosure and Other Regulations
Notice of proceeding, proposed trade regulation rules, statement of reason for proposed rules, invitation to propose disputed issues of fact for consideration in public hearings, and invitation to comment on proposed rules.

Notice is hereby given that the Federal Trade Commission, pursuant to the Federal Trade Commission Act, as amended, 15 U.S.C. 41, et seq., the Magnuson-Moss Warranty-Federal Trade Commission Improvement Act, 15 U.S.C. 2301, et seq., the provisions of Part 1, Subpart B of the Commission's procedures and rules of practice, 16 CFR 1.7, et seq., and section 553 of Subchapter II, Chapter 5, Title 5, U.S. Code (Administrative Procedure), has initiated a proceeding for the promulgation of Trade Regulation Rules concerning the disclosure of certain material information and other regulations concerning used motor vehicles offered for sale.

Accordingly, the Commission proposes the following Trade Regulation Rules and would amend Subchapter D. Trade Regulation Rules. Chapter 1 of CFR by adding a new Part 445 as follows:

PART 455-DISCLOSURE AND OTHER REGULATIONS CONCERNING THE SALE OF USED MOTOR VEHICLES

Sec.
455.1 Definitions.
455.2 Vehicle information disclosure.
455.3 "As is" disclosure.
455.4 Prohibition of contrary oral statements.
455.5 Retention of documents.

AUTHORITY: 38 Stat. 717, as amended, 15 U.S.C. 41, et seq.

§ 455.1 Definitions.

For the purpose of this Part, the following terms and definitions shall apply:

(a) "Person" means any individual, partnership or corporation.
(b) "Used motor vehicle dealer" means any person, partnership, or corporation, or any employee or agent thereof, engaged in the business of offering for sale, sale or distribution of any used motor vehicle to the general public.
(c) "Motor vehicle" means an automobile, truck, recreational vehicle or other motorized vehicle designed to transport not more than fifteen (15) individuals upon the public roads, streets and highways.
(d) "Used motor vehicle" means a motor vehicle which is offered for sale after:
  (1) A prior sale to a person who purchased the motor vehicle in good faith for a purpose other than resale; or
  (2) Use of the motor vehicle as a rental, driver education, or demonstration motor vehicle, or for the personal or business transportation of the manufacturer and/or dealer or any of their employees or for any use other than the limited use necessary in moving or road testing a vehicle prior to delivery to a customer.
(e) "Warranty" means:
  (1) Any written or oral affirmation of fact or promise made in connection with the sale of any used motor vehicle, which relates to nature of the material or workmanship of such used motor vehicle and or promises that such material or workmanship is free of any mechanical defect or will meet any specified level of performance over any specified period of time, or
  (2) Any written or oral undertaking made in connection with the sale of any used motor vehicle, to the effect that any person will refund, repair, replace or take other remedial action with respect to such used motor vehicle in the event said used motor vehicle fails to meet the specifications set forth in the undertaking, which written or oral affirmation, promise, or undertaking becomes part of the basis of the bargain between a used motor vehicle dealer and a buyer for purpose other than resale of such used motor vehicle.
(f) "Service contract" means a contract to perform, over any period of time or for any specified mileage, services relating to the maintenance or repair (or both) of any used motor vehicle.
(g) "Mechanical defect" means any defective or damaged part of the mechanical, electrical, or hydraulic system of any used motor vehicle including, but not limited to, the motor and transmission, and any defective or damaged part of the body, chassis, suspension or other part of said used motor vehicle.
(h) "Potential purchaser" means any person other than a used motor vehicle dealer, who expresses an interest or intention to purchase a used motor vehicle. Such person shall be of at least minimum legal driving age, possess sufficient credit worthiness to purchase the used motor vehicle under consideration and have no infirmities which would bar consummation of the sales transaction.

§ 455.2 Vehicle Information Disclosure.

In connection with the offering for sale, sale or distribution of any used motor vehicle to the public, in or affecting commerce as "commerce" is defined in the Federal Trade Commission Act, as amended, it is an unfair or deceptive act or practice for any used motor vehicle dealer to fail to affix to the right rear window of any used motor vehicle offered for sale a disclosure statement containing the following information in the order it appears below and in a clear, and conspicuous manner:

(a) The name, address, and chief executive officer of the used motor vehicle dealer.
(b) The make, model and year of manufacture of the used motor vehicle.
(c) The approximate odometer reading reflecting the amount of mileage the used motor vehicle has been driven.
(d) If known to the used motor vehicle dealer, the identity of any commercial or governmental entity which previously used, owned or leased the used motor vehicle and the nature of the principal prior use of such vehicle including but not limited to

FIGURE 7.2 A Proposed Regulation, continued

rental, lease, driver education, taxi and police vehicles.

(e) A description of any work (including reconditioning) performed by, or on behalf of the used motor vehicle dealer or otherwise known to such dealer and relating to any damaged or defective component (including bent frame) or condition (including flooding) of the used motor vehicle which may affect the performance or useful life of the vehicle or which exceeded one hundred dollars ($100.00) in dealer costs.

(f) A description of the extent of component coverage, allocation of costs and duration of any warranty or service contract provided with the used motor vehicle and a statement that the potential purchaser may obtain a copy of any warranty or service contract offered from the used motor vehicle dealer.

(g) If the used motor vehicle is sold without a warranty and the seller attempts to disclaim any implied warranty, the following statements shall appear:

"This vehicle is sold without any warranty. The purchaser will bear the entire expense of repairing or correcting any defects that presently exist and/or may occur in the vehicle unless the salesperson promises in writing to correct such defects." [Rule 11]

§ 455.3 "As is" disclosure.

In connection with the offering for sale, sale or distribution of any used motor vehicle to the public, other than to used motor vehicle dealers, in or affecting commerce as commerce is defined in the Federal Trade Commission Act, as amended, it is an unfair or deceptive act or practice for any used motor vehicle dealer to fail to disclose, in any sales contract, or any other writing used to evidence the sale of any used motor vehicle for which no warranty, either expressed or implied, is given, the following information in a clear, concise and conspicuous manner on the face of such document:

"AS IS

'THIS USED MOTOR VEHICLE IS SOLD AS IS WITHOUT ANY WARRANTY, EITHER EXPRESSED OR IMPLIED. THE PURCHASER WILL BEAR THE ENTIRE EXPENSE OF REPAIRING OR CORRECTING ANY DEFECTS THAT PRESENTLY EXIST OR THAT MAY OCCUR IN THE VEHICLE.' " [Rule 21

§ 455.4 Prohibition of contrary oral statements.

In connection with the offering for sale, sale or distribution of any used motor vehicle in or affecting commerce as 'commerce' is defined in the Federal Trade Commission Act, as amended, it is an unfair or deceptive act or practice for any used motor vehicle dealer:

(a) To make any statements or claims, written or oral, or engage in any practices which directly or by implication contradict, mitigate, disparage or detract from any printed disclosure required by §§ 455.2 and 455.3; or

(b) To make any false, misleading or deceptive representation, directly or by implication, of the quality, performance, reliability or lack of mechanical defects of any used motor vehicle offered for sale.

(c) To make any representation, directly or by implication, of the quality, performance, reliability or lack of mechanical defects of any used motor vehicle offered for sale without possessing at the time of such representation a reasonable basis. (Rule 3)

§ 455.5 Retention of Documents.

To assure compliance with the provisions of this part, it is an unfair practice for all used motor vehicle dealers subject to such provisions to fail to retain and make available for inspection by officials of the Federal Trade Commission, upon request, true and correct copies of the written disclosures required by § 455.2 for at least three (3) years after the date on which the used motor vehicle subject to the disclosure was sold, and a copy of any sales contract, or other agreement used to consummate the sale of a used motor vehicle containing the disclosure required by § 455.3 for at least three (3) years from the date the used motor vehicle subject to the disclosure was sold." [Rule 4]

Statement of Reason for the Proposed Rule

It is the Commission's purpose, in issuing this statement, to set forth its reasons for proposing this Trade Regulation Rule with sufficient particularity to allow informed comment. The precise format of such statements may vary from rule to rule depending on the complexity of the issues involved. In this proceeding the Commission has determined that meaningful comment by the public will be facilitated by presenting (1) a statement describing the basic factual and legal premises underlying the Commission's determination to propose the Rule, and (2) a series of questions designed to draw to the public's attention matters which the Commission deems particularly pertinent and on which is especially solicited.

The Commission emphasizes that neither the statement of factual and legal premises nor the questions set out in the materials accompanying the proposed Rule should be interpreted as a designation of disputed issues of fact. Such designations shall be made by the Commission or its duly authorized presiding official pursuant to the Commission's procedures and rules of practice.

Statement

The Commission has reason to believe that a substantial number of used motor vehicles, as that term is defined in the proposed rule, are offered for sale or sold to the general public with mechanical defects which affect the performance or reliability of the vehicles. Potential purchasers are not in a position to determine the mechanical condition of the used motor vehicles under consideration and dealers, who know or should know of the defects do not inform the prospective purchaser of such defects. In addition, some dealers misrepresent the mechanical performance and reliability of the vehicles they offer for sale.

The Commission also has reason to believe that used motor vehicle dealers frequently recondition the appearance of the vehicles they offer for sale. Such reconditioning, which includes body work, painting and cleaning eliminates signs of the vehicle's previous use and normal wear and tear. Because of reconditioning, consumers often make erroneous assumptions concerning the prior use and care and of the mechanical performance and reliability of the used vehicles which are offered for sale.

Inadequate Notice. Suppose that a federal agency publishes a notice in the *Federal Register* asking the public what changes it would like to see in a statute the agency enforces. Assume the agency plans to turn these suggestions over to Congress, hoping it will pass amendments to the act the agency enforces. However, after the agency starts receiving the public's suggestions, the agency instead promulgates a regulation dealing with the matter. This action saves the agency from having to go to Congress to get a statute passed.

A problem could arise with this procedure—the problem of *notice.* Remember the APA notice requirements for proposed regulations: A federal agency must first give notice of a proposed regulation by publishing either the regulation in draft form or information about it in the *Federal Register. National Tour Brokers Association v. United States* says that a regulation promulgated without a prior notice is invalid.

National Tour Brokers Ass'n v. United States

U.S. Court of Appeals (D.C. Cir.)
591 F.2d 896 (1978)

Background and Facts:

The National Tour Brokers Association (NTBA) was a group of travel agents. The NTBA sued the U.S. Interstate Commerce Commission (ICC). The ICC had promulgated regulations putting new, expensive duties on travel agents. The NTBA argued that the ICC did not first propose its regulations in the *Federal Register*, a requirement of the Administrative Procedure Act. The ICC did publish a *Federal Register* notice, but the notice did not mention any proposed regulation applying to tour brokers. The ICC argued that its action of publishing a general notice, asking for the public's ideas on how to limit tour brokers, was sufficient.

Body of Opinion

Judge Wilkey

A. *Constructive Notice*

The first clause of §553(b) provides for constructive notice: 'General notice of proposed rulemaking shall be published in the *Federal Register*.' We are unable to find that the Commission satisfied this requirement. It is true that the Commission published a general notice in the *Federal Register*, but it was not a notice of proposed rulemaking. A fair reading of that item clearly indicates that it was one looking toward the formulation of possible legislative amendments which might be proposed to Congress, not administrative rulemaking. It seems that the Commission changed its mind halfway through this proceeding and is now attempting to correct its procedural deficiencies by characterizing the proceeding *ex post facto* as informal rulemaking.

Agencies could in the future publish vague, ambiguous notices in the *Federal Register*, adverting obliquely to certain issues or proceedings, and then, months or years later, promulgate final rules and claim that constructive notice had been given. This cannot be the objective of the APA notice requirement.

The purpose of this (notice) requirement is clear—to put interested parties on notice that *administrative rulemaking* in certain areas is about to take place. We hold that the Commission failed to meet this requirement in this case. . . .

The legislative change sought in this case was basically an expansion of the authority of the ICC, while the administrative rules later issued addressed much more specific subjects such as territorial restrictions and bond amounts. . . .

B. *Actual Notice*

Section 553(b) allows the alternative of actual notice: ". . . unless persons subject thereto are named and either personally served or otherwise have actual notice thereof in accordance with law."

The Commission claims that actual notice was given to the parties at the oral hearing held 9 August 1976. The Commission's Chairman opened that hearing by outlining some of the questions the Commission hoped to resolve, among which was, "[I]f the Commission does decide that entry controls are no longer necessary, should we seek legislation or is some other course of action available?" This is clearly not a statement that a rulemaking proceeding is taking place. Rather, it is an inquiry asking whether it would be advisable to undertake a rulemaking proceeding. The statement of NTBA's counsel later at that hearing, in response to the Chairman's introductory remarks, was in conformity with this meaning. Counsel stated: Now, our position is this. We urge [the Commission] not to submit to Congress legislative recommendation for change in Section 211. We also urge that you not attempt a change in Section 211 administratively.

Counsel was simply stating that it did not think that an administrative rulemaking proceeding should be initiated.

It was not an implicit concession that a rulemaking proceeding was then underway....

Of even greater importance, though, is the purpose behind the requirement that the parties be able to comment on the rule while it is still in the formative or "proposed" stage. The purpose is both (1) to allow the agency to benefit from the expertise and input of the parties who file comments with regard to the proposed rule, and (2) to see to it that the agency maintains a flexible and openminded attitude towards its own rules, which might be lost if the agency had already put its credibility on the line in the form of "final" rules. People naturally tend to be more close-minded and defensive once they have made a 'final' determination.... The purpose of §553 is to "enable the agency promulgating the rule to educate itself before establishing rules and procedures which have a substantial impact on those regulated."...

The deficiencies in an approach whereby the agency issues final rules before it receives (and benefits from) comments and input from the parties is graphically illustrated in the instant proceeding. In its initial decision promulgating the final rules here in issue, the Commission stated that [i]n all but a few cases, such bonds [*i.e.*, tour broker surety bonds] will be written on a full collateral basis only, *i.e.*, the broker must post with the surety company the coverage amount in cash or acceptable investment bonds. Surety companies, even before issuing bonds on a full collateral basis, thoroughly investigate a bond applicant as to reputation, integrity, business ability, and financial stability. The possibility of questionable fly-by-night brokers is thereby all but eliminated.

As pointed out by petitioner the Commission may be in serious error about how tour broker surety bonding actually works....

Judgment and Result

The court invalidated the ICC's promulgated rules because the APA notice requirement had not been satisfied. The public had been denied its right to comment, and the ICC had thereby deprived itself of help from the public in understanding the business it was trying to regulate.

Questions

1. Did the agency (ICC) publish a notice of proposed rulemaking before it promulgated its rule? What effect did these actions have on the rule?
2. Because the ICC published a public notice in the *Federal Register* before promulgating the challenged regulation, how was the National Tour Brokers Association or any other member of the public harmed?
3. Did the court hold that the regulation in question was invalid because of what it did (a substantive flaw) or because of how the ICC promulgated it (a procedural defect)?

Step 5. The Public Comments

Step 5 in Figure 7.1—the comment period—is crucial from the public's standpoint. During this time, anyone, whether a private business, a teenager, a state government official, or another federal official, may submit comments to the agency proposing the regulation.

Time to Comment. A federal agency must usually give the public at least 30 days to comment on a proposed regulation before its effective date. As a practical matter, federal agencies often give the public a much longer time, sometimes months, between proposal and the end of the comment period.

Form for Comment. Comments do not have to follow any particular form; a simple letter directed to the proposing agency is sufficient. A member of the public could say several things in a comment. Comments are usually critical of agency-proposed regulations. Consider the comment letter submitted by the Virginia Independent Automobile Dealers Association (Figure 7.3) in response to the FTC's proposed regulation in Figure 7.2. Note that both comments are critical but in different ways. The car club comment believes the proposed regulation should exempt them. The used car dealers, who will bear the regulation's burden, believe the proposed regulation is too tough.

What Agencies Must Do with Comments. After the comment period, the APA directs the agency to "consider" the relevant material presented. This consideration could lead the agency to promulgate the rules as they were proposed or to modify the proposed regulations to take the comments into account, or withdraw the regulations.

FIGURE 7.3 A Comment to a Proposed Regulation

VIRGINIA INDEPENDENT AUTOMOBILE DEALERS ASSOCIATION

SUITE 113 NO. 1 KOGER EXECUTIVE CENTER
NORFOLK, VA. 23502 PHONE (804) 461-1038

March 19, 1976

Ms. Joan Z. Bernstein
Acting Director
Bureau of Consumer Protection
Federal Trade Commission
Washington, D.C. 20580

Dear Ms. Bernstein:

I have just finished reading and absorbing the contents of the proposed TRR concerning the Used Car Industry prepared by Mr. Edward Steinman and his staff. To say I feel chagrin would be the gross understatement of the century. I could hardly believe the proposal or the pseudo authority upon which it was reportedly based....

All through this proposal Mr. Steinman repeatedly refers to an article entitled "The Used Car Game" written by Joy Browne. Who is Joy Browne? By what stretch of the imagination does she qualify as an expert in the Used Car Industry? He also repeatedly refers to various newspaper articles written by innumberable reporters as a basis for the Commission to go along with this proposal. Again I ask by what authority do the authors of these various articles qualify as an "expert" in the Used Motor Vehicle Industry?...

Sincerely,

W.H. Wilcox

W.H. Wilcox
Executive Director
WHW/lfk

CC: Dr. G. Williams Whitehurst, Congressman Second Congressional District of Virginia

Why Comment. The principal importance of commenting lies in the public's ability to suggest changes in proposed regulations before they become law. In effect, the public is helping the agency write its regulations. As a practical matter, an agency need do nothing with public comments: The APA only tells agencies to consider comments. However, agencies do read, consider, and sometimes modify or even totally withdraw proposed regulations in response to comments. An example occurred when the Securities and Exchange Commission withdrew its proposed regulation that would have encouraged earnings projections in financial statements.[3] Public comments can significantly influence regulations.

Step 6. The Agency Promulgates, Modifies, or Withdraws the Regulation

After the public comment period closes, the APA tells the federal agency proposing the regulation to consider the comments. The APA does not require that the agency write letters to all the commenters with the agency's reaction to the comments, nor does the APA require that the agency promulgate the regulation.

An agency can do three basic things after the public comment period ends: promulgate the regulation, modify the regulation and either promulgate it as modified or repropose it for another round of public comments with an eye toward eventual promulgation, or withdraw the regulation. Let us examine each of these alternatives.

Promulgate Now. If the agency is making a regulation on a topic that is noncontroversial, is knowledgeable about the matter to be regulated, and has no staffing, budgetary, or other problems, the regulation would probably be promulgated as proposed after the comment period ends. For an example of the promulgated used car regulation, see Figure 7.4.

Modify and Repropose. Suppose the agency does not have a full understanding of the problem or the subject matter is controversial. In such cases the public comments could educate agency personnel by pointing out flaws in the proposed regulations. This process is a great help to federal agencies and could prevent an ineffective or overly burdensome proposed regulation from ever being promulgated. It may be the greatest service a business or member of the public could provide in the entire regulatory process, and it does not cost much to make a comment. Furthermore, the number and nature of public comments indicate the extent of interest in a problem. Strongly adverse or favorable public comments signal likelihood of future success to an agency for a regulatory program.

Withdraw. Comments to an agency's proposed regulation sometimes indicate overwhelming criticism. In effect, the proposal is a dud, a trial balloon shot down for one reason or another. The proposing agency may withdraw the proposed regulation and throw it out.

Step 7. Challenges in Court to the Promulgated Regulation

After an agency promulgates a regulation, it has the practical effect of law; however, legal ways are available to challenging a regulation after promulgation. According to the APA, such challenges can occur if the regulation does any of the following:

1. Violates the U.S. Constitution
2. Is arbitrary, capricious, an abuse of discretion, or otherwise not in accordance with law
3. Is beyond the authority (*ultra vires*) of the enabling act

[3] 41 *Fed. Reg.* 19,982 (1976).

FIGURE 7.5 Promulgated Used Car Regulation

PART 455-USED MOTOR VEHICLE TRADE REGULATION RULE

Sec.
455.1 General duties of a used vehicle dealer, definitions.
455.2 Consumer sales-window form.
455.3 Window form.
455.4 Contrary statements.
455.5 Spanish language sales.
455.6 State exemptions.
455.7 Severability.

Authority: 88 Stat. 2189, 15 U.S.C. 2309; 38 Stat. 717, as amended 15 U.S.C. 41 et seq.

§ 455.1 General duties of a used vehicle dealer; definitions.

(a) It is a deceptive act or practice for any used vehicle dealer, when that dealer sells or offers for sale a used vehicle in or affecting commerce as "commerce" is defined in the Federal Trade commission Act:
(1) To misrepresent the mechanical condition of a used vehicle;
(2) To misrepresent the terms of any warranty offered in connection with the sale of a used vehicle; and
(3) To represent that a used vehicle is sold with a warranty when the vehicle is sold without any warranty.

(b) It is an unfair act or practice for any used vehicle dealer, when that dealer sells or offers for sale a used vehicle in or affecting commerce as "commerce" is defined in the Federal Trade Commission Act:
(1) To fail to disclose, prior to sale, that a used vehicle is sold without any warranty; and
(2) To fail to make available, prior to sale, the terms of any written warranty offered in connection with the sale of a used vehicle.

(c) The Commission has adopted this Rule in order to prevent the unfair deceptive acts or practices defined in paragraphs (a) and (b). It is a violation of this Rule for any used vehicle dealer to fail to comply with the requirements set forth in §§ 455.2 through 455.5 of this part. If a used vehicle dealer complies with the requirements of §§ 455.2 through 455.5 of this part, the dealer does not violate this Rule.

(d) The following definitions shall apply for purposes of this part:
(1) "Vehicle" means any motorized vehicle, other than a motorcycle, with a gross vehicle weight rating (GVWR) of less than 8500 lbs., a curb weight of less than 6,000 lbs., and a frontal area of less than 46 sq. ft.
(2) "Used vehicle" means any vehicle driven more than the limited use necessary in moving or road testing a new vehicle prior to delivery to a consumer, but does not include any vehicle sold only for scrap or parts (title documents surrendered to the state and a salvage certificate issued).
(3) "Dealer" means any person or business which sells or offers for sale a used vehicle after selling or offering for sale five (5) or more used vehicles in the previous twelve months, but does not include a bank or financial institution, a business selling a used vehicle to an employee of that business, or a lessor selling a leased vehicle by or to that vehicle's lessee or to an employee of the lessee.
(4) "Consumer" means any person who is not a used vehicle dealer.
(5) "Warranty" means any undertaking in writing, in connection with the sale by a dealer of a used vehicle, to refund, repair, replace, maintain or take other action with respect to such used vehicle and provided at no extra charge beyond the price of the used vehicle.
(6) "Implied warranty" means an implied warranty arising under state law (as modified by the Magnuson-Moss Act) in connection with the sale by a dealer of a used vehicle.
(7) "Service contract" means a contract in writing for any period of time or any specific mileage to refund, repair, replace, or maintain a used vehicle, and provided at an extra charge beyond the price of the used vehicle, provided that such contract is not regulated in your state as the business of insurance.
(8) "You" means any dealer, or any agent or employee of a dealer, except where the term appears on the window form required by § 455.2(a).

§ 455.2 Consumer sales—window form.

(a) *General duty.* Before you offer a used vehicle for sale to a consumer, you must prepare, fill in as applicable and display on that vehicle a "Buyers Guide" as required by this Rule.
(1) Use a side window to display the form so both sides of the form can be read, with the title "Buyers Guide" facing to the outside. You may remove a form temporarily from the window during any test drive, but you must return it as soon as the test drive is over.
(2) The capitalization, punctuation and wording of all items, headings, and text on the form must be exactly as required by this Rule. The entire form must be printed in 100% black ink on a white stock no smaller than 11 inches high by 7¼ inches wide in the type styles, sizes and format indicated. . . .

Download the Buyer's Guide from www.ftc.gov/bcp/menu-auto.htm.

FIGURE 7.5 Promulgated Used Car Regulation, continued

When filling out the form, follow the directions in (b) through (e) of this section and § 455.4 of this part.

(b) *Warranties—(I) No Implied Warranty—"As Is"/No Warranty.* (i) If you offer the vehicle without any implied warranty, *ie.* "as is," mark the box provided. If you offer the vehicle with implied warranties only, substitute the disclosure specified below, and mark the box provided. If you first offer the vehicle "as is" or with implied warranties only but then sell it with a warranty, cross out the "As Is—No Warranty" or "Implied Warranties Only" disclosure and fill in the warranty terms in accordance with paragraph (b) (2) of this section. (ii) If your state law limits or prohibits "as is" sales of vehicles, that state law overrides this part and this rule does not give you the right to sell "as is." In such states, the heading "As Is—No Warranty" and the paragraph immediately accompanying that phrase must be deleted from the form, and the following heading and paragraph must be substituted: If you sell vehicles in states that permit "as is" sales, but you choose to offer implied warranties only, you must also use the following disclosure instead of "As Is—No Warranty."[1]

Implied Warranties Only

This means that the dealer does not make any specific promises to fix things that need repair when you buy the vehicle or after the time of sale. But, state law "implied warranties" may give you some rights to have the dealer take care of serious problems that were not apparent when you bought the vehicle.

(2) *Full/Limited Warranty.* If you offer the vehicle with a warranty, briefly describe the warranty terms in the space provided. This description must include the following warranty information:

(i) Whether the warranty offered is "Full" or "Limited." [2] Mark the box next to the appropriate designation.

(ii) Which of the specific systems are covered (for example, "engine, transmission, differential). You cannot use shorthand, such as "drive train" or "power train" for covered systems.

(iii) The duration (for example, "30 days or 1,000 miles, whichever occurs first").

(iv) The percentage of the repair cost paid by you (for example, "The dealer will pay 100% of the labor and 100% of the parts.").

(v) If the vehicle is still under the manufacturer's original warranty, you may add the following paragraph below the "Full/Limited Warranty" disclosure: MANUFACTURER'S WARRANTY STILL APPLIES. The manufacturer's original warranty has not expired on the vehicle. Consult the manufacturer's warranty booklet for details as to warranty coverage, service location, etc. If, following negotiations, you and the buyer agree to changes in the warranty coverage, mark the changes on the form as appropriate. If you first offer the vehicle with a warranty, but then sell it without one, cross out offered warranty and mark either the "As Is—No Warranty" box or the "Implied Warranties Only" box, as appropriate.

(3) *Service contracts.* If you make a service contract (other than a contract that is regulated in your state as the business of insurance) available on the vehicle, you must add the following heading and paragraph below the "Full/Limited Warranty" disclosure and mark the box provided.[3]

Service Contract

A service contract is available at an extra charge on this vehicle. If you buy a service contract within 90 days of the time of sale, state law "implied warranties" may give you additional rights.

(c) *Name and Address.* Put the name and address of your dealership in the space provided. If you do not have a dealership, use the name and address of your place of business (for example, your service station) or your own name and home address.

(d) *Make, Model, Model Year VIN.* Put the vehicle's name (for example "Chevrolet"), model (for example, "Vega"), model year, and Vehicle Identification Number (VIN) in the spaces provided. You may write the dealer stock number in the space provided or you may leave this space blank.

(e) *Complaints.* In the space provided, put the name and telephone number of the person who should be contacted if any complaints arise after sale.

§ 455.3 Window form.

(a) *Form given to buyer.* Give the buyer of a used vehicle sold by you the window form displayed under § 455.2 containing all of the disclosures required by the Rule and reflecting the warranty coverage agreed upon. If you prefer, you may give the buyer a copy of the original, so long as that copy accurately reflects all of the disclosures required by the Rule and the warranty coverage agreed upon.

(b) *Incorporated into contract.* The information on the final version of the window form is incorporated into the contract of sale for each used vehicle you sell to a consumer. Information on the window form overrides any contrary provisions in the contract of sale. To inform the consumer of these facts, include the following language conspicuously in each consumer contract of sale:

Magnuson-Moss Warranty Act does not apply to vehicles manufactured before July 4, 1975. Therefore, if you choose not to designate "Full" or "limited" for such cars, cross out both designations, leaving only "Warranty."

Violates the U.S. Constitution. A regulation that violates the U.S. Constitution is invalid. A regulation is presumed valid until a court decides otherwise. This standard applies whether it is a federal, state, or municipal regulation. Examples of an unconstitutional regulation are as follows:

1. At the federal level, the Internal Revenue Service's (IRS) promulgating a regulation that allows IRS agents to secretly enter private businesses without the owner's approval would violate the Fourth Amendment's unreasonable search and seizure prohibition.
2. At the state level, the state real estate licensing board's promulgating a regulation prohibiting people of Japanese ancestry from sitting for the state real estate licensing exam would violate the Fourteenth Amendment's equal protection clause.

Is Arbitrary, Capricious, Etc. The terminology "arbitrary, capricious, an abuse of discretion, or otherwise not in accordance with law" refers to several reasons why agency regulations could be invalid. Evidence must exist to support agency regulations. Courts use two tests to determine whether the studies and data that agencies use to justify regulations are sufficient: (1) arbitrary, capricious, an abuse of discretion, and (2) substantial evidence.

The arbitrary, capricious, and abuse of discretion (A-C-A) standard controls informal rulemaking. This standard is more lenient than the substantial evidence test. It allows agencies to makes rules with fewer data, and studies and less evidence than the substantial evidence standard. The substantial evidence (SE) test is used for hybrid and formal rulemaking and any other rulemaking where a statute specifically requires it.

Ethyl Corp. v. Environmental Protection Agency illustrates that the arbitrary, capricious, and abuse test applies when agencies promulgate regulations.

Ethyl Corp. v. Environmental Protection Agency

U.S. Court of Appeals (D.C. Cir.)
541 F.2d 1 (1976)

Background and Facts:

Lead "antiknock" compounds, when added to gasoline, dramatically increase the fuel's octane rating. Increased octane allows for higher compression engines, which operate with greater efficiency. Since 1923 antiknocks have been added to gasoline, and a large industry has developed to supply these compounds. Today, approximately 90 percent of motor gasoline manufactured in the United States contains lead additives, even though most 1975 and 1976 model automobiles are equipped with catalytic converters, which require lead-free gasoline. From the beginning, however, scientists have questioned whether the addition of lead to gasoline, and its consequent diffusion into the atmosphere from the automobile emission, poses a threat to public health.... The reasons for concern are obvious (and essentially undisputed by Ethyl Corp. and the other petitioners who challenge the no-lead regulations): (1) lead in high concentrations in the body is toxic; (2) lead can be absorbed into the body from the ambient air; (3) lead particulate emissions from gasoline engines account for approximately 90 percent of the lead in our air. Despite these apparent reasons for concern, hard proof of any danger caused by lead auto emissions has been hard to come by because of the multiple sources of human exposure to lead.

Lead is found in the land, in the sea, in plants, in animals, and, ultimately, in humans. Traces of lead ranging from 10 to 40 micrograms per 100 grams of blood (10-40 mg/100g) are found in everyone, including those living in environments with almost no atmospheric lead. [National Academy of Sciences Report or NASR]

Human body lead comes from three major sources. In most people, the largest source is the diet. EPA estimates daily dietary lead intake for adults average 200–300 mg per day, with a range of 100–500 mg a day.... Absorption of dietary lead into the bloodstream is estimated at about 10 percent, although in children absorption may be as high as 50 percent. Thus, the average adult adds 20–30 mg of lead to his/her bloodstream from his/her diet alone. This daily intake, which may be highly variable depending on individual diets . . . is generally regarded as, for all practical purposes, uncontrollable.

A second major source, ingestion of lead paint by children with pica (the abnormal ingestion of nonfood substances, a relatively common trait in preschool children, particularly ages 1–3), is generally regarded as "the principal environmental source in cases of severe acute lead poisoning in young children." [NASR] . . . Limited control has been achieved in that lead paints are now rarely used, and are frequently banned by statute for interior surfaces.

The last remaining major source of lead exposure for humans is the ambient air. This source is easily the most controllable, since approximately 90 percent of lead in the air comes from automobile emissions, and can be simply eliminated by removing lead from gasoline. . . . Once lead is in the body, its source becomes irrelevant; all lead in the bloodstream is essentially fungible. Thus, so long as there are multiple sources of lead exposure it is virtually impossible to isolate one source and determine its particular effect on the body. The effect of any one source is meaningful only in cumulative terms. . . .

For years the lead antiknock industry has refused to accept the developing evidence that lead emissions contribute significantly to the total human lead body burden. In the Clean Air Amendments of 1970 . . . Congress finally set up a legal mechanism by which that evidence could be weighed in a more objective tribunal. It gave the newly created EPA authority to control . . . any fuel additive whose emission "will endanger the public health or welfare." . . . It is beyond question that the fuel additive Congress had in mind was lead.

EPA published on January 31, 1971, advance notice of proposed rulemaking to regulate lead in gasoline. . . . Proposed regulations were issued one year later on February 23, 1972 supported by a document *Health Hazards of Lead*. Comments were invited for a 90-day period and were reopened for another 30 days. Public hearings were also held on these matters in Washington, D.C., Dallas, and Los Angeles. After a series of proposals and reproposals of no-lead regulations, the Natural Resources Defense Council [NRDC], a private environmental group, sued EPA to force it to promulgate the no-lead regulations pursuant to the Clean Air Act. Finally, on October 28, 1973, as a result of the NRDC lawsuit, EPA was ordered to publish a final decision as to whether lead additives should be regulated for health reasons. On November 28, 1973, EPA released its third health study on no-lead regulations and also promulgated its no-lead regulations. Lead additive manufacturers including Ethyl Corp. sued EPA on grounds that its no-lead regulations violated the Administrative Procedure Act's "arbitrary and capricious" standard.

Body of Opinion

Judge J. Skelly Wright

In promulgating the low-lead regulations . . . EPA engaged in informal rule-making. . . . Our review of the evidence . . . requires us to strike "agency action, findings, and conclusions" that we find to be "arbitrary, capricious, and abuse of discretion, or otherwise not in accordance with law." . . . This standard of review is a highly deferential one. It presumes agency action to be valid. . . . Moreover, it forbids the court's substituting its judgment for that of the agency . . . and requires affirmance if a rational basis exists for the agency's decision. . . .

This is not to say, however, that we must rubber-stamp the agency decision as correct. To do so would render the appellate process a superfluous (although time-consuming) ritual. Rather, the reviewing court must assure itself that the agency decision was "based on a consideration of the relevant factors." . . . Moreover, it must engage in a "substantial inquiry" into the facts, one that is "searching and careful." . . . This is particularly true in highly technical cases such as this one. . . .

There is no inconsistency between the deferential standard of review and the requirement that the reviewing court involve itself in even the most complex evidentiary matters. . . . The immersion in the evidence is designed *solely* to enable the court to determine whether the agency decision was rational and based on consideration of the relevant factors....It is settled that we must affirm decisions with which we disagree so long as this test is met. . . .

Thus, after our careful study of the record, we must take a step back from the agency decision. We must look at the decision not as the chemist, biologist or statistician that we are qualified neither by training nor experience to be, but as a reviewing court exercising our narrowly defined duty of holding agencies to certain minimal standards of rationality. . . . We must affirm unless the agency decision is arbitrary or capricious. . . .

Under Section 211(c)(1)(A) the Administrator may, on the basis of all the information available to him, promulgate regulations that

> control or prohibit the manufacture, introduction into commerce, offering for sale, or sale of any fuel or fuel additive for use in a motor vehicle or motor vehicle engine (A) if any emission products of such fuel additive will endanger the public health or welfare.

The Administrator cannot act under Section 211 . . . however, until after "consideration of all relevant medical and scientific evidence available to him, including consideration of other technologically or economically feasible means of achieving emission standards." . . .

In making his threshold determination that lead particulate emissions from motor vehicles "will endanger the public health or welfare," the Administrator provided his interpretation of the statutory language by couching his conclusion in these words: such emissions "present a significant risk of harm to the health of city children."...

Ethyl Corporation and other petitioners argue that the "will endanger" standard requires a high quantum of factual proof, proof of actual harm rather than of a "significant risk of harm."... Since, according to petitioners, regulations under section 211... must be premised upon actual proof of actual harm, the Administrator has, in their view, no power to assess risks or make policy judgments in deciding to regulate lead additives. Moreover, petitioners argue, regulation must be based on the danger presented by lead additives "in and of themselves," so it is improper to consider, as the Administrator did, the cumulative impact of lead additives on all other sources of human exposure to lead....

The Precautionary Nature of "Will Endanger." Simply as a matter of plain meaning, we have difficulty crediting petitioners' reading of the "will endanger" standard. The meaning of "endanger" is not disputed. Case law and dictionary definition agree that endanger means something less than actual harm. When one is endangered, harm is *threatened*; no actual injury need ever occur. Thus, for example, a town may be "endangered" by a threatening plague or hurricane and yet emerge from the danger completely unscathed. A statute allowing for regulation in the face of danger is, necessarily, a precautionary statute. Regulatory action may be taken before the threatened harm occurs; indeed, the very existence of such precautionary legislation would seem to *demand* that regulatory action precede, and, optimally, prevent the perceived threat. As should be apparent the "will endanger" language of Section 211... makes it such a precautionary statute.

The Administrator read it as such, interpreting "will endanger" to mean "presents a significant risk of harm."... We agree with the Administrator's interpretation. This conclusion is reached not only by reference to the plain meaning of the statute, but by juxtaposition of Section 211... with other sections of the Clean Air Act....

Summary of the Evidence From a vast mass of evidence the Administrator has concluded that the emission products of lead additives will endanger the public health. He has handled an extraordinarily complicated problem with great care and candor. The evidence did not necessarily always point in one direction and frequently, until EPA authorized research, there was no evidence at all. The Administrator reached his conclusion only after hearings spread over several months, consideration of thousands of pages of documents, publication of three health documents, three formal comment periods, and receipt of hundreds of comments. Each study was considered independently; its worth was assessed only after it was measured against any critical comments. From the totality of the evidence the Administrator concluded that regulation under Section 211... was warranted.

Judgment and Result

The U.S. Court of Appeals held that the arbitrary and capricious standard justified its upholding EPA's no-lead regulations.

Questions

1. What is the relation between the studies the regulator (EPA or the EPA Administrator here) uses to develop regulations and the arbitrary and capricious standard? Did EPA satisfy this standard when it regulated the lead in gasoline?
2. What would have to occur to the public's health if the Ethyl Corporation's interpretation of Section 211 of the Clean Air Act were followed? Would people have to actually experience illness before lead could be regulated? Who made the statutory decision to regulate lead in gasoline using the "will endanger standard"? Who made the regulatory decision? If someone wanted to blame EPA for regulating lead in gasoline hastily who should be assigned responsibility?
3. An environmental group (National Resources Defense Council) had to sue EPA to get it to perform its statutory duty to regulate lead under the Clean Air Act. What does this say about regulatory agencies? About the need for private environmental groups? Note in the Environmental Law chapter how many plaintiffs are private environmental groups.
4. Does lead have a helpful, harmful, or neutral effect on the human body? If the three major sources of lead in humans are diet, lead-based paint in the environment ingested by children, and air-born lead, as EPA concedes, why should the manufacturers of lead in gasoline be singled out for regulation? Is this not placing the burden for addressing a problem on one, albeit an important one, sector of society? How can this be justified?
5. How technically qualified are judges to assess the scientific studies that form the basis of regulations such as the no-lead regulations? Does the commenting process assist the judges in their job? How?
6. Of the several studies showing effects of lead on humans were these studies consistent in what they showed or was it simply a question of degree and not kind? Did EPA suppress these studies? How did it make them available to the public?

7. What was the nature of the rulemaking process that the EPA used to develop the no-lead regulations? The court at one point states that it was the informal rulemaking process and yet it notes that the EPA did hold public hearings during the rulemaking process. In so noting, what type of rulemaking actually was occurring?
8. What should happen to the evidentiary standard by which a regulation is judged if the regulation is, in fact, hybrid in nature? What evidentiary standard was used? Is there really any difference between the arbitrary and capricious standard as opposed to the substantial evidence test?

Is Beyond the Authority (Ultra Vires) of the Enabling Act. As discussed, an administrative agency may make a regulation only if the legislature gives it the power. Administrative agencies have no inherent power to make substantive regulations. A valid enabling act transferring regulation-making power from the legislature to the agency must exist.

An administrative agency acts *ultra vires* when it either makes regulations beyond the authority the enabling act grants or makes regulations where no enabling act exists at all. When an agency acts *ultra vires,* the courts discipline the agency by invalidating the regulation. *Ernst & Ernst v. Hochfelder* provides such an example. The enabling act in that case is the Securities Exchange Act of 1934. An important part of that act is Section 10b, which lets the Securities and Exchange Commission (SEC) make regulations covering fraud (which involves "scienter," meaning "intent"). However, Section 10b of the act does not empower the SEC to make regulations covering *negligent* misrepresentations. In the *Hochfelder* case the U.S. Supreme Court was asked whether part of SEC Rule 10b-5 was *ultra vires* (outside the power granted by) Section 10b of the Securities Exchange Act of 1934.

Ernst & Ernst v. Hochfelder

U.S. Supreme Court
425 U.S. 185 (1976)

Background and Facts:

Ernst & Ernst, an independent public accounting firm, audited a stockbroker. The stockbroker sold fraudulent securities to several investors, and the investors lost money on the securities. The investors sued the accounting firm under Section 10b of the Securities and Exchange Act and rule 10b-5 for negligently auditing the stockbroker. The investors claimed that if the accounting firm had audited the stockbroker properly, it would have uncovered the fraud. Rule 10b-5 made the accountants liable for negligent audits. The accountants argued that the enabling act (the SEC Act) prohibited fraud only, not negligence. Therefore, the accountants maintained that part of Rule 10b-5 was *ultra vires* the enabling act. As a result, they argued the rule was invalid when it tried to cover negligence.

Body of Opinion

Justice Powell

We have addressed, to this point, primarily the language and history of §10(b). The Commission contends, however, that subsections (b) and (c) of Rule 10b-5 are cast in language which—if standing alone—could encompass both intentional and negligent behavior. These subsections respectively provide that it is unlawful "[t]o make any untrue statement of a material fact or to omit to state a material fact necessary in order to make the statements made, in the light of the circumstances under which they were made, not misleading . . ." and "[t]o engage in any act, practice, or course of business which operates or would operate as a fraud or deceit upon any person. . . ."

Viewed in isolation the language of subsection (b), and arguably that of subsection (c), could be read as proscribing, respectively, any type of material misstatement or omission, and any course of conduct, that has the effect of defrauding investors, whether the wrong-doing was intentional or not.

We note first that such a reading cannot be harmonized with the administrative history of the Rule, a history making clear that when the Commission adopted the Rule it was intended to apply only to activities that involved scienter. More importantly, Rule 10b-5 was adopted pursuant to authority granted the Commission under §10(b). The rulemaking power granted to an administrative agency charged with the administration of a federal statute is not the power to make law. Rather, it is "the power to adopt regulations to carry into effect the will of Congress as expressed by the statute." Thus, despite the broad view of the Rule advanced by the Commission in this case, its scope cannot exceed the power granted the Commission by Congress under §10(b). For the reasons stated above, we think the Commission's original interpretation of Rule 10b-5 was compelled by the language and history of §10(b) and related sections of the Acts. . . . When a statute speaks so specifically in terms of manipulation and deception, and of implementing devices and contrivances—the commonly understood terminology of intentional wrong-doing—and when its history reflects no more expansive intent, we are quite unwilling to extend the scope of the statute to negligent conduct. . . .

Judgment and Result

Rule 10b-5 was partly invalid. Specifically, the part of the rule covering negligent acts was invalid because a rule must be within the authority of the enabling act. In this case, the enabling act was the Securities and Exchange Act of 1934. It let the SEC make rules covering fraud. It did not let the SEC make regulations covering negligence. Therefore, when Rule 10b-5 covered negligence, it went beyond the enabling act and was invalid to the extent it did so.

Questions

1. Had the public accounting firm (Ernst & Ernst) committed fraud when it audited the brokerage firm's books? Had it committed negligence?
2. Did the SEC's Rule 10b-5 cover negligence? Did the enabling act (Section 10(b) of the 1934 Securities Exchange Act) cover negligence? What is wrong with a regulation that covers more than its enabling act?

Step 8. An Agency Enforces Valid Reg Through Investigation, Prosecution, and Administration

The executive function of an administrative agency includes such matters as issuing permits and licenses. These tasks often involve testing for practitioner competence as realtors, engineers, or accountants. It also includes the agency's prosecution for violations of its statutes and regulations.

Permits and Licenses. Not all agencies issue permits or licenses; however, the essence of administering many agency statutes and regulations often involves permits. For example, much of the almost 100-page Clean Water Act boils down to getting a permit to discharge anything into U.S. waters.

Prosecuting. If a person, business, or other entity violates a permit or an administrative statute or regulation, the agency enforcing the act or regulation must generally prove the violation. In other words, people are innocent of administrative violations until proven guilty. Prosecutorial discretion applies here: Namely, the agency may prosecute whomever it chooses, subject only to its judgment about the strength of each case, staff resources, and other factors known only to prosecutors.

Searches and Investigations: Police and FBI. Agencies must gather evidence to prove regulatory or statutory violations. Many times, alleged regulatory violations occur on private property such as in a factory, home, or store. The Fourth Amendment to the U.S. Constitution says that warrantless searches by government officials are illegal; however, in certain exceptional cases, warrantless searches by law enforcement officials are allowed.

Administrative Searches Today. Do administrative officials, not police or the FBI, need search warrants to do administrative searches? In two cases, *Camara*[4] and *See*,[5] the Supreme Court decided that administrative officials must have search warrants to do health and other administrative searches of homes (*Camara*) and businesses (*See*),

[4] *Camara* v. *Municipal Ct.*, 387 U.S. 523 (1967).
[5] *See* v. *City of Seattle*, 387 U.S. 541 (1967).

unless the owner consents or an emergency exists. The Supreme Court modified its "administrators need a search warrant" rule in the later cases of *Colonnade*[6] and *Biswell*.[7] In those cases, the Court said that where a business is pervasively regulated (liquor in *Colonnade* and firearms in *Biswell*), the business expects no privacy. The Fourth Amendment's rule against warrantless searches does not apply; that is, warrantless searches of pervasively regulated businesses are legal. Then came the *Barlow's* case in 1978. In *Marshall v. Barlow's*, Bill Barlow demanded a search warrant before he would let the OSHA inspector onto his premises. The OSHA statute expressly allowed inspectors to enter private property without search warrants to see if OSHA regulations were being obeyed. Was the OSHA statutory right-of-entry provision for inspectors valid or invalid? The U.S. Supreme Court answered in *Marshall v. Barlow's*.

Marshall v. Barlow's, Inc.

U.S. Supreme Court
436 U.S. 307 (1978)

Background and Facts:

The Occupational Safety and Health Act (OSHA) lets government inspectors search nonpublic work areas of businesses to find OSHA violations. An OSHA inspector went to Barlow's, an electrical and plumbing business in Pocatello, Idaho. He asked Bill Barlow, the president and manager, if he could inspect the business's work areas. Barlow asked and found that there were no complaints and that the inspector had no search warrant. Barlow would not let the inspector enter. The government sued for and got an admission order. Barlow went to court to stop the inspector from entering. The court enjoined (stopped) the OSHA inspector's entry saying that the Fourth Amendment requires a warrant for this kind of search. The court held OSHA's warrantless search provision unconstitutional. The government (secretary of labor) appealed to the U.S. Supreme Court.

Body of Opinion

Justice White

The Secretary urges that warrantless inspections to enforce OSHA are reasonable within the meaning of the Fourth Amendment. Among other things, he relies on §8(a) of the Act, which authorizes inspection of business premises without a warrant and which the Secretary urges represents a congressional construction of the Fourth Amendment that the courts should not reject. Regrettably, we are unable to agree.

The Warrant Clause of the Fourth Amendment protects commercial buildings as well as private homes. To hold otherwise would belie the origin of that Amendment, and the American colonial experience. An important forerunner of the first 10 Amendments to the United States Constitution, the Virginia Bill of Rights, specifically opposed "general warrants, whereby an officer or messenger may be commanded to search suspected places without evidence of a fact committed." The general warrant was a recurring point of contention in the Colonies immediately preceding the Revolution. The particular offensiveness it engendered was acutely felt by the merchants and businessmen whose premises and products were inspected for compliance with the several parliamentary revenue measures that most irritated the colonists. "[T]he Fourth Amendment's commands grew in large measure out of the colonists' experience with the writs of assistance . . . [that] granted sweeping power to customs officials and other agents of the King to search at large for smuggled goods." Against this background, it is untenable that the ban on warrantless searches was not intended to shield places of business as well as of residence.

This Court has already held that warrantless searches are generally unreasonable, and that this rule applies to commercial premises as well as homes. In *Camara v. Municipal Court*, we held:

> [E]xcept in certain carefully defined classes of cases, a search of private property without proper consent is "unreasonable" unless it has been authorized by a valid search warrant.

On the same day, we also ruled:

> As we explained in *Camara*, a search of private houses is presumptively unreasonable if conducted without a warrant. The business man, like the occupant of a residence, has a constitutional right to go about his business free from unreasonable official entries upon his private commercial property. The

[6] *Colonnade Catering Corp.* v. *United States*, 397 U.S. 72 (1970).
[7] *United States* v. *Biswell*, 406 U.S. 311 (1972).

businessman, too, has that right placed in jeopardy if the decision to enter and inspect for violation of regulatory laws can be made and enforced by the inspector in the field without official authority evidenced by a warrant. *See v. Seattle.*

These same cases also held that the Fourth Amendment prohibition against unreasonable searches protects against warrantless intrusions during civil as well as criminal investigations. . . . The reason is found in the 'basic purposes of this Amendment . . . [which] is to safeguard the privacy and security of individuals against arbitrary invasions by governmental officials.' . . . If the government intrudes on a person's property, the privacy interest suffers whether the government's motivation is to investigate violations of criminal laws or breaches of other statutory or regulatory standards. It therefore appears that unless some recognized exception to the warrant requirements applies, *See v. Seattle* would require a warrant to conduct the inspection sought in this case.

The Secretary urges that an exception from the search warrant requirement has been recognized for "pervasively regulated business[es]," and for "closely regulated" industries long subject to "close supervision and inspection." These cases are indeed exceptions, but they represent responses to relatively unique circumstances. Certain industries have such a history of government oversight that no reasonable expectation of privacy could exist for a proprietor over the stock of such an enterprise. Liquor (*Colonnade*) and firearms (*Biswell*) are industries of this type; when an entrepreneur embarks upon such a business, he has voluntarily chosen to subject himself to a full arsenal of governmental regulation.

Industries such as these fall within the "certain carefully defined classes of cases," referenced in *Camara*, 387 U.S., at 528. The element that distinguishes these enterprises from ordinary businesses is a long tradition of close government supervision, of which any person who chooses to enter such a business must already be aware. "A central difference between those cases [*Colonnade* and *Biswell*] and this one is that businessmen engaged in such federally licensed and regulated enterprises accept the burdens as well as the benefits of their trade, whereas the petitioner here was not engaged in any regulated or licensed business. The businessman in a regulated industry in effect consents to the restrictions placed upon him." . . .

The clear import of our cases is that the closely regulated industry of the type involved in *Colonnade* and *Biswell* is the exception. The Secretary would make it the rule. Invoking the Walsh-Healey Act of 1936, the Secretary attempts to support a conclusion that all businesses involved in interstate commerce have long been subjected to close supervision of employee safety and health conditions. But the degree of federal involvement in employee working circumstances has never been of the order of specificity and pervasiveness that OSHA mandates. It is quite unconvincing to argue that the imposition of minimum wages and maximum hours on employers who contracted with the Government under the Walsh-Healey Act prepared the entirety of American interstate commerce for regulation of working conditions to the minutest detail. Nor can any but the most fictional sense of voluntary consent to later searches be found in the single fact that one conducts a business affecting interstate commerce; under current practice and law, few businesses can be conducted without having some effect on interstate commerce. . . .

The critical fact in this case is that entry over Mr. Barlow's objection is being sought by a Government agent. Employees are not being prohibited from reporting OSHA violations. What they observe in their daily functions is undoubtedly beyond the employer's reasonable expectation of privacy. The Government inspector, however, is not an employee. Without a warrant he stands in no better position than a member of the public. What is observable by the public is observable, without a warrant, by the Government inspector as well. The owner of a business has not, by the necessary utilization of employees in his operation, thrown open the areas where employees alone are permitted to the warrantless scrutiny of Government agents. That an employee is free to report, and the Government is free to use, any evidence of noncompliance with OSHA that the employee observes furnishes no justification for federal agents to enter a place of business from which the public is restricted and to conduct their own warrantless search. . . .

The Secretary submits that warrantless inspections are essential to the proper enforcement of OSHA because they afford the opportunity to inspect without prior notice and hence to preserve the advantages of surprise. While the dangerous conditions outlawed by the Act include structural defects that cannot be quickly hidden or remedied, the Act also regulates a myriad of safety details that may be amenable to speedy alteration or disguise. The risk is that during the interval between an inspector's initial request to search a plant and his procuring a warrant following the owner's refusal of permission, violations of this latter type could be corrected and thus escape the inspector's notice. To the suggestion that warrants may be issued *ex parte* and executed without delay and without prior notice, thereby preserving the element of surprise, the Secretary expresses concern for the administrative strain that would be experienced by the inspection system, and by the courts, should *ex parte* warrants issued in advance become standard practice.

We are unconvinced, however, that requiring warrants to inspect will impose serious burdens on the inspection system or the courts, will prevent inspections necessary to enforce the statute, or will make them less effective. In the first place, the great majority of businessmen can be expected in normal course to consent to inspection without warrant; the Secretary has not brought to this Court's attention any widespread pattern of refusal. In those cases where an owner does insist on a warrant, the Secretary argues that inspection efficiency will be impeded by the advance notice and delay. The Act's penalty provisions for giving advance notice of a search, . . . and the Secretary's own regulations, . . . indicate that surprise searches are indeed contemplated. . . . Nor is it immediately apparent why the advantages of surprise would be lost if, after being refused entry, procedures were available to the Secretary to seek an *ex parte* warrant and to reappear at the premises without further notice to the establishment being inspected.

Whether the Secretary proceeds to secure a warrant or other process, with or without prior notice, his entitlement to inspect will not depend on his demonstrating probable cause to believe that conditions in violation of OSHA exist on the premises. Probable cause in the criminal law sense is not required. For purposes of an administrative search such as this, probable cause justifying the issuance of a warrant may be based not only on specific evidence of an existing violation but also on a showing that "reasonable legislative or administrative standards for conducting an . . . inspection are satisfied with respect to a particular [establishment]." A warrant showing that a specific business has been chosen for an OSHA search on the basis of a general administrative plan for the enforcement of the Act derived from neutral sources such as, for example, dispersion of employees in various types of industries across a given area, and the desired frequency of searches in any of the lesser divisions of the area, would protect an employer's Fourth Amendment rights. We doubt that the consumption of enforcement energies in the obtaining of such warrants will exceed manageable proportions. . . .

Nor do we agree that the incremental protections afforded the employer's privacy by a warrant are so marginal that they fail to justify the administrative burdens that may be entailed. The authority to make warrantless searches devolves almost unbridled discretion upon executive and administrative officers, particularly those in the field, as to when to search and whom to search. A warrant, by contrast, would provide assurances from a neutral officer that the inspection is reasonable under the Constitution, is authorized by statute, and is pursuant to an administrative plan containing specific neutral criteria. Also, a warrant would then and there advise the owner of the scope and objects of the search, beyond which limits the inspector is not expected to proceed. These are important functions for a warrant to perform, functions which underlie the Court's prior decisions that the Warrant Clause applies to inspections for compliance with regulatory statutes.

We hold that Barlow's was entitled to a declaratory judgment that the Act is unconstitutional insofar as it purports to authorize inspections without warrant or its equivalent and to an injunction enjoining the Act's enforcement to that extent. The judgment of the District Court is therefore affirmed.

Judgment and Result

The Supreme Court said that OSHA warrantless searches are illegal unless the business consents. But the Supreme Court said the probable cause needed to obtain an OSHA search warrant is less than that required to get a *criminal* search warrant.

Questions

1. Did the Occupational Safety and Health Act give the OSHA inspector the right to enter businesses without a warrant? Why, then, did the U.S. Supreme Court say the OSHA inspector needed a search warrant?
2. If a business allows an OSHA inspector entry without a warrant, can the business later demand a warrant if the inspector finds several OSHA violations?

The General Rule. The *Barlow's* case sets out the general rule that search warrants are required before government inspectors can enter commercial facilities. But the *Colonnade* case (recognized in *Barlow's*) held that search warrants are not required in industries with a long history of pervasive regulation. Thus, in 1981 the U.S. Supreme Court held that federal mine safety inspectors needed no search warrant to inspect stone quarries. That case turned on whether the industry had a long history of government inspection. The U.S. Supreme Court said that it had. As a result, when government inspectors appear at a business, the manager must consider whether the particular business falls into the general rule of *Barlow's* (that is, the business can demand a search warrant before admitting the inspectors) or whether the business falls within the *Colonnade* exception (government inspectors may enter without a warrant when the industry has a long history of pervasive government regulation).

Practical Tip. As a practical matter, many businesses and individuals admit government inspectors into their factories, farms, and homes without a warrant. Sometimes they do it on the belief that a cooperative attitude will cause the inspectors to be forgiving as well as reasonable. The action also suggests nothing either to hide or to arouse suspicion. Finally, some agencies, such as the Occupational Safety and Health Administration (OSHA), will do courtesy inspections of a business before the official inspection to point out areas in which the business needs to improve its safety and health performance to comply with OSHA regulations and not be fined.

Administrative Sanctions. A final part of agency enforcement is punishing those who violate its regulations or statutes. Agencies do not have the power to punish someone criminally, mainly because agency procedures do not give defendants (called respondents) all of the constitutional protections courts provide, such as the right to jury trial. However, many regulatory statutes have criminal sanctions. Agencies such as the FTC must therefore ask the U.S. Justice Department to bring criminal charges when such statutes are violated. In such situations the Justice Department has prosecutorial discretion—the power to bring or not bring criminal charges.

Civil Penalties. Many statutes also give administrative agencies the power to assess civil penalties. They enable agencies to use the stick of punishment while avoiding the delay caused by all of the procedural protections given to criminal defendants.

In the *United States v. Ward* decision, the U.S. Supreme Court upheld the idea that federal administrative agencies can assess a civil penalty.

United States v. Ward

U.S. Supreme Court
448 U.S. 242 (1980)

Background and Facts:

The Clean Water Act prohibits the discharge of oil or hazardous substances into navigable U.S. waters. Violations can be punished with civil penalties of up to $5,000 per offense. The act also requires violators to report their violations to the U.S. Coast Guard, which sets the civil penalty for violators. Ward had an oil retention pit at a drilling site near Enid, Oklahoma. Oil escaped into Boggie Creek. Ward notified the Coast Guard of his violation. The Coast Guard (a federal agency in the Department of Transportation) imposed a civil penalty of $500 on Ward. Ward sued to stop collection of the penalty, claiming it violated his privilege against self-incrimination under the Fifth Amendment.

Body of Opinion

Justice Rehnquist

At the time this case arose §311(b)(3) of the act prohibited the discharge into navigable waters or onto adjoining shorelines of oil or hazardous substances in quantities determined by the President to be "harmful." Section 311(b)(5) of the Act imposed a duty upon "any person in charge of a vessel or of an onshore facility or an offshore facility" to report any discharge of oil or a hazardous substance into navigable waters to the "appropriate agency" of the United States Government. Should that person fail to supply such notification, he or she was liable to a fine of not more than $10,000 or imprisonment of not more than one year. Section 311(b)(5) also provided for a form of "**use immunity**," specifying that "[n]otification received pursuant to this paragraph or information obtained by the exploitation of such notification shall not be used against any such person in any criminal case, except a prosecution for perjury or for giving a false statement."...

Section 311(b)(6) provided for the imposition of a "civil penalty" against "[a]ny owner or operator of any vessel, onshore facility, or offshore facility from which oil or any hazardous substance is discharged in violation" of the Act. In 1975, that subsection called for a penalty of up to $5,000 for each violation of the Act. In assessing penalties, the secretary of the appropriate agency was to take into account "the appropriateness of such penalty to the size of the business or of the owner or operator charged, the effect on the owner or operator's ability to continue in business, and the gravity of the violation."...

On or about March 23, 1975, oil escaped from an oil retention pit at a drilling facility located near Enid,

Oklahoma, and eventually found its way into Boggie Creek, a tributary of the Arkansas River system. At the time of the discharge, the premises were being leased by respondent, L.O. Ward, who was doing business as L.O. Ward Oil & Gas Operations. On April 2, 1975, respondent Ward notified the regional office of the Environmental Protection Agency (EPA) that a discharge of oil had taken place. Ward later submitted a more complete written report of the discharge, which was in turn forwarded to the Coast Guard, the agency responsible for assessing civil penalties under §311(b)(6).

After notice and opportunity for hearing, the Coast Guard assessed a civil penalty against respondent in the amount of $500. Respondent filed an administrative appeal from this ruling, contending inter alia, that the reporting requirements of §311(b)(5) of the Act violated his privilege against compulsory self-incrimination. The administrative appeal was denied. On April 13, 1976, Ward filed suit in the United States District Court for the Western District of Oklahoma, seeking to enjoin the Secretary of Transportation, the Commandant of the Coast Guard, and the Administrator of EPA from enforcing §§311(b)(5) and (6) and from collecting the penalty of $500. On June 4, 1976, the United States filed a separate suit in the same court to collect the unpaid penalty. The District Court eventually ordered the two suits consolidated for trial.

Prior to trial, the District Court rejected Ward's contention that the reporting requirements of §311(b)(5), as used to support a civil penalty under §311(b)(6), violated his right against compulsory self-incrimination. The case was tried to a jury, which found that Ward's facility did, in fact, spill oil into Boggie Creek. The District Court, however, reduced Ward's penalty to $250 because of the amount of oil that had spilled and because of its belief that Ward had been diligent in his attempts to clean up the discharge after it had been discovered.

The United States Court of Appeals for the Tenth Circuit reversed.... Although admitting that Congress had labeled the penalty provided for in §311(b)(6) as civil and that the use of funds collected under that section to finance the administration of the Act indicated a "remedial" purpose for the provision, the Court of Appeals tested the statutory scheme against the standards set forth in *Kennedy v. Mendoza-Martinez*,... and held that §311(b)(6) was sufficiently punitive to intrude upon the Fifth Amendment's protections against compulsory self-incrimination. It therefore reversed and remanded for further proceedings in the collection suit.

The distinction between a civil penalty and a criminal penalty is of some constitutional import. The Self-Incrimination Clause of the Fifth Amendment, for example, is expressly limited to "any criminal case...." Similarly, the protections provided by the Sixth Amendment are available only in "criminal prosecutions...." Other constitutional protections, while not explicitly limited to one context or the other, have been so limited by decision of this Court. (Double Jeopardy Clause protects only against two criminal punishments); (proof beyond a reasonable doubt required only in criminal cases).

This court has often stated that the question whether a particular statutorily defined penalty is civil or criminal is a matter of statutory construction.... Our inquiry in this regard has traditionally proceeded on two levels. First, we have set out to determine whether Congress, in establishing the penalizing mechanism, indicated either expressly or impliedly a preference for one label or the other.... Second, where Congress has indicated an intention to establish a civil penalty, we have inquired further whether the statutory scheme was so punitive either in purpose or effect as to negate that intention. In regard to this latter inquiry, we have noted that "only the clearest proof could suffice to establish the unconstitutionality of a statute on such a ground."

As for our first inquiry in the present case, we believe it quite clear that Congress intended to impose a civil penalty upon persons in Ward's position. Initially, and importantly, Congress labeled the sanction authorized in §311(b)(6) a "civil penalty," a label that takes on added significance given its juxtaposition with the criminal penalties set forth in the immediately preceding subparagraph, §311(b)(5)....

We turn then to consider whether Congress, despite its manifest intention to establish a civil, remedial mechanism, nevertheless provided for sanctions so punitive as to "transfor[m] what was clearly intended as a civil remedy into a criminal penalty."... In making this determination, both the District Court and the Court of Appeals found it useful to refer to the seven considerations listed in *Kennedy v. Mendoza-Martinez*.... This list of considerations, while certainly neither exhaustive nor dispositive, has proved helpful in our own consideration of similar questions,...and provides some guidance in the present case.

Without setting forth here our assessment of each of the seven Mendoza-Martinez factors, we think only one, the fifth, aids respondent. That is a consideration of whether "the behavior to which [the penalty] applies is already a crime." In this regard, respondent contends that §13 of the Rivers and Harbors Appropriation Act of 1899, ...makes criminal the precise conduct penalized in the present case. Moreover, respondent points out that at least one federal court has held that §13 of the Rivers and Harbors Appropriation Act defines a "strict liability crime," for which the Government need prove no scienter.... According to respondent, this confirms the lower court's conclusion that this fifth factor "falls clearly in favor of a finding that §311(b)(6) is criminal in nature."...

While we agree that this consideration seems to point toward a finding that §311(b)(6) is criminal in nature, that indication is not as strong as it seems at first blush. We have noted on a number of occasions that "Congress may impose both a criminal and a civil sanction in respect to the same act or omission."... Moreover, in *Helvering*, where we held a 50% penalty for tax fraud to be civil, we found it quite significant that "the Revenue Act of 1928 contains two separate and distinct provisions imposing sanctions," and that "these appear in different parts of the statute...." To the extent that we found significant the separations of civil and criminal penalties within the same statute, we believe that the placement of criminal penalties in one statute and the placement of civil penalties in another statute enacted 70 years later tends to dilute the force of the fifth *Mendoza-Martinez* criterion in this case.

In sum, we believe that the factors set forth in *Mendoza-Martinez*, while neither exhaustive nor conclusive on the issue, are in no way sufficient to render unconstitutional the congressional classification of the penalty established in §311(b)(6) as civil. Nor are we persuaded by any of respondent's other arguments that he has offered the "clearest proof" that the penalty here in question is punitive in either purpose or effect....

Judgment and Result

The U.S. Supreme Court reversed the court of appeals decision. The Supreme Court decided the Clean Water Act's civil penalties provision was, in substance as well as in form, a *civil* not a *criminal* penalty. As such, the mandatory reporting of spills provision did not violate the Fifth Amendment's privilege against self-incrimination that applies to criminal acts.

Questions

1. Were the punishments applied to the defendant civil or criminal? Which did the defendant argue they were?
2. Does the Fifth Amendment's privilege against self-incrimination apply in civil cases?

Step 9. Agencies Hold Adjudicatory Hearings

Adjudication is the third major function of administrative agencies. (The other two functions are legislative and executive.) Adjudication means that agencies hold hearings similar to courtroom trials. The federal Administrative Procedure Act provides the basic rules for agency hearings.

The Hearing. To visualize an agency hearing, think of an ordinary courtroom trial and eliminate the jury. The agency is the moving party, or prosecutor, where someone is accused of breaking agency regulations. A private person, often a business, is the defendant, also called the respondent. A private party can be the moving party under certain circumstances. Notice of agency adjudicatory hearings must include the time and place of the hearing and tell what the hearing will be about.

Administrative Law Judge. The presiding official at an adjudicatory hearing is an administrative law judge, formerly called the hearing examiner. Technically, this person is independent of the agency personnel prosecuting the case, which keeps the administrative law judge off the agency's prosecutorial team.

Parties. Parties to an agency adjudication may introduce evidence, witnesses, and arguments to support their position. Settlement offers are allowed. In fixing the time and place of the hearing, the convenience and necessity of the parties are taken into account.

Step 10. Appeal of Administrative Law Judge's Decision

Once an administrative law judge makes a decision, it can be appealed.

Standing. The standing doctrine says that only the person injured may sue (has standing) to correct a wrong. This doctrine also applies to actions by administrative agencies. Therefore, a farmer whose land is flooded by a new Tennessee Valley Authority dam has standing to sue TVA, since the farmer is injured.

Exhaustion. Generally, a person must go through an agency's decision-making structure before taking an agency action to court. This procedure is called the exhaustion doctrine. Its purpose is to give an agency a chance to do its job and correct its own mistakes by having an appeal process within the agency itself. The exhaustion doctrine also saves the time and expense of suing in court. Consider the case of Mildred Smith, who retires at age 65 and files for Social Security benefits. The Social Security office mistakenly confuses her with another Mildred Smith and declares her ineligible. Mildred appeals to a higher level *within* the Social Security administration, which corrects the mistake. Mildred's Social Security checks are on the way without her having to go to court.

Exceptions to the Exhaustion Doctrine. At times the exhaustion doctrine does not apply. If agency action would cause irreparable injury, exhaustion is excused. Exhaustion is also excused when an agency acts beyond its jurisdiction and when going through agency channels would be a futile effort.

Appeals to the Courts. A person suffering a legal wrong by agency action may take the matter to court. For example, suppose the state real estate commission suspends a realtor's license after an adjudicatory hearing. The realtor may appeal this action to a court.

Appealable Agency Action. Generally, only an agency's *final* action may be appealed to a court. This practice gives an agency the opportunity to correct itself before the courts do.

Proper Court. Once a federal agency takes final action, the action may be appealed to a federal district court unless a special statute provides for appeal to another court, such as a U.S. court of appeals. For example, Securities and Exchange Commission and Federal Trade Commission adjudications are appealed to a U.S. court of appeals.

Courts of appeals are not trial courts. They have no juries and hear no witnesses. They accept the evidence developed at the agency adjudicatory hearing. On the other hand, federal district courts are trial courts. Witnesses are heard, and evidence is presented. Thus, an agency case that comes to a federal district court is usually entirely retried (a *de novo* review). *De novo* court review insults an administrative agency because it implicitly says, "What you [the agency] have done has to be all done over again because what you did in some way is not good enough." When the facts developed at agency adjudications are accepted by U.S. courts of appeals, stature is given to agencies, saving everyone's time and resources by not having to retry cases.

Ripeness. The term *ripeness* refers to an administrative agency's action being developed enough to give the court a clear understanding of the problem. In other words, the agency must have acted officially and not just sent up trial balloons about what it might do. Courts will not review an agency's action unless it is ripe—that is, what the agency has done must be final or complete enough for a court to say it is legal or illegal. Ripeness is therefore an argument made by one who does not want the agency action challenged. Often, this is the agency itself.

The following is an example of ripeness in an administrative agency action. The Securities and Exchange Commission (SEC) proposes a regulation requiring that securities sales people have a college degree in finance. The National Association of Securities Dealers (NASD) immediately sues the SEC to invalidate the proposed regulation. The SEC would argue that the matter is not yet ripe, because the regulation is only proposed, not promulgated. The SEC would win based on the ripeness doctrine, because the SEC has not taken any definite, concrete final action but has merely proposed a regulation. On the other hand, the ripeness defense would be weaker if NASD were to sue after the SEC promulgates the regulation. Promulgation is a definite, concrete, final agency action that a court can sink its teeth into.

Remedies a Court May Order for Agency Wrongdoings. A reviewing court may declare agency action illegal and either force it to act or stop it from acting when any of the following occur:

1. An agency has been arbitrary, capricious, abused its discretion, or otherwise not acted in accordance with the law.
2. An agency has acted contrary to constitutional right, power, privilege, or immunity.
3. An agency acts beyond its statutory authority.
4. An agency acts without observing legal procedures.
5. An agency acts without substantial evidence to support it.

In *Frank v. Chater,* a Soviet immigrant whose application for Social Security disability was denied by an administrative law judge appealed the matter to a U.S. District Court. His basic arguments were that APA adjudicatory hearing requirements were not satisfied. Before the adjudicatory hearing he acted pro se, meaning that he served as his own attorney. This approach is possible but not advisable in agency adjudications. Note that when he appealed the case, he did have an attorney.

Agency hearings thus must satisfy different rules (constitutions, statutes, and even regulations). The set of rules that controls depends in part on the case's facts and the arguments the parties make.

Frank v. Chater

U.S. District Court (E.D.N.Y.)
924 F.Supp. 416 (1996)

Background and Facts:

Frank, an attorney in the former Soviet Union for several years prior to coming to the United States, filed an application for Supplementary Security Income (SSI) benefits on October 1, 1991, claiming disability due to a heart condition and memory loss. The Department of Health and Human Services (HHS) which contains the Social Security Administration, denied Frank's application initially, and on reconsideration. In its reconsideration decision, HHS advised Frank regarding representation as follows: "In having your case heard, you can represent yourself or be represented by a lawyer, a friend, or any other person. Contact your Social Security office for names of organizations that can help you."

Frank then requested a hearing before an ALJ. HHS sent a subsequent notice informing Frank of the hearing date. The reverse side of the notification contained additional information regarding his options for obtaining representation.

On December 10, 1992, Frank appeared at the hearing without counsel. After Frank stated that he desired counsel and that he had not received the list of referral organizations from HHS, the ALJ adjourned the hearing to allow Frank to pursue free legal representation. At the subsequent hearing, held on January 14, 1993, Frank again appeared without counsel, but stated that he would like to proceed without the assistance of counsel even though he had an appointment with a legal aid organization later that day. The colloquy between Frank and the ALJ was as follows:

ALJ: We sent a letter on, on October 14, 1992, advising you of your right to representation. When you appeared on December 10, 1992, you were given an adjournment to obtain representation. You were not able to do it, you were not able to obtain representation?

Frank: They... gave me an appointment for today only but I would like to proceed today.

The ALJ then proceeded to conduct a brief hearing.

On June 15, 1993, the ALJ issued a short decision in which he determined principally that Frank's condition was not sufficiently severe to render him disabled and that, in any event, Frank was capable of performing his past relevant work as an attorney in the former Soviet Union. The ALJ's decision relied primarily on the opinion of a consulting physician, Dr. Antonio Deleon, who examined Frank once on February 12, 1992, at the request of HHS, and on the assessment of a vocational expert designated by HHS, Dr. Charles Plotz, who had never examined Frank and based his opinion on the medical record available at the time of the hearing even though the record was significantly supplemented after the hearing.

HHS sent Frank the ALJ's decision, which referred to Frank's options for obtaining legal representation if he chose to appeal. Frank's request for review of the ALJ's decision was denied by the Appeals Council on November 4, 1993, rendering the ALJ's decision the final decision of the HHS. Frank thereafter brought this action and is now represented by counsel. He seeks reversal or, in the alternative, remand arguing that: (1) the ALJ deprived Frank of a full and fair hearing by failing to adequately inform Frank of his right to counsel, conducting only a brief hearing with cursory examination of Frank, and failing to assist Frank as a pro se claimant in obtaining the relevant evidence for the record; (2) the ALJ's determination that Frank's alleged impairments did not meet or equal a listed impairment was not supported by substantial evidence; and (3) the ALJ's determination that Frank could engage in his past relevant work as an attorney in the former Soviet Union was erroneous as a matter of law.

Body of Opinion

Judge Block

Among HHS's basic responsibilities is the duty to provide a claimant with a full and fair hearing in accordance with the beneficent purposes of the Act and the regulations promulgated thereunder.... This obligation emanates from the unique nature of the benefits proceeding. Unlike the adversarial nature of a trial, where the primary responsibility for developing the facts rests with the parties, a benefits proceeding is essentially nonadversarial in nature and imposes an affirmative duty on the ALJ to develop the record to ensure that all claimants receive a fair hearing.... Among other things, this heightened duty provides the impetus for HHS and the ALJ's obligation to provide notification regarding the options for obtaining legal counsel in a benefits proceeding as well as the ALJ's responsibilities to ensure that there are no significant gaps in the record and to accord the appropriate weight to a treating physician's opinion.

...The Second Circuit has recognized the benefits of counsel by imposing a higher duty on the ALJ when a claimant proceeds *pro se*....

As an initial matter, it is necessary to clarify what the cases in this and other Circuits casually refer to as the "right to representation" in a benefits proceeding. This right does not rise to constitutional dimensions.... As such HHS is not obligated to provide counsel for the claimant...or even to "guarantee the availability of free legal services."... Rather, the "right to representation" articulated in these cases refers to a claimant's freedom to choose to be represented by counsel in a benefits proceeding.

...Thus, although the Act and accompanying regulations do not create an entitlement to counsel in a benefits proceeding, they do require that a claimant receive notification regarding the options for obtaining counsel. Once a claimant is provided with adequate notification, (s)he may effectively waive the option to proceed with counsel either in writing or on the record before the ALJ.

...In sum, the Court determines that HHS should provide written notice to a Social Security claimant, prior to an administrative hearing, containing information regarding the benefits of counsel, the possibility of free counsel or a contingency arrangement, and the limitation on direct fee payments in Title II cases and the fee approval process generally in both Title II and Title XVI cases. When a pro se claimant appears before an ALJ, the ALJ should verify that the claimant received such prior notification and, if the notification was inadequate, provide oral notification on the record at the hearing. The ALJ should also be sensitive to whether the claimant, once notified, has had a meaningful opportunity to secure counsel and, if not, to consider adjourning the hearing to provide that opportunity.

Given these precepts, the Court concludes that the notifications Frank received prior to the hearing described the fee approval process, they were inadequate insofar as they did not advise him of the benefits of counsel or the possibility of free legal services or a contingency arrangement....

Notwithstanding the importance of notification regarding legal representation, courts have nevertheless refused to remand in the absence of a showing that the claimant was prejudiced by the lack of counsel....

The ALJ here failed to adequately discharge his heightened duty to a pro se litigant as evidenced by gaps in the record which might have been obviated by the presence of counsel during the benefits proceeding.... Only six pages of the thirteen page hearing transcript were devoted to the questioning of Frank.... For example, the ALJ did not inquire into the circumstances surrounding Frank's hospitalization for heart problems in the former Soviet Union....

In general, the ALJ's examination of Frank focused on who treated him, how often he was treated, and what medications he was taking, but notably absent was any substantial inquiry into the nature of Frank's alleged impairments or their effect on his ability to work. The ALJ's cursory examination of Frank was insufficient considering the importance to be accorded a claimant's testimony....

Although the gaps in the record are themselves sufficient to warrant remand, the ALJ also discounted the opinion of Frank's treating physician, Dr. Cohen, without explanation. The Secretary [of the Department of Health and Human Services] must give a treating physician's opinion "controlling weight" if it is "well supported by medically acceptable clinical techniques and is not inconsistent with the other substantial evidence in... [the] case record."... Even where the treating physician's conclusions are contradicted by substantial evidence, they are still entitled to "some extra weight" although the "resolution of genuine conflicts between the opinion of the treating source, with its extra weight, and any substantial evidence to the contrary remains the responsibility of the fact-finder."...

Judgment and Result

The District Court remanded the case to the ALJ to decide whether sufficient evidence supported a finding of disability. The ALJ must evaluate Frank's physical and emotional ability to perform his past relevant work as an attorney in the former Soviet Union.

Questions

1. Did Mr. Frank have an attorney when he appeared before the administrative law judge? Did it present him with any problems at the hearing? Mr. Frank was represented by an attorney to appeal his case to the U.S. District Court.
2. What law covers the conduct of a federal agency hearing?
3. The District Court arrived at the seemingly counterintuitive conclusion that whether Mr. Frank was disabled depended on whether he could perform a profession (law practice in the old Soviet Union) that had no counterpart in the United States. Why should this result follow? To keep Social Security disability from becoming unemployment compensation? The court so held.

RECENT CHANGES IN RULEMAKING

In 1980 Congress amended the APA to improve informal (notice and comment) rulemaking by passing the **Regulatory Flexibility Act** (RF Act), which strengthens the APA's notice requirements. As a practical matter, most small business people and the public generally do not know that a publication called the *Federal Register* exists. Furthermore, many do not read it even when they are aware of its existence. Congress knew this when it enacted the Regulatory Flexibility Act. One of the act's provisions encourages federal agencies to publish proposed rules having a substantial impact on small entities (small hospitals, municipal governments, and small businesses) in journals likely to be obtained by those entities—journals in addition to the *Federal Register*. Whether affected people will read the proposed regulations and take the initiative by sending critical comments to the proposing agency is uncertain. At least the RF Act is a step in the right direction.

CONCLUDING POINTS ABOUT RULEMAKING

No Right to a Hearing

When a federal agency engages in informal rulemaking (notice and comment rulemaking), the U.S. Constitution's Fifth Amendment's due process clause does not require the agency to hold an evidentiary hearing. A practical effect for a business is that it never has a chance to hear the government's experts who gathered the evidence that was the basis for the agency's regulations. Therefore, the agency's experts are never cross-examined by business lawyers (helped by experts from outside the agency) who could point out weaknesses in the agency regulations. Any trial lawyer will point out that an important part of a trial is the right to cross-examine the opposition's witnesses.

A Warning

Although no Fifth Amendment right requires a hearing when an agency engages in informal rulemaking to make substantive regulations, specific agency statutes might require such a hearing. Even here, though, usually no provision to cross-examine opposing viewpoints is made. However, at least one U.S. court of appeals interprets the Administrative Procedure Act as allowing cross-examination on crucial administrative issues.

Reg-Neg: A Possible Future Direction for Federal Rulemaking

A statute enacted by the 101st U.S. Congress could have a significant impact on federal rulemaking. That law deals with what has come to be called **reg-neg**, regulations that are negotiated. Negotiated rulemaking differs from the "notice and comment" rulemaking discussed in this chapter. Basically it involves the appointment of a committee by an official of the agency responsible for the rule. The committee is made up of the different constituencies likely to be affected by the regulation, who meet, share information relevant to drafting the proposed regulation, come up with a report (possibly containing a draft regulation), and then submit it to the agency with authority to promulgate it. This draft report would be a basis for the agency to propose and promulgate the rule in an environment in which all affected parties have agreed on the particulars of the rule, thus cutting down on the time to make the regulation. The act does not restrict challenges to the regulation that emerge from this process.

Whether in fact agreement could be reached on highly controversial rules (such as the EPA's 1,000-year containment rule for nuclear waste disposal) remains to be seen. Also, the reg-neg law could simply add another layer of bureaucracy to the rulemaking process. Finally, this process could bury or hide controversial rules from the public. After all, how many people now know how regulations are made? If the process is made even more complex and is hidden from sight in a committee, is the public interest served?

Congress renewed in 1996 legal authority for negotiated rulemaking but later repealed it.

CHAPTER SUMMARY

Administrative agencies have three functions: executive, judicial, and legislative.

The three types of administrative rulemakings are formal, informal, and hybrid.

The chronological steps in an informal federal rulemaking are society perceives a problem; Congress studies the problem and enacts an enabling act; the agency studies the problem and develops a regulatory solution; the agency proposes the regulation in the *Federal Register*; the public comments on the proposed regulation; the agency promulgates, reproposes, or withdraws the proposed regulation; lawsuits challenge the regulation, which is either upheld or wholly or partially invalidated; a valid regulation is enforced; an adjudicatory hearing is held at which the alleged violation of the regulation is tried; an appeal from the ALJ hearing to the court system is possible.

Several recent modifications to the process by which federal regulations are made have been introduced by the Regulatory Flexibility Act and negotiated regulation ("reg-neg") process, which is set to expire unless renewed by Congress.

The executive function of an administrative agency covers investigation, prosecution, and administration.

Administrative searches by government officials are illegal unless the inspector has a search warrant or some exception to the search warrant requirement exists, such as closely regulated businesses.

Administrative agencies do not have the power to punish someone criminally. Federal administrative agencies may assess a civil penalty.

MANAGER'S ETHICAL DILEMMA

Tom Stebbins was the director of a conservatively run savings and loan (S&L) association in Grand Rapids, Michigan. Tom had always been careful to see that his S&L maintained ample capital, had a conservative loss ratio on total loans, and did not make high-risk loans. Now Tom learned the many failed S&Ls in other parts of the United States, particularly Texas, had not been managed as well. As a result the nation's S&L crisis was forcing federal regulators to impose added fees on the properly managed S&Ls, such as Tom's, to pay part of the cost of those that were poorly run. Tom felt the federal government was punishing the "good managers" to pay for the shenanigans of the "fast-buck" artists who had taken over S&Ls during the deregulation and weak regulation era of the late 1970s and 1980s.

Had weak regulation contributed to the S&L crisis of the 1990s, which threatened to cost the entire nation $500 billion over a period of years? Tom wondered whether good businesspeople do not actually benefit from tough regulations, because they follow the law anyway while the "fly-by-night operators" take deposits away from legitimate S&Ls by offering interest rates that well-managed S&Ls cannot match? Then well-managed S&Ls pay a second time by having to contribute extra fees to pay off insured deposits when poorly managed S&Ls "go under." Tom wondered, "Would not strong regulation really have been the friend of properly run S&Ls?"

Persons may challenge actions of administrative agencies in court. Requirements on those who seek to appeal agency actions to the courts include standing, primary jurisdiction, ripeness, and exhaustion.

Courts have a wide range of options in granting remedies for improper agency actions.

Discussion Questions

1. Is there value in letting citizens know what their government is doing? One attempt to let the public know what an agency is doing can be found using the internet. Describe the steps you would follow in finding regulations on cigarettes and smokeless tobacco. Would your answer be different if the regulations were merely proposed, but, as yet unpromulgated?
2. The secretary of transportation proposed an airport slot regulation. Northwest Airlines challenged that reg because the notice of *proposed* rulemaking did not say exactly what the *promulgated* reg would look like. Must the regulation itself be in the *Federal Register* notice when the agency proposes it? *Northwest Airlines, Inc. v. Goldschmidt,* 645 F.2d 1309 (1981)
3. What is informal rulemaking?
4. Give a disadvantage for small business people when a federal agency makes rules.
5. The proposed used car regulation in this chapter has had a lively existence. It was promulgated, then Congress, under authority of the enabling acts, legislatively vetoed it. A consumer group then sued Congress, claiming that Congress's legislative veto was unconstitutional. In 1983 the U.S. Supreme Court held that the two-house legislative veto was unconstitutional, making the used car regulation valid again. But this decision did not end the matter. The FTC, now headed by a Reagan-appointed committed to deregulation, then withdrew its promulgated used car regulation for further study. The used car reg was promulgated in 1984. The promulgated reg in Figure 7.5 is now in effect. A consumer group has again sued the FTC, claiming the reg is invalid for procedural reasons. That suit has now been decided in favor of the FTC (the rule is valid). Several enforcement actions have been brought by the FTC. The FTC also issued compliance guidelines in 1987 (52 *Fed Reg.* 18,552). Do you see why regulating is a *process* and not *static*?
6. The U.S. Environmental Protection Agency (EPA) proposed regulations setting air

pollution standards for new or modified cement plants. The EPA did not make available test results and methodology used (in part) as the basis for these regulations until *after* promulgation. The Portland Cement Association sued the EPA claiming it had a right to see data that partially formed the basis for the regulations before Portland filed comments to the proposed regulations. Was it right? The case is *Portland Cement Association v. Ruckelshaus* (1974).

7. Should an agency have a duty to disclose its complete data base, including studies supporting its final regulation?
8. Should commentators have a duty to disclose their database to the agency proposing a regulation?
9. Joseph Burger owned and operated a junkyard in Brooklyn, New York. His business involved dismantling cars and selling their parts. At about noon on November 17, 1982, Officer Joseph Vega and four other plainclothes officers, all members of the Auto Crimes Division of the New York City Police Department, entered Burger's junkyard to conduct an inspection under the New York statutes regulating vehicle dismantlers. The Auto Crimes Division conducted about 10 routine inspections daily. They asked to see Burger's vehicle-dismantling license and "police book," which state law required that such businesses keep. Burger did not have such a book. The officers then asked to inspect Burger's lot and he agreed, though the officers lacked a search warrant. They copied vehicle inspection numbers (VINs) from several cars and, after checking the police department computer, learned that several vehicles in Burger's possession had been stolen. The police arrested Burger. Burger moved to suppress the evidence the police seized during their search on grounds that New York's statute authorizing administrative searches of junkyards was unconstitutional. The police argued that Burger's junkyard was a pervasively regulated business for which no search warrant was required, particularly in view of the New York statutes permitting such inspections. The New York Court of Appeals basically agreed with Burger, and New York appealed to the U.S. Supreme Court. What was the result? *New York v. Burger*, 482 U.S. 691 (1987)
10. What does the exhaustion doctrine mean?
11. Immigration and Naturalization Service (INS) officials conduct surprise raids on factories to look for illegal aliens. The officials entered a factory after getting search warrants. Some officials stood at the doors while others went through the factory, asking workers about their immigration status. Workers who could not answer the INS officials satisfactorily or produce immigration papers were arrested, often as many as half the workers in certain California factories. The U.S. Court of Appeals for the Ninth Circuit held that these searches were unconstitutional. That court reasoned the surprise raids were unconstitutional seizures of the entire factory's workforce. It also said that INS officials could not question workers individually unless officials had a reasonable suspicion the worker was an illegal alien. The INS appealed to the Supreme Court. Were the surprise raids unconstitutional? *INS v. Delgado*, 466 U.S. 210 (1984)
12. When a regulator issues a license, is it performing an executive or a judicial function?
13. When can a regulator search a business without a search warrant?
14. Can a regulator impose a civil penalty? A criminal penalty?
15. Describe an agency adjudicatory proceeding. What is a main difference between it and a jury trial in a court?
16. A bill before Congress would impose a civil penalty of $100,000 on prohibited insider trading in an issuer's securities. Why would the enforcer (U.S. government) prefer a *civil* rather than a *criminal* penalty?
17. A veteran brought before the Veterans Administration a constitutional challenge to a federal law limiting lawyers' fees to $10 for representing veterans. The law was passed in the 1860s to protect Civil War vets from exploitation. The lower federal court upheld the law. The veteran appealed to the U.S. Supreme Court. What was the result? *Walters v. National Association of Radiation Survivors*, 473 U.S. 305 (1985)

Suggested Readings

Articles

CAMPBELL, "Revoking the 'Fishing License': Recent Decisions Place Unwarranted Restrictions on Administrative Agencies' Power to Subpoena Personal Financial Records," 49 *Vanderbilt Law Review* 395 (1996).

FISHER, "Controlling Government Regulation: Cost-Benefit Analysis Before and After the 'Cotton Dust' Case," 36 *Administrative Law Review* 179 (1984).

FISHER, "Is *New York v. Burger* a Threat to the Civil Liberties of Business?" 60 *New York State Bar Journal* 22 (1988).

HARTER, "Points on a Continuum: Dispute Resolution Procedures and the Administrative Process," 1 *Administrative Law Journal* 141 (1987).

HING, "Border Patrol Abuse: Evaluating Complaint Procedures Available to Victims," 9 *Georgia Immigration Law Journal* 757 (1995).

MASHAW, "Reinventing Government and Regulatory Reform: Studies in the Neglect and Abuse of Administrative Law," 57 *Pittsburgh Law Review* 405 (1996).

WILKIE, "Comment on a Positive Political Theory of Regulatory Instruments," 69 *California Law Review* 477 (1996).

Books

DAVIS, *Administrative Law Text* (1972).

GELHORN, *Administrative Law in a Nutshell* (1972).

GILBERT, *Administrative Law in a Nutshell* (1978).

SCHWARTZ, *Administrative Law* (1976).

TUCKER, *Administrative Law, Regulation of Enterprise and Individual Liberties* (1975).

CHAPTER

8

INTERNATIONAL BUSINESS: PUBLIC LAW

"THE WORLD IS YOUR OYSTER."

Shakespeare

POSITIVE LAW ETHICAL PROBLEMS

"I'm sorry, sir," said the U.S. immigration and passport official to a Canadian business executive. "I can't admit you to the United States."

"This is outlandish," replied Herbert Smith, the CEO of Mega-Industries. "Why not? I'm not a runaway crook or drug dealer."

"No, but your company, Mega-Industries bought property in Cuba, which formerly belonged to U.S. companies prior to Fidel Castro's takeover in 1959. The U.S. Congress has enacted the Helms-Burton Act which forbids entry into the United States of executives of companies that traffic in assets of U.S. firms confiscated by the Castro government."

Is the U.S. immigration official correct?

"We have been sued in New York for over 2,000 deaths and 200,000 other injuries that occurred in Bhopal, India," shouted one Union Carbide Corporation (UCC) executive to another. Thousands of Indians and the Indian government sued UCC, the U.S. parent of Union Carbide of India Limited, in New York City for the damages done in India. UCC thought that India was the place to bring the lawsuit. Who was right?

The one outstanding fact about international "law" is the absence of **positive law** in the international arena. That is, using John Austin's definition of law, no single sovereign or universal authority exists with the power to make rules binding on all persons, with sanctions imposed if the law is violated. Rather, in a crude sense, the law of the jungle—might makes right—prevails in international affairs. Of course, custom, fairness, private covenants, and treaties supplement the power ethic, but we should not forget that it is literally possible for nations to get away with what would be murder if committed by individuals—a sobering thought.

This chapter focuses on public institutional arrangements in international law under which business must operate. The following chapter examines business applications of international law.[1] This chapter will outline important treaties and institutions that influence commerce internationally,

[1] The authors acknowledge use of *Import Practice: Customs and International Trade Law* by David Serko and *International Trade for the Nonspecialist* by various authors for ALI/ABA in preparing this chapter.

including the WTO, UNCITRAL, the EU, the NAFTA, and OPIC. It begins with an overview of basic definitions concerning international trade in the U.S. economy.

DEFINITION AND SOURCES OF INTERNATIONAL LAW

When lawyers, international businesspersons, and diplomats refer to international law they are usually talking about treaties (also called conventions) between and among nations, customs, and recognized principles regulating independent nations in peace and war. Thus, Savigny's legal ethic of longstanding custom is important in the international area. We define international law, then, as the treaties, conventions, and customs nations observe in dealing with one another.

For information on treaties holdings of the United Nations, go to ***http://www.un.org/law***

http://

Treaties can be bilateral (between two nations) or multilateral (involving more than two nations). An example of a bilateral treaty is one between the United States and the People's Republic of China (PRC, or mainland China) authorizing certain trade between the two nations. An example of a multilateral treaty would be the World Trade Organization (WTO), successor to the General Agreement on Tariffs and Trade (GATT),[2] which now has over 130 signatory nations, including the United States. The North American Free Trade Agreement (NAFTA) has, at this writing, three parties—Canada, the United States, and the United Mexican States (Mexico).

International law should be distinguished from municipal law, which refers to the domestic law of a particular country. For example, the law governing the speed limits on interstate highways in the United States is considered municipal law, even though, technically, cities generally do not set interstate speed limits. International law refers to treaties and customs that nations recognize in dealing with one another.

NATURE AND EXTENT OF U.S. INTERNATIONAL TRADE

Economic isolationism results from passing laws that make it difficult or impossible for persons in the United States to buy and sell goods and services in foreign countries. High tariffs, quotas (limits on the number of goods that can be imported to the United States or exported from the United States), and trade barriers based on health, conservation, or other public policies are all examples of ways the legal system can stifle international trade. Isolationism is also referred to as protectionism.

The United States has learned the hard way that economic isolationism is a losing economic policy. The Tariff Act of 1930, known as the Smoot-Hawley Act, imposed extremely high tariffs on goods entering the United States. This act hurt foreign manufacturers, who in turn convinced their governments to retaliate by enacting high tariffs on U.S. goods. As a result of Smoot-Hawley and the resulting tariffs, international trade came to a standstill. Some say Smoot-Hawley even caused the Great Depression. Though its philosophy has been condemned, that act's structure is the basis for much of today's customs law, albeit in much amended form reflective of a less protectionist philosophy.

Other significant acts dealing with U.S. tariffs include the Reciprocal Trade Agreements Act of 1934, the Trade Act of 1974, and the Trade Agreements Act of 1979.

[2] GATT actually refers to two things: GATT, the agreement, and GATT, the organization. The agreement (covering only goods) supplemented by GATS (the General Agreement on Trade in Services) and TRIPS (the agreement on Trade-Related Aspects of Intellectual Property)(dealing with patents, copyrights, trademarks, trade secrets, and industrial designs) continues and is administered by the WTO. GATT, the organization, no longer exists because the WTO replaced it.

The 1934 act gives the president the power to negotiate lower tariffs with other nations, which quite obviously, was a reaction to Smoot-Hawley. The 1974 act authorized the president to negotiate reduction of nontariff barriers. With the 1979 act, Congress continued to focus on nontariff matters such as countervailing duties, antidumping, and subsidies.

Current Policy

Current U.S. policy generally favors international trade. The strongest evidence supporting this statement comes from the data in Figure 8.1. Despite the U.S. trade deficit for each of the past 10 years and its trend to increase, the United States generally has not raised tariffs on incoming goods; however, some significant exceptions should be noted. First an "off-the-books understanding" between Japanese and U.S. officials exists regarding the number of Japanese-made cars the United States will admit in any one year. In effect it is a voluntary quota, one of the most blatant forms of protectionism. Second, allegations persist that the U.S. dollar's decline against other currencies has been engineered by the U.S. government to create a trade barrier against foreign goods. The idea is that a cheap dollar makes foreign goods more expensive and hence less attractive for U.S. consumers. Third, even though the United States has approved the NAFTA, various concessions in the form of continued trade barriers against, among other things, Canadian peanut butter, were granted to gain U.S. congressional support for the NAFTA.

Most Favored Nations ("Normal Trade") Clauses in Treaties

Note in Figure 8.1 that the dollar amount of foreign goods imported into the United States is large. The United States imposes tariffs on many foreign goods. The United States also places different tariff rates on the same goods from different countries. Most favored nations (MFN) clauses, also called "normal trade," in treaties give citizens or subjects of the contracting nations privileges accorded by either party to those of the most favored nations. For example, if the United States and China have a treaty with a MFN clause, then the United States must give China the lowest tariff rate on a particular good that it gives to any nation. MFN treatment includes, but is not limited to, tariff rates. A principal effect of MFN clauses is to reduce tariffs, which promotes free trade.

MFN treatment is one of the key features of the WTO, which administers an international treaties to which over 130 nations are signatories or observe (the U.S. Senate, as of this writing has not ratified WTO, but the U.S. generally follows WTO provisions).

Some nations, such as Russia, do not have most favored nation status regarding shipping their goods into the United States. Other nations, such as the People's Republic of China, do have MFN status. Obviously, conferral of this status does not necessarily depend on whether the country involved is a communist or nondemocratic nation.

INSTITUTIONS AFFECTING INTERNATIONAL BUSINESS

Business professionals should be familiar with several laws and institutions that affect international business. Included here are the WTO, UNCITRAL, the EU, OPIC, and the NAFTA.

FIGURE 8.1 U.S. Exports and General Imports in Goods: 1970 to 1997

Year	Total Goods[1]			Manufactured Goods [2 3]			Agricultural Products			Mineral Fuels [3 5]		
	Exports	Imports	Balance	Exports	Imports	Balance	Exports	Imports	Balance	Exports	Imports	Balance
1970	43.8	40.4	3.4	31.7	27.3	4.4	7.3	5.8	1.6	1.6	3.1	-1.5
1971	44.7	46.2	-1.5	32.9	32.1	0.8	7.8	5.8	2.0	1.5	3.7	-2.2
1972	50.5	56.4	-5.9	36.5	39.7	-3.2	9.5	6.5	3.0	1.6	4.8	-3.2
1973	72.5	70.5	2.0	48.5	47.1	1.3	17.9	8.5	9.4	1.7	8.2	-6.5
1974	100.0	102.6	-2.5	68.5	57.8	10.7	22.3	10.4	11.9	3.4	25.5	-22.0
1975	109.3	98.5	10.8	76.9	54.0	22.9	22.1	9.5	12.6	4.5	26.5	-22.0
1976	117.0	123.5	-6.5	83.1	67.6	15.5	23.3	11.2	12.1	4.2	34.0	-29.8
1977	123.2	151.0	-27.8	88.9	80.5	8.4	24.2	13.6	10.6	4.2	47.2	-43.0
1978	145.9	174.8	-28.8	103.6	104.3	-0.7	29.8	15.0	14.8	3.9	42.0	-38.1
1979	186.5	209.5	-22.9	132.7	117.1	15.6	35.2	16.9	18.3	5.7	59.9	-54.2
1980	225.7	245.3	-19.5	160.7	133.0	27.7	41.8	17.4	24.3	8.2	78.9	-70.7
1981	238.7	261.0	-22.3	171.7	149.8	22.0	43.8	17.2	26.6	10.3	81.2	-70.9
1982	216.4	244.0	-27.5	155.3	151.7	3.6	37.0	15.7	21.3	12.8	65.3	-52.5
1983	205.6	258.0	-52.4	148.5	171.2	-22.7	36.5	16.5	19.9	9.8	57.8	-48.0
1983	205.6	258.0	-52.4	148.5	171.2	-22.7	36.5	16.5	19.9	9.8	57.8	-48.0
1984	224.0	330.7	-106.7	164.1	230.9	-66.8	37.9	19.3	18.6	9.7	60.8	-51.1
1985	218.8	336.5	-117.7	168.0	257.5	-89.5	29.3	19.5	9.8	10.3	53.7	-43.4
1986	227.2	365.4	-138.3	179.8	296.7	-116.8	26.3	20.9	5.4	8.4	37.2	-28.8
1987	254.1	406.2	-152.1	199.9	324.4	-124.6	28.7	20.3	8.4	8.0	44.1	-36.1
1988	322.4	441.0	-118.5	255.6	361.4	-105.7	37.1	20.7	16.4	8.5	41.0	-32.5
1989	363.8	473.2	-109.4	287.0	379.4	-92.4	41.6	21.1	20.5	9.9	52.6	-42.7
1990	393.6	495.3	-101.7	315.4	388.8	-73.5	39.6	22.3	17.2	12.4	64.7	-52.3
1991	421.7	488.5	-66.7	345.1	392.4	-47.3	39.4	22.1	17.2	12.3	54.1	-41.8
1992	448.2	532.7	-84.5	368.5	434.3	-65.9	43.1	23.4	19.8	11.3	55.3	-43.9
1993	465.1	580.7	-115.6	388.7	479.9	-91.2	42.8	23.6	19.2	9.9	55.9	-46.0
1994	512.6	663.3	-150.6	431.1	557.3	-126.3	45.9	26.0	20.0	9.0	56.4	-47.4
1995	584.7	743.4	-158.7	486.7	629.7	-143.0	56.0	29.3	26.8	10.5	59.1	-48.6
1996	625.1	795.3	-170.2	524.7	658.8	-134.1	60.6	32.6	28.1	12.4	78.1	-65.7
1997	689.2	870.7	-181.5	592.5	728.9	-136.4	57.1	35.2	21.9	13.0	78.3	-65.3

[1]Includes nonmonetary gold, military grant aid, special category shipments, trade between the U.S. Virgin Islands and foreign countries and undocumented exports to Canada. Adjustments were also made for carryover. Import values are based on transaction prices whenever possible ("f.a.s." for 1974-79 and Customs value thereafter). Import data before 1974 do not exist on a transaction price valuation basis. [2]Manufactured goods include commodity sections 5-9 under Schedules A and E for 1970-82 and SITC Rev. 3 for 1983-forward. Manufactures include undocumented exports to Canada, nonmonetary gold (excluding gold ore, scrap, and base bullion), and special category shipments. 3Data for 1970-80 exclude trade between the U.S. Virgin Islands and foreign countries. Census data concordances link the 1980-92 trade figures into time series that are as consistent as possible. Data for 1970-79 are not linked and are from published sources. Import values are "f.a.s." for 1974-79 and Customs value thereafter; these values are based on transaction prices while maintaining a data series as consistent as possible over time. Import data before 1974 do not exist on a transaction price valuation basis. 1991 imports include revisions for passenger cars, trucks, petroleum and petroleum products not included elsewhere. 4Agricultural products for 1983-forward utilize the latest census definition that excludes manufactured goods that were previously classified as manufactured agricultural products. 5Mineral fuels include commodity section 3 under SITC Rev. 1 for 1970-76, SITC REv. 2 for 1977-82 and SITC Rev. 3 for 1983-forward.

Source: *Statistical Abstract of U.S.*, 1998.

World Trade Organization (and GATT, its predecessor)

The General Agreement on Tariffs and Trade (GATT) took effect in 1947 and more than 130 nations now subscribe to its successor, the WTO. The WTO's main purpose is to reduce tariffs and trade restrictions. The WTO has had the practical effect of reducing http:// *Information about GATT can be accessed at the website for the World Trade Organization at* ***http://www.wto.org***

today's tariffs by more than 25 percent from what they were a generation ago. Nations take actions under the WTO at meetings called rounds, which first began in the late 1940s. The first five rounds mainly concerned themselves with reducing tariffs, while later rounds, such as the seventh in 1979, called the Tokyo round, focused on simplifying the trade procedures that proved stumbling blocks to international trade. The most recent round occurred in Uruguay and has had several deadlines that have been missed. Among the most important WTO (and GATT treaty) principles are:

1. The WTO outlaws tariff discrimination for WTO members and requires MFN treatment for WTO members
2. The WTO outlaws nontariff barriers; this provision plugs a loophole that could arise when member nations try to escape their obligations under item 1 by imposing quotas, health and safety standards, which actually are disguised trade barriers. The Dolphin case that follows, decided by a GATT panel, presented such a case. In that case, Mexico accused the United States of violating GATT's provision forbidding nontariff barriers when the United States required "dolphin friendly" labels (under the Dolphin Protection Consumer Information Act) on tuna cans sold in the United States and prohibited entry into the United States of foreign tuna caught under circumstances violating a U.S. law (the Marine Mammal Protection Act), which protects animals such as dolphins.
3. WTO/GATT places caps on tariffs (called "Schedules of Concessions" under Article II of GATT); according to this idea, WTO members commit themselves to limits on tariffs on particular items from other WTO members. However, member nations need not have tariff rates identical with other WTO member nations on the same products. Thus Mexico prior to the NAFTA, had higher tariffs on certain goods entering Mexico from the United States than the United States imposed on identical goods entering the United States from Mexico (on certain items this continues to be true even under the NAFTA although Mexican tariffs against certain U.S. agricultural products are scheduled to be phased out under the NAFTA). However, under MFN principles, Mexico may not impose higher tariff rates on U.S.-made widgets entering Mexico than on identical Canadian widgets entering Mexico, because all three nations are WTO/GATT (and now NAFTA) signatories.

A nation may receive MFN treatment from the United States without being a member of the WTO. Also membership in the WTO does not always entitle one to MFN treatment. Poland, a WTO member, for several years in the 1980s, was denied MFN treatment to induce domestic reforms designed to help the Polish people.

GATT Dispute Settlement Panel Report: United States—Restrictions on Imports of Tuna

1991 BDIEDL AD LEXIS 67 © American Society of International Law
Reproduced with permission from Basic Document of International Economic Law (a project of the American Society of International Law). (Not yet adopted as of March 1993.)

Background and Facts:

Purse-Seine Fishing of Tuna. The last three decades have seen the deployment of tuna fishing technology based on the "purse-seine" net in many areas of the world. A fishing vessel using this technique locates a school of fish and sends out a motorboat (a "seine skiff") to hold one end of the purse-seine net. The vessel motors around the perimeter of the school of fish, unfurling the net and encircling the fish, and the seine skiff then attaches its end of the net to the fishing vessel. The fishing vessel then purses the net by winching in a cable at the bottom edge of the net, and draws in the top cables of the net to gather its entire contents.

Studies monitoring direct and indirect catch levels have shown that fish and dolphins are found together in a number of areas around the world and that this may lead to incidental taking of dolphins during fishing operations. In the Eastern Tropical Pacific Ocean (ETP), a particular association between dolphins and tuna has long been observed, such that fishermen locate schools of underwater tuna by finding and chasing dolphins on the ocean surface and intentionally encircling them with nets to catch tuna underneath. This type of association has not been observed in other areas of the world; consequently, intentional encirclement of dolphins with purse-seine nets is used as a tuna fishing technique only in the Eastern Tropical Pacific Ocean. When dolphins and tuna together have been surrounded by purse-seine nets, it is possible to reduce or eliminate the catch of dolphins through using certain procedures.

Body of Opinion

Marine Mammal Protection Act (MMPA).

. . . The Marine Mammal Protection Act (MMPA) regulates . . . the harvesting of tuna by United States fishermen and others who are operating within the jurisdiction of the United States. The MMPA requires that such fishermen use certain fishing techniques to reduce the taking of dolphin incidental to the harvesting of fish. The United States authorities have licensed fishing of yellowfin tuna by United States vessels in the ETP on the condition that the domestic fleet not exceed an incidental taking of 20,500 dolphins per year in the ETP.

The MMPA also requires that the United States Government ban the importation of commercial fish or products from fish caught with commercial fishing technology which results in the incidental killing or incidental serious injury of ocean animals in excess of United States standards. Under United States customs law, fish caught by a vessel registered in a country is deemed to originate in that country. As a condition of access to the United States market for the yellowfin tuna or yellowfin tuna products caught by its fleet, each country of registry of vessels fishing yellowfin tuna in the ETP must prove to the satisfaction of the United States authorities that its overall regulatory regime regarding the taking of marine mammals is compatible to that of the United States. To meet this requirement, the country in question must prove that the average rate of incidental taking of marine mammals by its tuna fleet operating in the ETP is not in excess of 1.25 times the average incidental taking rate of United States vessels operating in the ETP during the same period.

The Panel noted that Mexico had argued that the measures prohibiting imports of certain yellowfin tuna and yellowfin tuna products from Mexico imposed by the United States were quantitative restrictions on importation under Article XI, while the United States had argued that these measures were internal regulations enforced at the time or point of importation under Article III:4 and the Note Ad Article III, namely that the prohibition of imports of tuna and tuna products from Mexico constituted an enforcement of the regulations of the MMPA relating to the harvesting of domestic tuna.

The Panel concluded from the above considerations that the Note Ad Article III covers only those measures that are applied to the product as such. The Panel noted that the MMPA regulates the domestic harvesting of yellowfin tuna to reduce the incidental taking of dolphin, but that these regulations could not be regarded as being applied to tuna products as such because they would not directly regulate the sale of tuna and could not possibly affect tuna as a product. Therefore, the Panel found that the import prohibition on certain yellowfin tuna and certain yellowfin tuna products of Mexico and the provisions of the MMPA under which it is imposed did not constitute internal regulations covered by the Note Ad Article III.

The Panel further concluded that, even if the provisions of the MMPA enforcing the tuna harvesting regulations (in particular those providing for the seizure of cargo as a penalty for violation of the Act) were regarded as regulating the sale of tuna as a product, the United States import prohibition would not meet the requirements of Article III. . . . Article III:4 calls for a comparison of the treatment of imported tuna as a product with that of domestic tuna as a product. Regulations governing the taking of dolphins incidental to the taking of tuna could not possibly affect tuna as a product. Article III:4 therefore obliges the United States to accord treatment to Mexican tuna no less favorable than that accorded to United States tuna, whether or not the incidental taking of dolphins by Mexican vessels corresponds to that of United States vessels.

Dolphin Protection Consumer Information Act (DPCIA).

The Panel examined the distinction between quantitative restrictions on importation and internal measures applied at the time or point of importation, and noted the following. While restrictions on importation are prohibited by Article XI:1, contracting parties are permitted by Article III:4 and the Note Ad Article III to impose an internal regulation on products imported from other contracting parties provided that it: does not discriminate between products of other countries in violation of the most-favored-nation principle of Article I:1; is not applied so as to afford protection to domestic production, in violation of the national treatment principle of Article III:1; and accords to imported products treatment no less favorable than that accorded to like products of national origin, consistent with Article III:4. . . .

The Panel noted that Mexico considered the labeling provisions of the DPCIA to be marking requirements falling under Article IX:1, which reads:

> Each contracting party shall accord to the products of the territories of other contracting parties treatment with regard to marking requirements no less favorable than the treatment accorded to like products of any third country.

The United States considered that the labeling provisions were subject not to Article IX but to the most-favored-nation and national-treatment provisions of Articles I:1 and III:4. The Panel noted that the title of Article IX is "Marks of Origin" and its text refers to marking of origin of imported products. The Panel further noted that Article IX does not contain a national-treatment but only a most-favored-nation requirement, which indicates that this provision was intended to regulate marking of origin of imported products but not marking of products generally. The Panel therefore found that the labeling provisions of the DPCIA did not fall under Article IX:1.

The Panel proceeded to examine the subsidiary argument by Mexico that the labeling provisions of the DPCIA were inconsistent with Article I:1 because they discriminated against Mexico as a country fishing in the ETP. The Panel noted that the labeling provisions of the DPCIA do not restrict the sale of tuna products; tuna products can be sold freely both with and without the "Dolphin Safe" label. Nor do these provisions establish requirements that have to be met in order to obtain an advantage from the government. Any advantage which might possibly result from access to this label depends on the free choice by consumers to give preference to tuna carrying the "Dolphin Safe" label. The labeling provisions therefore did not make the right to sell tuna or tuna products, nor the access to a government-conferred advantage affecting the sale of tuna or tuna products, conditional upon the use of tuna harvesting methods. The only issue before the Panel was therefore whether the provisions of the DPCIA governing the right of access to the label met the requirements of Article I:1.

The Panel noted that the DPCIA is based . . . on a finding that dolphins are frequently killed in the course of tuna-fishing operations in the ETP through the use of purse-seine nets intentionally deployed to encircle dolphins. The DPCIA therefore accords the right to use the label "Dolphin Safe" for tuna harvested in the ETP only if such tuna is accompanied by documentary evidence showing that it was not harvested with purse-seine nets intentionally deployed to encircle dolphins. The Panel examined whether this requirement applied to tuna from the ETP was consistent with Article I:1. According to the information presented to the Panel, the harvesting of tuna by intentionally encircling dolphins with purse-seine nets was practiced only in the ETP because of the particular nature of the association between dolphins and tuna observed only in that area. By imposing the requirement to provide evidence that this fishing technique had not been used in respect of tuna caught in the ETP the United States therefore did not discriminate against countries fishing in this area. The Panel noted that, under United States customs law, the country of origin of fish was determined by the country of registry of the vessel that had caught the fish; the geographical area where the fish was caught was irrelevant for the determination of origin. The labeling regulations governing tuna caught in the ETP thus applied to all countries whose vessels fished in this geographical area and thus did not distinguish between products originating in Mexico and products originating in other countries.

The Panel found for these reasons that the tuna products labeling provisions of the DPCIA relating to tuna caught in the ETP were not inconsistent with the obligations of the United States under Article I:1 of the General Agreement.

The Panel wished to underline that its task was limited to the examination of this matter "in the light of the relevant GATT provisions," and therefore did not call for a finding on the appropriateness of the United States' and Mexico's conservation policies as such.

The Panel wished to note the fact, made evident during its consideration of this case, that the provisions of the General Agreement impose few constraints on a contracting party's implementation of domestic environmental policies. The Panel recalled its findings . . . that under these provisions, a contracting party is free to tax or regulate imported products and like domestic products as long as its taxes or regulations do not discriminate against imported products or afford protection to domestic producers, and a contracting party is also free to tax or regulate domestic production for environmental purposes. As a corollary to these rights, a contracting party may not restrict imports of a product merely because it originates in a country with environmental policies different from its own.

. . . The Panel noted that the United States considered the prohibition of imports of certain yellowfin tuna and certain yellowfin tuna products form Mexico, and the provisions of the MMPA on which this prohibition is based, to be justified by Article XX(b) because they served solely the purpose of protecting dolphin life and health and were "necessary" within the meaning of that provision because, in respect of the protection of dolphin life and health outside its jurisdiction, there was no alternative measure reasonably available to the United States to achieve this objective. Mexico considered that Article XX(b) was not applicable to a measure imposed to protect the life or health of animals outside the jurisdiction of the contracting party taking it and that the import prohibition imposed by the United States was not necessary because alternative means consistent with the General Agreement were available to it to protect dolphin lives or health, namely international co-operation between the countries concerned.

Conclusions

The prohibition of imports of certain yellowfin tuna and certain yellowfin tuna products of Mexico and the provisions of the Marine Mammal Protection Act under which it is imposed are contrary to Article XI:1 and are not justified by Article XX(b) or Article XX(g).

The tuna labeling provisions of the Dolphin Protection Consumer Information Act relating to tuna caught in the Eastern Tropical Pacific Ocean are not inconsistent with the obligations of the United States under Article I:1 of the General Agreement on Tariffs and Trade.

Questions

1. Were the dolphins which the two U.S. statutes were attempting to protect in U.S. or international waters? How can U.S. statutes have extra-jurisdictional effect? If Mexico wants to export tuna caught in its waters or in international waters into the United States, is Mexico not imposing ITS environmental ideas on the U.S. consumers, that is, that dolphins should not be afforded much protection?
2. Was the Marine Mammal Protection Act attempting to protect U.S. citizens' health? Welfare?
3. What arguments did the United States advance to justify its limits on the importation of tuna? Animal rights? Did this relate to some feature of tunas? If it did not, how could the United States justify restricting the tuna if the purpose in so doing was to protect some other mammal not being imported into the United States?
4. How realistic is it for the GATT Panel to suggest that the United States could pursue its concern for dolphins by pursuing international cooperation between the two countries concerned? Is GATT not a form of international cooperation? Does GATT forbid countries from trying to protect marine mammals? If another country uses GATT to stymie protection of marine mammals, how likely is it to pursue cooperative efforts with the United States to achieve the same ends?
5. If the United States suddenly decided that goods could not be imported into the United States unless made under U.S. labor conditions (Fair Labor Standards Act for wages, Occupational Safety and Health Act for employment conditions, Workers' Compensation, ERISA, etc. protections), could it restrict imports of Mexican or any country's goods if not made under a comparable legal regime, according to the interpretation of GATT? What might be the legal justification the United States could advance to impose such a restriction? What would be the Mexican or other foreign nation legal challenge to such restrictions?
6. Does GATT completely disallow a member nation from protecting its citizens from harmful products entering its territory?
7. Are GATT panel deliberations open to the public? What legal ethics mentioned in Chapter 1 are or are not in evidence here?

UNCITRAL

The United Nations Commission on International Trade Law (UNCITRAL) had its first meeting in 1966. The commission is composed of representatives from only thirty-six countries from all regions of the world. This small number permits a group that is workable in size. The commission meets approximately one month per year. It aims to promote the unification and harmonization of international trade by drafting "model laws," which it presents to different nations with an eye toward encouraging each nation to enact them. The idea is that if each nation passes UNCITRAL's model statutes, eventually the goal of uniform national laws would be achieved. Presumably, trade barriers would decrease since trade laws would be similar from country to country. An example of a model act that UNCITRAL has drafted and the United Nations has approved is the Draft Convention on Contracts for the International Sale of Goods. This is patterned after Article 2 of the Uniform Commercial Code.

The website for United Nations Commission on International Trade Law, UNCITRAL is located at ***http://www.uncitral.org***

http://

European Economic Community (EEC)[3]

The Treaty of Rome created the European Economic Community (EEC), also known as the Common Market, in 1957. The EEC's main purpose is to promote tariff-free trade

[3] The authors acknowledge relying on Leonard's *Guide to the European Union* in preparing this and the Maastricht Treaty segments.

among its members and to have common tariffs for outsiders. Some see the EEC as a first step toward a politically united Europe. The EEC has legislative, executive, and judicial arms which in some ways have control of individual member nations. For example, the EEC's supreme court, called the Court of Justice, issues decrees that bind all member nations internally. In effect, this means that member nations are giving up a bit of their sovereignty. The Treaty of Rome's Articles 85 and 86 are laws forbidding anticompetitive acts by businesses within (and to some extent outside) the EEC, much as the antitrust laws do in the United States.

The following European nations belong to the ECC: Belgium, Denmark, France, Germany, Greece, Ireland, Italy, Luxembourg, the Netherlands, Portugal, Spain, and the United Kingdom. Several other nations (Austria, for example) as of this writing have sought EEC membership.

The Maastricht Treaty: Creating the European Union (EU)

The Maastricht Treaty establishes the European Union (EU), originally consisting of twelve member nations, but, as of this writing, consisting of the fifteen EC nations (with more seeking admission). The Maastricht Treaty is a significant development along the road to European unification. It amends the Treaty of Rome and, as such, carries forward that Treaty's efforts to unify Europe.

From this point forward the terms European Community and European Union will be used interchangeably. In a technical sense the EC became part of the EU when the Maastricht Treaty went into effect. The EU encompasses the European Commission (which has authority in matters such as education, health, culture, and consumer protection), the Council of Ministers, the European Parliament, and the Court of Justice.

When most people think of the Maastricht Treaty, they think of the unified currency (the Euro) for member states. However, that treaty has the far broader objective of European integration—politically, socially (with the Social Chapter), and economically (by establishing a European currency, the Euro, scheduled to take effect for the "person on the street" in the early 21st century).

An "opt out" provision permits Great Britain to stay out of the monetary union (Euro) and the Social Chapter. As of this writing, Great Britain has exercised its option to stay out of the European currency.

The NAFTA[4]

On August 12, 1992, then President Bush reported completion of negotiations for a North American Free Trade Agreement (NAFTA) among the nations of Canada, Mexico, and the United States. As of this writing NAFTA has not been ratified by all three countries, although the U.S. House of Representatives approved NAFTA on November 17, 1993. Canada is the United States' largest trading partner and Mexico is third. Much debate has surrounded the net economic effects of NAFTA, and readers are referred to other sources to assess the merits of the arguments pro and con. Here, attention is devoted to the some important NAFTA provisions.

Tariffs. All tariffs on products traded among the member nations are scheduled to be eliminated within 15 years of NAFTA's implementation. U.S./Canada trade will be duty-free by 1998. NAFTA will modify international trade rules that presently would allow Mexico to raise tariffs to as high as 50% (they presently range between 0-20% and on average are 2.5 times higher than U.S. tariffs on Mexican goods entering the

[4] The authors acknowledge reliance on U.S. State Department documents in preparing this segment.

United States). All Mexican tariffs on U.S. exports will disappear in 10 years except on corn and beans, which will be gone in 15 years.

Rules of Origin. NAFTA is designed to lower tariffs only on goods made in North America. Rules of origin determine whether a product is made in North America. The idea is to keep Mexico or Canada from being "export platforms" for shipment duty-free of, say, Japanese goods to the United States through, for example, Mexico.

Rules of origin are important under NAFTA because even after it takes effect, NAFTA members may still have different tariffs on goods coming into them from non-NAFTA countries such as Japan. Thus if the United States had a 10 percent tariff on Japanese cars and Mexico had a 1 percent tariff on Japanese cars, a clever importer could first import the Japanese cars into Mexico, "wash" them of their identity by superficially "finishing" them (such as installing cigarette lighters in Mexico), and exporting them as "Mexican" cars to the United States with no tariff, because tariffs among NAFTA members are to be phased out ultimately.

Goods entirely made in the United States, Mexico, or Canada of composed entirely of NAFTA components are given duty-free treatment within the NAFTA region (the area of the member nations). Goods having non-NAFTA region parts might be given duty-free treatment if they have undergone a specified change in tariff classification. Here the rules of product origin are crucial. Under the NAFTA, the U.S./Canada Free Trade Agreement's (a predecessor to the NAFTA) rules of origin will be used for U.S./Canadian trade.

NAFTA's Safeguards. NAFTA has at least two safeguards to prevent a member nation such as the United States being "overrun" with imports from another member such as Mexico. One bilateral safeguard is the snap-back provision, which allows pre-NAFTA tariff rates to be reimposed for up to three, and in some cases four, years if import surges from Mexico to the United States seriously injure U.S. firms or workers. A second global safeguard permits the United States to place quotas or tariffs on Canadian or Mexican products if multilateral action is taken in response to imports causing or threatening substantial injury.

NAFTA's Environmental Protections.[5] NAFTA provides that each member nation has the right to set what it thinks is the appropriate level of protection for people, animals, and plants life or health, technically called sanitary, which relates to humans and animals, and phytosanitary, which relates to plants. This right is qualified by disallowing arbitrary or unjustifiable life or health provisions that would result in arbitrary or unjustifiable discrimination against another party's goods or be, in effect, a disguised trade restriction. Also, when a nation deals with animal or plant life or health, cost effectiveness of alternative ways of limiting risks must be considered.

Two other qualifications significantly limit environmental measures in order for them to be valid under NAFTA: They must be "necessary" to protect human, animal, or plant life or health at the level the particular nation selects. For example, for a zero level of risk, it would be "necessary" to have a low level of pesticide residue on lettuce. Secondly, environmental measures to protect human, animal, or plant life or health must be "based on scientific principles." Commentators have noted that genetic engineering does not appear to be covered under this part of the NAFTA.

NAFTA is generally seen as more environmentally friendly than GATT for several reasons. First, NAFTA requires that a scientific study support a standard even though other studies might lead to an opposite conclusion. The Uruguay round of GATT

[5] The authors acknowledge reliance on Steve Charnovitz, "NAFTA: An Analysis of its Environmental Provisions," *Environmental Law Reporter*, (1993).

apparently would upset standards if contrary to "available scientific evidence," meaning that if several studies do not support the standard, the fact that one does support it would probably lead to the standard's being struck down. Secondly, GATT's Uruguay Round forces environmental standards to be the "least restrictive to trade, taking into account technical and economic feasibility." NAFTA does not force the environmental standards of nations to be so accommodating to trade. Third, GATT's Uruguay Round forces standards for humans as well as plants and animals life and health to meet cost and effectiveness standards, while the NAFTA requires cost and effectiveness only for animals and plants—not standards protecting humans. Fourth, GATT's Uruguay Round requires environmental standards to be consistent with "human health risks to which people voluntarily expose themselves." Thus, if the nation is one where everyone smokes and drinks alcohol heavily, it would appear inconsistent to have stringent environmental standards concerning pesticide residues in food, because people are voluntarily exposing themselves to greater risks by their lifestyle. NAFTA has no such consistency requirement between environmental standards and the population's lifestyle.

Overseas Private Investor Corporation (OPIC)

The Overseas Private Investor Corporation (OPIC) is a U.S. government agency. It provides insurance to citizens and businesses against certain risks associated with doing business abroad. Included are such risks as confiscation (a foreign government's taking a foreign business's property in violation of international law), insurrection, repatriation problems (the inability to take earnings "out" of a foreign country), war, and revolution. OPIC premiums are based on the risk involved.

U.S. INTERNATIONAL TRADE COMMISSION[6]

http://

View information about the International Trade Commission at ***http://www.usitc.gov***

In 1916 Congress established by statute the U.S. Tariff Commission. The name was changed in 1974 to the U.S. International Trade Commission (ITC). It provides studies, reports, and recommendations to the president, Congress, and other governmental bodies regarding tariffs and other international trade issues.

The ITC is an independent federal agency. It consists of six presidentially appointed commissioners who must be confirmed by the U.S. Senate. The commissioners' full terms are for nine years, although some commissioners serve only part of a term. The president designates the ITC chairperson and vice chairperson for two-year terms. Succeeding chairpersons may not be from the same political party. No more than three commissioners may be members of the same political party.

ITC Functions

The ITC must provide the president, the House Ways and Means Committee, and Senate Finance Committee with all information it has when requested. The ITC must also conduct investigations on matters of international trade requested by either the president or Congress.

[6] The authors acknowledge reliance on government documents in preparing material on the International Trade Commission.

Generalized System of Preferences

The president has the authority to lower U.S. tariffs, called *preferences*, on goods imported into the United States from certain developing countries. The ITC advises the president on the likely effect of such preferences on U.S. business and consumers.

Industry Adjustments to Import Competition

Suppose a particular business, a particular industry, a particular union, or other industrial representative believes that an imported good poses a serious threat to a U.S. business. This U.S. business may petition the ITC to investigate the matter. If the ITC finds the import does threaten serious injury to the U.S. industry, it can recommend that the president take corrective action. The president has discretion to increase tariff duties, impose a quota on the foreign goods, work out a marketing agreement of some sort, or assist U.S. workers, businesses, or communities adversely affected by the import.

Import Interference with Agricultural Programs

The president also has the authority to direct the ITC to investigate to determine whether articles being imported render Department of Agriculture programs for agricultural commodities or products ineffective or that would reduce the amount of any product processed in the United States from such commodities or products. The president can limit such imports by either fees or quotas.

Comparing Unit Labor Costs among Nations

A quiet but important war is occurring today: It is the fight for the consumer's money among businesses from all over the world. U.S. firms must sell goods that compete with goods from Japan, Germany, The Netherlands, Sweden, and many other nations. One basic cost in international competition is labor. Figure 8.2 compares U.S. unit labor costs with those of other nations. While labor is but one production cost, it is significant in most manufacturing enterprises.

Protecting U.S. Patents, Copyrights, and Trademarks Abroad: Special 301

The U.S. International Trade Commission (ITC) estimates that theft abroad of U.S. intellectual property costs its owners at least $43 billion in 1986 alone. Thieves in foreign countries pirate or counterfeit items such as computers, computer software, books, tapes, CDs, movies, auto parts, pharmaceuticals, and semiconductors. The pirates then sell copies of these items as the "real McCoy."

The 1988 Trade Act states that international protection of intellectual property rights is vital to the international competitiveness of individuals and businesses in the United States who rely on protection of intellectual property rights. That Act also recognizes that U.S. businesses must have access to foreign markets. Further, a section of the 1988 Act—**Special 301**—also states as its purpose the development of a strategy to protect intellectual property rights and to assume market access for U.S. business.

Special 301: A Major Purpose. Special 301, as stated by then President Reagan at the bill's signing, is to "strengthen the ability of U.S. firms to protect their patented, copyrighted, or trademarked goods and ideas from international thievery."

FIGURE 8.2 National Labor Costs in Selected Countries

Hourly compensation costs in U.S. dollars for production workers in manufacturing, 29 countries or areas and selected economic groups, selected years, 1975-97

Country or Area	1975	1980	1985	1990	1993	1994	1995	1996	1997
United States	$6.36	$9.87	$13.01	$14.91	$16.51	$16.87	$17.19	$17.70	$18.24
Canada	5.96	8.67	10.94	15.84	16.43	15.85	16.04	16.66	16.55
Mexico	1.47	2.21	1.59	1.58	2.40	2.47	1.51	1.54	1.75
Australia	5.62	8.47	8.20	13.07	12.49	14.02	15.05	16.52	16.00
Hong Kong SAR[1]	.76	1.51	1.73	3.20	4.29	4.61	4.82	5.14	5.42
Israel	2.25	3.79	4.06	8.55	8.82	9.19	10.54	10.99	12.05
Japan	3.00	5.52	6.34	12.80	19.21	21.35	23.82	20.91	19.37
Korea	.32	.96	1.23	3.71	5.64	6.40	7.29	8.09	7.22
New Zealand	3.21	5.33	4.47	8.33	8.01	8.93	10.11	11.03	11.02
Singapore	.84	1.49	2.47	3.78	5.25	6.29	7.33	8.32	8.24
Sri Lanka	.28	.22	.28	.35	.42	.45	.48	.48	-
Taiwan	.40	1.00	1.50	3.93	5.23	5.55	5.92	5.93	5.89
Austria	4.51	8.88	7.58	17.75	20.16	21.51	25.21	24.66	21.92
Belgium	6.41	13.11	8.97	19.17	21.44	23.07	26.65	25.89	22.82
Denmark	6.28	10.83	8.13	18.04	19.11	20.30	24.07	24.11	22.02
Finland	4.61	8.24	8.16	21.03	16.63	19.06	24.14	23.56	21.44
France	4.52	8.94	7.52	15.49	16.79	17.63	20.01	19.92	17.97
Germany[2]	6.31	12.25	9.53	21.88	25.32	27.03	32.22	31.79	28.28
Greece	1.69	3.73	3.66	6.76	7.23	7.73	9.14	9.59	-
Ireland	3.03	59.95	5.92	11.66	11.89	12.39	13.57	13.85	13.57
Italy	4.67	8.15	7.63	17.45	15.8	15.89	16.21	17.73	16.74
Luxembourg	6.50	12.03	7.81	16.74	18.74	20.33	23.35	22.55	-
Netherlands	6.58	12.06	8.75	18.06	20.08	20.80	24.02	23.08	20.61
Norway	6.77	11.59	10.37	21.47	20.21	20.97	24.38	25.05	23.72
Portugal	1.58	2.06	1.53	3.77	4.50	4.60	5.37	5.58	5.29
Spain	2.53	5.89	4.66	11.38	11.62	11.54	12.88	13.51	12.16
Sweden	7.18	12.51	9.66	20.93	17.59	18.62	21.44	24.37	22.24
Switzerland	6.09	11.09	9.66	20.86	22.63	24.91	29.30	28.34	24.19
United Kingdom	2.37	7.56	6.27	12.70	12.41	12.80	13.67	14.13	15.47

Dash means data not available.
[1]Hong Kong Special Administrative Region of China.
[2]Former West Germany.

Source: U.S. Department of Labor, Bureau of Labor Statistics (September 1998).

What Special 301 Requires. Special 301 tells the U.S. Trade Representative (USTR) to, within 30 days following publication of the *National Trade Estimate Report*, designate nations that deny "fair and equitable market access to U.S. persons who rely on intellectual property protection."

Identification of 301 Countries. The USTR must identify as "priority foreign countries" those whose acts, practices, or policies are the most onerous and have the most adverse economic effect on the United States and who are not trying to negotiate in good faith to correct deficient intellectual property protection. In this respect Congress determined that practices such as expropriation, restrictive licensing procedures, and "cultural sovereignty" barriers were undesirable. Once the USTR identifies priority foreign countries, it must investigate that nation's undesirable practices. The USTR must complete the investigation within six months and must also seek a bilateral solution with individual problem nations.

Sanctions. Assuming the offending nation refuses to cooperate, the USTR may sanction the country by raising duties or otherwise restricting imports from the problem country.

Other Aspects of Special 301. The USTR may add to the list of "priority foreign countries" at anytime. The USTR also has the power to revoke priority foreign country status anytime, provided detailed reasons are given for such revocation.

Special 301 should not be confused with Super 301, which is also designed to strengthen the hand of U.S. trade negotiators to liberalize trade with foreign countries. Super 301 was used to retaliate against countries hostile to U.S. trade. One difference between Super 301 and Special 301 is that Special 301 is permanent while Super 301 expired after 1990. Renewal of Super 301 is considered from time-to-time.

RESTRAINTS ON INTERNATIONAL BUSINESS

U.S. Antitrust Laws

Extraterritorial Effect. Suppose a German and Belgian firm agree to fix prices on radios sold in France. The U.S. antitrust laws do not apply to such conduct that has no effect or contact with the United States. To say otherwise would mean that the United States could set the speed limits or antitrust laws in Paris. However, U.S. antitrust laws (discussed in other chapters) can apply to international business; that is, they can have extraterritorial effect (outside the United States). The Sherman Act specifically states that it applies outside the United States.

U.S. Antitrust Law Control of Business Outside the U.S. U.S. antitrust laws apply if anticompetitive activities outside the United States have some substantial effect within the United States. Thus, if the German and Belgian radio firms agree to fix prices on radios shipped to the United States and this agreement has a substantial effect within the United States, the U.S. antitrust laws apply and make it illegal.

Who Can Sue for Extraterritorial Antitrust Violations. Another way of asking who can sue is to ask whom the antitrust laws protect. Foreign and U.S. governments, U.S. and foreign businesses, and any other person injured may sue for violations of U.S. antitrust laws outside the United States, which have a substantial effect within the United States.

Who Can Be Sued. Quite a number of categories of persons can be sued for breaking U.S. antitrust laws in international settings. Assuming the jurisdictional requirements are met, foreign governments, U.S. and foreign businesses, and any person who violates U.S. antitrust laws can be sued for alleged violations.

Antitrust Exemption. The Export Trading Company Act was passed in 1982 to encourage U.S. business to engage in international trade. The principal reason for encouraging U.S. trade, which was to help correct the trade deficit, can be understood by examining Figure 8.1 showing the U.S. merchandise trade balance from 1960 through 1997. Several figures stand out: the trend of the trade deficits over the past decade fluctuated up and down but have been worsening, particularly in the most recent years; the import value for petroleum fell sharply until 1986 (due at least in part to the decline in the world oil prices); the value of U.S. agricultural exports *fell* sharply between 1980 and 1986; and the United States consistently imports more in dollar terms of transportation equipment (autos, buses, and trucks) as it exports. All of these facts support efforts to encourage U.S. business to export more, while assuming that import restrictions will not frequently be imposed.

The Export Trading Company Act (ETCA) tries to encourage U.S. businesses to increase exports by letting competitors form Export Trading Companies (ETCs) without the threat of U.S. antitrust liability. The ETCA sets up a procedure for companies to get a certificate of antitrust compliance from the secretary of commerce and the Justice Department. To obtain such certification the applicant must show it will not (1) substantially lessen competition or restrain trade in the United States or substantially restrain export trade of a competitor; (2) cause unfair competition; (3) affect the prices of goods or services in the United States; or (4) sell for competition or resell the exported goods within the United States. Thus, the ETCA amended the Sherman and FTC Acts dealing with antitrust.

Antitrust in the European Union

The European Union (EU) has several provisions (especially Articles 85 and 86 of the Treaty of Rome, which established the EEC) that forbid anticompetitive business practices. Article 85 is similar to section 1 of the Sherman Act.

The Helms-Burton Act. Certain segments of the U.S. Congress and business community continue to feel hostility toward Fidel Castro and his communist revolution. In part this animus is due to the Cuban government's nationalization of assets of U.S. firms doing business in Cuba when Castro came to power in 1959.

In 1996 the U.S. Congress, led by Senator Jesse Helms of North Carolina and Congressman Dan Burton of Indiana, passed the Helms-Burton Act. This act has as its primary objective the economically isolating, in effect punishing, of Cuba for these earlier acts of confiscation. Helms-Burton attempts to achieve its objective by making certain acts illegal if done by a foreign business regarding such confiscated U.S. property. In other words, if a foreign business uses confiscated U.S. assets, that business is punished.

The punishment Helms-Burton imposes on foreign businesses takes several forms. One is the prevention of such foreign firms' executives from entering the United States. Also, foreign executives' families may not enter the United States to study or visit here. Another provision of Helms-Burton would allow U.S. firms whose Cuban property was seized by Castro to sue the company now using this property from Cuba in U.S. courts.

Helms-Burton is controversial. Many foreign governments and businesses have criticized Helms-Burton for violating principles of free economic trade. In fact, U.S. policy in general has favored free trade internationally since the 1930s, so, arguably, passage of Helms-Burton is at odds with U.S. trade policy. Critics point to the fact that the United States has robust trade with other communist nations, for example, the People's Republic of China (PRC), the largest communist nation and one of the most repressive governments in the world. The United States runs a trade deficit with the PRC of more than $50 billion per year. Critics of Helms-Burton also note that such laws invite other nations' retaliation against unpopular U.S. policies, which could ignite a series of international boycotts.

CHAPTER SUMMARY

International law refers to treaties, customs, and recognized principles nations use to regulate their relations in war and peace. In light of John Austin's positive law, international "law" cannot follow positive law because no sovereign entity rules over all nations.

International trade is extensive and has tended to grow. The important most-favored-nation status tends to reduce tariffs among nations.

MANAGER'S ETHICAL DILEMMA

Should the manager of a U.S. government agency help out the government of Iraq when it defaults on a loan at a time when Iraqi troops threatened U.S. servicemen and -women stationed in Saudi Arabia? This situation arose when the U.S. Government's Commodity Credit Corporation guaranteed $2.1 billion of a $2.8 billion loan made to the government of Iraq by an Atlanta, Georgia, branch of an Italian bank. The officials at the Atlanta bank only had authority from their Italian head office to loan up to $200 million, but they falsified their books and exceeded their lending authority, acts which eluded Georgia and federal bank examiners. The loans were made prior to the U.S. and Allied confrontation with Iraqi military in 1991. Iraq defaulted on $2 billion of the loan, and the Italian bank made the claim against the Commodity Credit Corporation, a federal agency which guaranteed repayment. U.S. officials, at a time when the United States was virtually, if not legally, at war with Iraq, were faced with paying the Italian bank approximately $2 billion because Iraq, the obligor on the loan, failed to repay the amount borrowed.

A number of institutions affect international trade, including the WTO, UNCITRAL, the EU, and OPIC.

U.S. antitrust laws can, under certain circumstances, regulate trade in foreign nations. The EU also in theory forbids certain anticompetitive practices.

The Helms-Burton Act aims to isolate Cuba in retaliation for seizure of U.S. firms' property during the communist takeover there in 1959. This law punishes certain foreign businesses using U.S. assets confiscated by the Castro government.

Discussion Questions

1. At least one candidate for the U.S. presidency in the past two presidential elections has pressed for a tightening of U.S. tariffs and quotas to protect "blue collar" jobs, which are being lost to labor in nations with much lower priced labor. What would be the pluses and minuses of such a proposal? Has this ever been tried before in the United States and what were the results?
2. What section of U.S. law would businesses with patents, trademarks and copyrights resort to if they felt their rights were being infringed?
3. In what way is Super 301 more potent that Special 301? Why is Super 301 less powerful than Special 301?
4. What relationship does the Generalized System of Trade Preferences have to tariffs?
5. What are the functions of the International Trade Commission?
6. What is the difference between GATT's basic philosophy and that of the EEC? Or do they share a basic "one world" approach?

Suggested Readings

Articles

ALVAREZ, "Critical Theory and the North American Free Trade Agreement, Chapter Eleven," 28 *University of Miami Inter-American Law Review* 303 (1996).

ALVAREZ, "Foreward: Why Nations Behave," 19 *Michigan Journal of International Law* 303 (1998).

BIRENBAUM, "The Omnibus Trade Act of 1988: Trade Law Dialectics," 10 *University of Pennsylvania Journal of International Business Law* 653 (1988).

BOEHMER and PALMER, "The 1992 EC Data Protection Proposal: An Examination of Its Implications for U.S. Business and U.S. Privacy Law," 31 *American Business Law Journal* 265 (1993).

CROLEY and JACKSON, "WTO Dispute Procedures, Standard of Review, and Deference to National Governments," 90 *American Journal of International Law* 193 (1996).

FARBER and HUDEC, "Free Trade and the Regulatory State: A GATT's-Eye View of the Dormant Commerce Clause," 47 *Vanderbilt Law Review* 1401 (1994).

FOX, "Securities Disclosure in a Globalizing Market: Who Should Regulate Whom," 97 *Michigan Law Review* 2498 (1997).

GOLDBERG, "A General Theory of Jurisdiction in Trademark Cases (Products Counterfeiting Survey)," 8 *Loyola of Los Angeles International and Comparative Law Journal* 611 (1986).

HOAGLAND, "The Act of State Doctrine: Abandon It," 14 *Denver Journal of International Law and Policy* 317 (1986).

HOFFMAN and MARCOU, "Combating the Pirates of America's Ideas," 7 *Computer Lawyer* 8 (1990).

HUDEC, "GATT/WTO Constraints on National Regulation: Requiem for an 'Aim and Effects' Test," 32 *International Lawyer* 619 (1998).

HUDEC, "Introduction and Overview: Symposium on the First Three Years of the WTO Dispute Settlement System," 32 *International Lawyer* 613 (1998).

HURD and ZOLLERS, "Product Liability in the European Community: Implications for United States Business," 31 *American Business Law Journal* 245 (1993).

LANSING and GABRIELLA, "Clarifying Gray Market Areas," 31 *American Business Law Journal* 313 (1993).

MAURER, "The United Nations Convention on Contracts for the International Sale of Goods," 15 *Syracuse Journal of International Law and Commerce* 361 (1989).

MAYER and HOCH, "International Environmental Protection and the GATT: The Tuna/Dolphin Controversy," 31 *American Business Law Journal* 187 (1993).

MORRISON, "The Future of International Adjudication," 75 *Minnesota Law Review* 827 (1991)

MORRISON, "The Significance of Nuremberg for Modern International Law," 149 *Military Law Review* 207 (1995).

MORRISON, "The United States and the World Court as a 'Supreme Court of the Nations': Dreams, Illusions, and Disillusion," 91 *American Journal of International Law* 396 (1997).

RAUENHORST, "Industrial Relations in Korea: The Backdrop to the Current Drama," 11 *Comparative Labor Law Journal* 317 (1990).

STOLTENBERG, "International Trade Law and Regulation in the Context of the Free Trade/Fair Trade Debate: A Review Essay," 31 *American Business Law Journal* 339 (1993).

CHAPTER 9

PRIVATE BUSINESS DEALINGS IN INTERNATIONAL CONTEXTS

"WHEN YOU ARE AT ROME LIVE IN THE ROMAN STYLE; WHEN YOU ARE ELSEWHERE LIVE AS THEY LIVE ELSEWHERE."

St. Ambrose (c 340–397)

POSITIVE LAW ETHICAL PROBLEMS

"If I have the U.S. copyrighted labels on my perfumes," said Jessica Wilson, a marketing executive of L'anza, a U.S. cosmetics manufacturer, "I have the right to stop someone from importing those products back into the United States." Wilson had sold her perfumes and other cosmetics to a British distributor for resale in Europe at a price far below what they sold to U.S. distributors. The British distributor had resold the perfumes and cosmetics to a Maltese distributor, who realizing how high the U.S. price was, resold to Quality King, a U.S. distributor unauthorized by L'anza to sell in the United States.

Wilson believed that because L'anza's U.S. copyrighted label was still affixed to the cosmetics when they were shipped back into the United States without L'anza's approval, L'anza had the right to stop Quality King's distribution in the United States. Was she correct?

Businesses are becoming international, even small businesses such as Art's Oriental Rug Shop. Because of this trend, the average person must possess some knowledge of laws affecting international business. This chapter is devoted to explaining how commercial transactions can occur in the international context. Because, as the prior chapter explained, no sovereign exists with the power to make uniform rules governing all nations, it is necessary for businesses to know how private individuals and businesses must and can operate in this environment of plural sovereigns.

This chapter starts with an anatomy of an international business deal. Included here is a discussion of letters of credit and bills of lading. Then the matter of gray market goods, a common phenomenon on the international scene, is noted. Business on the international scene is extremely competitive, and bribery of foreign governments to obtain business is, unfortunately, not unknown. The Foreign Corrupt Practice Act has a direct bearing on many international business transactions involving U.S. business, and its limits will be explored. Several avenues for dispute settlement are also addressed.

INTERNATIONAL BUSINESS DEALS

Art is an Atlanta, Georgia, rug dealer. He made a contract to buy 500 8-by-10-foot red, handwoven Turkish rugs for $200,000 from Ali, a rug maker in Ankara, Turkey. The Art-Ali contract presents many practical problems, including the following:

1. How can Ali be sure that he will be paid after shipping the rugs?
2. How can Art be certain that he will get the rugs after paying for them?
3. Can Art stop the deal if Ali sends rugs that are different from the ones that Art ordered?

http:// For valuable federal resources, as well as law firm and law school links, go to **http://www.findlaw.com**

You might look at the previous facts and say, "What's the problem? Art should simply mail Ali a check for $20,000, and Ali can send Art the rugs when the check clears." This scenario is possible. But what if Art is unsure that Ali will send the rugs once the check clears? What if Ali does not know if Art will pay? Art wants to keep the money until he gets the rugs. Ali wants to keep the rugs until he gets paid. If this standoff happens, the deal will never occur. Art and Ali mistrust each other.

Art and Ali's mistrust problem is solved by a letter of credit and a bill of lading. Both the letter of credit and the bill of lading use third parties, or banks for the letter of credit and transport companies for the bill of lading. Assume that Art and Ali trust banks and transport companies more than they trust each other.

Letters of Credit

A letter of credit is a bank's commitment to pay a definite amount of money or extend a certain amount of credit to a third person, called a *beneficiary*. The bank extends credit to the beneficiary because a customer (called the account party) pays the bank to do so. The bank extends credit to (pays) the beneficiary (Ali) when he gives the bank certain pieces of paper (often, bills of lading).

The Independence Principle. The general rule is that letters of credit are independent of the underlying contract (to buy rugs in the Ali-Art example). Therefore, if Ali sends blue rugs instead of red, the issuing bank must honor the letter of credit. It assumes that the beneficiary (Ali) presents the documents that the letter of credit requires, often a bill of lading. It also assumes that Ali (the seller) substitutes nonconforming goods (blue rugs instead of red) in good faith. *GATX Leasing Corp. v. DBM Drilling Corp.* illustrates the independence principle.

GATX Leasing Corp. v. DBM Drilling Corp.

Texas Court of Appeals
657 S.W. 2d 178 (Tex. App. 4th Dist. 1983)

Background and Facts:

DBM Drilling Corporation was the account party of an irrevocable letter of credit. DBM arranged with Frost National Bank to issue an irrevocable letter of credit to GATX Leasing Corporation to pay for a drilling rig. GATX presented documents to Frost National Bank as the letter of credit required. DBM, however, claimed that the oil rig itself did not live up to the contract DBM had with GATX. DBM sued to enjoin the Frost Bank from honoring the letter of credit.

Issue

May the account party on a letter of credit stop the issuing bank from paying the letter of credit when the goods do not conform to the underlying contract but the documents conform to the letter of credit?

Decision

No. The account party may not stop the issuing bank from paying an irrevocable letter of credit in the case of a mere breach of the underlying contract. It was not a case involving fraud or forgery by the beneficiary. Instead, the beneficiary and account party merely disagreed about whether the oil rig was being sold or leased.

Stopping Payment on Letters of Credit: Forgery. Assume that a letter of credit requires the seller to submit a bill of lading to get paid. If the seller submits a forged bill of lading and knows it, the buyer can stop payment on the letter of credit.

Stopping Payment on Irrevocable Letters of Credit: Fraud. The buyer can stop the issuer from paying a letter of credit if the beneficiary commits fraud in the underlying contract. *Sztejn v. J. Henry Schroder Banking Corp.* illustrates the rule.

Sztejn v. J. Henry Schroder Banking Corp.

Supreme Court Special Term, New York County
177 Misc. 719, 31 N.Y.S. 2d 631 (1941)

Background and Facts:

Sztejn, a U.S. businessman, contracted to buy bristles from Transea Traders Ltd., located in India. Sztejn arranged for a letter of credit to pay for the goods. Transea fraudulently sent 50 crates with cow hair and other rubbish instead of the bristles agreed upon. Transea presented documents conforming to those that the letter of credit required. The buyer tried to stop the issuing bank from paying Transea's drafts drawn on the letter of credit. Transea argued that the letter of credit was independent of the bristle contract. Therefore, Transea claimed that the buyer could not stop payment of the letter of credit. Instead, it should sue Transea for breach of contract (a costly, slow, uncertain process).

Issue

Can a buyer stop payment under an irrevocable letter of credit when the seller fraudulently ships nonconforming goods but presents documents (bills of lading) conforming to the letter of credit?

Decision

Yes. The letter of credit ordinarily is independent of the underlying contract. Therefore, if the seller presents documents that conform to what the letter of credit requires, a court will not enjoin payment on the letter of credit. Here, the seller's fraud was called to the issuing bank's attention before presentation of the drafts and documents for payment. In such a case, the idea that the letter of credit is independent of the underlying contract should not be extended to protect a fraudulent seller.

The court noted that the seller would have won if the buyer had notified the bank of the seller's fraud after the bank had paid the letter of credit.

Bill of Lading

Definition of a Bill of Lading. A bill of lading is a piece of paper a transport company gives to someone. It shows three things:

1. A receipt for goods
2. A contract to transport the goods
3. Title to or ownership of the goods

Example of an International Business Deal: The Art-Ali Contract

First, Art and Ali entered a contract for the rugs. (Recall Art is an Atlanta buyer; Ali is an Ankara, Turkey, seller.) Second, Art arranged with his Atlanta bank to issue a letter of credit to Ali, through which Art pays Ali (see Figure 9.1).

FIGURE 9.1 Anatomy of an International Business Deal Using a Letter of Credit and a Bill of Lading: The Art-Ali Contract

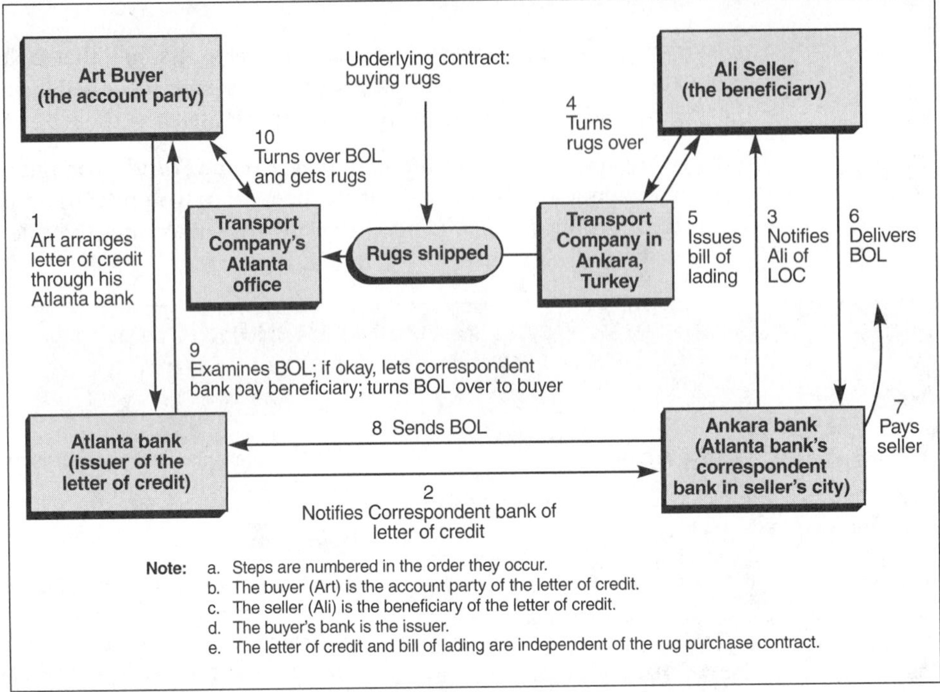

Often the bank issuing the letter of credit arranges for another bank, called a correspondent bank, in the seller's city to physically issue the letter of credit to the seller. (Assume that the Atlanta bank has a correspondent bank in Ankara.) The letter of credit will set out certain conditions that the foreign seller (Ali) must meet before the seller can draw on the credit. Drawing on the credit is how the seller is paid. It happens when the seller writes a draft (a check) on the letter of credit. It can be understood by comparing the letter of credit with a checking account that someone else sets up for you. You can then write checks using someone else's money. The same thing is true for the letter of credit that the buyer of goods has set up for the foreign seller.

Next, Ali delivers the rugs to a transport company in Ankara, Turkey. The transport company gives Ali a bill of lading for the rugs. Recall that the bill of lading is three things: a receipt showing that Ali actually turned something over to the shipper, a contract where the shipper agrees to transport the rugs to Art, and a title showing that whoever has the bill of lading owns the goods. Ali turns over the bill of lading to either Art's Atlanta bank or, more likely, the Atlanta bank's correspondent bank in Ankara.

When Ali turns the bill of lading over to the Ankara bank, it pays Ali. The Ankara bank could also delay paying Ali until the Atlanta bank determines that the bill of lading conforms to the letter of credit's requirements, which would be the more cautious way for the Ankara bank to pay Ali. The Ankara bank then sends the bill of lading to Art's Atlanta bank. The Atlanta bank checks the bill of lading to see that it meets the letter of credit's terms.

Notice that Art's Atlanta bank will not check the rugs—just the bill of lading for the rugs. The contract for the rugs is independent from the letter of credit and bill of lading. If the bill of lading meets the letter of credit's requirements, Art's Atlanta bank credits the Ankara bank's account.

Art's Atlanta bank charges Art for the letter of credit. It then gives Art the bill of lading. Art takes the bill of lading to the transport company's local office and gets the rugs. The deal is complete. Ali has his money, and Art has his rugs.

Harmonized Tariff Schedules

One crucial fact every business needs to know is whether the country where the good is to be imported imposes tariffs on such items, and, if they do, the amount. Tariffs can be very high—above 50 percent on some items or zero on other items such as original art works. It is interesting that a schoolteacher's wool coat purchased for $600 in Britain incurs a higher duty than a $50 million Picasso painting.

One can find what, if any, tariffs exist on goods shipped into the United States by consulting the Harmonized Tariff Schedule of the United States. The International Trade Commission publishes this book in loose-leaf form. It has tariff rates for virtually all items. This book can usually be found in larger libraries.

IMPORTING GRAY MARKET GOODS

Gray market goods refer to foreign-made goods bearing valid U.S. copyright, trademark, or other U.S. intellectual property protection that are imported into the United States without the consent of the U.S. trademark holder. At least three importing situations can give rise to gray market goods.

Case 1 Gray Market Goods

Here, a U.S. firm buys from an independent foreign firm both the rights to sell the foreign-made goods in the United States *and* the rights to register the foreign firm's trademark in the United States. Often the foreign manufacturer will have registered the foreign trademark in the United States. A U.S. firm would want to use the foreign firm's trademark because of the quality image associated with it. The gray market would arise if the foreign manufacturer exported its goods to the United States after having sold its trademark and the right to sell its goods in the United States to a particular U.S. firm. In such a case the U.S. firm would be forced into intrabrand competition with the very trademark it had purchased. Intrabrand competition could also arise if the foreign manufacturer sold its products outside the United States and a third party bought them there and imported them into the United States to compete once again with a valid trademark holder of those foreign goods. U.S. Customs Service regulations outlawing case 1 gray market goods were upheld by the U.S. Supreme Court in *Kmart Corp. v. Cartier, Inc.*

Case 2 Gray Market Goods

The second gray market situation occurs when a U.S. firm registers the U.S. trademark for goods made abroad by an affiliated manufacturer. In the most common case (called case 2a), a foreign parent firm controls U.S. distribution of its products by establishing a U.S. subsidiary. The subsidiary then registers a U.S. trademark under its own name, which is identical to the parent's foreign trademark. This type of gray market arises when a third party (such as K Mart) buys the foreign goods abroad either directly from the foreign parent or from another foreign source and imports them into the United

States. U.S. discount stores such as Kmart buy from foreign parents because they can often get lower prices when the U.S. dollar is stronger than foreign currencies. Two variations on case 2 occur when a U.S. firm sets up a manufacturing subsidiary abroad (case 2b) or its own unincorporated manufacturing division (case 2c) to make its U.S. trademarked goods, and then imports them for U.S. distribution. Then the foreign subsidiary or unincorporated foreign division may sell goods to U.S. companies that are not distributors of the U.S. parent firm. Importing of this type of gray market good by affiliates of the U.S. trademark holder is allowed under U.S. Customs regulations. Estimates are that as much as 98 percent of gray market goods enter the United States in a case 2 scenario. In *Kmart Corp. v. Cartier, Inc.*, the U.S. Supreme Court upheld Customs Service regulations authorizing case 2 gray market goods by foreign affiliates of U.S. firms.

Case 3 Gray Market Goods

The third type of gray market good occurs where a U.S. firm holding a U.S. trademark authorizes an independent foreign manufacturer the exclusive right to use the trademark in a particular foreign location, but it requires that the foreign manufacturer not import the trademarked goods into the United States. If the foreign manufacturer violates this agreement and ships the goods into the United States, or if a third party ships the goods into the United States, these foreign-made goods then compete in the United States with the U.S. manufacturer's domestic goods. This type of gray market good was declared illegal by the U.S. Supreme Court in *Kmart v. Cartier, Inc.*

1997 Supreme Court Case on Gray Market Goods

In 1997 the U.S. Supreme Court was again presented with situation akin to a gray market goods case, but this time the facts varied slightly: The gray market goods here were manufactured in the United States and had labels bearing valid U.S. copyrights. What made the goods "gray" was the fact that the U.S. copyright holder had originally shipped the goods to foreign countries on the assumption that they would be sold there at much lower prices than in the United States, where marketing costs contributed to and justified a much higher price. The U.S. copyright holder did not want the goods shipped back to the United States, which made the goods "gray," that is, improperly in the United States in the eyes of the U.S. manufacturer. Read the *Quality King Distributors v. L'anza Research International, Inc.* case to see whether the U.S. manufacturer was able to use the valid U.S. copyrighted labels as a basis for stopping the import of the goods. As you read the case, see whether you agree with Justice Stevens that this case is factually different enough from the *Kmart* case that it might not even involve "gray" market goods.

Quality King Distributors, Inc. v. L'Anza Research International, Inc.

U.S. Supreme Court
523 U.S. 135 (1997)

Background and Facts:

Respondent L'anza, a California manufacturer, sells its hair care products in this country exclusively to distributors who have agreed to resell within limited geographic areas and only to authorized retailers. L'anza promotes its domestic sales with extensive advertising and special retail training. In foreign markets, however, it does not engage in comparable advertising or promotion. Its foreign prices are substantially lower than its domestic prices. It appears that after L'anza's United Kingdom distributor arranged for the sale of several tons of L'anza products, affixed with U.S. copyrighted labels, to a distributor in Malta, that distributor sold the goods to Quality King Distributors, Inc. Quality King then imported the goods back into the United States without L'anza's permission and resold them at discounted prices to U.S. dealers unauthorized by L'anza to sell its products.

L'anza filed suit alleging that Quality King's actions violated L'anza's exclusive rights under the Copyright Act of 1976, sections 106, 501, and 602 to produce and distribute the copyrighted material in the United States. The federal district court rejected Quality King's "first sale" defense and entered judgment for L'anza. Concluding section 602(a), which gives copyright owners the right to prohibit the unauthorized importation of copies, would be "meaningless" if section 109(a) provided a defense, the Ninth Circuit Court of Appeals affirmed.

Body of Opinion

Justice Stevens

Section 106(3) of the Copyright Act of 1976 . . . gives the owner of a copyright the exclusive right to distribute copies of a copyrighted work. That exclusive right is expressly limited, however, by the provisions of sections 107 through 120. Section 602(a) gives the copyright owner the right to prohibit the unauthorized importation of copies. The question presented in this case is whether the right granted by section 602(a) is also limited by sections 107 through 120. More narrowly, the question is whether the "first sale" doctrine endorsed in section 109(a) is applicable to imported copies. . . .

In *Bobbs-Merrill v. Straus* . . . this court held that the exclusive right to "vend" under the copyright statute then in force applied only to the first sale of a copyrighted work. Congress subsequently codified Bobbs-Merrill's first sale doctrine in the Act. Section 106(3) gives the copyright holder the exclusive right "to distribute copies . . . by sale or other transfer of ownership," but section 109(a) provides: "Notwithstanding . . . section 106(3), the owner of a particular copy . . . lawfully made under this title . . . is entitled, without the authority of the copyright owner, to sell or otherwise dispose of the possession of that copy." . . . Although the first sale doctrine prevents L'anza from treating unauthorized resales by its domestic distributors as an infringement of the exclusive right to distribute, L'anza claims that section 602(a), properly construed, prohibits its foreign distributors from reselling its products to American vendors unable to buy from its domestic distributors.

The statutory language clearly demonstrates that the right granted by section 602(a) is subject to section 109(a). Significantly, section 602(a) does not categorically prohibit the unauthorized importation of copyrighted materials, but provides that, with three exceptions, such "importation . . . is an infringement of the exclusive right to distribute . . . under section 106. . . ." Section 106 in turn expressly states that all of the exclusive rights therein granted—including the distribution right granted by subsection (3)—are limited by sections 107 through 120. One of those limitations is provided by section 109(a), which expressly permits the owner of a lawfully made copy to sell that copy "notwithstanding the provisions of section 106(3)." After the first sale of a copyrighted item "lawfully made under this title," any subsequent purchaser whether from a domestic or a foreign reseller, is obviously an "owner" of that item. Read literally, section 109(a) unambiguously states that such an owner "is entitled, without the authority of the copyright owner, to sell" that item. Moreover, since section 602(a) merely provides that unauthorized importation is an infringement of an exclusive right "under section 106," and since that limited right does not encompass resales by lawful owners, section 602(a)'s literal text is simply inapplicable to both domestic and foreign owners of L'anza's products who decide to import and resell them here. . . .

The court finds unpersuasive the Solicitor General's argument that "importation" describes an act that is not protected by section 109(a)'s authorization to a subsequent owner "to sell or otherwise dispose of the possession of" a copy. An ordinary interpretation of that language includes the right to ship the copy to another person in another country. More important, the Solicitor General's cramped reading is at odds with section 109(a)'s necessarily broad reach. The whole point of the first sale doctrine is that once the copyright owner places a copyrighted item in the stream of commerce by selling it, he has exhausted his exclusive statutory right to control its distribution. There is no reason to assume that Congress intended section 109(a) to limit the doctrine's scope. . . .

Judgment and Result

The first sale doctrine is applicable to imported copies. Thus the U.S. copyright holder could not prevent the unauthorized import of the copyrighted goods here.

Questions

1. What section of the Copyright Act of 1976 was L'anza relying on to stop the reshipment of the cosmetics back into the United States? What section was Quality King relying on to limit L'anza's rights under section 602?
2. What is a gray market good? In a portion of the opinion omitted, Justice Stevens observes that ". . . we used those terms [gray market goods] to refer to the importation of foreign-manufactured goods bearing a valid U.S. trademark without the consent of the trademark holder. . . . We are not at all sure that those terms appropriately describe the consequences of an American manufacturer's decision to limit its promotional efforts to the domestic market and to sell

its products abroad at discounted prices that are so low that its foreign distributors can compete in its domestic market." Is Justice Stevens saying that the *Quality King Distributors, Inc. v. L'Anza Research International, Inc.* case might not be a gray market case? Why?

3. Does the *Quality King* case exemplify a philosophy in favor of or against restraints on importation of goods? What about the copyright holder's right to limit distribution including importation of copyrighted goods?
4. Had L'anza consigned (that is, kept title or ownership) the goods to foreign distributors and required that any foreign distributor not selling at retail in turn consign the goods to other distributors, do you think L'anza would have a stronger argument that it had the right to prevent shipment of the goods back into the United States? Why was it important to the Supreme Court that the title to the goods with the copyrighted labels had passed to the distributor? May a holder of a validly copyrighted label affixed to goods control who purchases the goods once they are sold? Why? What about consignments? What public policy is at work here?
5. What legal ethics are found in the *Quality King* decision?
6. Consider the following as a business ethics problem associated with gray market goods: Foreign manufacturers frequently sell their goods in different countries at different prices. Thus, for instance, a Japanese-made TV might be sold in Korea for $100 and in the United States for $200. In part this market differentiation is based on the various standards of living among countries. One consequence of this differentiated pricing is that consumers in the "upscale" countries, such as the United States, are subsidizing the consumers in the lower-income countries in the sense that a U.S. consumer is contributing a higher amount to the Japanese manufacturer's development costs than is the Korean consumer. Consider this problem from the standpoint of the business ethics noted in Chapter 1.

OTHER RULES GOVERNING INTERNATIONAL BUSINESS

The Foreign Corrupt Practices Act

In 1977 Congress passed the Foreign Corrupt Practices Act. It was amended in 1988. This act prohibits foreign corrupt practices by domestic concerns. Foreign corrupt practices are bribes. The act prohibits bribes to foreign officials (government employees) to influence official acts. For example, a U.S. company violates the act if it bribes an Iranian official to get oil drilling rights.

Businesses Covered. The Foreign Corrupt Practices Act (FCPA) covers businesses required to register their securities (called issuers) under the 1934 Securities Exchange Act. Covered businesses (issuers) can be corporations, partnerships, limited partnerships, business trusts, and unincorporated organizations. The FCPA also makes it illegal for any domestic concern to use the mails or interstate commerce to commit a foreign corrupt practice. Thus, the FCPA covers nonissuers of securities.

People Covered, Penalties, and Loopholes. People covered by the Foreign Corrupt Practices Act include an issuer's shareholders, officers, and directors who bribe to help the issuer. Violations of the Foreign Corrupt Practices Act are federal felonies. Punishments for certain individuals include five years in prison or a $100,000 fine or both. Covered business issuers violating the act can be fined up to $2 million.

The act does not apply to the following:

1. Small bribes (called grease payments) to foreign officials
2. Bribes to private (nongovernmental) foreigners
3. Extortion payments (when the foreign official first asks for a bribe and the issuer pays it)
4. Payments that are legal under the written laws of the foreign official's country.

Act of State Doctrine

The Act of State Doctrine says that U.S. courts should accept foreign governments' official acts at face value. For example, if Japan gives two people a marriage license, the United States should not question its validity. This rule generally applies to a government's official acts within its territory.

Reason for the Act of State Rule. The act of state rule keeps U.S. courts out of foreign affairs. Under the U.S. Constitution, Congress and the president—not the courts—run foreign affairs.

Business Example. Suppose the government of South Africa owns all the country's diamond mines. Suppose also that no company can mine diamonds unless it has a government permit. If the South African government gives deBoors Company such a permit, the U.S. courts cannot say that the permit is illegal. This matter is South Africa's business, not that of the U.S. courts.

State Securities Law Exception. In the following case, Mr. Riedel, an Ohio resident, deposited $100,000 in a Mexican bank. He later transferred his certificate of deposit (CD) to another Mexican bank to get the certificate payable in U.S. dollars instead of Mexican pesos (which were declining in value). After he got his dollar-denominated CD, the government of Mexico issued currency regulations forcing Mexican banks to pay back depositors both the interest and principal only in pesos. Later, the Mexican government nationalized all that nation's banks. When the CD matured, the Mexican bank sent Riedel a check in pesos, which turned out to be worth only $53,276.63—much less than what he had deposited. He sued the Mexican bank in Ohio claiming, among other things, that the CD was a security under Ohio law; thus, the security had to be registered, which it was not. The U.S. Court of Appeals agreed with Riedel.

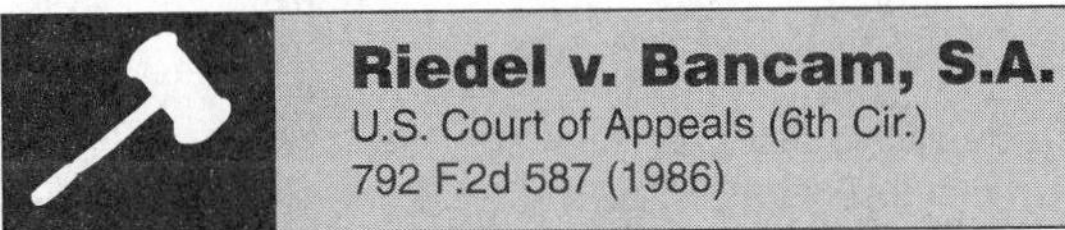

Riedel v. Bancam, S.A.

U.S. Court of Appeals (6th Cir.)
792 F.2d 587 (1986)

Background and Facts:

This appeal raises the question whether plaintiff-appellant, W. Christian Riedel, can maintain an action for alleged violations of Ohio securities law against defendant-appellee, Bancam, S.A. ("Bancam"), a Mexican bank that the Government of Mexico has nationalized. . . .

In January 1981, Riedel, a resident of the State of Ohio, asked Unibanco, S.A. ("Unibanco"), a Mexican bank, to transfer $100,000 to Banca Metropolitana, S.A. ("Bamesa"), another Mexican bank and a predecessor of Bancam, so that Riedel could purchase a dollar-denominated certificate of deposit from Bamesa. . . . On January 1, 1982, Bamesa and another Mexican bank merged, forming Bancam. On July 6, 1982, Riedel renewed the certificate for the last time and Bancam sent Riedel "Deposito de Dolares en Administracion a Plazo Fijo con Tasa Fija No. 077996" acknowledging an interest rate of 20.1737 percent per annum and a new maturity date of January 20, 1983. Neither Bamesa nor Bancam registered any of the certificates of deposit with either the Securities and Exchange Commission or the Ohio Division of Securities.

On August 13, 1982, the Government of Mexico issued rules governing the payment of bank deposits denominated in foreign currency which prohibited Mexican banks from using dollars to repay the holders of dollar-denominated certificates of deposit. The rules required Mexican banks to pay principal and interest on dollar-denominated deposits in pesos, at a rate of exchange substantially below the financial market exchange rate, rather than in dollars. On September 1, 1982, the Government of Mexico nationalized all privately owned Mexican banks. Consequently, Bancam, like every other banking institution in Mexico, became wholly owned by the Government of Mexico.

At maturity of the final renewal of the certificate of deposit, Bancam sent appellant a check in repayment of his certificate of deposit in the amount of 7,434,000 pesos in accordance with the exchange rate of 74.34 pesos to the dollar, the current legal exchange rate. Since the financial market exchange rate was approximately 149.5 pesos to the dollar, Riedel could only convert the 7,434,000 pesos to $53,276.63. Nevertheless, Riedel cashed the check.

On January 19, 1984, Riedel brought this action in the U.S. District Court for the Northern District of Ohio alleging violations of federal and Ohio securities laws. On June 7, 1984, Bancam filed a motion to dismiss the complaint.... Initially, Bancam argued that section 4(a) of the Foreign Sovereign Immunities Act of 1976 ("FSIA"), precluded the District Court from asserting personal or subject matter jurisdiction over the action. Second, Bancam argued that the "act of state doctrine" and the Articles of Agreement of the International Monetary Fund ("Fund Agreement") required dismissal for failure to state a claim upon which the District Court could grant relief because Riedel based the action solely on the Government of Mexico's actions in issuing and enforcing currency exchange rules which required banks to repay dollar-denominated certificates of deposit in pesos. Third, Bancam contended that the complaint failed to state a cause of action because the certificates of deposit were not "securities."... The District Court concluded that it lacked jurisdiction over the Ohio securities law and breach of contract claims. The District Court stated that 28 U.S.C. §1332 "does not permit a citizen of this state to sue a foreign government or agency thereof, in a federal district court."

This appeal raises several questions: (1) Whether the FSIA gives the District Court subject matter jurisdiction over Riedel's claims for breach of contract and violations of Ohio Revised Code ("ORC") Chapter 1707 ("Ohio securities law"); (2) Whether the act of state doctrine bars Riedel's claims against a Mexican bank that the Government of Mexico has nationalized.

Body of Opinion

Circuit Judge Cornelia G. Kennedy

In this appeal, Riedel does not challenge the District Court's conclusion that the certificates of deposit that Bancam issued are not "securities" under federal securities law. Instead, Riedel argues that the "act of state doctrine" does not bar his breach of contract and Ohio securities law claims. The District Court, however, did not refer to the "act of state doctrine" in denying Riedel's motion for a new trial. In addition to holding, as a matter of law, that the certificate of deposit involved in this case was not a "security" under federal securities law, the District Court ruled that it did not have jurisdiction over Riedel's breach of contract and Ohio securities law claims. The District Court concluded that: "Diversity jurisdiction pursuant to 28 U.S.C. Section 1332, does not permit a citizen of this state to sue a foreign government or agency thereof, in a federal district court."...

[W]e hold that the District Court properly concluded that it did not have jurisdiction under 28 U.S.C. §1332 over the breach of contract and Ohio securities law claims.

We conclude, however, that the District Court may have had jurisdiction over the breach of contract and Ohio securities law claims under FSIA. Although the FSIA ordinarily entitles foreign states to immunity from federal jurisdiction, 28 U.S.C. §1605(a)(2) creates a "commercial activity" exception to this immunity. Title 28 U.S.C. §1605(a)(2) provides in pertinent part:

> A foreign state shall not be immune from the jurisdiction of courts of the United States or of the States in any case...in which the action is based upon commercial activity carried on in the United States by the foreign state; or upon an act performed in the United States in connection with a commercial activity of the foreign state elsewhere or upon an act outside the territory of the United States in connection with a commercial activity of the foreign state elsewhere and that act causes a direct effect in the United States.

We agree and hold that the sale of the certificates of deposit in this case was a "commercial activity."...

Under the "act of state doctrine," courts exercise jurisdiction but prudentially "decline to decide the merits of the case if in doing so we would need to judge the validity of the public acts of a sovereign state performed within its own territory."

In *Callejo v. Bancomer, S.A., supra*, the Fifth Circuit concluded that the "act of state doctrine" precluded the court from inquiring into the validity of Mexico's currency exchange regulations.... We agree with the Callejos that these securities claims are not barred by the act of state doctrine, since they are based on Bancomer's initial failure to register the certificates of deposit, not on Bancomer's later breach of the certificates by complying with Mexico's exchange control regulations.... We dismiss these claims, however, on the ground that the certificates of deposit sold by Bancomer were not "securities" within the meaning of the federal and Texas securities laws.

We adopt the reasoning of the Fifth Circuit in *Callejo v. Bancomer, S.A.*, regarding the "act of state doctrine." Consequently, we hold that the "act of state doctrine" precludes the District Court from addressing Riedel's breach of contract claim. Accordingly, we affirm the portion of the District Court's order denying Riedel's motion for a new trial on the breach of contract claim. The "act of state doctrine," however, does not bar the Ohio securities law claim. Riedel bases that claim on Bancam's failure to register the certificate of deposit with the Ohio Division of Securities and not on Bancam's failure to repay dollars at the certificate's maturity.

We reject Bancam's contention that the certificates of deposit are not "securities" under ORC §1707.01(B). Accordingly, we reverse the portion of the District Court's order denying Riedel's motion for a new trial on the Ohio securities law claim.

Since the District Court may have had subject matter jurisdiction, we remand the Ohio securities law claim for further proceedings consistent with this opinion.

Judgment and Result

Accordingly, we affirm the portion of the District Court's order denying Riedel's motion for a new trial on the breach of contract claim, reverse the portion of the District Court's order denying Riedel's motion for a new trial on the Ohio securities law claim, and remand the Ohio securities law claim for further proceedings consistent with this opinion. (The U.S. Court of Appeals decided that despite the act of state doctrine, the plaintiff could question the legality of the Mexican government's rewriting the contracts under the Ohio securities law.)

Questions

1. What rate of interest was Mr. Riedel earning on his certificate of deposit (CD) in the Mexican bank? Why do you suppose he was promised such a high rate of interest?
2. Is a CD a "security" under Ohio law?
3. A foreign nation that nationalizes all the banks in the country and rewrites the local banks' CD contracts to require payment of interest and principal in pesos instead of U.S. dollars, this is the act of a foreign state, giving rise to the "act of state" doctrine. Does the *Riedel* case create a state securities law exception to the act of state doctrine?
4. Did the court of appeals find that some of the acts involved in the *Riedel* case did give rise to the "act of state" defense?

SETTLING INTERNATIONAL BUSINESS DISPUTES

Businesspersons who deal in the United States can often recite many problems that can ruin a business deal here. However, the difficulties increase dramatically when deals go international. Currency fluctuations, wars, confiscation, and economic boycotts all make dealing in foreign trade much riskier than conducting business domestically.

Ways of Settling Disputes

Here we consider three ways of settling international disputes. Then our attention turns to two problems concerning international lawsuits by and against businesses. One deals with the Foreign Sovereign Immunities Act (FSIA) in the context of a currency devaluation, and the other deals with the *forum non conveniens* doctrine in the Bhopal Gas Plant Disaster.

Private Settlement. If trouble occurs with an international business deal, a person can do several things. First, the parties can work out their problems themselves, which is the less expensive, faster way to settle contract disputes. For this approach to work, the parties must be reasonable and flexible. The legal system should be avoided if possible because international litigation is filled with uncertainty and it is expensive. Most important, it can destroy a business's goodwill.

Arbitration. Second, the parties can put an arbitration provision in their contract. An arbitration provision names a neutral third person to settle contract disputes. Arbitration is slower and costs more than a private settlement but is faster and less expensive than suing in a court.

Information about the American Arbitration Association can be found at ***http://www.adr.org***

http://

Lawsuit. A third approach is for the parties to sue each other in court, but this process is expensive and slow. Also, finding a court that will handle international business disputes is difficult. For example, the International Court of Justice in The Hague, Netherlands, is not available for private lawsuits. Only governments can sue governments there.

One business can sue another business in a country's courts, but to do so, the business suing must locate the business sued in a country where jurisdiction exists. The parties can specify in their contracts which country's rules will apply in the settlement of contract disputes.

Suing Foreign Governments

Foreign nations generally may not be sued. This is called the sovereign immunity doctrine. The U.S. Congress has enacted the Foreign Sovereign Immunities Act (FSIA), which makes foreign governments immune from suit in the United States. The FSIA has exceptions, however, which means that under certain circumstances, foreign governments *can* be sued in U.S. courts. These exceptions arise when (1) the foreign government waives (voluntarily gives up) the sovereign immunity defense, and (2) a foreign nation carries on a commercial activity in the United States.

Riedel v. Bancam, discussed earlier in this chapter, deals with the FSIA.

Forum Non Conveniens: Where to Sue When Things Go Wrong

http:// *When faced with international business problems, a good resource would be the lawyer directory at* ***http://www.martindale.com/locator/home.html***

The forum non conveniens doctrine is a rule of U.S. law that says that when a lawsuit may be brought in more than one court, the trial judge originally trying the case has the discretion to tell the litigants, "Go to another court; it is more convenient." The main factors the original judge should use in making that decision are matters of convenience, such as where the event giving rise to the suit occurred, where the witnesses are, and which court is more experienced in the type of litigation. In the *Bhopal* case, victims of an industrial disaster in India sued Union Carbide Corporation (UCC) in New York City rather than in India, where the events occurred. The U.S. Court of Appeals sent the case back to India on grounds of forum non conveniens.

A related issue in the *Bhopal* case discusses whether the U.S. courts would have to honor an Indian court judgment against Union Carbide Corporation property *in the United States* if an attempt is made to collect that Indian judgment in the United States. The case answers, "Yes," to that question, if Indian courts are impartial, their procedures are compatible with due process, and the Indian court has jurisdiction over the defendant.

Thus, U.S. courts often will enforce judgments from foreign countries' courts against U.S. businesses and individuals.

In Re Union Carbide Corp. Gas Plant Disaster

U.S. Court of Appeals (2d Cir.)
809 F.2d 195 (1987)

Background and Facts:

This appeal raises the question of whether thousands of claims by citizens of India and the Government of India arising out of the most devastating industrial disaster in history—the deaths of over 2,000 persons and injuries of over 200,000 caused by lethal gas known as methyl isocyanate which was released from a chemical plant operated by Union Carbide India Limited (UCIL) in Bhopal, India—should be tried in the United States or in India. The Southern District of New York, John F. Keenan, *Judge*, granted the motion of Union Carbide Corporation (UCC), a defendant in some 145 actions commenced in federal courts in the United States, to dismiss these actions on grounds of *forum non conveniens* so that the claims may be tried in India, subject to certain conditions. The individual plaintiffs appeal from the order and the court's denial of their motion for a fairness hearing on a proposed settlement. UCC and the Union of India (UOI), a plaintiff, cross-appeal. We eliminate two of the conditions imposed by the district court and in all other respects affirm that court's orders.

The accident occurred on the night of December 2–3, 1984, when winds blew the deadly gas from the plant operated by UCIL into densely occupied parts of the city of Bhopal. UCIL is incorporated under the laws of India. Fifty and nine-tenths percent of its stock is owned by UCC, 22% is owned or controlled by the government of India, and the balance is held by approximately 23,500 Indian citizens. The stock is publicly traded on the Bombay Stock Exchange. The company is engaged in the manufacture of a variety of products, including chemicals, plastics, fertilizers and insecticides, at 14 plants in India and employs over 9,000 Indian citizens. It is managed and operated entirely by Indians in India.

Four days after the Bhopal accident, on December 7, 1984, the first of some 145 purported class actions in federal district courts in the United States was commenced on behalf of victims of the disaster. On January 2, 1985, the Judicial Panel on Multidistrict Litigation assigned the actions to the Southern District of New York where they became the subject of a consolidated complaint filed on June 28, 1985.

In the meantime, on March 29, 1985, India enacted the Bhopal Gas Leak Disaster (Processing of Claims) Act, granting to its government, the UOI, the exclusive right to represent the victims in India or elsewhere. Thereupon the UOI, purporting to act in the capacity of *parens patriae*, and with retainers executed by many of the victims, on April 8, 1985, filed a complaint in the Southern District of New York on behalf of all victims of the Bhopal disaster, similar to the purported class action complaints already filed by individuals in the United States. The UOI's decision to bring suit in the United States was attributed to the fact that, although numerous lawsuits (by now, some 6,500) had been instituted by victims in India against UCIL, the Indian courts did not have jurisdiction over UCC, the parent company, which is a defendant in the United States actions. The actions in India asserted claims not only against UCIL but also against the UOI, the State of Madhya Pradesh, and the Municipality of Bhopal, and were consolidated in the District Court of Bhopal.

By order dated April 25, 1985, Judge Keenan appointed a three-person Executive Committee to represent all plaintiffs in the pretrial proceedings. It consisted of two lawyers representing the individual plaintiffs and one representing the UOI. On July 31, 1985, UCC moved to dismiss the complaint on grounds of *forum non conveniens*, the plaintiffs' lack of standing to bring the actions in the United States, and their purported attorneys' lack of authority to represent them. After several months of discovery related to *forum non conveniens*, the individual plaintiffs and the UOI opposed UCC's motion. After hearing argument on January 3, 1986, the district court, on May 12, 1986, 634 F.Supp. 842, in a thoroughly reasoned 63-page opinion granted the motion, dismissing the lawsuits before it on condition that UCC:

> (1) consent to the jurisdiction of the courts of India and continue to waive defenses based on the statute of limitations,
>
> (2) agree to satisfy any judgment rendered by an Indian court against it and upheld on appeal, provided the judgment and affirmance "comport with the minimal requirements of due process," and
>
> (3) be subject to discovery under the Federal Rules of Civil Procedure of the United States.

On June 12, 1986, UCC accepted these conditions subject to its right to appeal them; and on June 24, 1986, the district court entered its order of dismissal. In September 1986 the UOI, acting pursuant to its authority under the Bhopal Act, brought suit on behalf of all claimants against UCC and UCIL in the District Court of Bhopal, where many individual suits by victims of the disaster were then pending. . . .

India's interest is increased by the fact that it has for years treated UCIL as an Indian national, subjecting it to intensive regulations and governmental supervision of the construction, development and operation of the Bhopal plant, its emissions, water and air pollution, and safety precautions. Numerous Indian government officials have regularly conducted on-site inspections of the plant and approved its machinery and equipment, including its facilities for storage of the lethal methyl isocyanate gas that escaped and caused the disaster giving rise to the claims. Thus India has considered the plant to be an Indian one and the disaster to be an Indian problem. It therefore has a deep interest in ensuring compliance with its safety standards. Moreover, plaintiffs have conceded that in view of India's strong interest in its greater contacts with the plant, its operations, its employees, and the victims of the accident, the law of India, as the place where the tort occurred, will undoubtedly govern. In contrast, the American interests are relatively minor. Indeed, a long trial of the 145 cases here would unduly burden an already overburdened court, involving both jury hardship and heavy expense. It would face the court with numerous practical difficulties, including the almost impossible task of attempting to understand extensive relevant Indian regulations published in a foreign language and the slow process of receiving testimony of scores of witnesses through interpreters.

Having made the foregoing findings, Judge Keenan dismissed the actions against UCC on grounds of *forum non conveniens* upon the conditions indicated, after obtaining UCC's consent to those conditions subject to its right to appeal the order. After the plaintiffs filed their notice of appeal, UCC and the Union of India filed cross appeals.

Upon these appeals, the plaintiffs continue to oppose the dismissal. The Union of India, however, has changed its position and now supports the district court's order. UCC, as it did in the district court, opposes as unfair the condition that it submit to discovery pursuant to the

Federal Rules of Civil Procedure without reciprocally obligating the plaintiffs and Union of India to be subject to discovery on the same basis so that both sides might be treated equally, giving each the same access to the facts in the others' possession.

Upon argument of the appeal, UCC also took the position that the district court's order requiring it to satisfy any Indian court judgment was unfair unless some method were provided, such as continued availability of the district court as a forum, to ensure that any denial of due process by the Indian courts could be remedied promptly by the federal court here rather than delay resolution of the issue until termination of the Indian court proceedings and appeal, which might take several years. UCC's argument in this respect was based on the sudden issuance by the Indian court in Bhopal of a temporary order freezing all of UCC's assets, which could have caused it irreparable injury if it had been continued indefinitely, and by the conflict of interest posed by the UOI's position in the Indian courts where, since the UOI would appear both as a plaintiff and a defendant, it might as a plaintiff voluntarily dismiss its claims against itself as a defendant or, as a co-defendant with UCC, be tempted to shed all blame upon UCC even though the UOI had in fact been responsible for supervision, regulation and safety of UCIL's Bhopal plant.

Body of Opinion

Circuit Judge Mansfield

The standard to be applied in reviewing the district court's forum non conveniens dismissal was clearly expressed by the Supreme Court in *Piper Aircraft Co. v. Reyno*, . . . as follows:

> The *forum non conveniens* determination is committed to the sound discretion of the trial court. It may be reversed only when there has been a clear abuse of discretion; where the court has considered all relevant public and private interest factors, and where its balancing of these factors is reasonable, its decision deserves substantial deference.

Having reviewed Judge Keenan's detailed decision, in which he thoroughly considered the comparative adequacy of the forums and the public and private interests involved, we are satisfied that there was no abuse of discretion in his granting dismissal of the action. On the contrary, it might reasonably be concluded that it would have been an abuse of discretion to deny a *forum non conveniens* dismissal. . . . Practically all relevant factors demonstrate that transfer of the cases to India for trial and adjudication is both fair and just to the parties.

Plaintiffs' principal contentions in favor of retention of the cases by the district court are that deference to the plaintiffs' choice of forum has been inadequate, that the Indian courts are insufficiently equipped for the task, that UCC has its principal place of business here, that the most probative evidence regarding negligence and causation is to be found here, that federal courts are much better equipped through experience and procedures to handle such complex actions efficiently than are Indian courts, and that a transfer of the cases to India will jeopardize a $350 million settlement being negotiated by plaintiffs' counsel. All of these arguments, however, must be rejected. . . .

Although the plaintiffs' American counsel may at one time have been close to reaching a $350 million settlement of the cases, no such settlement was ever finalized. No draft joint stipulation in writing or settlement agreement appears to have been prepared, much less approved by the parties. No petition for certification of a settlement class under Fed.R.Civ.P. 23 has ever been presented. . . . Most important, the UOI, which is itself a plaintiff and states that it now represents the Indian plaintiffs formerly represented by American counsel, is firmly opposed to the $350 million "settlement" as inadequate. Under these circumstances, to order a Rule 23 "fairness" hearing would be futile. The district court's denial of the American counsels' motion for such a hearing must accordingly be affirmed. . . .

As the district court found, the record shows that the private interests of the respective parties weigh heavily in favor of dismissal on grounds of *forum non conveniens*. The many witnesses and sources of proof are almost entirely located in India, where the accident occurred, and could not be compelled to appear for trial in the United States. The Bhopal plant at the time of the accident was operated by some 193 Indian nationals, including the managers of seven operating units employed by the Agricultural Products Division of UCIL, who reported to Indian Works Managers in Bhopal. The plant was maintained by seven functional departments employing over 200 more Indian nationals. UCIL kept at the plant daily, weekly and monthly records of plant operations and records of maintenance as well as records of the plant's Quality Control, Purchasing and Stores branches, all operated by Indian employees. The great majority of documents bearing on the design, safety, start-up and operation of the plant, as well as the safety training of the plant's employees, is located in India. Proof to be offered at trial would be derived from interviews of these witnesses in India and study of the records located there to determine whether the accident was caused by negligence on the part of the management or employees in the operation of the plant, by fault in its design, or by sabotage. In short, India has greater ease of access to the proof than does the United States.

The plaintiffs seek to prove that the accident was caused by negligence on the part of UCC in originally contributing to the design of the plant and its provision for storage of excessive amounts of the gas at the plant. As Judge Keenan found, however, UCC's participation was limited and its involvement in plant operations terminated long before the accident. Under 1973 agreements negotiated at arm's-length with UCIL, UCC did provide a summary "process design package" for construction of the plant and the services of some of its technicians to monitor the progress of UCIL in detailing the design and erecting the plant. However, the UOI controlled the terms of the agreements and precluded UCC from exercising any authority to "detail design, erect and commission the plant," which was done independently over the period from 1972 to 1980 by UCIL process design engineers who supervised, among many others, some 55 to 60 Indian engineers employed by the Bombay engineering firm of Humphreys and Glasgow. The preliminary process design information furnished by UCC could not have been used to construct the plant. Construction required the detailed process design and engineering data prepared by hundreds of Indian engineers, process designers and subcontractors. During the ten years spent constructing the plant, its design and configuration underwent many changes.

The vital parts of the Bhopal plant, including its storage tank, monitoring instrumentation, and vent gas scrubber, were manufactured by Indians in India. Although some 40 UCIL employees were given some safety training at UCC's plant in West Virginia, they represented a small fraction of the Bhopal plant's employees. The vast majority of plant employees were selected and trained by UCIL in Bhopal. The manual for start-up of the Bhopal plant was prepared by Indians employed by UCIL.

In short, the plant has been constructed and managed by Indians in India. No Americans were employed at the plant at the time of the accident. In the five years from 1980 to 1984, although more than 1,000 Indians were employed at the plant, only one American was employed there and he left in 1982. No Americans visited the plant for more than one year prior to the accident, and during the 5-year period before the accident the communications between the plant and the United States were almost nonexistent.

The vast majority of material witnesses and documentary proof bearing on causation of and liability for the accident is located in India, not the United States, and would be more accessible to an Indian court than to a United States court. The records are almost entirely in Hindi or other Indian languages, understandable to an Indian court without translation. The witnesses for the most part do not speak English but Indian languages understood by an Indian court but not by an American court. These witnesses could be required to appear in an Indian court but not in a court of the United States. Although witnesses in the United States could not be subpoenaed to appear in India, they are comparatively few in number and most are employed by UCC which, as a party, would produce them in India, with lower overall transportation costs than if the parties were to attempt to bring hundreds of Indian witnesses to the United States. Lastly, Judge Keenan properly concluded that an Indian court would be in a better position to direct and supervise a viewing of the Bhopal plant, which was sealed after the accident. Such a viewing could be of help to a court in determining liability issues.

The first condition, that UCC consent to the Indian court's personal jurisdiction over it and waive the statute of limitations as a defense, are not unusual and have been imposed in numerous cases where the foreign court would not provide an adequate alternative in the absence of such a condition. . . . The remaining two conditions, however, pose problems.

In requiring that UCC consent to enforceability of an Indian judgment against it, the district court proceeded at least in part on the erroneous assumption that, absent such a requirement, the plaintiffs, if they should succeed in obtaining an Indian judgment against UCC, might not be able to enforce it against UCC in the United States. The law, however, is to the contrary. Under New York law, which governs actions brought in New York to enforce foreign judgments, . . . a foreign-country judgment that is final, conclusive and enforceable where rendered must be recognized and will be enforced as "conclusive between the parties to the extent that it grants or denies recovery of a sum of money" except that it is not deemed to be conclusive if:

> (1) the judgment was rendered under a system which does not provide impartial tribunals or procedures compatible with the requirements of due process of law;
>
> (2) the foreign court did not have personal jurisdiction over the defendant. . . .

UCC contends that Indian courts, while providing an adequate alternative forum, do not observe due process standards that would be required as a matter of course in this country. As evidence of this apprehension it points to the haste with which the Indian court in Bhopal issued a temporary order freezing its assets throughout the world and the possibility of serious prejudice to it if the UOI is permitted to have the double and conflicting staphhtus of both plaintiff and co-defendant in the Indian court proceedings. It argues that we should protect it against such denial of due process by authorizing Judge Keenan to retain the authority, after *forum non conveniens* dismissal of the cases here, to monitor the Indian court proceedings and be available on call to rectify in some undefined way any abuses of UCC's right to due process as they might occur in India.

UCC's proposed remedy is not only impractical but evidences an abysmal ignorance of basic jurisdictional principles, so much so that it borders on the frivolous. The district court's jurisdiction is limited to proceedings before it in this country. Once it dismisses those proceedings on grounds of *forum non conveniens* it ceases to have any further jurisdiction over the matter unless and until a proceeding may some day be brought to enforce here a final and conclusive Indian money judgment. Nor could we, even if we attempted to retain some sort of supervisory jurisdiction, impose our due process requirements upon Indian courts, which are governed by their laws, not ours. The concept of shared jurisdictions is both illusory and unrealistic. The parties cannot simultaneously submit to both jurisdictions the resolution of the pretrial and trial issues when there is only one consolidated case pending in one court. Any denial by the Indian courts of due process can be raised by UCC as a defense to the plaintiffs' later attempt to enforce a resulting judgment against UCC in this country.

Judgment and Result

For these reasons we direct that the condition with respect to the discovery of UCC under the Federal Rules of Civil Procedure be deleted without prejudice to the right of the parties to have reciprocal discovery of each other on equal terms under the Federal Rules, subject to such approval as may be required of the Indian court in which the case will be pending. If, for instance, Indian authorities will permit mutual discovery pursuant to the Federal Rules, the district court's order, as modified in accordance with this opinion, should not be construed to bar such procedure. In the absence of such a court-sanctioned agreement, however, the parties will be limited by the applicable discovery rules of the Indian court in which the claims will be pending.

As so modified the district court's order is affirmed. (The U.S. Court of Appeals transferred this case to India.)

Questions

1. Is it basically up to the discretion of the trial judge where the case is first brought to decide whether it should be sent to some other court because of forum non conveniens?
2. Where did the major event giving rise to the case occur? Where were the plant, the victims, and the witnesses?
3. What argument could be made for trying the Bhopal disaster case in New York City?
4. Would a New York or Bhopal jury be more likely to bring in a large damage verdict in the plaintiffs' favor?
5. What did the U.S. Court of Appeals do with the first condition, that Union Carbide Corporation (UCC) consent to the Indian court's personal jurisdiction over it and give up (waive) the statute of limitations as a defense? Do you think it is fair that a foreign nation such as India should be able to force a business to give up a defense it otherwise would have in the United States?
6. Why did the U.S. Court of Appeals knock out the trial court's second condition, that UCC must agree that an Indian court's judgment against UCC (should one be given) would bind UCC if the plaintiffs tried to enforce that judgment against UCC's property in the United States?
7. What reason did the U.S. Court of Appeals give for deleting the condition that UCC be subject to discovery in India according to United States—not Indian—rules of discovery? Can a U.S. court tell another nation's court system what procedural rules to use?
8. After this case the Indian government as representative of the victims filed a $3.3 billion lawsuit in an Indian court against UCC. That lower court rendered an interim decision against UCC in which UCC was told to pay immediately to the victims $270 million *before* final resolution of UCC's liability. UCC appealed this to an Indian appellate court, which on April 4, 1988, reduced to $195 million in immediate interim damages. In so doing the judge found UCC's liability adequately proven even though UCC argued that *no trial* had as yet determined that UCC was liable. Some see this decision as increasing the likelihood of a settlement. The $195 million award was to be divided as follows: $1950 each for the minor injury victims, $3900 each for the more seriously injured, and $7800 each for survivors of the deceased or those suffering the most serious injuries. About 520,000 claims have been filed, but UCC claims that many are fraudulent. Even though the appellate court in India reduced the verdict by $75 million, it apparently went further in declaring that there was more than a prima facie case against UCC. UCC has argued that sabotage caused the disaster.

In 1989 the government of India and Union Carbide entered an agreement capping UC's damages to all Indian victims at $470 million. This settlement occurred after the Supreme Court of India decreed the award.

Expropriation

Expropriation refers to a foreign government's seizing a business's assets in that country and giving less than fair value in return. This situation often happens following a foreign political revolution. The Iranian revolution in 1979 is an example. Millions, perhaps billions, of dollars of U.S. firms' assets were seized and inadequately paid for by the new Iranian government. Expropriation arises only if a U.S. company has a plant or property in a foreign country. Therefore, companies in the United States do not have to worry about foreign expropriation.

Repatriation

Repatriation means bringing back to the United States income and investments that U.S. businesses have earned or made in foreign countries. Many foreign countries lure U.S. businesses into them by telling of high profits that can be made there, sometimes forgetting to tell of limits on getting those profits back to the United States. U.S. businesses should make certain they ask whether a foreign country limits taking profits back to the United States.

CHAPTER SUMMARY

International business deals often use letters of credit and bills of lading to promote trust between the parties. Although letters of credit are independent of the underlying contract, under some circumstances courts will stop payment on "irrevocable" letters of credit.

Gray market goods refer to foreign-made goods bearing a valid U.S. trademark, which are shipped into the United States without the consent of the U.S. trademark holder. Most gray market goods are legally shipped into the United States. A Supreme Court decision tells us that U.S.-made goods with a copyrighted U.S. label may be shipped back into the United States without approval of the U.S. copyright owner if a legal "first sale" of the goods abroad has been transacted.

The Foreign Corrupt Practices Act makes it illegal for certain persons connected with U.S. corporations to use the mails or interstate commerce to bribe a foreign government official. This act exempts "grease" payments and certain other payments to foreigners.

MANAGER'S ETHICAL DILEMMA

Bill Foster knew that his job was on the line. He had been the top salesperson for Airpower Company in Seattle, Washington, for several years, but this year was terrible. He sold international jumbo jets for passenger services, mainly concentrating his efforts in the Middle East and Far Eastern markets. International competitors, especially the European consortium, Flybus, was somehow winning orders that Bob had formerly obtained. He learned of the underlying reasons for his competitors' success during a conversation in a hotel bar in Bahrain, when a friend remarked, "Bob, you've got to start playing ball with some of these foreign buyers."

"What do you mean?" asked Bob.

"Payola, old boy. It works every time," said Pierre Goldfinger of France. "You simply make the foreign buyer a "consultant" and he pushes his client—usually a government-run airline—to buy your product, even if it is more expensive."

"But why would a foreign buyer's agent purchase a product that is more expensive than the European model?" quizzed Bill.

"Oh, that's an easy one. Simply point out that your company has higher quality products. Foreign buyers don't want to have a plane crash on their hands with hundreds of angry relatives complaining that the government's procurement policies cost them their loved ones," rejoined Pierre.

"But Pierre, bribery of foreign government officials is illegal under U.S. law," Bill observed.

"Ah, you Americans are, how you say, 'hung up on legalities.' When in Rome, do as the Romans do, Bill. Everybody bribes a little, and it's for a good cause. Think of all of those American jobs you'd be saving in Seattle, to say nothing of your own. Further, if other nations' laws do not forbid bribery of government officials, why should you be put at a disadvantage by your own country?" asked Pierre.

Should Bill Foster "join the club" and bribe to get foreign government business as his foreign competitors appear to be doing?

Discussion Questions

1. This chapter quoted the *Kmart v. Cartier* case to define a gray market good as a foreign-made good bearing a valid U.S. trademark that is imported into the United States without the consent of the owner of that mark. What is it about the *Quality King Distributors, Inc. v. L'anza* case in this chapter that might make one hesitant to conclude that the Quality King case is a gray market case? If the term *gray market* is not statutorily defined but, rather, is federal common law, might not the term be subject to interpretation and consequently given a broader definition by a later case such as *Quality King*? How much did the Supreme Court rely on the term *gray market good* in *Quality King* to make its decision?
2. This chapter showed the mechanics of an international contract between a U.S. buyer and a foreign seller. Describe how the deal would work if the foreign business had bought and the U.S. business had sold. Who would arrange for the letter of credit? Who would draw on the letter of credit? Would would get the bill of lading? What would this person do with the bill of lading?
3. Suppose Art, the rug dealer in the scenario in this chapter, gets into a dispute with Ali, the Turkish rug seller. Why would Art not take the case to the International Court of Justice in The Hague, Netherlands?
4. What is a bill of lading?
5. Name the parties in a letter of credit and explain their function.
6. Why, as a practical matter, do people use letters of credit and bills of lading instead of dealing more directly with one another in international business?
7. If a beneficiary of a letter of credit presents fraudulent documents to the confirming bank to draw on the letter of credit, this act of fraud entitles an account party to get a court to enjoin payment under the letter of credit.

   A letter of credit covered shipments of sugar. The letter provided that drafts were to be drawn under it only when invoices and warehouse receipts showed the sugar's "net landed weight." The invoices and receipts were presented to the bank, and credit was sought. The sugar was not actually weighed until four days after the request for credit. The buyer sued to enjoin (stop) the bank from issuing credit under the letter of credit. The seller of the sugar, attempting to get credit under the letter of credit, claimed that the bank *had* to honor the letter of credit because the seller presented the bank with documents that the letter of credit required. The buyer of the sugar, on the other hand, argued that there was fraud because the letter of credit required the seller to have the sugar weighed and to present a weight certificate to the bank before credit would be given. Because the seller presented the weight certificate to the bank four days *before* the sugar was officially weighed, the buyer claimed that this action was clearly fraudulent, justifying a court in enjoining the confirming bank from giving credit under the letter of credit. Who was correct, buyer or seller? [*Old Colony Trust Co. v. Lawyers' Title and Trust Co.*, 297 F. 152 (2d Cir. 1924)]
8. Did Congress intend to do away with the act of state doctrine in private lawsuits where someone says that violations of the Foreign Corrupt Practices Act have occurred? In one case, Clayco Petroleum Corporation sued Occidental Petroleum Corporation (Oxy), claiming that Oxy's agents bribed a government official of the country of Umm Al Qaywayn unlawfully to obtain an offshore oil concession. Clayco claimed that in September 1969, Sheikh Ahmed (the ruler) told Clayco that it would get the oil concession. Clayco claimed that Oxy got the concession because Oxy bribed Ahmed. The Foreign Corrupt Practices Act prohibits corporations covered by the 1934 Securities Exchange Act or their agents from bribing foreign officials to get or keep business. Should Sheikh Ahmed's action in giving Oxy the oil concession be presumed legal as the act of state doctrine would require, or does the Foreign Corrupt Practices Act allow a U.S. court to examine the motives of a foreign government's giving the oil concession to Oxy? [*Clayco Petroleum Corp. v. Occidental Petroleum Corp.*, 712 F.2d 404 (9th Cir. 1983)]

Suggested Readings

Articles

BOEHMER and PALMER, "The 1992 EC Data Protection Proposal: An Examination of Its Implications for U.S. Business and U.S. Privacy Law," 31 *American Business Law Journal* 265 (1993).

BOGARDUS, "The GATT and the Environment: Irreconcilable Differences?" 5 *Dalhousie Journal of Legal Studies* 237 (1996).

FISHER, "The Ethical Consumer: A Rejecter of Positive Law Arbitrage," 25 *Seton Hall Law Review* 230 (1994).

HURD and ZOLLERS, "Product Liability in the European Community: Implications for United States Business," 31 *American Business Law Journal* 245 (1993).

LANSING and GABRIELLA, "Clarifying Gray Market Gray Areas," 31 *American Business Law Journal* 313 (1993).

MAYER and HOCH, "International Environmental Protection and the GATT: The Tuna/Dolphin Controversy," 31 *American Business Law Journal* 187 (1993).

STOLTENBERG, "International Trade Law and Regulations in the Context of the Free Trade/Fair Trade Debate: A Review Essay," 31 *American Business Law Journal* 339 (1993).

VON STERNBERG, "A Comparison of the Yugoslavian and Rwandan War Crimes Tribunals: Universal Jurisdiction and the 'Elementary Dictates of Humanity'," 22 *Brooklyn Journal of International Law* 111 (1996).

WILSON, "Barking Up the Wrong Tree: Proposals for Enhancing the Effectiveness of the International Tropical Tree Agreement," 10 *Temple International & Comparative Law* Journal 229 (1996).

MODULE

3

PRIVATE LAW AFFECTING ENTREPRENEURS

CHAPTER

10

TORTS: NEGLIGENCE, STRICT LIABILITY AND INTENTIONAL TORTS

"TORT LAW IS A LEGAL LABORATORY."

Prosser and Keeton, Torts, 5th ed.

Positive Law Ethical Problems

"Sarah Jones is cheating on her time sheets," said Fred McBay of Bullock's Department store to his supervisor, Denise Flynn. Ms. Flynn then dismissed Jones. Flynn called Jill Lansdale, Jones's superior at the store and told her Jones was being dismissed. Lansdale informed senior managers at Bullock's that Jones was dismissed for falsifying company documents. Jones then sued Bullock's for defamation. Can a company's managers discuss among themselves a possible theft by a company worker without becoming liable for slander?

"My ex-husband tricked me. Before we signed the property settlement as part of our divorce, he represented that he had much less property than he actually had. As a result I signed a property settlement agreement for about $500,000 less than I should have. But since I signed that agreement after my own attorney examined it, I guess that I am bound by it and can't get out of it," said Barbara Wilcox to her neighbor Beatrice Kayser. Is Ms. Wilcox correct?

"Texaco has just committed the largest wrong in the history of mankind," said a bystander to Mr. James Kinnear, President of Texaco. Mr. Kinnear was dumbfounded. A Texas jury had just returned a verdict of $10.53 billion, the largest verdict in the history of the law, against Texaco and in favor of Pennzoil. The jury had found that Texaco had wrongfully interfered with a contract Pennzoil had with Getty Oil. This history was not the kind Mr. Kinnear wanted to make. He told his lawyer to appeal the result because the trial had many questionable aspects, including the fact that the alleged Getty-Pennzoil contract was not even written and that the trial judge in the case had received a $10,000 campaign contribution from Pennzoil's attorney *after* the case had been assigned to the judge. Surely all of these facts would come out and would cause an appellate court to upset this outrageous miscarriage of justice, Mr. Kinnear thought. Was he right?

Today, businesses face billion-dollar judgments based on tort law. Tort law is a major area of legal theories where liability results mainly from judges' opinions. This chapter surveys three major common law tort categories: negligence, strict liability, and intentional torts. (Refer to Figure 2.2 in Chapter 2 to visualize how torts "fit" into the legal system.)

WHAT IS A TORT?

This website provides abstracts to law review articles on various topics including torts: ***http://www.LegalMinds.org***

A tort is a breach of a noncontractual civil duty for which a court will provide a remedy. The word *tort* comes from the French word meaning to twist. In other words, torts are wrongs, or actions that are not straight but twisted. Torts are *civil wrongs*. Slander, libel, negligence, and fraud are examples of civil wrongs, which individuals do to other individuals (as opposed to society as a whole, which are criminal and not civil wrongs).

PLACING TORTS IN GENERAL BUSINESS LAW

Figure 2.2 in Chapter 2 presents an overview of civil and criminal law. The negligence and strict liability areas show the placement of these torts. As you can see, such torts are civil, not criminal substantive law.

Tort law is mainly state law; however, the Federal Tort Claims Act (FTCA) allows persons to sue the United States government for certain torts that its agents commit. It is possible for something to be a tort in one state but not another; and even if a particular tort (such as slander) exists in all states, each of the 50 states could define it differently. Although this inconsistency creates the opportunity for great diversity, not much variation exists from state to state in their torts and how they are defined. Some states, such as California and New York, however, often recognize new legal wrongs sooner than others.

The common law tradition is that judges make most tort law; that is, judges decide what is a "wrong," or a tort, and thereby determine community standards of right and wrong.

Torts Compared with Crimes

Torts and crimes have differences and similarities and sometimes overlap. One similarity is that both try to stop wrongful conduct. An area of overlap is that some acts, such as striking another in anger, could be both a tort (battery) and a crime (criminal battery).

However, torts differ from crimes in several ways. First, a person owes tort duties to another person. A person owes a duty to society not to commit crimes. This distinction, however, is not completely satisfactory because one owes tort duties to all individuals, which in a sense is society. Another difference between torts and crimes is who enforces them. It is society's representative, such as the district attorney, who enforces criminal law, whereas the injured victim enforces tort law. Of course, government as a representative of society can sue a person in tort for damages to government property.

For a website supported by Stanford and Cornell Law Schools, which has abstracts on legal topics including torts, go to ***http://www.lawreview.org***

Tort and criminal law also differ in their objectives. One of the objectives of criminal law is to punish. Tort law is usually compensatory, designed to restore the victim's position prior to the commission of the tort. Occasionally, tort remedies include punitive damages designed to punish the person committing the tort.

Tort Law Is a Legal Laboratory

Tort law has been called a legal laboratory because courts' (judges') ideas change about what a tort is. For example, at one time invasion of privacy was not a tort but today it is. Also, certain torts apply to more situations now than they once did. For instance, strict liability first applied to water leaking onto another's property and causing damage. Today it also arises regarding defective products, handling wild animals, flying airplanes, and other situations.

Tort law has been a growing trend, part of a tendency within the courts to recognize new kinds of wrongs.

Tort Classifications

Torts can be classified in several ways. One classification—property torts and torts against the person—focuses on the victim.

Type of Victim: Property/Person. Property torts include trespass and conversion, while torts against persons include assault and battery. In a way, all torts are against people because people own property and sue if it is damaged.

Type of Wrong. Another tort classification looks at the type of wrong. Torts can involve carelessness (negligence), ultrahazardous activities (strict liability), or be intentional in nature.

This chapter discusses negligence, strict liability, and intentional torts.

NEGLIGENCE[1]

Negligence involves carelessness that injures others. It is a tort that can occur almost anywhere—while driving a car, doing an audit, or supervising one's children. Negligence has four parts: (1) duty, (2) breaking of the standard of care, (3) proximate cause, and (4) damages. All four parts must exist for negligence to occur.

http://

For a website that directs one to negligence cases, go to ***http://www.yahoo.com/government/law***

Duty

The duty part of negligence usually arises by "operation of the law," meaning that a court or legislature says a person owes a duty of care to others. People do not have to pay each other $2 per month to create these duties. The duty to drive carefully (as in most activities) arises automatically because a lawmaker says so.

Occasionally, however, the duty of care does arise by contract. For example, **malpractice** cases, which are, technically speaking, negligence suits, are brought against professionals such as physicians, lawyers, engineers, architects, veterinaries, and accountants who have not performed their contractual duties to their clients with requisite care. In other words, the duty to be careful *to the client* does generally arise by contract in the case of professionals, because the client *hired* the accountants, for example, to audit its financial statements. If the accountants did it carelessly and made many errors, the accountants have broken their duty of care to the client, who could recover against the accountants for negligence. However, what if the client had shown the poorly prepared financial statements to its bank to get a loan? The bank relies on the financial

[1] Negligence is also discussed in Chapter 23 on product liability.

statements, makes the loan, the business goes bankrupt and does not repay the bank, and the bank sues the accountants for negligently preparing the financial statements. Note the bank never hired the accountants, so the accountants will defend by invoking the **privity rule**. The privity rule says that accountants only have a duty of care to people who hire them. In recent times, however, courts have created exceptions to the privity rule making accountants liable for their negligence to more people than just their clients. Read the *First Florida Bank v. Max Mitchell & Co.* case to see what a major state's supreme court did when a third party (a bank) sued the accountants for negligently auditing its client's books, and the accountants raised the privity defense.

First Fla. Bank v. Max Mitchell & Co.

Supreme Court of Florida
558 So.2d 9 (Fla. 1990)

Background and Facts:

Max Mitchell is a certified public accountant and president of Max Mitchell and Company, P.A. In April of 1985, Mitchell went to First Florida Bank for the purpose of negotiating a loan on behalf of his client, C.M. Systems, Inc. Mitchell advised Stephen Hickman, the bank vice-president, that he was a certified public accountant and delivered to Hickman audited financial statements of C.M. Systems for the fiscal years ending October 31, 1983, and October 31, 1984, which had been prepared by his firm. The October 1, 1984, audited statement indicated that C.M. Systems had total assets of $3,474,336 and total liabilities of $1,296,823. It did not indicate that C.M. Systems owed money to any bank, and in a later conference with Hickman, Mithcell stated that as of April 16, 1985, C.M. Systems was not indebted to any bank. At that time, Mitchell asked Hickman to consider a $500,000 line of credit for C.M. Systems.

Over the next several weeks, Mitchell had numerous discussions with Hickman concerning various line items in Hitchell's audit of C.M. Systems. Mitchell represented that he was thoroughly familiar with the financial condition of C.M. Systems. On May 23, 1985, Hickman asked Mitchell for interim financial statements for the period which ended on April 30, 1985. Mitchell advised that they would not be available for several more weeks. Hickman asked Mitchell if there had been any material change in the company's financial condition since October 31, 1984, and Mitchell said that he was not aware of any material changes. On June 6, 1985, the bank approved the request for a $500,000 unsecured line of credit to C.M. Systems. Thereafter, C.M. Systems borrowed the entire amount of the $500,000 credit line, which it has never repaid.

Subsequently, the bank discovered that the audit of C.M. Systems for the fiscal year ending October 31, 1984, had substantially overstated the assets, understated the liabilities, and overstated net income. Among other things, the audit failed to reflect that as of October 31, 1984, C.M. Systems owed at least $750,000 to several banks. In addition, several material changes had occurred in the company's balance sheet after the audit but prior to the approval of the line of credit.

The bank filed a three-count complaint against Mitchell and his firm. Because of the absence of privity between either Mitchell or his firm and the bank, the trial court granted Mitchell summary judgment on the negligence and gross negligence counts. The bank voluntarily dismissed the count based on fraud. Believing itself bound by prior decisional law of the state, the district court of appeal affirmed. Recognizing the public policy implications of the issue and the erosion of the privity doctrine in other areas of the law, the court posed the certified question for our consideration.

Body of Opinion

Judge Grimes

The seminal case on this subject is *Ultramares Corp v. Touche*,... (1931), authored by Justice Cardozo. In that case the court held that a lender which had relied upon inaccurate financial statements to its detriment had no cause of action against the public accounting firm which had prepared them because of the lack of privity between the parties. In declining to relax the requirement of privity, the court observed:

> If liability for negligence exists, a thoughtless slip or blunder, the failure to detect a theft or forgery beneath the cover of deceptive entries, may expose accountants to a liability in an indeterminant [sic] amount for an indeterminant [sic] time to an indeterminant [sic] class. The hazards of a business conducted on these terms are so extreme as to enkindle doubt whether a flaw may not exist in the implication of a duty that exposes to these consequences.

...The court distinguished its earlier decision of *Glanzer v. Shephard*,... (1922), in which it had held that a public weigher was liable to the buyer of beans for the amount the buyer overpaid the seller in reliance on the weigher's erroneous certificate of weight. The court said that the use of the certificate was a consequence "which to the weigher's knowledge was the end and aim of the transaction," . . . and reasoned that, unlike the case before it, the bond between the weigher and the buyer "was so close as to approach that of privity, if not completely one with it." *Ultramares*. . . .

In purporting to reach a decision within the parameters of *Ultramares* and *Glanzer*, the New York Court of Appeals in *Credit Alliance Corp. v. Arthur Andersen & Co.*, . . . (1985), recently explained the circumstances under which recovery may be accomplished by persons in "near privity":

> Before accountants may be held liable in negligence to noncontractual parties who rely to their detriment on inaccurate financial reports, certain prerequisites must be satisfied: (1) the accountants must have been aware that the financial reports were to be used for a particular purpose or purposes; (2) in the furtherance of which a known party or parties was intended to rely; and (3) there must have been some conduct on the part of the accountants linking them to that party or parties, which envinces the accountants' understanding of that party or parties' reliance.

In the more than fifty years which have elapsed since *Ultramares*, the question of an accountant's liability for negligence where no privity exists has been addressed by many courts. There are now essentially four lines of authority with respect to this issue.

(1) Except in cases of fraud, an accountant is only liable to one with whom he is in privity or near privity. . . .

(2) An accountant is liable to third parties in the absence of privity under the circumstances described in section 552, *Restatement (Second) of Torts* (1976), which reads in pertinent part:

> **§552. Information Negligently Supplied for the Guidance of Others**
>
> (1) One who, in the course of his business, profession or employment, or in any other transaction in which he has a pecuniary interest, supplies false information for the guidance of others in their business transactions, is subject to liability for pecuniary loss caused to them by their justifiable reliance on the information, if he fails to exercise reasonable care or competence in obtaining or communicating the information.
>
> (2) Except as stated in Subsection (3), the liability stated in Subsection (1) is limited to loss suffered:
>
> (a) by the person or one of a limited group of persons for whose benefit and guidance he intends to supply the information or knows that the recipient intends to supply it; and
>
> (b) through reliance upon it in a transaction that he intends the information to influence or knows that the recipient so intends or in a substantially similar transaction.

(3) An accountant is liable to all persons who might reasonably be foreseen as relying upon his work product. . . .

(4) An accountant's liability to third persons shall be determined by the balancing of various factors, among which are the extent to which the transaction was intended to affect the plaintiff, the foreseeability of harm to him, the degree of certainty that the plaintiff suffered injury, the closeness of the connection between the defendant's conduct and the injury suffered, the moral blame attached to the defendant's conduct, and the policy of preventing future harm. . . .

Some of the competing interests involved in selecting the proper standard for accountants' liability to third parties are set forth in Annotation, *Liability of Public Accountant to Third Parties,* 46 A.L.R.3d . . . (1972):

> It is contended by those favoring such liability that accountants, due to their professional status and the respect they command, invite reliance on their work by the business community, and that investors and creditors do, in fact, rely upon their accuracy and integrity; on the other hand, it is pointed out that unlike members of other professions, accountants have no control over the identity or number of those who rely on their work, and that imposition of liability, in negligence to third parties would place an enormous potential burden on the profession. Those in favor of expanding liability argue that the accounting profession no longer needs the protection of nonliability in this area, due to its wealth, and contend that the cost of insurance protection could be passed on to the client, stating that the innocent relier should not be damaged because of the error of the negligent accountant. In reply, it is observed that the cost of such insurance protection is prohibitive and, in many cases, that such coverage is not available at any price; furthermore, it is said, such higher costs would tend to lead to dominance of the profession by the large national accounting firms and to a curtailment of the availability of accountancy services to small businesses. Nor, it is contended, does the argument for extended liability take into consideration the ever more acute shortage of qualified public accountants in private practice. Those in favor of expanding liability argue that liability could easily be limited by the increased use of disclaimers and limited certifications, pointing to the success of the British experience in this area. Opponents, however, observe that the use of such devices is a commercial impossibility unless all accountants follow this practice, since it tends to dissatisfy the client, who will then turn to the use of other accountants not following this practice.

Upon consideration, we have decided to adopt the rationale of section 552, *Restatement (Second) of Torts* (1976), as setting forth the circumstances under which accountants may be held liable in negligence to persons who are not in contractual privity. The rule shall also apply to allegations of gross negligence, but the absence of privity shall continue to be no bar to charges of fraud.

Because of the heavy reliance upon audited financial statements in the contemporary financial world, we believe permitting recovery only from those in privity or near privity is unduly restrictive. On the other hand, we are persuaded by the wisdom of the rule which limits liability to those persons or classes of persons whom an accountant "knows" will rely on his opinion rather than those he "should have known" would do so because it takes into account the fact that an accountant controls neither his client's accounting records nor the distribution of his reports. As noted by the North Carolina Supreme Court when it adopted a similar position in *Raritan River Steel Co. v. Cherry, Bekaert & Holland*, . . . (1988):

> We conclude that the standard set forth in the *Restatement (Second) of Torts* §552 (1977) represents the soundest approach to accountants' liability for negligent misrepresentation. It constitutes a middle ground between the restrictive *Ultramares* approach advocated by defendants and the expansive "reasonably foreseeable" approach advocated by plaintiffs. It recognizes that liability should extend not only to those with whom the accountant is in privity or near privity, but also to those persons, or classes of persons, whom he knows and intends will rely on his opinion, or whom he knows his client intends will so rely.

There remains the need to apply this rule to the facts at hand. At the time Mitchell prepared the audits for C.M. Systems, it was unknown that they would be used to induce the reliance of First Florida Bank to approve a line of credit for C.M. Systems. Therefore, except for the unusual facts of this case, Mitchell could not be held liable to the bank for any negligence in preparing the audit. However, Mitchell actually negotiated the loan on behalf of his client. He personally delivered the financial statements to the bank with the knowledge that it would rely upon them in considering whether or not to make the loan. Under this unique set of facts, we believe that Mitchell vouched for the integrity of the audits and that his conduct in dealing with the bank sufficed to meet the requirements of the rule which we have adopted in this opinion.

Accordingly, we answer the certified question in the affirmative. To the extent that they may conflict with this opinion, we disapprove the opinions in *Buchman*, *Investors Tax*, and *Gordon*. We quash the decision of the district court of appeal and remand the case for further proceedings.

Judgment and Result

The Florida Supreme Court held that an accountant, who does not exercise reasonable and ordinary care in preparing the client's financial statements and who personally presents the client's statements to the third party to induce the third party to make a loan to the client, is liable to the third party (the bank) for negligence. In so doing the Florida Supreme Court did *not* follow the privity rule.

Questions

1. If the privity rule says that accountants are not liable to people who do not hire them, why did the court in the *First Florida* case create an exception?
2. What is the rationale behind the privity rule? Does the privity rule make good sense in a fast-paced economy where third parties do not always have the time to examine financial statements in detail but who recognize the name of a prominent accounting firm known for its accuracy and integrity?
3. Should accountants be liable for their negligence to all third parties who might conceivably rely on the erroneous financial statements? What are the negatives of expanding the privity rule too much? What are the negatives in honoring the privity rule too much?
4. Would the following statement be an accurate rule to draw from the *First Florida* case? Accountants who audit a client's financial statements are liable to third persons for the client's business failure.

Standard of Care

People have duties to be careful in all their activities. But how careful? The degree is indicated by the standard of care. The exact standard of care is what the ordinary, reasonable, prudent (ORP) person would do in the same situation. It is an objective and not a subjective standard. Therefore, *reasonable* is determined by an ORP person and not by the person accused of negligence. An ORP person is just like each of us except that s/he is always reasonable and prudent. When we occasionally are not, we have broken the standard of care that we owe others; breaking this standard is being *careless* in a legal sense.

The standard of care is objective, but it takes many factors into account. For example, if a driver has a car accident, the amount of traffic, visibility, weather conditions, and other factors determine the standard of care. The actual driver's conduct is compared with these conditions to see whether it meets the ORP person standard of care.

Many states recognize the **negligence per se** doctrine. It helps plaintiffs prove defendants were careless. This doctrine says that a defendant breaks a duty of care by not obeying a statute (or regulation) setting a level of care (for example, speed limit laws) if the statute is intended to protect the plaintiff and prevent the type of loss the plaintiff suffers. *Munford, Inc. v. Peterson* illustrates negligence per se.

Munford, Inc. v. Peterson

Supreme Court of Mississippi
368 So.2d 213 (1979)

Background and Facts:

Justices Robertson, Walker, and Lee

The parents and brothers of Scott Peterson instituted suit in the Circuit Court, First Judicial District of Harrison County, against Munford, Inc. and Tommy Blankenship for damages accruing by reason of the wrongful death of Scott Peterson. The jury returned a verdict in favor of the Petersons for $100,000, judgment was entered against Munford, Inc., and in favor of Blankenship, and Munford, Inc. appeals.

On the afternoon of May 28, 1975, Scott Peterson and four other boys planned to get together after baseball practice. Peterson and one of the boys were to spend the night at the home of Blankenship. Later that evening, one of them took the keys to the family car, found some vodka, and took it with him to the appointed meeting place (another boy's home). They all went to the Majic Market (owned and operated by the appellant), where they bought some orange juice and later drank it with the vodka. One of the boys was fifteen years of age, three of them were fourteen, and one was thirteen. After drinking the vodka, they went back to the Majic Market and one of the fourteen-year-olds entered the establishment and purchased a six-pack containing 14-oz cans of beer. The woman operator asked him if he was eighteen years of age. He replied in the affirmative, but she made no effort to have him prove his age or identify himself. The record indicates that he looked no older than a fourteen-year-old boy.

The boys went to David Black's house (one of the party) and drank the beer. They then decided to return to the Majic Market for more beer. The seventeen-year-old sister of Black refused to let him leave because she knew they were drinking beer. The other four drove to the Majic Market where a different boy went in and bought a six-pack of beer (king-size). No inquiry was made concerning his age. They went out on a side road and drank the beer.

After consuming the second package of beer, the boys went back to the Majic Market where one of them again entered the place and bought another six-pack without any questions being asked about his age. They drove out on the side road, drank the beer and began to ride around. About 4 a.m., Blankenship was driving the automobile and was traveling west on U.S. Highway 90. A hard rain had fallen, there was water on the road, he lost control of the vehicle, crossed the median and south lanes of the highway, hit the seawall, the automobile hurdled fifty-seven feet through the air, landed on the beach, and turned over five times, traveling 337 1/2 feet. Scott Peterson was thrown out of the car and it rolled over him, fatally crushing his chest.

The declaration charged negligence against Munford, Inc. for selling beer to the boys in violation of the law, all of whom were under the age of eighteen years, and who became intoxicated as a result of drinking the beer. Blankenship was charged with negligence in the operation of the vehicle. . . .

Body of Opinion

Justice Lee

Under the common law, there is no action for damages in the selling or giving away of intoxicating liquors. The rule is stated in 45 AM.Jur.2d *Intoxicating Liquors* §553, at 852 (1969), as follows:

> At common law it is not a tort to either sell or give intoxicating liquor to ordinary able-bodied men, and it has been frequently held that in the absence of statute, there could be no cause of action against one furnishing liquor in favor of those injured by the intoxication of the person so furnished.

Where there is no statute pertaining to a subject, the common law prevails.

While the Wisconsin Supreme Court upheld the common-law principle stated above in *Garcia v. Hargrove*, 46 Wis.2d 724, (1970), (Wisconsin subscribes to the comparative negligence doctrine), the dissenting opinion of Chief Justice Hallows may have expressed a modern trend:

> The time has arrived when this court should again exercise its inherent power as the guardian of the

> common law and hold upon general principles of common law negligence a person, who, when he knows or should have known a person is intoxicated, sells or gives intoxicating liquor to such a person, is guilty of a negligent act; and if such negligence is a substantial factor in causing harm to a third person, he should be liable with the drunken person under our comparative-negligence doctrine. Conceded, the common law in this state for almost 100 years has been to the contrary... but the basis upon which these cases were decided is sadly eroded by the shift from commingling alcohol and horses to commingling alcohol and horsepower.

However, in the discussion of the two questions presented here, we do not look to, or decide, the application of the common law in view of our statutes. Mississippi Code Annotated Section 67-3-53(b) (1972) provides the following:

> In addition to any act declared to be unlawful by this chapter, or by sections 27-71-301 through 27-71-347, and sections 67-3-17, 67-3-27, 67-3-29 and 67-3-57, it shall be unlawful for the holder of a permit authorizing the sale of beer or wine at retail:
>
> (b) To sell, give, or furnish any beer or wine to any person visibly or noticeably intoxicated, or to any insane person, or to any habitual drunkard, or to any person under the age of eighteen (18) years.

The declaration charged, among other things, that appellant sold beer to the minors in violation of Mississippi law and that such negligence contributed to the wreck and to the death of Scott Peterson....

The principle that violation of a statute constitutes negligence per se is so elementary that it does not require citation of authority. When a statute is violated, the injured party is entitled to an instruction that the party violating the statute is guilty of negligence, and, if that negligence proximately caused or contributed to the injury, then the injured party is entitled to recover. The demurrer admitted that appellant violated the law and the evidence is undisputed that it did so. The demurrer was properly overruled and the peremptory instruction on negligence[2] was correctly given. The law is plain and unambiguous in prohibiting the sale, giving or furnishing beer or wine to any person under the age of eighteen years by the holder of such a permit. The method of determining a minor's age is for the proprietor to select. Suffice it to say, the responsibility is his to see that the law is not violated by him....

The evidence is uncontradicted that appellant sold to the minors involved a quantity of beer in violation of the statute.... The facts in this case raise a jury issue as to whether or not there was causal connection between the incompetence of the driver as a result of drinking the beer, and the accident. It is required only that the intoxication be a contributing cause to the accident, not the sole proximate cause. The evidence was sufficient to withstand a motion for directed verdict and the verdict was not against the overwhelming weight of the evidence.

Appellant contends the trial court erred in refusing instructions on contributory negligence and assumption of risk and in granting an instruction that plaintiff was not negligent as a matter of law.

The appellant requested an instruction on assumption of risk, which was refused by the court. The court committed no error in refusing same.

The co-defendant Blankenship, who received a favorable verdict from the jury, requested an instruction on contributory negligence which was refused. The appellant did not request such an instruction and cannot complain that the court erred in refusing that instruction to Blankenship.

The appellees requested and were granted the following instruction:

> The Court instructs the jury that as a matter of law in this case, the Plaintiffs' decedent was not negligent, nor at fault, nor to blame for his death; and cannot be charged with any negligence or fault.

Appellees seek the benefit of the statute to impose liability on appellant, yet argue that Scott Peterson was a member of a protected class and that he could not be guilty of negligence. We have stated hereinabove that the provision of the statute prohibiting sale of beer to persons under the age of eighteen years (and others named therein) is for the public safety.

The evidence is undisputed that Scott Peterson and the other boys pooled their money to buy the beer, that they were all together drinking it, that they all "felt no pain," that they were drinking the beer to make them feel good, and that Scott Peterson knew Blankenship had drunk a quantity of beer, in addition to drinking vodka. Appellant set up an affirmative defense of contributory negligence in its answer. The instruction directly contradicted the evidence and it precluded the jury from applying the law of comparative negligence, although the appellant did not request an instruction thereon, was highly prejudicial and constituted reversible error.

[The portion of the opinion upholding the admittedly "irregular" jury verdict is omitted. That verdict dismissed the case against defendant Blankenship, the driver of the car killing Peterson, while holding defendant/appellant Munford, Inc., liable. The Mississippi Supreme Court said this was not an error.]

Judgment and Result

The Mississippi Supreme Court said that when a person violates a statute, that person breaks the negligence

[2] "The Court instructs the jury in this case, the Defendant, Munford, Inc., was negligent as a matter of law."

standard of care. The parents of the deceased person stated a cause of action based on negligence. Trial court errors against the defendant/appellant justified a new trial.

Questions

1. How was the defendant business (Munford, Inc.) allegedly negligent? Did it drive the car that killed Peterson?
2. If a person violates a statute and injures a person the statute was intended to protect, is it negligence per se?
3. How do you explain the jury's refusal to hold liable the driver of the car while holding liable the business selling the beer?

Inference of Negligence. **Res ipsa loquitur** is a Latin phrase meaning "the thing speaks for itself." It is another legal idea helping a negligence plaintiff prove the defendant broke the standard of care. Courts apply the idea where three facts occur: first, only the defendant controls what caused the harm; second, the loss would not usually have happened except in the case of negligence; and third, the event must not have been due to any voluntary action or contribution by the plaintiff. If these three facts occur, res ipsa loquitur allows an **inference of negligence**, meaning that a plaintiff has proven negligence unless a defendant has some defense.

Proximate Cause

A plaintiff must prove that a defendant proximately caused a plaintiff's injuries. Proximate cause means that a defendant's carelessness in fact caused a plaintiff's damage; that is, but for a defendant's carelessness, a plaintiff would not have been injured. A defendant's carelessness also must be close in time and space to justify holding a defendant liable. Courts use words such as foreseeable to decide the proximate cause issue. **Proximate cause** in effect says that a defendant is not liable for all injuries that he or she causes. For example, a defendant's negligence results in his factory's burning down, and the flames spread from building to building until the entire town burns. Proximate cause says that a defendant is liable for the first building's burning but not the whole town's destruction. Factors such as wind conditions and the efficiency of the fire department could counteract a defendant's carelessness. Also, public policy favors limiting people's negligence liability.

The following famous case, *Palsgraf v. Long Island Railroad Co.*, holds that defendant was not liable for plaintiff's injuries because defendant's carelessness was not proximate to plaintiff's loss.

Damages

If a defendant owes a duty of care to a plaintiff and breaks that duty, this act alone does not let plaintiff recover. The breach of the duty must damage plaintiff, meaning that a defendant must have damaged plaintiff's person or property.

Palsgraf v. Long Island Railroad Co.

New York Court of Appeals
162 N.E. 99 (1928)

Background and Facts:

Ms. Palsgraf stood on a railroad platform awaiting a train. A man on the same platform ran to catch another departing train. He jumped toward the moving train car and in so doing appeared unlikely to make it so a railroad employee on the platform pushed him onto the car and another railroad employee on the car reached out to pull him aboard. In do doing, a package filled with explosives fell from the man's grasp onto the train tracks and blew up. The explosion in turn caused scales at the far end of the platform to fall onto Ms. Palsgraf. She sued the railroad for negligence and the railroad defended on grounds that it was not the proximate cause of her injuries.

Body of Opinion

Chief Judge Cardozo

. . . The conduct of the defendant's guard, if a wrong in its relation to the holder of the package, was not a wrong in its relation to the plaintiff, standing far away. Relatively to her it was not negligence at all. Nothing in the situation gave notice that the falling package had in it the potency of peril to persons thus removed. Negligence is not actionable unless it involves the invasion of a legally protected interest, the violation of a right. "Proof of negligence in the air, so to speak, will not do." . . . If no hazard was apparent to the eye of ordinary vigilance, an act innocent and harmless, at least to outward seeming, with reference to her, did not take to itself the quality of a tort because it happened to be a wrong, though apparently not one involving the risk of bodily insecurity, with reference to someone else. "In every instance, before negligence can be predicated of a given act, back of the act must be sought and found a duty to the individual complaining, the observance of which would have averted or avoided the injury." . . .

One who jostles one's neighbor in a crowd does not invade the rights of others standing at the outer fringe when the unintended contact casts a bomb upon the ground. The wrongdoer as to them is the man who carries the bomb, not the one who explodes it without suspicion of danger. Life will have to be made over, and human nature transformed, before prevision so extravagant can be accepted as the norm of conduct, the customary standard to which behavior must conform. . . .

What the plaintiff must show is "a wrong" to herself; i.e., a violation of her own right, and not merely a wrong to someone else, not conduct "wrongful" because unsocial, but not "a wrong" to any one. . . . The risk reasonably to be perceived defines the duty to be obeyed. . . . Here, by concession, there was nothing in the situation to suggest to the most cautious mind that the parcel wrapped in newspaper would spread wreckage through the station. If the guard had thrown it down knowingly and wilfully, he would not have threatened the plaintiff's safety, so far as appearances could warn him. His conduct would not have involved, even then, an unreasonable probability of invasion of her bodily security. Liability can be no greater when the act is inadvertent. . . .

One who seeks redress at law does not make out a cause of action by showing without more that there has been damage to his person. If the harm was not wilful, he must show that the act as to him had possibilities of danger so many and apparent as to entitle him to be protected against the doing of it though the harm was unintended. . . .

Judgment and Result

The New York Court of Appeals found for the defendant railroad.

Questions

1. Clearly if the defendant railroad's employees had not bumped the package from the one passenger's arms, the explosion would not have occurred. Therefore the railroad caused plaintiff's injuries. Why then was defendant not liable to plaintiff?
2. Why was defendant's negligence not the proximate cause of plaintiff's injuries?
3. If the man carrying the package had sued the railroad for its employees' negligence, would the railroad have been liable to him?
4. Does proximate cause excuse a person from liability for failure to live up to the appropriate standard of care? Why?

Defenses to Negligence

Even if a plaintiff proves the four parts of negligence, a defendant can raise affirmative defenses. If defendant can prove any one affirmative defense, plaintiff's negligence claim is defeated. Two affirmative defenses are contributory negligence and assumption of risk.

Contributory Negligence and Assumption of Risk. **Contributory negligence** means that a plaintiff's own carelessness partly caused his or her loss. Contributory negligence generally prevents a plaintiff from recovering anything. This rule is harsh, because a plaintiff could be only five percent contributorily negligent and yet recover nothing. To reduce this harshness, some states have **comparative fault**. Comparative fault schemes vary among the states, but ordinarily a contributorily negligent plaintiff recovers damages reduced by the amount of his or her contributing fault. For example, if a plaintiff's damages are $10,000 and a plaintiff is ten percent contributorily negligent, the plaintiff gets $9,000 if comparative fault applies.

Assumption of risk occurs when a plaintiff actually knows a risk exists and nonetheless engages in the activity. Spectators at baseball games probably assume the risk of being hit by a foul ball.

Damage Apportionment. Some states refine comparative fault by asking two questions. First, how much did plaintiff's fault contribute to the accident? Courts reduce plaintiff's recovery by this percentage. Second, how much did plaintiff's contributory negligence contribute to his or her damages? Courts reduce plaintiff's recovery again by this percentage. For example, a motorcyclist's failure to wear a protective helmet might contribute little to an auto collision; however, it might greatly increase his or her injuries.

STRICT LIABILITY

Strict liability means that a person is liable for harm proximately caused, even though no fault is shown. The defendant merely did or failed to do something that is close enough to a plaintiff's damages to justifiably hold the defendant liable.

Strict liability can occur in many situations. Persons engaged in ultrahazardous activities are strictly liable to persons whom they proximately injure. Examples of ultrahazardous activities include dynamiting, fumigation, flying airplanes, and keeping wild animals. Courts also apply strict liability to defective consumer goods. Chapter 23 discusses this issue.

Why Allow Ultrahazardous Activities?

If ultrahazardous activities are so risky, why allow them? The reason is that their social value outweighs prohibiting them. However, individuals participating in ultrahazardous activities are liable for any harm that they proximately cause no matter how careful they are. Strict liability encourages people in ultrahazardous activities to be careful.

Defenses to Strict Liability

Assumption of risk can be a defense to strict liability. However, contributory negligence is generally not a defense in strict liability cases. *Indiana Harbor Belt Railroad v. American Cyanamid* presents a contemporary strict liability scenario—a toxic chemical spill.

Indiana Harbor Belt Railroad Co. v. American Cyanamid Co.

U.S. District Court, Northern District of Illinois
517 F.Supp. 314 (1981)

Background and Facts:

American Cyanamid Company (Cyanamid) manufactured and shipped acrylonitrile, a hazardous, flammable, toxic substance. Cyanamid arranged for Missouri Pacific to transport acrylonitrile to Indiana Harbor Belt Railway's (Indiana Harbor) freight yard in Illinois. There the railroad car containing the substance was to be turned over to Conrail for delivery to Cyanamid in New Jersey. Upon arrival at Indiana Harbor's freight yard, substantial amounts of acrylonitrile leaked from the freight car. Indiana Harbor claims extensive damage to property, equipment, and the water supply over a two-mile area. The spill resulted in the evacuation of 3,000 people from their homes. It also caused extensive interference with railroad operations for a substantial time. Indiana Harbor spent much to fix its property. Indiana Harbor sued Cyanamid for its damages based on a strict liability theory. Cyanamid argued that even though acrylonitrile is a hazardous substance, strict liability only applies to ultrahazardous activities. Cyanamid claimed that common sense tells us that transporting a hazardous substance is not ultrahazardous or inherently dangerous.

Body of Opinion

District Judge Moran

Cyanamid argues that dismissal of plaintiff's strict liability counts is required because no cause of action has been stated under Illinois law. They maintain that strict liability standards apply to activities that are inherently dangerous and that naturally and probably result in harm despite the exercise of the utmost care. They argue that Illinois law has limited the ultrahazardous activity concept to cases involving blasting or explosives and it has not been extended to the circumstances alleged in this case. They note that regardless of acrylonitrile's qualities as a hazardous substance, strict liability cannot be applied unless it is a hazardous activity. Defendant contends that their activity was not inherently dangerous as a matter of common knowledge or otherwise.

Plaintiff Sanders applies the same legal standards as Cyanamid but believes that Cyanamid's conduct fits within them. They acknowledge that these facts raise a question of first impression but argue that the allegations "fit comfortably within the contours of the Illinois absolute liability doctrine."

Indiana Harbor argues that Illinois courts apply strict liability principles when a peril with potentially grave consequences is introduced into the community. As they believe shipping acrylonitrile is intrinsically dangerous regardless of how careful the shipper may be, plaintiff urges that this court apply strict liability standards. . . .

Neither party has cited any Illinois authority discussing whether shipment of acrylonitrile is an inherently dangerous activity. The Illinois cases in this area have focused largely on blasting activities though they have not expressly limited the concept to this activity. . . .

There are two opinions that this court believes provide persuasive rationales for finding liability in analogous circumstances. In *Chavez v. Southern Pacific Transportation Co.* . . . (E.D.Calif. 1976), Southern Pacific transported eighteen boxcars loaded with bombs. The bombs exploded in a railroad yard causing personal injury and property damage. The court imposed strict liability because the defendant was engaged in an ultrahazardous activity. The court focused on the relative positions of the parties and the desirability of properly distributing the loss. The court emphasized that one who intentionally acts with knowledge that their activity may cause harm, despite the exercise of due care, should "in all fairness be required to compensate the other for the damage done."

The risk distribution justification for imposing strict liability is well suited to claims arising out of the conduct of ultrahazardous activity. The victims of such activity are defenseless. Due to the very nature of the activity, the losses suffered as a result of such activity are likely to be substantial—an "overwhelming misfortune to the person injured" . . . . By indirectly imposing liability on those who benefit from the dangerous activity, risk distribution benefits the social-economic body in two ways: (1) the adverse impact of any particular misfortune is lessened by spreading its cost over a greater population and over a longer time period, and (2) social and economic resources can be more efficiently allocated when the actual costs of goods and services (including the losses they entail) are reflected in their price to the consumer. Both of these benefits may be achieved by subjecting Southern Pacific to strict liability.

Judgment and Result

The U.S. District court decided that strict liability applied to the facts of this case.

Questions

1. Does determining whether something is ultrahazardous depend on how much damage it causes? That is, is the ultrahazardous character known before or after a loss?
2. Might gas stations be ultrahazardous?

INTENTIONAL TORTS

Intentional Torts Compared with Crimes

Intentional torts are similar to and different from crimes. Both crimes and intentional torts are wrongs that usually involve some kind of intent; however, a few strict liability crimes do not involve intent. Both crimes and intentional torts are intentional wrongs, and indicate justification for punishing the wrongdoer. Also, the same act (assault and battery, for example) can be both an intentional tort and a crime.

The victims of intentional torts are individuals. Crimes, of course, have individual victims (the person robbed, for example). Because crimes are acts against general society, the punishment can be much greater, such as imprisonment or death. Society never sentences a person to prison or death for committing an intentional tort.

Intentional Torts Compared with Negligence

Intentional torts are both different from and similar to the tort of negligence. The main difference is that the "wrong" in negligence is carelessness, but the "wrong" in intentional torts concerns some kind of intent. Also, punitive damages are possible for intentional torts but not for negligence.

Intentional torts and negligence have several similarities. First, both are torts, which are civil wrongs. The victims are individuals not society in general. Second, victims can recover both nominal and compensatory damages for negligence and intentional torts.

Intentional Torts Compared with Contracts

Contracts and intentional torts are both areas of civil law; neither is a crime. A person injured by either a breach of contract or an intentional tort can possibly recover both nominal and compensatory damages.

An agreement does not have to be broken to recover for an intentional tort, but a broken contract is required before a person can recover contract damages. Also, intentional tort victims can recover punitive damages, which is not possible for victims of broken contracts.

Remedies for Intentional Torts

Basically, the two types of remedies for tort victims are legal and equitable.

Legal Remedies. Legal remedies include various kinds of damages—nominal, compensatory, and punitive damages—all of which are monetary.

Nominal damages are a small amount of money that a victim receives when his or her right is broken but no substantial harm occurs. For example, Norman could throw a Coke on Bruce (a battery), but what real harm does Bruce suffer? Nominal damages are proper because no real harm was suffered.

Compensatory damages refer to money needed to "make a victim whole." In other words, the victim has a physical or financial loss of some sort. For example, if Arthur slanders Tom's accounting book (by saying it has too many errors when it really does not), sales of Tom's book could fall. Therefore, Tom can receive compensatory damage.

Punitive damages punish wrongdoers when their conduct is particularly outrageous. For example, when Norman throws water on Bruce, it is proper to make Norman pay Bruce punitive damages.

Equitable Remedies. **Equitable remedies** include injunctions, specific performance, and accountings. Plaintiffs can recover these remedies only when their legal remedies are inadequate.

Injunctions are court orders to do or not do something. For example, a court might order a defendant not to trespass on a plaintiff's property.

Specific performance is basically a contract remedy, which orders a person breaking a contract to perform an obligation. This remedy is available only when legal remedies, such as money, are inadequate.

Accountings refer to court orders that direct someone, such as an agent, to present income and expense records to someone else. For example, if a former employee uses a former employer's trade secrets without authorization, the employee will have to account for (and turn over) any profits made.

Fraud[3]

Fraud is a misrepresentation of a material fact that the defrauding person knows about; the defrauding person intends to defraud, and the victim is damaged as a result of reasonably relying on the misrepresentations.

Fraud is one of the most frequently committed business torts and often occurs to persuade others to enter contracts. For example, if someone wants to sell a car, what better way to sell it than by lying about, or understating, its true mileage? However, lying in this situation may involve fraud, and the victim can escape the contract and recover damages.

Elements of Fraud. Because fraud is so common, a few other points should be noted.

First, the person misrepresenting must intend to defraud. If someone mistakenly misrepresents something, innocent misrepresentation—not fraud—occurs. The contract can be undone, but generally no damages can be recovered.

Second, either a buyer or seller (or both) can commit fraud in one contract.

Third, seller's talk, puffing, and opinions are different from misrepresentations of facts. Facts are objective, definite, or observable. For example, Jerry says his car will get 20 miles per gallon. This statement is a representation of fact because any person can determine its truth. If the statement is false, then it is a misrepresentation of fact. Puffing, opinions, or seller's talk are not misrepresentations of fact; they are subjective. For example, statements such as "This house is wonderful," "That car is the most stylish," or "That picture is beautiful" are subjective. Words such as wonderful, most stylish, and beautiful are opinion, not fact, and are unlike objective descriptions such as three feet or one carat. For fraud to exist, a misrepresentation of fact (not a misrepresentation of opinion) must be made.

Fourth, fraud can occur by **concealment**. That is, if a seller "keeps his or her mouth shut" instead of disclosing a material fact not easily discoverable by the other party, fraud can occur. In one case, a homeowner offered his house for sale. The other party bought the house but discovered later that the water was available only between 7 a.m. and 7 p.m. The seller had said that the buyer could have "all the water he wanted" and did not specify to the buyer that water would be available for "only half of the day." The court said this case involved fraud by concealment. The seller had a duty to disclose material facts not readily ascertainable.

Unfortunately half of the U.S. population will probably be a party to the type of agreement illustrated in the next case, because it involves a divorce property settlement. The case, *Hewlett v. Hewlett,* also shows that fraud can creep into such contracts.

[3] Fraud is also discussed in Chapter 22 under consumer protection.

Hewlett v. Hewlett
Missouri Court of Appeals
845 S.W.2d 717 (1993)

Background and Facts:

Robert T. and Patricia R. Hewlett were married on December 22, 1960, and they had three children during their 29-year marriage. Patricia worked as a full-time homemaker raising the couple's three children. Robert worked in the automobile sales industry for thirty years. He owned a partial interest in Bob Allen Ford Company and Bob Allen Investment Company, and also had certain other business and real estate interests. Robert handled all of the couple's financial matters. The Hewletts separated in January 1989. Robert filed for divorce on July 14, 1989. The parties signed a property settlement. The decree of dissolution was issued on January 2, 1990.

On December 21, 1990, Patricia filed a motion to set aside the judgment on the basis of her ex-husband's fraudulent representations incorporated in the property settlement. After an extensive hearing, the trial court made the following findings: That Robert incorrectly valued the marital assets and liabilities by at least $1,225,000; that Robert intended that Patricia rely upon his representations in negotiating the property settlement; that Patricia had a right to rely thereon; that Robert knew or should have known that these representations were false; and that Patricia was damaged by at least $500,000 as a result of her reliance upon Robert's representations. Based on these findings, the trial court set aside the decree of dissolution.

Body of Opinion

Judge Smart

The trial court found the following assets of Robert were undervalued: His ownership interest in Bob Allen Investment Company, his ownership interest in MidAmerican Insurance Company, a Connecticut General Insurance policy, his 401K plan, and an account at United Missouri Bank. The trial court found that two debts were overstated. ... Finally, the trial court found that Robert concealed the following assets: Stock in Kidder, Peabody; an interest in KCD Distributors; an interest in Transoceanic Casualty Company; a partnership interest in Hewlett-Wiegers Partnership; and facts related to the nature of the United Missouri Bank account and $24,000 spent from the account. ...

In asserting a claim of fraud, a party must prove the following elements: 1) a representation; 2) its falsity; 3) its materiality; 4) the speaker's knowledge of the falsity (or the speaker's awareness that s/he lacks knowledge of its truth or falsity); 5) the speaker's intent that the statement be acted upon by the other party in the manner contemplated; 6) that party's ignorance of the falsity; 7) reliance on the truth; 8) right to rely thereon; and 9) injury. ...

Mr. Hewlett owned a 50% interest in Bob Allen Investment Company. This company held as assets four parcels of real estate, an automobile dealership known as Metro Ford, and a leasing company known as Metro Leasing. The trial court found that Robert represented to Patricia and her counsel that his interest in the Bob Allen Investment Company had a value of $432,276, whereas, the court found, it was actually worth at least $1,400,000 even without inclusion of any factor for goodwill. Robert claims that he made no false representations regarding the value of the investment company. The record shows that he and his attorney provided Patricia and her attorney with many financial records. Robert stated that he relied on his accountant, Daniel Beattie, for the valuation of $432,276 and that the valuation was a statement of opinion, not one of fact. Robert states that Patricia and her attorney had the information, opportunity and means to obtain an appraisal of the business, and since she chose not to obtain an appraisal, she is now barred from claiming fraud. Patricia's attorney in the divorce case, Mr. Williams, testified that he examined the financial information provided, and he decided that the estimates of value seemed appropriate to him.

Patricia claims that Robert knew the value of the investment company was much higher than the valuation he provided. ... Patricia presented exhibits showing that prior to the dissolution hearing, Robert had valued the interest substantially higher in financial statements and corporate annual reports. Patricia presented the testimony of Mr. Beattie, who testified that he was never requested to formally appraise the investment company. Beattie stated that he was asked to prepare computations to enable Robert to find a formula for the purpose of valuing the dealership. Beattie testified that he did not know how the $432,276 value was determined by Robert, and that Robert's counsel told him the value was negotiated between the parties' counsel. Patricia presented as an expert Thomas Slack, who testified that Bob Allen Investment Company had a value of between $5,300,000 and $6,000,000. Slack valued the goodwill at $2,569,965.

Robert argues that the value he represented to Patricia ($432,276) was a statement of his opinion and not a statement of fact. A statement of value is ordinarily considered an opinion. The exception occurs when "the representing party has special knowledge and the other is ignorant in respect to the value which is known to the representing party and the representations are made with intention that they be relied on." *Alexander v. Sagehorn*... (Mo. 1980). ... Evidence was presented that Robert had special knowledge of the interest's value. Robert was actively involved in the auto dealerships as an executive as well as a major stockowner.

The second element, the representation's falsity, was shown by Slack's testimony as to the value of the interest and also by the tax returns and financial documentation presented at the hearing. ... The materiality of the representation is clear since the interest in the company is a substantial marital asset. Element four, Robert's knowledge of the falseness of the representation (or his awareness that he did not know whether it was true or false), is shown by the testimony of his accountant that Hewlett and his attorney did not ask the accountant to appraise his interest in the company, but instead sought information as to computations which might be used to determine a formula for ascertaining value. The trial court could have inferred that Robert did not want the accountant to value his interest because he desired to come up with his own figure, in order to mislead.

Robert argues that Patricia had no right to rely on his representations because she had an attorney and had ample opportunity to make her own determinations.

However, "[o]ne may act upon a positive representation of fact, notwithstanding that means of knowledge are open, particularly where the facts may be assumed to be within the knowledge of the person who declares it." *Alexander v. Sagehorn*. . . . If Robert had made no statement of value, Patricia may have taken some action to determine value, "but having been told by someone who purported to know, she relied on that figure." In this case, Patricia and her attorney had no obligation to determine value.

Judgment and Result

For the plaintiff. The court of appeals decided that substantial evidence supported the trial court's setting aside the decree of dissolution based on fraud in the husband's financial statements shown to her.

Questions

1. If a person misrepresents the value of something, is this act generally considered a representation of fact or opinion? Which would a defendant sued for fraud want it to be, fact or opinion? Why?
2. Was Patricia reasonable in her reliance on the figures Robert provided as to his net worth? Was her attorney reasonable in relying on the figures? Are attorneys supposed to be able to prepare financial statements? Did the accountant actually provide an appraisal of Robert's worth or just a formula for doing so? Does this excuse what the accountant did and put the blame for wrongdoing back on Robert's shoulders?
3. Would the scenario in the *Hewlett* case support or undercut the assertion made in Chapter 1, that positive law is the most one can expect of people in terms of ethical conduct?

False Imprisonment

False imprisonment occurs when one person totally restrains another for an "appreciable period of time," such as even a few minutes. The person restrained need not be physically harmed because the confinement or restraint itself is the harm. Most cases say that the victim must be aware of the confinement when it happens before he or she can be falsely imprisoned. The confinement need not be in a room, although it often is.

Remedies. Persons falsely imprisoned can recover nominal damages (a very small amount of money). Actual or compensatory damages (money to cover real losses or injuries) are also available. The victim can recover punitive damages where the wrongdoer had a bad intent or recklessly disregarded a plaintiff's interests. However, a plaintiff receives no punitive damages when a defendant made a good-faith error.

Defenses to False Imprisonment. One of the main defenses to false imprisonment is the "shopkeeper's privilege." Basically, this privilege allows a merchant with reasonable cause to detain a customer suspected of shoplifting for investigation, which must be conducted in a reasonable manner and time.

Invasion of Privacy

The intentional tort of **invasion of privacy** covers four loosely related but separate wrongs:

1. Intrusion upon a plaintiff's seclusion or into his or her private affairs
2. Public disclosure of private facts
3. Unauthorized appropriation of a person's name or likeness
4. Holding up a person in a false light

In other words, anyone who does any one of these four wrongs commits the tort of invasion of privacy.

Intrusion upon Solitude or Seclusion. **Intrusion upon solitude or seclusion** is one invasion of privacy. This invasion can occur if defendant sets up telescopes, listening devices, or snoops into a plaintiff's private life in a way that would be objectionable to a "reasonable person."

Unauthorized wiretapping of a plaintiff's private conversation has been held to be an intrusion upon a plaintiff's solitude and seclusion. An unauthorized photo of Herman using toilet paper for its intended purpose would usually invade his solitude or seclusion.

Public Disclosure of Private Facts. Public disclosure of private facts is a second type of invasion of privacy. The facts disclosed must be private. Courts have said that a person's personal finances and details about a personal part of the human body are private. Matters of public record, such as the amount of property taxes a homeowner pays, are not private facts.

Unauthorized Appropriation. The **unauthorized appropriation** of a plaintiff's name or likeness for a defendant's benefit frequently occurs in business cases. For example, Mace's Department Store advertises its dishes using Nancy Shurtz's name as a satisfied customer. The fact that Nancy uses Mace's dishes is no defense because Nancy's privacy is the protected interest.

False Light. Holding up a person in a **false light** in the public eye can arise in many situations. For instance, Ralph's illegitimate use of Michael Jackson's name to suggest Michael's connection with Ralph's product, book, or company is a false light case.

One famous false light case involved a defendant's unauthorized use of plaintiff's name on a telegram to the governor. The telegram asked the governor to act in a certain way on a pending law. The plaintiff actually did not agree with the telegram. Therefore, the telegram held the plaintiff up in a false light.

Defenses to Invasion of Privacy. No right of privacy exists in the following situations:

1. When the matter published is of public or general interest
2. When the matter is privileged under libel and slander laws
3. When the individual claiming privacy consents to publication

Harkey v. Abate is an invasion of privacy case, showing intrusion upon a person's solitude or seclusion.

Harkey v. Abate

Michigan Court of Appeals
346 N.W.2d 74 (Mich. App. 1983)

Background and Facts:

Plaintiff's original complaint, filed on August 28, 1981, alleged that plaintiff and her daughter were patrons at defendant's rollerskating rink on April 19, 1979, and that, while on the premises, they had utilized the women's restroom provided by the defendant for his patrons. Plaintiff thereafter discovered that the defendant had installed see-through panels in the ceiling of the restroom that permitted surreptitious observation from above of the interior, including the separately partitioned stalls. Plaintiff alleged that defendant had personally viewed plaintiff and her daughter while they used the restroom and claimed that the defendant's conduct constituted an invasion of their privacy, for which they seek damages.

Defendant moved for summary judgment, alleging there existed no genuine issue of fact. The motion was supported by an affidavit of defendant asserting he did not personally view the plaintiff and her daughter as alleged. Plaintiff conceded at the time of the hearing on the motion that there appeared to be no proof available that would establish that defendant had actually viewed plaintiff and her daughter in the restroom, but she asserted such proof is unnecessary to establish a prima facie case of invasion of privacy. The trial court apparently disagreed and granted summary judgment.

Body of Opinion

Judge Knoblock

The legally protected right of privacy has been variously defined as:

> [T]he right of an individual to be let alone, or to live a life of seclusion, or to be free from unwarranted publicity, or to live without unwarranted interference by the public about matters with which the public is not necessarily concerned, or to be protected from any wrongful intrusion into an individual's private life which would outrage or cause mental suffering, shame, or humiliation to a person of ordinary sensibility. 77 C.J.S., Right of Privacy, §1, pp 396, 397.

The type of invasion of privacy alleged in this case may be characterized as an "unreasonable intrusion upon the seclusion of another," 3 *Restatement of Torts*, 2d, §652A, p. 376, or more specifically an "[i]ntrusion upon the plaintiff's seclusion or solitude, or into his private affairs." A necessary element of this type of invasion of privacy is, of course, that there be an "intrusion." The issue presented for our resolution is whether the installation of the hidden viewing devices complained of can itself constitute a sufficient wrongful intrusion into the seclusion or solitude of plaintiff and her daughter so as to permit recovery. We hold that it can and that, therefore, the granting of summary judgment was improper. . . .

The installation of viewing devices as alleged by plaintiff is a felony in this state. Though this statute does not specifically impose civil liability for such conduct, nor does plaintiff's complaint assert liability based on its violation, it does constitute, at a minimum, a legislative expression of public policy opposed to such conduct.

The type of invasion of privacy asserted by plaintiff does not depend upon any publicity given to the person whose interest is invaded, but consists solely of an intentional interference with his or her interest in solitude or seclusion of a kind that would be highly offensive to a reasonable person. 3 *Restatement of Torts*, 2d, §652B, p. 378. Clearly, plaintiff and her daughter in this case had a right to privacy in the public restroom in question. In our opinion, the installation of the hidden viewing devices alone constitutes an interference with that privacy which a reasonable person would find highly offensive. And though the absence of proof that the devices were utilized is relevant to the question of damages, it is not fatal to plaintiff's case.

Plaintiff also claims on appeal that the trial court erred in denying her motion to amend the complaint. After the applicable statute of limitations had expired, plaintiff determined that the title to the rollerskating facility was held by a corporation, The Rink, Inc., and sought leave to add the corporate entity as a defendant. It appears from the record presented that defendant Abate is the resident agent for the corporate entity, that he is employed by it as manager of the rollerskating facility, that he is its sole officer, and that he had knowledge, both personally and in his representative capacity of the corporate entity, of this litigation and of plaintiff's intent to bring suit against the owner of the rollerskating facility. Based on these facts, we conclude the trial court abused its discretion in denying leave to amend.

Reversed and remanded.

Judgment and Result

The Michigan Court of Appeals said that the Harkeys' complaint stated a cause of action for invasion of privacy. The case was sent back to the trial court for further proceedings.

Questions

1. What part of the right of privacy did defendant allegedly violate?
2. Did plaintiff claim that defendant actually watched them use the restroom?
3. How can defendant protect the security of its restrooms without invading the customer's privacy?

Conversion

Conversion is the unauthorized and unjustified interference with the dominion and control of another's personal property. Personal property is anything movable; that is, things other than land and buildings can be converted.

Conversion is a wrong commonly called "stealing." Conversion is not a crime, however, but an intentional tort.

Interfering with another's personal property must be intentional. The intent does not have to be to harm—just interfere.

What Can Be Converted. Any tangible personal property—such as a horse, car, or diamond ring, for example—can be converted. Modern courts say that intangible personal property can be converted. The conversion is particularly true when there is a tangible symbol of an intangible right (such as a stock certificate representing a share of stock, an insurance policy representing insurance, or a savings bank book representing a savings account).

Land and buildings cannot be converted. Neither can gravel, trees, or crops. But once severed from the land, gravel, trees, and crops can be converted.

Examples of Conversion. A person who steals personal property commits conversion, but subtler forms of conversion exist. A person buying or selling stolen goods is considered a converter, even if unaware that the goods are stolen. A person who rightfully gets possession of goods but who refuses to give them to the owner is also a converter.

Abuse of Process

The essential parts of **abuse of process** are an ulterior purpose and the willful act in the use of the process not proper in the regular conduct of the proceeding.

Process refers to civil or criminal legal procedures. Arrest warrants and service of a summons and complaint in civil cases are examples of process. When process is used properly, no tort occurs. However, the intentional tort of abuse of process occurs when a person misuses process—that is, when process justified for one purpose is used for an improper purpose.

Generally, malice is not required for abuse of process. The case or matter also does not have to end in a plaintiff's favor. The crux of abuse of process is improper use.

Wrongful Interference with Contractual Relations

The elements of **wrongful interference with contractual relations** are as follows:

1. A valid, enforceable contract exists between B and C.
2. D, a third person, must know that the contract between B and C exists.
3. D must intentionally induce B or C to break the contract between B and C.

The intentional tort of wrongful interference with contractual relations makes contracts stable. This tort makes it wrong for a third person to upset an existing contract between two parties. Note that the defendant need not have either malice or bad faith.

Defenses to Wrongful Interference. Defenses to wrongful interference include lack of a part of the definition of this tort or justification. Justifications include moral, social, or economic pressures lawful in and of themselves. For example, if D's ads are so effective they cause B to break a contract with C, then it is considered economic justification.

In 1987 the Texas Court of Appeals decided *Texaco v. Pennzoil*. Pennzoil claimed that it had a contract to buy Getty Oil stock for a merger. After the alleged Getty-Pennzoil contract was formed, but before it was performed, Texas persuaded Getty to break its contract with Pennzoil and sell its stock to Texaco for a higher price. Pennzoil then sued Texaco on the theory that Texaco had wrongfully interfered with the Pennzoil-Getty contract. The result of this lawsuit in the Texas Court of Appeals follows.

Texaco, Inc. v. Pennzoil Co.

Texas Court of Appeals (1st Dist.)
729 S.W.2d 768 (1987)

Background and Facts:

This appeal concerns a judgment awarding Pennzoil damages for Texaco's tortious interference with a contract between Pennzoil and the "Getty entities" (Getty Oil Company, the Sarah C. Getty Trust, and the J. Paul Getty Museum).

The jury found, among other things, that:

(1) At the end of a board meeting on January 3, 1984, the Getty entities intended to bind themselves to an agreement providing for the purchase of Getty Oil stock, whereby the Sarah C. Getty Trust would own 4/7th of the stock and Pennzoil the remaining

3/7th; and providing for a division of Getty Oil's assets, according to their respective ownership if the Trust and Pennzoil were unable to agree on a restructuring of Getty Oil by December 31, 1984;

(2) Texaco knowingly interfered with the agreement between Pennzoil and the Getty entities;

(3) As a result of Texaco's interference, Pennzoil suffered damages of $7.53 billion;

(4) Texaco's actions were intentional, willful, and in wanton disregard of Pennzoil's rights; and,

(5) Pennzoil was entitled to punitive damages of $3 billion.

The main questions for our determination are: (1) whether the evidence supports the jury's finding that there was a binding contract between the Getty entities and Pennzoil, and that Texaco knowingly induced a breach of such contract. . . .

Though many facts are disputed, the parties' main conflicts are over the inferences to be drawn from, and the legal significance of, these facts. There is evidence that for several months in late 1983, Pennzoil had followed with interest the well-publicized dissension between the board of directors of Getty Oil Company and Gordon Getty, who was a director of Getty Oil and also the owner, as trustee, of approximately 40.2% of the outstanding shares of Getty Oil. On December 28, 1983, Pennzoil announced an unsolicited, public tender offer for 16 million shares of Getty Oil at $100 each.

Soon afterwards, Pennzoil contacted both Gordon Getty and a representative of the J. Paul Getty Museum, which held approximately 11.8% of the shares of Getty Oil, to discuss the tender offer and the possible purchase of Getty Oil. In the first two days of January 1984, a "Memorandum of Agreement" was drafted to reflect the terms that had been reached in conversations between representatives of Pennzoil, Gordon Getty, and the Museum.

Under the plan set out in the Memorandum of Agreement, Pennzoil and the Trust (with Gordon Getty as trustee) were to become partners on a 3/7ths to 4/7ths basis respectively, in owning and operating Getty Oil. Gordon Getty was to become chairman of the board, and Hugh Liedtke, the chief executive officer of Pennzoil, was to become chief executive officer of the new company.

The Memorandum of Agreement further provided that the Museum was to receive $110 per share for its 11.8% ownership, and that all other outstanding public shares were to be cashed in by the company at $110 per share. Pennzoil was given an option to buy an additional 8 million shares to achieve the desired ownership ratio. The plan also provided that Pennzoil and the Trust were to try in good faith to agree upon a plan to restructure Getty Oil within a year, but if they could not reach an agreement, the assets of Getty Oil were to be divided between them, 3/7ths to Pennzoil and 4/7ths to the Trust.

The Memorandum of Agreement stated that it was subject to approval of the board of Getty Oil, and it was to expire by its own terms if not approved at the board meeting that was to begin on January 2. Pennzoil's CEO, Liedtke, and Gordon Getty, for the Trust, signed the Memorandum of Agreement before the Getty Oil board meeting on January 2, and Harold Williams, the president of the Museum, signed it shortly after the board meeting began. Thus, before it was submitted to the Getty Oil board, the Memorandum of Agreement had been executed by parties who together controlled a majority of the outstanding shares of Getty Oil. The Memorandum of Agreement was then presented to the Getty Oil board, which had previously held discussions on how the company should respond to Pennzoil's public tender offer. A self-tender by the company to shareholders at $110 per share had been proposed to defeat Pennzoil's tender offer at $100 per share, but no consensus was reached.

The board voted to reject recommending Pennzoil's tender offer to Getty's shareholders, then later also rejected the Memorandum of Agreement price of $110 per share as too low. Before recessing at 3 a.m., the board decided to make a counterproposal to Pennzoil of $110 per share plus a $10 debenture. Pennzoil's investment banker reacted to this price negatively. In the morning of January 3, Getty Oil's investment banker, Geoffrey Boisi, began calling other companies, seeking a higher bid than Pennzoil's for the Getty Oil shares.

When the board reconvened at 3 p.m. on January 3, a revised Pennzoil proposal was presented, offering $110 per share plus a $3 "stub" that was to be paid after the sale of a Getty Oil subsidiary ("ERC"), from the excess proceeds over $1 billion. Each shareholder was to receive a pro rata share of these excess proceeds, but in any case, a minimum of $3 per share at the end of five years. During the meeting, Boisi briefly informed the board of the status of his inquiries of other companies that might be interested in bidding for the company. He reported some preliminary indications of interest, but no definite bid yet.

The Museum's lawyer told the board that, based on his discussions with Pennzoil, he believed that if the board went back "firm" with an offer of $110 plus a $5 stub, Pennzoil would accept it. After a recess, the Museum's president (also a director of Getty Oil) moved that the Getty board should accept Pennzoil's proposal provided that the stub be raised to $5, and the board voted 15 to 1 to approve this counterproposal to Pennzoil. The board then voted themselves and Getty's officers and advisors indemnity for any liability arising from the events of the past few months. Additionally, the board authorized its executive compensation committee to give "golden parachutes" (generous termination benefits) to the top executives whose positions "were likely to be affected" by the change in management. There was evidence that during another brief recess of the board meeting, the counteroffer of $110 plus a $5 stub was presented to and accepted by Pennzoil. After Pennzoil's acceptance was conveyed to the Getty board, the meeting was adjourned, and most board members left town for their respective homes.

That evening, the lawyers and public relations staff of Getty Oil and the Museum drafted a press release describing the transaction between Pennzoil and the Getty entities. The press release, announcing an agreement in principle on the terms of the Memorandum of Agreement but with a price of $110 plus a $5 stub, was issued on Getty Oil letterhead the next morning, January 4, and later that day, Pennzoil issued an identical press release.

On January 4, Boisi continued to contact other companies, looking for a higher price than Pennzoil had offered. After talking briefly with Boisi, Texaco management called several meetings with its in-house financial planning group, which over the course of the day studied and reported to management on the value of Getty Oil, the Pennzoil offer terms, and a feasible price range at which Getty might be acquired. Later in the day, Texaco hired an investment banker, First Boston, to represent it with respect to a possible acquisition of Getty Oil. Meanwhile, also on January 4, Pennzoil's lawyers were working on a draft of a formal "transaction agreement" that described the transaction in more detail than the outline of terms contained in the Memorandum of Agreement and press release.

On January 5, *The Wall Street Journal* reported on an agreement reached between Pennzoil and the Getty entities, describing essentially the terms contained in the Memorandum of Agreement. The Pennzoil board met to ratify the actions of its officers in negotiating an agreement with the Getty entities, and Pennzoil's attorneys periodically attempted to contact the other parties' advisors and attorneys to continue work on the transaction agreement.

The board of Texaco also met on January 5, authorizing its officers to make an offer for 100% of Getty Oil and to take any necessary action in connection therewith. Texaco first contacted the Museum's lawyer, Lipton, and arranged a meeting to discuss the sale of the Museum's shares of Getty Oil to Texaco. Lipton instructed his associate, on her way to the meeting in progress of the lawyers drafting merger documents for the Pennzoil-Getty transaction, to not attend that meeting, because he needed her at his meeting with Texaco. At the meeting with Texaco, the Museum outlined various issues it wanted resolved in any transaction with Texaco, and then agreed to sell its 11.8% ownership in Getty Oil.

That evening, Texaco met with Gordon Getty to discuss the sale of the Trust's shares. He was informed that the Museum had agreed to sell its shares to Texaco. Gordon Getty's advisors had previously warned him that the Trust shares might be "locked out" in a minority position if Texaco bought, in addition to the Museum's shares, enough of the public shares to achieve over 50% ownership of the company. Gordon Getty accepted Texaco's offer of $125 per share and signed a letter of his intent to sell his stock to Texaco, as soon as a California temporary restraining order against his actions as trustee was lifted.

At noon on January 6, Getty Oil held a telephone board meeting to discuss the Texaco offer. The board voted to withdraw its previous counterproposal to Pennzoil and unanimously voted to accept Texaco's offer. Texaco immediately issued a press release announcing that Getty Oil and Texaco would merge.

Soon after the Texaco press release appeared, Pennzoil telexed the Getty entities, demanding that they honor their agreement with Pennzoil. Later that day, prompted by the telex, Getty Oil filed a suit in Delaware for declaratory judgment that it was not bound to any contract with Pennzoil. The merger agreement between Texaco and Getty Oil was signed on January 6; the stock purchase agreement with the Museum was signed on January 6; and the stock exchange agreement with the Trust was signed on January 8, 1984....

The parties agree that in our review, we are required to apply the substantive law of New York and the procedural law of Texas....

Body of Opinion

Justice Warren

Texaco argues first that there was no evidence or there was insufficient evidence to support the jury's answers to Special Issue No. 1. The jury found that the Trust, the Museum, and Getty Oil Company intended to bind themselves to an agreement with Pennzoil containing certain enumerated terms at the end of the Getty Oil Company board meeting on January 3, 1984. Texaco claims that not only is there insufficient evidence of any intent to be found but also that the "agreement" referred to in Special Issue No. 1 is too indefinite to be a legally enforceable contract.

Texaco contends that under controlling principles of New York law, there was insufficient evidence to support the jury's finding that at the end of the Getty Oil board meeting on January 3, the Getty entities intended to bind themselves to an agreement with Pennzoil.

Pennzoil responds that the question of the parties' intent is a fact question, and the jury was free to accept or reject Texaco's after-the-fact testimony of subjective intent. Pennzoil contends that the evidence showed that the parties intended to be bound to the terms in the Memorandum of Agreement plus a price term of $110 plus a $5 stub, even though the parties may have contemplated a later, more formal document to memorialize the agreement already reached. Pennzoil also argues that the binding effect of the Memorandum of Agreement was conditioned only upon approval of the board, not also upon execution of the agreement by a Getty signator....

Thus, under New York law, the parties are given the power to obligate themselves informally or only by a formal signed writing, as they wish. The emphasis in deciding when a binding contract exists is on intent rather than on form. . . .

In its brief, Texaco asserts that, as a matter of black letter New York law, the "subject to" language in the press release established that the parties were not then bound and intended to be bound only after signing a definitive agreement, citing *Banking & Trading Corp. v. Reconstruction Finance Corp.* The court in that case stated that "if the agreement is expressly subject to the execution of a formal contract, this intent must be respected and no contract found until then." However, the court went on to say that where intent is less sharply expressed, the trier of fact must determine it as best he can. Although the intent to formalize an agreement is some evidence of an intent not to be bound before signing such a writing, it is not conclusive. The issue of when the parties intended to be bound is a fact question to be decided from the parties' acts and communications. . . .

Regardless of what interpretation we give to the conditional language in the press release, we conclude that it did not so clearly express the intent of the parties not to be bound to conclusively resolve that issue, as Texaco asserts. . . .

Texaco also contends that explicit language of reservation in drafts of Pennzoil's transaction agreement indicates the parties' expressed intent not to be bound without a signed writing. Texaco asserts that "Pennzoil's lawyers carefully stated that the parties' obligations would become binding only 'after the execution and delivery of this Agreement.'" . . .

A reasonable conclusion from reading the entire drafts is that the phrase "after the execution and delivery of this Agreement" was used chiefly to indicate the timing of various acts that were to occur, and not to impose an express precondition to the formation of a contract. Compare *Reprosystem* ("when executed and delivered," the agreement would become "a valid and binding agreement"). Again, the language upon which Texaco relies does not so clearly express an intent not to be bound to resolve that issue or to remove the question from the ambit of the trier of fact. . . .

Considering the type of action, the conduct involved, and the need for deterrence, we are of the opinion that the punitive damages are excessive and that the trial court abused its discretion in not suggesting a remittitur. Though our Texas guidelines are similar to those of New York, New York courts have adopted a more conservative stance on punitive damages. There is a point where punitive damages may overstate their purpose and serve to confiscate rather than to deter or punish. In this case, punitive damages of one billion dollars are sufficient to satisfy any reason for their being awarded, whether it be punishment, deterrence, or encouragement of the victim to bring legal action. We conclude that the award of punitive damages is excessive by two billion dollars.

Judgment and Result

If within thirty days from the date of this judgment, Pennzoil files in this Court a remittitur of two billion dollars, as suggested above, the judgment will be reformed and affirmed as to the award of $7.53 billion in compensatory damages and $1 billion in exemplary damages; otherwise the judgment will be reversed and remanded.

Questions and Comments

1. After the Texas Court of Appeals case, Texaco appealed to the Texas Supreme Court, which, in a *two-sentence* decision made without hearing oral argument, refused to upset the Texas Court of Appeals decision. Texaco earlier had tried to get the federal courts to enjoin Texas's enforcement of its appeal bond law, which would have required that Texaco post $10.53 billion *before* it could appeal to the Texas Court of Appeals or the Texas Supreme Court. Texaco was successful in its attempt to get the U.S. District Court in New York to enjoin the full use of the Texas appeal bonding requirement. The federal district court reduced the appeal bond to $1 billion. The U.S. Court of Appeals for the Second Circuit in New York basically upheld the district court. During this time Texaco was able to appeal to the Texas Court of Appeals. However, Pennzoil appealed the federal injunction decree to the U.S. Supreme Court which *reversed* the lower federal court decision on the appeal bond issue. This forced Texaco into bankruptcy on Sunday, April 12, 1987, so that it could appeal the Texas Court of Appeals decision to the Texas Supreme Court. As already noted, the Texas Supreme Court wasted little ink in affirming the court of appeals decision, and left Texaco with a last appeal on issues of federal law only. Before that happened Texaco and Pennzoil settled their wrongful interference with contractual relations suit for $3 billion in cash. This settlement forced Texaco to reorganize.
2. Who was the contract between in the *Texaco-Pennzoil* case? Who interfered with this contract? Are punitive damages possible for this type of tort?
3. Was the contract in question written or oral? Is it not odd that a billion-dollar merger would be oral?
4. If it is uncertain whether Pennzoil and Getty intended to have a contract before there was a writing, who decides this matter?
5. The Texas Court of Appeals found no judicial misconduct when the trial judge in the case received a $10,000 campaign contribution from Pennzoil's lead attorney *after* the judge had been assigned the case. The Court of Appeals said that judges have to run election campaigns, that they need money to do so, and that it is logical that the lawyers would be contributors to these election campaigns.

Intentional Infliction of Mental Distress

The tort **intentional infliction of mental distress** places liability on a person for intentionally causing severe emotional distress in situations where the actor's conduct goes beyond reasonable decency.

Intentional infliction of mental distress tries to protect people's peace of mind by allowing recovery if another person causes a plaintiff serious mental distress by an extremely outrageous act. An example would be wrapping a bloody dead rat in a loaf of bread and giving it to a sensitive person to open.

Intentional infliction of mental distress is a fairly new tort. Courts have for a long time given persons with physical injuries money for mental suffering "parasitic" (added on) to physical harm. The idea was that the victim was unlikely to be faking mental suffering if he or she had physical injuries.

Problems surround the whole notion of allowing recovery for mental injury without physical harm. First, mental suffering can be faked, allowing recovery for false claims. Second, this tort could flood the courts with lawsuits because of the large amount of mental stress in today's society. Third, this tort could encourage people to become crybabies, unable to stand the stress of modern life. Fourth, this tort could be a way for angry employees to get even with a boss who has properly disciplined them.

Defamation

Defamation has several key elements. First, a statement must be made by someone about another person. Second, the statement must hold up to ridicule, contempt, or scorn the person about whom the statement is made. Generally, favorable statements, such as "she is an intelligent person," are not defamatory because they fail to satisfy the holding up to ridicule, contempt, or scorn requirement. Third, the statement must be published. For defamation purposes, "publication" merely means that the statement is heard (if oral) or seen (if written) by at least one other person. Publication does not mean published in book form.

> http://
> *For help locating tort law, see* ***http://law2.house.gov***

Defamation as an intentional tort is designed to discourage abuse of reputations and to protect a person's relations with other people. This tort tries to make liable a person who says or writes untrue statements about another that hold up the person spoken about to ridicule, contempt, or scorn in the minds of others.

Defenses to Defamation. Several defenses to defamation include the following:

1. Truth
2. Lack of an element of the definition
3. Privilege (absolute or qualified)

Truth can be used as a defense. If, for example, Sally says something true to Maggie that makes Irene look ridiculous, contemptible, or scorned, most states say that this type of statement is not defamation.

Privilege means that, even though a defendant has uttered or written statements that would otherwise be defamatory, a defendant is not liable because of some superior public policy of free expression. The two types of privileges are absolute and qualified. **Absolute privilege** means that a person may make the defamatory remark maliciously or without necessity. **Qualified privilege** is a right to make defamatory statements limited by motive and manner in which the remarks were made. Some examples of absolutely privileged comments include remarks made on the floor of legislatures or at legislative hearings, executive communications, court or judicial hearings, husband-wife communications, and in publications consented to by the plaintiff.

The two types of defamation are libel and slander. Libel is written and slander is oral, although some difficult "in-between" areas exist. For example, are defamatory remarks spoken on television or radio slander or libel? Some courts have said that such remarks are libelous.

The *East v. Bullock's Inc.* case illustrates problems associated with alleged defamatory statements by an employer when evaluating an employee thought to have stolen from the employer. As you will see, the employer raised the qualified privilege defense.

East v. Bullock's Inc.

Federal District Court (D. Arizona)
34 F.Supp.2d 1176 (1998)

Background and Facts:

Melinda Ann East was employed at the Bullock's department store in Scottsdale, Arizona, from July 10, 1991, until she was terminated on March 29, 1995. During the course of her employment, she worked in various positions. Initially, she was hired as a sales associate and paid on an hourly basis. In April of 1992, she was promoted to manager of the Young Men's department and reclassified as a salaried employee. From February of 1993 through May of 1993, she worked as a merchandise trainer and was again paid hourly. In May of 1993 she was named manager of the Children's department and paid on a salaried basis. In December of 1993, she became an assistant manager in the Designer Ladies Dresses department and paid hourly. Thereafter, she assumed the position of selling manager in the Men's Polo department on a salaried basis. In November of 1994, Bullock's redefined the position of selling manager and, although East retained the title, she was reclassified as an hourly worker. She continued in this capacity until her March 1995 termination.

On October 30, 1994, Kerry McBay, the Human Resources Manager at Bullock's Scottsdale store, met with East to discuss problems relating to East's timekeeping. East had neglected to "clock in" and "clock out" on a regular basis as required by Bullock's rules of conduct.

Sometime in early 1995, another manager at the Scottsdale store reported that East was making additions or corrections to her time records after the fact, rather than on a real time basis. Thereafter, Bullock's security department placed East under surveillance. Video cameras recorded her entrances and exits. On several occasions, between March 15, 1995, and March 25, 1995, East's time records failed to match the times when she was observed entering and exiting the store.

On March 28, 1995, Security Chief Dale Lindgren interviewed East. When queried about the time discrepancies. East denied intentionally misrepresenting her hours. She apologized if she had made any inadvertent errors. She stated that her failure to punch in and out could be attributed to her frequent reclassification from hourly to salaried. Salaried employees are not required to record their time.

After East's interview, she was suspended by Mr. McBay. Mr. McBay then sought direction from Denise Flynn, Bullock's vice-president of Human Resources. Ms. Flynn instructed Mr. McBay to terminate East. East was terminated on March 29, 1995.

At the time of East's termination, Ms. Flynn called Jill Lansdale, the Scottsdale store manager, and advised her of East's termination. Ms. Lansdale informed the senior managers in the store that East had been terminated for falsifying company documents.

Based on the foregoing events East filed a number of claims against Bullock's including the defamation.

Body of Opinion

District Judge Ezra

. . . Count 3 of Plaintiff's Amended Complaint alleges defamation. Plaintiff argues that Ms. Lansdale, Bullock's vice-president of human relations, made statements to other managers that Plaintiff was terminated for falsifying company documents. Plaintiff attempts to characterize her termination as one for timekeeping theft and makes much of the fact that accusations of theft are per se defamatory. However, Plaintiff has not proffered any evidence that Ms. Lansdale said anything about theft.

Moreover, Plaintiff's defamation claim fails because Ms. Lansdale's statements were true, that is, Plaintiff was actually terminated for falsifying company documents, namely her time records. Although Ms. Lansdale did not independently investigate the grounds for Plaintiff's termination, she did not recklessly or negligently disregard the truth.

Finally, even if Ms. Lansdale's statements were not true, the statements were made in a meeting with other store managers. Bullock's argues that such statements fall within a qualified privilege under Arizona law. The Arizona Supreme Court recognized ... a two-part test for determining whether a qualified privilege exists. First, the court must examine the circumstances to determine whether a privileged occasion arose. Second, once a conditional privilege applies, a plaintiff must prove the privilege was abused by proving actual malice or by demonstrating excessive publication. Abuse through "actual malice" occurs when the defendant makes a statement knowing its falsity or actually entertaining doubts about its truth.... Abuse through excessive publication results from publication to an unprivileged recipient not reasonably necessary to protect the interest upon which the privilege is grounded.... Although the second part of the test is usually a question of fact for the jury, the court may decide the issue if there is no evidence of malice or excessive publication.

In this case, Ms. Lansdale's publication of Plaintiff's termination to other managers is entitled to a qualified privilege based on "common interest." Occasions in which "one is entitled to learn from his associates what is done in a matter in which he has an interest in common with them," warrant a qualified privilege.... Co-managers in a company would have a common interest in learning of an employee's termination. Furthermore, because there is no evidence of actual malice or excessive publication, the court finds that the conditional privilege has not been abused.

Judgment and Result

Statements by the store's vice-president of human relations that plaintiff was terminated for falsifying company documents were privileged from defamation action.

Questions

1. Does the decision acknowledge that managers have a broad privilege that extends to even saying untrue statements about company employees if done at company meetings where such matters are appropriately discussed? What limits does the court place on statements made even during closed meetings? Can such discussions take place at a company picnic where many employees unrelated to personnel matters, such as custodians and stockholders are present? What if family members who are not company employees are present at the picnic, what business do they have hearing about possible employee thefts of company property?
2. Does limited dissemination of allegedly defamatory remarks only within the affected organization tend to show the speaker's goodwill or is more required of supervisory personnel?
3. Are the arguments in favor of recognizing the qualified privilege doctrine especially strong today where employers are discovering that employee theft accounts for greater losses than those from shoplifters? If allegations that an employee is performing a given job unsatisfactorily prove to be untrue, does this error not stigmatize the employee? Does this type of incident not suggest that employers should be especially careful in appraising employee performance and corroborate allegations with *objective* evidence prior to making any allegations?
4. If East had shown that many other hourly employees of Bullock's routinely violated the "time clock rule" and were not disciplined at all, might this factor indicate that Bullock's was using East's violations as a pretext for dismissing her? Also, even if East and East alone were violating the time clock rule, might it not reveal prejudice against East IF it could be shown that East's sales performance far exceeded that of her co-workers?
5. Most states do require that plaintiff prove damages before recovering in a slander case unless it is slander per se. The lack of malice, however, can mitigate A's damages.
6. The *East* case speaks of defamation (slander) per se in which statements injuring a person in her trade, business, or professional calling are made. In such cases damages or malice is presumed. Why?

CHAPTER SUMMARY

Torts are breaches of noncontractual civil duties. Torts and crimes can overlap, but not all torts are crimes. Torts and contracts are both areas of civil law, but contract duties generally arise by agreements. Tort duties generally do not arise by agreement.

Remedies for torts include nominal, compensatory, and possibly punitive damages for intentional torts. Equitable remedies such as injunctions are also possible.

Torts can fall into the following categories: negligence, intentional torts, and strict liability torts.

Negligence involves duty, breach of the standard of care, proximately causing damages. Defenses to negligence include contributory negligence, assumption of risk, and lack of an element of the definition of negligence, for example, no duty.

MANAGER'S ETHICAL DILEMMA

Oscar Fuller could not stand it anymore. He had been sued again because his business, which ran a skating rink, had put "see through" ceilings in the women's restrooms for surveillance purposes. A woman customer had learned of it and accused Oscar of peeping at her, which he denied doing. Not only that, she successfully sued his business for the intentional tort of invasion of the right of privacy and won both compensatory and punitive damages. What really irked Oscar was that he had installed the ceilings after another woman patron had been robbed and raped while in the restroom and had successfully sued him for negligence in not supervising his restrooms more carefully.

Now Oscar saw an opportunity to get legal liability under control. A tort reform bill had been introduced in the state legislature. The bill contained the following provisions: (1) a "cap" on pain and suffering awards of $300,000 per incident; (2) a $250,000 cap on punitive damages; (3) a requirement that negligence claims against businesses be arbitrated before being allowed to go to court and, if such claims went to court and the jury award was less than 30 percent above the arbitrator's award, the party moving the case to court would have to pay both parties' attorney fees; and (4) a no-fault legal regime for negligence claims against vehicle drivers.

What ethical considerations might enter Oscar's decision on whether to support this bill?

Intentional torts include fraud, defamation, false imprisonment, conversion, wrongful interference with contractual relations, invasion of privacy, and abuse of process.

Discussion Questions

1. Compelled self-defamation, sometimes called "compelled self-disclosure," is a defamation doctrine that says the defamed person is forced by circumstances to reveal defamatory statements made about himself to third persons. For example, in applying for a job a person might be asked why they left a previous job. Suppose the former employer discharged the applicant for "theft of company property," but the employee disputes this claim. Nonetheless, rather than lying about it, the job applicant says, "My former employer dismissed me for allegedly stealing company property. I dispute his claim." The prospective employer decides not to hire the applicant believing the former employer. The applicant then bring a defamation action against his former employer arguing compelled self-disclosure ("I had to repeat my old employer's defamation to my new, prospective employer to be a truthful person.")

   Valencia made such a claim against Citibank International (Citibank) when she brought a defamation suit against Citibank. Specifically, Valencia alleged that Citibank's reasons for terminating her were false and that she was compelled to disclose the false reasons for her termination to prospective employers. Should the state of Florida (where this case arose) recognize the doctrine of compelled self-disclosure and permit the employee to sue the former employer for defamation when the former employer said nothing to anyone about why the former employee was terminated? [*Valencia v. Citibank International*, 728 So.2d 330 (Fla. Ct. App. 1999)].
2. Explain the difference between torts and crimes.
3. What does it mean to say that tort law is a legal laboratory?
4. List the four parts of the negligence definition.
5. How is the ORP person different from each of us?
6. Name two defenses to negligence.
7. What is the difference between intentional torts and crimes?
8. Is tort law generally state or federal law?
9. Define fraud.
10. A landlord had secretly installed a listening device in his tenants' bedroom. This device enabled him to monitor and record voices and sounds in the bedroom. The tenants did not claim that the landlord actually used the listening device. Did the tenants have a good

claim for invasion of their right of privacy? [*Hamberger v. Eastman*, 206 A.2d 239 (N.H.1964)].

11. Hallmark Builders, Inc., sued a local television station for defamation. The local television newscast reported on problems encountered by new home buyers, including defects in construction. Did a closeup camera shot of hairline masonry cracks in the house accurately represent the cracks or was this defamatory? [*Hallmark Builders Inc. v. Gaylord Broadcasting Co.*, 733 F.2d 1461 (11th Cir. 1984)].
12. A manufacturer's regional sales manager criticized a particular salesperson's job performance to the company president. The remarks related solely to the sales work for the company. Were these remarks privileged? [*Humphrey v. National Semiconductor Corp.*, 463 N.E. 2d 1197 (Mass. App. 1984)].
13. A motorcyclist was in an accident with a postal service jeep. The motorcyclist proved damages for injuries, medical expenses, pain and suffering, and disability and impairment amounted to $12,346.15. His negligence was 50 percent of the cause of the accident. The government showed that it sustained $589.67 in damages. The jurisdiction follows a comparative negligence scheme. What did each party recover? [*Wright v. United States*, 574 F.Supp. 160 (1983)].
14. Ernest Gortarez, age sixteen, and his cousin, Albert Hernandez, age eighteen, went to Smitty's store on January 2, 1979. About 8 p.m., Gortarez picked up a 59 cent vaporizer used to freshen the air in cars. He asked if he could pay for it in the front of the store when he finished shopping. The clerk said "Yes," but decided the request was suspicious and had a hunch that Gortarez would try to leave without paying. The two cousins finally left the store through an unattended checkout aisle. The clerk, Robert Sjulestad, had followed the two boys out of the store and had not seen them pay for or put down the vaporizer. Thus the clerk thought they had shoplifted it. Sjulestad told the security guard and store manager, "Those two guys just ripped us off." The assistant manager and two other store employees followed the boys into the parking lot, where the guard flashed his police badge (he was an off-duty policeman "moonlighting" as a security guard). The guard said, "I believe you have something you did not pay for." The guard then seized Hernandez, put his arms on the car, and began searching him. Hernandez offered no resistance even though Gibson did not ask for the vaporizer nor did Gibson say what he was looking for. Gortarez saw Gibson grab his cousin and was outraged at this behavior and used strong language to protest the detention and the search, yelling at Gibson to leave his cousin alone. Gortarez pushed Gibson away from his cousin. Gibson then put a choke hold on Gortarez for a period of time even after Gortarez had advised the store employees that the vaporizer had been left in the store. When a carry-out boy told the manager that he had found the vaporizer in a basket at the checkout lane, the two cousins were released. The cousins then sued Smitty's for false imprisonment. What was the result? [*Gortarez v. Smitty's Super Valu, Inc.*, 680 P.2d 807 (1984)].

Suggested Readings

Articles

ADAMS, "At the End of Palsgraf, There Is Chaos: An Assessment of Proximate Cause in Light of Chaos Theory," 59 *University of Pittsburgh Law Review* 507 (1998).

CHERRY, "Negligence: An Expanding Cause of Action Against Builders for Used Home Defects," 26 *American Business Law Journal* 167 (1988).

LANGVARDT, "A Principled Approach to Compensatory Damages in Corporate Defamation Cases," 27 *American Business Law Journal* 491 (1990).

LANGVARDT, "Defamation in the Employment Discharge Context: The Emerging Doctrine of Compelled Self-Disclosure," 26 *Duquesne Law Review* 227 (1988).

OAKLEY and MANSFIELD, "No-Fault Automobile Insurance in Georgia: Is Revision in Order?" 27 *Georgia State Bar Journal* 68 (1990).

Books

KEETON, *Prosser and Keeton on Torts* (1984).

CHAPTER

11

NATURE, DEFINITION, AND CLASSIFICATION OF CONTRACTS

"FREE TO CHOOSE"

Milton Friedman

POSITIVE LAW ETHICAL PROBLEMS

"I've been robbed," shouted William Story, Jr. His uncle had promised to pay him $5,000 if Junior did not smoke, drink, swear, or gamble at cards or billiards before becoming 21 years old. William had agreed, and his uncle had told William the money would be held at interest. When his uncle died two years later, William made a claim against his uncle's estate for the $5,000 plus interest. The estate argued that William should get nothing because he had given his uncle no "consideration" in return for the uncle's promise. Therefore, the uncle's estate argued that the uncle's promise was unenforceable. Was it?

"We don't have to go ahead with our option contract because it is unwritten," said Ken Garren, director of the Valdosta-Lowndes County Industrial Authority, which was sued for breach of contract for not selling the land to Firstline Corporation. Are options to sell realty required to evidenced by a signed writing to be enforceable and, if so, how detailed must the writing be?

With this chapter we survey the law covering contracts. We shall define contracts, discuss how contracts fit into the U.S. legal system, and examine contract classifications as well as the basic rules of contract formation.

HOW CONTRACTS FIT INTO THE MARKET ECONOMY

In introductory economics courses you learned about the market economy and the intersection of supply and demand curves, which set the price of goods and services. It is important to note that these supply and demand curves summarize not one but millions of **contracts**, which are agreements between buyers and sellers of all goods and services. In other words, contracts are the basis for the market economy. When people trade for money or exchange goods for goods (barter) they make contracts.

Trends in Contract Law

In the Middle Ages, people were born serfs or nobles. With a few exceptions, they kept their status of prince or serf for their entire lives. Serfs essentially were slaves with few rights; they had no freedom to enter contracts to work where they wanted in order to improve their economic and social status.

In the nineteenth and early twentieth centuries the market economy thrived, and individual freedom increased. People were free to work where they wanted and could own property in their own names. People could change their status by working and contracting. These freedoms continue today.

A site dealing with business law and providing information about contracts in particular can be found at **http://www.yahoo.com/government/law** **http://**

In the mid and late twentieth century, two trends have emerged in contract law. The first trend has been toward long-term contracts. For example, a utility company may enter a 10- or 20-year contract to buy coal. Second, since the late 1970s, a definite trend toward monopolies has developed, which concentrates economic power. This second trend was intensified by the merger "mania" of the 1980s and 90s. Because monopolies reduce the number of competitors, a few large businesses have great power to set contract terms. These terms include price, warranty, and quality standards.

Philosophies Found in Contract Law

Several philosophies, or beliefs, are found in contracts. First is the *libertarian* idea that people have freedom of choice. For example, people can contract for a particular job, buy or rent a house, buy a Ford or a Cadillac, and spend or save all or part of their paychecks. Because individuals are free to choose and shape their lives, they answer these questions on an individual basis.

Another philosophy found in contracts is the *utilitarian* concept of the greatest good for the greatest number. Again, each individual determines the "greatest good" personally. For example, a person who contracts to go to school to learn to be an insurance broker believes spending money on education is more valuable than spending it on a car or a vacation. Another person might do the opposite.

Finally, contracts are not positive law using John Austin's definition of positive law (a command of government with sanctions if it is broken). Instead, private people (not government) make their own contracts. However, contract law, as distinct from contracts, is made by courts and legislatures and, thus, is positive law. Note also that court-ordered remedies for breach of contract are a type of sanction, and thereby satisfy part of Austin's positive law definition.

Law Governing Contracts

The law governing contracts is generally state law, including state statutes or common law, or judge-made rules. Every state except Louisiana has passed the Uniform Commercial Code's (UCC) Article 2, which sets the rules for contracts dealing with goods. Real estate, services, and insurance contracts are controlled by common law and other state statutes.

For access to the Uniform Commercial Code, go to **http://www.law.cornell.edu/topics/contracts.html** **http://**

Contract Definitions[1]

Various legal scholars and authorities give us contract definitions. Members of the American Law Institute (ALI), a nongovernmental group of legal scholars including professors and practicing lawyers, read many cases and try to restate them in an easy-to-understand way. The ALI explains contracts in a set of books called the *Restatement, Second, Contracts*.

[1] This chapter is a survey, not an in-depth treatment of contract law. Other contract topics such as consideration, illegality, and unconscionability are covered later under the topics of consumer protection and product liability.

Restatement's *Contract Definition*. After reading thousands of cases, ALI scholars define a contract as follows: "A contract is a promise or a set of promises for the breach of which the law gives a remedy, or the performance of which the law in some way recognizes as a duty." Basically, this definition means that if a judge would make someone keep a promise, it is a contract. A problem with this definition is that a person has to sue to get a judge's decision.

***Common Definition of a Contract*.** The common definition of a contract is "an agreement between competent parties enforceable in court." An agreement involves an offer and acceptance. The offer and acceptance must be bargained for. "Competent parties" refers to the idea that minority age, insanity, and drunkenness on the part of one or more persons will result in an agreement that is void or voidable.

For additional information on contract law and business law in general, go to ***http://www.lawreview.org***

The "enforceable in court" part of the contract definition refers to several points. First, not all agreements are legally enforceable contracts. Social agreements (or "dates") are not contracts. For example, if Fred breaks a date with Marsha, Marsha *will* not get a judge to award her a remedy for breach of contract. Second, excited utterances (such as "I'll give a billion dollars to anyone who saves my drowning child," yelled by a mother to a crowd as she watches her child pulled under by an ocean current) do not give rise to contracts. Therefore, the hero who saves the woman's child is not entitled to a billion dollars given her excitement when she made the offer. Third, other problems (such as fraud, mistake, innocent misrepresentation, duress, unconscionability, or lack of a written contract where a writing is required) could make a contract unenforceable. Fourth, many contract definitions require that the parties give each other consideration. Consideration means that the contracting parties each have given up a right that was bargained for (asked for) by the other party. Consideration takes the form of a promise for a promise in a bilateral contract or a promise for an act in a unilateral contract.

The Objective Theory of Contracts

The **objective theory of contracts** means that contracts are determined by what people appear to have done (which is "objective"), not what they think they have done (which is "subjective"). This theory of contracts forces judges to point to evidence people can see, such as a signed contract, to decide whether a contract exists.

For example, Jim thinks he is playing a joke on Sarah. He pretends to offer his $35,000 Cadillac to her for $15,000 and signs a contract saying so. He does not actually intend to follow through on such an offer. However, based on appearances, any reasonable person would say Jim made an offer. Therefore, the objective theory of contracts says Jim and Sarah have a contract, even if Jim does not want one and assuming Sarah accepted.

CONTRACT CLASSIFICATIONS

We shall now examine five different contract classifications:

1. Bilateral and unilateral
2. Express and implied
3. Valid, voidable, void, and unenforceable
4. Executed and executory
5. Quasi-contracts

Bilateral and Unilateral Contracts

The basis for the bilateral and unilateral contract classification is the number of promises.

When two people exchange promises—one promise for another—they make a **bilateral contract**. For example, Irving says to Herman, "Promise to paint my house, and I'll promise to pay you $500." If Herman promises to do so, he has made a bilateral contract with Irving.

A **unilateral contract** consists of a promise and an act. A person makes a promise and also asks for an act in return. One example is: "I'll pay you $500 (the promise) if you paint my house" (the requested act). The promise is the offer, and the offeree's performance of the requested act is the acceptance. Only when the requested act is complete is there a contract.

Note the difference between bilateral and unilateral contracts. In a situation involving a unilateral contract, the offeror asks for a return act ("paint my house"), not a promise. However, if an offeror asks for a return promise, he or she wants to enter a bilateral contract. Only a return promise (not an act) will form the contract in a bilateral case.

One other point: A person does not have to use the word *promise* to make a promise. Any words showing you promise (such as "okay" "I agree") will do. *Davis v. Jacoby* examines the distinction between unilateral and bilateral contracts.

Davis v. Jacoby

Supreme Court of California
1 Cal. 2d 370, 34 P.2d 1026 (1934)

Background and Facts:

Caro Davis was the niece of Blanche and Rupert Whitehead, who were childless. The Whiteheads were very fond of Caro, who lived with them in California for a while. Then Caro married Frank Davis and moved to Canada.

When Mr. Whitehead became ill, he wrote to Caro and Frank. In the letter, he asked them to come to California and care for the Whiteheads until they died. In return for doing so, Mr. Whitehead promised to give Caro everything in his will (estimated at $150,000 in 1931). Frank Davis sent a return letter saying he and Caro accepted Mr. Whitehead's offer. The Davises prepared to leave Canada but before leaving, they received word that Mr. Whitehead had committed suicide.

The Davises went to California to care for Mrs. Whitehead until she died. Soon after, they learned that Mr. Whitehead's will did not give them anything. The estate argued Mr. Whitehead's letter was an offer requesting an act (an offer for a unilateral contract). Because the act (going to California and caring for the Whiteheads) was not done *before* Whitehead died, the estate executor argued there was no contract.

The Davises argued that Mr. Whitehead had asked for a *return promise* (not a return act). The Davises had made a return promise *before* Whitehead died.

Body of Opinion

The theory of the trial court and of respondents of this appeal is that the letter of April 12 was an offer to contract, but that such offer could only be accepted by performance and could not be accepted by a promise to perform, and that said offer was revoked by the death of Mr. Whitehead before performance. In other words, it is contended that the offer was an offer to enter into a unilateral contract, and that the purported acceptance of April 14 was of no legal effect.

The distinction between unilateral and bilateral contracts is well settled in the law. It is well stated in section 12 of the American Institute's *Restatement of the Law of Contracts* as follows: "A unilateral contract is one in which no promisor receives a promise as consideration for his promise. A bilateral contract is one in which there are mutual promises between two parties to the contract; each party being both the promisor and the promisee." This definition is in accord with the law of California.

In the case of unilateral contracts no notice of acceptance by performance is required. Section 1584 of the Civil Code provides: "Performance of the conditions of a proposal . . . is an acceptance of the proposal."

Although the legal distinction between unilateral and bilateral contracts is thus well settled, the difficulty in any particular case is to determine whether the particular offer is one to enter into a bilateral or unilateral contract. . . . By the provisions of the *Restatement of the Law of Contracts*, it is expressly provided that there is a presumption that the offer is to enter into a bilateral contract. Section 31 provides: "In case of doubt it is presumed that an offer invites the formation of a bilateral contract by an acceptance amounting in effect to a promise by the offeree to perform what the offer requests, rather than the formation of one or more unilateral contracts by actual performance on the part of the offeree." Professor Williston, in his *Treatise on Contracts*, volume 1 §60, also takes the position that a presumption in favor of bilateral contracts exists.

In the comment following section 31 of the *Restatement*, the reason for such presumption is stated as follows: "It is not always easy to determine whether an offeror requests an act or a promise to do the act. As a bilateral contract immediately and fully protects both parties, the interpretation is favored that a bilateral contract is proposed."

While the California cases have never expressly held that a presumption in favor of bilateral contracts exists, the cases clearly indicate a tendency to treat offers as offers of bilateral rather than of unilateral contracts.

Keeping these principles in mind, we are of the opinion that the offer of April 12 was an offer to enter into a bilateral as distinguished from a unilateral contract. Respondents argue that Mr. Whitehead had the right as offeror to designate his offer as either unilateral or bilateral. That is undoubtedly the law. It is then argued that from all the facts and circumstances it must be implied that what Whitehead wanted was performance and not a mere promise to perform. We think this is a non sequitur, in fact the surrounding circumstances lead to just the opposite conclusion. These parties were not dealing at arm's length. Not only were they related, but a very close and intimate friendship existed between them. The record indisputably demonstrates that Mr. Whitehead had confidence in Mr. and Mrs. Davis, in fact that he had lost all confidence in everyone else. The record indicates that Mr. Whitehead had become desperate, and that what he wanted was the promise of appellants that he could look to them for assistance. He knew from his past relationship with appellants that if they gave their promise to perform he could rely upon them. The correspondence between them indicates how desperately he desired this assurance. . . . "Will you let me hear from you as soon as possible—I know it will be a sacrifice but times are still bad and likely to be, so by settling down you can help me and Blanche and gain in the end." By thus specifically requesting an immediate reply Whitehead expressly indicated the nature of the acceptance desired by him, namely, appellants' promise that they would come to California and do the things requested by him. This promise was immediately sent by appellants upon receipt of the offer, and was received by Whitehead. It is elementary that when an offer has indicated the mode and means of acceptance, an acceptance in accordance with that mode or means is binding on the offeror.

Another factor which indicates that Whitehead must have contemplated a bilateral rather than a unilateral contract, is that the contract required Mr. and Mrs. Davis to perform services until the death of both Mr. and Mrs. Whitehead. It is obvious that if Mr. Whitehead died first some of these services were to be performed after his death, so that he would have to rely on the promise of the appellants to perform these services. It is also of some evidentiary force that Whitehead received the letter of acceptance and acquiesced in that means of acceptance. . . .

For the foregoing reasons we are of the opinion that the offer of April 12, 1931, was an offer to enter into a bilateral contract which was accepted by the letter of April 14, 1931. . . .

The judgment appealed from is reversed.

Judgment and Result

The California Supreme Court held that Mr. Whitehead's letter to the Davis's was an offer to enter a bilateral contract that Mr. Davis accepted by sending a letter of acceptance.

Questions

1. If A says to B, "Come to California and I'll pay you $500," and B says, "I promise to come," is there a contract?
2. How does one distinguish between a unilateral and bilateral contract?
3. Was it clear whether the contract sued upon here was unilateral or bilateral? Is there a preferred construction if there is doubt? Why?

Express and Implied Contracts

Express contracts are those having the terms completely stated in words. Such contracts can be either oral or written. A contract between a homeowner and a home buyer covering many details in selling a house is an example of an express, written contract. Calling the local pizza shop and ordering a 14-inch pizza with mushrooms and sausage to be delivered to your dorm room is an example of an express oral contract, if the pizza shop accepts the order.

Implied contracts can also be inferred from the parties' conduct even though nothing is said. Such contracts are implied in fact, meaning the facts justify assuming that the parties intend a contract. Two kinds of implied contracts are contracts implied in law and contracts implied in fact.

The following example involves an implied-in-fact contract. A student is in a bookstore, picks out a book, takes it to the cashier, and puts down the necessary money. The clerk makes change and bags the book. Nothing is said, yet the parties' conduct shows they intended to make a contract.

Valid, Voidable, Void, and Unenforceable Contracts

A contract is valid if it has no legal flaws. A **valid contract** is enforceable under virtually all circumstances.

Contracts are **voidable** when they have certain defects that could, but not necessarily will, make the contract unenforceable. At least one of the parties may escape voidable contracts by noting the defect. Defects making contracts voidable include fraud, innocent misrepresentation, and lack of contractual capacity (such as minority). For example, a 10-year-old who signs a contract to buy a Cadillac can avoid the contract because she or he is a minor.

Sometimes contracts have such serious flaws that they are called legally void. **Legally void** means no contract could have existed at all—ever. A contract can be void even though a piece of paper exists saying that it is a contract.

Factors that make an attempted contract void include illegality of the subject matter (such as contracts to commit murder), contracts against public policy, and attempts by persons adjudged legally insane to contract.

Unenforceable contracts are those failing to meet a procedural or formal requirement that makes them unenforceable. A *procedural flaw* would be not suing within the statute of limitations period. A *formal error* would involve making an oral contract when the statute of frauds requires a written one.

Executed and Executory Contracts

We can also classify contracts according to the degree to which they have been performed. Contracts partly performed or totally unperformed are **executory contracts**. Contracts fully performed by both parties are **executed contracts**.

It is possible for a contract to be fully performed (an executed contract) by one party and unperformed or partly performed (an executory contract) by the other party. For example, Claude Teagarden pays Bill Haymaker $10 to mow his lawn. Teagarden has fully executed his part of the contract, but Haymaker's part is executory until he finishes mowing.

Quasi-Contracts

A **quasi-contract** is not contracts but a legal idea that lets judges force a contract on parties even though they did not have one. The term *quasi-contract* means "like a contract." Quasi-contracts are also known as contracts implied in law, meaning a judge creates them.

Purpose of the Quasi-Contract Theory. The quasi-contract theory exists to prevent unjust enrichment. It applies in situations where one person confers benefits on another when it is reasonable to believe payment is expected, no gift is intended, and where no contract exists. A judge will tell the person receiving the benefits to pay the reasonable value, as set by the judge, of the benefits received.

Example of a Quasi-Contract. The following example involves a quasi-contract. Charles Walker calls Ace Painting Company (Ace) and tells them to paint his building. Ace mistakenly drives up in front of Bill Eshee's building and starts painting. Eshee sees the Ace truck and realizes they should be painting Walker's building next door. Eshee says nothing, hoping for a free paint job. When Ace finishes the job, Mr. Ace says to Eshee: "Well, Mr. Walker, how do you like the paint job?" Eshee replies, "It's great. But I'm Eshee. Walker's building is next door."

To allow Eshee to get a free paint job when he had reason to know that pay was expected would be unjust enrichment. Ace has no contract with Eshee. However, Ace can ask a judge to apply the quasi-contract idea to let Ace recover the reasonable value of the benefits Eshee got.

Limits on Quasi-Contracts. At times a judge will not allow a person to use the quasi-contract concept. If the person receiving benefits does not have a reasonable opportunity to reject the benefits before getting them, judges will not allow quasi-contract recovery. For example, suppose Ace Painting Company had painted Eshee's building, and Eshee had not known about the job until completion. Eshee would not have to pay on the basis of quasi-contract because he had no reasonable opportunity to reject the benefits.

A quasi-contract also does not apply when parties have a valid contract covering the matter. For example, suppose Ace Painting Company has a contract to paint Walker's building for $1,000. Mr. Ace does the job but discovers that the job costs are $2,000. He cannot use the quasi-contract concept to recover $2,000 because his contract for $1,000 controls.

The *Matter of Estate of Milborn* case gives an example of a quasi-contract.

Matter of Estate of Milborn

Illinois Appellate Court, Third District

122 Ill. App. 3d 688, 78 Ill Dec. 241, 461 N.E.2d 1075 (1984)

Background and Facts:

The plaintiffs, Paul and LaVon Campbell, filed combined claims against the estate of Gertrude Milborn, deceased, seeking $5,000 for services performed for the decedent.

The only evidence at trial consisted of the unrebutted testimony of the plaintiffs. LaVon Campbell stated that except for the last few months of decedent's life, all meals during a five-year period from 1977 until the decedent's death in 1982, came from the Campbells' kitchen. Mrs. Campbell also did the housecleaning for the decedent and most of the laundry. Both of the plaintiffs made sure that the decedent took her medicine every day and in the proper dosages.

Paul Campbell testified that he mowed the decedent's lawn, cared for the yard, and patched the roof. While the decedent was hospitalized during the last few months of her life, Mr. Campbell was given a power of attorney authorizing him to handle the decedent's financial matters. Mr. Campbell also provided transportation for the decedent when she needed to see out-of-town doctors.

Both plaintiffs testified that they expected compensation for most of the services they performed. The court, sitting without a jury, found that the plaintiffs had established an implied contract with the decedent and allowed their claim in the amount of $5,000. The executor appeals.

Body of Opinion

Justice Heiple

There are two kinds of implied contracts: contracts implied in law (also called quasi-contracts) and contracts implied in fact. The trial court found that there was an implied contract between the decedent and the plaintiffs but did not specify which kind. The executor contends that the plaintiffs failed to prove either type of implied contract.

A contract implied in fact is one whereby a contractual duty is imposed by reason of a promissory expression which may be inferred from the facts and circumstances and the expressions on the part of the promissor which show an intention to be bound. The record in the present case reveals no specific acts, conduct or circumstances which permit us to infer a promissory expression or intent to be bound. There is no evidence of mutual understanding between the parties or the implied terms of the alleged agreement. Thus, there was no contract implied in fact.

A contract implied in law differs from a contract implied in fact in that it arises by implication of law wholly apart from the usual rules relating to contracts and does not depend on an agreement or consent of the parties. A contract implied in law is equitable in nature, predicated on the fundamental principle that no one should unjustly enrich himself at another's expense. Where services are rendered by one person for another which are knowingly and voluntarily accepted, the law presumes that such services were given and received in the expectation of being paid for and implies a promise to pay their reasonable worth. When set in the context of a claim against a decedent's estate, the facts giving rise to a quasi-contract must be proven by clear and convincing evidence.

The executor does not deny that the plaintiffs performed services which were knowingly and voluntarily accepted by the decedent. In fact, the executor presented no evidence at all on behalf of the estate. The executor's argument is that there was no quasi-contractual liability because the plaintiffs failed to prove by clear and convincing evidence that the decedent requested and expected to pay for the plaintiffs' services.

The plaintiffs were not required to prove that the decedent requested their services. As previously stated, where useful services are knowingly and voluntarily accepted, the law presumes that such services were given and received in the expectation of being paid for and implies a promise to pay. It is true that a person who officiously confers a benefit upon another is not entitled to be compensated therefor. However, it is not the absence of a request which bars recovery but the officiousness of the claimant's conduct.

Officiousness is synonymous with meddlesomeness and can be described as volunteering one's services where they are neither asked for nor needed. *Webster's Third New International Dictionary* 1567 (1976). Despite the fact that the plaintiffs were not competent witnesses as to any request made by the decedent it would be unreasonable for us to assume, based on the nature of the work performed by the plaintiffs and the duration of their service, that the decedent made no request whatsoever. Furthermore, it cannot be said that the plaintiffs' services were unneeded.

According to Mrs. Campbell, the decedent lived alone and never cooked. She would only eat when food was brought to her. Doctors would prescribe medication for the decedent only if someone else would give it to her. Mr. Campbell performed all of the yard work and building maintenance. The decedent may not have required twenty-four hour nursing care, but it is obvious that she was unable to properly care for herself. In view of the fact that the plaintiffs were unable to obtain assistance from the decedent's family, their services were not only needed, they were essential and definitely not officious. Even without clear proof of a request by the decedent, her knowing and voluntary acceptance of the plaintiffs' necessary services over a five-year period raises a promise implied in law to pay the reasonable value of such services.

Next, the executor argues that the plaintiffs intended their services to be gratuitous. Gratuitous intent in cases of this type can be shown in one of two ways. The first is by the conduct of the claimant. With regard to the plaintiffs' intent and expectations, counsel for the executor made the following statement during closing argument: "I think that the testimony of the claimants show that one party expected to receive payment, that is the Campbells, certainly no contradiction at all on that." Based on the record, we agree with this conclusion. Having conceded that the plaintiffs' conduct did not demonstrate a gratuitous intent, the executor may not now argue to the contrary.

Gratuitous intent may also be presumed in certain cases. Where persons live together as members of one family, a promise to pay for services of one to another is not implied from the mere rendition and acceptance of such services. Absent a showing of an express or implied in fact contract for payment, the services are presumed to be gratuitous. Blood kinship is not necessary in order to raise the presumption. The rule rests upon the idea of mutual dependence between those who are members of one *immediate* family even though there may be no tie of blood or affinity.

The executor acknowledges that the plaintiffs are not related to the decedent by blood or marriage and did not share the same house as the decedent. Nonetheless, the executor asks us to extend the presumption of gratuitous intent because of the bond of friendship between the plaintiffs and decedent and because the plaintiffs loved the decedent and treated her as a member of the family.

A bond of friendship between parties who do not live as members of an immediate family is not regarded by the law as sufficient to raise a presumption of gratuitous intent. . . .

The final issue is whether the plaintiffs proved that their claim was worth $5,000. Mrs. Campbell testified that she arrived at a value of $5,000 based on the fact that her mother was paying $1,700 per month for nursing home care. Although the plaintiffs did not provide the decedent with twenty-four hour care as a nursing home, $5,000 is still a nominal figure which breaks down to approximately $60 per month for the plaintiffs' five years of service.

To recover under a quasi-contract, the plaintiffs are required to prove the reasonable value of their services. The executor certainly cannot argue that $60 per month is an excessive or unreasonable value to place on three meals per day, part-time nursing care, housecleaning, maintenance work and transportation. We find that $5,000 was a reasonable value to place on the plaintiffs' services and affirm the judgment of the circuit court of Hancock County.

Judgment and Result

The Court of Appeals held that the Milborn estate was liable on a quasi-contract theory to the Campbells for services rendered to Mrs. Milborn before she died.

Questions

1. Is a quasi-contract a contract that a court forces on a situation where the parties had no contract in fact? Why does the court impose a contract when none in fact existed?
2. If B, an unemployed painter, paints C's house during the night but C did not want the paint job, can B recover from C based on quasi-contract? How does this example differ from the *Milborn* case?

THE MAKING OF A CONTRACT: THE OFFER

A contract is a legally enforceable agreement between competent parties. Agreement means mutual assent. Courts usually say that agreements are made up of offers and acceptances. Therefore, the first step in making a contract is for one person to make an **offer** to another. The person making the offer is called the **offeror**. The person to whom the offer is made is called the **offeree**.

What is an offer? An offer is made when the offeror in some way tells the offeree that the offeror wants to enter a contract with the offeree. The offer indicates what the offeror will do and what is wanted in return from the offeree along with a definite willingness to commit. Offers can be made expressly or by implication. For example, an express offer occurs when a person signs a written contract to buy a house. An offer can also be made by implication. If, for example, Barbara Winslow enters Kmart, sees a blouse she likes, and takes it to the cashier, Winslow has made an offer by implication. The cashier then rings up the sale, puts the blouse in a bag, and hands it to Winslow. During this transaction, no words have been spoken, yet a contract has been made between Winslow and Kmart.

An easy way to think about making contracts is to remember the formula: offer + acceptance = contract.[2] The remainder of this chapter will examine offers and acceptances.

Intent Needed to Make an Offer

An offer must be made with **objective intent**, which is how something looks to a reasonable person. If a person *appears* to be making an offer, then an offer has been made—even if the offeror does not intend to make an offer. What a person personally thinks has occurred is called **subjective intent**. It is objective, not subjective, intent that decides whether a person has made an offer.

Unenforceable "Offers"

Jokes or Excited Utterances. If an offer is clearly made as a joke or **excited utterance**, it is not a legally enforceable offer at all. So if an offeree accepts an offer that obviously

[2] Keep in mind the *Restatement, Second's* definition of contract: "A contract is a promise or set of promises for the breach of which the law gives a remedy, or the performance of which the law in some way recognizes as a duty."

is a joke, no contract exists. Similarly, if in an excited moment a person shouts that a huge clearly unrealistic reward will be given, an offer has not been made. A person who accepts such an "offer" does not form a contract.

Social Offers. **Social offers** are not legally enforceable offers. For example, if Bill asks Mary to go to a party and then breaks the date, Mary cannot recover from Bill for breach of contract.

Agreements to Agree. **Agreements to agree** are not legally binding contracts. Rachael's statement to Bruce, "I agree that at some future time we shall make a contract to pay you a bonus for coming to work for my company," is not a legally binding contract because it provides no present commitment to an agreement.

Statements Showing Intent. Statements showing intent do not in and of themselves create contracts.

Sham Transactions. Sometimes people make what appear to be contracts to cheat creditors or the Internal Revenue Service. These transactions that are contracts in form but not in substance are referred to as **sham transactions**. For example, Harvey Slater, about to go bankrupt, contracts to sell his farm to his son Jim for $5, on the understanding that Jim would return the property to Harvey later; but Harvey's creditors can reclaim the farm from Jim because the contract was a sham or fraud on his creditors. No reasonable person viewing this arrangement would say objectively that intent to form a contract existed. Also, Harvey and Jim did not even subjectively intend to contract.

Invitations to Negotiate

When two people are negotiating, not all of their statements are offers, sometimes not even the first one. Instead, their first remarks are often **invitations to negotiate**. These invitations are not offers and, if accepted, do not become contracts. They are merely attempts to *feel out* the other party to strike the best deal if an offer and acceptance ever are made. They often take the form of questions, such as "Would you like to buy my Ford for $1,900?" Ads in newspapers and on television and radio are usually invitations to negotiate if they are general, incomplete, and not addressed to anyone in particular. Thus, it is usually the customer who comes into the store to make an offer, which the merchant may either accept or reject. If the rule were otherwise and merchants' ads were offers, merchants would have to carry huge inventories to avoid contract liability (if many customers accepted the offers in the ads).

Sometimes media ads are offers. If the ad is definite, complete, certain, and limited to certain specific items, it is more likely an offer than an invitation to negotiate.

Certainty

Generally, offers must be certain and definite. This rule helps courts decide the proper remedy if a contract is broken. An acceptance of an indefinite offer generally results in no contract. For example, an offer to lend money as a borrower's needs required was held too uncertain. Another offer stating that hay was to be measured according to government rule when several such rules existed was also held to be too indefinite.

The several exceptions to the rule that offers (acceptances and the resulting contracts) must be definite are as follows:

1. *Trade custom.* Trade custom can clear up an offer's indefiniteness. For example, failure to state a price when it is understood in the trade that market price at the time of delivery was intended will be considered definite.
2. *Previous dealings.* When parties have dealt with one another before and have followed a practice that clears up a vague contract term, courts hold that the offer and contract are not void for lack of definiteness.
3. *Implicit terms.* Some terms in an offer are not expressly stated, but courts nonetheless find them to be implicit. Thus, if a contract fails to state a required performance time, it has been held that performance is to be within a reasonable time.
4. *Open terms in sale of goods contracts.* The UCC allows contract terms such as price or quantity to be valid if a commercially reasonable way of filling them later is available.
5. *Contracts of indefinite length.* Offers for contracts whose performance covers an indefinite period are valid. Courts find the necessary definiteness by allowing either to cancel any time. For example, Sarah is to be Beatrice's cook as long as Beatrice lives, or as long as Sarah performs satisfactorily.
6. *Cost-plus contracts.* In cost-plus contracts, one person agrees to purchase something and pay another's costs plus a fee calculated on some other basis, such as a percentage of the cost. Even though Mike does not know the total cost of building the Empire State Building, his offer to pay Tom his costs plus 10 percent for the project is definite enough.
7. *Requirements and output contracts.* A requirements contract exists when one person agrees to buy all of its requirements from another. Requirements contracts are valid even when a party does not know the exact requirements when the contract is made. Thus, offers to buy all of one's requirements are definite enough. Similarly, output contracts that are offers to sell another all that one produces are definite enough for courts. The indefiniteness arises because no one knows exactly what the production output will be.
8. *Retainer contracts.* The following is an example of a retainer contract. Bob Wilson wants an attorney's services for one year. He offers George Blackstone $10,000 to be his attorney. If Blackstone accepts, this contract is valid even though neither Blackstone nor Wilson knows exactly what services Blackstone will perform in the coming year. In fact, Blackstone may do nothing, but courts usually require Blackstone to exercise good faith in deciding what actions he should take for Wilson.
9. *Incorporation of another writing.* An offer and resulting contract that are too uncertain can be made certain if it refers to another writing. In one case, a building contract lacked crucial terms such as square footage but referred to the building plans and specifications, which cleared up the indefiniteness.

Communication Requirement of Offers

Offers must be communicated before they are effective. For example, Marianne writes out an offer to Mike and puts it in her desk drawer. Mike secretly learns of the letter and calls Marianne to accept the offer. There is no contract in this case because the offer was not communicated to Mike by Marianne or her agent. Now assume Marianne has communicated her offer to Mike, the offeree. Mike then has the power to accept and thereby bind Marianne to a contract.

How Offers End

Offers end in a number of ways other than by acceptance, including the following:

1. Time lapse
2. Revocation
3. Rejection
4. Counteroffer
5. Death or insanity of the offeror or offeree
6. Destruction of essential subject matter
7. Intervening or subsequent illegality

Time Lapse. Because offers do not last forever, the offeror may state how long the offer will be open. The offer will remain open as long as the offeror states unless it is revoked or ended before that time. When the stated time ends, so does the offer.

If the offer does not say how long it will remain open, the offer lasts for a reasonable time. "Reasonable" takes into account the nature of the subject matter, any trade custom, and similar factors.

Revocation. Offerors revoke offers. **Revocation** means recalling or calling back an offer. Offerors generally may revoke an offer any time before acceptance. Revocations need not be in any particular form and take effect when communicated to the offeree. This communication can be indirect. If the offeree accepts before the offer's revocation, a contract exists and the later revocation has no effect on the contract. Public offers are usually revocable if made in a manner similar to the original offer. Revocations need not be communicated to all persons who read the original public offer. Once an offeror revokes an offer, the offeree's later acceptance does not form a contract.

If the offeror promises that the offer will remain open for a stated period of time, may the offeror revoke before that time expires? Yes, assuming no option or firm offer exists. *Gibbs v. American Savings & Loan Association* illustrates the revocation of an offer.

Exceptions to Revocation. **Options** are offers that stop the offeror from revoking the offer during the stated option period or until a certain date. The option is irrevocable for the option period because the offeree gives the offeror consideration (something of value). Options are an exception to the general rule that offers are revocable.

For example, if Ken Zeigler offers his farm to Tim Danielson for $100,000 and Danielson is interested but wants to think about it, an option is the answer. Assume Danielson offers Zeigler $500 if Zeigler will hold open his offer to sell the farm for 30 days, and Zeigler agrees. This arrangement is an option because Danielson has not yet bought the farm but he still has time to think about it. If Danielson exercises the option within the 30 days, he must pay Zeigler $100,000 in addition to the option price. (Sometimes the option amount is applied to the purchase price, sometimes not.) If Danielson thinks over the offer during the 30 days and decides not to exercise it, Zeigler keeps the $500 and the farm, and the offer to sell the farm ends.

Two last points: First, just because people call an offer an "option" does not mean it is an irrevocable offer. The offeree must give the offeror consideration (something of value) to turn an ordinarily revocable offer into an irrevocable option contract. Second, options can be given on anything, not just real estate.

Firm offers are a second exception to the general rule that offers are revocable at any time. A **firm offer** is a written offer made by a merchant for the sale or purchase of goods, assuring that the offer will be irrevocable for the period of time stated in the offer (up to a three-month maximum, which is renewable). The UCC is the law creating firm offers. Every state but Louisiana recognizes UCC firm offers. Note that the firm offer does not exist for realty or services.

Gibbs v. American Savings & Loan Association

California Court of Appeals, Second District
217 Cal. App. 3d 1372, 266 Cal.Rptr. 517 (Cal.App. 2 Dist. 1990)

Background and Facts:

In August 1984, James and Barbara Gibbs submitted an offer for $180,000 to American Savings to purchase a house in Woodland Hills, which American Savings had taken back through foreclosure. American Savings, through its employee, Dorothy Folkman, agreed that the Gibbs could move into the subject property and rent it until the close of escrow. No action was taken on this offer.

On March 27, 1985, pursuant to a request by Ms. Folkman, the Gibbs submitted a new offer because American Savings could not find their original offer. The purchase price was again $180,000. On the morning of June 6, 1985, the Gibbs received a counteroffer from American Savings containing several additional terms and conditions, but with no mention of purchase price. According to Barbara Gibbs, she immediately drove to her husband's job site where she and her husband signed this counteroffer. She drove to her office, typed an envelope with a certified mail tag, placed the counteroffer in the envelope, and before 10 o'clock that morning, she handed it to the mail clerk at her office, instructing him to mail it for her.

At approximately 11 a.m. that same morning, Barbara Gibbs had a telephone conversation with Dorothy Folkman in which Folkman said the counteroffer was in error, because American Savings had intended to increase the sales price to $198,000. Folkman also advised Gibbs that because of this error, the counteroffer was revoked.

American Savings took the position that no contract had been formed. The Gibbs insisted that they had accepted the counteroffer before it was revoked and that a contract thus existed. The Gibbs brought action for damages, specific performance, breach of contract, and declaratory relief. After trial, the court found that Barbara Gibbs did not place the acceptance of the counteroffer in the course of transmission when she gave it to the mail clerk in her office on June 6, 1985; thus there was no acceptance on that date. The postmark on the envelope was June 7, 1985. Dorothy Folkman's oral revocation of the counteroffer on June 6, 1985, preceded the Gibbs' acceptance of that counteroffer on June 7 and therefore no contract for sale of the property was ever formed. The Gibbs appeal judgment.

Body of Opinion

In a case such as this, where there is no request for a statement of decision, "it must be presumed that every fact essential to the judgment was proved and found by the court." ... In accordance with these well-established rules of appellate review, we find substantial evidence supports the trial court's judgment. Barbara Gibbs testified that she received the counteroffer from American Savings at about 8:45 or 9 a.m. on June 6, 1985. She and her husband signed the counteroffer at 9:39 a.m. that day. She then drove about one mile to her office, prepared an envelope and certified mail receipt, and gave the ready-to-mail, signed counteroffer to the mail clerk in her office for mailing. This purportedly occurred before 10 a.m. on June 6.

Barbara Gibbs further testified that the clerk brought the mail to the Woodland Hills Post Office and returned with her receipt by 10:15 a.m. on June 6. However, the certified mail receipt was not produced at trial, and the envelope in which the signed counteroffer was mailed to American Savings was postmarked June 7, 1985, not June 6. According to the Domestic Mail Manual of the United States Postal Service, section 144.471, the date shown in the meter postmark of any type of mail must be the actual date of deposit. Section 144.534 of the manual provides that metered mail bearing the wrong date of mailing shall be run through a canceling machine or otherwise postmarked to show the proper date. The postmarked envelope constitutes substantial evidence that the acceptance was mailed on June 7, not June 6.

Civil Code section 1583 provides: "Consent is deemed to be fully communicated between the parties as soon as the party accepting a proposal has put his acceptance in the course of transmission to the proposer," ... This rule has long been interpreted to require that the acceptance be placed out of the control of the accepting party in order to be considered "in the course of transmission." ... Typically, this is found when the acceptance is delivered to the post office.... California's "'effective upon posting'" rule, as codified in section 1583, thus holds that an acceptance of an offer is effective and deemed communicated upon its deposit in the mail....

The postmark on the counteroffer in the case before us shows such deposit occurred on June 7, 1985, not on June 6. The counteroffer was not placed in the course of transmission beyond the control of the offeree when Barbara Gibbs gave it to the mail clerk in her office with instructions to deliver it to the post office. It was placed in the course of transmission within the meaning of Civil Code section 1583 when it was deposited with the United States Postal Service on June 7, 1985.

It is basic contract law that any offer may be revoked any time prior to acceptance.... Both Barbara Gibbs and Dorothy Folkman from American Savings testified that they spoke together on the telephone on the morning of June 6, 1985. During that call, Folkman became aware of

American Savings' error in failing to include the $198,000 purchase price in the counteroffer, advised Barbara Gibbs of the error and stated that American Savings was revoking the counteroffer. Inasmuch as the counteroffer was revoked on June 6, prior to the Gibbs' acceptance, no contract was formed.

A similar result was reached in the Florida case of *Kendel v. Pontious* (Fla.App. 1971).... In *Kendel*, the buyers delivered their signed acceptance to their attorney who was to mail it to the seller. Before the attorney mailed the signed acceptance to the seller, the seller revoked the offer. The court held delivery to the buyers' attorney did not constitute posting. No contract was formed because the seller's revocation preceded the mailing of the acceptance.

We find no reason to depart from this well-reasoned law.

Judgment and Result

The court of appeals affirmed the trial court's finding that the seller had revoked its counteroffer before the buyer accepted it.

Questions

1. Who had made the first offer in this case? Why was it not accepted by American Savings?
2. Why was American Savings' correspondence on the morning of June 6, 1985, deemed a counteroffer if it was for the same price as the Gibbs' original offer?
3. May a written counteroffer be revoked orally?
4. If an offer is revoked before acceptance, does a contract exist? Is that the scenario that occurred here?

Offers to Form Unilateral Contracts

A unilateral contract is a promise requesting an act in return. If an offeror makes an offer requesting an act and the offeree starts performing the act, can the offeror revoke the offer before the offeree completes the act? Many courts say "No," allowing the offeree reasonable time to complete the requested act. They suspend the offeror's power to revoke during this period.

Rejection. A **rejection** is the offeree's unequivocal refusal of an offer communicated to the offeror. The legal effect of a rejection is to end the offer. Thus, a rejection followed by an acceptance does not form a contract. The following are rejections in response to offers: "No," "Never," "I don't want that," and words or indications of similar import. On the other hand, the offeree's questions to the offeror concerning the offer are not rejections and do not end the offer. Also, conditional acceptances (such as "I accept if you paint the fences") are rejections. Thus, they end offers, and are offers from the original offeree to the original offeror.

Counteroffer. Counteroffers end offers. Counteroffers are statements by offerees to offerors changing the terms in the original offer. Implicitly, a counteroffer amounts to an offeree's saying to an offeror, "I do not want your original offer, but I am making you this offer instead."

A counteroffer could be made even if an offeree tried to accept an offer. Common law says that any addition or change—even a small, unintentional one—of the offeree's acceptance turns an acceptance into a counteroffer. The UCC changes this rule somewhat when goods are involved. (See the "Acceptance" section for further discussion.)

Death or Insanity of the Offeror or Offeree. If either the offeror or offeree dies or becomes insane after the offer is made but before acceptance, the offer ends automatically.

Destruction of Essential Subject Matter. Destruction of the subject matter of an offer before acceptance ends the offer. For example, if Charles offers to sell Melinda his Ford and while Melinda is thinking about the offer the car burns up, the offer to sell the car ends. On the other hand, if the car's cigarette lighter is stolen before Melinda accepts the offer, this event would not end the offer because the cigarette lighter is not an essential subject matter of the offer.

Intervening or Subsequent Illegality. The following example involves intervening or subsequent illegality. Suppose John Sluck offers Ray Jordan 50 barrels of whiskey for $100 per barrel. If it becomes illegal to make and sell alcoholic beverages before Ray accepts, Sluck's offer would automatically end. If the contract becomes illegal after acceptance but *before* performance, the contract duties end due to illegality.

The next section discusses the second half of agreement—the acceptance.

THE MAKING OF A CONTRACT: THE ACCEPTANCE

Once the offeree has an offer, she or he has the power to accept it. Acceptance merges the offer and acceptance into a contract binding both the offeror and offeree. An **acceptance** is an assent by the offeree to the offer's terms. The acceptance can occur by word or act. The offeree must simply communicate the intent to accept to the offeror; she or he does not even have to use the word "accept."

Glover v. Jewish War Veterans examines the issue of intent to accept.

Glover v. Jewish War Veterans of the United States

Municipal Court of Appeals for the District of Columbia
68 A.2d 233 (1949)

Background and Facts:

The issue determinative of this appeal is whether a person giving information leading to the arrest of a murderer without any knowledge that a reward has been offered for such information by a nongovernmental organization is entitled to collect the reward. The trial court decided the question in the negative and instructed the jury to return a verdict for defendant. Claimant appeals from the judgment on such instructed verdict.

The controversy grows out of the murder on June 5, 1946, of Maurice L. Bernstein, a local pharmacist. The following day, June 6, Post No. 58, Jewish War Veterans of the United States, communicated to the newspapers an offer of a reward of $500 "to the person or persons furnishing information resulting in the apprehension and conviction of the persons guilty of the murder of Maurice L. Bernstein." Notice of the reward was published in the newspaper June 7. A day or so later Jesse James Patton, one of the men suspected of the crime, was arrested and the police received information that the other murderer was Reginald Wheeler and that Wheeler was the "boyfriend" of a daughter of Mary Glover, plaintiff and claimant in the present case. On the evening of June 11 the police visited Mary Glover, who in answer to questions informed them that her daughter and Wheeler had left the city on June 5. She told the officers she didn't know exactly where the couple had gone, whereupon the officers asked for names of relatives whom the daughter might be visiting. In response to such questions she gave the names and addresses of several relatives, including one at Ridge Spring, South Carolina, which was the first place visited by the officers and where Wheeler was arrested in company with plaintiff's daughter on June 13. Wheeler and Patton were subsequently convicted of the crime.

Claimant's most significant testimony, in the view that we take of the case, was that she first learned that a reward had been offered on June 12, the day after she had given the police officers the information which enabled them to find Wheeler. Claimant's husband, who was present during the interview with the police officers, also testified that at the time of the interview he didn't know that any reward had been offered for Wheeler's arrest, that nothing was said by the police officers about a reward and that he didn't know about it "until we looked into the paper about two or three days after that."

Body of Opinion

Associate Judge Clagett

We have concluded that the trial court correctly instructed the jury to return a verdict for defendant. While there is some conflict in the decided cases on the subject of rewards, most of such conflict has to do with rewards offered by governmental officers and agencies. So far as rewards offered by private individuals and organizations are concerned, there is little conflict on the rule that questions regarding such rewards are to be based upon the law of contracts.

Since it is clear that the question is one of contract law, it follows that, at least so far as private rewards are concerned, there can be no contract unless the claimant when giving the desired information knew of the offer of the reward and acted with the intention of accepting such offer; otherwise the claimant gives the information not in the expectation of receiving a reward but rather out of a sense of public duty or other motive unconnected with the reward. "In the nature of the case," according to Professor Williston, "it is impossible for an offeree actually to assent to an offer unless he knows of its existence." After stating that courts in some jurisdictions have decided to the contrary, Williston adds, "It is impossible, however, to find in such a case [that is, in a case holding to the contrary] the elements generally held in England and America necessary for the formation of a contract. If it is clear the offeror intended to pay for the service, it is equally certain that the person rendering the service performed it voluntarily and not in return for a promise to pay. If one person expects to buy, and the other to give, there can hardly be found mutual assent. These views are supported by the great weight of authority, and in most jurisdictions a plaintiff in the sort of case under discussion is denied recovery."

The American Law Institute in its *Restatement of the Law of Contracts* follows the same rule, thus: "It is impossible that there should be an acceptance unless the offeree knows of the existence of the offer." The *Restatement* gives the following illustration of the rule just stated: "A offers a reward for information leading to the arrest and conviction of a criminal. B, in ignorance of the offer, gives information leading to his arrest and later, with knowledge of the offer and intent to accept it, gives other information necessary for conviction. There is no contract."

We have considered the reasoning in state decisions following the contrary rule. Mostly, as we have said, they involve rewards offered by governmental bodies and in general are based upon the theory that the government is benefited equally whether or not the claimant gives the information with knowledge of the reward and that therefore the government should pay in any event. We believe that the rule adopted by Professor Williston and the *Restatement* and in the majority of the cases is the better reasoned rule and therefore we adopt it. We believe furthermore that this rule is particularly applicable in the present case since the claimant did not herself contact the authorities and volunteer information but gave the information only upon questioning by the police officers and did not claim any knowledge of the guilt or innocence of the criminal but only knew where he probably could be located.

Judgment and Result

The court of appeals agreed with the lower court's decision and found for the defendant. The plaintiff did not intend to accept the offer when she did the act the offer requested because she did not know the offer existed.

Questions

1. Must an offeree intend to accept when doing an act requested in an offer for a unilateral contract?
2. Is the rule different if the offeror of a reward is the government? Why?
3. If a person is asked for information, what should he or she do before answering?

The offeree usually has a choice about accepting or rejecting an offer. In a few cases (such as public accommodations, including motels, hotels, or restaurants), the federal Civil Rights Act of 1964 requires that hotels and restaurants accept customers' offers to use their facilities. This act assumes that the customer is able to pay and no public health, safety, or other laws would be broken. Years ago, the Waldorf-Astoria Hotel legally refused to house Fidel Castro because he insisted on bringing live chickens into his room—a clear breach of public health laws.

Also, a merchant's power to accept or reject a customer's offer may be limited by the FTC's regulations forbidding bait-and-switch advertising.

How to Accept

Acceptance must be done in the way the offeror requests. For example, if the offeror says, "Accept by mail," a telephoned acceptance is invalid and no contract results. If the offeror says, "Accept by return mail," the acceptance must be sent on the same day that the offer was received. If the offeror says, "Paint my house, and I'll pay you $500," a promise to paint the house is not acceptance; the offeror asked for painting, not a promise to paint. If the offeror does not specify a way to accept and the offeror mailed or telegraphed the offer, the offeree can use either to accept. The prior rule is common law, which applies to realty and services. In the case of goods, the UCC permits the parties or circumstances clearly to specify a way to accept. If neither the parties nor circumstances clearly indicate the medium (e.g., phone or mail) to use, the UCC permits any reasonable way in the situation. *Champagne Chrysler-Plymouth, Inc. v. Giles* examines the proper form of acceptance.

Champagne Chrysler-Plymouth, Inc. v. Giles

Florida Court of Appeals
388 So.2d 1343 (1980)

Background and Facts:

Judge Pearson

For a number of weeks prior to mid-January 1978, Champagne Chrysler-Plymouth Inc. advertised, in a thirty-second spot commercial on a Saturday television program called "Miami All Star Bowling," that it was giving away a new Plymouth Arrow to anyone who bowled a 300 game on the televised program that day. Giles unquestionably was aware of this advertising. Apparently believing that Champagne's offers could only be withdrawn by a revocation commensurate to the offer itself, Giles, in mid-February 1978, put up his pin money and entered the week-long tournament which culminated with the finals carried, as usual, on the "Miami All Star Bowling" television show of February 17, 1978. Giles qualified for the finals and, as the reader may have already surmised, threw twelve strikes in a row for a 300 game. Although otherwise rewarded with cash prizes, free Pepsi and the like, Giles called upon Champagne for his just desserts.

Not bowled over by this request, Champagne responded that it had made no offer of an automobile on February 17 and, for that matter, had not been offering such a prize for over a month of Saturdays. Its position, simply stated, was the Giles was aiming at the wrong pocket. Giles sued.

Champagne's defense was that its offer of a prize *on and for* a particular Saturday television show meant that it made an offer good for that show only. Since no such offer was made on February 17, the day Giles rolled a 300 game, Champagne had no liability. Giles responded that Champagne had placed mimeographed flyers and printed posters containing its offers in nearly every bowling alley, and some of this advertising was still posted as of February 17. The trial court, viewing Champagne's earlier offer unrevoked and outstanding as of February 17, and there being no doubt that Giles rolled a 300 game, entered summary judgment as to liability in favor of Giles.

Its bubble thus burst, Champagne appealed. We agree with Champagne that the mimeographed flyer offering a car as a prize for any 300 game bowled on the televised program, even if it remained posted on February 17, 1978, expired by its own terms. In the case of a unilateral contract:

> As the obligation is, before acceptance, on one side only, the proposer being bound to comply with his proposal, while the other party is under no obligation, and under no peril until acceptance, *the provision of the offer as to time of acceptance is viewed with strictness. C.W. Kitler v. Hotel Martinique*, 44 So. 2d 288, 291 (Fla.1950).

The television commercials and printed posters present a different problem. The present state of the record does not reflect whether these were unilateral offers limiting the time of acceptance by their express terms or were offers requiring revocation. While the trial court was correct that there was no genuine issue of material fact that appropriate revocation did not occur, the issue as to whether revocation was required remained. If, in fact, the television commercials were unilateral contracts, it would not have been necessary for Champagne to take any steps to revoke the offers made by it on prior television programs, since these offers would have expired by their own terms on the dates made and would not have been outstanding as of February 17, 1978. Since the record contains no clear and undisputed evidence of the words used on the cardboard poster (purportedly still displayed on February 17) and thus does not eliminate the distinct possibility that these were unilateral contracts requiring no revocation, it was error for the trial court to enter summary judgment for Giles. In this respect, as well as in respect to the issue of whether Giles believed the Champagne's offer of a car was outstanding as of February 17, we find that there were genuine issues of material fact still extant at the time of the entry of summary judgment.

Accordingly, we reverse the summary judgment entered in favor of Giles and remand this cause for further proceedings consistent with this opinion.

Judgment and Result

The Florida Court of Appeals decided that Giles did not accept the car dealer's offer since Giles did not bowl a 300 game on the Saturday the dealer specified (the offer's requirements).

Questions

1. Must an offeree accept an offer exactly for the acceptance to be effective? Why?
2. Why is not substantial performance by the offeree close enough to be acceptance?

Who Can Accept

Only the offeree can accept an offer. The offer could be directed to one person, a small group of people, or the general public.

What is the effect of an acceptance by someone to whom the offer was not directed? The acceptance is ineffective, and no contract results. However, the original offeree could treat this "acceptance" as an offer and accept it, thereby forming a contract.

Silence as Acceptance

Silence is generally not acceptance, which prevents an offeror from forcing the offeree to reply to an offer to avoid contract liability. For example, suppose a television store with a large inventory of new televisions sends out postcards describing in detail a particular model, offering it for $500, and providing that if the store has not heard from the customer in the next five days, it will treat the customer's silence as acceptance. Must the customer send in a postcard rejecting the offer to avoid a contract? No. Silence generally is not acceptance.

Two exceptions to the general rule that silence is not acceptance are trade customs and previous dealings. If failure to respond to an offer is regarded as acceptance in a particular trade, then the offeree must reject the offer to avoid contract liability. Previous dealings regarding silence refer to prior contracts that require the offeree to respond to avoid contract liability. For example, in some book and record clubs, members agree in advance to take the monthly selection unless they send in a stop order or rejection notice.

Unordered Goods in the Mail. Section 3009 of the federal Postal Reorganization Act of 1970 permits people receiving unordered goods in the mail from businesses to keep, use, discard, or dispose of the goods in any manner without any obligation whatsoever to the sender. It is also possible that the senders of unordered merchandise through the mails could be violating laws forbidding use of the mails to defraud and unfair methods of competition under the Federal Trade Commission Act.

Acceptances Adding to or Varying from the Offer: Common Law Exactness Rule

Is an acceptance effective if it adds to or changes a term in the offer? The answer depends on what was offered. If the offer was for realty, services, or insurance, acceptances must be exact, or the common law exactness or **mirror image** rule. The acceptance must exactly mirror what was offered to protect offerors from being forced into contracts they never intended, which would occur if offerees could add to or change the offer and have it bind the offeror.

The following is an example of the common law exactness rule. Tom Simon offers his house to Joe Blanc for $75,000. Blanc says, "I accept. Paint it white." Blanc accepted but added a new term, therefore, no contract is formed between Simon and Blanc for Simon's house because Blanc's acceptance was not exact. Putting it another way, Blanc's acceptance was *not* the mirror image of Simon's offer. To force Simon to sell a "white house" would force him into a contract his offer never suggested.

Acceptance Adding to or Varying from the Offer: The UCC Rule

The common law exactness or mirror image rule for acceptances is not followed when goods—distinguished from realty, services, or insurance—are involved. Acceptances of offers to buy or sell goods may add to or change the offer and still be acceptances forming contracts. For example, Sellit says to Buyit, "I'll sell you my car for $500." Buyit responds, "I'll take it; put new seat covers on it." Sellit clearly intended to sell the car but nothing in the offer mentions new seat covers. Is there a contract? If so, what are the terms?

The UCC sets out the rules for contracts dealing with goods. Acceptances with added terms are acceptances of the original offer *and* an offer back to the original offeror regarding the added term. In other words, a contract is formed regarding what the original offeror offered, such as in the situation with the car. The buyer is bound to the original offer only. The buyer's *added term* (the seat covers) in the acceptance is essentially a new offer made to the original offeror. The original offeror in the preceding example has sold his or her car and does not have to put seat covers on the car.

When Is an Acceptance Effective?

If an offeror says that an acceptance is effective only when received, it is effective only when the offeror receives it. If the offeror fails to say anything about an acceptance's effective date, a mailed acceptance is effective on the date it was sent with correct postage and address, also known as the **mailbox rule**; acceptance takes effect when the offeree drops the acceptance in the mailbox or other appropriate receptacle. This rule applies even if the letter of acceptance never reaches the offeror.

A telegraphed acceptance is effective when given to the telegraph office official. Again, if the offeror specifies that a telegraphed acceptance is effective only when received, this restriction must be observed.

The telephone can also be used to accept unless the parties involved say otherwise or state law requires a written contract.

Acceptances at an Auction

Who accepts and who offers at an auction? The auctioneer makes invitations to negotiate, and the audience's bids are offers. The auctioneer accepts these offers when his or her hammer falls to the auction block. Because a bid is an offer, the bidder may withdraw it any time before acceptance. If a bid is accepted, a contract results that binds both the bidder and auctioneer. If the bids are not high enough to satisfy the auctioneer, must the highest bid be accepted? The answer to that question depends on whether the auction is "with or without reserve." If an auction is "with reserve," the auctioneer may withdraw an item if the bids are too low. If the auction is "without reserve," the highest bidder's offer must be accepted no matter how low it is.

CONSIDERATION

We have already discussed the parts of a contract, which are the offer and the acceptance. This section of the chapter looks back at the agreement to determine whether it meets another test: Consideration. In a technical sense, consideration is a bargained for benefit to the promisor or a detriment to the promisee. Nontechnically, consideration means that both the offeror and offeree to the contract must bargain for and give up a right in order to make the other's promise or act enforceable.

Benefit to the Promisor. Consideration can be a benefit to the promisor. For example, B promises to pay A $500 if A promises to paint B's house. B's promise to pay A benefits A. B's promise is, therefore, consideration that makes A's promise to paint enforceable. The same is true about A's promise to paint: It makes B's promise to pay enforceable.

Detriment to the Promisee. A legal detriment means that someone gives up a right to do something. Referring to the painting example, B's promise to pay A $500 is a detriment to B, because B gives up the right to $500. Note that here B's giving A $500 is also a benefit to A in addition to being a detriment to B. A detriment to the promisee is consideration for the promise if the promisor bargained for it, which is true even if the promisor gets no benefit when the promisee does what the promisor bargained for. The *Hamer v. Sidway* case illustrates this type of consideration.

Hamer v. Sidway

Court of Appeals of New York
27 N.E. 256 (1891)

Background and Facts:

William E. Story, Sr., was the uncle of William E. Story, Jr. At a family dinner, the uncle promised to pay the nephew $5,000 if he would not drink, use tobacco, swear, play cards or billiards for money until the nephew became 21 years old.

The nephew followed the uncle's request. Upon reaching the age of 21, the nephew asked his uncle for the $5,000. The uncle sent the nephew a letter telling how hard he had worked for the money and went on to say that he hoped the nephew would not waste it. The uncle also said he was pleased that the nephew had followed his request. The uncle added, "You shall have the $5,000, as I promised you. I had the money in the bank the day you were 21 years old. You shall have the money certain. You can consider this money on interest."

The nephew agreed the money should stay with the uncle "on interest" as the letter described. Two years later the uncle died without having paid the nephew anything. The nephew sued the uncle's estate for the money. The estate argued that the uncle's promise was not binding because the nephew had given the uncle no consideration.

Body of Opinion

Judge Parker

...The defendant contends that the contract was without consideration to support it, and therefore invalid. He asserts that the promisee, by refraining from the use of liquor and tobacco, was not harmed, but benefitted; that that which he did was best for him to do, independently of his uncle's promise—and insists that it follows that, unless the promisor was benefited, the contract was without consideration—a contention which, if well founded, would seem to leave open for controversy in many cases whether that which the promisee did or omitted to do was in fact of such benefit to him as to leave no consideration to support the enforcement of the promisor's agreement. Such a rule could not be tolerated, and is without foundation in the law. The Exchequer Chamber in 1875 defined "consideration" as follows: "A valuable consideration, in the sense of the law, may consist either in some right, interest, profit, or benefit accruing to the one party, or some forbearance, detriment, loss, or responsibility given, suffered, or undertaken by the other."... Anson. Cont. 63. "In general a waiver of any legal right at the request of another party is a sufficient consideration for a promise."... Pollock in his work on Contracts (page 166), after citing the definition given by the Exchequer Chamber, already quoted, says: "The second branch of this judicial description is really the most important one. 'Consideration' means not so much that one party is profiting as that the other abandons some legal right in the present, or limits his legal freedom of action in the future, as an inducement for the promise of the first."

Now, applying this rule to the facts before us, the promisee used tobacco, occasionally drank liquor, and he had a legal right to do so. That right he abandoned for a period of years upon the strength of the promise of the testator that for such forbearance he would give him $5,000. We need not speculate on the effort which may have been required to give up the use of these stimulants. It is sufficient that he restricted his lawful freedom of action within certain prescribed limits upon the faith of his uncle's agreement, and now, having fully performed the conditions imposed, it is of no moment whether such performance actually proved a benefit to the promisor, and the court will not inquire into it; but, were it a proper subject of inquiry, we see nothing in this record that would permit a determination that the uncle was not benefited in a legal sense....

Judgment and Result

The nephew wins.

Questions

1. Consideration is said to be either benefit to the promisor or detriment to the promisee. Who was the promisor, the uncle or the nephew? Who was the promisee?
2. Does *Hamer v. Sidway find* that the uncle had benefitted from the nephew's failure to drink, smoke, etc.?
3. Did the nephew give up a legal right which, arguably, was not a benefit to the uncle? Is this situation what is meant by detriment to the promisee without there being benefit to the promisor?

Reason for the Consideration Rule

The reason for requiring consideration is to satisfy the basic natural law idea of fairness. Both sides of a contract should give something to the other to have a binding agreement.

"Bargained for" Part of the Consideration Definition

The "bargained for" part of the consideration definition means that the person receiving the benefit (or requesting the other party to suffer a detriment) must have requested or bargained for the benefit (or detriment). The idea is to stop the promisee from giving the promisor something she or he does not want to make the promisor's promise binding. For example, Bob says that he will pay Davy $500 if Davy promises to paint Bob's house. Instead of promising to paint, Davy promises Bob a fur cap. Davy's promising to give Bob the fur cap is a benefit to Bob but Bob did not bargain for (or want) the cap. Because Bob has "bargained for" the promise to paint and not the cap, only the promise to paint is consideration in this case.

Adequacy of Consideration

Adequacy of consideration means: Did you get "enough" under the terms of the contract or did you pay too much? Courts (judges) do not usually examine the adequacy of the consideration because of freedom of contract.

Freedom of contract means the parties to the contract, not a judge, decide what and how much consideration each gives the other. Each individual protects his or her own best interest. For example, suppose Ray Jordan agrees to pay Virginia Mosley $10,000 for her clunker of a car. After making the contract, Jordan has second thoughts and refuses to pay. Mosley sues him for breach of contract. Jordan defends by claiming that Mosley's car is worth $2,000, not $10,000. Said another way, Jordan claims Mosley's consideration is inadequate. However, this claim is no defense for Jordan. Jordan must bargain for the best price possible before entering the contract. If he cannot get a fair price, he should not buy the car. In a free market economy, Jordan, not a judge, protects Jordan's interest.

At times the courts will rule consideration is inadequate. Generally, the exceptions involve uneven exchanges suggesting duress or undue influence. For example, an uneven exchange of the same currency ($50 U.S. for $100 U.S.) will cause a court to say the consideration is inadequate.

When Contracts Should Be In Writing: The Statute of Frauds Rule

As a general business policy, it is good advice to write down and have both parties sign all contracts. Virtually all states have a **Statute of Frauds**, which requires that certain contracts dealing with certain subjects be evidenced by a signed writing. If contracts falling into these subject matter areas are oral, but the Statute of Frauds says they should be evidenced by a signed writing, the contract is said to be unenforceable. Then, the party trying to enforce the contract cannot enforce it if the defendant (person against whom the contract is asserted) raises the Statute of Frauds defense.

Statutes of Frauds are state laws and thus the exact coverage varies somewhat from state to state. The Uniform Commercial Code (UCC) also has a Statute of Frauds requirement for certain types of subject matter.

Reason for the Writing Requirement. The reason for the Statute of Frauds is to prevent persons from introducing fraudulent or perjured testimony to "prove" the formation of contracts dealing with important (realty), costly (expensive goods), complex (contracts that cannot be completed within one year), or unusual contracts (guaranty contracts or contracts in consideration of marriage). The thinking is that unless a writing signed by the party to be charged exists, contracts dealing with these matters should not be enforceable.

Categories of Contracts Required to Be Written. Generally, the areas in which contracts must be evidenced by a signed writing include: transfers of interests in real estate (generally including leases of over one year); contracts for the sale of expensive goods (the UCC sets the amount at $500 or more); guaranty contracts (contracts under which one person agrees to pay another's debts if the other does not pay); contracts that cannot by their terms be completed within one year; contracts in consideration of marriage.

Special Statute of Frauds Rules. Several refinements of the aforementioned Statute of Frauds rule should be noted. First, if a contract falls into any one of the aforementioned categories of contract, the contract must be evidenced by a signed writing. For example, a contract requiring an accounting firm to provide services for two years must be evidenced by a signed writing even though it is not for the sale of goods over $500. It is enough that one part of the Statute requires a writing to make the contract come within the Statute's terms.

A second point involves the signing. Ideally both parties should sign the contract, but the Statute of Frauds only requires that "the party to be charged"—the defendant—sign the contract. "Signing" can consist of a person's actual signature but can also be a stamped signature or even initials rather than one's full name. Note that if one party signs and the other does not, the contract would be enforceable against the signer but not against the nonsigner unless some exception to the signer rule applies. At least three important exceptions to the "signer" rule may affect the sale of goods between merchants. If two merchants orally negotiate a contract for the sale of goods and one of the merchants sends the other a written confirmation of the sale and the receiving merchant does not object to the confirmation within 10 days of receipt, the non-signing merchant is bound to the contract even though that merchant did not sign it. Note that this only applies in the case of the sale of goods under the UCC. A second exception to the writing requirement involves specially made goods. When a seller substantially starts to make specially ordered goods, no writing is required. A third exception involves part performance of a contract for goods costing $500 or more; an oral contract is enforceable for that part of the contract the buyer has paid for, but the remainder of the contract is unenforceable.

Another subtlety involves the sale of goods for $500 or more. What if a contract is for 500 widgets each of which cost $2, is this viewed as 500 contracts for $2 which obviously would not have to be written, or one contract for $1,000 that would have to be written? Courts often view it as one contract for 500 widgets, which, if over $500, requires a writing.

With respect to the provision requiring contracts that by their terms cannot be completed within one year to be written, the year starts to run from the date the contract is formed. Thus a contract for exactly one year whose performance starts the day the contract is formed need not be written to be enforceable. However, a contract formed on July 1, 2000, whose performance is to start September 1, 2000, and is to last until August 1, 2001, would have to be in a signed writing to be enforceable because the time from formation to finish of performance is 13 months. Also, some contracts appearing to last for more than a year actually are not required to be written. For example, a contract for Tom to be Fred's cook for the rest of Tom's life does not have to be written because Tom could die tomorrow (even though we hope he does not). This contract is exempt from the writing requirement even if Tom lives for more than one year.

Form of the Writing to Satisfy the Statute of Frauds. The writing to satisfy the Statute of Frauds must identify the parties and subject matter, indicate that a contract exists, and state essential terms (price, quantity, time of performance, credit terms). The UCC is quite liberal with respect to specific terms generally allowing a contract for goods to be enforceable if the quantity and parties are named and some sort of signature exists (for example, a stamped name anywhere on the document) even if the price is not, provided a mechanism, such as the market price, exists to "fill the gaps."

The following case indicates that not all courts will find the Statute of Frauds satisfied even where the contract is for a substantial amount.

Firstline Corporation v. Valdosta-Lowndes Indust. Auth.

Court of Appeals of Georgia
511 S.E.2d 538 (1999)

Background and Facts:

It is undisputed that in February 1997, Firstline Corporation submitted a "Project Eligibility Questionnaire," a formal request to purchase "approximately 20 acres" of undeveloped land from the Authority. According to the minutes of the March 18, 1997, meeting of the Authority, the members voted to give Firstline a 90-day purchase option for a 27.3 acre tract owned by the Authority priced at $10,000 per acre for 20 acres with no additional charge for 7.3 acres of wetland. Firstline did not provide any financial consideration to the Authority for this option. Nor did the Authority and Firstline execute a written agreement. The Authority ordered a survey and engaged an engineer to locate the wetlands.

Meanwhile, Standard Contractors applied to purchase 10 acres from the same tract. Ken Garren, the director of the Authority, informed Standard Contractors that 10 acres were not available because Firstline had been offered an option for 20 acres leaving only 7.35 acres available for purchase. On May 1, prior to the expiration of the option period, the Authority accepted Standard Contractors' offer to buy 7.35 acres. On May 2, Garren wrote Firstline offering to sell 20 acres at a price of $10,000 per acre for 16.67 acres with no additional charge for 3.33 acres of woodlands. The letter informed Firstline that the Authority had accepted another party's offer to purchase the remaining 7.35 acres. Garren enclosed a copy of the plat. Garren sent another letter on May 14 which showed some confusion about the terms: "This will acknowledge our recent telephone conversation in which you inquired into how it was determined which 20 acres of the approximate 27-acre tract... would be offered to you. At the March 1997 meeting, it was my understanding and the understanding of the Authority members present that you were being offered the upland or northernmost portion of the 27-acre tract with the southern boundary to be determined by a survey." Disregarding the May letters, on June 6, Firstline notified the Authority that it was accepting its "offer" and was agreeing to purchase 27.35 acres at the $10,000 per 20 acres price, citing the minutes of the March 18 meeting. Donald Murphy, Firstline's president, testified that prior to May 1, the Authority never suggested to him that the 27.35-acre tract would be subdivided or that Firstline would purchase only part of it.

Finding that no "meeting of the minds" had taken place as to the basic contract terms, the trial court granted summary judgment to the Authority and dismissed Firstline's claim against Standard Contractors. Firstline appealed both judgments.

Body of Opinion

Judge Harold Banke, Senior Appellate Judge

The threshold inquiry must be whether an enforceable

agreement existed. An option contract for the sale of realty comes within the Statute of Frauds, and, therefore, must: (1) be in writing, (2) identify the buyer and seller, (3) describe the subject matter of the contract, and (4) name the consideration.... An option agreement "must be complete within itself as to the essential elements."... A "valid, binding, and enforceable" contract for the sale of land "must describe the land to be sold with the same degree of certainty as that required of a deed conveying realty....

Here, the multiple documents including minutes of the March 18 meeting, questionnaire, tax maps, and letters were not sufficient to constitute a written contract of sale, since the land was not described with sufficient particularity. *Carver v. City of Moultrie*... Carley, J., concurring specially, (combination of correspondence and city council minutes failed to satisfy the Statute of Frauds because the subject land was not established by definite boundaries);... In these circumstances, the option was unenforceable....

Judgment and Result

The Court of Appeals affirmed the trial court's judgment. In so doing it held that the purported option agreement failed to describe the land subject to the option with sufficient particularity to satisfy the Statute of Frauds.

Questions

1. If no "meeting of the minds" took place between the Authority and Firstline, then was a contract formed? Why then did the Appeals Court bother to address the further issue of a writing sufficient to satisfy the Statute of Frauds? Does addressing the Statute of Frauds suggest that a contract had been formed, the only question being, "Is it in writing?"
2. Contracts for the sale of an interest in realty must be evidenced by a signed writing to satisfy the Statute of Frauds. Is an option to purchase land an interest in realty?
3. Why were not the minutes of the Authority meeting sufficient to satisfy the Statute of Frauds? Generally such minutes are signed.

CHAPTER SUMMARY

Contracts are the basis of the market economy.

A contract is an agreement between competent parties and is enforceable in court.

The *Restatement, Second, Contracts* definition of contracts is "a promise or set of promises for the breach of which the law gives a remedy, or the performance of which the law in some way recognizes as a duty."

Courts generally apply an objective test to decide whether a contract exists when the parties disagree as to whether they have formed a contract.

Classifications of contracts include bilateral and unilateral; express and implied; executed and executory; valid, void, voidable and unenforceable; and quasi-contracts.

The two major components of a contract are the offer and the acceptance. Offers are made by the offeror and can only be accepted by the person or persons to whom the offeror intended to make the offer.

Offers end in several ways, including death or insanity of the offeror or offeree before acceptance, destruction of an essential subject matter before acceptance, intervening illegality before or after acceptance but before performance, counteroffer before acceptance, and rejection of the offer before acceptance.

At common law, acceptances must mirror or exactly conform to the offer. The Uniform Commercial Code has liberalized the rules of acceptance. Sometimes courts will impose a contract on a situation in which one person has conferred benefits onto another under circumstances where the conferee knows or should know that compensation was expected and no gift was intended.

Consideration is generally required to make contracts enforceable. Consideration refers to the voluntary relinquishment of a known right that is bargained for in exchange for someone else's right.

The Statute of Frauds requires that contracts dealing with certain subject matter be evidenced by a signed writing to be enforceable.

MANAGER'S ETHICAL DILEMMA

Emil Tyden had a great idea. After many hours of experimenting in his laboratory, he developed a cure for baldness in men. He carefully tested his formula and, after repeated instances of success, he decided to approach the World Drug Company to see if it was interested in buying the formula. He met a Ms. Colgrove who asked Emil what he had discovered. He replied, "A cure for male baldness."

Ms. Colgrove expressed interest and asked to see his formula. Emil thought for a minute. He had worked hundreds of hours developing the formula. What assurances did he have that she would not write it down, tell him it was worthless, and then have World Drug Company start making it after claiming it had developed the product itself?

Discuss any of the material covered in the chapter that suggests a possible protection to assist Emil in deciding whether to reveal his information to Ms. Colgrove.

Discussion Questions

1. The arrival of the Internet and Internet auctions presents challenges for the legal system. An example occurred recently where a computer-sophisticated eighth grader logged on to an Internet auction site and bid on a Van Gogh painting, a Viking ship replica, and several other items. Although unsuccessful on the Van Gogh painting, the youngster was the high bid on a 1971 Corvette, a wrestling belt, and a bed belonging to Canada's first prime minister, Sir John A. Macdonald. Bidding was at $12,000 on the bed when the boy entered a winning bid of $900,000. The parents of the boy were reportedly about to suspend their son's Internet privileges (and hopefully not give him credit card privileges). What defenses might be available to the boy and his parents for such purchases?
2. Must an offer be written in all cases?
3. Give an example of a written offer.
4. Does a contract exist if a person offers to sell her car for $400, but really does not intend to follow through on the offer, and the offeree accepts?
5. Give an example of an invitation to negotiate.
6. Name some characteristics of offers.
7. Who can accept an offer?
8. If B offers his house to C for $40,000, and C says, "I accept. Paint the house before I move in," has C accepted?
9. Is contract law positive law, or are contracts positive law?
10. Is contract law more consistent with a market or planned economy?
11. A landowner listed certain land with a realtor. When the brokerage listing agreement expired, the broker called the owner to see whether the property was still available for sale. The owner replied that the property was still available, but the tenant leasing it had the first option to buy. Shortly after this conversation, the broker secured an offer to buy from a third party. However, the tenant exercised the first option to buy, which prevented the third party from buying. The broker sued the owner for the brokerage commission, arguing that the realtor had satisfied the brokerage contract's terms by producing a ready, able, and willing buyer. Was the landowner's conditional acceptance of the broker's offer accepted by the broker, thereby forming a contract? [*Arthur Rubloff & Co. v. Drovers Nat. Bank of Chicago*, 80 Ill. App. 3d 867, 36 Ill. Dec. 194, 400 N.E.2d 614 (1980)].
12. Golestaneh offered to sell his Florida condominium to Mintzberg. The offeror's terms were: selling price $200,000 cash; closing date beginning of October; broker's commission to be split evenly between the parties; price includes light fixtures, carpeting, and major appliances. The prospective buyer, Mintzberg, sent the following letter to the seller: "This will confirm that the October 1, 1979, closing date is acceptable with the understanding that Mr. Mintzberg would prefer an earlier closing date. I would appreciate a more detailed explanation of your advice to my secretary regarding the maintenance charges." Was the buyer's letter an acceptance of the seller's offer? [*Mintzberg v. Golestaneh*, 390 So.2d 759 (Fla. App. 1980)].

Suggested Readings

Articles

BURTON, "Good Faith in Articles 1 and 2 of the U.C.C.: The Practice View," 35 *William and Mary Law Review* 1533 (1994).

BURTON, "Racial Discrimination in Contract Performance: Patterson and a State Law Alternative," 25 *Harvard Civil Rights–Civil Liberties Law Review* 431 (1990).

BURTON and ANDERSEN, "The World of a Contract," 75 *Iowa Law Review* 861 (1990).

CHOMSKY, "Of Spoil Pits and Swimming Pools: Reconsidering the Measures of Damages for Construction Contracts," 75 *Minnesota Law Review* 1445 (1991).

EISENBERG, "The Responsive Model of Contract Law," 36 *Stanford Law Review* 1107 (1984).

FEINMAN, "The Meaning of Reliance: A Historical Perspective," 1984 *Wisconsin Law Review* 1373 (1984).

REIMANN, "Savigny's Triumph? Choice of Law in Contracts Cases at the Close of the Twentieth Century," 39 *Virginia Journal of International Law* 571 (1999).

"The $10.53 Billion Question—When Are the Parties Bound?: Pennzoil and the Use of Agreements in Principle in Mergers and Acquisitions," 40 *Vanderbilt Law Review* 1367 (1987).

WHITE, "Form Contracts Under Revised Article 2," 75 *Washington University Law Quarterly* 315 (1997).

WHITE, "How to Negotiate a Sales Contract," 19 *ALI-ABA Course Materials Journal* 47 (1995).

Books

CALAMARI and PERILLO, *The Law of Contracts* (1977).

FARNSWORTH, *Contracts* (1982).

CHAPTER

12 PROPERTY

"... THE RIGHT OF THE OWNER TO USE HIS LAND IS NOT ABSOLUTE."

Mr. Justice Brandeis, Pennsylvania Coal Co. v. Mahon, 260 U.S. 393 (1922)

Positive Law Ethical Problems

"How can it be?" said Terry Wine, a resident of Williamsburg Manor, a mobile home park.

"The preamble to the Williamsburg Manor rules and regulations states 'Williamsburg Manor is conceived as a community of neighbors living in harmony... not by rigid rules and regulations. The spirit behind this statement is the Golden Rule: Do unto others as you would have others do unto you. If this is so, why did Williamsburg Manor raise the monthly rent on our mobile home lots by 7 percent? It is wrong and illegal for a landlord to raise the rent on its tenants by so much," said Wine.

May landlords who state that they believe in the Golden Rule legally raise rents by a large amount without the tenants' consent?

"If a person pays $1 million for an artwork, shouldn't she get ownership of it?" said Ms. Goodly. She had purchased rare mosaics found in a Cyprus church and planned to resell them to a museum for $20 million. However Cypriot Church officials stepped forward and claimed that the mosaics were stolen from it and wanted them back. Who has better title to stolen property, the original owner from whom the property was taken or a later good faith purchaser from the thief?

At one time property law was the basis of the legal system. Today, as government has discovered ways to regulate and tax property, other rights, such as the right to one's job, are probably as important. This chapter surveys some basic property concepts such as title, property classifications, how property fits into the market economy, personalty, and realty. Also, given today's emphasis on entrepreneurship, ways to protect intellectual property are discussed.

DEFINITION OF PROPERTY

Property is the rights one person has regarding other people with respect to something. This definition may sound a bit obscure, so let's discuss it further. It is common to hear someone describe a car as property. Technically, this definition is wrong. A car is something in which one or more persons have rights. For example, the *owner* has the right to use the car, but often the owner will have borrowed from a credit union or bank to buy the car. That lender will have a security interest (a type of mortgage) on the car, which gives the lender the right to seize the car if the owner/borrower defaults on the loan. Occasionally, the car owner will take the car to a repair shop to have it worked on. The mechanic will have the right to use the car to test it and a limited right to keep the car until the bill is paid. So you can see that many different persons have rights—that is, property—in the car.

Property then means the rights a person or people have to something. The property is *not* the object or thing (house, car, fishing pole, etc.) but the *rights* to that thing. Thus, the owner of the car has greater rights to the car than a thief, but the owner who misses a payment may have less right to the car than the credit union that repossesses the car.

LEGAL PHILOSOPHIES REFLECTED IN PROPERTY LAW

Several legal ethics or philosophies are reflected in property law. Included here are positive law, historical jurisprudence, natural law, and Ehrlich's sociological philosophy of law. John Austin, who developed analytical positivism (discussed in Chapter 1), is credited with naming different property classifications. Such classifications are part of positive law even today. These classifications include personalty and realty.

The historic philosophy is evidenced by the idea that property rights are longstanding ideas that have been recognized since the ancient Greeks and Egyptians. Changing ideas of who can own property and what can be property reflect Ehrlich's sociological school of law, which emphasizes norms of conduct. For example, at one time slaves in the United States could not own property. Also, in the nineteenth century United States, African Americans could be property. Modern norms of conduct, however, reject the idea that only certain races can *own* property or that certain races can *be* property.

Natural law ideas of fairness found in the U.S. Constitution forbid government from taking property unless the government gives just compensation or fair market value to the owner.

PROPERTY LAW IS STATE LAW

Property law is generally state, not federal, law. Thus, in the area of constitutional lawmaking, property law is generally left to the individual states. For example, the state of Michigan makes the rules about who owns cars, land, and other things in Michigan. With 50 states, 50 different rules could exist about a particular property question. For example, the state of Maryland might say that oral wills are valid while Massachusetts might outlaw oral wills. Because of the federal system and the fact that each state makes its own property law rules, property law is quite complex.

Some federal laws do regulate property, however. The Fifth and Fourteenth Amendments say that property shall not be taken without due process of law. The U.S. Constitution also sets out the eminent domain rule, which means that private property may not be taken by the federal, state, or local governments or companies with eminent domain authority, without paying "just compensation"—fair market value. Several federal statutes also govern land sales contracts, including the Interstate Land Sales Full Disclosure Act (ILSFDA), which regulates the sale of undeveloped land by giving the buyer a three-day cooling-off period to escape the contract to buy.

TITLE AND TITLE DOCUMENTS

Title refers to ownership. If someone owns land, a car, or sweater, that person has **title** to it. Title is different from **title documents**. Title is ownership, but a title document is a piece of paper saying who owns the object. Most items do not have title documents. For example, if someone were to ask you to prove that you own the shirt or blouse you are wearing, it would probably be difficult to do (unless you saved the sales receipt) because our clothing, furniture, and most household goods do not have title documents.

However, we do have title documents called **deeds** for land. Also, cars and trucks have title documents called simply *titles*.

The state government issues title documents to autos and trucks, but private parties write deeds to land. Also, deeds should be recorded, or noted in a record book on land titles at the Courthouse in the county where the land is located.

PROPERTY CLASSIFICATIONS

Property can be classified in several ways. (Note that here we violate our earlier pure property definition that property is rights in some thing. Here we are treating property not as the rights but as the thing in which one has rights—the car, the land, the fishing pole.) One property classification includes realty, personalty, and fixtures. A second property classification refers to property as either tangibles or intangibles. A final classification is that of public and private property.

Personal Property

Personal property, also called **personalty**, refers to movables. (Things that cannot be moved are generally classified as realty.) Examples of personalty include clothing, automobiles, and furniture. This movable versus immovable distinction between realty and personalty is not perfect, because a shovelful of land can be moved and also the planet Earth moves through space, so arguably everything is always moving. Nonetheless the movable-immovable distinction is used here to distinguish personalty from realty.

Real Property

Real property, also called realty, refers to land and buildings. Realty is sometimes said to be immovable. A house is **realty,** as is a vacant lot. Realty also includes the air rights and subsurface rights to the land. A landowner who builds a skyscraper on her land would be using the air rights to her realty. Air rights are subject to the right of overflight by aircraft, which do not have to pay the realty owner for this right.

Realty owners have the rights to what is below their land, called *subsurface rights*. *Surface rights* can be sold separately from subsurface rights. A farmer does so by keeping the surface rights to raise crops and selling the subsurface rights to an oil company.

Trees, grass, and plants (called *fructus naturales*) that grow naturally on land without the help of humankind are part of the realty. Plants put on the land are also part of the realty. However, crops arising from vegetation helped partly by human effort (called *fructus industriales*) belong to whomever planted and grew them. Thus the tenant who planted the strawberries—not the landlord—would be entitled to them.

Fixtures

An in-between category of property is called fixtures. A **fixture** is personalty attached to realty with the intent that it will become a permanent part of the realty. An oven sitting in an appliance dealer's showroom is personalty. When built into the wall of a home, the oven becomes a fixture.

Fixtures can regain their identity as personalty if severed from the realty.

To decide whether personalty has become a fixture, four questions must be answered:

1. What does the person who owns the item (such as a microwave oven put in a wall cabinet) consider it to be—a fixture or personalty?
2. Who attached the item? If done by the realty owner, it is more likely a fixture.
3. How securely is the personalty attached to the realty? The more firmly attached the personalty is, the more likely it is a fixture. A sliding glass door, for example, would likely be a fixture, whereas a lamp nailed to the wall probably would remain personalty.
4. What function does the personalty have to the realty? A toilet is particularly and closely suited for use in a house. Thus it would be part of the realty.

Trade fixtures are an exception to the idea that fixtures become part of the realty. Items such as signs and counters, which are firmly attached to the realty, remain the tenant's personal property.

Tangible and Intangible Property

As already noted, all property is technically intangible because in a true sense, property refers only to rights in some thing. However, let us leave the world of pure property definitions. Instead, let us refer to property for the moment as the object (the car, land, or fishing pole) in which one has rights. Some property therefore is *tangible,* that is, can be seen, such as a car, land, or fishing pole. Other property—a patent, for instance—cannot be seen and is therefore *intangible.*

Public and Private Property

A third property classification is public and private property. This classification focuses on who owns the property. Your shirt or car would belong to one person. It therefore is private property. The Pentagon or the U.S. Supreme Court building would be public property because a government owns it.

TYPES OF REAL PROPERTY ESTATES

Owners of realty have **estates** in the land and buildings on the land. The word *estate* makes a person think of a huge house and large lawn, but estate here means something different. It refers to an interest in the realty.

Abstracts on various legal topics can be found at ***http://www.lawreview.org***

Fee Simple Absolute. The highest estate in land (the maximum rights the law allows) a person can have is called a **fee simple absolute**. Phrases such as "to A and his heirs" or "to A" create a fee simple absolute.

The owner of a fee simple absolute may sell, give, or devise (give by a will) the realty.

Life Estate. A **life estate** is an interest in realty for one's life but for no longer. When one dies, the realty belongs to someone else. Persons with life estates are called "life tenants." Because the life tenant has the realty only for his or her life, this estate may not be transferred by will. It can, however, be sold or given away for the life tenant's life.

Leaseholds. A person who leases another's realty has a **leasehold**, or leasehold interest. Persons with leaseholds are called *tenants*. Tenants do have only temporary rather than permanent rights to the realty. Leases may be for fixed periods or may run from period to period.

Easements. An **easement** is a nonpossessory right to use someone else's realty for some purpose. For example, the telephone company might have an easement to string a phone line over your land, or a neighbor might have a right to use your driveway to get to her property.

The property subject to the easement is called the **servient estate**. The property enjoying the benefit of the easement is the **dominant estate**.

Several kinds of easements are easements appurtenant, easements in gross, affirmative, and negative easements. **Easements appurtenant** benefit another piece of land, which is usually adjacent to the servient estate. **Easements in gross** benefit a certain person or business. A powerline easement for a utility would be an easement in gross. An **affirmative easement** would exist when someone is given a right to use someone else's land. A **negative easement** prevents someone from doing something on one's land, such as stopping the building of a structure if it would block the sunlight to the dominant estate.

Profits. **Profits** are a right to enter someone else's real estate to remove something, such as minerals, crops, or water.

Licenses. A **license** is not a real property interest. Instead it is a right to use another's realty, such as the use of a seat in a football stadium for the game only or a seat in a movie theater during operating hours.

WAYS TO HOLD TITLE TO REAL PROPERTY

Although it is certainly possible to own all the rights to real property, it is also possible to own rights with others. We shall now look at some types of joint realty ownership.

Tenants in Common

Tenants in common occurs where two or more people have title to an interest in realty. Tenants in common can give, sell, or devise by will their individual interests in the realty. Each tenant in common has a right to the whole realty. The tenants in common can have equal or unequal rights to the whole. An example of tenancy in common occurs if Mr. Sims deeds his house to his son Ronald and his daughter Beverly as tenants in common. Both Ron and Beverly would have equal right to use the house.

Joint Tenants

Joint tenants own realty together but with a **right of survivorship**. The right of survivorship refers to the idea that the joint tenants who die before other joint tenants lose all interest in the property. Thus, with three joint tenants, the last survivor takes all rights to the estate. When only one joint tenant left, the survivorship feature is gone. Obviously joint tenants may not convey their interest by will, which ends when they die, except for the last joint tenant. Joint tenancies are not favored because they involve a forfeiture, except for the surviving joint tenant.

However, joint tenants may convey their interest while they are alive. These transferees from a joint tenant become tenants in common regarding their share of the estate with the remaining joint tenants. To create a joint tenancy, however, the deed must specify that a joint tenancy exists.

Tenancy by the Entirety

Tenancy by the entirety is a specialized form of joint tenancy: The joint tenants must be spouses. It involves a right of survivorship, so the surviving spouse takes the entire estate. Not all states recognize tenancy by the entirety, however.

Tenancy in Partnership

The Uniform Partnership Act recognizes **tenancy in partnership**, which occurs when business partners own property—realty, personalty, or fixtures—together. This form of tenancy has the right of survivorship feature; that is, when a partner dies or departs from the business, the remaining partners take the departing partner's share.

Real Estate Syndications

Real estate syndications arise when several persons own property. The vehicle for the joint ownership could be a limited partnership, partnership, trust, or corporation. In other words, the individual investor owns a limited partnership share but the limited partnership itself owns the real estate. Similarly, if the corporate form is used for the syndication, the corporation owns the realty and the individual investors are shareholders in the corporation. The form the syndication takes governs what law controls these organizations. For example, if the syndication takes the form of a trust, trust law will govern matters of management and transferability of syndication interests.

Community Property

Community property exists in California, Arizona, Louisiana, Washington, Idaho, Nevada, Texas, and New Mexico. It only applies to the way married couples own property in those states. During the marriage when one spouse acquires property, half of it belongs to the other spouse, even if the deed specifically is made out only in the name of one spouse. During the marriage, community property may not be sold or mortgaged without both spouses' approval.

Condominiums

A **condominium** is a way individuals can own the space between the walls of their unit. "Condo" owners have equal interests in the common areas of the entire complex: grounds, swimming pool, tennis court, driveway, elevator, sidewalks, etc. Condo owners may sell or mortgage their interests subject to restrictions in the condo agreement, which sometimes can be very restrictive. Usually assessments or dues are charged monthly or annually to each unit to pay for maintenance and insurance on the common areas. In the case of high-rise condos, the owners actually own the bit of airspace their unit occupies.

HOW PROPERTY IS ACQUIRED

Property may be acquired in several ways. This discussion analyzes the following ways of acquiring both realty and personalty:

1. Theft
2. Gift
3. Capture
4. Finding
5. Inheritance
6. Trust
7. Manufacture
8. Confusion
9. Purchase

Theft

Personal property may not legally be acquired by stealing it. The original owner of property can reclaim it if found in the hands of a thief or a good-faith purchaser from a thief. Thus, if a thief steals Mary's ring and sells it to Betty, a good-faith buyer who pays $500 believing that the thief really owns it, and Mary tracks it down, Mary can recover it from Betty. (Betty must find the thief and sue her for breach of warranty of title.) A thief may not pass good title to personalty. A taker (buyer or donee) from a thief gets no better title than the thief had: nothing.

The following case deals with an art dealer who buys an object for more than $1 million in the international art market under suspicious circumstances, hoping to resell it for $20 million to a rich museum. Did that art dealer obtain good title?

Autocephalus Greek-Orthodox Church v. Goldberg
Federal District Court (S.D. Indiana)
717 F.Supp. 1374 (1989)

Background and Facts:

In this case the court is asked to decide the right of possession as between the plaintiffs, the Autocephalous Greek-Orthodox Church of Cyprus (Church) and the Republic of Cyprus and the defendants, Peg Goldberg (Goldberg) and Goldberg & Feldman Fine Arts, Inc., of four Byzantine mosaics created in the early sixth century. The mosaics, made of small chips of colored glass, were originally affixed to and for centuries remained in a church in Cyprus, a small island in the Mediterranean Sea. In 1974, Turkish military forces invaded Cyprus and seized control of northern Cyprus, including the region where the church is located. At some point in the latter 1970s, during the Turkish military occupation of Northern Cyprus, the mosaics were removed from their hallowed sanctuary. The plaintiffs claim that the Church has never intended to relinquish ownership of the mosaics, that the mosaics were improperly removed without the authorization of the Church or the Republic of Cyprus, and that the mosaics should be returned to the Church. The defendants, on the other hand, claim that export of the mosaics was authorized by Turkish Cypriot officials, and that in any event Goldberg should be awarded the mosaics because she purchased them in good faith and without information or reasonable notice that they were stolen.

Goldberg is president and majority shareholder of Goldberg & Feldman Fine Arts, Inc.... On July 1, 1988, Fitzgerald [another art dealer] informed Goldberg that he was aware of four early Christian mosaics that were for sale. Later that day, Fitzgerald introduced Goldberg to Michel van Rijn, a Dutch art dealer, and Ronald Faulk, an attorney from California. Goldberg knew very little about van Rijn or Faulk. She was told, however, that van Rijn was once convicted in France for forging Marc Chagall's signature to prints of that artist's work and that he also had been sued by an art gallery "for failure to pay money." . . . She also was aware that Faulk was in Europe to act as attorney for Fitzgerald and van Rijn.

At this July 1st meeting, van Rijn showed Goldberg photographs of the four Byzantine mosaics, and she immediately "fell in love" with them. . . . van Rijn told Goldberg that the seller of the mosaics was a Turkish antiquities dealer. In addition, he told her that the seller had "found" the mosaics in the rubble of an "extinct" church in northern Cyprus while serving as "an archaeologist from Turkey assigned to northern Cyprus." . . .

On July 3, 1988, while still in Amsterdam, Goldberg negotiated an agreement with van Rijn, Fitzgerald, and Faulk, whereby "the parties agreed to acquire the mosaics for their purchase price of $1,080,000 (U.S.)." . . . The agreement also provided that the parties would split the profits made on any future resale of the mosaics as follows: Goldberg & Feldman 50%,; Fitzgerald 22.5%; van Rijn 22.5%; and Faulk 5%. This agreement was executed on July 4th in Amsterdam. . . .

Goldberg intended to sell the mosaics. Beginning in the fall of 1988, she contacted at least two people in an attempt to market and sell the mosaics. By October 1988 Goldberg had discussed the sale of the mosaics with Dr. Geza von Habsburg, an art dealer operating out of Geneva and New York. In October of 1988 von Habsburg contacted Dr. Marion True of the Getty Museum in California and discussed whether it would be interested in purchasing the mosaics for $20 million. Dr. True explained that the Getty does not collect Byzantine art and told von Habsburg that because of her close working relationship with Cyprus, it would be necessary for her to contact her friend Dr. Vassos Karageorghis about the mosaics. Dr. True had developed a working relationship with Dr. Karageorghis, and he had often spoken to her of Cyprus's attempts to recover the mosaics. Dr. True then called Dr. Karageorghis, who told her that export of the mosaics was not authorized by Cyprus and that the mosaics she described were the mosaics which Cyprus had been so interested in recovering. Dr. True gave Dr. Karageorghis the name of Geza von Habsburg and how to contact him.

In November 1988, Dr. Karageorghis and others in conjunction with Cyprus's Director General of the Ministry of Foreign Affairs, contacted the Ambassador of Cyprus in Washington, D.C. They informed the Ambassador of the mosaics' existence in the United States and suggested that immediate and discreet action be taken to recover the mosaics. The embassy then began working with its attorneys, the plaintiffs' Washington law firm in this case, to determine the location and possessor of the mosaics. . . .

The plaintiffs and their attorneys eventually learned that the mosaics were in Goldberg's possession in Indianapolis. The plaintiffs wrote to Goldberg requesting the return of the mosaics. Upon the defendants' refusal, the plaintiffs instructed their attorneys to file suit to recover the mosaics. . . .

Body of Opinion

District Judge Noland

There are long-established rules of law in Indiana that a thief never obtains title to stolen items, and that one can pass no greater title than one has. . . . Therefore, one who obtains stolen items from a thief never obtains legal title to or right to possession of the item. . . .

In *Breckenridge v. McAfee* . . . (1876), one of the plaintiff's employees wrongfully and without the plaintiff's authorization took the plaintiff's wheat, sold it to defendants, and absconded with the money. The plaintiff sued for the return of the wheat, or if that was impossible, for money damages for the value thereof. At trial a jury returned a verdict for the plaintiff. The Indiana supreme court affirmed the judgment. . . .

Similarly, in *Torian v. McClure* . . . (1882) the thief rented a piano from the plaintiff. The thief then sold the piano to the defendant, a good faith purchaser for value. The plaintiff sued . . . for recovery of the piano. The trial court found for the plaintiff and ordered a return of the piano, or in the alternative money damages, and ordered money damages for the detention of the piano. The Indiana supreme court affirmed the judgment, including this conclusion of law:

> . . . that [the thief], at the time he sold the piano to the defendant, had no title thereto, and could confer none on the defendant, and that the plaintiff is the owner thereof.
>
> . . . This case as well stands for the proposition that a thief never acquires title to stolen property, and cannot pass any right to possession of stolen property to a subsequent transferee, including a *bona fide* purchaser for value.

Under Indiana law, as outlined, a thief obtains no title to or right to possession of stolen items and can pass no title or right to possession to a subsequent purchaser. The mosaics were stolen. For purposes of this analysis, it is of no significance whether Aydin Dikman originally stole the mosaics, or who originally stole them. Further, it matters not whether Goldberg purchased the mosaics from Dikman alone, or from only van Rijn and Fitzgerald. The evidence of theft and chain of possession under the facts of this case lead only to the conclusion that Goldberg came into possession of stolen property.

Judgment and Result

The court concludes that the defendants were in wrongful possession of the mosaics and had to relinquish them to the plaintiff Church.

Questions

1. If a person acquires goods from a thief but is unaware that the seller is a thief, can that person obtain valid title to the goods? Should the same rule apply to land (realty)? Why?
2. If a buyer acquires property from someone rightfully in possession but who wrongfully sells the property, does the buyer win over the property's original owner?
3. If a person rightfully in possession of another's goods wrongfully gives that property to an innocent person, does the original owner here win?
4. What business ethics noted in Chapter 1 are in evidence here? What legal ethics?

Voidable Title. A person who has voidable title to personalty may pass full title to a good faith purchaser for value. **Voidable title** means that someone got title to the goods by means that would permit O, the original owner, to recover the goods from T, the immediate transferee (the person with voidable title). Such means might include mistake, common nonphysical duress, fraud in the inducement, or sale by someone lacking contractual capacity. T, the immediate transferee from the owner, may pass good title on to G, a good faith purchaser for value if G takes before O rescinds (tries to recover) title. For example, if Mary goes to a jeweler and buys a diamond ring and pays for it with a bad check, Mary gets voidable title to the ring. If Mary sells the ring for value (say $400) to Betty, a good faith purchaser who does not know of the fraud, Mary may pass full title to Betty. If the jeweler later learns that Betty has the ring, he cannot recover it. The idea behind voidable title is to encourage commerce by letting good faith purchasers for value keep personalty even though the seller's title was somewhat flawed.

In cases where T still retains the goods, O may recover them from T. Where O bails (loans) goods to T, and T unauthorizedly sells the goods to G (a good faith purchaser for value), O may recover the goods from G. The reasoning is as follows: As between two innocent persons (O and G), the law asks who has legal title and says that person (in this case, O) owns the goods. O did not give T any title, voidable or otherwise, when she loaned the goods to T. T in such a case merely had possession of the goods, but no voidable title, and thus T could merely transfer what she had—possession, but not title—to G.

Buyer in the Ordinary Course of Business (BIOC). Section 2-403(2) of the Uniform Commercial Code, enacted in 49 states (but not Louisiana) gives merchants a voidable title to goods entrusted to them. Specifically, any entrusting of possession of goods to a merchant who deals in goods of that kind gives the merchant the power to transfer all rights of the entruster to a **buyer in the ordinary course of business (BIOC)**. Thus if Mary takes her diamond ring to the jeweler to be cleaned and the jeweler sells it to another customer (a BIOC), the BIOC keeps the ring even though Mary can find the ring and the BIOC. (Mary could sue the jeweler for the tort of conversion, but she may not legally recover the ring from the BIOC.) The reason for letting the BIOC prevail is to encourage buying from merchants without the fear that what they buy can be reclaimed by someone else.

Adverse Possession. Realty, meaning land and buildings, may in a real sense be acquired by theft, although the technical name is adverse possession. **Adverse possession** occurs where someone openly, adversely, and continuously claims the land that is officially titled in someone else's name. In *Pieper v. Pontiff*, one state supreme court named the following six elements of an adverse possession claim to land (the case discusses the elements):

1. Under a claim of right
2. Actual
3. Open, notorious, and visible
4. Exclusive
5. Continuous
6. Peaceful

A statutory period (typically ranging from 10–20 years) in each state determines how long a person must continuously claim someone else's realty to acquire title by adverse possession. The time starts to run once someone occupies and exclusively controls the property. The occupation has to be continuous, but not necessarily constant. Regular use is sufficient. If one adverse possessor holds the property for less than the statutory period and sells it to another adverse possessor, the successive adverse possessors' occupation periods can be added together (called *tacking*) to satisfy the statutory period. The adverse element does not mean fighting mad, just against and not subservient to the owner on the deed. For example, a tenant is subservient and not adverse to the landlord simply because of being a tenant. A person can mistakenly hold another's land and still be adverse, as in the case of a mistaken boundary line matter.

Pieper v. Pontiff

Supreme Court of Mississippi
513 So.2d 591 (1987)

Background and Facts:

On February 19, 1973, Mrs. Pontiff was conveyed a tract of land by her mother, Mrs. Hazel Reynolds, which was described in the warranty deed as having a northern boundary 289.7 feet along the south margin of a local road which intersects U.S. Highway 11. The land was also described as being located in the southeast quarter of the northwest quarter of Section 3, Township 2 North, Range 14 West, in Lamar County, Mississippi. On April 30, 1980, Mr. Pieper purchased property whose southern boundary was described as the south line of the northeast quarter of the northwest quarter of Section 3, Township 2 North, Range 14 West, in Lamar County, Mississippi. The above two described parcels of land overlap by 35 feet because the public road referred to in Mrs. Pontiff's deed is actually located in the northeast quarter of the northwest quarter and did not lie along the south line of the northeast quarter of the northwest quarter. The dispute as to ownership of this 35-foot strip of land arose when Mrs. Pontiff saw a "for sale" sign posted on the side of the road that she claimed as her property in December of 1982.

At trial Mrs. Pontiff testified that her mother, Mrs. Hazel Reynolds, bought property in 1942, which contains the property deeded to Mrs. Pontiff. Mrs. Reynolds' deed was also in evidence. Mrs. Pontiff also testified that Highway 11 dissects this larger tract of land and that her mother conveyed her, in 1973, the property on the east side of Highway 11, which includes the 35-foot strip now in dispute. Mrs. Pontiff testified that in 1942, on this east side of Highway 11 (the property deeded to her), there were remnants of an old cabin and that her father used the property to pasture his cows. She also testified that this land, including the 35-foot strip, was under fence in order to keep the cows in. She also testified that there was timber on this property, including the 35-foot strip in dispute. Mrs. Pontiff further testified that when she bought the property in 1973, the fence, although in deterioration, was still standing. In 1982, the time the controversy over this 35-foot strip of land arose, the fence was practically all torn down except for some remnants and fence posts.

Mr. Jordan, a certified land surveyor for state-aid roads in the county, testified from the survey he made of this property in 1973 for Mrs. Pontiff. In his testimony he stated that Mrs. Pontiff's property and Mr. Pieper's property were separated by a fence line and that this fence line ran along the south margin of the county road. He also testified that he had lived in Purvis all of his life and that he had never known anyone else to make use of this disputed property other than the Reynolds since World War II. He testified that the property had always been bounded by a fence or a fence line along the side of the road. He further testified that no one else besides the Reynolds family had ever claimed that 35 feet of property. Finally, he testified that the iron stake which marks the section line was probably placed there by a surveyor hired by Mr. Pieper in 1982, and that, indeed, the north boundary described in Mr. Pieper's deed did not run along the south margin of this road, but was described as being the section line. He speculated that the old fence was originally put up just outside the section line (so that it ran along the road) simply because the road is a natural boundary.

Two other witnesses, long-time residents of the area, testified that the disputed land had always been known as belonging to the Reynolds family, and that the property had been under fence since the early 1940s.

On cross-examination of these witnesses, the testimony focused on what use had been made of the land since 1973, when Mrs. Pontiff bought it from her mother. Mrs. Pontiff testified that the land had not been put to any use other than for her and her husband to walk on when they came from Texas to visit her mother. She also testified that they had planted trees on the property and specifically had planted a pear tree, which eventually died, on this 35-foot strip. The other three witnesses testified that, to their knowledge, the land had not been used for gardening, farming, cutting timber, or grazing cattle in the past nine years.

Mr. Pieper did not put on any witnesses of his own, and only offered his deed into evidence to prove the boundary lines of his property. At the end of oral testimony, both sides offered into evidence records of the taxes paid on this property from 1973 to the present.

Body of Opinion

We focus on the issue of adverse possession of the 35-foot strip of property in dispute.

Mr. Pieper incorrectly frames the issue in this case as to adverse possession. He correctly argues that there are six elements necessary to constitute an effective adverse possession claim: (1) under claim of right; (2) actual; (3) open, notorious and visible; (4) exclusive; (5) continuous and uninterrupted for ten years, and (6) peaceful. However, he incorrectly applies these elements to Mrs. Pontiff rather than to Mrs. Hazel Reynolds, Mrs. Pontiff's mother and predecessor in title. There was testimony throughout the trial that Mrs. Reynolds acquired her property through warranty deed in 1942 and that she and her family used the property deeded to Mrs. Pontiff, including the 35 feet in dispute, to graze cows. The disputed property was under fence for that purpose from 1942 until the mid-1960s, and the fence remained in repair "well enough to keep cattle" until at least 1972 when Mr. Jordan surveyed it. In 1945, in a quiet title action, the chancery court decreed that Mrs. Reynolds' property was bounded by the south margin of the public road. The decree assumed that the south margin of the road and the section line were one and the same. It was not until 1982, when Mr. Pieper hired a survey of the land pursuant to the boundaries set out in his deed, that the discrepancy came to light. Therefore, Mrs. Reynolds claimed the 35-strip from 1945 until she deeded it to Mrs. Pontiff in 1973.

The Reynolds family's use of this property was exclusive and peaceful, continuous for 41 years, actual, open and notorious and under claim of right, according to the evidence offered. In other words, there was much credible evidence that could lead the chancellor to conclude that title to the 35-foot strip of land had vested in Mrs. Hazel Reynolds by adverse possession before 1973, when it was deeded to Mrs. Pontiff.

It is upon the point of discrepancy in the 1945 decree of the chancery court that Mr. Pieper frames his second argument. He alleges that because Mrs. Pontiff's deed from her mother did not set out by legal quarter section that the disputed property was part of the deeded property, Mrs. Pontiff's claim to the property was ineffective. This Court held many years ago, and again more recently, that it does not matter whether land claimed under adverse possession be within or without the "call of the title deeds," *Evans v. Harrison*, (1922), or that it be in the same quarter section or section as the land lies which is described in the deed.

Finally, Mr. Pieper argues that the fence around the disputed property has been in disrepair since 1973, during Mrs. Pontiff's claim of right, and that, therefore, the fence was not enough to put anyone on notice that Mrs. Pontiff claimed the property. Again, Mr. Pieper applies the requirements of adverse possession to the wrong title claimant. Mrs. Pontiff's mother gave notice for more than forty years by a fence around the disputed property and by continued use of the property. Once title ripened by adverse possession in Mrs. Reynolds, it is not necessary that the fence be standing, or even in existence, when the suit is filed.

Once title to the disputed property ripened in Mrs. Reynolds by adverse possession, and once she conveyed the disputed property to her daughter, Mrs. Pontiff, Mr. Pieper could not divest Mrs. Pontiff of that title unless he adversely possessed against her, which he does not claim to have done. The chancellor did not err in quieting title to the disputed property in Mrs. Pontiff and dismissing Mr. Pieper's counterclaim.

Judgment and Result

Finding no error, we affirm the chancellor's order confirming and quieting title in Myrna Reynolds Pontiff.

Questions

1. Is it "fair," according to natural law principles, that one person should be able to "steal" another's land?
2. What are the six elements of adverse possession the Mississippi Supreme Court announces?
3. What legal ethics justify adverse possession?

Gift

A **gift** refers to the voluntary transfer of title to property where the transferor receives nothing in exchange for the transfer. The giver of the gift is called the **donor** and the person receiving the gift is called the **donee**. Title to both realty and personalty can be acquired by an *inter vivos* gift. Inter vivos gifts refers to gifts between living persons, to be contrasted with gifts one makes by will at one's death. A deed is necessary to convey realty by gift. Generally a valid delivery of the deed must occur in the giving of a gift of realty. The types of gifts are inter vivos and gifts *causa mortis*.

The elements of a valid inter vivos gift are (1) donative intent, (2) delivery, and (3) acceptance. **Donative intent** refers to the idea that the gift giver must presently intend to make a gift, not just want to give at some unspecified future time.

Delivery involves the present handing over of control to something from the donor to the donee. Delivery can be either actual (the donor's handing over a ring to the donee) or constructive (the donor's handing over something *representing* the item being given, such as the keys to a car when one is giving a car).

Acceptance refers to the donee's agreeing to take control over the item given. Acceptance is generally presumed except when the gift would impose a hardship on the donee (for example, if someone gave a friend a piece of land with a toxic waste dump that cost more to clean up than the land was worth).

Gift Causa Mortis. A **gift causa mortis** results when a donor thinks she or he is about to die, makes a gift because of this belief, and then actually dies because of the particular threat of death. The donor must die from that bout of that illness or operation that caused him or her to make the gift. For example, if the donor is about to undergo heart surgery, makes a gift in contemplation of this surgery, but survives, the gift is revoked. If the donor later undergoes heart surgery and dies, this event does not revive the gift causa mortis, unless of course the donor had again made such a gift.

Capture

The capture doctrine is a way to acquire title to animals in the wild, but not animals in captivity, as in a zoo. Capture occurs when one takes physical possession of wild animals, but federal and state conservation laws place restrictions on capturing some types of wild animals.

Finding

A person may acquire title to lost personalty by finding it. **Lost property** is personalty that has been unintentionally, involuntarily parted with by the owner. A **finder** is a person who locates lost property. The finder has a claim superior to all others except that of the owner who lost it.

Statutes on Finding. In some jurisdictions statutes set out procedures to be followed in claiming lost property. Usually such statutes require advertising the object in specific enough terms to notify the loser that the property has been found and awaits his or her claiming it, while allowing enough detail to be held back to enable the finder to test the claimant's ability to identify it.

Mislaid Property. Mislaid property differs from lost property. Mislaid property is personalty one intentionally parts with but which one cannot recall parting with. Mislaid property remains the property of the one who intentionally parted with it but forgot it. Mislaid property does not become the property of the finder.

Abandoned Property. Abandoned property is personalty someone has intentionally and permanently parted with by leaving it in no one's custody. The first one to take possession of abandoned personalty becomes its owner.

Inheritance

One way a person may acquire either realty or personalty is by inheriting it from the estate of a deceased person. Deceased persons' estates may transfer property to others either by the **statute of descent** or by **will**.

Statute of Descent. The statute of descent is a will made by the state legislature, which realizes that many people do not have wills (dying without a will is known as dying **intestate**) and so drafts a statute that distributes a decedent's property in accordance with the way the legislature thinks the decedent would want it distributed. The legislative determination of how most people would want their property distributed at their death may be entirely wrong. Nevertheless the statute of descent tells how a person's property is distributed unless that individual either dies without property or leaves a will.

Wills. A will is a piece of paper on which a **testator** (maker of the will) indicates the persons who will take his or her property when he or she dies. A will in the testator's (testatrix, if a woman) handwriting and signed by the testator is called a **holographic will**. It does not have to be witnessed to be valid in most states, but not all states recognize the validity of holographic wills. Wills that are not in the testator's handwriting generally have to be declared by the testator to be his or her will in the presence of two witnesses, who must sign in each other's presence. The testator must be the age specified by the legislature of the state in which she or he dies domiciled to be able to execute a valid will. The will requirement of witnesses, attestation, signing in the presence of witnesses, and being a certain age are referred to as **formal requirements**. If any one of them is lacking, the will is theoretically void. In practical terms, if a formal requirement is lacking, but no one challenges it, the will probably transfers property to the persons named in it.

Wills are **ambulatory**, meaning that they may be changed any number of times before the testator dies unless the testator has made a binding contract to make a will. If the testator has made a binding contract to make a will, it is a debt of the estate. One reason wills are ambulatory is that they do not take effect until the testator dies. Before that time a person named in the will merely has an expectancy, but no property rights in any of the testator's assets.

A testator's will may not be used to escape debts, even if the will does not mention the testator's wish to pay personal debts. The way the testator's creditors are assured of an opportunity to be paid is by the probate process. A **probate court** exists in virtually every county in the United States. The function of probate courts is to test the validity of deceased persons' wills. (Was it really her will?) Such courts also appoint administrators for estates of those dying without a will or without naming an executor. A person named in a will to manage and wind up the estate is called an **executor**. The executor's job is to collect all of the decedent's property, pay off his or her debts, and distribute any remaining property in accordance with the will or statute of descent. If the will names no one to be executor or if there is no will, the probate judge appoints someone—called an **administrator**—to wind up the estate as just described. After appointment of the executor or administrator, public notices are placed in newspapers of general circulation telling of the decedent's death and advising decedent's creditors where and when to present their bills for payment. Then a hearing is held, at which time creditors' claims can be presented, proven, and either allowed or disallowed by the probate court.

Allowed creditor claims are paid before bequests (personal property given by will) and **devises** (realty given by will) are made. It is possible that creditor claims could exhaust all of the decedent's property, in which case takers named in the will would get nothing.

Trusts

One can acquire property as a trustee or as a trust beneficiary.

Definition of Trust. A **trust** is a way of owning property with two titles (that is, with two owners at the same time). The two titles are beneficial title, sometimes called **equitable title**, and legal title. Putting it another way, a trust is a legal relationship consisting of a settlor (the person who sets up the trust), a *res* (the property subject to the trust), a trustee (the person having legal title who manages the res), and a beneficiary (the person who receives the trust benefits and who holds beneficial title to the res). An indication of the settlor's intent is necessary to establish a trust for a legally recognized trust purpose. Also, some states require following certain formalities (writings, etc.) to establish a trust.

Law Governing Trusts. State law governs the setting up of trusts. State law and federal estate and gift tax law play an understandably vital role in the operation of trusts.

Mechanics of Forming Trusts. Trusts may have either realty or personalty as their res. State statutes determine whether trusts have to be written. Generally such statutes require trusts to be written when realty is the res. At common law oral trusts with any kind of res are possible and, in a few states, is still the law. As a practical matter, it is best to have a written trust.

How Long Trusts Can Last. A trust can be set up to last for as long as possible provided that all interests the trust creates **vest** (take effect and become the property rights of someone) within any life (or lives) in being at the time the trust becomes effective, plus 21 years. This last statement is called the **rule against perpetuities**. It was announced in England hundreds of years ago to keep property from being tied up by any one person for an extended period of time. It is a populist idea, along the lines that every person should have a *shot* at becoming an owner of resources. This rule has been followed in the United States, much to the dismay of lawyers because it is difficult to draft documents to satisfy it. However, this rule does not apply to some statutory trusts for employee retirements.

Inter Vivos and Testamentary Trusts. Trusts created and taking effect during the settlor's life are called **inter vivos** trusts. Trusts that take effect at the settlor's death are **testamentary** trusts. The degree of formality (witnesses, writing, etc.) needed to create a trust is greater for testamentary trusts, because requirements for executing a will must be observed.

Reasons for Creating Trusts. The trust arrangement allows one person (the settlor) to give property to another (the beneficiary) even though that person is unable to manage it. For example, a minor child, insane person, or a person inexperienced in managing property would represent appropriate reasons for setting up a trust. The settlor confers legal title on the trustee, who manages the res for the benefit of the beneficiary.

Trustee's Duties. Trustees hold the legal title to the trust res. As such they have the duty to manage the res according to the terms set out in the instrument creating the trust. Trustees must not act negligently in managing the trust res. They must use the care and skill that ordinarily reasonable, prudent persons would use in managing their own affairs. Trustees are **fiduciaries**. As such they have the highest duty of good faith in managing the trust. They must avoid conflicts of interest, such as selling trust assets to themselves. Trustees must account to the trust beneficiaries. The duty to account provides a way to guard against the trustee's abusing the trust's terms.

Problems with the Trust. Disputes can arise when the trust beneficiary (often a young person) thinks the trustee (often a bank) is mismanaging the trust. If the beneficiary sues the trustee for mismanagement or violation of one of the trustee's duties, the suit takes place in an equity court, not law court.

Who Can Be a Trustee. Virtually any legal person, natural (an individual) or artificial (a corporation), private or governmental, can be a trustee.

How Trusts End. Trusts end when the instrument creating them says they end. It is usually a definite date or when some purpose has been accomplished. Trusts may also be ended if all parties to it agree.

Manufacture

A person may acquire ownership of property by manufacturing it from materials she or he owns; however, others' patents may limit what one may make and how one may make it. Also, trademarks can limit how something is marketed.

Confusion

Title to property may arise from a process known as **confusion** of fungible goods. **Fungible goods** are those that are uniform in size, shape, or nature, such as wheat or oil. If a grain elevator carelessly mixed a farmer's grain with others' grain, the farmer would have a claim on all of the grain needed to protect his or her interest.

Purchase

Purchase is perhaps the most common means of acquiring property, both real and personal. Purchase occurs as the result of a contract, covered in Chapter 10. Recall that a contract is an agreement between competent parties enforceable in court.

A person can acquire either personalty or realty by contracting to buy it. It is also possible to exchange goods for goods or goods for services in a **barter** transaction. Most property, however, is acquired in exchange for money.

Generally contracts can be oral unless realty or expensive goods valued at $500 or more are purchased, in which case *written* evidence of the contract, signed by the person against whom you are trying to enforce the contract, is necessary.

USES OF PROPERTY

One basic right property owners have is to use whatever property rights they have in whatever way they see fit. For example, if someone owns a sailboat, that person can use the boat on a sunny Sunday afternoon in July.

Bailment

Often owners of personalty will want to lend their property to some friend. This type of relationship is called a bailment. A **bailment** is the separation of title and possession of personal, not real, property. The bailor is the owner of the property and the bailee is the borrower. The loaned property is called the bailed property.

Types of Bailments. The law recognizes three types of bailments: bailment for the sole benefit of the bailor; bailment for the sole benefit of the bailee; and mutual benefit bailment.

A **bailment for the sole benefit of the bailor** benefits only the owner of the bailed property. It would occur when the owner of a fur coat asks a friend to keep it for no charge but not use it while the owner goes on vacation.

Bailments for the sole benefit of the bailee arise if the borrower only is benefitting from using someone else's property. For example, if a person asks her neighbor to borrow his lawnmower for no rental fee or other consideration and the neighbor agrees.

A **mutual benefit bailment** is created when Mary rents an auto from a car rental agency. Mary, the bailee, is getting use of the car. The car rental agency, the bailor, is getting money. Both bailee and bailor benefit, hence, the name mutual benefit bailment.

Significance of the Different Types of Bailment. The significance of the types of bailment is that the more a bailment benefits the bailee, the more care the bailee has to the bailed property. In a bailment for the sole benefit of the bailee, the bailee has a high standard of care. Under a mutual benefit bailment the bailee has the duty of ordinary care. In bailments for the sole benefit of the bailor, the bailee has a slight duty of care.

In addition to the previously described duties of care, the bailee must also return the bailed property at the end of the bailment.

Leases, Licenses, and Easements

Owners of real estate could let others use their realty. Such use of another's realty could be a license, an easement, or a lease. A license is the right extended to a person to enter onto another's realty for a limited time and purpose. A patron's sitting in a movie theater is a license. An easement is also a nonpossessory interest in someone else's realty. An easement that exists to benefit a particular person is called an easement in gross, while an easement benefitting adjacent land is an easement appurtenant. A lease is a right to possess and use someone else's realty for a limited time, frequently referred to as landlord-tenant law.

Kinds of Tenancies. Tenancies or landlord-tenant relationships include tenancy for years, tenancy for period (or periodic tenancy), a tenancy at will, and a tenancy at sufferance.

A tenancy for years is misleading because it refers to a lease for a period of time expressly stated in the lease contract. For example, a lease for one month (even though not a year) is, in fact, a tenancy for years and gives the tenant the right to occupy the premises for one month. Note that the period can be for any definite length, but if the lease is for more than one year, it must be written to be enforceable. When the period stated in the lease expires, the lease ends even if no notice is given. Renewal provisions (if they exist and are exercised) allow tenants to remain in possession.

A periodic tenancy arises by a lease but the lease does not state how long it lasts although periodic rent is required. Periodic tenancies are automatically renewed unless properly ended. A lease creating a periodic tenancy might read: "The tenant must pay rent to the landlord on the first of the month." The period can be any length—a week, a month, a year. Holdover tenants from a tenancy for years can become periodic tenants when they pay weekly or monthly rent if no express term exists and no renewal clause under the first lease was exercised. Landlords in periodic tenancy situations must give tenants proper notice (usually notice must be a period's length in advance) to end a periodic tenancy.

A tenancy at will exists if the lease is "for how long we make it." Both tenant and landlord have little security in this arrangement because either may end it at any time without even giving notice. Holdover tenants can also fall into this category until such time as they become periodic tenants.

Tenants at sufferance is actually not a tenancy, but, rather, someone who legally occupies someone else's property as a tenant for years, for example, and the lease expires and the tenant stays on wrongfully. In such a case the tenant becomes a tenant at sufferance.

Problem Areas in Landlord-Tenant Relations. Problem areas in landlord-tenant relationships include the following:

1. The amount of damage deposit the tenant is required to make when the lease is signed
2. The procedures to be followed to determine the amount of damages caused by the former tenant and by the present tenant (Is there a walk-through inventory by landlord and tenant at both the start and end of the lease?)
3. The date after the lease ends when the landlord has to refund the tenant's damage deposit
4. The uses to which the tenant may and may not put the premises
5. The degree to which the tenant must observe sanitation regulations in the apartment and in common areas
6. The extent of security protection the landlord must provide
7. The tenant's rights to deduct from rent amounts spent to make repairs the landlord must make
8. The tenant's rights to withhold rent payments and stay in or leave the premises free of any obligation if the premises become uninhabitable due to causes beyond the tenant's control
9. The extent to which class actions are allowable

Some Traditional Common Law Rules with Respect to Leases. These common law rules have been changed in some jurisdictions by statute.

1. If the tenant leases both a building and the land on which the building sits, and the building is destroyed, the tenant is liable for rent on both the building and land unless a lease clause or statute excuses the rent.
2. The tenant has a duty to make minor repairs to keep the premises livable, such as repairing a broken screen.
3. The tenant has a duty to pay rent.
4. The tenant may **sublet** or assign his or her lease unless the lease prevents it.
5. If the tenant, tenant's family member, or guest is injured on the leased premises, the landlord is generally *not* liable unless the injury resulted from some breach of a landlord's agreement to keep the premises in repair or the injury occurs in a common area (stairs, elevator, or deck) and is the result of the landlord's breaching a duty to maintain the premises.
6. The tenant has a duty not to commit waste on the premises.

The Uniform Residential Landlord Tenant Act (URLTA)

Landlord-tenant law is state law. About one-third of the states have passed the Uniform Residential Landlord Tenant Act (URLTA). As the name suggests, this law only covers residential leases, not those where a business leases space for its offices. URLTA strikes a balance between landlord and tenant rights that is generally more favorable to tenants than were the generally landlord-biased common law rules on this topic. Check your state code to determine whether your state has adopted URLTA.

Among the topics URLTA addresses are deposits, subleasing, habitability, landlord right of access, landlord rules governing tenants, general landlord and tenant rights and duties, unconscionability, and exculpatory clauses.

Deposits. Deposits refer to amounts of money the tenant is required to leave with the landlord to protect some landlord interest. Cleaning deposits cover landlord costs of cleaning the premises after the tenant vacates the premises. URLTA permits landlords to include cleaning deposits in residential leases. However, **BOLD** print must identify nonrefundable cleaning deposits.

Security deposits cover damage to the premises, theft of items belonging to the landlord, or tenant departure prior to termination of the lease. In effect, security deposits are damages the tenant pays in advance to cover any violations committed. URLTA caps the size of security deposits. These caps or limits vary from state to state; state codes set the exact amount. Many states (including some without URLTA) require that landlords place security deposits in a separate account, and some states even require that tenants earn interest on security deposits. Common law, on the other hand, allowed landlords to do what they wanted with security deposits.

Deposits for prepaid rent refers to amounts landlords require tenants to pay up-front (prior to entering the premises) to guarantee that rent will be paid. URLTA caps prepaid rent to one and one-half times the monthly rent.

Subleasing. A sublease occurs when a tenant transfers possession of the leased property to a third person for only part of the lease. The original tenant continues to pay rent to the original landlord in a sublease, and the sublessee becomes the tenant of the original tenant. The sublessee is not the tenant of the original landlord. The sublessee has no right to sue the original landlord if the original landlord fails to meet lease obligations. In such a case if the landlord breaches any obligations, the sublessee must sue the original tenant, who in turn must sue the original landlord.

An assignment of a lease differs from a sublease in several respects. In a lease assignment the original tenant turns over rights and duties to the assignee. The original tenant remains liable to the original landlord, but also the assignee is obligated to the tenant. Note also that the landlord remains liable to the original tenant and also becomes liable to the assignee. The assignee agrees to serve out the lease term and pay rent directly to the original landlord.

Common law rules allowed tenants to sublet or assign leases. The lease can, of course, take this right away from the tenant. A majority of states continue to allow tenants to sublet or assign the lease unless prohibited in the lease.

Habitability. Habitability requires that the leased property be "livable," that is, have functioning plumbing and heat, and be in good repair. Broken windows or leaky roofs would violate the habitability requirement. Amazingly, the common law did not impose a habitability requirement on the leased premises. Thus, the tenant could move into unlivable premises with no legal way of forcing the landlord to make repairs. Presumably only people in desperate financial situations or unaware of the poor condition of the premises would lease such property.

Unlike the common law, URLTA imposes a warranty of habitability on the landlord of residential property. Tenants now have a legal basis to sue landlords who fail to provide livable premises. For example, if the plumbing does not work, the tenant can sue the landlord for breaching the warranty of habitability.

URLTA makes it unconscionable (illegal) for landlords to eliminate the warranty of habitability in residential leases.

Landlord Right of Access. Even though tenants have leased the premises, landlords may legally enter them under certain circumstances. First, the tenant may allow the landlord to enter. Second, URLTA and a majority of states allow the landlord to enter after giving advance notice. For example, the landlord might want to check the premises for radon or some other health hazard. URLTA requires that the landlord give the tenant two days notice except in the case of an emergency, such as a fire, in which case no advance notice is required. Tenants must be told the reason a landlord needs access. URLTA says that repairing, decorating, and cleaning are appropriate reasons for entering the tenant's premises. Third, governmental inspectors may enter if they have a warrant. Landlords must obey such warrants covering tenants' premises. Should the warrant prove defective, the tenant has recourse against the government inspectors, not the landlord.

Landlord Rules. It is common for landlords to impose rules on tenants covering matters such as who can park in the apartment parking lot; who can use the apartment swimming pool; who can use the apartment laundry; whether pets are allowed; and what allowable noise levels are. URLTA and all jurisdictions allow such rules if they apply to all tenants, they are definite, tenants are aware of the rules when they sign the lease, tenants are notified of rules changes, and the rules' purposes are for the tenants' general welfare, convenience, or safety. Extra charges for rules violations are upheld by courts if the rules are reasonable even though the charge may amount to a large sum.

Landlord's Rights and Duties. The principal landlord right is to receive the tenant's rent on time. Tenants failing to pay their rent risk eviction, and landlords have the right to end the lease. URLTA requires that landlords give written notice that rent is overdue. If the tenant fails to pay rent within two weeks of receipt of an overdue notice, the lease is legally ended in thirty days. The *Lake County Trust Co. v. Vine* case illustrates a tenant's attempt to avoid paying a rent increase thought to be excessive.

Lake County Trust v. Vine

Court of Appeals of Indiana
704 N.E.2d 1035 (1998)

Background and Facts:

Williamsburg owns Williamsburg Manor, a residential community that provides mobile home lots for lease. The tenants of the park had executed written leases with Williamsburg that provided month-to-month tenancies. In November 1993, Williamsburg increased the rent for the lots from $221 to $236 per month, constituting a 7 percent increase. Many of the tenants vehemently protested the increase. Appellees, Terry and Sandra Wine, Ronald and Carol Niebauer, and other tenants of Williamsburg, paid their rent minus the increase; as a result, Williamsburg returned their checks with Notices to Quit. Several tenants were permitted to pay the required rent plus a late fee; however, the Niebauers and other ringleaders of the rent protest were not permitted to remain in Williamsburg under any circumstances. Williamsburg sued to evict the Niebauers, the Wines, and other tenants. The Wines' and Niebauers' eviction suits were consolidated. The

Wines and the Niebauers counterclaimed on behalf of themselves and the other tenants of Williamsburg for breach of contract (and other grounds here omitted). The trial court certified the action as a class action. Williamsburg moved for summary judgment on the Niebauer class counterclaims; additionally, Williamsburg moved the court to decertify the class action. The trial court denied both motions and let the appeal proceed before it rendered a decision.

Body of Opinion

Judge Robb

... Williamsburg argues that the trial court erred when it denied its motion for summary judgment on the Niebauers' class claim that a duty of good faith and fair dealing was expressly incorporated into the Williamsburg lease. Section 13 of the Williamsburg lease states that "the posted rules and regulations ... attached to this lease are part of this lease at the time of execution." ... The preamble to the rules and regulations states:

> Williamsburg Manor is conceived as a community of neighbors living in harmony... not by rigid rules and regulations.... When these standards are fair, reasonable and logical... when they are applied and complied with on an impartial basis... each resident can be assured a maximum of freedom, privacy, safety and comfort.... [T]he spirit behind this statement is the Golden Rule: "Do unto others as you would have others do unto you."

... The Neibauer class argues that the language of the preamble to the rules and regulations imposes a duty of good faith which is expressly incorporated into the rental agreement. We disagree.

Rules of construction of contracts apply to leases.... In Indiana, the duty of good faith is applied in contract law only under limited circumstances such as those involving insurance contracts.... Finally a contract may incorporate another unsigned writing when the contract expressly incorporates the terms of the writing....

The duty of "fairness" outlined in the rules and regulations does not apply to the lease; rather, this duty is expressly limited to the statement it precedes: the rules and regulations. The preamble to the rules and regulations states: "the spirit behind *this statement* is in the Golden Rule" [emphasis added]. Thus, even assuming the language of the preamble implies a contractual duty of good faith, the preamble limits itself to the rules and regulations and therefore does not apply to the conditions of the lease. Although the language of the lease incorporates the terms and conditions of the rules and regulations, the terms of each document retain their original meaning and will only effectuate the intent clearly contemplated by the language of said instruments. Thus, a statement which limits the effect and scope of a clause will retain its meaning when incorporated into another document.

In the alternative, the Neibauer class claims that the duty of good faith and fair dealing should apply to leases in general. In particular, it argues that a sophisticated landlord has undue influence in the execution of a lease. Thus, they claim that without a duty of good faith Williamsburg can arbitrarily and unfairly raise the monthly rent. In general, however, contract law does not require such a duty:

> It is not the province of courts to require a party acting pursuant to such a contract to be "reasonable," "fair," or show "good faith" cooperation. Such an assessment would go beyond the bounds of judicial duty and responsibility. It would be impossible for parties to rely on the written expressions of their duties and responsibilities....

The Niebauer class admits that Williamsburg had the right to raise rent; indeed, because the leases were month to month, Williamsburg and the tenants had the right to renegotiate the terms of the lease at the end of each successive tenancy....

Williamsburg gave all of the tenants over one month's notice of the new monthly rent; therefore, the terms of the leases were clear and unambiguous. Under Indiana law, a person is presumed to understand and assent to the terms of the contracts they sign.... Aside from the fact that Williamsburg is a "corporate landlord," the Niebauer class cannot point to any undue influence or unequal bargaining power exercised by Williamsburg in the execution of their respective leases; therefore, as a matter of law, we are unwilling to extend a duty of good faith and fair dealing to corporate landlords. Like all tenants, the residents of Williamsburg were free to execute a lease with a different landlord if the terms of the lease were unacceptable.

By asking the court to apply a duty of good faith to an unambiguous lease, the Niebauer class is effectively requesting this court to rewrite the terms of an agreement where the intent of the parties is clear. Such an exercise of our discretion is without the boundaries of our authority and in clear contravention of contract law as outlined by our Supreme Court....

Judgment and Result

The Court of Appeals would not apply a duty of good faith and fair dealing to tenants' unambiguous lease with the mobile home park.

Questions

1. Do rules of construction for contracts apply to leases?
2. Are persons who rent mobile home lots usually high or low income persons? Should the law protect

such persons from exploitation? In Indiana is a duty of good faith "read into" residential lease contracts where tenants are low income persons?

3. Williamsburg Manor's rules and regulations spoke of a community governed by the spirit of the Golden Rule. Did the court say this spirit of the Golden Rule applied to the lease? Would Kant (mentioned in Chapter 1 in connection with the categorical imperative) have approved of what the court did here?
4. Was there any legally recognized reason why Williamsburg Manor could not increase the tenants' rent? If landlords could not raise rents, is it not possible that they might not cover their costs and eventually go out of business? Then where would the tenants go?
5. What check do tenants have on a landlord who apparently arbitrarily raises rents too much? Go elsewhere? What if there is no other trailer park in the vicinity?

As noted earlier, landlords have duties under URLTA including keeping the premises habitable, providing a place for garbage disposal, keeping utilities safe as well as operable (assuming the tenants pay their utility bills), obeying building and safety codes, and keeping common areas safe and clean.

Tenants' Rights and Duties. Tenants have a duty to pay their rent on time and follow rules governing the leased premises. Failure to pay the rent or follow the rules entitles the landlord to end the lease or impose added charges.

The tenant has a number of rights including the right to habitable property and the right to repair and deduct the cost of repair from the rent payment. Under URLTA the landlord has 14 days to respond to tenants' demands to repair before the tenant can exercise self-help (repair them or hire someone to repair the problem). URLTA caps the amount of repairs tenants can engage in and deduct from the rent to the larger of $100 or half the month's rent. Amounts vary from state to state.

Occasionally the leased premises are in such disrepair that the tenants can assert that they have been *constructively evicted.* If constructive eviction occurs, the tenant has the right to leave the premises with no further liability on the lease. Exactly what amounts to constructive eviction will vary from case to case, but it could include, for example, lack of heat in a Boston apartment in January.

Unconscionability. Unconscionability means that a term in a contract such as a lease is unfair to the tenant to such an extent that a court will not enforce the provision. A provision could be unfair because the landlord had a much stronger bargaining position than the tenant, because the lease is offered on a "take it or leave it" basis, or because of some other factor. A lease that required that the tenant forfeit his car if he parked in the wrong parking spot would be unconscionable.

URLTA makes it unconscionable for landlords to deprive tenants of URLTA rights. Thus, it would be unconscionable for landlords to impose a lease provision taking away tenants' rights to have functioning plumbing.

Exculpatory Clauses. Perhaps you have heard of landlords who put terms in leases absolving the landlord from liability for tenant injuries or damages incurred during the lease. Generally courts refuse to honor exculpatory clauses that totally exempt landlords from their own negligence. The validity of such clauses generally turns on the amount of the landlord's culpability (blameworthiness) as well as the source and nature of the tenant's injury. For example, if the tenant's spouse throws a rolling pin at the tenant and puts out the tenant's eye, the landlord will not be liable because landlords are not responsible for tenants' marital bliss. On the other hand, if the tenant slips and falls because the landlord has not repaired loose tile after having been informed and after having had sufficient time to remedy the matter, the landlord will probably be liable for the tenant's damages even though the lease has an exculpatory clause exonerating the landlord from such liability.

The *Allison by Fox v. Page* case shows that at least one state's supreme court has held that landlords will not be liable for injuries to third persons caused by tenants' animals.

Allison by Fox v. Page

Supreme Court of Iowa
545 S.W.2d 281 (1996)

Background and Facts:

Robert L. Page and Clyda R. Page (landlords), owned a residential rental property. Their daughter and tenant, Julie Page, owned a dog that was allowed to run free in the fenced-in yard. In 1989, the dog injured a young girl visiting the tenant. The landlords learned of this incident shortly after it occurred.

Two years later the same dog bit appellant, Jordan Allison, when she entered the tenant's yard to retrieve a coat her sister had left there earlier. Jordan's mother, appellant, Shelley Fox, sued the landlords alleging a claim on behalf of Allison for her injuries, and a rule 8 claim for Fox's loss of consortium. Both claims were based upon a theory of premises liability, alleging the landlords knew or should have known the tenant's dog presented an unreasonable risk of danger to others.

The case was tried to a jury. The landlord moved for dismissal at the close of the plaintiffs' case and subsequently moved for a directed verdict; both motions were denied. The jury returned a verdict finding the landlords 25% at fault and Fox 75% at fault. It awarded damages of $60,000 to Allison and $16,580.68 to Fox.

Both parties appealed.

Body of Opinion

Justice Ternus

This case was tried under a theory of premises liability. We must decide whether a landlord is liable for an injury inflicted by a tenant's dog when the landlord knew or had reason to know that the dog was dangerous.

As a general rule, a landlord is not liable for injuries caused by the unsafe condition of the property arising after it is leased, provided there is no agreement to repair. ... However, this generality is subject to several exceptions. For example, if the landlord retains control of the property, the landlord may be held liable.... The landlord also has liability for unsafe conditions and defects in the common areas available to the public. ... Finally, implicit in the general rule is the conclusion that the landlord remains liable for any conditions existing before or at the time the property is leased.... The general rule and exceptions reveal a common principle: Liability is premised upon control.

We have never considered the applicability of these legal principles to a landlord whose tenant's dog has injured a third party. However, our court of appeals has addressed a similar issue concerning landlord liability for escaped farm animals owned by a tenant.... In *Byers*, swine owned by the tenant escaped onto an adjacent roadway.... The plaintiffs' vehicle collided with the swine and the injured parties sued the landlord claiming the landlord had a duty to exercise reasonable care in operating and managing the land.... The court of appeals ruled the landlord had no duty, reasoning that a landlord is not liable for injuries caused by dangerous conditions arising after a tenant takes possession.... The court noted that no exception to this rule applied because the landlord did not have any interest in or control over the swine....

We think the same analysis applies here: The landlords did not have any right to control the tenant's dog. The tenant's dog, to the extent it can even be categorized as a *condition of the premises*, came onto the land after the property was leased. Therefore, in the absence of any other applicable exception, the landlords have no liability for the injuries caused by their tenant's dog....

The plaintiffs claim, however, that keeping an animal on the leased premises is an *activity* for which liability may be imposed under *Restatement (Second) of Torts* section 379A:

> A lessor of land is subject to liability for physical harm to persons outside of the land caused by activities of the lessee or others on the land after the lessor transfers possession if, but only if,
>
> a) the lessor at the time of the lease consented to such activity or knew that it would be carried on, and
>
> b) the lessor knew or had reason to know that it would unavoidably involve such an unreasonable risk, or that special precautions necessary to safety would not be taken.

We decline the plaintiffs' invitation to apply section 379A to animals not owned or controlled by the landlord....

Under the common law, *owners or keepers* of animals could be held liable for injuries caused by their animals under certain conditions.... Mere possession of the land on which the animal is kept, however, did not give rise to liability.... A landlord who is not even in possession of the land, but merely owns the property on which a tenant keeps animals, is likewise not liable for injuries caused by the tenant's animals....

Judgment and Result

The landlord won. Because the landlords did not own the dog that bit Allison nor did the landlord have any right to control the dog, the landlord owed no duty to protect Allison from the dog.

Questions

1. Could persons coming onto leased premises who are injured by the tenant's dog possibly recover from the *tenant* who owned and had the right to control the dog?
2. The general, over-arching principle the court seems to focus on is control. For instance, what does the court say is the general rule about landlord liability for injuries caused by unsafe conditions arising after the property is leased where there is no agreement to repair? If the landlord retains control over the land, may the landlord be held liable? Do landlords have liability for unsafe conditions and defects in the common areas available to the public? Are landlords liable for any conditions existing before or at the time the property is leased?
3. Would holding a landlord liable for injuries caused by the tenant's dog be an extension or contraction of liability over the usual rule holding the tenant liable? Why would a person want to sue the landlord rather than the more obvious candidate for liability, the tenant?
4. Did the landlord know that the dog in the *Allison* case was dangerous? Why, then, was the landlord not liable? Could the landlord control the dog? Could the landlord have said, "No dogs" in its lease? Could it not be argued that because the landlord allowed dogs on the leased premises that it "controlled" dogs on the premises? Or is this simply stretching landlord liability too much? Other jurisdictions agreeing with the Iowa Supreme Court include Wisconsin, Arkansas, and Missouri.
5. Section 379A of the *Restatement of Torts* extends landlords' liability to "physical harm to third persons outside of the land caused by activities . . . on the land." Was the injured child here outside of the land? If not, was the court's refusal to apply 379A to this case based on the fact that 379A simply did not fit the facts?
6. Tenants do not enjoy having snoopy landlords micromanage their lives. Tenants want freedom to live their lives in the manner they select even if the property on which they live is leased as opposed to owned by the tenants. How could it be argued that the *Allison* decision is a tenants' rights victory? By reasoning that exonerating landlords from liability due to lack of control of the leased premises, are landlords encouraged to adopt a hands-off policy in controlling tenant conduct on the leased premises?

CHAPTER SUMMARY

Property is the bundle of rights one person has with respect to another person with respect to the thing. Property is not the thing, but the rights someone has in the thing.

Title refers to ownership of property. Title documents refer to pieces of paper that officially say who has property rights in something. Title documents exist for land, vehicles, and a few other things.

Property law is generally state law; thus, the rules of property law vary from state to state.

Property can be classified as realty, personalty, or fixtures.

Property can be acquired in a number of ways, including capture, manufacture, gift, purchase, theft (under some circumstances), as a trust beneficiary, finding, and confusion.

Property may be used in various ways including bailing property, leasing realty, or conveying an easement.

URLTA sets rules governing residential leases in some states.

MANAGER'S ETHICAL DILEMMA

Beatrice Kayser was the president of Smokey Mountain Realty of Knoxville, Tennessee. Beatrice prided herself on the fact that her firm had been in business for more than 25 years and had increased its sales volume each year. Customers trusted her firm and the salespeople worked hard. One day Beatrice received a report from the U.S. Environmental Protection Agency. The report noted a colorless, odorless gas called radon that seeps from underground uranium decays into radioactive particles which enter human lungs and cause cancer. EPA estimated that radon might be responsible for 5,000 to 20,000 lung cancer deaths per year (out of the total 140,000 annual deaths from lung cancer). Figure 12.1 was developed by EPA and shows the radon amounts and associated health risks.

According to the study, several states have much greater potential for harmful radon levels in the home. The states in which it is estimated that 25 percent or more of the homes have excessive radon levels in residences are Indiana, Pennsylvania, Wisconsin, Minnesota, North Dakota, Colorado, and Wyoming. States where 20–25 percent of the homes have radon levels above safe levels include Kansas, Rhode Island, and Massachusetts, while in Connecticut, Missouri, Tennessee, and Kentucky about 15–20 percent of the homes have unhealthy levels. In Michigan 10–15 percent of the homes have unsafe radon levels.

The study also indicated that radon risks increased up to 15 times for smokers than for nonsmokers. Thus, smoking in a house with elevated radon levels should not be allowed. The study recommended that homeowners test their homes for radon to see whether they exceed the level at which EPA recommends corrective action—4 picocuries per liter of air. This level is about equal to 200–300 chest X-rays per year or to smoking half a pack of cigarettes per day. Radon detection tests cost about $15 for each room. If excess radon is found, correction costs (involving ventilation and sealing cracks in the house's foundation and from underground pipes) range from $500 to $2,000 in most cases.

Beatrice realized she was selling real estate in a high-risk state for radon. None of her fellow realtors knew about this risk, nor did many homeowners. What should she do now that she is aware of it?

FIGURE 12.1 Health Risks Associated with Exposure to Radon

Radon Level pCI/l	Estimated Number of Lung Cancer Deaths Due to Radon Exposure (out of 1,000)	Comparable Exposure Levels	Comparable Risk
200	400–700	1,000 times average outdoor level	More than 60 times nonsmoker risk 4 pack-a-day smoker
100	270–630	100 times average indoor level 100 times average outdoor level	20,000 chest x-rays per year 2 pack-a-day smoker
20	60–210		1 pack-a-day smoker
10	30–120	10 times average indoor level	5 times non-smoker
4	13–50		200 chest x-rays per year
2	7–30	10 times average outdoor level	Non-smoker risk of dying from lung cancer
1	3–13	Average indoor level	20 chest x-rays per year
0.2	1–3	Average outdoor level	

Source: U.S. Environmental Protection Agency.

Discussion Questions

1. Great discussion today surrounds whether zoning of real property is necessary. At least one major U.S. city (Houston, Texas) has no zoning requirements. In effect, someone may legally put a chicken coop into an upscale residential neighborhood. On the other hand, zoning laws create, as well as destroy, property values by restricting what landowners can do with their land. Suppose you are a city council member of a medium-sized city that is considering revamping its zoning laws. Would you be in favor of more restrictive, less restrictive, or no zoning laws? Why?
2. If a person pays taxes on property that she claims by adverse possession and had occasionally mowed the land, is this enough to prove exclusive and adverse possession? [*Crowden v. Grantland*, 510 So.2d 238 (Ala. 1987)].
3. Is acceptance of a gift generally presumed? [*Smith v. Fleming*, 358 S.E.2d 900 (Ga.App. 1987)].
4. An owner of land bequeathed it to a Jesuit College. The college learned that a tenant operated an "adult" bookstore on the property and understandably wanted the tenant to leave. The tenant claimed that it had a 10-year oral lease. Could the college evict the tenant on grounds that no valid lease existed? [*William Henry Brophy College v. Tovar*, 619 P.2d 19 (1980)].
5. A lease agreement specified no animals, birds, pets, motorcycles, waterbeds, trucks, jeeps, or vans on the premises at any time. The lease also provided for a $50 fine for each violation. Berlinger had a motorcycle on his patio on October 10, 13, 24, and November 7, 1979. The landlord assessed a $200 fine for violating the lease's rule. Berlinger moved out without paying the fine, and the landlord tried to withhold $200 from his security deposit. Berlinger objected on grounds that the fine was excessive and the rule was arbitrary. Was it? [*Berlinger v. Suburban Apartment Management*, 454 N.E.2d 1367 (1982)].
6. Morton executed a will leaving most of his $55,000 property to a friend and to the First Presbyterian Church. He was 85 when he executed the will. Morton lived in a motel. He would go on walks and return with his pants soiled because he had voided in public. Morton forgot how to play checkers, and other evidence showed that he often forgot to pay his rent or would forget and pay twice. He left only $1,000 each to two nephews. They challenged Morton's will on grounds that he lacked the requisite mental capacity when he wrote the will. Did the nephews win? [*In Re Estate of Morton*, 428 P.2d 725 (1967)].
7. Charrier, an archeologist, discovered artifacts in graves of Tunica Indians on land owned by the State of Louisiana. He sold the artifacts to a university for $175,000. Louisiana claimed that it owned the property. Charrier argued that the artifacts were abandoned property. Who won? [*Charrier v. Bell*, 389 So.2d 155 (1979)].

Suggested Readings

Articles

CLINTON, "Private Property and the Limits of American Constitutionalism: The Madisonian Framework and Its Legacy," 19 *Policy Studies Journal* 173 (1990).

KURTZ, "The Transplant Paradox: Overwhelming Public Support for Organ Donation vs. Under-Supply of Organs: The Iowa Organ Procurement Study," 21 *The Journal of Corporation Law* 767 (1996).

POWELL, "The Seller's Duty to Disclose in Sales of Commercial Property," 28 *American Business Law Journal* 245 (1990).

WAGGONER, "Reforming the Law of Gratuitous Transfers: The New Uniform Probate Code," 55 *Albany Law Review* 871 (1992).

WAGGONER, "Spousal Rights in Our Multiple-Marriage Society: "The Revised Uniform Probate Code," 133 *Trusts and Estates* 18 (1994).

CHAPTER 13

INTELLECTUAL PROPERTY AND TECHNOLOGY

"AMERICA IS A LAND OF WONDERS, IN WHICH EVERYTHING IS IN CONSTANT MOTION AND EVERY CHANGE SEEMS AN IMPROVEMENT. THE IDEA OF NOVELTY IS THERE INDISSOLUBLY CONNECTED WITH THE IDEA OF AMELIORATION."

De Tocqueville, Democracy in America (1835).

POSITIVE LAW ETHICAL PROBLEMS

"You're a cybersquatter, and as such are diluting my trademark," said Ken Curry of Intermatic Corporation, which owned the valid trademark "Intermatic." Ken was talking to Mr. Toeppen, who had paid $100 to have the name "intermatic" registered as an Internet domain name.

"No I'm not. Nothing I've done is illegal under the federal trademark laws," replied Toeppen. "I registered the domain name 'intermatic' first, and because only one person may register a domain name on the Internet, I have the right to use the domain name 'intermatic' even though you have registered it as a trademark."

Who is correct?

"Chrysler is using my idea for an intermittent windshield wiper on its cars and is not giving me any royalty," complained Professor Kearns. Kearns was an engineering professor at Wayne State University. He had at least three patents on his invention, which allowed windshield wipers' speed to adjust depending on how much precipitation was falling.

"Patents are only valid for 17 years, and since we have been in litigation for that long, your patent is no longer valid," argued John Smith, a lawyer for Chrysler.

"Well, I'm betting that you are infringing and owe me over $15 million in lost profits and patent royalties. Further, I believe a court will see through your strategy of tying me up in court for 17 years so you can run out the clock on my patent," argued Kearns.

Who was right?

Ideas are the fodder of the entrepreneur. Ideas can rise to the form of personal property that the legal system will protect. Several devices protect these ideas including quasi-contracts, trade secrets, copyrights, trademarks, and patents. The following discussion examines each of these protections.

An idea of some kind is the basis of any business. The ability to conceive of an idea sufficiently novel, feasible from a cost standpoint, and offering market appeal is the basis for many fortunes. Consider, for example, Forbes' 1999 choice as the "richest person in the world": Bill Gates. Twenty years ago this man was a college dropout. But he had ideas and he knew how to exploit them.

http://
Federal and state codes and cases and links to law schools are available at **http://www.findlaw.com**

Once an idea is disclosed, however, competitors as well as customers learn of it and are not reluctant to "clone" it to profit themselves. The innovator of ideas has a need to protect the idea while at the same time disclosing it in order to enjoy the fruits of the innovation. Although the discussion here is geared to helping businesspersons exploit their inventions under the cover of some legal protection, we should not lose sight of the fact that some social justification must be present for legal protection in the first place. Hence, society is constantly balancing social costs of providing legal protection for ideas against the social benefits from developing legally protected ideas. The "law giveth and the law taketh away," and what protection society confers on an idea conceiver can be removed if the protection has been abused. What constitutes abuse of legal protection and what is creative use of the law is not always an easy matter to resolve as the cases in this chapter reveal.

http://
A free e-mail service providing legal information may be accessed through **http://www.lawnewsnetwork.com**

This chapter covers the legal protections of quasi-contracts, trade secrets, trademarks, copyrights, and patents. After examining these legal protections in detail, we briefly note some aspects of law as applied to e-mail and the Internet. Lastly, international protections for intellectual property is covered.

QUASI-CONTRACT

Quasi-contracts are not contracts at all. Rather, the judge says that something "like a contract," hence *quasi-contract*, will be regarded as existing in order to prevent unjust enrichment. The idea is that one person has received benefits for which she knows or should know that pay is expected and injustice would result by not holding her liable. If a judge decides in plaintiff's favor, the recovery is the reasonable value of the benefits conferred.

A simple example helps explain quasi-contract. Suppose an "Ace Painting Service" truck drives up in front of your house, and house painters say to you, "Hi, Mr. Smith, we'll have your house painted in no time." In fact, Smith lives next door. You say nothing because you are Mr. Jones, and the painter mistakenly starts to paint your house. You let him proceed knowing that he is painting the wrong house. He finishes and asks for pay. You then refuse, pointing out that Smith lives next door.

The judge will not let you cheat the painter. The judge will impose a quasi-contract to allow the painter to recover the reasonable value of the paint job. The reason? You knew that professional painters expect to be paid for their work; you had an opportunity to reject the benefits but you craftily decided to "be silent" and collect the benefits. The law will not allow you to wrongfully profit at the painter's expense.

But then you might ask, "What if you were not standing in front of your house when the painter drove up? What if the painter again mistakenly paints your house, and it looks great. Can the painter here assert quasi-contract as a way to "shake money out of your pockets"? Here, the answer is "No" because you were not in a position to reject the benefits. The benefits were being imposed without your knowledge. To hold otherwise would enable unemployed painters to sneak out to people's houses at night and foist all sorts of unwanted benefits on them in the hopes of using quasi-contract principles to recover. Here the circumstances do not justify paying the painter.

Quasi-Contract Compared to Contract Implied-in-Fact

Contracts implied by facts (or implied-in-fact) indicate that the parties actually intended for a contract to exist although their express language is not sufficient to create one. In the case of contracts implied in law (quasi-contracts), neither the facts nor the language indicate any intention of the parties to have a contract.

Applying Quasi-Contract to Business Ideas

As you might suspect, quasi-contract can help inventors. Consider the following example: Edison, an inventor, has worked on a unique toy doll that teaches children to speak French in a programmed way. He writes to Mega Company and asks whether they might be interested in hearing about a toy he believes has incredible market potential. A Mega executive writes back to Edison and asks for details about the toy explaining that he must know more about it prior to Mega's deciding whether to "sign Edison up."

If Edison discloses everything about his doll (including the years of development work and drawings), Mega might reject the idea and then copy it and manufacture it without giving Edison a dime of royalties. On the other hand, Mega might, in fact, be working on just such a device which, coincidentally, Edison was developing also. Deciding who is exploiting whom and thus who is entitled to quasi-contract protection in such a case is not easy as the following two cases demonstrate. In the first, the court said that quasi-contract protection might be appropriate. In the second, the court refused to apply the quasi-contract doctrine.

Kaplan v. Michtom

Federal District Court, S.D. N.Y.
17 F.R.D. 228 (1955)

Background and Facts:

The defendant Gillette Company seeks to dismiss a complaint in an action to recover the reasonable value of an idea for a doll with hair that could be given a permanent wave. Plaintiff claims that defendants wrongfully appropriated his idea after plaintiff confidentially disclosed it to him.

Plaintiff made his confidential disclosure to various representatives of the defendants in an attempt to sell his idea. He wrote a letter advising defendant he had an idea in which defendant might be interested and asking defendant whether it would like to know the details. Plaintiff received a reply, enclosing a "detailed statement of...policy on suggestions from outside sources," and advising him that if the terms were agreeable, he should complete and return the statement "and we will be happy to consider your suggestion." The letter expressed the hope that the writer would "hear from you again soon." It does not appear what the statement of policy provided or whether plaintiff signed it. Plaintiff then wrote a letter to the defendant in which he "communicated his idea" to it. The defendant did not answer his letter until about two months later, when it advised the plaintiff that a doll such as suggested had been planned for more than six months, to be manufactured by certain of the other defendants named in this suit.

This case is presently at the stage of the proceedings where a motion to dismiss the complaint has been made. The issue before the court is whether it appears to a certainty that the plaintiff would not be entitled to relief under any state or federal laws.

Body of Opinion

District Judge Edelstein

The main contention of the defendant is that the complaint is defective against it because of the absence of any allegation of "anything to limit the rights" of that defendant which I take to mean the absence of an express agreement. No express agreement is alleged. Nevertheless, the allegations of the complaint are sufficient to permit the plaintiff to adduce proof in support of his claim on the basis of which he would be entitled to recover....

Defendant cites *Williamson v. N.Y. Central R.R.*... for the proposition that there can be no protection of an "abstract idea" not reduced to a "concrete form" at disclosure in the absence of an express contract; and *Grombach Production v. Waring*... for authority that in a business idea case there can be no contract implied in law.... In view of the court's own definition of a contract implied in law, I have difficulty in understanding its conclusion that the jury could not be permitted to find such a contract based on the usage in the particular trade. It would seem that there has been a "curious admixture of the principles of quasi and implied-in-fact contracts."... 31 *Cornell Law Quarterly* 382, 389. Nevertheless, the decision in negation of the existence of a contract implied in law in the absence of an express contract was based upon "prior gratuitous, unsolicited disclosure." Whether the plaintiff's disclosure in the case at bar was gratuitous and unsolicited is a matter of proof. It is to be noted, moreover, that the *Grombach* case apparently involved an "abstract idea," communicated in telephone conversations, a written "presentation" having been rejected as evidence in the case. The decision of the Court of Appeals was not placed on the ground that the idea had not been reduced to "concrete form" at disclosure, nor is there any indication in the opinion that the issue ought to be treated as relevant. In any event it is impossible to determine from the complaint precisely what the form of the disclosure was in this case.

It is certainly proper for courts to be "assiduous in defeating attempts to delve into the pockets of business firms through spurious claims for compensation for the use of ideas. Thus to be rejected are attempts made by telephoning or writing vague ideas to business corporations and then seizing upon some later general similarity between their products and the motions propounded as a basis for damages."... But whether this is such a case cannot be determined from the complaint. It does not appear to a certainty that plaintiff will be unable to prove a state of facts giving rise to a right of recovery in quasi-contract....

Judgment and Result

The court refused to dismiss plaintiff's complaint. A trial could go forward at which plaintiff might be able to prove grounds for a quasi-contract recovery.

Questions

1. Did the judge in the *Kaplan* case allow the inventor to recover on a quasi-contract theory? What problems does the plaintiff face in proving his case?
2. Did the defendant solicit plaintiff's idea in *Kaplan*? If not, does the case suggest any reason why a court should be careful not to accept at face value plaintiff's quasi-contract claim?

The next case shows an unsuccessful attempt to raise the quasi-contract theory to recover for a business idea. Note that courts do not generally impose quasi-contracts where the parties have either an express or implied-in-fact contract. The reasoning is that if a judge imposes a quasi-contract in cases where a contract actually exists, it would amount to the court's substituting a new contract—in effect, changing the terms the parties themselves had agreed upon.

Wolfe v. American Airlines, Inc.

U.S. Court of Appeals (10 Cir.)
64 F.3d 670 (1995)

Background and Facts:

Plaintiff Howard Wolfe appeals from the district court's grant of summary judgment in favor of defendant American Airlines, Inc. The case comes from a suggestion plaintiff submitted to defendant under a company suggestion program. The issues on appeal are whether the district court correctly granted summary judgment by (1) holding defendant did not violate the terms of the suggestion program; (2) denying compensation on a quasi-contract basis; and (3) ruling that defendant did not unlawfully convert plaintiff's suggestion.

During plaintiff's employment with defendant as a mechanic, he developed a method to repair damaged aircraft parts. He submitted the concept to defendant pursuant to its company suggestion program, "IdeAAs in Action." Under the program, suggestions are classified as either quantifiable or unquantifiable. A quantifiable suggestion is one "whose monetary value to [defendant] can be calculated."... An unquantifiable suggestion is one "whose monetary value to [defendant] cannot be calculated, e.g., safety, product improvement without savings, appearance, schedule dependability, etc."... Suggestions that add impetus to act on an item management already has under review are considered "trigger" items and are classified as nonquantifiable for purposes of awards.... Quantifiable suggestions are eligible for a minimum of 30,000 and a maximum of 7,500,000 award credits; nonquantifiable suggestions are eligible for a flat 15,000 award credits. All award credits are redeemable for merchandise; participants who have accumulated $20,000 value in award credits in a year may elect to accept up to fifty percent of the value in cash....

Defendant initially rejected plaintiff's suggestion, but reevaluated it at his request. Analyst M. A. Mordecai made an estimate that defendant would avoid $963,060 in costs by adopting plaintiff's suggestion. However, according to Mordecai, neither the department responsible for implementing the suggestion nor the manager of the department whose budget would be affected agreed with his calculations.

The record contains several documents showing preliminary actions concerning plaintiff's suggestion. Ultimately, however, defendant categorized plaintiff's suggestion as a nonquantifiable trigger action item. It gave plaintiff 15,000 award credits.

On appeal the IdeAAs in Action Appeals Committee concluded that no actual savings could be quantified as a result of the suggestion, and closed their review. Plaintiff next complained to defendant's president without success.

Plaintiff then commenced a state court action for breach of contract and conversion of intellectual property. Defendant removed the case to federal court and moved to dismiss.... The district court concluded that the IdeAAs program documents granted defendant final authority over whether a suggestion was quantifiable, and the defendant had determined plaintiff's suggestion was a nonquantifiable trigger action item and paid plaintiff accordingly. The court also concluded that plaintiff's suggestion became defendant's property upon submission; consequently, defendant could not be held liable for conversion. Accordingly, the district court granted summary judgment for defendant.

Body of Opinion

Judges Tacha, Logan, and Briscoe.

The parties agree, for purposes of this case, that the IdeAAs program rules (AA Regulation 145-14) and program handbook constitute a contract. Plaintiff argues summary judgment was improper on his breach of contract claim because a factual issue exists concerning whether his suggestion was quantifiable.

Although the program rules provide that a suggestion is quantifiable if its "monetary value to [defendant] can be calculated,"... they also provide, "[d]ecisions of the company in determining eligibility, acceptance, or nonadoptions, and the amount of awards are final."... Further, the program handbook states "[t]he Appeals Committee will determine the final decision."...

Here it is irrelevant whether a trier of fact could find plaintiff's suggestion had monetary value; the Appeals Committee determined that no actual savings could be quantified. Under the terms of the contract, this decision was final.

Plaintiff relies on various rules of contract construction in an attempt to read out of the contract the language stating defendant makes the final decision on whether a suggestion is quantifiable. He argues that the contract should be construed against the drafter (i.e., the defendant) because it is ambiguous; that the contract should be construed to give effect to the parties' intent which, he claims (relying on an obsolete program handbook) was the buying and selling of ideas; and that the contract must be construed as a whole.

We conclude the contract, construed as a whole, is unambiguous on the essential issue: defendant makes the final decision whether a suggestion is quantifiable. Because the language is unambiguous, it is the only legitimate evidence of the parties' intent. The district court correctly granted summary judgment to defendant on the breach of contract claim.

Plaintiff also appears to argue that he is entitled to compensation under the theory of quasi-contract. A quasi-implied-in-law contract is a fictional contract imposed by law to adapt the case to a remedy.... No contract can be implied, however, where an express contract exists.... The parties agreed the IdeAAs program is an express contract; thus, the theory of quasi-contract is inapplicable. See *In re Penn Central Transp. Co.*, 831 F.2d 1221 (1987)...holding quasi-contract "may not be found if there is an express contract on the same subject." We hold plaintiff is not entitled to recover under the theory of quasi-contract.

Plaintiff asserts the district court erred when it granted summary judgment on the conversion claim. Conversion is an act of dominion "wrongfully exerted over another's personal property."...

The program rules provide that "[a]ll suggestions submitted become the sole and exclusive property of [defendant]."... The employee suggestion form on which plaintiff submitted his idea just above the signature line provides "I (we) understand the terms and rules and agree that [defendant] has the absolute and exclusive right to the suggestion."... Plaintiff contends that because defendant refused to pay him, it did not obtain an exclusive property interest in his suggestion. We disagree. Defendant fully complied with the contract by determining that plaintiff's suggestion was nonquantifiable and awarding plaintiff appropriate credits. Therefore, defendant acquired exclusive interest in plaintiff's suggestion.

Judgment and Result

Plaintiff lost. American Airlines was not liable for the employee's idea on a quasi-contract basis.

Questions

1. Was it a good idea from plaintiff's standpoint on the quasi-contract claim for plaintiff to admit that an express contract covering this dispute existed? Why?
2. Did the employer's IdeAAs program say anything about the fact that the Appeals Committee's (or the initial decision of the program referee of ideas submitted)

had to be rationally related to the facts presented and have a clearly articulated basis for the decision? Or could the Appeals Committee simply make a decision and refuse to explain why it rejected evidence that the idea in question here was apparently worth $963,060?

3. From American Airlines' standpoint, was the IdeAAs program a "well-drafted" suggestion program that protected the company? What were some provisions that could be cited supporting the idea that the program was well drafted?

4. The court dismisses the possibility that the employer might have converted plaintiff's idea. "Conversion" is defined as the unauthorized and unjustified interference with the dominion and control of another's personal property. It is commonly called stealing, but it is a civil, not criminal wrong. The torts chapter discusses conversion at greater length.

TRADE SECRETS

Trade secrets refer to information a person has that is used in a business and gives advantage over competitors who do not know or use it. Trade secrets can consist of formulas, patterns, devices, or compilation of information used in one's business. Two types of information that can be trade secrets are (1) product formulas, manufacturing processes, ingredient suppliers, and packaging suppliers that one uses in the manufacture of one's products; (2) customer lists and price information. The formula for Coca-Cola is a trade secret known by few persons.

Note recording or registering a trade secret is not required in obtaining this protection. However, one must take reasonable steps to keep the secret. In deciding whether to accord business information "trade secret" status, courts examine whether a business took substantial steps to keep the information secret. For example, having employees sign confidentiality agreements with respect to the secret information would be a definite step in furtherance of establishing trade secret status.

Trade secret law is common law, not statutory. Further, it is state, not federal, law so potential for variation exists among the states in terms of protection. Thus one should look to large, commercial states such as New York, which have many opportunities for making trade secret pronouncements. The *Geritrex* case is a New York decision.

Geritrex Corp. v. DermaRite Industries, LLC

U.S. District Court (S.D. N.Y.)
910 F.Supp. 955 (1996)

Background and Facts:

Geritrex was founded approximately 18 years ago by Madaio. Its manufacturing and sales operations are based at one site in Mount Vernon, New York. Geritrex currently has approximately 250 customers. Total sales for 1994 were $2.2 million and Madaio projected that sales for 1995 would total $1.8 million.

In April 1994, defendant Braunstein began working at Geritrex as its vice-president of sales. He left Geritrex in late March 1995. It is undisputed that while he was employed by Geritrex, he had access to its customer list and information concerning which customers purchased which products or received discounted prices. Braunstein currently owns a minority equity position in DermaRite, serves as its president, and runs its sales operations.

In August 1994, John Zimmerman joined Geritrex, where he served as production manager. He left Geritrex in late May 1995. While Zimmerman was employed by Geritrex, he was involved in all facets of production and had access to product formulations and to information about prices and suppliers of ingredients and packaging. Zimmerman began working for DermaRite in early June 1995. In addition to setting up DermaRite's manufacturing facility, his duties include formulating products, managing production, and obtaining ingredients and packaging.

DermaRite was formed in May 1995 by Braunstein and Israel Minzer, a businessman with contacts in the nursing home industry. Zimmerman testified that he completed the development of at least one DermaRite product by the end of August 1995 and finished work on the remainder of the twenty products in DermaRite's product line by the end of September 1995. According to Braunstein, DermaRite currently has about 35 customers, 12 of which were formerly Geritrex customers. Total sales as of the date of the preliminary injunction hearing were approximately $100,000. Braunstein offered testimony, as yet uncontroverted, that approximately $30,000 in sales is attributable to former Geritrex customers.

Plaintiff requests a preliminary injunction prohibiting defendants from competing with plaintiff for six months on the ground that Zimmerman and Braunstein signed confidentiality and noncompetition agreements during their employment with Geritrex. Plaintiff also asks for preliminary injunctions forbidding defendants from continuing to use its product formulations, manufacturing processes, supplier information, customer list, and price information on the ground that defendants have misappropriated plaintiff's trade secrets.

Body of Opinion

Judge Conner

Plaintiff... asserts that it is entitled to a preliminary injunction on the ground that DermaRite, Zimmerman, and Braunstein misappropriated information proprietary to Geritrex in order to develop and market DermaRite's products. To establish misappropriation of a trade secret, plaintiff must prove that: "1) it possessed a trade secret, and 2) [defendants are] using that trade secret in breach of an agreement, confidence, or duty, or as a result of discovery by improper means."... "A trade secret may consist of any formula, pattern, device or compilation of information which is used in one's business, and which gives him an opportunity to obtain an advantage over competitors who do not know or use it."... Plaintiff has identified two types of information that it alleges constitute trade secrets. The first is the product formulas, manufacturing processes, ingredient suppliers and packaging suppliers that it uses in the manufacture of its products. The second is its customer list and price information.

Although New York courts have identified a number of factors that courts may look to in determining whether information constitutes a trade secret,... the most important consideration is whether the information is kept secret.... Plaintiff must show that it took substantial measures to protect the secret nature of its information....

With respect to the information about plaintiff's manufacturing processes and product formulas, it is clear from the evidence before us that plaintiff did not take substantial measures to keep that information secret.... It is clear that the file copies [of batch records] were accessible, as cartons of batch products (some unsealed) were stored in several unlocked areas of the Geritrex facility.... Furthermore, nothing prevented an employee from copying a batch record while he or she was working with it. The batch records were not stamped confidential.... Zimmerman's uncontroverted testimony established that he regularly and quite openly took work, including batch records, home.... Michael Bernstein, the operations director, frequently worked on batch records in the cafeteria where any employee or visitor to the Geritrex plant could have had access to the records.... This evidence persuades us that plaintiff did not make substantial efforts to limit access to this information to employees who needed to know the product formulations.

Plaintiff contends that the Geritrex facility had only two doors, both locked, and that access to the building is limited to employees and escorted visitors. While this fact is indicative of some attempts at secrecy,..., it is not determinative in view of the overwhelming indications that plaintiff did not take substantial measures within the plant to protect the confidentiality of the product information from visitors or from employees who had no need to know it. Indeed, Madaio has admitted that he relied on the professional ethics of his production employees to keep Geritrex's product information secret, which simply does not constitute substantial efforts at secrecy.

We may make short shrift of plaintiff's argument that the source of the packaging for its products constitutes a trade secret. Anyone may easily determine the manufacturer of the containers for plaintiff's products by picking up the package and reading the manufacturer's name. Information that is readily ascertainable in this fashion does not constitute a trade secret.... Furthermore, plaintiff has presented no credible evidence at this time from which we could determine whether it has made substantial efforts to keep secret the sources of the ingredients used in its products.

Because Geritrex failed to take substantial measures to keep this alleged proprietary information secret, plaintiff has not demonstrated a likelihood of success on the merits, or even the existence of a serious question for litigation, on the issue of whether information regarding its product formulations, manufacturing processes, ingredient sources or packaging constitutes a trade secret.

Turning to plaintiff's contentions with respect to its customer argument is somewhat stronger though ultimately unsuccessful. Although there is no evidence before us at this time that this information was marked confidential or that access to it was limited to sales personnel, the members of the sales force had, for the most part, signed confidentiality and noncompetition agreements. Braunstein, whether he signed the agreement or not, admits that Madaio presented it to him. Braunstein was therefore aware that plaintiff sought to keep its customer list and price information confidential. Hence, there is at least some indication that plaintiff made efforts to keep its customer list and price information secret, and plaintiff may well succeed in establishing that this information constitutes a trade secret.

Even if we assume that Geritrex's customer list and price information are trade secrets, however, plaintiff has not presented convincing evidence that demonstrates that DermaRite has been using that information to compete for Geritrex customers. As head of sales for Geritrex, Braunstein undoubtedly had access to its customer list and price information. He has also acknowledged that while he worked for Geritrex, he added some business cards to the file of business contacts that he has developed over the course of his twenty-year career. Braunstein does not deny being aware of Geritrex's relationships with "a handful" of the customers that he has contacted, but he maintains that he has gathered his information about potential customers from a number of sources, including publicly available directories of nursing homes and hospitals and Minzer's apparently extensive contacts in the nursing home business. Indeed, Braunstein has testified that only 12 of DermaRite's 35 customers are former Geritrex customers. Braunstein has also offered uncontroverted testimony that DermaRite's two largest customers, responsible for approximately $60,000 in sales, were never Geritrex customers. Based on this evidence, we cannot find, at this juncture, that plaintiff is likely to succeed in demonstrating that defendants have used Geritrex's customer list and price information to lure away its customers. Plaintiff has, however, demonstrated that a serious question for litigation exists on this issue.

Judgment and Result

Plaintiff showed that a sufficiently serious question for further litigation existed (need for a trial) regarding whether one former employee had signed a noncompetition agreement. However, neither the product formulas and processes, the packaging suppliers, nor the ingredient sources were trade secrets. The plaintiff did show that a sufficiently serious question for litigation existed as to whether a competitor used a manufacturer's allegedly secret customer list and price information.

Questions

1. What items did plaintiff claim were trade secrets?
2. Why was plaintiff successful on some but not all of the trade secret claims?
3. What risks does society face if "too many things" are found to be trade secrets? Does such a finding stifle competition?
4. If, as the court says, the plaintiff relied on the "professional ethics" of the production employees to keep Geritrex's product formulas secret, which "simply does not constitute substantial efforts at secrecy," what does this judgment say about the court's regard for "ethics outside of the positive law"? Do they exist? Does your answer support the claims that positive law has risen to the status of an "ethic"?
5. Does a business need to register anything to claim trade secret protection?

COPYRIGHTS

Copyright law protects artistic, literary, or musical works. Thus if a person writes a play, a script for a movie, TV show, or commercial, it can be protected by copyrighting. Ideas alone may not be copyrighted. The expression of the idea, however, might be copyrighted, as the *Whelan* case that follows indicates.

http:// *For help with intellectual property matter or any legal matter in your community, access the attorney index at* ***http://www. martindale-hubbel lawyer locator***

Copyright owners have the exclusive right to sell, reproduce, or publish their copyrighted work for their lifetime plus 70 years, if the copyright arose *after* January 1, 1978. If someone wishes to use another's copyrighted material, he or she must obtain permission from the copyright owner. (The copyright term is 95 years for corporations if the copyright arose after January 1, 1978.) Copyrighted material used without permission is an infringement. Damages can be obtained from infringers, but no damages are allowed unless a © copyright symbol is on the material.

Copyright law is federal so if a person copyrights something, that protection is effective for the entire United States. Such protection makes it illegal for someone else to *copy* another's copyrighted material. However, if someone else *independently* develops exactly the same thing—admittedly, a highly unlikely occurrence—that is made without copying, it, too, could theoretically be copyrighted. This last point is highly academic because the likelihood of two authors writing the same song is remote.

Copyright protection has loopholes. For example, 51 years after an author dies, the copyrighted matter may be used without paying a royalty. Also, copying copyrighted material is allowed if done for "fair use." Fair use includes instruction, research, and criticism. *Whelan Associates v. Jaslow Dental Laboratory* holds that under some circumstances a custom computer program can be copyrighted.

Whelan Associates, Inc. v. Jaslow Dental Laboratory, Inc.

U.S. Court of Appeals Third Circuit
797 F.2d 1222 (1986)

Background and Facts:

Appellant Jaslow Dental Laboratory, Inc. is a Pennsylvania corporation in the business of manufacturing dental prosthetics and devices. Appellant Dentcom, Inc. is a Pennsylvania corporation in the business of developing and marketing computer programs for use by dental laboratories. Dentcom was formed out of the events that gave rise to this suit. Individual appellants Edward Jaslow and his son Rand Jaslow are officers and shareholders in both Jaslow Lab and Dentcom. Plaintiff-appellee Whelan Associates, Inc. is also a Pennsylvania corporation, engaged in the business of developing and marketing custom computer programs.

Jaslow Lab, like any other small or medium-sized business of moderate complexity, has significant bookkeeping and administrative tasks. . . .

Although Rand Jaslow had not had extensive experience with computers, he believed that the business operations of Jaslow Lab could be made more efficient if they were computerized. . . .

A few months later, . . . Rand Jaslow hired the Strohl Systems Group, Inc., a small corporation that developed custom-made software to develop a program that would run on Jaslow Lab's new IBM Series One computer and take care of the Jaslow's business needs. Jaslow Lab and Strohl entered into an agreement providing that Strohl would design a system for Jaslow Lab's needs and that after Strohl had installed the system Strohl could market it to other dental laboratories. Jaslow Lab would receive a 10% royalty on all such sales. The person at Strohl responsible for the Jaslow Lab account was Elaine Whelan, an experienced programmer who was an officer and half-owner of Strohl.

Ms. Whelan's first step was to visit Jaslow Lab and interview Rand Jaslow and others to learn how the laboratory worked and what its needs were. She also visited other dental laboratories and interviewed people there, so that she would better understand the layout, workflow, and administration of dental laboratories generally. After this education into the ways of dental laboratories, and Jaslow Lab, in particular, Ms. Whelan wrote a program called Dentalab for Jaslow Lab. Dentalab was written in a computer language known as EDL (Event Driven Language), so that it would work with IBM Series One machines. The program was completed and was operative at Jaslow Lab about March 1979.

Presumably with an eye towards exploiting the economic potential of the Dentalab program, Ms. Whelan left Strohl in November, 1979, to form her own business, Whelan Associates, Inc., which acquired Strohl's interest in the Dentalab program. Shortly thereafter, Whelan Associates entered into negotiations with Jaslow Lab for Jaslow Lab to be Whelan Associates' sales representative for the Dentalab program. Whelan Associates and Jaslow Lab entered into an agreement on July 30, 1980, according to which Jaslow Lab agreed to use its "best efforts and to act diligently in the marketing of the Dentalab package," and Whelan Associates agreed to "use its best efforts and to act diligently to improve and augment the previously successfully designed Dentalab package." The agreement stated that Jaslow Lab would receive 35 percent of the gross price of any programs sold and 5 percent of the price of any modifications to the programs. The agreement was for one year and was then terminable by either party on 30-days' notice.

The parties' business relationship worked successfully for two years. During this time, as Rand Jaslow became more familiar with computer programming, he realized that because Dentalab was written in EDL it could not be used on computers that many of the smaller dental prosthetics firms were using. Sensing a market for a program that served essentially the same function as Dentalab, Rand Jaslow began in May or June of 1982 to develop in his spare time a program in the BASIC language for such computers. The Dentcom PC program, when completed, became the alleged copyright infringer in this suit.

It appears that Rand Jaslow was sanguine about the prospects of his program for smaller computers. After approximately a year of work, on May 31, 1983, his attorney sent a letter to Whelan Associates giving one month notice of termination of the agreement between Whelan Associates and Jaslow Lab. The letter stated that Jaslow Lab considered itself to be the exclusive marketer of the Dentalab program which, the letter stated, "contains valuable trade secrets of Jaslow Dental Laboratory." The letter concluded with a thinly veiled threat to Whelan Associates: "I . . . look for your immediate response confirming that you will respect the rights of Jaslow and not use or disclose to others the trade secrets of Jaslow."

Approximately two months later, on about August 1, Edward and Rand Jaslow, Paul Mohr, and Joseph Cerra formed defendant-appellant Dentcom to sell the Dentcom program. At about the same time, Rand Jaslow and Jaslow Lab employed a professional computer programmer, Jonathan Novak, to complete the Dentcom program. The program was soon finished, and Dentcom proceeded to sell it to dental prosthetics companies that had personal computers. Dentcom sold both the Dentalab and Dentcom programs, and advertised the Dentcom program as "a new version of the Dentalab computer system."

Despite Jaslow Lab's May 31 letter warning Whelan Associates not to sell the Dentalab program, Whelan Associates continued to market Dentalab, which precipitated the present litigation. . . .

Body of Opinion

The elements of a copyright infringement action—To prove that its copyright has been infringed, Whelan Associates must show two things: that it owned the copyright on Dentalab, and that Rand Jaslow copied Dentalab in making the Dentcom program. Although it was disputed below, the district court determined, and it is not challenged here, that Whelan Associates owned the copyright to the Dentalab program. We are thus concerned only with whether it has been shown that Rand Jaslow copied the Dentalab program. . . .

It is well, though recently, established that copyright protection extends to a program's source and object codes. In this case, however, the district court did not find any copying of the source or object codes, nor did the plaintiff allege such copying. Rather, the district court held that the Dentalab copyright was infringed because the *overall structure* of Dentcom was substantially similar to the overall structure of Dentalab. The question therefore arises whether mere similarity in the overall structure of programs can be the basis for a copyright infringement, or, put differently, whether a program's copyright protection covers the structure of the program or only the program's literal elements, *i.e.*, its source and object codes.

Title 17 U.S.C. §102(a)(1) extends copyright protection to "literary works," and computer programs are classified as literary works for the purposes of copyright. The copyrights of other literary works can be infringed even when there is no substantial similarity between the works' literal elements. One can violate the copyright of a play or book by copying its plot or plot devices. . . . Defendants contend, however, that what is true of other literary works is not true of computer programs. They assert two principal reasons, which we consider in turn.

A. Section 102(b) and the dichotomy between idea and expression—It is axiomatic that copyright does not protect ideas, but only expressions of ideas. This rule, first enunciated in *Baker v. Selden* (1879), has been repeated in numerous cases. ("Unlike a patent, a copyright gives no exclusive right to the art disclosed; protection is given only to the expression of the idea—not the idea itself." The rule has also been embodied in statute. Title 17 U.S.C. §102(b) (1982) states:

> In no case does copyright protection for an original work of authorship extend to any idea, procedure, process, system, method of operation, concept, principle, or discovery, regardless of the form in which it is described, explained, illustrated, or embodied in such work.

The legislative history of this section, adopted in 1976, makes clear that §102(b) was intended to express the idea-expression dichotomy.

Defendants argue that the structure of a computer program is, by definition, the idea and not the expression of the idea, and therefore that the structure cannot be protected by the program copyright. Under the defendants' approach, any other decision would be contrary to §102(b). We divide our consideration of this argument into two parts. First, we examine the caselaw concerning the distinction between idea and expression, and derive from it a rule for distinguishing idea from expression in the context of computer programs. We then apply that rule to the facts of this case.

1. *A rule for distinguishing idea from expression in computer programs*—It is frequently difficult to distinguish the idea from the expression thereof. No less an authority than Learned Hand, after a career that included writing some of the leading copyright opinions, concluded that the distinction will "inevitably be *ad hoc*."

We begin our analysis with the case of Baker v. Selden, which, in addition to being a seminal case in the law of copyright generally, is particularly relevant here because, like the instant case, it involved a utilitarian work, rather than an artistic or fictional one. In *Baker v. Selden,* the plaintiff Selden obtained a copyright on his book, "Selden's Condensed Ledger, or Bookkeeping Simplified," which described a new, simplified system of accounting. Included in the book were certain "blank forms," pages with ruled lines and headings, for use in Selden's accounting system. Selden alleged that Baker had infringed Selden's copyright by making and selling accounting books that used substantially the same system as Selden's and that reproduced Selden's blank forms. No one disputed that Baker had the right to use and promulgate Selden's system of accounting, for all parties agreed that the system could not be copyrighted, although the Court opined that it might be patentable. Nor did the parties dispute that the text of Baker's book on accounting did not infringe Selden's copyright. The dispute centered on whether Selden's blank forms were part of the method (idea) of Selden's book, and hence non-copyrightable, or part of the copyrightable text (expression).

In deciding this point, the Court distinguished what was protectable from what was not protectable as follows:

> [W]here the art [*i.e.*, the method of accounting] it teaches cannot be used without employing the methods and diagrams used to illustrate the book, or such as are similar to them, such methods and diagrams are to be considered as necessary incidents to the art, and given to the public.

Applying this test, the Court held that the blank forms were necessary incidents to Selden's method of accounting, and hence were not entitled to any copyright protection.

The Court's test in *Baker v. Selden* suggests a way to distinguish idea from expression. Just as *Baker v. Selden* focused on the end sought to be achieved by Selden's book, the line between idea and expression may be drawn with reference to the end sought to be achieved by the work in question. In other words, *the purpose or function of a utilitarian work would be the work's idea, and everything that is not necessary to that purpose or function would be part of the expression of the idea.*

Although the economic implications of this rule are necessarily somewhat speculative, we nevertheless believe that the rule would advance the basic purpose underlying the idea/expression distinction, "the preservation of the balance between competition and protection reflected in the patent and copyright laws." As we stated above, *see supra* at 1231, among the more significant costs in computer programming are those attributable to developing the structure and logic of the program. The rule proposed here, which allows copyright protection beyond the literal computer code, would provide the proper incentive for programmers by protecting their most valuable efforts, while not giving them a stranglehold over the development of new computer devices that accomplish the same end.

The principal economic argument used against this position—used, that is, in support of the position that programs' literal elements are the only parts of the programs protected by the copyright law—is that computer programs are so intricate, each step so dependent on all of the other steps, that they are almost impossible to copy except literally, and that anyone who attempts to copy the structure of a program without copying its literal elements must expend a tremendous amount of effort and creativity. In the words of one commentator: "One cannot simply 'approximate' the entire copyrighted computer program and create a similar operative program without the expenditure of almost the same amount of time as the original programmer expended." According to this argument, such work should not be discouraged or penalized. A further argument against our position is not economic but jurisprudential; another commentator argues that the concept of structure in computer programs is too vague to be useful in copyright cases. He too would therefore appear to advocate limiting copyright protection to programs' literal codes.

Neither of the two arguments just described is persuasive. . . .

Judgment and Result

We hold that (1) copyright protection of computer programs may extend beyond the programs' literal code to their structure, sequence, and organization, and (2) the district court's finding of substantial similarity between the Dentalab and Dentcom programs was not clearly erroneous. The judgment of the district court that defendant infringed plaintiff's copyright will therefore be affirmed.

Questions

1. Can an idea be copyrighted?
2. What must a copyright holder prove to show its copyright has been infringed?
3. Who was the copyright holder in the *Whelan* case?
4. Was there copying of the source and object codes in *Whelan*? Was the overall structure of Dentcom substantially similar to Dentalab?
5. Does giving copyright protection beyond the literal computer code encourage entrepreneurs to develop computer programs?

TRADEMARKS

Trademarks refer to any word, letter, number, design, picture, or combination to designate someone's goods. Pepsi and Coke are examples of trademarks. Trademarks can fall into one of several categories: federal statutory trademarks, common law trademarks, and state trademarks.

Federal trademarks are created when one registers the mark under the Lanham Act. This law protects the mark for twenty years for marks registered before November 16, 1989; registrations granted after November 16, 1989, have a 10-year term that is renewable.

Anyone using the trademark without authorization **infringes** the mark and is liable for an accounting to the copyright holder for profits, destruction of the infringing copies and plates, and possibly an injunction. The Lanham Act permits services to be given **service marks**. The act permits the mark to be either *on* the goods or on the packaging, displays, tags, or product labels.

http://

To view the U.S. Patent and Trademark Office, go to ***http://www.uspto.gov***

Common law trademarks are created by use long enough so that the public associates the producer with that particular mark. Common law marks last as long as they are properly used. Although there is *federal* trademark law, the federal government has not preempted state law in this area. States control trademarks regarding matters solely within each state (intrastate commerce). State trademark law varies from state to state.

Public Service Co. of N.M. v. Nexus Energy Soft. illustrates an alleged federal trademark infringement where both firms compete on the Internet.

Public Service Co. of N.M. v. Nexus Energy Software, Inc.

U.S. District Court (D. Mass.)
36 F.Supp.2d 436 (1999)

Background and Facts:

Plaintiff Public Service Co. of New Mexico (PNM) sued Nexus Energy Software, Inc., because of Nexus's use of the mark "eNERGYplace" and the domain name "energyplace.com." PNM claims that Nexus's use of these marks infringes its service mark "Energy Place," Federal Registration No. 2,181,294.

PNM is a publicly traded utility company operating in New Mexico. In 1996, PNM developed its Energy Place information service. This service is a consumer hotline that, among other things, directs customers to vendors who supply energy efficient products. PNM's registration of "Energy Place" states that the use of the mark is for:

> . . . providing information services regarding the most efficient and cost-effective use of energy resources; providing energy audits for industrial, commercial, and residential consumers; energy consulting services; managing energy consumption for industrial and commercial consumers; promoting public awareness for the need for more efficient and cost-effective use of energy resources. . .

Energy Place operates on the Internet where it has received inquiries from throughout the United States. In addition to its Internet site, Energy Place advertises through television, radio, and the mail.

Nexus is a Massachusetts company founded in 1997. In April 1998, Nexus began operation of its Internet site, which offers consumers various services to analyze their energy needs. Nexus uses the mark "eNERGYplace" in connection with its site. Shortly thereafter, Nexus sought trademark protection for its "eNERGYplace" mark. In July 1998, PNM notified Nexus of its own mark "Energy Place"; one month after the Patent and Trademark Office (PTO) denied Nexus's trademark application citing the likelihood of confusion with PNM's mark. After settlement negotiations between the parties broke down, PNM filed this suit for a preliminary injunction against Nexus's use of the mark.

Body of Opinion

District Judge Harrington

To determine whether the plaintiff is likely to prevail on its claim of trademark infringement, the court must determine: 1) whether the trademark is valid; and 2) whether Nexus has infringed the mark. The court finds that PNM is likely to succeed on both points.

First, the court finds that Nexus is unlikely to succeed on its claim that PNM's trademark is invalid because it is generic or descriptive and therefore rules that the trademark is valid. Terms eligible for trademark protection lie on a spectrum of distinctiveness: on one end of the spectrum are generic terms that are not eligible for trademark protection; in the middle of the spectrum are descriptive terms that can be protected only if they have acquired a secondary meaning; at the far end of the spectrum are suggestive, arbitrary, or fanciful terms that are eligible for trademark without proof of secondary meaning. . . . Nexus argues that the term "Energy Place" is generic or, at most, descriptive.

The court's analysis begins with the fact that PNM's mark is registered, and, thus, is entitled to a presumption of validity. . . . This presumption "entitles the plaintiff to a presumption that its registered trademark is not merely descriptive or generic, or, if merely descriptive, is accorded secondary meaning." . . . Nexus can rebut this presumption by showing that the term is a generic name for goods or services or that the term is descriptive and has not acquired secondary meaning.

Nexus has produced no evidence showing that "Energy Place" is a generic term for consumer service relating to energy information, products, and services. The question of whether a term is generic is one of fact: do consumers associate the term with the product rather than the brand of a product? . . . Nexus' numerous exhibits indicate that many power companies have mailing addresses that include the term "Energy Place" and that some corporations have used energy place in their name, but this does not demonstrate that "Energy Place" is the generic term used by consumers for sites where they can find information regarding energy information, products, and services.

Having found that the term "Energy Place" is not a generic name for sites where consumers can find information regarding energy information, products, and services, the court must still address whether the term is merely "descriptive" of the product—in which case the trademark would be invalid without a showing of secondary meaning—or whether the term is suggestive, in which case the trademark is valid without any showing of secondary meaning. The court finds that the term "Energy Place" is "suggestive," and, thus, that the trademark is valid.

"A term is suggestive if it requires imagination, thought, and perception to reach a conclusion as to the nature of goods. A term is descriptive if it forthwith conveys an immediate idea of the ingredients, qualities, or characteristics of the goods." . . . Trademark law limits the protection accorded merely descriptive terms because they are a poor means of distinguishing between competing services and because descriptive terms are often necessary for a company to describe its services to consumers. . . . Given the wealth of synonyms in the English language, such concerns are reduced when the term is merely suggestive. . . .

Although the term "Energy Place" suggests that it is a place related to energy, it does not convey an immediate idea of the ingredients, qualities, or characteristics of the services PNM offers. . . . Moreover, competitors are left with a variety of terms to describe their competing services, one example being energy information services. Consequently, the court finds that the term "Energy Place" is not "merely descriptive," and that the trademark is valid.

The court also finds that Nexus' use of the mark "eNERGYplace" and the domain name "energyplace.com" likely infringes PNM's trademark. The essential element of a trademark infringement claim is likelihood of confusion. In assessing likelihood of confusion, the following factors guide the court: the similarity of the marks; the similarity of the goods; the relationship between the parties' advertising; the classes of prospective customers; evidence of actual confusion; the defendant's intent in adopting its mark; and the strength of the plaintiff's mark. . . .

In analyzing the above factors the court concludes that on balance they support a finding of likelihood of confusion:

1. Similarity of Marks: The two marks look virtually identical and sound identical.
2. Similarity of Services: Although there are some differences in the services offered, both parties offer consumers information relating to energy services.
3. Channels of Trade: Both parties compete on the Internet. Both parties are trying to lure the same customers, although there are some differences in the services offered and in the geographical regions served—PNM serves primarily New Mexico, while Nexus serves primarily customers in states that have deregulated their energy supplier (generally the Northeast).
4. Nexus's intent in adopting its Mark: Nexus apparently adopted its mark with no knowledge of PNM's mark; it has, however, knowingly continued to use PNM's trademark since July of 1998.
5. Evidence of Actual Confusion: PNM demonstrated that consumers trying to reach PNM's "Energy Place" site on the Internet are likely to be directed to a page that initially displays the term "eNERGYplace" that then fades to "eNERGYguide." Furthermore, information on this page tells consumers that the new name for "eNERGYplace" is "eNERGYguide."
6. Strength of PNM's Mark: PNM's mark is sufficiently distinct to warrant protection—it is registered, it has been used for over two years, and PNM has invested in various types of advertising of its mark, thus creating some goodwill.

In balance, the court finds that it is reasonably probable that PNM would succeed in proving a likelihood of confusion between its mark and Nexus's mark. . . .

Judgment and Result

The term "Energy Place" was not "merely descriptive," and the utility's trademark in that term was valid. Nexus's use of the mark "eNERGYplace" and the domain name "energyplace.com" likely infringed PNM's "Energy Place" trademark, warranting issuance of a preliminary injunction stopping Nexus's use of its mark and all variants of the terms that differ only in capitalization or italics and the domain name "energyplace.com" within 30 days of this order.

Questions

1. In determining whether PNM's trademark was valid, how important is its characterization as "generic"? Is it better for a trademark claimant that its mark is

descriptive? Can descriptive marks be valid? Does being suggestive help a descriptive mark become legally valid?
2. What value was it to PNM that its mark was already registered by the Patent and Trademark Office?
3. Once it is determined that a mark is valid, the next problem is to decide whether the other mark infringes it—that is, are the two marks likely to be confused? What were the six elements that the court of appeals relied on to resolve the "likelihood of confusion" issue in a trademark case? Does the ruling suggest that the trademark claimant must have actually have used its mark in order to claim trademark infringement?
4. Does the fact that defendant is in Massachusetts while plaintiff was thousands of miles away in New Mexico enter into the "likelihood that the parties do not compete"?
5. How can Nexus claim that it had no knowledge of plaintiff's mark if plaintiff's mark was already registered and the register is public? Wouldn't a trademark search have disclosed plaintiff's prior mark making defendant's claim that it did not know of plaintiff's prior mark at best negligent and at worst a lie?
6. Of the legal ethics noted in Chapter 1, which is/are most prominent here?

Trademark Dilution

Trademark dilution refers to the lessening of the capacity of a famous trademark to identify and distinguish goods or services, regardless of competition between the owner of the famous mark and other parties. Trademark dilution also can occur even without a likelihood of confusion, mistake, or deception between the protected mark and the allegedly diluting mark.

Trademark dilution finds its origin in a 1927 *Harvard Law Review* article written by Professor Frank I. Schechter. Schechter claimed that trademarks do more than identify the source of goods. Instead, he claimed trademarks can create consumer desire to purchase more if the marked goods are satisfying. Thus, even noncompeting goods could infringe a trademark by what is called *dilution* or a "whittling away" of the trademark by others.

In 1995 the Federal Trademark Dilution Act became law. It adopts Professor Schechter's ideas. The act only protects famous marks, based on their national recognition and the inadequate protection that the hodge-podge of state antidilution laws offer to trademark holders. To prove trademark dilution a plaintiff must establish that (1) it has a famous trademark, and (2) that defendant's use is commercial and in commerce and is likely to cause dilution.

Successful plaintiffs bringing antidilution actions may only get injunctive relief unless they can prove the defendant intended to trade on the owner's reputation or to cause dilution of the famous mark. States may also protect against dilution because the federal act does not preempt state antidilution laws. Noncommercial use of a mark is a defense to an antidilution suit.

The *Intermatic* case presents a dilution issue in the context of a cybersquatter—one who has registered an Internet domain name prior to a valid trademark holder's doing so.

Intermatic, Inc. v. Toeppen

U.S. District Court (N.D. Ill.)
947 F.Supp. 1227 (1996)

Background and Facts:

Intermatic, Inc., is a Delaware corporation having a place of business in Spring Grove, Illinois. Intermatic has been doing business under the name INTERMATIC since 1941. Intermatic has 37 offices throughout the United States and has been in business in Illinois since 1892. Intermatic manufactures and distributes a wide variety of electrical and electronic products, including computerized and programmable timers and other devices that are sold under the name and trademark INTERMATIC.

Intermatic's sales and advertising of INTERMATIC-labeled products have been continuous since the 1940s. Its products prominently bear the INTERMATIC name and trademark, and well over 100 million units have been installed in homes and businesses throughout the United States. In the last eight years, its sales in the United States have exceeded $850 million, with more than $16 million in advertising and promotional expenditures. Intermatic's co-op advertising consists of approximately 700 print ads per year, with each displaying the INTERMATIC mark. Intermatic also advertises and promotes its INTERMATIC products, marks, and name by way of tradeshows throughout the United States, magazines, point-of-purchase displays, brochures, radio, and television.

Defendant Toeppen resides in Champaign, Illinois, where he operates an Internet service provider business known as Net66. Toeppen has registered approximately 240 Internet domain names without seeking the permission from any entity that has previously used the names he registered, because he contends that no permission was or is necessary. Among the domain names he has registered are the following well-known business names:

deltaairlines.com	greatamerica.com
britishairways.com	neiman-marcus.com
crateandbarrel.com	northwest airlines.com
ramadainn.com	ussteel.com
eddiebauer.com	unionpacific.com

One of Toeppen's business objectives is to profit by the resale or licensing of these domain names, presumably to the entities who conduct business under these names.

Intermatic owns five incontestable trademark registrations issued by the U.S. Patent and Trademark Office for its INTERMATIC mark. Intermatic is the exclusive owner of the INTERMATIC trademark and trade name, with no known third party users. Prior to registering the intermatic.com domain name, Toeppen had never used the term *intermatic* for any purpose.

Domain names using the suffix ".com" are established by registration with an organization called Network Solutions, Inc. (NSI). Registration of the other available top-level domain names, "edu," "gov," and "net," is handled by other organizations. With some limitations, NSI will register any combination of up to 24 alphanumeric characters as a domain name on a first-come, first-served basis to anyone who has access to at least two domain name servers. A domain name server is a host computer with software capable of responding to domain name inquiries and accessible on a full-time basis to other computers on the Internet. Registering a domain name is the step that allows the top-level servers within the Internet to know where the domain name servers or hosts associated with those domain names are located in the Internet. The cost for a domain name registration is currently $100. Domain name service can be operated by the domain name holder or obtained from any entity with the proper computer equipment, including hundreds of Internet service providers.

Body of Opinion

Judge Williams (adopting magistrate Denlow's report and recommendation)

This case involves a dispute over the ownership of a highly prized Internet address. The issue is whether the owner of the Intermatic trademark may preclude the use of the trademark as an Internet domain name by defendant Toeppen, who had made no prior use of the Intermatic name prior to registering it as an Internet domain name. This case does not involve competing claims to the same name by parties who have actively used the same name in their businesses, such as the use of the term "United" by United Airlines, United Van Lines, United Mineworkers Union and the United Way.

Toeppen is what is commonly referred to as a cybersquatter. . . . These individuals attempt to profit from the Internet by reserving and later reselling or licensing domain names back to the companies that spent millions of dollars developing the goodwill of the trademark. While many may find patently offensive the practice of reserving the name or mark of a federally registered trademark as a domain name and then attempting to sell the name back to the holder of the trademark, others may view it as a service. Regardless of one's views as to the morality of such conduct, the legal issue is whether such conduct is illegal. Cybersquatters such as Toeppen contend that because they were the first to register the domain name through NSI it is theirs. Intermatic argues that it is entitled to protect its valuable trademark by preventing Toeppen from using "intermatic.com" as a domain name.

The practical effect of Toeppen's conduct is to enjoin Intermatic from using its trademark as its domain name on the Internet. Unlike the typical trademark dispute, where both parties are using the name simultaneously and arguing whether confusion exists, the current configuration of the Internet allows only one party to use the "intermatic.com" domain name. Because the Internet assigns the top-level domain name .com to commercial and noncommercial users, there does not currently appear to be a way in which both Intermatic and Toeppen can both use the intermatic.com name.

Congress and the states have been slow to respond to the activities of the cybersquatters. Some commentators take an extremely dim view of their activities. . . .

However, becoming rich does not make one's activity necessarily illegal. Speculation and arbitrage have a long history in this country....

Section 43(c) of the Lanham Act, also known as the Federal Trademark Dilution Act of 1995 (Act) became effective on January 16, 1996.... The new law benefits only "famous" trademarks. The "federal dilution statute is necessary because famous marks ordinarily are used on a nationwide basis and dilution protection is currently only available on a patch-quilt system of protection, in that only approximately 25 states have laws that prohibit trademark dilution."...

In order to state a cause of action under the Act a party must show that the mark is famous and that the complainant's [sic: probably meant "defendant's"] use is commercial and in commerce which is likely to cause dilution. The statute defines the term "dilution" to mean "the lessening of the capacity of a famous mark to identify and distinguish goods or services, regardless of the presence or absence of 1) competition between the owner of the famous mark and other parties, or 2) likelihood of confusion, mistake, or deception."...

As a matter of law the court finds that the Intermatic mark is famous within the meaning of [the act].... Therefore since Intermatic has established that its mark is famous, it need only show that Toeppen's use is a commercial use in commerce and that by his use dilution will likely occur.

Toeppen argues that there has been no violation of the Federal Trademark Dilution Act because his use of the Intermatic mark is not a commercial use. Intermatic asserts that Toeppen's use is commercial because the Internet designation ".com" is short for commercial and Toeppen used "intermatic.com" in connection with the sale of a computer software program.

The use of the first level domain designation ".com" does not in and of itself constitute a commercial use. The Internet is constantly changing and evolving. Currently the ".com" designation is the only one available for both commercial and private use. In the future perhaps other first level domain designations will be available solely for private or commercial uses. However, the court is not here to set policy guidelines for the Internet, but, rather, the court must apply the law to the Internet as it exists today. Therefore, the court holds that the ".com" designation alone does not establish commercial use.

...Toeppen's use of "intermatic.com" in connection with the software program does not constitute a commercial use because this particular commercial use terminated prior to the passage of the Act.

Toeppen's intention to arbitrage the "intermatic.com" domain name constitutes a commercial use. At oral argument Toeppen's counsel candidly conceded that one of Toeppen's intended uses for registering the Intematic mark was to eventually sell it back to Intermatic or to some other party. Toeppen's desire to resell the domain name is sufficient to meet the "commercial use" requirement of the Lanham Act....

Toeppen's use of the Internet satisfies the "in commerce" requirement of Section 43(c)....

Toeppen's use of "intermatic.com" is likely to cause dilution of its mark. For purposes of the Act, the "term dilution means the lessening of the capacity of a famous mark to identify and distinguish goods or services, regardless of the presence or absence of 1) competition between the owner of the famous mark and other parties, or 2) likelihood of confusion, mistake, or deception."... Toeppen's conduct has caused dilution in at least two respects. First, Toeppen's registration of the intermatic.com domain name lessens the capacity of Intermatic to identify and distinguish its goods and services by means of the Internet. Intermatic is not currently free to use its mark as its domain name.... This activity clearly violates the Congressional intent of encouraging the registration and development of trademarks to assist the public in differentiating products....

Second, Toeppen's conduct dilutes the intermatic mark by using the Intermatic name on its web page.... If Toeppen were allowed to use "intermatic.com", Intermatic's name and reputation would be at Toeppen's mercy and could be associated with an unimaginable amount of messages on Toeppen's web page. "It is the same dissonance that would be produced by selling cat food under the name 'Romanoff,' or baby carriages under the name 'Aston Martin.'"...

Judgment and Result

Toeppen diluted Intermatic's trademark under the Federal Dilution Act of 1995 and was permanently enjoined from using or infringing Intermatic's mark "INTERMATIC."

Questions

1. What is a cybersquatter? Had Toeppen used the name INTERMATIC in his business prior to registering it as a domain name? What difference do you think it would it have made if he had done so?
2. If someone has a famous trademark and another registers it as an Internet domain name, who has priority as to the trademark for use on the Internet?
3. Why must a trademark be "famous" prior to its being protected under the Trademark Dilution statute? Is "intermatic" famous for purposes of the Federal Trademark Dilution Act of 1995?
4. What are the other requirements to establish trademark dilution under the federal statute?
5. In 1999, Congress enacted the Anticybersquatting Consumer Protection Act which is described in detail later this chapter in the section on Internet Law on page 347.

PATENTS[1]

Patent protection is conferred exclusively by federal rather than state law. A **patent** is a legal monopoly conferred by the government (the patentor) on the private party (the patentee). The patent entitles the patentee to exclude anyone else from making, using, or selling the patented item for a period of 20 years from the date of the application. After a patent expires, the patentee loses rights to the invention. There is a proposal to change patent protection to 17 years from time of patent conferral to bring the United States in line with other nations.

An inventor may not obtain a valid patent if the invention was in public use or on sale in the United States for more than one year prior to the filing of the patent application. An inventor's own use and sale of the invention for more than a year before the patent application is filed bars rights to a patent just as effectively as though this use and sale had been by someone else. Patent protection under U.S. law is limited to the United States and does not extend beyond its borders.

The importance of patents was recognized early in the Constitution's statement of policy directed toward "promotion of science and the useful arts." A patent is, in effect, a contract between the government and the inventor. In return for a legal monopoly, the inventor discloses his idea to the public. Further refinements of a patent can extend its life beyond the original patent's 20 years. Because the patent rights accrue to the patentee and any heirs and assigns, the patentee may assign those rights. Patents are also inheritable.

Items that can be patented under section 101 of the Patent Act include "any new and useful process, machine, manufacture, or composition of matter, or any new and useful improvement thereof." Thus the Patent Act recognizes four categories of patentable inventions under section 101: (1) machines, (2) processes, (3) composition of matter, and (4) manufacture. Machines refer to any device, apparatus, or mechanism made up of coordinated parts that when placed in motion yield an intended result. "Machine" is broadly defined. "Process" covers chemical, mechanical, or mode of treatment of matter to produce a given result. A process might, for example, change something into a different state or matter. "Composition" includes mixtures and chemical unions that can take the form of gases, solids, and fluids. "Manufacture" is a catchall category that could cover items not specifically allowed by the other three categories.

> **http://** *Recent information on technology can be found at* ***http://www.corel.com/products/lawtalk_columns/index.htm***

Even if something is a machine, process, composition of matter, or manufacture, four other requirements must be met before something can be patented: novelty, utility, disclosure, and nonobviousness. First, in the novelty requirement for patents, *novel* means that something is not found in the store of common knowledge. Novel means new. The Patent Act lays out three conditions to decide whether something is new. First, the item must not be previously patented, described in U.S. or foreign publication, or known or used by someone else in the United States. Second, the item should not have been described in anyone else's previous U.S. patent application. The third condition for deciding whether something is new is that the item must not be U.S.-made by someone else who has not tried to abandon or hide the item.

The second major requirement for obtaining a patent is that the item must be useful (have utility or beneficial use). Most commentators regard this stipulation as easily satisfied.

[1] The authors acknowledge relying on Mark Holmes, "A Primer for Patents for the General Practitioner," 50 *Texas Bar Journal* 976 (1987).

Disclosure refers to the third requirement that the inventor tell the public how the item is made, how to make it, and the best uses of it.

Finally, the nonobviousness requirement means that the item when made was not readily seen by someone possessing average skill in the area of endeavor. The idea of nonobviousness is to advance the field. The *Minnesota Mining and Manufacturing v. Lake Country Manufacturing* case examines the nonobviousness requirement of patents.

Violation of Someone's Patent: Infringement

Infringement occurs when someone uses someone else's patent without permission. Infringement suits are brought only in federal court. One way for someone to avoid a patent infringement suit and still use the patented item is to obtain a **patent license** from the patent holder, which typically involves paying a royalty to the patentee.

The recovery that one can receive after proving patent infringement can be huge. However, the litigation costs to an individual inventor can "wipe out" most of any patent recovery. A large corporation can contest an inventor's patent for years during which time the clock on the patent is ticking away. Professor Kearns, a Wayne State University engineering professor, was able to recover millions of dollars from automobile manufacturers for infringement of his invention: the intermittent windshield wiper for autos. But was Kearns able to convince a court to "extend" his patent for a period equal to that during which auto makers challenged his patent? The *Kearns v. Chrysler Corp.* case provides an answer.

Kearns v. Chrysler Corp.

U.S. Court of Appeals (Fed. Cir.)
32 F.3d 1541 (1994)

Background and Facts:

In 1982, Kearns filed an action against Chrysler alleging infringement of U.S. patents 3,351,836, 3,564,374, 3,602,790, and 3,581,178, all relating to electronic intermittent windshield wipers (IWWs) for use in automobile vehicles. At the time the suit was filed, Kearns had three similar suits pending against other automobile manufacturers and distributors involving the same patents.

On October 22, 1982, proceedings in the Chrysler action were stayed pending resolution of the earlier filed suits. The stay was instituted pursuant to Chrysler's stipulation that it would be "bound by the judgment as to the validity of . . . U.S. patents Nos. . . ." in either Ford, Wood Motors, or SWF, whichever was the last to be adjudicated. The stipulation expressly provided, however, that Chrysler would "not be bound by any consent judgment."

In 1989, shortly before the Ford case went to trial, Chrysler renewed its stipulation regarding the issues of invalidity and unenforceability. Subject to continuation of the court-ordered stay, Chrysler agreed to be "bound by the judgment (excluding a consent judgment) in the *Kearns v. Ford* case, . . . as to the validity and enforceability of the patents involved in that action that are also involved in this action. . . .

The liability phase of the Ford case commenced on January 3, 1990. . . . On March 9, 1990, the district court entered partial judgment that the specified claims were valid, enforceable, and infringed by Ford. . . .

The damage phase of Ford was tried . . . in April 1990. The jury was unable to reach a unanimous verdict and a second trial on damages was held in July 1990. A second jury . . . returned a unanimous verdict in favor of Kearns awarding $5,163,842 for the period from April 3, 1978 through 1988. . . . Although damages for the period from 1972 to April 3, 1978 remained in dispute, Ford and Kearns eventually reached a settlement as to the total amount of liability. . . .

The Chrysler case returned to active status in early 1991. On February 20, 1991, the district court issued a pretrial order stating that the issues to be adjudicated at trial concerned "infringement, damages, and willfulness." On May 3, 1991, Chrysler filed a motion to have the pretrial order modified to add patent validity as an issue for trial. In support of its motion, Chrysler argued that the pretrial stipulations . . . did not bar Chrysler from challenging the patents. . . . Chrysler claimed that because the final judgment in *Ford* was entered pursuant to a settlement agreement between Ford and

Kearns, it was a "consent judgment" within the meaning of the stipulations.

The district court rejected Chrysler's argument noting that although a settlement had been reached in *Ford* on the issue of damages, the issue of validity was "hotly" contested by the parties at trial, resulting in a unanimous jury verdict and a final judgment in favor of Kearns....

By court order, the Chrysler action was split into separate jury trials on the issues of liability and damages. On December 10, 1991, the jury returned verdicts that Chrysler's accused IWW circuits, designated the "1977 Circuit" and the "1980 Circuit," infringed Kearns patents. On June 11, 1992, the same jury returned a verdict that Chrysler's infringement was not willful and assessed a reasonable royalty of $.90 per unit for a total of 12,564,107 infringing units. Pursuant to the jury's verdicts, the district court entered final judgment in favor of Kearns in the amount of $18,740,465.43, including prejudgment interest and costs.... Both Chrysler and Kearns appealed.

Body of Opinion

Circuit Judge Lourie

...Shortly before trial, Kearns expanded his claim for relief to include injunctive relief. Kearns believed that Chrysler's infringement deprived him of the "full value" of his patents during their respective terms by effectively extinguishing his exclusive right to sell his patented IWW systems to automobile manufacturers. Kearns urged that Chrysler should be enjoined from manufacturing infringing IWW systems for a period of sufficient duration "to put him in [a] position where the harm [caused by] past infringement during the terms of the patents in suit is rectified." The district court refused to grant such relief because the patents had already expired. The court concluded that "there is nothing in statute or common law giving Kearns the right to an injunction against practicing the disclosures in an expired patent."

In arguing that the district court erred in denying him post-expiration relief, Kearns claims that the $11 million damage award is not adequate to compensate him for the loss he sustained as a result of Chrysler's infringement. Kearns contends that Chrysler's infringement stripped him of "exclusive time" over his patents in violation of his rights under the U.S. Constitution and the patent laws, and that he is entitled to have that time restored to him. That contention, however, finds no basis in the statutory scheme governing patent infringement remedies.

Under the laws enacted by Congress, a patent grants the patent owner the right to exclude others from making, using, or selling the claimed invention in the United States for the term of seventeen years.... When that exclusive right is infringed, the patent owner is authorized to obtain compensation in the form of damages, measured, e.g., by lost profits or a reasonable royalty.... Moreover, the statute expressly provides for the grant of injunctions "in accordance with the principles of equity." ... In view of the fact that the principal right afforded by a patent is the "right to exclude," we have noted that "the nature of the patent grant... weighs against holding that monetary damages will always suffice to make the patentee whole." ... Indeed, while monetary relief is often the sole remedy for past infringement, it does not follow that a monetary award is also the sole remedy against future infringement." ... However, §283 relief is available only to "prevent the violations of any right secured by patent." Thus, when the rights secured by a patent are no longer protectable by virtue of expiration or unenforceability, entitlement to injunctive relief becomes moot because such relief is no longer available....

An invention claimed in a patent passes into the public domain upon termination of the patent's 17-year statutory term. Because the rights flowing from a patent exist only for the term of the patent, there can be no infringement once the patent expires. Here, all the asserted patents expired before the commencement of trial. Therefore, Kearns "can no longer obtain injunctive relief with respect to [those patents]." ... Granting the relief requested by Kearns would impermissibly extend the statutory term beyond that established by Congress. Congress has the power to provide for patent term extension in appropriate circumstances... but it has not done so here and we cannot legislate in its place.... The expiration of Kearns' patents precludes the grant of injunctive relief and the judgment for $11 million in damages thus amounts to adequate and full compensation under the law for Chrysler's past violation of his patent rights....

We sympathize with Kearns' complaint that his patents have expired without his ever being able to exclude others from practice of his invention, especially since he is an individual inventor contending with a multitude of giant corporations. While it is of course the essence of a patent that it provides the right to exclude, the same statute that grants that right also permits other parties, including accused infringers, to challenge the validity of a patent and to contest a charge of infringement.... Moreover, entitlement to an injunction implementing the right to exclude, as compared with only assessing damages against an infringer, in not absolute even during the life of a patent, but is discretionary.... Here, because Kearns' patents have expired, the district court certainly did not abuse its discretion in denying injunctive relief.

It is unfortunate that Kearns feels that he never enjoyed an exclusive status under his patents, but that is simply a consequence of the right of others to challenge his patents and the fact that his patents have expired. The patent statute does provide for increased damages and attorney fees as additional relief for aggrieved patent owners...but Kearns did not persuade the district court that he was entitled to such relief.

We therefore conclude that the district court properly granted summary judgment in favor of Chrysler on Kearns' request for post-expiration injunctive relief.

Kearns argues that the district court erred in granting Chrysler's motion for summary judgment on Kearn's claim for damages based on lost profits, rather than a reasonable royalty. A patent owner bears the burden of proof on damages.... Kearns has not carried that burden with respect to lost profits.

A lost profits award is appropriate only if the patent owner can prove there was a reasonable probability that "but for" the infringement, it would have made the infringer's sales.... Where, as here, a patent owner fails to prove lost profits, the court is left with no alternative but to have damages determined on the basis of a reasonable royalty....

Judgment and Result

Kearns was given no court order that would, in effect, have extended the life of his patent beyond the statutory period of 17 years (recently extended to 20 years). Evidence supported the finding of infringement and Kearns was entitled to a reasonable royalty, but not lost profits. Chrysler lost on the royalty issues. Kearns lost on the lost profit and post-patent injunctive relief issues.

Questions

1. Did Kearns recover lost profits from Chrysler? A reasonable royalty?
2. What was Kearns's argument that he was entitled to injunctive relief beyond the statutory period from the time he was granted the patent, that is, beyond 17 years (now 20 years)? Why did he fail on this issue? Is that answer troubling in light of the "little, but brilliant, guy" tied up in litigation with "corporate giants" for the period of his patent who was never able to exploit it to the extent he otherwise would have?
3. How much did Kearns recover from Chrysler? A footnote [omitted] pointed out that Kearns "fired several of his attorneys and attempted to conduct massive multiple suits pro se." Recall pro se suits mean Kearns acted as his own attorney. A newspaper account reported that Kearns spent almost all of his recoveries on attorney fees and actually netted little if anything from this litigation. How might the patent laws be amended to rectify this apparent injustice to inventors? Or was it injustice?
4. Why was the claim against Ford relevant in Kearns's suit against Chrysler?

In the next patent case, *Diamond v. Diehr,* the U.S. Supreme Court decided that computer programs meeting certain criteria are patentable.

Diamond v. Diehr

U.S. Supreme Court
450 U.S. 175 (1981)

Background and Facts:

Respondents filed a patent application claiming invention for a process for molding raw, uncured synthetic rubber into cured precision products. While it was possible, by using well-known time, temperature, and cure relationships, to calculate by means of an established mathematical equation when to open the molding press and remove the cured product, according to respondents the industry had not been able to measure precisely the temperature *inside* the press, thus making it difficult to make the necessary computations to determine the proper cure time. Respondents characterized their contribution to the art to reside in the process of constantly measuring the temperature inside the mold and feeding the temperature measurements into a computer that repeatedly recalculates the cure time by use of the mathematical equation and then signals a device to open the press at the proper time. The patent examiner rejected respondents' claims on the ground that they were drawn to nonstatutory subject matter under 35 U.S.C. §101, which provides for the issuance of patents to "[w]hoever invents or discovers any new and useful *process*, machine, manufacture, or composition of matter, or any new and useful improvement thereof...." The Patent and Trademark Office Board of Appeals agreed, but the Court of Customs and Patent Appeals reversed.

Body of Opinion

Justice Rehnquist

We have before us today only the question of whether respondents' claims fall within the §101 categories of possibly patentable subject matter. We view respondents' claims as nothing more than a process for molding rubber products and not as an attempt to patent a mathematical formula. We recognize, of course, that when a claim recites a mathematical formula (or scientific principle or phenomenon of nature), an inquiry must be made into whether the claim is seeking patent protection for that formula in the abstract. A mathematical formula as such is not accorded the protection of our patent laws, and this principle cannot be circumvented by attempting to limit the use of the formula to a particular technological environment. Similarly, insignificant postsolution activity will not transform an unpatentable principle into a patentable process. To hold otherwise would allow a competent draftsman to evade the recognized limitations on the type of subject matter eligible for patent protection. On the other hand, when a claim containing a mathematical formula implements or applies that formula in a structure or process which, when considered as a whole, is performing a function which the patent laws were designed to protect (e.g., transforming or reducing an article to a different state or thing), then the claim satisfies the requirements of §101. Because we do not view respondents' claims as an attempt to patent a mathematical formula, but rather to be drawn to an industrial process for the molding of rubber products, we affirm the judgment of the Court of Customs and Patent Appeals.

Judgment and Result

Respondents' claims recited subject matter that was eligible for patent protection under §101.

> (a) For purposes of §101, a "process" is "an act, or a series of acts, performed upon the subject-matter to be transformed and reduced to a different state or thing. If new and useful, it is just as patentable as is a piece of machinery. . . .
>
> (b) While a mathematical formula, like a law of nature, cannot be the subject of a patent, respondents do not seek to patent a mathematical formula, but instead seek protection for a process of curing synthetic rubber. Although their process employs a well-known mathematical equation, they do not seek to pre-empt the use of that equation, except in conjunction with all of the other steps in their claimed process. . . . The questions of whether a particular invention meets the "novelty" requirements of 35 U.S.C.§102 or the "nonobviousness" requirements of §103 do not affect the determination of whether the invention falls into a category of subject matter that is eligible for patent protection under §101.
>
> (c) When a claim containing a mathematical formula implements or applies the formula in a structure or process which, when considered as a whole, is performing a function which the patent laws were designed to protect (e.g., transforming or reducing an article to a different state or thing), then the claim satisfies §101's requirements.

Questions

1. When Congress amended the Patent Act in 1952 by replacing the word *art* with *process*, did Congress intend to expand or reduce the number of patentable items? Does this interpretation reflect a current legal norm, that is, the promotion of entrepreneurship?
2. Could Einstein have obtained a patent on his famous theory of relativity, $E = MC^2$? Why?
3. Are math formulas patentable? Would a math formula that is part of a process for molding raw, uncured synthetic rubber into cured precision products be patentable?

INTERNET, E-MAIL, AND SOME ASPECTS OF LAW AFFECTING THEM[2]

Few technologies have had the impact of the Internet (also known as the World Wide Web or "www") and the different, but also computer-associated, e-mail. Although the Internet was first developed in the 1960s in the United States so that defense contractors could communicate with each other, the Internet did not mature to the point where large numbers used it until the mid to late 1980s. Today the Internet and e-mail are available to anyone anywhere on Earth with access to a computer with a modem. The media through which the "net" and e-mail operate include telephone lines, coaxial cable, and radio waves using satellite transmission.

Congress and the courts have been active in making law regulating cyberspace. In 1997 the U.S. Supreme Court in *Reno v. A.C.L.U.* invalidated two parts of the Communications Decency Act (CDA) designed to protect minors from "obscene" and "indecent" material on the Internet. In so doing the Supreme Court ruled that the First Amendment's free speech protections, with attendant possible restraints, apply

[2] The authors acknowledge reliance on articles in the "Suggested Readings" section at the end of this chapter in preparing this segment.

to the Internet. Obscene speech and child pornography are not protected by the First Amendment.

Digital Millennium Copyright Act (DMCA)

The Digital Millennium Copyright Act (DMCA) was passed on October 28, 1998, and directed to be effective October 28, 2000. Part of its principal functions are to apply federal copyright law to the internet and to create four different safe harbors (areas of non-liability) for online service providers (OSPs) from primary federal copyright liability, contributory and vicarious copyright liability (see glossary for definitions of these).

One of the major concerns leading to passage of the DMCA was potential copyright liability of OSPs, such as America On Line, and web pages offering interactive bulletin board services (BBSs). When situations arise where third parties transmit or post copyrighted materials without authorization and without the OSP or BBS's knowledge or consent, the OSP or BBS could be subjected to contributory or vicarious copyright infringement.

The DMCA recognizes four distinct internet activities: (1) storing matter; (2) linking matter; (3) providing conduit service (e-mail); and (4) caching (storing matter for a short time). Any one of these four activities by third party users could involve an OSP or BBS in copyright infringement by transmitting infringing matter using the OSP or BBS. Hence, the DMCA provides four distinct safe harbors for OSPs and BBSs for each of the four functions.

Although each safe harbor is different, several steps are needed to qualify for any of them. First, defendants must implement a policy to terminate repeat offenders; and second, defendants must design their systems to accommodate copyright protection measures. After these initial steps, elaborate measures come into play to qualify for a particular safe harbor.

Generally speaking, OSPs are not liable under the DMCA for storing and linking copyright violations of their users if the OSP lacks actual knowledge of the infringement, if the OSP derives no financial benefit from the infringement, and the OSP has notice and "take down" procedures upon actually discovering infringement by a user. Other conditions exist for caching and conduit safe harbors.

The Anticybersquatting Consumer Protection Act (ACPA). In late 1999, the ACPA became law. It allows trademark owners to sue anyone who, with a bad faith intent to profit from a mark, registers, traffics in, or uses a domain name which, at the time of its registration, is (1) identical or confusingly similar to a distinctive mark; (2) dilutive of a famous mark; or (3) is a protected trademark, word, or name. The ACPA specifies factors a court may consider in determining bad faith intent of the cybersquatter. Such factors include the trademark or other intellectual property rights of the person in the domain name, the extent the domain name consists of the legal name of the cybersquatter, the cybersquatter's prior use of the domain name in connection with a bona fide business, and the cybersquatter's intent to divert consumers from the mark owner's online location to a site accessible under the domain name that could harm, tarnish, or disparage the mark.

The Act prohibits holding someone liable as a cybersquatter if the defendant believed, with reasonable grounds, that the use of the domain name was fair or otherwise lawful. Courts may order forfeiture or cancellation of the domain name or its transfer to the mark owner in appropriate cases.

Remedies under the ACPA include injunctions, recovery of defendant's profits, actual damages, attorneys fees, and statutory damages in an amount of at least $1,000 and up to $100,000 per domain name, as the court considers just.

INTERNATIONAL PROTECTION OF INTELLECTUAL PROPERTY[3]

Protection for intellectual property rights has existed since at least the mid-1800s with passage of the Paris Convention for the Protection of Industrial Property Rights and the Berne Convention for the Protection of Literary and Artistic Works. More recent treaties such as GATT/WTO and NAFTA require that signatories provide legal protection for intellectual property such as patents, trademarks, and copyrights.

The Uruguay Round of trade negotiations resulted in an agreement known as Trade-Related Aspects of Intellectual Property. One major feature of this agreement was to broaden former WTO coverage to now require that members provide legal protections for intellectual property. WTO provisions require that members must provide for trademark registration and renewal. WTO members must also provide for patent protection. WTO also creates a uniform term for protecting patents (20 years from the date of application). In late 1995 the United States amended its patent laws to conform to the WTO patent term. Two other GATT/WTO features that will affect intellectual property are reciprocity and most favored nation (MFN) status. Reciprocity refers to one nation's according nationals from other GATT/WTO signatories the same rights (such as intellectual property protections) that it gives its own nationals. Thus a foreign manufacturer would appear to be entitled to the same rights as a domestic manufacturer. With respect to MFN, GATT/WTO members must generally give other nations the same advantages it gives to a particular nation. This provision should drive down trade barriers to foreign trade enjoying intellectual property protection (such as patents for computer chips). Trade secret protections under GATT/WTO are recognized and are referred to as *undisclosed information*.

NAFTA also has provisions directed to intellectual property protection. It requires signatory nations to establish patent protection. NAFTA also recognizes trademarks and mandates an original term of at least 10 years, which is renewable. With respect to trade secrets, NAFTA precludes governmental disclosure of certain manufacturer data obtained under regulatory authority. For example, drug manufacturers' test data turned over to regulators would not be discoverable.

In addition to WTO/GATT and NAFTA protections, the United States unilaterally provides protection for intellectual property against foreign pirating under Special 301.

CHAPTER SUMMARY

Quasi-contracts are not contracts, but, instead, are judicially imposed devices "like" ("quasi-") contracts. They are designed to prevent unjust enrichment where benefits have been conferred under circumstances where the conferee knows or should know that pay is expected. They are usually not imposed if the parties have an express or implied-in-fact contract.

Trade secrets may consist of any formula, pattern, device, or compilation of information used in one's business, giving one an opportunity to obtain an advantage over competitors who do not know or use it. Examples of trade secrets include product formulas, manufacturing processes, customer lists, and price information.

Copyright protection affords protection for works expressed in a tangible medium, such as songs, books, plays, pictures, and movies. For works created after January 1, 1978, the length of protection is the life of the author plus 70 years. The criterion for obtaining copyright protection is originality.

[3] The authors acknowledge reliance on articles in the "Suggested Readings" section at the end of this chapter in preparing this segment.

MANAGER'S ETHICAL DILEMMA

Dennis Lilly had a device that would convert raw sewage into environmentally harmless and commercially viable fertilizer. He did not have the resources to develop and market his finding. He knows that patent, trademark, and copyright protection are available, but he wonders if it is worth pursuing such protections. He has a friend, Mr. Wollin, a successful entrepreneur, who is interested in his invention. What would you advise Lilly to do prior to seeking financial assistance from Wollin?

Trademarks can arise from federal protection. Trademarks are designed to distinguish goods (or services) from competing products. Such protection is available if one complies with federal statutes. Trademark protection lasts 10 years for marks granted after November 16, 1989 and is renewable. The test for trademark infringement is likelihood of confusion, mistake, or deception.

Functional patent protection, which is distinguished from design patents, is available to protect machines, processes, composition of matter, or manufactured items. Patent protection lasts for 20 years from the date of the application. Criteria for patent protection are that the item must be new, nonobvious, utilitarian, and disclosed. If someone other than the patent holder makes, sells, or uses items having the patented invention, he or she may be subject to infringement suits.

Internet domain names can obtain federal intellectual property protection such as trademark protection. A number of federal statutes aim to protect children in various ways from Internet abuses. Privacy of Internet users is also protected in various ways.

Discussion Questions

1. A celebrity named O.J. Simpson tried to register at the federal registry his name and nickname, including "O.J. Simpson," "O.J.," and "The Juice" for use with a broad range of goods, including figurines, trading cards, sportswear, medallions, coins, and prepaid telephone cards. After the marks were approved for registration by an examiner in the U.S. Patent and Trademark Office, the marks were published in the *Official Gazette* in accordance with federal law.

   William B. Ritchie filed oppositions to registration of these marks, asserting they were not registerable on either of two statutory grounds: first, that the marks are immoral or scandalous matter and should be denied registration under s 2(a) of the Lanham Act; and second, that one of the marks is primarily merely a surname and thus not registerable under s 2(e)(4) of the Lanham Act.

   Should a U.S. Court of Appeals allow Ritchie to challenge the registration, and did he establish a reasonable belief that he would be damaged by the registration? [*Ritchie v. Simpson*, 170 F.3d 1092 (1999)]
2. Must a newspaper claiming copyright ownership in an ad it wrote for someone else give a specific and separate copyright notice in the ad? Would a copyright notice properly affixed to the newspaper as a whole cover individual ads in that newspaper? [*Eastern Pub. and Advertising, Inc. v. Chesapeake Pub. and Advertising, Inc.*, 831 F.2d 488 (4th Cir. 1987)]
3. Can a telephone directory be copyrighted? [*Southwestern Bell Media, Inc. v. Trans Western Pub., Inc.*, 670 F.Supp. 899 (D. Kan. 1987)]
4. May a court award attorney fees to the winning party in a patent infringement suit? [*Afros S.p.A. v. Krauss-Maffei Corp.*, 671 F. Supp. 1402, reargument denied 671 F. Supp. 1458 (D. Del. 1987)]
5. Was a U.S. patent on double-sided floppy disc drives which had a fixed lower head infringed by an imported device with moveable lower heads, but which were more rigid than those of prior art? [*Tandon Corp. v. U.S. International Trade Com'n*, 831 F.2d 1017 (C.A. Fed. Cir. 1987)].
6. May someone prove that a competitor's patent is invalid? [*Afros S.p.A. v. Krauss-Maffei Corp.*, 671 F. Supp. 1402, reargument denied 671 F. Supp. 1458 (D. Del. 1987)]

7. If a word is generic it may not get trademark protection. Is the term *Gear* generic as applied to clothing? [*Gear, Inc. v. L.A. Gear California, Inc.*, 670 F. Supp. 508 (S.D. N.Y. 1987)]
8. A trademark acquires a secondary meaning when it is shown that the primary significance of the term in the minds of the consuming public is the producer not the product. Is the crux of the secondary meaning doctrine that the trademark comes to identify not only the goods but the source of the goods, even though the relevant consuming public might not know the producer's name? [*Centaur Communications Ltd. v. A/S/M Communications, Inc.*, 830 F.2d 1217 (2d Cir. 1987)]
9. Was a store owner's transmission of a radio broadcast, including music, in the workplace to benefit the employees a public performance subject to copyright control? [*Merrill v. County Stores, Inc.*, 669 F. Supp. 1164 (D. N.H. 1987)]

Suggested Readings

Articles

CHAUDHRY and WALSH, "Intellectual Property Rights: Changing Levels of Protection Under GATT, NAFTA, and the EU," 30 *Columbia Journal of World Business* 80 (1995).

EISENBERG, "Public Research and Private Development: Patents and Technology Transfer in Government-Sponsored Research," 82 *Virginia Law Review* 1663 (1996).

EISENBERG, "Technology Transfer and the Genome Project: Problems With Patenting Research Tools," 2 *Risk: Health, Safety & Environment* 163 (1995).

FRIEDMAN and BUONO, "Using the Digital Millennium Copyright Act to Limit Potential Copyright Liability Online," 6 *Richmond Journal of Law and Technology* 18 (2000).

HOWE, "Patentability of Pioneering Pharmaceuticals: What's the Use?" 32 *San Diego Law Review* 819 (1995).

IDLER, "Protecting Your Right to Privacy on the Internet," 138 *Trusts & Estates* 41 (1999).

JANIS, "Rethinking Reexamination: Toward a Viable Administrative Revocation System for U.S. Patent Law," 11 *Harvard Journal of Law & Technology* 1 (1997).

JANIS, "Second Tier Patent Protection," 40 *Harvard International Law Journal* 150 (1999).

JONES, "Wet Footprints? Digital Watermarks: A Trail to the Copyright Infringer on the Internet," 26 *Pepperdine Law Review* 559 (1999).

LIKOUREZOS, "A Case of First Impression: American Indians Seek Cancellation of the Trademarked Term 'Redskins'," 78 *Journal of Patent and Trademark Office Society* 65 (1996).

MILLER, "Washington's 'Spam-Killing' Statute: Does It Slaughter Privacy in the Process?", 74 *Washington Law Review* 453 (1999).

ROTHCHILD, "Protecting the Digital Consumer: The Limits of Cyberspace Utopianism," 74 *Indiana Law Journal* 893 (1999).

SEES, "Use of Another's Trademark in a Web Page Meta-Tag: Why Liability Should Not Ensue Under the Lanham Act for Trademark Infringement," 5 *Texas Wesleyan Law Review* 99 (1999).

SCULLY, "Markman and Hilton Davis: The Federal Circuit Strikes an Awkward Balance: The Roles of the Judge and Jury in Patent Infringement Suits," 18 *Hastings Commercial and Enterprise Law Journal* 631 (1996).

UPADHYE, "Rewriting the Lanham Trademark Act to Prohibit the Importation of All Gray Market Goods," 20 *Seton Hall Legislative Journal* 59 (1996).

YOCHES, "Patent Protection for Electronic Commerce and Other Internet Applications," 2 *Journal of Internet Law* 1 (1999).

Books

FRUCHTER, HIARING, and NEWBURY, *Understanding Basic Trademark Law 1999* (1999).

HARDING and VARNEY, *eCommerce: Strategies for Success in the Digital Economy* (1999).

MODULE

4

LAW AFFECTING THE BUSINESS HUMAN RESOURCES DEPARTMENT

CHAPTER

14

COMMON LAW RULES IN EMPLOYER-EMPLOYEE RELATIONS

"QUI FACIT PER ALIUM FACIT PER SE. (A PERSON WHO ACTS THROUGH ANOTHER IS LEGALLY RESPONSIBLE JUST AS THOUGH HE OR SHE HAD ACTED PERSONALLY."

Agency Principle

POSITIVE LAW ETHICAL PROBLEMS

"But the alleged acts—even if true—certainly do not bind us, the Boy Scouts—because scout masters receive no pay from us," said Mike Malloy, a Boy Scouts of America representative who was reviewing a complaint filed by a former Boy Scout alleging that a scout master had sexually molested him years earlier.

"Ah," replied the attorney for the alleged victim, "but principals are bound by the acts of agents even if they work for nothing."

"I doubt that. But even if it is true," continued Malloy, "the Boy Scouts clearly got no benefit from such allegedly outrageous conduct. It was beyond the scope of the scout master's duties."

Should a principal be liable for a volunteer agent's sexual molestation of a person the agent was charged with supervising, or does the outrageousness of such acts remove them from the scope of the job?

This chapter begins a series dealing with employer-employee relations. Chapter 14 examines common law rules governing employers' relations with individual employees. Chapters 15 and 16 look at statutes altering or adding to some of the common law rules. Chapter 17 examines federal labor law and dealing with employees on a collective basis.

EMPLOYER-EMPLOYEE LEGAL CLASSIFICATIONS

The terms **employer** and **employee** are helpful descriptions of functional relationships, but they do not have much legal significance. Rather, the archaic-sounding labels *master-servant, principal-agent,* and *employer-independent contractor* are the legal categories for most employer-employee relations.

A **master-servant relationship** arises when a person (the "master") employs another person (the "servant") to perform physical tasks not involving the making of contracts with third persons. The task is often a menial sort, such as gardening or cleaning. The **principal-agent relationship** occurs when one person (the principal) employs another (the agent) to enter business relations (usually contracts) with third persons. It differs from the master-servant situation in that the objective of a principal-agent relationship is to establish legal relations with third persons. The http:// The Congressional website at **http://thomas.loc.gov** provides links to state law and employment classifications

master-servant relationship does not have this objective. Legal relations, however, may result through a servant's torts, which injure a third person. (Recall that torts are breaches of civil duties, such as slander or assault.)

The **employer-independent contractor relationship** results when one person (the employer) hires another (the independent contractor) to work for the employer. In this relationship, the employer does not have the right to control the means by which the independent contractor performs the work. The principal or master in the agent or servant case, however, has the right to control both the *means* by which the job is to be done and the *end* or *object* of the work. In the independent contractor relation, the employer does retain the right to control the end or object of the work. Otherwise, independent contractors could choose to do nothing if they wished—certainly not something that someone would pay another to do.

An employee could be an agent or servant with respect to one part of the job and an independent contractor with respect to another part. For example, an insurance salesperson could be an agent with respect to the representations made to prospective customers in selling insurance policies but an independent contractor when driving to see a customer. Calling an employee an agent, servant, or independent contractor does not per se establish that relationship. Rather, courts will examine the substance of the relationship to determine which relationship exists.

Who May Be Principals

The general rule is that one who has the mental capability to act on one's own behalf may be a principal.[1] Minors may be principals if they are old enough to comprehend the nature and significance of the act undertaken on their behalf. Minors may also void a contract made on their behalf, as they could if they had acted for themselves. Because legally a corporation is considered a person, corporations may be principals. Partnerships and trusts may also be principals. However, legal incompetents, such as insane people, and unincorporated associations may not be principals.

Who May Be Agents, Servants, and Independent Contractors

One may be an agent, servant, or independent contractor for another person as long as one has the mental and physical capability to perform and understand the significance of the acts undertaken. Minors may be agents unless they are too young to meet the physical or mental requirements of the task. Corporations, trusts, and partnerships may be agents. All of the aforementioned people may be agents, assuming that the principal has in some way authorized the agent to act.

Effect of Different Employer-Employee Classifications

The basic common law classifications of employees are important because, generally, legal liability is greater for the employer when the employee is classified as an agent or servant rather than as an independent contractor. The principal in a principal-agent situation and a master in a master-servant context have the right to control the agent or servant to a greater extent than does an employer in an employer-independent contractor situation.

[1] Throughout the chapter, principal is treated as synonymous with master or employer in the case of an independent contractor.

Someone who commits a crime or a tort or breaks a contract is liable. Within the concept of vicarious liability, or **respondeat superior**, if one person does something, another is legally responsible. The respondeat superior concept applies across the board to agency or master-servant relations in private enterprise or governmental contexts. It does *not* usually apply to employer-independent contractor situations, except where the independent contractor performs **nondelegable duties** or engages in ultrahazardous activities for the employer. In the field of employer-employee relations, the exact category of that relationship—principal-agent or master-servant on the one hand or employer-independent contractor on the other—plays a large role in determining the employer's liability for the employee's acts.

Before illustrating the consequences of the various employer-employee classifications, let us look at the rule that agency relationships are consensual and usually contractual. **Consensual relations** are those that are entered by mutual consent but that do not necessarily possess all of the elements of a contract. As a practical matter, most agency arrangements are contractual, because agents want payment for their services. However, a neighbor or friend doing a good deed by running an errand for a sick friend would be a **gratuitous agent** if no pay were received for such help.

The respondeat superior rules establishing vicarious liability apply to both gratuitous as well as paid servant and agents. The *Lourim v. Swensen* case presents the respondeat superior concept in the context of a gratuitous servant/agent who supervised minor children as a Boy Scout leader. Given the fact that many families today have two wage earners who often must place their minor children in day care centers, the liability implications of the *Lourim* case are tremendous. One might further extrapolate beyond day care to primary schools, secondary schools, colleges, universities, and even churches. A segment of the opinion omitted dealt with Oregon's willingness to subject churches to vicarious liability for alleged sexual abuse by priests against children who attend church functions.

Note that in *Lourim* the question arose about whether the agent's allegedly outrageous acts were "outside the scope of employment," meaning they were not done "at work" resulting in no employer liability. The Supreme Court of Oregon decided, however, that the nature of the alleged acts—sexual molestation—did not render them beyond the scope of employment.

Lourim v. Swensen

Supreme Court of Oregon
977 P.2d 1157 (1999)

Background and Facts:

This case arises out of allegations by plaintiff that he was sexually abused by his Boy Scout leader, Swensen, approximately 30 years earlier, when plaintiff was a minor. In 1995, plaintiff brought the present action against Swensen as well as the Cascade Pacific Council and Boy Scouts of America (collectively, the Boy Scouts), claiming that Swensen had sexually abused him from 1965 until 1967. The complaint alleges that between 1965 and 1967, Swensen was a volunteer Boy Scout leader, duly authorized by the Boy Scouts to act as such. As part of his volunteer duties, he was directed to fulfill the role of troop leader or assistant troop leader to plaintiff's troop.

Plaintiff and his family became close to Swensen, and Swensen was a frequent guest in their home. Swensen gained the trust and confidence of plaintiff's family as a suitable friend, guide, mentor, and role model to plaintiff, then an adolescent. By virtue of that relationship, Swensen gained the support and permission to spend substantial periods of time alone with plaintiff. Swensen also won the friendship of plaintiff himself. He was plaintiff's mentor and role model. Swensen gained the opportunity to socialize with plaintiff and to spend time alone with him and together with other boys in remote places. Swensen used his position of trust to gain opportunity to touch plaintiff physically. Eventually, Swensen committed a series of sexual assaults on plaintiff when plaintiff was a minor. Plaintiff alleges Swensen's assaults were manipulations committed in connection with his duties as troop leader.

As against the Boy Scouts, the complaint alleges that the Boy Scout organizations are vicariously liable for Swensen's tortious conduct under the doctrine of respondeat superior.

The Boy Scouts moved to dismiss the action on the grounds that both claims are time-barred and that the complaint fails to state ultimate facts sufficient to constitute a tort claim for vicarious liability based on the doctrine of respondeat superior. The trial court granted defendants' motion as to all claims. Plaintiff appealed.

On appeal the Court of Appeals affirmed the decision of the trial court. That court concluded that plaintiff's complaint states no facts from which it reasonably could be concluded that Lourim's sexual assaults on plaintiff were within the scope of his employment.

The case was then appealed to the Oregon Supreme Court.

Body of Opinion

Justice Gillette

A complaint is sufficient to state a cause of action for vicarious liability based on the doctrine of respondeat superior if the allegations that it contains, if true, would establish that the employee's acts were committed within the scope of his or her employment.... In *Chesterman v. Barmon*... this court set out three requirements that must be met to establish that an employee's conduct was within the scope of employment: 1) the conduct must have occurred substantially within the time and space limits authorized by the employment; 2) the employee must have been motivated, at least partially, by a purpose to serve the employer; 3) the act must have been of a kind that the employee was hired to perform. Applying that framework to this case, the court of appeals held that the complaint failed to state a claim because

> "...there simply are no allegations of fact that satisfy all three of the elements of vicarious liability. In particular, there are no facts from which it reasonably could be concluded that Swensen's sexual assaults were acts 'of a kind [an] employee was hired to perform.'"

...Accepting the allegations in the complaint as true and drawing all reasonable inferences in the plaintiff's favor, a jury reasonably could infer that the sexual assaults were merely the culmination of a progressive series of actions that involved the ordinary and authorized duties of a Boy Scout leader.... A jury also reasonably could infer that Swensen's performance of his duties as troop leader with respect to plaintiff and his family was a necessary precursor to the sexual abuse and that the assaults were a direct outgrowth of and were engendered by conduct that was within the scope of Swensen's employment....

Notwithstanding that conclusion, the Boy Scouts argue that dismissal of the complaint is proper on a ground not considered by the court of appeals.... They assert that the doctrine of respondeat superior is premised on the existence of a master/servant relationship which, they argue, is not adequately alleged in the present complaint. For the following reasons, we disagree.

It is well established that one can be a servant even though the service is performed gratuitously.... The relevant inquiry in determining whether a master/servant relationship exists for respondeat superior purposes is whether the master has the right to control the actions of the servant.... We must determine whether plaintiff has adequately alleged that the Boy Scouts had the right to control Swensen's actions.

The complaint alleges that "at all relevant times, Swensen was a volunteer Boy Scout leader, duly authorized by the Boy Scouts and the Cascade Pacific Council to act in that capacity" and that "as part of his volunteer duties with the Boy Scouts and the Cascade Pacific Council, Swensen was directed to fulfill the role of troop leader or assistant troop leader to plaintiff's troop."...

A jury could reasonably infer from the allegation that "Swensen was directed to fulfill the role of troop leader or assistant troop leader to plaintiff's troop" that the Boy Scouts directed his activities and, thus, that the Boy Scouts had the right to control Swensen's activities.... In this regard, although the complaint does not contain a specific allegation setting forth the typical duties of a troop leader or what, specifically, Swensen was directed to do as a Boy Scout leader, such an allegation is unnecessary.

Judgment and Result

The Supreme Court of Oregon held that the plaintiff stated a cause of action in his complaint and if he could later prove at trial the allegations in his complaint, he could recover against Cascade Pacific Council and Boy Scouts of America for the alleged actions of the Boy Scout leader on grounds of respondeat superior.

Questions

1. How could the Boy Scouts of America be liable for actions of its scout master? Can a principal be liable for acts of an agent? What is the reason for the respondeat superior principle? Is it a new idea?
2. Must the person who injures the third party be a paid employee of the person sued under respondeat superior? Must the injured party work for the employer sued?
3. What tests did the court enunciate to determine whether the matter was within the scope of employment? Given the inflammatory nature of the alleged

actions of the agent/servant (scout master) here, how could it rationally be claimed that a scout master's sexually molesting a boy scout could ever be done for the benefit of the Boy Scouts of America?

4. What if the Boy Scouts could show that the alleged sexual assaults occurred at the scout master's home and not on Boy Scout premises, do you think this evidence removes the liability of the Boy Scouts on a respondeat liability basis? Obviously, given the nature of the alleged acts, no one other than the plaintiff and Swensen would have been present. Does the lack of witnesses present a problem in establishing that a wrong was committed? Does the fact that 30 years had elapsed since the alleged occurrence further complicate the matter? Why did the victim wait so long to bring this action? How can a suit 30 years later remedy any harm that might have been done to the plaintiff?
5. Comment on the paradox involved when masters are sued for intentional torts allegedly committed by their servants: That is, the more outrageous the alleged act of the servant, the more likely it is that the alleged act is beyond the scope of employment and the master is not liable. Note that in the *Lourim* case, it was never proven at this stage in the proceedings that the Boy Scout leader did anything improper.
6. Is respondeat superior a strict liability concept?
7. In a part of the opinion omitted, the Supreme Court of Oregon stated that the child abuse claim was not time barred even though it was raised 30 years after the alleged abuse. The court stated that the statute of limitations extended to "three years from when the plaintiff discovered the causal connection between the child abuse and his injuries." Might not psychological development injuries be undiscovered until a person entered professional counseling years after the child abuse thus justifying the extension of the statute of limitations?
8. If a court holds that an employee was not acting within the scope of his or her employment at the time the act was done, can the alleged victim recover from the alleged servant/agent? Why do alleged victims go against the master/principal as well as the servant/agent perpetrator?

Types of Agents

In a discussion of agents only—not servants or independent contractors—several types of agents should be noted. The **general agent** is someone having authority to act on another's behalf in many different types of transactions or to handle all matters involved with a particular business. When professional athletes appoint business managers to handle their endorsements, exhibitions, and media appearances, keep their books, and file their tax returns, the business managers are general agents. The manager of a neighborhood Kroger or Safeway supermarket is also a general agent.

A **del credere agent** is one who sells goods for another on credit and guarantees that, if the buyer does not pay, the agent will pay. This agent is similar to a guarantor, someone who agrees to pay the debt of another only if the primary obligor (debtor) does not pay. A guarantor can guarantee any type of obligation, but a del credere agent usually guarantees only a buyer's credit for goods purchased.

http:// *The Library of Congress website provides access to state law at* ***http://lcweb.loc.gov/global/state/stategov.html***

A **special agent** is one employed to accomplish a particular task. For example, if one desires to sell a particular oil painting, the agent employed to make such a sale is a special agent. The significance of terms such as *general agent* or *special agent* arises, for example, with respect to the ending notice that the principal must give third persons who have dealt with the principal through the agent. Actual notice of a general agent must be given by the principal to third persons who have dealt with a general agent in the past. No such actual notice would be required for third persons who have dealt with the principal through the special agent appointed to handle a particular transaction.

Why Employ an Independent Contractor

An important basic principle in employer-employee relations is that the employer and employee can play a large part in determining their legal relationship to one another.

They can put terms in their employment contract and conduct themselves in ways that have been legally recognized by courts in establishing the employer-employee relationship they desire. As long as the employer and employee put words in their agreement that accurately describe the legal relationship (principal-agent, master-servant, or employer-independent contractor) they want, *and* as long as they act as the words say, their relationship will most likely be recognized by the courts as what they claim it to be.

Many factors influence an employer's decision to employ a servant rather than an independent contractor. The employer's desire to exercise (or not exercise) control is a key factor. The more right to control that employers exercise over the means their employees use to do their work, the more likely a master-servant relationship exists. The advantage to the employer is that the work can be done exactly as the employer wishes. The disadvantages to the employer in hiring a servant instead of an independent contractor primarily involve cost.

The potentially higher cost of hiring an employee instead of an independent contractor comes from the employer's tort liability for the servant's acts while working. The employer is not liable for an independent contractor's torts committed while working on the employer's behalf unless the work is inherently dangerous. Many statutes impose taxes such as Social Security and workers' compensation on employers who hire employees *but* not on employers who hire independent contractors. Given the substantial (and increasing) Social Security liability for employers, the desire to minimize the impact of the Social Security tax is a significant consideration for an employer. *Toyota Motor Sales v. Superior Court* illustrates the employer's tort liability for servants as opposed to independent contractors. The tests for determining whether someone is a servant or independent contractor are the same in the tort and Social Security situations.

Toyota Motor Sales v. Superior Court

California Court of Appeals, Second District
220 Cal. App. 3d 864, 269 Cal.Rptr. 647 (1990)

Background and Facts:

[T]his case arises from a rear-end automobile accident that occurred on August 28, 1987, in the city of Torrance, California. The defendant Christopher Heard, while delivering a pizza from Numero Uno No. 12, a pizza franchise owned by Lee, so operated his vehicle as to cause it to collide with the rear of plaintiff's vehicle. As a result, plaintiff sustained damages that included $13,000 in medical expenses and $900 in property damage.

On July 8, 1988, plaintiff filed suit against Lee, Heard, and Toyota. She alleged that Heard was negligent in the operation of the vehicle and that Lee, as his employer, was vicariously liable under the doctrine of respondeat superior. The cause of action against Toyota alleged that it had defectively designed the seat belt installed in plaintiff's vehicle and that the belt's failure upon impact had contributed to her injuries.

Plaintiff made a demand upon the defendants for $500,000 to settle the entire case. Subsequently, Heard entered into a separate settlement with plaintiff for $100,000, which the court, on August 10, 1989, found to be in good faith within the meaning of section 877.6. The evidence in support of that determination included the fact that Heard was a 21-year-old student with few, if any, assets other than coverage for his car under his father's liability policy. The amount paid in settlement represented the full policy limits. Toyota did not object to the trial court's good faith determination with respect to this settlement.

Plaintiff then entered into a separate settlement with Lee in consideration of the payment of the sum of $15,000 which represented the full amount provided by Lee's liability policy. Over Toyota's objection the trial court found this settlement to be in good faith. Based thereon, Toyota's cross-complaint against Lee for comparative equitable indemnity was dismissed. Toyota then filed a timely petition for a writ of mandate.

Body of Opinion

It is clear from a review of the record, that the good faith determination made by the trial court was based on its conclusion that Heard was not an employee of Lee, but rather was an independent contractor. On that assumption Lee would have *no* liability to plaintiff, as the only theory against Lee asserted by plaintiff was based upon the doctrine of respondeat superior. There was no claim that Lee was independently negligent in hiring or using Heard's delivery services. In such circumstances, a settlement of $15,000 would clearly justify a finding that it was made in good faith. On the other hand, if Heard was an employee of Lee, acting in the course and scope of his employment at the time of the accident, then Lee might well be exposed to the potential of unlimited liability and the question of good faith would depend upon the trial court's evaluation of other factors (e.g., plaintiff's probable recovery and the extent of Lee's wealth) which were not reached or considered by the court. . . .

The evidence, relevant to the legal status of Heard, offered by Lee and apparently relied upon by the court, was that he (1) provided his own car, expenses and insurance, (2) was paid on a commission (10%) basis for each delivery, (3) agreed to pay his own payroll (FICA) and income taxes, (4) agreed to provide his own worker's compensation coverage, and (5) had signed a written agreement with Lee which acknowledged his status as an "independent contractor." Lee, in accordance with the agreement, paid Heard for his services each day in cash an amount equal to 10% of the total charges for the pizzas delivered.

The evidence emphasized by Toyota demonstrated that Heard (1) was requested by Lee to work between 5:00 p.m. and 9:00 p.m. each day, (2) delivered pizzas to Lee's customers who had called in orders, (3) delivered pizzas at the times and to the customers and in the quantities as directed by Lee, (4) collected the money indicated on the customer's bill prepared by Lee and returned it (with any "shortages" to be deducted from the commission), and (5) could be terminated by Lee at any time "For Any Reason Whatsoever" upon twenty-four hours written notice to him.

The most significant factor in determining whether the status of a person performing services for another is an employee or an independent contractor is the right to control the manner and means of accomplishing the result, that is, the details of the work. "If the employer has the authority to exercise complete control, whether or not that right is exercised with respect to all details, an employer-employee relationship exists". . . . Other factors are also to be considered. They, including the issue of employer control, are set forth in the *Restatement (Second)* of Agency section 220, as follows:

> (1) A servant is a person employed to perform services in the affairs of another and who with respect to the physical conduct in the performance of the services is subject to the other's control or right to control.
>
> (2) In determining whether one acting for another is a servant or an independent contractor, the following matters of fact, among others, are considered:
>
> (a) the extent of control which, by the agreement, the master may exercise over the details of the work;
>
> (b) whether or not the one employed is engaged in a distinct occupation or business;
>
> (c) the kind of occupation, with reference to whether, in the locality, the work is usually done under the direction of the employer or by a specialist without supervision;
>
> (d) the skill required in the particular occupation;
>
> (e) whether the employer or the workman supplies the instrumentalities, tools, and the place of work for the person doing the work;
>
> (f) the length of time for which the person is employed;
>
> (g) the method of payment, whether by the time or by the job;
>
> (h) whether or not the work is a part of the regular business of the employer;
>
> (i) whether or not the parties believe they are creating the relation of master and servant; and
>
> (j) whether the principal is or is not in business". . .

However, the cases which have recognized the *Restatement's* multiple factor enumeration have emphasized that employer control is clearly the most important and the others merely constitute "secondary elements." . . . Moreover, it is not the control actually exercised, but that which may be exercised which is determinative. . . .

> "One of the means of ascertaining whether or not this right to control exists is the determination of whether or not, if instructions were given, they would have to be obeyed." (*Press Pub. Co. v. Industrial Acc. Com.* [(1922) 190 Cal. 114, 121, 210 p. 820].) The real test has been said to be "whether the employee was subject to the employer's orders and control and was liable to be discharged for disobedience or misconduct; and the fact that a certain amount of freedom of action is inherent in the nature of the work does not change the character of the employment where the employer has general supervision and control over it." . . . "Perhaps no single circumstance is more conclusive to show the relationship of an employee than the right of the employer to end the service whenever he sees fit to do so." . . .

Indeed, the unlimited right to discharge at will and without cause has been stressed by a number of cases as a strong factor demonstrating employment. . . .

In light of such rules, it appears to us that the undisputed evidence in this case may be characterized very simply. Lee hired Heard to deliver pizzas to Lee's customers and directed and controlled (1) the number, nature and type of pizzas to be delivered, (2) the time when such deliveries would take place, (3) the persons and locations to whom they would be delivered and (4) the price to be charged for each pizza and the total amount of money to be collected from each customer. In short, Lee determined what would be delivered, when and to whom and what price would be charged.

What portion of Heard's work was left to his discretion and not subject to Lee's control? Did it include anything more than the route Heard would take to a customer's home or how fast he would drive? Such factors generally have been considered to be simply a freedom inherent in the nature of the work and not determinative of the employment relation.... Moreover, it is at least arguable that Lee had the right to control this aspect of Heard's work as well. It would be Lee's obvious purpose and desire, and thus clearly part of Heard's responsibility, to get the fresh warm pizza to the customer as soon as possible. Indeed, it will doubtless be argued at trial that Heard's preoccupation with the necessity for prompt delivery contributed in some manner to the accident which allegedly caused plaintiff's injuries.

Essentially, the only evidence offered in support of the claim that Heard was an independent contractor was that he provided his own car, expenses and insurance.... He was subject to Lee's total control as to all aspects of his job.... When Heard reported to work, how long he worked, when he made deliveries and to whom and for what purpose were all dictated and controlled by Lee. Heard was at no risk whatever with respect to Lee's business or any of the pizza sales which were the subject of Heard's delivery services (except that his commission was subject to a charge for any "shortages"). His only responsibility was to deliver, collect the money and return. Finally, Lee retained the express contractual right to terminate the relationship at any time and without cause.

The remaining factors relied upon by Lee are entirely self-serving or equivocal and are of little or no value on the issue. The fact that Heard was paid on a commission basis is equally consistent with employee status. The agreement characterizing the relationship as one of "client-independent contractor" will be ignored if the parties, by their actual conduct, act like "employer-employee".... Indeed, the attempt to conceal employment by formal documents purporting to create other relationships have led the courts to disregard such terms whenever the acts and declarations of the parties are inconsistent therewith....

Finally, the requirements that Heard pay his own payroll and income taxes and provide his own worker's compensation insurance are of no help whatever to Lee. These are merely the legal consequences of an independent contractor status, not a means of proving it. An employer cannot change the status of an employee to one of independent contractor by illegally requiring him to assume burdens which the law imposes directly on the employer.

Thus, given the undisputed facts which were presented to the trial court in this case, there was no substantial evidence to support its apparent finding that Heard was an independent contractor. In our view, there is no reasonable conclusion that can be drawn from this record except that Heard was Lee's employee. In the context of the good faith motion, Lee must be deemed exposed to the possibility of full vicarious liability to the plaintiff for any negligent act or omission of Heard occurring in the course and scope of his employment. That being so, it was an abuse of discretion for the trial court to find the settlement with Lee to be in good faith based on the unsupportable conclusion that no such liability existed....

Judgment and Result

The trial court judgment was modified. The Court of Appeals told the trial court to reexamine whether Lee's settlement with plaintiff was in good faith. This rehearing was necessary because the trial court had *incorrectly* decided that the pizza delivery boy (Heard) was an independent contractor and not a servant or agent. The Court of Appeals held the delivery boy was an agent or servant, not an independent contractor.

Questions

1. Why would Mr. Lee want his pizza delivery people to be independent contractors instead of agents or servants?
2. Who pays both the employer's and employee's Social Security taxes if the employee is an independent contractor? Is this a reason employers want employees to be independent contractors?
3. Who is liable for an independent contractor's torts committed on the job?

HOW AGENCY AUTHORITY IS CREATED

http:// *To search for various aspects of state law, go to* ***http://www.alllaw.com/state_resources/state_law_search***

Employees can obtain authority to do their work in at least four ways: express authority, implied authority, apparent authority, and ratification.[2] Each is discussed in detail in the following paragraphs. The points to watch are the formalities necessary to create the authority (if any), who creates the authority, when the authority is created, and how and when the authority ends.

[2] A few jurisdictions also recognize inherent authority. Inherent authority is such power an agent (or servant) has by virtue of the agency itself. This authority exists to protect people harmed by or dealing with the servant or agent claimed to have this authority. *Zanac v. Frazier Neon Signs* at the end of this chapter is an example.

Express Authority

Express authority is created when the employer (or principal or master) orally or in writing tells the employee (or agent, servant, independent contractor) to do something. Most agency situations have no formal requirements (writings or documents of appointment) for conferring express authority. An exception occurs in the case of real estate agents whose appointments as agents must be evidenced by a writing in many states. A rationale for the writing requirement in this case is that the transaction that a realtor enters on the principal's behalf (sale of realty) must be evidenced by a signed writing, as should the agency contract, because it is also of great legal significance. However, in many other situations in which the contract the agent enters with the third person on the principal's behalf is just as significant, the underlying agency contract does not have to be evidenced by a signed writing to satisfy most states' statute of frauds.[3] No writing is required to establish the principal-agent relationship.

As a matter of good business practice, the principal and agent (or master and servant, or employer and independent contractor) will want to have the terms of their employment relation spelled out in as much detail as possible to provide for contingencies. **Powers of attorney** refer to a particular kind of express authority that can be created only in writing. A person who is not a licensed attorney but who acts for another under a document called a power or letter of attorney is legally an **attorney in fact**, not an **attorney at law**. (The latter is the licensed professional attorney most people refer to as a lawyer.) Powers of attorney usually apply only with respect to future—not past—matters.

Implied Authority

An agent or servant receives **implied authority** by reasonable inference from the express authority, by conduct of the principal and agent, and by circumstances creating an emergency or necessity that the agent (servant) have such authority. What the principal and agent (or servant) do with respect to each other—not with respect to third persons—is a factor that in many cases decides whether the agent (or servant) has implied authority. Mere assumptions by a third person that an agent has implied authority to do something will not give implied authority to an agent (or servant). Without a special statute, mere relationships such as husband and wife, father and son, mother and daughter do not create implied authority to act as an agent or servant for the other party.

An example of implied authority's arising from express authority would be a principal's telling an agent to hire a secretary for the office. The principal's direction to the agent to hire a secretary is express authority. Implied authority, reasonably flowing from such express authority, would probably include the authority to offer a reasonable salary to a promising applicant. Implied authority would not allow the agent to hire two secretaries or promise a car to an applicant to induce acceptance. Neither act is implied from the express authority because it goes beyond what a reasonable person would infer is necessary to accomplish the express authority.

Implied authority arising from emergency or necessity occurs where an unexpected contingency creates a situation in which the agent is unable to contact the principal, and the principal has given no express instructions to the agent on how to handle the matter. The unexpected contingency must be an emergency requiring immediate attention to protect property or person.

[3] Equal dignity statutes exist in most states, however, and do require the contract between the agent and the principal to be written if the statute of frauds requires the contract the agent enters on the principal's behalf be written.

Apparent Authority

Apparent authority is authority an agent may acquire by words or conduct of the principal that leads a third person to believe that the agent has authority. The entire agency may be created by apparent authority. Also, agents with express authority may have their agency powers increased by apparent authority. The appearance must come from some act—or omission where the principal had a duty to act—of the principal and not of the agent.

For example, assume an employee has no express or implied authority to sell. If the boss watches the employee make a sale in front of a customer, the boss's failure to stop the employee creates the appearance (to the customer) that the employee has authority to sell. The *Northington* case illustrates an alarming apparent authority problem.

Northington v. Dairyland Ins. Co.

Supreme Court of Alabama
445 So.2d 283 (1984)

Background and Facts:

Appellant, Eunice Northington, appeals from the trial court's summary judgment in favor of Dairyland Insurance Company, Inc. in an action alleging breach of contract and fraud. We affirm.

In September 1981, Ms. Northington went to Mr. Leonard Wills and discussed the possibility of obtaining insurance for her automobile. Mr. Wills, who owns and operates Wills Realty and Insurance Company, Inc., is an independent insurance agent for various companies, including Dairyland, and is an insurance broker for other companies. On November 30, 1981, Ms. Northington gave Mr. Wills a cash payment of $80, and Mr. Wills advised her that she had full automobile insurance coverage on her automobile as of that date. Ms. Northington did not fill out an application for insurance or sign any other form at that time or at any subsequent time in connection with her insurance coverage.

Ms. Northington attempted to contact Mr. Wills subsequently to discuss the fact that she had never received her insurance policy papers. On the few occasions when she reached Mr. Wills, he maintained to Ms. Northington that she had full insurance coverage, but did not inform her of the particular insurance company through which she was allegedly insured.

On December 16, 1981, Ms. Northington was involved in a one-vehicle automobile accident. She made a claim to Mr. Wills for coverage of the damages under her alleged insurance policy. Mr. Wills advised her to get two estimates on the damage and not to worry.

In January 1982, following the accident, Mr. Wills informed Ms. Northington that she had insurance with Dairyland Insurance Company, Inc., and that this insurance would cover the damage to her automobile. In February 1982, Mr. Wills accepted a further payment of $37.55 from Ms. Northington to be applied to the cost of her insurance.

In fact, Mr. Wills never made application to Dairyland for insurance on Ms. Northington's behalf. Nor did Mr. Wills forward the premium payments from Ms. Northington or any notice of loss from the accident to Dairyland.

On April 8, 1982, Ms. Northington filed a complaint against Leonard Wills, Wills Realty and Insurance Company, Inc., and Dairyland Insurance Company. She alleged breach of contract and fraud against the defendants.

On January 27, 1983, Dairyland filed a motion for summary judgment. As grounds for the motion, Dairyland asserted that there was no material dispute as to the facts and that at no time did Dairyland write a policy of insurance for Ms. Northington, that at no time was Ms. Northington, prior to her accident, informed that she had a policy of insurance with Dairyland, and that the actions of Dairyland's agent, Mr. Wills, exceeded the scope of his authority.

The trial court granted Dairyland's motion for summary judgment. Ms. Northington appeals, alleging that the trial court erred in finding that there was no genuine issue of material fact as to Dairyland's liability. Her basic argument is that Dairyland is bound by the representations that she was fully insured made by Mr. Wills acting under apparent authority as a general agent for Dairyland. We do not agree.

Body of Opinion

Justice Faulkner

First, it is clear that Mr. Wills could not be considered an actual agent of Dairyland in his transactions with Ms. Northington, since he exceeded the scope of his actual authority as defined in the agency agreement existing between him and Dairyland. That agreement stated, in part:

> (1) Pursuant to request that the underwriting facilities of the Company be made available to the Agent, the Company hereby grants authority to the Agent to solicit proposals for insurance for such classes or risks as the Company from time to time may authorize to be solicited, and to collect, receive and receipt for premiums of insurance tendered by the Agent to and accepted by the Company subject, however, to restrictions placed upon such Agent by the laws of the state or states in which such Agent is authorized to write insurance business and to the terms and conditions hereinafter stated; provided, however, that the acceptance by the Agent of any premiums or the giving of a receipt therefor shall in no wise obligate the Company other than in accordance with the written instructions of the Company.

Agents shall have authority to bind insurance for classifications of risks and types of vehicles that are normally written by the Company. When a signed application is submitted, with a premium deposit of at least two months' premium, coverage is bound as of the time and date the application is signed by both the applicant and agent. All bound business must be submitted with cash and must be promptly forwarded to a Dairyland office.

Since Mr. Wills willfully breached the agency agreement by failing to follow the above procedures in securing insurance for Ms. Northington, he cannot be considered an actual agent so as to bind Dairyland in this case....

Ms. Northington, nevertheless, asserts that Dairyland is liable for Mr. Wills's representations under the doctrine of apparent authority and estoppel.

In *Roberts & Sons v. Williams,...* this court said:

> Where the evidence shows that the actor has been held out by the alleged principal, as being his agent or as possessing the authority assumed by such agent within the scope of the principal's business, the doctrine of apparent authority can be invoked by one who has been misled to his detriment....

The following was written in *Automotive Acceptance Corporation v. Powell*:

> The doctrine of apparent authority does not rest upon what one thinks an agent's authority may be, or what the agent holds out his authority to be; rather, the doctrine of apparent authority is based on the principal's holding the agent out to a third person as having the authority under which he acts. The following statement on the doctrine of apparent authority is found in Am.Jur.2d, Agency, Sec. 74, p. 476:
>
> 'The apparent power of an agent is to be determined by the acts of the principal, and not by the acts of the agent; a principal is responsible for the acts of an agent within his apparent authority only where the principal by his acts or conduct has clothed the agent with the appearance of authority, and not where the agent's own conduct and statements have created the apparent authority.'
>
> 'Apparent authority' is such as a principal knowingly permits an agent to assume or holds him out as possessing. It seems to be generally held that an agent's authority must be based upon the conduct of the principal and not of the agent.

These statements indicate that in order for a principal to be held liable under the doctrine of apparent authority and estoppel, the principal must have engaged in some conduct which led a third party to believe that the agent had authority to act for the principal. Reviewing the record, we find no evidence whatsoever that Dairyland indicated to Ms. Northington or led her to believe that Mr. Wills had authority to act for the company in the manner in which he acted. No one, other than Mr. Wills, made any representations to Ms. Northington or engaged in any conduct on behalf of Dairyland in this case. Since an agent's apparent authority must be based on conduct of the principal and not of the agent, and Dairyland engaged in no conduct which gave the impression of Wills's authority, we hold that Dairyland is not liable for Wills's representations.

Judgment and Result

As indicated above, Mr. Wills was not an agent for Dairyland in his transactions with Ms. Northington; he, therefore, had no authority to bind Dairyland by his representations. Accordingly, there was no genuine issue of material fact against Dairyland. Dairyland, therefore, was entitled to summary judgment. Affirmed.

Questions

1. Does apparent authority come from acts or omissions of the principal, which lead third persons to believe the agent had authority?
2. Why was Dairyland Insurance Co., the putative principal, not liable for failing to tell Ms. Northington that Mr. Wills was not its agent?
3. Does this case help explain why insurers have insureds send premiums directly to the company (the insurer) instead of paying the agent directly?

Ratification

An employer (or principal or master) may confer authority retroactively on a person for an act already done. This practice is known as ratification. **Ratification** is the acceptance by one of all benefits and burdens of an act done on one's behalf by another person who, at the time the acts were performed, had no authority to act for the ratifier. A simple example of ratification occurs when X, a customer, walks into S's furniture store and, without S's authority, sells a chair to C, another customer for $20 more than list price. If S soon learns of this sale and then approves of its terms (and, presumably, collects the purchase price from X), S is said to have ratified X's act of selling the chair.

The requirements for ratification are as follows:

1. One person without any authority or exceeding his or her authority purports to act for another.
2. The person for whom the acts were done was legally able to do those acts both at the time they were done and when they were ratified. In other words, the acts themselves were legal and not crimes, and the principal was not insane or drunk at the time of ratification.
3. The person for whom the acts were done has full knowledge of all material circumstances of the acts done on his or her behalf when ratification occurs.
4. The ratification occurs while the third person is a party to that contract; if the third person disclaims the contract before ratification, the principal will not be able to ratify.
5. Ratification is of the entire transaction done on the principal's behalf.
6. The person for whom the unauthorized act was done (the alleged principal), not the person who actually did the act, is the ratifying party.

COMMON LAW DUTIES THAT MASTERS OWE SERVANTS

Masters—employers of those who are legally termed servants—owe their employees several duties that arise automatically between the master and servant even without an express contract. One is the duty to provide a safe place to work, not necessarily a risk-free place to work but merely a relatively safe place. This duty attaches when employees are actually or constructively doing their jobs. Masters' common law duty to provide a relatively safe work place for employees applies irrespective of how many or how few servants masters have working for them. Remember this point when the discussion turns to state workers' compensation statutes for servants and agents, because many of these laws do not cover employers with fewer than a certain number of employees.

Masters generally have a duty to provide employees with tools with which to perform their work. The employers' common law duty extends to providing employees with safe tools as well. The master and servant might agree that the servant will provide the tools. If so, courts could rely on this factor in holding that the relationship is actually employer-independent contractor rather than master-servant. It could in turn mean that the independent contractor (the employee) is the only one liable for torts committed on the job—a favorable conclusion from the employer's standpoint and an unfavorable result from the employee's view.

The courts have generally imposed a duty on masters to pay their servants the reasonable value of their services, even if no specific mention is made of payment, providing the servant's services are of a type for which compensation is usually paid and inferring that compensation expected is reasonable under the circumstances.

COMMON LAW DUTIES THAT PRINCIPALS OWE AGENTS

In a gratuitous agency the agent agrees to work for nothing. Most agencies, however, are designed to pay the agent. Usually an agency contract—either written or oral—exists that will either specifically state an amount of pay for the entire period of the agency, provide a rate of pay if the agency has no definite term, or note conditions (such as production of a ready, able, and willing buyer for realty at the seller's asking price) on the contract.

If by chance the principal and agent neglect to mention the matter of the agent's pay, courts will examine the circumstances of the agency—matters such as the reasonable expectations of the parties, whether agencies of the sort at hand generally involve pay—to decide whether to infer a duty to pay the agent and in what amount. The failure to mention the agent's pay does not necessarily mean that the agent is not entitled to pay. Put another way, if nothing is said about paying the agent, the agency is not necessarily gratuitous. Also, if a person acts on another's behalf without authorization and that person ratifies the purported agent's acts, the agent is entitled to be paid. The duty to pay the agent, when such a duty is present, usually rests on the principal.

If an agent has a right to compensation, a number of actions can deprive the agent of this right. If the agent violates the fiduciary duty owed to the principal, fails to fulfill the conditions required of him or her by the agency contract, fulfills all the terms of an agency contract known to be illegal (such as a violation of the federal antitrust laws), waives[4] the right to pay, materially fails to follow instructions, or commits **fraud** or **conversion** against the principal, the agent loses the right to be paid. If the agent is careless in performing agency duties, thereby injuring the principal, the agent does not totally lose the right to be paid. Rather, the agent's compensation is reduced by the damage to the principal.

An **advance** is money an agent may obtain before making a sale. Although agents have no automatic right to advances, the agency contract can provide for them. A surprising number of cases allow an agent to keep all advances, even though sales commissions equal to advances were not made. An agent who represents both parties to a transaction is not entitled to be paid by either unless both parties are aware of the **dual agency** and approve of it.

Other common law obligations that a principal owes an agent are a **duty to reimburse** the agent for ordinary and necessary expenses incurred while performing agency duties. If an agent receives a fine or penalty for violation of the law in performing agency duties, the principal would not have to reimburse the agent for the violation, because it would not be ordinary and necessary to perform the agency duties. Except under exceptional circumstances, such as an emergency, the principal has no duty to reimburse the agent for expenses incurred resulting from a violation of the principal's instructions.

The principal owes agents a **duty to indemnify** them for losses sustained and for liabilities they incur in performance of agency duties. This obligation applies only if the agent is not breaching a duty to the principal. For example, if the agent fails to use proper care and injures a third person, the principal has no duty to indemnify the agent for the liability to the injured person.

As with masters and servants, the principals owe agents a duty of care. That duty of care is based on common law negligence principles. The elements of negligence are duty, breach of the standard of care, proximate cause, and damages. Defenses to negligence include contributory negligence, assumption of risk, the statute of limitations, and lack of an element of the definition of negligence, such as no duty.

[4] Voluntarily gives up a right.

COMMON LAW DUTIES THAT AGENTS OWE PRINCIPALS

Agents owe their principals a number of duties. Such obligations include the duty to use care and skill in performing for the principal, the duty to be faithful to the principal in performing agency functions and not self-deal (the fiduciary duty), and the duty to follow instructions. These duties arise automatically by establishment of the agency relation.

Duty to Account

The agent's duty to account arises either when the principal turns property over to the agent for use in performing agency duties or when a third person turns property over to the agent on the principal's behalf. The agent must not only account to the principal whenever the principal demands it, but the accounting must also be accurate. The agent has a duty to turn over property of the principal in the agent's possession when the principal demands it. If the agent refuses, the agent is liable to the principal for conversion. What satisfies the agent's duty to account? In one case, the agent's preparation of an income tax return covering the principal's business that the agent managed was said to satisfy the agent's duty to account.

Duty to Use Care and Skill

The duty to use care and skill in performing the principal's work is usually satisfied by using the standard of ordinary care in the occupation at hand. However, if the principal's project fails, the agent is not necessarily liable for failing to fulfill the duty and care or skill, because this duty does not make an agent an insurer. An agent can be an insurer of the principal's enterprise, although such an obligation will not be imposed under general agency law. The level of care and skill for gratuitous agents is often lower than that for compensated agents. Gratuitous agents are, however, liable for gross negligence and negligence in performing their agency duties.

Today's highly competitive business environment creates pressures on principals to keep agents' salaries low. Often this pressure means that employers must "churn" their employees so that they cannot develop seniority and make high incomes associated with seniority. In such environments, employees may be performing satisfactorily and yet be fired to keep costs down. How can this practice happen legally? If the level of skill and care that an employee must demonstrate is subjective, that is, dependent on what a particular employer says is appropriate, then the employee can, in effect, be fired anytime: the employer can simply make impossible demands on the employee, such as increase the employee's workload or assign ridiculous things, and when the employee makes an error, as is likely to happen when employee is overworked, or refuses the ridiculous request, the employer can, with a straight face, tell the employee that he or she is "not meeting standards." In answer to this problem, at least one court has applied an objective "reasonable person standard" to judge whether an agent is performing his or her job satisfactorily.

Duty to Follow Instructions

The agent has a duty to follow the principal's instructions. It has been said that this duty is not limited to reasonable instructions, but if the principal were to ask the agent to kiss every client who enters a contract with the agent on the principal's behalf, the agent would not have to perform. A kiss under such circumstances would probably amount to the tort of battery—a civil wrong. Agents have no duty to follow instructions if doing so constitutes a tort or crime. If an agent fails to follow the principal's legal instructions, the agent is liable for damages resulting from such breach of duty.

Fiduciary Duty

The most prominent of the agent's responsibilities to the principal is the fiduciary duty. A fiduciary is one who owes great faith, loyalty, and accountability to another. Some courts have included many of the agent's duties to the principal, such as the duty to account and the duty to follow instructions, under the umbrella term *fiduciary duty*. Here **fiduciary duty** is given a more limited scope, covering the agent's duty to act for only one principal, the duty not to profit at the principal's expense, the duty to communicate to the principal information relevant to the agency, and the duty not to act adversely to the principal's interests. If the agent violates the fiduciary duty, the principal may recover damages or obtain appropriate equitable relief. The fiduciary duty exists even in the case of gratuitous agents.

Some aspects of an agent's fiduciary duty extend beyond the time the agent ends the agency. For example, the agent's duty not to disclose trade secrets continues after an agent ceases employment for the principal who owns those secrets. This duty does not last interminably, but reasonable time and geographic parameters are read into it.

Of the duties agents owe principals, probably the one most involving ethics is the fiduciary duty. *American Express Financial Advisors, Inc. v. Topel* illustrates problems that can arise in this area.

American Express Financial Advisors, Inc. v. Topel

U.S. District Court (D. Colorado)
38 F.Supp.2d 1233 (1999)

Background and Facts:

For five years, Mr. Topel worked as a financial planner for American Express (AMEX) pursuant to a written contract with AMEX. Mr. Topel received copies of both his Planner Agreement and separate documents setting forth certain key terms of this contract prior to starting work as an agent for AMEX. Mr. Topel signed the Planner Agreement as a condition of his affiliation with AMEX. Pursuant to the Planner Agreement, Mr. Topel received training and what AMEX characterizes as confidential trade secret information, comprised of customer identities, addresses, financial holdings, investment objectives, and buying preferences.

The Planner Agreement, which Mr. Topel now seeks to avoid, prohibits him for a period of one year after resigning from AMEX, from soliciting or selling investments and financial services, directly or indirectly, to those AMEX customers in the territory he served or learned about through AMEX.

According to AMEX, after Mr. Topel tendered his resignation in late May 1997, it learned that he was violating the terms of his Planner Agreement and was actively soliciting and diverting the AMEX customers he serviced on its behalf. AMEX brought an action against Topel for, among other things, breach of his fiduciary duty to AMEX.

Body of Opinion

Judge Babcock

Colorado law provides that "unless otherwise agreed, an agent is subject to a duty to his principal to act solely for the benefit of the principal in all matters connected with the agency."... While an agent is entitled to make some preparations to compete with his principal after the termination of their relationship, an agent violates his duty of loyalty if he engages in pre-termination solicitation of customers for a new competing business. (See *Koontz v. Rosener*... by working to set up a competing business while still engaged by plaintiff, defendants violated their duty of loyalty); (see also *Community Counselling Serv., Inc. v. Reilly*... during period of employment, employee cannot solicit for himself future business which his employer requires him to solicit for his employer).

As the undisputed facts make clear, Mr. Topel solicited customers for his new venture while he was still affiliated with AMEX.... In some instances, there is evidence that Mr. Topel ignored his AMEX customers' requests to keep their investments with AMEX.... He also sent correspondence to his AMEX customers to solicit them for his new venture while he was still employed by AMEX and, in at least one instance, on an AMEX letterhead.... There is no genuine issue regarding whether Mr. Topel's activities violated his fiduciary duty of loyalty to AMEX. Therefore, AMEX is entitled to summary judgment on this claim.

Judgment and Result

The financial planner breached his fiduciary duty toward the corporation, his former employer.

Questions

1. How would you define fiduciary duty? What instances of violation of this duty were present in the *Topel* case?
2. Is the fiduciary duty owed by the agent to the principal? By the principal to the agent? Why not?
3. Is the fiduciary duty owed by servants to masters? By masters to servants? Why not?
4. What ethics mentioned in the first chapter are implicit in the fiduciary duty? Can you think of any way in which the fiduciary duty could be improved, that is, made more fair to both employees as well as employers?
5. Does the court acknowledge times when agents may do things that might not be entirely to the principal's benefit even though the employee is drawing a paycheck from the principal?

COMMON LAW DUTIES THAT SERVANTS OWE MASTERS

Generally, servants owe masters the same duties that agents owe principals. They owe masters a fiduciary duty, a duty to follow legal instructions, a duty to use ordinary care and skill in performance of servant duties, and a duty to communicate information to a master. The scope of the servant's duties is considerably narrower than an agent's because the servant by definition is one who may not enter contracts with third persons on the master's behalf. The last remark can easily mislead one into a false sense of certainty because determining who is a servant and who is an agent is often difficult, particularly when one realizes that courts have held that a person may be an agent with respect to one part of a job, a servant with respect to another part of a job, and an independent contractor with respect to yet another part of the same job.

AGENT OR SERVANT LIABILITY THIRD PERSONS: TORTS

An agent or servant is liable for torts committed against anyone regardless of whether the tort is committed within or beyond the scope of the agency. For example, if an agent commits fraud to induce a third person to enter a contract with the agent's principal, the agent would be liable for the fraud. This liability stands even if the principal ratified the contract by retaining the benefits of the agent's fraud. However, the tort victim may *not* obtain a double recovery (once from the agent and once from the principal). If the third person recovers once from the agent or servant, the third person is entitled to no further recovery against the principal.

The agent or servant would be entitled to be **indemnified** by the principal if the determination were made that the agent broke no duty owed to the principal at the time the agent was subjected to liability. The agent or servant would have no right of indemnity against the principal if the agent was not following instructions, was outside the scope of his or her authority during commission of the torts, or violated any of the duties owed the principal at the time the tort was committed.

The respondeat superior principle is the basis for subjecting one person to legal liability for the acts or omissions of another; that is, one person (principal or master) who does not personally commit a tort or enter a contract is held or sought to be held for a tort committed by another or a contract entered by another on that person's behalf. According to this doctrine, principals or masters are legally answerable for the acts or omissions of their servants or agents *within the scope of their employment*. The respondeat superior principle applies to both master-servant and principal-agent relationships. Recall, however, that the servant's express and implied authority is more limited than the agent's, because the servant has no authority to enter contracts on the master's behalf, while the agent does.

The **scope of employment** notion subjects a master or principal to liability for job-related acts or omissions of servants and agents. It is synonymous with authority concepts (express authority, implied authority, apparent authority, and ratification) introduced earlier, in that these authority bases set the employee's job parameters and, in so doing, establish the extent of the employer's liability for the employees.

The problem of determining where an agent's responsibilities end—the extent of the scope of employment—and where an agent's duty begins is difficult to ascertain in general terms. Consider the following. If a servant hired to deliver packages negligently drives too fast for road conditions and injures a third person, why should the master be liable? After all, the servant was hired to deliver packages, not to drive negligently into third persons. In other words, masters and principals could, and do, argue that the servant's or agent's committing a tort while performing duties in and of itself removes the act from within the scope of the agency. However, courts do not accept this categorical argument, because doing so would insulate masters and servants from liability in every tort situation. Yet, it must still be determined when a tort is within the scope of employment so as to subject the principal to vicarious liability. Generally, a case-by-case determination is necessary.

AGENT LIABILITY TO THIRD PERSONS: CONTRACTS

Agents may be subjected to liability to third persons with respect to contracts in three ways: on the contract, for the tort of fraud, or for **breach of warranty of authority**. All three legal theories will not be available in any single suit, although they would all likely be pleaded. Then, as the evidence develops to support one but not the others, some would be dropped.

A number of contract situations exist in which an agent will be held contractually liable to a third person. An agent for a **nonexistent principal** is liable on the contract to third persons who deal with the agent. The two most common nonexistent principal situations are a corporate promoter making contracts for a corporate principal that has not yet been legally organized and an agent entering a contract for an organization that is formed but is not a legal entity (an unincorporated fraternity, for example).

If an agent enters a contract with a third person on the principal's behalf and the agent acts within his or her authority, discloses the fact of agency and the principal's identity to the third person, and properly executes the contract, the principal and not the agent will be bound to the contract. The principal, and not the agent, will have the right to sue to enforce the contract that the agent entered on the disclosed principal's behalf.

Several situations exist, however, in which an agent may be liable to the third person when the agent enters a contract on behalf of the existing principal. On the mechanical side, the agent may improperly execute the contract. This problem generally involves a written contract. In such a case, a properly signed contract—one that binds only the principal—will identify the principal by name with the agent's name and the fact of agency disclosed, usually immediately below the principal's name as in the following example:

ABC Company
by John Johnson, Agent

A contract executed in this way would bind ABC Company and not John Johnson, even though Johnson signed the contract. The reason Johnson is not bound, assuming no special facts such as nonexistent principal, is that Johnson signed the contract in a representative capacity. However, what if John Johnson merely signs his name and nothing else to the contract, even though he intends to bind only his principal? In this **undisclosed principal** situation, the fact of agency and the principal's identity are both undisclosed to the third party. The cases dealing with the matter are not in agreement on whether Johnson should be held personally and exclusively, or whether extrinsic evidence (evidence outside of the contract) should be allowed to show that another person (the principal) is supposed to be bound. Some courts do not allow such evidence and some do.

The third person must elect which party—agent or principal—to subject to liability. Many cases allow the third person to elect to sue an agent and the principal when the principal becomes disclosed. Only one recovery, however, is allowed. Given this fact, the safest course to follow from the agent's position is to sign the principal's name and then the agent's name with an indication of agency. A **partially disclosed principal** exists where agents sign their names and identify themselves as agents but omit the principal's name. Generally, a third person may hold either the agent or the undisclosed (or partially disclosed, if that is the case) principal to the contract.

LIABILITY FOR CRIMES

Employee Liability

A person who commits a crime is liable for it. It makes no difference whether that person is an agent, employee, servant, or independent contractor when the crime occurs. People are *personally* liable for their crimes.

What if a boss orders employees to commit crimes as part of their work, and the employees obey the boss and are criminally prosecuted? Obedience to a boss's command is not a criminal defense. What if the boss threatens to fire employees who refuse to commit crimes as part of their jobs? For example, a truck dispatcher may set timetables for truckers at levels that are impossible to meet if highway speed limits are obeyed. Threat of job loss is not a criminal defense. Employees sometimes mistakenly believe that their bosses are ordering them to commit crimes, because employees think committing a crime is the only way to do the job. A clever employee might be able to do the job legally. For example, in our truck dispatcher example, the truck driver might have been able to meet timetables by taking a shorter route or by making shorter meal stops.

Employer Liability

If an employer personally commits a crime, the employer is criminally liable. Thus, if Mr. H. L. Box, an accountant, cheats on a client's income tax return to reduce the client's taxes, Box is criminally liable even though he committed the crime to help the client. Presumably, Box also intended to help his own business by committing the crime.

What if, instead of personally filling out a false tax return, Box tells his younger assistant, Jack Zeigler, to cheat on the client's return? Zeigler follows instructions, cheats, and is caught. Both Zeigler and Box are criminally liable. Zeigler, the employee, is liable because he personally committed the crime (following the boss's orders is no defense), and Box is liable based on criminal conspiracy rules. A **criminal conspiracy** is an agreement with an intent to commit an unlawful act or a lawful act in an unlawful way. Exactly how the intent to commit the unlawful act (or lawful act in an unlawful way) must be shown is not always clear. Often, a substantial act to carry out the illegal act shows the needed intent. In our tax evasion example, Zeigler's falsifying and filing a client's tax return would show intent. Thus, both Box and Zeigler would be liable for a criminal conspiracy to violate the income tax law.

Corporate Employers

What about corporate employers' liability for employee crimes? Corporations present special problems, because they are artificial persons who can act only through their employees. Corporate employers are liable for employee crimes on the following occasions: if a court applies the respondeat superior principle or (in many situations) if strict liability criminal statutes exist.

Respondeat Superior

The respondeat superior principle also applies to many crimes. Hence, a corporation is criminally liable for its employees' crimes committed on the job to benefit the corporation. For example, a corporate engineer who breaks a law against submitting a false pollution compliance report commits a crime. (The engineer would be criminally liable because the engineer did the act.) The corporate employer would also be liable because the crime was within the scope of the employee's job and was done on the employer's behalf.

The respondeat superior principle makes the corporate employer liable for employee crimes committed *within the scope of the employee's job* and for the employer's benefit. (In other words, the corporate employer is not answerable for employee crimes committed off-duty.) Corporate employers are liable under respondeat superior for employee on-duty crimes even if the corporate employer told the employee not to commit the crimes.

U.S. v. Gibson Products shows how a corporate employer was held criminally liable for an employee's crimes. The main reason for the respondeat superior in this case was that the employee performed the criminal acts within the scope of the agent's duties, which led the court to apply the respondeat superior doctrine to hold the corporation (but *not* the corporate president) criminally liable.

United States v. Gibson Products Co., Inc.

U.S. District Court Southern District of Texas
426 F.Supp. 768 (1976)

Background and Facts:

Defendant corporation, Gibson Products Company, Inc., in this consolidated action stands charged in 19 counts with knowingly making false entries on ATF Form 4473 in connection with the sale of firearms to foreign citizens. In Cr. No. 76-B-262, the defendant Pedro G. Alvarado was charged in five of said counts as a co-defendant with Gibson Products. Alvarado pled guilty to one count, and the other four counts in the indictment were dismissed as to him, thus removing him from this prosecution. In Cr. No. 76-B-393, this defendant, Gibson Products, was alone charged in the remaining 14 counts. These two consolidated actions were called for trial on November 8, 1976, and, a jury being waived, said actions proceeded to trial before the Court.

Body of Opinion

District Judge Cox

The Court, having heard all of the evidence, finds, beyond a reasonable doubt, that Gibson Products Company, Inc., has operated a department store located in McAllen, Texas, for many years. In January, 1969, Gibson Products Company applied for and was issued a license to be a dealer in firearms, other than destructive devices, or ammunition for other than destructive devices. The application for such license was made by Jack Hanshaw, who was identified as the corporation's president. Pedro G. Alvarado, a long-standing employee, had been placed in charge of the hardware and sporting goods department, and, on said application, was designated as "Sporting Goods Manager." While in such capacity and during the period of time from February 11, 1975, through November 14, 1975, the said Alvarado did manage the department, selling, among other items, guns (long guns and hand guns) and ammunition. There was no evidence to indicate that the designation originally given to Pedro G. Alvarado on the application had been changed and none to indicate that some other employee was in charge of the sporting goods department during the period in which the illegal gun sales were made.

The Court further finds, beyond a reasonable doubt, that Pedro G. Alvarado sold certain hand guns to foreign citizens and made false entries on ATF Forms 4473 in regard to each sale involved in this trial. Fictitious names and other fictitious information was entered on the forms. On a few occasions, Alvarado received a bribe or kick-back from the purchaser in connection with the illegal sales. However, such illegal activity and the receipt of kick-backs by Alvarado did not change his status as department head. Alvarado's actions in selling the aforementioned guns were in the course and scope of his employment, because that was his job. Alvarado deposited the full retail price of every gun sold in the store's cash register.

The Court also finds, beyond a reasonable doubt, that Hanshaw rarely went down on the sales floor. When he did audit the ATF 4473 Forms, he concerned himself only with inventory control of individual guns, not with proper completion of the statutorily required information.

In addition, the Court finds, beyond a reasonable doubt, that, in connection with several of the illegal sales, Alavardo received a benefit individually, either a small money kick-back or "ego satisfaction." However, since Alvarado was not himself knocking down, it goes without saying that all of the sales were also intended to benefit the corporation. It was the purpose of the store, and of Alvarado as manager of the department, to sell merchandise and encourage customers to return to the store. The major beneficiary of the sales was the corporation. Reference to gun sales as a "loss leader" does not change the situation. As the Court understands it, loss-leader merchandise is generally a part of the profit-making plan of a retail sales business. The Court concludes that Hanshaw was derelict in his supervision of the gun sales, especially in view of the fact that gun sales are strictly regulated by the United States government, and considering the potential for abuse given an unsupervised department.

In determining if the factual situation which existed in this case, as found by the Court beyond a reasonable doubt, constitutes a violation of 18 U.S.C. §922 (m), it is necessary to review the law applicable here.

Criminal liability for the commission of certain offenses may be imputed to a corporate defendant. . . . Because corporations act only through human agents, the requisite level of intent, here, a "knowing" act, must be imputed to the corporation. This theory, known in civil tort as *respondeat superior*, can be applied to corporate defendants in criminal cases. . . .

The Court must determine whether this corporate defendant, under the facts found by the Court, had the requisite intent, and whether the evidence shows beyond a reasonable doubt that the acts were done deliberately and with knowledge. . . . The circuit courts have required that a finding of intent to benefit the corporation is necessary to hold the corporation criminally liable for illegal acts. The acts must also have been performed in the scope of the agent's duties. . . .

Defendant argues that the corporate president gave specific instructions to Alvarado and to all gun sales personnel, prohibiting them from making false entries on the Form 4473. This argument is no legal persuasion to the Court. . . .

The Court concludes that the evidence, as the Court has found it, beyond a reasonable doubt, establishes that Alvarado acted within the scope of his employment, and with an intent to benefit the corporation, when he made the illegal entries on Form 4473. The Defendant Gibson's Products Company, Inc., is therefore guilty of Counts 1 through 5 in Criminal Action No. 76-B-262 and is guilty of Counts 1 through 14 in Criminal Action No. 76-B-393.

Judgment and Result

The federal district court held *both* Pedro Alvarado, the employee who committed the crime, *and* Gibson Products Company, Inc., the corporate employer, liable for the crime of falsifying the government form regarding gun sales.

Questions

1. What reasons did the court give for subjecting the corporate employer to criminal liability for the employee's crimes?
2. Is it possible to imprison a corporate employer held criminally responsible for an employee's on-the-job crimes?

Some Limits on Corporate Criminal Liability. The **superior agent rule** says that corporations are liable only for crimes of high-level employees (superior agents). This rule limits corporate criminal liability to some extent. It is justified in part by the basic fairness of holding corporations for crimes by employees close enough to the corporate inner circle to say the corporation itself knew. Although this idea has some appeal, strictly speaking, corporations cannot know anything, because they are artificial persons. Also, problems exist in defining how high in the corporate structure employees must be before they can be called superior agents. These and other problems have led some jurisdictions to reject the superior agent rule.

A second limit on corporate criminal liability for employee crimes is the requirement that the crime be within the scope of the employee's job and done for the corporation's benefit. Consider an extreme example. A small incorporated supermarket has a deliveryman. While delivering groceries to a customer, the deliveryman rapes the customer. Because this crime would be beyond the scope of the employee's job and not for the corporate employer's benefit, the deliveryman's corporate employer would not be criminally liable for the rape. The employee's crime must relate directly to the employee's duties and be intended as part of or incident to the employee's job before the corporate employer will be criminally liable.

HOW AGENCIES END

An agency relationship may end in many ways. An initial distinction should be made between the power and the right to end an agency relation. An agency relationship is a voluntary, consensual relationship. In addition, courts refuse to enforce personal service contracts because, among other things, they violate the U.S. Constitution's Thirteenth Amendment slavery prohibition; therefore a principal or agent always has the power—not necessarily the right—to end agency arrangements. If an agent or principal ends an agency relationship without the right to do so, the principal or agent breaking the contract will be liable to the other for contract damages and whatever other remedies are appropriate in the situation. Thus, agencies may end at any time by either the principal's or agent's decision to end the arrangement.

Probably the usual way agencies end is by finishing the work the agent was hired to do or by arrival of the date at which the contract calls for the agency to end. The principal and agent may voluntarily agree between themselves to end the agency at any time, irrespective of what the agency agreement may say about the termination date.

The death of either the principal or agent ends the agency by **operation of law**, as does insanity of either principal or agent. Bankruptcy of the principal, and in some cases the agent, will end the agency. If the agent becomes physically or legally incapacitated (for example, loss of a professional license), the agency terminates. If it becomes impossible to perform due to loss or destruction of essential subject matter, the agency relation ends. Illegality of the agency's object or even sudden shifts in the economy (e.g., economic depression) or in the political climate (e.g., war) may result in an agency's ceasing.

Many of the prior observations made about an agency's ending apply with equal force to ending master-servant and employer-independent contractor arrangements.

Ending the Employment Relationship: Employment At-Will

About 55 percent of the nonfarm workforce in the United States is not protected by union contracts or by civil service statutes. Many of these workers legally operate as at-will employees; that is, they have no written contract for a definite term. In at-will employment situations, the general rule has traditionally been that either the employer or the employee may end the working relationship any time for almost any (or no) reason. (Dismissals for protected union activities are prohibited, and are discussed in Chapter 17; dismissals prohibited by the civil rights laws are discussed in Chapter 16.)

On the surface, the employment at-will rule appears fair to both workers and employers. After all, both have the power to end the employment relationship. In practice, the rule generally favors employers, especially when jobs are scarce. Thus, the rule gives employers a strong disciplinary tool against employees. Used constructively, the employment at-will rule helps employers enforce their common law right to have workers follow instructions. Obedience can help production and harmony. If an employee at-will disobeys a direct order, the employer can fire that worker immediately.

Unfortunately, some employers lean on at-will employees to induce them to do questionable, unethical, or even illegal things. Also, some employers are not above terminating employees in questionable circumstances, such as just before an employee would be entitled to a large bonus. Such wrongful firings represent the negative or dark side of the at-will rule.

Wrongful Dismissal Lawsuits in General. Lawsuits based on wrongful dismissals have become common in most states. Two studies of California (generally a leader in legal developments) wrongful dismissal cases indicated that plaintiffs win between 90–95 percent of the cases going to the jury. Damage awards averaged $450,000 and $548,000 in the two studies.

Employee Actions Causing Wrongful Dismissals. Employee actions prompting dismissals run the gamut, including major blunders. In the *Mau* case, an employee of 28 years who had worked his way up to be head mailroom clerk was fired for neglecting to send out 300 retirees' pension checks.[5] He lost his wrongful dismissal suit in the Nebraska Supreme Court. Employee actions are sometimes heroic. Recall the *Geary* case in Chapter 1 where Geary, a U.S. Steel salesman, went over his immediate boss's head to report a defect in a company product.[6] The company later withdrew the product from the market. U.S. Steel then fired Geary, who sued unsuccessfully in the Pennsylvania Supreme Court. *Geary* was a 1974 case, and *Mau* was decided in 1980. Both follow the traditional common law rule that an employer may fire an at-will employee any time for almost any reason.

Legal Limits on Wrongful Dismissals. The at-will rule remains, but it is being modified by statutes and judicial decisions. Several states have private sector whistleblower statutes protecting against wrongful dismissal. Although no federal statute forbids wrongful dismissals in all situations, specialized federal laws such as the National Labor Relations Act and Title VII of the Civil Rights Act of 1964 do give some protections in limited circumstances.

Courts in at least 30 states now provide some rights against wrongful dismissal. (In 1979 only about 15 states gave this protection.) Reasons for judicial relief can be grouped under contract and public policy headings.

If an employer and employee have an express contract covering the subject of grounds for dismissal, generally courts will honor its terms. For example, the contract could simply recite the general at-will rule allowing dismissal any time for almost any reason, or it could list the grounds for dismissal, such as insubordination or theft of company property.

---

[5] *Mau v. Omaha Nat. Bank*, 207 Neb. 308, 299 N.W.2d 147 (1980).
[6] *Geary v. U.S. Steel Corp.*, 456 Pa. 171, 319 A.2d 174 (1974).

Problems arise when no written contract exists or when the written contract either ignores, partially covers, or is ambiguous on the dismissal. Courts can then do one of several things. First, they can uphold the firing by citing the general rule. Second, more than twenty states allow recovery on an implied contract basis. Under this idea, courts interpret vague language in recruitment brochures, company manuals, and the like as meaning that the employer will dismiss employees only for "good cause." Third, courts can refuse to allow at-will employee terminations on the grounds that they violate a strong public policy. In one case, *Petermann v. International Brotherhood of Teamsters*, an employee was subpoenaed to testify before a state legislative committee.[7] The employer told him to give false testimony. The employee disobeyed, told the truth, and was fired. The employee won his claim for wrongful dismissal, even though the employment relationship was at-will. The Supreme Court of California reasoned that coercing perjury is "patently contrary to public policy." Fourth, some courts rely on promissory estoppel to hold an employer liable for promises made in company personnel manuals regarding dismissal procedures. Promissory estoppel holds a promisor liable for promises made when the promisee justifiably relies on the promise, the promisor knows or should know the promisee will act or forebear in reliance, and substantial injustice can be prevented only by holding the promisor liable.

The *Wlasiuk v. Whirlpool Corp.* case illustrates an attempt by an employer to escape promises made in an employee handbook. Note that the court here decides that it is an issue for the jury—a fact question rather than a legal question to be decided by a judge. Read the *Wlasiuk* case to see if the employer was able to escape liability.

Wlasiuk v. Whirlpool Corp.

Court of Appeals of Washington
914 P.2d 102 (1996)

Background and Facts:

Joe Wlasiuk began working for Whirlpool Corporation in 1976. In the mid-1980s, Wlasiuk received a "Whirlpool Corporate Salaried Employees Handbook." The handbook included a section entitled "The System Works," in which the president and chief operating officer of Whirlpool emphasized Whirlpool's commitment to ethical behavior. The handbook section on ethics was consistent with the Whirlpool company ethic Wlasiuk had learned previously; he was taught that ethical treatment of dealers was paramount. The handbook also included provisions relating to discipline and termination procedures.

On Friday, January 27, 1989, Wlasiuk met one of his dealers, Bill Long. Long told Wlasiuk that he had information that could affect Whirlpool, but Long did not want it known that he was the source of the information. Wlasiuk told Long he would "honor his confidentiality." Long said that a second dealer had found a Whirlpool price sheet for appliance dealer Jack Roberts, and that some of Jack Roberts's prices were lower than those given by Whirlpool to other dealers. Long refused to identify the dealer who had found the price sheet.

Wlasiuk immediately called his supervisor, Fred Huggins, who wanted to know what dealer had given him the information. Wlasiuk told Huggins that he had promised not to divulge the dealer's name. Huggins then said that unless Wlasiuk revealed the name of the dealer, he would be placed on probation. Wlasiuk declined to breach his promise to the dealer, believing that to do so would destroy the trust with the dealer, which was essential to his job.

Later that day, Wlasiuk went to the office to meet with Huggins. The meeting concluded with Wlasiuk declining to violate his promise to the dealer. Huggins then suspended Wlasiuk, followed him to his home, and removed Whirlpool materials from Wlasiuk's home office. Huggins instructed Wlasiuk not to contact any dealers or any Whirlpool personnel.

On the following Monday morning, Huggins called Bill Long and learned that Long was the dealer who told Wlasiuk about the missing price sheet. Long confirmed that he had asked Wlasiuk not to reveal his name. Long again refused to reveal the name of the dealer with the price sheet. Wlasiuk met with Huggins the next day to help Huggins determine which dealer actually had the price list. For the next few days, Wlasiuk stayed around home because he was told by someone "from Corporate. . . to be available."

7 174 Cal. App. 2d 184, 344 P.2d 25 (1959).

On Friday, February 3, Wlasiuk went to the office expecting to meet with someone from Whirlpool's Human Resources Department. Instead, he was told that he was terminated. At the time of his termination, Wlasiuk was 50 years old, had worked for Whirlpool for more than 12 years, and was the top retail sales territory manager in the Seattle office.

Wlasiuk sued Whirlpool and Huggins claiming age discrimination, wrongful termination in violation of public policy, breach of contractual and/or promissory obligations under the employee handbook, and, against Huggins only, tortious interference with a business relationship. The claims against Huggins were dismissed on summary judgment. The remaining claims were tried to a jury. At the close of plaintiff's case, the trial court dismissed the age discrimination claim. The jury then returned a verdict in favor of Wlasiuk on his claim of wrongful discharge under the employee handbook, but in favor of Whirlpool on the claim of discharge in violation of public policy. Each party appealed.

Body of Opinion

Judge Ellington

Generally, unless an employment contract specifies the length of time during which an employee will be employed, either party may terminate the contract at any time, for any reason.... However, an employee handbook or manual may modify the terminable-at-will relationship if it creates an atmosphere of job security and fair treatment by promising specific treatment in specific situations, thereby inducing the employee to remain on the job, and not seek other employment....

Where an employee handbook promises specific treatment in specific situations, an employer may disclaim any intent to be bound by the handbook, and if such a disclaimer is effectively communicated, employees may not justifiably rely upon the handbook provisions.... Therefore, we first consider whether Whirlpool's disclaimer effectively communicated that Whirlpool did not intend to be bound by its handbook.

At minimum, a "disclaimer must state in a conspicuous manner that nothing contained in the handbook, manual, or similar document is intended to be part of the employment relationship and that such statements are instead simply general statements of company policy."... A disclaimer also must be effectively communicated to the employee, who must have reasonable notice that the employer is disclaiming an intent to be bound by what appear to be promises. Whatever the language, the effect of a disclaimer may be negated by inconsistent representations and practices. The disclaimer must be considered in light of the surrounding circumstances, including the parties' representations and conduct. The effect of a disclaimer in an employee manual is a question of fact....

Whirlpool's disclaimer was as follows:

> This booklet is a general outline of Whirlpool Corporation's Corporate Administration and Marketing Group personnel policy and certain employee benefit programs. Additional policies and benefits may apply to you which are not included in this summary. In many instances the policy matters summarized in this booklet are covered by specific detailed policy statements. Details of employee benefits are specified by the various legal documents providing for such benefits. Strict interpretation of company policies and benefits as they pertain to individual cases will, in all cases, be based upon actual underlying policy statements and plan documents and must be the concern of your supervisor and the Human Resources Department. Nothing contained herein shall be deemed to constitute all of the conditions of employment or a contract of employment or to confer or modify any specific employee benefit.

The disclaimer's statement that nothing in the handbook "shall be deemed to constitute... a contract of employment" is "manifestly unclear," because even terminable-at-will employees have a contract of employment.... The statement "nothing contained herein shall be deemed... to confer or modify any specific employee benefit" is ambiguous in a paragraph which also states that the booklet is only a "general outline" and that "additional benefits and policies may apply." In context, these statements in the disclaimer could reasonably be read to mean that the handbook is incomplete and that other policies or benefits may be found elsewhere. Wlasiuk testified that he did not recall reading the disclaimer, nor had company officials called his attention to it. He had not signed anything acknowledging the disclaimer....

Whether an employee manual contains a promise of specific treatment in specific situations, whether the employee justifiably relied upon the promise, and whether the employer breached the promise are questions of fact for the jury.... These questions may be decided as a question of law only if reasonable minds could reach but one conclusion....

Judgment and Result

The jury here determined that Whirlpool promised specific treatment in specific situations in its employee handbook, that Wlasiuk relied upon those promises and that Whirlpool breached those promises. The trial court decision favoring Wlasiuk was affirmed.

Questions

1. How can the court reason that the employee handbook's language stating that nothing in the handbook "shall be deemed to constitute... a contract of employment" is manifestly unclear? What is unclear?

Must statements in employee handbooks be read "in context," that is, the circumstances of the handbook's issuance and the entire employment situation? Can context make an otherwise "clear" statement "unclear?"

2. If an employer's handbook promises specific treatment in specific situations, may the employer disclaim any intent to be bound by such statements if such a disclaimer is effectively communicated to the employees? If so, as this court says, what does this disclaimer do to employee trust in employer statements about ethics? If an employee has to sue an employer to get it to do the right thing, does this fact support the notion that positive law has risen to the stature of ethics? That is, in today's environment is the most one can expect in the way of "proper" or "ethical" conduct that which the positive law requires?
3. How important is it that an employee actually read the handbook an employer gives to employees? How can an employee who is hired and later dismissed logically claim that she or he relied on a statement in a handbook if she or he never read the handbook?
4. Why would an employer make promises it never intends to keep?

Notice of the Agency's Ending. Sometimes an agency ends with bad feelings between the principal and agent. This animosity may cause a disgruntled agent to enter unauthorized contracts on the principal's behalf merely to even the score against the former principal. It is also possible that the agent may forget or carelessly enter a transaction after the agency relationship has ended. Is the principal bound by an agent's contracts made on the principal's behalf after the agency has ended?

The answer depends on the type of agency, whether the third person who enters the contract after the agency ended ever had previous dealing with the principal through the agent, the manner in which the agency ends, and whether the principal gives the third person notice of the agency's termination.

Considering the most significant of these factors—notice to the third person of the agency's termination—the principal must give actual notice to third persons who have dealt with the principal through the agent. **Actual notice** is a phone call, personal visit, or letter. Of these methods, a certified letter probably provides the best evidence that the third person has received actual notice, although large certified mailings can be costly. **Constructive notice** is to be contrasted with actual notice. Constructive notice of any agency's termination must be given to people other than those who have dealt through the agent. A paid advertisement in a newspaper or trade journal giving public notice of an agency's termination is an example of constructive notice.

No notice of any kind need be given to third persons upon termination of a special agent hired to accomplish a particular task. If the agency ends by the principal's death, the agent's authority ends at that time in most cases. This situation can create hardship for an agent who, while in good faith not knowing that principal has died, enters a contract with a third person on the principal's behalf. Generally, the agent will be liable on the contract, even though it was understood the agent was acting only in an agency capacity in entering the contract. One effective lobbying group—commercial banks—has succeeded in reversing this rule regarding their ability to pay checks written by a depositor before death but presented for payment after death. Since the bank is viewed as an agent of people with checking accounts, the death ending the agent's authority rule does not apply here according to Section 4-405 of the Uniform Commercial Code (the law in the District of Columbia and 50 states).

CHAPTER SUMMARY

Employers' relations with their employees generally fall into one of the following categories: master-servant, principal-agent, and employer-independent contractor. The terms employer-employee are generally not recognized by the courts as a separate legal category.

The respondeat superior principle establishes the idea that one person can be liable for another's actions if the nonactor has the right to control the means and ends of the actor's job. Respondeat superior applies in principal-agent situations to hold principals liable for their agent's actions within the scope of their jobs. Respondeat superior also holds masters liable for their servants' actions within the scope of their employment. Respondeat superior does not generally apply in the case of employers and independent contractors.

The rules permit almost anyone to be an agent, servant, or independent contractor who demonstrates the mental and physical capability to perform and understand the significance of the acts undertaken. Corporations, trusts, and partnerships can be agents.

The ways of creating authority in an agent or servant include conferring express authority, implied authority, apparent authority, and ratification.

Masters and principals owe their employees several duties including the duty to provide safe working conditions, the duty to instruct, the duty to pay, and the duty to provide tools to perform their jobs. Principals also owe agents the duty to reimburse them for reasonable expenses incurred in carrying out the agency as well as the duty to indemnify agents for losses sustained in the agency.

Agents owe principals the duty to account, the duty to use care and skill, the duty to follow instructions, and the fiduciary duty. The fiduciary duty is broad and covers such matters as being honest and avoiding conflicts of interest with one's principal.

Agents who are authorized to contract on their principal's behalf are generally not personally liable on such contracts if the agent signs in a representative capacity and the principal's identity is known to the other contracting party.

Employees who commit crimes on the job are personally liable for them. Employers can be liable for their employees' crimes if courts apply the respondeat superior doctrine or the criminal conspiracy doctrine. Generally, corporate executives are not criminally liable for their employees' crimes if the executives did not authorize or know of the crimes. Defenses to employers prosecuted for employee crimes include the superior agent rule and the scope of employment doctrine.

When agencies end, the principal should notify third parties. Actual notice of the agency's ending should be given to third persons with whom the principal has dealt through the agent, and constructive notice given to other third parties.

The employment at-will doctrine permits either the employer or employee to end an employment relationship at any time for almost any reason. Exceptions to the employment at-will rule tend to protect the employee. Such exceptions include the tort of wrongful dismissal, implied contract limits on employers' dismissal rights, public policy exceptions, and the promissory estoppel theory.

Discussion Questions

1. A real estate agent may not lie to would-be purchasers if asked whether the former occupant of a home had AIDS, because so doing would be fraud or misrepresentation. On the other hand, the agent has a fiduciary duty to the seller, whom the agent represents, to attempt to sell the property as well as not to disclose unauthorized information.

   In California a realtor representing a seller was sued by a buyer on grounds that the realtor failed to disclose that, in the previous five years, five murders had taken place in the house the realtor sold. The customer said the brokers should disclose matters related to the house that would have a psychological impact on the buyer. Do you agree? [*Reed v. King*, 145 Cal. App. 3d 261 (1983)].
2. Michael Auston, a shift supervisor at the A.B.P. Midwest, Inc., allegedly asked Sharon Paul, an employee at A.B.P., "What are you two lesbians doing tonight?" It was uncontested that the persons referred to as "two

MANAGER'S ETHICAL DILEMMA

John Schreiner was crushed between his parked automobile and the colliding vehicle owned and driven by the appellant, Clay Fruit. As a result of the accident, Schreiner's left leg was amputated and the muscle tissue of the right leg so destroyed as to leave him crippled and permanently disabled.

At the time of the accident, Fruit, a life insurance salesman, was attending a sales convention of his employer, Equitable Life Assurance Society. The annual convention was being conducted at the resort location of Land's End near Homer on July 10–13, 1969. Sales employees of the company were required to attend the convention. After discussing with district managers the possibility of transporting the Anchorage insurance salesmen to the convention by bus, the agency manager decided that participants should travel by private transportation, and that they would be reimbursed a lump sum for their expenses. Clay Fruit chose to drive his own automobile, accompanied by his wife, another insurance agent, and the wife and child of the latter.

A business meeting on Friday morning proceeded on schedule followed by a cocktail party and hors d'oeuvres in the room and adjoining spaces of the agency manager. Fruit went to the room of an out-of-state guest with whom he talked business and had drinks. Testimony indicates that by mid-afternoon Fruit was asleep on the floor. That evening, a scheduled cocktail party and seafood dinner on the beach proceeded without Fruit who was still asleep in a room adjacent to that of the out-of-state guest.

At some time between 10:00 and 11:30 p.m. following the seafood dinner other members of the group awoke Fruit who, accompanied by his wife and two couples, walked to the Salty Dawg Bar and returned shortly. The others were tired and went to bed but Fruit decided to go to Homer as he was under the impression that the out-of-state guests were at the Waterfront Bar and Restaurant. Fruit then drove his car to Homer but departed when he did not find any of his colleagues.

His return route to Land's End took him past the Salty Dawg Bar where Schreiner's automobile was disabled on or immediately off the side of the road opposite Fruit's lane. While the facts of the particular moment of the accident which occurred at approximately 2:00 a.m. on July 12, 1969, are unclear, it appears that Fruit applied his brakes and skidded across the dividing line of the highway, colliding with the front of Schreiner's car. The hood of Schreiner's automobile had been raised and Schreiner was standing in front of his car. The collision crushed his legs.

The subsequent amputation and crippling of Schreiner was exacerbated by a urinary disorder resulting from exploratory surgery necessitated by the accident. Schreiner sued Fruit and his employer, Equitable, for damages including pain and suffering, mental anguish, interference with normal activities, continuing medical expenses, loss of income and financial losses incurred from the forced sale of his home, a lot, and securities. The jury found on special interrogatories that Fruit's negligence was the proximate cause of the accident; that he was acting within the course and scope of his employment for Equitable; that Equitable was directly negligent in planning and conducting the convention, which negligence was a proximate cause of the accident; and that Schreiner was not contributorily negligent. The jury awarded damages of $635,000 against both defendants. Both moved for a judgment notwithstanding the verdict and presently appeal from the respective denials of the motions. . . .

What result on appeal?

lesbians" were Sharon Paul and Norma Mae O'Brien. When Auston made this allegedly defamatory statement, was he acting within the scope of his employment? [*O'Brien v. A.B.P., Inc.*, 814 F.Supp. 766 (D. Minn. 1992)]

3. The common law rules controlling the employer-employee relationship were developed many years ago when employers and employees often knew each other personally and took a personal interest in each other. Is this familiarity true today? Why? Do you think this shift in some way explains why statutes have supplemented the common law rules?
4. What are some of the common law duties employers owe employees? Do these rules tend to favor either the employer or the employee, or are they neutral in operation?
5. What are the advantages and disadvantages to employers in having agents or servants instead of independent contractors?
6. What legal ethics discussed in Chapter 1 are served by holding an employer criminally answerable for an employee's on-the-job

crimes? What legal ethics support holding an employer civilly liable for damages resulting from an employee's work-related crimes?

7. When an employer wrongfully discharges an employee by breaking an unexpired employment contract, the employee may sue the employer and recover damages. However, the employee has a duty to mitigate damages. Therefore, the employee must actively seek other employment. When an Indiana school board wrongfully dismissed an untenured teacher for filing a grievance, she sued the school board for damages. The board claimed the teacher did not try hard enough to find other work and thereby failed to fulfill her duty to mitigate her damages, and her damages should therefore be reduced. The teacher had unsuccessfully applied for teaching jobs at several other school systems in the area in which she lived. She argued this satisfied her duty to mitigate damages. The school board, on the other hand, argued that she had to either take a job of a substantially different character or grade, or move to another community to find comparable work to fulfill her duty to mitigate damages. Who was correct? [*Board of Sch. Trustees v. Indiana Ed. Employment Relations Bd.*, 412 N.E.2d 807 (Ind. App. 1980)]
8. The question of the employer's right to dismiss an employee in an employment at-will arrangement is hotly contested today. One key issue is whether the employer has an unconditional right to dismiss without having or stating a reason. In one case, a woman sued her employer for an alleged breach of an oral employment contract. She was hired for factory work in 1968 at $1.84 per hour. She allegedly was told that if she worked well, she would get better jobs with better pay. She claimed that she was harassed by her foreman because she refused to go out with him. His hostility, condoned—if not shared—by the company personnel manager, resulted in her being fired. A jury trial produced a $2,500 verdict. The employer appealed to the New Hampshire Supreme Court. What was the result? [*Monge v. Beebe Rubber Co.*, 114 N.H. 130, 316 A.2d 549 (1974)].
9. An assistant manager authorized repair work on a restaurant's neon sign. The restaurant owner refused to pay the repair bill. He argued that the assistant manager had authority only to take bids on the job, not contract for it. Did the assistant manager bind the restaurant based on inherent authority? [*Zanac, Inc. v. Frazier Neon Signs, Inc.*, 134 Ga.App. 501, 215 S.E.2d 265 (Ga.App. 1975)]

Suggested Readings

Articles

CROLEY, "Vicarious Liability in Tort: On the Sources and Limits of Employee Reasonableness," 69 *Southern California Law Review* 1705 (1996).

DWORKIN and NEAR, "Whistleblowing Statutes: Are They Working?" 25 *American Business Law Journal* 241 (1987).

GREEN and REIBSTEIN, "Counseling the Employer on Recruitment Liability," 36 *Practical Lawyer* 25 (1990).

HURD, "Use of the Polygraph in Screening Job Applicants," 22 *American Business Law Journal* 530 (1985).

KUSKE and GUNZ, "The Letter of Engagement," 16 *Journal of Legal Studies Education* 297 (1998).

MALIN, "Protecting the Whistleblower from Retaliatory Discharge," 16 *Michigan Journal of Law Reform* 277 (1983).

MASSINGALE, "At-Will Employment: Going, Going . . ." 24 *University of Richmond Law Review* 187 (1990).

PRENTICE and WINSLETT, "Employee References: Will a 'No Comment' Policy Protect Employers against Liability for Defamation?" 25 *American Business Law Journal* 207 (1987).

SMITH, "AIDS and the Law: Protecting the HIV-Infected Employee from Discrimination," 57 *Tennessee Law Review* 539 (1990).

ST. ANTOINE, "Employment-at-will: Is the Model Act the Answer," 23 *Stetson Law Review* 179 (1993).

CHAPTER

15

IMPORTANT STATUTES IN EMPLOYER–EMPLOYEE RELATIONS

POSITIVE LAW ETHICAL PROBLEMS

"I got my hair sucked into a drive shaft and suffered horrific injuries because the OSHA inspectors performed a negligent inspection," said Gail Irving.

"No one would argue that," responded a lawyer for OSHA. "But put yourself in our shoes: We have limited resources and a limited number of inspectors who must of necessity 'spot check' the thousands of employers subject to OSHA regulations. It is unreasonable to expect that OSHA inspectors will be able to spot every conceivable safety hazard in every employer's workplace."

"Well what good is OSHA if the inspectors can simply 'pick and choose' what things to inspect?" answered Irving. "Your theory of 'spot checking' condones negligence and entitles me to recover against the federal government under the Federal Tort Claims Act because the OSHA inspector performed a negligent inspection resulting in my being seriously injured."

Was Irving right?

"My employer wants me to give up an age discrimination claim as a condition to getting increased retirement benefits," said Beatrice Kayser.

"Well, what's wrong with that?" ask Denise Bern, Kayser's co-worker.

"Just this," answered Kayser, "my employer is chiseling me out of a good claim that could be worth several thousand dollars in exchange for a few bucks more a month in retirement benefits. I think that ERISA [Employee Retirement Income Security Act] forbids employers from using retirement benefits as a bargaining chip to cheat hard-working employees out of their valid claims." Was Kayser correct?

"DURING 1998 OVER 44 MILLION PERSONS—ONE IN SIX—RECEIVED OVER $375 BILLION IN BENEFITS OUT OF A 1998 FEDERAL BUDGET OF $1.667 TRILLION."

Statistical Abstract of the United States

In Chapter 14 we saw some common law (judge-made) rules affecting employer-employee relations. Federal and state statutes have reshaped the entire area of employer-employee relations over the past 50 years. Such statutes address two major employee concerns: on-the-job safety and financial security. This chapter divides the statutes into two major areas. The first, job safety and statutory recovery, discusses *preventive* law (dealt with in the Occupational Safety and Health Act (OSHA), and a *compensatory* law, or workers' compensation. The second area, workers' financial security, covers the Employee Retirement Income Security Act of 1974 (ERISA), the Social Security Act, the Fair Labor Standards Act, unemployment compensation, the Family and Medical Leave Act of 1993, and plant closing legislation. Figure 15.1 presents a historical overview of statutes in the employer-employee area.

JOB SAFETY AND STATUTORY RECOVERY

Workers' Compensation

In the early part of the twentieth century, state legislatures started establishing workers' compensation systems. The objective of these systems is to pay workers (or their dependents) for work-related injuries, diseases, or death. Employers are liable for all such employee harm, even though the employer was not to blame. Put another way, employers are insurers of job-related harm to employees.

Early laws tended to cover only hazardous work, and even then they were not always welcomed. For example, Maryland enacted a law in 1902 setting up a cooperative accident fund for miners. It was held unconstitutional. Montana had a similar experience with its 1909 miners' compensation act. Although New York's 1910 compulsory workers' compensation act covered only a few hazardous jobs, it was likewise declared unconstitutional.

Finally, in 1917 the U.S. Supreme Court held that workers' compensation laws were valid exercises of a state's police power in *New York Central Railroad v. White* (243 U.S. 188). The *White* decision broke state resistance to workers' compensation. By 1920, only eight states were without a workers' compensation law. Today all states have workers' compensation laws, covering hazardous and most nonhazardous jobs.

Common Law Fault. Before workers' compensation laws, workers injured on the job recovered if they showed that employer **fault** (negligence) had injured them. It was a common law basis of recovery. Furthermore, even if employer fault were shown, the employer could escape liability by proving any *one* of the following defenses: (1) the injured employee's **contributory negligence** (that is, the employee's own fault contributed to the employee's loss); (2) the worker's **assumption of risk** (that is, the

FIGURE 15.1 Significant Statutes Affecting Employer–Employee Relations

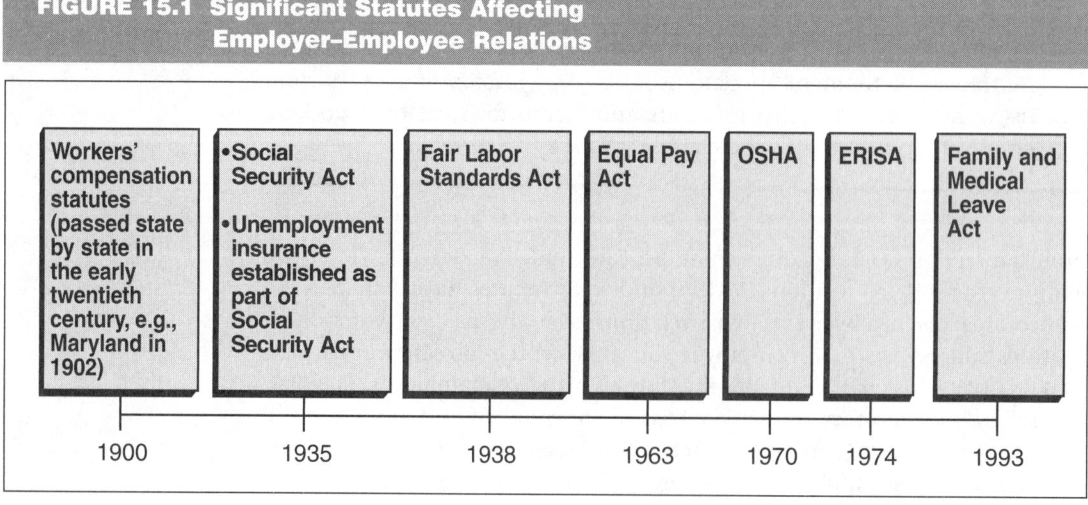

worker voluntarily performed a job knowing of the risk involved and was injured by this risk); or (3) a fellow servant's carelessness injured the worker, called the **fellow servant rule.**

The common law negligence rules just described prevented many injured workers or deceased workers' dependents from recovering for job-related injuries or death. The employers' argument on behalf of common law rules was essentially cost: common law rules kept worker claims low. Common law rules placed a large part of the cost of industrial injuries on the victims and their families and, indirectly, on society. For example, if an employee broke her back at work due in part to her own carelessness (contributory negligence), she recovered nothing.

Shift to Workers' Compensation. Common law rules were often harsh on injured and deceased workers' families. Many believed that using common law's fault idea was too crude to allocate the burden of industrial injury, disease, and death in a complex economy. To such people, these costs were simply part of the good or service produced and should be borne irrespective of fault by the party in the best position to administer them—the business producing the good or service. The business in turn passed this cost on to the consumers of the product or service.

Workers' compensation insurance is the mechanism for imposing these human costs on employers. Workers' compensation abandons common law fault principles in deciding who bears the cost of work-related injuries, diseases, and deaths. It makes the employer the insurer of these risks.

Key Features of Workers' Compensation Statutes. Workers' compensation statutes are state laws. And although they vary from state to state concerning the accidents and diseases covered, beneficiaries, and procedures, these laws have many similarities.

Work-Related Requirement. A worker (or dependent) may recover only for injuries, diseases, and death occurring on the job. For example, if an employee carelessly places a ladder against a wall at work, falls and sustains injuries, workers' comp pays. If that same accident had happened at home, workers' comp would not pay since the injuries would not be job-related.

Courts tend to construe the work-related requirement liberally. If doubt exists whether an injury occurred on or off the job, courts tend to say that "gray area" cases are work-related, allowing the worker to recover from workers' comp. For example, an accountant working for a large public accounting firm attended a day-long firm outing at a country club. On the way home at midnight, he was killed in an auto accident. A court held that this death was work-related, enabling the accountant's family to recover under workers' comp. If heart attacks are work-related, the claimant may recover even if the worker had a preexisting heart condition. Also, others cases have held that heart attacks at work resulting from psychic upset are recoverable.

Generally, workers' comp statutes do not allow employees to recover for self-inflicted injuries. This rule attempts to stop malingering (pretending one has a covered injury to collect benefits). Suicides present exceptional cases because malingering is unlikely. In one Delaware Supreme Court case (*Delaware Tire Center v. Fox*), the court indicated that certain suicides were compensable. According to *Fox*, a suicide is not willful for workers' comp purposes if an industrial accident was the main factor triggering the worker's suicide. Suicides are, thankfully, rare in the workplace. Back injuries are not. The most common worker compensation claims arise from back injuries. The *Cormier v. Resthaven Nursing Home* case illustrates the difficulty of proving that an employee with a back injury is "faking" such a claim.

Cormier v. Resthaven Nursing Home

Court of Appeal of Louisiana
670 So.2d 233 (1996)

Background and Facts:

On October 19, 1993, Cormier filed a disputed claim for compensation benefits, seeking weekly indemnity and medical benefits. She contended that she had injured her left shoulder, left side, and back on October 7, 1993, while moving furniture to clean at the Resthaven Nursing Home.

After the August 25, 1994, hearing, the worker's compensation hearing officer issued judgment that claimant was entitled to all worker's compensation benefits. Defendant Resthaven appeals, asserting that the hearing officer erred in determining that claimant was entitled to worker's compensation benefits. Cormier answered the appeal, assigning as error the hearing officer's failure to award statutory attorney's fees and penalties.

Body of Opinion

Judge Woodard

To be entitled to receive worker's compensation benefits, a claimant must first establish by a preponderance of the evidence that she has received "personal injury by an accident arising out of and in the course of... employment."... Under the Lousiana Worker's Compensation Act, "accident" is defined as "an unexpected or unforeseen actual, identifiable, precipitous event happening suddenly or violently, with or without human fault, and directly producing at the time objective findings of an injury which is more than simply a gradual deterioration or progressive degeneration."...

On appeal, Resthaven argues that the hearing officer erred in accepting claimant's testimony about the occurrence of the accident. The hearing officer's determination as to whether the claimant's testimony was sufficient to discharge the burden of proof constitutes a factual determination. Consequently, the resolution of this issue will not be disturbed on review absent error. We will only set aside the hearing officer's factual finding if the record demonstrates that this finding is clearly wrong.... Additionally, the hearing officer's determination as to whether a claimant's testimony was sufficient proof of the occurrence of an accident is necessarily a credibility call and demands great deference on review because "only the fact finder can be aware of the variations in demeanor and tone of voice that bear so heavily on the listener's understanding and belief in what is said."...

A claimant's testimony alone can satisfy the preponderance of the evidence burden of proof that an accident occurred, provided two elements are met: (1) no other evidence discredits or casts *serious* doubt on the worker's version of the accident, and (2) the claimant's testimony is corroborated by circumstances following the alleged accident....

In her reasons for judgment, the hearing officer found that claimant had sustained her burden of proving a work-related accident by "a very bare preponderance of the evidence" because the evidence did not cast doubt on claimant's version of the accident and that her version of events was corroborated by circumstances immediately after the accident; namely, that claimant reported the accident to her employer, and the day after the accident, she sought medical treatment from Dr. Young Kang. While there were inconsistencies in claimant's testimony from her deposition, she explained that she had suffered a similar accident on July 29, 1993, and had confused the details. Claimant's accident data filed with the Office of Worker's Compensation reflects that she reported the accident to her supervisor, Linda Benoit, on October 7, 1993. Also the record reflects that claimant's injuries were present.

The hearing officer had a rational basis for her finding; therefore, we cannot say that she was clearly wrong.... Accordingly, we affirm on this issue....

Cormier had been under the treatment of Dr. R. Dale Bernauer, an orthopedic surgeon, from October 13, 1993, through the date of the hearing. By letter dated June 7, 1994, Dr. R. Dale Bernauer wrote that claimant's "problem with her neck and back is directly related to her accident." Accordingly, Cormier met her burden of proving that she sustained a work-related accident. Thus, she is entitled to medical benefits.

Regarding weekly indemnity benefits, a claimant is entitled to total temporary disability benefits if she meets the burden of proving her disability, or her inability to engage in any employment, by clear and convincing evidence.... After Cormier's October 8, 1993, visit to Dr. Kang, she was taken off work indefinitely and referred to a specialist. On October 13, 1993, Dr. R. Dale Bernauer, orthopedic surgeon, examined her and found that her neck and lumbar spine showed a decreased range of motion; thoracic spine showed compression sign positive and distraction positive; straight leg raising was negative; neurological exam and x-rays were normal. He diagnosed her with cervical, thoracic, and lumbar strain, placed her on physical therapy, and issued a slip stating that she was unable to return to work. By a letter to Thomas Filo, Cormier's attorney, dated October 18, 1993, he wrote that he thought claimant was suffering from cervical, thoracic and lumbar strain, and on December 30, 1993, he issued another off-work slip: "Glenda Cromier is a patient I am currently treating for a cervical, thoracic and lumbar strain. She is unable to do any type of gainful employment and cannot work." And, on May 23, 1994, Dr. Bernauer wrote to Alexsis Risk Management, Resthaven's worker's compensation insurance carrier, that: "Glenda Cormier has continued neck pain and left arm pain. I have attempted to schedule an MRI. Her examination showed weakness on triceps on the left and grip strength on the left. She has signs of a herniated disc in her neck. I think an MRI is medically necessary at this time." In another letter to Thomas Townsley, Cormier's attorney, dated June 7, 1994, Dr. Bernauer noted that claimant complained of pain and stated that he ordered a CT scan on February 2, 1994, but it was not performed due to Resthaven's worker's compensation carrier's refusal to authorize payment; that he had ordered an MRI on April 25, 1994, but it had not been done; and that claimant's "problem with her neck and back is directly related to her accident. I think she needs an MRI done. She may have a herniated disc in her neck, if so, she may need surgery on this."

On February 7, 1994, Cormier was examined by Dr. Thomas Ford, an orthopedic surgeon, at Resthaven's request. His physical examination was normal. He could find no physiological reason for her complaints of tenderness along her left side; no objective reason why she cannot work as a nurse's aide; and no reason why her activities as a nurse's aide require restriction, noting that her x-rays showed mild degenerative changes. He notified Cindy McMahon, in a letter dated February 9, 1994, that: "I am unable to explain the complaints on a physical basis. The bizarre complaints of hemi-dysesthesias is [sic] not compatible with an anatomical lesion aside from a brain tumor. It is my opinion this patient is capable of working."

At the hearing, Cormier testified that she was unable to work because of pain and numbness on her left side from head to toe. She stated that she was unable to perform household chores. Yet, Resthaven produced a surveillance tape of her moving around and occasionally bending while at the flea market where her husband works.

To satisfy the clear and convincing standard, it must be established that "the existence of the disputed fact [is] highly probable, that is, much more probable that its non-existence."...

Furthermore, as this court recently held... there must be *objective* medical evidence to carry the burden of proving disability by clear and convincing evidence. The testimony of a patient's treating physician should ordinarily be afforded more weight than that of an examining physician.... Additionally, positive feelings as to the existence of an injury are to be afforded more weight than negative findings....

Judgment and Result

After careful examination of the record, we find that Cormier satisfied her burden that she is temporarily and totally disabled. [The court also awarded Cormier's attorney fees of $8,000 and penalized Resthaven for not investigating her claim.]

Questions

1. How did the Cormier case define "accident" for workers' compensation purposes?
2. Why would an appellate court defer to a trial court's (or workers' compensation hearing officer, as here) decision as to whether a workers' compensation claimant proved that her back injury in fact existed and that she was not merely malingering to win?
3. One hundred thousand dollars invested at six percent interest earns $6,000 per year or $500 per month. In effect, if someone wins a $500 per month workers' compensation award is it not the equivalent of winning one hundred thousand dollars?
4. Often workers' compensation claims hinge on expert witness testimony, such as that of a physician. What was the expert testimony here as to Cormier's back condition? Of what relevance was the surveillance tape showing Cormier "bending while at the flea market"? Do you suppose that Cormier bent over to go to the toilet? Thus, can occasional "bending over" necessarily negate Cormier's claim?

Certain But Limited Recovery. One feature of workers' comp is the certain recovery given to all covered employees. If an employee has an injury, a schedule sets dollar values for many specific losses. For example, the schedule may allow $5,000 for a hand, $7,500 for an arm, and $10,000 for an eye. For unscheduled losses, a percentage of disability is determined. This partial (or total) disability recovery is related to an employee's earnings. In either case, employees are handed checks for the amount the workers' comp benefit schedule says they get—no more, no less. Thus, this recovery is certain. It does not depend on winning a jury verdict. The common law defenses of contributory negligence, the fellow servant rule, and assumption of risk are not available to employers under workers' comp because the employer is an insurer (presumed liable provided the worker loss relates to the job). Fault is not an issue as it is in negligence cases.

Exclusivity of Remedy. Workers' comp statutes eliminate employee common law and statutory claims against employers, making the workers' comp statute the *only* legal basis for an employee to recover from the employer, co-workers, and employer's executives for job-related injuries, diseases, or death. The employee is guaranteed a workers' comp recovery for these events.

What if the employee's actual expenses or losses from a work-related accident are more than what workers' comp allows? The injured employee recovers *only* the scheduled amount, because workers' comp statutes are bargains between employees and employers. Even if a harm is worth more to one person than to another, an employee cannot forego the workers' comp recovery and sue on common law principles instead. Employees are limited to workers' comp recovery for work-related injuries, disease or death, even if a particular employee's real losses are far greater than what workers' comp allows. This limited exclusive remedy is a major benefit to employers. Such a benefit is greater in inflationary times because workers' comp benefits are usually not inflation indexed. Also, workers' comp benefits are often conservative, partly because they try to project mythical average employees' losses (in calculating, for example, the value of an arm).

Workers' comp's exclusive remedy rule applies only to employee lawsuits against their employers. In other words, workers' comp says its recoveries are the only ones available against an employer. However, it does *not stop* an employee from suing a *third party* on common law or other statutory principles for job-related injuries, disease, or death. For example, employees of insulation installers have sued the manufacturer of asbestos insulation for diseases caused by inhaling asbestos fibers. One such manufacturer, the Manville Corporation, entered bankruptcy due to such third-party claims.

Nonapplication to Independent Contractors. Most state workers' compensation statutes apply only to employees (agents and servants), not to independent contractors. This limitation has great financial consequences for business. Specifically, business would prefer to have independent contractors rather than employees (agents and servants) because it does not directly pay their workers' comp insurance costs. Workers' comp costs are high and rising because of increased medical and hospital costs and the pressures to expand job relatedness to include more employee injuries and disease under workers' comp coverage. One Wall Street investment firm's 1976 study on workers' comp costs showed an increase from $3.9 billion to $6.4 billion in three years.

Funding. Virtually all state workers' comp systems force employers to pay for industrial injuries, accidents, and deaths in one of three ways: by purchasing insurance from industrial insurers, by **self-insuring** (large employers set up contingency funds to cover risks to workers), or by using a state fund to which covered employers contribute.

Administration. Workers' comp systems are run by state administrative agencies. Such names as "industrial commissions" are common for such bodies. These agencies **adjudicate** worker claims (for example, they decide whether a disease is job-related). No juries are involved, only an administrative law judge. Decisions of such industrial boards may be appealed to the courts. The agencies also enforce the law by making sure required employers have workers' comp coverage.

Employees Covered. State workers' compensation laws cover most employees. However, farm workers, workers in the home, and federal workers (covered by federal laws) are not covered by state workers' comp laws.

Mandatory or Elective. State workers' comp laws are either elective or mandatory. In the case of mandatory statutes, a state could require employers having a certain minimum number of employees (three is a common number) to have workers' comp coverage. Many states allow employers to elect workers' comp coverage or common law negligence. If an employer chooses the latter, the defenses of contributory negligence, assumption of risk, and the fellow servant rule are not available. One advantage to the employee if an employer elects not to have workers' comp coverage is that the workers' comp recovery limit does not apply. An injured employee may recover at common law all provable damages. Because of its limited benefit schedule, full recovery is often not true where workers' comp controls.

Occupational Safety and Health Act (OSHA)

The Occupational Safety and Health Act is a federal law passed in 1970. In the four years before OSHA was passed, more U.S. workers were killed at work than were killed in the Vietnam War. About two million were disabled each year by work-related accidents. The *President's Report on Occupational Safety and Health* (1972) estimated that 100,000 deaths per year were attributable to occupational diseases and illnesses from exposure to chemical and physical hazards. Congress tried to stop this carnage in the workplace when it passed OSHA. President Nixon signed it into law on December 29, 1970, and OSHA took effect on April 28, 1971.

For regulations, inspections, and processes of the Occupational Safety and Health Administration, go to ***http://www.osha.gov***

http://

OSHA's Objectives. OSHA tries to make the workplace safe and healthy for workers and to preserve the country's human resources. When OSHA became law, it covered about 57 million workers in about four million businesses, large and small, affecting interstate commerce.

OSHA Administration and Records. The Occupational Safety and Health Administration (also known as OSHA) administers and enforces the act.

OSHA puts a record-keeping burden on employers. Four types of records must be kept:

1. Enforcement records
2. Research records
3. Job-related injury and accident records
4. Records of job hazards

OSHA Standards. How does OSHA propose to accomplish its objective of making the workplace safer and healthier? The answer is familiar: by regulations. The three types of OSHA standards are interim, permanent, and temporary emergency. The *interim standards* were applicable for two years after the act's passage. The secretary of labor was allowed to use any national consensus standard of a nationally recognized standards setting organization (e.g., professional engineering groups' standards) for this purpose. The *permanent standards* are the basic OSHA regulations setting workplace safety and health requirements. Permanent standards may be set any time after consulting with the OSHA Advisory Committee. *Temporary emergency standards* last only six months and provide some protection while OSHA develops a permanent standard. For instance, OSHA has imposed an emergency standard for vinyl chloride (a carcinogen).

OSHA regulations vary from industry to industry. The regulations detail how to carry on work to avoid accidents and promote health. For example, hearing loss results from overexposure to job noise. An OSHA regulation (found in 29 CFR §1926.101) tells when and which earplugs must be used in construction work.

OSHA standards come from several places. OSHA got many of its standards from private organizations such as the American National Standards Institute and the National Fire Protection Association. Such privately developed standards were called national consensus standards. They were advisory occupational safety and health standards from federal standards already established under prior federal laws. (An example is the Walsh-Healey Act, which forbids the federal government from buying more than $10,000 of goods made under unsanitary or hazardous working conditions.)

National Institute of Occupational Safety and Health (NIOSH). The National Institute of Occupational Safety and Health (NIOSH) is a research institute that develops **criteria documents**, which are studies telling how much of a substance causes diseases, how much noise causes deafness, and so on. A few OSHA standards (specific numbers, amounts, levels, and the like) are based partly on criteria documents.

State OSHAs (SOSHAs). OSHA lets states develop standards and plans to regulate job safety and health. If a state assures it will regulate its plan as effectively as the federal plan, the state—not the OSHA—regulates workplace safety and health in that state. At least half of the states have assumed OSHA administration and enforcement.

Steps in OSHA's Operation. Figure 15.2 details how OSHA works. In step 1, Congress passed the Occupational Safety and Health Act. This delegated rulemaking authority from Congress to the Occupational Safety and Health Administration (actually the secretary of labor). The act also sets out a general duty standard for employers based on common law principles. It provides: "Each employer shall furnish to each of his

FIGURE 15.2 How OSHA Works

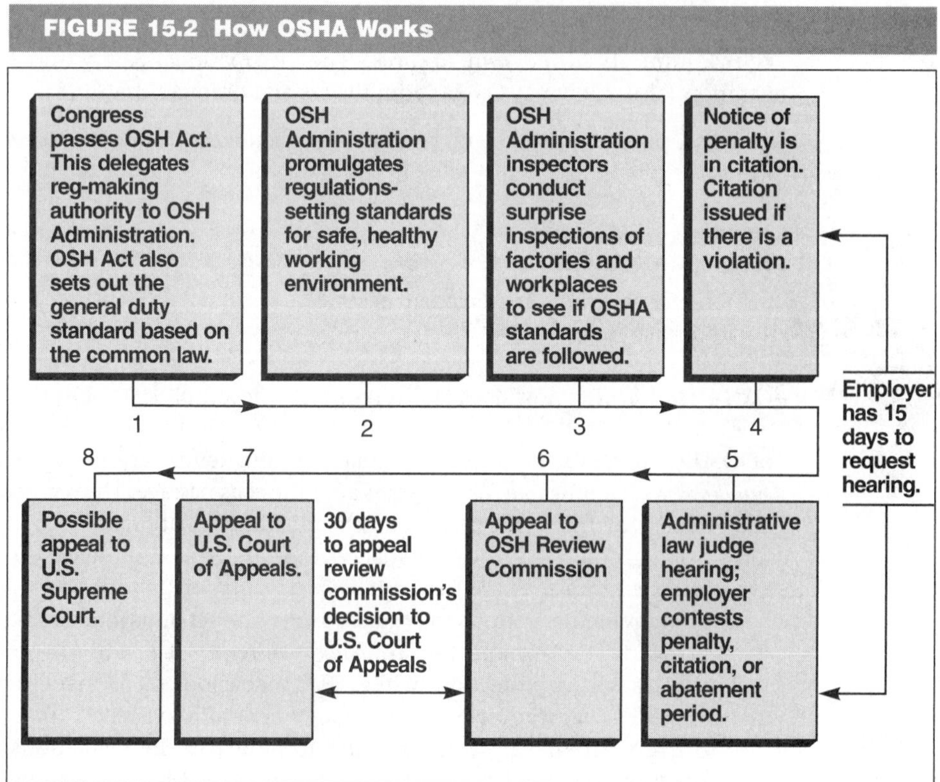

employees employment and a place of employment which are free from recognized hazards that are causing or are likely to cause death or serious physical harm to his [or her] employees."

The act itself (OSHA) creates only one workplace safety and health standard, the **general duty standard** just quoted. The OSH Act is an *enabling* act. It is a delegation of regulation-making authority from Congress to an administrative agency. OSH Administration worker safety and health standards are promulgated as regulations by the secretary of labor as part of the Department of Labor.

Reread Chapters 6 and 7 on the anatomy of a federal regulation if you do not recall how notice and comment regulation making takes place (step 2 in Figure 15.2). In *Whirlpool Corp. v. Marshall*, the U.S. Supreme Court upheld an OSHA regulation that lets employees refuse to do their work if they reasonably believe death or serious injury will result *and* if they believe they have no less dangerous way of doing the job.

In step 3, OSH Administration inspectors conduct surprise inspections of factories and other workplaces that the OSH Act covers. These inspections are designed to see whether a business follows OSHA standards. Recall from Chapter 8 that a business person has a right of privacy. This protection lets a business demand a search warrant from the OSHA inspector before admitting that person. The act allows an employer and an employee representative to walk with the OSHA official during an inspection.

Step 4 in OSHA's operation is the possible issuance of an OSHA citation. An OSHA citation lists alleged employer violations of OSHA. It also contains a notice of penalties for the various alleged violations as well as an abatement period. The **abatement period** tells an employer how much time it has to correct an OSHA violation.

Employer penalties for OSHA infractions exist for nonserious violations or for serious, nonwillful violations. If a violation is willful and repeated, penalties up to $10,000 are possible. Additionally, a six-month period of imprisonment is possible if an employee death results from an OSHA violation.

In step 5 of OSHA's operation, an employer receiving an OSHA citation has 15 days to contest the citation, penalty, or abatement period. Such a challenge takes place before an administrative law judge, who is basically a federal judge. (Refer to Chapters 6 and 7 on enforcement of a federal regulation if you need to recall how an administrative hearing differs from a trial court.) The administrative law judge hears witnesses, other evidence, and legal arguments, decides factual and legal issues, and enters an order.

Step 6 in OSHA's operation involves a possible appeal of the administrative law judge's order to the Occupational Safety and Health Review Commission, which is an appellate administrative review. Once the Occupational Safety and Health Review Commission enters its order, an employer or the secretary of labor has 30 days to appeal to a U.S. Court of Appeals. Twelve of these courts are spread throughout the United States. Their decisions can possibly be taken to the U.S. Supreme Court (steps 7 and 8 in OSHA's operation). A leading OSHA practicing lawyer suggests that employers appeal Occupational Safety and Health Review Commission orders to U.S. courts of appeals. This lawyer reported that about half of the time the courts of appeals reverse Review Commission orders.

Criticisms of OSHA. OSHA is hated by many businesses for several reasons. First, OSHA has many vague regulations. For example, OSHA had a regulation requiring "all places of employment, passageways . . . be kept clean and orderly." What is "clean and orderly" to a businessperson may not be so to an OSHA inspector. In one case, a business was cited for violating this regulation.

Second, other OSHA regulations are quite detailed about trivial matters. One U.S. Secretary of Labor (Ray Marshall) has called OSHA regulations nit-picking. No detail is too small for OSHA regulations. For example, 29 CFR §1910.25(b)(1)(ii) of the 1977

OSHA regulations contain detailed requirements for permissible irregularities in western hemlock used for ladder construction.

Third, business has to pay for OSHA's requirements. No matter how great OSHA may be, the one who pays has less enthusiasm. Fourth, some of OSHA's enforcers were allegedly arrogant and high-handed, with an adversarial rather than supportive attitude toward business. "We are out to get you" rather than "we are out to help you improve" was the perception some businesses had of OSHA. Whether this assessment was accurate or just an excuse attempting to divert attention from OSHA violations probably cannot be answered the same way in all cases.

Fifth, many have questioned OSHA's judgment in regulating trivial matters having little bearing on worker safety and health. For example, one early OSHA regulation (later amended) prohibited ice in drinking water. Because OSHA has always had a limited enforcement staff, its job of improving workplace safety and health has been allegedly shortchanged by its spending excessive time on trivia.

OSHA Changes. In the Appropriations Act of 1977, Congress told OSHA to get rid of "nuisance standards" (trivial regulations or those unrelated to OSHA's safety and health objectives). President Carter also told executive departments (such as Labor, which houses OSHA) to reduce and simplify regulations. OSHA got these messages on October 24, 1978, when OSHA published a final rule in the *Federal Register* (43 F.R. 49726) revoking about 900 OSHA regulations.

Other suggestions for OSHA improvement include more frequent inspection of high-risk industries (such as construction) and less frequent inspection of less hazardous workplaces (such as real estate offices), *de minimis* (little) notices (or warnings) for small or technical standards violations with no direct bearing on health and safety, simplified standards, further reduction of unneeded standards, and increasing help to businesses so they can comply with the standards.

One of the most persistent areas of controversy under OSHA concerns workplace inspections. Employers frequently complain that OSHA inspectors are officious and lack judgment resulting in employer fines for what are, essentially, trivial regulations infractions.

On the other hand, employees complain that employers have complained to the point that OSHA inspectors now "look the other way," often ignoring serious safety violations with resulting hazardous conditions for workers. The *Irving v. U.S.* case presents an interesting twist on this theme: while workers are not entitled to sue employers for injuries sustained by OSHA violations, could workers bring a Federal Tort Claims Act case against the OSHA when OSHA inspectors negligently inspect an employer's workplace proximately causing a worker's injury?

Irving v. United States

U.S. Court of Appeals (1st Cir.)
162 F.3d 154 (1998)

Background and Facts

In 1979, Somersworth Shoe Company operated a manufacturing plant in New Hampshire. On October 10 of that year, the plaintiff Gail Merchant Irving, a Somersworth employee, was stamping innersoles by means of a marker machine. At one point, she went behind her workbench to obtain materials from the die rack. In the process, she dropped a glove. When she stooped to retrieve it, her hair was drawn into the vacuum created by the high speed rotation of a drive shaft that delivered power to an adjacent "die-out" machine. She sustained horrific injuries.

Irving sued the United States under the Federal Tort Claims Act (FTCA) claiming that inspectors employed by the Occupational Safety and Health Administration (OSHA) negligently performed their duties and thereby proximately caused her injuries. The case traveled an inexcusably long and tortuous route to a decision on the merits—a route that included four detours to the U.S. Court of Appeals for the First Circuit. Ultimately, the district court, proceeding under a legal framework established by a panel of the First Circuit, concluded that the FTCA's discretionary function exception did not bar Irving's claim; that the OSHA inspector acted negligently; and that such negligence was actionable under applicable state law.

A divided panel of this court affirmed the judgment... but the full court, acting sua sponte [on its own motion] withdrew the opinion and ordered rehearing en banc, principally to review the important question of whether the FTCA's discretionary function exception foreclosed the plaintiff's negligent inspection claim.

Body of Opinion

Circuit Judge Selya

...In this instance, the plaintiff claims that workplace inspections, negligently performed by OSHA compliance officers, proximately caused her injuries. In analyzing the nature of this conduct, we begin with the language of the OSH Act because "it will most often be true that the general aims and policies of the controlling statute will be evident from its text"... and, in turn, these aims and policies will offer valuable insights into the nature of the conduct.

In relevant part, the OSH Act authorizes the Secretary of Labor to "inspect and investigate during regular working hours and at other reasonable times, and within reasonable limits and in a reasonable manner, any such place of employment and all pertinent conditions, structures, machines, apparatus, devices, equipment, and materials therein."... Under this authority, OSHA conducts both programmed general administrative inspections—known in the bureaucratic argot that OSHA so readily attracts as "full-scope" or "wall-to-wall" inspections—and more focused efforts pinpointed to threats of imminent danger. Aside from a reasonableness limitation on the time and manner of inspections, the statute places virtually no constraint on the Secretary's discretion to conduct such inspections in any way that she deems fit....

It [Congress] left the scope and detail of OSH Act inspections to the Secretary's discretion. Had Congress wished to impose upon OSHA an obligation to inspect every corner of every plant that it visited, we think it is highly likely that Congress would have expressed its intention by choosing language comparable to that which it used in crafting the [Federal Mine Safety Act].

We recognize that, by its plain terms, the OSH Act confers discretion only upon the Secretary, not upon compliance officers—and it is the latter's conduct that concerns us. Nevertheless, the legislative rules governing the authority of compliance officers mimic the statute and grant these officials broad discretion over the scope, manner, and detail of general administrative inspections. The regulations' stated goal is "to set forth general policies for enforcement of the inspection, citation, and proposed penalty provisions of the Act."... Echoing the language of... the Act], section 1903.3 of the regulations confers upon compliance officers the unbridled power, subject only to limits of reasonableness, to enter workplaces, inspect any piece of equipment or other pertinent item, and interview any person in order to carry out the Secretary's statutory mission....

To be sure, the regulations contain a sprinkling of mandatory directives.... (obligating compliance officers, inter alia, to present their credentials at the start of an inspection, to use "reasonable precautions" when taking photographs and samples, to wear appropriate protective clothing, to avoid "unreasonable disruption" of the workplace, and to "confer with the employer" in order to inform him of "any apparent safety or health violations disclosed by the inspection"). Save for these and, for our purposes, other similarly innocuous details, the regulations neither mandate a particular modus operandi for conducting inspections nor otherwise materially restrict compliance officers' flexibility. Of particular importance, the regulations do not prescribe any specific regimen governing the scope or detail of general administrative inspections performed by compliance officers....

The function of an OSHA compliance officer is an integral part of OSHA's enforcement policies. When conducting inspections under the auspices of an administrative plan, OSHA compliance officers are expected to study the layout of the facility they are about to investigate, to review its health and safety records, and to interview employer and employee representatives during the inspection about working conditions. One might expect that as a result of such study, OSHA inspectors will make daily judgments about what risks and safety issues most urgently require their attention. At bottom, OSHA inspectors must visit numerous workplaces, all of which present different challenges and issues, and they simply cannot be expected to inspect every item in every plant. The day-to-day decisions made by compliance officers thus further OSHA's enforcement policy of ensuring adequate safety in workplaces with a view toward efficient and effective use of limited resources, and are thus grounded in policy....

We are not persuaded by plaintiff's contention that all inspections ought to be painstakingly comprehensive because individual companies rely on OSHA inspections to improve their health and safety conditions. The OSH Act, in no uncertain terms, places primary responsibility for workplace safety on employers, not on the federal government....

Judgment and Result

Plaintiff loses. The Federal Tort Claims Act does not allow tort claims such as plaintiff's negligent OSHA inspection claim, which are based on discretionary functions. The manner of conducting OSHA inspections is discretionary.

Questions

1. Is the OSH Act mandatory meaning that it forces the government to do certain things and if it does not it can be sued for not doing them? Or is the OSH Act discretionary, meaning that the act essentially lets the OSHA do whatever it wants in carrying out the Congressional mandates and thus the OSHA is immune from suit if it does not observe the OSH Act? Note that this mandatory/discretionary characterization was essential to the success of plaintiff's suit.

   Did the court admit that the OSHA really is a hodge-podge of mandates and discretion?
2. When conducting OSHA inspections under an administrative plan, what are OSHA inspectors expected to do? Anything?
3. Under OSHA, who has the primary responsibility for workplace safety—employers or the Occupational Safety and Health Administration? Why? Is this reasonable in light of employers' desire to "cut costs to the bone" and thereby skimp on safety if at all possible?

WORKERS' FINANCIAL SECURITY

Fair Labor Standards Act

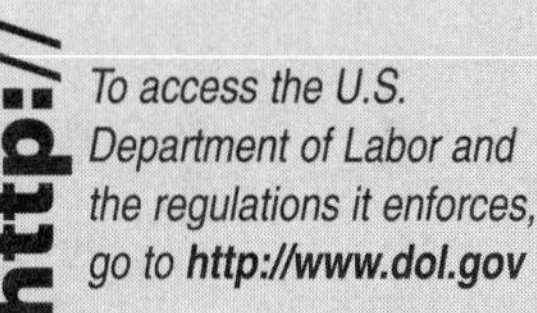

Congress enacted the Fair Labor Standards Act (FLSA) in 1938. The act's purpose was to eliminate labor conditions that did not allow employees to maintain minimum living standards. The belief was that substandard wages and working hours impaired employee health and welfare. Thus, Congress declared that poor labor conditions burdened commerce and led to unfair competition among the states.

Two of the FLSA's main provisions direct employees to pay their workers at least minimum wages and limit the hours employees can work unless they are paid overtime (higher) wages. The FLSA also establishes equal pay, record-keeping, and child labor standards. These rules affect more than 50 million full-time and part-time workers.

The FLSA has recently been criticized as causing unemployment in certain labor sectors. Some maintain that such unemployment reflects that minimum wage rates are set above the value of the services these people have to offer.

Covered Workers. The FLSA covers workers in interstate commerce (such as interstate bus drivers) and workers producing goods for interstate commerce (such as the employees in Hastings, Michigan, who make piston rings for shipment throughout the United States). The following businesses are covered by the FLSA:

1. Laundries or dry cleaners
2. Construction firms
3. Hospitals
4. Schools (including higher education) whether public or private
5. Retail or service businesses with certain levels of annual gross incomes
6. Any other business having annual gross sales or business of certain levels

A business whose *only* regular employees are the owner or members of the owner's immediate family is not covered by the FLSA.

Federal employees are subject to the FLSA's minimum wage, overtime, child labor, and equal pay provisions. State and local government employees are covered by the FLSA's child labor and equal pay provisions only if they are in traditional governmental activities. (The U.S. Supreme Court indicates that schools, hospitals, parks, fire prevention, police protection, sanitation and public health, and recreation are considered traditional governmental activities.) Minimum wage and overtime provisions do not apply to state and local traditional governmental activities. Thus, for example, equal pay would have to be given to male and female state park employees doing the same work, but the state park does not have to pay the minimum federal wage or abide by the federal maximum working hours. (However, about three-fourths of the states have state wage and hour laws that could apply to state government employees.)

Some employees who do not work for businesses covered by the FLSA might still get the FLSA's minimum wage, maximum hours (overtime pay), equal pay, and child labor protections if they individually engage in interstate commerce. Such employees include those who regularly cross state lines in their work.

FLSA Wage Standards. Workers covered by the FLSA have a legal right to $5.15 per hour starting September 1, 1997. Covered workers also have a right to overtime pay at no less than one and one-half times the employees' regular rate after 40 hours of work in the work week.

Covered employers may sometimes pay less than the minimum wage. Learners, apprentices, and handicapped workers may, under certain circumstances, be paid less than the minimum wage. Full-time students in retail or service businesses, agriculture, or higher education institutions may be paid less than the minimum federal wage. (Keep in mind that most states have minimum wage laws that might cover students and others not federally protected.) Special certificates issued by the Department of Labor's wage and hour administrator must be obtained to pay these groups subminimum wages.

Industry wage orders may set minimum rates below the generally applicable FLSA minimum wage in Puerto Rico, the Virgin Islands, and American Samoa.

FLSA Exemptions. Despite being employed by a covered firm, some employees are not covered by the FLSA's minimum wage provisions. Others are not protected by the overtime sections. Still others get no wage or hour protection at all. The following jobs are exempt from both the FLSA's minimum wage and overtime provisions:

1. Executive, administrative, and professional employees, including teachers and academic administrative employees in elementary and secondary schools; outside salespeople are also included
2. Employees of certain individually owned and operated small retail or service establishments not part of a covered enterprise
3. Employees of certain seasonal amusement or recreational establishments, employees of certain small newspapers, switchboard operators of small telephone companies, workers/sailors employed on foreign vessels, and employees engaged in fishing operations
4. Farm workers employed by anyone who used no more than 500 person-days of farm labor in any calendar quarter of the preceding calendar year
5. Casual babysitters and people employed as companions to the elderly

Certain workers are exempt from the FLSA's overtime provisions only (although many make beyond the minimum wage, and that protection is not worth much to them anyway).

As noted, executive and administrative employees are exempt from both the FLSA's minimum wage and overtime provisions. Is an assistant manager at a Burger King restaurant an executive? Read *Donovan v. Burger King Corporation* to find out.

Donovan v. Burger King Corp.

U.S. Court of Appeals (2d Cir.)
675 F.2d 516 (1982)

Background and Facts:

The plaintiff Secretary of Labor brought this action under 28 U.S.C. §217 alleging defendant Burger King's failure to pay overtime compensation to certain employees and to keep related records as required by the Fair Labor Standards Act (FLSA). . . . Burger King raised as an affirmative offense a claim that the employees, designated Assistant Managers, are "*bona fide* executive" employees under 29 U.S.C. §213(a)(1) and exempt from both overtime and recordkeeping requirements.

Burger King operates a chain of fast food restaurants, which employ hourly employees, one salaried manager and two salaried assistant managers. During substantial periods of time an assistant manager is the sole supervisor in the restaurant. Among the duties performed by assistant managers are assigning hourly employees to particular tasks and monitoring their performance; determining the quantity of food to be prepared; ordering supplies and maintaining sufficient inventory; dealing with customer complaints; and auditing cash receipts. The assistant managers also spend time performing the same work as hourly employees, such as preparation and service of food. To assist the managers and assistant managers in the running of the restaurant, Burger King has prepared a "Manual of Operating Data." The manual prescribes and explains standardized practices relating to the operation of the restaurant.

After a court trial, Judge Sifton held that assistant managers earning less than $250 per week were not exempt and made a backpay award. He ordered Burger King to comply with the overtime provisions of the FLSA as to all such employees in defendant's New York region and to keep records as to their allocation of work time between production and managerial tasks. Judge Sifton also found that assistant managers earning $250 or more were exempt under §213(a)(1) from the FLSA overtime provisions. Burger King appeals from the backpay award and injunction, while the Secretary appeals from the determination that assistant managers earning $250 per week are exempt.

Body of Opinion

Before Circuit Judges Oakes, Newman, and Winter

Chief Judge Ralph K. Winter, Jr.

This case turns upon the meaning and application of regulations promulgated by the Secretary of Labor... which define which employees are *bona fide* executives. Employees earning less than $250 per week must satisfy the so-called "long test" criteria of 29 C.F.R. §541.1 (1981): their "primary duty" must be management; they must regularly direct the work of two or more other employees; they must have "authority to hire and fire" or have their personnel recommendations accorded "particular weight"; they must regularly exercise "discretionary powers"; they must not devote more than 40% of their workweek to activities "not directly and closely related" to management. Employees earning $250 or more must satisfy the requirements of the so-called "short test": their "primary duty" must be management, and they must regularly direct the work of two or more other employees. The regulation thus establishes different legal tests according to salary level, employees earning less than $250 being subject to the "long test" while those earning $250 or more are governed by the "short test."

The "Long Test" Assistant Managers

Judge Sifton found as a fact that the Burger King assistant managers "spent at least half of their time doing the same work as the hourly employees." This was a direct consequence of a deliberate corporate policy at the regional level which dictated "ideal" ratios of hourly labor to production and thereby required Assistant Managers to serve as an "extra hand" during high volume meal periods. Were the assistant managers to abstain from production work, more hourly employees would be needed, "thereby 'blowing payroll'—that is, spending more than the stores' budgeted amount for hourly labor."

Under the "long test," a finding that more than 40% of an employee's worktime in one week is spent on non-exempt work is dispositive. Judge Sifton thus held the "long test" assistant managers subject to the FLSA.

Burger King's attack on these findings is unpersuasive. First, it argues that assistant managers often do two things at once, *e.g.*, prepare a hamburger while directing an hourly employee to clean an area. This claim was fully explored in the testimony before Judge Sifton and provides no grounds for us to disturb his findings as to allocation of time between production and managerial tasks, particularly since Burger King bears the burden of proof on this issue.

Second, Burger King relies on an express written policy of the corporation and admonitions made during the training period at Whopper College forbidding assistant managers from spending in excess of 40% of their time on production tasks. The District Judge, however, rightly looked to what Burger King did rather than what it said. He found that the "ideal" ratio of hourly labor to production was inconsistent with the ostensible restrictions on assistant managers' doing of production work and that Burger King's district managers, knowing of the inconsistency, nevertheless continued to enforce the personnel/output ratio. The record supports the finding as to Burger King's actual practices, in contrast to its public declarations.

The "Short Test" Assistant Managers

The regulations provide a different test for employees earning at least $250 per week. Such employees are exempt if their "primary duty consists of management of the enterprise . . . or of a . . . subdivision thereof . . . and includes the customary and regular direction of the work of two or more employees."

Because Judge Sifton denied exemption for the "long test" Assistant Managers solely on the grounds that they devote 40% of their time to non-exempt work, he had to make separate findings as to those assistant managers who earn $250 or more. Concluding that their primary duty is, in fact, managerial, he held them exempt from the Act's overtime provisions.

Since all the assistant managers in question do identical work, the result reached by Judge Sifton is anomalous. The anomaly, however, is a result of the Secretary's regulations, which provide a dispositive, mechanical test for employees earning less than $250, while calling for a judgmental decision in the case of higher paid employees. Because the threshold distinction made by the regulations is between salary levels rather than job responsibilities, they clearly permit differing legal conclusions in the case of employees doing identical work. While anomalous, such results are not necessarily irrational. Salary ranges and allocation of time to different tasks are relevant to whether an employee's primary duty is managerial. Where salary is low and a substantial amount of time is spent on non-exempt work, the inference that an employee is not an executive is quite strong and the savings in enforcement costs afforded by the mechanical test may offset whatever is lost in accuracy in aberrational cases. At higher salaries, no such inference can be drawn and the need to weigh and balance a range of factors is more compelling.

We agree with Judge Sifton that the "short test" assistant managers have, as their "primary duty," managerial responsibilities. The regulation lists five factors to be weighed in determining an employee's primary duty: (1) time spent in the performance of managerial duties; (2) relative importance of managerial duties; (3) the frequency with which the employee exercises discretionary powers; (4) the employee's relative freedom from supervision; and (5) the relationship between the employee's salary and the wages paid employees doing similar non-exempt work.

As to (1), §541.103 offers as a "rule of thumb" or "useful guide" the proposition that "primary duty" means that work which occupies over 50% of an employee's time. Judge Sifton found that assistant managers spend "at least half their time" on non-exempt work, but §541.103 expressly states that "time alone . . . is not the sole test" and that an employee may "nevertheless have management as his primary duty if the other pertinent factors support such a conclusion." His finding as to allocation of work time is thus not dispositive, albeit that it weighs against Burger King's position.

The other "pertinent factors," however, support that position. As to (2), for example, the record fully supports Judge Sifton's finding that the principal responsibilities of assistant managers, in the sense of being most important or critical to the success of the restaurant, are managerial. Many of the employees themselves so testified and it is clear that the restaurants could not operate successfully unless the managerial functions of assistant managers, such as determining amounts of food to be prepared, running cash checks, scheduling employees, keeping track of inventory, and assigning employees to particular jobs, were performed. For that reason, as well as the fact that much of the oversight of the operation can be carried out simultaneously with the performance of non-exempt work, we believe the principal or most important work of these employees is managerial.

Such employees also exercise discretionary powers, criterion (3). They schedule work time for employees according to estimates of business based on factors such as weather and local events and assign them to particular work stations. They have the power, which they exercise, to move employees from task to task and to see that they are performing their jobs. They represent management in dealings with employees when they are in charge of the restaurant and, while they do not exercise the power to hire and fire frequently, there are some instances thereof in the record. Given that the ten to twenty-five employees under their direction are teenagers, many on their first job, this supervision is a not insubstantial responsibility. . . . Finally, they must deal with cash or inventory irregularities. . . . We fully recognize that the economic genius of the Burger King enterprise lies in providing uniform products and service economically in many different locations and that adherence by assistant managers to a remarkably detailed routine is critical to commercial success. The exercise of discretion, however, even where circumscribed by prior instruction, is as critical to that success as adherence to "the book." . . .

We conclude that assistant managers satisfy all the criteria suggested by the Secretary, save (1), for determining whether an employee's "primary duty" is managerial.

It was argued before us that the Secretary's view of the meaning of his regulations and interpretive guidelines is entitled to weight. Even according it such weight, however, we are not free to apply the regulations in a way which we regard as a distortion solely because the

Secretary has initiated litigation. If the Secretary believes that the underlying legislation was intended to cover employees such as Burger King's assistant managers, or that employees doing identical work for an employer should have identical legal status so far as overtime is concerned, he should reconsider the regulations as issued.

Judgment and Result

Assistant managers earning $250 or more per week are held to be "executives" and therefore exempt from FLSA overtime and record-keeping requirements. Burger King was told that it had to pay overtime to "long test" managers in weeks when they spend more than 40 percent of their time in nonsupervisory work. Also, Burger King had to keep records on long-test assistant managers.

Questions

1. Did the secretary of labor (Donovan) argue that Burger King assistant managers were executives or regular hourly employees?
2. Why do Department of Labor regs establish a longer test for assistant managers making under $250 per week?
3. Even if more than half of a long-test assistant manager's time is spent as a regular employee, how much must the employee be paid for such work?

FLSA Child Labor Provisions. The FLSA child labor provisions are partly designed to keep children in school and out of work that is harmful to their health or well-being. The U.S. Secretary of Labor publishes lists of hazardous farm and nonfarm occupations in which minors may not work. Department of Labor regulations controlling youth nonfarm jobs differ somewhat from those covering farm jobs.

FLSA Record Keeping. The FLSA requires employers to keep records on wages and hours. Most of the information is of the kind generally maintained by employers for other laws. These records do not have to be in any particular form. Time clocks need not be used.

FLSA Enforcement. The U.S. Department of Labor's Wage and Hour Division administers and enforces the FLSA against business. It also enforces the FLSA against state and local governments, federal employees of the Library of Congress, U.S. Postal Service, Postal Rate Commission, and the Tennessee Valley Authority. The U.S. Civil Service Commission enforces the FLSA for all other federal employees.

To see that the FLSA is followed, the Department of Labor's Wage and Hour Division has authority to investigate and gather data from an employer on wages, hours, and other employment conditions or practices. The division can tell an employer to change its way of operating so that it obeys the FLSA.

FLSA Sanctions. Willful violations of the FLSA are crimes carrying fines up to $10,000. Second criminal convictions may result in imprisonment. Civil penalties are possible for violators of the FLSA's child labor provisions. It is an FLSA violation to fire or in any other manner discriminate against an employee who files a complaint or participates in an FLSA proceeding.

Recovery of Back Wages. One of the FLSA's remedies for workers is the possibility of recovering amounts they were underpaid. The statute of limitations is two years for recovery of back pay. If a willful violation occurs, the statute of limitations is three years. Workers can recover unpaid minimum or overtime wages in several ways:

1. The Department of Labor's Wage and Hour Division may supervise such payments.
2. The Secretary of Labor may sue for back wages *and* an equal amount as liquidated damages.
3. An employee may file a private suit for back pay *and* an equal amount as liquidated damages, plus attorney's fees and court costs.
4. The Secretary of Labor may get an injunction to stop anyone from violating the FLSA, including wrongful withholding of the proper minimum wages.

Equal Pay Act

The Equal Pay Act of 1963 amends the Fair Labor Standards Act (FLSA) and is part of the FLSA. The Equal Pay Act makes it illegal to pay different wages based on sex to men and women doing substantially the same work. If the jobs require equal skill, effort, and responsibility, and if working conditions are similar, pay to men and women must be equal. Because the act is federal law, it applies in all states to all businesses affecting interstate commerce, meaning that the Equal Pay Act applies to most businesses and labor unions as well. It also covers federal, state, and local government employees. The Equal Pay Act applies to most employees subject to the FLSA, including executive, administrative, professional, and outside sales personnel.

If a bank has two tellers—one a man, the other a woman—and each has slightly different tasks, the bank must pay them the same wages. Jobs do not have to be identical for the Equal Pay Act to apply. It is enough that they are substantially equal. Otherwise employers could easily defeat the Equal Pay Act's purpose to pay men and women the same amount for the same work by creating some small difference in their jobs and basing differences in pay on this inequality. If an employer violates the Equal Pay Act, it may not lower an employee's wages to eliminate the differential.

Suppose a wage difference is only partly based on sex. The difference is totally illegal. However, the Equal Pay Act does allow wage differences between men and women if based on factors other than sex. Such factors as bona fide seniority systems, merit systems, or systems rewarding productivity do not violate the act.

Unemployment Compensation

The Social Security Act of 1935 established today's federal-state unemployment insurance system. The U.S. Supreme Court upheld its constitutionality in 1937. The system's basic idea is to pay workers something so that they can survive when they lose their jobs because of adverse business conditions.

From Where Does the Money Come. The money to pay unemployment compensation comes from federal payroll taxes imposed on employers. If states have unemployment insurance programs meeting federal requirements, employers pay state rather than federal unemployment taxes. (This state tax is credited against federal unemployment taxes.) By 1938, every state had enacted an unemployment compensation act.

Which Employers Are Covered. Any employer with one or more employees who worked some part of 20 or more weeks per year must pay federal (or state) unemployment taxes. Also covered are employers paying wages of $1,500 or more in any calendar quarter. The preceding are federal minimums that all state unemployment programs must meet. States may force more employers to pay unemployment taxes. A few do; for example, at least four states cover domestic employees who are not covered federally. Certain employers are exempt from unemployment taxes: employers of labor for educational, religious, and charitable institutions; employers of certain farm labor; employers of federal or state government labor; and employers of labor for the family.

Which Employees Are Covered. The unemployment system provides benefits only for employees working for covered employers (those paying unemployment taxes). In other words, if an employee works for an exempt employer and loses a job, no unemployment benefits are available.

Both federal and state law set unemployment eligibility requirements. Federal law sets certain coverage floors, or minimums. States may set how long a person must have worked to be eligible for unemployment benefits. For example, a person joining the labor force from high school who has never worked and is immediately unemployed is not entitled to unemployment benefits. States set earnings requirements before a person is entitled to unemployment benefits. Federal law does not set either earnings or minimum work requirements.

Amount of Benefits. The length and amount of unemployment benefits vary from state to state. All states give at least 26 weeks' coverage. Some go as high as 39 weeks. Additionally, various federal laws provide supplemental unemployment income when state unemployment income runs out. In some instances, this supplement (when added to state benefits) has lasted for as long as 65 weeks. Refer to Table 15.1 for data concerning the various states' unemployment benefits.

Generally, only certain causes entitle one to collect unemployment benefits. For example, economic recessions or depressions causing a person to be laid off generally entitle the person to benefits. If another job with someone else opens up, the unemployed person cannot turn it down and draw unemployment until his old job reappears. Every state unemployment compensation law requires that a person be available for, seeking, and able to work to collect benefits. If a person voluntarily quits a job without good cause, refuses suitable work, or is dismissed for improper conduct at work, he or she has no right to unemployment compensation.

Most state laws refuse to give unemployment benefits to workers on strike. The state of New York is an exception. The employer in the following case sued the state, claiming that this law violates the federal Constitution because it is **preempted** by the federal Social Security Act and the National Labor Relations Act. The U.S. Supreme Court said that the New York Unemployment Compensation Act is constitutional in *New York Telephone Company.*

TABLE 15.1 State Unemployment Insurance by State and Other Area: 1997

State and other area	Beneficiaries first payments (1,000)	Benefits paid (mil. dol.)	Avg. weekly unemployment benefits (dol.)	State and other area	Beneficiaries, first payments (1,000)	Benefits paid (mil. dol.)	Avg. weekly unemployment benefits (dol.)	State and other area	Benefi ciaries, first payments (1,000)	Benefits paid (mil. dol.)	Avg. weekly unemployment benefits (dol.)
Total	7,325	19,735	193	KY	114	222	176	OH	254	691	208
AL	135	194	145	LA	69	141	133	OK	41	86	177
AK	44	121	176	ME	42	98	152	OR	137	362	198
AZ	69	144	147	MD	107	332	196	PA	430	1,430	228
AR	93	182	198	MA	178	725	263	RI	49	151	224
CA	1,073	2,628	152	MI	348	912	222	SC	92	169	169
CO	64	162	213	MN	110	355	242	SD	9	16	156
CT	114	367	211	MS	61	114	142	TN	165	305	163
DE	21	68	194	MO	140	275	154	TX	345	943	196
DC	21	79	233	MT	27	56	166	UT	34	75	193
FL	246	646	192	NE	27	51	163	VT	21	49	174
GA	180	279	162	NV	64	175	204	VA	101	187	179
HI	38	164	269	NH	18	34	165	WA	198	698	240
ID	45	94	187	NJ	283	1,144	259	WV	56	133	180
IL	320	1,165	217	NM	30	75	158	WI	211	463	188
IN	121	257	186	NY	490	1,754	204	WY	11	27	182
IA	79	179	205	NC	201	357	198	PR	132	229	94
KS	49	128	204	ND	19	38	176	VI	2	6	166

Source: U.S. Employment and Training Administration, *Unemployment Insurance Financial Handbook,* annual.

New York Tel. Co. v. New York St. Dept. of Labor

U.S. Supreme Court
440 U.S. 519 (1979)

Background and Facts:

A New York statute authorizes the payment of unemployment compensation after one week of unemployment, except that if a claimant's loss of employment is caused by a strike in the place of his employment the payment of benefits is suspended for an additional 7-week period. Pursuant to this statute, petitioners' striking employees began to collect unemployment compensation after the 8-week waiting period and were paid benefits for the remaining five months of the strike. Because New York's unemployment insurance system is financed primarily by employer contributions based on the benefits paid to former employees of each employer in past years, a substantial part of the cost of these benefits was ultimately imposed on petitioners (employers). Petitioners brought suit in District Court seeking a declaration that the New York statute conflicts with federal law and is therefore invalid.... The District Court granted the requested relief, holding that the availability of unemployment compensation is a substantial factor in the workers' decision to remain on strike and has a measurable impact on the progress of the strike and that the payment of such compensation conflicted "with the policy of free collective bargaining established in the federal laws and is therefore invalid under the Supremacy Clause." The Court of Appeals reversed, holding that although the New York statute conflicts with the federal labor policy, the legislative histories of the National Labor Relations Act (NLRA) and Social Security Act (SSA) indicate that such conflict was one which Congress has decided to tolerate. *Held*: The judgment is affirmed....

Mr. Justice Stevens, joined by Mr. Justice White and Mr. Justice Rehnquist, concluded that Congress, in enacting the NLRA and SSA, did not intend to pre-empt a State's power to pay unemployment compensation to strikers.... This case does not involve any attempt by the State to regulate or prohibit private conduct in the labor-management field but rather involves a state program for the distribution of benefits to certain members of the public.... Although the class benefited is primarily made up of employees in the State and the class providing the benefits is primarily made up of employers in the State, and although some members of each class are occasionally engaged in labor disputes, the general purport of the program is not to regulate the bargaining relationship between the two classes but instead to provide an efficient means of insuring employment security in the State.... Rather than being a "state la[w] regulating the relations between employees, their union, and their employer," as to which the reasons underlying the pre-emption doctrine have their "greatest force," ... [t]he New York statute is a law of general applicability. Since it appears that Congress has been sensitive to the importance of the States' interest in fashioning their own unemployment compensation programs and especially their own eligibility criteria... it is appropriate to treat New York's statute with the same deference that this Court has afforded analogous state laws of general applicability that protect interests "deeply rooted in local feeling and responsibility." With respect to such laws, "in the absence of compelling congressional direction," it will not be inferred that Congress "had deprived the States of the power to act."...

In an area in which Congress has decided to tolerate a substantial measure of diversity, the fact that the implementation of this general state policy affects the relative strength of the antagonists in a bargaining dispute is not a sufficient reason for concluding that Congress intended to preempt that exercise of state power....

Judgment and Result

The U.S. Supreme Court in a nonmajority opinion decided that the New York statute letting striking union workers collect unemployment insurance was not preempted (invalidated) by the National Labor Relations Act (NLRA) or the federal Social Security Act (SSA).

Questions

1. Who was paying for the unemployment benefits used by the strikers? Who passed the statute allowing strikers to qualify for unemployment insurance?
2. What was the argument in favor of denying states the right to pass statutes that let strikers draw unemployment compensation?
3. Does the logic of the *New York Telephone Company* case support or undercut states' rights?

Experience Rating. An employer may reduce its unemployment tax liability if its employees are unemployed less than the average. This reduction occurs because of the experience rating factor. **Experience rating** relates a particular employer's unemployment tax rates to employment rates. If an employer has steady levels of employment so that its workers are seldom out of work, it will have a low experience rating, which means lower unemployment taxes for that particular employer. Experience ratings are affected by all employers' employment levels. During high unemployment, all employers pay higher unemployment taxes, because more people are drawing from the unemployment fund.

Exhaustion of Unemployment Benefits. When unemployment benefits (both state and supplemental federal benefits) run out, a worker is left to public works employment (if it is available), welfare, charity, or the generosity of friends and relatives to survive.

Social Security[1]

Marv Wollin had been a tool and die worker with American Machine Company for 45 years. He started work at age 20 after serving three years in the U.S. Army. Marv had managed to put his two children through college at State University and had fully paid for his house. He was planning to retire the next year. Both he and his wife were in good health and they hoped to move to Florida. Marv started calculating his retirement, knowing he would receive a monthly retirement check from the company retirement fund. He also knew he would start getting a Social Security check but was uncertain whether his Social Security income would be taxed. He also wondered whether his Social Security income would be cut, because he had heard the Social Security system was going bankrupt. He was concerned that his working part-time might cause him to lose his monthly Social Security income.

Let us examine the answers to these uncertainties.

Background. The Social Security Act took effect in 1935. Its original purpose was to provide a minimal income for retired workers. The original act did not provide for survivors of a worker who died in the prime of life, leaving a family. In 1939, an amendment to the act increased coverage to pay dependents of a worker who died. The 1935 act gave only the worker—no dependents—money to live on in retirement. The 1939 amendments gave a retirement income to certain of the worker's dependents.

The 1935 act gave nothing to workers who were totally disabled. It was not until July 1957 that Social Security Act disability insurance benefits were first given to workers who lost income due to total disability.

In 1965, the Social Security program was amended to include Medicare, which assures hospital and medical insurance protection to people 65 and over. Since 1973, Medicare coverage has been available to people under age 65 entitled to disability checks for two or more consecutive years. The 1973 amendments also cover people with permanent kidney failure who need dialysis or kidney transplants. Additional medical problems are added to the coverage from time to time.

Workers Covered. In 1935 the Social Security program covered only workers in industry and commerce. The 1950s saw the program expand to cover household and farm employees, people in the U.S. armed forces, members of the clergy, most self-employed people, and most state and local employees. Today, most workers in the United States (nine out of ten, according to the U.S. Department of Health and Human Services) are covered by Social Security.

[1] The authors acknowledge the assistance of Social Security Administration brochures in preparing this section.

Administration. The Social Security program is run by the Social Security Administration in the U.S. Department of Health and Human Services. Employers and the self-employed send in periodic (monthly or more frequent) Social Security taxes to a Federal Reserve bank or designated commercial bank.

Employers must keep records for Social Security purposes. Employee names, earnings, Social Security numbers (no two are alike), and other information must be kept for four years after the taxes are due. Government officials may inspect employer Social Security records.

Types of Social Security Benefits. About one out of six persons in the United States gets some form of Social Security benefit. Retirement checks are what most people think of when the term *Social Security* is mentioned. People today can start receiving retirement benefits at age 62. People who wait until age 65 before retiring draw larger benefits than those retiring earlier. Even after early retirees reach age 65, they draw less than those who waited. After workers retire, what kind of benefits can they expect? Three factors influence the size of retirement benefits: (1) the average yearly earnings covered by Social Security, (2) the age at retirement, and (3) the number of dependents.

The Social Security Act provides, in addition to retirement benefits, disability and survivors' benefits. A worker becoming severely disabled before age 65 can receive disability checks under Social Security. Disability for Social Security purposes exists if a person has a severe physical or mental condition that prevents working and is expected to last (or has lasted) for at least 12 months or is expected to end in death. Blindness is an example. Disability checks start on the sixth full month of a worker's disability and continue as long as the disability lasts. Severely disabled workers (for example, those totally blinded) can get benefits even if they manage to do *some* work. The size of the disability benefit is currently tied to one's age and work credit.

The number of disabled workers in 1998 receiving benefits (according to the most recent data in the *Statistical Abstract of the United States*) was 4,698,000, the average monthly benefit was $733, and children of disabled workers also received an additional $208 per month. Additionally, disabled children (such as persons diagnosed as child schizophrenics), who number 705,000 in total receive in aggregate $4.0 billion per year (in 1997—most recent year) (an average of $5,673.76 each per year). A monthly benefit of $733 might not seem like much, but keep in mind that it would take more than $100,000 in 30–year U.S. Treasury bonds to generate a monthly income of $733 per month. Thus, conferring a monthly benefit of $733 on someone is like giving that person income from over $100,000 in U.S. Treasury bonds—a significant amount.

For adults, one of the most frequent disabilities is back injuries. The following case presents a common claim for Social Security disability payments and provides a flavor of the problems associated with such claims.

Schmidt v. Apfel

Federal District Court (D. Kansas)
39 F.Supp.2d 1291 (1999)

Background and Facts:

Vera Schmidt applied for disability benefits on July 11, 1994, stating that she had become disabled on February 16 of that year. The claim was denied initially and on reconsideration. An administrative law judge (ALJ) denied her claim on January 26, 1996. He determined that Schmidt was unable to return to her former employment, but that she could perform other work in the national economy. Schmidt's appeal from this decision was denied on February 12, 1997. She then instituted the present action.

At the time of the hearing before the ALJ, Schmidt was 53 years old. She had a high school education, and had worked as a print shop worker, a bookkeeper, and a gas station attendant. After the date of her alleged disability, she briefly returned to the print shop on a part-time basis. She was not engaged in any substantial gainful activity at any time since February 16, 1994.

On February 7, 1994, Schmidt saw a chiropractor, Stephen Dent, complaining of pain in the thoracic and lumbar areas. Dent reported a "decreased" range of motion in these areas, and wrote in his notes that Schmidt had "acute moderate thoracic strain." He prescribed ice packs and scheduled Schmidt for another visit in two days. Schmidt continued to see Dent on several occasions up to January 20, 1995. Schmidt contacted Dr. Ted R. Cook, her family physician, on March 8, 1994. Dr. Cook reported that "Vera is in today wanting an evaluation of her back for Workman's Comp." He noted that Schmidt had been seeing Dent who was treating a rib between her scapula, "usually getting the rib popped back in place when she is in his office but as soon as she gets home she does something and it pops right back out." She reported back pain, but stated that it "seems to be much better" since she began taking Flexeril, which she took at night because it made her drowsy. Dr. Cook examined Schmidt and found "very tender areas" near the spine. He found no neurological deficits and no paresthesia. He prescribed Lodine 300 mg. for Schmidt to take with the Flexeril.

Dr. Cook saw Schmidt on a number of occasions during 1994. On March 11, Dr. Cook reported that Schmidt stated she was continuing to see Dent for her lumbar strain and that she was "60 to 70% improved." Dr. Cook's examination indicated "moderate spasm" in the lumbar region, and that Schmidt has "good range of motion." He advised her to modify her work activities so that she didn't have to lift so much and to exercise. On May 2, he reported that Schmidt showed "significant spasm" in the thoracic region, but did not show any tenderness in the joints or lumbar region.

On May 4, 1994, Schmidt had seen orthopedist Dr. Jay Stanley Jones. Dr. Jones found Schmidt's x-rays showed some thoracic area spinal degeneration. He wrote that Schmidt had "a chronic overuse syndrome seeing that she gets better over the weekends and then when she returns to work she gets worse." He decided to keep Schmidt off work for a week and prescribed Feldene. "If this improves her symptomatology," he wrote, "I am going to recommend a job change."

In May Schmidt reported to Dr. Jones that there was little change in her condition, although she was a "little bit better." On June 22, she saw Dr. Jones complaining of "increasing back pain" which was "localized over the scapula."

In August, Schmidt reported that her back condition hadn't changed, that she felt it was "as good as she is going to be" and that she wanted to schedule a functional capacity examination. On September 29, Dr. Jones wrote that Schmidt should sit at a desk or stand in one position for "brief periods" only. She should not use a keyboard or do bookkeeping or other repetitive work with her hands. However, Dr. Jones indicated that Schmidt's "impairment rating" for her back was only 8%.

The hearing before the ALJ was conducted on September 27, 1995. Subsequent to the hearing, on November 1, 1995, Dr. Jones summarized his findings regarding Schmidt in a letter to her attorney. He wrote that Schmidt was being seen for severe shoulder pain, as well as carpal tunnel syndrome. He concluded that he did not believe Schmidt could perform even sedentary work because of her pain, which limited her to sitting for 10 minutes, and then standing or walking for 10 minutes. She could lift 5 to 10 pounds frequently, and 20 pounds occasionally. She had an "impingement syndrome" which restricted her ability to perform grasping, gripping, and reaching motions with her hands."

Schmidt testified at the hearing, stating that her pain is a dull pain in the upper part of her back. Schmidt testified that the pain becomes a stabbing pain when she stands for 10 minutes, does dishes, sits in a work position for 10 to 15 minutes, or lifts too much. When this happens, she sits in her recliner for 45 minutes to an hour. She can then resume work for a shorter period of time than she would have been able to perform but for the onset of the stabbing pain.

She also gets headaches that begin in her neck and move up. She treats these headaches with over-the-counter medicines and sitting in her recliner. She spends approximately 5 hours a day in her recliner.

Her hands and fingers get tingly and numb on occasion. Her hands hurt when her back hurts or when she has been using them. She often drops things and can no longer crochet. She continues to needlepoint, which she can do for 45 minutes, after which she relaxes in her recliner for 15 to 20 minutes before resuming. She prepares supper three times a week, each of which requires an hour of preparation. She no longer goes boating or fishing, or plays ball. She can read in her recliner, and goes to her son's basketball games. She can lift 30 pounds, although she has found it difficult because it causes a sharp pain in her back. She can lift 15 pounds comfortably but not reliably. She takes medications only on an as-needed basis.

On a scale of one to ten, she has described her pain as an eight, when it has been aggravated by an activity such as doing dishes. After steroidal treatment, she testified that her pain diminished to a level of four or five for two or three weeks. None of her physicians has recommended surgery on her back or hands nor have they prescribed electronic pain blockers or back braces.

A vocational expert, Cindy Younger, also testified at the hearing. Younger testified that a person with Schmidt's vocational characteristics and residual function capacity (RFC) could lift 10 pounds frequently and 15 to 30 pounds occasionally and perform the job of bookkeeper, one of Schmidt's previous jobs. The ALJ asked Younger about the effect of a hypothetical RFC which would limit Schmidt to the frequent lifting of only nominal weights, occasional lifting of 10 to 15 pounds, with a limitation on standing no more than 2 to 4 hours per 8-hour shift.

Younger testified that such an RFC would not preclude working as a bookkeeper. She stated that Schmidt had acquired the skills to work in such a job from her previous employment, and could work in the position of reception clerk, of which there were 2,630 positions in Kansas and 900 in the Wichita area.

The ALJ determined that there was no evidence Schmidt met or exceeded a listed impairment, that she could not return to work due to her medical condition, but that she could perform other work in the national economy. However the ALJ also determines that Schmidt's claim of total inability to work was not credible. He noted several factors in reaching this conclusion: (1) that the objective medical records established "only minimal degenerative changes of the thoracic spine; (2) that there was a contradiction between the level of incapacity claimed by Schmidt and her normal daily activities.

Body of Opinion

Under... [the U.S. Code] "the finding of the Secretary as to any fact, if supported by substantial evidence, shall be conclusive." Substantial evidence is more than a scintilla and is that evidence which a reasonable mind might accept as adequate to support a conclusion....

This deferential standard of review does not apply to the Secretary's application of the law.... In determining whether the decision of the Secretary is based on substantial evidence, the court is not to re-weigh the evidence or substitute its judgment for that of the Secretary.... However, the court will not simply "rubber stamp" the decision of the Secretary.

The qualifications for disability insurance benefits under the Social Security Act are that the claimant meets the insured status requirements, is less than 65 years of age, and is under a "disability."... An individual "shall be determined to be under a disability only if his physical or mental impairment or impairments are of such severity that he is not only unable to do his previous work but cannot, considering his age, education, and work experience, engage in any other kind of substantial gainful work which exists in the national economy."...

The burden is on the claimant to prove the existence of a disability that prevents him from engaging in his prior work or a continuous period of twelve months.... If the claimant makes such a showing, the Secretary must show the claimant is able to do other work in jobs present in the national economy....

The Secretary employs a five-step process in determining the existence of a disability... a process which ends at any point if the Secretary determines the claimant is disabled or not. The steps, in order, require determinations of whether the claimant: 1) is currently engaged in substantial gainful activity; 2) has a medically severe impairment or combination of impairments; 3) has an impairment equivalent to one of a number of extremely severe impairments listed in 20 C.F.R. Part 404, Subpt. P, App. 1; 4) is unable due to the impairment to perform past work; and 5) has the residual functional capacity to perform other work available in the national economy, considering age, education, and past work experience....

The ALJ's decision correctly states and applies the relevant standards.... While Schmidt points to other indicia of physical impairments, it remains true that none of the impairments is more than minimal in nature.... In her appeal, Schmidt repeatedly argues that a person need not be completely disabled to be entitled to benefits. This is certainly true but it misses the point here, which is that Schmidt's credibility as to her assertions of nearly complete disability—for instance, that she cannot perform sedentary work because she cannot hold a pen or pencil—are directly undermined by evidence that, for example, she performs needlework for as much as 45 minutes at a time. She also shops, cooks, keeps house, and attends her son's basketball games. Schmidt argues that the ALJ erred in not explicitly considering facts which would buttress her credibility. Schmidt fails to show any error, however. The ALJ concluded that Schmidt's claims were partially credible, finding that she did suffer some moderate, non-disabling degree of pain. The allegedly corroborative evidence does not alter the inconsistencies noted in Schmidt's claims which were noted by the ALJ....

Judgment and Result

Schmidt loses. The ALJ's decision was affirmed.

Questions

1. Does someone who has never been employed qualify for Social Security disability payments?
2. What is "RFC" and how does it relate to qualifying for Social Security disability payments?
3. If a worker is able to engage in some other job for which he or she is qualified, but not his or her original work, does it mean that he or she cannot recover Social Security disability income?
4. How common are back injuries? If a more relaxed standard of qualification applied to Social Security disability payments, what would happen to the Social Security budget and Social Security taxes? Given the elusiveness of objectively measuring whether someone has a back injury, does this play into the decision to have a "tough" test for such disability payments, as exemplified by the *Schmidt* case? How important

Building Work Credits. Work credit refers to a minimum amount of time a person must work (covered by Social Security) before becoming eligible for benefits. Social Security work credit is measured in quarters of coverage. A worker can earn no more than four quarters of coverage for a year. The amount of covered earnings needed for a quarter of coverage will increase automatically in the future to keep pace with average wages.

If a worker does not work enough quarters to qualify for Social Security benefits, the worker gets no benefits. Also, such workers do not get back the Social Security tax they or their employer paid while they worked. However, work credit that workers earn stays on their records. Thus, if a person without enough work credit to qualify for Social Security returns to work, that person can add to work credit already earned and eventually could qualify for benefits.

The amount of Social Security benefits one eventually gets depends on average earnings during one's working years and on one's personal situation (for example, being married with two dependents versus being single). Once the minimum work credits to qualify for Social Security are earned, working has no effect on the size of one's Social Security benefits. One's personal situation (for example, marital status and number of dependents) then affects benefit size.

Financing Social Security. The employer and the employee pay equal Social Security taxes for the employee. The tax rate schedule for employers and employees is shown in Figure 15.3. Note that it was set at 7.15 percent each (or 14.3 percent total) of the employee's gross wages or salary for 1987 and rose to 7.65 percent each (or 15.3 percent total) of the employee's gross salary in 1990.

Self-employed people now pay the same rate for Social Security as do employers and employees combined, because the benefits are the same for the self-employed as for employees. Figure 15.4 shows Social Security tax rates for self-employed people. The maximum salary taxable is the same for employees and the self-employed.

Social Security Features. Social Security has a number of significant points.

1. Social Security *benefits* are not subject to state or local income taxes. However, a worker earning $20,000 pays a Social Security tax on the entire $20,000, even though that worker takes home less than $20,000 because of federal income taxes and other deductions. Thus, the worker is taxed (by the Social Security tax) on tax (the amount of the federal income tax taken from the worker's paycheck).
2. Social Security payments may not be garnished by the beneficiary's creditors.
3. Social Security benefits (of all types) increase if the cost of living increases.
4. A person must survive to get Social Security retirement benefits. Those who die before retirement will reap no personal benefit from their years of contributions, although their survivors, if any, might draw benefits.

FIGURE 15.3 Tax Rate Schedule for Employees and Employers

Percent of covered earnings

Years	For Retirement, Survivors, and Disability Insurance	Hospital Insurance	Employee and Employer Rate	Total
1988–89	6.06	1.45	7.51	15.02
1990 and later	6.20	1.45	7.65	15.30

Source: Social Security Administration.

FIGURE 15.4 Tax Rate Schedule for Self-Employed People

Percent of covered earnings			
Years	For Cash Benefits	For Hospital Insurance	Total
1984	11.40	2.60	14.00
1985	11.40	2.70	14.10
1986–87	11.40	2.90	14.30
1988–89	12.12	2.90	15.02
1990 and after	12.40	2.90	15.30

Social Security Changes. The following changes were made to the Social Security system in 1983:

1. The COLA (cost of living adjustment) was modified to make inflows and outflows to the system more nearly equal.
2. People who first became federal workers on January 1, 1984, or later are now part of the system.
3. Social Security beneficiaries in certain cases now pay federal income taxes on their benefits. (Single retirees making more than $25,000 and couples receiving $32,000 from other sources can have as much as 85 percent of their Social Security benefits taxed.)

Current Issue: Social Security Equity. A matter not corrected in 1983 was the serious intergenerational wealth transfer now occurring under Social Security. Specifically, current retirees withdraw all they have paid into Social Security within 18–24 months after retiring. These retirees then continue to draw Social Security benefits even if they have no financial need. In fact, millionaires may draw Social Security retirement benefits even after receiving all they have paid in. Further, current retirees will on the average draw four dollars in benefits for every one dollar they paid into Social Security. Who pays the missing three dollars? The working people who currently pay Social Security taxes. Thus, the intergenerational wealth transfer is away from the younger generation (who generally have a greater financial need) to the retirees, who often are doing well financially.

Natural law principles of fairness plus sound public policy suggest that Social Security benefits should be fine tuned to take account of the following:

1. Social Security should be recognized for what it is—a social program that transfers wealth from the better-off to the less fortunate, particularly after a recipient of benefits has been paid more than she or he has paid in.
2. Some retirees need increased Social Security benefits since they lack enough income from all sources to survive.
3. Present retirees receiving in excess of some indexed income figure—say, $35,000 from all sources—should receive zero Social Security benefits once such persons withdraw what they have paid into the system (including interest).
4. In 1999, Social Security was running a surplus of about $70 billion. A surplus is expected to continue until the "baby boomers" begin retiring in five to ten years. Because Social Security is part of the federal budget, the surplus from Social Security helps cut the overall federal deficit, which most agree is still too high. Thus, the reluctance to cut Social Security taxes stems from the logic that

to do so would either increase the federal deficit or necessitate raising the federal income tax rates. Also, cuts now in Social Security taxes could jeopardize benefits for baby boomers in the "out years"—five to ten years in the future.

Regulation of Employee Pensions

Sara Coleman had contributed six percent of her weekly take-home pay to her employer's retirement plan for the past five years. She wondered what was being done with the money. Was it in safe or risky investments? She also was thinking of changing jobs. If she went to work for a new employer, would she lose her pension contributions, or would they follow her to her new job (that is, were they "portable")? She also asked her employer for information about the retirement plan. The employer refused to give her any information. Was Sara entitled to anything?

Retirement Plans. Private retirement plans, which are separate from Social Security, involve billions of employee (and often employer) dollars. If an employer sets up a qualified employee retirement plan, employer contributions are tax deductible from the employer's standpoint. Income earned on pension contributions while it accumulates, before it is paid out, is not subject to federal income taxation, and usually not to state and local taxes, either. When a person retires, however, amounts received from a qualified pension plan are taxed by federal, state, and local income tax laws. The assumption is that a retired worker will then be in a lower tax bracket, and the taxes paid will thus be lower.

The U.S. Internal Revenue Code sets the rules for establishing qualified employee retirement plans. The **coverage requirement** means that a certain percentage of all employees must be part of the retirement program. This requirement forces top management to spread benefits to lower-level employees.

In addition to the terms just discussed, you should be aware of several other pension-related terms. First, pensions can be *noncontributory* (where only the employer pays into them for the employees' retirement) or *contributory* (where the employees each pay at least part of the contribution). Second, in **defined contribution** plans, the periodic payment into the pension plan is fixed, whereas in **defined benefit** plans, the periodic payment into the plan varies so that the benefits ultimately received will be a definite—often indexed—dollar amount. Generally, defined contribution plans are more favorable to employers because the amounts employers must pay into such plans are fixed, while amounts paid into defined benefit plans tend to increase as inflation makes it necessary to maintain benefit levels. Of course, if the plan's investment experience is favorable, the employer's contributions can decrease in a defined benefit plan so it can benefit employers.

Employee Retirement Income Security Act of 1974 (ERISA)

Many employees, such as Sara Coleman in the previous story, pay money into an employer-established retirement plan. Many, like Sara, wonder what protections the law provides for employee retirement plans. Congress enacted ERISA to deal with just those concerns to see that employee retirement plans provide the retirement income they are supposed to when they are supposed to.

Fiduciary Duties. ERISA tries to protect employee retirement plans in several ways. Although ERISA imposes other restrictions on employee retirement plans, the main ones are as follows. First, it creates *fiduciary duties* for plan managers and advisors. Second, it requires plan records and reports. Third, it sets plan investment restrictions.

Fourth, it creates a federal corporation to insure employee benefits should the plan fail. Fifth, ERISA requires vesting of both employee and employer contributions. Sixth, it places funding requirements on certain plans.

ERISA's fiduciary duties for plan managers and advisors place the law's highest duty of care and good faith on such people. Specifically, plan managers and advisors should use the care that prudent people would use in managing their own assets. This high level of duty exists because employee retirement plans must be protected to make sure retirement income is available. Furthermore, plan managers and advisors have millions, sometimes hundreds of millions or even billions, of employee dollars under their control. The temptation to abuse this control is great; therefore, the deterrent against such abuse must also be great. The ERISA fiduciary duty applies to both retirement plan managers (those exercising control over the plan) and plan advisors who charge for their services.

The following case addresses the matter of self-dealing or the conflict of interest provision of ERISA. Specifically, ERISA forbids employers' retirement committees from causing their plan to engage in transactions that directly or indirectly transfer plan assets to parties in interest. In other words retirement plan managers should not sell plan assets to themselves (presumably at bargain prices) or force the plan to buy assets from the managers' personal assets (undoubtedly at inflated prices). The idea is that plan managers should avoid conflicts of interest. What if an employer promises employees increased retirement benefits if they forego age discrimination and ERISA claims against the employer? Is this transaction benefitting a party in interest (here the employer) prohibited?

Lockheed Corporation v. Spink

U.S. Supreme Court
116 S.Ct. 1783 (1996)

Background and Facts:

Paul Spink was employed by Lockheed Corporation from 1939 until 1950, when he left to work for one of Lockheed's competitors. In 1979, Lockheed persuaded Spink to return. Spink was 61 years old when he resumed employment with Lockheed. At that time, the terms of the Lockheed Retirement Plan for Certain Salaried Individuals (Plan), a defined benefit plan, excluded from participation employees who were over the age of 60 when hired. This exclusion was expressly permitted by ERISA.

Congress later passed the Omnibus Budget Reconciliation Act of 1986 (OBRA). Section 9203(a) of OBRA repealed the age-based exclusion provision of ERISA, and the statute now flatly mandates that "[n]o pension plan may exclude from participation (on the basis of age) employees who have attained a specified age." Sections 9201 and 9202 of OBRA amended ERISA and ADEA (the Age Discrimination in Employment Act) to prohibit age-based cessations of benefit accruals and age-based reductions in benefit accrual rates.

In an effort to comply with these new laws, Lockheed ceased its prior practice of age-based exclusion from the plan, effective December 25, 1988. As of that date, all employees, including Spink, who had previously been ineligible to participate in the plan due to their age at the time of hiring became members of the plan. Lockheed made clear, however, that it would not credit those employees for years of service rendered before they became members.

When later faced with the need to streamline its operations, Lockheed amended the plan to provide financial incentives for certain employees to retire early. Lockheed established two programs, both of which offered increased pension benefits to employees who would retire early, payable out of the plan's surplus assets. Both programs required as a condition of the receipt of benefits that participants release any employment-related claims they might have against Lockheed. Though Spink was eligible for one of the programs, he declined to participate because he did not wish to waive any ADEA or ERISA claims. He then retired, without earning any extra benefits for doing so.

Spink brought this suit, in his individual capacity and on behalf of others similarly situated, against Lockheed and several of its directors and officers. Among other things, the complaint alleged that Lockheed and the members of the board of directors violated ERISA's duty of care and prohibited transactions provisions by amending the plan to create the retirement programs. Relatedly, the complaint alleged that the members of Lockheed's Retirement Committee, who implemented the plan as amended by the board, violated those same parts of ERISA. For these alleged ERISA violations, Spink sought monetary, declaratory, and injunctive relief pursuant to ERISA's enforcement provisions. Lockheed moved to dismiss the complaint for failure to state a claim, and the District Court granted the motion.

The Court of Appeals for the Ninth Circuit reversed. That court held that the amendments to the plan were unlawful under ERISA §406(a)(1)(D), which prohibits a fiduciary from causing a plan to engage in a transaction that transfers plan assets to a party in interest or involves the use of plan assets for the benefit of a party in interest. The court reasoned that because the amendments offered increased benefits in exchange for a release of employment claims, they constituted a use of plan assets to "purchase" a significant benefit for Lockheed. Though the court found a violation of §406, it decided that there was no need to address Lockheed's status as a fiduciary. The Supreme Court issued a writ of certiorari (the way to appeal a case to the Supreme Court).

Body of Opinion

Justice Thomas

Nothing in ERISA requires employers to establish benefits plans. Nor does ERISA mandate what kind of benefits employers must provide if they choose to have such a plan.... ERISA does, however, seek to ensure that employees will not be left empty-handed once employers have guaranteed them certain benefits.... Accordingly, ERISA tries to "make as certain as possible that pension fund assets [will] be adequate" to meet expected benefits payments....

To increase the chances that employers will be able to honor their benefits commitments—that is, to guard against the possibility of bankrupt pension funds—Congress incorporated several key measures into the Act. Section 302 of ERISA sets minimum annual funding levels for all covered plans...and creates tax liens in favor of such plans when those funding levels are not met....Sections 404 and 409 of ERISA impose respectively a duty of care with respect to the management of existing trust funds, along with liability for breach of that duty, upon plan fiduciaries....Finally, §406 of ERISA prohibits fiduciaries from involving the plan and its assets in certain kinds of business deals.... It is this last feature of ERISA that is at issue today.

Congress enacted §406 "to bar categorically a transaction that [is] likely to injure the pension plan."... That section mandates, in relevant part, that "[a] fiduciary with respect to a plan shall not cause the plan to engage in a transaction, if he knows or should know that such transaction constitutes a direct or indirect... transfer to, or use by or for the benefit of a party in interest, of any assets of the plan."...The question here is whether this provision of ERISA prevents an employer from conditioning the receipt of early retirement benefits upon the participants' waiver of employment claims. For the following reasons, we hold that it does not.

Spink...alleged that the members of Lockheed's Retirement Committee who implemented the amended Plan violated §406(a)(1)(D).... [T]he court of appeals erred in holding that the Retirement Committee members violated the prohibited transaction section of ERISA without making the requisite finding of fiduciary status. It is not necessary for us to decide the question whether the Retirement Committee members acted as fiduciaries when they paid out benefits according to the terms of the amended Plan, however, because we do not think that they engaged in any conduct prohibited by §406(a)(1)(D).

The "transaction" in which fiduciaries may not cause a plan to engage is one that "constitutes a direct or indirect...transfer to, or use by or for the benefit of a party in interest, of any assets of the plan."...Spink reads §406(a)(1)(D) to apply in cases where the benefit received by the party in interest—in this case the employer—is not merely a "natural incident of the administration of pension plans."... Lockheed, on the other hand, maintains that a plan administrator's payment of benefits to plan participants and beneficiaries pursuant to the terms of an otherwise lawful plan is wholly outside the scope of §406(a)(1)(D)....We agree with Lockheed.

Section 406 (a)(1)(D) does not in direct terms include the payment of benefits by a plan administrator. And the surrounding provisions suggest that the payment of benefits is in fact not a "transaction" in the sense that Congress used the term in §406 (a). Section 406 (a) forbids fiduciaries from engaging the plan in the "sale," "exchange," or "leasing" of property...; the "lending of money" or "extension of credit,"...the "furnishing of goods, services, or facilities,"...; and the "acquisition...of any employer security or employer real property,"...with a party in interest.... These are commercial bargains that present a special risk of plan underfunding because they are struck with plan insiders, presumably not at arms-length....What the "transactions" identified in §406 (a) thus have in common is that they generally involve uses of plan assets that are potentially harmful to the plan....The payment of benefits conditioned on performance by plan participants cannot reasonably by said to share that characteristic.

According to Spink and the Court of Appeals, however, Lockheed's early retirement programs were prohibited transactions within the meaning of §406 (a)(1)(D) because the required release of employment-related claims by participants created a "significant benefit" for Lockheed.... Spink concedes, however, that among the "incidental" and thus legitimate benefits that a plan sponsor may receive from the operation of a pension plan are attracting and retaining employees, paying deferred compensation, setting or avoiding strikes, providing increased compensation without increasing wages, increasing employee turnover, and reducing the likelihood of lawsuits by encouraging employees who would otherwise have been laid off to depart voluntarily....

We do not see how obtaining waivers of employment-related claims can meaningfully be distinguished from these admittedly permissible objectives. Each involves, at bottom, a quid pro quo between the plan sponsor and the participant: that is, the employer promises to pay increased benefits in exchange for the performance of some condition by the employee.... By Spink's admission, the employer can ask the employee to continue to work for the employer, to cross a picket line, or to retire early. The execution of a release of claims against the employer is functionally no different; like these other conditions, it is an act that the employee performs for the employer in return for benefits. Certainly, there is no basis in §406 (a)(1)(D) for distinguishing a valid from an invalid quid pro quo. Section 406 (a)(1)(D) simply does not address what an employer can and cannot ask an employee to do in return for benefits.... Furthermore, if an employer can avoid litigation that might result from laying off an employee by enticing him to retire early, as Spink concedes, it stands to reason that the employer can also protect itself from suits arising out of that retirement by asking the employee to release any employment-related claims he may have.

In short, whatever the precise boundaries of the prohibition in §406 (a)(1)(D), there is one use of plan assets that it cannot logically encompass: a quid pro quo between the employer and plan participants in which the plan pays out benefits to the participants pursuant to its terms. When §406 (a)(1)(D) is read in the context of the other prohibited transactions, it becomes clear that the payment of benefits in exchange for the performance of some condition by the employee is not a "transaction" within the meaning of §406 (a)(1)(D); it also would provide little guidance to lower courts and those who must comply with ERISA.

Judgment and Result

The payment of benefits under an amended retirement plan regardless of what the plan requires of the employees in return for those benefits, does not constitute a prohibited transaction under ERISA.

Questions

1. ERISA makes it illegal for retirement plan fiduciaries to self-deal, that is, engage in transactions that are "direct or indirect ... transfers to, or use by or for the benefit of a party in interest, of any assets of the plan." Why is the employer's conditioning an employee's right to retirement benefits on the employee's giving up an age discrimination or ERISA claim the employee would otherwise have against the employer not considered self-dealing? After all, is the employer not using plan assets to benefit the employer by "buying off" litigation claims?
2. Is perhaps the key to the *Lockheed* case that the employer was not taking away employee retirement benefits that had already vested but, rather, was *increasing* retirement benefits for those who relinquished their otherwise valid employment claims against Lockheed?
3. The Lockheed Plan was a defined benefit plan. What does such a plan entail?

Records and Reports. ERISA imposes records and reports requirements. The plan manager must record each individual plan participant's length of employment and the amount of **vested benefits**. An explanation of the retirement plan must be given to each employee. This explanatory brochure of the retirement plan must be simple enough for the average person to understand. It might include such things as circumstances causing loss of plan benefits, claims procedures, and eligibility requirements. Each employee retirement plan must prepare an annual report with opinions from both an independent actuary and an independent certified public accountant. Employees and the public have a right to see the retirement plan's annual report. Although ERISA imposes disclosure requirements, some suggest they are not as tough as those under the 1933 and 1934 federal securities acts.

Investment Restrictions. ERISA investment restrictions limit what the retirement plan manager can do with the millions or billions of dollars in the plan. Transactions between the plan manager and the plan are illegal. For example, the plan manager cannot sell his or her hula hoop factory to the plan because it would be a conflict of interest. Loans by the plan to the employer are also illegal. The plan can, however, own the employer's securities. For example, Sears' employee retirement plan is the largest stockholder in that company.

Pension Benefit Guaranty Corporation. ERISA created the Pension Benefit Guaranty Corporation (PBGC), designed to make sure employees get vested retirement benefits if the plan fails. Both the plan and the employer are required to repay amounts the PBGC has to pay employees, but limits exist on an employer's liability to repay the PBGC.

Vesting. An important ERISA reform is its *vesting requirements*. Vesting refers to rights that cannot legally be taken away. For example, workers who have vested pension rights cannot lose them by changing jobs. Often, both employees and employers pay toward an employee retirement plan. Before ERISA, employer contributions often did not vest until just before a worker retired. If a worker changed jobs, was fired, or for some other reason stopped working before vesting, the worker lost the entire employer retirement contribution (which might be 40 years' accumulation in extreme cases). Before ERISA, if a large number of employees were fired just before vesting at retirement, the employer would get back all employer contributions for all such employees. The amounts would be used to pay benefits for other employees who remained until retirement, thus reducing the employer's retirement costs. Most scholars viewed this practice as inequitable, assuming employer contributions are a type of deferred pay (instead of a gift or tip from the employer). Employers argued that late vesting of their contributions reduced employee retirement costs.

ERISA requires 100 percent immediate vesting of employee pension contributions. After December 31, 1988, ERISA requires that employers' contributions must vest at least as rapidly as either one of the following vesting schedules:

1. Five-year "cliff" (all at once) vesting; that is, employees who have worked five years or more must be 100 percent vested regarding the employer's contribution to their retirement plan; or
2. Three- to seven-year graduated vesting; this approach requires that employees have the right to the employer's contribution to the employee's retirement plan according to the following schedule:

Years of service	Percentage Vested
3	20
4	40
5	60
6	80
7	100

Does ERISA prevent a private employer's retirement plan from reducing retirement benefits by amounts received from other benefit plans? The *Alessi v. Raybestos-Manhattan Inc.* case says, "No."

Alessi v. Raybestos-Manhattan, Inc.

U.S. Supreme Court
451 U.S. 504 (1981)

Background and Facts:

In two suits initiated in New Jersey state court, retired employees who had received workers' compensation awards subsequent to retirement challenged the validity of provisions in their employers' pension plans reducing a retiree's pension benefits by an amount equal to a workers' compensation award for which the retiree is eligible. Those private pension plans are subject to federal regulation under the Employee Retirement Income Security Act of 1974 (ERISA). The employers independently removed the suits to Federal District Court, where the judges in each suit held that the pension offset provisions were invalid under a provision of the New Jersey Workers' Compensation Act prohibiting such offsets; that Congress had not intended ERISA to pre-empt such state laws; that the offsets were prohibited by ERISA's provision, prohibiting forfeitures of pension rights except under specified conditions inapplicable to these cases; and that a Treasury Regulation authorizing offsets based on workers' compensation awards were invalid. The Court of Appeals consolidated appeals from the two decisions and reversed.

Body of Opinion

Justice Marshall

1. Congress contemplated and approved the kind of pension provisions challenged here.

Pension plan provisions for offsets based on workers' compensation awards do not contravene ERISA's nonforfeiture provisions. While (ERISA) prohibits forfeitures of vested rights, with specified exceptions that do not include workers' compensation offsets, nevertheless other provisions make it clear that ERISA leaves to the private parties creating the pension plan the determination of the content or amount of benefits that, once vested, cannot be forfeited. The statutory definition of "nonforfeitable" pension benefits... assures that an employee's claim to the protected benefit is legally enforceable, but it does not guarantee a particular amount or a method for calculating the benefit.... It is particularly pertinent that Congress did not prohibit "integration," a calculation practice under which benefit levels are determined by combining pension funds with other public income streams available to the retired employee. Rather, Congress accepted the practice by expressly preserving the option of pension fund integration with benefits available under both the Social Security Act and the Railroad Retirement Act. Offsets against pension benefits for workers' compensation awards work much like the integration of pension benefits with Social Security or Railroad Retirement payments, and thus the nonforfeiture provision has no more applicability to the former kind of integration than it does to the latter.

Although neither ERISA nor its legislative history mentions integration with workers' compensation, ERISA does not forbid the Treasury Regulation permitting reductions of pension benefits based on awards under state workers' compensation laws, or Internal Revenue Service rulings to the same effect. There is no merit in the argument that integration of pension funds with workers' compensation awards, which are based on work-related injuries, lacks the rationale behind ERISA's permission of integration of pension funds with Social Security and Railroad Retirement payments, which supply payments for wages lost due to retirement. Both the Social Security and Railroad Retirement Acts also provide payments for disability, and ERISA permits pension integration with such benefits as well as with benefits for wages lost due to retirement. Moreover, when it enacted ERISA, Congress knew of the IRS rulings permitting integration with workers' compensation benefits and left them in effect.

The New Jersey statute in question is preempted by federal law insofar as it eliminates a method for calculating pension benefits under plans governed by ERISA. The provision of ERISA, stating that the Act's provisions shall supersede any state laws that "relate to any [covered] employee benefit plan," demonstrates that Congress meant to establish pension plan regulation as exclusively a federal concern. Regardless of whether the purpose of the New Jersey statute might have been to protect the employee's right to workers' compensation disability benefits rather than to regulate pension plans, the statute "relate[s] to pension plans" governed by ERISA because it eliminates one method for calculating pension benefits—integration—that is permitted by federal law, and the state provision thus is an impermissible intrusion on the federal regulatory scheme. It is of no moment that New Jersey intrudes indirectly, through a workers' compensation law, rather than directly, through a statute called "pension regulation," since ERISA makes clear that even indirect state action bearing on private pensions may encroach upon the area of exclusive federal concern. Moreover, where, as here, pension plans emerge from collective bargaining, the additional federal interest in precluding state interference in labor-management negotiations calls for preemption of state efforts to regulate pension terms.

Judgment and Result

The U.S. Supreme Court held that ERISA does not stop a private pension plan from reducing retirement benefits by the amount of money obtained from workers' compensation awards received after retirement.

Questions

1. Does ERISA have a provision that stops retirement plans from forfeiting pension benefits?
2. What is meant by *integration* with respect to retirement plans? Does integration reduce a person's retirement benefits or merely calculate those payments by taking into account benefits from other sources?
3. If state law prohibits pension offsets and ERISA allows them, which prevails? Why?
4. Explain what a pension offset provision is.

ERISA Preemption. Recall from Chapter 5 that federal preemption refers to a federal statute's (or regulation's) preventing state or local laws from dealing with a particular matter. For example, does ERISA preempt states from passing laws that affect employee benefit plans?

ERISA does have a specific preemption provision designed to promote national uniformity in employee pensions and other benefits. (ERISA covers employee benefits other than pensions.) However, states argue that ERISA's preemption provision is only partial, which would mean that states could regulate *some* areas of employee benefit programs.

In 1985 the U.S. Supreme Court decided *Metropolitan Life v. Massachusetts.* Massachusetts and 11 other states require private insurers to include mental health coverage in group insurance policies. Two private insurers, Metropolitan Life and Travelers Insurance Company, argued that ERISA preempted the states on this matter; that is, if each state could tell insurers what to put into their group policies, ERISA's national goal of uniformity would be lost. The Supreme Court decided that ERISA does *not* preempt state law on this matter. In other words, state law can force group insurers to cover certain risks such as alcoholism, drug treatment, and infant care.

Reversion of Excess Plan Assets. Employers sometimes go out of business. If they fully fund present and future liabilities under the employee benefit plan, the plan sometimes has excess assets (money left over after all obligations are paid. In one case, an employer amended its pension plan (before going out of business) to allow any excess plan assets to go to the employer. ERISA has an exclusive benefit rule which says that plans are only supposed to benefit participants and their beneficiaries plus pay reasonable plan administration costs.

In *Washington-Baltimore Newspaper Guide Local 35 v. The Washington Star Co.*, a federal court of appeals held that an employer's plan amendment allowing excess assets to revert to the employer did not violate ERISA's exclusive benefit rule.

Family and Medical Leave Act of 1993[2]

The authors acknowledge reliance on readings at the end of this chapter in preparing this segment.

http:// *The Family and Medical Leave Act of 1993 can be found on the Library of Congress website at* ***http://thomas.loc.gov***

In 1993 the first major piece of legislation President Clinton signed into law was the Family and Medical Leave Act of 1993. This law was passed in recognition of several demographic shifts in the workforce over the past three or four decades: first, the influx of women into the workforce, and second, the increase in single-parent families. This act aims to accommodate such new members of the workforce by mandating that employers provide leaves of absence to employees when leave is requested for certain family purposes including birth of a child, placing a child for adoption or in foster care, the employee's ill health, or the ill health of an employee's family member.

Two important requirements of this law are that employers must give up to 12 weeks of leave in a calendar year to employees covered by the act's family or medical purposes. Employers do not have to pay employees during the leave, but employers must continue to provide health insurance during the leave. However, if the employee usually has to pay part or all of the health coverage while at work, then this requirement continues during the leave. Secondly, the employees are entitled to get their jobs back (or an equivalent job) at the end of the leaves.

[2] The authors acknowledge Deloitte, Haskins, & Sells *DH&S Review* in preparing this segment.

Employees must provide employers with a 30-day advance notice of the request for a leave when need for such a leave is foreseeable. Obviously, a pregnancy is foreseeable, although predicting the exact time is problematic, and the required notice must be "practicable" in such cases.

Employers have a legal obligation to provide employees with written guidance as to the rights and obligations the FMLA requires.

Certain limitations affect coverage of the FMLA. It does not apply to employers who have just opened their business, because employees have no rights under the act until they have worked at least one year. Also employers must have 50 or more employees before the FMLA applies.

Enforcement of the FMLA is similar to the federal Fair Labor Standards Act. Remedies for violating the FMLA include employment, reinstatement, and promotion. The Secretary of Labor may bring actions seeking injunctions against employers. Class actions under the act are allowed.

Plant Closing Legislation

As plants across the United States close, particularly in the "rust belt" states of the Midwest and also in the Northeast, thousands of workers lose their jobs. Additionally, communities with unemployed workers suffer because the community's tax base can decline along with schools and other public services. To soften the shock of sudden plant shutdowns, several states (including Maine, Wisconsin, Massachusetts, Maryland, Michigan, and Connecticut) and cities (Philadelphia and Vacaville, California) have passed laws at one time or another that require some type of preclosing notice to workers. Several features of the notice can vary.

1. The size of the business it applies to (often it only covers employers with 100 or more employees)
2. How much advance notice of closing must be given (60 days is common, although the longer the notice, the more protection there is)
3. The sanction for noncompliance (Wisconsin's sanction was at one time only $50 per worker—hardly a deterrent)
4. Whether the notice is mandatory or voluntary (in some states such as Michigan, the notice has been voluntary with little if any compliance)

Federal Plant Closing Statute.[3] On August 4, 1988, federal plant closing legislation requiring advanced notice of certain layoffs and closings became law without President Reagan's signature. This law requires employers with more than 100 employees to give 60 days advanced notice if 50 or more employees at one site will lose their jobs because of a plant closing. A layoff notice must be given if 50 workers at one site will lose jobs and they are 33 percent or more of the work force. Notice is also required if 500 or more employees are to be laid off no matter what the circumstances.

In the *Fort Halifax Packing Company v. Coyne* case, the U.S. Supreme Court upheld the Maine plant closing legislation when challenged on grounds that ERISA and the National Labor Relations Act preempted it.

CHAPTER SUMMARY

A number of statutes passed in the twentieth century affect employees' job safety and financial security.

[3] The authors acknowledge Deloitte, Haskins, & Sells, *DH&S Review*, in preparing this segment.

Workers' compensation statutes provide money to workers who suffer on-the-job injuries, diseases, or death. These statutes impose no-fault liability on employers. Defenses to workers' comp claims include the fact that the employee intentionally caused the injury or was not at work at the time of the loss.

The federal OSHA statute tries to prevent injury and loss to employees while at work.

The Fair Labor Standards Act is the federal law that sets maximum hours and hourly wage minimums employers must pay their employees who affect interstate commerce. Some employees are exempt from either or both the maximum hours and minimum wage requirements.

The Equal Pay Act amends the Fair Labor Standards Act. The Equal Pay Act prohibits employers from paying different wages based on sex to men and women who do substantially equal work.

Unemployment compensation is a federal and state program designed to provide unemployed individuals with some support while they are unemployed. The money for this program comes from a federal payroll tax placed on employers. State unemployment taxes can be credited against the employer's federal unemployment tax liability if the state law meets federal requirements. Not all employees are covered by unemployment compensation.

Social Security taxes are imposed on employers and employees. Independent contractors pay both the employer's and employees' share of this tax. Social Security taxes are paid on an employee's gross income before income taxes are deducted.

ERISA is a federal statute designed to regulate private pension plans. ERISA imposes vesting requirements, imposes duties on retirement plan managers, and establishes the Pension Benefit Guaranty Corporation to insure plan benefits. ERISA does not require that employers have retirement plans.

The Family and Medical Leave Act of 1993 requires certain employers to provide leaves of absence when requested to certain employees for up to 12 weeks during each calendar year to take care of certain family and medical problems. Covered employees taking such leaves are entitled to get their jobs (or equivalent) back and to keep health insurance during the leave.

Plant closing statutes in a number of states require that employers give employees advance notice if plants are about to close. In 1988 a federal plant-closing statute became law.

Discussion Questions

1. "In 1992, petitioners, a group of probation officers, filed suit against their employer, the State of Maine, in the United States District Court for the District of Maine. The officers alleged the State had violated the overtime provisions of the Fair Labor Standards Act of 1938 (FLSA), . . . and sought compensation and liquidated damages." Should state employees be able to recover against a state that violates the federal Fair Labor Standards Act or does the Eleventh Amendment, which explicitly refers to states' immunity from suits by "Citizens of another State, or by Citizens or Subjects of any Foreign State," immunize states from suits brought by their own citizens? Note that the Eleventh Amendment literally does not immunize states from suits brought against them by their own citizens. [*Alden v. Maine*, 119 S.Ct. 2240 (1999)]
2. What are the principal benefits of the Fair Labor Standards Act? How could it be argued that the Fair Labor Standards Act causes unemployment among young workers who tend to have low skill levels? Does this argument suggest a possible modification in the FLSA? What are some arguments against exempting young workers from the FLSA's protections?
3. Who benefits from the Equal Pay Act? How can it be argued that men benefit from this law? What employers does it cover? Why should the Equal Pay Act cover governmental units?

MANAGER'S ETHICAL DILEMMA

Dee Leacoca, the CEO (chief executive officer) of the Leacocá Motor Company of Detroit, Michigan, discovered that 16 percent of the cost of the cars his firm built was made up of employee health care costs. Dee wanted to reduce this cost and thereby make his cars more competitive with foreign manufacturers. Most foreign manufacturers operated in countries having national health insurance systems. Their workers' health costs were paid for by society (the country's government) rather than directly by the foreign manufacturer. Although foreign manufacturers had to pay taxes to support their governments' programs (including national health insurance), this cost was spread over the entire society rather than being concentrated on the employers. This system, in turn, made it relatively cheaper for foreign manufacturers to produce cars.

A bill that several car manufacturers wanted to be introduced in Congress was placed on Dee's desk for his reaction. The bill proposed establishing a national health care agency in the United States. Under the bill physicians would be made federal employees and would receive subsidized medical school education (as they do now), and would receive starting salaries of \$50,000 per year, which would rise to as high as \$150,000 per year depending on the physician's expertise, medical specialty, and years of experience, and scarcity of medical practitioners in the geographic region (SMSA, standard metropolitan statistical area). The federal health care agency would provide offices, nurses, hospitals, and staff. Also, liability limits of \$500,000 per operation would be imposed for physician malpractice under this scheme, with arbitration rather than jury trials of malpractice claims in order to control medical costs.

Dee wondered whether he should throw his support behind this bill. What legal and business ethics mentioned in Chapter 1 are involved here? What would you do if you were in Dee's position?

4. What objectives does OSHA have? In what ways does OSHA achieve them? How does it not achieve its goals? In this regard, how can the reduction of OSHA regulations increase the likelihood of OSHA's success?
5. Does the "integration principle" announced in the *Alessi* case suggest a way to reduce the cost of employer retirement programs? Should the *Alessi* principle be extended to allow any (private or public) pension plan to reduce benefits by taking into account amounts received from other retirement plans? If all pension plans could be reduced, what would they be reduced to—some absolute dollar level?
6. Workers' compensation generally covers only injuries, disease, or death at work. Did the following death occur at work? An electric utility company's line foreman supervised correction of a power outage. He corrected the problem at 9:00 A.M. but remained subject to call. He headed home in a company car, did some personal shopping, and stopped at several bars. At 4:00 P.M., while drunk, he got into the company car, continued on his way home, and was killed in a two-car accident. Evidence showed the collision occurred when he turned to avoid hitting a pedestrian. His widow and children sued to recover workers' compensation. Was he at work when killed? [*Oakes v. W.C.A.B.*, 79 Pa. Cmwlth. 454, 469 A.2d 723 (1984)]
7. HPL Ohio, Inc., was cited for a serious violation of OSHA regulations requiring handrails on platforms higher than four feet. HPL's platform was seven feet high and did not have handrails. It was used for storage. Employees climbed on it about every three months. HPL argued that the violation was nonserious. Was it? [*HPL Ohio, Inc.*, 7 OSHC 21512 (1974)]
8. Employers Temporary Service, Inc. (E.T.S.) was an employment service. A 15-year-old applied for employment but misrepresented his age as 19 on the employment application. E.T.S. told the boy he would have to prove his age at his next visit to the hiring hall. No such proof was ever requested or offered. E.T.S. found the boy work at R.A. Young Industries, Inc. While running a power press there, the boy suffered amputation of two fingers and part of his hand. The boy sued the employers Young and E.T.S. for negligence. They defended by arguing the boy's exclusive remedy was under workers' compensation. The boy argued that people illegally employed (here, child labor) were not "employees" covered by workers' comp. (The workers' comp remedy would probably have been smaller than a judgment in a

negligence suit, which would benefit the employers.) Who was right? [*Allossery v. Employers Temporary Serv., Inc.*, 88 Mich. App. 496, 277 N.W.2d 340 (1979)]

9. Employees are generally unable to collect unemployment insurance benefits if they voluntarily quit work. Brousseau was convicted of drunken driving, and a judge suspended Brousseau's driver's license. As a result, his employer fired Brousseau from his job as a truck driver and warehouse worker. Did Brousseau involuntarily lose his job so as to be eligible for unemployment compensation, or did his voluntary act of drunkenness disqualify him from unemployment benefits? [*Brousseau v. Maine Employment Security Com'n*, 470 A.2d 327 (Me. 1984)]
10. Social Security benefits are available for several disabled workers under age 65. In one case, a 47-year-old drywall finisher suffered from heart disease, hypoglycemia, vertebrovascular insufficiency, mental depression, and possible emphysema. Was this condition a "slight neurosis, slight impairment of hearing and sight" not entitling him to Social Security disability benefits? [*Brady v. Heckler*, 724 F.2d 914 (11th Cir. 1974)]

Suggested Readings

Articles

BALLAM, "The Occupational Safety and Health Act's Preemptive Effect on State Criminal Prosecutions of Employers for Workplace Deaths and Injuries," 26 *American Business Law Journal* 1 (1988).

BALLAM, "The Workers' Compensation Exclusivity Doctrine: A Threat to Workers' Rights Under State Employment Discrimination Statutes," 27 *American Business Law Journal* 95 (1989).

BIBLE, "Employee Urine Testing and the Federal Appeals Courts," 26 *American Business Law Journal* 219 (1988).

BROCKHOEFT, "AIDS in the Workplace: Legal Limitations on Employer Actions," 26 *American Business Law Journal* 255 (1988).

GABEL and MANSFIELD, "Practicing in the Evolving Landscape of Workers' Compensation Law," 14 *The Labor Lawyer* 73 (1998).

GABEL, MANSFIELD, and KLEIN, "The New Relationship Between Injured Worker and Employer: An Opportunity for Restructuring the System," 35 *American Business Law Journal* 403 (1998).

LINDER, "I Gave My Employer a Chicken That Had No Bone: Joint Firm-State Responsibility for Line-Speed-Related Occupational Injuries," 46 *Case Western Reserve Law Review* 33 (1995).

MANSFIELD, BAER, and HOPE, "Insurance Gaps on AIDS-Related Healthcare Costs: Will the ADA Fill the Gap Created by ERISA," 14 *Georgia State University Law Review* 601 (1998).

PINCUS and TROTTER, "The Disparity Between Public and Private Sector Employee Privacy Rights for Private Sector Workers," 33 *American Business Law Journal* 51 (1995).

RIGLER, "Analysis and Understanding of the Family and Medical Leave Act of 1993," 45 *Case Western Reserve Law Review* 457 (1995).

WIDISS, "What's Wrong with the ERISA 'Vacuum'? The Case Against Unrestricted Freedom for Employers to Terminate Employee Health Care Plans and to Decide What Coverage Is to Be Provided When Risk Retention Plans Are Established for Health Care," 41 *Drake Law Review* 635 (1992).

CHAPTER

16

EMPLOYMENT DISCRIMINATION

POSITIVE LAW ETHICAL PROBLEMS

Karen Sutton and Kimberly Hinton are twin sisters. Both are extremely near-sighted. Each woman's uncorrected vision is 20/200 or worse in her right eye and 20/400 or worse in her left eye. But both Karen and Kimberly are correctable down to 20/20 or better with the use of corrective lenses. Without corrective lenses, on the other hand, neither woman can see to conduct numerous activities such as driving a vehicle, watching television, or shopping in public stores. In 1992, Karen and Kimberly applied to United Airlines for employment as commercial airline pilots. After submitting their applications, both women were invited to an interview and to flight simulator tests. However, both were told during their interviews that a mistake had been made in inviting them to interview because they did not meet United's minimum vision requirement, which was uncorrected vision of 20/100 or better.

Karen and Kimberly later sued United for disability discrimination under the Americans with Disabilities Act (ADA). United's position was that, because their vision was correctable, Karen and Kimberly were not disabled and thus were not covered by the act. The two women responded that this reading of the ADA irrationally gave United the power to discriminate against people like themselves whose vision was correctable, but *not* against people whose vision was uncorrectable. In other words, they maintained that United's reading of the ADA let employers discriminate where discrimination could not be justified, but forbade discrimination where it might be justified. Who was right?

This chapter discusses the most important federal laws forbidding discrimination in employment. Before the 1960s, few if any federal statutes regulated employment discrimination. During the 1960s and 1970s, however, that pattern changed dramatically. As a result, business now confronts a maze of employment discrimination regulations. Those regulations have continued to increase through the 1990s. Today, federal law prohibits discrimination on the bases of age, gender, race, color, national origin, religion, and disability. Figure 16.1 summarizes the types of discrimination forbidden by the most important federal employment discrimination laws.

"A PRACTITIONER IN THE [EMPLOYMENT DISCRIMINATION] AREA, BE IT STUDENT, ATTORNEY, BUSINESSPERSON, EMPLOYEE, GOVERNMENT OFFICIAL, OR UNION LEADER, CANNOT CONCENTRATE ALL ENERGIES ON ONE SOURCE OF RIGHTS OR REMEDIES. A POTENTIAL PLAINTIFF HAS A QUIVER OF REMEDIAL ARROWS; A POTENTIAL DEFENDANT MANY FLANKS TO COVER."

M. Player, Federal Law of Employment Discrimination, 2d ed. (1981)

FIGURE 16.1 Major Federal Employment Discrimination Laws

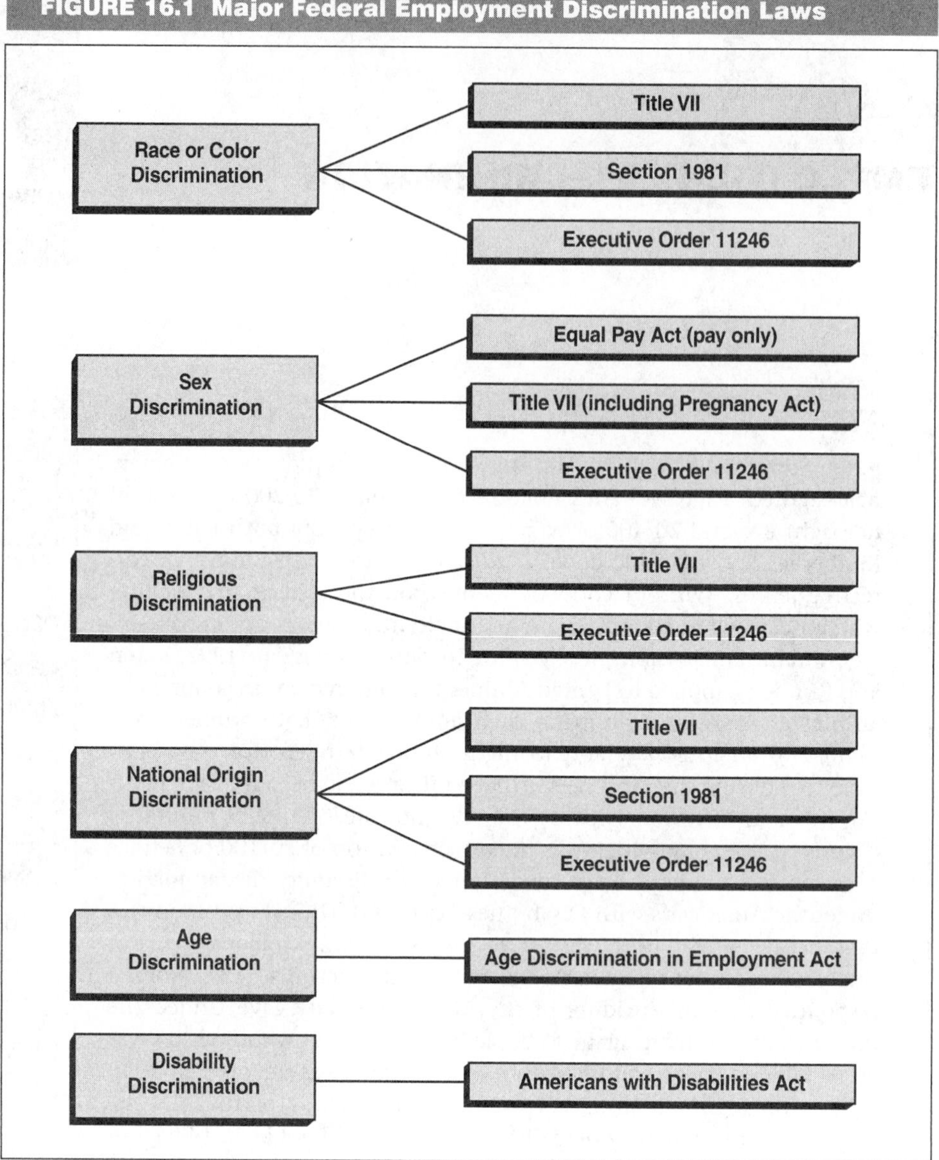

EQUAL PAY ACT

The Equal Pay Act of 1963 (EPA) is an employment discrimination provision of limited scope. The EPA forbids sex discrimination regarding pay only. It commands that men and women performing equal work receive equal pay. The EPA was passed as an amendment to the Fair Labor Standards Act (FLSA), and its coverage is similar to that of the FLSA[1]. Unlike the FLSA, however, the EPA protects executive, administrative, and professional employees.

[1] The FLSA is discussed in Chapter 15.

Elements of an Equal Pay Act Case

Although the Equal Pay Act forbids pay discrimination against both men and women, the usual EPA case involves an aggrieved woman. To recover, a woman must show that she has received lower pay than a male employee who performed substantially equal work for the same employer. Two jobs are substantially equal when they involve each of the following: (1) equal effort, (2) equal skill, (3) equal responsibility, and (4) similar working conditions. As the following *Fowler* case suggests, however, courts often do not consider these factors one by one.

The effort associated with a job is the amount of physical or mental exertion it requires. Skill involves the experience, training, education, and ability required by a job, not the skills the male and female employees actually possess. Responsibility (or accountability) refers to such things as the importance of the decisions made in a particular job or the degree of supervision the job requires. For example, bank employees whose loan decisions must be reviewed by a superior when the loan exceeds $10,000 probably are not equal to bank employees who can approve loans of up to $50,000 at their own discretion. Finally, working conditions refers to the quality of the employee's physical surroundings; the hazards the job creates; and factors such as heat, cold, inside or outside work, and exposure to fumes or toxic substances. Note that the working conditions for the positions being compared need only be similar, not equal.

EPA Defenses

Once a plaintiff establishes the elements of an EPA claim, the defendant loses the case unless it proves that the pay disparity is justified by one of the act's four defenses. These defenses are (1) seniority, (2) merit, (3) quality or quantity of production (e.g., a piecework system), and (4) any factor other than sex. To successfully use the first three defenses, employers ordinarily cannot rely on discretionary, subjective employee evaluation systems that might permit sex-based criteria to influence their decisions. Instead, employers usually must demonstrate that they used an organized system with fairly precise criteria that apply equally to employees of each sex and are communicated to all employees. The catchall any-factor-other-than-sex defense may include practices such as shift differentials or bonuses paid because a position is part of a training program.

EPA Remedies

Because the Equal Pay Act is part of the FLSA, its remedies resemble the FLSA remedies discussed in Chapter 15. In an EPA case, therefore, successful plaintiffs generally recover the amount of back pay lost because of the employer's discrimination. In addition, such plaintiffs may receive an equal amount as liquidated damages. Unlike the FLSA, however, the EPA is enforced by the Equal Employment Opportunity Commission (EEOC) rather than the Labor Department.[2] The EPA differs from many of the employment discrimination measures discussed later by not requiring private plaintiffs to submit their claims to the EEOC or a suitable state agency before a lawsuit may take place.

> http://
> The EEOC's web site is at **http://eeoc.gov**

[2] The EEOC is an independent federal agency with a sizable staff and many regional offices. It enforces most of the employment discrimination laws discussed in this chapter. It also interprets those laws by issuing regulations and guidelines.

Fowler v. Land Management Groupe, Inc.

United States Court of Appeals for the Fourth Circuit
978 F.2d 158 (1992)

Background and Facts:

In 1987, the Land Management Groupe, Inc. (LMG) hired Barbara Fowler as a project manager at a starting salary of $32,000 per year. Fowler worked for LMG for approximately three years, until she was laid off in February 1990. During her three years with LMG, Fowler attained the title of Vice-President of Building Development. Her salary at the time of her termination was $60,000.

After her departure from LMG, Fowler sued the firm in federal district court under the Equal Pay Act. After a jury trial, the jury entered a verdict in her favor. The court, however, granted LMG's motion for judgment notwithstanding the verdict (JNOV). Fowler appealed this ruling.

Body of Opinion

Chief Judge Ervin

Under [the Equal Pay Act], a female plaintiff bears the burden of proof of establishing . . . that: (1) her employer pays her a lower wage than a male counterpart (2) for equal work on jobs the performance of which requires equal skill, effort and responsibility. . . . The burden [then] shifts to the defendant to show, by a preponderance of the evidence, that the wage differential resulted from one of the allowable causes enumerated by the statute.

In reviewing a JNOV, we must view the evidence in the light most favorable to the non-moving party [Fowler]. JNOV is appropriate only when there is no legally sufficient evidentiary basis for a reasonable jury to have found for the non-moving party. . . .

The evidence shows that another Vice-President of the company, Bruce Reese, was hired six months after Fowler. Reese's starting salary was $62,000 (compared to Fowler's $32,000). At the time LMG terminated Fowler's employment, Reese's annual salary was $73,500 (compared to Fowler's $60,000). . . .

LMG points to various aspects of the trial testimony which established that: (1) Reese had certain professional qualifications that Fowler did not possess (he possessed an engineer's license and a surveyor's license); (2) Reese had greater practical experience; (3) Reese's expertise in site preparation and zoning were more useful to the company than Fowler's expertise in building construction because the majority of LMG's properties were not yet undergoing construction; (4) Reese's activities generated a greater share of the company's profits than did Fowler's activities; and (5) Reese was considered a more important employee of LMG.

While these justifications are persuasive, we do not believe they rise to such an overwhelming level that no reasonable jury could find that the pay differential was unjustified. Contradicting LMG's position, several LMG employees testified that they discerned no difference in the respective tasks performed by Reese and Fowler or in the degree of authority that they appeared to exercise on behalf of the company. . . . Furthermore, there is no evidence that Reese was ever called upon to use his engineering or surveying licenses while in the employ of LMG. Viewed in the light most favorable to Fowler, we believe the evidence adequately supports the jury's verdict.

Judgment and Result

District court's grant of judgment notwithstanding the verdict to LMG reversed; jury verdict for Fowler stands.

Questions

1. Did the court of appeals say that it would have reached the same result the jury did had the case been tried before it?
2. How did the court dispose of the assertion that Reese's engineering and surveying licenses made his job and Fowler's job unequal? Was it right to do so?

TITLE VII OF THE 1964 CIVIL RIGHTS ACT

Due mainly to its scope, Title VII of the 1964 Civil Rights Act is the most important federal employment discrimination statute. Title VII prohibits employment discrimination based on race, color, religion, sex, and national origin. It forbids such discrimination in a wide range of employment contexts, and thus covers most significant terms, conditions, and benefits of employment.

Coverage

Another portion of Title VII covers employment discrimination in the federal government. For more on this subject, see ***http://eeoc.gov***

http://

Covered Entities. Title VII basically covers employers employing 15 or more employees and engaging in an industry affecting interstate commerce. The term *employer* includes individuals, partnerships, corporations, labor unions (regarding their own employees), employment agencies (regarding their own employees), and state and local governments. Title VII also prevents unions and employment agencies from discriminating against their members and clients, respectively. For Title VII to apply in these two cases, the union usually must have 15 or more members, and the employment agency must service an employer with 15 or more employees. Note that the latter test differs from the test applied where an employment agency discriminates against its own employees. For example, a three-person employment agency is covered by Title VII if it discriminates against African-Americans when making job referrals to IBM, but Title VII would not cover the agency's refusal to hire a secretary because of his or her race.

Exclusions from Coverage. Certain employers, employees, and employment relationships are specifically excluded from Title VII's coverage. First, Title VII does not apply to employer discrimination against independent contractors.[3] Second, Title VII's definition of the term *employer* specifically excludes Native American tribes and certain bona fide tax-exempt private clubs. Third, Title VII allows religious educational institutions to employ individuals of that religion to carry on their activities.

Covered Decisions. Recall that the Equal Pay Act forbids sex discrimination regarding pay only. The range of decisions covered by Title VII is much broader. Its sweeping provisions against employer, employment agency, and union discrimination cover almost all of the ways that these parties might disadvantage employees, clients, or members because their race, color, sex, religion, or national origin. Title VII also has a broad antiretaliation provision forbidding discrimination against any employee who has opposed an employment practice made illegal by Title VII; has exercised his Title VII rights; or has participated in any investigation, proceeding, or hearing under Title VII. Finally, Title VII forbids discrimination on the bases of race, color, sex, religion, or national origin in notices or advertisements.

Procedures

For directions on how to file a charge with the EEOC, see ***http://eeoc.gov***

http://

Private parties alleging a violation of Title VII cannot simply sue their employers at any time they desire. Instead, they must comply with certain procedures before doing so. The general aim of these procedures is to give the EEOC or state employment discrimination agencies the opportunity to settle the dispute or to sue in their own right in lieu of the private party's suit. The details of these complex procedures are beyond the scope of this text, but a few points should be kept in mind. First, the complaining party (complainant) must file a *charge* with a state fair employment agency or (if no suitable state agency is available) with the EEOC within a specified time period after the alleged violation. This requirement gives the state agency or the EEOC the opportunity to take such action as it deems appropriate. Second, the EEOC's or the state agency's failure to take

[3] The employee-independent contractor distinction is discussed in Chapter 14.

action satisfactory to the complainant ordinarily does not prevent the complainant from suing on his or her own behalf. In most such cases, the EEOC eventually issues a right-to-sue letter, which gives the claimant the power to sue.

Proving a Title VII Violation

For there to be a violation of Title VII, a private plaintiff or the government must *prove* that the employer acted for discriminatory reasons when making the challenged employment decision. Proof of discrimination is easy where the employer has an express policy that discriminates on one of the bases forbidden by Title VII. The *Johnson Controls* case later in the chapter is an example. Proving discrimination also poses few problems when direct evidence of discrimination, such as testimony or documents, establishes a discriminatory motive.

However, if Title VII were limited to cases of this sort, it would be a paper tiger in the struggle against employment discrimination. Often, employers can discriminate without leaving such obvious evidence in their wake. Thus, various other methods of proving a Title VII violation are available. The most important are Title VII's disparate treatment and disparate impact theories. The details of these theories are critical in determining Title VII's impact, and those details have changed from time to time in response to political pressures. Because Title VII's disparate treatment and disparate impact rules may change again by the time you read this chapter, and because each theory has become increasingly complicated, we describe them in general terms only.[4]

Disparate Treatment. Title VII's **disparate treatment theory** is most often used where a single plaintiff or a small number of plaintiffs allege some isolated instance or instances of discrimination that cannot be proven by direct evidence. The disparate treatment theory involves a three-stage order of proof.

1. First, the plaintiff must establish a **prima facie case**: a case strong enough to require some rebuttal by the defendant. The evidence needed to establish a prima facie case varies from situation to situation, but usually it creates few problems for plaintiffs. In discriminatory hiring cases, for example, the plaintiff must show that: (1) he is within one of Title VII's five protected classes; (2) he applied for, and was qualified to perform, a job for which the employer was seeking applicants; (3) he was denied the job; and (4) the employer continued to seek applicants for the position after his rejection.
2. Once the plaintiff has established a prima facie case, the defendant must produce evidence that the challenged employment decision was made for legitimate, nondiscriminatory reasons or it will lose the case. In a hiring case, for example, the employer might claim that the reason for its refusal to hire the plaintiff was a lack of qualifications for the job.
3. If the defendant produces legitimate, nondiscriminatory reasons, the burden is on the plaintiff to show that discrimination actually occurred. Although it no longer guarantees victory, a plaintiff who can show that the employer's allegedly legitimate, nondiscriminatory reasons were only a pretext for a decision actually made with a discriminatory motive is usually in good shape. For instance, a black plaintiff might show that the employer's job qualifications were applied only to African American job seekers and not to their white counterparts.

[4] This chapter reflects the state of the law as of late 1999.

Disparate Impact. Unlike the disparate treatment theory, Title VII's **disparate impact** (or adverse impact) **theory** is most often used in cases involving a large number of plaintiffs. This theory proceeds in three steps.

1. First, the plaintiffs must show that the employment practice they are challenging has an adverse impact (or disparate impact) on the basis of race, color, religion, sex, or national origin. The most common examples are employer rules such as testing, high school diploma, height, weight, and strength requirements that are neutral on their face, but that obviously can have a disproportionate adverse effect on certain groups protected by Title VII. Height and weight requirements for a particular job, for example, might well have this effect on people of certain national origins. In addition, the Supreme Court has held that the disparate impact theory includes subjective employer practices such as hiring and promotion systems that permit discretionary, qualitative judgments.
2. Once the plaintiffs demonstrate adverse impact, the employer must show that the challenged practice is job-related for the position in question and consistent with business necessity. For example, an employer might argue that physical size is important for the proper performance of certain jobs. If the employer fails to make the necessary showing, it loses the case.
3. If the employer makes the previous showing, the plaintiffs ordinarily will lose. But they have an alternate route to victory: showing that the employer's legitimate business needs can be advanced by an alternative employment practice that is less discriminatory than the challenged practice, and that the employer has failed to adopt such a practice. National origin groups disadvantaged by a height or weight requirement, for instance, might argue that the employer's needs would be better met by a strength test and that such a test also would be less disadvantageous to them.

Defenses to Title VII Claims

Even if a violation of Title VII is proven, an employer still emerges victorious if it can establish one of Title VII's various defenses. Title VII's most important defenses break down into three groups.

Bona Fide Occupational Qualification. Sometimes, one's gender, religion, or national origin is a genuine qualification for a particular job. In such cases, the **bona fide occupational qualification (BFOQ)** defense protects defendants from Title VII liability. As the following *Johnson Controls* case makes clear, however, the BFOQ defense is a narrow one. For one thing, it applies mainly to hiring and referral decisions. Also, the defense has no application to race or color discrimination.

More importantly, for a BFOQ defense to exist, sex, religion, or national origin must be necessary for effective job performance. Thus, female gender is not a BFOQ for the job of airline flight cabin attendant. However, a firm that requires men to work as attendants in men's washrooms, or employs only women as fitters for women's undergarments, should not violate Title VII.

Seniority. An employer is not liable under Title VII if its alleged discrimination resulted from the operation of a bona fide seniority system. To be bona fide, a seniority system must at least treat all employees equally on its face, have been created for nondiscriminatory reasons, and operate in a nondiscriminatory fashion.

Various Merit Defenses. Title VII gives employers a defense if their alleged discrimination resulted from the operation of a bona fide merit system or a system that measures earnings by quality or quantity of production (e.g., a piecework system). Like their Equal Pay Act counterparts, these systems must be organized, communicated, and neutrally applied in order to protect employers. Title VII also protects employment decisions made as the result of a professionally developed ability test. Of course, such tests generally must be job-related. The EEOC has promulgated detailed guidelines on employee selection procedures for determining the validity of ability tests.

Auto Workers v. Johnson Controls, Inc.

U.S. Supreme Court
499 U.S. 187 (1991)

Background and Facts:

Johnson Controls, Inc. manufactures batteries. Lead is a primary ingredient in its manufacturing process. Exposing female employees to lead creates a risk of harm to any fetus they may carry. For this reason, Johnson Controls excluded pregnant women or women who are capable of bearing children from jobs that involve exposure to lead.

A number of plaintiffs began a federal district court class action alleging that Johnson Controls' policy was illegal sex discrimination under Title VII. After the district court entered a summary judgment for Johnson Controls and the court of appeals affirmed, the plaintiffs appealed to the U.S. Supreme Court.

Body of Opinion

Justice Blackmun

The bias in Johnson Controls' policy is obvious. Fertile men, but not fertile women, are given a choice as to whether they wish to risk their reproductive health for a particular job. [The] policy explicitly discriminates against women on the basis of their sex....

[But] an employer may discriminate on the basis of "religion, sex, or national origin in those certain instances where religion, sex, or national origin is a bona fide occupational qualification reasonably necessary to the normal operation of that particular business or enterprise." The BFOQ defense is written narrowly, and this Court has read it narrowly....

Johnson Controls argues that its fetal-protection policy falls within the so-called safety exception [of] the BFOQ. Our cases have stressed that discrimination on the basis of sex because of safety concerns is allowed only in narrow circumstances. In *Dothard v. Rawlinson* (1977),... we allowed the employer to hire only male guards in contact areas of maximum-security male penitentiaries only because more was at stake than the individual woman's decision to weigh and accept the risks of employment. We found sex to be a BFOQ inasmuch as the employment of a female guard would create real risks of safety to others if [rape-related] violence broke out because the guard was a woman. Sex discrimination was tolerated because sex was related to the guard's ability to do the job—maintaining prison security. We also required in *Dothard* a high correlation between sex and ability to perform job functions, and refused to allow employers to use sex as a proxy for strength although it might be a fairly accurate one.

Similarly, some courts have approved airlines' layoffs of pregnant flight attendants... on the ground that the employer's policy was necessary to ensure the safety of passengers. In two of these cases, the courts pointedly indicated that fetal, as opposed to passenger, safety was best left to the mother.

Our case law, therefore, makes clear that the safety exception is limited to instances in which sex or pregnancy actually interferes with the employee's ability to perform the job.... [Thus,] we have no difficulty concluding that Johnson Controls cannot establish a BFOQ. Fertile women, as far as appears in the record, manufacture batteries as efficiently as anyone else. Johnson Controls' professed moral and ethical concerns about the next generation do not suffice to establish a BFOQ of female sterility. Decisions about the welfare of future children must be left to the parents who conceive, bear, support, and raise them rather than to the employers who hire those parents.

Judgment and Result

Judgment in favor of Johnson Controls reversed; case returned to the lower courts for further proceedings consistent with the Supreme Court's opinion.

Questions

1. Why did the plaintiffs have an easy time proving a Title VII case here?
2. How did the Court distinguish its decision in *Dothard v. Rawlinson*?

Remedies for Title VII Violations

Courts can order a wide range of remedies once the government or a private plaintiff wins a Title VII suit. If intentional discrimination results in lost wages, a private plaintiff can obtain back pay accruing from a date two years prior to the filing of the charge. Successful private plaintiffs may also recover attorney's fees at the court's discretion. Victims of intentional discrimination who suffer harms such as emotional distress, sickness, loss of reputation, and denial of credit also can obtain compensatory damages. Victims of intentional discrimination also can recover punitive damages in cases where the defendant was malicious or recklessly indifferent to the victim's rights. However, the sum of the plaintiff's compensatory and punitive damages cannot exceed certain amounts stated in the statute. These amounts vary with the size of the employer.

Title VII also gives courts much discretion to formulate equitable remedies appropriate to the violation. For example, a court might order that a private plaintiff be hired, reinstated, or given retroactive seniority. In addition, courts sometimes impose various "affirmative action" orders: for example, injunctions compelling active steps to recruit minorities, including the ordering of quota-like preferences for minorities—and occasionally for women—in the employer's future hiring and promotion. For example, a court might order an employer with a long history of systematic discrimination to hire minorities at a certain rate until the minority percentage of the employer's work force equals the minority percentage in some relevant local population. In general, such remedies are permissible where they are needed to eliminate the effects of pervasive, persistent, and/or severe discrimination; they do not excessively or unnecessarily restrict the employment prospects of white people; and they do not require that unqualified people be hired or promoted. This is true even if the favored minority people were not themselves victims of illegal employment discrimination.

Quota-like remedial minority preferences favoring nonvictims also may appear in consent decrees that courts issue following the settlement of a Title VII suit. In fact, the Supreme Court has stated that the preferential relief agreed to in a consent decree sometimes can be broader than the relief a court could order on its own after a violation of Title VII.

As discussed in Chapter 5, however, the Supreme Court has decided that reverse racial discrimination by the federal government now gets the same full strict scrutiny as racial discrimination against minorities. In the future, this may create a new obstacle to remedial orders and consent decrees containing minority preferences.

Race and Color Discrimination

Thus far, we have been discussing certain basic rules that apply to any Title VII suit. Now we examine in greater detail Title VII's prohibited bases of discrimination—race and color, sex, national origin, and religion. Title VII's ban on race and color discrimination includes discrimination against blacks or African Americans, other racial minorities, Eskimos, and Native Americans. In such cases, plaintiffs can use the various methods of proving a Title VII violation.

Title VII also forbids racial discrimination against whites. Does this mean that voluntary employer preferences favoring racial minorities cannot stand under Title VII? These voluntary racial preferences differ from the racial preferences discussed previously. Here, the question is whether a *private employer* violates Title VII when it institutes such a preference. Earlier, the question was whether a court could order such a preference *as a remedy* after it was shown that an employer had violated Title VII by discriminating against racial minorities, or could approve a racially preferential consent decree following Title VII litigation. In a 1979 case, the Supreme Court said that voluntary employer preferences survive a Title VII attack if they (1) are intended to open opportunities for minorities by admitting them to job categories in which they have been underrepresented, (2) do not unnecessarily trammel upon the interests of white employees, (3) are not an absolute bar to the advancement of white employees, and (4) are only temporary.

Sex Discrimination

Although Title VII's ban on sex discrimination protects men as well as women, most Title VII sex discrimination cases involve female claimants. Because this provision was added to Title VII in a late amendment, little legislative history assists courts in its interpretation. Clearly, however, Title VII's prohibition of sex discrimination applies only to gender-based discrimination. Thus, Title VII does not forbid discrimination on the bases of sexual orientation or transsexuality (although some states forbid the former). Finally, Title VII's various methods of proof are available to plaintiffs in sex discrimination cases.

Title VII's ban on sex discrimination involves a number of more or less distinct topics. They include:

Sexual Stereotyping. Sexual stereotyping is employer behavior that discriminates against women by either (1) assuming that women can behave only in a stereotypically "female" fashion, or (2) requiring that they behave in such a fashion. For example, an employer might violate Title VII if it denies a female employee a job opportunity because it assumes that she is unaggressive, or instead penalizes her for acting aggressively.

Preferences Favoring Women. In 1987, the Supreme Court held that a voluntary county wide affirmative action plan covering public employees did not violate Title VII even though the plan favored female employees over male employees in promotion decisions. In doing so, it applied the tests for voluntary racial preferences described earlier. Of course, the Court reformulated those tests to reflect gender rather than race.

Pregnancy Discrimination. The Pregnancy Discrimination Act, which became effective in 1978, amended Title VII to make discrimination based on pregnancy, childbirth, or related medical conditions illegal. Thus, women are protected from such practices as being fired or refused a job merely because of pregnancy, childbirth, or related conditions. The act also says that pregnancy and related conditions must be treated like other ailments similarly affecting an employee's ability to work. For example, an employer's sick leave, disability insurance, and health insurance policies must treat pregnancy like other ailments similarly affecting the ability to work.

Sexual Harassment. Since the 1970s, two general theories of Title VII recovery for sexual harassment have emerged.5 Both cover many kinds of unwelcome sex-related behavior, including sexual advances, requests for sexual favors, and other verbal or physical conduct of a sexual nature.

The first sexual harassment theory is called **quid pro quo sexual harassment**. As its name suggests, this form of sexual harassment involves some kind of linkage, connection, or trade between the employee's submission to sex-related behavior and tangible job consequences. This linkage can be either express or implied. Thus, a male supervisor who fires a female subordinate because she refused to have sexual

[5] Similar principles apply to race, color, religion, or national origin harassment.

relations with him (or refused to submit to other kinds of sex-related conduct) violates Title VII. This would be true regardless of whether he expressly told the subordinate that she would be fired for refusing to submit. The same result would occur where submission is expressly or implicitly linked to other tangible job consequences such as promotions, raises, and performance evaluations. Many courts, however, require that the plaintiff show some tangible job detriment, usually one with financial consequences, in order to recover for quid pro quo sexual harassment. Thus, this form of liability is unlikely where an employee rejects a supervisor's advances and "nothing happens."

However, neither a quid pro quo nor a tangible job consequence is necessary when an employee sues for **work environment sexual harassment**. This is sexually related behavior that is so severe or pervasive that it creates an intimidating, hostile, or offensive working environment. Work environment sexual harassment may be individual or group behavior. For example, a supervisor might deluge a female subordinate with sexual propositions, touchings, and so forth; or co-workers might subject a female employee to a barrage of sex-related touchings, inquiries, jokes, comments, and general abuse. Liability for work environment sexual harassment may arise even if the employee is treated fairly regarding compensation, promotion, fringe benefits, and so forth. Because such behavior must be unwelcome, however, a female employee may not recover if she instigated the alleged harassment or willingly participated in it. More importantly, the harassment must be severe or pervasive for liability to exist.

Although most sexual harassment cases involve male perpetrators, men clearly can sue for sexual harassment by women. The courts are split on the question whether Title VII allows sexual favoritism suits. In these cases, an employee sues his or her employer because another employee has obtained an unfair employment advantage by submitting to sexual harassment or freely giving sexual favors. In the following *Oncale* case, the Supreme Court held that Title VII applies to same-sex sexual harassment.

Oncale v. Sundowner Offshore Services, Inc.

U.S. Supreme Court
523 U.S. 75 (1998)

Background and Facts:

Joseph Oncale was employed by Sundowner Offshore Services on a Chevron oil platform in the Gulf of Mexico. He worked as a roustabout on an eight-man crew. On several occasions, Oncale was forcibly subjected to sex-related, humiliating conduct by certain crew members in the presence of the rest of the crew. Also, two of the crew members physically assaulted Oncale in a sexual manner, and one threatened him with rape. Oncale's complaints to supervisory personnel produced no remedial action. Oncale eventually quit his job with Sundowner, asking that his pink slip reflect that he "voluntarily left due to sexual harassment and verbal abuse." When later asked why he left Sundowner, Oncale stated "I felt that if I didn't leave my job, that I would be raped or forced to have sex."

Oncale then sued Sundowner in federal district court, alleging sex discrimination in employment. The district court held that, as a male, Oncale had no cause of action under Title VII for harassment by male co-workers. On appeal, the Fifth Circuit Court of Appeals affirmed. Oncale then appealed to the U.S. Supreme Court.

Body of Opinion

Justice Scalia

This case presents the question whether workplace harassment can violate Title VII's prohibition against "discrimination . . . because of . . . sex," when the harasser and the harassed employee are of the same sex. . . . Title VII of the Civil Rights Act of 1964 provides, in relevant part, that "it shall be an unlawful employment practice for an employer . . . to discriminate against any individual with respect to his compensation, terms, conditions, or privileges of employment, because of such individual's race, color, religion, sex, or national origin." We have held that this not only covers "terms" and "conditions" in the narrow contractual sense, but "evinces a congressional intent to strike at the entire spectrum of disparate treatment of men and women in employment." "When the workplace is permeated with discriminatory intimidation, ridicule, and insult that is sufficiently severe or pervasive to alter the conditions of the victim's employment and create an abusive working environment, Title VII is violated." Title VII's prohibition of discrimination "because of... sex" protects men as well as women.... In *Johnson v. Transportation Agency, Santa Clara County* (1987), a male employee claimed that his employer discriminated against him because of his sex when it preferred a female employee for promotion. Although we ultimately rejected the claim on other grounds, we did not consider it significant that the supervisor who made that decision was also a man. If our precedents leave any doubt on the question, we hold today that nothing in Title VII necessarily bars a claim of discrimination "because of... sex" merely because the plaintiff and the defendant (or the person charged with acting on behalf of the defendant) are of the same sex.

Courts have had little trouble with that principle in cases like *Johnson*, where an employee claims to have been passed over for a job or promotion. But when the issue arises in the context of a hostile environment sexual harassment claim, the state and federal courts have taken a bewildering variety of stances. Some, like the Fifth Circuit in this case, have held that same-sex sexual harassment claims are never cognizable under Title VII. Other decisions say that such claims are actionable only if the plaintiff can prove that the harasser is homosexual (and thus presumably motivated by sexual desire). Still others suggest that workplace harassment that is sexual in content is always actionable, regardless of the harasser's sex, sexual orientation, or motivations. We see no justification in the statutory language or our precedents for a categorical rule excluding same-sex harassment claims from the coverage of Title VII. As some courts have observed, male-on-male sexual harassment in the workplace was assuredly not the principal evil Congress was concerned with when it enacted Title VII. But statutory prohibitions often go beyond the principal evil to cover reasonably comparable evils, and it is ultimately the provisions of our laws rather than the principal concerns of our legislators by which we are governed....

[The defendant claims] that recognizing liability for same-sex harassment will transform Title VII into a general civility code for the American workplace. But that risk is no greater for same-sex than for opposite-sex harassment, and is adequately met by careful attention to the requirements of the statute. Title VII does not prohibit all verbal or physical harassment in the workplace; it is directed only at "discrimination... because of... sex." We have never held that workplace harassment, even harassment between men and women, is automatically discrimination because of sex merely because the words used have sexual content or connotations. The critical issue, Title VII's text indicates, is whether members of one sex are exposed to disadvantageous terms or conditions of employment to which members of the other sex are not exposed. Courts and juries have found the inference of discrimination easy to draw in most male-female sexual harassment situations, because the challenged conduct typically involves explicit or implicit proposals of sexual activity; it is reasonable to assume those proposals would not have been made to someone of the same sex. The same chain of inference would be available to a plaintiff alleging same-sex harassment, if there were credible evidence that the harasser was homosexual. But harassing conduct need not be motivated by sexual desire to support an inference of discrimination on the basis of sex. A trier of fact might reasonably find such discrimination, for example, if a female victim is harassed in such sex-specific and derogatory terms by another woman as to make it clear that the harasser is motivated by general hostility to the presence of women in the workplace. A same-sex harassment plaintiff may also, of course, offer direct comparative evidence about how the alleged harasser treated members of both sexes in a mixed-sex workplace....

There is another requirement that prevents Title VII from expanding into a general civility code: the statute does not reach genuine but innocuous differences in the ways men and women routinely interact with members of the same sex and of the opposite sex. The prohibition of harassment on the basis of sex requires neither asexuality nor androgyny in the workplace; it forbids only behavior so objectively offensive as to alter the conditions of the victim's employment. Conduct that is not severe or pervasive enough to create an objectively hostile or abusive work environment—an environment that a reasonable person would find hostile or abusive—is beyond Title VII's purview. We have always regarded that requirement as crucial, and as sufficient to ensure that courts and juries do not mistake ordinary socializing in the workplace—such as male-on-male horseplay or intersexual flirtation—for discriminatory conditions of employment.

We have emphasized, moreover, that the objective severity of harassment should be judged from the perspective of a reasonable person in the plaintiff's position, considering all the circumstances. In same-sex (as in all) harassment cases, that inquiry requires careful consideration of the social context in which particular behavior occurs and is experienced by its target. A professional football player's working environment is not severely or pervasively abusive, for example, if the coach smacks him on the buttocks as he heads onto the field—even if the same behavior would reasonably be experienced as abusive by the coach's secretary (male or female) back at the office. The real social impact of workplace behavior often depends on a constellation of surrounding circumstances, expectations, and relationships which are not fully captured by a simple recitation of the words used or the physical acts performed. Common sense, and an appropriate sensitivity to social context, will enable courts and juries to distinguish between simple teasing or roughhousing among members of the same sex, and conduct which a reasonable person in the plaintiff's position would find severely hostile or abusive.

Judgment and Result

The Supreme Court concluded that same-sex sexual harassment is actionable under Title VII. Therefore, it reversed the Fifth Circuit, and remanded the case for proceedings consistent with its opinion.

Questions

1. Under the Supreme Court's opinion, is Title VII's ban on same-sex sexual harassment limited to homosexual harassment, or does it extend further?
2. Why is same-sex sexual harassment even considered sex discrimination at all? What does it have to do with gender?

National Origin Discrimination

Title VII's ban on national origin discrimination includes discrimination based on: (1) a person's country of origin; (2) a person's ancestors' country of origin; or (3) a person's possession of physical, cultural, or linguistic characteristics shared by people of a certain national origin. For example, an employee has a Title VII case if he suffers discrimination because he was born in Germany. He would also have a Title VII case if he suffers discrimination because his parents were born there. Where discrimination is based on the employee's possession of physical, cultural, or linguistic traits, moreover, neither the employee nor his ancestors need have been born in a particular country for a Title VII claim to exist. Thus, a person of pure Brazilian ancestry might recover if she suffers discrimination because she looks like, behaves like, or speaks like a German.

The various Title VII proof rules apply in national origin discrimination cases. In addition, the EEOC has promulgated various guidelines on national origin discrimination. An employer's citizenship requirement, for example, violates Title VII if it has the purpose or effect of discriminating against an individual on the basis of national origin. Thus, if a northwest Montana logging company imposes a U.S. citizenship requirement for hiring lumberjacks, this could be a Title VII violation against Canadian lumberjacks.

Because formally neutral employer selection procedures such as tests, educational requirements, and interviews can disproportionately affect certain national origin groups, these procedures may violate Title VII. The EEOC's detailed guidelines on employee selection procedures set the standards such selection criteria must meet. However, a special rule applies to employer height and weight requirements. Because such requirements tend to exclude individuals on the basis of national origin, an employer must evaluate them for adverse impact, even if the employer's total selection process has no adverse impact on national origin groups. The EEOC also has stated that it will carefully evaluate national origin discrimination charges involving requirements that employees be fluent in English.

Finally, because job safety and efficiency often require that employees be competent in English and communicate in that language, the EEOC does not flatly ban speak-English-only rules in the workplace. Where such a rule is applied at all times in the workplace, the Commission presumes that it violates Title VII and closely scrutinizes it. Where such a rule is applied only at certain times, it is permissible if the employer can justify it by business necessity.

Discrimination Based on Religion

Title VII prohibits most employment discrimination based on a person's religion. As you saw earlier in the chapter, however, religious educational institutions usually are immune from Title VII when they discriminate on the basis of religion. Occasionally, religion also may be a BFOQ. The usual methods for proving a Title VII case apply in the religious discrimination context.

Title VII's definition of religious discrimination is broad. Although not all courts might agree, the EEOC says that the term *religion* includes almost all moral beliefs that are sincerely held with the strength of traditional religious views. Indeed, Title VII forbids employment discrimination against atheists because of their atheism. Besides forbidding discrimination based on religion as such, Title VII also prohibits discrimination based on religious observances or practices. Examples include grooming, apparel, and the refusal to work on the Sabbath. Some observances or practices, however, may interfere with an employer's business operations. Thus, discrimination based on such practices is justified if the employer demonstrates that it cannot reasonably accommodate the religious practice without undue hardship. An accommodation creates undue hardship if it imposes more than a minimal burden on an employer.

SECTION 1981

The Civil Rights Act of 1866 was a post–Civil War statute designed to protect the civil rights of the newly freed slaves. A portion of the act called "Section 1981" has frequently been used to attack employment discrimination. Section 1981 mainly covers racial discrimination, but it also applies to discrimination against people of racially defined national origin such as Germans or Mexicans, and ethnic groups such as gypsies and Jews.

Section 1981 obviously protects fewer groups than does Title VII. Due to a 1991 amendment, however, it now covers almost all the ways in which an employer might discriminate against the groups it does protect. Where it applies, moreover, section 1981 has proven useful to plaintiffs. Title VII's methods of proving discrimination generally apply in section 1981 suits. More importantly, plaintiffs in section 1981 suits need not comply with Title VII's complex procedural requirements and may have more time in which to sue. In addition, Title VII's limits on compensatory and punitive damages do not apply in section 1981 cases. For these reasons, section 1981 has proven a useful supplement or alternative to Title VII, and plaintiffs sometimes include a section 1981 count alongside a Title VII claim.

EXECUTIVE ORDER 11246

Originally issued in 1965, Executive Order 11246 forbids race, color, national origin, religion, and sex discrimination by certain federal contractors. The order is enforced and administered by the Office of Federal Contract Compliance Programs (OFCCP) of the Department of Labor, which has issued regulations to implement it. On occasion, Executive Order 11246 has been the basis for affirmative action plans preferring racial minorities.

AGE DISCRIMINATION IN EMPLOYMENT ACT

The aim of the Age Discrimination in Employment Act of 1967 (ADEA) is to prohibit arbitrary age discrimination against employees and to ensure that employees are evaluated on the basis of ability rather than age. The act protects those who are at least 40 years of age, with no upper age limit. As the following *O'Connor* case makes clear, someone within that 40-and-over age group can recover for age discrimination regardless of whether the favored employee was inside or outside the group. In addition, a person age 40 or over probably can recover for age discrimination that favors either a younger or an older individual. Finally, those who are less than 40 years old receive no protection against age discrimination under the ADEA.

Like Title VII, the ADEA prohibits employer discrimination regarding almost all terms, conditions, and benefits of employment. The ADEA also resembles Title VII in forbidding employer retaliation against those who object to illegal age discrimination, file charges, or otherwise assist or participate in proceedings under the act.

Entities Covered

The ADEA covers employer discrimination by individuals, partnerships, employment agencies (regarding their own employees), labor organizations (regarding their own employees), and corporations that (1) are engaged in an industry affecting interstate commerce, and (2) employ 20 or more persons. The act no longer applies to state and local governments. In addition, it covers referral activities by employment agencies of any size if they make referrals to a covered employer. Finally, the ADEA applies to labor unions in their role as employee representative.[6]

Procedures

Like Title VII, the ADEA sets up a complex procedural path that private parties with age discrimination claims must follow. These procedural requirements, whose details are beyond the scope of this text, resemble Title VII's requirements but differ in a few particulars. The EEOC also can sue to enforce the act, and an EEOC suit blocks private suits involving the same alleged violation. For all ADEA actions, suit must be filed within two years of an alleged nonwillful violation, and within three years of an alleged willful violation.

Proving an ADEA Violation

The methods of proving an ADEA violation resemble the Title VII methods discussed earlier. Proving age discrimination is easy where the defendant has an express policy treating people differently because of their age. Other direct evidence of age bias such as testimony or documents obviously can be useful to plaintiffs as well. The ADEA also permits disparate treatment suits that resemble Title VII disparate treatment suits. Finally, some courts have used Title VII's disparate impact theory in ADEA suits.

ADEA Defenses

Even if the plaintiff manages to prove unlawful age discrimination, the defendant triumphs if it can establish one of the ADEA's defenses. The act has a seniority defense that resembles the corresponding defense under Title VII. The ADEA also allows the employer to use age criteria in bona fide employee benefit plans such as retirement, pension, and insurance plans. In addition, the ADEA allows an employer to discharge or otherwise penalize an employee for good cause. It also allows employers to use

[6] Here, the labor union usually must have 25 or more members.

reasonable factors other than age in their employment decisions. Finally, the ADEA has a bona fide occupational qualification (BFOQ) defense that applies when age is reasonably necessary to effective job performance. Possible examples include age limits on school bus drivers, airplane and helicopter pilots, police, and firefighters.[7]

ADEA Remedies

A successful ADEA plaintiff can recover unpaid back wages resulting from the discrimination. If the discrimination was willful, the plaintiff obtains an additional equal amount as liquidated damages. Generally, courts do not permit punitive damage recoveries, or recoveries for consequential damages such as pain, suffering, and emotional distress. Equitable remedies are also possible under the ADEA; they include court orders requiring hiring, reinstatement, and promotion.

O'Connor v. Consolidated Coin Caterers Corp.

U.S. Supreme Court
517 U.S. 308 (1996)

Background and Facts:

At the age of 56, James O'Connor was fired from his job with the Consolidated Coin Caterers Corporation. O'Connor's replacement was 40 years old. Alleging that he was fired because of his age, O'Connor sued Consolidated under the ADEA. After the federal district court granted Consolidated's motion for summary judgment and O'Connor appealed, the court of appeals affirmed. It did so because O'Connor's replacement was inside, rather than outside, the ADEA's protected 40-and-over age group. O'Connor appealed to the U.S. Supreme Court.

Body of Opinion

Justice Scalia

[T]here must be at least a logical connection between each element of the [plaintiff's] prima facie case and the illegal discrimination for which it establishes a legally mandatory, rebuttable presumption. The element of replacement by someone under 40 fails this requirement. The discrimination prohibited by the ADEA is discrimination because of an individual's age, though the prohibition is limited to individuals who are at least 40 years of age. This language does not ban discrimination against employees because they are aged 40 or older; it bans discrimination against employees because of their age, but limits the protected class to those who are 40 or older. The fact that one person in the protected class has lost out to another person in the protected class is thus irrelevant, so long as he has lost out *because of his age*. Or to put the point more concretely, there can be no greater inference of *age* discrimination... when a 40-year-old is replaced by a 39-year-old than when a 56-year-old is replaced by a 40-year-old. Because it lacks probative value, the fact that an ADEA plaintiff was replaced by someone outside the protected class is not a proper element of the... prima facie case.

Judgment and Result

Court of appeals decision in Consolidated's favor reversed; O'Connor's age discrimination case allowed to proceed.

Questions

1. Does the Supreme Court's decision mean that O'Connor wins his suit against Consolidated?
2. Although the Court's opinion does not consider the point, do you think that O'Connor should win in a case where his replacement is 65?

AMERICANS WITH DISABILITIES ACT

For a long time, the major federal law dealing with employment discrimination against handicapped people was the Vocational Rehabilitation Act of 1973, which mainly

[7] Also, a 1996 amendment to the ADEA says that employers do not violate the act when they discharge or refuse to hire certain firefighters and law enforcement officers.

applies to federal contractors and to programs receiving federal financial assistance. But this pattern of limited federal protection changed dramatically in 1990, when Congress enacted Title I of the Americans with Disabilities Act (ADA). Title I's procedures and remedies are the same as those for Title VII and it is enforced by the EEOC.

Entities Covered

Title I of the ADA covers employers that are engaged in an industry affecting interstate commerce and that have 15 or more employees. The ADA's employers are basically the same as for Title VII; they include individuals, partnerships, corporations, colleges and universities, labor unions (with respect to their own employees), employment agencies (with respect to their own employees), and state and local governments. Not covered, however, are the U.S. government and corporations it wholly owns, Native American tribes, and certain tax-exempt private clubs. Like Title VII, the ADA also covers discrimination by unions against their members, and by employment agencies against their clients.

Prohibited Discrimination

Under Title I, the covered entities just described may not discriminate against qualified individuals with a disability because of that disability. The act forbids such discrimination in a wide range of employment contexts, including hiring, firing, pay, promotions, job training, and many others. It also has an antiretaliation provision that resembles Title VII's antiretaliation provision.

The ADA's protected disabilities are (1) physical or mental impairments that substantially limit one or more of a person's major life activities, (2) any record of such an impairment, and (3) a person's being regarded as having such an impairment. The last two categories include people who have earlier been misdiagnosed as having some impairment, have recovered from an earlier impairment, or are regarded by others as having an impairment even though they might not. However, those who suffer discrimination due to their current use of illegal drugs are not considered "qualified individuals with a disability." Also, homosexuality, bisexuality, transvestism, transsexualism, pedophilia, exhibitionism, voyeurism, compulsive gambling, kleptomania, pyromania, and certain other conditions or disorders are not disabilities. Furthermore, entities covered by the act may prohibit workplace drug or alcohol use, may require that employees not be under the influence of drugs or alcohol at the workplace, and may hold drug users or alcoholics to the same standards as other employees. As the following *Sutton* case makes clear, finally, the ADA does not protect people whose medical conditions or other "disabilities" are correctable.

To be a *qualified* individual with a disability, a disabled job applicant or employee must be able to perform the essential functions of the job he or she desires or holds, either *with or without reasonable accommodation*. Thus, the ADA forbids handicap discrimination against impaired people who can perform the essential functions of the relevant job without any extra assistance from their employers. But it also requires that employers make reasonable accommodation to those who could perform the job's essential functions with such accommodation.

What is a reasonable accommodation? The ADA's definition of the term includes acts such as making facilities accessible and usable by people with disabilities; job restructuring; part-time or modified work schedules; reassignments; adjustments to equipment, examinations, and training materials; and others. But as the *Nesser* case later in the chapter states, even if a reasonable accommodation is available, the employer need not provide it if it would impose an *undue hardship*. Undue hardship is defined as an act requiring significant difficulty or expense. Among the factors for determining whether an accommodation involves such difficulty or expense are its cost, the covered entity's financial resources, and the accommodation's effect on its business operations.

Figure 16.2 recapitulates these points.

ADA Defenses

Certain factors already mentioned—for example, undue hardship, the plaintiff's use of illegal drugs, and others—effectively operate as defenses to an ADA suit. In addition, the act lists certain specific defenses. For example, it says that covered entities may use standards, tests, or selection criteria that disadvantage people with protected disabilities, if those standards, tests, or criteria are job-related and consistent with business necessity, and if no reasonable accommodation is possible. The ADA also lets employers require that an employee not pose a direct threat to the health and safety of other employees.

FIGURE 16.2 Finding Your Way Through the ADA

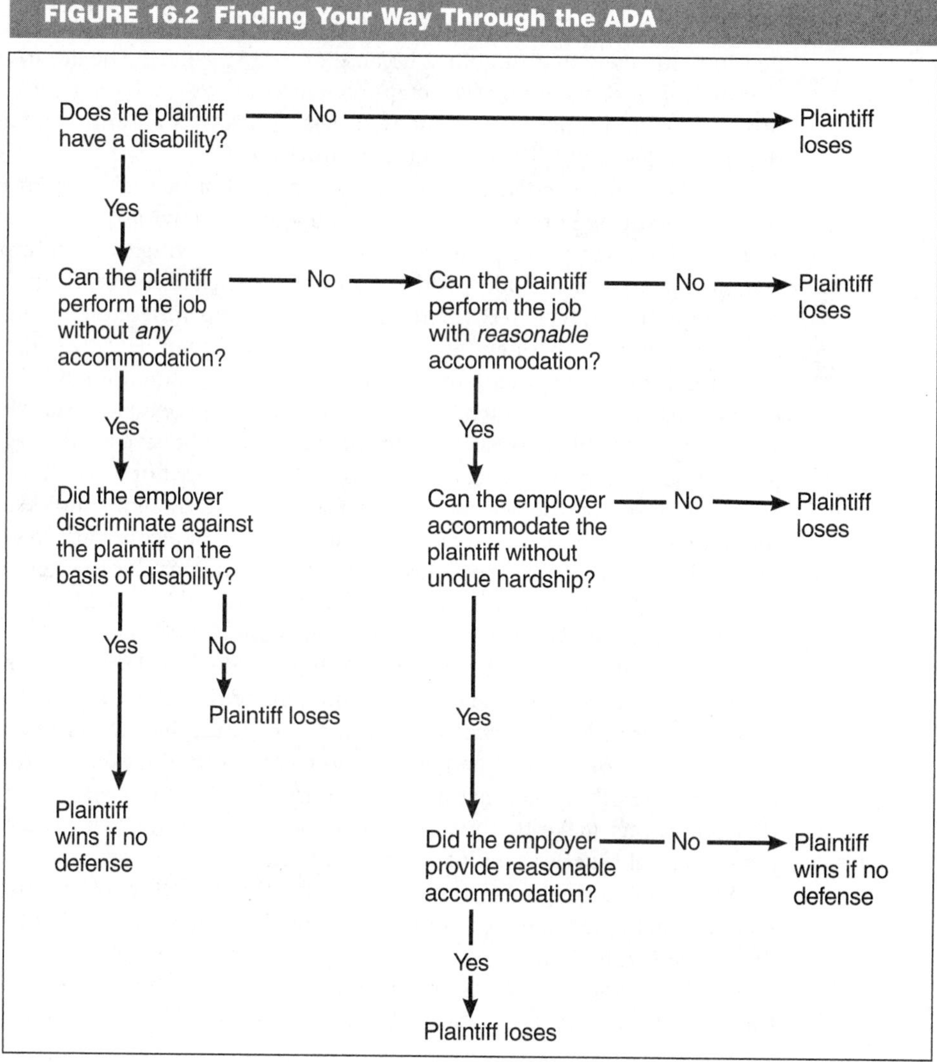

Sutton v. United Airlines

U.S. Supreme Court
119 S. Ct. 2139 (1999)

Background and Facts:

Karen Sutton and Kimberly Hinton, who are twin sisters, both have severe myopia. Each woman's uncorrected vision is 20/200 or worse in her right eye and 20/400 or worse in her left eye. But with the use of corrective lenses both women have vision that is 20/20 or better. Without corrective lenses, on the other hand, Karen and Kimberly effectively cannot see to conduct numerous activities such as driving a vehicle, watching television, or shopping in public stores. But with corrective measures both function identically to individuals without a similar impairment.

In 1992, Karen and Kimberly applied to United Airlines for employment as commercial airline pilots. After submitting their applications, both women were invited to an interview and to flight simulator tests. Both were told during their interviews, however, that a mistake had been made in inviting them to interview because they did not meet United's minimum vision requirement, which was uncorrected visual acuity of 20/100 or better. Due to their failure to meet this requirement, neither Karen nor Kimberly was offered a pilot position.

The two women then sued United in federal district court, alleging disability discrimination under the ADEA. The district court dismissed their complaint for failure to state a claim upon which relief could be granted. After the court of appeals affirmed, the two women appealed to the U.S. Supreme Court.

Body of Opinion

Justice O'Connor

The ADA prohibits discrimination by covered entities, including private employers, against qualified individuals with a disability. . . . A qualified individual with a disability is identified as "an individual with a disability who, with or without reasonable accommodation, can perform the essential functions of the employment position that such individual holds or desires." In turn, a "disability" is defined as: (A) a physical or mental impairment that substantially limits one or more of the major life activities of such individual; (B) a record of such an impairment; or (C) being regarded as having such an impairment. . . .

We turn to the question whether petitioners have stated a claim under subsection (A) of the disability definition, that is, whether they have alleged that they possess a physical impairment that substantially limits them in one or more major life activities. Because with corrective measures [the women's] vision is 20/20 or better, they are not actually disabled within the meaning of the act if the disability determination is made with reference to these measures. Consequently, with respect to subsection (A) of the disability definition, our decision turns on whether disability is to be determined with or without reference to corrective measures. . . .

We conclude that the approach that persons are to be evaluated in their hypothetical uncorrected state is an impermissible interpretation of the ADA. Looking at the Act as a whole, it is apparent that if a person is taking measures to correct for, or mitigate, a physical or mental impairment, the effects of those measures—both positive and negative—must be taken into account when judging whether that person is "substantially limited" in a major life activity and thus "disabled" under the act. . . . Three separate provisions of the ADA, read in concert, lead us to this conclusion. The act defines a disability as "a physical or mental impairment that substantially limits one or more of the major life activities of an individual." Because the phrase "substantially limits" appears in the Act in the present indicative verb form, we think the language is properly read as requiring that a person be presently—not potentially or hypothetically—substantially limited in order to demonstrate a disability. A disability exists only where an impairment "substantially limits" a major life activity, not where it "might," "could," or "would" be substantially limiting if mitigating measures were not taken. A person whose physical or mental impairment is corrected by medication or other measures does not have an impairment that presently "substantially limits" a major life activity. To be sure, a person whose physical or mental impairment is corrected by mitigating measures still has an impairment, but if the impairment is corrected it does not "substantially limit" a major life activity.

The definition of disability also requires that disabilities be evaluated "with respect to an individual" and be determined based on whether an impairment substantially limits the "major life activities of such individual." Thus, whether a person has a disability under the ADA is an individualized inquiry. . . . The [other] approach would often require courts and employers to speculate about a person's condition and would, in many cases, force them to make a disability determination based on general information about how an uncorrected impairment usually affects individuals, rather than on the individual's actual condition. For instance, under this view, courts would almost certainly find all diabetics to be disabled, because if they failed to monitor their blood sugar levels and administer insulin, they would almost certainly be substantially limited in one or more major life activities. A diabetic whose illness does not impair his or her daily activities would therefore be considered disabled simply because he or she has diabetes. Thus, the guidelines approach would create a system in which persons often must be treated as members of a group of people with similar impairments, rather than as individuals....

Finally, and critically, findings enacted as part of the ADA require the conclusion that Congress did not intend to bring under the statute's protection all those whose uncorrected conditions amount to disabilities. Congress found that "some 43,000,000 Americans have one or more physical or mental disabilities, and this number is increasing as the population as a whole is growing older."... The 43 million figure reflects an understanding that those whose impairments are largely corrected by medication or other devices are not "disabled" within the meaning of the ADA....By contrast, nonfunctional approaches to defining disability produce significantly larger numbers. The 1986 National Council on Disability report estimated that there were over 160 million disabled under the "health conditions approach." Indeed, the number of people with vision impairments alone is 100 million. And there were approximately 50 million people with high blood pressure.... Had Congress intended to include all persons with corrected physical limitations among those covered by the Act, it undoubtedly would have cited a much higher number of disabled persons in the findings. That it did not is evidence that the ADA's coverage is restricted to only those whose impairments are not mitigated by corrective measures.... Applying this reading of the Act to the case at hand, we conclude that the court of appeals correctly resolved the issue of disability in United's favor....Because we decide that disability under the Act is to be determined with reference to corrective measures, we agree with the courts below that petitioners have not stated a claim that they are substantially limited in any major life activity.

Judgment and Result

Court of appeals decision affirmed; Sutton and Hinton lose.

Questions

1. Suppose that United's 20/100 vision requirement was completely irrational as applied to the plaintiffs in this case. If that were the case, could they recover under the ADA?
2. What do you think really motivated the Court's decision in this case?

Nesser v. Trans World Airlines

U.S. Court of Appeals, 8th Circuit
160 F.3d 442 (1998)

Background and Facts:

Charles Nesser began working for TWA on March 29, 1993 as a Reservation Sales Agent in the Frequent Flyer Department. On April 4, 1994, Nesser transferred to a position as a Rate Desk Agent in the Sales Department. Nesser's duties as a Reservation Sales Agent and a Rate Desk Agent included extensive computer work and some telephone work. In December 1995, Nesser was awarded a position as a Customer Services Agent in the Air Cargo Department. Nesser's duties in the Air Cargo Department included assisting passengers and other customers with air transportation of packages and other cargo. Nesser remained in this position until TWA terminated his employment on January 9, 1996 for excessive absenteeism.

Nesser suffers from Crohn's Disease, which is an inflammatory bowel disorder that produces a thickening of the intestinal wall, a narrowing of the bowel channel, and a variety of symptoms including abdominal pain, fever, diarrhea, flatulence, fatigue, extreme pain, and dehydration. TWA granted Nesser numerous medical leaves of absence for treatment and recovery, but to no avail. Nesser was absent from work six days in 1993, 43 or 44 days in 1994, and 175 days in 1995. Nesser did not work in 1996 prior to his termination on January 9, 1996, and never reported to work for his new position in the Air Cargo Department. Throughout this period, TWA regularly notified Nessen that his lack of regular attendance at work was unacceptable.

After some preliminary notices to Nesser, TWA held a discharge hearing on January 4, 1996. At the hearing, Nesser requested that he be allowed to return to his former position as a Reservation Sales Agent and to work from home. However, Nesser presented no evidence that a position was available in that department. TWA denied Nesser's request and he was terminated on January 9, 1996 for excessive absenteeism. Nesser then sued TWA under the ADA, alleging that his employment was terminated on the basis of his disability and that he was not provided with reasonable accommodations. The federal district court granted TWA's motion for summary judgment, and Nesser appealed.

Body of Opinion

Circuit Judge Kelly

It is clear that Nesser, who suffers from Crohn's disease, is disabled within the meaning of the ADA, and that he suffered an adverse employment action because of his disability. Nesser failed to establish, however, that he was qualified to perform the essential functions of his job with or without accommodation. Nesser did not establish that he could perform the essential functions of his job without accommodation because he was unable to attend work on a regular basis. We have recognized that attendance at work is a necessary job function. An employee who is unable to come to work on a regular basis is unable to satisfy any of the functions of the job in question, much less the essential ones. Other circuits have also held that regular and reliable attendance is a necessary element of most jobs. TWA considered attendance to be an essential function of each of Nesser's positions with TWA.... An employer's identification of a position's essential functions is given some deference under the ADA. Nesser was absent from work 43 or 44 days in 1994, and 175 days in 1995. Because of Nesser's frequent absences, he was unable to meet the essential functions of his position without accommodation.

Because Nesser's disability prevents him from fulfilling an essential function of his job, the ADA requires TWA to reasonably accommodate his disability, unless the accommodation would impose an undue hardship on TWA. Nesser was required to make a facial showing that reasonable accommodation was possible, and then the burden would have shifted to TWA to show that it was unable to accommodate him. Nesser failed to make a facial showing that reasonable accommodation was possible. Nesser had voluntarily transferred to a new position as a Customer Service Agent just prior to his termination. This position involved face-to-face contacts between Nesser and customers, and could not be performed from Nesser's home. Because his Customer Service Agent position required him to be present at TWA, he suggested that TWA transfer him back to his former position as a Reservation Sales Agent and allow him to work from home. The ADA states that reassignment may be a reasonable accommodation if a vacant position is available. Because Nesser did not present any evidence that a vacant position was available in the Reservation Sales Department, he did not establish that a reasonable accommodation was available. Therefore, we need not consider whether denying an employee's request to work at home can ever be a violation of the ADA's reasonable accommodation requirement.

Judgment and Result

The court of appeals affirmed the district court's summary judgment in favor of TWA. Nesser loses.

Questions

1. Trace the path of Nesser's arguments and TWA's counterarguments in Figure 16.2. At what point did Nesser's claim fail?
2. Suppose that Nesser had established that a vacant position was available in the Reservation Sales Department. What would have happened then?

STATE EMPLOYMENT DISCRIMINATION LAWS

A great many states have laws resembling Title VII and the ADEA, and many have statutes protecting the handicapped. Some of these measures impose tougher standards on employers than their federal counterparts. Also, some states go beyond federal law regarding the types of discrimination they forbid. Some, for example, prohibit unfavorable employment decisions based on a person's marital status, physical appearance, sexual orientation, political affiliation, off-the-job smoking, and AIDS infection.

In addition, some states and localities have enacted "pay equity" laws that could be regarded as **comparable worth** provisions. Most such laws apply only to public employment. Often they say that the relevant government unit(s) should not discriminate in pay between female-dominated jobs and male-dominated jobs, if those jobs have comparable overall worth to the employer. The worth of different jobs frequently is determined by giving the jobs point ratings under variables resembling the Equal Pay Act's equal work components (skill, responsibility, effort, and working conditions), totalling the point ratings, and comparing those totals. Once, indications were that Title VII would become a vehicle for comparable worth claims, but that possibility has receded over the years.

CHAPTER SUMMARY

This chapter examines the major federal laws forbidding employment discrimination. It opens by discussing the Equal Pay Act, which forbids sex discrimination regarding pay. America's most important employment discrimination provision is Title VII of the 1964 Civil Rights Act. Title VII forbids all sorts of employment discrimination on the bases of race, color, religion, sex, and national origin. Executive Order 11246 forbids certain federal contractors from discriminating on the same bases. A post-Civil War antidiscrimination statute called section 1981 also has been enlisted in the fight against employment discrimination. Section 1981 covers some kinds of racial, ethnic, and racial/national origin discrimination.

The Age Discrimination in Employment Act forbids age discrimination against those age 40 and up.

Finally, the Americans with Disabilities Act forbids employment discrimination against qualified individuals with disabilities.

The states frequently forbid these and other forms of employment discrimination as well.

Discussion Questions

1. Opponents of the 1991 amendments to Title VII charged that planned changes to the disparate impact method of proof would make Title VII a "quota bill." What they meant was that the changes would force employers to hire the "right numbers" of African Americans and other racial minorities to head off possible Title VII liability. Although this criticism may not apply to the legislation that actually emerged, how could the disparate impact method lead employers to "hire by the numbers"? *Hint:* check out the second part of the disparate impact test and consider what might happen if it imposed a genuinely tough burden of proof on employers. On the other hand, what is likely to happen if the second portion of the disparate impact test is easy on employers?

   Finally, assuming solely for the sake of argument that the 1991 amendments force employers to prefer minorities in hiring and elsewhere, what would happen if they are sued by white people who suffer racial discrimination because employers have felt compelled to favor minorities?
2. What are the arguments for and against the quota-like minority preferences (or reverse discrimination) discussed in this chapter? First, consider some of the common criticisms of such practices. Are they consistent with the idea that individuals should be treated solely on the basis of their ability to perform the job in question? Are such practices fair to white employees or job applicants? What other objections to these preferences can you think of?

   Also consider what might be said in favor of such practices. Do minorities deserve reparations for the generations of discrimination they have suffered? (Here, note that some beneficiaries of minority preferences may not themselves be victims of discrimination.) Would a system in which all employment decisions are made on a perfectly neutral color-blind basis really treat minorities fairly and equally? In answering this question, consider America's long history of prior discrimination against racial minorities, and the effect this discrimination may have had on their ability to compete equally in the employment market. Could minority employment preferences help give future generations of minorities the ability to compete on an equal basis, so that such preferences eventually become unnecessary? Would abandoning the present system of minority preferences endanger social harmony in future years? Are these preferences valuable because they promote workforce diversity? (But is diversity valuable in itself? Or is it supposed to be valuable because it furthers some of the policies just discussed? Does it promote any other important values?) What other arguments might support

MANAGER'S ETHICAL DILEMMA

You are the president of Computerex, Inc., a medium-sized firm in a highly competitive segment of the computer industry. Right now, Computerex is the leading firm in this segment, and its profitability is outstanding. The firm's success is due in large measure to Jim Sloan, Computerex's director of research. Jim's abilities have made him essential to the firm's continuing success.

In at least one respect, however, Jim is something less than the model manager. In recent years, Jim has had sexual relations with many of Computerex's female employees. It is difficult to say whether Jim's behavior really constitutes sexual harassment of either the quid pro quo or the work environment variety. For one thing, he is a very attractive and personable individual. For another, he is discreet. Also, Jim's "victims" seem to get more than their share of good raises, promotions, choice assignments, and so forth. Thus, these women are unlikely to complain about Jim's actions, or even to admit that they had sex with him.

By now, though, some of Computerex's other male and female employees have begun to get wind of what's going on. As a result, employee morale is beginning to suffer. Even if they have a claim under Title VII or state law, however, none of these suspicious employees could prove anything. Nonetheless, some of them are beginning to voice their suspicions both inside and outside the firm.

It is probably within your formal power to get Jim fired. Doing so, however, would hardly do Computerex or its shareholders any good. Worse yet, Jim has sufficient clout within the firm and on its board of directors that taking action against him could put your neck on the line. Even if Jim were canned, moreover, any one of Computerex's competitors would snap him up in an instant, probably even if they discovered the reason for his firing. Needless to say, Jim would vastly improve the competitive position of any firm acquiring his services.

Despite all the disadvantages of taking action against him, Jim's behavior still bothers you. What should you do?

the preferential treatment of minorities in employment?

3. How do the various arguments and counter-arguments made in the previous question apply to employment preferences in favor of women?
4. In the Manager's Ethical Dilemma above, what kind of Title VII suit might the disgruntled employees conceivably be able to mount? What are their chances of success? Is it a good idea to allow such suits under Title VII? *Hint*: check out the concluding portions of this chapter's discussion of sexual harassment.
5. Employment discrimination law recognizes the employer's need to run the business in an efficient and effective manner. In particular, it recognizes the employer's interest in ensuring that its employees be competent in performing their jobs. What rules discussed in the chapter specifically recognize these interests?
6. What do you think about the *Sutton* case? Is it saying that employers can irrationally discriminate against people whose problems are correctable, but that employers must be careful with people who really do have problems and thus may really be unable to perform? If so, isn't this crazy? On the other hand, check out the numbers toward the end of the Supreme Court's opinion. Do you think that Congress really wanted to assert such great control over employers' prerogatives? *Should* it exercise such control?

Suggested Readings

Articles

BENNETT-ALEXANDER, "The State of Affirmative Action in Employment: A *Post-Stotts* Retrospective," 27 *American Business Law Journal* 565 (1990).

BLACK, "Personality Screening in Employment," 32 *American Business Law Journal* 69 (1994).

BOEHMER, "The Age Discrimination in Employment Act—Reductions in Force as America Grays," 28 *American Business Law Journal* 379 (1990).

BROCKHOEFT, "AIDS in the Workplace: Legal Limitations on Employer Actions," 26 *American Business Law Journal* 255 (1988).

FRANKE, "Retroactivity of the Civil Rights Act of 1991," 31 *American Business Law Journal* 483 (1993).

HIPP, "Now You See It, Now You Don't: The 'Hostile Work Environment' after *Meritor*," 26 *American Business Law Journal* 339 (1988).

MOORE and BRASWELL, "The Probative Value of Multiple Regression Analysis in Title VII Litigation," 27 *American Business Law Journal* 251 (1989).

PAETZOLD and O'LEARY-KELLY, "Continuing Violations and Hostile Environment Sexual Harassment: When is Enough, Enough?" 31 *American Business Law Journal* 365 (1993).

PATTISON and VARCA, "The Resurrection of the Disparate Impact Theory?" 29 *American Business Law Journal* 451 (1991).

SCHNEYER, "Talking about Judges, Talking about Women: Constitutive Rhetoric in the *Johnson Controls* Case," 31 *American Business Law Journal* 117 (1993).

Books

PLAYER, *Employment Discrimination Law* (1988).

PLAYER, *Federal Law of Employment Discrimination in a Nutshell,* 3d ed. (1992).

LINDEMANN, GROSSMAN, and CANE, *Employment Discrimination Law,* 3d ed. (1997)

CHAPTER 17

FEDERAL LABOR LAW: UNIONIZATION AND COLLECTIVE BARGAINING

"EMPLOYEES HAVE AS CLEAR A RIGHT TO ORGANIZE AND SELECT THEIR REPRESENTATIVES FOR LAWFUL PURPOSES AS THE RESPONDENT HAS TO ORGANIZE ITS BUSINESS AND SELECT ITS OWN OFFICERS AND AGENTS."

Chief Justice Charles Evans Hughes in NLRB v. Jones & Laughlin Steel Corp., 301 U.S. 1 (1937)

POSITIVE LAW ETHICAL PROBLEMS

"We are more skilled than cashiers and therefore we should have our own union," said David Bern, a meat cutter at KMart's superstore.

"You're no different than the other KMart employees and should be part of the same union representing all employees at KMart's superstore," replied Beatrice Wollin, a KMart store manager. "If we let you meat cutters have your own union, the next thing you know, the automotive department will want its own union. Where will it end?"

Who was right? Who decides whether a KMart superstore should be considered one bargaining unit represented by one union or whether the meat department should be a separate bargaining unit with its own union?

This chapter deals with the federal law of union organization and collective bargaining and focuses on three federal statutes: the National Labor Relations Act of 1935 (also called the Wagner Act), the Taft-Hartley Act (also known as the Labor-Management Relations Act of 1947), and the Landrum-Griffin Act (or Labor-Management Reporting and Disclosure Act of 1959).

DEVELOPMENT OF LABOR LAW

In the 1800s the labor organization was treated by state law as a criminal conspiracy, a combination of employees withholding services from their employers. This rule gradually changed by the late 1800s when the legality of union efforts was judged by the ends it sought to achieve and the means used to reach these ends. Throughout the century, the court injunction was used to control unions.

The year 1890 witnessed the passage of the Sherman Act, which declared combinations in restraint of trade illegal. The effect of the Sherman Act on unions was soon felt when the *Danbury Hatters* case applied that act to union boycotting activities. Injunctive relief was used to stop picketing and strike activity and to kill the strike entirely. During this period and for a considerable time thereafter, the judiciary identified with ownership interests and consequently showed its hostile attitude toward unions by interpreting statutes to curb unions.

After an unsuccessful attempt in the Clayton Act of 1914 to exempt union activity from the antitrust laws, the Norris-LaGuardia Act was passed in 1932. Rather than outlawing the injunction against lawful union activity, the Norris-LaGuardia Act removed jurisdiction to enjoin peaceful labor disputes from the federal courts. The effect of this was to keep federal courts out of the process of regulating unions. (Note that state courts may issue injunctions in labor disputes.)

In 1926, prior to enactment of the Norris-LaGuardia Act, the Railway Labor Act was passed. As the name suggests, the function of the act was to regulate labor in the railroad industry.

The National Labor Relations Act became law in 1935. At that time it had two functions: (1) to provide a way for employees to say if they wanted a union, and (2) to set forth a code of unfair labor practices binding on employers only, with no prohibitions on unions.

From the management viewpoint, this last feature of the NLRA was a shortcoming, and in 1947, with the conservative trend in the country, the Taft-Hartley Act (the Labor-Management Relations Act) was passed. It rewrote the original NLRA and provided a new code of unfair labor practices applicable to unions. It also outlawed **secondary boycotts**,[1] enforced collective bargaining agreements, and provided for a resolution of disputes affecting national health and welfare. It also backed these provisions up with an 80–day injunction before a strike could be called, to encourage collective bargaining for the period.

Further reduction of union power came in 1959 in the Landrum-Griffin amendment to the Labor Management Relations Act. For the first time, Congress provided for federal regulation of the internal affairs of labor unions. Also, further restrictions were placed on secondary boycotts and picketing during organizational campaigns.

In the 1980s the largest single factor affecting labor was the presidency of Ronald Reagan. Although once a union member and even a union president, Mr. Reagan pursued labor policies generally opposed by union leaders. Some evidence, however, indicates that union members supported him.

Specifically, the president's power to appoint individuals who shared his union views to the federal judiciary and the National Labor Relations Board (NLRB) may affect labor law years after his presidency. Labor law cases today reflect an increasingly hostile attitude toward unions. For example, in 1984 the U.S. Supreme Court decided *NLRB v. Bildisco & Bildisco*, holding that employers may legally file a Chapter 11 bankruptcy petition and immediately dishonor an existing collective bargaining agreement without first talking to the union. Congress then modified the *Bildisco* decision by amending the bankruptcy code. The code now sets up a consultation process that employers must follow with the union and the bankruptcy court before seeking bankruptcy relief from collective bargaining agreements.

A second example of an increasingly hostile attitude of the law toward unions concerns the NLRB's reversal of its earlier ruling on a multiplant employer's shifting work from a high to a low labor cost plant, often in another state. The NLRB had declared this action illegal in the 1982 case of *Milwaukee Spring Division of Illinois Coil Spring Company*. In 1984, after two Reagan appointees had joined the NLRB, the board reversed its 1982 decision. An employer may now legally switch work from a union plant covered by a collective bargaining agreement to a nonunion plant, solely because of lower labor costs. The employer in the *Milwaukee Spring* case did bargain

[1] *Secondary boycotts* refer to a bargaining technique and generally refer to requiring or forcing someone to stop handling another's products or doing business with another person. Put another way, a secondary boycott is any combination whose purpose and effect are to force customers or suppliers of an employer with which the union has a dispute to stop doing business with that employer. The union is one of the parties to the combination, and the other party is a customer or supplier of the employer.

with the union to an impasse before shifting work to the other plant. Thus, the employer must apparently consult with the union before shifting work.

Finally, although unions have faced hard times legally and economically in recent years, society still benefits from well-paid workers. They are consumers and taxpayers. Who buys the products that businesses make? Who pays the taxes that support public schools and other public services? Working men and women—not robots. Labor must be competitively employed to maximize social welfare. Nonetheless, as U.S. business becomes increasingly internationalized, labor must recognize that pay levels are being set on a worldwide basis. Wage demands that are out of step with the world labor market run the risk of driving employers to lower cost domestic or foreign markets.

NATIONAL LABOR RELATIONS BOARD (NLRB)[2]

The National Labor Relations Board was established by the National Labor Relations Act. The NLRB is a federal administrative agency whose function is to administer rights and duties arising under the NLRA and its subsequent amendments. More specifically, its two main jobs are to prevent unfair labor practices and to settle representation questions.

The NLRB has jurisdiction to the maximum extent allowable under the U.S. Constitution's commerce clause. The NLRB does not initiate its own proceedings; anyone except the NLRB may initiate proceedings pursuant to its powers.

Two types of proceedings can be initiated with the NLRB. One is the **complaint case** (C case), which alleges that an unfair labor practice has been committed. Unfair labor practices (ULPs) can be committed by the company or by the union. The second is the **representation case** (R case) in which a union seeks NLRB recognition as the employees' bargaining representative. Anyone but the NLRB can initiate R proceedings. In the C case, a charge can be filed by anyone except the NLRB. The complaint issues from the NLRB general counsel's employee. No power to review the general counsel's decision not to issue an order is currently available.

http://

For more information about the National Labor Relations Board, go to ***http://www.nlrb.gov***

NLRB Jurisdiction

The National Labor Relations Board, not a state or federal court, is the forum for trying unfair labor practices created under the National Labor Relations Act. In other words, when it holds a hearing before an administrative law judge, the NLRB is similar to a court. The NLRB is an administrative agency and thus performs other functions. This new forum was created to escape what many labor leaders perceived to be an employer-biased judiciary. Because the unions were dissatisfied with the businessperson's forums (courts), they created their own forum—the NLRB—which was generally sympathetic to unions until the 1980s.

The NLRB has exclusive jurisdiction over unfair labor practices in and affecting interstate commerce. However, staff shortages and budgetary constraints have forced the NLRB to limit its jurisdiction over unfair labor practices in interstate commerce to those involving larger businesses.

Certain employers are exempt by the NLRA, including federal, state, and municipal governments. Certain employees are also exempt by the NLRA, including supervisors, managers, agricultural workers, independent contractors, domestic workers (such as maids and housekeepers), people who work for parents or spouses, and workers covered by the Railway Labor Act.

[2] The authors acknowledge reliance on government publications in preparing this segment.

The *Holly Farms Corp. v. NLRB* case shows how the U.S. Supreme Court has upheld an NLRB interpretation of the NLR Act by covering "chicken catchers" and other workers closely allied to the agriculture industry. Recall that the NLRA specifically exempts farm workers from its protections.

Holly Farms Corp. v. NLRB

U.S. Supreme Court
517 U.S. 392 (1996)

Background and Facts:

Holly Farms Corporation is a wholly owned subsidiary of Tyson Foods, Inc. Holly Farms is a vertically integrated poultry producer headquartered in Wilkesboro, North Carolina. Holly Farms' activities include hatcheries, a feed mill, an equipment maintenance center, and a processing plant.

"Broiler" chickens are birds destined for human food markets. Holly Farms hatches broiler chicks at its own hatcheries and immediately delivers the chicks to the farms of independent contractors. The contractors then raise the birds into full-grown broiler chickens. Holly Farms pays the contract growers for their services, but retains title to the broilers and supplies the food and medicine necessary to their growth.

When the broilers are seven weeks old, Holly Farms sends its live-haul crews to reclaim the birds and ferry them to the processing plant for slaughter. The live-haul crews—which typically comprise nine chicken catchers, one forklift operator, and one live-haul driver—travel in a flat-bed truck from Holly Farms' processing plant to the farms of the independent growers. At the farms, the chicken catchers enter the coops, manually capture the broilers, and load them onto the bed of the truck, and the live-haul driver returns the truck, with the loaded cases and crew, to Holly Farms' processing plant. There, the birds are slaughtered and prepared for shipment to retail stores.

In 1989, the Chauffers, Teamsters and Helpers, Local 391, filed a representation petition with the National Labor Relations Board, seeking an election in a proposed unit that included live-haul employees working out of Holly Farms' Wilkesboro processing plant. Over Holly Farms' objection, the Board approved the bargaining unit, ruling that the live-haul workers were "employees" protected by the NLRA rather than "agricultural laborers" excluded from the Act's coverage. The U.S. Court of Appeals for the Fourth Circuit enforced the Board's order. Other Federal Courts of Appeals have held that live-haul workers employed by vertically integrated poultry producers are engaged in "agriculture." The Supreme Court agreed to hear the case.

Body of Opinion

The NLRA's protections extend only to workers who qualify as "employee[s]" under . . . the Act. The term "employee," NLRA . . . states [does] not include any individual employed as an agricultural laborer." No definition of "agricultural laborer" appears in the NLRA. But annually since 1946, Congress has instructed, in riders to Appropriations Acts for the Board: "Agricultural laborer" for NLRA purposes, shall derive its meaning from the definition of "agriculture" supplied by the Fair Labor Standards Act. . . .

This definition includes farming in both a primary sense, which encompasses practices "performed by a farmer or on a farm as an incident to or in conjunction with such farming operations." When a statutory prescription is not free from ambiguity, the Board must choose between conflicting reasonable interpretations. Courts, in turn, must respect the judgment of the agency empowered to apply the law to varying fact patterns.

The Court confronts no contention that the live-haul crews are engaged in primary agriculture. Thus, the sole question the Court addresses and decides is whether the chicken catchers, forklift operators, and truck drivers are engaged in *secondary* agriculture. The live-haul activities are not "performed by a farmer." When an integrated poultry producer contracts with independent growers for the care and feeding of chicks hatched in the producer's hatcheries, the producer's status as a farmer ends with respect to those chicks. The producer does not resume farmer status when its live-haul employees arrive on the independent farms to collect broilers for carriage to slaughter and processing. This conclusion entirely disposes of the contention that the truck drivers are employed in secondary agriculture, for Holly Farms acknowledges that these crew members do not work "on a farm."

The more substantial question is whether the catching and loading of broilers qualifies as work performed "on a farm as an incident to or in conjunction with" the independent growers' farming operations. Holly Farms' position that this work is incident to the raising of poultry is a plausible, but not an inevitable, construction of the Fair Labor Standards Act. Hence, a reviewing court must examine the Board's position only for its reasonableness as an interpretation of the governing language.

The Board concluded that the collection of broilers for slaughter, although performed "on a farm," is not incidental to farming operations. Rather, the Board determined, the live-haul crews' work is tied to Holly Farms' processing operations. This is a reasonable interpretation of the statute. Once the broilers have grown on the farm for seven weeks, the growers' contractual obligation to raise the birds ends, and the work of the live-haul crew begins. The growers do not assist the crews in catching or loading the chickens, and the crews play no role in the growers' performance of their contractual undertakings. Furthermore, the live-haul employees all work out of the Wilkesboro processing plant, begin and end each shift by punching a timeclock at the plant, and are functionally integrated with other processing-plant employees. It was also sensible for the Board to home in on the status of the crews' *employer.*

The Board's decision adheres to longstanding NLRB precedent... and is supported by the construction of the Fair Labor Standards Act by the Department of Labor, the agency responsible for administering the FLSA. The Labor Department's regulations accord with the Board's conclusion that the live-haul crews do not engage in secondary farming and further demonstrate that the FLSA's meaning is not so plain [as to "agricultural laborer"] as to bear only one permissible construction....

Judgment and Result

The Supreme Court upheld the NLRB's interpretation of "employees" in the NLRA to cover live haul workers as a bargaining unit. Such workers were not exempt as "agricultural workers."

Questions

1. The NLRA exempts from its coverage agricultural workers but does cover employees of employers in interstate commerce. Is it obvious or ambiguous that chicken catchers, forklift operators, and live-haul drivers fall into one category instead of the other type of worker?
2. Who has the primary responsibility for interpreting and administering the NLRA, the courts or the NLRB? Did the Supreme Court here seem to support the NLRB's interpretation of the National Labor Relations Act? Did this decision benefit unions or employers?
3. As an economic matter, will the Court's opinion in Holly Farms likely increase or decrease the cost of chickens for consumers?

Unfair Labor Practices

The Wagner Act (NLRA) defined unfair labor practices (ULPs) and is one of the NLRA's main accomplishments. When passed in 1935, only employers could commit ULPs. In 1947 the Taft-Hartley Act added ULPs that unions could commit.

An **unfair labor practice** is a legal wrong that gives rise to a cause of action. The NLRA, as amended by the Taft-Hartley Act, created several new causes of action based on wrongs that unions or employers can commit.

Employer ULPs. Section 8(a) of the NLRA sets out five specific wrongs or ULPs that employers can commit under the NLRA:

1. Employer interference with, restraint, or coercion of employees in their rights to form, join, and assist unions [§8(a)(1)]
2. Employer dominance or interference with the formation or administration of any labor organization, or giving financial or other support to it [§8(a)(2)]
3. Employer discrimination regarding hire or tenure or any term or condition of employment to encourage or discourage union membership [§8(a)(3)]
4. Employer discharge or other discrimination against an employee because the employee has filed charges or testified under the NLRA [§8(a)(4)]
5. Employer refusal to bargain collectively with employees [§8(a)(5)]

The Landrum-Griffin Act amended the Wagner Act and added a sixth employer ULP—an employer's entering any contract or agreement, express or implied, with a union to commit a secondary boycott [§8(e)].

The remedies available if an employer commits a ULP include damages and injunctions (court orders telling someone to stop doing something).

Union ULPs. The Taft-Hartley amendments to the NLRA in 1947 added the following union ULPs:

1. Restraining or coercing employees in the exercise of their rights to form, join, or assist unions [§8(b)(1)]
2. Causing or attempting to cause an employer to discriminate against an employee in violation of §8(a)(3) or causing or attempting to cause an employer to discriminate against an employee denied union membership for a reason other than nonpayment of union dues or fees [§8(b)(2)]
3. Refusing to bargain with an employer [§8(b)(3)]
4. Engaging in a secondary strike or picketing activity [§8(b)(4)]
5. Requiring as a condition to union membership a discriminatory or excessive fee [§8(b)(5)]
6. Causing or attempting to cause an employer to pay anything of value for service not performed (also known as the anti-featherbedding provision) [§8(b)(6)]

The 1959 Landrum-Griffin Act added two more union ULPs:

1. Picketing against any employer where an object thereof is forcing an employer to recognize or bargain with an uncertified union [§8(b)(7)]
2. Entering an agreement with an employer to engage in a secondary boycott [§8(e)]

Generally, state courts handle labor disputes that otherwise would be unfair labor practices but that do not qualify under the NLRB's jurisdictional tests. They do so by applying state common law (to the extent it exists) to resolve the matter. Because the concept of an unfair labor practice as developed under the National Labor Relations Act is unknown in most states, the law that courts hand out in this complex area of union-management relations is unsatisfactory. Also, the state court judges, many of whom hold antiunion biases, administer their own form of justice in labor disputes.

Steps in ULP Cases. An unfair labor practice (ULP) case (see Figure 17.1) begins when someone contacts the National Labor Relations Board and makes a charge against an employer or a union or both. A six-month statute of limitations exists on unfair labor practice charges, which means that filing of the complaint and service on the defendant must occur within six months after the alleged unfair labor practice has occurred. The NLRB gives priority to certain cases, including the secondary boycott, **hot cargo contract**,[3] organizational and recognition picketing, and discrimination against individual employees.

ULP charges filed by an individual can be disposed of short of issuance of a complaint by (1) **adjustment**, which is settlement informally or formally, (2) **dismissal**, which may be appealed to the NLRB general counsel, whose decision is final, or (3) **withdrawal** of the complaint.

If one of the aforementioned events does not occur, a complaint will issue from the NLRB. In certain rare instances the NLRB may get a temporary injunction or restraining order in a U.S. district court against an unfair labor practice. If the NLRB has reason to believe the charge is true, a mandatory injunction may issue. After the party accused of committing an unfair labor practice answers the complaint, the administrative law judge (ALJ) holds a hearing at which the charging party, as well as the

[3] Hot cargo contracts are made when a neutral employer (someone not involved in the labor dispute) agrees with the union to exert pressure on the employer with which the union has the dispute to help the union. Hot cargo refers to goods made or handled by an employer with whom the union has a dispute.

FIGURE 17.1 Possible Steps in ULP Cases

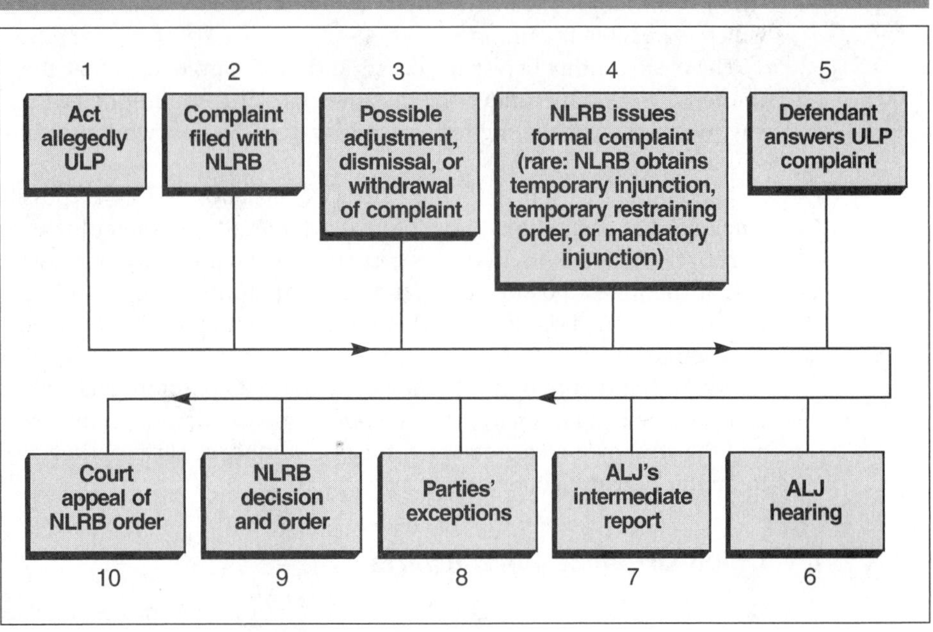

respondent (defendant) and the general counsel of the NLRB, may participate. The judge at these hearings is the ALJ. Presentation of argument is similar to that followed in federal trial courts.

The ALJ makes an intermediate report with recommendations to which the parties may file exception. If none is filed, the NLRB adopts the intermediate report as its decision. If exceptions are filed, the NLRB considers the written records, usually without oral argument.

The level of proof by which one must establish one's case before the NLRB or one of the ALJs is the same as in most civil cases—preponderance of the evidence. If the NLRB determines that an unfair labor practice has been committed, it makes fact findings and issues a cease-and-desist or affirmative action order.

NLRB orders are reviewable by any one of three federal courts of appeals—the one where the firm does business, the District of Columbia court of appeals, or the court of appeals where the ULP occurred. If the NLRB's order is not enforced by the court of appeals, the NLRB may still issue a similar order and resist the court of appeals decision until the U.S. Supreme Court speaks or until enough courts of appeals prove antagonistic to the NLRB order.

UNION-EMPLOYER CONFLICTS AND COMMON GROUNDS

Chapter 1 discussed the legal ethic of power. Nowhere is the power ethic more apparent than in labor law. Employees unite to make one contract (collective bargaining agreement) with their employer to cover all of them. Previously, each made a separate contract with the employer but had no bargaining power as individuals. If one worker quit in disgust over low wages or poor working

> http://
> *The home page for International Brotherhood of Electrical Workers can be found at* ***http://www.IBEW.org/IBEWhome.htm***

conditions, the employer was not affected. Thus, workers combined to get the strength of numbers. Few employers can afford to lose their entire workforce at once, which is possible if a union strikes.

The basic conflict between workers and their employer is that the employer wants the most work done under the cheapest working conditions at the lowest possible pay. Workers want the highest possible wages, the best working conditions, and the shortest hours.

The employer's job is to keep the cost of labor as low as possible because the employer has competitors (possibly both domestic *and* foreign) who are also fighting to keep their costs low. All of this cost control benefits consumers, who can buy products at the lowest possible price and in the quantities they want. (Compare this system with planned economics, where prices do not reflect market reality and shortages are common.)

Workers and employers do, however, share a common goal—preservation of the company, which represents jobs, incomes, and dividends. To the extent that workers and the employer consume the company product or service, they also share a desire to produce quality goods or services.

Union Organizational Efforts

Consider the following example. Jack Driver, a former professional golfer who won the Masters and U.S. Open golf tournaments, made $3 million while on the pro golf tour. When Jack realized his playing days were numbered, he bought a Cincinnati, Ohio, company that manufactured golf clubs. The company had five clerical employees (two accountants and three secretaries), two full-time sales representatives, one club designer, and 25 production and maintenance employees.

Jack had ideas about how golf clubs should be designed. He thought there should be one style of club for pros and another for average players. Jack then built clubs incorporating these ideas. The sales of Jack's company tripled the year after the new clubs came on the market. Company profits tripled. Jack doubled his and the designer's salaries. He gave the sales reps $50,000 bonuses, and the clerical, production, and maintenance employees got merit increases of 20 percent that year. At a Christmas party at his house, Jack gave each employee a set of golf clubs and a Christmas card with a $100 bill while everyone watched videotapes of Jack's U.S. Open victory.

For more information and history of the AFL/CIO, go to **http://www.aflcio.org/home.htm**

Jack subsequently expanded his plant and doubled the number of production employees. He hired an MBA from State University to handle personnel problems, which had formerly been taken care of by Jack. The next year, Jack had too many employees to entertain at his house. Instead of a party, he put an extra $25 in everyone's Christmas cards. Some employees grumbled about the company's getting too big.

One day several of Jack Driver's employees discussed forming a union. Jack regarded this as ingratitude and became angry. He learned who the pro-union employees were and fired them for their beliefs. This action is an employer ULP [specifically, a Section 8(a)(1) violation]. The fired employees are entitled to reinstatement with back pay and seniority rights.

If Jack were to decide to preempt the union issue by setting up a union financed by the company, he would commit an employer ULP [specifically, a Section 8(a)(2) violation]. Employers may not give financial or other support to labor unions. **Checkoff** of union dues by an employer is an exception. An employer may petition the NLRB for a representation election if at least one union claims to represent its employees.

Three Ways to Unionize. Jack's employees can unionize in at least three ways:

1. By voting in a union at a representation election
2. By signing authorization cards
3. By the NLRB's ordering the employer to bargain with a union

The usual way to unionize is by voting at a representation election (R election) run by the NLRB. The employees vote by secret ballot. A majority vote is needed for union certification. What prompts the NLRB to hold an R election for a particular employer's workers is a request, or petition, from the employees, an outside union who wants to represent such employees, or the employer. Employers cannot make a request for an R election unless at least one outside union has sought to represent the employees.

Employees or outside unions may not request an election without a **showing of employee interest** in a union in which at least 30 percent of the employees support a vote. Usually the employees' showing of interest comes by their signing authorization cards saying they want an R election or that they want a particular union as their collective bargaining representative. Employers often complain that unions tell employees that the authorization cards merely request an election when actually the cards authorize a particular union to represent the workers. Workers, employers claim, do not read what they sign. Workers may by authorization card designate a union as collective bargaining agent subject to an NLRB check for accuracy and authenticity.

When the NLRB receives an R petition accompanied by the required showing of employee interest, its regional director decides whether it has jurisdiction over the employer. Recall from the discussion earlier that the NLRB may not or may refuse to take jurisdiction over many smaller businesses or certain other employers.

If the regional NLRB director concludes that it has jurisdiction over a particular employer, an attempt is made to hold a consent representation election. Sometimes employers claim, for example, union misrepresentation in obtaining employee authorization cards. If this claim is raised, the NLRB regional director will order a hearing on these objections. At the end of the hearing, the regional director will either order or not order a representation election.

One of the areas where the National Labor Relations Board has considerable discretion lies in deciding what is the appropriate bargaining unit for a particular employer. For example, a KMart superstore might have several departments where employees in some departments might desire one union's representation for the entire store while employees in another department—such as the meat cutters—might want a separate union because they are more skilled and could command higher wages. Is the bargaining unit the entire KMart store or the meat department? The *KMart Corp. v. NLRB* case below tells us that the NLRB decides what the appropriate bargaining unit is.

KMart Corp. v. NLRB

U.S. Court of Appeals (7th Cir.)
174 F.3d 834 (1999)

Background and Facts:

KMart owns and operates Super KMart Centers throughout the United States. Much larger than a traditional KMart store, Super KMart Centers are vast, one-stop shopping centers open 24 hours per day, seven days per week. Each Super KMart Center is organized into four divisions: (1) customer service, which includes cashiers, cash and general offices, and invoicing; (2) hardlines, which include items such as electrical appliances, toys, camera equipment, garden equipment, and sporting and automobile equipment; (3) softlines, which include items such as clothing, accessories, and jewelry; and (4) food, which includes items such as grocery, dairy, meat, produce, bakery, deli, health and beauty, as well as pet products and a food court. The food sections comprise approximately one-third of the total selling space in the store.

KMart owns and operates two such stores in Bradley and Broadview, Illinois. Both of these stores include food divisions that consist of meat, deli, produce, and bakery departments. The Bradley meat department unit consists of some 23 people, including six meat cutters and a total of 13 meat wrappers and perishable service associates (PSAs), while the meat department at the Broadview store employs 14 individuals, including four meat cutters and a total of eight meat wrappers and PSAs. The meat departments in both stores handle three varieties of meat products, including prepackaged products requiring no processing whatsoever, boxed fresh meat, and ground beef.

Meat cutters' responsibilities include preparing premixed ground beef for sale by running it through a patty machine which forms the beef into patties as well as preparing boxed meat by partitioning large pieces of meat enclosed in shipping boxes, known as *primals*, into either subprimal cuts, steaks, or roasts through repetitive slicing and trimming tasks. According to the record, the meat cutters use specialized meat cutting skills.

The employees classified as meat cutters receive wages of approximately $17.50 per hour, more than three times as high as other employees in the Bradley and Broadview stores.

Meat wrappers operate wrapping machines and package and price the meat after it has been cut by the meat cutters. The meat wrappers earn wages slightly higher than the $5.50 per hour starting wages paid to meat department PSAs. The PSAs are responsible for continually stocking fresh and frozen meat counters, staffing gourmet and seafood counters, and preparing products such as meatloaf and shish kabob, and their wages are equal to that of other employees in the store.

On October 10, 1996, Local 546 of the United Food and Commercial Workers Union (Local 546) filed a petition with the NLRB's regional office, seeking certification as the exclusive bargaining representative of the meat department's employees at the Broadview store, while on December 16, 1996, Local 1540 of the United Food and Commercial Workers Union (Local 1540) filed a petition with the NLRB's regional office seeking certification as the exclusive bargaining representative of all of the meat department employees at the Bradley store. The regional director for the two geographic regions ruled that the employee units petitioned for were appropriate. The director ruled specifically that those employees assigned to the two respective meat departments shared a "community of interests" separate from other employees at the two super KMart Centers. Furthermore, the director found that the meat department employees utilized special skills, had separate daily supervision, and worked in physically separate areas. The director ordered the representation elections be conducted among and limited to the meat department employees for both stores to determine whether they wished to be represented by the locals.

Following successful votes for unionization in the respective meat departments, the NLRB certified Local 1540 as representative of the meat department of the Bradley store and Local 546 as representative of the meat department employees at the Broadview store. After KMart refused to recognize Local 1540 and Local 546 as representatives in the respective stores, each filed charges with the NLRB alleging that the refusals constituted unfair labor practices. The general counsel of the NLRB issued an unfair labor practice complaint against KMart Later the NLRB issued decisions granting the unions' motions for summary judgment finding unfair labor practices by KMart by refusing to bargain with the respective locals. KMart appealed to the U.S. Court of Appeals.

Body of Opinion

Circuit Judge Coffey

On appeal, we consider whether the NLRB reasonably determined that units consisting of meat department employees in two KMart stores constituted appropriate bargaining units and therefore properly found that KMart violated the National Labor Relations Act by refusing to bargain with the duly certified collective bargaining representative of the employees.

In reviewing the matter under consideration, we will sustain the Board's factual findings if the record as a whole provides substantial evidence to support them, even if we might justifiably have reached a different conclusion as a matter of first impression. . . .

This court recognizes that "the selection of an appropriate bargaining unit lies largely within the discretion of the Board, whose decision, 'if not final, is rarely to be disturbed. . . .'" . . . Accordingly, this court recognizes that the Board's unit determinations should not be reversed unless they are arbitrary or unreasonable. . . . To disqualify a unit, the employer must establish "not that another unit is more appropriate, but that the unit selected is utterly inappropriate." . . . Furthermore, the court may not substitute its judgment for a rationally supported position adopted by the NLRB . . . and underlying factual findings must be upheld if they are supported by substantial evidence. . . .

. . . We defer "to reasonable NLRB conclusions in analyzing its application of the law to particular facts, in recognition of the Board's special function of applying the general provisions of the Act to the complexities of industrial life." . . . Therefore we are of the opinion that the NLRB, in applying the traditional community of interest factors, including skills, experience, integration, supervisory structure, employee interchange, and wage rates, reasonably determined that a separate meat department bargaining unit was appropriate. . . .

KMart contends that the Board's decision in this case amounts to improper "gerrymandering" of collective bargaining units because the Board should have accorded greater weight to evidence that store-wide, or "wall-to-wall" units are appropriate. The Board properly rejected this evidence because it was simply not relevant to the issue of whether the meat department units in the instant case are appropriate. The Board is not charged with determining the most appropriate unit, or required to engage in comparative analysis of the relative appropriateness of various potentially bargaining units. On the contrary, the employer must establish "not that the other unit is more appropriate, but that the unit selected is utterly inappropriate," . . . and KMart has failed to do this in this case. . . .

Judgment and Result

The U.S. Court of Appeals upheld the NLRB's decision to recognize the meat department as a bargaining unit separate from the rest of the KMart Superstore.

Questions

1. What legal body makes the initial decision as to what is an appropriate bargaining unit? If evidence supports another decision as to the appropriate bargaining unit, will the court of appeals reverse the decision of the NLRB? In effect, does this tendency make the NLRB the determiner of what an appropriate bargaining unit is?
2. What factors did the NLRB examine to determine whether the meat department was an appropriate bargaining unit?
3. The "gerrymandering" referred to in the opinion is a practice of arbitrarily drawing lines for congressional and other electoral offices in public elections to achieve political advantage for the one drawing the lines. By analogy, if the NLRB decides that a superstore can be divided into many different bargaining units, some wanting unions and others not, when, arguably, the majority of all workers storewide do not want a union, is not KMart correct that this division is gerrymandering? After all, if you were a KMart store manager, would you rather deal with the unionization issue on a storewide basis or a department-by-department basis?

Preelection Campaign Statements

Assuming the NLRB orders a representation election (R election), what may an employer say to its employees to influence the election? The NLRA recognizes that the employer has a free speech right created by the First Amendment of the U.S. Constitution and implemented by Section 8(c) of the NLRA. This right allows the employer to state its legal position and its views, arguments, or opinions on what unionization will mean, provided that no threats of reprisal or force or promises of benefits are made violating the NLRA's Section 8(a)(1) discussed previously. The idea is that R elections should be conducted in **laboratory conditions**—that is, they should take place in a clinical, dispassionate atmosphere for employees to judge whether to unionize.

The following *NLRB v. Vemco, Inc.* case illustrates employer remarks to employees prior to a representation election. It shows that the employer may legally predict that it might have to cut workers or suffer a layoff.

http://
For more information about the United Auto Workers, go to ***http://www.uaw.org***

NLRB v. Vemco, Inc.

U.S. Court of Appeals, Sixth Cir.
989 F.2d 1468 (1993)

Background and Facts:

In 1989 the United Auto Workers (UAW) filed charges with the NLRB alleging that Vemco, Inc., was engaging in certain unfair labor practices in violation of the NLRA during the course of the UAW's campaign to organize Vemco's employees. After hearings, an administrative law judge (ALJ) found that Vemco had engaged in numerous unfair labor practices related to the UAW's organizing efforts. He therefore ordered Vemco... to reinstate with back pay employees laid off allegedly because of union activity and to bargain on request with the UAW. On review, the NLRB affirmed the ALJ's decision with only slight modification.

Vemco, Inc., located in Grand Blanc, Michigan, supplies the automotive industry with large plastic exterior car parts requiring injection molding and sophisticated paint application. Vemco's executive management consists of Larry Winget, principal owner and president, Michael Torakis, vice president of finance and administration and secretary/treasurer, and James Schutz, vice president of manufacturing. . . .

Vemco's three operations are molding, paint, and assembly. The paint plant is considered state of the art. For the 1989 model year, the paint plant itself was subdivided into cladding and fascia lines, with the fascia line further split into a masking area and a paint area.

At the time it opened its doors and throughout the 1989 automotive year, Vemco had only one customer, Buick-Oldsmobile-Cadillac Division of General Motors (BOC). BOC contracted with Vemco for fascias and claddings for several of its car models. The contract called for delivery to commence in August 1988, with projected quantity requirements to increase weekly over the fall of the year as BOC increased its own manufacturing. The contractual penalty for a failure to deliver according to the industry practice of just-in-time (JIT) shipping causing downtime on a BOC assembly line ran as high as $25,000 per minute of downtime.

Vemco's high-tech paint system did not function as planned when Vemco began operations because of major technical problems in many of the components of the system. The company that designed and built the paint system eventually walked off the project, leaving Vemco to identify and correct these problems with its own personnel and other outside contractors. Ultimately, the system had to be redesigned and rebuilt at the same time BOC's increasing delivery requirements had to be met.

As a result of its technical problems, Vemco was unable to produce a product that consistently met quality standards the first time through and had to rework enormous numbers of unacceptable parts. Because of the severe economic consequences of a failure to timely deliver to BOC, Vemco ended up with many more employees working longer hours than originally forecast. By mid-December, Vemco was running a second shift on both the fascia and cladding lines, partially to relieve the 60- to 84-hour weeks its employees had been working and partially in anticipation of orders from Ford Motor Company, which, if obtained, would have required a fully trained second shift to produce.

By early 1989, Vemco succeeded in "debugging" in part its paint operation. As a result, workhours decreased and productivity increased. These productivity gains resulted in a shortage of workhours for Vemco's employees. By mid-January, both shifts on the fascia lines were reduced to a four-day workweek, and Vemco considered going to a three-day workweek. At this point, employees expressed unhappiness with the sharp decline in hours and apprehension over further hourly reductions and possible layoffs.

Vemco has a non-union philosophy that is clearly expressed in its Personnel Policies Handbook that all employees receive and sign for at the time of their orientation. Some Vemco employees, however, became interested in unionizing soon after the company opened and by late September employees made telephone inquiries of the UAW. An initial union meeting was held in early October 1988, attracting 50 employees. Periodic meetings were held thereafter, including more or less weekly gatherings between January and March of 1989. Both Schultz and Torakis were aware of general union activity by October 1988. Line supervisors, who were also aware of this general union activity, committed unfair labor practices during the period between Vemco's start-up and the March 1989 mass layoff.

Body of Opinion

Senior Circuit Judge Rosen

. . . We examine the violations that may rely on protected speech before reviewing the evidence as a whole to determine whether a bargaining order is appropriate.

The violations that Vemco claims rely on protected speech related to predictions made to employees and the media, both verbal and written, that if the company were required to reinstate employees laid off on March 17, it might have to cut workhours or suffer another layoff because of lack of work. In discussing protected speech, the Supreme Court set forth its views on employer conduct in the course of an organizing campaign:

> An employer is free to communicate to his employees any of his general views about unionism or any of his specific views about a particular union, so long as the communications do not contain a "threat of reprisal or force or promise of benefit." He may even make a prediction as to the precise effects he believes unionization will have on his company. In such a case, however, the prediction must be carefully phrased on the basis of objective fact to convey an employer's belief as to demonstrably probable consequences beyond his control. . . . If there is any implication that an employer may or may not take action solely on his own initiative for reasons unrelated to economic necessities and known only to him, the statement is no longer a reasonable prediction based on available facts but a threat of retaliation based on misrepresentation and coercion, and as such is without the protection of the First Amendment [as implemented by section 8 (c) of the NLRA]. *Gissel*, 395 U.S. at 617-19.

First, we note that it is not at all clear whether the Vemco prediction at issue is a prediction of the consequences of company unionization or, instead, a prediction of the consequences of an impending NLRB decision that might mandate reinstatement of the laid-off employees, regardless of the outcome of the organizing campaign. If the latter, it is not a violation of the Act; if the former, we believe it satisfies the *Gissel* prediction standard for the reasons discussed below. Thus, it is protected speech which must be excluded in a review of the record to determine the propriety of a rerun election. ...

There was nothing to suggest that the predicted shortage of work was within Vemco's control and there was no implication that Vemco would implement a cutback in hours or a layoff solely on its own initiative for reasons unrelated to the economic necessity of adjusting to a shortage of work. Given the severe consequences of a failure to deliver according to JIT, it hardly seems likely Vemco would cut back if it had the work. Vemco therefore made a reasonable prediction based on available facts, and not a threat of retaliation based on misrepresentation and coercion. This prediction is protected employer speech under section 8(c) and will not be used to determine whether a rerun election should be ordered.

The remaining violations are summed up as follows:

1) Threat to close plant for non-economic reasons in the face of an organizing campaign and to later reopening with new employees;

2) Threat of harsher personnel decisions;

3) Promise of benefits relating to the institution of recall rights and advance notice of weekend overtime;

4) Confiscation of union literature;

5) Solicitation of grievances; and

6) Overly broad no-solicitation rule and threats of discriminatory discharge involving employee Hall.

These undisputed violations are sufficient to support the traditional remedy of a rerun election. They do not, however, warrant a bargaining order under either category set forth in *Gissel*.

Judgment and Result

The court here decided that the employer committed ULPs while the employees were considering whether to unionize and this justified a rerun representation election. However, the employer's statements that it might have to cut workers if required to reinstate laid off employees was protected employer speech and not a threat.

Questions

1. What test did the court follow to distinguish threats from employer's predictions of things to come?
2. What, if any, free speech rights does an employer have to tell its side of the story when confronting employee unionization efforts?
3. If an employer commits unfair labor practices during unionization efforts, what remedies are available?

If an employer commits ULPs in pre-R election campaign statements, several outcomes are possible. If the union wins the election, probably nothing will happen other than union certification as the employees' collective bargaining agent. If the union loses the election, the election could be rerun. Thus, an employer who has a good chance of winning an R election should either make no preelection statements to employees or be cautious about what is said. (If the union loses a close election, it will often claim that the employer statements were ULPs destroying the election laboratory conditions.) Another possibility if the employer commits preelection ULPs is that the NLRB will simply order the employer to bargain with the union. In effect, the NLRB administratively declares the union a winner even though it has not won an R election. The reason is that the employer has so tainted the election atmosphere that laboratory conditions are impossible to achieve. This remedy is ordered where a majority of the employees signed cards authorizing the union to be their bargaining agent.

In 1969 the Supreme Court decided the *Gissel* case, which is the leading case on NLRB remedies if employer preelection ULPs taint the R election. In *Gissel*, the U.S. Supreme Court had to decide whether a union could become the employees' NLRB certified representative solely by producing union authorization cards signed by a majority of employees. The Court said it was possible. The Supreme Court also had to decide whether the union could gain certification as the collective bargaining representative solely by NLRB certification where employer preelection ULPs made holding an R election in laboratory conditions impossible. The Supreme Court also said that this remedy was an NLRB option.

COURT REVIEW OF NLRB UNION CERTIFICATION

Suppose a representation election is held and the NLRB certifies a union as the employee bargaining representative. The employer may not go directly to court for a review of the certification. The employer may, however, refuse to bargain with the union. This refusal would probably be challenged as a ULP, would first go to the NLRB, and could later be appealed. At the court of appeals, the employer could raise the union certification issue as a defense to its refusal to bargain. As a result, the employer can indirectly get court review of NLRB certification of unions. Unions, on the other hand, may not get court review of the NLRB refusal to certify the union as the employees' collective bargaining agent.

Frequency of Representation Election

Election Bar Rule. Suppose an NLRB-run representation election is held and the union loses. What, if anything, stops the union from getting the required 30 percent showing of interest (by having employees sign authorization cards) the next week and petitioning the NLRB to hold another representation election? The answer is the **election bar rule**. The NLRA prevents an R election if one was held within the previous 12 months and the union was defeated. The NLRB has held that the 12-month bar also applies if the union wins.

Several reasons support the election bar rule. First, it forces the employees to reflect soberly before initially voting for a union. Second, it reduces the disruption of the employer's business that R elections cause. Third, it reduces the drain on NLRB administrative resources that occurs whenever R elections are held.

Contract Bar Rule. Once a certified union and employer agree on a collective bargaining agreement, the NLRB will dismiss any attempt (such as another union's) to have a representation election while the contract is in effect. This is the **contract bar rule**. The reason for the rule is to preserve stable relations between labor and management. In effect, the contract bar rule stops workers from getting rid of or changing unions while a contract exists between an employer and the union certified by the NLRB as the employees' collective bargaining agent.

The contract bar rule has several exceptions.

1. The collective bargaining contract is longer than three years.
2. A union schism exists, or the union is defunct.
3. The employer has greatly expanded its operations.

The three-year exception is easily understood. A union in a shaky position as the employees' bargaining representative might try for long-term employer-union contracts to protect its position as bargaining agent. The NLRB thus limits the contract bar period to three years.

Schism—the second exception to the contract bar rule—means that top union officials have a conflict or a split over fundamental union policy. A schism could occur if union leaders allegedly embezzle union assets. Related to schism is union **defunctness**, which refers to situations in which the union no longer operates. For instance, a union's not holding meetings or presenting employee grievances to management is evidence of defunctness. If a schism or defunctness occurs during the life of a collective bargaining agreement, a representation election can be held.

A great expansion or change in an employer's operations is a third exception to the contract bar rule and includes several things. First, if fewer than 30 percent of the current employees were at work when the present contract was entered, the contract bar rule does not apply. Second, the contract bar does not apply if either a merger of two or more operations creates an entirely new operation with major personnel changes *or* operations are resumed with new employees after the firm has been closed down for an indefinite period.

Runaway Shop

Shortly after the union wins an R election, Jack decides to shut down his Cincinnati, Ohio, plant and open a newer factory in Sarasota, Florida. This action may or may not be legal under the NLRA. If Jack moves his plant solely to get economic advantages of lower taxes and a lower area wage scale in Sarasota, Florida, he does not commit a ULP. However, if he moves his plant to escape or discourage unions, he does commit a ULP [specifically, a Section 8(a)(3) violation]. These distinctions create the problem (or opportunity, depending on one's viewpoint) of avoiding illegality by simply stating reasons for plant relocation solely on economic grounds.

What sanction is applied if Jack relocates solely to escape a union? The NLRB will not order Jack to move his plant back to Cincinnati (his original location from which he fled). However, Cincinnati unionized employees will be offered first opportunity on jobs at the new location in Sarasota and will be awarded relocation expenses if they take the new jobs.

Employers often have several plants—some union, some nonunion. Shifting work from high-cost unionized plants to lower-cost nonunion plants is tempting. Unions argue that such shifts made while a collective bargaining agreement is in effect amounts to the employer's breaking the agreement.

Bankruptcy to Escape Collective Bargaining Agreements

Bankruptcy is sometimes available to escape union contracts. See the section, "Development of Labor Law," earlier in the chapter for discussion of this topic.

Going Out of Business

The U.S. Supreme Court has held that employers may shut down a plant completely (forever) without committing a ULP, provided the employer does not have the intent to discourage unionization elsewhere (at plants in other locations, for instance). Thus, if Jack Driver's Cincinnati, Ohio, plant unionizes, Jack may legally close the plant permanently if he does not want to deal with the union.

Duty to Bargain

U union is NLRB certified as the collective bargaining representative of Jack Driver's production employees. The U representative approaches Jack to talk about entering a collective bargaining agreement. Jack says, "I don't believe in unions. I refuse to talk with you. My employees each have individual employment contracts. This suits me just fine. Get out." Jack has committed a ULP because employers have a duty to bargain, as do unions.

What does "duty to bargain" mean? Could Jack meet once with the union representative, listen to the representative, and leave without saying anything? He may not. The NLRB and courts have added "good faith" to the "duty to bargain," meaning that Jack must meet and discuss wages, hours, and working conditions with an open mind. The parties do not have to agree on anything, however.

In *NLRB v. American National Insurance* (1952), the U.S. Supreme Court said that an employer's presenting a comprehensive "management functions" clause to a union did *not* amount to a refusal to bargain in good faith. The clause in question kept standards for work schedules flexible at management's option. Nor was management's refusal to budge from its position a refusal to bargain in good faith. However, the employer did bargain over some terms in the union proposals in *American National*. If the employer had come to the bargaining table and claimed the right to control *every* aspect of the employees' jobs and adamantly refused to bargain or yield, this action would be a ULP [Section 8(a)(5) violation].

The Supreme Court has also held that employers and unions can bring economic pressures (strikes and lockouts, for example) against each other before, during, and after meeting to bargain and still be bargaining in good faith, and hence not committing ULPs.

Often during bargaining, an employer will claim that it cannot afford a union demand. If the union asks the employer to prove this claim, the employer must document the claim or it violates the duty to bargain in good faith. However, the union demand for proof of employer inability to pay must be narrow and must not impose unreasonable demands on the employer.

An employer may not increase employee wages or employment terms without first bargaining with the union. To do so violates the duty to bargain in good faith, because it undercuts the negotiating process. However, employers may change wages or benefits after bargaining with the union over them, even if no agreement is reached.

Boulwareism is a violation of the duty to bargain in good faith. Boulwareism is an employer's careful study of all bargaining issues before meeting the union, and presenting its best offer to the union immediately on a take-it-or-leave-it basis. This process was developed by a General Electric Company executive. Although it eliminates the low-offer posturing that characterizes negotiations, it suggests a closed mind at the start of negotiations, which is apparently a fatal flaw.

Bargaining Topics

The NLRA requires that an employer bargain about wages, hours, and working conditions. If an employer refuses, it commits a ULP, but some items are not mandatory subjects of bargaining. In *NLRB v. Borg-Warner* (1958), the employer's insistence on a clause excluding the international union as a party was held not to be a mandatory subject of bargaining. Therefore, the employer's continued insistence about this point was a refusal to bargain in good faith.

The *Fibreboard v. NLRB* case holds that an employer's decision to end part of its operation and contract it out is a mandatory subject of bargaining. Therefore, employer's contracting out maintenance work (formerly done by unionized company employees) without first discussing it with the union was a ULP—a refusal to bargain about a mandatory subject of bargaining. Justice Stewart pointed out in a concurring opinion in *Fibreboard* that *any* management decision, such as how to market the company's product, could affect the employees' wages, hours, and working conditions. Does this decision mean the union must be consulted about all such managerial decisions? Stewart thought not, but he raised an interesting question about the limits of mandatory subjects of bargaining.

The *Radisson Plaza Minneapolis v. NLRB* case shows an employer's refusal to bargain in good faith.

Radisson Plaza Minneapolis v. NLRB

U.S. Court of Appeals, Eighth Circuit
987 F.2d 1376 (1993)

Background and Facts:

This case arose following allegations by unions representing Radisson's employees that the employer had failed to bargain with the union in good faith. The opinion contains specific examples that formed the basis for the charges filed with the NLRB. The NLRB essentially agreed with the union charges. Radisson appealed to the U.S. Court of Appeals.

Body of Opinion

Section 8(a)(5) of the Act makes it an unfair labor practice for an employer "to refuse to bargain collectively with the representatives of his employees." ... Section 8(d) of the Act defines the duty to bargain collectively as the mutual obligation of the employer and union "to meet at reasonable times and confer in good faith with respect to wages, hours, and other terms and conditions of employment, or the negotiation of an agreement. ..."

Although the duty of bargaining in good faith does not require that the parties make particular concessions, it envisions "a sincere, serious effort to adjust differences and to reach an acceptable ground"... Thus, an employer engages in bad faith or surface bargaining by conducting negotiations "as a kind of charade or sham, all the while intending to avoid reaching an agreement."...

In determining the existence of bad faith bargaining, we examine "the employer's conduct in the totality of the circumstances in which the bargaining took place."... Moreover, we have noted that "the Board not only looks to the employer's behavior at the bargaining table but also to its conduct away from the table that may affect the negotiations."... We have recognized that "the question of good faith bargaining is for the Board's expertise more than ours."... Consequently, we will affirm a finding by the Board of an employer's bad faith bargaining if it is supported by substantial evidence on the record as a whole."...

The Board based its finding that Raddison failed to bargain in good faith upon Radisson's engaging in unfair labor practices "away from the table," and surface bargaining during the sessions. We examine these contentions in turn.

The Board found that Radisson unlawfully refused to bargain with the unions concerning changes in employee working conditions. In September 1988, Radisson changed job assignments and schedules of some unit employees. In March 1989, Radisson unilaterally increased the base wage rate for sixty-five percent of unit employees. Radisson does not dispute that it rebuffed the unions' request for bargaining after the changes were made. Under the Act, wages, hours, and other terms and conditions of employment are mandatory subjects of bargaining, and any unilateral change in these items by a company, when accompanied by a refusal to deal with the incumbent union, constitutes a violation of the Act. ...

Radisson responds that it bargained over the changes before it made them. Further, it argues that the wage increase was exempt from the duty to bargain because it was a continuation of an established company practice.

Radisson's first argument is without merit. Radisson cites evidence that the parties had generally discussed company policies on wages and working conditions during the negotiations. Mere evidence of company policies concerning employment conditions, without more, however, is not the equivalent of notice to the union of specific changes or of bargaining to impasse over a specific proposal. Accordingly, Radisson may not claim that it bargained over the changes.

Second, Radisson's argument that the wage increase was exempt from the duty to bargain is misplaced. The Board applies this exemption only in cases where the wage increase is automatic and does not involve the exercise of a company's discretion. ... Here the Board found that Radisson exercised substantial discretion in determining both the timing and amount of the increases. Radisson granted the increases at irregular intervals, and only after a preliminary determination that its budget and competitive requirements would sustain the increase. Consequently, the Board correctly found that the wage and schedule changes were mandatory subjects of bargaining and that Radisson committed an unlawful labor practice by unilaterally altering them without notification to the unions.

Moreover, Radisson does not contest two of the Board's findings: 1) that Radisson violated 8(a)(5) and (1) of the Act by refusing the unions' March 14 request for information for an updated list of the unit employees' names, addresses, wages, and social security numbers and 2) that Radisson and its parent corporation violated section 8(a)(1) of the Act by maintaining a rule in its employee handbook prohibiting employees from discussing their wages with anyone other than management. Consequently, we accord these findings summary enforcement. ... Moreover, these findings remain relevant in determining whether Radisson bargained in bad faith. ...

Thus, the Board properly found that Radisson's conduct away from the bargaining table supported an inference that Radisson failed to bargain in good faith. Radisson treated the unions as irrelevant with respect to issues of vital significance, including wage and schedule changes, and then refused to provide the unions with basic information concerning unit employees.

Likewise, Radisson's conduct during the bargaining sessions supported the Board's finding that Radisson engaged in surface bargaining. First, the Board found that Radisson's chief negotiator, attorney Stokes, engaged in a pattern of dilatory conduct. Stokes cancelled three bargaining sessions, terminated five of eleven meetings significantly earlier than planned, and refused the unions' requests for more frequent sessions without explaining why he was unavailable.... As a result, the parties had only seven meetings over eight months.

Additionally, the Board found that Stokes had engaged in obstreperous conduct during the meetings calculated to deter consensus. First, Stokes engaged in frequent filibusters in collateral matters, such as Secretary Califano's book on health care, the nature of unions in Sweden, and the character of a hotel in Williamsburg, Virginia. Second, Stokes continually reminded unions of their slim margin of victory, questioned whether they enjoyed majority support, and cited allegations of the unions' international affiliate's linkage to organized crime without any reference to how this purported affiliation was related to the negotiations.

Last, Stokes insisted on extreme gambits during bargaining sessions that the Board found supported the charges of surface bargaining. During the March 27 meeting, Stokes requested that the contract contain a clause relieving Radisson of its obligation to bargain should either of the unions be found to be "dominated by organized crime." Second, Stokes insisted at more than one meeting that the handbook form the basis of the agreement. The handbook contains a clause, however, permitting Radisson "to amend, modify, or discontinue any of the information or benefits contained herein." In the light of this provision, the unions' acceptance of Stokes's proposal would have permitted Radisson to unilaterally change working conditions whenever it pleased or to require the union to renegotiate working conditions at its whim.

The use of such tactics by Radisson provide substantial evidence to support the Board's finding that Radisson engaged in surface bargaining during the negotiation sessions. Thus the Board reasonably found that the totality of Radisson's conduct, both at and away from the bargaining table violated sections 8(a)(1) and (5) of the Act.

Judgment and Result

The court found that Radisson failed to bargain in good faith.

Questions

1. What specific single act constituted failure of the employer to bargain in good faith? Or was it a series of acts?
2. How can a situation in which an employer unilaterally raises employees' wages without first discussing it with the union be considered a failure to bargain in good faith?
3. If an employer has a duty to bargain in good faith, is a failure to reach an agreement with the union considered a breach of the duty to bargain in good faith?
4. Do unions also have a duty to bargain in good faith?

Collective Bargaining Agreements

A collective bargaining agreement (CBA) is what a union negotiates with an employer on behalf of the employees. It is a contract that can have any number of terms in it, such as management function clauses, union recognition clauses, arbitration clauses, and no-strike clauses.

The U.S. Supreme Court decided in 1962 the case of *Sinclair Refining v. Atkinson.* This case held that a no-strike clause in a union-employer contract could not be enforced by injunctive relief in a federal district court. The main reason for the *Sinclair* decision was the **Norris-LaGuardia Act**, which prohibits federal courts from issuing injunctions in labor disputes. It was unsuccessfully argued in *Sinclair* that the situation was not a labor dispute about strikes because the union had signed the agreement containing the no-strike clause.

As noted earlier in this chapter, the injunction had been an effective employer weapon against unions before the 1930s. Since passage of the Norris-LaGuardia Act in 1932, the federal courts have been understandably reluctant to issue injunctions against union activity. However, the Norris-LaGuardia Act as amended does not preclude federal courts from issuing injunctions against labor unions in all situations. For example, the Taft-Hartley Act allows a federal district court to issue a back-to-work order for 80 days when a union strike has been called that threatens the national health or safety.

In the *Boys Markets* case (1970) the U.S. Supreme Court again looked at the enforceability of a no-strike clause contained in a union-employer collective bargaining agreement. The agreement there called for *binding arbitration* of the dispute causing the strike. The Supreme Court overruled the *Sinclair* case by saying that the federal district court could issue an injunction to enforce a no-strike clause where the collective bargaining agreement (CBA) had a binding arbitration clause covering the dispute. The idea behind the *Boys Market* decision was to promote arbitration. The importance of the arbitration clause became apparent in 1976 when the Supreme Court was again called upon in the *Buffalo Forge* case to enforce a no-strike clause where the arbitration clause in the CBA did not cover the dispute. The Supreme Court refused to enforce the no-strike clause because arbitration would not be furthered by doing so. Thus, if an employer negotiates a no-strike clause in the CBA, it should also seek an arbitration clause so the no-strike clause can be enforced in federal court.

Employer Attempt to Disavow Collective Bargaining Agreements

One of the main objectives of the National Labor Relations Act is maintaining industrial peace and stability. Collective bargaining agreements support this NLRA objective because they encourage continuity of labor management relations.

Recently, however, employers have sought to play "hardball" with unions. One technique is by attempting to disavow collective bargaining agreements shortly after they have been entered. Employers use this technique when they sense that union members are unhappy with collective bargaining agreement terms, for example, wage increases might be small or employers might reduce fringe benefits. In such cases, union members feel their unions are charging them dues for which members are getting nothing. Read the following *Auciello* case to see an instance of employer attempts to disavow a day-old collective bargaining agreement.

Auciello Iron Works, Inc. v. NLRB

U.S. Supreme Court
517 U.S. 781 (1996)

Background and Facts:

Auciello Iron Works of Hudson, Massachusetts, had 23 production and maintenance employees during the period in question. After a union election in 1977, the NLRB certified Shopmen's Local 501, AFL-CIO, as the collective bargaining representative of Auciello's employees. Over the following years, the company and the Union were able to negotiate a series of collective bargaining agreements, one of which expired on September 25, 1988. Negotiations for a new one were unsuccessful throughout September and October 1988, however, and when Auciello and the Union had not made a new contract by October 14, 1988, the employees went on strike. Negotiations continued, nonetheless, and on November 17, 1988, Auciello presented the Union with a complete contract proposal. On November 18, 1988, the picketing stopped, and nine days later, on a Sunday evening, the Union telegraphed its acceptance of the offer. The very next day, however, Auciello told the Union that it doubted that a majority of the bargaining units employees supported the Union, and for that reason disavowed the collective bargaining agreement and denied it had any duty to continue negotiating. Auciello traced its doubt to knowledge acquired before the Union accepted the contract offer, including the facts that 9 employees had crossed the picket line, that 13 employees had given it signed forms indicating their resignation from the Union, and that 16 had expressed dissatisfaction with the Union.

Judgment and Result

The Supreme Court found for the National Labor Relations Board. Auciello's attempted disavowal of the day-old collective bargaining agreement was an unfair labor practice.

Questions

1. How does the *Auciello* case holding further the objectives of the National Labor Relations Act?
2. Suppose an employer negotiates a collective bargaining agreement that is generous to its unionized workforce and shortly thereafter realizes its mistake. Does *Auciello* encourage such employers to carefully consider making collective bargaining agreements they will not be able to escape on "good faith belief" that the union suddenly has lost majority status?

Collective Bargaining Agreements: Arbitration Provisions

Arbitration provisions are put into collective bargaining agreements by employers and unions to settle labor disputes by using a neutral third party (the arbitrator) to resolve differences without going to court. Courts and Congress both favor arbitration of labor disputes (rather than lawsuits in court) because this method enables private settlement of disputes. Because the arbitrator is selected by the parties and draws his or her authority from the collective bargaining agreement, courts give great weight to what the arbitrator decides. Thus, arbitrators' awards may be appealed to courts, but courts will not tamper with the award if no arbitrator fraud or misconduct is indicated.

The *Misco* case is a U.S. Supreme Court decision upholding an arbitrator's award when an employer challenged it in court.

United Paperworkers International Union v. Misco, Inc.

U.S. Supreme Court
484 U.S. 29 (1987)

Background and Facts:

Misco's (the employer) collective bargaining agreement with United Paperworkers union authorizes the submission to binding arbitration of any grievance that arises from the interpretation or application of the agreement's terms, and reserves to management the right to establish, amend, and enforce rules regulating employee discharge and discipline and setting forth disciplinary procedures. One of respondent's rules listed as causes for discharge the possession or use of controlled substances on company property. Isiah Cooper, an employee covered by the agreement who operated a hazardous machine, was apprehended by police in the backseat of someone else's car in respondent's parking lot with marijuana smoke in the air and a lighted marijuana cigarette in the front-seat ashtray. A police search of Cooper's own car on the lot revealed marijuana gleanings. Upon learning of the cigarette incident, respondent discharged Cooper for violation of the disciplinary rule. Cooper then filed a grievance which proceeded to arbitration on the stipulated issue whether respondent had just cause for the discharge under the rule and, if not, the appropriate remedy. The arbitrator upheld the grievance and ordered Cooper's reinstatement, finding that the cigarette incident was insufficient proof that Cooper was using or possessed marijuana on company property. Because, at the time of the discharge, respondent was not aware of, and thus did not rely upon, the fact that marijuana had been found in Cooper's own car, the arbitrator refused to accept this fact into evidence. However, the District Court vacated the arbitration award and the Court of Appeals affirmed, ruling that reinstatement would violate the public policy "against the operation of dangerous machinery by persons under the influence of drugs." The court held that the cigarette incident and the finding of marijuana in Cooper's car established a violation of the disciplinary rule that gave respondent just cause for discharge.

Judgment and Result

1. The Court of Appeals exceeded the limited authority possessed by a court reviewing an arbitrator's award entered pursuant to a collective-bargaining agreement.

(a) Absent fraud by the parties or the arbitrator's dishonesty, reviewing courts in such cases are not authorized to reconsider the merits of the award since this would undermine the federal policy of privately settling labor disputes by arbitration without governmental intervention. The parties having agreed to submit all questions of contract interpretation to the arbitrator, the reviewing court is confined to ascertaining whether the award draws its essence from the contract and does not simply reflect the arbitrator's own notions of industrial justice. As long as the arbitrator is even arguably construing or applying the contract and acting within the scope of his authority, the court cannot overturn his decision simply because it disagrees with his factual findings, contract interpretations, or choice of remedies.

(b) The Court of Appeals was not free to refuse enforcement of the award simply because it considered the cigarette incident ample proof that the disciplinary rule had been violated, since no dishonesty is alleged here, and since improvident fact finding is hardly a sufficient basis for disregarding what the arbitrator appointed by the parties determined to be the historical facts. Nor is the arbitrator's refusal to consider the evidence of marijuana in Cooper's car a sufficient basis for nonenforcement, since the collective-bargaining agreement largely left evidentiary matters to the arbitrator, whose decision on this point was consistent with the practice followed by other arbitrators of refusing to admit evidence which a discharging party did not rely upon. Assuming that the arbitrator did err on this point, his error was not in bad faith or so gross as to amount to affirmative misconduct. Moreover, his decision not to consider the disputed evidence did not forever foreclose respondent's use of that evidence as a basis for discharge. Even if it were open to the court to find a disciplinary rule violation on the basis of that evidence, the court could not properly set aside the award because in its view discharge was the correct remedy, since arbitrators normally have wide discretion in formulating remedies. Although the agreement here may have limited the arbitrator's remedial discretion by giving respondent the unreviewable right to discharge violators of the disciplinary rule, the proper course would have been to remand to the arbitrator for a definitive construction of the contract in this respect.

2. The Court of Appeals erred in setting aside the arbitral award on public policy grounds. A court's refusal to enforce an arbitrator's *interpretation* of a collective-bargaining agreement is limited to situations where the contract as interpreted would violate "some explicit public policy" that is "well defined and dominant, and is to be ascertained by reference to the laws and legal precedents and not from general considerations of supposed public interests." *W. R. Grace & Co. v. Rubber Workers*, 461 U.S. 757, 766. An alleged public policy must be properly framed under the approach set out in *W. R. Grace*, and the violation of such policy must be clearly shown. Here, the court made no attempt to review existing laws and legal precedents, but simply formulated a policy against the operation of dangerous machinery under the influence of drugs based on "general considerations of supposed public interests." Even if that formulation could be accepted, no violation of the policy was clearly shown, since the assumed connection between the marijuana gleanings in Cooper's car and his actual use of drugs in the workplace is tenuous at best. It was inappropriate for the court itself to draw that inference, since such fact finding is the task of the arbitrator chosen by the parties, not the reviewing court. Furthermore, the award ordered Cooper's reinstatement in his old job or an equivalent one for which he was qualified, and it is not clear that he would pose a threat to the asserted public policy in every such alternative job.

Questions

1. Whose idea was it to have an arbitrator resolve disputes between the employer and the workers?
2. Was the arbitrator dishonest or did the arbitrator commit fraud in deciding the case?
3. Does *Misco* support or undercut arbitrators' decisions?
4. Which legal ethics support the *Misco* result?
5. Do any business ethics suggest *Misco* is the correct result?

Successor Liability for Collective Bargaining Agreements. Employers frequently try to escape collective bargaining agreements. For example, suppose Company X negotiates a collective bargaining agreement generous to the union and extravagant from X's standpoint. X soon realizes that it made a mistake in signing the agreement because its labor costs put it at a competitive disadvantage. Suppose X sells out to Y. Does Y, called a successor employer, have to honor X's CBA? A successor employer has an obligation to bargain in good faith with the union representing employees of the predecessor employer, assuming substantial continuity is demonstrated between the predecessor and successor employers. However, the successor employer is not bound to the substantive provisions of the predecessor CBA.

Devices Affecting Union Security

Four devices affecting union security are state right-to-work laws, closed shops, union shops, and agency shops.

Right-to-Work Laws. Right-to-work laws are state laws that let individuals working for unionized employers refuse to join the union and also not pay union dues or fees.

Unions must represent all employees in the bargaining unit, even non-dues-paying, nonunion employees, called "free riders." The **state right-to-work laws** are permitted by Section 14(b) of the NLRA. About half of the states have such laws.

State right-to-work laws are not union security devices. Right-to-work laws undercut unions and, depending on one's point of view, can be either condemned or supported. Familiarity with right-to-work laws helps one understand the union security devices of closed shops, union shops, and agency shops.

Closed Shops. The closed shop protects unions by requiring that employers hire only union member job applicants. In other words, before an employer can consider hiring a job applicant, the employer must first determine whether that applicant is a union member. If the applicant is not a union member, the person may not be hired.

Closed shops arise from closed-shop clauses put in union-employer collective bargaining agreements. The NLRA [in Sections 8(a)(3) and 8(b)(2)] now makes the closed shop illegal.

Union Shops. Union shops require an employee to join a union after a specified time frame (often 30 days) after going to work for a unionized employer. Collective bargaining agreements with union shop clauses create union shops. Union shops are legal under the NLRA.

Agency Shops. Agency shops originate from clauses put in union-employer collective bargaining agreements. Agency shops require that a person pay to the union an amount equal to union dues and fees after going to work for a unionized employer. This arrangement is legal. Agency shops do not require that an employee join the union—only that the employee pay to the union the dollar value of union dues and fees. In states with right-to-work laws so providing, employees do not even have to pay the equivalent of dues and fees (they can be free riders), and the union still has a duty to represent them.

If employees pay the equivalent of union dues and fees, why should they not join the union? The answer lies in the enforceability of union rules. If an employee is a union member, the employee must follow union rules. If union members violate these rules, they can be fined. These fines are enforceable in court (civilly, not criminally). However, employees who do not join the union but merely pay the equivalent of dues and fees are not subject to union fines. This fact is not well known, and it can affect union discipline.

Strikes and Lockouts

Strikes and lockouts are devices that unions and employers use to pressure one another to enter collective bargaining agreements with terms favorable to them. **Strikes** are used by unions. In a **lockout**, the employer temporarily refuses to let employees work. Thus, a lockout is an employer device to pressure employees. With some limits, strikes and lockouts are legal under the NLRA.

Whipsaw strikes refer to union strikes against one or a few, but not all, employers in a multiemployer bargaining group while union labor continues to work for one or a few employers. The union attempts to pressure the struck employers to agree to bargaining demands by putting them at a competitive disadvantage. Whipsaw strikes are legal. Employers in a multiemployer bargaining group often respond to whipsaw strikes with lockouts. Lockouts neutralize what would otherwise be the competitive disadvantage of whipsaw strikes. Lockouts in response to whipsaw strikes are also legal.

Employers may hire temporary or permanent replacements for employees on **economic strikes**. Economic strikers are entitled to full reinstatement when their permanent replacements leave unless strikers get equivalent work elsewhere. However, if employees strike in response to an employer ULP, the employer may only temporarily replace them. If the ULP strikers unconditionally offer to return to work, the employer must reinstate them fully.

Secondary Boycotts

Secondary boycotts generally refer to requiring or forcing someone to stop handling another's products or doing business with another person. Either unions or employers can commit them. Usually the NLRA makes secondary boycotts unfair labor practices and hence illegal. The NLRA condemns secondary boycotts essentially because it wants to confine labor disputes to the immediate parties (the employer and union directly involved). Thus, the NLRA legalizes direct economic weapons, called **primary activities**, by the union against the employer, such as primary strikes, and by the employer against the union, such as the lockout. However, the NLRA has a general policy forbidding unions or employers from involving third parties in their disputes. Again, the reason is to confine the dispute and minimize economic disruptions accompanying union-employer strife.

A secondary boycott could occur in the following manner. U union has a labor dispute with Jack Driver's golf company. Jack is the primary employer. If U union forces KMart to stop buying golf clubs from Jack's company, it is engaging in a secondary boycott. KMart is the secondary employer. U union's conduct violates the NLRA's prohibition on secondary boycotts. Jack, the primary employer, can sue and recover damages from U union. Jack may not get injunctive relief to stop this illegal boycott, although the NLRB could.

Another example of a secondary boycott prohibited by the NLRA Section 8(e) occurs if U union induces Jack to sign a collective bargaining agreement not to deal with any employer with whom U union has a dispute. The two exceptions to such agreements are on-site construction and the garment industry. These exceptions let employers agree with unions not to handle certain products of people with whom the union has a dispute.

In the *Woodwork Manufacturers Association v. NLRB* case, a question at issue was whether the carpenter's union committed a secondary boycott by refusing to handle prefitted doors (those not finished at the job site). The basis for the alleged secondary boycott was a "will not handle" clause in the union-building contractor collective bargaining agreement. [Recall that Section 8(e) of the NLRA makes it illegal for employers and unions to agree to boycott others' products.] The U.S. Supreme Court in the *National Woodwork Manufacturers* case refused to hold that the union's actions were a prohibited secondary boycott, because the clause was designed to preserve carpenters' on-site work, not to expand carpenters' work. The union's intent in including the "will not handle" clause was not aimed at a secondary party (door manufacturers) but rather was to preserve work with the primary employer (the building contractors).

VOTING OUT THE UNION: DECERTIFICATION ELECTIONS

Suppose Jack Driver's employees have had a union for three years. After assessing their costs (union dues, having to attend union meetings and pay attention to how the union is run, and lost work time from strikes) and benefits (higher wages and better working conditions), they decide that having a union is not worth the costs. Can they get rid of the union? Yes.

One way employees can eliminate an existing union is through a **decertification election**. One or several employees or another person or union acting for the employees may file a decertification petition with the NLRB. Along with the decertification petition, at least 30 percent of the employees must indicate that they want decertification. The NLRB then conducts a decertification election by secret ballot. If a majority of employees vote to decertify the union, it no longer is the collective bargaining agent.

Employers may *not* file decertification petitions. If Jack Driver learns that some of his employees are unhappy with their union and encourages or helps them to file a decertification petition, he commits a ULP [Section 8(a)(1) violation].

UNIONS FOR GOVERNMENT EMPLOYEES

The National Labor Relations Act does not cover employees in the public sector (government employees). The sovereignty doctrine, which says that the federal government is the supreme lawgiver (although in a democracy, the people are the ultimate source of lawmaking power), explains why federal workers are treated differently from private sector employees regarding unions. State and municipal governments (in addition to the national or federal government) also give their workers fewer collective bargaining rights than business workers have.

Labor Laws Covering Federal Employees

When Congress passed the Civil Service Reform Act of 1978 it set up the Federal Labor Relations Authority. This body hears unfair labor practice complaints from federal workers. It also can hear requests that bargaining be allowed for certain issues. The catch is that, unlike employees who work for private businesses, federal workers may *not* bargain about wages, hours, and fringe benefits. Federal agencies (the employers) may, however, bargain about some aspects of their employees' jobs, such as work equipment, the number and grades of "job slots," and certain work rules. Federal employees (including postal workers) have no right to strike.

Labor Laws Covering State and Municipal Government Employees

Most states allow public employees to form unions. However, even though these states allow state workers to unionize, they do not let such workers strike, thus weakening state employee unions. A few states allow certain government workers to strike in limited circumstances. However, public workers, such as teachers, do occasionally have illegal strikes. As with businesses whose employees illegally strike, state and municipal governments sue for injunctions to order the employees back to work.

CHAPTER SUMMARY

Labor unions in the United States were at one time treated as criminal conspiracies designed to restrain trade in the labor market. Over time, courts and the legislatures have recognized labor unions' legal right to exist. In recent years, however, labor union membership in the United States has declined both in absolute numbers and as a percentage of the nonfarm workforce.

The Supreme Court ruled in the *Danbury Hatters* case that labor unions were subject to the Sherman Act.

The Clayton Act in 1914 unsuccessfully tried to exempt labor unions from the federal antitrust laws.

In 1932 the Norris-LaGuardia Act removed federal court jurisdiction to issue injunctions in peaceful labor disputes.

The National Labor Relations Act, passed in 1935, established the National Labor Relations Board (NLRB) and defined unfair labor practices that employers, but not unions, could commit.

Employer unfair labor practices include restraining or coercing employees in their right to form, join, and assist unions; employer dominance of labor organizations; employer discrimination regarding hire or tenure to encourage or discourage union membership; employer discrimination against an employee who has filed charges or testified under the NLRA; employer refusal to bargain with employees; and an employer commission of secondary boycotts.

In 1947 Congress enacted the Labor-Management Relations Act, also known as the Taft-Hartley Act. This act outlined for the first time unfair labor practices labor unions could commit.

Two types of cases can come before the National Labor Relations Board: R (representation) cases and C (complaint) cases.

Three ways an employer's workers can unionize are by (1) voting in the union at a representation election; (2) employees signing cards authorizing that the union represent them; and (3) the NLRB ordering the employer to bargain with the union.

The election bar and contract bar rules limit the frequency of representation elections. Employers may move their operations if their reasons for doing so are solely economic and not motivated by anti-union animus. Employers who do move their plants to encourage or discourage unions commit an unfair labor practice.

Under certain circumstances an employer may enter bankruptcy to escape collective bargaining agreements.

Devices affecting union security include right-to-work laws, closed shops, union shops, and agency shops.

Lockouts refer to employer actions to temporarily refuse to let employees work. Strikes occur when workers withhold their services from employers.

MANAGER'S ETHICAL DILEMMA

Neel Warren owned a company in Wisconsin that made auto seat covers. Neel became alarmed at his labor costs, particularly because his foreign competitors paid their employees only one-third to one-half of what Neel paid his employees. Labor was a sizable component of his costs of production.

One day Neel decided to call the governors of Tennessee, Georgia, Mississippi, and Alabama to see whether they would be interested in having a 300–person factory relocated there. The response was instantaneous and uniform: Each governor leaped at the opportunity! The different governors put forth packages offering Neel tax incentives (low or forgiven real property taxes, low unemployment taxes, low workers' compensation costs) and free buildings for several years. What ethical considerations (refer to Chapter 1) should Neel consider in deciding whether to remain in Wisconsin or relocate in another state?

Discussion Questions

1. Why do you think labor union membership has dropped so significantly in the past 20 years? Notice a further trend in the United States: Medical doctors and psychologists, feeling the pinch of government constraints on permissible fee reimbursements, have recently taken steps to unionize. Thus while the blue collar workforce is becoming less unionized, the white collar workforce is in the process of becoming more unionized. What ethics discussed in Chapter 1 might account for this trend?
2. Why do you suppose a separate "court" system has been established for the trial of unfair labor practices? The name of that court system is the National Labor Relations Board with its network of administrative law judges. How does the NLRB law judge (ALJ) hearing differ from the usual trial court? Is a jury ever part of an administrative hearing? Who benefits most in this setting? Who loses?
3. What evidence indicates that federal labor law has not always treated union and employer alike? When did employer unfair labor practices come into being? When were union unfair labor practices created?
4. Currently intense employer pressure is present to decertify unions as collective bargaining agents. What factors in the business environment could account for their motivation? Are company-sponsored unions legal? What realities have unions run into in their incessant efforts for improved wages, hours, and working conditions?
5. How true do you think the following statement is? "The union movement in the United States prevented the country from becoming communistic."
6. In *Dal-Tex*, which follows, what was so threatening about the employer's remarks? Explain what we mean when we say that the atmosphere surrounding representation elections is supposed to be one of laboratory conditions.

   In *Dal-Tex Optical* [132 NLRB 1782 (1962)], the NLRB held that the following employer statements were threats and hence exceeded the free speech right:

   Two years ago the I.U.E. Union tried to organize this plant. They went to every length to cause trouble. They misrepresented all of the facts. They conducted a vicious campaign. They did not then, nor do they now, represent any optical laboratory in Texas. Our employees were not fooled and voted against the Union by a large majority. The Union lost the election. This election was conducted by a secret ballot and was a fair election, but the Union could not stand being beaten and attempted to set aside the election. They introduced evidence before the Board, which I considered then, and do now consider, to be false and perjured. A year and a half after the election the National Labor Relations Board, based upon such evidence, decided that the election should be set aside and a new one held. After another six months the Board then decided to hold another election next week. The Company does not agree with the Board, and has maintained and is going to maintain that the election held two years ago was a valid election. And the Courts are going to have to decide whether this first election was valid. In the meantime, the Company is permitting the holding of this new election on Company property on September 22nd, because it feels that your rights can be better protected. If the Union should win this election, which I don't think it can, the Courts are still going to have to determine whether the Board was right or wrong. If the Board was wrong, which I firmly believe, the election to be held on September 22nd will not mean a thing if the Union wins it. My guess is that it will be another couple of years before this matter is settled. In the meantime we will go on just as we are without any Union. I am explaining all of this to you so you will understand that wild promises by this Union of what is going to happen here if the Union wins don't mean a thing. I believe in law and order. When the Courts decide the matter I will abide by the decision of the Courts.

   [After detailing some of the benefits employees were receiving:]

   So, why should you want a Union to represent you? Is it because you believe they can get you more than you now have, or have you been told the Union will run this plant? I have made it a practice of giving back in increased wages all efficiency gains during the year. During the year 1959 there were 270 individual raises given. During the year 1960 there were 298 raises given, and during this year already there have been 349 raises given.

These are merit raises. These are raises that you get in addition to your profit sharing and pension plans. I not only provide for your old age and your family in case of your death, but as the efficiency improves you get the benefit of it in increased wages. Do you want to gamble all of these things? If I am required by the Court to bargain with this Union, whenever that may be, I will bargain in good faith, but I will have to bargain on a cold-blooded business basis. You may come out with a lot less than you have now. Why gamble because agitators make wild promises to you? If I am required to bargain and I cannot agree there is no power on earth that can make me sign a contract with this Union, so what will probably happen is the Union will call a strike. I will go right along running this business and replace the strikers. There has been a lot of talk about your being skilled workers. You only do one operation and in a short period I can train anybody to do any of these operations, as we trained most of you. I am not afraid of a strike. It won't hurt the Company. I will replace the strikers. They will lose all of their benefits. Strikers will draw no wages, no unemployment compensation and be out of a job. The Union won't pay you wages. The Union has nothing to lose. You do all of the losing. No employee is so important that he or she cannot be replaced. I am not afraid of threats. Before the last election this Union tried everything. Before this election is over, you will see how dirty the Union will get. It has no responsibility. It is not reasonable to believe that you would give up your individual rights to outside agitators and not be able to come to me as you have in the past with your problems. I cannot believe you want to change to the cold-blooded bargaining basis that must follow.

[In the September 19 speech he stated, among other things:]

Will the union get you more wages? No, who pays the wages? I do. I built this plant. I invest the capital. I see to it that it runs 52 weeks a year. I see that the orders come in. I have consistently turned back to you in increased wages all efficiency gains made by the Company. I give hundreds of increase[s] in wages that are merited. In 1960 I gave 349 raises. This year I have already given 442 raises. This is the right way to handle wages. The result is that you have the highest wages in the industry. This I can assure you, it is my position now, and it will be my position at all times, that you will get merit raises just as I have been giving them over the years. If you don't merit them, you will not get them. This is nothing new. It is the system I have operated on from the beginning. I do not have to, nor will I change it. If you believe promises the Union makes you, you will find out the Union doesn't pay wages. I do. The Union doesn't give raises. I do. Now, please remember you have to compare your wages with those of other optical laboratories in Dallas, Texas. We are at the top. It does not make any difference what Collins Electric pays or any other industry. It is what is paid in our industry. No Union and no company in our industry in Texas can match our wages and benefits.

7. Suppose a union does an ineffective job of representing its members during collective bargaining talks. To what standard does the U.S. Supreme Court hold unions in representing their members? The *Air Line Pilots Association v. O'Neill* case 111 S.Ct. 1127 (1991) provides an answer.

Suggested Readings

Articles

CUNNINGHAM, "The North American Free Trade Agreement: The Sale of U.S. Industry to the Lowest Bidder," 10 *Hofstra Labor Law Journal* 413 (1993).

GOTTESMAN, "Rethinking Labor Law Preemption: State Laws Facilitating Unionization," 7 *Yale Journal on Regulation* 355 (1990).

GREGORY, "The Right to Unionize in the United States, Canada, and Mexico: A Comparative Assessment," 10 *Hofstra Labor Law Journal* 537 (1993).

PALEWICZ, "Attacking the Body Corporate: Union Corporate Campaigns," 26 *Maryland Bar Journal* 34 (1993).

PARIGI et al., "Labor Law and the Future of Organized Labor Under the Clinton Administration," 44 *Labor Law Journal* 313 (1993).

ST. ANTOINE, "How the Wagner Act Came to Be: A Prospectus," 96 *Michigan Law Review* 2201 (1998).

ST. ANTOINE, "Mandatory Arbitration of Employee Discrimination Claims: Unmitigated Evil or Blessing in Disguise?" 15 *Thomas M. Cooley Law Review* 3 (1998).

ST. ANTOINE, "Divergent Strategies: Union Organizing and Alternative Dispute Resolution," 45 *Labor Law Journal* 465 (1994).

SCHUPP, "Employer Property Rights Versus Union Right to Access," 44 *Labor Law Journal* 361 (1993).

TWOMEY, "The *Hammondtree* Challenge to the NLRB's Deferral Policy," 23 *Business Law Review* 225 (1990).

Books

LESLIE, *Labor Law in a Nutshell*, 3rd ed. (1992).

MODULE

5

LAW AFFECTING BUSINESS FINANCING

CHAPTER

18

BUSINESS ORGANIZATIONS

"TIS THE ONLY COMFORT OF THE MISERABLE TO HAVE PARTNERS IN THEIR WOES."

Cervantes, Don Quixote

"IF THERE WERE A READING PUBLIC NUMEROUS, DISCERNING, AND IMPARTIAL, THE SCIENCE OF ETHICS, AND ALL THE VARIOUS SCIENCES WHICH ARE NEARLY RELATED TO ETHICS, WOULD ADVANCE WITH UNEXAMPLED RAPIDITY."

John Austin

POSITIVE LAW ETHICAL PROBLEMS

In 1965 CPC Corporation thought that the Ott Corporation looked like a good investment. CPC incorporated a wholly owned subsidiary to purchase the assets of Ott Chemical Company. Prior to CPC's takeover and in the course of its operations, Ott had polluted the land it operated on. In 1972 CPC sold the Ott facility to Story Chemical Company, which operated the facility in a manner that polluted the environment until its bankruptcy in 1977, when Aerojet-General Corporation created a wholly owned subsidiary to buy the highly polluted property. In 1981 the U.S. Environmental Protection Agency sought to have CPC (among others) pay tens of millions of dollars for the environmental cleanup of the land its subsidiary corporation formerly owned. Can a parent corporation ever be liable for environmental cleanup costs of its corporate subsidiary?

"The board of directors' action in accepting the lower bid for corporate assets violates the directors' duty to shareholders to maximize shareholder value," shouted Fred Pittman, a minority shareholder in Forest Manor, Incorporated. Forest Manor, Inc., was a corporation whose main asset was a nursing home. A majority of the board decided to sell the nursing home. Two bids were received, one from Alexandria Investments for $4.8 million and the other from Group 2, for $4.896 million. The board accepted the *lower* bid. Did this action violate any board duty to the minority shareholders who wanted the board to accept the higher bid?

This chapter's objective is to survey the legal forms a business can take and to point out some advantages of each. A business can select from a wide variety of legal forms, including the sole proprietorship, business trust, partnership, limited partnership, limited liability partnership (LLP), limited liability company, (LLC) and corporation.

SOLE PROPRIETORSHIPS

A sole proprietorship is simply any person in business to make a profit for himself or herself alone. According to the *Statistical Abstract of the United*

States (1999 edition), for the year 1996 an estimated 16,956,000 nonfarm sole proprietorships filed federal tax returns in the United States. The same source estimated total business receipts from sole proprietorships for 1996 as $844 billion, with total net income of $177 billion.

Legal Form

A **sole proprietor** owns the business and its property in her or his individual name but may have employees to help in the business. The sole proprietor may operate under an assumed or fictitious name. For example, Jane Keeling may own a drugstore called "Arrow Pharmacy." States have fictitious name statutes, which require registry of assumed names; generally, the penalties for noncompliance with fictitious name statutes are not severe.

Reasons for Sole Proprietorships

Reasons for having sole proprietorships include simplicity, control, convenience, and privacy. Few legal formalities must be observed to form a sole proprietorship, although some rules apply. For example, a retailer must obtain a sales tax license and secure an occupational license before doing certain types of work. The state of Illinois, for example, requires licenses for more than 180 occupations ranging from florist to insurance broker.[1] The lack of such a license can mean that contracts entered by persons in such professions are unenforceable or void.

The *Brady v. Fulghum* case shows what can occur when a building contractor does not have an occupational license.

Brady v. Fulghum
Supreme Court of North Carolina
308 S.E.2d 327 (1983)

Background and Facts:

Plaintiff brought this action for monies allegedly due under a contract for construction of a private dwelling. In affirming summary judgment for defendants, the Court of Appeals concluded that plaintiff, a general contractor, had not complied "substantially" with the statutory licensing requirements.

In February 1980, plaintiff agreed with defendants by written contract to construct their house for a price of approximately $106,850. Plaintiff began construction on or about 13 March 1980. Neither during the negotiation of this contract nor when he began performance was plaintiff licensed as a general contractor as required by North Carolina law.

Plaintiff was awarded his builder's license on 22 October 1980, having passed the examination on his second attempt. At that time, he had completed two-thirds of the work on defendants' house. Defendants paid plaintiff $104,000. Plaintiff by this legal action seeks an additional $2,850 on the original contract and $28,926.41 for "additions and changes" requested by defendants during construction.

Body of Opinion

Justice Exum

The legislature has provided a mechanism for certification of general construction contractors.... This process...protects the public by insuring confidence and integrity within the construction industry.... Although the statute does not expressly preclude an unlicensed contractor's suit against an owner for breach of contract, *Builders Supply v. Midyette*... held the contractor may not recover on the contract or in quantum meruit when he has ignored the protective statute.

After *Midyette*, the Court of Appeals decided several cases including the one at bar, in terms of whether the contractor had "substantially" complied with the licensing statutes....

[1] A complete list is published in Conard, Knauss, and Siegel, *Enterprise Organization* (Mineola, NY: Foundation Press, 1972), pp. 10–11.

Generally, contracts entered into by unlicensed construction contractors, in violation of a statute passed for the protection of the public, are unenforceable by the contractor.... A majority of jurisdictions adhere to this interpretation.... Reading these statutes as being designed to protect the public from irresponsible contractors, ... most state courts find "no legal remedy for that which is illegal itself."... General contractors have been precluded from maintaining actions if they must rely on their illegal act to justify their recovery.... The unenforceability of such contracts by the contractor stems directly from their conception in the contractor's illegal act.

The express language of the North Carolina licensing statute indicates that it is designed to insure competence within the construction industry.... The legislature seeks to guarantee "skill, training and ability to accomplish such construction in a safe and workmanlike fashion."... In tandem, these requirements "protect members of the general public without regard to the impact upon individual contractors."...

In examining the licensing statute in question, we recognize the distinction between legislation designed to produce revenue and to protect the public. In the former situation, the legislature exercises its taxing authority. In the latter, it exercises its police power. Accordingly, when a legislature invokes its police power to provide statutory protection to the public from fraud, incompetence, and irresponsibility, as ours has done with the contractor licensing statutes, courts impose greater penalties on violators.... Making contracts unenforceable by the violating contractor produces "a salutary effect in causing obedience to the licensing statute."... These public policy considerations militate against permitting unlicensed general construction contractors to enforce their contracts....

In recognition of the essential illegality of an unlicensed contractor's entering into a construction contract for which a license is required and in order to give full effect to the legislative intent to furnish protection to the public by strict licensing requirements, we reject the doctrine of substantial compliance, cognizant that harsh consequences may sometimes fall on those who do contracting work without a license....

We do recognize the minority rule, adhered to by our Court of Appeals, is not without some support. California applies the doctrine of substantial compliance in certain cases to avoid unnecessarily harsh results on unlicensed contractors who perform well....

We agree that the existence of a license at the time the contract is signed is determinative and attach "great weight to the significant moment of the entrance of the parties into the relationship."... Accordingly, we adopt the rule that a contract illegally entered into by an unlicensed general construction contractor is unenforceable by the contractor. It cannot be validated by the contractor's subsequent procurement of a license....

In this circumstance there can be no substantial compliance with the licensing statutes. Neither may the contractor recover for extras, additions or changes made during construction commenced pursuant to the contract. Such a contract is not, however, void. Others not regulated by the licensing statutes passed for their protection do not act illegally in becoming parties to such a contract. The policy underlying the licensing statutes would not be served by preventing enforcement by those for whose protection the statutes were passed. These parties may enforce the contract against the unlicensed contractor.... Further, if a licensed contractor's license expires, for whatever reason, during construction, he may recover for only the work performed while he was duly licensed. If, in that situation, the contractor renews his license during construction, he may recover for work performed before expiration and after renewal. If, by virtue of these rules, harsh results fall upon unlicensed contractors who violate our statutes, the contractors themselves bear both the responsibility and the blame.

Plaintiff was unlicensed at the time he negotiated and contracted with the defendants to construct their house. He illegally entered into the contract; it is, therefore, unenforceable by him. His subsequent procurement of a valid license cannot validate or make legal that which was illegal in its inception.

Judgment and Result

Plaintiff loses. Failure to have the occupational license was fatal to the sole proprietor's recovery on the contract to build the house. His subsequent obtaining of the license did not make legal what was illegal at its inception.

Questions

1. Did the contractor have an occupational license to build houses at the time he signed the contract to build the house? Did he obtain such a license after the house in question was built?
2. What is the purpose of occupational licenses? Note that the case mentions two types of occupational licenses—revenue raising and policing (governing practitioner ethical and technical qualifications). Which type of license was the contractor's license in the preceding case?
3. The plaintiff builder in the preceding case was a sole proprietor. Can it be said that sole proprietors have no restrictions on them with respect to entering certain businesses and making contracts?
4. Does the "substantial compliance" doctrine, which states that if one meets most, but not all, of a statute's requirements that the individual may recover under the statute, help one not in full compliance with the positive law? Did the court in the preceding case adopt or reject the substantial compliance doctrine?
5. Was anything structurally wrong with the house that plaintiff built? Could one argue that natural law (justice) lost to positive law (the licensing law) in this case?

PARTNERSHIPS

The 1999 edition of the *Statistical Abstract of the United States* reports an estimated 1,654,000 partnership tax returns were filed in the United States for 1996. Partnership gross receipts for 1995 (the most recent year for statistics) were estimated at $1,042 billion, operating at a total net income of $145 billion. The strengths of using the partnership as one's legal form of business arise from combining the broader talents and material resources of two or more people. The partnership form also has other advantages.

Partnership Advantages

A partnership is easy to form and does not require state approval. Property (real and personal) may be held and transferred by the partnership itself. The partnership may be ignored for federal income tax purposes. In such a case, the partnership income is divided among the partners according to the partnership agreement and taxed as part of their personal incomes. This procedure eliminates "double taxation."

Partnership Disadvantages

A major disadvantage of partnerships is liability exposure, meaning that if a partner or partnership employee (while at work) harms a third person, the victim can seize all the partnership's property as well as each individual partner's assets to pay the damages. For example, if two doctors are partners and one commits malpractice against a patient, the victim can take all the partnership's assets (as well as each partner's individual assets) to pay the loss.

Second, partners must keep minutes of meetings and business records. This requirement is imposed by the Uniform Partnership Act (UPA). Also, partnerships selling partnership interests interstate may have to register such interests as securities under the Federal Securities Act.

Partnership Definition

The UPA's definition of a **partnership** is an "association of two or more persons to carry on, as co-owners, a business for profit." The UPA is the law in all but one state.

If two or more persons do not intend to carry on the business on a long-term basis, it probably is not a partnership. If two or more persons do charitable work, the association is not a partnership because it does not intend to make a profit. The fact that two or more people try but fail to make a profit in a business is irrelevant with respect to the partnership's existence. What is crucial is whether they *intend* to operate a business for profit. If they do, and they intend to do so over a period of time, they are partners.

Partnership Existence

No express agreement is needed between two or more people for a partnership to exist. In other words, the law may hold that two or more people are in a partnership even when they do not intend there to be one. Also, the fact that the parties have said their relationship is not a partnership is not conclusive. The courts use an objective, rather than subjective, test to determine the parties' intent to form a partnership.

Example of the Objective Test. One example in which two parties are partners (even though they did not intend to be partners) occurs when a corporation is defectively organized. Its "shareholders" are treated as partners even though the clear subjective intent that they desired shareholders' limited liability rather than general partners' unlimited liability.

Proving a Partnership's Existence. The burden of proving that a partnership exists is on the party claiming that it exists. Courts look at a number of factors to determine whether a partnership exists. Two of the most important factors are joint right to manage the business and sharing profits and losses.

Profit Sharing. Section 7 of the UPA declares that a person sharing the profits of a business with another is prima facie evidence that she or he is a partner in the business. **Prima facie** evidence means that the evidence is strong enough to allow a judge in a jury trial to let the partnership issue go to the jury, and it can justify (but does not require) a jury's finding that a partnership exists. However, the UPA goes on to say that no prima facie inference that a person is a partner shall be drawn if business profits are received in any of the following ways:

1. As a debt repayment by installments or otherwise
2. As wages of an employee or rent to a landlord
3. As an annuity to a widow or representative of a deceased partner
4. As interest on a loan, although the amount of payment varies with the business's profits
5. As consideration for the sale of a business's goodwill or other property by installments or otherwise

The sharing of gross returns (gross income before expenses are deducted to arrive at a profit figure) does not create a prima facie presumption of partnership. Sharing gross returns also does not establish a partnership's existence, regardless of whether the persons sharing them have a joint interest in property from which the returns are obtained. As these points suggest, the fact that two or more persons jointly own property does not necessarily mean they are partners. However, joint property ownership does not necessarily preclude the joint owners from being partners. Joint ownership is a neutral fact in determining partnership existence.

Right to Manage. The right to share in business management is one of the basic partnership attributes. However, a partnership agreement may confer the management power on one partner only, without destroying the business's legal nature as a partnership. On the other hand, proof that a person has a right to share in partnership management does not establish that he or she is a partner; however, when this fact is coupled with the additional fact of profit sharing, the presumption is that a person is a partner.

Partnership as an Entity. The law treats partnerships as legal entities for some purposes but not others. Partnerships are entities for bankruptcy, suing and being sued (in many states), and owning property. On the other hand, partnerships are not entities for liability purposes. Thus, if someone sues the partnership and gets a judgment that uses up and exceeds all the partnership's assets, individual partners' assets must go toward payment of the debt.

Forming Partnerships

A partnership may be formed between two persons or among three or more persons. Good business practice suggests that the partnership contract be written. If a partnership agreement cannot by its terms be completed within one year, most states' statutes of frauds would require that the partnership agreement be written to be enforceable. For example, if two accountants agree to form a partnership for three years, this partnership agreement cannot be performed within one year and thus would have to be evidenced by a writing signed by the partners to be enforceable. If a partner does not want to honor a partnership agreement, courts will not force him or her into a partnership. In other words, specific performance will not be awarded for breach of a partnership agreement. Damages, however, are given when appropriate.

The *Dalton v. Austin* case shows some problems in determining if a partnership exists.

Dalton v. Austin

Supreme Judicial Court of Maine
432 A2d. 774 (1981)

Background and Facts:

Justice Nichols

The Plaintiff, Emily Dalton (formerly Emily Ruebsamen), appeals from a judgment for the Defendant, Whitney W. Austin, Sr., entered by the Superior Court in Penobscot County after a jury-waived trial on her complaint for conversion of certain financial contributions she had made to a business in Bangor known as The Small Change Restaurant, of which Austin was originally the sole proprietor.

In March of 1974, the Plaintiff and Defendant reached an oral agreement concerning the business, the exact terms of which were the subject of conflicting testimony at trial. The Plaintiff, who had had prior experience in the restaurant business, testified that she and the Defendant agreed to be equal partners in the restaurant and that, in consideration of certain financial contributions she was to make to the business, the Defendant agreed to incorporate the business, turn those business assets to which he had title over to the corporation, and distribute stock to the Plaintiff and himself. It appears, however, that the Plaintiff did not expect the business to be incorporated until after she became involved in its operation.

The Defendant testified that he and the Plaintiff agreed to become partners and that in consideration for being made a partner, the Plaintiff initially contributed her automobile to the business. The Defendant's understanding of the agreement differed from the Plaintiff's, however, in that he did not recall promising to turn assets over to the corporation, or to have stock issued and distributed. Rather, his testimony suggests that the agreement contemplated that the Plaintiff would ultimately purchase the restaurant, thus leaving him "free and clear" of the business, a circumstance the Defendant desired for reasons of health and overwork. In response to questions posed by opposing counsel as to whether the Defendant agreed to transfer assets in his name to the corporation and distribute stock to the Plaintiff, the Defendant testified that he did not remember or understand the agreement but thought the heart of the agreement to be the Plaintiff's ultimate purchase of the entire business.

After the agreement was made, the Defendant no longer took an active part in management of the restaurant; the Plaintiff, on the other hand, operated the business on a day-to-day basis for several months. In the months that she managed the restaurant, the Plaintiff made major financial contributions to the business totalling $18,214.89. She made these contributions by directly paying the debts and operating expenses of the business. The Defendant testified that he had no knowledge of the nature or extent of her payments on behalf of the business and that he never personally received them.

Under Plaintiff's management, business income declined dramatically. After operating the business for several months, the Plaintiff finally asked the Defendant to distribute the stock and transfer the assets. The record does not disclose whether the business was ever incorporated. Stock, however, was never distributed, and the Defendant's testimony suggests that ownership of business-related assets was never transferred to a corporation. Instead, a closing date for sale of the restaurant to the Plaintiff was set. On the advice of her attorneys, however, she ultimately refused to purchase the business from the Defendant and he eventually closed the business when its management totally failed. Thereafter, he made several attempts to lease profitably the business and finally sold it to a lessee. The proceeds from the sale, according to the Defendant's testimony, were used to pay mortgagees and creditors whose claims apparently exceeded the gain from the sale. The Defendant claims to have paid the balance out of personal funds.

At trial, after testimony by the two parties was heard, the presiding justice found for the Defendant. The justice specifically found that the parties were partners and that their original agreement created a partnership. From that finding, he concluded that neither party had a cause of action for restitution or conversion. In response to the request of the Plaintiff's counsel for a specific finding on whether an agreement existed between the parties in which the Defendant was obliged to transfer assets to the corporation and distribute stock, the court declined to rule on the specifics of any such agreement. Rather, the court limited its ruling to finding generally that a partnership agreement existed and that any controversy over the business arising out of the partnership was properly the subject of an action for an accounting between partners.

On appeal here, the Plaintiff contends the Superior Court erred in finding a partnership and in concluding that an action for conversion or money had and received was inappropriate....

The Plaintiff argues that the Superior Court erred in concluding a partnership existed because no evidence of co-ownership or sharing of profits appears on the record.

Under the Uniform Partnership Act...which Maine adopted in 1973, as under the common law, the existence of a partnership is an inference of law based on established facts.... Under the Act, a partnership is defined as "an association of 2 or more persons...to carry on as co-owners a business for profit."

Evidence relevant to the existence of a partnership includes evidence of a voluntary contract between two persons to place their money, effects, labor, and skill, or some or all of them, in lawful commerce or business with the understanding that a community of profits will be shared.... No one factor is alone determinative of the existence of a partnership, but the record before us supports the finding of the Superior Court.

While the specifics of the agreement were in dispute, evidence of an agreement between the parties existed. That agreement clearly related to operation of a business. Assets used in the business and capital contributions to the business were made by both parties. They consistently testified that both regarded themselves as partners. Finally, the Plaintiff actively managed the business for several months.

The Plaintiff contends, nevertheless, that there is no evidence of co-ownership or a sharing of profits. Under the Uniform Act, the concept of co-ownership does not necessarily mean joint title to all business assets. Rather, as the commentary to the Uniform Act suggests, the right to participate in control of the business is the essence of co-ownership.... Contrary to this Plaintiff's contention, then, the record sufficiently supports the existence of co-ownership inasmuch as it reveals that she actively managed the business for several months without the supervision of the Defendant. While the record is devoid of evidence that the parties shared profits, sharing is not required if, as the evidence shows in this case, the agreement itself implies that the parties contemplated the sharing of profits. In the case before us evidence of actual sharing of profits was naturally absent, given the financial straits of the business.

We conclude that the Superior Court did not err in concluding that Austin and Dalton were engaged in a partnership.

The Plaintiff also argues that the Defendant is liable to her for conversion under theories of unjust enrichment or quasi-contract. The Superior Court clearly rejected this argument on grounds that the controversy between the parties over monies spent by Dalton for the business arose out of the partnership itself, and thus the only appropriate remedy under Maine law was an action for accounting.

Under the Uniform Partnership Act, partners have a fiduciary responsibility toward the partnership which obliges them to account for disposition of partnership property. Section 302 of the Act, in pertinent part, gives any partner the right to an account in a wide variety of circumstances, many of which closely resemble the circumstances of the instant case. In particular, section 302(1) gives a partner who has been "wrongfully excluded from the partnership business or possession of its property by his copartners" a right to a formal account. Similarly, section 302(3) gives any partner the right to an account pursuant to the fiduciary duties of every partner set forth in §301. Section 301 provides in part as follows:

> Every partner must account to the partnership for any benefit and hold as trustee for it any profits derived by him without the consent of the other partners from any transaction connected with the formation, conduct or liquidation of the partnership or from any use by him of its property.

These provisions reflect a strong legislative preference, borrowed from the common law, for efficient settlement of partnership disputes involving complex and multifarious aspects in a single proceeding....

Thus, other courts have consistently held that an action derived from the common law brought by one partner against another is inappropriate when the subject matter of the action is directly related to partnership business or property.... In particular, this rule has been applied to actions for conversion of partnership property, actions necessarily involving breaches of fiduciary duty....

In the case before us, the appropriateness of resolving the dispute between the parties through an action for an accounting is clear. The Superior Court concluded that a partnership agreement existed between the parties and that the restaurant business was conducted in the form of a partnership. Once an agreement to form the partnership was struck and business proceeded accordingly, it is apparent that the money the Plaintiff sought to recover in this action was funds spent by her in the course of conducting the partnership business. The circumstance that the parties may have agreed to do business in the corporate form at some later date does not alter the essential character of the form of the business association....

The Plaintiff attempts to distinguish her action from the general rule precluding independent actions on grounds that it rests on a separate legal obligation arising out of the Defendant's alleged promise to incorporate the business, turn assets over to the corporation and distribute stock. In so arguing, she is suggesting that her claim falls within a select group of exceptions to the rule limiting a partner's remedies to an accounting.

Actions by one partner against another in tort or for restitution on a theory of implied contract or unjust enrichment have been allowed by courts in other jurisdictions when the wrong which a plaintiff alleged constituted an injury to an individual in contrast to a partnership interest. Similarly, independent actions have been allowed when the affairs of a partnership are really wound up and the issues before the court can be resolved without extensive study of the partnership accounts.... The record before us indicates that the basis of this Plaintiff's claim is intimately related to partnership affairs. Moreover, the record is replete with confusion and ambiguity concerning the winding up of the partnership as well as the manner in which the partnership property was ultimately liquidated. These circumstances both suggest the prudence of settling the dispute between these two litigants in one comprehensive proceeding for an accounting and provide adequate support for the finding below that an independent action was inappropriate.

Judgment and Result

We conclude that there was no error when the Superior Court entered judgment for the Defendant. The Supreme Judicial Court of Maine agreed with the lower court that Dalton and Austin had a partnership even though no written partnership agreement existed, there was no sharing of profits, and business assets were not jointly owned.

Questions

1. What factors were relied on by the Supreme Judicial Court of Maine to hold that a partnership existed between Dalton and Austin?
2. How did the court answer Dalton's specific arguments that no partnership existed?
3. Assuming Dalton and Austin agreed to organize the business in corporate form at a future date, did their agreement necessarily mean they did not have a partnership before that time?
4. Why are partners not allowed to sue each other for torts or breaches of contract in connection with the partnership? Are such wrongs one partner commits against another corrected in one lawsuit for an accounting?

Aspects of the Partners' Relationship

The Uniform Partnership Act sets out a number of rights and duties partners have with respect to one another. These rights and duties include the following:

1. The right to be repaid the partner's contribution and to share equally in the partnership profits after partnership debts are paid
2. The duty to contribute toward partnership losses (capital or other) according to the partner's share in the profits
3. The right to be indemnified respecting personal liabilities reasonably incurred by a partner in the ordinary and proper conduct or preservation of the partnership business or property
4. The right to be repaid with interest any payment or advance beyond the amount of capital contribution
5. The right to manage the partnership along with the other partners
6. The duty to keep partnership books and the right to inspect and copy such books
7. The duty to render information to copartners regarding all things affecting the partnership
8. A fiduciary duty to copartners much the same as that owed by an agent to a principal

9. The right to a formal account as to partnership affairs if a partner is wrongfully excluded from the partnership business or possession of its property by the copartners or if the right to account is provided in the partnership agreement or any other circumstances rendering an accounting just and reasonable

If the partnership is for a fixed term, say, two years, and the partnership continues beyond the term without any express agreement, the UPA declares that the rights and duties of the partners remain the same as before expiration of the term.

Partners' Agreements. The Uniform Partnership Act allows partners' rights and duties to be varied by their partnership agreement. For example, partners could agree that only one of them has the right to manage the partnership business. Another variation frequently encountered adjusts the profits to which each partner is entitled on the basis of capital contribution or time devoted to managing the partnership affairs.

Suppose, for example, a three-person partnership is composed of A, B, and C, with A and B each contributing 25 percent of the partnership capital and C contributing 50 percent. Even if A, B, and C all devote equal amounts of time to managing the partnership, C might be justified in insisting on a provision in the partnership agreement that gives him 50 percent of the profits. If no such provision is included, the partners will divide the profits equally, even though C paid in twice as much as A and B.

Partners are understandably optimistic about their business prospects. They therefore tend to speak only of dividing profits, neglecting to mention losses. If no mention is made of dividing losses but only of profit division, losses are divided in the same way as profits. C, therefore, should try to insert an additional sentence dividing losses equally (or even more favorably from his standpoint). Profits and losses, in other words, do not have to be divided equally among partners, nor do losses have to be divided in the same way as profits. However, if no partnership agreement on the point is specified profits and losses are divided equally.

Partners' Salaries. The UPA general rule is that partners are not entitled to salaries. This rule also exists where the UPA is not the law. The rule, however, may be changed to allow partners to receive salaries for partnership work if the partnership agreement so provides. A reason for the usual no-salary rule is that each partner is entitled to share partnership profits, presumably a salary substitute.

Partners' Suits against One Another. Partners may not sue one another on partnership matters except to end the partnership. This prohibition includes violations of the partnership rights and duties listed previously. The logic of this rule is similar to that of rules generally precluding a husband and wife from suing one another for certain torts: If they cannot get along, they should end their relationship permanently and not expect courts to resolve their differences. Thus, the partners should talk out their disagreements or sue to dissolve the partnership. They can then have one another's violation of partnership rights and duties taken into account in settling partnership accounts when the partnership is brought formally to an end.

Partners' Liability for Copartners' Contracts and Torts. Every partner is an agent of the partnership for the purpose of its business, which sounds as though the partnership is the party from whom recovery is ultimately sought and that the partnership is an entity. However, the UPA drafters generally rejected the idea that a partnership is an entity. The partners—both the one who injured another or entered the contract on the partnership's behalf and the other partners who were not involved—will be sought to be held by the third party. The question will often be, "Did the acting partner have authority to commit a tort or to contract on the other partners'—not the partnership's—behalf?" If the partner committing the tort had the authority to act, the nonacting partner will also be liable.

Partners' Authority. Partners can obtain authority from copartners through express, implied, and apparent authority, or through ratification. Partners may empower each other to act by expressly saying so orally or in a document. Written **express authority** is easier to prove than oral express authority. **Implied authority** arises from express authority and amounts to those acts that are reasonably necessary to accomplish the express authority but that cannot, as a practical matter, be elaborately described. For example, partners selling autos will authorize a copartner to sell the cars, but they will not in detail say, "Open the hood and show the prospect the engine. Describe the engine size. Open and shut the car door to show how solid the car is. Turn on the lights, windshield wipers, and radio to demonstrate how well they work." The assumption is that a thorough salesperson will do all of these things, but seldom will instructions be so elaborate as to mention all of these matters.

Apparent authority arises from some act or omission of a copartner, not the acting partner, that reasonably leads a third person to conclude that the partner has authority to act on a particular matter. The UPA notes that the "act of a partner which is not apparently for the carrying on of the business of the partnership in the usual way does not bind the partnership unless authorized by the other partners." The UPA also notes certain acts by a partner that would not bind the other partners unless the business has been abandoned or all other partners agree. Such acts include assigning partnership property in trust for creditors or on the assignee's promise to pay the debts of the partnership, disposing of the partnership's goodwill, confessing a judgment, submitting a partnership claim or liability to arbitration or reference, or doing any other act that would make it impossible to carry on the ordinary business of the partnership.

Ratification occurs when a partner commits an act unauthorized by the other partners, and the other partners later learn of the act and approve it. The legal effect of this after-the-fact authority is to bind the person ratifying.

The matter of a partner's liability for a copartner's tort is also addressed by the UPA. It states that any wrongful act or omission of any partner acting in the ordinary course of the business of the partnership or with the authority of the copartners and causing loss or injury to any third person subjects the acting partner and all other partners to joint and several liability. Under **joint and several liability**, a partner could be forced to pay the entire tort judgment obtained against a copartner who injured others within the scope of the partnership. All partnership property and all of each individual partner's property may be seized to pay the tort judgment against the individual partner who commits the tort if it is within the scope of the partnership.

A partner's liability for partnership torts is joint and several. In jurisdictions that have abolished contributory negligence in favor of a comparative fault system in tort law, this system could modify partners' tort liability to one of comparative negligence. A partner's liability for partnership contracts is joint.

Partnership Property

Land and buildings (realty) and personalty,[2] such as typewriters, automobiles, and calculators, are used by partnerships to generate income. Partnerships may own property in the partnership name, although partnership property may be held in a partner's

[2] Personalty is a property classification and generally refers to movables. It is to be contrasted with realty (land and buildings, typically) and fixtures (things permanently attached to realty).

name. It is one way partnerships are regarded by the Uniform Partnership Act as entities, because only entities may own property. Not all property has a title document (a piece of paper officially recognized as evidence of ownership). Realty and automobiles do have title documents (called *deeds* in the case of realty), and statutes require recording of titles before their validity is recognized in many circumstances. However, most other less substantial property (e.g., desks, chairs, computers, office equipment) do not have title documents. One way to establish who owns nontitle-bearing property is by retaining the invoice issued by the seller when the item is purchased. Often the invoice contains the purchaser's name. The partnership's name on the purchase invoice would be evidence that the property belonged to the partnership.

The Uniform Partnership Act defines partnership property as all property originally brought into the partnership or later acquired on the partnership's account. The last clause suggests that keeping the purchase invoice for property without a title document is vital in establishing its identity as partnership property. If property is purchased with partnership funds, it is presumed to belong to the partnership unless a contrary intention appears.

Realty may be acquired in the partnership name. At the same time, realty titled in a partner's individual name is presumed to be partnership property if purchased with partnership funds. This presumption is rebuttable. If the partnership realty is in the partnership's name, it can be transferred only in the partnership name. Where title to partnership realty resides in a partner or partners and not in the partnership, the partner in whose name the realty is titled may convey it to a third person, and this act will bind the partnership if the third person is a good-faith purchaser for value without knowledge of any limit on the conveying partner's authority to transfer it. If the third person knows of the conveying partner's lack of authority to convey the realty or does not give fair value, the other partners may recover the property for the partnership.

Individual Partner's Property Rights. Assuming for a moment that property used by the partnership is partnership property, what rights does an individual partner have in it? The UPA identifies a partner's property rights as being three: rights in specific partnership property, an interest in the partnership, and the partner's right to take part in partnership management. The UPA further says that a partner is a co-owner with his or her partners of specific partnership property as a **tenant in partnership**.

Tenants in partnership have equal rights with other partners to possess specific partnership property for partnership purposes. This right may be modified or eliminated by the partnership agreement. However, a partner has no right to possess partnership property for any nonpartnership purpose unless the other partners agree. Thus, a partner in an insurance firm may not drive the partnership Buick up to Cape Cod for an extended weekend unless the other partners agree.

A partner's **interest in the partnership** is his or her share of the profits and surplus. It is personal property. A partner may sell or convey this interest in the partnership. Doing so does not of itself dissolve the partnership, nor does it make the buyer of the partnership interest a partner. Thus, the buyer of a partner's partnership interest is entitled to the assigning partner's share in the partnership profits, not to share or to manage the business, inspect partnership books, or require any information on account of partnership transactions.

The partnership's continuity and viability as a business is to some extent protected from creditors of individual partners by the UPA's rule that a partner's right in specific partnership property is not subject to attachment or execution. Partnership creditors may attach and execute against partnership property to receive payment for partnership debts, however. Interestingly, homestead and other **exemptions** are not available to the partnership when its creditors seek **execution** against partnership property for partnership debts. Also, the UPA provides that a partner's right in specific partnership property may not be subjected to **dower** (claims by a wife against her husband's realty simply because she married him), **curtesy** (a husband's claim to his wife's realty simply because he married her and they had a child), or other claims of widows, heirs, or next of kin.

Partnership by Estoppel

Partnership by estoppel is a legal theory that a plaintiff will raise against a defendant to attempt to hold him or her for obligations of a partnership of which she or he actually is not a member. Partnership by estoppel applies when the defendant has by words or actions led the plaintiff to believe that the defendant is a partnership member, the plaintiff changes his position in reliance, and the plaintiff sustains damages as a result of relying on such partnership membership. In short, partnership by estoppel has three elements: reasonable reliance that another is a partnership member, change of position in reliance, and damages. The person asserted to be a partner by estoppel is not, in fact, a partner. Yet, if these three elements of partnership by estoppel can be established, the defendant is estopped (stopped) to say that he or she is not a partner, making the defendant liable to the plaintiff for the partnership obligation in question.

LIMITED PARTNERSHIPS

Sometimes a person wishes to join another in a business but does not want to take an active role in managing the business or be subject to unlimited liability for partnership claims greater than the original capital contribution. Short of incorporating (with attendant double taxation, increased red tape in filing annual state reports, and the problems of qualifying to do intrastate business in other states), what, if anything, can be done to satisfy such a person?

The limited partnership is a possible answer to the problem just posed. The limited partnership is made possible because of the Uniform Limited Partnership Act (or the Revised Uniform Limited Partnership Act), which is the law in all states except Louisiana,[3] plus the District of Columbia and the Virgin Islands. The Uniform Limited Partnership Act (ULPA) lists certain requirements for forming a limited partnership. A filing of the articles of limited partnership (partnership agreement) or a specified information document with a public office is required by each state's ULPA. Documentation requirements vary among the states' ULPAs, particularly with respect to the forms to be filed and the place of filing.

Partners in Limited Partnerships

Any limited partnership must have at least one **general partner**. This person's (or persons') liability for all the obligations of the limited partnership is unlimited. The **limited partner** (or partners) is liable, however, only for the amount of capital contribution he or she agreed to make.

Limited Partner Registry

Ordinary partnerships do not and may not have limited partners; only limited partnerships may do so. The reason for allowing the limited partnership to exist is to help

---

[3] Louisiana recognizes by statute the partnership in commendam, which is essentially the same thing as the limited partnership (and in some respects is the first legal recognition of the limited partnership in the United States. See 55 *Tulane Law Review* 515).

the partnership attract investors. The limited partnership creditors are protected (from being misled into believing they are extending credit to a partner who has unlimited liability) by the registration of the limited partnership articles in a public office. Potential creditors of the limited partnership should go to such a registry to see whether the partnership is listed as limited. In the case of a limited partnership, note should be taken of which partners are limited.

Limited Partners Are Passive

The limited partner is supposed to be passive with respect to management of the limited partnership business. The more active a limited partner is in managing the firm's business, the greater the risk that the limited partner will become a general partner. If this situation occurs, the partner has unlimited liability.

The Revised Uniform Limited Partnership Act (RULPA) permits limited partners to engage in certain management functions while retaining their limited partner status. Among such actions are serving as an agent, contractor, or consultant for the limited partnership; serving as a surety for the limited partnership; approving or disapproving amendments to the limited partnership agreement; voting on dissolution, winding up, or transferring all or most of the limited partnership assets to others; changing the business in which the partnership is engaged; or removing a general partner.

The *Obert v. Environmental Research & Development* case raises several issues concerning limited partnerships including the following: May a corporation be a general partner in limited partnership? May the limited partners carry on the partnership following the discharge of the general partner for cause? Do a majority of the limited partners have a fiduciary duty to the general and remaining limited partners not notified of proposed action of removing the general partner? May the limited partners act without holding a meeting?

Obert v. Environmental Research & Development

Supreme Court of Washington
112 Wash. 2d 323, 771 P.2d 340 (1989)

Background and Facts:

Plaintiffs are approximately 50 entities and individuals all of whom are limited partners of the Campus Park Associates Limited Partnership, a Washington limited partnership. The defendant, ERADCO, is a Washington corporation whose stock is owned entirely by Patrick and Rosemary Easter.

The primary asset of the Campus Park LP is an 83-acre parcel of rural land located in Federal Way, Washington, which was purchased for $2,472,333 in December 1978. In 1978, ERADCO sold limited partnership units of the Campus Park LP to the plaintiffs through the use of a private placement memorandum. At the time of the purchase of the partnership units, each of the Campus Park LP limited partners and ERADCO entered into a limited partnership agreement.

ERADCO acted as the general partner of Campus Park LP from its inception in 1978 until May 5, 1984. In May 1984, 74.4 percent of the ownership of Campus Park LP amended the limited partnership agreement and voted by proxy to remove ERADCO as general partner, electing the Pace Corporation (Pace), a Washington corporation, as successor general partner. On or about May 5, 1984, an amended certificate of limited partnership was filed with the State of Washington amending the limited partnership agreement and replacing ERADCO with Pace as the new general partner. A King County Superior Court Judge confirmed the replacement of ERADCO by Pace on November 27, 1984. A later amendment to the certificate of limited partnership was made, naming Robert Gerend as an additional cogeneral partner of the Campus Park LP.

At the bench trial, the court found that prior to its removal, ERADCO had breached several fiduciary duties owed to the Campus Park LP limited partners, specifically:

(a) ERADCO failed to provide audited financial statements as required by the Limited Partnership

Agreement. Some financial statements were eventually produced, but they were not timely....

(b) ERADCO failed to pay real estate taxes on the Campus Park property for the years 1979, 1980, 1981 and 1982 until late 1982. This was contrary to the terms of the Deed of Trust, placing the limited partnership in default of its deed to its seller.

(c) Defendants failed to keep a reserve account as set forth in the Limited Partnership Agreement for the payment of taxes and assessments.

(d) Defendants failed to keep adequate land management time records for the "actual time" it alleges it spent in managing the limited partnership property. This timekeeping requirement was provided for in the Limited Partnership Agreement and represented in the Private Placement Memorandum. ... Finally, some of the entries were fictitious, leaving an overall lack of confidence in ERADCO's attention to this fiduciary duty.

(e) Defendants borrowed monies from the limited partnership's bank, Westside Federal Savings and Loan, for its own purposes and pledged as collateral the separate limited partnership savings accounts of Campus Park. Also used as collateral to secure their borrowings were the Limited Partnership accounts of other limited partnerships. Also as part of the collateral agreement with the bank, ERADCO and Easter agreed to restrict the use of those limited partner accounts for the duration of its loans. The monies were kept in a five and one-half percent (5-1/2%) interest bearing account rather than being placed in an account earning interest at the current market rate of at least twelve percent (12%) or more. This practice started in May 1981 with the Campus Park account and terminated May 1982 at the request of the Campus Park limited partners. ERADCO continues to use other limited partnership savings accounts as collateral for its separate borrowings. The State Securities Division asked ERADCO and Easter to stop this practice but it has continued the loans against the limited partnership savings accounts. [The trial court found that the amount of damage to the limited partners in lost interest as a result of these actions was $2,100.]

(f) In December 1983 ERADCO commingled the separate monies of the Campus Park limited partnership with its own monies in its corporate account at the First Interstate Bank. One Hundred Fifty-five Thousand Dollars ($155,000) of limited partnership funds were transferred from the Campus Park savings account at Westside Federal Savings and Loan into an ERADCO corporate checking and savings account, which account had approximately One Hundred Fifty Dollars ($150) of other funds in it. ERADCO commingled Campus Park limited partnership funds with its own with the clear purpose of inflating ERADCO's own financial statement for its own borrowings. This commingling was not disclosed to the limited partners at the time and was not reflected in any audited or unaudited financial statements of either ERADCO or Campus Park. It also subjected those funds to unlimited risk as ERADCO had not paid its withholding taxes to the IRS, which had begun action to collect the overdue taxes.

In addition, the trial court found that ERADCO was unable to substantiate approximately 75 percent of its land management fees that the limited partners had already paid ERADCO, an amount totalling $127,181.32.

Despite these breaches, ERADCO did make capital contributions to the Campus Park LP in the amount of $24,076.83, a portion of the amount required under the limited partnership agreement. Accordingly, the trial court found that ERADCO was entitled to recover its capital contribution, plus interest in the amount of $4,700.50. In further compliance with the limited partnership agreement, ERADCO performed "program management activities" and "land management activities," and also attempted to market the Campus Park LP real property. The trial court found that in performing its management duties, ERADCO advanced $169,790 in expenses on behalf of the Campus Park LP that are recoverable from the Campus Park limited partners under paragraph 9 of the limited partnership agreement. Finally, the trial court confirmed a total of $1,800 in terms against ERADCO awarded throughout the litigation.

The trial court concluded as a matter of law that the Campus Park general partner could be removed for cause upon a 66 percent vote, and thus confirmed the previous court order confirming ERADCO's removal and Pace's replacement as general partner. Further, the trial court held that as a result of ERADCO's fiduciary breaches it was not entitled to specific performance of the limited partnership agreement. Specifically, the trial court refused to enforce paragraphs 8 and 14 of the limited partnership agreement, denying defendant its 25 percent share of the profit.

The trial court ordered that the sums due each party should be offset against the other, with a net judgment entered in favor of ERADCO in the amount of $67,486.01, that was to be a lien against the property of the Campus Park LP, and paid in five equal annual payments commencing September 18, 1986. The trial court found that ERADCO did not violate the Washington State Securities Act or the Consumer Protection Act.

The Court of Appeals reversed in part when it held that pursuant to RCW 25.10.440 upon the removal of ERADCO as general partner, the failure of the limited partners *unanimously* to elect a successor general partner resulted in the dissolution of the partnership. Further, the court reversed the $169,790 award to ERADCO for reimbursement of advanced expenses as not supported by the findings of the trial court. The court also held that ERADCO had violated the Securities Act, and thus remanded for an award of attorney fees attributable to proving those violations. Finally, the court remanded for a determination of whether ERADCO had violated the Consumer Protection Act....

As to the present status of the limited partnership, plaintiffs represent in their petition for review:

> Since May, 1984 to the present, the Pace Corporation has managed the [Campus Park LP] property and acted in all respects as the [General Partner]. *No Motion for Stay of this authority has ever been proposed by ERADCO.* Indeed, Pace by its President, Robert Gerend, personally guaranteed a $260,000 loan from Puget Sound Bank to the partnership in reliance on the court's ruling and the vote of the limited partners that he was the legal [General Partner].... The partnership is presently solvent and well managed.

Body of Opinion

Justice Pearson

...ERADCO contends the trial court abused its discretion when it denied ERADCO's prayer for specific performance of the profits clause in the Agreement, even though ERADCO breached its fiduciary duty to the limited partners.

Paragraph 8.5 of the Agreement provided for ERADCO to receive a subordinated 25 percent interest in the net profits of the Campus Park LP:

> The General Partner shall receive a subordinated interest of 25% of the net cash proceeds from sale or refinancing of the property, provided, that said fee shall be postponed until all the partners have received cash distributions equal to 100% of their original investment.

This provision was to hold true even in an instance where the general partner was removed for cause:

> In the event of, and upon the removal of the General Partner as provided in subparagraph 14.2.1 of this paragraph [Removal of the General Partner for cause], the General Partner shall receive in cash prior to said removal full payment of the subordinated interest as defined in paragraph 8.5 hereof... The subordinated interest shall be calculated as set forth in paragraph 8.5 above, with the exception that the sales price shall be determined by an independent M.A.I. appraisal, or a bona fide offer to purchase, whichever figure may be the greater, and shall further be treated as if the sale were a cash sale, and the General Partner shall receive his fee forthwith....

Essentially, this provision converts ERADCO's subordinated profit, as provided for in paragraph 8.5, into a preferential profit on the occasion of a breach by ERADCO, and then, subsequently rewards ERADCO upon its removal for cause. While this is not immediately at issue, we note that the propriety of this paragraph is highly questionable, given the nature of the fiduciary relationship. *See Note, Partnership—Disclosure, Fairness and Substantive Administrative Regulation of a General Partner's Fiduciary Duty in a Real Estate Limited Partnership*, 50 Wash.L.Rev. 977 (1975). According to ERADCO's own calculations, this 25 percent subordinated interest is valued at approximately $634,000. This figure is based upon the trial court's finding that the value of the property was $7,000,000 on the date ERADCO was removed as the general partner.

Upon finding that ERADCO had breached its fiduciary duty to the limited partners, the trial court refused to invoke its equitable power to order specific performance of the Agreement and denied ERADCO its contractual 25 percent interest in the profits:

> Paragraph 14 and paragraph 8 of the Limited Partnership Agreement, specifically as they relate to payment of twenty-five percent (25%) of the subordinated profits on sale of the property to the General Partner even when the General Partner is removed for cause, are against public policy as they operate as a disincentive to the limited partners to pursue an action for breach of fiduciary duty against the General Partner. A court acting in equity cannot reward a general partner who breaches its fiduciary duty and breaches the contract by awarding it a profit it has not earned.

We affirm the ruling of the trial court, and hold that it did not abuse its discretion in denying ERADCO's prayer for specific performance of the subordinated profit contractual provision.

Not unexpectedly, ERADCO argues to the contrary. First, ERADCO attempts to minimize the severity of the fiduciary breaches it committed by focusing on the lack of actual damage done to the limited partners. Second, ERADCO contends that since the nature of the fiduciary breaches it committed are unrelated to its contractual right to the 25 percent compensation under the Agreement, the trial court should have no discretion to deny ERADCO its profit. Nevertheless, we find ERADCO's analysis unpersuasive. In point of fact, such arguments attempt to equate a breach of a fiduciary duty to a mere breach of contract. Such is not the law, and a disservice to the law would be done were we to ignore the very real distinctions between the two:

> Not honesty alone, but the punctilio of an honor the most sensitive, is then the standard of behavior. *As to this there has developed a tradition that is unbending and inveterate. Uncompromising rigidity has been the attitude of courts of equity when petitioned to undermine the rule of undivided loyalty by the "disintegrating erosion" of particular exceptions. ... Only thus has the level of conduct for fiduciaries been kept at a level higher than that trodden by the crowd....*

ERADCO incorrectly argues that *Cogan* stands for the proposition that a breaching fiduciary forfeits only those profits related to the breach. On its face, this argument boldly ignores the above quoted language from *Cogan*. It further ignores the trial court's power of discretion regarding the employ of specific performance. Finally, it fails to recognize that all of the profits arising out of the fiduciary relationship with the plaintiff in *Cogan* were denied. In that case, a real estate broker earned a secret commission by representing two parties in a transaction. The court disallowed all of the profit the fiduciary gained from the plaintiff, the party to whom the fiduciary breached its obligation. Nonetheless, the broker was allowed to retain the other principal's commission, an individual not a party to the action. In the case at hand, ERADCO's claim to 25 percent of the profits arises out of the agreement with the parties to whom it owed, and against whom it breached, a fiduciary duty.

This court has held that a denial of specific performance, in an instance of a fiduciary's breach, is in the sound discretion of the court:

> *The Restatement (Second) of Agency* §469 (1958) provides: "An agent is entitled to no compensation for conduct which is disobedient or which is a breach of his duty of loyalty."...

Therefore, once it determined a fiduciary breach had occurred, it is apparent the trial court did not err when it refused to consider the extent of the breaches, or the extent of the damage suffered by the plaintiffs as a result of those breaches. As reflected, *supra*, the court credited ERADCO the amount of its capital contribution plus interest.

Granting it breached its fiduciary obligation, ERADCO argues that the 74.4 percent of the limited partners who voted for ERADCO's removal and Pace's replacement as general partner breached their fiduciary duty by failing to hold a meeting and failing to notify ERADCO and the remaining limited partners of the proposed action. ERADCO's sole basis for this claim is a sentence in paragraph 14.6 of the agreement that provides: "The laws of the State of Washington pertaining to corporate proxies shall govern all Partnership proxies." ERADCO then cites a section of the Washington Business Corporation Act to support its position.

> Any action required by this title to be taken at a meeting of the shareholders of a corporation, or any action which may be taken at a meeting of the shareholders, may be taken without a meeting if a consent in writing, setting forth the action so taken, is signed by all of the shareholders entitled to vote with respect to the subject matter thereof....

The Court of Appeals correctly held that the language of the Agreement, and the inapplicability of this statute, defeated ERADCO's claim.

As previously quoted, the Agreement provides:

> 14.2 Limited Partners shall only have the right to vote upon the following matters affecting the basic structure of the Partnership:
>
> 14.2.1 Removal of the General Partner for cause;
>
> 14.2.2 Election of a successor General Partner...

Additionally, the Agreement provides that a majority vote, defined as 66 percent shall effect passage of the action. Paragraph 14.6 provides: "Each unit holder entitled to vote may do so either in person *or by written proxy*."

There is absolutely nothing in the Agreement, however, that requires a meeting be held when a vote is taken by the limited partners. In fact, the language of paragraph 14.6 suggests otherwise when it allows a *written* proxy. Absent a required meeting, RCW 23A.08.265 is inapplicable. Accordingly, we affirm the Court of Appeals on this issue....

Judgment and Result

Accordingly, we reverse the Court of Appeals holding that the Campus Park LP was dissolved. We affirm the trial court's denial of specific performance of the subordinated profits clause. We affirm the Court of Appeals holding that the limited partners did not breach their fiduciary duties when they removed and replaced ERADCO. Finally, we remand to the trial court for consideration of those issues ruled upon by the Court of Appeals, but not raised in the petitions for review.

Questions

1. What evidence indicated that the general partners were managing the partnership poorly? How serious is it if someone fails to pay real property taxes for three straight years?
2. May a corporation be a general partner? Does allowing a corporation to be a general partner defeat the purpose of requiring someone to be unlimitedly liable?
3. What danger is present in having a unanimity requirement for removal of the general partner by the limited partners? Explain.

BUSINESS TRUSTS

It is possible to understand the business trust by first examining the trust device. A trust involves a settlor, a trustee, a beneficiary, and a res. The **settlor** has property that is to be the **res** (the subject matter of the trust). The **beneficiaries** are the person or persons who are to receive the benefits from the trust. The **trustee** is the person or institution that manages the trust property. A peculiar feature of a trust is that it has two titles (owners)—a legal title and a beneficial title. The trustee holds the legal title, and the beneficiary has the beneficial title (also called the *equitable title*). The beneficiary is usually unable or unwilling to manage property. A trust arrangement lets someone else (the trustee) manage the trust property, while another (the beneficiary) receives its benefits. With this background, we now turn to business uses and variations of the trust, including the business trust, the Massachusetts trust, and the real estate investment trust (REIT).

In a **business trust**, the managers are trustees and the shareholders are beneficial owners. The basic feature of the business trust is that property is placed in the hands of trustees who manage and deal with it for the use and benefit of the shareholders (who are the beneficiaries). The similarities to the trust are apparent. It is a specialized application of the conventional trust applicable to a business's organizational form.

The **Massachusetts trust** is a business organization where property is legally owned by trustees who manage the trust property for the benefit of holders of trust certificates, which are similar to stock certificates. The Massachusetts business trust is an unincorporated association organized under Massachusetts law for investing in real estate in much the same way as a mutual fund invests in corporate securities.

A **real estate investment trust** (REIT) is a financial device in which investors buy shares in a trust and the trust res is invested in real estate. The REIT has been both in and out of favor as an investment device in the past decade.

LIMITED LIABILITY PARTNERSHIPS (LLPs)

The proliferation of lawsuits directed at professionals, such as physicians, has led to the creation of a new legal form, the **limited liability partnership (LLP)**. These entities are creatures of state law, so individual state statutes must be consulted. Generally, however, LLP statutes are patterned after the Uniform Partnership Act with the exception that liability is limited for professional malpractice only. Thus, if five physicians are organized as an LLP and one physician removes a client's liver instead of appendix, only the physician who commits the malpractice will be liable to the injured patient or survivors. On the other hand, if the partnership fails to pay its phone bill, this liability is joint and several among all physician partners.

LLP statutes generally require annual reports to state officials.

LIMITED LIABILITY COMPANIES (LLCs)

A recent development in business organizations is the **limited liability company** (LLC). A number of states have passed laws creating variations of the LLC. Such laws are designed to attract business into a state authorizing the LLC, but given the fact that most states now allow such organizations, this objective is likely to be unrealized.

The LLC is a hybrid form of legal organization, taking some of the most advantageous attributes of partnerships *and* corporations and combining them to form the LLC. Specifically, the LLC is an entity similar to a corporation and has shareholders (called "members") as does a corporation. LLC members have limited liability as do corporate shareholders. Usually at least two members are required but this format permits an unlimited number of LLC members (unlike subchapter S corporations). Also, few restrictions are placed on the type of members, and therefore even a corporation could be a "member."

The federal income tax treatment of LLCs is flexible. In 1996 the U.S. Treasury Department and the Internal Revenue Service (IRS), decided to adopt a "check the box" policy for federal income tax treatment of LLCs. Simply put, this regulation would allow LLCs (as well as unincorporated businesses) to decide whether they want to be treated as a corporation or a partnership for such taxes. Formerly, elaborate tests were used to decide whether a business fell into the "partnership" or "corporation" pigeonhole for federal income tax purposes. This new treatment cuts red tape.

However, some state income tax schemes tax LLC income. This problem is an entirely separate legal issue because states are separate sovereigns under federalism principles.

LLCs, however, do have disadvantages. LLC memberships are not freely transferable. This major limitation explains why LLCs have little future for large enterprises where investors often want to "exit" their investments quickly. Also, as already noted, some states treat LLCs as corporations and impose state income taxes on LLC income—clearly an unfavorable development. Finally, LLCs organized in states allowing such organizations may not have their legal status as LLCs recognized in other states not allowing such organizations.

CORPORATIONS

Corporations play a major role in our economic and political life. The 1999 edition of the *Statistical Abstract of the United States* estimates that in 1996 (the latest year for which figures are available) 4,631,000 federal tax returns were filed from U.S. corporations. Total receipts for such corporations for the same year were $14.890 trillion, and with income of $806 billion.

Definition of a Corporation

The word *corporation* derives from the Latin word *corpus,* which means "body." A **corporation** is a legal person, body, or entity. It is intangible. True, many of the assets owned by the corporation, such as the corporate office building, are visible and tangible, as are the corporate officers, directors, and shareholders. They are not, however, the legal corporation.

What, then, is this legal person, body, or entity called a corporation? It is a **legal fiction**. It is made up, a notion created by the law to satisfy certain social and economic needs. The corporate form allows the small investor to participate in capitalism by dividing up corporate ownership into many small pieces, or **shares**. These shares are then sold to the members of the general public. People who purchase corporate shares are known as **shareholders** or **stockholders**. Although the corporate assets and the total stockholder interest in them can be huge, the shares are often sold at comparatively small prices, having no relation to the size of the corporation.

Limited Liability and Transferable Shares

Another feature of corporations that encourages public purchasing of shares and enables the small investor to participate in corporations is the **limited liability** concept. This idea is an outgrowth of the concept that the corporation is an artificial, legal person. Because a corporation is an entity or a legal person, it can enter contracts. It may be a principal and as such is liable for its agents' or servants' torts committed and contracts entered on its behalf within the scope of their employment. However, the shareholders as shareholders generally are not liable for corporate obligations. This rule has some exceptions, but the important point is that one can purchase corporate stock and not be liable for any greater amount to the corporation or corporate creditors. In other words, the financial risk involved in purchasing corporate stock consists only in the amount one agrees to pay for the stock. If the corporation later goes insolvent, the corporate creditors may not seize the shareholders' individual assets to pay the corporate debt.

One other feature promoting popular participation in stock investment is **transferability of shares**. Although restricting share ownership is possible, most large corporations do not. By allowing transfer of its shares, a corporation enables the investor to sell the stock to another, thereby protecting the investor from being locked in to the corporation.

Professional Corporations

At one time, professionals such as physicians, attorneys, CPAs, architects, and engineers could not organize in the corporate form. However, today many states allow professionals to create a different type of corporation called a professional corporation because all of the shareholders are required to be members of the same profession. Such corporations are often identified with the letters P.A. (professional association), P.C. (professional corporation), or S.C. (service corporation) as part of their name.

One of the major objectives behind professional corporations was to confer limited liability to the professionals/shareholders for the acts of other corporate employees (but not the actor herself or himself) while providing some flexibility in operating the profession or business.

Professionals such as CPAs who are shareholders in a P.C. have limited liability for the P.C.'s debts, with some exceptions. One area presenting an exception involves professional malpractice—negligence related to practicing as a professional. The tort liability of professionals, such as CPAs (who throughout this discussion will be used to represent professionals in general) who are shareholders in a professional corporation, depends on the approach taken by the state's P.C. statute. First, under a conventional corporate approach, one CPA shareholder is not liable for the professional torts of another CPA shareholder. However, some state P.C. statutes make CPA shareholders liable for both their own professional torts and those professional torts of those they supervise. Also, the Model Professional Corporation Act Supplement offers three alternatives, any one of which a state may adopt: (1) treat CPA shareholders as partners for purposes of professional torts (which would make the CPA shareholders vicariously liable for the professional torts of all coworkers); or (2) treat CPA shareholders as they would be treated under conventional corporation statutes (that is, the CPA shareholder would not be liable for other CPA shareholders' professional torts or those of other P.C. employees); or (3) "cap" the CPA shareholders' personal professional liability to an amount by which the P.C. shows financial responsibility (by insurance or surety bond). Suppose a receptionist negligently spills hot coffee on a client. If this act by a P.C. employee is regarded as a professional tort (as incident to the professional service), the CPA shareholder would not be liable if alternative 2 were followed. However, the CPA shareholder would be liable under alternative 1. If alternative 3 were in effect in the state, the CPA shareholder would be liable up to the statutory cap on damages.

A second exception to limited liability concerns a CPA shareholder's vicarious liability for corporate employees' torts; liability will depend on when and where the tort occurred. Of course a CPA shareholder is personally liable for his or her own torts. Generally, CPA shareholders are liable for for coworkers' on-the-job torts but not their off-the-job torts. Thus, if after work, an assistant accountant negligently runs down a little girl while driving to the Kroger store, the assistant accountant, but not the CPA shareholder, would be liable because the tort did not happen on the job.

Corporations' Constitutional Rights

A corporation, being a legal person or entity, is a "person" for purposes of both the U.S. and state constitutions. As discussed in Chapter 5, a corporation is a "person" entitled to due process and equal protection of the laws, which extend to people only. Also, corporations are protected by the Fourth Amendment to the U.S. Constitution, which includes the "right of the *people* to be secure in their persons, houses, papers, and effects, against unreasonable searches and seizures" (emphasis added).

However, corporations are not given all the protections possible under the federal Constitution. Corporations are not "citizens" within the language of the Constitution conferring on citizens "all privileges and immunities of citizens of the several states." The significance of this distinction lies in the fact that a corporation does not legally exist outside of the state that creates it if *intra*state (local) business is transacted in a second state. Corporations do exist outside the creating state regarding *inter*state business.

A corporation organized under the laws of California does not exist legally in Nebraska for purposes of doing intrastate business in Nebraska. The people trying to so operate would legally be a partnership unless they *qualified* to do intrastate business as a corporation in Nebraska. Although it is not exactly the same as reincorporating in Nebraska, certain documents must be filed with Nebraska state officials to enable the California corporation to transact intrastate business in Nebraska.

Law Governing Corporations

The previous discussion points out a significant fact: Almost all business corporations are creations of state, not federal, law. Some are corporations federally chartered, such as the Tennessee Valley Authority. Some interest in passing a federal corporation statute pursuant to the national government's power to regulate interstate commerce continues to be mentioned. As of now, such a proposal is merely talk, but from a business standpoint, the advantage of uniformity and being a corporation in all states with one federal incorporation is apparent.

Currently, even though a corporation is created pursuant to one state's corporation law, other states and the national government may have the power to regulate that state's corporation. For example, if the corporation sells its securities in interstate commerce, the federal securities laws require the registration of securities to be sold. Also, as just discussed, if a corporation is organized in one state and does business in another, it will have to qualify to do intrastate business in the other state.

http://

For an example of a large corporation, visit the website for General Motors at ***http://www.gm.com***

Basic Corporate Definitions

A **domestic corporation** is organized under the state corporation law of the state in which it is located. For example, a corporation organized under the laws of the state of Michigan is a domestic corporation to the state of Michigan. It is contrasted with a **foreign corporation**, which is a corporation organized under the laws of a state other than the state it is in. For example, a corporation organized under Indiana law would be a foreign corporation in Michigan. The foreign-domestic distinction is unrelated to the physical location of a corporation's assets. Many corporations are Delaware corporations, even though they have little in the way of physical plants or equipment there.

Governmental corporations refer to organizations, such as the Federal Deposit Insurance Corporation, that have no profit motive but exist for a social goal. **Municipal corporations** refer to cities and towns that have been given charters by the state to govern a geographic area. **Corporations for profit** are to be contrasted with **corporations not for profit**. Profit corporations are those that may divide profits among shareholders; they do not necessarily have to earn a profit to be so classified. Nonprofit corporations are those that may not turn over earnings to their members. (Nonprofit corporations have no shareholders, merely members.) **Professional corporations** refer to corporations organized by members of certain professions (e.g., physicians, accountants, dentists, and attorneys). The professional corporation is relatively new and offers certain tax advantages and fringe benefits to professionals.

Model Business Corporation Act

The committee on Corporate Laws of the Section of Corporation, Banking, and Business Law of the American Bar Association is responsible for drafting the **Model Business Corporation Act** (hereinafter called the Model Act or MBCA). The Model Act is, as its name suggests, an attempt to give state legislatures ideas for desirable features their state corporation statutes should include. It is up to the legislatures of the individual states whether to adopt the Model Act in whole or in part. Thus far, about half of the states have adopted, at least partially, the MBCA.

Why are states adopting the Model Act? In part, to do what the states of Delaware and New Jersey have long engaged in—attracting firms from other states to incorporate under their tax laws so the state can generate revenue from corporate franchise taxes. The Model Act is a liberal act from management's viewpoint. It gives management considerable power, arguably at the expense of corporate shareholders and creditors. For example, shareholders are given the right to examine corporate books and records but are discouraged from exercising this right by requiring that the shareholder either have been a shareholder for at least six months before requesting to see the books or own five percent of all outstanding corporate stock. Further, the shareholder must submit a request to see the book in writing and state the reason for the request. The corporation may then grant the shareholder's request at a reasonable time, if the shareholder's request is proper (determined in the first instance by corporate officials). Still, not all provisions of the Model Act are designed to place the shareholders and corporate creditors at the mercy of the corporate directors who are the legal managers of the corporation.

> **http://**
> The Wall Street Journal *provides access to present and past business news at* **http://www.wsj.com**

An example of a provision in the Model Act that better provides a means for corporate creditors to sue the corporation is the **registered agent**. The Model Act requires the continuous maintenance of a registered agent for each corporation formed in a state having that act. In practical terms, this provision benefits the creditor of small, elusive corporations, of which there are many. Trying to find these corporations when one wants to sue them is difficult and frustrating because the corporation may have moved its principal place of business from the address given on the charter filed with the secretary of state. The Model Act says each corporation must maintain a registered agent. One might ask, "Why can't the corporate officials simply fail to designate a registered agent?" In the first instance, they must designate a registered agent as a condition to getting the secretary of state to file their charter so they may legally act as a corporation. Then one might ask, "Why can't the corporate officials let the registered agent resign or retire, or just fire the registered agent?" The Model Act provides that if for any reason the person indicated on the publicly filed document as being the registered agent cannot be located, the secretary of state will be the registered agent and may be served with process to sue the evasive corporation. The practical problem turns to collecting a default judgment against the corporation, but at least the Model Act provides some help to previously distressed litigants who sued corporations.

How Corporations Are Formed

Unlike sole proprietorships and partnerships, corporations may be formed only with official government, usually state, authorization. The state authorization takes the form of granting a **charter** or officially filing articles of incorporation.

Before the 1900s, corporations were formed when a state legislature passed a special statute that granted certain people a corporate charter. As one might suspect, the inducements that led legislators to introduce charter bills in state legislatures for particular people were not always honorable. Bribes to legislators for this purpose were not unusual. However, starting in 1811 in the state of New York, and by the start of the twentieth century in most other states, the general **corporate enabling act** became common.

A general corporate enabling act is a state statute that establishes a procedure by which anyone who complies may become incorporated. The democratization of the ability to incorporate removed much corruption associated with corporate formation, although correspondingly reducing some state legislators' unofficial source of income. Today, virtually all states have general business, corporate enabling statutes that permit anyone to form a business corporation for any lawful purpose. (Sometimes, though, states require three natural persons to incorporate.) Some special requirements, often established by other state corporation statutes, impose stricter formation requirements than do general corporation acts. Businesses supposedly having a strong public interest, such as banks and insurance companies, must usually meet these more stringent formation and operational requirements.

The job of generating the idea and enthusiasm for forming a new corporation belongs to the **corporate promoter**. This person usually sells corporate **share subscriptions** to the corporation to be organized, purchases property, hires employees, and makes necessary leases so that when the corporate existence begins, it will be relatively ready to do business.

Promoters' Preincorporation Legal Duties

Promoters of corporations about to be organized face number of legal problems. If a promoter misrepresents facts about the corporation she or he is forming, the promoter may be liable on either a fraud or breach of fiduciary duty basis to people subscribing for shares in corporations in the organization stage. The promoter who enters preincorporation contracts on behalf of the corporation may face legal problems. The problem is that the contract is between the promoter and the third party (a building lessor, for example); the corporation must be substituted for the promoter on that preincorporation contract after the corporation comes into existence. Four legal theories have been used to effect this substitution: novation, continuing offer, adoption, and ratification.

Novation. The novation theory assumes that a new contract is formed between the corporation and the third party once the corporation comes into existence. The promoter drops out of the scene and does not become a party to the new contract. Also, the old contract between the promoter and third party is ended by mutual agreement. If the corporation never comes into existence, or if the corporation comes into existence and does not enter a new agreement with the third person, the promoter is liable for such contracts.

Continuing Offer. The continuing offer is another way to hold a corporation liable on a promoter's preincorporation contract. The promoter induces the third person to make an offer to the planned corporation, which can be accepted or rejected when the corporation comes into existence.

Adoption. The adoption theory holds a corporation liable on a preincorporation contract made on the yet-to-be-formed corporation's behalf if the corporation's directors, after the corporation comes into existence, approve of the contract and adopt it as their own. Adoption legally takes effect when the corporation approves the preincorporation agreement. Adoption does not relieve the promoter of liability to the third party, however, because basic contract law holds that two persons (in this case, the promoter and the corporation after it comes into existence) may not extinguish a third person's contract rights without his or her consent (in this case, the third party with whom the promoter made the preincorporation contract). What third person will give up a claim against a promoter when he or she does not have to? Thus, adoption is not entirely satisfactory from the promoter's standpoint, although later performance by the corporation on the contract relieves the promoter of liability.

Ratification. Ratification is an agency theory. It holds that if a person without authority acts as another's agent in a transaction, and the person for whom the act was done later learns fully of the act and approves it, this person will be bound. In ratification, the purported agent is given retroactive authority to act and is relieved of personal responsibility to the third person for his or her previously unauthorized act. Because ratification relates back in time, the act of the agent is the principal's act when the agent did it, and not later, when the principal ratifies it. The principal's ratification relieves the agent of liability and subjects only the principal to liability to the third person. Thus, in the promoter's reincorporation contract situation, he or she would prefer a jurisdiction that follows the ratification theory rather than the adoption theory of holding corporations for preincorporation contracts made on their behalf. Unfortunately for the promoters, most jurisdictions follow the adoption notion, partly because of the rule that, to have ratification, the principal must exist when the act was done on its behalf. By definition, a preincorporation contract occurs when the corporation does not exist. In such a case, ratification is not possible.

Corporate Existence

Knowing when corporate existence begins can prevent many problems. The Model Business Corporation Act states that corporate life starts when the responsible public official (often the secretary of state of incorporation) issues the certificate of incorporation. In *Robertson v. Levy* a note was signed in the corporation's name before the corporation came into being. The incorporator was held personally liable on the note in that case.

Another extensive corporate website is General Electric's at ***http://www.ge.com***

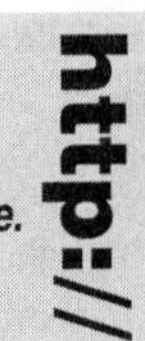

Disregard of Corporateness

Occasionally, someone will follow all of the rules for forming a corporation and a court will nonetheless say that a corporation does not exist. Several legal names indicate this situation, including *alter ego, piercing the corporate veil,* and *disregarding corporateness.*

Why would a court say no corporation exists if the rules for forming a corporation have been followed? Because:

1. The corporation may be used to commit a fraud.
2. The corporation may be used contrary to public policy.
3. The people running the corporation may be mingling their business with the corporation's so the corporation actually is not a separate entity.

The *United States v. BestFoods* case illustrates an attempt to pierce the corporate veil to hold a parent corporation liable for a subsidiary's toxic cleanup responsibility under CERCLA.

United States v. BestFoods

U.S. Supreme Court
118 S.Ct. 1876 (1998)

Background and Facts:

In 1957 Ott Chemical Co. (Ott I) began manufacturing chemicals at a plant near Muskegon, Michigan, and its intentional and unintentional dumping of hazardous substances significantly polluted the soil and groundwater at the site. In 1965 CPC International Inc. incorporated a wholly owned subsidiary to buy Ott I's assets in exchange for CPC stock. The new company, also dubbed Ott Chemical Co. (Ott II), continued chemical manufacturing at the site, and continued to pollute its surroundings. CPC kept the managers of Ott I, including its founder, president, and principal shareholder, Arnold Ott, on the board as officers of Ott II. Arnold Ott and several other Ott II officers and directors were also given positions at CPC, and they performed duties for both corporations.

In 1972, CPC sold Ott II to Story Chemical Company, which operated the Muskegon plant until its bankruptcy in 1977. Shortly thereafter, when the Michigan Department of Natural Resources (MDNR) examined the site for environmental damage, it found the land littered with thousands of leaking and even exploding drums of waste, and the soil and water saturated with noxious chemicals. MDNR sought a buyer for the property who would be willing to contribute toward its cleanup, and, after extensive negotiations, Aerojet-General Corp. arranged for transfer of the site from the Story bankruptcy trustee in 1977. Aerojet created a wholly owned California subsidiary, Cordova Chemical Company, to purchase the property and Cordova/California in turn created a wholly Michigan subsidiary, Cordova Chemical Company of Michigan, which manufactured chemicals at the site until 1986.

In 1981 the federal Environmental Protection Agency had undertaken to see the site cleaned up, and its long-term remedial plan called for expenditures well into the tens of millions of dollars. To recover some of that money, the United States filed this action under §107 of the Comprehensive Environmental Response Compensation and Liability Act (CERCLA) in 1989 naming five defendants as potentially responsible parties: CPC, Aerojet, Cordova/California, Cordova/Michigan, and Arnold Ott. By that time Ott I and Ott II were defunct. After a first phase of a trial on the liability issue under CERCLA, a second phase turned to issues of whether CPC and Aerojet, as parent corporations of Ott II and the Cordova companies had "owned or operated" the facility within the meaning of §107 of CERCLA.

The District Court said that operator liability may attach to a parent corporation both directly, when the parent itself operates the facility, and, indirectly, when the corporate veil can be pierced under state law. Applying that test to the facts of this case, the District Court held both CPC and Aerojet liable as operators. As to CPC, the court found it particularly telling that CPC selected Ott II's board of directors and populated its executive ranks with CPC officials, and that a CPC official played a significant role in shaping Ott II's environmental compliance policy.

Applying Michigan veil-piercing law, the Court of Appeals decided that neither CPC nor Aerojet was liable for controlling the actions of its subsidiaries, since the parent and subsidiary corporations maintained separate personalities and the parents did not utilize the subsidiary corporate form to perpetrate fraud or subvert justice. The U.S. Supreme Court granted certiorari.

Body of Opinion

Justice Souter

When (but only when) the corporate veil may be pierced, a parent corporation may be charged with derivative CERCLA liability for its subsidiary's actions in operating a polluting facility. It is a general principle of corporate law that a parent corporation (so-called because of control through ownership of another corporation's stock) is not liable for the acts of its subsidiaries. CERCLA does not purport to reject this bedrock principle, and the Government had indeed made no claim that a corporate parent is liable as an owner or an operator under §107 simply because its subsidiary owns or operates a polluting facility. But there is an equally fundamental principle of corporate law, applicable to the parent-subsidiary relationship as well as generally, that the corporate veil may be pierced and the shareholder held liable for the corporation's conduct when, among other things, the corporate form would otherwise be misused to accomplish certain wrongful purposes, most notably fraud, on the shareholder's behalf. CERCLA does not purport to rewrite this well-settled rule, either, and against this venerable common law backdrop, the congressional silence is audible.

CERCLA's failure to speak to a matter as fundamental as the liability implications of corporate ownership demands application of the rule that, to abrogate a common law principle, a statute must speak directly to the question addressed by the common law.

A corporate parent that actively participated in, and exercised control over, the operations of its subsidiary's facility may be held directly liable in its own right, under §107 of CERCLA as an operator of the facility.

Derivative liability aside, CERCLA does not bar a parent corporation from direct liability for its own actions. Under the plain language of §107, any person who operates a polluting facility is directly liable for the costs of cleaning up the pollution, and this is so even if that person is the parent corporation of the facility's owner. Because the statute does not define the term "operate," however, it is difficult to define actions sufficient to constitute direct parental "operation." In the organizational sense obviously intended by CERCLA, to "operate" a facility ordinarily means to direct the workings of, manage, or conduct the affairs of the facility. To sharpen the definition for purposes of CERCLA's concern with environmental contamination, an operator must manage, direct, or conduct operations specifically related to the leakage or disposal of hazardous waste, or decisions about compliance with environmental regulations.

The Sixth Circuit correctly rejected the direct liability analysis of the District Court, which mistakenly focused on the relationship between parent and subsidiary, and premised liability on little more than CPC's ownership of Ott II and its majority control over Ott II's board of directors. Because direct liability for the parent's operation of the facility must be kept distinct from derivative liability for the subsidiary's operation of the facility, the analysis should instead have focused on the relationship between CPC and the facility in itself, i.e., on whether CPC "operated" the facility, as evidenced by its direct participation in the facility's activities. That error was compounded by the District Court's erroneous assumption that actions of the joint officers and directors were necessarily attributable to CPC, rather than Ott II, contrary to time-honored common law principles.

The District Court's focus on the relationship between parent and subsidiary (rather than parent and facility), combined with its automatic attribution of the actions of dual officers and directors to CPC, erroneously, even if unintentionally, treated CERCLA as though it displaced or fundamentally altered common law standards of limited liability. The District Court's analysis created what is in essence a relaxed, CERCLA-specific rule of derivative liability that would banish traditional standards and expectations from the law of CERCLA liability. Such a rule does not arise from congressional silence, and CERCLA's silence is dispositive.

Nonetheless, the Sixth Circuit erred in limiting direct liability under CERCLA to a parent's sole or joint venture operation, so as to eliminate any possible finding that CPC is liable as an operator on the facts of this case. The ordinary meaning of the word "operate" in the organizational sense is not limited to those two parental actions, but extends also to situations in which, e.g., joint officers or directors conduct the affairs of the facility on behalf of the parent, or agents of the parent with no position in the subsidiary manage or direct activities at the subsidiary's facility. Norms of corporate behavior (undisturbed by any CERCLA provision) are crucial reference points, both for determining whether a dual officer or director has served the parent in conducting operations at the facility, and for distinguishing a parental officer's oversight of a subsidiary from his control over the operation of the subsidiary's facility. There is, in fact, some evidence that an agent of CPC alone engaged in activities at Ott II's plant that were eccentric under accepted norms of parental oversight of a subsidiary's facility: The District Court's opinion speaks of such an agent who played a conspicuous part in dealing with the toxic risks emanating from the plant's operation. The findings in this regard are enough to raise an issue of CPC's operation of the facility, though this Court draws no ultimate conclusion, leaving the issue for the lower courts to reevaluate and resolve in the first instance.

Judgment and Result

The U.S. Supreme Court vacated the Court of Appeals' disposition of the case and returned the case to the district court with instructions. The Supreme Court held that when a corporation's veil may be pierced, a parent corporation may be charged with derivative CERCLA cleanup liability for its subsidiary's actions. The Supreme Court further held that a participation and control test looking to the parent's supervision of the subsidiary cannot be used to identify operation of a facility resulting in direct parental liability under CERCLA.

Questions

1. As a matter of general corporate law, is a parent corporation legally responsible for a subsidiary's actions solely because the parent owns the subsidiary's stock?
2. For what reasons may a corporation's veil be pierced and the stockholder (here, a parent corporation) be held liable for the subsidiary's actions?
3. Does the exercise of control that stock ownership gives to the stockholders create liability on the part of a parent corporation for the act of a subsidiary corporation? Assume "control" includes the election of the subsidiary's directors, the making of bylaws, and the doing of all other acts incident to the legal status of stockholders.
4. Does duplication of some or all of the directors or executive officers create liability on the part of the parent corporation for acts of the subsidiary corporation?
5. According to the case opinion, can the corporate veil ever be "pierced" so that the parent corporation is held liable for the subsidiary's CERCLA cleanup costs? Is this liability pursuant to state corporate law or federal law? Isn't corporate law a state law matter? Or do the issues in the *BestFoods* case transcend business organization law and go to national health policy and bring into play federal preemption?
6. Does the *BestFoods* decision give a definitive result as to whether this particular parent corporation is liable for this particular subsidiary's environmental harm?

Corporate Directors

The Model Business Corporation Act declares that the directors are the corporate managers. However, the Model Act permits the charter to vary this requirement by naming another person or persons as corporate managers.

The directors do not have to be residents of the state of incorporation, nor do they have to be shareholders unless the charter so requires. The charter or bylaws may prescribe other director qualifications. The directors have authority to fix their compensation unless the charter provides otherwise.

Number. The number of directors may be as few as one or it may be (and usually is) more. The number of directors is fixed in the manner provided by the charter or bylaws, except that the first board of directors is fixed by the charter. The number of directors may be increased or decreased by periodically amending the charter or bylaws. A decrease in the number of directors may not shorten the term of an incumbent director.

First Board. The names and addresses of the first board of directors are stated in the charter. The first board of directors holds office until shareholders at the first annual shareholders' meeting elect directors. After that point, directors are normally elected at each annual meeting of the shareholders. A shareholder, unless stipulated otherwise in a special charter or bylaw provision, has as many votes as he or she has shares.

Term. A director, after the first board, has a term of office as provided for in the charter or bylaws (often from 1–3 years). A director holds office until the successor has been elected and qualified.

Vacancies. Vacancies on the board of directors may be filled by an affirmative vote of a majority of the remaining directors even if it is less than a quorum. A director so elected to fill a vacancy occupies this position only for the unexpired term of the predecessor.

A director ceases being a director through expiration of the term of office, death, corporate dissolution, or removal by shareholders. In the case of director removal by shareholders, any director or all directors may be removed with or without cause by a majority vote of shares (not shareholders) entitled to vote in an election of directors. If the corporation has **cumulative voting**, a director or directors may not be removed if the vote cast against removal would be sufficient to elect such director if cumulatively voted at an election of the entire board.

Quorum. A majority of the number of directors established by the charter or bylaws is a quorum to transact business unless the charter or bylaws require more. Once a quorum is established at a directors' meeting, a majority of the quorum is the act of the board unless the charter or bylaws require more.

Bylaws. One of the directors' important tasks is the adoption of the first set of corporate bylaws, a set of rules governing internal operation of the corporation. Bylaws regulate who writes salary checks, who signs corporate contracts, how long officers hold office, what sort of notice is appropriate for directors' meetings, and many more equally mundane matters. The bylaws may contain any provision for the regulation and management of corporate affairs not inconsistent with the charter, applicable state and federal statutes, and state and federal constitutions.

Meetings. Directors usually hold meetings to decide matters relating to corporate management. Directors' meetings may be held anywhere. Time and place of regular board meetings are usually prescribed in the corporate bylaws. Notice need not be given to directors for regular board meetings. Notice is required, per the bylaws, for special directors' meetings. If a director attends a directors' meeting, notice of such meeting is waived unless the director attends for the sole purpose of objecting to the notice's inadequacy. The business to be discussed or transacted at a regular or special directors' meeting does not have to be mentioned in the meeting notice unless the bylaws require it.

The Model Act, in a sensible departure from tradition, makes it possible for directors to act without holding a meeting if they act unanimously and in writing. The logic of holding meetings is to fully discuss the issues. However, if all agree on a matter, considerations of speed and economy seem to suggest the wisdom of dispensing with meetings.

A question arises as to the validity of director meetings where notice and other procedural rights are not observed. Generally, the answer turns on where the notice requirements are found and against whom nonobservance of them (and, hence, invalidity of the corporate action) is asserted.

Dividends. From the shareholders' standpoint, few actions that directors take are as important as declaring dividends. The general rule is that the matter of dividend declaration is solely within the directors' discretion. In some cases a court has passed on the question of whether directors can ever abuse their authority to declare dividends. Dividends may be declared and paid in cash or other property. A distillery once paid its dividends in whiskey. One limit on dividend declarations by directors is the requirement that **unrestricted, unreserved earned surplus** be available. Dividends may be declared and paid using **treasury shares**. After a dividend has been declared, but before its payment, the shareholders are creditors to the extent of the dividend declared. A stock dividend is merely a movement from the **capital surplus account** to the **paid in capital account** and the corporation's issuance of new pieces of paper (shares) to show that the equity remains the same after declaration and payment of a **stock dividend**, as does each shareholders' pro rata portion of corporate equity. A **stock split** (which entails no movement in the corporate capital accounts but rather a further division of the corporate equity) is not regarded legally as the same thing as issuance of a stock dividend.

Conflicts of Interest. A problem associated with corporate directors is that of conflicts of interest. Unlike corporate officers, directors are not agents of the corporation. Thus, directors have no fiduciary duties arising from an agency relationship. They do, however, owe the corporation a duty to avoid conflicts of interest. The Model Business Corporation Act takes a fairly liberal view in favor of upholding transactions in which an interested director transacts business with his or her corporation. The Model Act does not invalidate such transactions provided disclosure of the directors' interest has been made to the other board members (or the shareholders, if they are the approving authority in the matter) and the interested director's vote is not needed to approve the transaction *or* if the contract or transaction is, in fact, fair and reasonable to the corporation. An interested director (or directors) may be counted in calculating the presence of a director's quorum when action is taken on the transaction in question.

The board of directors may delegate its managerial authority to an executive committee if the charter or bylaws allow and a resolution by a majority of the corporate directors allows. If this delegation of authority is done, such action does not relieve the directors of their legal responsibility for corporate management.

Duty of Care. Corporate directors have a legal duty to the corporation and its shareholders to exercise independent judgment in making decisions charting the corporation's course in the seas of commerce. Thus, agreements with a shareholder or shareholder group in which directors try to precommit themselves to a particular course of action are invalid. The directors also owe a duty of care in exercising their independent judgment. One case stated this duty of care in the following way: "Corporate directors are not liable for honest mistakes made in the exercise of their authority if they exercise reasonable care and business judgment."

This standard of director care does not obligate directors to insure the success of their decisions; if it did, directors would become too conservative and not venturesome. The encouragement of risk taking with other people's (corporate) property is called the **business judgment rule**. It protects both corporate directors and officers from damage liability to the corporation and shareholders for good-faith business mistakes. For example, the decision to develop the Edsel automobile was reputedly a $250 million error for the Ford Motor Company, yet no executive was held liable by shareholders or the Ford Motor Company for that blunder.

Another case, *Levine v. Smith*, presented in Discussion Questions at the end of this chapter, showed how the business judgment rule protected the General Motors board of directors when GM shareholders challenged the buyout of GM's largest shareholder, H. Ross Perot.

Another situation giving rise to allegations of corporate mismanagement involves sale of corporate assets for less than their apparent market value. When the purchasers are dominated by majority shareholder interests, the legal matters are particularly sensitive. The *Pittman v. Beebe* case is an illustration.

Pittman v. Beebe

Court of Appeals of Louisiana
670 So.2d 761 (1996)

Background and Facts:

Dr. Marcus Pittman and Dr. Michael Pittman were minority shareholders in Forest Manor, Inc. (Old Forest Manor), a Louisiana business corporation that owned and operated a nursing home in Covington, Louisiana. On April 20, 1994, two offers were made to the shareholders of Old

Forest Manor to purchase all of the operating assets of Old Forest Manor. Alexandria Investments, Inc., made an offer of $4.8 million. The Pittmans were part of a group that made a counteroffer of $4.896 million. The offer of Alexandria Investments was accepted. The Pittmans filed written notices dissenting from that acceptance.

The Pittmans were served with formal notice on June 2, 1994, that Old Forest Manor would be sold to Forest Manor, L.L.C. (New Forest Manor), the assignee of Alexandria Investments, Inc., for the sum of $4.8 million. The Pittmans made written demand for the cash value of their shares in Old Forest Manor. They each owned 750 shares of the 6000 outstanding shares. They asserted that the fair cash value was $960 a share or $720,000 total to each of them. In accordance with the procedure required by Louisiana law relating to dissenters' rights, they deposited their shares into an escrow account with Hibernia National Bank of Alexandria. The response to that demand was an offer of $360 a share for a total of $270,000 to each.

The Pittmans filed this suit seeking the fair cash value of their stock and damages due to breach of fiduciary duty. They sued W. R. Bryant, Marvin Bryant, H. H. Holloway, Debra Norman, Charles Holloway, and Stuart Johnson, the other shareholders who voted against selling Forest Manor to the Pittman Group. The Pittmans also named as defendants Elton Beebe, who owned part of Alexandria Investments, and Leonard Bossier, described in the petition as the "control person" of Alexandria Investments. The Pittmans alleged that Beebe and Bossier conspired to buy Old Forest Manor through Alexandria Investments to subsidize their joint venture seed business that had been losing money. In addition to these individual defendants, the suit named Old Forest Manor, Forest Manor L.L.C., and Alexandria Investments, Inc.

All defendants filed an exception of no cause of action alleging that the plaintiffs' sole cause of action was for dissenter's rights against Old Forest Manor pursuant to... [Louisiana statutes]. The trial court maintained the exception of no cause of action as to all defendants except the cause of action against Old Forest Manor for dissenters' rights pursuant to... [Louisiana statutes]. The suit against the other defendants was dismissed. It is from the second judgment maintaining the exceptions of no cause of action that the Pittmans appealed.

Body of Opinion

Judge Yelverton

The suit is one for harm the Pittmans claim that they suffered individually. They exercised their dissenters' rights pursuant to... [Louisiana statutes]. The Pittmans additionally claim that they suffered personal injury and have a right to recover under the provisions of... [Louisiana statutes].

In well-written reasons for judgment the trial court concluded that the Pittmans did not have a contract or a legally protected interest with Old Forest Manor to purchase its assets, and that, accordingly, there could not be a tortious interference with a contract.... The trial court found that any damage suffered by the Pittmans as a result of the alleged action of the defendants was a reduction in the value of their stock.... The trial court concluded that the decline in the value of a stock was an indirect damage and had to be asserted through a derivative action. The trial court therefore maintained defendants' exceptions of no cause of action as to all defendants except Old Forest Manor, as to which there remained a cause of action based on dissenters' rights....

Three of the shareholders named in the suit as defendants became the new board of directors elected at the April 20, 1994, meeting: They were W. R. Bryant, Marvin Bryant, and H. H. Holloway. In their amended petition, the Pittmans alleged that this board of directors refused the Pittman Group's second offer as the higher bid in violation of their fiduciary duty to minority shareholders.

Officers and directors of a corporation stand in a fiduciary relation to the corporation's shareholders as well as to the corporation itself.... A shareholder of a corporation does not generally have a right to sue personally for the alleged losses sustained by a corporation due to mismanagement and/or breach of fiduciary duties.... Rather, a shareholder may only sue to recover losses to a corporation resulting from mismanagement and breaches of fiduciary duties secondarily through the shareholder's derivative suit. ...

The directors' action in rejecting the higher bid allegedly damaged the Pittmans; if it damaged the Pittmans, it damaged the rest of the shareholders as well. As a result of accepting the lower bid, there was allegedly a decline in the value of the stock. As the first circuit stated... "if a shareholder suffers only an indirect loss in the form of a decline in the value of his stock resulting from a loss sustained by the corporation due to mismanagement and/or breaches of fiduciary duty, that shareholder may only bring a derivative action on behalf of the corporation." Therefore, the Pittmans were limited to a derivative action against the directors for breach of fiduciary duty for this alleged damage. They did not assert a derivative claim but instead sued only for themselves.

Pursuant to... [Louisiana statutes], the shareholder, upon filing a demand for the value of his shares, shall cease to have any rights of a shareholder except the rights accorded by that section. Also, in the present case, Old Forest Manor had already sent notice of disagreement on the value of the shares, so the plaintiffs' demand could not have been withdrawn. As this court stated in *Armand v. McCall*... "The filing of a demand by the petitioners for the value of their shares was tantamount to an acceptance of the merger. Once they had elected not to contest the merger but had chosen to pursue an increased valuation of the cash payment for shares, the petitioners ceased 'to have any of the rights of a shareholder except the rights accorded by this section."... These latter rights referred to, of course, are the rights to demand a greater value than that offered. Consequently, the right to pursue a derivative action is also forfeited....

Although that case dealt with a merger, as opposed to the sale of all the corporation's assets, the same reasoning applies in this case. Therefore, the Pittmans could not have asserted a derivative action on behalf of the shareholders even if they had wanted to....

Judgment and Result

The minority shareholders lost on their claim that they have a right to sue directors personally for alleged corporate losses due to mismanagement and breach of fiduciary duty.

Questions

1. If a board of directors takes an action that harms all shareholders, may minority shareholders sue the directors on the corporation's behalf? Did the plaintiffs (Pittmans) do that in the preceding case?
2. Do officers and directors of a corporation generally have a fiduciary duty to the corporation's shareholders? To the corporation itself?
3. Does an individual corporate shareholder have the right to sue the corporate board or its directors for losses sustained by the corporation?
4. Is the *Pittman v. Beebe* case simply a "pleading error," that is, should the Pittmans have couched their complaint as that of the corporation instead of merely themselves? Or by seeking the value of their shares did they also forfeit their shareholder rights to bring a derivative suit on behalf of themselves and other shareholders?
5. Corporate directors and officers have a duty not to seize corporate business opportunities. Why was this duty not pursued here?
6. "Squeeze outs," that is, actions by majority shareholders to force minority shareholders out at share prices below their fair market value are not unheard of. Could the preceding case be so characterized? What remedies are available to minority shareholders in such cases?

Director Loans. A corporation may not loan money or use its credit to assist its directors unless shareholders authorize such acts in the particular matter at hand. However, corporate loans (or credit assistance) are permitted to help any corporate employee (including a director) if a board decides the loan or credit assistance may benefit the corporation. Thus, a corporation-supported credit union for its employees would, no doubt, pass legal muster, but a loan to a director for the purchase of a new sports car would probably not.

Illegal Acts. A number of particular problems involve director liability. The first concerns director declarations and authorizations of dividend payments that are contrary to the corporate statutes, charter, or bylaws. If directors engage in such conduct, they are liable to the corporation for such dividends to the extent they exceed what legally could have been declared and paid.

A director is not liable for an illegal dividend if he or she relies and acts in good faith upon the corporate financial statements represented to him or her by the corporate president or officer in charge of the accounting books or presented in a written report by an independent public or certified public accountant fairly to reflect the corporation's financial condition. This reliance assumes the director in good faith determined that the amount was available for any dividends.

Another question of director liability arises where it is unclear how a director voted on a particular matter whose legality is in question. If a director is present at a meeting, he or she is presumed to have agreed with the action taken unless his or her objection is entered in the minutes of the meeting or a written objection is filed at or immediately after the meeting. A director who voted openly for an action at the meeting may not later disclaim liability by filing a dissent to the action taken.

Corporate Stockholders

A person who owns a share of corporate stock is called a *stockholder*. A share of stock is illustrated in Figure 18.1. When a corporation first issues stock to stockholders, they

FIGURE 18.1 Corporate Share Certificate

must pay the corporation the full amount for which the shares were issued. Persons who buy, are given, or to whom stock is transferred in good faith and without knowledge the corporation never got full consideration, are not personally liable to the corporation or its creditors for the unpaid part of the consideration.

> **http://** *A great deal of information investors and stockholders can use can be found at the website for CNBC, cable TV's business channel at* ***http://www.cnbc.com***

Each outstanding share of stock has one vote on each matter voted at a shareholder meeting. However, the corporate charter (articles of incorporation) may give more or less than one vote for any share on any matter. Stockholders may vote their shares either in person or by stock proxy. A **stock proxy** is a shareholder's written authorization to someone else to vote the shares. Proxies last for a maximum of eleven months unless the proxy says otherwise. Figure 18.2 provides an example of a proxy.

Corporate Officers

Corporate officers consist of a president, one or more vice-presidents as may be prescribed by the bylaws, a secretary, and a treasurer. Any person may hold more than one office at a time, but the offices of president and secretary must be held by different people. The board of directors selects the president, vice-president, secretary, and treasurer. The time and manner of officer selection is usually found in the corporate bylaws. Any other officers, assistant officers, or agents who are necessary may be elected or appointed by the board or chosen as the bylaws prescribe.

Agency law determines the relationship between a corporation and its officers. The corporation is the principal, and the officer is the agent. The types of agent's authority

FIGURE 18.2 Corporate Stock Proxy

DU PONT

E. I. DU PONT DE NEMOURS AND COMPANY
THIS PROXY IS SOLICITED BY ORDER OF THE BOARD OF DIRECTORS

P R O X Y

The undersigned hereby appoints W. S. Carpenter, Jr., L. du P. Copeland, C. H. Greenewalt, and C. B. McCoy, or any of them, each with power of substitution, as proxies for the undersigned to attend the annual meeting of stockholders of said Company to be held in the Ballroom of the Hotel du Pont, Wilmington, Delaware, at 12 o'clock noon, on April 12, 1971, and thereat, or at any adjournment thereof, to vote and act with respect to all shares of the Common Stock of said Company which the undersigned is entitled to vote upon the election of directors, and upon the proposals set forth in the proxy statement for said meeting, and, in their discretion, upon any matters not known to the management at the time of the solicitation of this proxy which may properly come before the meeting; hereby ratifies and confirms all that said proxies or any of them or any substitute may lawfully do or cause to be done by virtue thereof, and hereby revokes all proxies heretofore given.

The undersigned instructs such proxies to vote FOR ☐ or NOT VOTE ☐ for the election of directors. The undersigned also instructs such proxies to vote as directed on the reverse side with respect to the nine proposals. If no direction is given, the shares represented by this proxy will be voted "For" the election of directors and "For" Proposal 1 and "Against" Proposals 2 through 9 as set forth in the Proxy Statement on the pages indicated.

The Board of Directors favors a vote "For" Management Proposal No. 1: NO.066568

No. 1 (Page 10 of Proxy Statement) **For** ☐ **Against** ☐

The Board of Directors favors a vote "Against" Stockholder Proposals Nos. 2 through 9:

No. 2 (Page 10 of Proxy Statement)	**For** ☐	**Against** ☐	No. 6 (Page 14 of Proxy Statement)	**For** ☐	**Against** ☐
No. 3 (Page 12 of Proxy Statement)	**For** ☐	**Against** ☐	No. 7 (Page 15 of Proxy Statement)	**For** ☐	**Against** ☐
No. 4 (Page 13 of Proxy Statement)	**For** ☐	**Against** ☐	No. 8 (Page 15 of Proxy Statement)	**For** ☐	**Against** ☐
No. 5 (Page 13 of Proxy Statement)	**For** ☐	**Against** ☐	No. 9 (Page 16 of Proxy Statement)	**For** ☐	**Against** ☐

PLEASE SIGN, DATE AND RETURN THIS PROXY, USING THE ENCLOSED POSTAGE PREPAID ENVELOPE

BRUCE D FISHER
1101 MONTVIEW DRIVE
KNOXVILLE TENN 37914

30 SHARES

066568

⑈066568⑈
Number used for machine counting of the vote

Dated__________1971. SIGN HERE__________
When signing as attorney, executor, administrator, trustee or guardian, please give full title as such. If the signer is a corporation, sign in the full corporate name by duly authorized officer

discussed in Chapter 14—express, implied, and apparent authority and ratification—apply to corporate officers. The express authority (and duties) of corporate officers and agents comes at least in part from the corporate bylaws. Also, board resolutions, which are formal acts of corporations and other official bodies, may spell out in greater detail the powers given to specific officers. For example, the bylaws may empower the corporate treasurer to handle the corporation's financial affairs.

A board resolution might further say that the treasurer may sign payroll checks if countersigned by the president. Implied authority for officers is that which is usual and necessary to carry out the express authority. Reference would have to be made to the express authority to determine the nature and extent of implied authority. Apparent authority comes from corporate officials' acting in an official capacity, which reasonably leads a third person to believe the officers have authority to engage in a task. Ratification occurs if the corporate principals (most likely, the directors) retroactively approve an act by an officer for which the officer had no authority to perform.

The length of time that a corporate officer holds office is determined by the corporate bylaws or the officer's employment contract. A principal always has the power, but not necessarily the right, to end an agent's employment. Thus, a corporation could always fire an officer, but it would be liable to the officer for breach of contract. The board of directors is the "person" having the authority to remove corporate officers.

COMPARING BUSINESS FORMS

Corporations are inevitably compared with sole proprietorships, partnerships, and limited partnerships as organizational forms for carrying on business. Which is the best legal form for a business? The answer depends on the business and the businesspeople's objectives. Each has advantages and disadvantages based on their ease of formation, ease of operation (for example, absence of government red tape), attractiveness of the form as an investment vehicle, tax considerations, privacy, and control.

Corporations

The corporate form scores well on attractiveness as an investment vehicle. Its limited liability feature for shareholders and its divisible share ownership whereby investors are not obligated to manage the corporation are attractive to the financially well-heeled and lazy investor. At best, the corporate form earns mediocre grades for ease of formation and ease of operation. Corporate formation has been eased by the Model Business Corporation Act, which requires only one incorporator, shareholder, and director for a one-person corporation. However, state approval is required, minimum capitalization is mandatory ($1,000, according to many state corporation laws), and reports to state government are necessary. All these factors hinder operation as a corporation. Corporate tax considerations likewise do not all cut unfavorably or favorably. Corporations are subject to federal, state, and municipal taxes. Corporations must also pay annual franchise taxes to the creating state government. (Workers' compensation tax, Social Security tax, and unemployment taxes must be paid by an employer regardless of the employer's legal form.)

Two taxing events arise when a corporation earns net income and distributes part or all of that income to its shareholders. The corporation itself pays a tax on that income, and the shareholder recipients of dividends pay a tax on the dividend income. Critics of the tax system refer to this as double taxation. However, practically speaking, this double taxation can be and frequently is eliminated in **close corporations** (corporations with few shareholders) where the shareholders and officers are the same people. In such situations, generous expense accounts and inflated salaries are given to corporate officers so that the profit or net taxable corporate income is low. Then little taxable income for the corporation and few taxable dividends for the shareholders remain.

Based on the hypothesis that the corporate officers and shareholders are the same people, giving officers the inflated salaries and expense accounts is a way to give them their dividends so that they are tax deductible to the corporation. A warning is in order: the Internal Revenue Service is aware of this gimmick and limits corporate salaries to reasonable levels. Considerable manipulation and straining are done to establish a salary as reasonable. Also, certain small corporations may qualify for federal income taxation as Subchapter S corporations, which also eliminates double taxation. In larger corporations that are not close corporations, the ability to inflate corporate officers' salaries and expense accounts is also present, but its effect is negligible due to the comparatively small portion that officers' salaries and expense accounts take from total corporate profits.

Privacy and control are generally negative factors with respect to the corporate form. If a corporation's securities are registered for purposes of the Securities Act of 1933 or the Securities Exchange Act of 1934, the firm's financial statements are available to any member of the public. Also, corporate annual and quarterly reports are available to any shareholder in the company, no matter how small the holding. Thus, to learn what any corporation's net income is and other aspects of its operations, all a person has to do is buy one share of its stock. All annual reports with summaries of the firm's financial operations would be forthcoming. A limit on such availability of corporate information is the availability of its shares. If shares in a corporation are not for sale, they then are not a source of information. Stocks unlisted on a securities exchange are often unavailable for public purchase.

Control is a controversial area of corporate law. Legally, shareholders (the corporation's owners) are separated from management (the board of directors) which is not to say that shareholders may not be directors. Rather, directors are not required under corporate law to be shareholders. Directors thus do not have to own enough stock to elect themselves to the board. They merely have to win the votes of enough shares of owners to elect them to the board. A number of commentators have discussed this phenomenon of separation of corporate ownership from control. Some commentators see a danger in this phenomenon in that accountability and efficiency are possibly lost when property owners do not control or decide matters concerning their property. The separation of ownership and control in corporations is not inevitable. Certainly, in close corporations the shareholders and directors are the same people. This separation is present in the largest corporations that produce the bulk of the nation's goods.

Sole Proprietorships

Sole proprietorships get favorable marks on ease of formation (no government approval or forms are required to organize them), ease of operation (books are legally not required except for income tax purposes, and no annual reports need be sent to owners or government agencies except tax officials), and privacy (no reports are filed with regulatory agencies and therefore are not available to those who want to know how much money one makes). Sole proprietors also have, by definition, sole control of operation of their business. This control is a plus for this legal form. Sole proprietorships get fair marks on taxation, particularly federal income taxation, because net income is taxable once to the sole proprietor, eliminating the double taxation present with corporation income. Also, various tax shelters such as annuities and Keogh plans are available to sole proprietors to diminish their federal income tax liability. Sole proprietors pay Social Security tax on net income over a certain minimum dollar amount at a certain percentage rate (15.30 percent in 1990 and beyond). It can actually be an advantage for a sole proprietor to pay some Social Security tax because to qualify for some of the preretirement disability benefits that are part of Social Security, a person must have paid Social Security taxes for a certain minimum number of quarters.

The factor on which sole proprietorships receive their least favorable mark is probably attractiveness to investors, because sole proprietorships are not designed to be joint or group undertakings. Any investment in the equity or capital of the business would likely turn the sole proprietorship into a partnership. Also, sole proprietors are vulnerable to unlimited personal liability to business creditors.

Partnerships

Partnership pros and cons are mentioned here briefly in relation to the six criteria used to compare partnerships to other business forms. Partnerships are easy to form. No written partnership agreement is necessarily required for most partnerships. No government permission is needed to organize them, nor is any legal minimum capital necessary. Also, only two persons are required to form a partnership, although it may include more. Ease of operation is high for partnerships, owing to the general absence of government supervision. However, partnerships are unattractive to potential investors (as partners, at least) due to the unlimited personal liability each partner has for all partnership debts.

Tax considerations are usually favorable for partnerships. The double taxation present for many corporations is lacking in partnerships. A partnership generally is not an entity for federal income tax purposes. Such federal taxes fall only once on partners, not on the partnership, as a general rule. Also, tax shelters such as Keogh plans and tax-sheltered annuities are available to partnerships. Privacy is generally great in a partnership, owing to the unavailability of public reports on partners' activities. Control likewise does not have to be shared with shareholders, although other partners have a right to manage, unless this right is given up as part of the partnership agreement.

Limited Partnerships

From the limited partner's standpoint, many of the attributes of limited partnership bear close resemblance to the corporation's. Thus, a limited partnership is an attractive investment vehicle in terms of potential liability to the limited partner, because his or her liability is limited to the amount contributed to the business. On the other hand, a limited partnership requires a state statute allowing such organizations to be formed. State approval must be obtained before forming these organizations, which means filling out forms and dealing with red tape.

The number of reports limited partnerships must file is not as great as with corporations. Tax ramifications for limited partnerships are generally about the same as for partnerships. Limited partnerships offer less privacy than partnerships, owing to the public filing of information pursuant to forming the limited partnership.

The control that a limited partner has in a limited partnership could be less than that of a shareholder, because the shareholder has a right to be a corporate director if she or he is able to muster sufficient votes to win a directorship. In a small corporation, being voted a director is a distinct possibility. This opportunity fades as corporate size increases. Thus, a shareholder could exercise some control over corporate management. In contrast, limited partners have no right to manage a limited partnership's assets, and if they do, their character as limited partners is lost, and with it they become personally liable for all the partnership's obligations. Figure 18.3 compares sole proprietorships, partnerships, and corporations as legal forms for business.

CHAPTER SUMMARY

The U.S. legal system offers businesses a variety of legal forms in which to organize, including the sole proprietorship, the partnership, the limited partnership, the business trust, and the corporation.

In recent years sole proprietorships in the United States numbered more than 16 million. Few legal formalities are involved in setting up sole proprietorships. Obtaining occupational and sales tax licenses are two requirements. However, sole proprietorships must obey the OSHA, Social Security, environmental, and many other laws that regulate businesses organized in other forms.

Partnerships in the United States number more than 1.58 million. Partnerships are associations of two or more persons to carry on as co-owners a business for a profit. The Uniform Partnership Act, which is the law in virtually all 50 states, governs the formation, operation, and termination of partnerships. Several persons can have a

FIGURE 18.3 Comparing Legal Forms of Business

Business Organiz-ational Form	Ease of Formation	Ease of Operation	Liability Exposure	Tax Consid-erations	Privacy	Control
1. **Sole propri-etorship**	Easy to form; no agreement required.	Simplest form, except for governmental reports.	Unfavorable; unlimited personal liability.	No double taxation, but sole proprietor's income is subject to federal income taxation.	Yes; some reports.	Sole proprietor controls except for governmental regulation.
2. **Partnership**	Easy to form; no written agreement required, but one is advisable; two or more carrying on as co-owners a business for profit; could have a partnership and not be aware of it; possible partnership share subject to registration as a security.	Easy to operate, except for governmental reports.	Unfavorable; unlimited personal liability for each partner for all partnership debts; any change in partnership membership dissolves partnership.	No double taxation; partnership income not taxed at partnership level but passes to individual partners, where it is taxed at individual tax rates.	Yes, except possible reports filed with governmental agencies may be public records.	Each partner has equal right to manage regardless of capital contribution unless contrary agreement.
3. **Corporation**	Need state authorization (charter); possible need to register corporate securities before offering to public.	Neutral to poor; many governmental reports possible.	Favorable; shareholder liability limited to share subscription or share amount; shareholder not personally liable for corporate debts unless guarantor of them.	Favorable to poor depending on number of shareholders; double taxation (two taxing events) possible when corporate income taxed and shareholder dividend income taxed; Subchapter S corporation avoids double taxation.	Least private business form; corporate charter (articles of incorporation) is public record; various reports filed with federal agencies may be public records.	Management control of proxy system results in shareholder loss of control of board of directors in corporations with large number of shareholders.

business partnership but be unaware that they are in one. An objective test is used to decide whether a partnership exists. Partners are personally liable for copartners' and partnership employees' torts committed within the scope of the partnership. Agency rules apply in determining whether partners have authority to act for the partnership. Partnerships can own property in the partnership name. Property used in a partnership can also be owned by individual partners.

Limited partnerships can be formed if states have statutes permitting their organization. Virtually all states have such statutes. Limited partnerships must have at least one general partner (who has unlimited liability for partnership obligations) and may have any number of limited partners (who have limited personal liability for the partnership's debts).

Corporations are legal, artificial persons. Most business corporations are created under state corporation statutes. Corporate shareholders generally have limited personal liability for corporate debts. The corporate charter (also known as the articles of incorporation) must be filed with and approved by the state of incorporation. A business corporation generally may incorporate in any state. Corporations can have perpetual life. The business judgment rule provides some protection for corporate management from damage liability to corporate shareholders and the corporation when management decisions prove financially unsuccessful.

When comparing the different forms of business organization, an entrepreneur should consider factors such as ease of formation, ease of operation, liability exposure, tax considerations, privacy, and control.

MANAGER'S ETHICAL DILEMMA

"I think it's wrong," said Harmon Wilcox. Harmon had loaned $1 million to his friend, Eddie Dow, or rather, Eddie's corporation, Dow Oldsmobile, Inc. Auto sales had fallen after gasoline prices had shot up following the Mid-East crisis. Consequently, Dow Olds, Inc. was unable to repay the loan. Now Harmon went to Eddie Dow and said, "Look, Eddie, we've been friends for years. You repay the loan your corporation obtained from me."

Eddie replied, "Harmon, look, I didn't borrow anything from you. My corporation did. It owes you the money—not me."

Harmon would hear none of that legal mumbo jumbo. "You borrowed the money. The law looks at substance, not form. No corporation walked into my office and asked for the loan. You did. Now you pay up."

What ethics are involved here?

Discussion Questions

1. H. Ross Perot was a General Motors (GM) director because he was GM's largest shareholder and thus could elect himself to the board of directors. He was publicly critical of GM's management. GM decided to remove Perot from its board by offering to buy his GM shares for almost $750 million—a "giant premium." Mr. Grobow and certain other GM shareholders thought GM's board was paying Perot "hush mail" in making the offer. They sued the GM board and Perot for wasting corporate assets in making such an offer. The GM board claimed that the "business judgment rule" made its offer to Perot legal. Who was correct? [*Levine v. Smith*, 591 A.2d 194 (1991)]
2. Which factors should a businessperson consider in selecting a legal form? Which factor is the most important? Is it advisable to answer the preceding question without knowing the nature and particulars of a person's business?
3. Jim Wheeler believed he had a great idea—turn used newspaper into cattle feed. He bought the necessary equipment, leased a building, and hired several employees. He signed contracts for these items as an agent for Delta Corporation. Delta had not yet been legally organized. Later it came into existence as a Texas corporation. What is Jim's personal liability for Delta's preincorporation contracts?
4. A creditor sued a person he claimed was a partner, for partnership debts. The person the creditor claimed was a partner said he had no voice in partnership management even though he had cosigned a partnership note. Was the cosigner of a partnership note a partner? [*J.M. Schultz Seed Co. v. Roberts*, 451 N.E.2d 62 (Ind. App. 1983)]
5. Defendants loaned money to the KNK partnership. They put a number of terms in the loan agreement designed to ensure that KNK would be able to repay the loan.
   a. A statement was included in the agreement to the effect that defendants as creditors

specifically said that they were creditors and not the borrowers' partners.
b. Debtors were to receive their loan repayment from sharing their debtors' profits.
c. Defendants had the option to become the borrowers' partners at a future date.
d. Defendants called themselves trustees rather than partners.
e. Defendants loaned securities instead of money.
f. The securities that defendants loaned were not to be commingled with the borrowers' property.
g. Defendants were at all times to be kept informed regarding transactions affecting the defendants' loan.
h. Defendants were to receive all dividends and income accruing from the loaned securities.
i. Defendants' borrowers could, with defendants' consent, substitute securities of equal value for any of the securities loaned.
j. Borrowers could, with defendants' consent, sell any of the securities loaned to them if the proceeds went to the defendants.

Another creditor of the KNK partnership claimed this loan agreement contained enough partnership elements to make the creditors partners in the KNK partnership. Was this creditor correct? [*Martin v. Peyton*, 246 N.Y. 213, 158 N.E. 77 (1927)]

6. A limited partnership agreement was signed by all the "partners." However, no one filed a limited partnership certificate with the appropriate public office. Did a limited partnership exist? [*Blow v. Shaughnessy*, 68 N.C. App. 1, 313 S.E.2d 868 (1984)]
7. Is use of a person's name in a business with that person's knowledge enough to justify finding the person was "held out" as a partner to establish liability under the doctrine of partnership estoppel? [*Brown v. Gerstein*, 460 N.E.2d 1043, 17 Mass.App.Ct. 558 (1984)]

Suggested Readings

Articles

ARONOVSKY and FULLER, "Liability of Parent Corporations for Hazardous Substance Releases Under CERCLA," 24 *University of South Florida Law Review* 421 (1990).

ELFIN, "Revision of the Uniform Partnership Act, An Analysis and Recommendations," 23 *Indiana Law Review* 655 (1990).

ELFIN, "Suggested Revisions of the Law Pertaining to the Dissolution of Partnerships and Close Corporations," 25 *American Business Law Journal* 93 (1987).

EISENBERG, "Bad Arguments in Corporate Law," 78 *Georgetown Law Journal* 1551 (1990).

FOX, "The Political Economy of Statutory Reach: U.S. Disclosure Rules in a Globalizing Market for Securities," 97 *Michigan Law Review* 696 (1998).

GASS, "Departing Directors, Officers, and Employees and the Limits of Their Fiduciary Duties," 72 *Michigan Bar Journal* 650 (1993).

HANSEN, "The Duty of Care, the Business Judgment Rule, and the American Law Institute Corporate Governance Project," 48 *Business Lawyer* 1355 (1993).

HENNING, "The Conundrum of Corporate Criminal Liability: Seeking a Consistent Approach to the Constitutional Rights of Corporations in Criminal Prosecutions," 63 *Tennessee Law Review* 793 (1996)

MILLER, "Breaking Through the Glass Ceiling: Some Personal Reflections on Women's Climb Toward Partnership," 10 *California Lawyer* 34 (1990).

NOTE, "Corporate Criminal Liability for Homicide: The Need to Punish Both the Corporate Entity and Its Officers," 92 *Dickinson Law Review* 193 (1987).

OSWALD, "Bifurcation of the Owner and Operator Analysis Under CERCLA," 72 *Washington University Law Quarterly* 223 (1994).

SCHIPANI, "Integrating Corporate Law Principles with CERCLA Liability for Environmental Hazards," 18 *Detroit Journal of Corporate Law* 1 (1993).

SCHIPANI, "Should Bank Directors Fear FIRREA: The FDIC's Enforcement of the Financial Institutions Reform, Recovery and Enforcement Act," 17 *Journal of Corporate Law* 739 (1992).

SWINSON, "Partner v. Partner: Actions at Law for Wrongdoing in a Partnership," 9 *Georgia State University Law Review* 905 (1993).

WENSINGER, "The Revised Uniform Partnership Act Breakup Provisions: Stability or Headache?" 50 *Washington & Lee Law Review* 905 (1993).

WHITE, "Corporate Judgment Proofing: A Response to Lynn LoPucki's 'The Death of Liability,'" 107 *Yale Law Journal* 1363 (1996).

CHAPTER

19

SECURITIES REGULATION

"TICKER TAPE AIN'T SPAGHETTI."

Fiorello LaGuardia

POSITIVE LAW ETHICAL PROBLEMS

"I didn't do anything wrong when I bought Pillsbury stock because I wasn't representing Grand Met in its takeover bid for Pillsbury," said O'Hagan, a lawyer at Dorsey & Whitney, a law firm advising Grand Met on its takeover bid for Pillsbury Corp.

"But," replied a federal prosecutor, "you as a corporate 'outsider' violated section 10-b of the Securities and Exchange Act of 1934. The 'misappropriation' theory says that you owe a duty to the source of the information, which you broke when you bought Pillsbury stock and options with the confidential information you got through your firm."

Did the 1934 Securities Exchange Act outlaw O'Hagan's conduct?

"How large must an error be in a corporation's SEC registration statement before it is 'material'?" asked Mary Barker. Mary had just lost money on BarChris Corp's bonds. She had invested after having read BarChris's financial statements included in the registration statement.

Ralph Foster, Mary's lawyer, replied, "Well, if the error would deter you, a reasonable investor, from putting your money in this company at the time you invested, it is 'material.' What sort of 'errors' were in BarChris's financials?"

"The registration statement said that the earnings per share were 75 cents when they were actually 65 cents. Annual earnings of BarChris were said to be \$9.1 million when, in fact, they were \$8.5 million—an overstatement of over \$600,000. Contingent liabilities were said to be \$750,000, when they actually were \$1.1 million—about a 50% error."

Were these errors significant enough to be considered "material" entitling investors to recover their losses from BarChris directors?

Federal securities laws are controversial. Investors' feelings vary. Some say, "These laws are great because they give me information to invest and protection if something goes wrong." Other investors are ignorant about the protections that such laws provide.

Businesses subject to federal securities laws also have mixed feelings about them. Some firms see such laws as evidence of the heavy hand of government regulation. They claim such rules add compliance costs and slow securities marketing. They also say that such laws give the average investor more information than needed to make an investment decision. Other businesses accept securities regulation as a fact of life. They see it as necessary to keep out scoundrels and to maintain public confidence in the many reputable securities businesses.

FEDERAL SECURITIES LAWS

When we speak of the federal securities laws, we are referring to 11 federal laws—six passed between 1933 and 1940, one enacted in 1968, two enacted in the 1970s, one enacted in 1984, and one enacted in 1995:

1. The Securities Act of 1933
2. The Securities Exchange Act of 1934
3. The Public Utility Holding Company Act of 1935
4. The Trust Indenture Act of 1939
5. The Investment Company Act of 1940
6. The Investment Advisers Act of 1940
7. The Williams Act of 1968
8. The Securities Investor Protection Act of 1970
9. The Foreign Corrupt Practices Act of 1977
10. The Insider Trading Sanctions Act of 1984
11. The Private Securities Litigation Reform Act of 1995

http:// The Wall Street Journal *website is a good place to keep up-to-date on federal securities laws and SEC rulings:* **http://www.wsj.com**

We look at each of these laws briefly and then examine in depth the Securities Act of 1933, the Securities Exchange Act of 1934, and the Foreign Corrupt Practices Act of 1977 (an amendment to the 1934 act).

Securities Act of 1933. The Securities Act of 1933 (SA) sets out the rules for selling securities to the investing public. It basically deals with the **primary market** (the sale of new or just issued securities). Its main requirement is that securities be registered with the federal Securities and Exchange Commission before they are offered or sold.

Securities Exchange Act of 1934. The SA deals with the primary markets (*new* securities). Regulating all of the old securities bought and sold daily (the **secondary markets**) is a job of the Securities Exchange Act of 1934 (SEA). The SEA also created the Securities and Exchange Commission (SEC) to administer and enforce the federal securities laws.

Public Utility Holding Company Act of 1935. The Public Utility Holding Company Act of 1935 (PUHCA), administered by the SEC, aims to stop abuses in the financing and operations of gas and electric public utility holding companies.

Trust Indenture Act of 1939. The Trust Indenture Act of 1939 (TIA) regulates sale of debt securities (such as bonds) to the public. The law requires debt securities registered under the SA to satisfy TIA requirements as well. The TIA requires that the debt contract (trust indenture) contain certain provisions (which the SA does not require) to protect investors. Some debt arrangements have a trustee who is supposed to look out for the lenders' (creditors') interest. The TIA requires that the trustee be independent of obligations other than those of the investors that the trustee is supposed to represent.

Investment Company Act of 1940. The Investment Company Act of 1940 (ICA) lets the SEC regulate publicly owned companies that invest and trade in securities. Who can be managers, how much management can be paid, how large sales charges can be, what their investment strategies can be, and other such matters are controlled by authority of the ICA.

Investment Advisors Act of 1940. The Investment Advisors Act of 1940 (IAA) gives the SEC the authority to regulate investment advisors (people who tell others where to invest their money).

Williams Act of 1968. The Williams Act attempts to regulate tender offers (corporate takeovers brought about by the purchase by one corporation of another corporation's stock). Congress passed the Williams Act in 1968 in response to the increasing number of **hostile tender offers** in which the corporation targeted to be taken over does not want to be taken over.

The Williams Act sets requirements in two basic areas. First, it requires the offeror (person trying to take over a corporation) to file a statement disclosing information about the offer. Second, the Williams Act sets out procedural rules on tender offers (for instance, whether stockholders who tender their shares to the offeror may later withdraw their offer).

Individual states have also passed statutes that attempt to limit takeovers. These laws have been challenged on the grounds that, among other things, the Williams Act preempts them. In 1987 the U.S. Supreme Court held in *CTS Corporation v. Dynamics Corporation* that state statutes regulating tender offers are valid if they do not frustrate the Williams Act's purposes. In other words, it is possible that both state and federal statutes could regulate corporate takeovers.

Securities Investor Protection Act of 1970. The Securities Investor Protection Act of 1970 (SIPA) set up a federal corporation (Securities Investor Protection Corporation, or SIPC) to administer the liquidation of brokerage firms having financial problems. For example, investors whose stockbrokers are forced out of business by financial problems would present their claims to the SIPC for payment.

Foreign Corrupt Practices Act of 1977. The Foreign Corrupt Practices Act of 1977 (FCPA) grew out of revelations in the 1970s that U.S. businesses would sometimes have to bribe foreign government officials, political parties, or political candidates to get business. The FCPA prohibits certain bribes to foreign officials and requires that certain businesses set up systems of internal control to enable responsible managers to know if such activity is going on. Greater discussion of this important law comes later in the chapter. The FCPA was amended in 1988.

Insider Trading Sanctions Act of 1984. In recent years scandals have occurred involving corporate insider trading. Such trading undermines public confidence in the securities markets. To increase the risk to those engaging in insider trading, Congress enacted the Insider Trading Sanctions Act of 1984. This law significantly increases the possible punishment for those caught trading on inside information.

Private Securities Litigation Reform Act of 1995. Prior to passage of the Private Securities Litigation Reform Act of 1995 Congress found considerable evidence that abusive and meritless lawsuits were threatening the U.S. capital markets. These lawsuits were being generated by aggressive plaintiffs' attorneys, who would find investors who had lost money in high-risk companies such as computer technology firms or bio-tech companies and convince them that they could sue such companies alleging errors in documents filed with the SEC (such as registration statements). If such errors were found (or even alleged), often the companies found it cheaper to settle rather than fight the matter out in court where litigation costs can be astronomical.

http://

Current financial news and analysis can be found at CNN Financial network; go to http://www.cnbc.com

In response to such perceived exploitative litigation, Congress passed the Private Securities Litigation Reform Act over President Clinton's veto. Some of the more significant features follow. First, this act replaces joint and several liability with proportionate liability in certain cases under the Securities Act of 1933 and Securities Exchange Act of 1934 . Specifically, under section 11 of the 1933 Act (which covers "primary offerings"), the joint and several liability rule no longer covers "outside directors." Under the 1934 SE Act (covering secondary offerings), joint and several liability no longer applies with respect to almost any defendant. Therefore, defendants' liability in such cases is limited to only the harm they caused the defendants. Prior to this change, a public accounting firm, for example, could be held liable for the entire loss plaintiff suffered even if the accounting firm were only 5 percent at fault. Exceptions to the elimination of "joint and several" liability include defendants who "knowingly" violate the securities laws.

Secondly the Act limits private class actions. The biggest protection here is a requirement that the "lead plaintiff" be the "most adequate plaintiff" for all shareholders. A judge determines who the lead plaintiff is, usually the largest shareholder in the class. Before this act, a "professional plaintiff" could buy a share of stock in the company to be sued, join with an "entrepreneurial attorney," and if they were the first to file the class action, they effectively controlled the entire class of stock. Now, professional plaintiffs are limited to major shareholders certified by a court.

Thirdly, the act establishes penalties for abusive litigation. Courts have the authority to shift defendants' attorney fees to plaintiffs for defenders against litigation held by a court to be without merit.

Fourth, the act limits damages. Under the 1934 SE Act the damages are limited to the difference between the purchase or sales price paid and the mean trading price of the security over a 90-day period starting when the alleged misstatements about the security were given to the market.

Fifth, the act imposes whistle-blowing duties on independent public auditors who examine firms subject to federal securities acts. Public auditors must bypass the issuer's management and whistle-blow directly to the board of directors if management has not taken appropriate action to remedy an illegal act reasonably likely to materially affect the issuer's financial statements. Also, the board must notify the SEC one business day after receiving the auditors' report and send a copy of the notice to the auditors. If they do not get this directors' notice to the SEC within one business day, the auditors must resign or themselves notify the SEC.

Sixth, securities fraud is not a Racketeer Influenced Corrupt Organization Act (RICO) offense. This provision has favorable damage implications for securities act defendants who have committed certain other offenses within a 10-year period.

Seventh, the act creates a "safe harbor" for certain forward-looking statements that issuers may wish to make concerning future earnings. A problem with such statements in the past has been that potential investors rely too heavily on issuers' rosy earnings projections only to be disappointed when future profits do not appear and share prices drop. Disappointed investors are inclined to sue under the securities laws alleging they were misled by material statements or omissions in registration statements.

Forward-looking statements (such as earnings projections) by the issuer are legal if identified by the issuer as "forward-looking" and accompanied by cautionary statements that identify important factors that could cause actual results to differ materially from the forward-looking statement. Forward-looking statements can be oral or written. No duty requires that forward-looking statements later be updated.

The 1995 Act exempts forward-looking statements made by the issuer, a person acting on the issuer's behalf, an outside reviewer retained by the issuer to "tout" the issue, or an underwriter with respect to information provided by the issuer or derived from such information. This safe harbor rule does not apply if the issuer was convicted of certain felonies or has been subject to judicial decrees relating to securities law violations. Also, the safe harbor for forward-looking statements is unavailable for such statements regarding blank check companies, issues of penny stocks, and going private transactions. Additionally not covered by the safe harbor for forward-looking statements are such statements in financial statements conforming with generally accepted accounting principles, representations in registration statement made in connection with tender offers or initial public offerings, and certain other situations.

Definition of a Security

What is a security? The term *security* might mean different things in different statutes. To be safe, one should see if and how *security* is defined in the statute with which one is dealing.

The website for CNBC, NBC's business channel, provides a wealth of securities information and analysis at ***http://www.cnbc.com***

http://

Securities Act of 1933 Definition The Securities Act of 1933 provides a broad definition of *security*, similar to that found in other federal laws and in a number of state laws:

> Any note, stock, treasury stock, bond debenture, evidence of indebtedness, certificate of interest or participation in any profit-sharing agreement, collateral-trust certificate, pre-organization certificate or subscription, transferable share, investment contract, voting trust certificate, certificate of deposit for a security, fractional undivided interest in oil, gas, or other mineral rights, or, in general, any interest or instrument commonly known as a "security," or any certificate of interest or participation in, temporary or interim certificate for, receipt for, guarantee of, or warrant of right to subscribe or purchase, any of the foregoing.

Substance, Not Form. The term *security* defined usually includes shares of stock. In one case, however, the U.S. Supreme Court held that shares of stock in a cooperative housing corporation were not securities. It reasoned that the incentive for buying was solely to get low-cost housing; it was not to invest for a profit. The Supreme Court emphasized that form should be disregarded for substance and that economic reality should be stressed. Thus, something being called "stock" does not conclusively mean that it is a security for purposes of a particular federal securities statute. The word *security* is not limited to equity or ownership interest.

Howey *Case Definition*. One problem area in defining the word *security* is in defining investment contracts. Often, a piece of paper called a security or stock is not involved, yet courts have often said that investment contracts are securities. In *SEC v. W. J. Howey Co.* [328 U.S. 293 (1946)], the U.S. Supreme Court said that the test whether an investment contract is a security is whether "the person invests his money in a common enterprise and is led to expect profits solely from the efforts of the promoter or a third party." That case held that separate rows of orange trees accompanied by contracts to cultivate, pick, and sell the oranges were securities under the Securities Act of 1933. Other investment contracts that have been declared securities in given situations include whiskey warehouse receipts, merchandise marketing programs, oil drilling investment programs, farmlands and animals, and condominiums.

Cutback in Securities Protection. In past years, the changed composition of the U.S. Supreme Court has led to a narrower definition of *security*. The *Daniel* case was evidence of this trend. There, the U.S. Supreme Court decided a noncontributory, compulsory pension plan was not a security for purposes of either the Securities Act of 1933 or the Securities Exchange Act of 1934.

Recent Supreme Court Case Applications of Security Definition

Generally speaking, when one thinks of a security, the first thing that comes to mind is a share of stock. However, when Congress passed the Securities Act of 1933 and the Securities Exchange Act of 1934, it was primarily concerned with transactions in securities traded in public markets. Thus Congress did not intend the federal securities laws to apply to "the private sale of a substantial ownership interest" in a business simply because the transaction was structured as a sale of stock instead of assets. Thus arose the "sale of a business" exception to federal securities registration requirements. The *Landreth* case indicates that it is not always easy to determine whether something is a sale of a business involving a stock transfer or an investment in stock.

Landreth Timber Co. v. Landreth

U.S. Supreme Court
471 U.S. 681 (1985)

Background and Facts:

Respondents father and sons, who owned all of the common stock of a lumber business that they operated, offered their stock for sale through brokers. The company's sawmill was subsequently damaged by fire, but potential purchasers were told that the mill would be rebuilt and modernized. Thereafter, a stock purchase agreement for all of the stock was executed, and ultimately petitioner company was formed by the purchasers. Respondent father agreed to stay on as a consultant for some time to help with the daily operation of the mill. After the acquisition was completed, the mill did not live up to the purchasers' expectations. Eventually, petitioner sold the mill at a loss and went into receivership. Petitioner then filed suit in Federal District Court for rescission of the sale of stock and damages, alleging that respondents had violated the registration provisions of the Securities Act of 1933 and the antifraud provisions of the Securities Exchange Act of 1934. The court granted summary judgment for respondents, holding that under the "sale of business" doctrine, the stock could not be considered a "security" for purposes of the Acts because managerial control of the business had passed into the hands of the purchasers, who bought 100% of the stock. The court concluded that the transaction thus was a commercial venture rather than a typical investment. The Court of Appeals affirmed.

Judgment and Result

Held: The stock at issue here is a "security" within the definition of the Acts, and the "sale of business" doctrine does not apply.

(a) Section 2(1) of the 1933 Act defines a "security" as including "stock" and other listed types of instruments. Although the fact that instruments bear the label "stock" is not of itself sufficient to invoke the Acts' coverage, when an instrument is both called "stock" and bears stock's usual characteristics as identified in *Forman*, a purchaser justifiably may assume that the federal securities laws apply. The stock involved here possesses all of the characteristics traditionally associated with common stock. Moreover, reading the securities laws to apply to the sale of stock at issue here comports with Congress' remedial purpose in enacting the legislation to protect investors.

(b) When an instrument is labeled "stock" and possesses all of the traditional characteristics of stock, a court is not required to look to the economic substance of the transaction to determine whether the stock is a "security" within the meaning of the Acts. A contrary rule is not supported by this Court's prior decisions involving unusual instruments not easily characterized as "securities." Nor were the Acts intended, as asserted by respondents, to cover only "passive investors" and not privately negotiated transactions involving the transfer of control to "entrepreneurs."

(c) An instrument bearing both the name and all of the usual characteristics of stock presents the clearest case for coverage by the plain language of the definition. "Stock" is distinguishable from most if not all of the other listed categories, and may be viewed as being in a category by itself for purposes of interpreting the Acts' definition of "security."

(d) Application of the "sale of business" doctrine depends on whether control has passed to the purchaser.

Even though the transfer of 100% of a corporation's stock normally transfers control, the purchasers here had no intention of running the sawmill themselves. Moreover, if the doctrine were applied here, it would also have to be applied to cases in which less than 100% of a company's stock was sold, thus inevitably leading to difficult questions of line-drawing. As explained in *Gould v. Ruefenacht*, coverage by the Acts would in most cases be unknown and unknowable to the parties at the time the stock was sold. Such uncertainties attending the applicability of the Acts would be intolerable.

Questions

1. What was sold in *Landreth* was clearly "stock." How could any questions arise concerning its status as "security" requiring registration under the 1933 Securities Act?
2. When someone sells the assets of a business—rather than the stock that represents those assets—is it a "sale of a business" (and not a "sale of a security"), which is exempt from registration under the securities laws?
3. Why did the court refuse to apply the "sale of business" exception to the securities laws here? Is it because the buyer did not in fact manage ("hands on") the business and hence treated the business as an investment?
4. Does treating something as covered by the securities laws when it arguably might not be covered promote any business ethics noted in Chapter 1?
5. Of the legal ethics noted in Chapter 1, which one or two are most in evidence in the *Landreth* case?

SECURITIES ACT OF 1933

Figure 19.1 provides an overview and summary of the Securities Act of 1933.

The main objective of the Securities Act of 1933 (SA) is to provide the public with full and fair disclosure about new securities offered for sale.

Main Provisions

Issuers of new securities must register them with the SEC before offering them to the public. Registration takes place when a person files a **registration statement** with the SEC and the SEC approves the registration statement as a full and fair disclosure. Offering or selling securities in interstate commerce or by use of the mails is illegal unless one first registers them.

A registration statement consists of two parts: a **prospectus** and Part II. A copy of the prospectus must be given to the security buyer before or when the purchase occurs. It contains detailed information about the issuer, its officers, directors, assets, liabilities, and the business. As a practical matter, many buyers never ask for or read the prospectus before placing an order with their broker. By not reading a prospectus, the investor throws away a large part of the SA's protection. Undoubtedly, many investors do not want to wade through the detail that a prospectus contains. Instead, they rely on their broker's judgments and the implied threat of withholding future business if the broker makes a mistake. Part II of the registration statement (containing various exhibits) need not ever be given to the investor. It is available for public inspection at the SEC.

Registering Securities under the SA. An issuer files information with the SEC in a proposed registration statement. Many professionals (accountants, lawyers, underwriters, geologists, and engineers, among others) might contribute to a particular registration statement. An issuer may not offer a security for sale until the registration statement becomes effective, which automatically occurs 20 days after the issuer files the proposed registration statement with the SEC. (This 20-day period is called the **waiting period**.) However, the SEC may accelerate or delay the registration statement's effective date. Delays occur when the SEC believes the registration statement is misleading or omits or falsely states information that investors need to evaluate the security.

FIGURE 19.1 Overview of Securities Act of 1933

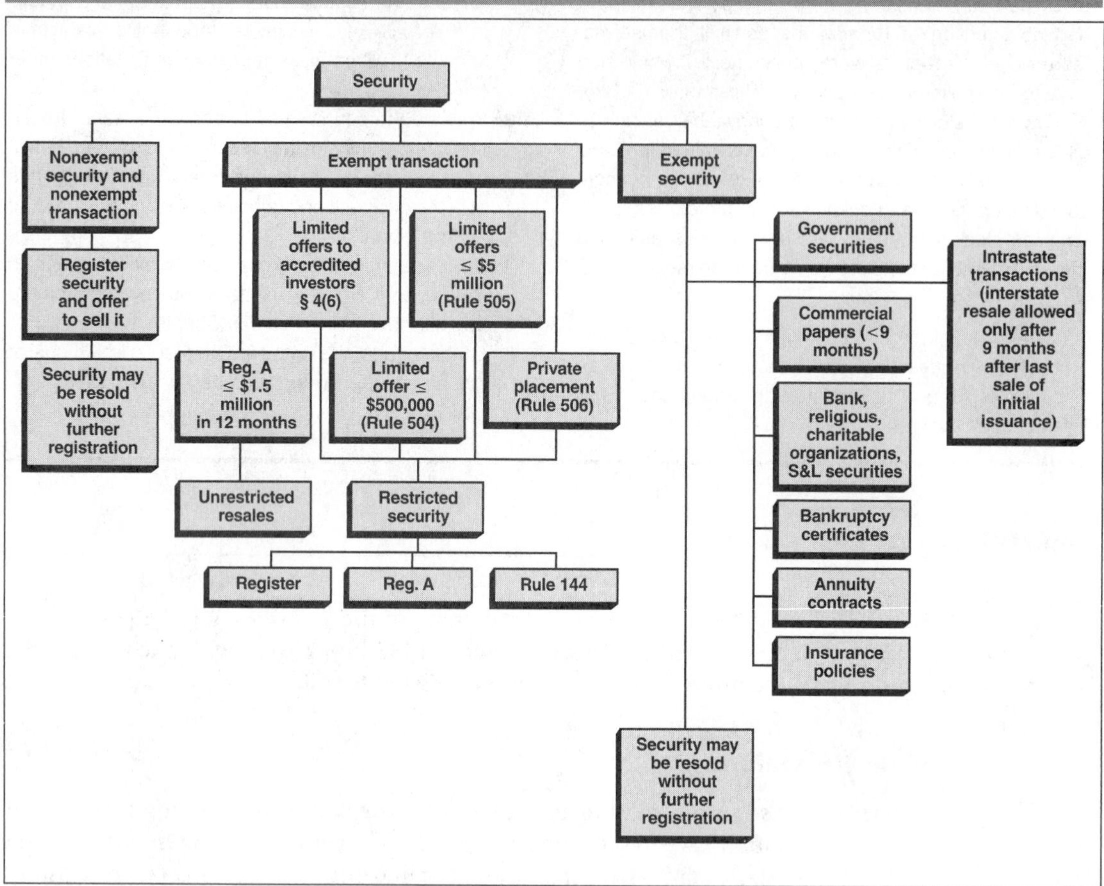

The Meaning of Registration. The SEC does not judge a security's merits as an investment—that is, the SEC does not stamp a security "a good buy" or "fools' gold." Instead, the SEC merely determines whether the registration statement gives prospective investors full and fair disclosure of facts pertinent to making an investment decision. If it does, a registration statement for garbage could be offered for sale. It cannot be stressed too strongly that a security registered with the SEC does not signify that the SEC thinks it is a good investment.

Steps in Registration. The registration process involves several steps. Who is involved in each step, and when can a security be offered and sold to the public? Figure 19.2 briefly describes the registration process under the SA of 1933. Keep in mind that a different registration is required under the Securities Exchange Act of 1934.

Prefiling Period. In the prefiling period, no offers to buy, offers to sell, or sales to the public may be made. During the prefiling period, the issuer may state preliminary negotiations or reach agreements with underwriters, because offers to underwriters are not covered by the act. An **underwriter** is a large, usually national, securities firm that buys the entire securities issue. Often, several underwriters are involved in a syndicate for a large issue. The underwriter distributes the security through a network of securities dealers throughout the country. These dealers sell to the investing public. During the prefiling period, underwriters may not offer to sell securities to dealers, and dealers may not offer to buy securities.

FIGURE 19.2 Security Registration under SA of 1933

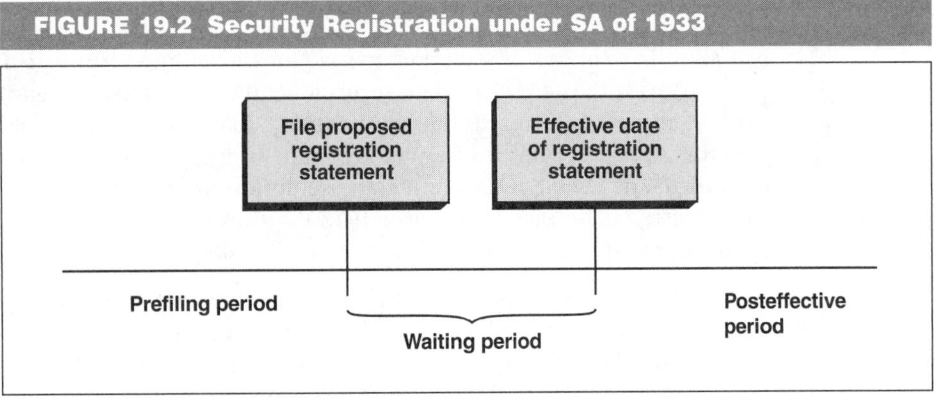

Waiting Period. The waiting period is the period between the filing and the registration statement's effective date. The period is 20 days unless accelerated or delayed. Registration statements may be amended during this time. If the SEC does not ask for the amendment and an issuer files an amendment, the waiting period starts anew.

During the waiting period, contracts to sell the security are illegal; however, offers to sell or buy are allowed. Such offers may be written or oral, and oral offers are unrestricted. A written offer is technically a prospectus, which must contain certain information that is unavailable between filing and the effective date.

Two devices evade the limits on written offers during the waiting period: the **tombstone ad** and the **red herring prospectus**. A tombstone ad, so named because of its black borders, is a written ad for a security about to be issued that does not have enough information to make it a legal offer. The SEC requires that the tombstone ads contain certain language designed to tell the public that they are not legal offers. Various financial publications such as *Fortune* magazine or the financial sections of newspapers often carry tombstone ads. A red herring prospectus is a prospectus with red printing that does not contain the price and certain other information. A red herring prospectus allows distribution of written information to investors during the waiting period without meeting all the technical requirements of a prospectus. Neither a tombstone ad nor the red herring prospectus is an offer. Either may be made in the waiting period. Neither is required to be made.

Posteffective Period. No limits are placed on offers or sales of securities after a security's registration statement takes effect. Generally, when investors buy a newly issued security, they must be given a prospectus (not the red herring prospectus, but the final, completed prospectus).

Shelf Registration. Two major problems that issuers face in selling new securities are timing and red tape. Timing refers to a time lag of several days usually occurring between an issuer's presenting a registration statement to the SEC and the SEC's approving it, which permits a public offering. The registration process reduces an issuer's flexibility in responding to rapidly changing securities markets. Red tape occurs when a securities issuer must prepare a registration statement (a lengthy, detailed report) before offering securities to the public.

The SEC has recently developed **shelf registration** to deal with these timing and red tape problems. Shelf registration permits an issuer to prepare one registration statement covering any securities offering by the issuer for two years. Thus, an issuer can prepare a registration statement, receive SEC authorization for it, put securities "on the shelf" until the market is receptive, and sell them immediately.

Exemptions from the Securities Act of 1933

Not all new securities or securities transactions have to go through the full registration process with the SEC. Certain securities and transactions in securities are exempt from all or part of the registration requirement. Exemptions are valuable because they save the issuer the time, money, and red tape of registration. Exemptions are strictly construed, and the person claiming an exemption has the burden of proving all facts to establish it. The Securities Act of 1933 (SA) has two types of exemptions: exempt transactions and exempt securities.

The Meaning of Exemptions. As a general rule, before newly issued securities can be offered or sold, they must be registered with the SEC as required by the Securities Act of 1933. Each time a sale of (or offers to sell) a new security is made, a registration statement has to be filed with the SEC unless exemptions apply. Exemptions excuse an issuer from filing a registration statement with the SEC, which is desirable for the issuer.

Two Kinds of Exemptions. The two general kinds of exemptions under the Securities Act of 1933 are exempt securities and exempt transactions. **Exempt securities** never have to be registered with the SEC before being offered for sale or before being sold.

An **exempt transaction** means that, when a particular sale (a transaction) of a security occurs, the seller does not have to register the security. However, before buyers of the first round of sales resell, they must file registration statements for later sales unless another exemption applies. In other words, a transaction exemption lasts for only one sale or round of sales. Therefore, a transaction exemption does not last as long as an exemption of a security.

Exemption Trade-offs. An important point about exemptions is that they are costly for business because they slow up selling securities and raising capital. On the other hand, exemptions generally lower investor protection, because information about the issuer and the security is generally not available in a government report.

Exempt Transactions under the Securities Act of 1933

Secondary Trading. Sales by people other than the issuer or underwriter are exempt. The issuer is the source of the security, such as the corporation that issues its own stock. The underwriter is someone who buys from the issuer or the person who controls the issuer, such as the issuer's chief executive officer, a major stockholder, or several directors, with a view to distributing the security, usually by sale to the public. In other words, this exemption covers sales by securities dealers (stockbrokers) to the public and situations in which members of the public sell to their brokers.

Generally, this exemption is for secondary trading. The SA deals almost entirely with newly issued securities—the so-called primary market. Most securities sold daily on stock exchanges and over the counter involve secondary trading, that is, sales of already issued securities. New issues, although not unusual in a strong securities market, make up only a small fraction of daily trading. This loophole in the SA was plugged by the Securities Exchange Act of 1934, discussed later in this chapter.

Private Placements. Private placements occur when an issuer sells directly to a buyer without a public offering. Billions of dollars worth of securities are sold this way each year. An example is Chrysler Corporation's sale of bonds to an insurance company.

Intrastate Offerings. The intrastate offering exemption is for securities offered and sold within one state. The mails, telephone, or other interstate means of communication may be used if the issuer and all offerees and buyers are residents of one state. If a single offeree lives in another state, the entire exemption is lost.

Regulation A. The SEC promulgated Regulation A by authority of Section 3(b) of the Securities Act of 1933. This regulation relieves small security issues from the usual lengthy registration statement requirements by permitting short-form registration. It consists of a notice and offering circular filed with the SEC at least 10 days before the public offering. The SEC currently defines a small issue as $1,500,000 or less in any 12-month period.

Integration rules treat several small securities issues of the same kind within a 12-month period as being one issue (integrated, or one). Thus, three $700,000 issues sold three months apart do not qualify as a small issue. The integration rules treat this as one $2,100,000 issue not qualifying for the small issue exemption, because it exceeds $1,500,000.

Regulation D. Regulation D exempts limited offerings from the Securities Act of 1933. Even though they are exempt, sellers of limited offerings must still give some notice to the SEC. Regulation D contains Rules 501 through 506.

Rule 501. The term *accredited investor* is used in limited offering exemptions. It includes the following:

1. Any bank, insurance company, investment company, or employee benefit plan
2. Any business development company
3. Any charitable or educational institution with assets of more than $5 million
4. Any director, executive officer, or general partner of the issuer
5. Any person buying at least $150,000 of the securities if the purchase is 20 percent or less of the person's net worth
6. Any person with a net worth of more than $1 million
7. Any person with an annual income of more than $200,000

The idea is that accredited investors are sophisticated and rich and do not need securities law protection as much as do smaller investors.

Rule 502. Rule 502 deals with three Regulation D matters: (1) integration, (2) information, and (3) manner of offering and limits on resale. **Integration** in securities law means that securities sold at different times are treated as one offering. Integration can destroy a small issue or limited offering exemption. In other words, if the maximum amount that can be sold and still keep the exemption is $500,000, two separate $270,000 securities sales might be treated as one (integrated) $540,000 sale. Because this value exceeds the exemption amount, the securities have to be registered unless some other exemption applies. Securities offerings separated by more than six months are not part of one offering. Therefore, a sale of $400,000 in securities on January 5, 2000, and $400,000 in securities on July 10, 2000, are not integrated. Each would come within the $500,000 exemption.

No special information requirements must be satisfied when an issuer offers or sells securities under Rule 504 or only to accredited investors. If sales are made to unaccredited investors under Rule 505 or 506, all buyers must get certain information (a short-form prospectus) about the issuer.

Limits are placed on offering and resale of securities that are exempt under Regulation D. It is illegal to make a general offer or general solicitation of such exempt securities. Securities bought under Regulation D cannot be resold without registration unless another exemption is available.

Rule 503. Sellers must give notice to the SEC of any sales under Regulation D. Therefore, Regulation D does not totally eliminate red tape.

Rule 504. Rule 504 creates another exemption from the 1933 Securities Act's registration requirement. To qualify, the issuer must not sell more than $1 million of securities in any 12-month period. These sales may be to any number of purchasers, accredited or unaccredited. Rule 504 does not require giving any information to investors. Figure 19.3 illustrates rules 504, 505, and 506.

Rule 505. Under Rule 505 an issuer may sell up to $5 million of securities in any 12-month period to an unlimited number of accredited investors and up to 35 unaccredited investors. If any investors are unaccredited, all buyers must get certain information (a short-form prospectus) about the issuer.

Rule 506. An issuer can sell an unlimited amount of securities to accredited investors and up to 35 unaccredited investors. This rule assumes the seller reasonably believes the unaccredited investors can assess the risks before investing. If any investors are unaccredited, all buyers must get certain information (a short-form prospectus) about the issuer.

Section 4(6). Another exemption under the Securities Act of 1933 is Section 4(6). It exempts securities offerings up to $5 million when made only to accredited investors.

Exempt Securities under the Securities Act of 1933

The previous discussion covers exempt transactions. Even if a particular transaction is not exempt, the securities themselves might be exempt from the SA's registration and disclosure requirements. Note that exempt securities are not exempt from the SA's antifraud and civil liability provisions—only from the disclosure and registration parts. In other words, anyone who commits fraud to sell an exempt security violates the SA. Also, keep in mind that a security exempt under the SA may not be exempt under the Securities Exchange Act of 1934.

The following securities are exempt from the SA's disclosure and registration requirements:

1. Securities issued or guaranteed by federal, state, or municipal governments, such as U.S. bonds and state securities
2. Commercial paper (promissory notes with a maturity of under nine months)
3. Bank, religious and charitable organizations, and savings and loans securities
4. Securities of common carriers subject to the Interstate Commerce Commission
5. Bankruptcy certificates
6. Annuity contracts
7. Insurance policies

FIGURE 19.3 Regulation D Exemptions

	Rule 504	Rule 505	Rule 506
Number of buyers	Unlimited	Unlimlited for accredited; 35 for unaccredited	Unlimited for accredited; 35 for unaccredited
Amount	$1 million	<$5 million	Unlimited
Disclosure required	None	Disclosure to all, if any, unaccredited investors	Disclosure to all, if any, unaccredited investors

Civil Liability under the Securities Act of 1933

People can be held civilly liable under the Securities Act of 1933 (SA) if they offer to sell unregistered securities (a violation of Section 5 of the SA) or if the registration statement has material omissions or misstatements (violations of Section 11 of the SA). Section 11 violations deal only with securities registered under the SA. Section 12 of the SA puts civil liability on those committing fraud in the sale or offer of any security even if not registered under the SA. The remainder of this section deals with Section 11 violations—material omissions or misstatements in the registration statements.

Section 11 Claims. Section 11 of the SA allows those acquiring a security covered by a registration statement to recover damages if they show the following:

1. They acquired the security.
2. A registration statement covers the security.
3. The registration statement has a material misstatement or omission.
4. They lost money on the security.

Note that the investors need not show that they relied on the registration statement.

Section 11 Defendants. The following individuals can be sued in a Section 11 claim:

1. Signers of the security's registration statement (The issuer, the issuer's chief executive, financial and accounting officers, and a majority of the board all must sign the registration statement; therefore, they all may be sued.)
2. All directors
3. All people who agree to be directors
4. Experts agreeing to be named as having prepared all or part of the registration statement (which might include, among others, geologists, lawyers, accountants, and engineers)
5. All underwriters

Extent of Liability and Recent Changes. All the previously mentioned individuals may not only be sued on a Section 11 claim, but some may also be jointly and severally liable for the claim. Thus, if an investor lost $100,000 and a director signed the registration statement, the individual director could be forced to pay the entire $100,000. Assuming the director paid the entire claim, the director would have a right of contribution from others liable for their proportionate share of the loss. Experts are liable only for the material omissions or misstatements in the part of the registration statement with which they were involved.

As noted earlier in this chapter, the 1995 Private Securities Litigation Reform Act exempts outside directors from joint and several liability. They are only **proportionately liable** for the harm they caused unless they knowingly violate the securities laws. For example, the dean of State University's business school who sits on the board of a local company that issues securities covered by a registration statement under the 1933 Act would not be jointly and severally liable for investors' losses but only proportionately liable for his negligence that may have contributed to the investors' loss. Obviously, such a provision encourages prominent citizens who are not employees of the issuer ("outsiders") to become directors. This practice is good public policy because it encourages a "fresh look" at the company's affairs by someone not closely associated with it on a day-to-day basis.

Defenses to Section 11. Given the great liabilities facing a wide variety of people under Section 11, the following defenses are available:

Due Diligence. Most defendants can raise the due diligence defense; however, the issuer may not, because it is liable in virtually all cases for material omissions or misstatements. **Due diligence** means that the individuals sued met a standard of care regarding information in their part of the registration statement. If the individuals are experts, such as lawyers, they have to meet the due diligence of their professions.

Immateriality. An omission or misstatement in the registration statement that is **immaterial** (a matter that the average prudent investor ought not to know before buying the security) is a defense. Part of the plaintiff security buyer's case is to show that the omission or misstatement was material. The defendant can, however, rebut this claim.

Purchaser Knowledge. The defendant's ability to show that the purchaser knew of the omission or misstatement when the security was bought is a defense.

Other Causes of Damages. A defendant can escape liability under Section 11 by showing that the plaintiff's loss was from causes other than the material omission or misstatement. For example, a general economic recession could account for a decline of the stock of all firms in an industry, aside from omissions or misstatements in the registration statement.

No Reliance. A Section 11 plaintiff need not prove reliance on the material error or omission. The defendant may, however, escape liability by proving that the plaintiff did not rely on the error or omission—an almost impossible task. However, if the plaintiff bought the security after the issuer released an income statement covering a period of a year or more after the registration statement took effect, the plaintiff must show reliance on the omission or misstatement.

Statute of Limitations. A peculiar 1–3-year statute of limitations exists for SA civil violations. Suits must be started one year after discovering the violation but in no case later than three years after the violation.

Escott v. BarChris Construction Corporation is the leading case interpretation of Section 11 of the Securities Act of 1933.

Escott v. BarChris Construction Corporation

U.S. District Court (S.D. N.Y.)
283 F.Supp. 643 (1968)

Background and Facts:

Some investors bought bonds that BarChris Construction Corporation issued. BarChris's executives, attorneys, accountants, and underwriters prepared and filed a registration statement for the bonds. On May 16, 1961, the registration statement took effect. BarChris sold the bonds in May 1961 and used the money in its business, which was building bowling alleys. However, by 1962 it was obvious that there were too many bowling alleys. In October 1962, BarChris filed for bankruptcy. It defaulted on the bonds it had sold just a year earlier. Bond investors lost their money and pointed out the following errors in the bond registration statement.

Summary

For convenience, the various falsities and omissions discussed in the preceding pages are recapitulated here.

1. 1960 Earnings
   (a) Sales

Per prospectus	$ 9,165,320
Correct figures	8,511,420
Overstatement	$ 653,900

   (b) Net Operating Income

Per prospectus	$ 1,742,801
Correct figure	1,496,196
Overstatement	$ 246,605

(c) Earnings per Share

Per prospectus	$ .75
Correct figure	.65
Overstatement	$ .10

2. 1960 Balance Sheet Current Assets

Per prospectus	$ 4,524,021
Correct figure	3,914,332
Overstatement	$ 609,689

3. Contingent Liabilities as of December 31, 1960, on Alternative Method of Financing

Per prospectus	$ 750,000
Correct figure	1,125,795
Understatement	$ 375,795
Capitol Lanes should have been shown as a direct liability	$ 325,000

4. Contingent Liabilities as of April 30, 1961

Per prospectus	$ 825,000
Correct figure	1,443,853
Understatement	$ 618,853
Capitol Lanes should have been shown as a direct liability	$ 314,166

5. Earnings Figures for Quarter Ending March 31, 1961

(a) Sales

Per prospectus	$ 2,138,455
Correct figure	1,618,645
Overstatement	$ 519,810

(b) Gross profit

Per prospectus	$483,121
Correct figure	252,366
Overstatement	$230,755

6. Backlog as of March 31, 1961

Per prospectus	$ 6,905,000
Correct figure	2,415,000
Overstatement	$ 4,490,000

7. Failure to Disclose Officers' Loans Outstanding and Unpaid on May 16, 1961 $ 386,615
8. Failure to Disclose Use of Proceeds in Manner Not Revealed in Prospectus *Approximately* $ 1,160,000
9. Failure to Disclose Customers' Delinquencies in May 1961 and BarChris's Potential Liability with Respect hereto *Over* $ 1,350,000
10. Failure to Disclose the Fact that BarChris Was Already Engaged and Was About to be More Heavily Engaged in the Operation of Bowling Alleys

The investors who bought BarChris bonds and lost money sued the following:

1. BarChris's directors
2. BarChris's executive officers
3. BarChris's controller
4. BarChris's attorney
5. People who signed BarChris's registration statement for the bonds
6. The bond underwriters
7. Independent auditors who prepared financial statements that became part of the registration statement

Investors based their claim on Section 11 of the Securities Act of 1933. Section 11 allows buyers of securities covered by a registration statement to recover damages if they show the following:

1. They bought the security.
2. A registration statement covers the security.
3. The registration statement has a material misstatement or omission.
4. They lost money on the security.

Key Points

[What follows are a number of the rulings the court made in the *BarChris* case.]

1. The provision of the Securities Act of 1933 imposing civil liability for material false statements and omissions in securities registration statement on directors of issuing corporation and others imposes liability upon director regardless of how new he is; presumption is that director knows his responsibility when he becomes a director, and he can escape liability only by using that reasonable care to investigate the facts which a prudent man would employ in management of his own property.

2. The evidence in this representative action by debenture buyers against the issuing corporation's nonofficer director who became a director on eve of the debenture financing, for damages resulting from false statements and material omissions in prospectus contained in registration statement for debentures was not sufficient to establish his due diligence defense.

3. The evidence in this representative action by debenture buyer against issuing corporation's "outside" director, who was a civil engineer, for damages resulting from false statements and material omissions in prospectus contained in registration statement for debentures failed to sustain his burden of proving his due diligence defense as to portions of statement other than audited 1960 figures.

4. The purpose of provision of Securities Act of 1933 imposing civil liability for false securities registration statement is to protect investors, and the "reasonable investigation" required of underwriters as one of prerequisites to avoid liability required more than mere accurate reporting in prospectus of data presented to them by corporate issuer; underwriters had to make some reasonable attempt to verify data submitted to them.

5. The extent to which underwriters must go in verifying data submitted to them by issuing corporation to avoid civil liability for false securities registration statement is one of degree and a matter of judgment in each case.

6. The evidence in this representative action by debenture buyers against the underwriters of debentures for damages resulting from false statements and material omissions in prospectus contained in registration

statement for debentures established that the underwriters' counsel did not make a reasonable investigation of truth of prospectus which had not been made on authority of auditor as an expert.

7. The debenture underwriters whose counsel did not make a reasonable investigation of truth of portions of prospectus, contained in registration statement for debentures, not made on authority of auditor as an expert were bound by counsel's failure.

8. The evidence in this representative action by debenture buyers against the underwriters of debentures for damages resulting from false statements and material omissions in prospectus contained in registration statement for debentures failed to establish the underwriters' due diligence defense.

9. Under the Securities Act of 1933 the provision that no one shall be liable for false statements or omissions in securities registration statement as to part "not purporting to be made on the authority of an expert" if he had reason to believe that statements were true and that material facts were not omitted, only portions of debenture registration statement purporting to be made by issuing corporation's auditors constituted the expertised portions.

10. For purposes of "due diligence" defenses in this representative action by debenture buyers against the issuing corporation and others for false statements and omissions in the prospectus contained in registration statement for debentures, only consolidated balance sheet of corporation and its subsidiaries as of December 31, 1960, and statement of earnings and retained earnings for the five years then ended constituted the expertised portion, where corporation's auditors purported to certify only that portion.

11. The issuing corporation's executive vice president who was, in effect, the corporation's chief executive officer had no due diligence defenses ... where vice president knew all relevant facts and could not have believed that there were no untrue statement or material omissions in prospectus.

12. The liability of an issuing corporation's director who signed securities registration statement for damages sustained as a result of false statements or material omissions in statement for the securities does not depend upon whether director read statement or, if he did, whether he understood what he was reading.

13. For purposes of the prospectus contained in the registration statement for bowling alley construction corporation's debentures, inclusion of bowling alley contract price as part of "scheduled," "unfilled orders" on corporation's books on designated date was erroneous and misleading, where contract was not signed until subsequent date, contract was canceled, and alley was never built.

14. The statement in the prospectus, contained in registration statement for bowling alley construction corporation's debentures, that $1,745,000 of proceeds of sale of debentures was to be utilized as "additional" working capital in "expansion" of bowling alley construction was false and misleading, where over 60% of the sum was immediately expended in other ways, primarily to pay prior debts incurred as result of bowling alley construction already undertaken.

15. The statement in the prospectus, contained in the registration statement for this bowling alley construction corporation's debentures, that, since the designated date, this corporation had been required to repurchase less than one-half of one percent of its customers' notes discounted by unaffiliated financial institutions was literally true but impliedly false and misleading, where outstanding notes of defaulting customers substantially exceeded the percentage, but immediate repurchase had not been demanded.

16. The omission of any reference to operation of bowling alleys in statement, in prospectus contained in registration statement for corporation's debentures, that corporation was engaged in design, manufacture, construction, installation, modernizing, and repair of bowling alleys and manufacture and sale of related equipment rendered the description of this corporation's business incomplete and, therefore, misleading, even though this corporation actually operated only one alley prior to the date of this prospectus, in view of other bowling operations then intended or anticipated.

17. A materiality of false statement in, or omission from, a registration statement for a security is a prerequisite to liability in damages for such false statement or omission.

18. Under the Securities and Exchange Commission regulation defining the word "material" as meaning "matters as to which an average prudent investor ought reasonably to be informed," refers to matters which an investor needs to know before he can make an intelligent, informed decision as to whether to buy the security involved.

19. As a prerequisite to civil liability for false statements in or omissions from security registration statements, a "material fact" is one which, if it had been correctly stated or disclosed, would have deterred or tended to deter average prudent investor from purchasing the securities in question.

20. For purposes of the prospectus contained in the registration statement for debentures issued by bowling alley construction corporation, sales, the net operating income, and earnings per share were overstated for year 1960. This was because profit had been claimed on alleys completed but not sold, money loaned had been improperly included in contract price and carried into profits, and alleys not completed had been treated as completed in applying the percentage of completion method in allocating sales to year 1960.

21. $50,000 of $125,000 due corporation as down payment on bowling alley constructed and sold by

corporation constituted an overstatement of the corporation's current assets in the balance sheet included in the prospectus contained in the registration statement for the corporation's debentures, despite security given corporation. This was because that payment was overdue on both the down payment and on the notes given in payment of balance of purchase price.

22. The current assets of this bowling alley construction corporation were not grossly overstated in balance sheet included in prospectus contained in registration statement for corporation's debentures. This was because at most the net current assets should have been reduced by $609,689, which would have made them total $3,914,332 instead of $4,524,021.

23. As to prospectus contained in the registration statement for the corporation's debentures, the inclusion in the amount of this corporation's net sales for the three-month period of a figure constituting contract prices for bowling alleys constructed by the corporation and operated without sale by corporation's subsidiary during the period was improper.

24. The treatment of the bowling alley construction contract as a scheduled, unfilled order on the bowling alley construction corporation's books for purposes of the prospectus contained in the registration statement for the corporation's debentures was inaccurate and misleading. This was because as of the date mentioned in the prospectus, the construction contract had not been signed, and no firm commitment existed.

25. In this representative action by debenture buyers against the issuing corporation's auditor for damages resulting from false statements and material omissions in prospectus contained in registration statement for debentures, the auditor had the burden of proving the due diligence defense.

26. Accountants should not be held to a standard higher than that recognized in their profession.

27. In regard to civil liability for a false securities registration statement, the accountant's S-1 review made, with reference to debenture registration statement, to ascertain whether material changes had occurred in the issuing corporation's financial position subsequent to the date of the certified balance sheet was not sufficient where accountant failed to take the steps prescribed by his employer or to spend adequate time on the task and was too easily satisfied with glib answers to his inquiries.

28. The evidence of this representative action by debenture buyers against the issuing corporation's auditor for damage resulting from false statements and material omissions in the prospectus contained in the registration statement for debentures failed to establish the auditor's due diligence defense.

29. The evidence in this representative action by debenture buyers against issuing corporation and others... failed to establish that the entire damage suffered by every plaintiff had been caused by decline in bowling industry in which corporation was involved, rather than errors and omissions in registration statement for which defendants were responsible.

Judgment and Result

The court decided evidence indicated material misrepresentations and omissions in the registration statement. Its finding meant the bond buyers could recover from the accountants, directors, signers, and certain others if they did not establish a defense.

Questions

1. Had the plaintiffs in the *BarChris* case bought BarChris bonds? How had they been damaged? Whom did the plaintiffs sue?
2. What does the fact that the plaintiffs were not repaid interest and principal on their bonds have to do with the registration statement?
3. Do the plaintiffs suing under the 1933 Securities Act for a material mistake or omission in the registration statement have to prove they relied on the registration statement's error to prove their case? What if the defendant shows that the plaintiff did not rely on the error?
4. What is the connection between a registration statement and the security?
5. What defenses were raised in *BarChris*?

Criminal Punishment under the Securities Act of 1933

The Securities Act of 1933 (SA) has criminal sanctions. Committing fraud in the sale of securities (whether exempt or nonexempt) or willfully violating the SA is a crime. Possible punishment is up to five years in prison, a maximum fine of $10,000 or both.

SECURITIES EXCHANGE ACT OF 1934

Figure 19.4 summarizes the Securities Exchange Act of 1934 (SEA). The SEA covers many different securities areas, unlike the Securities Act of 1933, which requires registration of

FIGURE 19.4 Overview of Securities Exchange Act of 1934 (SEA)

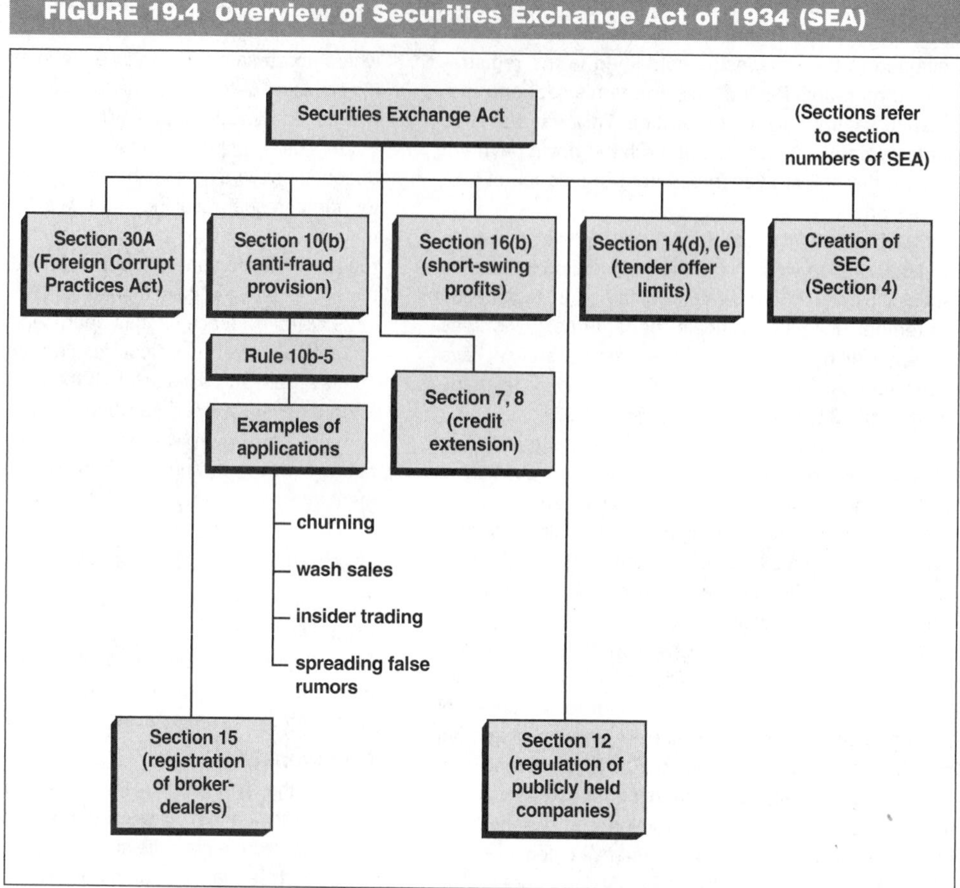

new issues. The SEA concentrates on the secondary (used) securities and their markets. Among matters covered in the SEA are establishing the Securities and Exchange Commission and regulating the securities exchanges, dealers, and brokers, as well as publicly held companies.

As noted earlier in this chapter, the Private Securities Litigation Reform Act of 1995 substantially amended the 1934 SE Act. Refer to that discussion for particulars. One of the most significant amendments was changing the "joint and several" liability rule to "proportionate liability." Unlike the 1933 Act (where proportionate liability only applies to outside directors) the proportionate liability rule applied to all 1934 Act cases in which liability can be based on nonknowing (basically, negligent) conduct.

The purposes of the Securities Exchange Act of 1934 include the following:

1. Regulating securities markets
2. Regulating securities traded in securities markets
3. Registering and regulating broker-dealers, municipal securities dealers, securities, information processors, clearing agencies, and transfer agents
4. Regulating publicly held companies
5. Requiring public disclosure

Main Provisions

The main provisions of the SEA are as follows:

1. Creation of the Securities and Exchange Commission
2. Registration requirements
3. Reporting requirements
4. Proxy solicitation rules
5. Regulation of credit in securities markets
6. Antifraud provisions
7. Insider trading information
8. Tender offer limits

The Securities and Exchange Commission

The Securities and Exchange Commission (SEC) is the leading enforcer of the federal securities laws. It enforces the Securities Act of 1933, the Securities Exchange Act of 1934, the Public Utility Holding Company Act of 1935, the Investment Company Act of 1940, the Investment Advisers Act of 1940, and the Trust Indenture Act of 1939. Interestingly, the SEC was established in 1934 by the Securities Exchange Act of 1934, one year after the first major federal act regulating securities—the Securities Act of 1933—became law. The Federal Trade Commission enforced the 1933 Act during its first year. This responsibility was transferred from the FTC to the SEC upon the SEC's establishment.

For more on the regulations and operations of the Securities and Exchange Commission, go to ***http://www.sec.gov***

http://

The SEC promulgates rules and regulations, enforces them, and adjudicates cases where rules and regulations are allegedly violated. If this description sounds familiar, it should. The SEC is a federal administrative agency and performs most of the agency functions described in chapters 6 and 7.

SEA Registration Requirements

To achieve the SEA's purposes of regulating securities and the securities markets, the SEA imposes registration requirements. Securities exchanges, security broker-dealers, municipal securities dealers, and certain securities must be registered with the Securities and Exchange Commission.

Securities Registration. The SEA requires that certain securities be registered with the SEC. Any security (bonds or equity security) traded on any national securities exchange must be registered unless it is exempt. Also, any company with 500 or more shareholders and more than $10 million in assets must register its equity (not debt) securities if they are traded in interstate commerce. Thus, securities traded over the counter (not on an exchange) must be registered if the issuer has more than $5 million in assets and 500 or more shareholders. It cannot be emphasized too strongly that SEA registration is in *addition* to registration under the Securities Act of 1933, discussed earlier.

Reporting Requirements. The Securities Exchange Act of 1934 requires that certain reports be filed with the SEC by issuers of securities registered under the SEA. (Recall that these securities are not necessarily the same as those registered under the SA.) Some of the more important reports a securities issuer must file with the SEC are as follows:

1. The 10-K report is an annual report on the issuer's operations. It is similar in some ways to the annual report that the issuer's management submits to shareholders. The 10-K must be audited by independent auditors.
2. The 10-Q report is an unaudited quarterly report of operations.
3. The 8-K report, known as the current report, is filed during the first 10 days of the month following the happening of certain material events, such as a change in directors or an increase in authorized shares.

SEA Proxy Restrictions

A proxy is a person who acts for another. In a corporation, a common practice for shareholders is to give the right to vote their shares to incumbent management or to a challenging group. When someone solicits proxies of shares registered under the SEA, the SEA and its rules and regulations impose certain requirements.

Proxy Statement Requirements. A proxy statement must accompany any proxy solicitation sent by the mails or in interstate commerce. The proxy statement contains facts about the person seeking the proxy. For example, if management asks for proxies when it wants to reelect itself (incumbent directors), the proxy statement will contain information about director shareholdings, salaries, and occupations. Each separate management proposal, such as approval of the independent accountants, and any shareholder proposals must be listed separately so that each can be voted on by the person whose proxy is sought. Management solicitation of proxies must include shareholder proposals if the shareholder owns one percent of the voting shares or $1,000 in market value of a voting security for at least one year. Limits are imposed on what shareholders can put in proxies. Proxies must have a space for the date and signature of the person giving them. The proxy, proxy statement, and accompanying material must be submitted to the SEC if the shares are registered under the SEA.

SEA Credit Restrictions

Securities buyers are sometimes greedy. They want to give themselves leverage by putting a small amount down on a securities purchase and borrowing the rest, hoping the security swings wildly in value—in their favor. Such buying on margin contributed to the stock market crash of 1929. To control speculation the Federal Reserve Board sets margin requirements for securities dealers and brokers. These requirements determine how much credit a broker can extend to a securities buyer. For example, a 70 percent margin requirement means that the securities buyer must pay 70 percent of the security's price and can finance only 30 percent.

Other credit restrictions include prohibitions on brokers' hypothecating (using as collateral) a customer's securities unless the customer owes the broker for the securities. A customer who buys securities and wishes to take physical delivery of them (instead of holding them in a "street name") sometimes does not receive the securities for weeks. Understandably, the customer wonders whether the broker is using the securities as collateral for personal dealings.

Short-Swing Profits

Insiders. An officer, director, or large shareholder (holder or beneficial owner of more than 10 percent of an equity class) is an insider for Section 16(b). Insiders often know a great deal more about the issuer than the market does. They could profit from this knowledge by trading in the issuer's securities. At one time trading on such knowledge was thought to be a fringe benefit of being an insider. Then Congress enacted Section 16(b) of the Securities Exchange Act of 1934, its short-swing profits rule.

Section 16(b). Section 16(b) says that an insider must return to the issuer any profit from any sale and purchase or purchase and sale of the issuer's equity securities occurring within a six-month period. The intent of the insider is irrelevant. In other words, if the prohibited acts occurred within the six-month period, the insider is presumed to have used inside information to make the gain even if the insider actually had no information not known by the market. The idea behind the rule is to put all investors on the same footing by eliminating special advantages for insiders.

Insider Reports. Insiders must file reports of their holdings of the issuer's equity securities with the SEC and the securities exchange involved. Any change must be reported to the SEC within twenty days. Note that this requirement does not stop insiders from trading in the issuer's stock and keeping the profits. Also, this rule does not stop an insider from trading in another company's stock and making a profit within a six-month period, because the investor, by definition, is not an insider in the other issuer.

Exceptions. The short-swing profit rule has exceptions for odd-lot transactions (fewer than one hundred shares) and transactions involving low dollar amounts.

Straw People. Insiders may not act through "straw people" (friends or relatives); nor may insiders pass on information to friends or relatives so they can act for themselves. Such gains are recoverable by the issuer.

Section 10(b) and Rule 10b-5

Rule 10b-5 is aimed at preventing fraud in buying and selling securities. The rule's language clearly says that it applies to "any person," meaning corporate insiders and outsiders. In this way, Rule 10b-5 is broader than Section 16(b). On the other hand, it is similar to Section 16(b) because it can stop profit taking in the firm's securities by corporate insiders who have inside information that is unavailable to the general public.

Examples of Rule 10b-5 Violations. Some specific fraudulent acts include knowingly spreading false rumors about securities issuers to affect the issuer's securities prices, matching buy and sell orders from different people (such as two brokers from the same firm), a broker's "churning" a customer's account, or one person's simultaneously buying and selling the same security (wash sales) to give the appearance of market activity in the stock. The list is unlimited. *Zaretsky v. E.F. Hutton & Co.* illustrates **churning**.

Zaretsky v. E. F. Hutton & Co., Inc.

U.S. District Court (S.D. N.Y.)
509 F. Supp. 68 (1981)

Background and Facts:

On February 14, 1977, Betty and Mort Zaretsky opened a brokerage account with E. F. Hutton & Co. (Hutton). Their account executive was Tom Hanlon. The Zaretskys told Hanlon they were placing their entire $25,000 life's savings in his care. They told him they wanted conservative investment to help in their retirement. On May 12, 1978, the Zaretskys shifted their account to Advest, Inc., to follow Hanlon, who had changed firms. They continued to trade through Hanlon until November 1978. By then, Hanlon had made 147 separate purchases and sales for their account. They owed or had paid $24,664.24 for commissions, fees, taxes, and margin interest ($15,715.18 was allegedly incurred for similar charges at Advest). The account had made an $11,755.10 profit while at E.F. Hutton. The Zaretskys sued E. F. Hutton, alleging that Hanlon had churned their account while there.

Body of Opinion

The elements that must be proved to make out a claim for churning are: (1) that the broker dealer or his agent engaged in excessive trading in light of the character of the account; and (2) that the broker effectively exercised control over the account. Factors relevant to the element of control include the discretion given the broker-dealer, the age, education, intelligence, and business and investor experience of the client, the relationship between client and broker, and the reliance placed by the customer on his broker. . . .

In the instant complaint, plaintiffs allege: All of the aforesetforth securities trading activity was based upon the initiation and recommendation of defendant Hanlon who exercised effective control over the account.

In support of that allegation, they maintain that, when they opened the Hutton account, they "informed defendant Hanlon that they were placing their entire life's savings of some $25,000 into his care for the purpose of conservative investment and to generate some extra income." . . . They also maintain that Hanlon promised that they would "make good money on options;" that he would make money for them; and that he was "the best in the business." . . .

Defendant's objection that the complaint fails to allege the manner in which Hanlon exercised control of the account is not persuasive. It is sufficient in this case that Hutton has received notice of the particular account in issue, the relevant time period, the specific securities transactions, and the identity of the Hutton representative allegedly in control of the account.

Judgment and Result

Section 10(b) and Rule 10b-5 of the Securities Exchange Act of 1934 view *churning* as a fraudulent act. Churning occurs when (1) the broker trades excessively in light of the type of account, and (2) the broker effectively controls the account. Factors relevant to the control element of the account include the discretion given the broker-dealer, the age, education, intelligence, and business and investor experience of the client, the relationship between the client and the broker, and the customer reliance on the broker. The court said that the plaintiff's allegation was supported when they told Hanlon they were placing their entire life's savings of $25,000 into his care for the purpose of conservative investment and to generate some extra income. The plaintiffs also claimed that Hanlon had promised that they would "make good money on options," that Hanlon said he would make money for them, and that he claimed he was the "best in the business." The court said that this supported the plaintiff's claim that Hanlon controlled the account.

Questions

1. What must the plaintiff prove to establish a claim for churning?
2. What factors are relevant in proving that the broker controlled the account?
3. Is it possible that a churning claim could be based on one broker's conduct while working at different brokerage houses?

Rule 10b-5 Applies to All Securities. Virtually any fraud in connection with the sale or purchase of any security where the mails or an instrumentality of interstate commerce is involved is covered by Rule 10b-5. Rule 10b-5 applies even to securities otherwise exempt, such as government bonds. The rule applies even if the securities do not have to be registered under the SEA (because, for instance, the issuer has fewer than 500 stockholders). Unlike Section 16(b), only a sale or purchase (not both) of securities is required to violate Rule 10b-5.

Example. Rule 10b-5 makes illegal any device, scheme, or artifice to defraud; any untrue statement, or any act, practice, or course of business that operates as a fraud in connection with the sale or purchase of a security. In the *Texas Gulf Sulphur* case, a mineral company drilled core samples in Canada that suggested a lucrative strike. The company was unsure whether the samples gave a true or misleading indication of the extent of minerals in the area. It issued an ambiguous press announcement about the matter. Later, it made a press announcement telling of a profitable strike. Between these announcements, corporate officers and their relatives bought or placed orders to buy company stock, which zoomed up in price after the news of the strike was publicly announced. Was the first ambiguous press announcement followed by the insider buying a device, scheme, or course of business operating as a fraud in connection with the sale or purchase of securities in violation of Rule 10b-5? Read the next case to find out.

SEC v. Texas Gulf Sulphur Co.

U.S. Court of Appeals (2d Cir.)
401 F.2d 833 (1968)

Background and Facts:

Texas Gulf Sulphur Company (TGS) explored for minerals in Canada. Preliminary drilling on November 12, 1963, suggested that TGS had found a rich mineral deposit. Between November 12, 1963, and April 16, 1964, before the extent of the discovery was confirmed, various TGS officers, directors, and employees used this material inside information to buy TGS stock in the open market. They did not disclose the Canadian find to the public before their purchases. Word of the TGS Canadian find spread on Wall Street. On April 12, 1964, TGS issued a press release designed to lower public expectations about the nature and extent of the Canadian discovery. During this time, various TGS directors, officers, and employees continued to buy TGS stock. On April 16, 1964, TGS held a press conference where it announced a discovery of at least 25 tons of ore (very good news). Twenty minutes later, Coates, a TGS director, bought 2,000 shares for family trusts through his broker son-in-law, who also bought 1,500 shares for himself and his customers. TGS stock rose from 17-3/8 on November 8, 1963, to 37 on April 16, 1964, the day of the public announcement of the Canadian mineral find. The SEC sued TGS officers, directors, and employees under Section 10(b) of the Securities Exchange Act of 1934 (SEA) and Rule 10b-5. The SEC accused the insiders of trading in TGS stock based on material inside information undisclosed to the general investing public or the particular sellers.

Body of Opinion

Circuit Judge Waterman

This action was commenced in the United States District Court for the Southern District of New York by the Securities and Exchange Commission (the SEC) pursuant to Sec. 21(e) of the Securities Exchange Act of 1934 (the Act), against Texas Gulf Sulphur Company (TGS) and several of its officers, directors and employees, to enjoin certain conduct by TGS and the individual defendants said to violate Section 10(b) of the Act, and Rule 10b-5 (the Rule), promulgated thereunder, and to compel the rescission by the individual defendants of securities transactions assertedly conducted contrary to law. The complaint alleged (1) that defendants Fogarty, Mollison, Darke, Murray, Huntington, O'Neill, Clayton, Crawford, and Coates had either personally or through agents purchased TGS stock or thereon from November 12, 1963, through April 16, 1964, on the basis of material inside information concerning the results of TGS drilling in Timmins, Ontario, while such information remained undisclosed to the investing public generally or to the particular sellers; (2) that defendants Darke and Coates had divulged such information to others for use in purchasing TGS stock or calls or recommended its purchase while the information was undisclosed to the public or to the sellers; that defendants Stephens, Fogarty, Mollison, Holyk, and Kline had accepted options to purchase TGS stock on Feb. 20, 1964, without disclosing the material information as to the drilling progress to either the Stock Option Committee or the TGS Board of Directors; and (3) that TGS issued a deceptive press release on April 12, 1964. The case was tried at length before Judge Bonsal of the Southern District of New York, sitting without a jury. Judge Bonsal in a detailed opinion decided, *inter alia*, that the insider activity prior to April 9, 1964, was not illegal because the drilling results were not "material" until then; that Clayton and Crawford had traded after that date; that Coates had committed no violation as he did not trade before disclosure was made; and that the issuance of the press release was not unlawful because it was not issued for the purpose of benefiting the corporation, there was no evidence that any insider used the release to his personal advantage and it was not "misleading, or deceptive on the basis of the facts then known." ... Defendants Clayton and Crawford appeal from that part of the decision below which held that they had violated Sec. 10(b) and Rule 10b-5 and the SEC appeals from the remainder of the decision which dismissed the complaint against defendants TGS, Fogarty, Mollison, Holyk, Darke, Stephens, Kline, Murray, and Coates.

[What follows are a number of the rulings the court made in the *Texas Gulf Sulphur* case. The case is the leading interpretation of Rule 10b-5.]

1. The essence of the rule of the Securities and Exchange Commission providing that it is unlawful for any person, directly or indirectly, by use of any means or instrumentality of interstate commerce, or of mails, or of any facility of any national securities exchange, to engage in any act which operates as fraud or deceit is that anyone who, trading for his own account in securities of his corporate employer, has access, directly or indirectly, to information intended to be available only for corporate purpose and not for personal benefit of anyone may not take advantage of such information knowing it is unavailable to the investing public.

2. Not only are directors or management officers of corporation "insiders" within rule of Securities and Exchange Commission, so as to be precluded from dealing in stock of corporation, but any one in possession of material inside information is an "insider" and

must either disclose it to investing public, or, if he is disabled from disclosing it in order to protect corporate confidence, or he chooses not to do so, must abstain from trading in or recommending securities concerned while such inside information remains undisclosed.

3. Individuals, who were insiders within meaning of rule of Securities and Exchange Commission precluding insiders from dealing in stock of corporation without disclosing material inside information, were not justified in engaging in insider activity because disclosure of material inside information was forbidden by legitimate corporate activity of acquisition by the corporation of options to purchase land surrounding mineral exploration site, and if information was material, individuals should have kept out of the stock market until disclosure of inside information was accomplished.

4. An insider, within meaning of the rule of the Securities and Exchange Commission, is not always foreclosed from investing in his own corporation merely because he may be more familiar with corporation's operations than are outside investors, and the duty of the insider to disclose information or duty to abstain from dealing in corporation's securities arises only in those situations which are essentially extraordinary in nature and which are reasonably certain to have substantial effect on the market price of the security if extraordinary situation is disclosed.

5. An insider is not obligated by the rule of the Securities and Exchange Commission to confer on outside investors the benefit of his superior financial or other expert analysis of the value of securities of a corporation by disclosing his educated guesses or predictions, and the only regulatory objective is that access to material information be enjoyed equally, and such objective requires nothing more than disclosure of basic facts so that outsiders may draw on their own evaluative expertise in reaching their own investment decisions with knowledge equal to that of insiders.

6. The basic test in determining whether information of insider is "material inside information," so that insider must disclose information or refrain from dealing with stock or securities of corporation, is whether a reasonable man would attach importance to information in determining his choice of action in transaction in question, and that encompasses any fact which in reasonable and objective contemplation might affect value of corporation's stock or securities.

7. "Material inside information" which insider is required by rule of Securities and Exchange Commission to disclose before dealing in stock and securities of corporation includes not only information disclosing earnings but also those facts which affect the probable future of the corporation and those which may affect desire of investors to buy, sell, or hold corporation's securities.

8. Whether facts in possession of insider are material inside information within rule of Securities and Exchange Commission, so that insider cannot deal in stock without disclosing information, when facts known to insider relate to particular event and are undisclosed will depend at any given time on balancing of both, indicated probability that event will occur and anticipated magnitude of event in light of totality of corporation's activity.

9. Knowledge by corporation and certain of its officers and employees of remarkably rich ore drill core was "material inside information" within meaning of rule of Securities and Exchange Commission so that they were required to divulge such information before purchasing stock of corporation.

10. The core of rule of Securities and Exchange Commission providing that it shall be unlawful to use any means or instrumentality of interstate commerce, or of mails, or of any facility of any national securities exchange to make untrue statement of material fact or to omit such statement is implementation of congressional purpose that all investors should have equal access to rewards of participation in securities transactions, and that all members of investing public should be subject to identical market risks, including risk that one's evaluative capacity or one's capital available to put at risk may exceed another's capacity or capital.

11. Even if insiders were in fact ignorant of broad scope of Securities and Exchange Commission and purchased stock as to which they had material inside information under mistaken belief as to applicable law, such ignorance did not insulate them from consequences of their acts in purchasing the stock without first disclosing the material inside information.

12. Insider violated rule of Securities and Exchange Commission and Securities Exchange Act by "tipping" outsider individuals or "tippees" concerning the material inside information about remarkably rich ore drill core made by corporation.

13. Insider, who knew that corporation drilled a core to determine whether ore was present, though he did not know that drilling disclosed remarkably rich ore, but who thereafter participated in program of corporation for acquisition of land surrounding site of drilling, and who then purchased for the first time a call on 100 shares of stock of corporation, possessed material "inside information" so as to make his purchase violative of rule of Securities and Exchange Commission and Securities Exchange Act.

14. Effective protection of the public from insider exploitation of advance notice of material information in violation of rule of Securities and Exchange Commission and Securities Exchange Act in purchase of stock by insider requires that time that insider places an order for stock, rather than time of its ultimate execution, be determinative, otherwise insiders would be able to beat the news of the material inside information to the public.

15. Insider, who had knowledge of remarkably rich ore discovery by corporation, and who telephoned his orders for stock in corporation to broker with instructions

to buy at opening of midwest stock exchange the morning that material inside information was disclosed to the public, beat the news and violated rule of Securities and Exchange Commission and Securities Exchange Act.

16. Before insiders may act on material inside information about corporation by purchasing stock in corporation, such information must have been effectively disclosed to the public in a manner sufficient to insure availability of information to investing public, or there is a violation of rule of Securities and Exchange Commission and Securities Exchange Act.

17. Where formal announcement to entire financial news media has been promised by corporation in prior official release known to news media, all insider activity with respect to stock of corporation must await dissemination of promised official announcement or there is violation of rule of Securities and Exchange Commission and Securities Exchange Act.

18. Insider, who knew of remarkably rich ore discovery by corporation, and who placed his telephone order for stock of corporation about 20 minutes after official news release by corporation of the material inside information violated rule of Securities and Exchange Commission and Securities and Exchange Act, since public did not have equal opportunity to make informed investment judgments by time insider ordered stock.

19. Beliefs of certain insiders, who purchased stock of corporation after learning inside material information that corporation had made a rich ore discovery, that news of ore strike was sufficiently public at time they ordered stock were of no avail to them and did not prevent their purchases of stock from violating rule of Securities and Exchange Commission and Securities Exchange Act, if those beliefs of insiders were not reasonable under circumstances.

20. A member of the top management of a corporation was under duty, before accepting stock option, to disclose any material inside information he may have possessed concerning rich ore discovery by corporation, and rescission of stock option would be directed, where he did not disclose such information to option committee.

21. Dominant Congressional purposes underlying Securities Exchange Act of 1934 were to promote free and open public securities markets and to protect investing public from suffering inequities in trading, including specifically, inequities that follow from trading that has been stimulated by publication of false or misleading corporate information releases.

22. Phrase "in connection with purchase or sale of any security" by deceptive device within meaning of rule of Securities and Exchange Commission and Securities Exchange Act making such purchase or sale unlawful means that device employed whatever it might be, be of a sort that would cause reasonable investors to rely thereon, and, in connection therewith, so relying cause them to purchase or sell corporation's securities....

23. Congress by Securities Exchange Act intended to protect investing public in connection with purchases or sales on exchanges from being misled by misleading statements promulgated for or on behalf of corporations irrespective of whether insiders contemporaneously traded in securities of corporation and irrespective of whether corporation or its management had an ulterior purpose or purposes in making official public release....

24. When materially misleading corporate statements or deceptive insider activities have been uncovered, courts should broadly construe phrase "in connection with purchase or sale of any security" by deceptive device as used in rule of Securities and Exchange Commission and Securities Exchange Act.

25. The rule of Securities and Exchange Commission forbidding misleading corporate statements is violated whenever assertions are made by corporation in manner reasonably calculated to influence investing public, by means of financial news media, if such assertions are false or misleading or are so incomplete as to mislead irrespective of whether issuance of release was motivated by corporate officials for ulterior purposes.

26. If corporate management demonstrates that it was diligent in ascertaining information issued by means of financial media was the whole truth and that such diligently obtained information was disseminated in good faith there is no violation of rule of Securities and Exchange Commission forbidding deceptive statements by corporations....

27. Choice by corporation of ambiguous general statement concerning ore discovery rather than summary of specific facts could not reasonably be justified by corporation by any claimed urgency due to rumors, in order to defend charge that corporation violated rule of Securities and Exchange Commission and Securities Exchange Act.

28. Choice by corporation of ambiguous general statement concerning ore discovery rather than summary of specific facts could not be justified on ground that corporation desired to avoid liability under rule of Securities and Exchange Commission and Securities Exchange Act for misrepresentation in event that mining project failed.

29. Choice by corporation of ambiguous general statement of ore discovery rather than summary of specific facts could not be justified on ground that explicit disclosure of facts might have encouraged rumor mill which corporation was seeking to allay, in order to avoid violation of rule of Securities and Exchange Commission and Securities Exchange Act.

Judgment and Result

[The court held that certain insiders violated Section 10(b) and Rule 10b-5.] For reasons which appear below, we decide the various issues presented as follows:

1. As to Clayton and Crawford, as purchasers of stock on April 15 and 16, 1964, we affirm the finding that they violated 15 U.S.C. §78j(b) and Rule 10b-5 and remand, for a determination of the appropriate remedy.

2. As to Murray, we affirm the dismissal of the complaint.

3. As to Mollison and Holyk, as recipients of certain stock options, we affirm the dismissal of the complaint.

4. As to Stephens and Fogarty, as recipients of stock options, we reverse the dismissal of the complaint and remand for a further determination as to whether an injunction should issue.

5. As to Kline, as a recipient of a stock option, we reverse the dismissal of the complaint and remand with directions to issue an order rescinding the option and for a determination of any other appropriate remedy in connection therewith.

6. As to Fogarty, Mollison, Holyk, Darke, and Huntington, as purchasers of stock or calls thereon between November 12, 1963, and April 9, 1964, we reverse the dismissal of the complaint and find that they violated 15 U.S.C. §78j(b) and Rule 10b-5, and remand, for a determination of the appropriate remedy.

7. As to Clayton, although the district judge did not specify that the complaint be dismissed with respect to his purchase of TGS stock before April 9, 1964, such a dismissal is implicit in his treatment of the individual appellees who acted similarly. Consequently, although Clayton is named only as an appellant, our decision with respect to the materiality of K-55-1 (a core drilling sample) renders it necessary to treat him also as an appellee. Thus, as to him, as one who purchased stock between November 12, 1963, and April 9, 1964, we reverse the implicit dismissal of the complaint, find that he violated §78j(b) and Rule 10b-5, and remand, for a determination of the appropriate remedy.

8. As to Darke, as one who passed on information to tippees, we reverse the dismissal of the complaint and remand, for a determination of the appropriate remedy.

9. As to Coates, as one who on April 16th purchased stock and gave information on which his son-in-law broker and the broker's customers purchased shares, we reverse the dismissal of the complaint, find that he violated [the 1934 Securities Exchange Act] and Rule 10b-5, and remand, for a determination of the appropriate remedy.

10. As to Texas Gulf Sulphur, we reverse the dismissal of the complaint and remand for a further determination by the district judge in the light of the approach taken in this opinion....

Questions

1. Who are insiders for purposes of Section 10(b) of the Securities Exchange Act and Rule 10b-5?
2. If a person is an insider, how does that status affect that person's ability to deal in the issuer's securities?
3. What does the insider trading rule apply to? Stocks? Bonds? Puts? Calls? Anything else?
4. Does the insider trading rule apply only to corporate issuers?
5. How long after inside information becomes public must an insider wait before dealing in the firm's security?

Almost 30 years after the *Texas Gulf Sulphur* case, the U.S. Supreme Court was presented with the question of whether an "outsider" could be liable to the source for misappropriating inside information under section 10b and Rule 10b-5. *United States v. O'Hagan* deals with this issue.

United States v. O'Hagan

U.S. Supreme Court
521 U.S. 642 (1997)

Background and Facts:

After Grand Metropolitan PLC (Grand Met) retained the law firm of Dorsey & Whitney to represent it regarding a potential tender offer for the Pillsbury Company's common stock, respondent O'Hagan, a Dorsey & Whitney partner who did no work on the representation, began purchasing call options for Pillsbury stock, as well as shares of the stock. Following Dorsey & Whitney's withdrawal from the representation, Grand Met publicly announced its tender offer, the price of Pillsbury stock rose dramatically, and O'Hagan sold his call options and stock at a profit of more than $4.3 million. A Securities and Exchange Commission (SEC) investigation culminated in a 57 count indictment alleging, among other things, that O'Hagan defrauded his law firm and its client, Grand Met, by misappropriating for his own trading purposes material, nonpublic information regarding the tender offer. The indictment charged O'Hagan with securities fraud in violation of §10(b) of the Securities Exchange Act of 1934 and SEC Rule 10b-5.... A jury convicted O'Hagan on all counts, and he was sentenced to prison. The Eighth Circuit reversed all of the convictions, holding that §10(b) and Rule 10b-5 liability may not be grounded on the "misappropriation theory" of securities fraud on which the prosecution relied. . . .

Body of Opinion

Justice Ruth Bader Ginsburg

This case concerns the interpretation and enforcement of §10(b) . . . and rules made by the Securities and Exchange Commission pursuant to these provisions, Rule 10b-5. . . . Two prime questions are presented. The first relates to the misappropriation of material, nonpublic information for securities trading; [the second is omitted here]. In particular, we address and resolve these issues: 1) Is a person who trades in securities for personal profit, using confidential information misappropriated in breach of a fiduciary duty to the source of the information, guilty of violating §10(b) and Rule 10b-5? . . . [The second, not involving §10(b) is omitted.] Our answer to the first question is yes. . . .

The Eighth Circuit rejected the misappropriation theory as a basis for §10(b) liability. We hold, in accord with several other Courts of Appeals, that criminal liability under §10(b) may be predicated on the misappropriation theory. . . .

Under the "traditional" or "classic theory" of insider trading liability, §10(b) and Rule 10b-5 are violated when a corporate insider trades in securities of his corporation on the basis of material, nonpublic information. Trading on such information qualifies as a "deceptive device" under §10(b), we have affirmed, because "a relationship of trust and confidence [exists] between the shareholders of a corporation and those insiders who have obtained confidential information by reason of their position with that corporation." . . . That relationship, we recognized, "gives rise to a duty to disclose [or to abstain from trading] because of the necessity of preventing a corporate insider from . . . taking unfair advantage of . . . uninformed . . . stockholders.'" . . . The classic theory applies not only to officers, directors, an other permanent insiders of a corporation, but also to attorneys, accountants, consultants, and others who temporarily become fiduciaries of a corporation . . .

The "misappropriation theory" holds that a person commits fraud "in connection with" a securities transaction, and thereby violates §10(b) and Rule 10b-5, when he appropriates confidential information for securities trading purposes, in breach of duty owed to the source of the information. . . . Under this theory, a fiduciary's undisclosed, self-serving use of a principal's information to purchase or sell securities, in breach of a duty of loyalty and confidentiality, defrauds the principal of the exclusive use of that information. In lieu of premising liability on a fiduciary relationship between company insider and purchaser or seller of the company's stock, the misappropriation theory premises liability on a fiduciary turned trader's deception of those who entrusted him with access to confidential information.

The two theories are complementary, each addressing efforts to capitalize on nonpublic information through the purchase or sale of securities. The classic theory targets a corporate insider's breach of duty to shareholders with whom the insider transacts; the misappropriation theory outlaws trading on the basis of nonpublic information by a corporate "outsider" in breach of a duty owed not to the trading party, but to the source of the information. The misappropriation theory is thus designed to "protect the integrity if the securities markets against abuses by 'outsiders' to a corporation who have access to confidential information that will affect the corporation's security price when revealed, but who owe no fiduciary or other duty to that corporation's shareholders."

In this case, the indictment alleged that O'Hagan, in breach of a duty of trust and confidence he owed to his law firm, Dorsey & Whitney, and to its client, Grand Met, traded on the basis of nonpublic information regarding Grand Met's planned tender offer for Pillsbury common stock. This conduct, the Government charged, constituted a fraudulent device in connection with the purchase and sale of securities.

We agree with the Government that misappropriation as just defined, satisfies §10(b)'s requirement that chargeable conduct involve a "deceptive device or contrivance" used "in connection with" the purchase or sale of securities. We observe, first that misappropriators, as the Government describes them, deal in deception. A fiduciary who "pretends loyalty to the principal while secretly converting the principal's information for personal gain," . . . "dupes" or defrauds the principal. . . .

We turn next to the §10(b) requirement that the misappropriator's deceptive use of information be "in connection with the purchase or sale of a security." This element is satisfied because the fiduciary's fraud is consummated, not when the fiduciary gains the confidential information, but when, without disclosure to the principal, he uses the information to purchase or sell securities. The securities transaction and the breach of duty thus coincide. This is so even though the person or entity defrauded is not the other party to the trade, but is, instead, the source of the nonpublic information. . . . A misappropriator who trades on the basis of material, nonpublic information, in short, gains his advantageous market position through deception, he deceives the source of the information and simultaneously harms members of the investing public. . . .

The misappropriation theory targets information of a sort that misappropriators ordinarily capitalize upon to gain no risk profits through the purchase or sale of securities. Should a misappropriator put such information to other use, the statute's prohibition would not be implicated. The theory does not catch all conceivable forms of fraud involving confidential information; rather, it catches fraudulent means of capitalizing on such information through securities transactions.

The Government notes another limitation on the forms of fraud §10(b) reaches: "The misappropriation theory would not... apply to a case in which a person defrauded a bank into giving him a loan or embezzled cash from another, and then used the proceeds of the misdeed to purchase securities."... In such a case, the Government states, "the proceeds would have value to the malefactor apart from their use in a securities transaction, and the fraud would be complete as soon as the money was obtained."... In other words, money can buy, if not anything, then at least many things; its misappropriation may thus be viewed as sufficiently detached from a subsequent securities transaction that §10(b)'s "in connection with" requirement would not be met....

The misappropriation theory comports with §10(b)'s language, which requires deception "in connection with the purchase or sale of any security," not deception of an identifiable purchaser or seller. The theory is also well tuned to an animating purpose of the Exchange Act: to insure honest securities markets and thereby promote investor confidence....

Judgment and Result

O'Hagan violated the Securities and Exchange Act's section 10(b).

Questions

1. Was O'Hagan an "insider" trading on insider information? If not, how could he be liable under section 10(b)?
2. If O'Hagan's conduct violated section 10(b), a misrepresentation must have occurred. Where was the misrepresentation by O'Hagan here? His failure to disclose his personal trading to the persons from whom he bought Pillsbury shares? Or his failure to disclose to Grand Met and his law firm—the source of the information? Was his misrepresentation an affirmative misrepresentation or misrepresentation by concealment?

Tippees. A tippee is someone getting material nonpublic information about an issuer from an insider. Is tippee trading in the company's security illegal? Not always. If the insider breaks a fiduciary duty to the issuer by disclosing the information to the tippee, it is illegal for the tippee to trade in the issuer's securities unless the tippee discloses the tip before trading. On the other hand, if the insider is not breaking a fiduciary duty by disclosing information to the tippee, the tippee may trade or act on the information. The *Dirks v. SEC* case so held.

Insider Trading Sanctions Act

In 1984 Congress enacted the Insider Trading Sanctions Act to regulate insider trading. That act has the following provisions:

1. *Civil penalties.* The SEC is authorized to seek civil penalties in federal court against anyone buying or selling securities while possessing material nonpublic information.
2. *Triple damages.* Damages of up to three times the profit made (or loss avoided) by using nonpublic information are possible. (Before this statute, recovery was limited to giving up any profits.)
3. *Criminal penalties.* Criminal penalties for insider trading are increased from $10,000 to $100,000.
4. *Stock options.* Insider trading in stock options is explicitly stated as being illegal.
5. *Aiders and abettors.* The SEC can sue anyone aiding and abetting someone else who communicates material nonpublic information. No triple damages are available against aiders and abettors.
6. *Statute of limitations.* This statute contains a five-year statute of limitations.
7. *No definition.* The act does not define insider trading or material nonpublic information.

Takeover Bids (Tender Offers)

Definitions. A takeover bid, or tender offer, occurs when someone publicly offers to buy stock from a corporation's shareholders at a set price. Shareholders can then tender their stock to the offeror. Shareholders do not have to tender their stock. The offeror must give all who tender the same price. Acceptance of tendered stock is sometimes conditioned on a certain percentage—often a controlling percentage—of the stock being tendered. Shareholders may withdraw tendered stock for the first seven days of a tender offer. They may also withdraw their tendered shares if they are not purchased after 60 days following the start of the offer.

Tender offers are one way a person (including a corporation) or group can take control of a corporation. The corporation whose stock is sought is called the **target corporation**. The one offering to buy the securities is the **tender offeror**.

Federal Regulation. The Securities Exchange Act of 1934 (SEA) and the Williams Act of 1968 (amending the SEA) regulate tender offers. If a tender offer would result in the offeror's owning more than five percent of a class of securities registered under the SEA, the offeror must file with the SEC and furnish each offeree certain data. That data must have five items:

1. The offeror's background
2. Where the offeror gets the money to make the offer
3. Why the tender offer is made
4. How many shares are owned
5. Any relevant contracts, arrangements, and understandings

Also, any person who acquires more than five percent of any security registered under the SEA must file the prior five-point report with the SEC and the target corporation 10 days after getting more than five percent ownership.

Purpose of Regulating Tender Offers. Tender offers can be friendly to the target corporation's management. Often, however, the target's management sees tender offers as threats to their jobs. This perception has led to **golden parachutes**—contracts with high severance pay that existing managers give themselves if a takeover is successful and the new owners fire them.

In an unfriendly takeover bid, the tender offeror often tells the target's shareholders that existing management is stupid and lazy. The tender offeror then may offer the target's shareholders much more than market value for their stock. Existing managers, in turn, caution shareholders not to sell because they feel that the tender offerors would ruin the company and its communities by closing plants and firing hard-working employees. Federal law (the SEA) helps target shareholders get the facts from both sides in such a takeover fight by letting existing management know that its corporation is a target.

Misstatements. Misstating or omitting a material fact, or engaging in any fraudulent, deceptive, or manipulative acts in connection with a tender offer, is unlawful. In the following case, a shareholder of a target company claimed that a series of tender offers which resulted in her not benefiting as much as she would have had the first tender offer been the only one, which violated the Williams Act's prohibition against fraudulent, deceptive, or manipulative acts or practices. Read the *Schreiber* case to see whether the Supreme Court agreed with her.

Schreiber v. Burlington Northern, Inc.

U.S. Supreme Court
472 U.S.1 (1985)

Background and Facts:

On December 21, 1982, Burlington Northern, Inc., made a hostile tender offer for El Paso Gas Co. Through a wholly owned subsidiary, Burlington proposed to purchase 25.1 million El Paso shares at $24 per share. Burlington reserved the right to terminate the offer if any of several specified events occurred. El Paso management initially opposed the takeover, but its shareholders responded favorably, fully subscribing to the offer by the December 30, 1982, deadline.

Burlington did not accept those tendered shares; instead, after negotiations with El Paso management, Burlington announced on January 10, 1983, the terms of a new and friendly takeover agreement. Pursuant to the new agreement, Burlington undertook, *inter alia*, to (1) rescind the December tender offer, (2) purchase 4,166,667 shares from El Paso at $24 per share, (3) substitute a new tender offer for only 21 million shares at $24 per share, (4) provide procedural protections against a squeeze-out merger[1] of the remaining El Paso shareholders, and (5) recognize "golden parachute" contracts between El Paso and four of its senior officers. By February 8, more than 40 million shares were tendered in response to Burlington's January offer, and the takeover was completed.

The rescission of the first tender offer caused a diminished payment to those shareholders who had tendered during the first offer. The January offer was greatly oversubscribed and consequently those shareholders who retendered were subject to substantial proration. Petitioner Barbara Schreiber filed suit on behalf of herself and similarly situated shareholders, alleging that Burlington, El Paso, and members of El Paso's board of directors violated §14(e)'s prohibition of "fraudulent, deceptive or manipulative acts or practices... in connection with any tender offer." She claimed that Burlington's withdrawal of the December tender offer was a "manipulative" distortion of the market for El Paso stock. Schreiber also alleged that Burlington violated §14(e) by failing in the January offer to disclose the "golden parachutes" offered to four of El Paso's managers. She claims that this January nondisclosure was a deceptive act forbidden by §14(e).

The District Court dismissed the suit for failure to state a claim. The District Court reasoned that the alleged manipulation did not involve a misrepresentation, and so did not violate §14(e). District Court relied on the fact that in cases involving alleged violations of §10(b) of the Securities Exchange Act, this Court has required misrepresentation for there to be a "manipulative" violation of the section.

The Court of Appeals for the Third Circuit affirmed.

Body of Opinion

Chief Justice Burger

We are asked in this case to interpret §14(e) of the Securities Exchange Act. The starting point is the language of the statute. Section 14(e) provides:

> It shall be unlawful for any person to make any untrue statement of a material fact or omit to state any material fact necessary in order to make the statements made, in the light of the circumstances under which they are made, not misleading, or to engage in any fraudulent, deceptive, or manipulative acts or practices, in connection with any tender offer or request or invitation for tenders, or any solicitation of security holders in opposition to or in favor of any such offer, request, or invitation. The Commission shall, for the purposes of this subsection, by rules and regulations define, and prescribe means reasonably designed to prevent, such acts and practices as are fraudulent, deceptive, or manipulative.

Petitioner relies on a construction of the phrase, "fraudulent, deceptive, or manipulative acts or practices." Petitioner reads the phrase "fraudulent, deceptive or manipulative acts or practices" to include acts which, although fully disclosed, "artificially" affect the price of the takeover target's stock. Petitioner's interpretation relies on the belief that §14(e) is directed at purposes broader than providing full and true information to investors....

She argues, however, that the term *manipulative* takes on a meaning in §14(e) that is different from the meaning it has in §10(b). Petitioner claims that the use of the disjunctive *or* in §14(e) implies that acts need not be deceptive or fraudulent to be manipulative. But Congress used the phrase "manipulative or deceptive" in §10(b) as well, and we have interpreted manipulative in that context to require misrepresentation. Moreover, it

---

[1] A "squeeze-out" merger occurs when Corporation A, which holds a controlling interest in Corporation B, uses its control to merge B into itself or into a wholly owned subsidiary. The minority shareholders in Corporation B are, in effect, forced to sell their stock. The procedural protection provided in the agreement between El Paso and Burlington required the approval of non-Burlington members of El Paso's board of directors before a squeeze-out merger could proceed. Burlington eventually purchased all the remaining shares of El Paso for $12 cash and one-quarter share of Burlington preferred stock per share. The parties dispute whether this consideration was equal to that paid to those tendering during the January tender offer.

is a "familiar principle of statutory construction that words grouped in a list should be given related meaning." *Securities Industry Assn. v. Board of Governors, FRS* (1984). All three species of misconduct, i.e., "fraudulent, deceptive, or manipulative," listed by Congress are directed at failures to disclose. The use of the term *manipulative* provides emphasis and guidance to those who must determine which types of acts are reached by the statute; it does not suggest a deviation from the section's facial and primary concern with disclosure or congressional concern with disclosure which is the core of the Act.

Our conclusion that *manipulative* acts under §14(e) require misrepresentation or nondisclosure is buttressed by the purpose and legislative history of the provision.

The expressed legislative intent was to preserve a neutral setting in which the contenders could fully present their arguments. The Senate sponsor went on to say:

> We have taken extreme care to avoid tipping the scales either in favor of management or in favor of the person making the takeover bids. §510 is designed solely to require full and fair disclosure for the benefit of investors. The bill will at the same time provide the offeror and management equal opportunity to present their case.

To implement this objective, the Williams Act added §§ 13(d), 13(e), 14(d), 14(e), and 14(f) to the Securities Exchange Act. Some relate to disclosure; §§ 13(d), 14(d), and 14(f) all add specific registration and disclosure provisions. Others—§§13(e) and 14(d)—require or prohibit certain acts so that investors will possess additional time within which to take advantage of the disclosed information.

Section 14(e) adds a "broad antifraud prohibition," *Piper v. Chris Craft Industries, Inc.*, modeled on the antifraud provisions of §10(b) of the Act and Rule 10b-5. It supplements the more precise disclosure provisions found elsewhere in the Williams Act, while requiring disclosure more explicitly addressed to the tender offer context than that required by §10(b). . . .

Nowhere in the legislative history is there the slightest suggestion that §14(e) serves any purpose other than disclosure, or that the term *manipulative* should be read as an invitation to the courts to oversee the substantive fairness of tender offers; the quality of any offer is a matter for the marketplace.

To adopt the reading of the term *manipulative* urged by petitioner would not only be unwarranted in light of the legislative purpose but would be at odds with it. Inviting judges to read the term *manipulative* with their own sense of what constitutes "unfair" or "artificial" conduct would inject uncertainty into the tender offer process. An essential piece of information—whether the court would deem the fully disclosed actions of one side or the other to be *manipulative*—would not be available until after the tender offer had closed. This uncertainty would directly contradict the expressed congressional desire to give investors full information.

Judgment and Result

1. *Manipulative* acts under §14(e) require misrepresentation or nondisclosure. To read the term *manipulative* in §14(e) to include acts that, although fully disclosed, "artificially" affect the price of the takeover target's stock, conflicts with the normal meaning of the term as connoting conduct designed to deceive or defraud investors by controlling or artificially affecting the price of securities.

2. This interpretation of the term *manipulative* as used in §14(e) is supported by the provision's purpose and legislative history. The purpose of the Williams Act, which added §14(e) to the Securities Exchange Act, was to ensure that public shareholders who are confronted with a tender offer will not be required to respond without adequate information. Nowhere in the legislative history is there any suggestion that §14(e) serves any purpose other than disclosure, or that the term "manipulative" should be read as an invitation to the courts to oversee the substantive fairness of tender offers; the quality of any offer is a matter for the marketplace.

3. Applying the above interpretation of the term *manipulative* to this case, respondents' actions were not manipulative. (Plaintiff lost.)

Questions

1. What are the objectives of the Williams Act, which governs tender offers?
2. Do sections 14(e) and 10(b) of the 1934 SEA have similar purposes?
3. Describe how plaintiff was wronged by the tender offer process.
4. Was it possible for the Supreme Court to find *for* plaintiff? Why did it refuse to do so?
5. To whom does the tender offeror owe a duty not to be manipulative—to its own shareholders or to the target's shareholders?
6. What is the natural law philosophy in the Williams Act?

Criminal Violations of SEA

Violations of the SEA or its rules and regulations must be willful to be crimes. Section 32 of the SEA makes criminal the willful and knowing making of a statement in a required report, application, or document that is false or misleading in any material respect. An example of a Section 32 violation is an accountant's signing a corporation's financial statements as being fair representations of the firm's financial status when the accountant knows they are not. Accountants have been convicted for committing this federal felony.

Penalties. Punishment can be up to five years in prison, up to a $100,000 fine, or both for SEA criminal violations. Conviction for a criminal violation prevents certain benefits under the securities laws (for example, use of the small issue exemption under the Securities Act of 1933 or association with a registered investment company).

Foreign Corrupt Practices Act

Internal Reports. The Foreign Corrupt Practices Act (FCPA) has three principal sections: 102, 103, and 104. Section 102 establishes internal reporting requirements for companies subject to the FCPA. These requirements are designed to put management in a position to know whether bribes are being paid directly or indirectly to foreign officials or political parties or candidates.

Foreign Corrupt Practices. Section 103 prohibits foreign corrupt practices—bribes—by issuers. An issuer is any firm required to register its securities under the 1934 Securities Exchange Act. The FCPA also makes it illegal for any U.S. citizen or domestic concern to use the U.S. mail or interstate commerce to commit a foreign corrupt practice. As such the FCPA covers nonissuers of securities.

Penalties. Violations of the FCPA are federal felonies. An issuer committing prohibited foreign corrupt practices is subject to a fine of not more than $2,000,000. The fine could be a substantial deterrent to small firms. For large concerns, the stigma of a conviction would be more adverse than the size of the fine. Any officer or director of an issuer or stockholder acting on the issuer's behalf who willfully violates the corrupt practices applicable to issuers can be fined not more than $100,000, imprisoned for not more than five years, or both. The same penalties apply to domestic concerns, officers, directors, and shareholders acting on behalf of domestic concerns who bribe foreign officials or political party officials, or any person with reason to know his or her bribe will end up in the hands of a foreign official, foreign political candidate, or party official. (For more about the FCPA, see Chapter 9.)

State Securities Regulation

http:// *To check out individual state securities laws go to http://www.prairienet.org/~scruffy/f.htm*

Each individual state has the power to regulate securities within its borders. The federal constitutional basis for such state authority is found in the Tenth Amendment to the U.S. Constitution, which reserves power to the states that is not expressly given to the national government or retained by the people. The specific reserved power that the states invoke to regulate securities is the police power—the power to regulate to promote the health, safety, morals, and general welfare of the state.

Some states were in the securities regulation business long before the federal government was. In 1911, Kansas was the first state to attempt to regulate securities. Other states have adopted securities laws, called **blue-sky laws**, designed to prevent sale by unscrupulous people of securities that represent nothing more than an interest in the blue sky. About half the states have passed the Uniform Securities Act as their blue-sky law.

Other states have their own blue-sky laws, which are usually of three types: licensing, disclosure, and fraud. The licensing type requires sellers of securities to obtain state licenses before engaging in the securities business. Such laws impose a duty on licensed sellers to disclose to prospective purchasers information germane to the security. The disclosure type of blue-sky law is akin to the philosophy of the Federal Securities Act of 1933, which is also one of full and fair disclosure. The idea is that the investor should be provided with all relevant facts about the issues before deciding whether to invest. People who provide facts are liable for falsity or omission of material facts. A registration statement similar to that filed under the Securities Act of 1933 furnishes investors with facts relevant to their decision to invest. The fraud type of blue-sky law forbids misrepresentation in the sale of securities. A violation of such statutes usually results in civil (damages and injunctions) and criminal sanctions.

State regulation of securities has been uneven. In some states, saying that such regulation exists is a joke, even though statutes are on the books. In other states—and they constitute a minority—regulation does exist. In fairness to the states, the same securities being regulated once by the feds and once by the states no doubt has caused a number of states not to regulate securities, even though they have the constitutional authority to do so.

The 1995 Private Securities Litigation Reform Act has amended the 1933 Securities Act as well as the 1934 Securities Exchange Act. A major change this act affects is the introduction of proportional liability (rather than joint and several liability) in certain situations.

CHAPTER SUMMARY

A number of federal laws attempt to regulate the sale of securities. Two of the most important such laws are the Securities Act of 1933 and the Securities Exchange Act of 1934.

The Supreme Court defines *security* by using the *Howey* case definition. According to this definition, an investment in a common enterprise for profit expectation from third-party efforts qualifies something as a security. Courts examine the substance, not form, of an investment to determine whether it is a security.

The main objective of the Securities Act of 1933 is to provide full and fair disclosure of new securities offered for sale. This act does not require the government to tell the public whether an investment is good or bad. The 1933 Securities Act requires that nonexempt securities be registered with the SEC.

The Securities Exchange Act of 1934 created the Securities and Exchange Commission (SEC). The SEC is charged with administering many laws that regulate the securities markets.

The Securities Exchange Act of 1934 regulates the secondary market, made up of "used" or already issued securities. The 1934 Act requires that certain securities be registered unless exempt. The 1934 Act also imposes proxy statement requirements, credit restrictions, short-swing profit prohibitions, and antifraud provisions. Civil and criminal sanctions may be brought for violations of the 1934 Securities Exchange Act.

The Insider Trading Sanctions Act imposes civil and criminal sanctions.

State laws also regulate the sale of securities.

MANAGER'S ETHICAL DILEMMA

"I got information from a company whistleblower, who said the company had nonexistent assets, so I advised clients to short the stock (sell stock they did not own and buy such stock to cover later when the stock price hopefully is lower) and when the company collapsed, my clients made money," said Ray Dirks, a securities analyst.

"But Ray," said a friend, "that's illegal. You were a tippee, and tippees who receive any information from insiders are strictly prohibited from trading in the stock."

"Oh, no," replied Dirks. "I was neither an 'insider' nor a 'tippee' from an insider who was violating any duty owed to the issuer. Therefore, I could trade in the issuer's stock using insider information."

"That's hogwash," said the friend. "There is an absolute prohibition on tippees' trading in an issuer's stock."

What do you think? Should a tippee trade in an issuer's stock?

Discussion Questions

1. Discussion is currently ongiong about the creation of a new body to regulate both commodities exchanges, presently regulated by the Commodities Futures Trading Commission (CFTC), and the securities exchanges, now regulated by the SEC (Securities and Exchange Commission). What do you see as the pros and cons of such a proposal?
2. In 1986 and 1988, the Colorado Springs-Stetson Hills Public Building Authority issued a total of $26 million in bonds to finance public improvements at Stetson Hills, a planned residential and commercial development in Colorado Springs. Central Bank served as the bond trustee for the bond issues.

   The bonds were secured by landowner assessment liens, which covered about 250 acres for the 1986 bond issue and about 272 acres for the 1988 bond issue. The bond covenants required that the land subject to the liens be worth at least 160 percent of the bonds' outstanding principal and interest. The covenants required AmWest Development, the developer of Stetson Hills, to give Central Bank an annual report containing evidence that the 160 percent test was met.

   In January 1988, AmWest provided Central Bank an updated appraisal of the land securing the 1986 bonds and of the proposed liens to to secure the 1988 bonds. The 1988 appraisal showed land values almost unchanged from the 1986 appraisal. Soon afterwards, Central Bank received a letter from the senior underwriter for the 1986 bonds. Noting that property values were declining in Colorado Springs and that Central Bank was operating on an appraisal over 16 months old, the underwriter expressed concern that the 160 percent test was not being met.

   Central Bank asked its in-house appraiser to review the updated 1988 appraisal. The in-house appraiser decided that the values listed in the appraisal appeared optimistic considering the local real estate market. He suggested that Central Bank retain an outside appraiser to conduct an independent review of the 1988 appraisal. After an exchange of letters between Central Bank and AmWest in early 1988, Central Bank agreed to delay independent review of the appraisal until the end of the year, six months after the June 1988 closing on the bond issue. Before the independent review was complete, however, the Authority defaulted on the 1988 bonds.

   First Interstate and Jack Naber had purchased $2.1 million of the 1988 bonds. After the default, First Interstate and Naber sued the Authority, the 1988 underwriter, a junior underwriter, an AmWest director, and Central Bank for violations of section 10b of the Securities Exchange Act of 1934. The complaint alleged that the Authority, the underwriter defendants, and the AmWest director had violated section 10b for its conduct in aiding and abetting the fraud. A federal district court found for defendant Central Bank (the bond trustee). The U.S. Court of Appeals for the Tenth Circuit reversed holding that there is a section 10b aiding and abetting civil claim when: (1) there is a primary violation of 10b; (2) there is recklessness by an aider and abettor (here,

Central Bank, the bond trustee for failure to update the appraisal in a timely fashion); and (3) substantial assistance is given to the primary violator by the aider and abettor (i.e., would the 1988 bond issue have been marketable had the trustee reappraised the land that secured the bond issue?).

The bond trustee (Central Bank) appealed to the U.S. Supreme Court arguing that section 10b of the 1934 Act coupled with a federal aiding and abetting statute does not create a private aider and abettor cause of action. Who won? [*Central Bank v. First Interstate Bank*, 114 S.Ct. 1439 (1994)]

3. Winans was coauthor of a *Wall Street Journal* investment advice column that, because of its perceived quality and integrity, had an impact on the market prices of the stocks it discussed. Although he was familiar with the *Journal's* rule that the column's contents were the *Journal's* confidential information prior to publication, Winans entered into a scheme with Felis and another stockbroker who, in exchange for advance information from Winans as to the timing and contents of the column, bought and sold stocks based on the column's probable impact on the market. They then shared their profits with Winans. On the basis of this scheme, Winans and Felis were convicted of criminal violations of section 10b of the Securities Exchange Act of 1934. The Court of Appeals affirmed. Winans appealed to the U.S. Supreme Court arguing that the alleged fraud victim, the *Journal*, was not a buyer or seller of the stocks traded and thus the fraud was not covered by section 10b of the Securities Exchange Act, because it requires fraud "in connection with the purchase or sale of any security." What was the result? [*Carpenter v. United States*, 108 S.Ct. 316 (1987)]
4. Securities brokers get commissions whenever a customer buys or sells a security (even if the customer loses money). Commissions may tempt brokers to urge customers to buy and sell securities frequently, even if such sales or purchases are not in the customer's best interests. Such frequent broker-encouraged trades are called *churning*. Is churning a violation of the Securities Exchange Act of 1934; that is, is it considered a fraud in connection with the purchase and sale of securities? [*Costello v. Oppenheimer & Co., Inc.*, 711 F.2d 1361 (7th Cir. 1983)]
5. Are punitive damages recoverable under a Rule 10b-5 claim? [*Meyers v. Moody*, 693 F.2d 1196, rehearing denied 701 F.2d 173 (5th Cir. 1983)]
6. A newspaper financial columnist bought stock in a company. He then wrote a column advising people to buy that stock. He did not mention in his column that he owned stock in the recommended company. The column appeared, the stock rose, and the columnist sold his stock, making a profit. Does this conduct (known as scalping) violate Section 10(b) of the Securities Exchange Act of 1934 and Rule 10b-5? [*Zweig v. Hearst Corp.*, 594 F.2d 1261 (9th Cir. 1979)]
7. Michael Moss owned 5,000 shares of Deseret Pharmaceutical Company. Warner-Lambert Company wanted to buy Deseret stock to take over the company. Warner hired Morgan Stanley, Inc. to recommend an appropriate price to offer Deseret's shareholders. Courtois, a Morgan Stanley employee, learned of the possible Warner purchase of Deseret. On November 30, 1976, Courtois and two friends, Newman and Antoniu, bought 11,700 shares of Deseret (including Moss's stock) at $28 per share. The next day, December 1, 1976, the New York Stock Exchange stopped trading in Deseret for six days when Warner announced it would buy Deseret stock for $38 per share. Newman, Courtois, and Antoniu sold their 11,700 shares and made a big profit. Did they violate Section 10(b) of the 1934 Securities Exchange Act and Rule 10b-5 by buying Deseret stock knowing of Warner-Lambert's upcoming offer and without telling existing Deseret stockholders about it when they bought their stock? [*Moss v. Morgan Stanley, Inc.*, 719 F.2d 5 (2d Cir. 1983)]
8. A securities broker was making a sales pitch to Edna Brown. Edna was not sure whether buying stock in the recommended company was a good investment. The broker pulled out a prospectus that the company had filed with the SEC and said, "Edna, the SEC has registered this stock. Therefore, you can bet your last dollar that it's a good investment." Do you agree? When the SEC registers a new security under the 1933 Securities Act, what is the SEC saying?
9. Sometimes one corporation will try to buy another corporation's stock from existing shareholders to take control of the corporation. This offer is called a tender offer. The tender offer price per share is usually above the share's existing market price. The company to be taken over is called the target

company. The target company's management gets nervous when another firm tries to take it over. Why? Because one of the first things the buyer does is fire the target firm's existing management. Can the target company's management get a court to stop a takeover by showing that the group making the tender offer did not disclose material financial information about two members of the takeover group? [*Pabst Brewing Co. v. Kalmanovitz*, 551 F. Supp. 882 (D.C. Del. 1982)]

10. Must people making a tender offer disclose their general business philosophy to the target corporation's shareholders? Existing management of Pabst Brewing Company argued that Kalmanovitz, who owned a competing brewery, planned to shut down several Pabst plants if his takeover bid succeeded. Pabst management thought Pabst shareholders should know of Kalmanovitz's plan before they sold their stock to Kalmanovitz. [*Pabst Brewing Co. v. Kalmanovitz*, 551 F. Supp. 882 (D.C. Del. 1982)]
11. Suppose Sally Morgan is an insider under Rule 16(b). She buys and sells 100 shares of her company's stock within a five-month period, making $1,000 on the deal. Assume that she did not actually use any inside information when she made her purchase and sale. Has she violated Rule 16(b), and can the company recover the $1,000? [*Smolowe v. Delendo Corp.*, 136 F. 2d 231 (2d Cir. 1943)]
12. Why should management know if one of its employees is violating the Foreign Corrupt Practices Act? (See Section 102 of the Foreign Corrupt Practices Act.)
13. Mr. Chiarella worked as a markup man in Pandick Press's New York composing room. Chiarella handled announcements of corporate takeover bids. When a corporation delivered these documents to Pandick Press, the names of the acquiring and target corporation were hidden by either fake names or blank spaces. The corporations sent the true names on the night of the final printing. Mr. Chiarella figured out the target companies' names (the companies being bought) before the final printing from other information in the documents. Without telling anyone what he knew, Chiarella bought stock in the target companies. He then sold it soon after the takeover attempts became publicly known. He made more than $30,000 through this method over fourteen months. The SEC investigated him, and he agreed to return the profits to the people from whom he had bought the stock. His employer fired him, and he was later indicted for violating Section 10(b) of the Securities Exchange Act of 1934 and Rule 10b-5. Chiarella was convicted. He appealed first to the court of appeals, which affirmed his conviction. He then appealed to the U.S. Supreme Court, arguing that his failure to inform sellers of the stock in target companies he had bought was not a fraud under Rule 10b-5 of the Securities Exchange Act of 1934. Does a duty to disclose under Section 10(b) arise just because Chiarella had nonpublic information? [*Chiarella v. United States*, 445 U.S. 222 (1980)]
14. The SEC charged that Texas International Company's (TI) president, George Platt, while in the stands at a track meet, told his son and Barry Switzer, University of Oklahoma football coach, that TI was going to sell a company (Phoenix Resources) it controlled. Platt and Switzer allegedly bought stock in Phoenix Resources and sold it at a profit. Did Platt intentionally tip Switzer in violation of his (Platt's) fiduciary duty to Phoenix Resources shareholders, making Switzer's action illegal tippee trading? [*SEC v. Platt*, 565 F. Supp. 1244 (W.D. Okl. 1983)]

Suggested Readings

Articles

AALBERTS and POON, "The New Prudent Investor Rule and the Modern Portfolio Theory: A New Direction for Fiduciaries," 34 *American Business Law Journal* 39 (1996).

ALDAVE, "Misappropriation: A General Theory of Liability for Trading on Nonpublic Information," 13 *Hofstra Law Review* 101 (1984).

ATHANUS, "Texas Gulf Sulphur Revisited: Fiduciary Duty Becomes Federal Law, 23 *Business Law Review* 1 (1990).

BAGBY, "The Evolving Controversy over Insider Trading," 24 *American Business Law Journal* 571 (1987).

BURGUNDER and HARTMANN, "Soft Dollars and Section 28(e) of the Securities Exchange Act of 1934: A 1986 Perspective," 24 *American Business Law Journal* 139 (1986).

DOTY, "Regulatory Expectations Regarding the Conduct of Attorneys in the Enforcement of the Federal Securities Laws: Recent Development and Lessons for the Future," 48 *Business Lawyer* 1543 (1993).

FERRERA, "Corporate Board Responsibility under the Foreign Corrupt Practices Act of 1977," 18 *American Business Law Journal* 259 (1980).

FOX, "SEC Rule 10b-5: Tippee Liability Revisited," 22 *American Business Law Journal* 38, (1984).

LEVINE, "Compliance with GAAP and GAAS: Its Proper Use as an Accountant's Defense in a Rule 10b-5 Suit," 1993 *Columbia Business Law Review* 109 (1993).

SIEDEL, "Internal Accounting Controls under the Foreign Corrupt Practices Act: A Federal Law of Corporations?" 18 *American Business Law Journal* 443 (1981).

TIDWELL, "Teaching Rules of Insider Trading," 9 *Journal of Legal Studies Education* 85 (1990).

WHITE, "Outside Directors Under the Federal Securities Laws: Fraudulent Actors or Innocent Victims?" 21 *Securities Regulation Law Journal* 297 (1993).

Books

RATNER, *Securities Regulation in a Nutshell*, 4th ed. (1992).

MODULE

6

LAW AFFECTING THE MARKETING DEPARTMENT

CHAPTER

20

ANTITRUST LAW

"PEOPLE OF THE SAME TRADE SELDOM MEET TOGETHER, EVEN FOR MERRIMENT AND DIVERSION, BUT THE CONVERSATION ENDS IN A CONSPIRACY AGAINST THE PUBLIC, OR IN SOME CONTRIVANCE TO RAISE PRICES."

Adam Smith, The Wealth of Nations (1776)

POSITIVE LAW ETHICAL PROBLEMS

Barkat U. Khan had long wanted to run a gas station, but when he got his chance, things didn't work out. Khan contracted with State Oil Company to lease and operate a gas station and convenience store owned by State Oil. The contract said that Khan would get his gasoline supply from State Oil at a price equal to a suggested retail price set by State Oil, minus a margin of 3.25 cents per gallon. Khan could charge his station's customers any gasoline price he wanted, but if the price charged was higher than State Oil's suggested retail price, the excess was to be rebated to State Oil. Khan also could sell gasoline for less than State Oil's suggested retail price, but any such decrease would reduce his margin.

About a year after Khan began operating the gas station, he fell behind in his lease payments. State Oil then gave notice of its intent to terminate the agreement and began a state court proceeding to evict Khan. But Khan had a plan to avoid this fate. Khan sued State Oil in federal court, alleging that, by its contract with him, State Oil had fixed prices in violation of Sherman Act section 1. Had the agreement with State Oil not existed, Khan claimed, he could have charged different prices based on the different grades of gasoline he offered, thereby achieving increased sales and profits.

Assuming that State Oil really had fixed his resale prices, Khan's antitrust argument seemed solid. The courts had long held that so-called *vertical price-fixing* (price-fixing down the chain of distribution, usually between a supplier and a retailer) automatically violates Sherman Act section 1. The main reason is that such price-fixing stifles *intrabrand competition*—competition among sellers of the same brand—which hurts consumers of that brand. But at least in part, the contract about which Khan was complaining fixed *maximum* prices. How does this hurt consumers? Does it make sense to read section 1 as automatically barring the fixing of maximum prices?

Free-market economies tend to be more efficient and productive than other kinds of economies. This is primarily due to the economic competition they foster. Yet the very freedom that helps promote competition also can frustrate it. Business firms sometimes restrain competition in order to increase their own profits. For example, competitors may agree to fix artificially high prices or to suppress competition by dividing territories among themselves. Also, one competitor may come to dominate its market, and then use the resulting economic power to hurt consumers, its remaining competitors, or other firms. For example, a business that monopolizes its industry may be able to maximize its profits by raising prices and restricting output.

Businesses have used these and other *restraints of trade* for centuries. Over those same centuries, the law sometimes has tried to prevent such anticompetitive behavior. The common law, for instance, has long prohibited certain trade restraints and other anticompetitive practices. In late nineteenth-century America, however, the common law was increasingly perceived as an inadequate tool for containing anticompetitive behavior. The main reason was the array of problems created by the unprecedented growth in the size and power of business organizations. In response, Congress enacted the **antitrust laws**.[1] This chapter examines the body of law courts have created as they fleshed out these statutes.

THE EMERGENCE OF ANTITRUST LAW IN THE UNITED STATES

The emergence of large corporations and industrial combines during the latter part of the nineteenth century was accompanied by various economic abuses. For example, railroads often charged high rates to customers with little economic power and low rates to powerful shippers (sometimes through secret rebates). Such abuses led to passage of the Interstate Commerce Act of 1887, which established the Interstate Commerce Commission to regulate railroads in general and their rates in particular.

Regulated industries such as railroads often are *natural monopolies*: industries in which a particular market is most economically served by one firm. (Electrical power generation is another example.) In such cases, the antitrust laws are inappropriate because they seek to promote competition and competition is not socially beneficial where a genuine natural monopoly exists. By the late nineteenth century, however, industries other than natural monopolies also were beset by abuses. At that time, lines of business such as fuel oil, cotton, and sugar were dominated by combinations of several firms called *trusts*.[2] The tactics trusts used to gain and hold power in their industries—for example, below-cost pricing and business espionage—provoked widespread criticism. Also, many felt that the economic concentration the trusts created and the private power they exerted were inconsistent with freedom and democracy. At a minimum, trusts that subdued their competitors gained some freedom to raise prices above competitive levels. At worst, some believed, they would dominate the political processes and create a social environment in which large groups dominate and the individual counts for nothing.

The public outcry against the trusts and their abuses eventually led to enactment of the federal antitrust laws. The first of these laws, the **Sherman Act**, was passed by Congress in 1890. Section 1 of the Sherman Act forbids "[e]very contract, combination in the form of trust or otherwise, or conspiracy, in restraint of trade or commerce among the several States, or with foreign nations." Section 1 covers many different anticompetitive practices. Section 1 also requires *joint action*: collaboration by two or

[1] Many of the states also have antitrust laws. Because the federal antitrust laws are more important, and because the state laws vary, the latter are not discussed here.

[2] A trust might be defined as a property right held by one party for the benefit of another. Typically, the person holding the right, called the *trustee*, manages the property for the benefit of someone else, the *beneficiary*. For the trusts in question here, stockholders in several different companies transferred their shares to a set of trustees, in exchange for certificates entitling them to a percentage of the combined earnings of the jointly managed companies.

more parties. Section 2 of the Sherman Act says that "[e]very person who shall monopolize, or attempt to monopolize, or combine or conspire with any other person or persons, to monopolize any part of the trade or commerce among the several States, or with foreign nations, shall be deemed guilty of a felony." Basically, section 2 forbids monopolization and attempts to monopolize. Notice that unlike section 1, section 2 has no joint action requirement; action by one party can violate section 2.

Responding to perceived inadequacies in the Sherman Act, Congress supplemented it by enacting the **Clayton Act** in 1914. Section 3 of the Clayton Act makes it unlawful to sell or lease commodities (goods) where the sale or lease is made on the condition that the buyer or lessee not use or deal commodities sold or leased by a competitor of the seller or lessor, and where the effect of the sale or lease may be to substantially lessen competition or tend to create a monopoly. Section 3 mainly applies to three kinds of potentially anticompetitive behavior: tying contracts, exclusive dealing contracts, and requirements contracts. Section 7 of the Clayton Act governs mergers. Like Clayton Act section 3, section 7 requires that the merger or other allegedly illegal behavior substantially lessen competition or tend to create a monopoly. Section 8 of the act forbids interlocking corporate directorates: situations in which one person serves on competing corporations' boards of directors.

Clayton Act section 2 prohibited price discrimination, or charging similarly situated buyers different prices for a product. In 1936, section 2 was amended by the **Robinson-Patman Act**. We examine the Robinson-Patman Act's prohibitions on price discrimination and related offenses later in the chapter. Finally, the year 1914 also witnessed Congress's passage of the **Federal Trade Commission Act**. Chapter 21 discusses this act in detail.

THE DEBATE OVER ANTITRUST POLICY

Many antitrust provisions are vague, and the legislative history behind them does not clearly fix their meaning either. Thus, the formulation of antitrust law is largely up to the courts. What general views about the purposes of antitrust law should guide courts in this endeavor? In recent years, two general approaches have dominated the antitrust policy debate. Although they go by various names, we will call them the "Chicago School" view and the "traditional" view.

According to the Chicago School view, the primary, if not the sole, purpose of the antitrust laws is to promote economic efficiency. This, Chicago School theorists assume, maximizes the economic welfare of consumers. The traditional view, on the other hand, says that the antitrust laws should promote other values in addition to efficiency. Some traditionalists remain attached to the ideal of an economy dominated by small entrepreneurs. Some say that concentrated economic power is inconsistent with democracy and liberty in the long run, and that for this reason the antitrust laws should be used to break up such concentrated power. These values should prevail, some traditionalists maintain, even if they involve losses in economic efficiency. To the Chicago School theorists, on the other hand, size and economic concentration are not necessarily bad as long as competition exists and efficiency is maximized. In their view, the traditionalists' position often boils down to protecting competitors rather than promoting competition.

Clashes between Chicago School and traditionalist views of antitrust will be described at various points in this chapter. Nonetheless, it might be useful to sketch the different practical implications of the two views at this point. Three implications stand out. First, the traditionalists favor more antitrust enforcement than does the Chicago School. Specifically, the traditionalists regard more kinds of business behavior as violations of the antitrust laws. Secondly, the traditional view is very concerned about economic concentration, while the Chicago School is less bothered by it. To the Chicago School, a firm's large size often is its reward for being a superior competitor, and to punish size is to discourage competitive activity. The traditionalists, on the other hand, worry about the economic and political power possessed by large firms and the uses to which it will be put. Finally, the Chicago School is less concerned about so-called vertical restraints (restraints down a firm's chain of distribution) than is the traditionalist camp. This view reflects the Chicago School position that, for example, price-fixing between manufacturers and retailers or agreements whereby manufacturers assign territories to particular retailers are not necessarily anticompetitive on balance.

THE SHERMAN ACT: PRELIMINARIES

The Act's Reach

Congress's power to enact the Sherman Act comes from the U.S. Constitution's commerce clause, which enables it to regulate commerce among the states. As discussed in Chapter 5, Congress's commerce clause regulatory power includes intrastate matters that have a substantial impact on interstate commerce. Thus, the Sherman Act extends to (1) activities that interfere with the flow of commerce among the states, and (2) activities inside a particular state that substantially affect commerce among the states. As a practical matter, the Sherman Act probably reaches most anticompetitive activities that occur solely within a particular state.

In addition to regulating anticompetitive conduct that involves or affects interstate commerce, the Sherman Act also regulates conduct that restrains trade or commerce with foreign nations. Like the former assertion of regulatory power, the latter has its basis in the commerce clause, which also allows Congress to regulate foreign commerce. To oversimplify a complex subject, the Sherman Act's regulation of foreign commerce basically covers anticompetitive activities that affect the U.S. economy. These activities may be undertaken by (1) foreign firms within the United States, (2) foreign firms outside the United States, or (3) U.S. firms outside the United States. Various statutes and judicial doctrines further refine and/or limit the Sherman Act's application to foreign commerce. In all such cases, finally, the U.S. government or a private plaintiff must get personal jurisdiction over the defendant.

Criminal Prosecutions

Liability for violations of the Sherman Act may be both criminal and civil. Criminal prosecutions are initiated by the Antitrust Division of the Justice Department.[3] The maximum fine for a corporation found guilty of a Sherman Act criminal violation is $10 million. Individuals are punishable by fines of up to $350,000 and jail sentences of up to three years.

A Sherman Act criminal defendant can enter one of three pleas—guilty, not guilty, or *nolo contendere*. A defendant who pleads nolo contendere can be criminally punished to the same degree as a defendant who pleaded guilty or who was proven guilty following a not-guilty plea. But unlike a defendant who pleads guilty, a defendant who pleads nolo contendere neither admits nor denies the criminal charges. Thus, the plea cannot be used to prove liability in a private

[3] The Federal Trade Commission also enforces the antitrust laws. See Chapter 21.

plaintiff's subsequent civil suit against the defendant. When the defendant pleads guilty or is found guilty after a not-guilty plea, on the other hand, a private plaintiff can use the previous criminal conviction to help make its civil case. This feature of the nolo contendere plea naturally makes it attractive to alleged antitrust violators, and settlements of criminal antitrust cases often involve such pleas.

Civil Suits

Both the Justice Department and private parties may sue antitrust violators civilly. The courts have broad injunctive powers in cases of this kind. For example, they may order the defendant to cease business and sell its assets (called *dissolution*), to sell its own stock or assets or those of an acquired firm (called *divestiture*), or to separate itself from some functional level of its operations such as retailing (called *divorcement*). An antitrust violator might also be enjoined to refrain from certain conduct in the future. If the parties settle the case, the court or the Justice Department completes a legally enforceable consent decree approving the terms of the settlement. Typically, a consent decree obligates the defendant to do something to remedy the effects of its anticompetitive behavior, or to refrain from such behavior in the future. Like a plea of nolo contendere, a consent decree does not constitute an admission of guilt or liability, and does not prove liability in subsequent civil litigation.

In addition, private parties who win a civil Sherman Act case recover **treble damages** plus attorney's fees from the defendant. This means that a successful private plaintiff gets three times its actual damages (plus attorney's fees). One reason for awarding treble damages is to supplement government enforcement of the antitrust laws by giving private parties an incentive to sue. Because such suits can be abused, however, courts have limited the availability of private treble damage claims. To be awarded damages, a private plaintiff must show that the defendant's conduct harmed its business or property. In addition, that harm must constitute *antitrust injury*. This means that the defendant's allegedly unlawful conduct must cause injury of the type the antitrust laws were intended to prevent. For example, a private plaintiff cannot recover damages when the defendant's allegedly unlawful conduct increases the competition the plaintiff must face. Here, there may be harm to business or property, but that harm is not an antitrust injury because the antitrust laws aim to promote competition, not to prevent it.

The antitrust laws' **standing** requirements are another important obstacle to private suits. Standing rules appear in many different legal contexts; the general idea uniting them is that there must be a fairly direct and tangible connection between the alleged violation and the injury the plaintiff suffered. In other words, standing is a question of the plaintiff's proximity to the violation.

In *Illinois Brick Co. v. Illinois* (1977), the state of Illinois sued Illinois Brick and other concrete block manufacturers for price-fixing. Because Illinois Brick had not sold directly to the state but instead to masonry subcontractors who then sold to the state, the Supreme Court held that the state lacked standing to sue. This was true even though the subcontractors had passed on the costs created by the defendants' price-fixing, costs that probably constituted harm to business or property and antitrust injury. *Illinois Brick* at least means that only direct purchasers from members of an illegal price-fixing conspiracy have standing to sue. One justification for this rule is the possibility of multiple recoveries where several indirect purchasers buy from a direct purchaser; another is the difficulty of apportioning damages among the various parties affected by the price-fixing. Nonetheless, later cases suggest that an indirect purchaser has standing where (1) it buys from the direct purchaser under a fixed-quantity, cost-plus contract enabling the direct purchaser to pass on any price increases and obligating the indirect purchaser to buy a fixed quantity despite the price increase, or (2) the indirect purchaser owns or controls the direct purchaser.

SHERMAN ACT SECTION 1

Section 1 of the Sherman Act forbids every contract, combination, or conspiracy in restraint of trade. This language presents two initial problems. First, what is a "contract, combination, or conspiracy" and how is its existence proven? Second, does the word "every" mean that *all* contracts, combinations, and conspiracies in restraint of trade are illegal?

Joint or Concerted Action

Sherman Act section 1's "contract, combination, or conspiracy" language requires *joint action* or *concerted action*. Purely unilateral action is insufficient for a section 1 violation. In other words, section 1 requires collaboration between two or more parties. Who or what counts as a separate party for this purpose? Under section 1, a corporation cannot engage in joint action with itself or its employees. Also, a firm's employees cannot jointly act among themselves unless they collaborate with some independent party. In a 1984 case, furthermore, the Supreme Court held that a corporation cannot engage in concerted action with a wholly owned subsidiary. However, this rule may not cover all partially owned subsidiaries. One justification for all these rules is that in each case, the participants in the joint action are not completely distinct from one another. Also, collaboration among these participants probably creates less threat to competition than collaboration among parties who are genuinely distinct from one another, and who may be competitors.

Assuming that the participants in illegal concerted action are distinct from one another, how does a private plaintiff or the government prove the necessary contract, combination, or conspiracy? This question is important because sophisticated business managers do not make express agreements to restrain trade, or leave few tracks if they do. Therefore, courts sometimes must infer or imply concerted action from the parties' behavior and other relevant facts and circumstances. Most of the cases considering such inferences have involved alleged *horizontal* collaboration: joint action among competitors.

Where it exists, of course, direct evidence of an agreement such as documents or testimony often makes it easy to prove concerted action. In other cases, the question is what circumstantial evidence will do the job. Courts generally agree that without anything more, mere "conscious parallelism"—identical or similar conduct by competitors—does not prove an agreement to engage in that conduct. In a competitive market, for example, one might expect two competitors to charge identical or nearly identical prices at any particular point in time. But joint action may be found when conscious parallelism is accompanied by certain "plus factors." These include whether the defendants have a rational economic interest in conspiring, whether the defendants' parallel behavior is improbable without an agreement, whether the defendants committed past antitrust violations, and whether they took action to further the alleged conspiracy after directly communicating with each other. Related to this last factor is another consideration that sometimes has led to section 1 liability: exchanges of information between competitors, especially price information.

Rule of Reason and Per Se Violations

Section 1 expressly states that *every* contract, combination, or conspiracy in restraint of trade is illegal. Finding this standard impractical, in 1911 the Supreme Court held that section 1 only forbids *unreasonable* restraints on trade. This **rule of reason** approach means that courts consider the economic impact of particular restraints on a case-by-case basis. Naturally, they look for evidence that the defendants' joint action had anticompetitive effects. But they also consider whether that behavior had a procompetitive impact or produced some social benefit such as increased efficiency. Of course, it is unclear just what balance of competitive over anticompetitive effects suffices to make a trade restraint unreasonable.

The rule of reason approach enables courts to make sensitive, case-by-case determinations about the anticompetitive effects of particular business behavior. But it is questionable whether courts can do this difficult job well. Even if the rule of reason standard does not strain judges' abilities, it certainly consumes their time. In addition, that standard obviously gives little guidance to business. For these reasons, the Supreme Court has fashioned **per se rules** under Sherman Act section 1. Under the per se approach certain kinds of anticompetitive conduct are *conclusively presumed* to violate section 1. Issues such as standing and antitrust injury aside, that is, in a per se case the only thing necessary for section 1 liability is that the plaintiff or the government prove the relevant concerted action. The idea behind per se violations is that some kinds of business conduct are so often anticompetitive and without redeeming social value that it is useless and wasteful to consider their effects on a case-by-case basis. The virtues of per se rules mirror the disadvantages of the rule of reason approach: (1) per se rules are relatively easy, quick, and inexpensive for courts to apply; and (2) they give businesses more definite guidance about what they can and cannot do. Because per se rules are relatively clear, they also may deter antitrust violations. The main disadvantage of per se rules is their inflexibility.

Therefore, section 1 of the Sherman Act recognizes two kinds of antitrust violations: (1) rule of reason violations, and (2) per se violations. In a rule of reason case, a private plaintiff or the government must (1) prove the concerted action in question; and (2) convince the court that its anticompetitive effects are sufficiently great, and its countervailing virtues sufficiently few, to justify liability. In a per se case, the plaintiff or the government need only prove the relevant joint action.

Per Se Violations

The rule of reason is the "default rule" under Sherman Act section 1. Unless the challenged economic behavior fits within one of the "per se" categories described next, it is handled under the rule of reason. Now we consider the types of conduct that are said to be illegal per se under Sherman Act section 1. Their number has been dwindling over the past 20–30 years. Moreover, some of these "per se rules" resemble the rule of reason.

Vertical Price-Fixing. Since 1911, **vertical price-fixing** or **resale price maintenance** (RPM) has been a per se violation. The main reason is that such agreements inhibit *intrabrand* competition. Suppose that the Wonder Widget Company requires all its Philadelphia-area dealers to sell at or above a certain price. How much price competition will there be for Wonder Widgets in the Philadelphia area?

Traditionally, the per se rule for vertical price-fixing has not covered two kinds of behavior that resemble vertical price-fixing. First, the per se rule generally has not applied to price-fixing in **consignment** arrangements. In a consignment, the seller (the consignor) retains another party (the consignee) to act as its agent in selling its goods, while retaining title to those goods. Because the seller/consignor keeps title, and because an owner should have the right to sell its own goods at its own price, a price-fixing agreement between consignor and consignee should not violate section 1. Over the years, courts have nibbled away at this rule, but for the most part it still stands.

Second, due to the need to prove joint action, certain kinds of *suggested retail prices* and *refusals to deal* do not violate section 1. A manufacturer that merely suggests a retail price to its distributors does not engage in vertical price-fixing—even if the distributors follow the suggestion. The same is true of a manufacturer that announces that it will terminate any distributor who fails to follow its suggested prices, and then backs up the threat. In each case, the courts say, there is insufficient evidence of concerted action. A refusal to deal, moreover, represents the kind of free choice our system usually seeks to protect. However, joint action may be found if, in addition to the threatened refusal to deal, the manufacturer engages in some collaborative behavior to get its distributors to comply. For example, illegal vertical price-fixing may exist where a manufacturer enlists complying dealers to help police the price-fixing scheme. However, a manufacturer's termination of a price-cutting retailer after complaints from other retailers, without more, probably does not violate section 1.

Supreme Court cases of the past 20-odd years cast some doubt on the continued per se illegality of vertical price-fixing. In its 1977 *Sylvania* decision, the Supreme Court moved vertical *territorial* restraints—i.e. manufacturers' assigning their retailers to territories—from the per se category to the rule of reason category. In doing so, the Court showed the influence of the Chicago School economic ideas discussed at the beginning of the chapter. It conceded that vertical territorial restraints inhibit intrabrand competition. But, the Court added, they may also promote interbrand competition. For example, vertical territorial restraints may enable manufacturers to attract competent and aggressive retailers, and may give such retailers an incentive to heavily promote the product and to offer good service. All these things may stimulate competition among brands and thereby benefit consumers. Without the territorial restraint, though, another retailer (called a *free-rider*) might benefit from a "good" retailer's promotional and service activities while stealing its business because, by not doing those things itself, it can offer lower prices. Without the territorial restriction, therefore, no one may have a sufficient incentive to engage in such valuable activities as promotion and service. The bottom line, said the Court, is that vertical territorial restrictions involve a complex mix of effects: they may inhibit intrabrand competition while sometimes promoting interbrand competition. Because the latter effect may sometimes predominate, vertical territorial restrictions should be examined under the flexible rule of reason standard rather than a rigid per se rule.

Why does the law on vertical territorial restraints matter here? It matters because the arguments just made probably apply to vertical price-fixing as well as to vertical territorial restraints. A vertical price-fixing scheme, that is, may help manufacturers attract superior retailers and give those retailers the incentive and the means to give good service and aggressively promote the product. Like vertical territorial restrictions, therefore, vertical price-fixing may present a complex mix of effects and be better treated under the rule of reason.

With all this in mind, perhaps it is not surprising to see the following *Khan* case make vertical maximum price-fixing a rule of reason violation rather than a per se violation. Vertical minimum price-fixing, however, remains a per se violation.

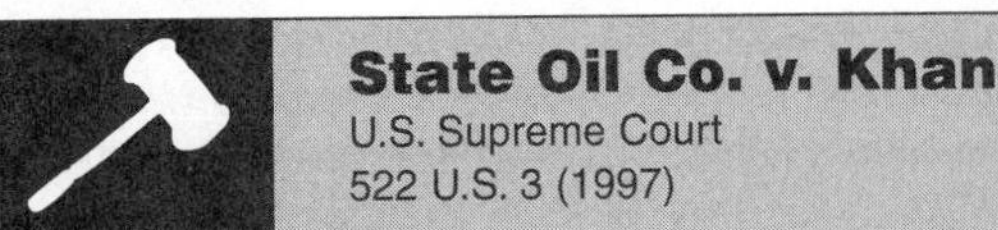

State Oil Co. v. Khan

U.S. Supreme Court
522 U.S. 3 (1997)

Background and Facts:

Barkat U. Khan and his corporation contracted with State Oil Company to lease and operate a gas station and convenience store owned by State Oil. The agreement provided that Khan would obtain the station's gasoline supply from State Oil at a price equal to a suggested retail price set by State Oil, less a margin of 3.25 cents per gallon. Under the agreement, Khan could charge any amount for gasoline sold to the station's customers, but if the price charged was higher than State Oil's suggested retail price, the excess was to be rebated to State Oil. Khan could sell gasoline for less than State Oil's suggested retail price, but any such decrease would reduce his margin. About a year after Khan began operating the gas station, he fell behind in his lease payments. State Oil then gave notice of its intent to terminate the agreement and began a state court proceeding to evict Khan.

Khan then sued State Oil in federal court, alleging that State Oil had fixed prices in violation of Sherman Act section 1 by preventing Khan from raising or lowering retail gas prices. But for the agreement with State Oil, Khan claimed, he could have charged different prices based on the different grades of gasoline he sold, thereby achieving increased sales and profits. The district court granted State Oil's motion for summary judgment, but the court of appeals reversed. State Oil appealed to the U.S. Supreme Court.

Body of Opinion

Justice O'Connor

Although the Sherman Act, by its terms, prohibits every agreement in restraint of trade, this Court has long recognized that Congress intended to outlaw only unreasonable restraints. As a consequence, most antitrust claims are analyzed under a "rule of reason," according to which the finder of fact must decide whether the questioned practice imposes an unreasonable restraint on competition, taking into account a variety of factors, including specific information about the relevant business, its condition before and after the restraint was imposed, and the restraint's history, nature, and effect. Some types of restraints, however, have such predictable and pernicious anticompetitive effect, and such limited potential for procompetitive benefit, that they are deemed unlawful per se. Per se treatment is appropriate once experience with a particular kind of restraint enables the Court to predict with confidence that the rule of reason will condemn it. Thus, we have expressed reluctance to adopt per se rules with regard to restraints imposed in the context of business relationships where the economic impact of certain practices is not immediately obvious....

Albrecht v. Herald Co. (1968)... involved a newspaper publisher who had granted exclusive territories to independent carriers subject to their adherence to a maximum price on resale of the newspapers to the public.... The Court concluded that it was per se unlawful for the publisher to fix the maximum resale price of its newspapers. The Court acknowledged that maximum and minimum price fixing may have different consequences in many situations, but nonetheless condemned maximum price fixing for substituting the perhaps erroneous judgment of a seller for the forces of the competitive market.... In a vigorous dissent, Justice Harlan asserted that the majority had erred in equating the effects of maximum and minimum price fixing. Justice Harlan pointed out that, because the majority was establishing a per se rule, the proper inquiry was "not whether dictation of maximum prices is *ever* illegal, but whether it is *always* illegal."

....[O]ur reconsideration of *Albrecht's* continuing validity is informed by several of our decisions, as well as a considerable body of scholarship discussing the effects of vertical restraints. Our analysis is also guided by our general view that the primary purpose of the antitrust laws is to protect interbrand competition. Low prices, we have explained, benefit consumers regardless of how those prices are set, and so long as they are above predatory levels, they do not threaten competition. Our interpretation of the Sherman Act also incorporates the notion that condemnation of practices resulting in lower prices to consumers is especially costly because cutting prices in order to increase business often is the very essence of competition. So informed, we find it difficult to maintain that vertically imposed maximum prices could harm consumers or competition to the extent necessary to justify their per se invalidation.

We recognize that the *Albrecht* decision presented a number of theoretical justifications for a per se rule against vertical maximum price fixing. But criticism of those premises abounds. The *Albrecht* decision was grounded in the fear that maximum price fixing by suppliers could interfere with dealer freedom. In response, as one commentator has pointed out, the ban on maximum resale price limitations declared in *Albrecht* in the name of "dealer freedom" has actually prompted many suppliers to integrate forward into distribution, thus eliminating the very independent trader for whom *Albrecht* professed solicitude.... The *Albrecht* Court also expressed the concern that maximum prices may be set too low for dealers to offer consumers essential or desired services. But such conduct, by driving away customers, would seem likely to harm manufacturers as well as dealers and consumers, making it unlikely that a supplier would set such a price as a matter of business judgment. In addition, *Albrecht* noted that vertical maximum price fixing could effectively channel distribution through large or specially advantaged dealers. It is unclear, however, that a supplier would profit from limiting its market by excluding potential dealers. Further, although vertical maximum price fixing might limit the viability of inefficient dealers, that consequence is not necessarily harmful to competition and consumers. Finally, *Albrecht* reflected the Court's fear that maximum price fixing could be used to disguise arrangements to fix minimum prices, which remain illegal per se. Although we have acknowledged the possibility that maximum pricing might mask minimum pricing, we believe that such conduct—as with the other concerns articulated in Albrecht—can be appropriately recognized and punished under the rule of reason. . . .

After reconsidering *Albrecht's* rationale and the substantial criticism the decision has received, we conclude that there is insufficient economic justification for per se invalidation of vertical maximum price fixing. That is so not only because it is difficult to accept the assumptions underlying *Albrecht*, but also because *Albrecht* has little or no relevance to ongoing enforcement of the Sherman Act. Moreover, neither the parties nor any of the amici curiae have called our attention to any cases in which enforcement efforts have been directed solely against the conduct encompassed by *Albrecht's* per se rule. Khan argues that reconsideration of *Albrecht* should require persuasive, expert testimony establishing that the per se rule has distorted the market. His reasoning ignores the fact that *Albrecht* itself relied solely upon hypothetical effects of vertical maximum price fixing. Further, *Albrecht's* dire predictions have not been borne out, even though manufacturers and suppliers appear to have fashioned schemes to get around the per se rule against vertical maximum price fixing. In these circumstances, it is the retention of the rule of *Albrecht*, and not, as respondents would have it, the rule's elimination, that lacks adequate justification. . . .

Judgment and Result

[T]he court of appeals noted that the district judge was right to conclude that if the rule of reason is applicable, Khan loses. . . . [Nonetheless], the matter should be reviewed by the court of appeals in the first instance. We therefore vacate the judgment of the court of appeals and remand the case for further proceedings consistent with this opinion.

Questions

1. Suppose it could be proven beyond a doubt that the three leading U.S. computer manufacturers agreed to fix maximum prices for the computers they sell. Does *Khan* mean that this behavior would be tested under the rule of reason?
2. Does *Khan* mean that vertical maximum price-fixing is always legal under section 1?

Horizontal Price-Fixing. Horizontal price-fixing is concerted action to fix prices by competitors at the same level. Its effect is to defeat interbrand competition: competition among brands of the same product. For this reason, and because its procompetitive effects seem few, horizontal price-fixing is the classic Sherman Act section 1 per se violation. Horizontal price-fixing also includes agreements among competitors on matters that affect price—for example, agreements on the amount of goods the competitors will make, sell, or buy. Despite the *Khan* case, section 1's per se ban on horizontal price-fixing most likely still includes the setting of maximum prices as well as the setting of minimum prices.

Horizontal price-fixing cases often involve a problem discussed earlier: proving concerted action. The courts generally agree that simple "price parallelism"—a situation in which competitors are following the same price—does not violate section 1 unless other evidence indicates joint action to fix prices. (In a competitive market, after all, one would expect competitors to be charging roughly the same price at any point in time.) The courts also have agreed that simply following an industry "price leader," without more, does not violate section 1. (In the automobile and steel industries, for example, competitors traditionally would follow price increases announced by those industries' price leaders at the time, General Motors and U.S. Steel.) Although it is difficult to generalize about this subject, exchanges of price information also probably do not violate section 1 by themselves. As discussed earlier, the additional considerations—the "something more"—which might render any of the above a section 1 violation include the defendants' possession of a rational economic interest in conspiring, parallel behavior that is unlikely without an agreement, any past antitrust violations by the defendants, and the defendants' taking action to further the alleged conspiracy after directly communicating with each other.

Horizontal Division of Markets. Agreements by competitors to divide markets can take many forms. Perhaps the most common example is concerted action dividing territories among competitors, such as an agreement that each competitor will sell only in its own particular region. But competitors might also agree to divide customers: for example, competitors A and B might agree that A will sell only to retailers, while B will sell only to wholesalers. In addition, competitors might divide product types—for example, competitors X, Y, and Z might agree that each will sell different sizes of ball bearings. In such cases, of course, the plaintiff or the government will have the now-familiar problem of proving joint or concerted action.

The division of territories, customers, or products reduces interbrand competition. (Sometimes, in fact, such an agreement may give one firm an effective monopoly within a particular territory or for a particular product.) For this reason, such agreements are per se violations of Sherman Act section 1. However, some lower federal courts and some commentators have held or suggested that the rule of reason should apply in cases where the conspiring competitors lack market power and/or their agreement has positive procompetitive benefits. For example, suppose that three widget firms agreeing to allocate territories form ten percent of the national market, and that each faces powerful competitors within its territory. Or suppose that, as part of their agreement to develop a new jet aircraft, two co-venturers agree that each will sell the plane to different customers. If the plane is valuable and it would not be developed without the division of customers, should the agreement be per se illegal?

Group Boycotts. A group boycott might be defined as joint action involving a refusal to deal with a particular firm or firms. (As we saw earlier, however, a purely unilateral refusal to deal does not violate section 1.) Group boycotts can assume various forms. Perhaps the most common and most harmful example is an agreement by firms within an industry not to deal with suppliers or customers who deal with a competitor. For example, Firms A, B, and C in the widget industry might agree not to sell to retailers who market widgets manufactured by a competitor, Firm D. If the boycott works, D might be weakened or forced out of business, which would mean less competition in the widget industry. On the other hand, the boycott might make D cooperate with A, B, and C in some other anticompetitive conduct. Suppose for example that A, B, and C had initiated their boycott because D refused to join their price-fixing scheme.

Boycotts such as those just described are per se illegal. But this might not be true where the conspiring firms lack market power (what if A, B, and C together had ten percent of the widget market?), or where the boycott might promote efficiency or some other important value. In such cases, the rule of reason applies. In the following *Nynex* case, the Supreme Court basically limited the per se ban to horizontal boycotts among direct competitors.

NYNEX Corp. v. Discon, Inc.

U.S. Supreme Court
525 U.S. 128 (1998)

Background and Facts:

Discon, Inc., sold "removal services"—the removal of obsolete telephone equipment—to Materiel Enterprises Company, a subsidiary of the NYNEX Corporation, and ultimately to the New York Telephone Company, another NYNEX subsidiary. After Materiel Enterprises began buying removal services from AT&T Technologies, rather than from Discon, Discon sued, alleging that Material Enterprises, NYNEX, and New York Telephone (the petitioners) had engaged in unfair, improper, and anticompetitive activities. The district court dismissed the complaint for failure to state a claim upon which relief could be granted.

The Second Circuit Court of Appeals affirmed, but with one exception. One of Discon's allegations was that Materiel Enterprises paid AT&T Technologies more than Discon would have charged because AT&T Technologies could pass the higher prices on to New York Telephone, which could then pass them on to telephone consumers through higher regulatory-agency-approved service charges; that Materiel Enterprises would receive a year-end rebate from AT&T Technologies and share it with NYNEX; that Materiel Enterprises would not buy from Discon because it refused to participate in this fraudulent scheme; and that Discon therefore went out of business. All this, Discon continued, stated a claim under section 1 of the Sherman Act. The Second Circuit asserted that Discon may have alleged a cause of action under the antitrust rule set forth in *Klor's, Inc. v. Broadway-Hale Stores, Inc.* (1959), which held that group boycotts are illegal per se. This last claim was the main issue before the Supreme Court after the petitioners appealed.

Body of Opinion

Justice Breyer

As this Court has made clear, the Sherman Act's prohibition of "every" agreement in restraint of trade prohibits only agreements that unreasonably restrain trade. Yet certain kinds of agreements will so often prove so harmful to competition and so rarely prove justified that the antitrust laws do not require proof that an agreement of that kind is, in fact, anticompetitive in the particular circumstances. An agreement of such a kind is unlawful per se. The Court has found the per se rule applicable in certain group boycott cases.... Thus, in *Fashion Originators' Guild of America, Inc. v. FTC* (1941), this Court considered a group boycott created by an agreement among a group of clothing designers, manufacturers, suppliers, and retailers. The defendant designers, manufacturers, and suppliers had promised not to sell their clothes to retailers who bought clothes from competing manufacturers and suppliers. The defendants wanted to present evidence that would show their agreement was justified because the boycotted competitors used "pirated" fashion designs. But the Court wrote that it was not error to refuse to hear the evidence offered—evidence that the agreement was reasonable and necessary to protect against the devastating evils of design pirating—for that evidence is no more material than would be the reasonableness of the prices fixed by a price-fixing agreement.

In *Klor's* the Court also applied the per se rule. The Court considered a boycott created when a retail store, Broadway-Hale, and ten household appliance manufacturers and their distributors agreed that the distributors would not sell, or would sell only at discriminatory prices, household appliances to Broadway-Hale's small, nearby competitor, namely, Klor's. The defendants had submitted undisputed evidence that their agreement hurt only one competitor (Klor's) and that so many other nearby appliance-selling competitors remained that competition in the marketplace continued to thrive. The Court held that this evidence was beside the point. The conspiracy was not to be tolerated merely because the victim is just one merchant. The Court thereby inferred injury to the competitive process itself from the nature of the boycott agreement. And it forbade, as a matter of law, a defense based upon a claim that only one small firm, not competition itself, had suffered injury.

The case before us involves *Klor's*. The Second Circuit did not forbid the petitioners to introduce evidence of justification. To the contrary, it invited the petitioners to do so, for it said that the per se rule would apply only if no pro-competitive justification were to be found. Thus, the specific legal question before us is whether an antitrust court considering an agreement by a buyer to purchase goods or services from one supplier rather than another should (after examining the buyer's reasons or justifications) apply the per se rule if it finds no legitimate business reason for that purchasing decision. We conclude that no boycott-related per se rule applies and that the plaintiff here must allege and prove harm, not just to a single competitor, but to the competitive process, i.e., to competition itself.

Our conclusion rests in large part upon precedent, for precedent limits the per se rule in the boycott context to cases involving horizontal agreements among direct competitors.... The agreement in *Fashion Originators' Guild* involved what may be called a group boycott in the strongest sense: a group of competitors threatened to withhold business from third parties unless those third parties would help them injure their directly competing rivals. Although *Klor's* involved a threat made by a single powerful firm, it also involved a horizontal agreement among those threatened, namely, the appliance suppliers, to hurt a competitor of the retailer who made the threat.... This Court subsequently pointed out specifically that *Klor's* was a case involving not simply a vertical agreement between supplier and customer, but a case that also involved a horizontal agreement among competitors. And in doing so, the Court held that a vertical restraint is not illegal per se unless it includes some agreement on price or price levels. This precedent makes the per se rule inapplicable, for the case before us concerns only a vertical agreement and a vertical restraint, a restraint that takes the form of depriving a supplier of a potential customer. Nor have we found any special feature of this case that could distinguish it from the precedent we have just discussed. We concede Discon's claim that the petitioners' behavior hurt consumers by raising telephone service rates. But that consumer injury naturally flowed not so much from a less competitive market for removal services, as from the exercise of market power that is *lawfully* in the hands of a monopolist, namely, New York Telephone, combined with a deception worked upon the regulatory agency that prevented the agency from controlling New York Telephone's exercise of its monopoly power.

To apply the per se rule here—where the buyer's decision, though not made for competitive reasons, composes part of a regulatory fraud—would transform cases involving business behavior that is improper for various reasons, say, cases involving nepotism or personal pique, into treble-damages antitrust cases. And that per se rule would discourage firms from changing suppliers—even where the competitive process itself does not suffer harm. The freedom to switch suppliers lies close to the heart of the competitive process that the antitrust laws seek to encourage. At the same time, other laws, for example, unfair competition laws, business tort laws, or regulatory laws, provide remedies for various competitive practices thought to be offensive to proper standards of business morality. Thus, this Court has refused to apply per se reasoning in cases involving that kind of activity.

Judgment and Result

The Supreme Court vacated the Second Circuit's decision and remanded the case for further proceedings consistent with its opinion. Discon probable will lose.

Questions

1. Why did this case not involve a horizontal agreement among competitors?
2. Why did the alleged conspiracy among the petitioners and its effect on consumers not much matter to the Supreme Court?

Tying Contracts. A **tying contract** (or tie-in) is a contract in which a seller conditions the buyer's purchase of one product (the **tying product**) on the buyer's purchase of another product sold by the seller (the **tied product**). For example, a firm might condition the sale of its copiers (the tying product) on the purchase of its copier paper (the tied product). Under section 1 of the Sherman act, the tied or tying "product" might be a service as well.[4] The main justification for suppressing tying contracts is that they distort competition in the tied product market. In the previous example, competition in the copier paper market might be distorted if consumers want the seller's copiers badly enough.

Courts apply a modified rule of per se illegality to tying contracts in which a tying contract is per se illegal if certain tests are met: (1) the tying and tied products are distinct items; (2) the seller has required the buyer to buy the tied product in order to obtain the tying product (the tie-in); (3) the seller has market power in the tying product market; and (4) the tie-in affects a substantial amount of commerce in the tied product market. The *Eastman Kodak* case in the next section states and applies this test. The test's most important element, the market power requirement, might be satisfied by showing that the seller has a large share of the tying product market, or a patent in the product.

One Chicago School argument against the per se rule for tying contracts says that if the seller has market power in the tying product, it can distort competition in other ways than by using a tying contract. For example, such a seller might simply use its market power to charge a higher price for the tying product, rather than by linking it to something else. In other words, a seller can derive only so much "monopoly profit" from its market power in the tying product, and it matters little how the seller chooses to exercise that power. The apparent implication of the argument is that cracking down on tie-ins only treats a symptom, and does not address the source of the problem: the seller's market power in the tying product. When

[4] Under Clayton Act section 3, however, both the tied and the tying products must be commodities (i.e., goods).

might that power be sufficient to violate the antitrust laws? The answer is found in section 2 of the Sherman Act.

SHERMAN ACT SECTION 2

Sherman Act section 2 forbids monopolization and attempts to monopolize.[5] We now consider each of these subjects in turn.

Monopolization

Monopolies reduce consumer welfare because monopolists can raise prices above free-market levels, usually restricting output in the process. Who qualifies as a monopolist under section 2 of the Sherman Act? First, note that section 2 does not require—and seldom involves—concerted action. Normally, that is, a single firm violates section 2. This happens when (1) the firm has *monopoly power* in (2) the relevant *product and territorial market*, and (3) the firm acquired or exercised that monopoly power with *intent to monopolize*.

In economic terms, **monopoly power** might be defined as the ability to raise prices above the competitive level for a sustained time period, and to profit by doing so. Courts interpreting section 2, however, define it as a percentage. The most commonly stated number is 70 percent of sales in the product-territorial market. In other words, if the ratio of the defendant's sales in the product-territorial market to total sales in that market equals or exceeds 70 percent, the monopoly power test probably is met.

But what is the product-territorial market? The **product market** depends heavily on the question of substitutability: whether reasonable substitutes are available for the specific product the defendant sells. For example, suppose that the XYZ Corporation, with 100 percent of the widget market, tries to charge a monopoly price for its widgets. This strategy obviously will fail if gidgets are perfect substitutes for widgets, and if buyers can readily obtain all the gidgets they need. So why define the product market as merely involving widgets rather than widgets plus gidgets? And why worry if XYZ lacks monopoly power in the combined widget-gidget market?

In determining which substitutes to include in the product market, courts examine several factors. To illustrate them, consider the Supreme Court's 1956 decision in *United States v. E.I. du Pont de Nemours & Co.* (the "cellophane case"), where the Court concluded that other flexible wrapping materials such as aluminum foil, wax paper, and saran wrap were reasonable substitutes for cellophane. Du Pont's 20 percent share of this broader product market meant that it was not liable under section 2 even though it had almost 75 percent of the cellophane market. The Court concluded that many of the substitutes had qualities—for example, flexibility, transparency, and permeability—similar to those consumers sought in cellophane. The Court also found that, because one or more of the substitutes competed with cellophane in each of its uses, the substitutes were functionally interchangeable with it. Finally, the Court judged that there was "cross-elasticity of demand" between cellophane and its substitutes; for example, an increase in the price of cellophane would cause increased demand for the substitutes.

In addition to determining the product market, courts in section 2 cases also must determine the **territorial market** (or geographic market). The territorial market is that region of the country in which a firm can increase its price without drawing in new competitors and without losing sales to competitors outside the region. Suppose that

[5] Section 2 also forbids conspiracy to monopolize. Because this offense requires concerted action, and because most conspiracies to monopolize probably violate Sherman Act section 1 in some way or another, this book does not discuss the subject.

the relevant product market is widgets and that the ABC Corporation has 10 percent of widget sales nationally, but 85 percent of sales in the Rocky Mountain region. But is the Rocky Mountain region the correct territorial market? To make such a determination, courts look at several factors. For example, if transportation costs are high, maybe widgets will not flow from other parts of the country to the Rockies once XYZ raises prices. Also, if price movements within the Rocky Mountain area do not correlate with price movements elsewhere, maybe we have reason to think that this area is a self-contained market. On the other hand, maybe consideration of such factors (and others) would force a court to conclude that the geographical market is the whole United States, or some segment of the country besides the Rocky Mountain region.

By itself, monopoly power in an appropriate product-territorial market is not enough for liability under section 2. The defendant also must have an intent to monopolize. In theory, this intent is absent, and section 2 liability does not exist, when a firm acquires its monopoly innocently. For example, a company might get a monopoly simply by offering better products and services, or by historical accident (e.g., the last survivor in a dying industry).

Today, intent to monopolize means an intent either to *acquire* or to *maintain* monopoly power. Each kind of intent normally is inferred from the defendant's behavior. Intent to acquire monopoly power is easy to prove where the defendant has acquired its monopoly through practices such as below-cost pricing. A monopoly obtained through the acquisition of competitors probably meets the test as well. Intent to maintain monopoly power almost certainly exists where a monopolist engages in monopolistic pricing. In the famous *Alcoa* case, where Alcoa had 90 percent of the U.S. market for virgin aluminum ingot, the court held that Alcoa intended to maintain monopoly power because it maintained excess production capacity, grabbed every new opportunity to make or sell aluminum, and thus kept new competitors from entering the industry. *Alcoa* may come close to holding that the mere possession of monopoly power proves intent to monopolize. For those whose primary worry is what firms will do once they acquire monopoly power, such a rule might make sense. But under that rule, would the fear of section 2 liability deter superior firms from socially valuable competitive activity?

Eastman Kodak Co. v. Image Technical Services, Inc.

U.S. Supreme Court
504 U.S. 451 (1992)

Background and Facts:

The Eastman Kodak Company manufactured and sold high-volume photocopier equipment and micrographic equipment (e.g., scanners, microfilm viewers, and other such items). Kodak's equipment and the parts for that equipment were not compatible with competitors' machines and parts. Kodak provided its customers with service and parts for its machines. It made some of the parts itself; the rest were made to order for Kodak by independent original equipment manufacturers. Beginning in the 1980s, 18 independent service organizations (ISOs) began servicing Kodak equipment. In response, Kodak instituted a policy of selling replacement parts only to buyers of its equipment who used Kodak service or repaired their own machines. It also got the original equipment manufacturers to sell parts only to Kodak. Due to these and other steps taken by Kodak, the ISOs could not obtain Kodak parts and some went out of business. Also, customers were forced to switch to Kodak service even though they preferred the ISOs' service.

The ISOs then sued Kodak in federal district court. They alleged that Kodak violated Sherman Act section 1 by tying the sale of Kodak service to the sale of Kodak parts, and that Kodak also violated Sherman Act section 2 by monopolizing the parts and service markets for Kodak machines. The district court granted Kodak's motion for summary judgment, but the court of appeals reversed this decision. Kodak appealed to the U.S. Supreme Court.

Body of Opinion

Justice Blackmun

Because this case comes to us on petitioner Kodak's motion for summary judgment, the evidence of the ISOs is to be believed, and all justifiable inferences are to be drawn in their favor. . . . A tying arrangement is an agreement by a party to sell one product but only on the condition that the buyer also purchases a different (or tied) product, or at least agrees that he will not purchase that product from any other supplier. Such an arrangement violates section 1 of the Sherman Act if the seller has appreciable economic power in the tying product market and if the arrangement affects a substantial volume of commerce in the tied market. Kodak did not dispute that its arrangement affects a substantial volume of interstate commerce. . . .

For the ISOs to defeat a motion for summary judgment on their claim of a tying arrangement, a reasonable trier of fact must be able to find, first, that service and parts are two distinct products, and, second, that Kodak has tied the sale of the two products. For service and parts to be considered two distinct products, there must be sufficient consumer demand so that it is efficient for a firm to provide service separately from parts. Evidence in the record indicates that service and parts have been sold separately in the past and still are sold separately to self-service equipment owners. Indeed, the development of the entire high-technology service industry is evidence of the efficiency of a separate market for service. . . . [Also,] the ISOs have presented sufficient evidence of a tie between service and parts. . . .

Market power is the power to force a purchaser to do something that he would not do in a competitive market. It has been defined as the ability of a single seller to raise price and restrict output. The existence of such power normally is inferred from the seller's possession of a predominant share of the market.

The ISOs contend that Kodak has more than sufficient power in the parts market to force unwanted purchases of the tied market, service. The ISOs provide evidence that certain parts are available exclusively through Kodak. The ISOs also assert that Kodak has control over the availability of parts it does not manufacture. . . . The ISOs also allege that Kodak's control over the parts market has excluded service competition, boosted service prices, and forced unwilling consumption of Kodak service. . . . [T]his evidence [is] sufficient to entitle the ISOs to a trial on their claim of market power. . . . We therefore affirm the denial of summary judgment [to Kodak] on the ISOs' section 1 claim.

The ISOs also claim that they have presented genuine issues for trial as to whether Kodak has monopolized . . . the service and parts markets in violation of section 2 of the Sherman Act. The offense of monopoly under section 2 of the Sherman Act has two elements: (1) the possession of monopoly in the relevant market; and (2) the willful acquisition or maintenance of that power, as distinguished from growth or development as a consequence of a superior product, business acumen, or historical accident.

The existence of the first element, possession of monopoly power, is easily resolved. As had been noted, the ISOs have presented a triable claim that service and parts are separate markets, and that Kodak has the power to control prices or exclude competition in service and parts. Monopoly power under section 2 requires, of course, something greater than market power under section 1. The ISOs' evidence that Kodak controls nearly 100% of the parts market and 80% to 95% of the service market with no readily available substitutes is, however, sufficient to survive summary judgment under the more stringent monopoly standard of section 2.

Kodak also contends that, as a matter of law, a single brand of a product or service can never be a relevant market under the Sherman Act. We disagree. The relevant market for antitrust purposes is determined by the choices available to Kodak equipment owners. Because service and parts for Kodak equipment are not interchangeable with other manufacturers' service and parts, the relevant market from the Kodak equipment owner's perspective is composed of only those companies that service Kodak machines. . . .

The second element of a section 2 claim is the use of monopoly power to foreclose competition, to gain a competitive advantage, or to destroy a competitor. If Kodak adopted its parts and service policies as part of a scheme of willful acquisition or maintenance of monopoly power, it will have violated section 2. . . . The ISOs have presented evidence that Kodak took exclusionary action to maintain its parts monopoly and used its control over parts to strengthen its monopoly share of the Kodak service market. Liability turns, then, on whether valid business reasons can explain Kodak's actions. . . . Factual questions exist, however, about the validity and sufficiency of each claimed justification, making summary judgment inappropriate. . . .

In the end, of course, Kodak's arguments may prove to be correct. . . . But we cannot reach these conclusions as a matter of law on a record this sparse.

Judgment and Result

The court of appeals decision denying Kodak's motion for summary judgement is affirmed. The case continues in the district court.

Questions

1. What was the tying product here? What was the tied product?
2. In which market or markets was Kodak said to have market power?
3. Why did the Court's marketpower determination on the tying contract issue not necessarily bind it on the question of monopoly power under the section 2 claim?

Attempts to Monopolize

The paradox of Sherman Act section 2—that preventing anticompetitive market structures may mean deterring good competitors—also arises when we consider attempts to monopolize. In a 1993 case, the Supreme Court held that liability for an attempt to monopolize requires (1) that the defendant has engaged in predatory or anticompetitive conduct, (2) with a specific intent to monopolize, and (3) a dangerous probability of achieving monopoly power. A dangerous probability of achieving monopoly power is unlikely to exist if the defendant's market share is less than 50 percent. In some cases, the defendant's predatory or anticompetitive conduct might prove a specific intent to monopolize. One possible example of such conduct is below-cost pricing.

CLAYTON ACT SECTION 3

Clayton Act section 3 forbids the selling or leasing of commodities (goods) on the condition that the buyer or lessee not use or deal commodities sold or leased by a competitor of the seller or lessor, where the effect of this sale or lease may be to substantially lessen competition or tend to create a monopoly in any line of commerce. Section 3 mainly applies to tying contracts, exclusive dealing contracts, and requirements contracts. (Because section 3 requires a sale or a lease, it does not govern consignment arrangements.) We consider requirements and exclusive dealing contracts together.

Tying Contracts

Section 3 of the Clayton Act governs tying contracts only when both the tied and the tying products are commodities. Today, most courts impose the same requirements for tying contract liability under both Sherman Act section 1 and Clayton Act section 3. Thus, when considering tying contracts under Clayton Act section 3, the four-part test discussed earlier is applicable.

Exclusive Dealing and Requirements Contracts

An **exclusive dealing contract** is a sales contract in which the buyer agrees to deal only in the seller's goods and/or not to deal in the goods of the seller's competitors. For example, a gas station might agree to sell only gasoline produced by a certain oil company, and not to sell gasoline produced by other oil companies. In a **requirements contract**, the buyer agrees to purchase all its requirements of a particular commodity from the seller. For example, an electrical utility might agree to buy all the coal required for one of its generating stations from a particular coal company, thus preventing other coal companies from competing for its business.

Both exclusive dealing contracts and requirements contracts inhibit interbrand competition by preventing the seller's competitors from competing for the buyer's business. In our previous examples, the effect of the exclusive dealing or requirements contract is to prevent other oil companies or coal companies from competing for the gas station's or the utility's business. However, because firms have rational motives for entering requirements contracts, which ensure them a source of supply, maybe their business would never have been the competitors' to obtain. Furthermore, because they may reduce a manufacturer's sales and distribution costs, attract good retailers, and give them an incentive to push the product, exclusive dealing and requirements contracts may sometimes enhance competition and efficiency. But on other occasions they simply are imposed by a powerful seller that wants to foreclose competition.

In addition to creating possible section 3 liability, exclusive dealing and requirements contracts may also be rule of reason violations under Sherman Act section 1. The standards for liability are basically the same under each act. Today, the most important factor courts consider is the degree to which the contract forecloses competition in the relevant market. This basically involves the percentage market share taken up by the challenged contract (so-called "qualitative substantiality"), not the absolute dollar value of the contract (so-called "quantitative substantiality"). If the foreclosure is less than 20–30 percent, liability probably will not exist. (Of course, this factor may require difficult product and territorial market determinations.) Another factor is the duration of the agreement. Exclusive dealing or requirements contracts with shorter time periods and/or easy-to-use termination provisions are more likely to escape liability than contracts of longer duration that cannot easily be terminated. A third factor is the presence or absence of entry barriers to the affected market; the easier that market is to enter, the less likely that the exclusive dealing or requirements contract will violate section 3.

CLAYTON ACT SECTION 7

Section 7 of the Clayton Act forbids the acquisition of a firm's stock or assets, where the effect of this acquisition is to substantially lessen competition or tend to create a monopoly. In effect, section 7 forbids certain mergers. A merger might be said to exist where one firm buys enough of another firm's stock or assets to give the buying firm control over the firm that is bought. Defined narrowly, a merger occurs when two or more firms combine, with one of these firms continuing to exist while the other becomes part of (merges into) the survivor. Defined more broadly, the term *merger* also includes situations where one corporation buys a controlling interest in another corporation's stock but both corporations continue to exist; here, the buyer (the parent firm) controls the seller (the subsidiary) because the parent elects the subsidiary's board of directors. Finally, the term *merger* can include a consolidation, in which two or more corporations combine to form a new business entity. In this chapter, all these various combinations will be treated as mergers and as potentially subject to Clayton Act section 7.

General Policy Considerations

One reason for Sherman Act section 1's concern with joint action is that joint action usually poses a greater threat to competition than purely unilateral behavior. At first glance, this threat to competition seems to compound when two businesses not only act jointly, but merge. Contracts, combinations, and conspiracies may eventually end as each of the once-collaborating firms goes its own way, but mergers create a more permanent union between businesses. For this reason, one might expect the courts to announce per se rules against mergers. As we will see, however, some mergers pose little threat to competition. Others may have social benefits that offset their potential to harm competition. For example, mergers can enhance efficiency by creating economies of scale, and by enabling the acquiring firm to make better use of the acquired firm's assets. Also, the threat of a takeover can force managers to behave efficiently. If the takeover in question is per se illegal, this threat—and its benefits—would disappear.

For the reasons just suggested, courts must exercise some discretion in merger cases. Thus, the "law" under section 7 is less a matter of definite rules to be followed than of factors to be considered on a case-by-case basis. The resulting indefiniteness is more acute now than it has been in the past, in part because many recent merger cases have been settled and the Supreme Court has not issued a major section 7 decision for some time.

Over that period, moreover Chicago School ideas have gained influence. Were the Court to decide an important merger case today, therefore, it might well give more weight to economic efficiency concerns than in the past, and less to political values such as the desire to limit corporate size. Further increasing the uncertainty faced by firms that contemplate a merger are the inevitable changes in FTC and Justice Department enforcement policy that accompany the arrival of a new administration in Washington.[6]

Types of Mergers

Mergers come in three basic varieties. A **horizontal merger** is a merger between two (or more) competitors. In a **vertical merger**, a firm acquires either a customer (called *forward integration*) or a supplier (called *backward integration*). The term **conglomerate merger** covers all other kinds of mergers. Perhaps the most common kind of conglomerate merger, one sometimes called a "pure" conglomerate merger, occurs when the merging firms do not compete and have no evident economic relationship. Another type of conglomerate merger, the product extension merger, involves firms that make different products which nonetheless involve similar manufacturing or marketing techniques. In a geographic extension merger, finally, the two firms make the same product, but in different geographical markets. As the preceding definitions should suggest, merger cases often require that courts determine product and territorial markets. The considerations relevant to such determinations are much the same as in Sherman Act section 2 cases.

http://

For some information on premerger notification, see **http://www.ftc.gov**

Horizontal Mergers. Horizontal mergers threaten competition for at least three reasons. First, they obviously eliminate competition between the merging firms. Second, the firm resulting from the merger may have enough market power to distort competition. Third, the merger may increase concentration in the industry, making it easier for industry members to collude.

During the 1960s and early 1970s, the Supreme Court apparently thought that horizontal mergers were a serious threat to competition. The court in the following *Baker Hughes* case may be only slightly exaggerating when it says that during this period the Court used section 7 to invalidate almost any horizontal merger. In particular, the Court sometimes struck down mergers that did not greatly increase industry concentration. Perhaps the best example is the Court's 1966 decision in *United States v. Von's Grocery Co.*, where the third largest retail grocery chain in the Los Angeles market (with 4.7 percent of all sales) acquired the sixth largest firm in that market, and the resulting firm accounted for only 7.5 percent of sales in the market. Since the mid-1970s, however, the Supreme Court has relaxed its horizontal merger standards. As *Baker Hughes* suggests, the lower federal courts have tended to continue this relaxation. Whenever the Supreme Court again decides a horizontal merger case, the results may differ considerably from those of the 1960s.

---

[6] Because they are not law and because they further complicate an already-complicated subject, this text does not discuss the Justice Department's 1984 Merger Guidelines and the 1992 Justice Department/FTC Horizontal Merger Guidelines. The former basically state the Justice Department's enforcement policy for nonhorizontal mergers, and the latter the Justice Department's and the FTC's enforcement policy for horizontal mergers.

Under the Hart-Scott-Rodino Antitrust Improvements Act of 1976, furthermore, certain mergers require premerger notification to the FTC and the Justice Department. The act also creates a waiting period during which these agencies decide whether to challenge the merger. If the agencies decide not to attack the merger, they are unlikely to challenge it after it has been consummated. The tests for triggering the premerger notification requirement involve matters such as net sales and net assets of the acquired and acquiring firms, and the price or value of the acquisition.

Regardless of how they view the subject, what factors commonly influence courts in horizontal merger cases? Heading the list is the market share of the firm resulting from the merger. But as *Baker Hughes* suggests, even a high market share might be overcome by other considerations. Another important factor is the market structure of the industry. For example, a merger creating a firm with a 20 percent market share is more worrisome in a highly concentrated market than in an unconcentrated one, because the opportunities for anticompetitive collaboration are greater in the first case. For similar reasons, courts also look for a trend toward greater (or lesser) concentration in the industry. In particular, they are concerned about the increase in concentration resulting from the merger itself. Yet another factor is the nature of the acquired firm. That firm may have special competitive advantages; on the other hand, it may be a failing company whose market share overstates its strength.

As *Baker Hughes* makes clear, however, even where the firm resulting from the merger has a high market share in a concentrated industry, other factors may make section 7 liability inadvisable. Due to instability and changes in the industry, the market share figures may be misleading. Buyers of the industry's products may be sufficiently powerful and sophisticated to foil any attempt at anticompetitive behavior. Low barriers to entry for the industry may mean little reason to worry about anticompetitive behavior such as price-fixing because such behavior will attract new competitors. In fact, the presence of such potential competitors may keep existing competitors from cooperating to thwart competition in the first place. As we have seen, finally, some horizontal mergers may mean greater efficiency.

United States v. Baker Hughes, Inc.

D.C. Circuit Court of Appeals
908 F.2d 981 (1990)

Background and Facts:

Tamrock AG, a subsidiary of a Finnish corporation, proposed to acquire Eimco Secoma, S.A., a French subsidiary of Baker Hughes, Inc. Both firms manufactured and sold hardrock hydraulic underground drilling rigs (HHUDRs) in the United States and around the world. The U.S. government challenged the merger under Clayton Act section 7. After a bench trial, a federal district court dismissed the government's claim. The government then appealed.

Body of Opinion

Circuit Judge Thomas

The basic outline of a section 7 horizontal acquisition case is familiar. By showing that a transaction will lead to undue concentration in the market for a particular product in a particular geographic area, the government establishes a presumption that the transaction will substantially lessen competition.[7] The burden of producing evidence to rebut this presumption then shifts to the defendant. If the defendant successfully rebuts the presumption, the burden of producing additional evidence of anticompetitive effect shifts to the government, and merges with the ultimate burden of persuasion, which remains with the government at all times.

By presenting statistics showing that combining the market shares of Tamrock and Secoma would significantly increase concentration in the already concentrated United States HHUDR market, the government established a prima facie case of anticompetitive effect. The district court, however, found sufficient evidence that the merger would not substantially lessen competition to conclude that the defendants had rebutted this prima facie case. The government did not produce any additional evidence showing a probability of substantially lessened competition, and thus failed to carry its ultimate burden of persuasion. . . .

I

It is a foundation of section 7 doctrine, disputed by no authority cited by the government, that evidence on a variety of factors can rebut a prima facie case. These factors include, but are not limited to, the absence of significant entry barriers in the relevant market. . . . The district court in this case considered at least two factors in addition to entry: the misleading nature of the statistics

[7] The parties in this case do not seriously contest the district court's definition of the relevant markets. The court defined the geographic market as the entire United States, and the relevant product as three types of HHUDRs [court's footnote].

underlying the government's prima facie case and the sophistication of HHUDR consumers. These nonentry factors provide compelling support for the court's holding that Tamrock's acquisition of Secoma was not likely to lessen competition substantially. . . .

With respect to the first factor, the statistical basis of the prima facie case, the court accepted the defendants' argument that the government's statistics were misleading. . . . In 1986, for instance, only 22 HHUDRs were sold in the United States. In 1987, the number rose to 43, and in 1988 it fell to 38. Every HHUDR sold during this period thus increased the seller's market share by two to five percent. A contract to provide multiple HHUDRs could catapult a firm from last to first place. . . . While acknowledging that the HHUDR market would be highly concentrated after Tamrock acquired Secoma, the court found that such concentration in and of itself would not doom competition. High concentration has long been the norm in this market. For example, only four firms sold HHUDRs in the United States between 1986 and 1989. Nor is concentration surprising where, as here, a product is esoteric and its market small. Indeed, the trial judge found that concentration has existed for some time in the United States HHUDR market but there is no proof of overpricing, excessive profit, or any decline in quality, service, or diminishing innovation.

The second nonentry factor that the district court considered was the sophistication of HHUDR consumers. HHUDRs currently cost hundreds of thousands of dollars, and orders can exceed $1 million. These products are hardly trinkets sold to small consumers who may possess imperfect information and limited bargaining power. HHUDR buyers closely examine available options and typically insist on receiving multiple, confidential bids for each order. This sophistication . . . [is] likely to promote competition even in a highly concentrated market. . . .

II

The existence and significance of barriers to entry are frequently, of course, crucial considerations in a rebuttal analysis. In the absence of significant barriers, a company probably cannot maintain supracompetitive pricing for any length of time. The district court in this case reviewed the prospects for future entry into the United States HHUDR market and concluded that, overall, entry was likely, particularly if Tamrock's acquisition of Secoma were to lead to supracompetitive pricing. The government attacks this conclusion, asserting that, as a matter of law, the court should have required the defendants to show clearly that entry would be quick and effective. We reject this novel and unduly onerous standard. . . .

That the "quick and effective" standard lacks support in precedent is not surprising, for it would require of defendants a degree of clairvoyance alien to section 7. . . . A defendant cannot realistically be expected to prove that new competitors will "quickly" or "effectively" enter unless it produces evidence regarding specific competitors and their plans. Such evidence is rarely available; potential competitors have a strong interest in downplaying the likelihood that they will enter a given market. . . . Furthermore, the supposed "quick and effective" entry requirement overlooks the point that a firm that never enters a given market can nevertheless exert competitive pressure on that market. If barriers to entry are insignificant, the threat of entry can stimulate competition in a concentrated market, regardless of whether entry ever occurs. . . .

Having rejected the "quick and effective" entry standard itself, we turn briefly to the government's more general argument that the district court's findings regarding ease of entry failed to support its conclusion that the defendants had rebutted the prima facie case. The district court in this case discussed a number of considerations that led it to conclude that entry barriers to the United States HHUDR market were not high enough to impede future entry should Tamrock's acquisition of Secoma lead to supracompetitive pricing. First, the court noted that at least two companies . . . had entered the United States HHUDR market in 1989, and were poised for future expansion. Second, the court stressed that a number of firms competing in Canada and other countries had not penetrated the United States market, but could be expected to do so if Tamrock's acquisition of Secoma led to higher prices. . . . Third, these firms would exert competitive pressure on the United States HHUDR market even if they never actually entered the market. Finally, the court noted that there had been a tremendous turnover in the United States HHUDR market in the 1980s. . . . In sum, we see no error—legal or factual—in the district court's determination that entry into the United States HHUDR market would likely avert anticompetitive effects from Tamrock's acquisition of Secoma. . . .

III

Finally, we consider the strength of the showing that a section 7 defendant must make to rebut a prima facie case. . . . The government argues that the [district] court erred by failing to require the defendants to make a "clear" showing. . . . We conclude that a "clear" showing is unnecessary, and we are satisfied that the district court required the defendants to produce sufficient evidence.

The government's "clear showing" language is by no means unsupported in the case law. In the mid-1960s, the Supreme Court construed section 7 to prohibit virtually any horizontal merger or acquisition. At the time, the Court envisioned an ideal market as one composed of many small competitors, each enjoying only a small market share; the more clearly a given market approximated this ideal, the more competitive it was presumed to be. This perspective animated a series of decisions in which the Court stated that a section 7 defendant's market share measures its market power, that statistics alone establish a prima facie case, and that a defendant carries a heavy burden in seeking to rebut the presumption established by such a prima facie case....

Although the Supreme Court has not overruled these section 7 precedents, it has cut them back sharply.... [It has produced] a line of decisions differing markedly in emphasis from... [its] antitrust cases of the 1960s.... In the aftermath of... [these cases], a defendant seeking to rebut a presumption of anticompetitive effect must show that the prima facie case inaccurately predicts the relevant transaction's probable effect on future competition. The more compelling the prima facie case, the more evidence the defendant must present to rebut it successfully. A defendant can make the required showing by affirmatively showing why a given transaction is unlikely to substantially lessen competition, or by discrediting the data underlying the initial presumption in the government's favor....

The appellees in this case presented the district court with considerable evidence regarding the United States HHUDR market. The court credited the evidence concerning the sophistication of HHUDR consumers and the insignificance of entry barriers, as well as the argument that the statistics underlying the government's prima facie case were misleading. This evidence amply justified the court's conclusion that the prima facie case inaccurately depicted the probable anticompetitive effect of Tamrock's acquisition of Secoma. Because the government did not produce sufficient evidence to overcome this successful rebuttal, the district court concluded that it is not likely that the acquisition will substantially lessen competition in the United States either immediately or long-term. The government has given us no reason to reverse that conclusion.

Judgment and Result

The court of appeals affirmed the district court's decision holding that the Tamrock-Secoma merger did not violate Clayton Act section 7.

Questions

1. The *Baker Hughes* opinion was written by Judge Clarence Thomas, now a Supreme Court Justice. It was joined by Judge Ruth Bader Ginsburg, who now is on the Supreme Court as well. What does this tell you about the likely future evolution of section 7 horizontal merger law?
2. The court conceded that the merger would increase concentration in an already-concentrated industry. Why then did it not hold for the government?

Vertical Mergers. Vertical mergers have at least three possible anticompetitive effects. First, they may block competitors' access to a share of some market. For example, if a retailer acquires a supplier, competitors of the supplier will not be able to compete for the retailer's business. Similarly, if a supplier acquires a retailer, the supplier's competitors cannot compete for the retailer's business. Secondly, vertical mergers can eliminate a potential competitor from the acquired firm's market. This potential competitor is the acquiring firm itself, which might have entered the acquired firm's market on its own if the merger had not occurred. A third, and related, effect of vertical mergers is to eliminate the benefits of threatened competition in the acquired firm's market. In our previous example, the threat that the acquiring firm will enter the acquired firm's market might prevent the acquired firm and its competitors from making the industry look more attractive to potential entrants by colluding to raise prices.

The main factor courts consider in vertical merger cases is the share of the relevant market in which, due to the merger, competition no longer occurs. In a merger between supplier S and retailer R, for example, courts may condemn the merger if R's share of the relevant retail market is sufficiently large. Of course, courts also examine the other considerations just discussed, where they are important. They may also consider historical trends in the industry (e.g., is it becoming more or less concentrated?), as well as the acquiring firm's history (e.g., has it made similar acquisitions in the past?). Over the past 20 years or so, courts have come under some criticism for not considering the possible efficiency gains resulting from vertical mergers. If nothing else, such mergers usually reduce transaction costs.

Conglomerate Mergers. Two important factors courts consider in conglomerate merger cases have already been discussed. First, such a merger obviously eliminates the possibility that the acquiring firm might have entered the acquired firm's market on its own, thereby increasing competition in that market. Second, such a merger makes it impossible for the acquiring firm's potential entry to keep the acquired firm and its competitors from colluding to raise prices. Conglomerate mergers might also give the acquired or acquiring firm too great an edge over their competitors. For example, accessing the acquired the firm's resources and/or expertise may enable the acquiring firm to dominate its market and to deter new entrants to that market. The first two factors have usually been the most important considerations in conglomerate merger litigation. Other considerations include such now-familiar issues as the acquired firm's market share, the degree of concentration in its market, and barriers to entering that market.

THE ROBINSON-PATMAN ACT

The Robinson-Patman Act is primarily concerned with price discrimination: a seller's charging different prices to different buyers of the same product. Why is this practice a problem? One cause for concern is that large buyers might overcome their smaller competitors by using their market power to extract price concessions from suppliers. For example, concessions from food processors might enable a supermarket chain to undersell local "Mom and Pop" grocery stores. Because they represent less business to food suppliers than the chain does, the smaller groceries typically could not get a similar deal. This scenario is one example of **secondary line price discrimination**, which involves economic injury to competitors of the favored *buyer*. A similar phenomenon, called **tertiary line price discrimination**, involves economic injury to competitors of the *favored buyer's buyers*. For example, suppose that a large food wholesaler gets price concessions from a food processor, passes those savings on to its customers, and these grocery stores thereby get an edge over their competitors.

Another form of price discrimination, called **primary line price discrimination**, involves economic injury to competitors of the *discriminating seller*. For example, a large manufacturer might finance its low prices in areas where it faces strong competition by charging higher prices in areas where competition is weak. As a result, it may obtain a significant advantage over its competitors. For most of its history, the Clayton Act's original section 2 was primarily concerned with primary line price discrimination. In 1936, however, section 2 was amended by the Robinson-Patman Act. As its legislative history makes abundantly clear, the Robinson-Patman Act's main aim was to protect small retailers against their bigger and more powerful competitors by forbidding price discrimination in those competitors' favor. Thus, the act forbade secondary and tertiary line price discrimination as well as primary line discrimination. As we will see, the Robinson-Patman Act also prohibits discrimination regarding matters other than price.

The Robinson-Patman Act has been controversial ever since the time of its consideration and passage. To see why, first observe that the price discrimination forbidden by the act often benefits consumers. A major reason that chain stores have prospered, for example, is that they offer consumers lower prices. Indeed, the standard criticism of the Robinson-Patman Act is that it protects competitors rather than protecting competition. To this criticism, a defender of the act might reply that competitors who overcome their rivals by offering lower prices may then become oligopolists or even monopolists, or at least may get the market power to engage in anticompetitive practices. But in theory, at least, the other provisions of the antitrust laws can deal with such behavior. Due in part to such misgivings, government enforcement of the

Robinson-Patman Act has been minimal for at least 15 years. Thus, private suits are now the main vehicle for enforcing the act's provisions.

Jurisdictional Reach

The Robinson-Patman Act applies only to price discrimination and other acts that occur "in commerce," which normally means that one of the sales involved in the price discrimination or other discrimination must cross state lines. Thus, an Indiana manufacturer probably would not violate the act if it sold at different prices to two or more Indiana customers.

Price Discrimination

Price discrimination is forbidden by section 2(a) of the Robinson-Patman Act. In addition to the in-commerce requirement, section 2(a) liability requires the following:

1. *A sale.* Not included are offers to sell, leases, consignment arrangements, and refusals to deal.
2. *Of commodities* (or goods). Thus, sales of services, real estate, and intangibles are not covered.
3. *Of like grade and quality.* A difference in grade or quality, of course, can justify a difference in price. Such a difference must be based on a physical difference that affects the commodity's acceptability to buyers. By themselves, differences in a product's brand name or label are not sufficient.
4. *To different competing customers at a different price or prices.* Normally, it is permissible to charge different prices to wholesalers than to retailers, or to buyers who do not compete in the same geographic market.
5. *Probable injury to competition.* This element varies with the type of price discrimination at issue. Primary line discrimination requires the greatest probability of injury to competition. If the following *Brooke Group* case is any guide, injury to a competitor—for example, lost sales—is insufficient for liability in a primary-line discrimination case. In all likelihood, the motives of the price-discriminating firm are not the critical thing either. Rather, liability requires some fairly significant actual or potential detriment to competition.

Secondary- and tertiary-line discrimination, however, require less likelihood of injury to competition. Here, it is generally sufficient for liability if the prices a seller charges competing buyers display sustained and substantial differences. Minor or short-term differences, however, may not be sufficient for liability.

Brooke Group Ltd. v. Brown & Williamson Tobacco Corp.

U.S. Supreme Court
509 U.S. 209 (1993)

Background and Facts:

In 1980, the Liggett Corporation (later renamed the Brooke Group Limited) introduced a line of economy generic cigarettes called "black and white" cigarettes. As the market for these economy cigarettes expanded, other cigarette manufacturers began their own offerings in this segment. Among them was the Brown & Williamson Tobacco Corporation (BW), which competed with Liggett by offering discriminatory volume discounts to wholesalers. This practice triggered a rebate war in the economy segment, a war BW apparently was winning. By the end of the war, Liggett claimed, BW was selling its black and whites at a loss.

Eventually, Liggett sued BW, alleging that BW's rebates constituted illegal price discrimination under section 2(a) of the Robinson-Patman Act. Liggett claimed that BW's below-cost sales amounted to predatory pricing that was intended to force Liggett to raise its prices on generic cigarettes. This, Liggett further contended, would narrow the difference between generic and branded cigarette prices, thus restraining the growth of the economy segment and preserving BW's excessive profits on its branded cigarettes. Liggett also claimed that, to avoid prolonged losses on the generics that had become its main line of business, it had to go along with BW's scheme.

After a 115-day trial, the jury returned a $49.6 million treble damages verdict in Liggett's favor. The district court, however, decided that BW was entitled to judgment as a matter of law and therefore set aside the jury's verdict. After the court of appeals affirmed this decision, Liggett appealed to the U.S. Supreme Court.

Body of Opinion

Justice Kennedy

By its terms, the Robinson-Patman Act condemns price discrimination only to the extent that it threatens to injure competition.... Liggett contends that BW's discriminatory volume rebates to wholesalers threatened substantial competitive injury by furthering a predatory pricing scheme designed to purge competition from the economy segment of the cigarette market. This type of injury, which harms direct competitors of the discriminating seller, is known as primary-line injury. We last addressed primary-line injury over 25 years ago, in *Utah Pie Co. v. Continental Baking Co.* (1967).... *Utah Pie* has often been interpreted to permit liability for primary-line price discrimination on a mere showing that the defendant intended to harm competition or produced a declining price structure. The case has been criticized on the grounds that such low standards of competitive injury are at odds with the antitrust laws' traditional concern for consumer welfare and price competition.... As the law has been explored since *Utah Pie*, it has become evident that primary-line competitive injury under the Robinson-Patman Act is of the same general character as the injury inflicted by predatory pricing schemes actionable under section 2 of the Sherman Act.... Accordingly, whether the claim alleges predatory pricing under section 2 of the Sherman Act or primary-line price discrimination under the Robinson-Patman Act, two prerequisites to recovery remain the same. First, a plaintiff seeking to establish competitive injury resulting from a rival's low prices must prove that the prices complained of are below an appropriate measure of its rival's costs.... The second prerequisite to holding a competitor liable... is a demonstration that the competitor had a reasonable prospect... of recouping its investment in below-cost prices. For the investment to be rational, the predator must have a reasonable expectation of recovering, in the form of later monopoly profits, more than the losses suffered.... That below-cost pricing may impose painful losses on its target is of no moment to the antitrust laws if competition is not injured: it is axiomatic that the antitrust laws were passed for the protection of *competition*, not *competitors*....

These prerequisites to recovery are not easy to establish, but they are not artificial obstacles to recovery; rather, they are essential components of real market injury. As we have said in the Sherman Act context, predatory pricing schemes are rarely tried, and even more rarely successful.... It would be ironic indeed if the standards for predatory pricing liability were so low that antitrust suits themselves became a tool for keeping prices high....

There is... sufficient evidence in the record from which a reasonable jury could conclude that for a period of approximately 18 months, BW's prices on its generic cigarettes were below its costs, and that this below-cost pricing imposed losses on Liggett that Liggett was unwilling to sustain.... Liggett has failed to demonstrate competitive injury as a matter of law, however, because its proof is flawed in a critical respect: the evidence is inadequate to show that in pursuing [its] scheme, BW had a reasonable prospect of recovering its losses from below-cost pricing through slowing the growth of generics....

Based on Liggett's theory of the case and the record it created, there are two means by which one might infer that BW had a reasonable prospect of producing sustained supracompetitive pricing in the generic segment adequate to recoup its predatory losses: first, if generic output or price information indicates that oligopolistic price coordination in fact produced supracompetitive prices in the generic segment; or second, if evidence about the market and BW's conduct indicate that the alleged scheme was likely to have brought about tacit coordination and oligopoly pricing in the generic segment, even if it did not actually do so.

In this case, the price and output data do not support a reasonable inference that BW and the other cigarette companies elevated prices above a competitive level for generic cigarettes.... Not only does the evidence fail to show actual supracompetitive pricing in the generic segment, it also does not demonstrate its likelihood. At the time BW entered the generic segment, the cigarette industry as a whole faced declining demand and possessed substantial excess capacity. These circumstances tend to break down patterns of oligopoly pricing and produce price competition.... Tacit coordination is facilitated by a stable market environment, fungible products, and a small number of variables upon which the firms seeking to coordinate their pricing may focus. Uncertainty is an oligopoly's greatest enemy. By 1984, however, the cigarette market was in an obvious state of flux. The introduction of generic cigarettes in

1980 represented the first serious price competition in the cigarette market since the 1930s. This development was bound to unsettle previous expectations and patterns of market conduct and to reduce the cigarette firms' ability to predict each others' behavior. The larger number of product types and pricing variables also decreased the probability of effective parallel pricing. In order to coordinate in an effective manner and eliminate price competition, the cigarette companies would have been required, without communicating, to establish parallel practices with respect to each of these variables, many of which, like consumer stickers or coupons, were difficult to monitor. . . .

Even if all the cigarette companies were willing to participate in a scheme to restrain the growth of the generic segment, they would not have been able to coordinate their actions and raise prices above a competitive level unless they understood that BW's entry into the segment was not a genuine effort to compete with Liggett. If even one other firm misinterpreted BW's entry as an effort to expand share, a chain reaction of competitive responses would almost certainly have resulted, and oligopoly discipline would have broken down, perhaps irretrievably. . . . Liggett argues that the means by which BW signalled its anticompetitive intent to its rivals was through its pricing structure. According to Liggett, maintaining existing list prices while offering substantial rebates to wholesalers was a signal to the other cigarette firms that BW did not intend to attract additional smokers to the generic segment by its entry. But . . . [t]he likelihood that BW's rivals would have regarded its pricing structure as an important signal is low, given that Liggett itself, the purported target of the predation, was already using similar rebates. . . .

Judgment and Result

Court of appeals decision in BW's favor affirmed. Liggett's Robinson-Patman claim fails and BW wins.

Questions

1. What were the two requirements Liggett had to meet in order to demonstrate the necessary probability of injury to competition? Which one did it fail to satisfy? Why?
2. Why does below-cost pricing suggest predatory intent?
3. Make an argument that Liggett's motives for suing BW were anticompetitive.

Two Defenses to Price Discrimination. There are two accepted defenses to price discrimination.

1. *Cost Justification.* Section 2(a) permits otherwise-illegal price discrimination where the price differential is due to differences in the commodity's cost of manufacture, sale, or delivery that result from the different methods or quantities in which the commodity is sold. To prove this defense, the defendant must group its customers into different categories according to their buying characteristics, and show that this grouping justifies its price differentials. Despite the difficulties such proof creates, the defense still can allow sellers to escape Robinson-Patman liability in cases where the price differential reflects genuine differences in the costs of servicing particular customers. Quantity discounts are one possibility.
2. *Meeting Competition.* Section 2(b) of the Robinson-Patman Act insulates a seller from liability where its price discrimination took place "in good faith to meet an equally low price of a competitor." The aim of this defense is to prevent normal price competition from violating the Robinson-Patman Act. The standard for granting the defense is whether a reasonable person would believe that charging the lower price would meet the equally low price of a competitor. Although this test requires that the seller have some more or less reliable information about the competitor's price, it does not demand absolute certainty. Note, however, that a seller normally cannot undersell a competitor, but only meet its price.

Buyer Inducement of Discrimination

Robinson-Patman Act section 2(f) makes it illegal for a buyer to knowingly induce or receive a discriminatory price that violates section 2(a). The aim of section 2(f) is to penalize not only sellers who charge discriminatory prices, but the buyers who demand them. However, such buyers are not liable under section 2(f) if the seller has a valid defense to price discrimination liability.

Other Forms of Seller Discrimination

Sellers can discriminate among customers in other ways than by the prices they charge. Thus, the Robinson-Patman Act penalizes three other ways in which sellers might discriminate among buyers. Unlike section 2(a) liability, in all three cases no harm to competition is necessary for liability.

Section 2(c) of the act forbids sellers from paying, and buyers from accepting, commission or brokerage payments that are not in compensation for services rendered in connection with the sale or purchase of goods. Section 2(c)'s aim is to prevent indirect price discrimination in the form of fake commissions or brokerage payments to the buyer or its agents. Robinson-Patman Act section 2(d) makes it illegal for a seller to pay a customer "for any services or facilities furnished by or through such customer" in connection with the sale of the product, unless the payment is available on proportionately equal terms to all competing customers. For example, a manufacturer cannot pay one of its retailers to advertise the product unless it offers essentially the same deal to its other retailers. Section 2(e) imposes a similar restriction on sellers who themselves furnish such services or facilities to their buyers. Note that unlike section 2(c)'s ban on discriminatory commission or brokerage payments, the buyer is not liable under sections 2(d) and 2(e). Also, a "meeting competition" defense is available under sections 2(d) and 2(e).

INTERLOCKING DIRECTORATES AND OFFICERS

"Competitors" that share officers and directors may be competitors in name only. Clayton Act section 8 says that no person shall serve as a director, or as an officer chosen by the directors, of two corporations that: (1) each have capital, surplus, and undivided profits aggregating more than $10 million; and (2) are so situated that an anticompetitive agreement between them would violate the antitrust laws. However, section 8 does not govern banks, banking associations, and trust companies. Also, the $10 million figure is adjusted yearly by an amount equalling the percentage increase or decrease in the gross national product (GNP).

In addition, section 8 does not prohibit simultaneous service by an officer or director if (1) the "competitive sales" of either corporation are less than $1 million; (2) the "competitive sales" of either corporation are less than two percent of that corporation's total sales; or (3) the "competitive sales" of *each* corporation are less than four percent of that corporation's total sales. "Competitive sales" are the gross revenues for all products and services sold by one corporation in competition with the other. Like the $10 million figure, the $1 million figure is adjusted yearly according to the percentage change in the GNP. This provision's apparent aim is to allow people to serve as officers or directors of two firms that are small or do not compete to any significant extent even though they meet the basic tests for section 8 liability.

ANTITRUST EXEMPTIONS

Many activities are exempt from the antitrust laws. Most of these exemptions are explicitly stated in a statute, while some result from judicial decisions. Speaking generally, these exemptions reflect the notion that in some cases, the procompetitive policies underlying the antitrust laws should be superseded by other values. (Of course, self-interested political forces may also explain some exemptions.) The following list of antitrust exemptions is not exhaustive.

The State Action Exemption

In *Parker v. Brown* (1943), the Supreme Court held anticompetitive activities by private raisin growers and packers exempt from the antitrust laws because those activities were authorized by state regulation. Federalism was the basis for this state-action exemption. However, the state regulation protected by *Parker v. Brown* may sometimes reflect the political influence of private firms that desire to avoid competition. To minimize this possibility, the Court has formulated two criteria for the state-action doctrine's application. First, the restraint on competition must be clearly articulated and affirmatively expressed as state policy. Second, that policy must be actively supervised by the state.

The point of the first test is to assure that the state actually has intended to displace competition in a particular area. It includes situations in which a state has clearly permitted, but not commanded, some anticompetitive practice. The "active supervision" test requires that the state exercise sufficient independent judgment and control over the allegedly anticompetitive practices that their details are the product of deliberate state intervention, rather than the result of private agreements. In the case where it enunciated this test, the Court found that price-fixing by state-regulated title insurance companies violated the Sherman Act, in part because the states essentially ratified the companies' rates, instead of setting them or at least scrutinizing them more carefully.

So far, we have been considering regulation by the state itself. What about anticompetitive behavior sanctioned by such local units of government as cities, counties, and townships? Here, state action immunity exists only if the subdivision acts under a state mandate and the challenged anticompetitive practice was a clearly foreseeable consequence of that mandate. However, it is not necessary that the state actively supervise the local unit's implementation of the mandate. Under these tests, the anticompetitive consequences of local zoning regulation probably would be shielded from the antitrust laws, while the anticompetitive consequences of a city's home-rule powers might not.[8]

Petitioning the Government

In 1961, the Supreme Court held that the antitrust laws do not prohibit two or more people from associating together to persuade the government to enact a law with an anticompetitive impact. The reason was that the antitrust laws should not regulate political activity—even political activity with anticompetitive aims—because such activity implicates First Amendment values. However, this exemption does not cover "sham" political action that really is an attempt to suppress competition. In one such case, for example, the Supreme Court refused to exempt a group of large trucking firms that routinely opposed all applications by smaller truckers before state and federal agencies.

---

[8] Due to fear that application of the antitrust laws to local governments might result in crippling treble damage liability, Congress passed the Local Government Antitrust Act of 1984. The act bars federal antitrust damage suits against local governments, their officials and employees (when acting in their official capacity), and private persons (for actions directed by a local government). However, injunctive relief remains available.

Union Activity

Trade unions may seek to monopolize the labor supply within a particular market, and strikes arguably resemble group boycotts. For this reason, organized labor's well-being might be endangered were the antitrust laws applicable to unions and their activities. Thus, labor unions, most union activities, and collective bargaining agreements generally are exempt from the antitrust laws. However, the exemption does not apply if a union engages in anticompetitive activity with a nonlabor group.

Other Exemptions

Many regulated industries such as insurance; banking; airline and rail transportation; electric, gas, and water services; financial services; and others are exempt from the antitrust laws to a greater or lesser extent. Often, the administrative bodies regulating such industries deal with matters that otherwise would be antitrust issues. Federal law also exempts certain agricultural cooperatives from antitrust regulation. Federal law further exempts certain joint export activities by U.S. companies, as long as they do not affect prices within the United States. The aim of these combinations is to help U.S. firms better compete against foreign cartels.

CHAPTER SUMMARY

All parties to the debate over antitrust law agree that, at least in part, it exists to thwart anticompetitive business behavior that diminishes consumer welfare. The most important of the federal antitrust laws is the Sherman Act. Sherman Act section 1 forbids various contracts, combinations, or conspiracies in restraint of trade.

Some of these violations are per se violations, which only require proof of the offending behavior. Section 1 per se violations include horizontal and vertical price-fixing, the horizontal division of markets, group boycotts, and tying contracts.

Other potentially anticompetitive contracts or combinations are called rule of reason violations. Here, in addition to proof of the offending behavior, an individualized inquiry into the economic effects of that behavior is necessary before section 1 liability will exist.

Section 2 of the Sherman Act forbids monopolization and attempts to monopolize. Monopolization requires (1) a firm with monopoly power, in (2) the relevant product and territorial market, and (3) the firm's acquisition or exercise of that monopoly power with intent to monopolize.

Section 3 of the Clayton Act forbids the sale or lease of commodities on the condition that the buyer or lessee not use or deal commodities sold or leased by a competitor of that seller or lessor, where this would substantially lessen competition or tend to create a monopoly. Section 3 applies mainly to tying contracts, exclusive dealing contracts, and requirements contracts.

Clayton Act section 7 forbids mergers that substantially lessen competition or tend to create a monopoly. Its discretionary standards vary depending upon whether a horizontal merger, a vertical merger, or a conglomerate merger is present. Clayton Act section 8 forbids interlocking directorates and officers.

The Robinson-Patman Act mainly concerns price discrimination, which may be of the primary line, the secondary line, or the tertiary line variety. It also forbids a buyer's inducement to discrimination, discriminatory commission or brokerage payments, discriminatory payments to a customer, and the discriminatory furnishing of services or facilities to customers.

MANAGER'S ETHICAL DILEMMA

"Those chiropractors are stealing our patients," said Dr. Edward to Dr. Simpson. "And they're not doing them much good, either." Both Edward and Simpson are medical doctors. Due to their concerns, they sent letters to their lobbying groups and to the American Medical Association. Their letters urged that these groups pressure Congress and the state legislatures to enact tougher education requirements for chiropractors, tougher chiropractor licensing standards, and fee caps for chiropractic services. Drs. Edward and Simpson also joined a large group of medical doctors who agreed not to refer patients to chiropractors even in situations where they felt that chiropractic treatment might do those patients some good. Instead, they agreed to send their patients to fellow MDs specializing in orthopedics.

Are these actions ethical behavior on the two doctors' part? What factual question will definitely affect your answer? *Note:* this scenario is loosely based on *Wilk v. American Medical Association*, 895 F.2d 352 (7th Cir. 1990).

Many kinds of behavior are exempt from the antitrust laws. The most important antitrust exemptions are (1) the state action exemption, (2) a "political action" exemption, and (3) an exemption for union activity.

Discussion Questions

1. The *Alcoa* case discussed under section 2 of the Sherman Act probably came close to inferring the intent to acquire or exercise monopoly from its possession by the defendant. Is this a good or a bad thing? What are monopolists—even innocent monopolists—likely to do with monopoly power once they get it? On the other hand, might they not face new entrants to the industry if they try these things? Or will barriers to entry always or nearly always prevent new competitors from entering the industry? Finally, will firms' competitive juices flow more weakly if they know that the ultimate reward of competitive effort—domination of an industry—will only get them in legal trouble under section 2?
2. The chapter states the arguments made by the Supreme Court in the 1977 *Sylvania* case, where it held that vertical territorial restrictions should be treated as rule-of-reason violations rather than per se violations. Do you find these arguments persuasive? If so, should they be extended to justify rule-of-reason status for the vertical fixing of minimum prices?
3. As the chapter should make clear, "Chicago School" thinking is coming to dominate the antitrust laws. Go through the chapter and identify as many examples as you can. In each case, say *why* the development in question exemplifies Chicago School thinking.
4. All things considered, do you believe that the Chicago School approach is preferable to the more liberal traditional approach? Or is it the other way around?
5. Does the Robinson-Patman Act protect competitors more than it protects competition? How much does it protect competition at all? Should it be repealed? Why is it unlikely to be repealed any time soon?
6. Is the state action exemption a good idea? Whose interests do the "state policies" protected by the exemption tend to serve? Is federalism just a fig leaf here?

Suggested Readings

Articles

CANN, "Vertical Restraints and the 'Efficiency' Influence—Does Any Room Remain for More Traditional Antitrust Values and More Innovative Antitrust Policies?" 24 *American Business Law Journal* 483 (1987).

KOVALEFF, "A Symposium on the 100th Anniversary of the Sherman Act and Upon the 75th Anniversary of the Clayton Act," 35 *Antitrust Bulletin* 1 (1990).

OSTAS, "Municipal Antitrust Liability under the State Action Exemption," 24 *American Business Law Journal* 643 (1987).

WERDEN, "Challenges to Horizontal Mergers by Competitors under Section 7 of the Clayton Act," 24 *American Business Law Journal* 213 (1986).

Books

GELLHORN and KOVACIC, *Antitrust Law and Economics in a Nutshell*, 4th ed. (1994).

CHAPTER

21

FEDERAL TRADE COMMISSION ACT, FRANCHISING, AND UNFAIR COMPETITION

"THE OBJECTIVE OF THE FEDERAL TRADE COMMISSION IS TO MAINTAIN COMPETITIVE ENTERPRISE AS THE KEYSTONE OF THE AMERICAN ECONOMIC SYSTEM, AND TO PREVENT THE FREE ENTERPRISE SYSTEM FROM BEING FETTERED BY MONOPOLY OR RESTRAINTS ON TRADE OR CORRUPTED BY UNFAIR OR DECEPTIVE TRADE PRACTICES. IN BRIEF, THE COMMISSION IS CHARGED WITH KEEPING COMPETITION BOTH FREE AND FAIR."

U.S. Government Manual, 1998–1999

POSITIVE LAW ETHICAL PROBLEMS

The price inflation that afflicted the United States during the 1970s had definite consequences for the Orkin Exterminating Company. From 1966 until 1975, Orkin had offered its customers contracts for "lifetime" termite protection and control. These contracts said that this guarantee would remain in effect for the lifetime of the covered structure, so long as the customer continued to pay the annual renewal fee. After increasing costs made the contracts too expensive, Orkin decided that it had to get out of them. In 1980, therefore, the firm began notifying its 1966–1975 "lifetime" customers that it was going to increase its annual renewal fees by about 40 percent. Despite many complaints, most customers accepted the increase. One reason they caved in was that signing on with Orkin's competitors often left them no better off than under Orkin's revised plan. Also, Orkin instituted an "accommodation program" in which it explained its changed position to complaining customers and thereby mollified some of them. Although a few persistent customers did escape the rate increase through the program, most complaining customers were not made aware of this possibility.

Was Orkin's behavior ethical? In any event, was it legal? The Federal Trade Commission (FTC) thought not. In 1984, the FTC issued an administrative complaint charging that Orkin had committed an unfair act or practice in violation of FTC Act section 5. Did the Commission wins its case?

The previous chapter explained how the Sherman, Clayton, and Robinson-Patman Acts forbid various anticompetitive practices. Section 5 of the Federal Trade Commission Act of 1914, which prohibits unfair methods of competition, does much the same. By forbidding unfair or deceptive acts or practices, moreover, section 5 also protects consumers. Both of these missions—promoting competition and protecting consumers—are entrusted to the Federal Trade Commission (FTC), created by the FTC Act in 1914.

This chapter opens by examining the FTC, its enforcement devices, and its role in attacking anticompetitive behavior. The chapter's main concern, however, is the Commission's regulation of deceptive and unfair business conduct, especially deceptive advertising. The chapter then outlines some of the remedies the FTC employs in advertising cases, as well as its regulation of franchising. The chapter concludes by considering a federal statute—section 43(a) of the Lanham Act—that provides a civil remedy for false or deceptive advertising and certain other kinds of unfair competition.

FEDERAL TRADE COMMISSION

The Federal Trade Commission (FTC) is an independent federal administrative agency. It is not part of the executive branch of government and is not so subject to political control as agencies located within the executive branch. The FTC is headed by five commissioners, appointed by the president and confirmed by the Senate for staggered seven-year terms. The president also designates one of the commissioners as chairman of the FTC.

Figure 21.1 describes the FTC's internal organization. As the figure suggests, the Commission has several regional offices. These offices are the usual starting point for businesses or consumers wishing to contact the FTC about possible violations of the laws it enforces. The addresses and territorial coverage of the FTC's regional offices can be found on their website.

http://

For up-to-date information on the FTC's regional offices, see ***http://www.ftc.gov***

Functions

Today, the FTC's main functions can be grouped under two headings: (1) maintaining economic competition, and (2) consumer protection. In other words, the FTC tries to encourage business competition that is both free and fair. The Commission promotes free competition by enforcing both the antitrust statutes discussed in Chapter 20 and FTC Act section 5's ban on unfair methods of competition. The FTC's consumer protection mission has three main components. First, section 5 enables the Commission to regulate *deceptive* acts or practices by businesses. The most important example is deceptive advertising. Second, section 5 also gives the Commission the power to regulate *unfair* acts or practices. Third, the FTC enforces a number of specific federal consumer protection measures, some of which are discussed in the next chapter. The Commission also enforces various other miscellaneous federal statutes.

http://

For a full list of all the federal acts the FTC enforces or administers, see ***http://www.ftc.gov/ogc/stats.htm***

FTC Regulation under Section 5

FTC Act section 5 is worded in a broad and general fashion. One reason for its vagueness is that there are too many kinds of unfairness and deception for Congress ever to specify in a single statute. Another reason is that the ingenuity of unscrupulous businesspeople continually produces novel forms of deception, unfairness, and anticompetitive activity. Thus, Congress probably had little choice but to announce general standards, and to delegate the power to enforce those standards to an agency such as the FTC.

This necessary flexibility, however, comes at a price. Due to section 5's generality, businesses sometimes have difficulty determining whether their activities will run afoul of the FTC. As you will see shortly, however, the FTC has taken a number of steps to address this problem.

FIGURE 21.1 The Federal Trade Commission

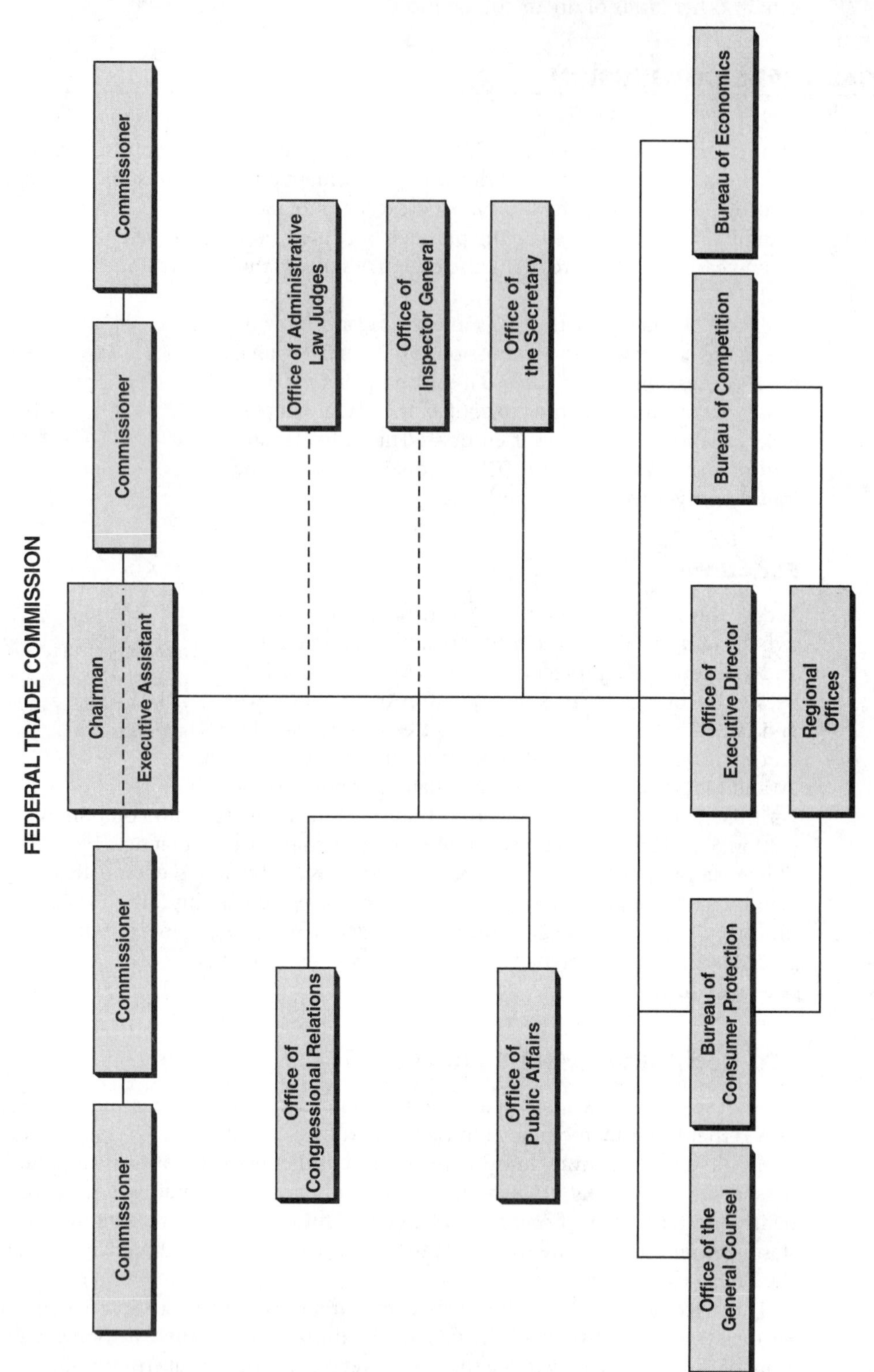

Source: *U.S. Government Manual*, 1998–99.

Another implication of section 5's generality is that the FTC has considerable freedom to determine how aggressively it regulates business misbehavior. In fact, the FTC's conception of its role—and thus its effect on business activity—has varied considerably over the years. This is because the economic philosophies of the commissioners and the political allegiances of the administrations appointing them go some way toward determining the FTC's course. In the 1970s, for example, the Commission was an activist agency that constantly attempted to define and enforce stricter rules against business misconduct. During the 1980s, on the other hand, the FTC tended to be more skeptical about the virtues of government regulation and to stress the economic costs of such regulation.

FTC RULES, GUIDES, AND OTHER STANDARDS

Due to the generality of FTC Act section 5 and some other laws the Commission enforces, businesses need authoritative guidance about what is legal and illegal under these provisions. To supply such guidance, the FTC uses three procedures called **advisory opinions**, **industry guides**, and **trade regulation rules**. Neither advisory opinions nor industry guides have the force of law. Trade regulation rules, however, are legally binding. Advisory opinions and industry guides try to promote voluntary compliance by business. Trade regulation rules have the same aim, but violation of these rules can lead to FTC sanctions as well.

Advisory Opinions

Although it is not obligated to do so, the FTC often responds to business queries about the legality of proposed conduct by issuing an advisory opinion. For example, a firm contemplating a particular marketing technique may be able to get an advisory opinion giving it some idea whether the FTC will act to block the use of that technique. Advisory opinions do not bind the FTC, because the Commission may later reconsider and revoke the opinion if the public interest so requires. But in such situations the FTC must give the recipient of the opinion notice of the revocation and an opportunity to cease actions taken in good faith reliance on the opinion before it can proceed against the recipient for such actions.

Industry Guides

Another way the FTC tries to promote voluntary, cooperative business compliance is by issuing industry guides. Industry guides are FTC interpretations of the laws it enforces. They are stated in lay language and are not legally binding. Thus, the FTC cannot proceed against a business just because its behavior violates an industry guide. However, such behavior often violates some other, more authoritative, standard such as a trade regulation rule.

Trade Regulation Rules

Like industry guides, FTC trade regulation rules interpret the statutes the Commission enforces. For example, they may specify particular practices that the FTC deems deceptive or unfair. Unlike industry guides, however, trade regulation rules are written in legalistic language and have the force of law. Thus, violations of trade regulation rules can trigger FTC enforcement efforts.

FTC ENFORCEMENT DEVICES

The primary way that the FTC enforces its statutes and rules is through formal administrative action. After considering FTC administrative enforcement in some detail, we briefly consider some other enforcement devices at the Commission's disposal.

Formal FTC Action

Initiation of Proceedings. Sometimes the initiative for FTC administrative action comes from the FTC's own investigations of possible illegal activity. On other occasions, the action is initiated by an informal complaint. Examples of the latter include a business that complains about a competitor's anticompetitive conduct, a consumer who argues that certain advertising is deceptive, or another government body that tips off the FTC about illegal private behavior. No special form is needed for an informal complaint. A letter stating the relevant facts in detail, accompanied by all supporting evidence in the complaining party's possession, is enough. It is the FTC's policy not to disclose the identity of any complainant, except as required by law.

After it receives an informal complaint, the FTC must decide whether to investigate the matter. Within the limits of its resources, the Commission will investigate in situations where its goals of maintaining competition and protecting consumers are most directly involved. Upon completion of the investigation, a staff recommendation is submitted for final Commission action. The staff may recommend that the case be closed. It may also recommend that the Commission settle the case. Finally, the FTC may issue a formal complaint against the alleged violator (the respondent).

FTC Administrative Hearings. Even after a formal complaint is issued, the FTC and the respondent still may settle the case. If the case is not settled, it goes to an FTC administrative hearing (also called an adjudicative proceeding). The hearing resembles a court trial. It is presided over by an administrative law judge, without a jury. After hearing the testimony and the legal arguments made by counsel for the respondent and the FTC, the administrative law judge issues an initial decision.

Commission Orders. An initial decision against the respondent in an FTC administrative proceeding typically is accompanied by an order. The most common such order is called a **cease and desist order**, or C&D order. As its name suggests, a C&D order basically is a command ordering the respondent to cease from certain behavior. However, Commission orders sometimes go beyond a simple command to cease and desist. The FTC may, for example, compel a respondent to make affirmative disclosures, to divest itself of certain assets or stock, or to make restitution to injured parties. In cases involving deceptive or unfair advertising, the Commission may also issue the affirmative disclosure, corrective advertising, and all-products orders described later in the chapter. Parties who violate the terms of a Commission order are subject to civil penalties of up to $10,000 per violation. Where the violation continues, each day of its continuance is a separate violation.

As noted earlier, the FTC may settle a case with the alleged violator either before or after the issuance of a formal complaint. Such settlements involve a **consent order**. Where a consent order is worked out, the FTC agrees not to pursue the case further, in return for the respondent's promise to refrain from engaging in certain behavior. The respondent need not admit any violation of the law. The penalties for failure to obey a consent order are the same as for the failure to observe a normal Commission order.

Further Review. Where no settlement occurs, the administrative law judge typically decides for or against the respondent. This initial decision usually becomes the decision of the full Commission at the end of 30 days unless (1) the Commission decides to review it, or (2) either party appeals to the full Commission. When the FTC's five commissioners review the initial decision, they may (1) sustain the decision, (2) modify it, or (3) reverse it. If an administrative law judge's decision against the respondent is sustained or modified, the Commission issues an order against the respondent. (If a decision against the respondent is reversed, of course, no order is issued.) Once the full Commission issues an order, the respondent has 60 days to appeal it to the appropriate U.S. Court of Appeals. Either party may appeal the court of appeals' decision to the U.S. Supreme Court.

Other Enforcement Devices

C&D orders and consent orders are the primary methods used by the FTC to enforce its statutes and trade regulation rules. But the Commission also has a few other enforcement devices at its disposal. In various situations, the FTC may sue for **injunctive relief** in federal district court. Also, the Commission may obtain federal district court **civil penalties** in certain cases involving unfair or deceptive acts or practices. This can happen where (1) a private party knowingly violates a trade regulation rule defining such acts or practices, or (2) a private party knowingly violates a C&D order involving such acts or practices, even if the order involved some other party. In each case, the penalty cannot exceed $10,000 per violation. To illustrate the second situation, suppose that the FTC orders a manufacturer to cease making certain untrue advertising claims. If a competitor of the manufacturer makes the same untrue claims with knowledge of the order, the FTC may sue to impose a civil penalty.

In two other situations involving unfairness or deception, the FTC may sue in state or federal court for **redress** to consumers or other injured parties. A business may be required to make such redress where it (1) violates any trade regulation rule defining such acts or practices, or (2) violates a C&D order imposed on it because of such acts or practices. The redress available to injured parties may include the rescission or reformation of contracts, the refund of money, the return of property, payment of damages, or public notice of the unfair or deceptive practice.

THE FTC AND ANTICOMPETITIVE BEHAVIOR

As we have stressed, one of the FTC's missions is to promote free economic competition. The main kinds of anticompetitive behavior with which the FTC is concerned are the orthodox antitrust violations described in Chapter 20. The FTC has specific statutory authority to enforce the Clayton Act and the Robinson-Patman Act.[1] In addition, FTC Act section 5's broad "unfair methods of competition" language covers all behavior made illegal by the Sherman Act.

Section 5 also lets the FTC attack anticompetitive conduct outside the letter or spirit of the other antitrust statutes. In one such case, the Supreme Court held that the Sperry and Hutchinson Company's attempt to suppress trading stamp exchanges that dealt in its S&H Green Stamps violated section 5, even though the attempt did not violate either the letter or the spirit of the antitrust laws. Finally, section 5 gives the FTC the power to proceed against potential or incipient violations of the antitrust laws.

---

[1] Also, companies planning certain kinds of mergers are required to give premerger notification to the FTC and the Justice Department, and supply certain information to these agencies as well.

The following *California Dental Association* case involves advertising—one of the FTC's chief regulatory responsibilities. But the Court is concerned with the anticompetitive effect of an advertising scheme, not its deceptiveness or its unfairness to consumers. The main issue in the case is the approach courts should adopt in such situations.

California Dental Ass'n v. Federal Trade Commission

U.S. Supreme Court
526 U.S. 756 (1999)

Background and Facts:

The California Dental Association (CDA) is a voluntary nonprofit association of local dental societies to which some 19,000 dentists belong, including about three-quarters of those practicing in the state. The dentists who belong to the CDA agreed to abide by a Code of Ethics (Code), which included certain restrictions on advertising. Responsibility for enforcing the Code rested in the first instance with local dental societies, to which applicants for CDA membership had to submit copies of their advertisements. The local societies also actively sought information about potential Code violations by applicants or CDA members. Applicants who refused to withdraw or revise objectionable advertisements might be denied membership; and members who remained similarly recalcitrant were subject to censure, suspension, or expulsion from the CDA.

The FTC brought a complaint against the CDA, alleging that it applied its guidelines so as to restrict truthful, nondeceptive advertising, and so violated section 1 of the Sherman Act and section 5 of the FTC Act. The complaint alleged that the CDA had unreasonably restricted two types of advertising: price advertising (particularly discounted fees) and advertising relating to the quality of dental services. An administrative law judge found a violation of section 5, and the full Commission agreed. The Ninth Circuit Court of Appeals affirmed the Commission's decision, and the CDA appealed to the U.S. Supreme Court.

Body of Opinion

Justice Souter

[In] "quick-look" analysis under the rule of reason, an observer with even a rudimentary understanding of economics could conclude that the arrangements in question would have an anticompetitive effect on customers and markets. In [one case], the league's television plan expressly limited output (the number of games that could be televised) and fixed a minimum price. In [another], the restraint was an absolute ban on competitive bidding. In [a third], the restraint was a horizontal agreement among the participating dentists to withhold from their customers a particular service that they desire. As in such cases, quick-look analysis carries the day when the great likelihood of anticompetitive effects can easily be ascertained.

The case before us, however, fails to present a situation in which the likelihood of anticompetitive effects is comparably obvious. Even on Justice Breyer's view that bars on truthful and verifiable price and quality advertising are prima facie anticompetitive and place the burden of procompetitive justification on those who agree to adopt them, the very issue at the threshold of this case is whether professional price and quality advertising is sufficiently verifiable in theory and in fact to fall within such a general rule. Ultimately our disagreement with Justice Breyer turns on our different responses to this issue. Whereas he accepts... that the restrictions here [are] like restrictions on advertisement of price and quality generally, it seems to us that the CDA's advertising restrictions might plausibly be thought to have a net procompetitive effect, or possibly no effect at all on competition. The restrictions... are, at least on their face, designed to avoid false or deceptive advertising in a market characterized by striking disparities between the information available to the professional and the patient....

The explanation proffered by the court of appeals for the likely anticompetitive effect of the CDA's restrictions on discount advertising began with the unexceptionable statements that price advertising is fundamental to price competition, and that restrictions on the ability to advertise prices normally make it more difficult for consumers to find a lower price and for dentists to compete on the basis of price. The court then acknowledged that, according to the CDA, the restrictions nonetheless furthered the legitimate, indeed pro-competitive, goal of preventing false and misleading price advertising. The court of appeals might, at this juncture, have recognized that the restrictions at issue here are very far from a total ban on price or discount advertising, and might have considered the possibility that the particular restrictions on professional advertising could have different effects from those normally found in the commercial world, even to the point of promoting competition by reducing the occurrence of unverifiable and misleading across-the-board discount advertising....

The court of appeals was comparably tolerant in accepting the sufficiency of abbreviated rule-of-reason analysis as to the nonprice advertising restrictions. The court began with the argument that "these restrictions are in effect a form of output limitation, as they restrict the supply of information about individual dentists' services. . . ." [But it] gave no weight to the countervailing, and at least equally plausible, suggestion that restricting difficult-to-verify claims about quality or patient comfort would have a procompetitive effect by preventing misleading or false claims that distort the market. It is, indeed, entirely possible to understand the CDA's restrictions on unverifiable quality and comfort advertising as nothing more than a procompetitive ban on puffery. The point is not that the CDA's restrictions necessarily have the procompetitive effect claimed by the CDA; it is possible that banning quality claims might have no effect at all on competitiveness if, for example, many dentists made very much the same sort of claims. And it is also of course possible that the restrictions might in the final analysis be anticompetitive. The point, rather, is that the plausibility of competing claims about the effects of the professional advertising restrictions rules out the indulgently abbreviated review to which the Commission's order was treated. The obvious anticompetitive effect that triggers abbreviated analysis has not been shown.

Saying here that the court of appeals' conclusion at least required a more extended examination of the possible factual underpinnings than it received is not, of course, necessarily to call for the fullest market analysis. Although we have said that a challenge to a naked restraint on price and output need not be supported by a detailed market analysis in order to require some competitive justification, it does not follow that every case attacking a less obviously anticompetitive restraint (like this one) is a candidate for plenary market examination. The truth is that our categories of analysis of anticompetitive effect are less fixed than terms like "per se," "quick look," and "rule of reason" tend to make them appear. We have recognized, for example, that there is often no bright line separating per se from rule of reason analysis, since considerable inquiry into market conditions may be required before the application of any so-called per se condemnation is justified. . . . As the circumstances here demonstrate, there is generally no categorical line to be drawn between restraints that give rise to an intuitively obvious inference of anticompetitive effect and those that call for more detailed treatment. What is required, rather, is an enquiry meet for the case, looking to the circumstances, details, and logic of a restraint. The object is to see whether the experience of the market has been so clear, or necessarily will be, that a confident conclusion about the principal tendency of a restriction will follow from a quick (or at least quicker) look, in place of a more sedulous one. And of course what we see may vary over time, if rule-of-reason analyses in case after case reach identical conclusions. For now, at least, a less quick look was required for the initial assessment of the tendency of these professional advertising restrictions.

Judgment and Result

Because the court of appeals did not scrutinize the assumption of relative anticompetitive tendencies, we vacate the judgment and remand the case for a fuller consideration of the issue.

Questions

1. How is "quick look" analysis supposed to work? How different is it from the per se analysis described in Chapter 20?
2. The Court describes the approach taken by Justice Breyer's opinion in this case (which we do not present here). What is it?
3. Anyone can see that restrictions on advertising may help stifle competition and thus enrich the parties who enact the restriction. Why, then, did the Court not immediately conclude that the CDA's advertising restrictions violated section 5?
4. In this abbreviated version of the Court's opinion, at least, how much guidance did it give lower courts in handling cases of this kind? Would you like to be a federal court of appeals judge trying to follow the guidance given here?

DECEPTIVE AND UNFAIR ACTS OR PRACTICES

Section 5's prohibition of deceptive and unfair acts or practices gives the FTC power to regulate a wide range of activities harmful to consumers, especially deceptive advertising. When the Commission attacks business behavior under this portion of section 5, it may do so on either of two bases. It may argue that the act or practice violates section 5 because it is deceptive, or because it is unfair. This section considers each of these standards in turn, and then examines some matters that specifically pertain to advertising.

Deception

Many deceptive advertising cases apply standards found in the Commission's 1983 policy statement on that subject. The standards say that, to violate section 5 on grounds of deceptiveness, advertising and other allegedly deceptive behavior must involve (1) a material (2) representation, omission, or practice that is likely to mislead (3) a consumer acting reasonably under the circumstances.

Representation, Omission, or Practice Likely to Mislead Consumers. Many kinds of business behavior can violate section 5's ban on deceptive acts or practices. Often, a seller's advertisements or other statements involve express claims that can be proven false. In addition, false claims can sometimes be implied from the circumstances. Implied representations can arise from the product's physical appearance, the circumstances of the transaction, the seller's express representations, and ordinary consumer expectations. For example, a product that looks new but actually is used may create an implied representation that it really is new. In one case, moreover, the FTC found an implied assertion that Listerine mouthwash can prevent and cure colds and sore throats because the following two representations appeared close together in Listerine's advertising: "Kills Germs by Millions on Contact" and "For General Oral Hygiene, Bad Breath, Colds, and Resultant Sore Throats." Sellers also can deceive by omitting significant facts. For example, claims that a product cures baldness may violate section 5 if they are not accompanied by a statement that most forms of baldness cannot effectively be treated.

In all of these situations, the express statement, implied statement, omission, or practice must be likely to mislead consumers. (Actual deception, however, is not necessary.) Often, this test requires the FTC to determine the truth or falsity of the respondent's express and implied claims. In addition, the Commission may require sellers to substantiate objective claims about their products by showing that they have a reasonable basis.

The "Reasonable Consumer" Test. To violate section 5, deceptive behavior also must be likely to mislead consumers who have acted reasonably under the circumstances. The reason for this requirement is to protect sellers from all the ignorant, foolish, or outlandish misconceptions to which some consumers are subject. As the FTC put it more than 20 years ago:

> "Some people, because of ignorance or incomprehension, may be misled by even a scrupulously honest claim. Perhaps a few misguided souls believe, for example, that all 'Danish Pastry' is made in Denmark. Is it therefore an actionable deception to advertise 'Danish Pastry' when it is made in this country? Of course not."[2]

Due to the "reasonable consumer" test, many familiar kinds of advertising statements usually do not violate section 5. Statements of opinion are one example. Subjective claims such as taste, feel, appearance, and smell are another. The same is true for obviously exaggerated statements that amount to sales talk or "puffing." The Commission also may be reluctant to proceed against deceptive advertising where the consumer easily can evaluate the product or service, it is inexpensive, and it is frequently purchased. In such situations, sellers have little incentive to misrepresent because they want to encourage repeat purchases.

---

[2] *Heinz v. W. Kirchner*, 63 F.T.C. 1282, 1290 (1963).

Critics of the Commission's approach toward deception have argued that the reasonableness standard may protect some unscrupulous advertising schemes aimed at the unsophisticated, naive, and gullible. Although this criticism could be true, the Commission has indicated that when advertising is targeted toward a specific audience, it will examine the ad's effect on a reasonable member of that audience. Ads claiming miracle cancer cures, for example, are not judged from the perspective of a healthy person. On the other hand, a similar advertisement aimed at the medical profession would be judged in light of the knowledge and sophistication possessed by a reasonable member of that group.

Materiality. Insignificant forms of deception, one would think, should be of little concern to the FTC. Thus, the Commission has declared that only *material* misrepresentations, omissions, or practices violate section 5's ban on deceptive acts or practices. Material information is information that is important to reasonable consumers and is likely to affect their conduct regarding a product or service, especially their decision to purchase it. Examples include statements or omissions regarding a product's cost, safety, purpose, effectiveness, performance, quality, durability, or warranties. In addition, the Commission has said that express claims are material.

Federal Trade Commission v. Patriot Alcohol Testers, Inc.

U.S. District Court for the District of Massachusetts
798 F. Supp. 851 (1992)

Background and Facts:

Patriot Alcohol Testers, Inc. marketed a coin-operated blood alcohol measuring device known as the "Model 5000." To use the Model 5000, people would deposit fifty cents, blow through a straw into the machine, and then receive a blood alcohol reading. Patriot marketed the Model 5000 by telling potential distributors that they could make money by placing it in bars, nightclubs, and restaurants for use by patrons of those establishments. Among the representations made by Patriot were the following: (1) that distributors' annual income from the Model 5000 would be $130 per week per device; (2) that it is easy to get bars and other drinking establishments to place the Model 5000 on their premises; and (3) that such establishments could obtain substantial discounts in their liability insurance upon installing a blood alcohol testing device like the Model 5000.

Claiming that these and other representations were deceptive under FTC Act section 5, the Commission sued Patriot in federal district court, apparently for injunctive relief. Then it moved for partial summary judgment.

Body of Opinion

Senior District Judge Caffrey

Section 5 of the FTC Act provides that "unfair or deceptive acts or practices in or affecting commerce are declared unlawful." To establish that an act or practice is "deceptive" under section 5, the FTC must establish three required elements. First, the FTC must establish that there is a representation, omission, or practice. Second, the FTC must establish that the representation, omission, or practice is likely to mislead consumers acting reasonably under the circumstances. Third, the FTC must establish that the representation, omission, or practice is material.

The first element simply requires a showing that the defendant made some representation. With respect to the second element, a court must consider whether the representation is likely to mislead a reasonable consumer by viewing it as a whole, without emphasizing isolated words or phrases apart from their context. In addition, a court must focus on the impression created by the advertisement, not its literal truth or falsity. With respect to the third element, a material representation is one that involves information that is important to consumers and hence likely to affect their choice of, or conduct regarding, a product. Express representations that are shown to be false are presumptively material. Assuming that the plaintiff satisfies the three elements, the fact that an advertiser may have acted without an intent to deceive is not a defense to a violation of section 5. Nor is an advertiser's good faith a defense. . . .

Average Weekly Income. With respect to the first prong of the [deception] standard, there is no genuine issue as to whether the defendants made the representation that distributors' average weekly income from the Model 5000 is $130 per device. . . . The second prong of the standard requires the FTC to show that the representation is likely to mislead consumers acting reasonably under the circumstances. Based on the record before this court, the claim that the Model 5000 earns an average of $130 per week appears to have been an exaggeration.... No affidavit submitted by the defendant reported an average weekly income per device of greater than $100. If the FTC's affidavits were taken into consideration, the average would drop substantially lower; the highest average weekly income per device reported in the FTC's affidavits was twenty dollars. Thus, given the wide disparity between defendant's representations regarding the device's average weekly income and the actual earnings of distributors who submitted affidavits, the only conclusion that a reasonable finder of fact could reach is that the representations were false and likely to mislead consumers acting reasonably under the circumstances....

The third element... requires the FTC to show that the representation is material. Express representations that are shown to be false are presumptively material. In the instant case, defendant's representation that Model 5000s earn an average of $130 per week per device was express, and the court has concluded that there is no genuine issue of fact that the representation is false. Therefore, the representation is presumptively material. Thus, the FTC has satisfied all three of the required elements for establishing that the representation is deceptive under section 5....

Ease of Placement. There is no genuine issue that the defendant made representations concerning the ease with which distributors could convince bar and restaurant owners to have Model 5000s placed at their establishments.... As for the second element, however, there is a genuine issue of fact as to whether these representations were likely to mislead consumers acting reasonably.... Some distributors report in their affidavits of having had great difficulty finding locations that would accept placement of the Model 5000. Many other distributors, however, report having had no difficulty.... [T]herefore, the FTC is not entitled to summary judgment with respect to these representations.

Insurance Discounts. There is no genuine issue that defendant represented that bars and other drinking establishments are able to obtain substantial discounts on their liability insurance based on their installation of alcohol testing devices.... Nor is there a genuine issue of material fact with respect to the second prong. The defendant's representations regarding insurance discounts would mislead consumers acting reasonably under the circumstances because the representations were clearly false.... Moreover, since the representations have been found to be false, they are presumptively material. Therefore, the FTC has satisfied the third prong as well as the second.

The defendant argues, however, that... it merely repeated representations made to it by insurance agents and companies. In essence, defendant argues that it did not know that the representations were false. But a violation of section 5 can occur even absent an intent to deceive, and an advertiser's good faith does not shield it from liability.... The FTC is entitled to summary judgment that defendant violated section 5 by representing that drinking establishments are able to obtain substantial insurance discounts based on the installation of alcohol testing devices.

Judgment and Result

The FTC's motion for partial summary judgment was granted in part and denied in part.

Questions

1. What common factor did the court consider in determining whether each of the representations was likely to mislead a consumer acting reasonably under the circumstances?
2. Regarding the ease-of-placement representation, why did the court not have to consider the deception standard's third prong?

Unfairness

Many unfairness cases proceed under standards promulgated by the FTC in 1980. These standards require that the offending practice cause injury to consumers and that this injury be (1) substantial, (2) not outweighed by any offsetting consumer or competitive benefits the practice produces, and (3) not reasonably avoidable by consumers. *Substantial harm* includes monetary losses and unwarranted health and safety risks to consumers, but it is unlikely that emotional distress or the perceived offensiveness of an advertisement qualify.

The second element of the test—that the harm the challenged practice causes not be outweighed by its benefits to consumers or to competition—requires the FTC to balance the practice's costs against its benefits. Only when the practice is injurious in its net effects does it satisfy this second test. For example, a seller's failure to disclose complex technical data about its products might not be unfair if the data are of marginal usefulness to consumers and disclosure would significantly raise the product's price.

Finally, the FTC considers an injury not reasonably avoidable when the challenged act or practice significantly interferes with consumers' ability to make informed decisions that would have prevented the injury. Such interference can occur where a seller fails to disclose important performance data regarding its product, and the buyer lacks sufficient information to meaningfully compare the product with other products. The Commission has also suggested that this test is met when sellers exercise undue influence over highly susceptible consumers—as, for example, when questionable cures are marketed to seriously ill cancer victims.

Orkin Exterminating Co. v. Federal Trade Commission

U.S. Court of Appeals (11th Circuit)
849 F.2d 1354 (1988)

Background and Facts:

From 1966 until 1975, the Orkin Exterminating Company offered its customers contracts for "lifetime" termite protection and control. The contracts said that the guarantee would remain in effect for the lifetime of the covered structure, as long as the customer paid the annual renewal fee. After inflation and increasing costs made the contracts too expensive, Orkin decided that it had to get out of them. In 1980, therefore, the firm began telling its 1966-75 "lifetime" customers that it would increase its annual renewal fees by about 40 percent. Despite many complaints, most customers accepted the increase. One reason they did so was that signing on with Orkin's competitors often left them no better off than under Orkin's revised plan. Also, Orkin instituted an "accommodation program" in which it explained its new position to complaining customers and thereby mollified some of them. While a few persistent customers escaped the rate increase through the program, most complaining customers were not made aware of this possibility.

In 1984, the FTC issued an administrative complaint charging that Orkin had committed an unfair act or practice in violation of FTC Act section 5. The administrative law judge found against Orkin, issuing an order requiring it to roll back the fees in its pre-1975 contracts to the levels originally stated in those contracts. The full Commission affirmed this decision, and Orkin appealed to the Eleventh Circuit Court of Appeals.

Body of Opinion

Circuit Judge Clark

Section 5 declares that "unfair or deceptive acts or practices in or affecting commerce" are unlawful; it also empowers the Commission to prevent certain entities from engaging in behavior that constitutes "unfair or deceptive acts or practices."... In 1980, the Commission promulgated a policy statement containing an abstract definition of "unfairness" which focuses upon unjustified consumer injury. Under the standard enunciated in this policy statement:

> To justify a finding of unfairness the injury must satisfy three tests. It must be substantial. It must not be outweighed by any countervailing benefits to consumers or competition that the practice produces; and it must be an injury that consumers themselves could not reasonably have avoided.

... The first prong of the unfairness standard requires a finding of substantial injury to consumers. In finding that Orkin's conduct had caused the requisite harm, the Commission said: "The harm resulting from Orkin's conduct consists of increased costs for services previously bargained for and includes the intangible loss of the certainty of the fixed price in the contract." The Commission's finding of substantial injury is supported by the undisputed fact that Orkin's breach of its pre-1975 contracts generated, during a four-year period, more than $7,000,000 in revenues from renewal fees to which the company was not entitled. As the Commission noted, although the actual injury to individual customers may be small on an annual basis, this does not mean that such injury is not substantial.

As for the second prong of the unfairness standard, the Commission noted that "conduct can create a mixture of both beneficial and adverse consequences." But because the increase in the fee was not accompanied by an increase in the level of service provided or an enhancement of its quality, the Commission concluded that no consumer benefit had resulted from Orkin's conduct....

With regard to the third prong of the unfairness standard, the Commission concluded that consumers could not have reasonably avoided the harm caused by Orkin's conduct. ... The Commission determined that "neither anticipatory avoidance nor subsequent mitigation was reasonably possible for Orkin's pre-1975 customers." Anticipatory avoidance through consumer choice was impossible because these contracts give no indication that the company would raise the renewal fees as a result of inflation, or for any other reason.

As for mitigation of consumer injury, the Commission concluded that the company's "accommodation program" could not constitute an avenue for avoiding injury because relief from Orkin's conduct was available only to those customers who complained about the increases in the renewal fees.... The Commission also rejected the claim that customers could have avoided their injuries by electing to transfer their business to one of Orkin's competitors.... [S]ome of Orkin's competitors did testify that they would assume the company's pre-1975 contracts at the renewal fees stated therein. Yet there is no evidence that Orkin's pre-1975 customers could have contracted with competitors for a renewal fee that would be subject to increase only upon structural modifications of the subject property. Because Orkin failed to present such evidence, it was not error for the Commission to rule summarily that this purported avenue of relief did not create a real choice to consumers who might seek to avoid their injuries.

Judgment and Result

The Circuit Court of Appeals affirmed the Commission's decision and its order.

Questions

1. By charging higher renewal fees, Orkin broke the contracts it had made with its "lifetime" customers, making the promises contained in those contracts worthless. Why did the FTC not treat this action as deception (rather than unfairness) under section 5?
2. How did the Commission and the court deal with the argument that because the harm to each individual consumer was relatively low, no "substantial injury" occurred?

Remedies in Advertising Cases

Several types of orders are possible after successful Commission administrative action against deceptive or unfair advertising. The FTC may simply order the respondent to cease and desist from certain advertising claims. The Commission also may condition the respondent's resumption of such claims upon its obtaining proper scientific evidence to support them. The Commission also may order the inclusion of certain statements in subsequent advertising through either affirmative disclosure of information or corrective advertising. A corrective advertising requirement demands disclosure in future ads regardless of their content; an affirmative disclosure requirement demands disclosure only when the ad makes certain specific claims. In addition, the FTC may issue an all-products order extending to products or services other than the products or services covered by the original offending advertisement. In certain cases, finally, the FTC may also seek the civil penalties or consumer redress discussed earlier in the chapter.

First Amendment Considerations

As discussed in Chapter 5, commercial advertising receives an intermediate degree of constitutional protection that is less strong than the protection afforded political speech. Because Commission orders under FTC Act section 5 restrict commercial speech, constitutional challenges to the Commission's regulation of advertising are possible. However, such challenges have not seriously affected the FTC's regulation of advertising. The main reason for giving constitutional protection to commercial speech is to remove government-created obstacles to the flow of commercial information, and thus to promote informed consumer choice. This is consistent with the FTC's mission of eliminating deceptive and unfair advertising. In fact, the Constitution does not protect false or misleading advertising. This insulates much of the FTC's regulation of advertising from constitutional attack. Occasionally, however, courts may modify or narrow the scope of a Commission order on constitutional grounds.

FTC REGULATION OF FRANCHISING

The term ***franchise*** is not consistently defined. It might be described as a relationship in which one party (the **franchisee**) gets the right to sell another party's (the **franchisor's**) goods or services under a marketing plan substantially dictated by the franchisor. Often, the franchisor gives the franchisee assistance in setting up the business, and allows the franchisee to operate under its trademark or trade name. Typically, the franchisee pays a purchase price for these benefits, and may also have to pay the franchisor a percentage of its income or its sales. Common examples of franchised businesses include fast-food restaurants, hotel and motels, hair styling salons, gas stations, employment agencies, motor vehicle dealerships, and farm equipment distributors.

Franchising has enjoyed tremendous growth over the past 20–30 years. It has been estimated that more than 500,000 franchises operated in the United States during the mid-1990s, and that they accounted for more than one-third of the nation's total retail sales. It also has been claimed that the number of people working for franchised outlets rose from a 3.5 million in 1975 to about 7 million in the early 1990s. The reasons for franchising's growth seem obvious. The relationship gives franchisors a relatively easy method for expanding into new markets, while at the same time receiving payments from franchisees. For franchisees, the relationship provides a chance to run "their own" business, while benefitting from the franchisor's resources, expertise, and brand name.

Franchise agreements usually are standard-form contracts drafted by the franchisor and offered to the franchisee on a take-it-or-leave-it basis. They typically cover subjects such as the royalties the franchisee must pay, any financing the franchisor might provide, whether or when the franchisor can terminate the franchisee, the franchisee's duty not to compete after the relationship ends, and many others. Many people believe that, on average, franchisors have greater bargaining power than do franchisees. It probably is safe to say that the typical franchisor's understanding of the agreement's terms exceeds that of the typical franchisee. Also, franchisors may often have a greater choice of potential franchisees than would-be franchisees have of franchisors. On the other hand, franchisors have little rational incentive to mistreat capable, efficient, and productive franchisees.

State Regulation of Franchising

The perceived imbalance in power between franchisor and franchisee had led to increasing regulation of the relationship. The starting point for determining these two parties' legal relationship, of course, is the contract between them. To protect franchisees, some courts have supplemented or modified such contracts in various ways. A few have allowed franchisees to recover for the breach of fiduciary duties owed them by the franchisor (for example, a duty to terminate the relationship only for good cause). A few courts have found that the franchise contract contains an implied covenant of good faith and fair dealing running from the franchisor to the franchisee (and perhaps vice versa). This covenant might be breached when, for example, the franchisor opens a new franchised outlet too near an existing outlet. Several courts have taken a more targeted approach, requiring only that the franchisor show good cause when terminating a franchisee.

In general, state statutory regulation of franchising is more significant than the common law doctrines just described.[3] Many states require the disclosure of certain

[3] Some states have so-called "business opportunity" statutes that may or may not cover franchising. A "business opportunity" typically involves a sale of goods or services enabling the buyer to start a business. Examples including vending machine routes and businesses involving the assembly of parts in one's home.

information to potential franchisees. Many such disclosures may be required; our following discussion of FTC regulation provides numerous possibilities. Many states also require that franchisors register with state authorities. As part of the registration process, franchisors usually must file various documents with the state. Examples include filings regarding the franchisor's business, officers and directors, litigation and bankruptcy history, intellectual property, and finances, as well as documents explaining many aspects of the franchisor's relationship with its franchisee. Finally, many states regulate the ongoing franchise relationship after it has been formed. The most common examples are the numerous state statutes that block franchisors from terminating or refusing to renew franchisees unless the termination or nonrenewal was for good cause. Other subjects that may be regulated include the notice required before termination, the duration of the franchise term, franchisor discrimination against particular franchisees, franchisee covenants not to compete after the relationship ends, and exclusive franchisee territories.

The FTC's Franchising Rule

The FTC's response to the problems posed by franchising came in the form of a 1979 trade regulation rule.[4] The FTC rule preempts inconsistent state regulation of franchising. For the most part, however, it is only a disclosure regulation.

The rule defines the term *franchise* as any continuing commercial relationship in which a franchisee offers or sells goods or services, where the relationship meets either of the two following descriptions. In each case, the franchisee must be required to pay the franchisor a fee of $500 or more within the first six months of the business's operation or the rule does not apply. The two descriptions are:

1. A franchisee offers or sells goods or services that are (a) identified by the franchisor's trademark, trade name, or other commercial symbol, or (b) required to meet the franchisor's quality standards (where the franchisee operates under the franchisor's trademark, trade name, or other commercial symbol). For the FTC rule to apply in either case, the franchisor also must either (a) exert significant control over the franchisee's method of operation, or (b) give the franchisee significant assistance in its method of operation. Thus, the Benson Bicycle Company is covered by the FTC's rule if it exerts significant control over its franchisees or gives them significant assistance, and if (a) the franchisees sell its "Voyageur" bikes, or (b) the franchisees bear the "Benson" name and sell bikes that are not identified with Benson but that do have to meet Benson's quality standards.
2. A franchisee offers or sells goods or services supplied by the franchisor, or by someone dictated by the franchisor. Here, the FTC rule applies only if the franchisor secures retail outlets, accounts, vending machine sites, rack displays, or other sales displays for the franchisee. Note that in this case the franchisee is not selling products or services identified with the franchisor or subject to the franchisor's quality standards.

The FTC rule says that a franchisor can commit an unfair act or practice under FTC Act section 5 in any of the following ways, among others. The usual section 5 remedies and enforcement devices apply in such cases.

[4] 16 C.F.R. part 436 (1998).

1. *Failing to furnish any prospective franchisee with certain written information.* The voluminous information required by the Commission includes the following: the franchisor's name, address, and principal place of business; the trademarks, trade names, and other commercial symbols identifying the goods or services offered to the franchisee; the business experience of the franchisor's directors and officers; certain crimes of which these people may have been convicted; certain civil judgments that may have been obtained against them; any bankruptcies they have suffered; a factual description of the franchise being offered; the total and recurring charges the prospective franchisee will have to pay; the people with whom the franchisee will have to deal; property or other things the franchisee will have to lease or rent; a description of any financing arrangement offered by the franchisor; any limitations on the products or services the franchisee may sell, the customers to whom she or he may sell, or the territory within which she or he may sell; the duration of the agreement and the conditions under which its renewal, termination, or modification may occur; the franchisee's post-termination rights and obligations; details concerning any training program offered by the franchisor; and the franchisor's balance sheet statement for the most recent fiscal year. This list is incomplete; the relevant disclosures fill approximately four pages in the *Code of Federal Regulations* and more than seven pages on the FTC's website.

    All the disclosures required by the rule must be contained in a single disclosure statement or prospectus. The cover of this prospectus must bear the following statement:

    Information for Prospective Franchisees Required by Federal Trade Commission

    * * *

    To protect you, we've required your franchisor to give you this information. *We haven't checked it, and don't know if it's correct.* It should help you make up your mind. Study it carefully. While it includes some information about your contract, don't rely on it alone to understand your contract. Read all of your contract carefully. Buying a franchise is a complicated investment. Take your time to decide. If possible, show your contract and this information to an advisor, like a lawyer or an accountant. If you find anything you think may be wrong or anything important that's been left out, you should let us know about it. It may be against the law.

    There may also be laws on franchising in your state. Ask your state agencies about them.

    FEDERAL TRADE COMMISSION
    Washington, D.C.

2. *Making any representations that state a specific level of potential sales, income, or profit for the prospective franchisee, UNLESS* (a) there is a reasonable basis for the representations, the franchisor has material demonstrating their reasonableness, and it makes that material available to prospective franchisees or to the FTC upon demand; and (b) the representations and the assumptions underlying them are set forth in a single written document that is furnished to each prospective franchisee to whom the representations are made. In addition to stating certain specific information detailed in the regulations, this document must include the following statement.

CAUTION

These figures are only estimates of what we think you may earn. There is no assurance you'll do as well. If you rely upon our figures, you must accept the risk of not doing as well.

3. *Making any representations to a prospective franchisee that state a specific level of sales, income, or profit for existing outlets of the franchise business being offered.* However, such representations are permissible if conditions like those already stated are met. Here, though, the FTC requires the following statement:

CAUTION

Some outlets have [sold] [earned] this amount. There is no assurance you'll do as well. If you rely upon our figures, you must accept the risk of not doing as well.

4. *Failing to include the following statement on the cover sheet of the written documents required by items 2 and 3 already listed:*

INFORMATION FOR PROSPECTIVE FRANCHISEES ABOUT FRANCHISE [SALES] [INCOME] [PROFIT] REQUIRED BY THE FEDERAL TRADE COMMISSION

To protect you, we've required the franchisor to give you this information. *We haven't checked it and don't know if it's correct.* Study these facts and figures carefully. If possible, show them to someone who can advise you, like a lawyer or an accountant. Then take your time and think it over.

If you find anything you think may be wrong or anything important that's been left out, let us know about it. It may be against the law.

There may also be laws on franchising in your state. Ask your state agencies about them.

FEDERAL TRADE COMMISSION
Washington, D.C.

LANHAM ACT SECTION 43(a)

Deceptive or unfair advertising cases under FTC Act section 5 often are begun by the respondent's competitors. The best this tactic can achieve, however, is a C&D order against the respondent. How might the injured party obtain damages for the offending advertisement as well? Perhaps the best option is to sue under section 43(a) of the Lanham Act.

The language of section 43(a) is too complicated for easy restatement. Its most important provision allows civil recoveries for advertising statements that misrepresent the nature, attributes, or geographic origin of goods or services. The goods or services in question can be either the advertiser's goods and services or a competitor's goods and services. For instance, the Wisdom Widget Company might use section 43(a) to sue Wonder Widgets both for false advertising claims Wonder makes about its own widgets, and for Wonder's false advertising claims about Wisdom's widgets. In addition to false statements, section 43(a) creates liability for ads that are likely to deceive purchasers. The section probably covers deceptive omissions as well. However, statements of opinion do not create section 43(a) liability.

In addition to false or misleading advertising, section 43(a) also covers several other kinds of commercial misbehavior. Indeed, the section might be said to create a federal law of unfair competition. Thus, section 43(a) permits civil claims for:

- *Trademark infringement.* This includes both registered and unregistered trademarks.
- The form of invasion of privacy that involves *appropriating another's name or likeness for commercial purposes.* One example of this would be a manufacturer of golf clubs that uses Tiger Woods's name or likeness to promote its clubs without Woods's permission.
- *Trade dress infringement.* A product's trade dress might be defined as its overall appearance and sales image. Section 43(a) allows firms to recover against competitors who use a substantially similar trade dress to promote their products, where this is likely to cause confusion about the origin of the products. The following *Gallo* case involves alleged trade dress infringement.
- *"Palming off"* or *"passing off"*. These terms include all sorts of falsehoods designed to make consumers believe that one's own goods are those of a competitor. For example, a firm might imitate a popular competitor's packages, labels, containers, trademarks, trade names, and so forth.

Kendall-Jackson Winery, Ltd. v. E. & J. Gallo Winery

U.S. Court of Appeals for the Ninth Circuit
150 F.3d 1042 (1998)

Background and Facts:

Kendall-Jackson is a California winery that has a reputation for producing high-quality, mid-priced wines. By 1994, Kendall-Jackson was selling over $100 million worth of its Vintner's Reserve wine a year, and its chardonnay was the number one selling chardonnay in the United States. During this time, Kendall-Jackson tried to distinguish its Vintner's Reserve wine by packaging the wine in recognizable bottles. The Vintner's Reserve bottles, which came in one of two shapes ("burgundy-style" or "bordeaux-style"), had a rounded flange, a visible cork with printed leaves on it, a brown or burgundy neck label with gold lines on the top and bottom that form an oval in the back, and an off-white label featuring the multicolored leaf design.

Gallo is also a successful California winery. Unlike Kendall-Jackson, however, Gallo has a reputation for producing lower-priced, nonpremium wines. In 1992, Gallo considered entering the premium wine market. For three years, Gallo conducted extensive market research, much of which was directed at the success of the market leader—Kendall-Jackson Vintner's Reserve. Through its market research, Gallo determined that consumers associate the name "Gallo" with "jug wine" rather than premium wine. In accordance with these results, Gallo introduced in the fall of 1995 a line of premium wine that did not use the Gallo name and that came in either a burgundy-style bottle or a bordeaux-style bottle and featured a rounded flange, a visible cork with printed leaves on it, a brown or burgundy neck label with gold lines on the top and bottom that form an oval in the back, and an off-white label with a prominent, downward-pointing, stylized grape leaf design in various shades of green, yellow, orange, red, and brown.

Six months after Gallo introduced its new line, Kendall-Jackson sued Gallo in federal district court for trade dress infringement under the Lanham Act. Gallo then moved for summary adjudication of Kendall-Jackson's claim. After the court denied Gallo's motion, the claim then went to a jury, which decided that Gallo's trade dress did not infringe Kendall-Jackson's trade dress. The district court entered judgment for Gallo, and Kendall-Jackson appealed.

Body of Opinion

Circuit Judge Pregerson

Section 43(a) of the Lanham Act makes actionable the deceptive and misleading use in commerce of "any word, term, name, symbol, or device" on any goods or in connection with any goods. For a number of years after this section was enacted, courts construed it narrowly to include only two kinds of wrongs: false advertising and the common-law tort of "passing off" one's goods as those of another. But over time section 43(a) has been expanded to create, in essence, a federal law of unfair competition. Section 43(a) now protects both trademarks and trade dress from infringement. To state an infringement claim under section 43(a)—whether it be a trademark claim or a trade dress claim—a plaintiff must meet three basic elements: (1) distinctiveness, (2) nonfunctionality, and (3) likelihood of confusion....

Marks are often classified in one of five categories of increasing distinctiveness: (1) generic, (2) descriptive, (3) suggestive, (4) arbitrary, or (5) fanciful. The latter three categories of marks, because their intrinsic nature serves to identify a particular source of a product, are deemed inherently distinctive. These three categories of marks therefore meet the distinctiveness element automatically. At the other end of the spectrum are generic marks, which can never meet the distinctiveness element. Marks that are descriptive fall in the middle of these two extremes. Descriptive marks are not inherently distinctive and hence do not initially satisfy the distinctiveness element. But descriptive marks can acquire distinctiveness if the public comes to associate the mark with a specific source. Such acquired distinctiveness, which is referred to as "secondary meaning," allows section 43 to protect descriptive marks that otherwise could not qualify for protection as trademarks. Thus, an identifying mark is distinctive and is capable of being protected if it either: (1) is inherently distinctive or (2) has acquired distinctiveness through secondary meaning.

But distinctiveness is only the first of three elements for liability under section 43(a). A plaintiff trying to establish liability under section 43(a) must also prove nonfunctionality and likelihood of confusion. A product feature is functional and cannot serve as a trademark if the product feature is essential to the use or purpose of the article or if it affects the cost or quality of the article, that is, if exclusive use of the feature would put competitors at a significant, non-reputation-related disadvantage. This doctrine prevents trademark law, which seeks to promote competition by protecting a firm's reputation, from instead inhibiting legitimate competition by allowing a producer to control a useful product feature. Under the functionality doctrine, competitors can reasonably replicate important non-reputation-related product features.

The last element—likelihood of confusion—is the most important element of all. Likelihood of confusion exists when customers viewing the mark would probably assume that the product or service it represents is associated with the source of a different product or service identified by a similar mark. Evidence of actual confusion is persuasive proof that future confusion is likely. So is evidence that the defendant intentionally copied the plaintiff's mark....

Kendall-Jackson argues that the district court erred when it refused to grant Kendall-Jackson judgment as a matter of law on the nonfunctionality and distinctiveness elements of its trade dress claim.... Although Kendall-Jackson presented evidence that could support a jury's finding that the trade dress was nonfunctional and distinctive, that evidence did not compel such a conclusion. Gallo presented contrary evidence that a jury could reasonably believe.... A reasonable jury could conclude from this evidence that Kendall-Jackson's trade dress as a whole is functional and nondistinctive. For instance, a reasonable jury could conclude that these features—an exposed cork, a rounded flange, and a neck label—constitute a significant part of Kendall-Jackson's trade dress and that granting Kendall-Jackson exclusive use of this combination of features would put competitors at a significant non-reputation-related disadvantage. Such conclusions would support a finding that the trade dress as a whole is functional. Likewise, a jury could conclude from this evidence that the "California-look" tells consumers what the product is or at least describes a characteristic of the product, namely that it is wine from California. This conclusion would support a finding that the trade dress was generic or descriptive and therefore nondistinctive. The fact that Kendall-Jackson's grape-leaf design is distinctive does not necessarily mean that the entire trade dress is distinctive because, as Kendall-Jackson itself emphasizes, trade dress must be analyzed as a whole. Thus, there were genuine issues of fact about whether Kendall-Jackson's trade dress was distinctive and nonfunctional. The district court therefore properly let the jury decide these issues....

Kendall-Jackson's final complaint is that the district court mishandled the jury instructions of likelihood of confusion.... Although there was some risk of ambiguity in the phrasing [of the instructions], considered in context, we do not believe that the jury could have been misled. The jury was properly instructed on the factors for determining likelihood of confusion, and Gallo introduced a survey that showed that although some people might be confused by Gallo's trade dress, a significant portion of the general public is not likely to be confused.

Judgment and Result

The court of appeals affirmed the district court decision holding for Gallo on Kendall-Jackson's trade dress claim.

Questions

1. Although the opinion does not say, what do you think the court meant by a generic mark?
2. Did the court say that the jury's decision in favor of Gallo was clearly correct? What was it saying?

CHAPTER SUMMARY

The Federal Trade Commission enforces many federal statutes involving competition and consumer protection. The most important of these laws is section 5 of the FTC Act, which empowers the Commission to regulate unfair methods of competition and unfair and deceptive acts or practices.

In enforcing all these various measures, the FTC may issue advisory opinions, industry guides, and trade regulation rules. An example of the latter is the Commission's rule on franchising. It also may enforce these measures through its own administrative proceedings. The most common remedy issued after a successful FTC proceeding is a cease-and-desist order.

Although FTC Act section 5 reaches beyond the antitrust laws, the FTC mainly attacks the orthodox antitrust violations described in Chapter 20, when it employs section 5's "unfair methods of competition" language. Section 5 "deceptive acts or practices" liability exists when (1) a material representation, omission, or practice (2) is likely to mislead a consumer (3) acting reasonably under the circumstances. This part of section 5 applies mainly to deceptive advertising.

Section 5's "unfair acts or practices" jurisdiction covers all kinds of actions that harm consumers. For liability to exist under this part of section 5, the act or practice must produce consumer injury that is (1) substantial, (2) not outweighed by any consumer or competitive benefits the practice produces, and (3) reasonably avoidable by consumers.

The FTC also regulates franchising—primarily the disclosures that the franchisor makes to the franchisee before the relationship is formed. Many states regulate franchising in a more comprehensive fashion.

Section 43(a) of the Lanham Act provides a federal civil remedy for deceptive advertising. The section also covers unfair competitive tactics such as palming off one's goods as another's, imitating a competing product's trade dress, infringing another's trademarks, and appropriating another's name or likeness for commercial purposes.

Discussion Questions

1. Suppose that the manipulative advertising described in the Manager's Ethical Dilemma (following page) really works, and that it has all the bad effects Nelson claims. What does FTC regulation of advertising, as presently constituted, do about it?
2. Philosophers sometimes distinguish between *deontological* ethical theories and *consequentialist* ethical theories. Extreme (or strict) deontological theories say that certain actions are intrinsically right or wrong, irrespective of their consequences. Extreme consequentialist theories say that in evaluating the goodness or badness of an action, its consequences are all that matter. The main example is a moral theory called *utilitarianism*, which says that the criterion for evaluating actions is the amount of net pleasure, happiness, or satisfaction they produce. In the following Manager's Ethical Dilemma, which paragraph expresses strict deontological views? Where are utilitarian views expressed?
3. Assuming that it works, manipulative advertising often is said to have two bad effects. First, it makes people buy the wrong products for their needs (e.g., a Ford rather than a Chevy or vice versa), and thus to leave them with less utility per dollar spent. Second, it makes people too obsessed with material things and thereby stimulates lots of needless consumption of those things. Pick out the places in the following dialogue where Nelson makes each of these arguments. Pick out the place where Tom seems to concede the first argument while maintaining that people get extra utility even when they are manipulated.

   Can one of these two effects of manipulative advertising exist alone without the other?

   Finally, do you think that manipulative advertising works as well as both Tom and Nelson think it works?
4. Is the FTC's "reasonable consumer" test for deception cases a good idea? Will it block

Manager's Ethical Dilemma

Nelson Eiland, a college professor, and Tom Neilson, an executive at a major advertising agency, are brothers-in-law. Over Christmas dinner one year, Nelson initiates a familiar exchange between himself and Tom.

NELSON: "Well, Tom, tell me: How many poor fools have you hoodwinked this year?"

TOM: "Nelson, we've been through this before. Firms that 'hoodwink' people with their advertisements can get in trouble with the FTC."

NELSON: "And you know that's not what I'm talking about. The problem isn't illegal behavior; the problem is what's perfectly *legal*. You guys spend all your time dreaming up ways to manipulate people into buying things they don't need, and the law does nothing about it."

TOM: "Hey, people can always turn off the set if they don't like what's in our ads. No one's forcing them to do anything."

NELSON: "Come off it. The whole point of a lot of modern advertising is to overcome people's will and reason through 'hidden persuaders' of all kinds. And it works."

TOM: "If only it were that easy."

NELSON: "False humility will get you nowhere. If that kind of advertising is so useless, why have so many corporations spent so much money on it for so long?"

TOM: "Because they don't know whether it works or not, and they don't want to take a chance. Didn't you ever hear that old business lament: 'Half our advertising budget is wasted, but we don't know which half.'"

NELSON: "But you admit that *some* of it works. That means that in some cases people buy Product A when Product B would better suit them, or buy things that they don't really want or need at all. And that means that people don't get the most value for their hard-earned dollars. Worse yet, it means that, for society as a whole, money is diverted from pressing public needs like better schools and a decent environment, and instead funneled toward stupid consumer baubles."

TOM: "Aha! Just like I always suspected! You think you know better. You think *you* know what people *really* want and need. You *know* they'd really be happier driving a Honda Civic than a five-series BMW. Or using public transportation rather than driving cars at all."

NELSON: "What I'm trying to do is to distinguish between ads that appeal to the intrinsic merits of the product and ads that appeal to irrational drives. Like hidden and half-hidden sexual pitches, for instance. By associating a product with sexual titillation, you make people more likely to buy it. And you also steer social resources toward consumption and away from better things. So people wind up with a product that meets their needs less well than some alternative expenditure of the money, *and* we wind up with misallocated societal resources. And the guy who buys the BMW doesn't get the girl either."

TOM: "Like it or not, sometimes they do. And even if they don't, maybe that guy who buys the Beemer *thinks* he can attract good-looking women, so he's a little happier."

NELSON: "Oh my God! And you accused *me* of paternalism! Happiness and the good life courtesy of Madison Avenue! Why not just wire the electrodes to the pleasure centers in our brains and have done with it?"

TOM: "Hey, why not?"

NELSON: "*Human dignity* is why not. Immanuel Kant said that we should treat people as *ends* and not just as means to our own ends. By that he meant that we shouldn't *use* people, and that we should appeal to their reason when we're trying to persuade them to do something—not employ manipulative techniques on them. So you shouldn't use manipulative techniques on people to get them to buy things, even if that somehow would make them happier."

TOM: "You can't eat 'reason' and 'dignity.'"

Who do think has gotten the better of this exchange? Why?

FTC action in cases where unscrupulous parties prey upon human weaknesses such as greed, gullibility, and lack of business sophistication? Examples include hard-sell pitches for get-rich-quick schemes such as the purchase of oil and gas leases, jewels, or real estate that are claimed to be valuable but in fact are nearly worthless. Can the purchasers in such cases generally be said to have acted reasonably? If not, should the FTC try to protect fools from their folly, or should it take the attitude that in such cases people simply have to take care of themselves?

5. Is the First Amendment protection of commercial speech (discussed in Chapter 5) a good idea? If the doctrine were ever seriously applied to FTC regulation of deceptive and unfair advertising, might it not block such regulation? In that event, wouldn't advertisers have more freedom to deceive and manipulate consumers? Thus, isn't the doctrine potentially an unjustified boon to business?

   On the other hand, the First Amendment protection of commercial speech has never been a big impediment to FTC regulation of advertising. And, as we asked earlier, how well does advertising deceive and manipulate consumers in any event? As Chapter 5 makes clear, furthermore, the doctrine tends to *promote* competition in many cases. It does so mainly by knocking down advertising bans in professions such as law and accounting. (Note that unlike the advertising rules in the *California Dental Association* case, these rules are governmental. Should that make a difference?)

   In any event, which of the two general views presented here strikes you as more correct?

Suggested Readings

Articles

BAILEY and PERTSCHUK, "The Law of Deception: The Past as Prologue," 33 *American University Law Review* 849 (1984).

EMERSON, "Franchise Termination: Legal Rights and Practical Effects When Franchisees Claim the Franchisor Discriminates," 35 *American Business Law Journal* 559 (1998).

EMERSON, "Franchise Contract Clauses and the Franchisor's Duty of Care Toward Its Franchisees," 72 *North Carolina Law Review* 905 (1994).

EMERSON, "Franchising and the Collective Rights of Franchisees," 43 *Vanderbilt Law Review* 1503 (1990).

FREDERICKSON, "Recovery for False Advertising under the Revised Lanham Act: A Methodology for the Computation of Damages," 29 *American Business Law Journal* 585 (1992).

KARNS, "The Federal Trade Commission's Evolving Deception Policy," 22 *University of Richmond Law Review* 399 (1988).

PETTY, "FTC Advertising Regulation: Survivor or Casualty of the Reagan Revolution?" 30 *American Business Law Journal* 1 (1992).

PRESTON, "Data-Free at the FTC? How the Federal Trade Commission Decides Whether Extrinsic Evidence of Deceptiveness Is Required," 24 *American Business Law Journal* 359 (1986).

PRESTON and RICHARDS, "A Role for Consumer Belief in FTC and Lanham Act Deceptive Advertising Cases," 31 *American Business Law Journal* 1 (1993).

REED, "Should the First Amendment Protect Joe Camel? Toward an Understanding of Constitutional 'Expression,'" 32 *American Business Law Journal* 311 (1995).

Books and Services

BUREAU OF NATIONAL AFFAIRS, *Antitrust and Trade Regulation Report.*

CHAPTER

22

CONSUMER PROTECTION

"THERE'S A SUCKER BORN EVERY MINUTE."

P. T. Barnum

POSITIVE LAW ETHICAL PROBLEMS

"I'm going to have to turn you down for medical treatment," said Dr. Blade to Goodly, an indigent person applying for treatment at Blade's clinic.

"You're just turning me down because I'm a welfare recipient," replied Goodley, who was on Medicaid, a federal and state program to provide health care for the indigent. "I believe that persons who receive Medicaid cannot be denied treatment under the Equal Credit Opportunity Act (ECOA)."

"Oh yes they can," replied Dr. Blade. "You see, the ECOA only protects welfare recipients who are 'applicants' from discrimination in credit applications and you are not an 'applicant.' You see, our state—Ohio—pays my clinic directly, and not you, for services I render to Medicaid patients. You are a third-party beneficiary of the state of Ohio's contract with me to provide the poor with medical treatment. As such you are not a credit applicant under the ECOA, and thus when I deny you treatment I am not violating the ECOA." Was Dr. Blade correct?

Total retail trade in the United States amounted to $2.696 trillion in 1998 according to the 1999 *Statistical Abstract of the United States*. Although most purchases result in satisfied customers, some purchases produce consumer agony

Tension exists between consumers and business. Business would like to produce goods with a short life (so the market is constantly rejuvenated), to sell goods at the highest price, and to forget the consumer once the purchase is made. The consumer, on the other hand, wants the highest quality, lowest-priced goods and services, trouble free, but if anything goes wrong, everyone in the production and distribution cycle should be eternally responsible.

DEFINING A CONSUMER

A consumer is any person who buys goods or services for personal consumption. A widow who buys aluminum siding for her house is a consumer, as are a five-year-old who buys an ice cream cone and Bill Gates (reputedly the richest American) when he buys a new suit. We are all consumers in our personal capacities.

Arguments Favoring Consumer Protection

Why protect consumers? First, natural law with its basic notions of fairness suggests an equalization of economic power. The law has traditionally said it at least protects the weak from the strong. In this view, consumers are small, defenseless people pitted against industrial giants like Exxon and General Motors. According to this argument, they therefore deserve protection.

A second reason for protecting consumers is to protect businesses. This rationale seems strange when consumers and businesses are often seen as adversaries. However, the key word *honest* must be added before *businesses*. If a consumer buys inferior goods or is cheated by *one* business, sales could be diverted from a more ethical merchant. By establishing standards, consumer protection protects honest merchants who offer value to consumers. It does so in two ways. First, it makes life difficult for scoundrels. Second, it encourages people to buy more and with less hesitation, because they know that if their purchases are unsatisfactory, they are protected.

Arguments Against Consumer Protection

Many reasons exist for *not* protecting consumers. The first reason is the cost. Consumer protection can raise the price of goods and services if merchants pass the price increase along to their buyers. How would consumer protection raise prices? One way is by requiring producers to test products more thoroughly before selling them. Increased testing means increased cost, which often means that consumer goods would increase in price.

A second reason for not protecting consumers is suggested by the *caveat emptor* doctrine. Are people helpless babies? No. They vote, have sex, smoke, and drink at increasingly younger ages. The theory is that turnabout is fair play. If people are mature and self-reliant in those areas, they can watch out for their own pocketbook interests.

Sources of Consumer Protection Law

Consumer protection rules are made by courts, legislators, and administrative agencies. Furthermore, consumer protection occurs at federal, state, and municipal levels.

The many sources of consumer law yield complexity. For example, 50 different state statutes can govern a consumer's right to revoke acceptance of a contract with a door-to-door salesperson. Such a situation obviously could complicate life for the sales manager of a national magazine publisher selling door-to-door.

FEDERAL TRADE COMMISSION (FTC)

No federal consumer protection agency is officially called a "consumer protection agency." However, because one of the Federal Trade Commission's (FTC's) main jobs is consumer protection, practically speaking it is, in part, a federal consumer protection agency. The FTC, discussed in Chapter 21, was established in 1914 to regulate trade to keep markets competitive. The focus of FTC activity was not directly on consumers but rather on preserving competition. To the extent that the market is competitive, consumers benefit through lower prices, better service, and higher quality products.

> **http://** *To access the major federal agency responsible for protecting consumers, go to* ***http://www.ftc.gov***

Consumerism

In the 1930s Congress amended the FTC Act to allow the FTC to inform and protect consumers directly. Since that time, the FTC has conducted studies of many industries—life insurance, funeral homes, and auto repair, among others—with an eye toward pointing out how consumers are not getting the "biggest bang for their buck." For example, the life insurance industry study pointed out that term insurance provides the most life insurance protection per dollar of premium cost. In effect, it is a better buy than whole life insurance. Yet, life insurance companies market whole life insurance as more desirable than term insurance. The FTC believed consumers were being misled by the life insurance industry. Factors such as building up savings, rather than the amount of low-cost insurance protection per dollar, support buying whole life insurance.

Putting aside the relative merits of term versus whole life insurance, the FTC's studies of the insurance industry and certain other industries have produced hostility toward the FTC from certain businesses. No business likes to have its practices questioned, particularly those who are pulling their own weight through productive activities in a free competitive market economy. Competition is the regulator that keeps prices low, service good, and quality high. If competition cannot force businesses to produce a cheaper, higher quality, and better serviced product, the theory maintains, it cannot be done. If government tries to do it, what happens? Costs can get out of control, and the product or service does not reflect what consumers are willing to pay, given the market discipline of keeping costs within market price.

Thus, the FTC's cracking the whip on businesses is seen by some as misplaced. They ask, "Why not crack the whip on welfare recipients and other nonproductive beneficiaries of government benefits?" An answer to this question is that the FTC tries to protect honest, efficient businesses (as well as consumers) by informing consumers about who are the honest, efficient producers and what are the best buys. Remember the FTC costs society money. The question becomes, "Does the FTC save consumers more than it costs taxpayers?" If it does, it is cost-justified.

FTC Consumer Protection Regulations

http://
http://www.consumer.gov *provides a gateway to many sites of interest to consumers.*

Since the FTC consumer protection laws are discussed extensively in Chapter 21, here we discuss only five FTC consumer protection regulations. The FTC has authority under the Federal Trade Commission Act to promulgate regulations preventing unfair competition and unfair or deceptive acts and practices. The FTC has promulgated many consumer protection regulations. Four important regulations discussed here are the bait-and-switch regs, the reg modifying the holder-in-due-course rule, the mail-order merchandise reg, the three-day cooling off reg for door-to-door sales, and the telemarketing rule.

Bait and Switch. Robert Berry sat dejectedly in his appliance store. He had 50 expensive color console TVs in his inventory that he had to sell because it was costing him a bundle to floor plan them (finance them at the local bank). Richard May, one of Robert's hotshot salespeople, suggested that Robert aggressively advertise new black-and-white portable TVs for $10 each. Richard told Robert to do one of three things when a customer came in. Robert was to say that he had just sold the last $10 set, or he was to say he could not find the $10 sets, or he was to bad-mouth the $10 sets and direct the customer to the expensive color consoles, which the store would sell at a rock-bottom price. Should Robert approve Richard's idea?

Richard's idea as stated violates the FTC regs, "Guides on Bait Advertising." **Bait advertising** occurs when a business advertises goods or services at a low price to attract buyers into the seller's business. The seller then switches the buyer to more expensive products or services. Among practices prohibited by the FTC regs are having salespeople refuse to show the low-priced, bait item; indicating that the bait item will not be available for a long time; having an inadequate supply of the bait item; or telling employees to sell items other than the bait item when a customer seeks the bait item.

Modification of the Holder-in-Due-Course Rule. Bill Vanderpuddle was excited. He had just bought a new microwave oven from E-Z Appliance Company. Bill did not have the full $500 purchase price, but E-Z had him sign a **negotiable note** for $400 plus interest and pay $100 down. Bill took the oven home, used it a couple of times, but discovered it took ten times as long to cook foods as it was supposed to. Bill returned the oven to E-Z but got the runaround. ("It will take a month to get the parts and another two weeks to get it repaired.") Bill told the E-Z manager he would stop making his installment payments on the oven unless he got better service. The E-Z manager told Bill the negotiable note he had signed had been sold to City Bank, and, since the bank was a **holder in due course**, it was not subject to Bill's claim against E-Z. (A holder in due course is a good-faith purchaser for value without notice of any personal defenses such as the breach of warranty Bill might have against E-Z.) The E-Z manager told Bill that his claims (such as Bill's warranty claim that the oven did not work) were personal (between Bill and E-Z only) and could not be asserted by Bill when the bank tried to collect monthly payments on the installment note. Bill was angry. He bought a defective oven and had lost his bargaining power with the seller (the ability to stop monthly payments) because the seller had sold to a holder in due course the negotiable note Bill used to buy the oven. It did not seem fair.

What happened in this fictional story occurred daily before the FTC promulgated its reg changing the holder-in-due-course (HIDC) rule. The **HIDC rule** is of common law origin. It was later codified (made part of a lengthy commercial law statute) in the Uniform Commercial Code (UCC). The purpose of the HIDC rule is to encourage people to buy negotiable instruments (commercial **promissory notes** and other **commercial paper** having a certain form). The HIDC rule encourages buying commercial paper because it is a "courier without luggage"—someone or something that is not weighed down by personal defenses between the person who issued the commercial paper and the only one originally accepting it as payment. The idea is to make commercial paper the same thing as money.

The HIDC rule made commercial paper a money equivalent, but it did so at the expense of consumers like Bill Vanderpuddle. The same problem occurs when consumers enter installment contracts with a **waiver-of-defenses clause** in which third parties, such as banks, who buy an installment contract, even though not involving a negotiable instrument, are free of the consumer-buyer's defenses against the sellers. This waiver-of-defenses clause has the same effect on finance companies and banks who buy seller's installment contracts as does the HIDC rule: It frees them from defenses the consumer has against the seller.

To correct the perceived injustice to consumers caused by the HIDC rule and defense waiver clauses, the FTC promulgated a reg in 1976 that to a limited extent changed the HIDC rule and defense waiver clauses. Banks and consumer finance companies who buy commercial paper on consumer installment contracts with defense waiver clauses and who would otherwise have been holders in due course are now subject to consumer claims and defenses against the seller. Bill Vanderpuddle now has a claim (probably breach of warranty) against the bank that justifies his stopping payments until the oven is fixed.

Several points need to be made about the FTC reg modifying the HIDC rule and defense waiver clauses. First, the reg applies only to individual consumers, not to businesses that purchase goods or services. Second, it applies to consumer purchases or leases of either goods or services. Third, it does not apply to credit card issuers. Therefore, if Bill buys an oven at KMart with a Visa card and the oven doesn't work, he must still pay Visa for the oven. He has lost his bargaining power with KMart because the oven has been paid for by Visa.

***Mail-Order Merchandise*.** Carl Johnson had always wanted to win the Lake St. Helen annual fishing contest. He received his spring copy of the famous L.L. Toadstool Sporting Goods catalog, advertising a set of dry flies for $15.95, a fly rod for $60, and fishing tackle for $20. He sent in his order on April 1. It was received by L.L. Toadstool on April 5. L.L. Toadstool knew on April 10 that it would be unable to fill Carl's order until June 1, due to a run on fishing equipment, but L.L. Toadstool did not tell Carl of this delay. On May 15, Carl still had not received his fishing gear. The Lake St. Helen's contest was almost over. What rights (if any) does Carl have against L.L. Toadstool?

The Federal Trade Commission Act outlaws unfair methods of competition and unfair or deceptive acts and practices. This act gives the FTC power to promulgate regulations declaring certain specific acts unfair methods of competition and unfair or deceptive acts and practices. Thus, the FTC has made a **30-day regulation governing mail-order merchandise**. The rule makes it an unfair method of competition and an unfair or deceptive act and practice for a seller to solicit orders for merchandise from the buyer through the mails unless the seller reasonably expects to be able to ship the goods within 30 days (or less if the seller promises a shorter time) after getting a properly completed order. In other words, mail-order companies cannot entice buyers to order and send their money and then sit on the orders. Sellers must ship promptly (within 30 days).

If sellers cannot ship mail-ordered merchandise within a 30-day period, they must tell buyers that they may either cancel their orders and receive a prompt refund or get delayed shipment. The sellers must tell buyers about such delays within a reasonable time after the seller realizes a delay is likely.

What happens if sellers break this FTC 30-day rule? The FTC can issue a formal or informal complaint against the alleged reg breaker. An FTC administrative hearing possibly followed by an appeal to a federal court of appeals is then possible. Only the courts have the power to punish violators of FTC regs. The FTC can issue a cease-and-desist (C&D) order against reg breakers. Court-ordered civil penalties up to $10,000 per violation of FTC C&D orders are possible. The FTC 30-day mail-order rule exempts the following transactions:

1. Subscriptions (such as magazines sales) ordered for serial delivery after the first shipment complies with this reg
2. Orders of seeds and growing plants
3. COD (cash on delivery) orders (delay is tolerated here because the consumer has not sent in any money)

The FTC's 30-day mail-order rule does not preempt state or municipal laws that are not inconsistent with it or that put equal or greater burdens on mail-order sellers. The FTC rule does replace state or municipal rules that put lesser duties on mail-order sellers.

***Cooling-Off Period for Door-to-Door Sales*.** The doorbell rings. The homeowner goes to the door. There stands a smiling aluminum siding salesperson. Such people hypnotize consumers with talk. Before the homeowner knows it, he has signed a contract to have aluminum siding installed for $1,000. He has agreed to pay five days later when the siding is installed. As the consumer lies in bed the night of the purchase, he realizes he could have the same job done at half the cost by a carpenter friend. What can consumers do in situations such as this one?

First, they should ask the seller to release them from the contract. Unperformed contracts can be ended by the parties' agreement anytime before both finish performing. This scenario is possible but unlikely to happen. Second, many state statutes provide three-day cooling-off periods in such cases. They usually apply only to door-to-door salespeople who call on consumers. (In other words, consumers do not have three days to escape contracts they make in stores.) These state laws are discussed later in the chapter under the heading "State Statutes Protecting Consumers." A third suggestion involves a Federal Trade Commission regulation that makes it an unfair and deceptive act or practice for any door-to-door seller not to furnish a buyer with a fully completed receipt or contract copy with substantially the following notice:

> You, the buyer, may cancel this transaction at any time prior to midnight of the third business day after the date of this transaction. See the attached notice-of-cancellation form for an explanation of this right.

The completed receipt or contract copy must also contain a completed notice-of-cancellation form. This form helps the buyer cancel any contract made with a door-to-door salesperson. The cancellation right must be exercised within three business days after making the contract. The contract, receipt, and notice-of-cancellation form must all be in the same language (all in Spanish, for example, for Spanish-speaking people).

This FTC rule applies to the sale, lease, or rental of consumer goods or services with a purchase price of $25 or more.

The following sales are *not* covered by the FTC rule:

1. Sales made by prior negotiations when the buyer visited the seller's permanent showroom
2. Sales wherein the buyer has the right to rescind the transaction under the Consumer Credit Protection Act or its regs
3. Sales wherein the buyer first contacted the seller, and the goods or services are needed for the buyer's personal emergency, and the buyer gives the seller a separate, signed statement in the buyer's handwriting describing the situation and waiving the right to cancel within three business days
4. Sales made and completed entirely by phone or mail and without any other contact between the buyer and seller's agent before delivery or performance
5. Sales of realty (houses, buildings, and land), insurance, or securities or commodities from a broker registered with the Securities and Exchange Commission
6. Sales wherein the *buyer* first contacted the *seller* and asked the seller to visit the buyer's home for repair or maintenance purposes

Door-to-door sellers who do not give the receipt or contract and notice-of-cancellation form as required break FTC regs, resulting in a possible court-imposed $10,000 civil penalty.

Telemarketing Rule. The Federal Trade Commission regulates telemarketing. Telemarketing refers to a plan, program, or campaign conducted to induce the purchase of goods or services by one or more telephones and involves more than one interstate telephone call. The FTC has promulgated a telemarketing rule setting out the requirements for telemarketers.

The FTC rule covers both goods and services sold over the telephone, but not Internet sales. The FTC rule covers only marketing initiated by the telemarketer/seller but not when the buyer first contacts the seller. The FTC rule does not cover marketing that consists only of intrastate telephone calls.

When the FTC telemarketing rule applies, the seller must disclose to the customer in a clear/conspicuous manner before the customer pays the following information:

- Total costs
- Material conditions/limits/restrictions to buy/lease the goods/services
- Any policy or not refunding, exchanging, cancelling, repurchasing, and stating all material terms regarding that policy
- Disclosure of prize promotion scheme odds of receiving the prize and whether the odds are not calculable in advance, factors used in calculating the odds; that no purchase or payment is necessary to win a prize or participate in the prize promotion, with instructions on how to participate or an address or local or toll-free telephone number to which customers may write or call for information on how to participate.

If the FTC telemarketing rule applies to the marketing plan, telemarketers may not make any calls before 8 A.M. or after 9 P.M. local time.

Several things are not considered telemarketing under the FTC rule. One of these is solicitation of sales through the mailing of a catalog that describes or illustrates the goods or services offered for sale. Thus, a mail-order catalog company that merely conducts a mailing encouraging consumers to call the company in response to the catalog would not be subject to the FTC's telemarketing rule, even if the mail order company provides the caller with further information about products or attempts to sell callers other products.

TRUTH-IN-LENDING ACT

The Truth-in-Lending Act is actually a major part of the Consumer Credit Protection Act. It became federal law on May 29, 1968. The purpose of the Truth-in-Lending Act is to better inform consumers about credit terms. The act enables consumers to learn the cost of credit and helps them compare credit costs from different sources.

Truth-in-Lending does not set maximum or minimum credit charges. (However, state usury laws, which vary from state to state, do limit what creditors may charge.) Truth-in-Lending ensures that the customer is advised of all costs and conditions of credit.

Regulation

Truth-in-Lending is not fully self-executing. In other words, a federal agency (the Board of Governors of the Federal Reserve Board) has authority under the act to promulgate regulations spelling out the act's requirements in detail. The basic Truth-in-Lending regulations make up **Regulation Z**. The Truth-in-Lending Act went into effect July 1, 1969. From that date forward, all covered creditors have had to comply with the act and Regulation Z.

Types of Credit Covered

Only certain types of credit are covered by Truth-in-Lending's requirements. Basically, it covers only credit not exceeding $25,000 that is extended to individuals for personal, family, household, or agricultural purposes. However, all real estate credit extended to individuals for personal, family, household, or agricultural purposes is covered, no matter what the amount.

Some forms of credit are exempt from Truth-in-Lending. Loans to businesses are exempt, as are loans to federal, state, and local governments. However, if a governmental unit—federal, state, or local—extends credit to an individual for personal, family, household, or agricultural purposes, it must comply with Truth-in-Lending. Another Truth-in-Lending exemption exists for transactions in securities or commodity accounts with a broker-dealer registered with the Securities and Exchange Commission. A third exemption exists for some types of transactions under regulated public utility tariffs. Finally, consumer loans exceeding $25,000 are also exempt (except for real estate).

The *In Re Hill* case illustrates the sanctions that can be applied to lenders who fail to disclose fully to borrowers in real estate transactions.

In Re Hill

U.S. Bankruptcy Court (D. Maryland)
213 B.R. 934 (1996)

Background and Facts:

Ms. Veda T. Hill is a Chapter 13 bankruptcy debtor who seeks to rescind and avoid the mortgage of Allright Mortgage Co. on her home, to reduce Allright's claim by offset, to be awarded statutory damages, and to obtain other related relief. The complaint asserts three alleged violations of the Federal Truth-In-Lending Act (TILA). Based on these alleged violations, plaintiff seeks a determination that she has properly rescinded Allright's security interest on her home and that Allright's mortgage is avoided. Plaintiff granted the mortgage to secure a loan for home improvements and bill consolidation. Plaintiff has also objected to Allright's secured claim on the same grounds. The two matters have been consolidated.

Three three alleged violations of TILA are as follows: (1) Allright improperly disclosed (and it charged plaintiff twice for) a $236.11 advance interest payment; (2) Allright improperly failed to disclose to plaintiff a $15 courier fee as a Finance Charge, and it should not have calculated the fee as part of the Amount Financed, resulting in an understatement of the Annual Percentage Rate (APR) disclosed to plaintiff; and (3) Allright improperly failed to disclose to plaintiff that a $2,000 broker's fee was a Finance Charge, and it should not have included the fee as part of the Amount Financed, causing a further understandment of the APR disclosed to plaintiff.

Allright loaned the borrowers $25,000. Material disclosures on Ms. Hill's Federal Loan Disclosure Statement were: APR—20.7320%; Amount Financed—$24,250.00; Finance Charge—$55,018.71; and Total Payments—$79,268.71. The term of the loan was 180 months with monthly payment of $439.07, and a call provision after 5 years. Settlement on the mortgage loan occurred on April 9, 1992. From the gross amount of $25,000, defendant deducted. . . "Brokers' fees" of $2,000 and a fee of $15 for a "Courier to record documents." Interim interest of $236.11 was not deducted. Allright escrowed $10,500 for the home repairs, and $9,956.87 was left and described as "Cash to Borrower."

Body of Opinion

. . . The first alleged violation of TILA upon which plaintiff seeks judgment involves an interim interest charge of $236.11 that was paid by plaintiff prior to its due date and deducted from the amount distributed to Ms. Hill. Plaintiff alleges that Allright collected the $236.11 as a prepaid Finance Charge, as part of the Amount Financed, and again by deducting it from the proceeds that were distributed to plaintiff.

The parties do not dispute that Allright was entitled to charge plaintiff the $236.11 in interest that was due on May 1. The expense was properly allocated as a Finance Charge. . . . However, by deducting the charge from the proceeds but not from the Amount Financed, Allright was collecting the $236.11 twice—first as a Finance Charge and second, in part, as interest. In other words, Allright collected interest on prepaid interest, and this increased collection extends over the life of the loan. A prepaid Finance Charge should be subtracted from, and not included in, the Amount Financed. . . . The fact that borrowers made a voluntary choice makes no different. . . . Therefore the interim interest charge was improperly disclosed under TILA.

The second violation of TILA that plaintiff was alleged is that the fee for courier service charged by the attorney handling the settlement was a Finance Charge. It is undisputed that plaintiff was charged a $15 fee for having a courier record the mortgage documents. Further, this was not reimbursement for an actual cost, but was an approximation based on a standard charge. This expense was deducted from the Amount Financed rather than disclosed as a Finance Charge, and plaintiff has alleged that this allocation was improper and violated TILA. . . .

The court concludes that Allright did not act improperly in deducting the courier fees from the Amount Financed as such charges are not a Finance Charge. Mr. Rubenstein as settlement attorney, made the courier charge to cover, on the average, his costs. Allright did not require or retain his charge for itself.

[W]hether a particular expense constitutes a Finance Charge under TILA... must be examined. Certain charges may be excluded as Finance Charges if they are bona fide, reasonable in amount, and relate to one of the following:

> 1) fees for title examination, abstract of title, title insurance, property survey, and similar purposes.
> 2) fees for preparing deeds, mortgages, and reconveyance, settlement, and similar documents.
> 3) notary, appraisal, and credit report fees.
> 4) amounts required to be paid into escrow or trustee accounts if the amounts would not otherwise be included in the finance charge....

However, fees are Finance Charges if the creditor either requires the fee or retains a portion of the fee for itself....

Where a broker is required, as in the instant case, the broker's fee must be included as a Finance Charge. ... It does not matter that the lender does not retain part of the broker's fee for itself, especially when the lender benefits from the broker's services....

While it is true that plaintiff contacted Mr. Hyleigh of her own volition and not through Allright, it was acknowledged that Allright only made loans through brokers, except for 2 or 3 refinancings over 15 years, and that this arrangement benefitted Allright in many ways.... The fact that Allright did not expressly require plaintiff to use a particular broker... does not alter the court's conclusion. United Mortgage brokered about 20% of Allright's loans....

Because Allright required plaintiff to use the services of a broker, the broker's fee charged to plaintiff was required by TILA to be included as a Finance Charge.... Moreover, a recent amendment to TILA supports the court's conclusion by expressly including as an example of finance charges "borrower-paid mortgage broker fees, including fees paid directly to the broker or the lender (for delivery to the broker) whether such fees are paid in cash or financed."... These amendments are not, however, applicable to this case because this action was commenced before June 1, 1995.... They are referred to here merely as not expressing an intent contrary to the court's conclusions.

For these reasons, the court finds that Allright violated TILA by not disclosing the $2,000 broker's fee as a Finance Charge, and by including the broker's fee in the Amount Financed....

A potential problem for plaintiff is that her right to rescind the transaction was limited by a three-year statute of limitations period after Allright failed to disclose material information properly to plaintiff. ... The limitations period commenced running on the date the transaction was consummated....

In the instant case, the loan transaction was consummated on April 9, 1992.... Plaintiff did not give Allright notice of her intent to rescind based on the improper broker's fee until October 10, 1995, more than three years after the loan had settled....

Plaintiff's first attempt to rescind the transaction, however, via letter to Allright, occurred within three years, on March 6, 1995, although it did not mention the broker's fee. Similarly, plaintiff filed the complaint initiating this action on April 7, 1995, also within three years, but it also did not raise the broker's fees issue. Nevertheless, on February 5, 1996, the court granted plaintiff's motion to amend her complaint and her objection to Allright's claim that she filed on April 24, 1995, without objection from Allright. Plaintiff's amended complaint related back to the date of the timely original pleading because the added material concerning the broker's fee arose out of the same conduct, transaction, or occurrence....

In the alternative, plaintiff may raise her TILA violation claims at any time as a matter of defense by way of recoupment or setoff....

In the TILA context, courts have held that a defense based upon TILA can be raised in a foreclosure or other proceeding at any time.... Allright chose to file a foreclosure against Ms. Hill in state court. Ms. Hill then instituted this bankruptcy action. Following that, Allright sought to collect on the alleged debt by filing a proof of secured claim. Ms. Hill filed an objection to the proof of claim raising her TILA claims defensively.

Specifically, in the bankruptcy context, courts have held that when the creditor files a proof of claim, the debtor may defend against that claim by raising TILA as a defense at any time.... Thus, Ms. Hill's defense to the proof of claim based on TILA is not time-barred.

Contrary to Allright's contention, Ms. Hill did prove actual damages at trial. The method of measuring the actual damages under TILA is the amount by which the Finance Charge is understated.... Ms. Hill presented proof from Mr. Rubenstein that he did not disclose the broker fee in the Finance Charge. Thus, the Finance Charge was understated by $2,000. In addition, two statutory penalties of $1,000 each are invoked for the disclosure violations and for the failure to honor the rescission....

Allright is entitled to judgment in its favor regarding the $15 courier fee; because of Allright's failure to disclose the $2,000 broker's fee as a Finance Charge was a violation of TILA, plaintiff is entitled to rescind the loan transaction, avoid the deed of trust, and cancel interest and settlement cost charges; and for the TILA violations plaintiff should recover actual damages of $2,000 for the broker's fee and $2,000 statutory damages. These remedies should be implemented by way of recoupment or set off....

Judgment and Result

The court finds that (1) the $236.11 interim interest charge was incorrectly classified and double charged; (2) Allright did not violate TILA with respect to the $15 courier fee; and (3) plaintiff is entitled to judgment for a violation of TILA involving the $2,000 broker's fee.

Questions

1. How did plaintiff/borrower get around the three-year statute of limitations for raising TILA violations?
2. What rate of interest did plaintiff pay on her home improvement and cash advance loan? Does the federal TILA set a federal maximum rate of permissible interest on consumer loans? How, then, can a loan be rescinded if the consumer/debtor agreed up front to the loan? What if the loan terms were not clearly disclosed up front as "Finance Charges"?
3. What were the most egregious nondisclosures of the loans here: the "double interest," the courier charges, or the broker's fee?
4. What charges may be excluded as Finance Charges: title examination fees; title abstract fees; title insurance; property survey; deed preparation fees; mortgage preparation fees; reconveyance fees; settlement fees; notary fees; credit report fees; amounts required to be paid into escrow or trustee accounts if the amounts would not otherwise be included in the finance charge?
5. Putting aside the legalities of plaintiff's loan, what do you think about the financial wisdom of the terms of this loan? Does the fact that plaintiff ended up in bankruptcy suggest an answer to this question?

Types of Creditors Covered

Any person or business regularly extending or arranging for credit to individuals for personal, family, household, or agricultural purposees must comply with Truth-In-Lending. Banks, savings and loan associations, department and other retail stores, credit card companies, automobile dealers, credit unions, consumer finance companies, and mortgage bankers are covered. Some less obvious individuals or businesses covered by Truth-in-Lending are hospitals, doctors, physicians, dentists, plumbers, and electricians who regularly extend or arrange for credit.

Disclosing Credit Terms

As mentioned, one of Truth-in-Lending's main aims is to increase consumer credit information. Regulation Z requires consumer credit information to be clear, conspicuous, and written. Truth-in-Lending and Regulation Z require disclosure of charges consumers must pay to get credit, including, in most cases, the finance charge and the annual percentage rate.

Finance Charge and Annual Percentage Rate

Disclosure of the **finance charge** and disclosure of the **annual percentage rate (APR)** are the two most important ideas coming from Truth-in-Lending. These requirements tell consumers at a glance how much they are paying for credit in two ways—in dollar terms (the finance charge) and as a percentage of the loan (the annual percentage rate, or APR). The APR and finance charge must appear on the face of the periodic statement that creditors send to consumers.

The words *finance charge* and *annual percentage rate* must stand out clearly. In some transactions involving the sale of dwellings, that total dollar finance charge need not be stated, but the annual percentage rate must be disclosed.

Neither Truth-in-Lending nor Regulation Z sets maximum, minimum, or any charges for credit (state usury laws control this). Both require creditors to show consumers any finance charges and whatever annual percentage rate is charged. The annual percentage rate must be accurate to the nearest one-quarter of one percent.

Credit Cards

The Truth-in-Lending Act and Regulation Z also cover the **credit card**—a single credit device used to get money, property, labor, or services on credit.

Credit cards may not be issued except in response to a request or application or as a renewal of, or substitute for, an accepted credit card. An **accepted credit card** is a credit card that the cardholder has requested or applied for and received, has signed or used, or has authorized another person to use. Any credit card issued in renewal of, or in substitution for, an accepted credit card becomes an accepted credit card when received by the cardholder.

The "accepted credit card" concept means only that the person who accepts a card is liable for its use. However, Truth-in-Lending limits a cardholder's liability for unauthorized use to $50 or to the amount of money, property, labor, or services obtained by unauthorized use before the card issuer is notified, whichever is lower. As a matter of goodwill, some credit card companies do not subject cardholders to even the $50 amount for unauthorized card use.

Unauthorized credit card use occurs, for example, when someone loses his wallet containing his credit cards, and someone finds it and makes charges on the cards. The cardholder would be liable up to only $50. What if spouses separated? Might one become liable for the other's use of credit cards obtained while they were happily married? The following case gives an answer.

Oclander v. First Nat. Bank of Louisville

Kentucky Court of Appeals
700 S.W.2d 804 (1985)

Background and Facts:

Appellant, Monica Oclander, appeals from the summary judgment of the Jefferson Circuit Court against her in the sum of $11,319.43 with 12% interest from March 23, 1983, and costs on the appellee bank's suit on credit card charges made on appellant Monica's Mastercard open end credit plan with the bank. We affirm.

We need not burden this opinion with a detailed factual presentation of this case inasmuch as its facts are of record and the parties and their counsel are familiar with them. We recite only those necessary to this appeal.

The credit card charges in question were made by Bonifacio Aparicio, appellant's estranged husband and co-defendant. The account was opened October 20, 1981, with cards issued to both. The credit limit was $400. In July 1982, Monica notified the bank that she was separated from Bonifacio. It "blocked" the account from additional charges and by letter forwarded to her advised her how to apply for and use its standard divorce and separation affirmation form to be completed and returned to the bank to restore her credit. She completed and returned them on August 9, 1982, indicating she had destroyed one of the two credit cards issued to her and Bonifacio and retained the other. Relying on this representation, the bank "unblocked" the account under the impression it was for her credit alone. Apparently she had not destroyed the one because various charges were made on the account ostensibly by Bonifacio in Spain between October 29, 1982, and November 30, 1982, the card's expiration date.

Congress recognized some time ago that the area of credit card liability needed to be dealt with in a uniform manner. Accordingly, 15 U.S.C.A. §1643 provides protection for a card holder against "unauthorized" charges made on an account. Obviously, this was to protect the card holder in cases where the card had been stolen or lost and was being used to make "unauthorized" charges. §1643 limits the liability of a card holder where there has been "unauthorized use." Title 15 U.S.C.A. §1602(o) defines the term "unauthorized use" to mean "a use of a credit card by a person other than the card holder who does not have actual, implied, or apparent authority for such use and from which the card holder receives no benefit." If the person using the card has either actual, implied, or apparent authority then the charges are authorized and the limitations imposed by §1643 do not apply and Ms. Oclander would be liable for all charges made on the account as set out under the "Terms of Agreement." Thus, the issue of liability turns on whether the charges made by Bonifacio Aparicio were authorized.

Apparent authority exists where a person has created such an appearance of things that it causes a third person to reasonably and prudently believe that a second party has the power to act on behalf of the first person.

In the present case, the Bank had sent a "Divorce and Separation Affirmation" along with a letter setting out what needed to be done to release Ms. Oclander from liability. The letter was specific and stated as follows:

> Be advised that signing this in no way releases either party at this time, that the individual to be responsible must complete the application in full, both to update our file and to determine whether or not they qualify for an account in their name alone. If they do qualify for credit in this manner, the other party's name will be dropped. Otherwise, no charges are to be made on this account and both parties are responsible until the balance is reduced to zero.

The Bank then stated that it had "blocked" the account and that no further charges were to be made until the conditions in the above letter were met. Obviously, the intention of the Bank was to protect both itself and its customer from the abuses that have occurred in this case. Ms. Oclander stated that she was in possession of both the cards and destroyed one and retained the other for her use. Relying on these statements, the Bank removed the "block" from the account and Ms. Oclander was allowed to continue making charges on the account. What the Bank requested of Ms. Oclander was not unreasonable and would have protected all concerned if Ms. Oclander's statements had been accurate. . . . Bonifacio Aparicio did in fact have a card in his possession with his name on it as a joint card holder and presented the card to merchants who had no reason to question his authority to use it. Mr. Aparicio was in possession of a card which was a representation to merchants (third parties) to whom they were presented that he (second parties/card bearers) was authorized to make the charges. This is not a case where charges were made on an expired card, or the card was obtained through fraud or other wrongdoing. Mr. Aparicio was actually in possession of one of the cards and at all times was ostensibly authorized to make charges on the account. If Ms. Oclander had accurately explained the situation to the Bank and told them that Mr. Aparicio was in possession of one of the cards, or at the very least, that she did not have possession of both cards, then the Bank would have maintained the "block" it had originally placed on the account in July, and none of the charges made during Mr. Aparicio's buying spree would have been chargeable to the Bank.

The Bank did not even require that the cards be surrendered but only that they be accounted for by Ms. Oclander. Ms. Oclander failed to do so, and as a result the Bank has suffered damages for which she should be held accountable.

We find no merit to Monica's argument that there is a material dispute of fact over the bank's delay in placing an "overseas block" on the account. We find none. It placed the "block" as soon as it could after it became apparent something was amiss.

Judgment and Result

The lower court's judgment is affirmed. The bank wins.

Questions

1. Do people who obtain credit cards have potentially unlimited liability for unauthorized use of their credit cards? Why or why not?
2. Did the court in the *Oclander* case interpret the charges there as authorized?
3. Would any business ethics support the *Oclander* result?
4. Of the legal ethics noted in Chapter 1, which supports the result in *Oclander*?

Credit Advertising

Advertising of credit is covered by Truth-in-Lending. No ad for credit may tell consumers that a specific down payment, installment plan, or amount of credit can be arranged unless the creditor usually arranges terms of that type.

Creditors cannot tell consumers of a specific credit term unless all other terms are clearly and conspicuously stated. This rule applies to newspaper, TV, and radio advertising. It also covers all other ads, such as those in magazines, leaflets, flyers, catalogs, public address system announcements, direct mail literature, window displays, and billboards.

Penalties

Criminal and civil penalties can be imposed for violating the Truth-in-Lending Act. Fines up to $5,000, prison terms up to one year, or both are possible for willful violators of Truth-in-Lending or its regulations. The injured consumer may also sue civilly and recover twice the amount of the finance charge (but not less than $100 or more than $1,000) plus court costs and reasonable attorney fees.

Creditor Records

Creditors must save their papers for at least two years from the transaction date to prove compliance with Truth-in-Lending and its regulations. Government enforcement agencies have the right to inspect creditors' records to see that they are complying with the act and its regs.

Enforcers

The two enforcement groups for Truth-in-Lending and its regs are private and public. Private enforcers are consumers whose rights under the act are violated.

Which agency enforces the act depends on what type of creditor allegedly violated it. In other words, no single federal agency enforces the act, making it confusing for consumers to know to which agency to complain.

FAIR CREDIT REPORTING ACT

The Fair Credit Reporting Act (FCRA) is a federal law passed in 1970. Its main purpose is to provide accurate current information about consumers, but not about businesses. Consumer credit information used to get a job, insurance, or credit is covered by the act. The FCRA also makes illegal the disclosure of consumer credit information to third parties with no legitimate need to know the information.

How the FCRA Works

Suppose Mike Harrison tries to charge a purchase at Mace's department store but is turned down. Mike asks why and is told an unfavorable credit report has been filed on him. Mike cannot think of any reason for having a bad credit report; he has always paid his bills on time. He asks Mace's department store, who supplied the credit report, but the store refuses to tell him unless he pays $10. What are Mike's rights?

Under the Fair Credit Reporting Act, consumers have the right to know the credit reporting agency that turns in reports that are the basis for the denial of credit. Furthermore, the consumer has a right to the information in any credit report the business relies on in this matter. Because the information must be given free of charge to the consumer, Mace's must give Mike the information in the credit report it used to evaluate his creditworthiness and may not charge him $10. Mike does not, however, have a right to the report itself.

Suppose that after Mace's gives Mike the free credit report, Mike finds the credit reporting agency has confused him with a Mike Harrimon. He can then force the credit reporting agency to correct the credit report and notify any credit or insurance recipient of the report for the six months before the error. If the erroneous credit concerned employment, Mike is entitled to have the correction sent to any potential employer receiving the incorrect report within the past two years.

The Fair Credit Reporting Act also entitles consumers to stop credit reporting agencies from disclosing accurate credit information if the requester wants it for noncommercial reasons.

Sanctions

The Fair Credit Reporting Act lets consumers sue anyone violating it. Damages, attorney fees, and court costs are recoverable. Also, the Federal Trade Commission has authority to enforce the Fair Credit Reporting Act. The *Houghton* case illustrates the FCRA in operation.

Houghton v. Ins. Crime Prevention Institute

U.S. Court of Appeals (3d Cir.)
795 F.2d 322 (1986)

Background and Facts:

On November 29, 1984, Joseph M. Houghton filed a complaint alleging that defendants, the Insurance Crime Prevention Institute (ICPI), an organization funded by property and casualty insurance companies, and John Andrew Hoda, an employee of ICPI, violated the FCRA by obtaining under false pretenses information on a consumer from a consumer reporting agency. The complaint alleged that on or about July 6, 1982, Hoda, on behalf of ICPI, an agency which seeks to investigate suspected fraudulent claims, submitted to the Mid-East Index Bureau, a division of Central Index Bureau (CIB), card files stating that Houghton was involved in an accident on October 15, 1980, and that he had made a claim with Kemper Insurance Company regarding the accident. Houghton contends this information was false and fraudulent, because he was not involved in an accident on that date, had made no claim with Kemper as of that time, and had no bodily injury claim pending with Kemper at that time. The complaint alleges that defendants knew or should have known that this information was false and fraudulent and that defendants submitted the information to CIB so that, in return, defendants could obtain from CIB its accumulated confidential medical records, documents and information from other insurance carriers about Houghton.[1]

The complaint alleges that defendants had no permissible purpose under FCRA to obtain the information from CIB, a consumer reporting agency within the meaning of the Act, and that defendants disseminated to others the information received with the specific intent to discredit and harass plaintiff and to interfere in his personal affairs. Houghton sought compensatory and punitive damages, attorneys' fees and costs.

Defendants filed an answer on January 14, 1985, denying the material allegations in the complaint and asserting an affirmative defense that the complaint was barred by the two-year applicable statute of limitations set forth in FCRA. Since the action complained of took place on July 6, 1982, it is apparent that the complaint filed November 29, 1984 was not filed within the two-year period.

Houghton then amended the complaint to include the following paragraph:

> Plaintiff did not become aware of the existence of said [index] card . . . prior to October 24, 1983, when a copy of said card was forwarded to plaintiff's counsel by the Secretary and Counsel of the American Insurance Association. . . . Moreover, plaintiff exercised all due diligence in obtaining said card and could not have obtained said card sooner, as plaintiff on numerous occasions prior to October 24, 1983, demanded of CIB all cards and reports in their possession regarding plaintiff, but said card was either inadvertently or intentionally withheld until October 24, 1983.

By this amendment, Houghton sought to invoke the discovery rule to toll application of the two-year statute of limitations until his discovery of the relevant facts.

The district court then granted the motion to dismiss, holding:

> Plaintiff's amended complaint is barred by the two-year statute of limitations in the Fair Credit Reporting Act, and does not come within the "discovery" exception therein since the disclosure was not one required to be disclosed by defendants to plaintiff and the Central Index Bureau, which made the disclosure to its subscribers, is not a defendant.

Body of Opinion

Circuit Judge Sloviter

The Fair Credit Reporting Act was passed in 1970 to insure that consumer reporting agencies exercise their "grave responsibilities" regarding the "assembling and evaluating [of] consumer credit and other information on consumers" with "fairness, impartiality, and a respect for the consumer's right to privacy."

Congress found that the "banking system is dependent upon fair and accurate credit reporting" and that an

---

[1] The parties explained at oral argument that CIB works under a cooperative arrangement permitting access to its information only to those who provide it with information.

"elaborate mechanism [had] developed" concerning the credit and general reputation of the consumer.

The Act provides that a consumer reporting agency may furnish a consumer report in certain enumerated circumstances and no other. The Act provides for both criminal penalties and civil liability, which may include compensatory and punitive damages, costs and attorneys' fees. The United States district courts have jurisdiction over suits brought under the statute.

The Act contains a statute of limitations, limiting suit to two years from the date the liability arises, with one exception. The applicable section provides:

> An action may be brought within two years from the date on which the liability arises, except that where a defendant has materially and willfully misrepresented any information required under this subchapter to be disclosed to an individual and the information so misrepresented is material to the establishment of the defendant's liability to that individual under this subchapter, the action may be brought at any time within two years after discovery by the individual of the misrepresentation.

Since the complaint was admittedly filed more than two years after the alleged violation of the Act, the only basis appellant argues to overturn the dismissal is by application of the discovery rule to the statute of limitations. Appellant cites to various state cases which, in the consumer context, have tolled the limitations statute until discovery by plaintiff of the wrongful act.

Appellant contends that these cases are applicable to the facts at bar since, despite due diligence, he did not become aware, nor would he have become aware, of the fraudulent submission of a false report until CIB finally released the report to him, which was October 24, 1983. His suit was filed within two years of that date. He argues that as a matter of policy, and in the interest of justice, the time in which an injured party should have the right to sue for the wrongful submission of false information to a consumer reporting agency should be counted from the date of discovery.

If Houghton prevails on his legal position that a plaintiff has two years from the discovery of the violation, it would be irrelevant that in this case he would have had sufficient time to have filed his action in the period between October 1983 when the information was released to him and July 1984 when the statute of limitations barred the action. If a discovery rule is not applied, other plaintiffs would be barred from suit even if they were unaware of the relevant facts throughout the entire statutory period. Nonetheless, we cannot accept the extension of the discovery rule to this statute. . . .

In examining the statute of limitations set forth in the FCRA, the plain language of the Act shows Congress' intent to permit tolling of an FCRA action only in a precisely defined situation. By its terms, it only permits tolling in the case of a material and willful misrepresentation by a defendant of information required to be disclosed under the Act which is material to defendant's liability. Plaintiff does not challenge the district court's holding that the statutory tolling provision does not apply to these defendants because none of the disclosure provisions of the Act imposed an obligation on these defendants to disclose to plaintiff the information pertinent here. CIB, the one entity which arguably had such an obligation, an issue we do not decide here, was not made a defendant in this lawsuit.

If we construe the statute as permitting us to imply a discovery exception to circumstances other than the one which Congress explicitly set forth, we would be rendering superfluous the discovery exception which Congress did set forth. This we may not do. The Supreme Court has stated that where Congress has enunciated an exception to a general prohibition, "additional exceptions are not to be implied in the absence of evidence of a contrary legislative intent." In this case, the statutory language clearly evidences the legislative intent. If the discovery rule is to be made generally applicable to FCRA cases, it must be done by congressional action.

Judgment and Result

District Court judgment dismissing plaintiff's complaint is upheld. Houghton loses.

Questions

1. How long did Mr. Houghton wait after discovering the allegedly improper submission of the information here before starting his suit?
2. Was Mr. Houghton wronged by an apparent violation of the Fair Credit Reporting Act here?
3. Does the *Houghton* case represent a triumph of procedural law over substantive law?
4. What do you think of the business ethics of Mr. Hoda of the Insurance Crime Prevention Institute?
5. What legal ethic(s) support what Mr. Hoda allegedly did?

EQUAL CREDIT OPPORTUNITY ACT

The Equal Credit Opportunity Act (ECOA) was passed in 1974 and took effect in 1975. As a federal law, it applies in all 50 states.

Five revelations were made during consideration of the ECOA bill.

1. Getting credit is harder for single women than it is for single men.
2. When women marry, creditors make them reapply for credit in their husbands' names; men do not have to do the same thing.
3. Creditors will not loan money to a married woman in her own name.
4. Creditors will usually not consider a married working woman's income when a married couple applies for a loan.
5. Divorced or widowed women find it difficult to reestablish credit.

The ECOA responded to these concerns by placing requirements on financial institutions and other firms extending credit on a regular basis. Covered lenders must make credit available to all creditworthy customers without regard to sex or marital status. A 1976 amendment to the ECOA prohibits credit discrimination by commercial lenders based on an applicant's national origin, race, religion, color, or age. The ECOA also makes it unlawful for any creditor to discriminate against any applicant with respect to any aspect of a credit transaction, because all or part of the applicant's income derives from any public assistance program. *Barney v. Holzer Clinic, Ltd.* deals with this aspect of the ECOA.

ECOA Applications

Firms in the business of extending credit may not ask credit applicants about their marital status. This rule has exceptions. A lender may ask credit applicants about their marital status to determine its rights and remedies regarding a particular loan. For example, the lender could ask a woman if anyone else is going to be a co-obligor on the debt, or it could inquire about a woman's income sources. If she says she has no source of income except for her husband's income, questions about her marriage would then seem appropriate. Also, creditors may consider state property laws (such as community property in the southwestern states) directly or indirectly affecting creditworthiness.

Lenders may not deny credit to married women who apply for it individually (without their husbands). Lenders may ask a married woman only about the sources of income she intends to rely on in applying for credit (including income from a part-time job that is income producing on a regular basis, welfare, alimony, separate maintenance payments, or child support). Just because the creditor must take these sources of income into account does not mean a loan must be made. If credit applicants fail to meet creditworthiness requirements, the ECOA does not require that the creditor extend them credit.

The ECOA prohibits discrimination in credit extension based on age. A creditor may ask a credit applicant's age if it is to be used to determine the amount and probable continuance of income levels or credit history. Similarly, a creditor does not violate the ECOA by asking or considering the age of an elderly applicant when the age of such an applicant is to be used by the creditor in extending credit in favor of such an applicant. Using an empirically derived credit system that considers age is permissible if the system complies with Federal Reserve regs. However, an elderly applicant's age may not be given a negative value in such system.

Asking credit applicants whether their income comes from any public assistance program does not violate the ECOA if it is done to determine the amount and probable continuance of income levels or to determine credit history. Welfare payments and government benefits must be taken into account by creditors in determining a credit applicant's income, which does not mean a creditor must loan money to applicants who are otherwise not creditworthy.

The ECOA prohibits discrimination in extending credit based on race. For example, suppose Harvey Slater, an African American mail carrier, is turned down by a savings and loan association for a home loan. The stated reason is the "instability of real estate in that part of town." This categorical refusal to finance real estate purchases in declining neighborhoods (called **redlining**) violates the ECOA's prohibition if race is the real reason for the credit rejection.

Note several aspects about the ECOA.

1. It restricts only commercial lenders (not friends, family, or those making loans who are not in the credit business).
2. It preserves lenders' rights to reject loan applicants because they are not creditworthy. For example, "slow-pay, no-pay" debtors can still be turned down for loans.
3. It does not require lenders to make loans.
4. It limits the basis for which creditors can turn down loan applicants.

Other ECOA Provisions

Creditor Deadline. The ECOA requires a creditor to notify an applicant of its action on a credit application within 30 days of receiving a completed application.

Specificity Requirement. The ECOA requires creditors to be specific in telling credit applicants why they are denied credit. Creditors may not deny credit simply because the applicant "is not creditworthy" or because the applicant did not meet a minimum score on the lender's application test. Credit rejections may be oral if the creditor did not act on more than 150 credit applications in the prior year.

ECOA Enforcement. Private parties and administrative agencies make up the two general categories of ECOA enforcement.

ECOA Remedies. Damages, punitive damages designed to punish intentional violators, and injunctions are possible remedies when a private party sues an alleged violator. Court costs and attorney fees can be assessed against violators of the ECOA. Lawsuits by private parties must be started within two years of an ECOA violation (or within one year after an enforcement agency sues).

Barney v. Holzer Clinic, Ltd. alleges an ECOA violation.

Barney v. Holzer Clinic, Ltd.

U.S. Court of Appeals (6th Cir.)
110 F.3d 1207 (1997)

Background and Facts:

Plaintiff/appellants Teresa and Randy Barney and Bonita Waldron are all residents of Vinton County, Ohio, who receive Aid to Families with Dependent Children and are therefore eligible for medical treatment under Medicaid. Defendant/appellee Holzer Clinic is a "for-profit physician's organization which generally provides non-emergency medical services and treatment in various Ohio and West Virginia counties." The clinic presently has a policy under which it will accept new patients under the Medicaid program only if those patients live in counties in which Holzer Clinic has clinics. Holzer Clinic does not have any facilities in Vinton County and admits that "plaintiffs were not accepted as patients who live in Vinton County."

Plaintiffs brought this action in federal district court claiming Holzer, by refusing to treat them, had denied them incidental credit because they received public assistance, in violation of the Equal Credit Opportunity Act (ECOA). The complaint requested injunctive and declaratory relief as well as compensatory and punitive damages. The district court granted Holzer's motion to dismiss for failure to state a claim under the ECOA.

Body of Opinion

Circuit Judge Moore

The ECOA makes it "unlawful for any creditor to discriminate against any applicant, with respect to any aspect of a credit transaction . . . because all or part of the applicant's income derives from any public assistance program." . . . Plaintiffs argue that Holzer is a creditor under the ECOA because it regularly extends "incidental credit" to patients by providing them with medical services and billing them later. They further argue that because Holzer will treat privately insured residents of Vinton County, but will not accept new Medicaid patients from that county, it thereby discriminates against them because part of their income derives from public assistance. We need not address either of these propositions, however, because plaintiffs are not "applicants" under the ECOA and therefore cannot invoke the Act's protections.

The ECOA defines an "applicant" as "any person who applies to a creditor directly for an extension, renewal, or continuation of credit, or applies to a creditor indirectly by use of an existing credit plan for an amount exceeding a previously established credit limit." . . .

Plaintiffs do not argue that they were granted a right "to defer payment of a debt" or to "incur debt and defer its payment"; indeed, they seem to concede that if debt were a prerequisite for the ECOA's protections they would fall outside the Act's scope. . . . They argue instead that the requisite credit transaction occurs when Holzer extends to patients a right to "purchase . . . services and defer payment therefor." . . . Plaintiffs, however, have not asked Holzer to give them a right to purchase anything or to defer payment. Rather, as discussed below, they have asked the clinic to provide them with medical services under an agreement between Holzer and the State of Ohio, to which plaintiffs are third party beneficiaries. This is not a request for credit under the ECOA, and that Act's protections do not apply.

Congress created Medicaid in 1965 to provide medical services to families and individuals who would otherwise not be able to afford necessary care. . . . The federal law allows states considerable discretion in administering the program; so long as a state's program meets federal statutory and regulatory standards, the federal government provides the bulk of the program's funding. . . .

Ohio has chosen to participate in the Medicaid program. . . . Under federal law, medical service providers must accept the state-approved Medicaid payment as payment-in-full, and may not require that patients pay anything beyond that amount. . . .

Federal law allows states to pay either the provider or, in some circumstances, the patient. . . . In Ohio, however, all Medicaid payments flow from the state directly to the medical provider; a provider is absolutely barred from requesting any payment from patients for treatment provided under the program. . . . Medical providers may not bill patients for treatment under the program. . . .

Under Ohio law, then, Holzer Clinic could never grant patients requesting medical services under Medicaid the right to purchase those services and defer payment therefor. Patients who receive treatment under Medicaid are not granted a right to defer payment; where there is no duty to pay, there cannot be a right to defer payment. Similarly, although the ECOA does not define "purchase," it is clear that any definition of the term must include some sort of exchange between the parties as an element. Holzer and the state have entered into a provider agreement, a "contract between the Ohio department of human services and a provider of medical assistance services," under which Holzer provides services to Medicaid-eligible patients and then receives reimbursement from the state. . . . The provision of medical treatment under this program is not a credit transaction, either under the technical language of the ECOA or in the more common sense of the term, any more than is a court-appointed attorney's agreement to represent an indigent defendant.

Judgment and Result

The court of appeals decided that plaintiffs did not state a cause of action under the ECOA.

Questions

1. Does the ECOA forbid creditors from discriminating against applicants because they receive all or part of their income from a public assistance program? Did the applicants here not receive all or part of their income from Medicaid, a public assistance program? Why, then, were plaintiffs found not to be applicants under the ECOA?
2. What is the purpose of the ECOA? By interpreting the word "applicant" narrowly, is the court advancing the purpose of the ECOA?
3. How can the decision in the *Barney* case be defended? To keep down the costs of health care for the poor? To help the state of Ohio balance its budget?
4. What philosophies of law mentioned in Chapter 1 are evidenced in the *Barney* decision?

FAIR CREDIT BILLING ACT

Suppose your name is John W. Smith—a common name. Suppose further that you have Visa and MasterCard credit cards. Given your name, being billed for someone else's purchases would not be impossible. If your monthly MasterCard statement (or billing from any business using credit cards) contains errors, what can you do?

Billing Errors

The Fair Credit Billing Act of 1975 establishes a way for consumers to do something about credit card billing errors. It applies only to credit cards, not to other billing arrangements. Because it is a federal law, it applies in all states. If a consumer sends a written billing complaint to a creditor within 60 days of receiving the allegedly erroneous bill, that creditor must acknowledge the consumer's complaint within 30 days. The consumer's complaint to the credit card issuer must be written. The credit card issuer must either explain the alleged error in writing or correct the error within two billing cycles, but in no case more than 90 days after receiving the cardholder's complaint.

Discounts

The Fair Credit Billing Act deals with credit card purchases. It allows a retailer who accepts credit cards to offer discounts to cash customers (those not using credit cards). This option recognizes the service fee that merchants pay to credit card companies. However, the act forbids merchants who honor credit cards to raise retail prices for cardholders over what cash customers pay without the discount. Note that the act does not require discounts for cash customers.

Credit Reporting

The Fair Credit Billing Act restricts a card issuer's reporting past due payments to third parties (for example, credit bureaus). Federal law requires a credit card issuer to inform the cardholder if and to whom it discloses a credit cardholder's past due amounts.

FAIR DEBT COLLECTION PRACTICES ACT

The Fair Debt Collection Practices Act, which took effect on March 15, 1978, is a federal law and therefore applies in all states, the District of Columbia, and U.S. territories. The general purpose of the Fair Debt Collection Practices Act is to end abusive, deceptive, and unfair debt collection practices by debt collectors. It tries to see that people are treated fairly by debt collectors. The law does not permit debt collectors to use unjust means to collect debts. However, this act does not cancel consumer debts.

What Debts Are Covered

Only personal, family, and household debts are covered by the Fair Debt Collection Practices Act. For example, if Juan Rodriguez buys a stereo on credit for home use, his debt is a consumer debt covered by the act. However, if Juan Rodriguez buys a stereo on credit to play music in the waiting room of his advertising firm, the debt is not a consumer debt because the stereo is used for business and not personal consumption purposes. The Fair Debt Collection Practices Act does not protect business debtors. Presumably, business debtors can protect themselves.

Debt Collectors

A debt collector (for purposes of this act only) is anyone other than the creditor who regularly collects debts for others. In other words, the Fair Debt Collection Practices

Act does not apply to creditors who collect their own debts. Today it covers the creditor's attorney's collection efforts, although formerly it did not. The exception for creditors is a loophole in the Fair Debt Collection Practices Act, which is justified because of the belief that the creditor fears losing the debtor's goodwill and future business and will therefore civilize the creditor's debt collecting. Because debt collectors who collect others' debts and sell nothing themselves have no goodwill to protect, the act applies to them.

Contacting a Debtor. A debt collector may contact a debtor in person or by mail, telephone, or telegram. The contact may not occur at inconvenient or unusual hours, such as before 8:00 A.M. or after 9:00 P.M., or at inconvenient or unusual places unless the debtor agrees. A debt collector may not contact a debtor at work if the debtor's employer disapproves.

Within five days after the debt collector first contacts the debtor, the debt collector must send the debtor written notice telling the amount the debtor owes, who the creditor is, and what the debtor should do if the debtor believes the money is not owed.

A debt collector may not contact a debtor if the debtor sends a letter within thirty days after first being contacted, saying that no money is owed. However, a debt collector may start to collect again if the debtor is sent proof of the debt, for example, a copy of the bill.

A debt collector must stop contacting a debtor if the debtor says to do so in writing. Once a debt collector is told not to contact a person, the debt collector may no longer do so, except to confirm no further contact. Also, the debt collector may notify a debtor that some specific action may be taken, such as suing the debtor to collect, but only if the debt collector or creditor usually takes such action, that is, actually sues.

Contacting Others about a Debtor's Bills. Debt collectors may contact any person to locate a debtor. Debt collectors may tell people they contact only that they want to locate the debtor, not why they want to locate the debtor. The debt collector must not tell anyone that the debtor owes money. Also, the debt collector must not use a postcard or an envelope identifying the writer as a debt collector when contacting anyone while trying to locate the debtor.

Prohibited Collection Practices. A debt collector may not harass, oppress, or abuse any person. Examples of prohibited practices include the following:

1. Using threats of violence to anyone or anyone's property or reputation
2. Publishing lists of consumers' names, saying that the consumers refuse to pay their debts (except to a credit bureau)
3. Using obscene or profane language
4. Repeatedly using the telephone to annoy anyone
5. Telephoning any person without identifying the caller
6. Advertising the debtor's debt
7. Using false statements to collect a debt, such as falsely implying that the debt collector is a U.S. or state government official or an attorney; falsely implying that the debtor committed a crime or that the creditor will seize, garnish, attach, or sell the debtor's property unless the debt collector or creditor intends to do so and it is legal to do so; saying that an action will be taken against the debtor if it can't legally be taken
8. Giving false credit information about the debtor to anyone else
9. Sending the debtor anything that looks like an official document, such as a summons and complaint, that might be sent by any court or U.S. agency, such as the Federal Trade Commission, or any state or municipal court or agency

10. Using any false name
11. Being unfair in debt collection, including the following examples:
    a. Collecting any amount greater than what the debtor owes
    b. Depositing any postdated check before the date on that check
    c. Making the debtor accept collect calls or pay for telegrams
    d. Contacting the debtor by postcard
    e. Taking or threatening to take the debtor's property unless allowed by statute
    f. Putting anything on an envelope other than the debt collector's name and address, even the debt collector's name may not be used if it shows it is about collection of a debt

Again, the prohibited practices listed apply only to **debt collectors** as defined by the act. A creditor is not a debt collector and thus is not prohibited by the act from doing any of the listed practices. However, other laws do prohibit some of these acts by creditors.

Debtor Control over Specific Debts

Aside from paying legal debts, the debtor has some control under the Fair Debt Collection Practices Act. If the debtor owes several debts to a single creditor, any payment made must be applied as the debtor directs. For example, the debtor may owe money for one purchase having a higher carrying charge than do other purchases. The debtor may have the creditor apply the payment to the debt with the higher carrying charge. A creditor may not apply a debtor's payment to a debt that the debtor believes is not owed.

Debtor Remedies

If the debt collector breaks the Fair Debt Collection Practices Act by doing one or more of the prohibited acts listed, the debtor may sue the creditor in state or federal court. The statute of limitations is one year. The debtor can recover damages, attorney fees, and court costs. If the creditor violates the act and injures several debtors, the act allows class actions with damage recovery up to $500,000.

Debtor Complaints

The debtor can complain instead of suing. If a debt collector breaks the Fair Debt Collection Practices Act or a debtor has questions about it, the debtor may write to the FTC. The following case illustrates the Fair Debt Collection Practices Act.

Venes v. Professional Service Bureau, Inc.

Court of Appeals of Minn.
353 N.W.2d 671 (1984)

Background and Facts:

Robert and Jane Venes are farmers living in Waukon, Iowa. Their farm suffered heavy financial losses. From 1975–1976, [the] Venes were forced to assign all of their income except $300 a month to the mortgage holder of the farm to prevent foreclosure. The farm operation started improving in 1977.

The Venes had major medical expenses not covered by insurance, including the birth of children in 1976 and 1978. In addition they paid bills for extended cancer treatment for both Robert Venes's father and brother. The brother died in 1978 and the father in 1980. By 1978 Venes were unable to keep up with payments owed to the Mayo Clinic for family medical bills.

The Mayo Clinic assigned a balance of $552.40 to PSB for collection. The clinic has a long-standing policy of not charging patients interest and did not authorize PSB to collect interest on the Venes account. PSB employees made a series of collection calls to Venes, starting in September 1979 and following at approximately two-week intervals.

Jane Venes testified that she received at least four calls although she told the first caller that her family did not deal with collection agencies. She hung up on one caller when his questions became detailed and prying. He immediately called back. She said the calls disrupted her work schedule and left her with the impression that PSB's object was to keep her on the telephone as long as possible to interrupt her day as much as possible.

Robert Venes received six calls. He told callers that he had not received notice of the assignment and would deal only with Mayo Clinic. During one call a PSB employee who identified himself as "Mr. West" became abusive. He called Venes a "deadbeat" and threatened, "If you know what's good for you and your family, you'll stay out of the state of Minnesota." West refused to reveal his real name in that or subsequent calls, although Robert Venes repeatedly requested it.

In April 1980, PSB brought an action against Venes in Minnesota. The complaint sought interest on the account balance from December 14, 1977. Due to a communication problem between Venes and their Minnesota attorney, they failed to answer the complaint. A default judgment for $690, including $107 interest, was obtained and filed in Venes's home county in Iowa.

Robert Venes paid the principal amount to the Mayo Clinic and traveled to Rochester to hire another attorney to reopen the interest issue. Venes incurred attorney fees of $3,827.40 in vacating the judgment and bringing a motion for summary judgment to prevent collection of the interest. The trial court dismissed PSB's interest claim on the grounds that the Mayo Clinic does not charge patients interest as a matter of policy and that PSB has no greater rights than its assignor.

Venes subsequently brought action against PSB for violation of the Fair Debt Collection Practices Act based on the calls and PSB's suit to collect interest.

At trial Robert Venes testified that PSB's conduct had been irritating, insulting, and threatening and had angered him. He said he always had been a nervous person. He claimed the stress of the calls and the litigation aggravated his preexisting medical problems, such as migraines, ulcers, and his spastic bowel syndrome. Jane Venes confirmed that calls irritated her husband's nervous condition.

The jury awarded Venes $1,000 for out-of-pocket expenses, $3,900 for attorney fees for the prior action, and $6,000 for emotional distress. In addition, the trial court awarded $2,000 statutory damages and $1,500 attorney fees for the instant action. PSB appealed the damage awards for emotional distress, for out-of-pocket expenses, and for attorney fees incurred in the prior action.

Body of Opinion

First, PSB challenges the award of damages for emotional distress. A consumer injured by a debt collector's failure to comply with the provisions of the Fair Debt Collection Practices Act is entitled to recover actual damages, including damages for intentional infliction of emotional distress.

The jury, by special verdict, found that PSB violated 15 U.S.C. §1692f by attempting to collect interest not due the underlying creditor. It also found that PSB harassed Venes in violation of one or more subdivisions of 15 U.S.C. §1692d:

> (1) The use or threat of use of violence or other criminal means to harm the physical person, reputation, or property or any person.
>
> * * *
>
> (5) Causing a telephone to ring or engaging any person in telephone conversation repeatedly or continuously with intent to annoy, abuse, or harass any person at the called number.
>
> * * *
>
> (6) . . . [T]he placement of telephone calls without meaningful disclosure of the caller's identity.

The jury awarded $6,000 damages for emotional distress suffered as a result of these violations.

PSB argues that even if it violated the act, its actions were inadequate as a matter of law to justify an award of damages for emotional distress. Although the question may be a close one, we find that the evidence considered in the light most favorable to the Venes was sufficient to sustain the award. . . .

In this case PSB made a series of calls to Venes. In one a PSB employee became abusive, called Robert a "deadbeat" and threatened him to "stay out of Minnesota if you know what's good for you and your family." PSB argues that the caller's conduct was at worst in bad taste. We disagree. It was a fact question for the jury whether PSB's conduct was simple bad taste or extreme and outrageous. The jury reasonably could have found it was extreme and outrageous, particularly in light of Robert's medical problems.

In addition, PSB sought to collect interest from Venes even though the Mayo Clinic, the assigning creditor, did not charge patients interest and did not authorize PSB to do so. PSB attempted to collect interest on Venes' account even after it received notice that the principal amount was paid in full.

There was evidence at trial that each year the Mayo Clinic assigned approximately 1,500 accounts averaging $1,000 each to PSB for collection. The clinic has a published policy of not charging patients interest. It did not authorize PSB to charge interest on accounts assigned for collection. PSB was aware of the Mayo Clinic policy on interest. PSB did not inform the clinic that it was charging interest. It did not pay the clinic any of the interest it collected. PSB has continued to charge interest on some clinic accounts despite a court ruling that it is entitled to no more than its assignor.

A creditor has a right to urge payment of a just debt and to resort to proper legal procedures to enforce such payment. In this case, the jury could find that PSB exceeded its legal rights and recklessly or intentionally inflicted severe emotional distress upon Robert Venes.

Second, PSB contends that the trial court erred in submitting attorney fees for the first action to the jury as an element of actual damages in this case. The company admits that the legal fees incurred in the first action were the result of its violation of the Fair Debt Collection Practices Act, but argues: (1) Venes waived the right to collect attorney fees by not seeking them in the prior action, and (2) there is no statutory authority for treating attorney fees as actual damages. . . .

The purpose of the act, as reflected in 15 U.S.C. §1692, is to eliminate abusive debt collection practices, to protect consumers and redress their injuries. Civil suits will deter abusive practices only if it is economically feasible for consumers to bring them. Unless consumers can recover attorney fees it may not be possible for them to pursue small claims. As Venes' attorney argued forcefully to the jury, unscrupulous collection agencies have little to fear from such suits if consumers must pay thousands of dollars in attorney fees to protect hundreds. Congress recognized this problem and specifically provided for the award of attorney fees to successful plaintiffs. 15 U.S.C. §1692k(a)(3). It would be unfair to deny Venes attorney fees simply because they were incurred in a prior action which established the violation rather than in the instant proceeding.

Judgment and Result

We affirm the verdict that PSB violated two provisions of the Fair Debt Collection Practices Act and affirm the award of damages for emotional distress, out-of-pocket expenses, and attorney fees for the prior action establishing one of the violations.

Questions

1. What specific acts allegedly violated the Fair Debt Collection Practices Act?
2. What business ethics are reflected in the FDCPA?
3. How is the legal ethic of realism shown in the case?
4. Who benefits and who loses as a result of the FDCPA?

ELECTRONIC FUND TRANSFER ACT

The U.S. Treasury Department makes millions of Social Security payments using electronic fund transfers (EFTs). Thousands of automated tellers process on average 2,000 transactions per month. A number of financial institutions have pay-by-phone services. All of these devices to transmit money are referred to as electronic fund transfers.

EFTs include several banking and payment systems that use computers and electronic technology. Such systems eliminate checks and reduce paper steps in transmitting funds, which greatly reduce transaction costs.

In 1978 Congress passed the Electronic Fund Transfer Act (EFTA), which went into effect in 1979. The EFTA, along with the regulations the Federal Reserve system promulgates under it, set out the liability rules governing EFTs. The EFTA itself defines such transfers as

> [A]ny transfer of funds, other than a transaction originated by check, draft, or similar paper instrument, which is initiated through an electronic terminal, telephonic instrument, or computer or magnetic tape so as to order, instruct, or authorize a financial institution to debit or credit an account. Such term includes, but is not limited to, point-of-sale transfers, automated teller machine transactions, direct deposits or withdrawals of funds, and transfers initiated by telephone.

The definition does not include check guarantee and authorization services, and check systems involving electronic processing.

General Consumer Protections

If a consumer receives EFT services, the financial institution must disclose all of the terms, including the following:

1. The customer's liability for unauthorized transfers caused by loss or theft of the card, code, or other access device
2. Whom to call and the phone number in case of theft or loss
3. The charges for using the EFT system
4. What systems are available, including limits on frequency and dollar amounts
5. The consumer's rights to see transactions in writing
6. Ways to correct errors
7. The consumer's rights to stop payments
8. The financial institution's liability to the consumer
9. Rules concerning disclosure of account information to third parties

Records. The EFTA sharply reduces, but does not eliminate, the amount of paper in fund transfers. Financial institutions must give customers periodic statements describing types, amounts, dates, transferees, and locations of transfers. Timing of the periodic statements depends on the account activity and nature of the account.

Financial institutions must also notify consumers if an automatic deposit is not made as scheduled. This provision helps consumers avoid overdrawing their accounts.

Unauthorized Use. If the access device to the EFT system is lost, stolen, or misplaced, the EFTA limits the consumer's liability to $50 if the consumer notifies the financial institution within two business days of learning of such loss or theft. Liability limits climb to $500 if notification happens after the second business day. Finally, the consumer can have unlimited liability if notification does not occur within 60 days after receiving a periodic statement reflecting the unauthorized transfer.

Mistakes. Consumers discovering errors in their periodic statements must notify the financial institution within 60 days after receiving the statement. The notice can be oral or written. It must contain the following information:

1. The consumer's account number and name
2. The statement that an error has been made, along with an indication of the amount of the alleged error
3. The reasons the consumer believes an error has been made

The financial institution has ten days to investigate the alleged error and report to the consumer, or the financial institution may credit the consumer's account and take 45 days to investigate. If an error is discovered, the financial institution has one day to adjust the consumer's account. If no mistake has been made, however, the financial institution has to give the consumer a full, written report with conclusions.

Financial institutions failing to make transfers according to account terms are liable for all damages that the errors proximately caused. This provision assumes the account had sufficient funds to otherwise make the transfer.

Sanctions and Damages. If a financial institution violates the EFTA, a consumer may recover the following:

1. Actual damages
2. Punitive damages of not more than $1,000 in a single action nor less than $100; in class actions the limit is the lesser of $500,000 or one percent of the financial institution's net worth

The EFTA has criminal sanctions. It is a federal misdemeanor for a financial institution to violate the EFTA. A $5,000 fine and up to one year's imprisonment are possible. It is a federal felony for people to fraudulently use EFT devices. Sanctions in such cases include a $10,000 fine and ten years' imprisonment.

Criticism of the EFTA

The banking community has criticized the EFTA. The criticism centers on the absence of a fault standard in the EFTA's liability provisions. That is, even if the consumer negligently loses the EFT access device, the consumer's maximum loss is $50, assuming timely notice is given. Banks argue that consumers' incentive to be careful would increase if they had to bear the full loss for their own negligence. As it is, the financial institution incurs this loss unless it passes it on to all EFT users, in which case careful users pay for mistakes of the careless.

In the *Ognibene* case the bank transferred money from a customer's account to a con man to whom the customer had loaned its card for purposes of seeing whether the automated teller machine worked. In fact the con man worked a scam, withdrawing money from the customer's account unbeknownst to the customer. Was this transfer authorized, where the customer bore the loss, or an unauthorized transfer where the bank sustained the loss? (The con man had disappeared.) Read the *Ognibene* case to see the result.

Ognibene v. Citibank, N.A.

Civil Court of the City of New York, Small Claims Part.
446 N.Y.S.2d 845 (1981)

Background and Facts:

Plaintiff seeks to recover $400 withdrawn from his account at the defendant bank by an unauthorized person using an automated teller machine. The court has concluded that plaintiff was the victim of a scam which defendant has been aware of for some time.

Defendant's witness, an assistant manager of one of its branches, described how the scam works: A customer enters the automated teller machine (ATM) area for the purpose of using a machine for the transaction of business with the bank. At the time that he enters, a person is using the customer service telephone located between the two automated teller machines and appears to be telling customer service that one of the machines is malfunctioning. This person is the perpetrator of the scam and his conversation with customer service is only simulated. He observes the customer press his personal identification code into one of the two machines. Having learned the code, the perpetrator then tells the customer that customer service has advised him to ask the customer to insert his Citicard into the allegedly malfunctioning machine to check whether it will work with a card other than the perpetrator's. When a good samaritan customer accedes to the request, the other machine is activated. The perpetrator then presses a code into the machine, which the customer does not realize is his own code which the perpetrator has just observed. After continuing the simulated conversation on the telephone, the perpetrator advises the customer that customer service has asked if he would try his Citicard in the allegedly malfunctioning machine once more. A second insertion of the cards permits cash to be released by the machine, and if the customer does as requested, the thief has effectuated a cash withdrawal from the unwary customer's account.

Plaintiff testified that on August 16, 1981, he went to the ATM area at one of defendant's branches and activated one of the machines with his Citibank card, pressed in his personal identification code and withdrew $20. While he did this a person who was using the telephone between plaintiff's machine and the adjoining machine said into the telephone, "I'll see if his card works in my machine." Thereupon he asked plaintiff if he could use his card to see if the other machine was working. Plaintiff handed it to him and saw him insert it into the adjoining machine at least two times while stating into the telephone, "Yes, it seems to be working."

Defendant's computer records in evidence show that two withdrawals of $200 each from plaintiff's account were made on August 16, 1981, on the machine adjoining the one plaintiff used for his $20 withdrawal. The two $200 withdrawals were made at 5:42 P.M. and 5:43 P.M.

respectively; plaintiff's own $20 withdrawal was made at 5:41 P.M. At the time, plaintiff was unaware that any withdrawals from his account were being made on the adjoining machine.

The only fair and reasonable inferences to be drawn from all of the evidence are that the person who appeared to be conversing on the telephone observed the plaintiff enter his personal identification code into the machine from which he withdrew $20 and that he entered it into the adjoining machine while simulating a conversation with customer service about that machine's malfunctioning. It is conceded in the testimony of defendant's assistant branch manager that it would have been possible for a person who was positioned so as to appear to be speaking on the telephone physically to observe the code being entered into the machine by plaintiff. Although plaintiff is not certain that his card was inserted in the adjoining machine more than twice, the circumstances indicate that it was inserted four times. No issue of fraud by plaintiff or anyone acting in concert with him has been raised by defendant. Having observed plaintiff's demeanor, the court found him to be a credible witness and is of the opinion that no such issues exist in this case.

Body of Opinion

Judge Mara T. Thorpe

The basic rights, liabilities and responsibilities of the banks which offer electronic money transfer services and the consumers who use them have been established by the federal legislation contained in 15 U.S.C.A. 1693 et seq., commonly called the Electronic Fund Transfers Act (EFT). Although the EFT Act preempts state law only to the extent of any inconsistency... to date New York State has not enacted legislation which governs the resolution of the issues herein. Therefore, the EFT Act is applicable.

The EFT Act places various limits on a consumer's liability for electronic fund transfers from his account if they are "unauthorized." Insofar as is relevant here, a transfer is "unauthorized" if 1) it is initiated by a person other than the consumer and without actual authority to initiate such transfer, 2) the consumer receives no benefit from it, and 3) the consumer did not furnish such person "with the card, code or other means of access" to his account....

In an action involving a consumer's liability for an electronic fund transfer, such as the one at bar, the burden of going forward to show an "unauthorized" transfer from his account is on the consumer. The EFT Act places upon the bank, however, the burden of proof of any consumer liability for the transfer.... To establish full liability on the part of the consumer, the bank must prove that the transfer was authorized. To be entitled to even the limited liability imposed by the statute on the consumer, the bank must prove that certain conditions of consumer liability,... have been met and that certain disclosures mandated... have been made.

Plaintiff herein met his burden of going forward. He did not initiate the withdrawals in question, did not authorize the person in the ATM area to make them, and did not benefit from them.

However, defendant's position is, in essence, that although plaintiff was duped, the bank's burden of proof on the issue of authorization has been met by plaintiff's testimony that he permitted his card to be used in the adjoining machine by the other person. The court does not agree.

The EFT Act requires that the consumer have furnished to a person initiating the transfer the "card, code, or other means of access" to his account to be ineligible for the limitations on liability afforded by the Act when transfers are "unauthorized." The evidence establishes that in order to obtain access to an account via an automated teller machine, both the card and the personal identification code must be used. Thus, by merely giving his card to the person initiating the transfer, a consumer does not furnish the "means of access" to his account. To do so, he would have to furnish the personal identification code as well. See 12 C.F.R. 205.2(a)(1), the regulation promulgated under the EFT Act which defines "access device" as "a card, code or other means of access to [an]... account *or any combination thereof*" [emphasis added].

The court finds that plaintiff did not furnish his personal identification code to the person initiating the $400 transfer within the meaning of the EFT Act. There is no evidence that he deliberately or even negligently did so. On the contrary, the unauthorized person was able to obtain the code because of defendant's own negligence. Since the bank had knowledge of the scam and its operational details (including the central role of the customer service telephone), it was negligent in failing to provide plaintiff-customer with information sufficient to alert him to the danger when he found himself in the position of a potential victim. Although in June 1981, after the scam came to defendant's attention, it posted signs in its ATM areas containing a red circle approximately 2-1/2 inches in diameter in which is written "Do Not Let Your Citicard Be Used For Any Transaction But Your Own," the court finds that this printed admonition is not a sufficient security measure since it fails to state the reason why one should not do so. Since a customer of defendant's electronic fund transfer service must employ both the card and the personal identification code in order to withdraw money from his account, the danger of loaning his card briefly for the purpose of checking the functioning of an adjoining automated teller machine would not be immediately apparent to one who has not divulged his personal identification number and who is unaware that it has been revealed merely by virtue of his own transaction with the machine.

Since the bank established the electronic fund transfer service and has the ability to tighten its security characteristics, the responsibility for the fact that plaintiff's code, one of the two necessary components of the "access device" or "means of access" to his account, was observed and utilized as it was must rest with the bank.

For the foregoing reasons and in view of the fact that the primary purpose of the EFT Act and the regulation promulgated thereunder is the protection of individual consumers . . . , the court concludes that plaintiff did not furnish his code to anyone within the meaning of the Act. Accordingly, since the person who obtained it did not have actual authority to initiate the transfer, the transfer qualities as an "unauthorized" one under 15 U.S.C.A. 1693a(11) and the bank cannot hold plaintiff fully liable for the $400 withdrawal.

To avail itself of the limited liability imposed by the Act upon a consumer in the event of an "unauthorized" transfer, the bank must demonstrate 1) that the means of access utilized for the transfer was "accepted" and 2) that the bank has provided a way which the user of the means of access can be identified as the person authorized to use it. . . . One definition of "accepted" under the Act is that the consumer has used the means of access. . . . Both of the foregoing conditions of liability have been met here since plaintiff used the means of access to his account to withdraw the $20 and had been given a personal identification code.

Additionally, the bank must prove that it disclosed to the consumer his liability for unauthorized electronic fund transfers and certain information pertaining to notification of the bank in the event the consumer believes that an unauthorized transfer has been or may be effected. . . . Defendant did not establish that it made such disclosures to plaintiff. Accordingly, it is not entitled to avail itself of the benefit of the limited liability for unauthorized transfers imposed upon consumers by the Act.

For the foregoing reasons, judgment shall be for plaintiff in the sum of $400.

Judgment and Result

Plaintiff wins $400 from Citibank because Citibank transferred money from plaintiff's account without authorization.

Questions

1. Was state or federal law the basis for regulating electronic fund transfers?
2. Must a consumer prove that an unauthorized transfer from his account has occurred? Must the bank or consumer prove the consumer authorized the transfer?
3. When the consumer turned his card over to the crook, who used it to withdraw from the consumer's account, hadn't the customer authorized the withdrawal?

BANKRUPTCY

In our consumption-oriented society, advertising, credit availability, and peer pressure encourage us to buy in excess. Consumers overindulge. How do consumers spell relief? B-A-N-K-R-U-P-T-C-Y. Bankruptcy provides a type of consumer protection by offering a fresh start to people in debt.

The Bankruptcy Reform Act of 1978 (Bankruptcy Code) took effect on October 1, 1979. It is the first complete revision of federal bankruptcy law since 1938. (States have no bankruptcy laws.) The Bankruptcy Code provides two general types of relief for consumer debtors: (1) straight bankruptcy, which can be voluntary or involuntary, and (2) adjustment of debts of individuals with a regular income.

Straight Bankruptcy

Straight bankruptcy (filed as Chapter 7 bankruptcy) refers to the process by which people turn over their property to the trustee in bankruptcy, and in return the bankruptcy court cancels their debts. This relieves people of their debts and allows them to get a fresh start. A **straight bankruptcy** lets consumer-debtors avoid their debts. These bankruptcies provide a safety valve; a relief from bad luck, bad economic conditions, bad management, or a combination of these.

Straight bankruptcy can be voluntary or involuntary. Debtors may voluntarily enter bankruptcy by filing a petition for relief. Creditors may put a debtor into involuntary bankruptcy if the debtor owes at least $5,000 in unsecured debt. Specifically, three creditors with unsecured claims of at least $5,000 can put someone into involuntary bankruptcy if 12 or more creditors have made claims, and one creditor with at least $5,000 in unsecured claims can do so. If the debtor is unable to pay debts as they mature, a court will order relief in an involuntary bankruptcy.

In straight bankruptcies, debtors turn all of their **nonexempt property** over to the bankruptcy trustee (an official of the bankruptcy court). The Bankruptcy Code lets debtors keep their **exempt property**. People can determine whether their property is exempt in bankruptcy through the federal Bankruptcy Code (law), which lists what property is exempt for bankruptcy or permits alternative state exemptions. Thus, the code lets states replace the **federal exemptions** with **state exemptions**; more than 30 states have done so thus far. State exemptions are usually less favorable to the debtor than the federal exemptions.

The debtor's nonexempt property is divided among the creditors. Not all creditors have equal rights to share the debtor's remaining property. A pecking order exists, which requires all claims at a particular level to be fully paid before anything is paid to the next lower level of creditors. That order is as follows:

1. Secured creditors (those with secured claims on particular property of the debtor have first claim on that property)
2. Bankruptcy administration costs
3. Debts that the debtor's business incurs in the ordinary course of the debtor's business after an involuntary case starts but before an order for relief or trustee's appointment
4. Employee wage, salary, and commission claims (with a maximum of $2,000 multiplied by the number of employees) earned within 90 days before filing for bankruptcy
5. Claims for contributions to employee benefit plans arising from employee services within 180 days of filing for bankruptcy (maximum of $2,000 per employee)
6. Unsecured claims of grain farmers against grain elevators for grain or grain proceeds. Also, unsecured claims of $2,000 or less per individual of U.S. fishers against fish storage or fish processing plants
7. Consumer prepayments or deposits (maximum of $900 per consumer)
8. Taxes
9. General creditors (for example, those selling to the debtor on open account)

After all the creditors' claims are examined, the trustee distributes the debtor's property in accordance with these priorities. General creditors usually fare poorly, receiving about a nickel for every dollar the debtor owes them. At the end of the process, the bankruptcy judge enters an order discharging all dischargeable debts. The debtor (consumer) now has a fresh start.

Bankruptcy Consumer Protections

The new Bankruptcy Code provides certain protections for consumers but also places some limits on consumer bankruptcy.

Discharge. The **discharge** in effect cancels the debtor's debts. Technically, it bars the creditor from enforcing the debt unless the debtor reaffirms the debt. As the main reason for going bankrupt, it was a key provision under prior bankruptcy laws and is part of the new Bankruptcy Code.

Few Limits on Who Can Go Bankrupt. A consumer may voluntarily enter bankruptcy. Farmers may now file for voluntary bankruptcy.

Difficulty in Reaffirmation of Debts. Debtors do not want to reaffirm debts discharged in bankruptcy. When a person goes bankrupt and gets a debt discharged, a creditor often will not sell to that debtor again without a promise to pay the debts discharged in bankruptcy. This demand kills the main reason for going bankrupt. Although this tactic once was allowed and still is permitted under the new Bankruptcy Code, more procedural protections are given to the debtor. The purpose of these protections is to discourage reaffirmation.

Under the recent bankruptcy changes, the reaffirmation can take place only after the debtor's rights and the effects of reaffirmation have been fully explained to the debtor by the judge in a bankruptcy court hearing after the judge finds that reaffirmation does not impose an undue hardship on the debtor or a dependent of the debtor. Reaffirmation itself must occur before a debtor receives a bankruptcy discharge. Furthermore, the debtor may rescind the reaffirmation within 60 days after making it.

Bankruptcy for Less-Than-Honest Debtors. Under prior law, if a debtor lied in a loan application, got the loan, and later tried to go bankrupt to discharge the loan, bankruptcy was denied. The old rule required a debtor to be completely honest to go bankrupt. The new Bankruptcy Code limits this rule by letting the debtor go bankrupt but denying discharge for the debts about which the debtor lied to obtain, while allowing discharge for other debts.

Limited Utility Service Cutoff. When a debtor does not pay utility bills, the utilities cut off power or telephone service. The new Bankruptcy Code requires the bankruptcy trustee to deposit money with the utility within 20 days after entry of an order for relief. If the trustee does not provide a deposit, the utility may stop service.

Nullification of Bankruptcy Clauses. Bankruptcy clauses are put into contracts such as leases and provide that if a debtor files for bankruptcy, the debtor's property interest, lease, or contract ends automatically. These clauses are now invalid under the new Bankruptcy Code—another debtor protection.

Waiver of Exemptions Not Allowed for Nonpurchase Money Security Interests. Recall that certain of the debtor's property (exempt property) may not be taken by creditors to pay the debtor's bills. If a debtor borrows money and uses as collateral property the debtor already owns, a nonpurchase money loan is made. In other words, the debtor is not using the borrowed money to buy the collateral. If the collateral is exempt property (such as a car), creditors often require debtors to waive their exemption in the collateral as a condition to getting the loan, which is called an *exemption waiver*. It hurts debtors and helps creditors. To protect consumer debtors, the Bankruptcy Code invalidates exemption waivers when exempt property is used as collateral for nonpurchase money loans.

The Perez Doctrine. The Perez doctrine says that state law is invalid if it penalizes or punishes people for exercising their federal bankruptcy rights. This doctrine arose from a 1965 case in which Adolpho Perez, an uninsured motorist, had an auto accident in Tucson, Arizona, which injured Miss Pinkerton. She sued him and won a $2,425.98 judgment. Perez immediately went bankrupt to escape his debts, including the accident judgment. Arizona had a statute suspending the driver's license of anyone going bankrupt to escape debts arising from auto accidents. Perez claimed that this statute violated the federal supremacy clause. The U.S. Supreme Court agreed with Perez saying in effect that state law may not penalize a person for exercising the federal right to go bankrupt. This doctrine obviously benefits consumers.

Bankruptcy Limits

The new Bankruptcy Code is not entirely debtor oriented. It places some limits on bankruptcy as a consumer protection. First, a consumer may obtain a straight bankruptcy only once every six years. Second, certain debts are nondischargeable—that is, they cannot be gotten rid of by going bankrupt. Such debts include taxes (state, federal, and municipal) under certain circumstances, educational loans coming due within five years of filing for bankruptcy, intentional tort judgments (if, for example, the debtor is sued for an intentional tort such as assault, battery, libel, slander, or fraud and loses, such judgments cannot be gotten rid of by going bankrupt), child support or alimony obligations, liability for breach of a trust or fiduciary duty, fines owed to governments, and unscheduled debts (that is, the debtor does not list them as being owed).

"Loading Up" With Luxury Purchases Immediately Before Filing for Bankruptcy. Typically, before an individual files for bankruptcy he or she is emotionally depressed. What better way to fight "the blues" than by going on a spending spree? Buy that Cadillac, that new suit, that Caribbean cruise, and expensive meals with the idea that one is going bankrupt anyway, so these debts will be cancelled too. The Bankruptcy Code stops this practice by prohibiting discharge of a debtor from any debt for money, property, or services if this debt was obtained by false pretenses, false representation, or actual fraud other than a statement respecting the debtor's financial condition. Consumer debts owed to a single creditor (such as a credit card company) and aggregating more than $500 for "luxury goods or services" incurred by an individual debtor on or within 40 days before filing an order for relief are presumed nondischargeable. "Luxury goods or services" do not include goods or services reasonably acquired for the support or maintenance of the debtor or a dependent of the debtor.

The following case presents the "loading up" problem by an individual debtor who made 38 separate purchases totalling $1,017.17 on her MasterCard within the 40-day period before the bankruptcy court entered the order for relief. Read the case to see which, if any, of these debts were discharged.

In Re Tondreau

U.S. Bankruptcy Court (N.D. Indiana)
117 B.R. 397 (1989)

Background and Facts:

On April 27, 1985, Marie Madeleine Tondreau (the debtor) completed an Application for MasterCard and Cardholders Agreement requesting a MasterCard with a credit limit of $500. The Credit Union approved Marie's application on May 17, 1985, and thereafter issued a MasterCard to her. Between May 1985 and July 1986, the Credit Union raised the limit on the debtor's MasterCard account from $500 to $1,000. On July 8, 1986, the Credit Union issued a letter to her informing her that her MasterCard account exceeded the assigned limit of $1,000 by $166.83. The Credit Union further notified her that it would revoke her MasterCard privileges if she failed to bring the account within the assigned spending limit by July 18, 1986. On July 21, 1986, after the date set for revoking the debtor's credit card privileges, the Credit Union issued notice to Marie informing her that it had decided to terminate her credit card and asked her to return the MasterCard to the Credit Union. The notice listed the reasons for its action as "MasterCard Overlimit and Loan Delinquent." Marie testified at trial that she received both the July 8, 1986, letter and the termination notice from the Credit Union. She testified that upon receiving the notice from the Credit Union she understood that her MasterCard privileges were revoked.

Following the termination of her credit card privileges, the statements concerning Marie's MasterCard account reflect the following activity:

August 25, 1986 Statement	
Payments	-0-
New Activity	61.77
Finance Charge	16.71
New Balance	$1,165.47

September 23, 1986 Statement	
Payments	270.00
New Activity	-0-
Finance charge	14.86
New Balance	910.33

October 23, 1986 Statement	
Payments	-0-
New Activity	404.07
Finance charge	14.82
New Balance	1,329.22

November 24, 1986 Statement	
Payments	-0-
Credits	375.54
Adjustments	10.00
New Activity	988.64
New Balance	1,952.32

At trial the debtor testified that the transactions recorded on the October 23, 1986, and November 24, 1986, statements were charge purchases for ordinary living expenses for herself, such as groceries, gasoline, cigarettes, household toiletries, car parts/service, shoes, prescriptions, eye glasses, and lumber for repairing the porch on her home. Marie had no dependents at the time she made the credit card purchases although her boyfriend lived with her off and on during 1986 and therefore may have used some of the items purchased. Marie stated that her boyfriend made some of the purchases himself using her credit card but indicated that he did so with her permission. She explained that throughout 1986 she worked at St. Paul's Retirement Community and earned a salary of approximately $15,000 annually. She further testified that her income was sufficient to cover her living expenses until September of 1986 when she contacted an attorney about the possibility of filing a bankruptcy petition. She testified that her attorney informed her that once she filed for bankruptcy, she should no longer use any of her credit cards. Marie filed her bankruptcy petition on October 28, 1986.

Body of Opinion

Robert K. Rodibaugh, Senior Bankruptcy Judge

The issue before the court is whether any portion of the debtor's obligation to the Credit Union on her MasterCard account may be excepted from the debtor's discharge under section 523(a)(2). This section provides in relevant part:

a) A discharge . . . does not discharge an individual debtor from any debt—
   2) for money, property, services, or an extension, renewal, or refinancing of credit, to the extent obtained by—
      A) false pretenses, a false representation, or actual fraud, other than a statement respecting the debtor's or an insider's financial condition;...
      C) for purposes of subparagraph A) of this paragraph, consumer debts owed to a single creditor and aggregating more than $500 for "luxury goods or services" incurred forty days before the order for relief . . . are presumed to be nondischargeable; "luxury goods or services" do not include goods or services reasonably acquired for the support or maintenance of the debtor or a dependent of the debtor. . . .

The exception to discharge provided by section 523 a)2)A) is construed liberally in favor of the debtor and strictly against the party asserting the exception. . . . To have a debt declared nondischargeable in bankruptcy under section 523 a)2)A), the burden is on the plaintiff to prove each of five elements including:

1) that the debtor made the representations;
2) that at the time the representations were made he knew them to be false;
3) that the representations were made with the intention and purpose of deceiving the creditor;
4) that the creditor reasonably relied on the representations;
5) that the creditor sustained the alleged injury as a proximate result of the representations having been made. . . .

The standard of review is that of clear and convincing evidence. . . . If plaintiff, however, is able to show that the debtor's obligation falls within section 523 a)2)C), the debt is presumed to be nondischargeable.

Reviewing the debtor's testimony and the other evidence presented herein, the court finds that the Credit Union has met its burden of showing that the obligations incurred on her MasterCard from September 20, 1986, to October 27, 1986, should be excepted from the debtor's discharge. The court notes that the debtor made four small purchases on her MasterCard in July of 1986. Thereafter on August 27, 1986, and September 19, 1986, the debtor made two payments on her MasterCard account in the amounts of $170 and $100 which apparently brought the account current and within the designated credit line of $1,000. Then, beginning on September 20, 1986, the debtor made 38 separate purchases totalling $1,017.17 on her MasterCard within the 40-day period before the court entered the order for relief in her case. . . . The debtor made the purchases at a variety of businesses including Osco's, Baker's Shoes, Saveway Shoes, Super America, 9 West, South Bend Clinic, Joseph's Shoes, The Ridge Company, Auto Works, Seven Eleven, Hub Cap Annie, Rainbow Muffler, Williams Home Center and C&B Optical. These transactions, although individually quite small in amount (all under $50.00 but one) doubled the outstanding balance on the debtor's MasterCard account bringing it $952.32 over her $1,000 line of credit.

Considering the nature of the items purchased, the court concludes that most of them would not qualify as "luxury goods or services" under section 523 a)2)C). Hence, the presumption of nondischargeability set forth in section 523 a)2)C) does not apply to most of the items purchased. This conclusion, though, does not end the court's inquiry in this case. The Credit Union still has the opportunity to prove that the debtor knowingly made false representations in order to obtain an extension of credit on her MasterCard account. The court believes that the Credit Union has met its burden with respect to this issue.

Courts have considered various factors in determining whether a debtor's use of a credit card amounts to a false representation which should be excepted from the discharge under section 523 a)2)A). These factors include:

1) The length of time between the credit card charges and the filing of the petition in bankruptcy.
2) Whether the debtor consulted an attorney about bankruptcy before making the charges.
3) The number of charges made.
4) The amount of the charges.
5) Whether the debtor made several charges on the same day or at the same store below the amount at which the seller would seek approval of the charges.
6) Whether the charges represent an abrupt change in the debtor's use of the credit card.
7) Whether the charges exceeded the credit limit of the account.
8) The debtor's financial circumstances when the charges were made.
9) Whether the debtor was employed at the time.
10) Whether the debtor had reasonable prospects for employment or a reasonable expectation of additional income.
11) The debtor's financial sophistication.
12) Whether the items charged were superflous.

...Another important factor to consider is whether the debtor used the credit card after receiving notice that it had been revoked.

In this case the court finds that each time the debtor used her MasterCard after she had notice that the Credit Union had revoked her account privileges, she falsely represented that she was entitled to use the MasterCard. In order to facilitate her use of the MasterCard after the Credit Union suspended her credit card privileges and her balance was well above her line of credit, the debtor made purchases under $50 which were unlikely to be detected immediately by the Credit Union since most businesses are not required to get authorization for purchases under $50. Using this system the debtor generated a total new debt to the Credit Union of $1,017.17 in just over one month's time often making several charges on the same day at the same store in amounts below $50. In doing so, the court finds the debtor knowingly violated the terms of her MasterCard account....

The court believes the Credit Union has come forward with sufficient evidence to show that the debtor falsely represented the status of her MasterCard account to the various businesses where she made purchases on her MasterCard after her account had been closed.

Judgment and Result

The bankruptcy court refused to allow the credit card purchases made within the 40-day period prior to the court's entering the order for relief to be discharged in bankruptcy. Such purchases were deemed to be made by a debtor who falsely represented that she was entitled to use her credit card, with intent to deceive the creditor, and the businesses that sold items to the debtor reasonably relied on such false representations.

Questions

1. Were the purchases of shoes under $50 "luxury goods"? How then could the court say that such purchases were nondischargeable?
2. Was it really the "false pretense" aspect of using a credit card whose privileges had been terminated that rendered these rather small purchases nondischargeable?
3. Why should purchases made after consulting an attorney become suspect and possibly less likely to be dischargeable?
4. Does this case and bankruptcy law in general support the authors' assertion that "positive law has become the ethical ceiling in our society"?

Debt Adjustment (Chapter 13 Bankruptcy)

In addition to allowing straight bankruptcy, the Bankruptcy Code allows individuals to adjust their debts in which the amount owed all creditors is reduced, maturities are extended, or some combination of the two is followed. Courts sometimes let debtors adjust their debts by paying only 15 percent (or occasionally less) of their debts as payment in full. Unlike straight bankruptcy no express limit is placed on the frequency of debt adjustment. However, bankruptcy judges have discretion to deny this type of relief.

Any individual with a regular income (even welfare or alimony income), with less than $100,000 in *unsecured* debt (no mortgage or security interest) and less than $350,000 in *secured* debt (a mortgage or security interest), qualifies for a debt adjustment under the Bankruptcy Code. Thus, a small, sole proprietorship (as well as a consumer) could adjust its debts.

The preceding discussion covers only some aspects of the federal Bankruptcy Code as it applies to consumers. The Bankruptcy Code's treatment of business and municipalities will not be discussed.

1984 Amendments Affecting Consumers

In 1984 Congress amended the Bankruptcy Code. The amendments affect consumers going bankrupt in several ways. First, consumer-debtors owing mainly consumer debts and entering Chapter 7 (straight bankruptcy) must be advised of the availability of Chapter 13 as an alternative.

Second, the bankruptcy court has the power to dismiss Chapter 7 petitions if a debtor has demonstrated a prior or substantial abuse of the bankruptcy process.

Third, motor vehicle drivers becoming liable while legally intoxicated (drunken drivers) can no longer have such judgments discharged in bankruptcy.

Fourth, consumer-debtors who "load up" (buy luxury goods and services or obtain $1,000 or more in credit card cash advances right before filing for bankruptcy to maximize use of the exemptions) will find it harder to get debts for such purchases discharged. Specifically, if a debtor incurs consumer debts owed to a single creditor and aggregating more than $500 for luxury goods or services within 40 days before filing for bankruptcy, such debts are presumed nondischargeable. Also presumed nondischargeable are cash advances aggregating more than $1,000 under an open-end credit plan obtained by an individual debtor on or within 20 days before filing for bankruptcy.

Fifth, in Chapter 13 cases unsecured creditors now have a veto over the plan in certain circumstances.

In early 2000, Congress considered amending the bankruptcy code to make it tougher in certain situations for consumers earning a substantial income to go bankrupt and escape certain debts. President Clinton promised to veto such amendments arguing that low income persons need the escape valve that bankruptcy provides.

CHAPTER SUMMARY

A number of situation-specific consumer protection laws have been developed by Congress, the Federal Trade Commission, the courts, and the states.

The Federal Trade Commission has promulgated several regulations designed to protect consumers, including the bait-and-switch reg, the modification of the holder-in-due-course rule, the mail-order merchandise rule, the regulation establishing a cooling-off period for door-to-door sales, and the telemarketing rule.

Congress passed a number of statutes that protect consumers, including the Truth-in-Lending Act, the Fair Credit Reporting Act, the Equal Credit Opportunity Act, the Fair Debt Collection Practices Act, the Electronic Fund Transfer Act, and the federal bankruptcy code.

MANAGER'S ETHICAL DILEMMA

Sanford Frederickson worked for E.F. Hutton, a company that sold investment securities in many states. Frederickson would draft a prospectus describing the investment and would then send it out to prospective investors in all 20 states. In order to make one investment opportunity more attractive, Frederickson negligently misrepresented the risk involved in certain tax shelter investments offered to Henry Blankenheim and Philip Kaefer. Frederickson stated the investments were "good"; that he had placed other clients in an earlier investment with the same people, and it was doing well; that he had his own money in this venture; that the forms Blankenheim and Kaefer were to sign to buy this stock were just administrative formalities and meant nothing; and that the reason the buyers needed to sign the purchase forms was because neither Frederickson nor E.F. Hutton was receiving commissions on this sale. The purchase forms the buyers signed contained "hold harmless" provisions according to which the buyers agreed to exonerate the sellers from any loss buyers incurred on the investments and also agreed that the sellers made no representations to the buyers about the securities. The buyers bought about $230,000 in these securities from E.F. Hutton.

The investments proved unsuccessful, and Blankenheim and Kaefer lost all they had put into the tax shelters. They sued E.F. Hutton and Frederickson on a misrepresentation theory because the investments did not live up to Frederickson's representations. Frederickson and Hutton pointed out to Blankenheim and Kaefer that they were sophisticated businesspeople who knew they had signed a hold-harmless agreement. Should hold-harmless agreements exonerate businesses that negligently misrepresent what they sell to the buyers? [*Blankenheim v. E.F. Hutton & Co., Inc.*, 266 Cal. Rptr. 563 (Cal. App. 6 Dist. 1990)]

Discussion Questions

1. You are Sally Cotter, a vice-president at First National Bank, a multistate bank that is considering expanding its offerings to small consumers. George Miracle, a new MBA, has come forward with the following proposal: First National Bank has a large consumer credit card operation. He proposees offering an insurance policy to each of these credit cardholders for $19.95 per year, which if all accepted, would generate almost $20 million in revenue for the bank. Specifically, Miracle's plan would offer to protect existing and new credit cardholders from losses if their credit cards were stolen or used without the authorization of the person whose name is on the card. His proposal would hold harmless from liability cardholders for losses above $50 if they notified the bank within three days of discovering unauthorized use of the credit card. As Miracle's superior, what do you say in response to his proposal?
2. What legal institutions have been most active in the consumer protection movement? Would a business prefer that a court, a legislature, or an administrative agency develop consumer rights? Which legal institution is generally more capable of producing sweeping, immediate social and economic changes?
3. What are the costs of consumer protection? What are the possible costs of consumer protection that consumers must bear? For example, does business have compliance costs with credit disclosure and more restrained debt collection? Who pays these costs? What would be the costs (and who would bear them) of not having consumer protection laws? Are consumer protection costs a factor no matter what is done or not done?
4. Which consumer protection laws are enforced by consumers? Which by courts? Which by administrative agencies? Of these enforcers, which is likely to be most effective? Why?
5. Consumer protection has been criticized by some as paternalistic, that is, someone or some agency is looking out for consumer interests. Should consumers look out for their own interests? Realistically, can consumers protect themselves when dealing with large businesses? Which does consumer protection help or hurt more—the ethical, fair-dealing businesses, or the unethical?
6. The Federal Bankruptcy Code protects consumers by allowing them to turn over their property to a bankruptcy trustee and in

exchange receive a discharge of their bad debts. Not all debts are dischargeable through bankruptcy. For example, educational loans are not dischargeable unless they cause an undue hardship on the debtor. In one straight bankruptcy case, the debtors, Mr. and Mrs. Rice, owed $3,025 in student loans. Their monthly payment on these loans was $36. Mrs. Rice attended college for one-half semester. Mr. Rice attended college for one and one-half semesters. The Rices quit college because they lacked money and had family responsibilities. They made no effort to repay their loans. The Rices were married with four children ages 17, 15, 14, and 12, who lived at home. The children did not work. Mr. Rice was a maintenance man. Mrs. Rice was a psychiatric aide. Their combined monthly take-home pay was $1,268. Their budget showed $1,237 in expenses, leaving them $31 per month surplus if the $36 per month educational loan payment were not made. If the student loan payments were made, their monthly budget showed a $5 deficit. Should the educational loan be discharged as creating an undue hardship on the debtor? [*In re Rice*, Bankr. S.D. 13 B.R. 614 (1981)]

7. The Fair Credit Reporting Act is a federal law designed to stop the reporting of obsolete credit information used in obtaining jobs, insurance, or consumer credit. In one case brought under this act, Mr. Fite, a youth, had been convicted in 1972 in federal court of stealing government property. He was sentenced under the Youth Corrections Act, a federal law. The sentence was suspended, and he was put on one year's probation. Before the year was up Mr. Fite was unconditionally discharged and his conviction was automatically set aside. In August 1973, Mr. Fite was hired as an insurance salesman. His employer obtained a credit report from the Retail Credit Company that fairly and accurately reported Mr. Fite's arrest, conviction, and the setting aside of the conviction. He lost his job. He then tried to obtain a court order under the Fair Credit Reporting Act stopping the Retail Credit Company from reporting his arrest, conviction, and its setting aside to its customers and from maintaining any record of such facts. What was the result? [*Fite v. Retail Credit Company*, 386 F.Supp. 1045 (D. Mont. 1975)]
8. Sharpstown Dodge, Inc. sold Thornhill a van. Thornhill financed the van through Chrysler Credit Corporation. The amount financed was $4,292.38. The finance charge was $1,403.26. The total was to be repaid in 42 monthly installments. Thornhill claimed (correctly) that Sharpstown and Chrysler charged him 42 cents too much interest (that is, one penny per month too much interest). Thornhill claimed he was entitled to recover a statutory forfeiture under Texas law because of the interest overcharge. What result? [*Thornhill v. Sharpstown Dodge Sales, Inc.*, 546 S.W.2d 151 (1976)]
9. On May 27, 1980, a salesman for City Home Service, a siding and home repair company, called on Arelenar and William James at their home in Canton, Mississippi. After giving his sales pitch for vinyl siding, the salesman completed some, but not all, blanks in an installment sales contract. The Jameses signed the contract despite its omissions and the fact that some handwritten parts could not be read. Two days later, the salesman returned with another contract. In it all blanks were filled in and readable. The Jameses signed this substitute contract covering the same siding purchase as the previous contract. After making two payments on the siding, the Jameses sued for penalties and to cut off the contract. They argued that the defects in the first contract violated the Truth-in-Lending Act. Specifically, the Jameses said the act requires contract terms to be disclosed when the contract is signed. City Home Service defended by saying the second contract signed two days later was part of one continuous deal (covering three days). City Home claimed the second contract cured any disclosure defects in the first contract. The district court agreed with City Home. The Jameses appealed. What result? [*James v. City Home Service, Inc.*, 712 F.2d 193 (5th Cir. 1983)]
10. Should a manufacturer be liable for the violation of a consumer protection regulation on the ground that the manufacturer failed to monitor the retailer's marketing practices? The parents of a two-year-old boy sued the manufacturer of a "lawn dart" made and distributed by Regent Sports Corporation under the name "Slider Jarts." The plaintiff, a little boy, was injured when the point of a lawn dart penetrated his skull and entered his brain when he walked away from his parents (unsupervised) and into the path of a lawn dart thrown by an eight-year-old girl. The dart was sold two days before this event by a

Walgreen Drug store. Plaintiffs charged Regent Sports Corporation with liability under the Consumer Product Safety Act for manufacturing and distributing a product labeled "hazardous" under federal regulations. What result? [*Aimone by Aimone v. Walgreen's Co.*, 601 F.Supp. 507 (E.D. Ill. 1985)]

Suggested Readings

Articles

ANDERSEN, "Good Faith in the Enforcement of Contracts," 73 *Iowa Law Review* 299 (1988).

BIXBY, "Judicial Interpretation of the Magnusen-Moss Warranty Act," 22 *American Business Law Journal* 125 (1984).

BURKHART, "Third-Party Defenses to Mortgages," 1998 *Brigham Young Law Review* 1003 (1998).

BURTON, "Good Faith in Articles 1 and 2 of the U.C.C.: The Practice View," 35 *William and Mary Law Review* 1533 (1994).

FISHER, "The Federal Exemption Scheme: Delayed Until 1983 for Ohio Bankrupts," 49 *University of Cincinnati Law Review* 791 (1980).

FOX, "New Hope for Harassed Consumers: The Federal Fair Debt Collection Practices Act," 18 *American Business Law Journal* 19 (1980).

GREEN, "Cipollone Revisited: A Not-So-Little Secret About the Scope of Cigarette Preemption," 82 *Iowa Law Review* 1257 (1997).

HARRELL and LUCAS, "Update on the Federal Debt Collection Practices Act," 45 *Business Lawyer* 2001 (1990).

HIGHSMITH and HAVENS, "Revocation of Acceptance and the Defective Automobile: The Uniform Commercial Code to the Rescue," 18 *American Business Law Journal* 303 (1980).

MAURER, "Common Law Defamation and the Fair Credit Reporting Act," 72 *Georgetown Law Journal* 95 (1983).

MEYERSON, "The Efficient Consumer Form Contract: Law and Economics Meets the Real World," 24 *Georgia Law Review* 583 (1990).

NOTE, "New York's Used Car Lemon Law: An Evaluation," 35 *Buffalo Law Review* 971 (1986).

TARANTINO, MCKAY, and RUSSO, "Unfair Trade Practices and Consumer Protection Acts: Do They Apply to the Practice of Law?" 23 *Suffolk U. L. Review* 249 (1989).

ZOLLERS, "The Power of the Consumer Product Safety Commission to Levy Civil Penalties," 22 *American Business Law Journal* 551 (1985).

MODULE

7

LAW AFFECTING THE MANUFACTURING DEPARTMENT

CHAPTER 23

PRODUCT LIABILITY

"THE 19TH CENTURY LAW OF PRODUCT LIABILITY, SUCH AS IT WAS, EMBODIED THE PRINCIPLE OF *CAVEAT EMPTOR*: 'LET THE BUYER BEWARE.' TODAY THIS PRINCIPLE STRIKES MANY AS INHUMANE. PERHAPS FOR THIS REASON, 20TH-CENTURY PRODUCT LIABILITY LAW EMBODIES THE OPPOSITE PRINCIPLE—*CAVEAT VENDITOR* OR 'LET THE SELLER BEWARE.' AS WE ARE INCREASINGLY LEARNING, HOWEVER, THIS ISN'T TOO WONDERFUL EITHER."

Anonymous

POSITIVE LAW ETHICAL PROBLEMS

Roberto Martinez knew perfectly well that is dangerous to try to put a 16-inch tire on a 16.5-inch rim. And even if he had not known, the prominent warning on the 16-inch Uniroyal Goodrich tire he was installing would have told him about the danger. Due to what may have been an understandable mistake, however, Martinez tried to install the 16-inch Uniroyal Goodrich tire on a 16.5-inch rim. As the warning predicted, the tire exploded when Martinez made the attempt, and he was injured.

Martinez then sued Uniroyal Goodrich for his injuries. His theory was that Goodrich could have designed the tire so as to avoid the risk he faced, and that its failure to do so made it liable. Goodrich responded by claiming, among other things, that its very conspicuous warning was sufficient to protect installers like Martinez, and should likewise protect it from liability. Who is right? That is, should the presence of an adequate warning be allowed to compensate for a less-than-safe design? Assume that a safer design was possible, and do not worry about any contributory fault on Martinez's part.

Product liability law determines when manufacturers and sellers of defective goods are civilly liable to purchasers of those goods or other parties harmed by the defect.[1] Although product liability often is regarded as a consumer matter, many product liability suits are brought by businesses against other businesses that sold them defective products. After sketching the historical evolution of product liability law, this chapter examines the most important **theories of product liability recovery**. These theories of recovery are legal rules stating the things a plaintiff must prove in order to recover damages from a seller of defective goods; sometimes plaintiffs employ several of these theories simultaneously. The chapter then discusses several legal problems that are common to the most important theories of recovery, but that often are resolved differently from theory to theory. We begin with theories of product liability recovery based on contract reasoning.

[1] Chapter 22 discusses some state and federal regulations that police various aspects of consumer transactions but do not involve the recovery of damages for defective goods.

CONTRACT THEORIES OF PRODUCT LIABILITY RECOVERY

Nineteenth-century contract law was highly individualistic. One example was freedom *of* contract—the parties' ability to set their own terms. Another was freedom *from* contract—a tendency to bind parties contractually only when they clearly expressed their willingness to be bound. For instance, sellers usually were bound only on those terms to which they had expressly assented. Indeed, some states made sellers contractually liable for defective goods only if they used words such as "warrant" or "guarantee" while describing those goods. Today things are quite different. Now sellers can be bound on the basis of implied promises about their goods—promises created not by words, but by operation of law. When this happens, government denies traditional freedom of contract by dictating contract terms. In addition, now it is much easier for sellers to be bound on express statements that they make. In fact, the range of things considered "express statements" has expanded considerably. For all these reasons, modern sellers are less "free from" contractual liability too.

Today, there are three important contract-based theories of product liability recovery. Each involves a product **warranty**: a promise regarding the nature of the product sold. In a breach-of-warranty suit, the plaintiff claims that the product failed to conform to the seller's promise. Today this promise may be express (made in words or in some behavior from which a verbal promise can be inferred) or implied (created by operation of law). Thus, we have an **express warranty** theory of recovery and two implied warranty theories—the **implied warranty of merchantability** and the **implied warranty of fitness for a particular purpose**.

Each of these three warranty theories is created by Article 2 of the Uniform Commercial Code (UCC, or Code). The UCC is a uniform act drafted by legal scholars and practitioners and eventually enacted in much the same form by the state legislatures. Article 2 of the Code governs the **sale of goods**; other transactions usually are controlled by the common law of contracts. Goods basically are movable things. Services and real estate do not qualify, although most kinds of farm products and other foodstuffs are regarded as goods. In determining whether a contract is for the sale of goods, various borderline situations arise. One problem concerns services in which goods play a role—for example, hair or beauty treatments, or the installation of an automobile battery. In such cases, the test for applying Article 2 is whether the good is the dominant part of the transaction. The installation of a car battery, for instance, probably is a sale of goods, but in the case of a hair or beauty treatment the service element probably predominates.

Express Warranty

The term *express warranty* usually means a warranty that the seller states in actual words, whether written or oral. The Code's express warranty provision, however, also includes certain conduct from which a verbal promise can be inferred. UCC section 2-313(1) says that a seller can create an express warranty by (1) making any affirmation of fact or promise regarding the goods sold, (2) making any description of such goods, or (3) providing a sample or model of such goods. A seller is liable for breach of express warranty when its products fail to conform to an affirmation, description, sample, or model it has made or given.

Affirmations and Descriptions. Any affirmation of fact or promise involving the goods can create an express warranty. For example, a seller who states or promises that a truck can or will handle a 5,000-pound load normally creates an express warranty to that effect. Closely related to this first means of creating an express warranty is the second: making a description of goods sold. A description includes statements that goods are of a certain brand, type, or model (e.g., that a vehicle is a "Toyota 4-Runner"); descriptive adjectives characterizing the product (e.g., "radial" tires); and drawings, blueprints, or technical specifications. Also, the statement in the following *Daughtrey* case probably is best classed as a description. Neither an express warranty by fact or promise nor an express warranty by description requires that the seller use such formal words as "warrant" or "guarantee." Also, each warranty can be either written or oral.

Although the line between the two groups is hazy, it is important to distinguish: (1) affirmations of fact or promise and descriptions from (2) statements of value or opinion and statements that amount to puffery or sales talk. Statements of the second kind are not express warranties. For example, a seller who represents a boat's value by telling the buyer that "You could resell this boat next year for $5,000" or who says "In my opinion, this boat will hold up for five years" normally is not liable if the statement turns out to be false. Similarly, sellers do not make express warranties when they say things like: "I know you'll be happy with this boat" or "Boats like this one have traditionally been known for quality." Also, as *Daughtrey* suggests, courts are more likely to conclude that an express warranty exists if the seller is knowledgeable about the goods sold and the buyer is not.

Samples and Models. The third way for a seller to create an express warranty is by giving a sample or model of the goods to be sold. A sample is an object taken from the actual collection of goods that the seller intends to sell, while a model is a replica offered for inspection when the actual goods are not available. Where either a sample or a model is given, there is an express warranty that the remaining goods conform to the sample or the model.

The Basis-of-the-Bargain Requirement. All three express warranties identified by section 2-313(1) must be "part of the basis of the bargain." The meaning of this phrase is unclear. Before enactment of the UCC, the buyer had to actually—and strongly—rely on the warranty in order to recover. Some courts still interpret the UCC's basis-of-the-bargain test as requiring some significant degree of reliance by the buyer. Others only require that the warranty be a factor in the buyer's decision to purchase. Presumably, this means some lesser degree of reliance than required by pre-Code law. The *Daughtrey* case does not require any reliance on the buyer's part; it seems to bind the seller to all statements that otherwise qualify as express warranties.

Advertisements and the Like. Statements in advertisements, catalogs, brochures, and so forth can be express warranties. But they may not be part of the basis of the bargain where it is unclear whether or how much the buyer relied on the statement in making the purchase—for example, where an ad appeared well before the sale. Also, advertisements often are filled with sales talk.

Daughtrey v. Ashe

Supreme Court of Virginia
413 S.E.2d 336 (1992)

Background and Facts:

W. Hayes Daughtrey contacted Sidney Ashe, a jeweler, about the purchase of a diamond bracelet for his wife. Ashe showed Daughtrey a diamond bracelet which he offered to sell for $15,000. His only description of the bracelet when talking to Daughtrey was to call it "nice." When Daughtrey later phoned Ashe to say that he would buy the bracelet, Ashe completed an appraisal form containing the following language:

DESCRIPTION	APPRAISED VALUE
platinum diamond bracelet, set with 28 brilliant full ct diamonds weighing a total of 10 carats. H color and v.v.s. quality	$25,000

The term v.v.s. is one of the highest quality ratings for diamonds.

Daughtrey eventually bought the bracelet. However, he never saw the appraisal form before the sale, because Ashe placed it inside the box containing the bracelet. Later, Daughtrey discovered that the diamonds in the bracelet were not of v.v.s. quality. He demanded that Ashe replace the bracelet with a bracelet containing diamonds of that quality, but Ashe only offered to refund the purchase price upon Daughtrey's return of the bracelet. Because diamonds had increased in value since the sale, Daughtrey refused. Instead he sued Ashe for breach of an alleged express warranty that the bracelet contained v.v.s. diamonds. The trial court denied Daughtrey's claim. Daughtrey appealed.

Body of Opinion

Justice Whiting

Ashe contends that his statement of the grade of the diamond is a mere opinion and thus cannot qualify as an express warranty.... However, here, Ashe did more than give a mere opinion of the value of the goods; he specially described them as diamonds of "H color and v.v.s. quality." Ashe did not qualify his statement as a mere opinion. And if one who has superior knowledge makes a statement about the goods sold and does not qualify the statement as his opinion, the statement will be treated as a statement of fact. Nor does it matter that the opinions of other jewelers varied in minor respects. All of them said, and the trial judge found, that the diamonds were of a grade substantially less than v.v.s. ... Given these considerations, we conclude that Ashe's description of the goods was more than his opinion; rather [it was] a statement of fact.

Next, Ashe maintains that because the description of the diamonds as v.v.s. quality was not discussed, Daughtrey could not have relied upon Ashe's warranty, and thus it cannot be treated as "part of the basis of the bargain." In our opinion, the "part of the basis of the bargain" language of UCC section 2-313 does not establish a buyer reliance requirement. Instead, this language makes a seller's description of the goods that is not his mere opinion a representation that defines the obligation.... We conclude from the language used in section 2-313 and the Official Comment thereto that the drafters of the Uniform Commercial Code intended to modify the traditional requirement of buyer reliance on express warranties.... We note that "induce" and "reliance" appear nowhere in section 2-313, as contrasted with the reference to buyer reliance in the subsequent section, UCC section 2-315, dealing with an implied warranty of fitness for a particular purpose....

Ashe introduced no evidence of any factor that would take his affirmation of quality out of the agreement. Therefore, his affirmation was a part of the basis of the bargain. Accordingly, we hold that Daughtrey is entitled to recover for his loss of bargain.

Judgment and Result

Trial court judgment in Ashe's favor reversed. Case returned to the trial court for a determination of Daughtrey's damages.

Questions

1. Why was Ashe not liable for his statement that the bracelet was "nice?"
2. According to the Virginia Supreme Court, what does the basis-of-the-bargain requirement mean?
3. Do you agree with the court's definition of the basis-of-the-bargain requirement and its application to this case? Why should Daughtrey be able to recover for breach of a promise on which he did not rely?

Implied Warranty of Merchantability

An implied warranty is a contractual promise arising by operation of law. Implied warranties represent government intervention to dictate the terms of a contract; they exist because the law says they exist. Implied warranties regarding the sale of goods have been created because legislatures and courts believe that consumers need additional legal protection against sellers with whom they cannot deal on equal terms. One important implied warranty in Article 2 of the UCC is the implied warranty of merchantability created by section 2-314. That section states that "a warranty that the goods shall be merchantable is implied in a contract for their sale if the seller is a merchant with respect to goods of that kind."

The Merchant Requirement. Note from the language just quoted that for the implied warranty of merchantability to exist, the seller must be a **merchant** rather than a casual, one-time seller. For our purposes, the term *merchant* includes two kinds of sellers. The first involves those who regularly deal in products of the kind at issue in the case. Drug stores, hardware stores, and car dealers are examples. Thus, a business law professor who sells a used car does not make the implied warranty of merchantability. The second kind of merchant includes people who regularly perform services involving the provision or installation of goods. Electricians, plumbers, carpenters, and heating supply contractors are examples.[2] In both cases, finally, the seller must be a merchant with respect to goods of the *kind sold*. For instance, section 2-314 does not cover the sale of a used car by a sporting goods store.

What Is Merchantability? If the seller is a merchant with respect to the goods sold, the seller's goods carry an implied warranty that they are merchantable. What qualities must the goods possess in order to meet this test? UCC section 2-314(2) states that such goods must at least (1) pass without objection in the trade under the contract description; (2) in the case of fungible goods, be of fair average quality; (3) be fit for the ordinary purposes for which such goods are used; (4) be of even kind, quality, and quantity within each unit (e.g., case, package, or carton) and among all such units; (5) be adequately contained, packaged, and labeled as the agreement may require; and (6) conform to any promises or affirmations of fact made on the container or label. The following *Keaton* case involves the third and fifth of these requirements.

The most important merchantability requirement is section 2-314's command that the goods be fit for the ordinary purposes for which such goods are used. This requirement often is interpreted to mean that the goods must meet the reasonable expectations of the average consumer. This type of broad, discretionary test is almost inevitable given the wide range of products sold today and the even wider range of defects they can present. As a result, implied warranty of merchantability cases often are decided on the basis of their particular facts.

Sometimes it is easy to determine whether goods satisfy the reasonable-consumer-expectation test. This is most true where they fail to perform properly or have harmful side effects in their ordinary uses. For example, an adhesive that fails to bind or that corrodes the things it touches is not merchantable. On the other hand, goods do not have to be perfect to be merchantable. In some cases, courts rely on prevailing industry practices or government health and safety regulations in formulating the merchantability standard. Finally, some courts, like the *Keaton* court following, say that there is no implied warranty of merchantability recovery for obvious or reasonably discoverable defects.

Other situations present more difficult problems. One such problem arises where the harm caused by the defect is improbable. In cases involving an allergic reaction to the product, for example, courts often find that there was a breach of the implied warranty of merchantability where it was reasonably foreseeable that an appreciable number of people would suffer the reaction. Another problem involves sales of contaminated food or drink. Here, different courts have applied different merchantability standards. Under the foreign-natural test, the plaintiff recovers when the thing causing the injury is foreign to the food product in question (e.g., an open safety pin in a serving of fish), but not when it is natural to the food product (e.g., a fishbone in a serving of fish). Today, however, most courts use the standard reasonable consumer expectations test in this situation.

---

[2] However, note that the problem of Article 2's application to mingled goods/services situations may arise here.

Keaton v. A.B.C. Drug Co.

Georgia Supreme Court
467 S.E.2d 558 (1996)

Background and Facts:

Marilyn Keaton entered an A.B.C. Drug Company (ABC) store to buy laundry detergent and liquid bleach. After picking up some detergent, she proceeded to the bleach aisle, where bottles of bleach were stacked to a height above her eye level. Keaton reached up, grasped the handle of a half-gallon bottle of bleach, and began pulling it down from the shelf. As she did so, bleach splashed onto her face, causing injury to one of her eyes. The cause of the injury was a loose cap on the bottle. Keaton did not see that the cap was loose.

Keaton sued ABC under the implied warranty of merchantability in a Georgia trial court. After the jury found in her favor, the trial court denied ABC's motion for judgment notwithstanding the verdict. However, a Georgia intermediate court of appeals reversed the trial court's decision. Keaton then appealed to the Georgia Supreme Court.

Body of Opinion

Chief Justice Benham

Keaton alleged a claim of breach of implied warranty under [UCC section 2-314(2)(c)], asserting that the bleach container was not fit for the ordinary purposes for which it was intended. There was evidence presented at trial regarding the elements required to prove a claim under subsection (c), but also regarding the elements required to prove a claim under subsection (e), which provides a claim for breach of implied warranty if a product is defective via its container or packaging. We conclude that the jury was authorized to find that ABC, as a merchant of bleach, was required to adequately contain and package the bleach that it sold. Because bleach which spills via a loose cap is not adequately contained or packaged, a claim under subsection (e) is supported. Because we hold that the evidence presented at trial supported a claim under subsection (e), under the right-for-any-reason theory, it is unnecessary for us to review the claim under subsection (c).

Contrary to ABC's contentions, Keaton's claim . . . is not defeated by virtue of an alleged lack of privity. . . . [T]aking possession of merchandise with the intent to purchase it establishes such privity. . . . Keaton's actions of grasping the product and beginning to take the product from the shelf with the intent to purchase it sufficiently constituted possession of the product, establishing privity between Keaton and ABC.

Keaton's claim . . . is not defeated by an alleged failure to exercise care for her own safety. . . . The [Georgia] Court of Appeals has held that the law of implied warranty will not avail against patent defects, nor against latent defects which are either disclosed or are discoverable by the exercise of caution on the part of the purchaser. [But] the bleach in this case was located at a height above Keaton's eye level, and it is undisputed that the top was not off [and that there was nothing] noticeably wrong with the bottle. Therefore, there was no patent or obvious defect. It was a jury question whether Keaton failed to exercise caution for her own safety.

Judgment and Result

Intermediate appellate court decision reversed; Keaton wins.

Questions

1. What would the result have been if Keaton had seen the loose bottle cap? What result if she should have seen it?
2. Which two merchantability definitions did the court consider here? On which did it base its decision? Did the court say that Keaton could not recover under the version it rejected?
3. For Article 2 of the UCC to apply, a *sale* of goods must occur. How did the court deal—or try to deal—with this problem here? Are you persuaded?

Implied Warranty of Fitness

UCC section 2-315 provides that "[w]here the seller at the time of contracting has reason to know any particular purpose for which the goods are required and that the buyer is relying on the seller's skill or judgment to select suitable goods, there is . . . an implied warranty that the goods shall be fit for such purpose." Section 2-315 first requires that the seller have reason to know of the particular purpose for which the buyer desires the goods. In many 2-315 cases, the buyer clearly makes his needs known. But because the test is the seller's reason to know, the seller may be liable where the buyer's purpose is evident from the surrounding facts and circumstances even though it is not openly disclosed. Second, the seller must have reason to know that the buyer is relying on the seller's skill or judgment to select suitable goods. Third, a Code drafters' comment to section 2-315 states that the buyer must actually rely on the seller's skill or judgment. Once these tests are met, the goods then carry an implied warranty that they are fit for the buyer's particular purposes.

The last two requirements pose few problems where the buyer asks for a product that will perform in certain ways and declares that it is up to the seller to select such a product. However, they are difficult to satisfy where the buyer is more knowledgeable than the seller, insists upon a certain brand, submits specifications for the goods to be purchased, or actually selects them. As the following *Trans-Aire* case makes clear, recovery also is unlikely where the buyer conducts its own tests of the product and bases its purchase decision on those tests.

How does the implied warranty of fitness differ from the implied warranty of merchantability? For one thing, the seller must be a merchant for the implied warranty of merchantability to exist, but the implied warranty of fitness has no merchant requirement.. Secondly, the implied warranty of merchantability requires only that the goods be fit for their *ordinary* purposes, while the fitness warranty says that the goods must be fit for the buyer's *particular* purposes. For example, if a novice camper goes to a sporting goods store, requests a sleeping bag suitable for temperatures as low as -20° Fahrenheit, and is sold a bag perfectly suitable for normal use but not for the requested temperature, an implied warranty of fitness claim can be made, but not a claim based on the implied warranty of merchantability. However, if the sleeping bag is totally defective and thus worthless for any purpose, the plaintiff should be able to use both implied warranties. Finally, the implied warranty of fitness arises in a less common situation than the implied warranty of merchantability: basically, the case where the buyer has put himself in the seller's hands by making his needs known and requesting that the seller select suitable goods.

Trans-Aire International, Inc. v. Northern Adhesive Co.

U.S. Court of Appeals (Seventh Circuit)
882 F.2d 1254 (1989)

Background and Facts:

Trans-Aire International, Inc. converts automotive vans into recreational vehicles. As part of that process, Trans-Aire once used a 3M Company adhesive to fasten interior carpet and ceiling fabrics. After experiencing problems with the 3M adhesive, Trans-Aire contacted Northern Adhesive Company in an effort to obtain a replacement adhesive. Trans-Aire informed Northern of the purposes for which it needed an adhesive, but never requested a specific adhesive by name. In response, Northern sent several adhesive samples to Trans-Aire. It also told Trans-Aire that one of its adhesives, Adhesive 7448, was a "match" for the 3M product with which Trans-Aire had had problems.

Trans-Aire then tested the sample adhesives, but did so in a cool plant rather than the hot conditions under which the 3M product had failed. As a result of the testing, Trans-Aire determined that Adhesive 7448 was superior to its 3M counterpart. Thus, it ordered several shipments of Adhesive 7448 from Northern. Thereafter, Trans-Aire experienced the same problems with Adhesive 7448 that it had experienced with the 3M adhesive. For this reason, it sued Northern under the implied warranty of fitness for a particular purpose in federal district court. After dismissing portions of Trans-Aire's complaint, the district court granted Northern's motion for summary judgment on the remaining claims. Trans-Aire appealed.

Body of Opinion

Circuit Judge Kanne

[W]e hold that the district court correctly concluded that no warranty of fitness for a particular purpose existed. We agree with the district court that Trans-Aire cannot demonstrate that it relied upon Northern's skill or judgment in deciding to purchase Adhesive 7448, even assuming Northern knew of the purpose for which Trans-Aire needed the adhesive.

Trans-Aire's chief engineer, Fribley, expressly stated in a deposition that he did not rely upon Northern's skill or judgment when Trans-Aire decided to purchase Adhesive 7448. Trans-Aire asserts that Fribley was not authorized to, and did not, negotiate the purchase of Adhesive 7448; and therefore his testimony is not dispositive of the issue whether Trans-Aire relied upon Northern's judgment. However, Trans-Aire's President, Higgins, clearly did make the final purchase decision, and the record supports Northern's assertion that Higgins relied upon Fribley's recommendation. Furthermore, it is undisputed that Fribley's recommendation and Higgins's final decision were based upon the tests which Fribley conducted, not any express or implied representations made by Northern. We therefore must agree with the district court that Trans-Aire cannot demonstrate that an implied warranty of fitness for a particular purpose existed.

Judgment and Result

District court decision affirmed; Trans-Aire's suit fails.

Questions

1. Did Northern have reason to know the particular purpose for which Trans-Aire desired an adhesive?
2. Did Northern have reason to know that Trans-Aire was relying on its skill or judgment to select a suitable adhesive?

TORT THEORIES OF PRODUCT LIABILITY RECOVERY

Besides freedom of contract and limited liability, nineteenth-century economic individualism also had implications for tort law. The most important such implication was the principle of "no liability without fault." Like the contract tendencies discussed earlier, this meant limited liability for sellers of defective goods. Another reason for this limited liability, some say, was the perceived need to promote industrialization by protecting infant manufacturing industries. If such industries had been required to pay their way by compensating everyone injured by their products, the argument runs, their profitability would have been endangered, their survival imperiled, and the country's industrialization retarded.

By now, however, the industrial system's survival is not an issue and the old no-liability-without-fault mentality has bitten the dust. The most important example of this new mentality is the emergence of **strict liability**—liability without fault—in the product liability sphere. But there are other reasons for strict liability's emergence—reasons represented by the terms ***risk spreading*** and ***socialization of risk***. Imposing strict product liability on sellers and manufacturers helps protect consumers, but it also imposes additional costs on these businesses. As a result, they are required to pay more to self-insure or to purchase liability insurance. But if most competitors are in roughly the same boat, they can pass on these costs to consumers in the form of higher prices. Thus, the economic losses caused by defective goods are spread out or "socialized" by imposing those costs on the people who benefit from strict liability.

Negligence law has long been available to parties who sue for injuries and other losses caused by defective goods. Beginning mainly in the 1960s, however, negligence was supplemented by the emergence of strict product liability.[3] The most important version of strict product liability is the rule stated by section 402A of the *Restatement (Second) of Torts*.[4] Section 402A was promulgated by the American Law Institute in 1965, and adopted by many states thereafter. In 1998, the American Law Institute published a *Restatement (Third) of Torts—Products Liability*. The new *Restatement* apparently wishes to avoid traditional labels such as *negligence* and *strict liability*. Because

[3] Negligence and strict liability are discussed in Chapter 10.

[4] The *Restatements* are statements of common law (and occasionally statutory) rules authored by the American Law Institute, a body of distinguished legal scholars and practitioners. The *Restatements* are not legally binding by themselves, but they often influence courts. It is not uncommon for state courts to adopt *Restatement* rules within their states.

most states still adhere to negligence and section 402A, however, we discuss these traditional theories first. Then we examine the *Restatement (Third)*, which may represent the future evolution of product liability law.

Negligence

In product liability cases based on a seller's or manufacturer's alleged **negligence**, plaintiffs must prove a **breach of duty** on the defendant's part. A breach of duty normally means that the defendant failed to act as a reasonable person would have acted under the circumstances. In product liability cases, this most often happens where the defendant failed to (1) properly manufacture, package, or handle the goods, (2) make an adequate inspection of the goods, (3) provide an adequate warning of hazards associated with the goods, or (4) properly design the goods.

Improper Manufacture, Packaging, Handling, or Inspection. Negligence suits alleging the manufacturer's careless construction, handling, or inspection of the goods often pose problems for plaintiffs, because evidence of the breach usually is under the defendant's control. However, the doctrine of **res ipsa loquitur** discussed in Chapter 10 sometimes may help plaintiffs establish a breach of duty.

Cases alleging a wholesaler's or retailer's negligent failure to inspect involve different considerations. Most states hold that such intermediaries have no duty to inspect goods sold them by another party, unless they knew or had reason to know of defects in those goods. In addition, there generally is no duty to inspect where this would be unduly difficult, burdensome, or time-consuming. Unless a defect is obvious or virtually certain to occur, therefore, there is no duty to inspect a product that is packaged in a sealed container which is not to be opened before the sale.

However, where an intermediary is not merely a conduit for the goods but is actively involved in their preparation or installation, it is liable for a failure to spot defects that are reasonably discoverable from the preparation or installation work done. A car dealer, for example, may be liable for the failure to discover defects that are reasonably apparent from a test drive or a routine mechanical check of an automobile. Absent unusual circumstances, however, the dealer is not required to disassemble the car to see whether every component part is in proper condition.

Finally, where either manufacturers or intermediaries have a duty to inspect and a reasonably discoverable defect exists, other duties may arise. Depending on the circumstances, such defendants may be required to warn purchasers of the defect, to repair the product, or simply not to sell it.

Duty to Warn. Courts consider many factors when determining whether a seller or manufacturer has a duty to give buyers and users of its products a suitable warning of risks associated with those products. The first and most important is whether harm is foreseeable. Another is the severity of this foreseeable harm. Yet another is whether a warning is likely to be effective in reducing the risk of harm. A further factor is the burden that providing a warning imposes on the seller or manufacturer. Finally, courts often consider whether the buyer or user is likely to realize the danger. For this reason, there ordinarily is no duty to warn about obvious product dangers. A sporting goods store, for example, need not warn buyers that hunting knives are dangerously sharp.

A warning's suitability is decided on a case-by-case basis. This same is true for a related question: which parties must the seller warn? For example, is a drug manufacturer required to warn physicians, patients, or both? Finally, in two situations even a perfectly adequate and thoroughly communicated warning may not protect a seller from negligence liability. First, the warning may be of no avail if the seller could feasibly make the product safe for its foreseeable uses. Second, a warning may not protect a seller who markets a product that is extremely unsafe even with the warning.

Design Defects. Even if a product is manufactured according to specifications, it may pose an unacceptable risk of harm because of its faulty design. Thus, manufacturers generally have a duty to design their products so that they are safe for any reasonably foreseeable use. However, other factors besides the reasonable foreseeability of harm and the severity of that harm help determine the manufacturer's design duty. One factor working in the defendant's favor in design defect cases is the product's compliance with government product safety standards. Another is the design's similarity to the design of similar products in the industry at the time of the sale. Yet another is that the product embodies the contemporary state of the art (the state of existing scientific and technical knowledge). A further consideration benefitting manufacturers is the product's social utility. Defendants sometimes escape liability in situations where making the product safer would cause a significant reduction in its social value. In some cases of this kind, courts may consider the safety and effectiveness of alternative designs and the cost of safer designs.

Strict Liability

Strict liability is liability irrespective of fault. By now, some form of strict product liability has been adopted by most states. These states usually employ section 402A of the *Restatement (Second) of Torts*. Section 402A exemplifies the demise of the nineteenth-century principle of no liability without fault. Where sellers and manufacturers are able to pass on the costs section 402A imposes, it also facilitates risk-spreading or socialization of risk.

The Requirements of Section 402A. Section 402A states, "One who sells any product in a defective condition unreasonably dangerous to the user or consumer or to his property is subject to liability . . . if (a) the seller is engaged in the business of selling such a product, and (b) it is expected to and does reach the user or consumer without substantial change in the condition in which it is sold." This rule applies even though "the seller has exercised all possible care in the preparation and sale of his product." Thus, section 402A imposes strict liability on certain product sellers. If the section's tests are met, those sellers are liable no matter how careful their behavior, and plaintiffs need not prove a breach of duty.

However, section 402A applies only in certain circumstances. First, the seller must be engaged in the business of selling the product that harmed the plaintiff. This test resembles UCC section 2-314's merchant requirement. Thus, section 402A does not cover occasional sales by those not regularly selling the product as a business. A housewife's twice-a-year sales of home-grown vegetables or a used car dealer's sale of camping equipment, for instance, are not within section 402A. Second, the product must be one that is expected to reach the consumer without substantial change in its condition, and in fact does reach the consumer without undergoing any such change. This requirement protects sellers from liability where their products were substantially modified before reaching the plaintiff and the modification helped cause the plaintiff's injury.

The key problem under section 402A is determining whether the product was in a defective condition that made it unreasonably dangerous to the user or consumer or to his property. The defective condition requirement, which resembles UCC section 2-314's test of fitness for the goods' ordinary purposes, often is defined by the reasonable expectations of the average consumer. But for section 402A to apply the product also must be unreasonably dangerous, meaning that it must have some significant and unexpected capacity to cause personal injury or property damage. For instance, butter is not unreasonably dangerous because it contains cholesterol, but it would be so regarded if it is contaminated with lead. Due to the unreasonably dangerous requirement, section 402A covers a narrower range of product defects than the implied warranty of merchantability. A coffee maker that simply fails to operate should not create 402A liability, but a coffee maker that short-circuits and causes a fire probably would. However, some courts have dispensed with the unreasonably dangerous requirement, or blurred it together with the defective condition requirement in various ways. In the *Bredburg* case, however, the court followed section 402A's literal language.

Design Defects and Failure to Warn. Courts routinely allow failure-to-warn and design defect cases to be brought under section 402A. The factors considered in such cases resemble those considered in negligence cases involving an alleged failure to warn or defective design, even though section 402A is supposed to be a strict liability provision for which the defendant's fault is irrelevant.

Unavoidably Unsafe Products. Should strict liability apply where the defendant markets a product that is likely to harm a certain number of people, but that also does considerable good and that cannot be made safer without sacrificing that utility? Examples might include some of the drugs used to treat cancer or AIDS. In such cases, defendants may be able to use the "unavoidably unsafe product" defense set out in comment k to section 402A. Comment k says that such "unavoidably unsafe products," if properly prepared and accompanied by proper directions and warning, are not defective or unreasonably dangerous. Under the "learned intermediary" doctrine, drug manufacturers normally may rely on the prescribing physician to warn the ultimate consumer about the risks of a prescription drug.

Wholesalers and Retailers. Section 402A covers wholesalers, retailers, and other parties down the chain of distribution when they sell products that are unreasonably dangerous because of manufacturing defects, even if such parties were in no way at fault. However, some states protect such intermediaries by statute. Typically, such laws immunize them from liability if (1) the plaintiff can get state court jurisdiction over the responsible manufacturer; and (2) the manufacturer is neither insolvent nor likely to become so.

Bredburg v. PepsiCo, Inc.

Supreme Court of Iowa
551 N.W.2d 321 (1996)

Background and Facts:

After leaving Joyce's Food Land grocery store, Michael Bredburg proceeded to purchase one bottle of Diet Mountain Dew from a soft drink machine owned by Joyce's. Bredburg inserted change into the machine, and then pushed the Diet Mountain Dew button. After some delay, Bredburg testified, the following events transpired:

> I didn't see the bottle anywhere around so I . . . bent down and lifted up the thing and [saw] the bottle. . . . It had come down on its neck and was wedged into the left hand side of the machine, so then I reached in there and . . . pulled the bottle out. . . . I had the bottle [of Diet Mountain Dew] in my right hand by the neck. I put it in my left hand where it started to get fat and I turned around to walk over to the other machine. *It started slipping out, so I slid down on the bottle for a better grip . . . and caught it . . . and that's when it exploded.*

This alleged explosion caused severe and permanent injuries to Bredberg's left hand. The broken bottle was swept up and thrown away after this incident.

Bredburg sued, among others, PepsiCo, Inc. (PepsiCo) and Pepsi Cola General Bottlers, Inc. (Pepsi Cola) on strict liability grounds. PepsiCo owns the formula and trademarks associated with Diet Mountain Dew, and issues licenses to bottlers, such as Pepsi Cola, granting them the right to bottle and distribute Pepsi Cola products, such as Diet Mountain Dew. Pepsi Cola purchases Diet Mountain Dew concentrate from PepsiCo, and mixes, bottles, and sells the product to Pepsi customers. The bottler is required to mix the concentrate pursuant to a formula provided by PepsiCo. Decisions pertaining to container alternatives, such as returnable/nonreturnable containers, aluminum cans and plastic, are left to the bottler.

At trial, the defendants vigorously denied that the bottle had really exploded. Nonetheless, the jury found for Bredberg. Then the defendants moved for judgment notwithstanding the verdict. They argued that Bredberg did not present sufficient evidence that the bottle of Diet Mountain Dew was unreasonably dangerous or in a defective condition at the time it entered the stream of commerce. The trial court denied this motion, but an intermediate appellate court reversed this decision. Bredberg appealed to the Iowa Supreme Court.

Body of Opinion

Chief Justice McGivern

We review the district court's denial of a motion for judgment notwithstanding the verdict for correction of errors at law. Our only inquiry in assessing such a motion is to determine whether there is sufficient evidence to justify submitting the case to the jury. In making this assessment, . . . we view the evidence in the light most favorable to the party against whom the motion was made, taking into consideration every legitimate inference that may fairly and reasonably be made. The motion should be denied if there is substantial evidence to support each element of the plaintiff's claims. . . . Evidence is not made insubstantial merely because more than one conclusion can be reached by the evidence presented. Substantial evidence is that which a reasonable person would find adequate to reach a conclusion (in this case, that the bottle and/or Diet Mountain Dew were defective and unreasonably dangerous).

Plaintiff's case against PepsiCo and Pepsi Cola was rooted in strict liability, not negligence. Strict liability claims rooted in *Restatement (Second) of Torts* section 402A generally involve factual issues to be resolved by a jury or other trier of fact. PepsiCo and Pepsi Cola are in different positions concerning the production of Diet Mountain Dew. PepsiCo is the designer and licensor of the finished product. . . . Pepsi Cola, on the other hand, is a manufacturer, bottler, and distributor of the product claimed by plaintiff to be defective and unreasonably dangerous. PepsiCo and Pepsi Cola contend that plaintiff presented no proof that the bottle, Diet Mountain Dew concentrate, or Diet Mountain Dew final product were defective at the time they left defendants' individual control. After an examination of the record, the evidence appears sufficient for us to conclude that the Diet Mountain Dew concentrate here was not damaged by any extraneous force after delivery to Pepsi Cola. PepsiCo does not dispute plaintiff's claim that it shipped the Diet Mountain Dew concentrate to Pepsi Cola for mixing, filling, and distribution. Pepsi Cola does not dispute that it mixed the concentrate, bottled the product, and shipped the product to Joyce's Food Land, a retail customer, for sale and consumption. [With this issue resolved,] it was plaintiff's burden to prove by a preponderance of the evidence that defendants PepsiCo and Pepsi Cola were strictly liable for plaintiff's injuries because, among other things, the bottle and/or product were in a defective condition and were unreasonably dangerous at the time the products left the possession of each defendant.

Defective condition. In our view, plaintiff's testimony, . . . that the bottle exploded can be weighed by a jury as circumstantial evidence that the bottle and/or its contents were in a defective condition at the time they were placed into the stream of commerce. Assuming the bottle exploded, as we must in this case, it appears that either the bottle or the pressurized product inside was in a defective condition. Therefore, we conclude that plaintiff's evidence as to product defect generated a jury question as against both the designer (PepsiCo) and manufacturer (Pepsi Cola) of the allegedly defectiveproduct.

Unreasonably dangerous. In addition to showing product defect, plaintiff must also present substantial evidence that the product was unreasonably dangerous in order for plaintiff's strict liability claims against PepsiCo and Pepsi Cola to be submitted to the jury. Without hesitation, we believe an exploding bottle of Diet Mountain Dew is unreasonably dangerous as the defect which causes the explosion is not "one contemplated by the user or consumer which would be unreasonably dangerous to him in the normal and intended use or consumption thereof."

Defendants had every right to, and did, argue to the jury that the facts did not support plaintiff's strict liability claims, specifically that plaintiff did not prove that its products were either in a defective condition or unreasonably dangerous at the time they left defendants' possession. Plaintiff, however, met his burden to support his claims. Because we believe Bredberg presented substantial evidence on all of the strict liability elements, including the defective condition and unreasonably dangerous elements against both PepsiCo and Pepsi Cola, we believe a jury question was generated on the strict liability claims and the district court properly [denied] PepsiCo's and Pepsi Cola's motions for directed verdict and denied their post-trial motions for judgment notwithstanding the verdict.

Judgment and Result

The Supreme Court vacated the decision of the intermediate appellate court and affirmed the trial court's decision. Bredberg wins.

Questions

1. The jury in this case originally set Bredberg's damages at $112,134.70. Then it knocked that figure down to $56,067.35. Why do you think that it did so? Check out the section on product liability defenses later in this chapter.
2. Why were both defendants "seller[s] engaged in the business of selling such a product," as section 402A requires?
3. What was the Iowa Supreme Court really saying about the jury verdict? That it definitely was correct? Something else?

The *Restatement (Third)*

Section 1 of the *Restatement (Third): Product Liability* states its basic rule: "One engaged in the business of selling or otherwise distributing products who sells or distributes a defective product is subject to liability for harm to persons or property caused by the defect." Notice that, unlike section 402A, the *Restatement (Third)* does not require that the product be unreasonably dangerous. However, it resembles 402A by only covering manufacturers and commercial sellers who are engaged in the business of selling the kind of product that injured the plaintiff. Also like 402A, section 1 covers not only manufacturers but other sellers down the product's chain of distribution.

The *Restatement (Third)* has special rules governing sales of product components, prescription drugs, medical devices, food products, and used goods. But its most important specific rules come in its section 2, which elaborates on section 1 by defining the term *product defect*. Section two identifies three such defects:

1. *Manufacturing Defects*. A product contains a manufacturing defect when it departs from its intended design. Examples include products that fail to meet specifications because they are incorrectly assembled, physically flawed, or damaged. For liability to exist, the product must have been in such a condition when it left the defendant's hands.
2. *Inadequate Instructions or Warnings*. Liability for manufacturing defects is strict; it applies even though all possible care was exercised in the preparation of the product. Under the *Restatement (Third)*, however, liability for the other two kinds of product defects involves something more like negligence. *Restatement* section 2 says that a product is defective due to inadequate instructions or warnings when reasonable instructions or warnings could have reduced the product's foreseeable risks of harm, the seller failed to provide such instructions or warnings, and this omission made the product not reasonably safe. Here, manufacturers and sellers are only liable for reasonably foreseeable harms; they are not required to protect against every conceivable risk that their products might present. Most likely the other failure-to-warn factors discussed earlier apply under the *Restatement (Third)* as well. As also was true under negligence and 402A, there is no duty to warn about obvious and generally known risks. As before, finally, courts have to consider various factors and circumstances in determining both the reasonableness of the instructions or warnings, and the parties other than the immediate buyer who are entitled to such instructions or warnings.
3. *Design Defects*. According to the *Restatement (Third)*, a product is defective in design when the foreseeable risks of harm it poses could have been reduced or avoided by a reasonable alternative design, and the omission of the alternative design makes the product not reasonably safe. The plaintiff must prove that such a reasonable alternative was, or reasonably could have been, available at

the time of sale. How do courts determine whether an alternative design is reasonable and whether the product is unsafe without it? They consider and weigh a broad range of factors, most of which are stated in the following *Martinez* case. These factors resemble the factors used in design-defect cases under section 402A. As *Martinez* also makes clear, the *Restatement (Third)* takes the position that a warning does not substitute for the provision of a reasonably safe design.

Uniroyal Goodrich Tire Co. v. Martinez

Texas Supreme Court
977 S.W.2d 328 (1998)

Background and Facts:

Roberto Martinez was injured while installing a Uniroyal Goodrich tire on a motor vehicle. The injury occurred when the 16-inch tire exploded while Martinez was attempting to mount it on a 16.5-inch rim. He made the attempt despite the presence of a prominent warning label on the tire. The warning specifically stated that one should never mount a 16-inch tire on a 16.5-inch rim, and that doing so could cause severe injury or death because the tire would explode.

Martinez sued Goodrich under strict liability in a Texas trial court. His theory was not that the warning was inadequate, but rather that the exploding tire was defective because Goodrich had failed to use a safer alternative bead design that would have kept it from exploding. The jury found for Martinez, awarding him $5.5 million in actual damages and $11.5 million in punitive damages. After reducing the punitive damages award pursuant to a settlement agreement between the parties, the trial judge awarded Martinez about $10.3 million. A Texas appeals court upheld the trial court's award of actual damages, but reversed its punitive damages award. Goodrich appealed to the Texas Supreme Court.

Body of Opinion

Chief Justice Phillips

We must decide whether a manufacturer who knew of a safer alternative product design is liable in strict products liability for injuries caused by the use of its product that the user could have avoided by following the product's warnings....

This court has adopted the products liability standard set forth in section 402A of the *Restatement (Second) of Torts*. . . . To prove a design defect, a claimant must establish, among other things, that the defendant could have provided a safer alternative design. Implicit in this holding is that the safer alternative design must be reasonable, i.e., that it can be implemented without destroying the utility of the product. The newly released *Restatement (Third) of Torts: Product Liability* carries forward this focus on reasonable alternative design. . . . To determine whether a reasonable alternative design exists, and if so whether its omission renders the product unreasonably dangerous (or, in the words of the new *Restatement*, not reasonably safe), the finder of fact may weigh various factors bearing on the risk and utility of the product. One of these factors is whether the product contains suitable warnings and instructions. The new *Restatement* likewise carries forward this approach:

> A broad range of factors may be considered in determining whether an alternative design is reasonable and whether its omission renders a product not reasonably safe. The factors include, among others, the magnitude and probability of the foreseeable risks of harm, the instructions and warnings accompanying the product, and the nature and strength of consumer expectations regarding the product, including expectations arising from product portrayal and marketing. . . . The relative advantages and disadvantages of the product as designed and as it alternatively could have been designed may also be considered. Thus, the likely effects of the alternative design on production costs; the effects of the alternative design on product longevity, maintenance, repair, and aesthetics; and the range of consumer choice among products are factors that may be taken into account. . . .

Goodrich urges this court to depart from this standard by following certain language from comment j of the *Restatement (Second) of Torts*. Comment j provides in part: "Where warning is given, the seller may reasonably assume that it will be read and heeded; and a product bearing such a warning, which is safe for use if it is followed, is not in defective condition, not is it unreasonably dangerous." The new *Restatement*, however, expressly rejects the comment j approach. . . . "[I]nstructions and warnings may be ineffective because users of the product may not be adequately reached, may be likely to be inattentive, or may be insufficiently motivated to follow the instructions or heed the warnings. However, when an alternative design to avoid risks cannot reasonably be implemented, adequate instructions and warnings will normally be sufficient to render the product reasonably safe. Warnings are not, however, a substitute for the provision of a reasonably safe design."

Goodrich argues that . . . it is still entitled to judgment as a matter of law because no safer alternative was available. In response, Martinez points to the evidence that Goodrich's competitors, and eventually Goodrich itself, adopted [a safer tire bead design]. Goodrich counters that this alternative design is not in fact safer because if the tire is matched to the wrong rim size, the bead will never seat on the rim and it will inevitably explode during use. . . . Martinez, however, offered some evidence that his alternative design not only would have prevented the injury, but also that it would not have introduced other dangers of equal or greater magnitude. . . . [The] evidence does not conclusively prove that the [new design] would have introduced into the product other dangers of equal or greater magnitude. There was thus an issue of fact regarding whether a reasonable alternative design existed, which the jury resolved in favor of Martinez.

Judgment and Result

The Texas Supreme Court affirmed the decision of the intermediate appellate court. Martinez wins.

Questions

1. Why did the court hold that a suitable warning cannot insulate the defendant from liability where a better alternative design is available?
2. Did the court hold that the presence or absence of a suitable warning is irrelevant to determining liability in design-defect cases?
3. Should this case be taken as holding that manufacturers must adopt the safest possible design, no matter what the cost?
4. Due in part to extenuating circumstances not presented here, the Texas Supreme Court also rejected Goodrich's contention that Martinez was guilty of contributory negligence. But suppose that Martinez actually was contributorily negligent. Would his negligence necessarily have defeated his claim? See the section on defenses toward the end of this chapter.

Figure 23.1 provides a summary of the major product liability theories and their characteristics.

FIGURE 23.1 The Major Product Liability Theories Compared

Theory	Tort or Contract?	Type of Defendant	Nature of Product
Express warranty	Contract	Seller of goods	Not as expressly warranted
Implied warranty of merchantability	Contract	Merchant for goods sold	Most often, not fit for ordinary purposes for which such goods used
Implied warranty of fitness	Contract	Seller of goods	Not fit for buyer's particular purposes
Negligence	Tort	Seller of goods	Defective due to seller's failure to behave like reasonable person in manufacturing, inspecting, designing, and giving warnings about the product
Section 402A	Tort	Seller engaged in business of selling product sold	Defective and unreasonably dangerous
Restatement (Third)	Tort	One engaged in the business of selling product	Defective

OTHER THEORIES OF PRODUCT LIABILITY RECOVERY

The Magnuson-Moss Act

Look for the FTC regulations accompanying the Magnuson-Moss Act at ***http://www.ftc.gov***

The federal Magnuson-Moss Warranty Act of 1975 contains many consumer protection provisions. Here, we focus on the act's provisions concerning warranty liability for sellers. Other portions of the act impose requirements regarding the full, fair, timely, and conspicuous disclosure of warranty terms to consumers.

The Magnuson-Moss Act says that where sellers of a consumer product costing more than $10 per item give a written warranty covering that product, they must designate the warranty as either full or limited. A consumer product is tangible personal property normally used for personal, family, or household purposes. Sellers who give a *full warranty* must (1) obligate themselves to remedy or repair the product in case of a defect, and (2) enable the consumer to obtain either a replacement product or a refund of the purchase price after a reasonable number of unsuccessful attempts to remedy the defect. Any other written warranty given by a seller of consumer products costing more than $10 per item should be designated as a limited warranty. In this case, sellers are only bound to whatever they promise in the warranty. Note that nothing in the act requires that sellers give a written warranty, and that sellers can avoid the previous requirements simply by not giving such a warranty.

Misrepresentation

Product liability law has long allowed consumers and other parties to recover for misrepresentations made by sellers of products they buy. Section 9 of the *Restatement (Third)* continues this tradition. Its rule applies only to merchant-like sellers engaged in the business of selling or otherwise distributing the product in question. The section includes fraudulent, negligent, or innocent misrepresentations made by such sellers. The misrepresentation must involve a material fact concerning the product—a fact that would matter to a reasonable buyer. Thus, inconsequential misstatements, sales talk, and statements of opinion do not create liability. However, section 9 does not require that the product be defective. Unlike past law, moreover, section 9 does not require that the misrepresentation be made to the public, or that the plaintiff have justifiably relied upon it. However, the misrepresentation must have caused the plaintiff to suffer personal injury or property damage.

INDUSTRYWIDE LIABILITY

All the product liability theories just discussed require that the product defect cause the injury or other loss the plaintiff has suffered. However, some courts have dispensed with this causation requirement in certain cases. In doing so, they have held defendants liable where it is unclear whether they manufactured the specific product that caused the plaintiff's injury. This liability has occurred where the plaintiff was injured by a standardized product manufactured by many firms and is unable to prove which of several possible defendants actually was responsible for the injury. Several cases of this sort have involved DES, an anti-miscarriage drug causing various delayed diseases in the daughters of women to whom it was administered. A similar approach has been used in some decisions involving claims based on long-term exposure to asbestos.

In such cases, the courts in question apportion liability among the firms in the industry that might have produced the product that harmed the plaintiff, usually on the basis of market share. These courts often differ on the legal rationales for their decisions, and on many other more specific points. However, some courts considering the question have followed traditional causation rules and have rejected this whole approach to the problem. In such states, a plaintiff generally must prove that a particular defendant's product caused the harm of which she complains.

DAMAGES

At this point in the chapter, we shift our focus from the theories of product liability recovery to some important problems that cut across the theories, and that may be resolved differently from theory to theory. These problems often are important factors in determining whether a plaintiff will recover. The following discussion only considers how these problems affect the six most important theories of recovery already discussed.

One of the most important considerations affecting a plaintiff's choice of a product liability theory is the type(s) of damages that can be recovered under that theory. In addressing this question, we first consider the kinds of damages that might be recoverable in the normal product liability case. Then we consider which such damages can be obtained under each of the six major theories of recovery. After that, the text briefly examines some recent statutory measures reducing the damages plaintiffs can recover.

The Types of Damages

The damages a plaintiff might recover in a product liability case break down into three general categories, one of which has several subcategories. It is possible for a single product liability suit to involve all these types of damages. The general categories are:

1. *Basis-of-the-Bargain Damages* (also called direct economic loss or harm to the product itself). These damages compensate buyers for the "lost" or "missing" value of defective goods. They are measured by the value of the goods as contracted for (generally the value as warranted, the sale price, or some reasonably anticipated value), minus the value of the goods as received.
2. *Consequential Damages*. These damages comprise various harms that result from a product defect, but that are more remote from the defect than basis-of-the-bargain damages. Consequential damages include **personal injury**, **property damage**, and **indirect economic loss**. Personal injury most often means bodily harm of some kind. Often included under the personal injury heading are losses attributable to pain and suffering, mental distress, inconvenience, loss of companionship and consortium, injury to reputation, lost earnings, and so forth. Property damage is damage to property of the plaintiff other than the defective product that she purchased. As its name suggests, indirect economic loss covers a wide range of economic harms resulting from the product defect. Uusally these harms are business losses of some kind. Examples include lost profits and loss of business goodwill.
3. *Punitive Damages*. Punitive damages are not awarded to compensate plaintiffs for harm they have suffered. Instead, they are imposed as an extra penalty for especially bad behavior by the defendant, and as a deterrent to such behavior by the

defendant and by others. The behavior justifying a punitive damages award usually involves an intentional or reckless disregard for the safety of those likely to be affected by the goods. Examples include concealing known product dangers, consciously violating government or industry product safety standards, and maintaining grossly inadequate testing or quality control procedures.

Damages under the UCC

Because they traditionally have been unavailable in contract cases, punitive damages usually cannot be obtained in express and implied warranty suits. Determining the other damages to which successful warranty plaintiffs are entitled, however, can be a complex matter. An important factor affecting this question is whether there was **privity of contract**—a direct contractual relationship—between the plaintiff and the defendant.

Plaintiffs who dealt directly with—who are "in privity" with—the defendant collect basis-of-the-bargain damages. In addition, such plaintiffs can recover the various types of consequential damages if certain tests are met. UCC section 2-715(2)(b) allows a buyer to recover for personal injury and property damage proximately resulting from his seller's breach of warranty. Although the Code does not define the term *proximately*, it probably refers to personal injury or property damage that is a reasonably foreseeable consequence of the breach. Section 2-715(2)(a)'s test for recovery of indirect economic loss is the seller's reason to know about the buyer's needs and requirements for the goods. For example, if a seller is familiar with his buyer's business and thus has reason to know how goods sold to the buyer will be used, the seller should be liable for indirect economic loss caused by defects in those goods.

What happens when there is no privity of contract between plaintiff and defendant? As you will see in the next section, plaintiffs who did not deal directly with the defendant sometimes cannot recover anything at all under the UCC. Even where such plaintiffs can recover, moreover, the types of damages available to them are limited. In general, such plaintiffs are (1) quite likely to recover for personal injury, (2) fairly likely to recover for property damage, (3) unlikely to recover basis-of-the-bargain damages, and (4) quite unlikely to recover indirect economic loss.

Tort Damages

As the following *Alloway* case suggests, tort theories are best suited for obtaining personal injury, property damage, and (where appropriate) punitive damages. These theories are fairly poor vehicles for recovering indirect economic loss and basis-of-the-bargain damages. Despite a few differences, negligence law, section 402A, and the *Restatement (Third)* generally speak with the same voice on these questions.

Tort Reform Measures

The policies of risk spreading and socialization of risk discussed earlier have not been trouble-free. Over the past 20-odd years, many have claimed that there is a crisis in the tort system generally, and in product liability law particularly. Attention has centered on the greater ease with which plaintiffs have been able to recover, and the increasing recoveries they have received. The resulting economic burden on sellers and manufacturers, it is claimed, makes it more difficult and more expensive for them to obtain liability insurance. Firms that cannot obtain insurance and that cannot self-insure might be wiped out by a single huge product liability judgment. For those who can get insurance, its greater costs have become increasingly difficult to pass on. Where these costs can be passed on, consumers have less money to spend. Consumers may also suffer as manufacturers fearful of massive product liability suits are deterred from worthwhile product innovations.

The preceding scenario has not persuaded everyone. For example, some people have blamed the increase in insurance premiums on the industry itself. Still, perceptions like those just described have created a so-called tort reform movement. Its aim is to scale back the explosion in product liability and thus to reduce the economic pressure on firms and their insurers. To date, the movement has not had a big impact on product liability law. In particular, none of the many federal product liability reform measures has passed Congress.

The states, however, have been more active as reformers. Most of their tort reform measures have tried to scale back damage recoveries. For example, some states have limited recoveries for noneconomic loss, most often by putting a definite dollar cap (e.g., $250,000 or $500,000) on such recoveries. Also, many states restrict punitive damage recoveries in various ways. They may do so by capping punitive damages at some definite dollar figure (e.g., $250,000), or at some multiple of the plaintiff's compensatory damages (e.g., three times compensatory damages). Some states also bifurcate, or separate, the procedure for determining whether to award punitive damages and the procedure for determining their amount.

Alloway v. General Marine Industries

Supreme Court of New Jersey
695 A.2d 264 (1997)

Background and Facts:

In July of 1990, Samuel Alloway purchased a new 33-foot Century Grande XL boat from the Mullica River Boat Basin, which in turn had purchased it from General Marine Industries (GMI). The cost was $61,070. Due to a defective seam in the boat's swimming platform, it sank three months later while docked at a marina. After Alloway paid $2,490 of the $2,500 deductible under his insurance policy, the insurer spent an additional $40,106.63 to repair the boat.

Then, Alloway sued Mullica and GMI under various theories. He eventually assigned most of those claims to his insurer. But he retained tort claims against GMI for the $2,490 and for the difference between the boat's $62,070 purchase price and the boat's market value in its defective condition. A New Jersey trial court granted GMI's motion to dismiss for failure to state a claim, but an intermediate appellate court reversed. An appeal to the New Jersey Supreme Court followed.

Body of Opinion

Justice Pollock

The issue is whether the plaintiff may rely on theories of strict liability and negligence to recover damages for economic loss resulting from a defect that caused injury only to the boat itself.... The question reduces to whether plaintiff may use tort theories to recover the lost benefit of [his] bargain from [GMI]....

Allocation of economic loss between a manufacturer and a consumer involves assessment of tort and contract principles in the determination of claims arising out of the manufacture, distribution, and sale of defective products. Generally speaking, tort principles are better suited to resolve claims for personal injuries or damage to other property. Contract principles more readily respond to claims for economic loss caused by damage to the product itself. Various considerations support the distinction. Tort principles more adequately address the creation of an unreasonable risk of harm when a person or other property sustains accidental or unexpected injury. When, however, a product fails to fulfill a purchaser's economic expectations, contract principles, particularly as implemented by the UCC, provide a more appropriate analytical framework. Implicit in the distinction is the doctrine that a tort duty of care protects against the risk of accidental harm and a contractual duty preserves the satisfaction of consensual obligations....

By enacting the UCC, the legislature adopted a comprehensive system for compensating consumers for economic loss arising from the purchase of defective products. The UCC represents the legislature's attempt to strike the proper balance in the allocation of the risk of loss between manufacturers and purchasers for economic loss arising from injury to a defective product. Consequently, the UCC provides for express warranties regarding the quality of goods, as well as an implied warranty of merchantability and an implied warranty of fitness for a particular purpose. When a seller delivers goods that are not as warranted, the buyer may recover the difference between the value of the defective goods and their value if they had been as warranted....

The vast majority of courts across the country have concluded that purchasers of personal property, whether commercial entities or consumers, should be limited to [economic loss] recovery under contract principles.... Scholars likewise have criticized the extension of strict liability to include claims for purely economic loss.... Following the majority rule, the American Law Institute's proposed *Restatement (Third) of Torts: Products Liability* defines economic loss to exclude recovery under tort theories for damage to a product itself....

In addition to the right to recover under the UCC, victims of fraud or unconscionable conduct possess substantial rights to recover for common-law fraud or for violations of various state and federal statutes. The UCC expressly provides that "unless displaced by the particular provisions of this Act, the principles of law and equity, including the law merchant and the law relative to capacity to contract, principal and agent, estoppel, fraud, misrepresentation, duress, coercion, mistake, bankruptcy or other validating or invalidating cause shall supplement its provisions."... Additionally, the legislature has adopted the Consumer Fraud Act, which provides generous protection to defrauded consumers.... Another [New Jersey] statute, the Truth-In-Consumer Contract, Warranty and Notice Act protects consumers by requiring that consumer contracts be clearly written and understandable.... Congress has provided further protection for consumers. For example, the Magnuson-Moss Warranty Act... offers consumers a basis in federal law for recovering damages.... In sum, judicial decisions and statutory enactments, including the UCC, protect consumers from overreaching. Against this background, a tort cause of action for economic loss duplicating the one provided by the UCC is superfluous and counterproductive....

Over thirty years ago, before the adoption of the UCC, this court, concerned about the ability of consumers to reach remote parties in a chain of distribution, perceived the need to provide those consumers with a tort action. In the interim, the UCC has taken effect.... Under the UCC, as construed by this court, moreover, the absence of privity no longer bars a buyer from reaching through the chain of distribution to the manufacturer.

Judgment and Result

Intermediate appellate court decision reversed; trial court decision dismissing Alloway's claims reinstated. Alloway cannot recover in tort for economic loss.

Questions

1. Of the types of damages discussed in the text, which one is Alloway pursuing in this case?
2. Suppose that when the boat sank, damaged along with it was a new $3,000 computer that Alloway planned to use in his home. Does the New Jersey Supreme Court's opinion rule on this particular loss?
3. What is the significance of the court's reference to privity in the last paragraph of the decision? *Hint*: Is it easier to recover outside privity under the UCC or under tort theories? Check the next section of this chapter.

WHO CAN RECOVER AGAINST WHOM? THE NO-PRIVITY DEFENSE

Yet another manifestation of the individualism that underlay much nineteenth-century law was the traditional rule of no liability outside privity of contract. **Privity of contract** is the existence of a direct contractual relationship between two parties. The attitude underlying the rule was that manufacturers and sellers only had duties toward the parties with whom they directly dealt, and not remote parties down the product's chain of distribution. The traditional rule may also have reflected the perceived need to protect infant manufacturing industries. Manufacturers obtained such protection because under the no-privity rule, plaintiffs injured by defective goods had to sue their immediate seller, with suits proceeding up the chain of distribution until they reached the guilty manufacturer. In part because the various intermediaries may have been relatively blameless, manufacturers sometimes could escape liability for the consequences of their defective products.

Over the past century, the old no-privity defense has lost most of its importance in the product liability area. Among the reasons for its decline are the increased feelings of interdependence that have replaced traditional economic individualism, the achievement of a viable industrial order, and the emergence of longer and longer chains of distribution marked by greater and greater distances between injured plaintiffs and the party that caused their injuries. Despite its diminished importance, however, the old no-privity rule still retains some influence, especially in cases arising under the UCC. Our discussion of the rule's contemporary impact uses the illustrative chain of distribution in Figure 23.2. Suits between parties in the normal contractual chain of distribution (e.g., consumer-wholesaler) often are described as involving vertical privity. Suits between a party who is not part of this contractual chain (e.g., a family member or bystander) and one who has sold the goods (e.g., a retailer) often are said to involve horizontal privity.

Privity under the UCC

The effect of the no-liability-outside-privity defense in cases brought under the Uniform Commercial Code is a confused subject. The first part of the discussion focuses on three versions of the provision (UCC section 2-318) that are supposed to govern this question. Then, it describes the factors that often influence courts when they decide whether the plaintiff can recover against a remote defendant under the UCC.

Most states' versions of section 2-318 can be found at ***http://www.law.cornell.edu***

http://

UCC section 2-318 comes in three alternative versions from which the states can choose. Alternative A extends the seller's express or implied warranty to any natural person who is in the family or household of his (the seller's) buyer or who is a guest in the buyer's home, if it is reasonable to expect that such a person would use, consume,

FIGURE 23.2 A Hypothetical Chain of Distribution

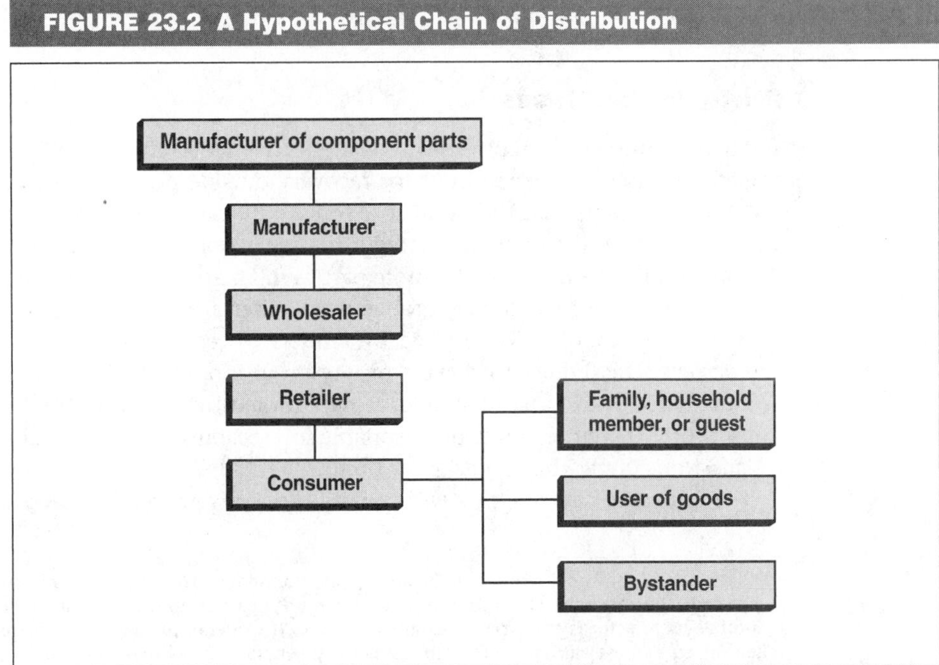

or be affected by the goods and if that person suffers personal injury from a breach of the warranty. Alternative A does not significantly extend the seller's liability to parties outside privity of contract. In Figure 23.2, for example, its only real impact is to raise the possibility that a family or household member or a guest may be able to sue the retailer for personal injury.[5]

Alternatives B and C go much further. Alternative B extends the seller's express or implied warranty to any natural person who may be reasonably expected to use, consume, or be affected by the goods and who suffers personal injury from a breach of the warranty. Alternative C is much the same, but it allows recovery by any person (not just natural persons) who is "injured" (not just injured in person) by the breach. In an appropriate case, liability under Alternatives B and C might extend from the component parts manufacturer to the bystander in Figure 23.2.

The literal language of section 2-318's three alternatives is not much of a guide to the courts' behavior in UCC cases where privity is absent. Alternatives B and C obviously are flexible on their face. And while Alternative A is fairly precise, a Code drafters' comment to section 2-318 suggests that the courts are free to extend the seller's liability beyond Alternative A's explicit limits. To add to the confusion, some states have departed from section 2-318 by adopting their own privity provisions.

Among the states as a whole, therefore, considerable uncertainty exists regarding the UCC plaintiff's ability to recover outside privity. Several factors, however, make such recovery more or less likely.[6] The first such factor, one suggested by the "reasonable to expect" language of section 2-318, is the reasonable foreseeability that a party like the plaintiff would suffer harm from the product defect in question. The second factor is suggested by the "natural person" language of Alternatives A and B. This factor is the status of the plaintiff. On the whole, ordinary consumers stand a better chance of recovering outside privity than do business concerns. The third factor is the type of damages the plaintiff has suffered. This factor was discussed in the preceding section. To review, a UCC plaintiff who lacks privity of contract with the defendant is most likely to recover for personal injury and property damage, in that order. However, recoveries for basis-of-the-bargain damages are infrequent and recoveries for indirect economic loss rare.

Privity in Tort Cases

Today the no-privity defense usually is ineffective when the plaintiff sues in tort. In negligence cases, the general test for recovery outside privity is whether it was reasonably foreseeable that the product defect would cause harm of the sort suffered to a plaintiff of the sort injured. Although the results of this test vary with the facts of the case, it allows suits against remote parties in an appropriate situation. Only rarely does section 402A pose privity problems of either a horizontal or a vertical nature. Indeed, many courts have allowed bystanders to recover under section 402A. The *Restatement (Third)* does not have a privity provision, but it does say that whether a product defect caused harm should be determined by the prevailing rules on causation in tort. Therefore, a test of reasonable foreseeability should usually govern privity questions under the *Restatement (Third)*.

The following case grapples with privity problems under UCC section 2-318.

---

[5] Of course, the consumer also would be able to sue the retailer. Under a literal reading of Alternative A, however, the consumer would not be able to sue other parties up the vertical chain of distribution.

[6] Another such factor is the type of warranty at issue. In general, plaintiffs outside privity who have relied on an express warranty made to them by advertising, brochures, and so forth have a better chance of recovery than implied warranty plaintiffs.

Minnesota Mining & Manufacturing Co. v. Nishika, Ltd.

Supreme Court of Minnesota
565 N.W.2d 16 (1997)

Background and Facts:

James Bainbridge and Daniel Fingarette [the claimants] established a plan for a three-dimensional photography business through four independent companies. In January 1988, Bainbridge met with officials of the Minnesota Mining & Manufacturing Company (3M) to seek assistance with the three-dimensional film development process. Bainbridge testified that he told 3M all about his planned business, including his need for quality emulsion and backcoat sauce to process the film. In mid-1989, 3M formulated a new emulsion that it claimed would work well with the film development process. 3M apparently understood that this emulsion would be used in combination with a backcoat sauce that 3M had also developed.

In December 1989, 3M began selling the new emulsion and backcoat sauce components to two of the claimants' four companies, but not to the two others. After Bainbridge and Fingarette began using 3M's new emulsion in December 1989, a problem emerged with the film development process. Specifically, the photographs faded, losing their three-dimensional effect. By early 1990, the claimants experienced a significant decline in camera sales. 3M eventually solved the problem, but the claimants' business ultimately failed.

The claimants' four companies sued 3M in a Texas trial court alleging, in part, breach of express and implied warranties. They argued that the photographic fading was caused by the incompatibility of 3M's new emulsion and its old backcoat sauce, which in turn undermined confidence in their business. The jury concluded that 3M breached an express warranty for the emulsion and implied warranties for the emulsion and the backcoat sauce. Applying Minnesota law, the trial court awarded the four firms $29,873,599 in lost profits. An intermediate appellate court upheld this award. The Texas Supreme Court withheld final judgment and certified the following question to the Minnesota Supreme Court: "For breach of warranty under [Minnesota's version of UCC section 2-318], is a seller liable to a person who never acquired any goods from the seller, directly or indirectly, for pure economic damages (e.g., lost profits), unaccompanied by any injury to the person or the person's property?" This question was relevant to the two plaintiff companies that had not dealt directly with 3M, but had suffered lost profits due to its various breaches of warranty. In the following opinion, the Minnesota Supreme Court answers the question.

Body of Opinion

Chief Justice Keith

The certified question asks this court to consider whether a seller may be held liable for breach of warranty to a plaintiff, who never used, purchased, or otherwise acquired goods from the seller, for lost profits unaccompanied by personal injury or property damage. Unlike the other two plaintiffs, [two of them] did not deal directly with 3M nor did they use, purchase, or otherwise acquire the 3M goods at issue.... Hence, [they] premise their recovery of lost profits on the statutory extension of warranty protection to certain noncontracting parties ("third-party beneficiaries"). The third-party beneficiaries provision of Minnesota's Uniform Commercial Code addresses the reach of express and implied warranties to "injured" parties lacking privity of contract with the seller. Essentially, the provision broadens the reach of warranties by narrowing the lack-of-privity defense: "A seller's warranty whether express or implied extends to any person who may reasonably be expected to use, consume or be affected by the goods and who is injured by breach of the warranty. A seller may not exclude or limit the operation of this section." The term "person" includes corporations and other business organizations.... Minnesota's current version [of section 2-318] is somewhat broader than the broadest of three options recommended by the drafters of the model UCC in 1966.... Alternative C is identical to current Minnesota law, but allows a seller to exclude or limit the operation of the provision if injury to the person is not involved. We agree with 3M that the statute is not so clear and free from ambiguity that we may disregard legislative intent... or the consequences of a particular construction. The unadorned term "injured" is not defined in the UCC, nor is it used elsewhere in the text of Article 2. As applied to [two of the plaintiffs], the reach of [the] section is unclear....

Under [this] section, this court has sanctioned the recovery of lost profits (one form of economic loss) by a third-party beneficiary whose damages arose from a remote seller's breach of warranty. We have also indicated that plaintiffs who never used, purchased, or otherwise acquired defective goods may qualify as third-party beneficiaries when they suffer property damage. But this court has never gone so far as to hold that [the] section reaches a plaintiff who is seeking lost profits unaccompanied by physical injury or property damage and who never used, purchased, or otherwise acquired the goods in question. To do so, we believe, would expand warranty liability well beyond the limits contemplated by the legislature....

Our understanding of the background and aims of [Minnesota's privity provision] leads us to conclude that the scope of a seller's liability for breach of warranty should recede as the relationship between a "beneficiary" of the warranty and the seller's goods becomes more remote.... [T]hose who purchase, use, or otherwise acquire warranted goods have standing to sue for purely economic losses. Those who lack any such connection to the warranted goods must demonstrate physical injury or property damage before economic losses are recoverable.... Any other result implies almost unlimited liability for sellers of warranted goods. If [the] section were interpreted as the plaintiffs advocate, it seems that [their] individual employees, or perhaps even their families, would have standing to sue 3M for causing the loss of their jobs or even a decline in their wages.... The plaintiffs appear to advocate warranty recovery as a catch-all alternative for plaintiffs with no viable legal basis for suit. The risk, however, is that the fortuitous existence of a warranty—between some seller and some buyer, somewhere—would allow remote yet foreseeable parties to recover for their hampered expectations, while others in similar circumstances—but who could not identify a warranty—would not. Confronted with liability of this magnitude, sellers would be encouraged to attempt to disclaim warranties or exclude consequential damages remedies—affecting both the immediate buyer and third-party beneficiaries alike. We therefore reject the plaintiffs' reading of the statute—an interpretation that would likely lead to a variety of unreasonable, unjust, and absurd results that we cannot imagine were intended by the legislature. In light of the statute's language and purpose, and consistent with the legislature's apparent intent, the best reading of [the] section is that noncontracting parties who never used, purchased, or otherwise acquired the seller's warranted goods may not seek lost profits, unaccompanied by physical injury or property damage, for breach of warranty under the statute.

Judgment and Result

The Minnesota Supreme Court answered the Texas Supreme Court's certified question in the negative; two of the four plaintiff corporations could not recover lost profits. In *Minnesota Mining & Manufacturing Co. v. Nishika, Ltd.*, 953 S.W.2d 733 (Tex. 1997), the Texas Supreme Court applied the present case to deny these two firms recovery.

Questions

1. Look at the text's three factors for determining privity questions under the UCC and apply them to the facts in this case. In which direction does each of the factors pull?
2. How is this case different from the other cases in which the Minnesota Supreme Court let the plaintiff recover outside privity of contract?

LIABILITY DISCLAIMERS

A product liability **disclaimer** is a sales contract provision attempting to eliminate or modify the seller's liability for product defects under one or more theories of recovery.[7] Where a disclaimer is enforceable, it erases or reduces the seller's liability under a particular theory or theories of recovery. The main policy argument for enforcing disclaimers is freedom of contract. Also, because goods accompanied by an effective disclaimer are likely to be cheaper than other goods, enforcing disclaimers can increase the choices available to buyers. By enforcing disclaimers, courts effectively give buyers a choice between paying a higher price and getting an "insurance policy" against defects (the seller liability that is likely without a disclaimer), or paying a lower price while accepting a greater risk of an uncompensated defect (because the disclaimer would block recovery).

Today, these freedom of contract-based arguments pack less weight than they did a century ago. As a result, disclaimers often are not enforced. The main reason why these arguments tend to be unpersuasive is that disclaimers sometimes are imposed rather than freely bargained and accepted. Often, a disclaimer is offered on a standardized, take-it-or-leave-it basis by a seller of superior business sophistication, and is

[7] As used here, the term *disclaimer* includes limitations on the duration of a warranty. For example, a seller might include contract language attempting to limit the implied warranty of merchantability's coverage to one year from the sale or to the duration of an express warranty.

accepted without dissent by a consumer who has not read or understood the disclaimer prior to making the purchase. However, where the buyer is a knowledgeable business entity that has understood and freely bargained a disclaimer, these observations are much less valid and courts are more likely to enforce disclaimers.

As you will see shortly, the legal rules on the enforceability of disclaimers are complicated. One reason for this complexity is that the law often tries to make case-specific decisions regarding disclaimers, enforcing them when it appears that they resulted from a free, equal, and knowing bargaining process, and invalidating them in other cases. Another reason for this complexity is that some theories of recovery—mainly the UCC's two implied warranties—are more hospitable to disclaimers than other theories. We begin our discussion of this subject by considering some relatively easy cases. Then we turn to the complex rules governing implied warranty disclaimers.

The Easy Cases

Express Warranty Disclaimers. It is difficult to disclaim an express warranty. UCC section 2-316(1) says that an express warranty and language negating or limiting it should be read consistently if possible, but that the negation or limitation is "inoperative to the extent that such construction is unreasonable." Because an express warranty is a freely made contractual promise, disclaiming it usually is unreasonable. By successfully disclaiming, the seller would effectively be taking away with one hand what it freely and openly gave with the other.

Disclaimers and Tort Liability. Disclaimers of negligence liability can be regarded as contractually created forms of the negligence defense known as **assumption of risk**. As you will see later in the chapter, assumption of risk protects defendants from liability if the plaintiff's acceptance of the risk (here, the disclaimer) is knowing and voluntary. Today, it is difficult for a negligence disclaimer to meet these tests, and such disclaimers rarely are effective. Any disparity in bargaining power between plaintiff and defendant often leads courts to say that the voluntariness test has not been met. Inconspicuous disclaimers and disclaimers failing to state that *negligence* liability is being disclaimed often fail to satisfy the knowledge standard. Thus, disclaimers of negligence liability rarely succeed in consumer cases, and may fail in many other situations as well. However, such disclaimers often are enforced in commercial deals between business parties of relatively equal bargaining power, if the disclaimer clearly refers to negligence liability and it is evident that the parties actually negotiated it.

Disclaimers usually are ineffective in 402A cases, especially where the plaintiff is an ordinary consumer. However, some courts have upheld disclaimers of 402A liability in situations similar to those where negligence disclaimers are enforced.

The *Restatement (Third)* says that disclaimers are ineffective in cases involving personal injury, but declines to state a rule for property damage and indirect economic loss cases. Although the new *Restatement* does not specifically address the subject, it is difficult to believe that it would block disclaimers negotiated in commercial deals between business parties of relatively equal sophistication and bargaining power.

Implied Warranty Disclaimers

Figure 23.3 outlines the inquiries courts may be required to make in cases where the enforceability of implied warranty disclaimers is at issue. Our presentation basically follows Figure 23.3.

FIGURE 23.3 The Enforceability of Implied Warranty Disclaimers

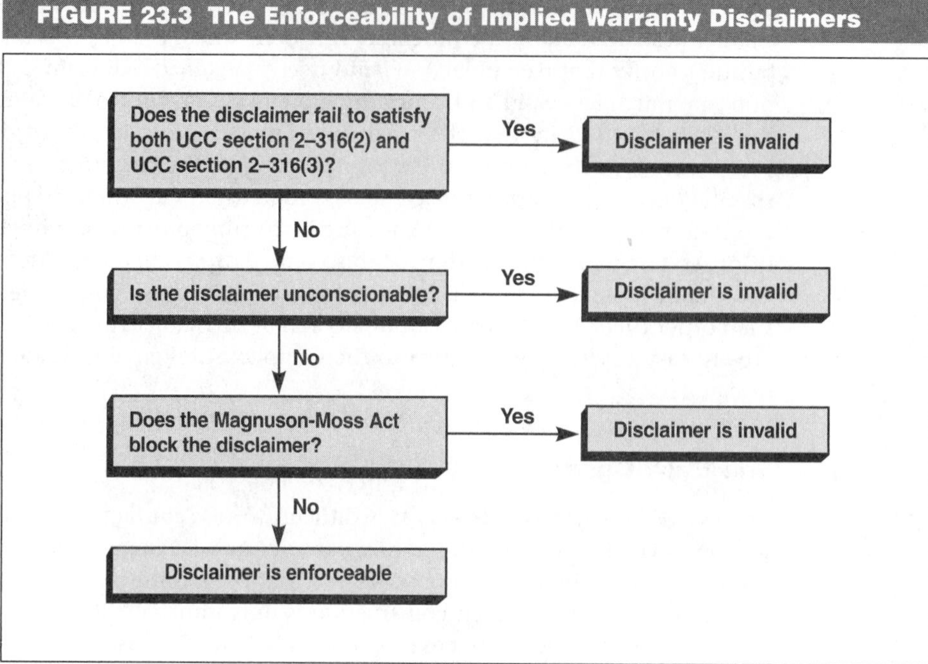

The Basic Tests. UCC section 2-316(2)'s basic tests for the enforceability of implied warranty disclaimers seem to make it easy for sellers to disclaim implied warranties. To disclaim the implied warranty of merchantability, the seller must use the word *merchantability*, and the disclaimer must be conspicuous if it is in writing. To disclaim the implied warranty of fitness for a particular purpose, the disclaimer must be in writing and must be conspicuous. The general test for conspicuousness is whether a reasonable person ought to have noticed the disclaimer. Usually, disclaimers written in capital letters, bold face, larger type, or type of a contrasting color meet this test. Note that unlike a fitness warranty disclaimer, a disclaimer of the implied warranty of merchantability may be oral. Note also that while all disclaimers of the latter warranty must use the word *merchantability*, no special form is needed to disclaim the implied warranty of fitness. A statement such as "THERE ARE NO WARRANTIES WHICH EXTEND BEYOND THE DESCRIPTION ON THE FACE HEREOF" suffices to disclaim that warranty.

Additional Ways to Disclaim Implied Warranties. UCC section 2-316(3) states some additional ways in which an implied warranty can be disclaimed. The first is by using phrases such as "as is," "with all faults," and "as they stand." Although the Code does not expressly say so, many courts have held that such terms must be conspicuous to be effective as disclaimers.

Section 2-316(3) also provides that if the buyer inspects the goods and fails to discover a reasonably apparent defect, he will not have an implied warranty suit for the defect. Also, if the seller requests that the buyer inspect, the buyer refuses, and such an inspection would have revealed a reasonably apparent defect, the buyer will not have an implied warranty suit for that defect. Finally, an implied warranty can be disclaimed by course of dealing (previous conduct between the parties), course of performance (the parties' previous conduct under the contract in question), and usage of trade (a commercial practice having wide acceptance in the relevant locality or business).

Unconscionability. The discussion thus far may lead one to think that disclaiming implied warranty liability is easy for any seller (or seller's attorney) who takes the time and trouble to use the proper legal boilerplate. The following *Myers* case may reinforce this conclusion. Even if a disclaimer meets section 2-316's lenient tests for enforceability, however, it can still be invalid if it is found to be unconscionable. UCC section 2-302 gives a court broad powers to invalidate or modify contract provisions it concludes are unconscionable. The Code does not define the term *unconscionable*; in practice, it means little more than "grossly unfair." Courts using section 2-302 have considerable discretion to determine whether a particular contract or contract term is unconscionable.

In exercising this discretion, courts consider a wide range of factors. They usually examine the substantive terms of the contract—those contract provisions creating the parties' rights and duties—and their tangible impact on the buyer. Disclaimers, which clearly are substantive contract terms, often leave the buyer without a legal remedy for defective goods. Sometimes this is an important factor influencing courts to find them unconscionable. Courts also consider procedural factors such as differences in bargaining power; one party's lack of education, intelligence, or experience; the seller's use of high-pressure sales tactics or "sales hype"; and technical, confusing, well-hidden, or inconspicuous contract language. Such factors obviously can assume importance in cases involving implied warranty disclaimers. However, disclaimers that meet section 2-316(2)'s tests should at least be conspicuous.

Courts frequently find implied warranty disclaimers unconscionable in consumer cases, especially when a consumer has suffered personal injury. In cases where the plaintiff is a business or commercial entity, however, many courts still refuse to apply section 2-302, or find disclaimers conscionable even if they do apply the section. Even in this situation, though, a few courts have held disclaimers unconscionable. The *Fargo* case at the end of the next section, which involved a remedy limitation rather than a disclaimer, suggests how such courts proceed.

The Impact of Magnuson-Moss. Like the Code's unconscionability doctrine, the Magnuson-Moss Act also blocks the enforceability of certain otherwise-valid implied warranty disclaimers. The act does so by restricting a seller's ability to disclaim implied warranties or limit their duration where it gives a written warranty to a consumer for the sale of a consumer product costing more than $10 per item. If the seller gives a full warranty, it cannot disclaim, modify, or limit any implied warranty. If the seller gives a limited warranty, it cannot disclaim or modify any implied warranty. But it can limit the implied warranty's duration to the duration of the written warranty if this is done conspicuously, the limitation is for a reasonable time period, and the limitation is not unconscionable. These rules are a significant restriction on sellers' ability to disclaim implied warranties in consumer cases. However, sellers can avoid the Magnuson-Moss Act's restrictions by simply refusing to give a written warranty. In such situations, the disclaimer probably could be placed on some other writing.

Myers v. A.O. Smith Harvestore Products, Inc.
Court of Appeals of Idaho
757 P.2d 695 (1988)

Background and Facts:

Dale and Ila Myers operated a dairy farm near New Plymouth, Idaho. They purchased a "feed storage and delivery system" manufactured by A.O. Smith Harvestore Products, Inc. (AOS). The system consisted of a silo and a power-operated unloading unit. The Myerses' silo allowed the hay it contained to deteriorate. The result was decreased milk production and lost profits.

The Myerses sued AOS in an Idaho trial court under various theories of recovery, among them the implied warranties of merchantability and fitness. The trial court granted AOS's motion for summary judgment on these claims, and the Myerses appealed.

Body of Opinion

Chief Judge Walters

[AOS] asserts that as a matter of law [the implied] warranties were disclaimed.... Ordinarily, to be effective an implied warranty disclaimer must comply with UCC section 2-316(2), which provides:

> (2) Subject to subsection (3) [not applicable here], to exclude or modify the implied warranty of merchantability or any part of it the language must mention merchantability and in the case of a writing must be conspicuous, and to exclude or modify any implied warranty of fitness the exclusion must be by a writing and conspicuous. Language to exclude all implied warranties of fitness is sufficient if it states, for example, that "There are no warranties which extend beyond the description on the face hereof."

"A term or clause is conspicuous when it is so written that a reasonable person against whom it is to operate ought to have noticed it. A printed heading in capitals is conspicuous.... Language in the body of a form is 'conspicuous' if it is in larger or other contrasting type or color." UCC section 1-201(10).

Here, [the Myerses'] order form or purchase contract directed and required the buyer's signature not on the front of the form but on its reverse side. The side of the form upon which the signatures appear included the following bold heading and paragraph:

> SECOND DISCLAIMER
>
> NO OTHER WARRANTY, EITHER EXPRESS OR IMPLIED AND INCLUDING A WARRANTY OF MERCHANTABILITY AND FITNESS FOR A PARTICULAR PURPOSE HAS BEEN OR WILL BE MADE BY OR IN BEHALF OF THE MANUFACTURER OR THE SELLER OR BY OPERATION OF LAW WITH RESPECT TO THE EQUIPMENT AND ACCESSORIES OR THEIR INSTALLATION, USE, OPERATION, REPLACEMENT OR REPAIR.

Dale and Ila Myers signed this form and initialed an "ACKNOWLEDGMENT AND RELIANCE" to [this] effect:

> I HAVE READ AND UNDERSTOOD THE TERMS AND CONDITIONS OF THIS PURCHASE ORDER INCLUDING THE WARRANTIES, DISCLAIMERS AND TERMS AND CONDITIONS HEREIN GIVEN TO ME, EITHER BY THE MANUFACTURER OR THE SELLER. I RELY ON NO OTHER PROMISES OR CONDITIONS AND REGARD THAT AS REASONABLE BECAUSE THESE ARE FULLY ACCEPTABLE TO ME.

[T]he question whether the disclaimer statement and acknowledgement was sufficiently conspicuous to effect a waiver is a question of law for the court. The language quoted above is *labelled* as a disclaimer in large, bold, capital letters, and also is *written* in bold, capital letters. We hold that the disclaimer was conspicuous and that the language effectively excluded implied warranties of merchantability and fitness for a particular purpose. Our holding is in accord with the conclusions reached by other courts which have examined nearly identical documents.

Even if [it is] conspicuous, the Myerses suggest [that] the disclaimer clause should not be effective because a [sales] representative told Dale Myers that the side of the form containing the parties' signatures did not relate to his purchase. However, upon examining the referenced testimony we find a slightly different account of the execution of the document. On direct examination, Dale Myers testified:

> Q: [T]here was [sic] some statements made by Mr. Collette concerning the back of this contract. What were those statements?
>
> A: To the best of my recollection, Mr. Collette said that "That part of this contract has nothing to do with the equipment you're purchasing, the price of that equipment or anything of that nature. The back of this contract is the fine print, and you can read it." He handed me a pencil.
>
> I started to read it, and to me, it's small print, I did not read the whole thing. And he says, "When you get through, you can initial it here and sign it here."
>
> That's what I done [sic].

Here, the disclaimer was *not* part of the small print also appearing on the signature page. We find little in this testimony to suggest that Dale Myers was directed to ignore the disclaimer. On the contrary, he apparently was allowed to read it. Finding no reason to refuse to enforce the clause, we hold that the implied warranty claims were barred by the disclaimer.

Judgment and Result

Trial court decision on the implied warranty claims affirmed; the Myerses lose on those claims.

Questions

1. Compare AOS's disclaimer to the language of section 2-316(2). Why did the disclaimer successfully insulate AOS from implied warranty liability?
2. What legal doctrine might the Myerses' attorney have used to attack AOS's disclaimer? Under that doctrine, what arguments could he or she have made? On the facts of this case, however, what objection to the use of this doctrine would many courts still make?
3. Why did the court not have to consider the Magnuson-Moss Act here?
4. Read the *Fargo* case that concludes the next section. Do you think that the court in that case would have decided this case in the same way it was decided here?

REMEDY LIMITATIONS

Immediately following the implied warranty disclaimer in the *Myers* case, the following language appeared: "NEITHER THE MANUFACTURER NOR THE SELLER SHALL BE LIABLE BY VIRTUE OF THIS WARRANTY, OR OTHERWISE, FOR ANY SPECIAL OR CONSEQUENTIAL LOSS OR DAMAGE.... RESULTING FROM THE USE OR LOSS OF THE USE OF EQUIPMENT AND ACCESSORIES." This statement is a **remedy limitation**. Unlike disclaimers, which attack the plaintiff's theory of recovery, an enforceable remedy limitation prevents plaintiffs from recovering certain damages while leaving the theory of recovery intact. Thus, damages that have not been excluded by a remedy limitation still can be recovered by the plaintiff as long as all liability under that theory has not been disclaimed. For example, suppose that a seller fails to properly disclaim the implied warranty of merchantability but does manage to exclude liability for consequential damages. Here, a buyer with a good implied warranty of merchantability claim still could recover basis-of-the-bargain damages. Like the contract provision in the following *Fargo* case, most remedy limitations attempt to exclude consequential damages. Often, such exclusions are coupled with contract language limiting recovery to the repair or replacement of defective products or parts.

In tort cases, the tests for enforcing remedy limitations resemble those previously discussed for disclaimers. Under the UCC, remedy limitations are handled under different provisions than those governing disclaimers. UCC sections 2-719(1) and 2-719(3) allow the seller to limit the buyer's remedies in express and implied warranty cases. Section 2-719(3), however, raises the possibility that a limitation of consequential damages will be unconscionable. It suggests that such a limitation may be unconscionable where the plaintiff's loss is "commercial." It is unclear what Code means by this term, but it might include all kinds of damages except personal injury and punitive damages. Where the loss is deemed commercial, courts presumably must make case-by-case determinations under the criteria described in the previous section. Section 2-719(3) also states that a limitation of consequential damages is prima facie unconscionable where the plaintiff has suffered personal injury resulting from the sale of consumer goods (goods used for personal, family, or household purposes). The "prima facie" language probably means that the limitation of consequential damages is presumed to be unconscionable unless the seller can demonstrate otherwise.

Construction Associates, Inc. v. Fargo Water Equipment Co.

Supreme Court of North Dakota
446 N.W.2d 237 (1989)

Background and Facts:

Construction Associates, Inc. contracted to construct a pipeline for the city of Breckenridge, Minnesota. As part of the job, Construction bought a large supply of polyvinyl pipe manufactured by the Johns-Manville Sales Corporation (J-M) from the Fargo Water Equipment Company. Some time after the pipe was installed and the job was completed, the pipe began to develop leaks. After Construction spent considerable sums repairing the leaks, it sued Fargo and J-M under the UCC in a North Dakota trial court. The court found for Construction, awarding it $140,000 in damages for its expenses in repairing the pipeline. The court also held that J-M had to indemnify Fargo for its share of Construction's recovery. J-M then appealed.

Body of Opinion

Chief Justice Erickstad

J-M asserts that the trial court erred in concluding that a clause limiting the remedies available upon a breach of its warranty and specifically excluding liability for consequential damages was unconscionable.... On page 3 of

[J-M's] installation guide, [it] expressly warranted the pipe to be free from defects in workmanship and materials. A limitation of liability clause was also included:

> Limitation of Liability
>
> It is expressly understood and agreed that the limit of J-M's liability shall be the resupply of a like quantity of nondefective Product and that J-M shall have no such liability except where the damage or claim results solely from breach of J-M's warranty. IT IS ALSO AGREED THAT J-M SHALL NOT BE LIABLE FOR ANY INCIDENTAL, CONSEQUENTIAL, OR OTHER DAMAGES FOR ANY ALLEGED NEGLIGENCE, BREACH OF WARRANTY, STRICT LIABILITY, OR ANY OTHER THEORY, OTHER THAN THE LIMITED LIABILITY SET FORTH ABOVE.

Courts... have construed [UCC] sections 2-302 and 2-719 together in holding that a general limitation of remedies clause, including those limiting liability to repair or replacement, may be subject to unconscionability analysis under the Code. Because we are dealing with a limitation of remedies, rather than a disclaimer of warranty, we need not address UCC section 2-316.... Courts and commentators have generally viewed the Code's unconscionability provision within a two-pronged framework: procedural unconscionability, which encompasses factors relating to unfair surprise, oppression, and inequality of bargaining power; and substantive unconscionability, which focuses upon the harshness or one-sidedness of the contractual provision in question....

Procedural Unconscionability. This case presents a commercial, rather than a consumer, transaction. Although courts have generally been more reluctant to find unconscionability in purely commercial settings, under appropriate circumstances a contractual provision may be found unconscionable even in a commercial setting. Courts' general skepticism of unconscionability claims in purely commercial transactions stems from the presumption that businessmen possess a greater degree of commercial understanding and substantially stronger economic bargaining power than the ordinary consumer. Some courts, however, have recognized that disparity of bargaining power may exist even in traditional commercial transactions....

The circumstances presented in this case demonstrate a substantial inequality in bargaining power between J-M and Construction Associates. Construction Associates is a relatively small local construction firm, while J-M is part of an enormous, highly diversified international conglomerate. The limitation of remedies... [was] part of a preprinted installation guide included with all shipments of J-M pipe.... It is obvious that there is no room for bargaining or negotiation as to the warranty provisions.

We also note that the facts in this case demonstrate an actual lack of negotiation coupled with elements of unfair surprise.... The [limitation] clause [was] included on page 3 of a preprinted installation guide expressly directed to the worker in the field, rather than to the officers of Construction Associates. Construction Associates was not apprised at the time of contracting that [its] remedies were being limited or excluded. It would be within J-M's [ability] to do so by, for example, requiring its dealers to accept orders for pipe only upon a J-M form which included the limitations and which required the purchaser's signature....

Substantive Unconscionability. Substantive unconscionability focuses upon the harshness of the particular contractual terms.... [T]he Official Comment to section 2-719 of the Code stresses that contractual provisions which would deprive a party of minimum adequate remedies for breach will not be enforced.... The clause at issue here would limit Construction's remedy for J-M's breach to a like quantity of replacement pipe, with no recovery of consequential damages. Construction argues, with support in the evidence, that replacement pipe is not used when making repairs to leaking joints on a completed underground water pipeline.... [Thus,] the trial court determined that J-M's limited remedy amounted to "nothing whatsoever." J-M has not pointed to any evidence which refutes Construction's contention.

Numerous courts... have held limitations unconscionable when they leave the nonbreaching party with no effective remedy. This is particularly true where the defect in the product is latent, so that the buyer is unable to discover the defect until additional damages are incurred. In this case, Construction did not discover the defects until the pipe was assembled and placed underground....

The circumstances of this case demonstrate elements of procedural and substantive unconscionability which, when viewed in totality, adequately support the trial court's conclusion that the clause limiting remedies and excluding consequential damages was unconscionable.

Judgment and Result

Trial court decision in Construction's favor affirmed.

Questions

1. Why did the court not have to determine whether the limitation was sufficiently conspicuous to satisfy UCC section 2-316?
2. How convincing is the court's argument that J-M had superior bargaining power? Does superior bargaining power necessarily follow from superior size? Assuming that the "weaker" party knows the terms the "stronger" party is offering (which apparently was not the case here), what is to prevent the "weaker" party from simply walking away? Would your conclusion on these questions change if Construction had no alternative source of supply, or if every seller in the industry limited remedies in the same way that J-M did?

TIMING PROVISIONS

Product liability law puts several limitations on the time period within which suit must be brought. Here, we divide these restrictions into statutes of limitations and statutes of repose.

Statutes of Limitations

Product liability suits under the UCC are governed by section 2-725(1), which states that "An action for breach of any contract for sale must be commenced within four years after the cause of action has accrued."[8] Section 2-725(2) says that the normal time of a cause of action's accrual is the time the breach occurs, and makes this the time the seller offers to deliver the defective goods to the buyer. However, section 2-725(2) changes the time of accrual to the time when the breach was or should have been discovered where "a warranty explicitly extends to future performance of the goods and discovery of the breach must await the time of such performance." Determining when this exception applies can be difficult. For example, the later date of accrual may apply if the goods are sold with a "Lifetime Guarantee" or are warranted for "25,000 miles or five years."

In tort suits, the applicable statutes of limitations typically are shorter than the UCC statute of limitations. However, this shorter period normally begins to run only at the time of the injury, or the time the plaintiff discovered or should have discovered the defect. For this reason, the tort standard often is more favorable to the plaintiff.

Some states also have special statutes of limitations that override their regular UCC and tort statutes of limitations where they apply. Examples include special limitations for delayed manifestation injuries, such as those caused by long-term exposure to asbestos, and for cases involving death, personal injury, and property damage.

Statutes of Repose

Statutes of repose try to limit seller and manufacturer liability for products that have been used for extended time periods. A statute of repose normally begins to run at the time the product is sold to the first purchaser in the chain of distribution who is not buying for resale (thus excluding intermediaries), and usually continues for 10–12 years thereafter. In a state with a 10-year statute of repose, a buyer who buys the product for purposes other than resale and never resells it cannot recover for losses occurring more than 10 years after the purchase, even if the suit was commenced quickly enough to satisfy the applicable statute of limitations.

Closely resembling statutes of repose are the useful safe life statutes created by some states. These laws prevent recovery for losses occurring after the product's "useful safe life" has passed. A product's useful safe life is the period during which it is normally likely to perform in a safe manner. Some states follow a presumption that the useful safe life ceases 10–12 years after the product is delivered to the first buyer who does not purchase for resale. In such states, the useful safe life defense resembles a statute of repose.

[8] The Code also requires that the plaintiff notify the seller of any breach of warranty within a reasonable time after the buyer discovered or should have discovered that breach. Usually no notice is required in tort cases involving defective goods.

DEFENSES INVOLVING THE PLAINTIFF'S BEHAVIOR

In a broad sense, the term *defense* refers to any legal argument a defendant uses to defeat a plaintiff's claim. In a product liability suit, for example, a defendant might allege the plaintiff's failure to comply with a statute of limitations, the absence of privity, or the existence of an enforceable disclaimer. Here, however, we discuss defenses that involve the plaintiff's behavior. Traditionally, product liability law has recognized three such defenses: product misuse (or abnormal use), contributory negligence, and assumption of risk. These defenses overlap to some degree. Increasingly moreover, these traditional categories are breaking down. The *Restatement (Third)*, for example, has a broadly worded "comparative responsibility" provision that apportions liability among the plaintiff, the seller, and distributors. This text limits itself to the apportionment of liability between the plaintiff and the seller under doctrines called **comparative fault** and **comparative negligence**. Before that, however, we must examine the traditional defenses.

The Traditional Defenses

Product Misuse. Product misuse or abnormal use occurs when a product is used in some unusual, unforeseeable way, and this causes the injury or loss for which the plaintiff sues. Examples of product misuse include mishandling the product, materially altering it, and failing to follow the manufacturer's instructions. Abnormal use has been a complete defense for the defendant in warranty, negligence, and 402A cases. However, the defense is not available where the defendant has reason to foresee the misuse and fails to take reasonable precautions to protect against it.

Contributory Negligence. Contributory negligence is the plaintiff's failure to exercise reasonable care for her or his own safety. If the plaintiff fails to exercise such care and this failure causes the injury or loss for which she sues in negligence, the defendant has a defense to that suit. In product liability cases, many kinds of behavior can qualify as contributory negligence. Perhaps the most common example is the simple failure to notice a dangerous but plainly apparent product defect. Many forms of product misuse also amount to contributory negligence.

Traditionally, contributory negligence has been a complete defense even where the plaintiff's carelessness was relatively slight. This rule has long worked to the advantage of defendants in negligence suits. It has also created an all-or-nothing situation in which slightly careless plaintiffs recovered nothing, while plaintiffs who were only somewhat more careful obtained a large damage award. In response to these perceived injustices, most states have enacted some form of **comparative negligence**. All systems of comparative negligence require that the factfinder determine the degree to which each party's negligence caused the injury, and state it in percentage terms. Then, the court allocates damages on this basis by reducing the plaintiff's recovery in proportion to his or her percentage share of the negligence causing the injury. In a *pure* system of comparative negligence, this allocation of damages occurs no matter what the plaintiff's and the defendant's relative shares of the negligence causing the injury. Thus, a plaintiff suffering losses of $10,000 would recover $4,000 if the factfinder determines that the defendant's share of the negligence causing the injury was 40 percent and the plaintiff's share was 60 percent. In states with a *mixed* system of comparative negligence, however, this percentage allocation of losses operates only where the defendant's share of the negligence causing the injury is greater than (or greater than or equal to) 50 percent. Under this comparative negligence system, the plaintiff in the preceding example would recover nothing.

Traditional contributory negligence always is a defense in negligence cases. Some states have allowed contributory negligence in warranty suits, and some have not. Contributory negligence usually has not been a defense in 402A cases. Although comparative negligence obviously is available in a negligence suit, it is difficult to generalize about its application to other theories. Here, much may depend on how the state's comparative negligence statute is written—whether, for example, it only applies to negligence suits.

Assumption of Risk. Assumption of risk is the voluntary acceptance of a known risk of harm. It differs from contributory negligence because it involves a subjective test: actual knowledge of the risk. Suppose that the plaintiff consumes a soft drink containing a plainly visible decomposed mouse. If the plaintiff simply failed to notice the condition of the drink, only contributory negligence could be raised as a defense. But if the plaintiff was aware of the defect and consumed the drink anyway, assumption of risk would be available to the defendant. Like product misuse, assumption of risk has been a defense in negligence, warranty, and 402A cases.

The Movement Toward Comparative Fault

Although not all states have joined the bandwagon, recent years have witnessed a general movement toward a system of comparative fault in product liability cases. Although comparative negligence and comparative fault are often used interchangeably, they probably should be distinguished. Technically, comparative negligence only compares the plaintiff's and the defendant's *negligence*, while comparative fault compares all kinds of fault, such as negligence, contributory negligence, assumption of risk, product misuse, and others. Comparative fault operates much like comparative negligence, except that it considers all these kinds of fault, and not just the parties' negligence. Like comparative negligence, comparative fault may operate in either a pure or a mixed fashion. However, it is not always clear which theories of recovery permit a comparative fault defense.

CHAPTER SUMMARY

Today, the six most important theories of product liability recovery are (1) express warranty (made by affirmation of fact or promise, description, sample, or model); (2) implied warranty of fitness for a particular purpose (made when the seller has reason to know the buyer's needs and that the buyer was relying on the seller's skill or judgment); (3) implied warranty of merchantability (made by merchants who sell goods); (4) negligence (which assumes many forms); and (5) strict liability (mainly under section 402A of the *Restatement (Second) of Torts*, which applies when merchant-like sellers sell products that are defective and unreasonably dangerous).

A few minor theories of recovery exist as well. To all these theories, add the new scheme of recovery created by the *Restatement (Third) of Torts: Product Liability*.

Several problems cut across the theories of recovery just described and are resolved differently from theory to theory; they include (1) the damages obtainable; (2) the effect of the old no-liability-outside-privity-of-contract defense; and (3) the effect of disclaimers and remedy limitations.

The states' various limitations on the time within which suit can be brought also vary somewhat from theory to theory.

Finally, the traditional defenses of assumption of risk, contributory negligence, and product misuse vary somewhat in their effect from theory to theory. Currently, however, there is a broad movement toward comparative fault in this area.

Manager's Ethical Dilemma

Fred Smith, an in-house attorney for one of the firms in the farm equipment market, apparently is having a mid-life crisis. He is discussing his feelings with Norma Thomas, a hotshot young MBA with the company.

FRED: Year after year, we take these poor farmers to the cleaners with our standard-form implied warranty disclaimers, and it's beginning to get me down.

NORMA: Why? It's legal, isn't it?

FRED: What's legal isn't always what's right. Sometimes businesses have to recognize moral obligations that go beyond just obeying the law.

NORMA: Well, I don't know about that. But even assuming you're right, what's so awful about implied warranty disclaimers? They're in the contract, aren't they? And don't they have to be conspicuous, too? So why can't people just take a walk if they don't like our terms?

FRED: Every firm in our industry uses the same standard-form implied warranty disclaimers.

NORMA: So that must mean that they're acceptable. Don't you think some competitor would offer different terms if it thought it could get an edge that way?

FRED: Good God, Norma! Who ever reads that those things? I don't, and I'm a lawyer! Do *you* read them? Besides, some of those clauses are so filled with legalese that they're not so easy to read and understand. And to tell you the truth, some of our customers probably can't read very well. Even if they could and even if they made the effort, would they understand what an implied warranty is and what it means to disclaim it?

NORMA: So you seem to be saying that courts should never enforce implied warranty disclaimers. But doesn't that deprive consumers of an important option? An implied warranty is a lot like an insurance policy, because it says that if the goods are defective, you can recover against the seller. But why shouldn't consumers have the option to buy a product without this insurance policy and pay a lower price? Shouldn't a "moral" company give people that choice?

FRED: But you've missed my whole point! Usually, our buyers don't have the foggiest idea what they're getting! But maybe you have a point—we could try harder to make our customers aware. For example, we might have our salespeople explain the disclaimer in everyday language and thus give our customers a clear choice.

NORMA: I wonder how many firms would or could operate that way. For example, your system probably would make it tougher to predict our liability exposure, so we might need more insurance coverage. Also, we'd need better internal recordkeeping. Stuff like this probably would increase our internal costs, cut our profits, and generally make us less competitive.

FRED: It's not a question of what corporations *would* do, but what they *should* do. People are more important than profits!

NORMA: But profit-seeking activity in truly competitive markets promotes economic efficiency. And *everyone* benefits from a more efficient economic system.

FRED: I don't know what the world's coming to. Young people used to be concerned and idealistic.

NORMA: Wake up and smell the coffee. The '60s are long gone, Fred.

Who do you think has gotten the best of this exchange? Why?

Discussion Questions

1. One general trend within twentieth-century product liability law has been the blurring of the line between tort and contract. From the materials in this chapter, identify some instances where the requirements established by particular tort and contract theories are similar.

2. Is the implied warranty of merchantability a good idea? If it did not exist, would buyers probably be paying less for the products they buy, or more? In the former case, why shouldn't they have the choice of getting less legal protection in exchange for a lower price, or paying more to get the "insurance policy" the implied warranty of merchantability affords them? Or should certain minimum obligations of commercial responsibility apply to sellers regardless of what deal they might make with their buyers? If not, finally, what body of rules discussed in this chapter make it theoretically possible for buyers to distinguish sellers who offer implied warranty protection from sellers who do not?
3. The applicable product liability rules often vary considerably depending on whether the plaintiff is an ordinary consumer, or a business entity. Review this chapter and identify as many examples of this divergence as you can. Why does the law make this distinction? Should this distinction be made in all cases involving "business" plaintiffs? For example, should a gas station operated as a sole proprietorship be treated the same as the IBM Corporation?
4. In strict liability cases, the sellers and manufacturers are liable regardless of whether they were at fault. Is this morally right? On the other hand, is it right to allow a seriously injured plaintiff to receive no compensation for injuries caused by a defective product? How does the risk-spreading strategy balance these competing moral concerns?
5. What do you think about the *Martinez* case earlier in the chapter? Leaving aside the question of Martinez's contributory fault, why shouldn't a seller who gives an adequate warning of risks associated with the product be allowed to escape liability? On the other hand, consider the likely real-world effects if other courts follow the rule in the *Martinez* case. What will manufacturers have to do?
6. What do you think about the tort reform movement? Is it a praiseworthy effort to scale back the ridiculous excesses of the product liability explosion? Or is it a cynical ploy to allow businesses to evade their moral responsibilities and increase their profits? Does the truth lie somewhere between these extremes?

Suggested Readings

Articles

BIXBY, "Judicial Interpretation of the Magnuson-Moss Warranty Act," 22 *American Business Law Journal* 125 (1984).

DAVIS, "Different Treatment of Marketing and Design Defects in Pure Risk-Utility Balancing: Who's the Villain?" 27 *American Business Law Journal* 41 (1989).

KEGLEY and HILLER, "'Emerging' Lemon Car Laws," 24 *American Business Law Journal* 87 (1986).

OSTAS, "Predicting Unconscionability Decisions: An Economic Model and an Empirical Test," 29 *American Business Law Journal* 535 (1992).

PHILLIPS, "Unconscionability and Article 2 Implied Warranty Disclaimers," 62 *Chicago-Kent Law Review* 199 (1985).

RAZOOK, "Legal and Extralegal Barriers to Federal Product Liability Reform," 32 *American Business Law Journal* 541 (1995).

RAZOOK, HORRELL, and ROBLYER, "A Descriptive and Analytical Matrix for Product Liability Defenses," 30 *American Business Law Journal* 69 (1992).

VOLZ and FAYZ, "*McBride v. General Motors*: Judicial Response to Constitutional Challenges in a Product Liability Punitive Damage Limitation Statute," 29 *American Business Law Journal* 367 (1991).

Books

J. WHITE and R. SUMMERS, *Handbook of the Law under the Uniform Commercial Code*, 3d ed. (1988).

J. WHITE and R. SUMMERS, *Uniform Commercial Code: Sales* (1998).

AMERICAN LAW INSTITUTE, *Restatement of the Law Third, Torts: Products Liability* (1998).

CHAPTER

24

ENVIRONMENTAL LAW

"A RIVER IS MORE THAN AN AMENITY, IT IS A TREASURE."

Justice Oliver Wendell Holmes, Jr., in New Jersey v. New York, *283 U.S. 336 (1931)*

ELEVEN PERCENT OF ALL U.S. WOMEN WILL CONTRACT BREAST CANCER DURING THEIR LIVES.

Advertisement by General Electric.

APPROXIMATELY ELEVEN PERCENT OF ALL MEN IN THE U.S. WILL CONTRACT PROSTATE CANCER DURING THEIR LIVES.

Statistical Abstract of the United States.

POSITIVE LAW ETHICAL PROBLEMS

"You are kidding," shouted David Mihalic, superintendent of Glacier National Park Service, when told that an environmental group had sued to stop his agency from building a parking lot to accommodate the hundreds of people who wanted to see the beauty of Glacier National Park. "The people now park illegally on the shoulder of the road. They risk being struck by other cars when they get out to enjoy the view. Our agency prepared an Environmental Assessment, issued a FONSI (Finding of No Significant Impact), and now some environmental group is claiming we did not properly take account of the environment in our parking lot plan. No court will ever agree that building a parking lot is a 'major federal action' requiring a full EIS (Environmental Impact Statement)." Was Mihalic right?

It is difficult to speak about environmental law without falling victim to the high-sounding platitudes used by commencement speakers. For example, "The problems we face in this area will be with us for thousands of years." "Our solutions to these problems could determine the future of humanity." Unfortunately, in the case of environmental law, many of these observations are true.

This chapter surveys several federal statutes addressing various environmental problems: water and air pollution, waste disposal, and extinction of life forms. The chapter ends with a glimpse at environmental trends.

THE ENVIRONMENTAL ETHIC

While recognizing the flaws in the words ***conservative*** and ***liberal***, we might say that environmental law shares both aspects. It is conservative because it aims to maintain and improve the quality of the air, water, and life generally and to strike an appropriate balance between present consumption and maintenance for future generations of the earth. However, liberals also have seized upon environmental and resource scarcity as areas that demand social control.

Environmental law has been criticized by both the politically conservative and liberal sectors. Conservatives point out that the estimated $1 trillion cost of toxic waste cleanup in the United States has bankrupted many "names" in Lloyds of London, which has insured toxic cleanups in the United States. As the sector that will immediately be called on to spend this amount, business conservatives rightfully ask, "Is environmental control worth it?" Thus, such persons often demand a cost-benefit analysis. If benefits outweigh costs, then the argument is settled. One problem, though, is that cleanup costs are definite, while benefits are not. How much is it worth to reduce the incidence of breast cancer in women, which studies have linked to environmental causes? How much is it worth to reduce emphysema, bronchitis, and heart disease, all of which have been linked to environmental causes? What is the value of a blue sky? We rightfully ask these questions when we are called upon to spend billions to cope with environmental problems. Ultimately, society pays in poorer health, property damage, and possible long-term habitat destruction, on the one hand, or in high environmental cleanup and maintenance costs, on the other. Table 24 1 presents the cost-benefit trade-off associated with a variety of health and safety regulations.

Some political liberals (in particular, certain poverty and minority groups) criticize the environmental movement as elitist. They see environmentalism as an attempt to prevent lower socioeconomic classes from enjoying the good life already enjoyed by many environmentalists. The good life, as they see it, necessitates some environmental degradation and resource exhaustion. They say it is is not fair to prevent them from enjoying the material things that economically privileged middle and upper classes have had for years.

AN IMPROVEMENT IN CALCULATING GDP

Gross domestic product (GDP) is the prime measure of national economic welfare. Until 1994, GDP did not measure all positive environmental benefits such as cleaner air and water, fewer health problems, and less property damage. Following 1994, efforts to take pollution control into account were made.

OVERVIEW OF ENVIRONMENTAL LAW

Before examining specific environmental statutes, consider the following observations about environmental law. First, if the number of environmental laws on the books is any indication of environmental concern, then the United States is environmentally concerned. The following list includes some important environmental laws:

1. National Environmental Policy Act of 1969
2. Clean Water Act (formerly known as the Federal Water Pollution Control Act, or simply the FWPCA)
3. Clean Air Act
4. Federal Noise Control Act of 1972
5. Resource Conservation and Recovery Act of 1976 (RCRA)
6. Federal Insecticide, Fungicide, and Rodenticide Act (FIFRA)
7. Toxic Substances Control Act (TOSCA)
8. Marine Protection, Research, and Sanctuaries Act of 1972
9. Energy Supply and Environmental Coordination Act of 1974
10. Endangered Species Act
11. Safe Drinking Water Act of 1974
12. Nuclear Waste Policy Act
13. Comprehensive Environmental Response Compensation and Liability Act (CERCLA)

TABLE 24.1 Risks and Cost-Effectiveness of Selected Regulations, By Cost Per Premature Death Averted

Regulation*	Year Issued	Health or safety	Agency	Baseline mortality risk per million exposed	Cost per premature death averted
					million $
Unvented Space Heater Ban	1980	S	CPSC	1,890	0.1
Aircraft Cabin FireProtection Std.	1985	S	FAA	5	0.1
Auto Passive Restraint/SeatBelt Std.	1984	S	NHTSA	6,370	0.1
Steering Column Protection Std.**	1967	S	NHTSA	385	0.1
Underground Construction Stds.***	1989	S	OSHA-S	38,700	0.1
Trihalomethane Drinking Water Stds.	1979	H	EPA	420	0.2
Aircraft Seat Cushion Flammability Std.	1984	S	FM	11	0.4
Alcohol and Drug Control Stds.***	1985	H	FRA	81	0.4
Auto Fuel-System Integrity Std.	1975	S	NHTSA	343	0.4
Stds. for Servicing Auto Wheel Rims***	1984	S	OSHA-S	630	0.4
Aircraft Floor Emergency Lighting Std.	1984	S	FAA	2	0.6
Concrete & Masonry Construct. Std.***	1988	S	OSHA-S	630	0.6
Crane Suspended Pers. Platf'm Std.***	1988	S	OSHA-S	81,000	0.7
Passive Restraints—Truck & Bus (P)	1989	S	NHTSA	6,370	0.7
Side-Impact Stds. for Autos (Dynamic)	1990	S	NHTSA	na	0.8
Children's Sleepwear Flam'lity Ban****	1973	S	CPSC	29	0.8
Auto Side Door Support Stds.	1970	S	NHTSA	2,520	0.8
Low-Alt. Windsh'r Equip. & Train. Std.	1988	S	FAA	na	1.3
Electrical Equip't Stds. (Metal Mines)	1970	S	MSHA	na	1.4
Trenching & Excavation Stds.***	1989	S	OSHA-S	14,310	1.5
Traffic Alert & Collision Avoidance Sys.	1988	S	FAA	na	1.5
Hazard Communication Std.***	1983	S	OSHA-S	1,800	1.6
Side-ImpactTruck, Bus, & MPV (P)	1989	S	NHTSA	na	2.2
Grain Dust Explosion Prev'n Stds.***	1987	S	OSHA-S	9,450	2.8
Rear Lap/Shoulder Belts for Autos	1989	S	NHTSA	na	3.2
Radionuclides—Uran. Mines Stds.***	1984	H	EPA	6,300	3.4
Benzene NESHAP (Fugitive Emis'n)	1984	H	EPA	1,470	3.4
Ethylene Dibromide Drinking Water Std.	1991	H	EPA	na	5.7
Benzene NESHAP(Coke By-Prod.)***	1988	H	EPA	na	6.1
Asbestos Occup'l Exposure Limit***	1972	H	OSHA-H	3,015	8.3
Benzene Occup'l Exposure Limit***	1987	H	OSHA-H	39,600	8.9
Electrical Equip. Stds. (Coal Mines)***	1970	S	MSHA	na	9.2
Arsenic Emis'n Stds.—Glass Plants	1986	H	EPA	2,660	13.5
Ethylene Oxide Occup'l Expos. Limit***	1984	H	OSHA-H	198	20.5
Arsenic/Copper NESHAP	1986	H	EPA	63,000	23.0
Haz Waste List—Petrol. Refin. Sludge	1990	H	EPA	210	27.6
Cover/Move Uran. Tail'gs (Inact. Sites)	1983	H	EPA	30,100	32.0
Benzene NESHAP (Trans. Oper'ns)	1990	H	EPA	na	33.0
Cover/Move Uran. Tailings (Act. Sites)	1983	H	EPA	30,100	45.0
Acrylonitrile Occup'l Expos. Limit***	1978	H	OSHA-H	42,300	52.0
Coke Ovens Occup'l Expos. Limit***	1976	H	OSHA-H	7,200	64.0
Lockout/Tagout***	1989	S	OSHA-S	4	71.0
Asbestos Occup'l Expos. Limit***	1986	H	OSHA-H	3,015	74.0
Arsenic Occup'l Expos. Limit***	1978	H	OSHA-H	14,800	107.0
Asbestos Ban	1989	H	EPA	na	111.0
Diethylstilbestrol (DES) Cattlefeed Ban	1979	H	FDA	22	125.0
Benzene NESHAP (Waste Oper'ns)	1990	H	EPA	na	168.0
1,2-Dichloropropane Drink. Water Std.	1991	H	EPA	na	653.0
Haz Waste Land Disposal Ban (1st 3rd)	1988	H	EPA	2	4,190.0
Municipal Solid Waste Landfill Std. (P)	1988	H	EPA	<1	19,107.0
Formaldehyde Occup'l Expos. Limit***	1987	H	OSHA-H	31	86,202
Atrazine/Alachlor Drinking Water Std.	1991	H	EPA	na	92,070
Haz Waste List—Wood Preser. Chems.	1990	H	EPA	<1	5,700,000

Source: J.F. Morall, III, "A review of the record." Regulation, vol. 10, no. 2, p. 30. Updated by the authors and published in Executive Office of the President, The Budget for Fiscal Year 1992. CEQ, *Environmental Quality.*

continued

FIGURE 24.1 *continued*

Notes: *=70-year lifetime exposure assumed unless otherwise specified; **=50-year lifetime exposure; ***=45-year lifetime exposure; ****=12-year lifetime exposure; na=not available. Abbreviations—CPSC: Consumer Product Safety Commission; MSHA: Mine Safety and Health Administration; EPA: Environmental Protection Agency; NHTSA: National Highway Traffic Safety Administration; FAA: Federal Aviation Administration; FRA: Federal Railroad Administration; FDA: Food and Drug Administration; OSHA-H: Occupational Safety and Health Administration, Health Standards; OSHA-S: Occupational Safety and Health Administration, Safety Standards. Potential benefits other than avoiding premature death are not included. Other benefits could include avoiding risks that are not life threatening and benefits that are not related to health.

The list is long but not complete. International environmental law includes treaties (such as the Antarctic Treaty), international conventions (such as the International Convention for the Regulation of Whaling), and international agreements (such as the Agreement on the Conservation of Polar Bears). On the state level, environmental protection statutes and municipal ordinances are designed to maintain environmental quality (such as "green belt" ordinances around municipalities designed to limit growth and be buffer zones against unsightly urban sprawl).

> *The website to one of the oldest environmental groups, the Sierra Club, can be found at* ***http://www.sierraclub.org***
>
> **http://**

While space limits prevent comments on every environmental law, this chapter will survey some of the more important or popular acts: the National Environmental Policy Act of 1969 (NEPA), the Clean Water Act, the Clean Air Act, RCRA, TOSCA, CERCLA, the Nuclear Waste Policy Act, and the Endangered Species Act. Suggested readings at the chapter's end provide good sources if readers want more information on other acts or greater detail on the acts covered here.

PRINCIPAL ACTORS OR INSTITUTIONS

No single institution exists in the development of environmental law. Instead, a number of sectors in society have shaped such law, including private environmental groups, the U.S. Environmental Protection Agency (EPA), other federal administrative agencies (including the Department of Interior), the president, Congress, state administrative agencies, and the courts (mainly federal but increasingly state).

> *The website for the U.S. Environmental Protection Agency is found at* ***http://www.epa.gov***
>
> **http://**

The Council on Environmental Quality (CEQ) formerly oversaw federal agency compliance with the environmental impact statement requirement. Additionally, CEQ used to issue an annual report on the state of the environment. The Clinton administration has essentially eliminated the CEQ by cutting its staff to almost zero. Thus other organizations, such as citizen groups, must now monitor federal agency compliance with the EIS requirement as well as issue annual reports documenting environmental welfare.

> *The Environmental Defense Fund, a private environmental organization, has a website at* ***http://www.edf.org***
>
> **http://**

NATIONAL ENVIRONMENTAL POLICY ACT

The National Environmental Policy Act of 1969 (NEPA) was signed into law on January 1, 1970, by President Nixon. The act's name is misleading because it sounds like a law to correct all sorts of environmental harm. However, it does no such thing, directly. NEPA does three things.

1. It establishes the Council on Environmental Quality (CEQ), which as of this writing is scheduled to be eliminated and its functions transferred elsewhere.
2. It requires federal agencies to take environmental concerns into account when they take certain actions.
3. It requires federal agencies to prepare detailed environmental statements (popularly called environmental impact statements, or EISs) in certain situations.

Before NEPA was passed, one federal agency (the old Atomic Energy Commission, or AEC) tried to take environmental factors into account in licensing a nuclear power plant. The AEC was successfully sued for doing so, the argument being that taking environmental concerns into account was *ultra vivres* (beyond the power of) the AEC. Soon thereafter, NEPA was passed to correct this issue by requiring federal agencies to consider environmental harms from the project *before* it is started and to reduce the harshness of environmental impacts wherever possible.

NEPA declares the following to be a *continuing* national environmental policy:

> [The Federal Government is] to use all practicable means and measures, including financial and technical assistance, in a manner calculated to foster and promote the general welfare, to create and maintain conditions under which man and nature can exist in productive harmony, and fulfill the social, economic, and other requirements of present and future generations of Americans.

To put this national environmental policy into operation, NEPA recognizes some specific federal responsibilities:

1. To fulfill the responsibilities of each generation as trustee of the environment for succeeding generations
2. To assure for all Americans safe, healthful, productive, and esthetically and culturally pleasing surroundings
3. To attain the widest range of beneficial uses of the environment without degradation or risk to health or safety
4. To preserve important historic, cultural, and natural aspects of our national heritage
5. To achieve a balance between population and resources permitting a high standard of living
6. To enhance the quality of renewable resources and to help enable the recycling of depletable resources

Note that these federal responsibilities are not required. NEPA qualifies the federal agency duty to achieve with "all practicable means" language. In other words, federal agencies must use all means to promote recycling, resource-balancing, population preservation, historic preservation, and the other responsibilities, if they are practicable.

Environmental Rights

NEPA does not give people any national right to a healthy environment. If polluted air causes lung cancer or carcinogenic water causes bladder cancer, NEPA is not violated. NEPA merely says that each person *should* enjoy (not *will* enjoy or has a right to enjoy) a healthful environment. NEPA is not a potent statute in many ways.

Environmental Impact Statements

NEPA requires all federal agencies to prepare environmental impact statements (EISs) in two cases: (1) when the agency sends a proposed law to Congress, and (2) whenever the agency proposes major federal action significantly affecting the quality of the human environment. NEPA requires that five items be contained in an EIS:

1. The environmental impact of the proposed action
2. Any adverse environmental effects of the proposed action
3. Alternatives to the proposed action
4. The relation between short-term uses of the environment and the maintenance and enhancement of long-term productivity
5. Any irreversible and irretrievable resource commitments involved in an agency action about to be implemented

Most lawsuits dealing with NEPA have concerned EISs. As the core of NEPA, the EIS requirement is called the action-forcing part of NEPA because it requires federal agencies to prepare an EIS.

Failure to Prepare an EIS. Nothing happens if a federal agency fails to prepare an EIS unless someone sues the agency. If someone takes the agency to court and the court decides the agency should have prepared an EIS, the court enjoins (stops) the project until an EIS is prepared. Generally, if an EIS is adequate, with all five items that all EISs must contain, a federal project can go ahead.

Length of EIS. Under new Council on Environmental Quality (CEQ) regulations, EISs are supposed to be no longer than 150 pages in ordinary circumstances. Extraordinary circumstances justifying longer EISs would be "super-colossal" projects, such as the Alaskan pipeline (that EIS was 12,000 pages).

Inadequate EIS. A federal agency can be sued if its EIS is inadequate, and the project can be stopped. For example, if the EIS fails to consider alternatives to the proposed project or if the EIS lacks any of the other five items an EIS should contain, a court will stop the project until the agency makes the EIS adequate.

The Public and an EIS. A member of the public can obtain an EIS. Recall that a federal agency prepares a separate EIS for each of its major federal actions significantly affecting the quality of the human environment. Thus, anyone may ask the particular federal agency for a copy of an EIS for a particular federal project.

The public also has a right to participate in writing an EIS. The CEQ regulations set out steps a federal agency must follow in writing an EIS. The agency writes a draft EIS and submits copies to CEQ and any other federal agencies with expertise on the project. For example, the Army Corps of Engineers would have expertise in a TVA dam proposal. How the public would learn about a draft EIS is uncertain, because CEQ's EIS regulations do not require *Federal Register* notice of a particular project's EIS availability.

After receiving agency and public comments, the agency writing the EIS considers the comments, might modify the EIS to take account of the comments, and then publishes the final EIS. If significant changes are made in the final EIS after comments are received, the changes are submitted for public and agency comment again before the final EIS is published. This entire EIS public and agency commenting process is similar to the proposal-comment-promulgation process for federal regulations discussed in Chapter 7. The public helps to write EISs by making comments in response to proposed EISs.

Substantive Requirements. NEPA's action-forcing EIS requirement originally was procedural. That is, as long as a major agency action affecting the environment was accompanied by an EIS document containing the five basic EIS requirements, courts tended to say that NEPA's EIS requirements were met. However, the courts now generally look at the substance of the EIS and what it actually says to see whether NEPA's requirements have been met.

Interest of Business in EIS. Federal agency actions could require an EIS, such as EPA's issuing NPDES permits[1] to sources, the Interior Department's issuance of grazing permits on western land, and the Interior Department's leasing federal land (one-third of U.S. land belongs to the U.S. government) to oil and other companies for mineral exploration. Unless an agency prepares an EIS, the agency's conferrals of a permit to a business could be invalid. Thus, business has a dollar-and-cents interest in EISs. The *Public Citizen v. U.S. Trade Representative* case shows how the entire U.S. business community can be affected by an EIS issue. Even though NAFTA's passage was undoubtedly a major federal action significantly affecting the quality of the human environment, a federal court of appeals held that no EIS was required for NAFTA. The court reasoned that the president was not a federal "agency" for NEPA purposes and that there was no "final" agency action when the president submitted NAFTA to Congress for approval. Therefore, no EIS was required for NAFTA. Do you think the court caved in to political pressures to have NAFTA take effect?

On a smaller level, NEPA issues affect businesspeople such as land developers and timber harvesters. Often a federal agency such as the National Park Service (part of the Department of the Interior) is called upon to determine whether "cutting 200 ancient trees to build a parking lot in a national park will have "major" environmental effects. The *Coalition for Canyon Preservation v. Slater* case illustrates the problem and shows how agencies go about deciding such matters.

Coalition for Canyon Preservation v. Slater

U.S. District Court (D. Montana)
33 F.Supp.2d 1276 (1999)

Background and Facts:

This case involves a challenge to a decision by the National Park Service (NPS) to construct a parking lot on the east side of the Going to the Sun Road (GTSR) at the Avalanche Creek area of Glacier National Park. The NPS issued an Environmental Assessment (EA) in April of 1996 for the project. A little over one year later, the service issued a Finding of No Significant Impact (FONSI) in July of 1997. The Coalition seek a declaratory judgment that defendants have violated the National Environmental Policy Act (NEPA).... The Coalition also wants an injunction barring defendants from construction of the proposed parking lot and access road unless and until they have complied with the National Environmental Policy Act.... The Avalanche Creek Area is located at the confluence of Avalanche and McDonald Creeks several miles upstream of McDonald Lake adjacent to the Going to the Sun Road (GTSR). Currently, the east side of the GTSR in the the area contains a campground. It has an asphalt and handicapped accessible boardwalk through the Trail of the Cedars. It is the trailhead for the two-mile hike to Avalanche Lake. The Trail of the Cedars and Avalanche Lake are both popular with Glacier visitors.

The west side of the GTSR in the Avalanche area has a 12-table picnic area, restrooms, and 20 parking spaces that abut the southbound lane of traffic of the GTSR. Because the Trail of the Cedars and the trailhead to Avalanche Lake are on the east side of the road, and the parking to the west, there is considerable pedestrian traffic across the GTSR. Additionally, automobiles create roadside parking along both shoulders of the GTSR in order to visit the popular area. Some of this parked traffic is illegal.

[1] NPDES stands for National Pollutant Discharge Elimination System, the permit scheme set up to implement EPA regulations limiting what people may dump into the nation's waters.

Responding to the increased visitor use and the perceived need to find a long-term solution, the National Park Service conducted and completed an Environmental Assessment (EA) for a parking lot on the east side of GTSR in 1984.... The lack of funding meant no action was taken on the 1984 plan.

Finding a solution for the congestion in the Avalanche Creek area was revisited by the National Park Service in 1995–1996. That consideration culminated in the Environmental Assessment and FONSI which are the subject of this case.... The Environmental Assessment resulted in the designation of a preferred alternative by the National Park Service which calls for a parking lot on the east side of GTSR in the Avalanche Creek area. The Coalition charges that too much is at stake to go forward without benefit of a full-blown Environmental Impact Statement.

Body of Opinion

District Judge Molloy

The heart of the controversy is the impact the parking lot might have on the vegetation at the site where the proposed alternative is to be constructed. It is a forest classified as cedar-devil's club habitat with trees dating to 1517. It is an area with vegetation that the Environmental Assessment admits is rare and vulnerable to extinction. The cedar-devil's club habitat in the Avalanche Creek area is the largest in Montana. It is significant in other ways because it marks the eastern-most location of cedar-devil's club habitat in the North American continent....

The Draft Environmental Assessment supporting the current proposal characterized the effects of development of the parking facility as follows: Further permanent loss of this rare and unique habitat, whether it be mature or successional forest constitutes a long-term significant impact."... Curiously, the Final Environmental Assessment omitted this language, but did note that the habitat "is an extremely significant resource due to its age, rarity (and) biogeograhic uniqueness."... The language of the draft implies the need for an Environmental Impact Statement while the final language is somewhat less demanding but it too implies the need for an EIS to consider the project's impact on an extremely significant resource.

... Public comment on the Environmental Assessment also focused on the anticipated removal of trees from the old-growth forest to accommodate the parking lot. The public comment was nearly universally against the proposed parking lot....

The National Environmental Policy Act (NEPA) requires agencies to prepare an Environmental Impact Statement (EIS) for each "major Federal action significantly affecting the quality of the human environment. ... The policy behind NEPA is "to ensure that an agency has at its disposal all relevant information about environmental impacts before the agency embarks on the project."...

An Environmental Assessment (EA) is a first step under NEPA to determine whether or not projected impacts of a project may be "significant."... Based on the significance determination made in the EA, the agency must then prepare an EIS or FONSI.... Here, the National Park Service made a determination of no "significant impact" and issued a FONSI. A Finding of No Significant Impact is reviewed under the arbitrary and capricious standard.... This standard requires that the "court must ensure that the agency has taken a 'hard look' at the environmental consequences of its proposed action."...

A court may reverse an agency decision when it offers an explanation for its decision that runs counter to the evidence before the agency....

In reviewing agency decisions not to prepare an Environmental Impact Statement, the inquiry by the district court centers on the reasonableness of the Finding of No Significant Impact. "If substantial questions are raised regarding whether the proposed action may have a significant effect on the human environment, a decision not to prepare an Environmental Impact Statement is unreasonable."...

Agencies may reach a FONSI if mitigation measures are proposed that directly address the impacts identified in the Environmental Assessment.... Here, the National Park Service proposes to remove the picnic area on the west side of GTSR to allow for restoration of the habitat there. It then argues that this undertaking mitigates the impacts that will result from constructing the parking lot on the east side of the road. However, the Environmental Assessment is deficient in yet another way. There is insufficient scientific analysis that the area to the west will regenerate, or that its regeneration is sufficient mitigation to the loss of the habitat to the east. The National Park Service conclusion that it will regenerate is speculative. Finally, there is no dispute that regeneration, if successful, would take centuries. The measure of mitigation would be nearly half of the next millenium....

The mitigation resolution here proposed does not meet the test.

Judgment and Result

The District Court granted the injunctive relief sought by the Canyon Coalition. The agency had to prepare an EIS.

Questions

1. What did the court in this case say were NEPA's purposes? Had the National Park Service (and other agencies) prepared an EIS or merely an EA? Who initially decides whether a federal action is "significant" from an environmental standpoint?

2. How does an EA relate to an EIS and a FONSI?
3. Who decides to make an EA and FONSI? Do "development-oriented" agencies tend to ignore EIS requirements as "just another form to fill out" before getting on with the important activity of development?
4. Did the court determine that the National Park Service had taken a "hard look" at the plaintiffs' environmental concerns? Notice who the plaintiffs were in the case. Does their involvement support the notion that private environmental groups—not CEQ—are the main enforcers of NEPA?

CLEAN WATER ACT

The Environmental Protection Agency tries to control water pollution by keeping unwanted matter out of the rivers, lakes, and streams of the United States. The Clean Water Act (formerly the Federal Water Pollution Control Act, or FWPCA) first set goals in stages: swimmable, fishable waters by 1983 zero discharge of pollutants by 1985. The act tries to stop water pollution by making it illegal to discharge pollutants from point sources into waters of the United States without an NPDES permit.

Let us look more closely at the elements of this definition. A pollutant could be anything foreign to water in its natural state (such as heat, sewage, or any chemical). "Waters of the United States" is so broad a phrase that, technically speaking, a person pouring Scotch into water needs an NPDES permit. It is called a commerce clause definition of water. Recall from Chapter 5 that the federal government may regulate almost anything *affecting* interstate commerce. Because all water in some way affects interstate commerce, anytime anyone puts a pollutant into water, an NPDES permit may be needed.

An NPDES permit is a piece of paper every discharger from a **point source** (a discrete point such as a pipe or outlet as opposed to general runoff) needs before it is legal to put any pollutant into any lake, river, or stream in the United States (even a lake, river, or stream on one's own land). Such a permit must be obtained from the EPA before one can legally discharge anything into U.S. waters. In the permit, the EPA sets limits on what the permit holder can put into the water.

How does the EPA decide what amounts of which pollutants can be put into the water? Recall the steps in how a regulation is made, discussed in Chapter 7. The Clean Water Act is an enabling act. It directs the EPA to conduct studies that tell which pollutants are harmful and how harmful they are. From these studies EPA proposes and promulgates regulations limiting harmful amounts of pollutants.

The Clean Water Act set out phases of pollution control for point source dischargers to meet. Municipalities were to meet secondary treatment levels by 1977, which involved letting the large items settle out and chlorinating the rest. **Best practicable treatment control** (BPT) levels were to be met by 1983. Industrial dischargers were held to stricter discharge limits—BPT by 1977 and **best available treatment** (BAT) control levels by 1983. These industrial limits apply only to businesses that dump pollutants directly into U.S. waters (as opposed to those discharging into sewers).

Understanding the EPA's water pollution regulations requires knowledge of two other aspects: **effluent guidelines** and **effluent limitations**. The Clean Water Act puts all direct industrial dischargers into U.S. waters into a number of categories. The EPA then set ranges of discharge for each of the industrial groups. Within an industrial group (textile mills, for example) a particular plant dumping waste directly into a stream would have an effluent limitation set for it. (The word *effluent* refers to waste dumped into the water.) This effluent limit for a particular textile mill would be taken from the range of limits in the effluent guidelines for all textile mills. The effluent limit for the particular mill would be put into an NPDES permit.

Every direct point source discharger into U.S. waters, including municipalities, businesses, farms, and all other point source dischargers, must have an NPDES permit.

Many industries discharge into municipal sewers, but municipal treatment plants were not equipped to filter out heavy metals and other toxic substances common in industrial discharge.

Some things are not point sources and do not need NPDES permits. For instance, general runoff from a farmer's field at no particular point needs no NPDES permit. Pollutants from general land runoff are treated by **area-wide waste treatment programs** under the Clean Water Act. An example of such a program might be a buffer zone of grass or vegetation next to a stream to filter the runoff before it goes into the water. Starting on October 1, 1993, storm water runoff on land will require a permit under the SWPPP (Storm Water Pollution Prevention Plan) and such runoff must be treated to remove pollutants before being discharged from one's land.

Midcourse Corrections

Between 1972 (when the present Clean Water Act's structure and goals were set) and 1985 (by which time the act's goals were to be attained), the act called for midcourse corrections (adjustments in the act) through the 1977 amendments to the Clean Water Act. They moved some compliance dates from July 1, 1983, to July 1, 1984.

The midcourse corrections tried to toughen treatment of extremely dangerous water pollutants (toxins) and loosen up on less harmful pollutants by establishing three broad groups of pollutants: conventional, nonconventional, and toxic. A discharger has to treat pollutants in a discharge according to the group into which it falls. **Best conventional treatment** (BCT) control is required for conventional pollutants. Best available treatment (BAT) control (the strictest standard) is required for both toxins and nonconventional pollutants (a catchall category).

The moving back of the dates, the loosening of pollution control requirements on some pollutants, and the tightening up on toxins were in recognition of the huge costs of water pollution control, the large number of noncompliers with the July 1, 1977, phase one deadline, and the need to control deadly pollutants.

The new midcourse correction standards provided in the 1977 amendments to the Clean Water Act are applied to individual business and municipal dischargers through NPDES permits issued to each discharger by the EPA. The 1972 act required the same thing. As of February 12, 1980, individual point source dischargers in the United States had been issued 58,907 NPDES permits (43,512 to nonmunicipal entities such as businesses and 15,395 to municipalities).

The 1977 amendments also expanded the regulatory framework by authorizing EPA to issue **best management practices** regulations to control certain parts of the plant operations to restrict toxic runoff and hazardous materials. An example of the best management practice might be a tarp put over a coal pile to limit rain from washing off untreated impurities into the streams or sewers. EPA has discretion about whether to require best management practices and how stringent to make them. Table 24.2 provides information on water pollution levels.

Criticisms

A primary criticism of the Clean Water Act is its cost to public and private sectors. The 1997 Statistical Abstract sets the public sector cost at $26.9 billion and the private sector cost at $78.3 billion for the year 1993 alone. The inevitable question is, what would the quality of water be if we did not spend this money to clean it?

Another criticism of water pollution control is the inflexibility of the regulators. For example, why should all discharge pipes in a factory have to meet the same effluent limits if it is cheaper to eliminate pollutants entirely from some pipes and to let

TABLE 24.2 National Ambient Water Quality in Rivers and Streams—Violation Rate: 1980 to 1995

POLLUTANT	VIOLATION LEVEL	1980	1985	1989	1990	1991	1992	1993	1994	1995
Fecal coliform bacteria	Above 200 cells per 100 ml	31	28	30	26	15	28	31	28	35
Dissolved oxygen	Below 5mg per liter	5	3	3	2	2	2	(Z)	2	1
Phosphorus, total, as phosphorous	Above 1.0 mg per liter	4	3	2	3	2	2	2	2	4
Lead, dissolved	Above 50 μg per liter	(Z)	(Z)	(Z)	(Z)	(Z)	(Z)	(NA)	(NA)	(NA)
Cadmium, dissolved	Above 10 μg per liter	1	(Z)	(Z)	(Z)	(Z)	(Z)	(NA)	(NA)	(NA)

NA Not available. Z Less than 1.

(**In percent.** Violation level based on U.S. Environmental Protection Agency water quality criteria. Violation rate represents the proportion of all measurements of a specific water quality pollutant which exceeds the "violation level" for that pollutant. "Violation" does not necessarily imply a legal violation. Data based on U.S. Geological Survey's National Stream Quality Accounting Network (NASQAN) data system; for details, see source. Years refer to water years. A water year begins in Oct. and ends in Sept. μg=micrograms; mg=milligrams.)

Source: U.S. Geological Survey, national-level data, unpublished; state-level date, *Water-Data Report*, annual series prepared in cooperation with the state governments.

others discharge more? As long as the total amount of pollutants discharged from all the plant's outlets is the same as if each individual outlet discharged exactly the same amount, society is not hurt. This idea is reflected in the **bubble policy**. Think of an entire factory as having a bubble over it. The factory is viewed as having an allowable discharge limit, but individual factory pipes discharging pollutants may dump different levels of pollutants as long as the total plant's discharge does not exceed the plant limit. The bubble concept has been tried for air pollution, but its application to water pollution is in the developmental stages.

One evidence of flexibility in the Clean Water Act was the extension of phase two deadlines (the July 1, 1983, dates of BAT for industry and BPT for municipalities) to July 1, 1984, and in some cases mid-1987. Another bit of flexibility was the 1977 amendments' new pollutant classifications (conventional, nonconventional, and toxic), which set different pollution control levels based on the harm each causes—that is, more treatment for more harmful pollutants such as toxins, less treatment for less harmful conventional pollutants. Table 24.3 provides some information on the various levels of waste water treatment.

TABLE 24.3 Wastewater Treatment Facilities: 1988 to 1996

	NUMBER OF FACILITIES			1996		
				Present design capacity	Number of persons served	
LEVEL OF TREATMENT	1988	1992	1996		Number	Percent of U.S.
Total	**15,591**	**15,613**	**16,024**	**42,225**	**189,710,899**	**71.8**
Non-discharge[1]	1,854	1,981	2,032	1,421	7,660,876	2.9
Less than secondary	1,789	868	176	3,054	17,177,492	6.5
Secondary	8,536	9,086	9,388	17,734	81,944,349	31.0
Greater than secondary	3,412	3,678	4,428	20,016	82,928,182	31.4

[1] Facilities that do not discharge effluent to surface waters.

[Covers treatment facilities, which are structures designed to treat wastewater, storm water, or combined sewer overflows prior to discharge to the environment. Treatment is accomplished by subjecting the wastewater to a combination of physical, chemical, and/or biological processes that reduce the concentration of contaminants.]

Source: U.S. Environmental Protection Agency, Office of Wasterwater Management, *1996 Clean Water Needs Survey Report to Congress.*

Enforcement

The Clean Water Act has both civil and criminal sanctions. Either private parties or the governmental bodies (the EPA, the U.S. Justice Department, or state government if it has assumed administration of the NPDES permit program) can enforce the act. The governmental units may bring either civil suits (for example, to enjoin or stop dumping of pollutants into streams) or criminal suits.

Violators of the Clean Water Act are liable for damages, civil penalties, cleanup costs, fines, and prison terms. *General Motors v. EPA* illustrates that businesses holding NPDES permits have a limited time to challenge the discharge parameters set in such permits.

General Motors v. EPA

U.S. Court of Appeals (D.C. Cir.)
168 F.3d 1377 (1999)

Background and Facts:

Section 402 of the Clean Water Act (CWA) establishes the National Pollutant Discharge Elimination System (NPDES), a permitting program through which the EPA and the several states implement various regulatory limits upon the discharge of pollutants into navigable waters. Forty-two states, including Michigan, administer the NPDES program within their borders. Although those states assume responsibility as the primary permitting authority, the U.S. EPA retains the power to enforce state-issued permits in federal court.

In 1984 GM applied to the Michigan Department of Natural Resources (MDNR) for an NPDES permit to discharge stormwater from a point source, known as "Outfall 002," at a plant in Pontiac, Michigan. The MDNR initially advised GM that it would not act upon the application until later that year, when GM would be applying to renew its NPDES permit for the other point sources at the plant. Upon receiving the renewal application, however, the MDNR decided not to address the stormwater permit application for Outfall 002 but rather to revisit that matter "when EPA finalizes stormwater discharge permit regulations." In 1987 the Congress put a stop to the EPA's ongoing attempt to craft stormwater discharge permit regulations by prohibiting, except in limited circumstances, "the Administrator or the State... [from requiring] a permit under this section for discharges composed entirely of stormwater."

In June 1988 the MDNR issued GM a stormwater NPDES permit for Outfall 002 based upon its 1984 application. The permit advised GM that if aggrieved by its terms the Company could petition the MDNR for review but that the agency "may reject any petition filed more than 60 days after issuance as being untimely." The permit, which specified limits upon GM's discharge of copper, lead, and zinc was to be in effect through October 1, 1990. GM could renew the permit by submitting the appropriate forms "no later than 180 days prior to the date of expiration." GM did not challenge the terms of the permit. Meanwhile, in August 1988, the Pontiac plant ceased operating.

As required by its permit, GM began to submit to the MDNR periodic discharge monitoring reports (DMRs) for Outfall 002. Beginning in May 1989 the DMRs revealed that water discharged at Outfall 002 contained levels of metals in excess of the limits set in the permit. GM determined that those levels were the result not of cross-connections to the plant's idled operations but of some combination of metals present in the rain and metals leached from the roofs of buildings and from copper gutters.

In 1991 the EPA twice ordered GM to come into compliance with the terms of its permit. GM responded by coating most of the roofs and gutters, which lowered the concentrations of metals in the discharges, but did not bring GM into full compliance with the terms of its permit. In 1993 the U.S. EPA filed an administrative complaint against GM under the Clean Water Act alleging 92 violations of its NPDES permit and seeking the maximum administrative penalty ($125,000) allowed.

After a hearing, an administrative law judge (ALJ) held that GM had violated the terms of its permit.... The ALJ assessed GM a civil penalty of $62,500, half the amount sought by the EPA, because GM's violations were not willful and because but for the Company's apparently unique status as holder of an NPDES permit for discharges of stormwater it likely would have faced no penalty at all.

Body of Opinion

Circuit Judge Ginsburg

...In this case GM claims there is no substantial evidence that it violated its permit because the evidence demonstrates that the permit was invalid from the outset, but the EPA refused to hear this attack upon the validity of the permit. The question now before us, therefore, is whether the EPA erred in interpreting the [Clean Water Act] CWA to limit the grounds upon which GM may challenge the validity and applicability of its permit in this federal enforcement proceeding....

GM... argues that the CWA allows a collateral attack upon a state-issued NPDES permit in an enforcement proceeding because... [the CWA]... prohibits only collateral attacks against "actions of the Administrator [of EPA] with respect to which review could have been obtained under... [the CWA]" of which one is "issuing or denying any [NPDES] permit." A state-issued NPDES permit, GM points out, is neither an action of the Administrator nor otherwise made reviewable under... [the CWA]; therefore, the argument goes, the prohibition of collateral attacks in... [the Act] does not bar its challenge in this federal proceeding to the validity of its state-issued permit....

The failure of the Congress in... [the Act] expressly to forbid collateral attacks upon state permits is of no import, therefore. That is, not having authorized any review of state permits in the first place, the Congress simply had no reason to single out and prohibit collateral review of state permits....

Presumably, the EPA would not find a permit violation if a permit holder could demonstrate that a state court had previously decided that the permit was void ab initio; certainly we would not find reasonable an interpretation of the CWA that precluded such a challenge to an EPA enforcement action. GM can point to no such decision, however, because it declined to take advantage of available state procedures to challenge its permit.... And the EPA persuasively argues that it reasonably interpreted the Act to prevent GM from doing in a federal enforcement proceeding what the Company had declined to do before the MDNR (Michigan Department of Natural Resources) and the Michigan state courts.

First, the Clean Water Act assigns to the participating states the primary role in administering the NPDES permitting program.... As the EPA states, precluding collateral attacks ensures that "the States [have] the opportunity as a threshold matter to address objections" to the permits they issue. Moreover, when a permit has been issued by a state agency, it alone will have the information pertinent to an attack upon the decision-making process that led to the issuance of that permit. Not only would the EPA have to expend considerable resources to obtain the information from the state agency; it would also be second-guessing that agency, which is inconsistent with the primary role of the states under the Act.

Judgment and Result

GM was not permitted to contest the validity of an NPDES permit in an enforcement proceeding even though the permit in question was based on questionable legal validity.

The time for challenging the permit was limited to a short period after issuance. GM had not challenged during that time and thus was barred from later challenging the permit in an enforcement hearing.

Questions

1. What act is the NPDES permit system designed to implement?
2. Who administers the NPDES permit system, the states or the federal [EPA] government? What is the argument for allowing a state to limit the amount of time in which a permittee can challenge its permit after which time the permit is treated as valid?
3. If runoff water from an abandoned factory roof goes into a sewer or other body of water must there be an NPDES permit for it? If Congress ended EPA's authority to regulate stormwater runoff via the NPDES permit system, how could GM be fined for violating its NPDES permit for discharging polluted storm water runoff?
4. What government issued GM's NPDES permit? What limits were there on GM's right to attack the permit's terms? Is the mistake GM made "not challenging the initial state-issued NPDES permit" when issued on grounds that the state/EPA had no authority under the CWA to regulate storm water runoff? A collateral attack occurs when a legal challenge to an official act, such as permit issuance, is first raised in a different proceeding, such as an enforcement of the permit.
5. Would the ultra vires doctrine have helped GM here? If an enabling act vanishes, how can a valid reg/permit regulate the matter?

1987 Amendments

In the space of approximately 83 pages, Congress comprehensively amended the Clean Water Act (CWA) with the passage of the Water Quality Act of 1987. Essentially these amendments fine-tune the CWA and do not make major structural changes to it.

Aspects of the CWA Left Unchanged. The principal part of the Clean Water Act for controlling direct discharges from point sources into the nation's waters is the NPDES permit system. This system remains after the 1987 Act subject only to "fine-tuning." Similarly, the Act retains the concepts of point source discharges, nonpoint source discharges, and publicly owned treatment works (POTW).

Specific Features of the CWA the 1987 Act "Fine-Tunes". First, the 1987 Act alters criminal penalties. For negligent violations of NPDES permits or negligently introducing any pollutant or hazardous substance into a sewer system a person knows or reasonably should have known could cause personal injury or property damage, fines are at least $2,500 to a maximum of $25,000 per day or one year in prison, or both. For repeat offenders, punishment for negligent violations can be double the maximum for first violations.

Second, **knowing violations** of an NPDES permit or a pretreatment program result in fines of no less than $5,000 per day and not more than $50,000 per day or imprisonment of three years, or both.

Third, a fine of up to $250,000 or imprisonment up to 15 years or both is possible for the offense of **knowing endangerment**. This violation involves an entity with an NPDES permit knowingly placing another person in imminent danger of death or serious bodily injury. Organizations can be fined not more than $1 million under this provision. Sanctions for repeat offenders are doubled for both fines and imprisonment.

Fourth, any person who knowingly makes any material false statement in a report, record, or document filed under the act can be fined not more than $10,000 or imprisoned up to two years, or both.

Fifth, civil penalties for certain violations are increased from a maximum of $10,000 per day to $25,000 per day. Good-faith efforts to comply may be considered in setting the amount of these penalties.

Sixth, administrative penalties can be assessed by the administrator of EPA for NPDES violations.

Seventh, a new provision referred to as **anti-backsliding** prevents reissuance of an NPDES permit with less stringent limits than the permit it replaces. The intent of anti-backsliding provisions is to maintain pollution control; unfortunately, some exceptions are permitted.

CLEAN AIR ACT[2]

Pre-Federal Air Pollution Control

The first statutory attempts to control air pollution were made by the states. Uneven standards and enforcement were common. Various common law doctrines, such as nuisance, were also available to private party plaintiffs, but these were inadequate for broad pollution control efforts.

Federal Air Pollution Control

In 1955, for the first time, a federal statute dealt with air pollution. It merely authorized research and federal technical and financial assistance. In 1963, Congress passed the Clean Air Act, the first federal attempt to regulate by controls applicable directly to polluters. The statute had two main flaws: it did not define air pollution, merely saying that it was designed to prevent and control air pollution; and enforcement was hampered by a requirement that courts were to give consideration to the practicability and physical and economic feasibility of stopping pollution.

[2] The authors acknowledge reliance on government documents in preparing this segment.

1965 Amendments

The 1965 amendments to the Clean Air Act attacked the problem of air pollution caused by automobiles and trucks by authorizing emission standards for mobile sources. The U.S. Public Health Service was to set the number. Again, however, economic and technical feasibility conditions affecting the development of such standards curbed development of meaningful emission controls.

1967 Amendments

The Clean Air Act was again amended in 1967. The theory behind these amendments was that air cleanup requires a national effort but that states should keep the primary authority for doing so. The 1967 amendments required that states establish **ambient air quality standards** for air quality control regions that are state and federally determined. After the air quality standards were determined, states were required to establish **state implementation plans** to achieve ambient air quality standards.

From the environmental viewpoint, weaknesses of the Clean Air Act after the 1967 amendments included the continued failure to define air pollution, the economic and technical feasibility conditions to the standards, the absence of private suit provisions, the lack of citizen surveillance, and excessive discretion in the act's administration.

1970 Amendments

The 1970 amendments to the Clean Air Act provided a definition of air pollution and eliminated the economic and technical feasibility loophole that previously existed. However, this law was still not strong. It had two functional elements—programs to furnish technical and financial help, and regulatory authority. A puzzling feature of the 1970 amendments was their continued declaration that the prevention and control of air pollution was the primary responsibility of the states, clearly a holdover from the 1955 act. Even though technical research is the heart of good air pollution regulations, the pattern has been to underfund air pollution research by about one third of its statutory authorization. Short-funding a regulatory program with criminal penalties has serious adverse implications, because judicial challenge is often directed to the scientific evidence behind the regulations.

Three objectives of the 1970 amendments were to establish the nondeterioration principle, primary air quality standards, and secondary air quality standards. **Primary air quality standards** are ambient or general environmental standards that outdoor air must meet to protect the public health. The time set for achievement of primary air quality standards was 1975. The **secondary standards** are designed to protect public welfare, including the avoidance of any adverse effects on any human-made or aesthetic aspects of the environment. They were to be achieved within a "reasonable" time after 1975. Some ambient standards were set by the 1967 amendments and others by the 1970 amendments. Since its establishment in 1970, the EPA's administrator is the party legally authorized to determine ambient air quality standards through promulgating regulations that set forth numbers indicating the amount of a particular air pollutant that will be legally tolerated.

Pollutants Covered

Only about six pollutants are covered by the ambient air quality standards: hydrocarbons, carbon monoxide, sulfur dioxide, nitrogen oxides, particulates, and photochemical oxidants. Actually, more than six substances are now covered because hydrocarbons, particulates, and photochemical oxidants are generic, embracing more than one element. The Clean Air Act allows expansion of the list of air pollutants. Additionally, the 1970 amendments further authorize the EPA administrator to establish **direct emission standards** for any stationary source emitting substances designated by the administrator as hazardous, which may cause or contribute to mortality or irreversible or incapacitating illness). Vinyl chloride, asbestos, beryllium, mercury, and benzene have thus far been designated hazardous pollutants. Finally, the 1970 amendments give the EPA administrator authority to set **standards of performance** for new sources that contribute significantly to air pollution or endanger the public health or welfare.

Basic Concepts

At this point, noting some basic air pollution concepts under the Clean Air Act may be helpful. The first is the **air quality control region** (AQCR). The entire area of the United States is divided into 247 air quality control regions, as designated by the EPA administrator, often consisting of several states having common topography, climactic, and air pollution characteristics. The AQCR has not proven successful as an air pollution cleanup technique mainly due to political reasons. For example, governors of some western and midwestern states see other governors, particularly those of eastern states, as wanting to clean up the air in eastern states at a cost of western and midwestern jobs. The second air pollution concept is that of criteria documents—scientific studies that set forth parameters for primary and secondary ambient air quality standards. They provide the support for the administrator's decision to set ambient air quality standards at a particular level and prevent accusations that the administrator pulled numbers out of thin air.

The heart of the federal air pollution control program—and the third important term in air pollution control under the Clean Air Act—is the state implementation plan (SIP). Each state submits a plan (SIP) to the EPA administrator to achieve the federally set primary and secondary air quality standards. **Nondeterioration standards** were made a mandatory part of the SIP after the Sierra Club successfully sued the EPA administrator to force such an inclusion. States were given until January 31, 1972, to submit proposed SIPs to EPA for approval. The EPA could either approve or disapprove all or part of the SIP. If EPA approved a SIP, it became part of federal law. The EPA may amend a SIP to conform to federal ambient air criteria.

The SIPs contain a compilation of state air pollution statutes, regulations plus municipal ordinances, emission limits, schedules and timetables for compliance, land use controls, and transportation control plans.

Enforcement

Enforcement under the Clean Air Act has several aspects. Elaborate information-gathering provisions authorize the EPA administrator to require any emission source to install, use, and maintain monitoring equipment and to establish and maintain air pollution records. EPA officials are given a right of entry onto the premises of pollution sources. All information the administrator requires of pollution sources is publicly available, except for trade secrets. However, in the case of emission data, no trade secret protection is available.

Violations of the Clean Air Act can lead to civil penalties or criminal sanctions. The act also includes authority for citizen suits against any person (including the U.S. government) allegedly in violation of the Clean Air Act. This provision is the basis for a number of environmental group suits against the EPA to force promulgation of regulations. On a number of occasions the EPA has failed to meet statutory deadlines for promulgation of regulations or has promulgated weak regulations.

The EPA has emergency power to go to court to shut down any source or combination of sources that presents imminent, substantial danger to health. This power was used in 1971 in Birmingham, Alabama, to close steel mills, among other things.

Mobile sources account for slightly more than 50 percent of the air pollution in the United States. The EPA has emission standard authority for two general moving sources: all new vehicles, and engines in vehicles used on streets, as well as aircraft engines. Additionally, the EPA has the authority to regulate vehicular fuel, since this affects vehicular emissions.

In the following case, Virginia sued the federal government claiming that the Clean Air Act's enforcement mechanisms against the states violate federalism. See what a U.S. Court of Appeals did with this claim.

Commonwealth of Virginia v. United States

U.S. Court of Appeals
74 F.3d 517 (4th Cir. 1996)

Background and Facts:

Virginia says that this dispute arises out of two major ongoing disputes with EPA regarding the Commonwealth's compliance with the federal Clean Air Act (CAA). One dispute, according to the complaint, involves Virginia's alleged failure to develop and submit to EPA an approvable vehicle inspection and maintenance (I and M) program and a volatile organic compound (VOC) reduction plan for Northern Virginia and Richmond. The other dispute involves Virginia's alleged failure to submit to EPA an approvable Title V stationary source operating permit program.

The chief mischief-maker here is ozone, the pollutant that most often causes a particular region's air to violate federal standards. Ozone is one of the primary components of smog. In sufficiently high concentrations, ozone causes chest pains, coughing, nausea, irritation of the throat and increased susceptibility to respiratory infection. Excessive ozone can also damage forests and crops.

Ozone is formed when volatile organic compounds (VOCs) react with nitrogen oxides in the presence of sunlight and heat. . . . "VOC is the collective name given to pollutants that [contain carbon and] are gases at room temperature." Automobile exhaust is a VOC source. Although most nitrogen oxides are made naturally, automobile exhaust increases atmospheric nitrogen oxide levels. Thus, auto exhaust, as a source of both VOCs and nitrogen oxides, is a major cause of increased ozone levels. Because by 2010 the number of miles driven in the United States will increase by an estimated 60 percent, the nation faces a real potential for ever-increasing amounts of pollution from automobile exhaust.

The CAA authorizes the EPA Administrator to promulgate national ambient air quality standards (NAAQS). An area that does not meet the minimum level of air quality mandated by the NAAQS is considered to be a "nonattainment area." With respect to the pollutant ozone, an area's degree of nonattainment may be classified as marginal, moderate, serious, severe, or extreme.

By 1989 more than 90 of the nation's urban areas were in nonattainment of the NAAQS for ozone, raising a health concern for as many as 95 million Americans. As a result, Congress in 1990 extensively amended the CAA in an effort to cope with the increasingly severe problem of unhealthy ozone levels throughout the country.

The CAA's complex statutory and regulatory scheme calls upon the states to shoulder a large portion of the difficult task of cleaning up the nation's air. The 1990 amendments extended deadlines (that had existed under earlier versions of the CAA) for states to reach full attainment with respect to ozone levels and set new deadlines for states to achieve lesser (but still maintaining) reductions of ozone. The 1990 amendments also encourage states to design and implement an operating permit program intended to regulate stationary sources of air pollution, such as factories and power plants.

Body of Opinion

Court of Appeals Judge Michael

Under Title I of the CAA, if a state has an area within it that EPA has classified as being in moderate, serious or severe nonattainment with respect to ozone, the state must devise and implement a "state implementation plan" (SIP) that reduces VOC emissions within the area by 15 percent ("a 15% Plan"). . . . The SIP must include a program of vehicle inspection and maintenance that will reduce automobile exhaust's contribution to air pollution (an "I & M Program").

Title I imposes sanctions on states that fail to comply with its provisions. States may, for example, be prevented from spending federal highway money in nonattainment areas.... This loss of highway money is automatic and mandatory if the state fails to implement an adequate SIP within 24 months of EPA's finding that a proposed SIP is deficient.... Even before this two-year period expires, EPA may (after first going through a notice-and-comment rulemaking proceeding) block the state from spending federal highway funds in nonattainment areas.... However, highway money may not be blocked—under either the mandatory or the discretionary sanction provisions—for projects that "likely will result in a significant reduction in, or avoidance of, accidents."...

Nor may money be blocked if it is to be spent on transportation projects that would encourage conservation and that would tend to result in less pollution from automobiles, i.e., public transit programs, development of park-and-ride facilities, construction of high-occupancy vehicle lanes and the like....

The state's failure to submit a valid SIP also causes the EPA to subject private industry to more stringent permitting requirements.... This sanction is mandatory after 18 months and (as with the highway sanction) is discretionary at any time after EPA has found a proposed SIP to be inadequate....

Finally, if two years pass after a SIP is first found to be deficient or the state's submission of a proposed SIP to EPA is found to be administratively incomplete, EPA must impose a "federal implementation program" (FIP) on those areas of a state that are in nonattainment.... "The FIP provides an additional incentive for state compliance because it rescinds state authority to make the many sensitive technical and political choices that a pollution control regime demands."...

Title V of the CAA requires states to administer permitting programs intended to regulate stationary sources of air pollution....

Once EPA rejects a proposed Title V permitting program, the state has 18 months to correct any problems EPA has with the proposed plan. If the state does not correct the problems within 18 months, EPA must impose either the highway sanction or the permitting sanction described above.... Six months later, if the problems remain uncorrected, EPA must impose the remaining sanction.... In addition, EPA may impose these sanctions earlier, but (as in the Title I context) it first must go through a notice-and-comment rulemaking proceeding.... Finally, if EPA has not approved a state's Title V Program by November 15, 1995 (five years after enactment of the 1990 Amendments), EPA must promulgate and administer a federal Title V permitting program (a FIP) within the state.

Judgment and Result

Virginia lost. The Court of Appeals held that the CAA's provision denying states the right to appeal EPA decisions to federal district courts, requiring instead appeals directly to the Court of Appeals, was valid. The Court of Appeals only decided this jurisdictional issue, not whether Congress, through the EPA, could impose environmental mandates on states.

Because the Northern Virginia area has been in "serious" nonattainment with respect to ozone levels, and because the Richmond area has been in "moderate" nonattainment, Virginia is subject to Title I. Virginia is also subject to Title V.

EPA took final action by letter on January 20, 1994, finding that Virginia's Title I (I & M and 15% Plan) submissions were incomplete, in part because Virginia only submitted draft regulations to EPA instead of final, permanent regulations. On December 5, 1994, EPA took final action disapproving on substantive grounds Virginia's Title V Program,...in part because Virginia limited judicial review of permitting decisions to those litigants who could prove that they had a "pecuniary and substantial interest" in the outcome of the litigation....

EPA's actions prompted Virginia to file on January 9, 1995, under...[the U.S. Code] a three-count complaint against EPA in the United States District Court for the Eastern District of Virginia, asking that certain CAA provisions be declared unconstitutional on their face....

A reading of the complaint thus leaves no doubt that Virginia seeks to reverse final EPA action. Because jurisdiction under [the CAA] turns on whether final agency action is the target of the challenger's claim, it is of no consequence that Virginia has armed itself with the Constitution....

It is settled that "when Congress has chosen to provide the circuit courts with exclusive jurisdiction over appeals from agency [actions], the district courts are without jurisdiction over the legal issues pertaining to final [actions]—whether or not those issues arise from the statutes that authorized the agency action in the first place."...CAA...channels review of final EPA action exclusively to the courts of appeals, regardless of how the grounds for review are framed....

Virginia makes several points in contending that [the CAA]...does not, or at least should not be allowed to, restrict final action review to the circuit courts.

Because Congress wanted prompt and conclusive review in air quality controversies, it channeled (to the courts of appeals) all challenges, regardless of their basis, of EPA rules and final actions. See *Palumbo*... "exclusive jurisdiction in the court of appeals avoids duplicative review."

Questions

1. Did the Court of Appeals actually make a decision on the politically sensitive issue of whether Congress can command (under the Clean Air Act) states to set up I & M (inspection and maintenance) programs? Or did the Court duck the issue?
2. One of the judges in the *Virginia v. U.S.* case was former U.S. Supreme Court Justice Lewis Powell of

Virginia. He sat on the case during oral argument but did not participate in the decision of the case. Why would a Virginian sit on such a case?

3. Was the gist of Virginia's constitutional and jurisdictional argument this: That if the CAA is unconstitutional and the CAA says that challengers to it must go to the Court of Appeals and not the District Courts, then the District Courts really do have jurisdiction because the entire CAA (including the jurisdictional route by-passing the District Court) is invalid? Or that constitutional claims should be handled in the district courts and review of agency actions should be dealt with as the CAA prescribed, in the Courts of Appeal? Did either of these arguments prevail?
4. Despite the court's unwillingness to answer many questions the *Virginia* case raises, the opinion does contain a good discussion of SIPs, FIPs, nonattainment areas, and NAAQSs. How does each of these Clean Air Act concepts try to clean up the nation's air? How far were Northern Virginia and Richmond out of compliance with the 1990 amendments that were passed five years before this suit? What does this indicate about the air quality in these areas?
5. What development does the Court cite as likely to occur by the year 2010 with respect to air pollution caused by vehicle emissions in the United States? That the number of miles driven is likely to increase by 60%? What does this mean regarding air pollution? That even if we produce vehicles emitting less ozone and other pollutants, that gains will be offset by increased driving? Table 24.4 provides air pollution concentration levels.

CONTROVERSIAL ISSUES

Before the 1977 amendments to the Clean Air Act, several controversial legal issues had to be settled: whether automobile emission standards should be extended or postponed; whether air quality in regions already cleaner than ambient air quality standards should be allowed to deteriorate so that economic development could occur; whether new construction and hence increased population sources and expansion of old sources would be allowed in areas that had not yet attained ambient air quality standards; and whether faster and more effective enforcement of the act could be achieved.

TABLE 24.4 National Ambient Air Pollutant Concentrations: 1990 to 1997

POLLUTANT	UNIT	Monitoring stations, number	Air quality standard	1987	1990	1993	1994	1995	1996	1997
Carbon monoxide	ppm	368	[2]9	6.71	5.8	4.9	5.0	4.5	4.2	3.9
Ozone	ppm	660	[3].12	0.124	0.112	0.108	0.107	0.112	0.105	0.105
Sulfur dioxide	ppm	486	.03	0.009	0.008	0.007	0.007	0.006	0.006	0.005
Particulates (PM-10)[4]	µg/m³	845	50	(NA)	29.5	26.2	26.2	25.1	24.2	24.0
Nitrogen dioxide	ppm	224	.053	0.021	0.020	0.019	0.020	0.019	0.018	0.018
Lead	µg/m³	195	[5]1.5	0.16	0.09	0.05	0.05	0.04	0.04	0.04

NA Not available. [1] Refers to the primary National Ambient Air Quality Standard that protects the public health. [2] Based on 8-hour standard of 9 ppm. [3] Based on 1-hour standard of .12 ppm. [4] The particulates (PM-10) standard replaced the previous standard for total suspended particulates in 1987. [5] Based on 3-month standard of 1.5 µg/m³.

[Data represent annual composite averages of pollutant based on daily 24-hour averages of monitoring stations, except carbon monoxide is based on the second-highest, non-overlapping, 8-hour average; ozone, average of the second-highest daily maximum 1-hour value; and lead, quarterly average of ambient lead levels. Based on data from the Aerometric Information Retrieval System. µg/m³=micrograms of pollutant per cubic meter of air; ppm=parts per million]

Source: U.S. Environmental Protection Agency, *National Air Quality and Emissions Trends Report*, annual.

1977 Amendments

In August 1977 President Carter signed the Clean Air Act amendments into law. The amendments further extended the auto emissions reduction deadline (originally set for 1975 and later postponed to 1978) for unburned hydrocarbons to 1980 and for carbon monoxide to 1981. The nitrogen oxide standard was relaxed from 0.4 to 1.0 gram per mile.

The 1977 amendments require studies of excess sulfates from catalyst-equipped cars that had shown some early problems in this area. EPA measurements of sulfate concentrations along the Los Angeles freeway system during a two-year study indicate the problem is less serious than at first feared. The 1977 amendments also extended National Academy of Sciences health studies of auto pollutants.

The 1977 Clean Air Act amendments deal with the second major problem—**prevention of significant deterioration** of air cleaner than ambient standards—by saying, in general, that some deterioration may take place but in different amounts in different areas. The 1977 amendments divide areas having cleaner than national standards into three classes. Class I areas are those in which little deterioration may take place. Mandatory Class I areas are international parks, national wilderness areas exceeding 5,000 acres, national memorial parks exceeding 5,000 acres, and national parks exceeding 6,000 acres. In Class II areas, only moderate air quality deterioration will be allowed. In Class III areas, significant deterioration will be allowed but may not exceed national ambient standards.

The principal practical issue involved in nondeterioration is whether western states' pristine air will give way to development of the region's coal resources. An answer to this question will be provided by the states' governors, because, according to the 1977 amendments, all clean air areas are Class II (except parks and wilderness areas designated by Congress as Class I in the amendments) unless the governor designates them as Class I or Class III. Thus, the 1977 amendments confer considerable power on a western state governor to promote air quality or economic development.

The third major air pollution problem addressed by the 1977 amendments involves nonattainment areas—areas that do not meet ambient air quality requirements. Because many areas presently do not meet national ambient air quality standards (NAAQS), and because each state SIP contains a **preconstruction review mechanism** to ensure that new source construction will not interfere with attainment or maintenance of NAAQS, it is questionable whether any new construction or expansion of existing facilities should be allowed in "dirty air" areas. EPA has proposed an **emission offset policy** that would allow new air pollution in present dirty air areas, provided that the net effect of the new emissions, together with reductions from existing sources below SIP requirements, does not worsen PAQSs (primary air quality standards) but contribute to reasonable progress in attaining such standards.

The 1977 amendments adopted the proposed EPA emission offset policy in modified form by allowing new sources in dirty air areas "only if they attain the lowest achievable emission rates" and if other sources in the state under the same ownership or control are in compliance with relevant emission control provisions. The state must reduce emissions in the dirty air area each year and make progress toward meeting the 1982 or 1987 deadline for attainment of NAAQS.

Improving Clean Air Act compliance and enforcement is the fourth major area tackled by the 1977 amendments. In an unusual attempt to gain industry's compliance with air pollution control regulations, the amendments establish a scheme that sets an economic penalty equal to the economic benefit of being out of compliance. Among the other new enforcement provisions is a requirement of **economic impact statements** (EIS) for new regulations under the Clean Air Act, including an evaluation of employment losses resulting from new regulations and studies of potential employee dislocation that the act will cause. Energy-related or economic emergencies will provide temporary relief from the act's regulations.

Air Pollution Costs and Benefits[3]

In its 1980 annual report, the Council on Environmental Quality (CEQ) estimates that $299.1 billion will be spent on air pollution control alone between 1979 and 1988. Given the magnitude of past and projected expenditures on air pollution, what are the resulting benefits? Probably the major benefit—improved public health—will never be known, because we can only speculate about what might have been had no pollution abatement occurred.

According to a recent CEQ annual report, scrubbers designed to control sulfur dioxide and particulate control systems have reduced violations of standards for those pollutants. However, increased emphasis on coal as an energy source could cause other **noncriteria pollutants** such as nitrates, trace metals, and organic carcinogens to increase.

Carbon monoxide and photochemical oxidants are the principal air pollution problems in U.S. cities. The areas having ozone standard violations are large cities. Ozone has several known adverse health effects.

Global air pollution problems include the carbon dioxide greenhouse effect, the turbidity effect, and potential depletion of the ozone layer. The **greenhouse effect** refers to the increased temperatures at lower atmospheric levels caused by increased carbon dioxide, which tends to retain solar energy in the lower atmosphere. The projection is that if we use up fossil fuels at an accelerated rate, the CO_2 level will double by 2025 and will be seven to eight times the present level by 2100. A doubling of the CO_2 level would raise global temperature 2° to 3° C, a major environmental threat. **Turbidity**—the presence of microscopic particulates in the air—tends to counteract the CO_2 greenhouse effect somewhat. Analyses since 1970, however, show no clear global cooling or heating trend. Depletion of the ozone layer is caused at least in part by use of flourocarbons (propellants for certain aerosols such as hair sprays). The depletion of the ozone layer continues. One result is increased susceptibility to skin cancer.

Chevron v. National Resources Defense Council is a Supreme Court interpretation of the Clean Air Act dealing with the bubble policy. This case deals with a stationary air pollution source. Following the *Chevron* case is *United States v. Haney*, which deals with mobile sources of air pollution.

Chevron v. National Resources Defense Council

U.S. Supreme Court
467 U.S. 837 (1984)

Background and Facts:

The Clean Air Act amendments of 1977 impose certain requirements on states that have not achieved the national air quality standards. The U.S. Environmental Protection Agency established those standards under earlier laws. The Clean Air Act requires that "nonattainment" states set up a permit program regulating "new or modified major stationary sources" of air pollution. Generally, a permit may not be issued for such sources unless stringent conditions are met. EPA regulations promulgated in 1981 to implement the permit requirement allow a state to adopt a plantwide definition of the phrase "stationary

[3] Table 24.5 lists pollutant standard values for the five major criteria pollutants.

source." Under this definition, an existing plant that contains several pollution-emitting devices may install or modify one piece of equipment without meeting the permit condition if the alteration will not increase the total plant emissions. Thus, a state may treat all of the pollution-emitting devices within the same industrial grouping as though they were encased within a single "bubble."

The National Resources Defense Council (NRDC) filed a petition for review in the court of appeals. That court set aside the regulations that allowed the bubble concept. The court of appeals recognized that the amended Clean Air Act does not explicitly define what Congress envisioned as a "stationary source" to which the permit program would apply. The court of appeals also noted that the issue was not squarely addressed in the legislative history. It concluded that in view of the purpose of the nonattainment program to improve rather than merely maintain air quality, a plantwide definition was "inappropriate." Chevron appealed to the U.S. Supreme Court.

Body of Opinion

Justice Stevens

The legislative history of the portion of the 1977 Amendments dealing with nonattainment areas does not contain any specific comment on the "bubble concept" or the question whether a plantwide definition of a stationary source is permissible under the permit program. It does, however, plainly disclose that in the permit program Congress sought to accommodate the conflict between the economic interest in permitting capital improvements to continue and the environmental interest in improving air quality. Indeed, the House Committee Report identified the economic interest as one of the "two main purposes" of this section of the bill. It stated:

> Section 117 of the bill, adopted during full committee markup establishes a new section 127 of the Clean Air Act. The section has two main purposes: (1) to allow reasonable economic growth to continue in an area while making reasonable further progress to assure attainment of the standards by a fixed date; and (2) to allow States greater flexibility for the former purpose than EPA's present interpretative regulations afford. . . .

We are not persuaded that parsing of general terms in the text of the statute will reveal an actual intent of Congress. We know full well that this language is not dispositive; the terms are overlapping and the language is not precisely directed to the question of the applicability of a given term in the context of a larger operation. To the extent any congressional "intent" can be discerned from this language, it would appear that the listing of overlapping, illustrative terms was intended to enlarge, rather than to confine, the scope of the agency's power to regulate particular sources in order to effectuate the policies of the Act.

In August 1980, however, the EPA adopted a regulation that, in essence, applied the basic reasoning of the Court of Appeals in this case. The EPA took particular note of the two then-recent Court of Appeals decisions, which had created the bright-line rule that the bubble concept should be employed in a program designed to *maintain* air quality but not in one designed to *enhance* air quality. Relying heavily on those cases, EPA adopted a dual definition of "source" for nonattainment areas that required a permit whenever a change in either the entire plant, or one of its components, would result in a significant increase in emissions even if the increase was completely offset by reductions elsewhere in the plant. The EPA expressed the opinion that this interpretation was "more consistent with congressional intent" than the plantwide definition because it "would bring in more sources or modifications for review" but its primary legal analysis was predicated on the two Court of Appeals decisions.

In 1981 a new administration took office and initiated a "Government-wide reexamination of regulatory burdens and complexities." In the context of that review, the EPA reevaluated the various arguments that had been advanced in connection with the proper definition of the term "source" and concluded that the term should be given the same definition in both nonattainment areas and PSD areas.

In explaining its conclusion, the EPA first noted that the definitional issue was not squarely addressed in either the statute or its legislative history and therefore that the issue involved an agency "judgment as how to best carry out the Act." It then set forth several reasons for concluding that the plantwide definition was more appropriate. It pointed out that the dual definition "can act as a disincentive to new investment and modernization by discouraging modifications to existing facilities" and "can actually retard progress in air pollution control by discouraging replacement of older, dirtier processes or pieces of equipment with new, cleaner ones." Moreover, the new definition "would simplify EPA's rules by using the same definition of 'source' for PSD, nonattainment new source review and the construction moratorium. This reduces confusion and inconsistency." Finally, the agency explained that additional requirements that remained in place would accomplish the fundamental purpose of achieving attainment with NAAQS as expeditiously as possible. These conclusions were expressed in a proposed rulemaking in August 1981 that was formally promulgated in October.

In this Court respondents (NRDC) expressly reject the basic rationale of the Court of Appeals' decision.

That court viewed the statutory definition of the term "source" as sufficiently flexible to cover either a plantwide definition, a narrower definition covering each unit within a plant, or a dual definition that could apply to both the entire "bubble" and its components. It interpreted the policies of the statute, however, to mandate the plantwide definition in programs designed to improve air quality. Respondents place a fundamentally different construction on the statute. They contend that the text of the Act requires the EPA to use a dual definition—if either a component of a plant, or the plant as a whole, emits over 100 tons of pollutants, it is a major stationary source. They thus contend that the EPA rules adopted in 1980, insofar as they apply to the maintenance of the quality of clean air, as well as the 1981 rules which apply to nonattainment areas, violate the statute.

In addition, respondents argue that the legislative history and policies of the Act foreclose the plantwide definition, and that the EPA's interpretation is not entitled to deference because it represents a sharp break with prior interpretations of the Act.

Based on our examination of the legislative history, we agree with the Court of Appeals that it is unilluminating. The general remarks pointed to by respondents "were obviously not made with this narrow issue in mind and they cannot be said to demonstrate a Congressional desire...."

The arguments over policy that are advanced in the parties' briefs create the impression that respondents are now waging in a judicial forum a specific policy battle which they ultimately lost in the agency and in the thirty-two jurisdictions opting for the bubble concept, but one which was never waged in the Congress. Such policy arguments are more properly addressed to legislators or administrators, not to judges....

Judges are not experts in the field, and are not part of either political branch of the Government. Courts must, in some cases, reconcile competing political interests, but not on the basis of the judges' personal policy preferences. In contrast, an agency to which Congress has delegated policymaking responsibilities may, within the limits of that delegation, properly rely upon the incumbent administration's views of wise policy to inform its judgments. While agencies are not directly accountable to the people, the Chief Executive is, and it is entirely appropriate for this political branch of the Government to make such policy choices—resolving the competing interests which Congress itself either inadvertently did not resolve, or intentionally left to be resolved by the agency charged with the administration of the statute in light of everyday realities.

Judgment and Result

We hold that the EPA's definition of the term "source" is a permissible construction of the statute which seeks to accommodate progress in reducing air pollution with economic growth. "The regulations which the Administrator has adopted provide what the agency could allowably view as... [an] effective reconciliation of these twofold ends...." The judgment of the Court of Appeals is reversed.

Questions

1. Where did the idea for the bubble policy come from—Congress or the EPA?
2. Whom does the bubble policy help? How does it help?

Much air pollution is the result of motor vehicles. The *Haney* case illustrates the temptation to tamper with cars' pollution control equipment.

United States v. Haney Chevrolet, Inc.

U.S. District Court (M.D. Fla.)
371 F.Supp. 381 (1974)

Background and Facts:

The United States alleges that on or about July 26, 1972, Haney Chevrolet, Inc., an automobile dealer in Orlando, Florida, sold a new 1972 Chevrolet Corvette, Model LT-1, to William L. Ellis of Orlando, Florida. The United States further alleges that on or about August 23, 1972, Haney Chevrolet, Inc., violated [the Clean Air Act] by knowingly removing the original carburetor and its accompanying idle speed solenoid from that Corvette and replacing the carburetor without replacing the idle speed solenoid and knowingly rendering inoperative the transmission-controlled spark system on the Corvette. (The United States consolidated for trial these two devices or systems into one count.) Each of these devices or systems is alleged to be an emission control device or element of design which was installed on the Corvette by the manufacturer in compliance with the regulations promulgated by the Administrator of the Environmental Protection Agency pursuant to Title II of the Clean Air Act.

Prior to trial the parties stipulated... the following facts....

1. The defendant, Haney Chevrolet, Inc., is a corporation organized under the laws of the State of Delaware... and is engaged in the sale and distribution of new Chevrolet motor vehicles within the Middle District of Florida.

2. On... July 26, 1972, Haney Chevrolet, Inc. sold the 1972 Chevrolet Corvette... to William L. Ellis for personal use and not for resale, and... William L. Ellis [took] delivery of [the] 1972 Chevrolet Corvette....

3. On... August 23, 1972, Donald McDowell, on instructions given him by Douglas Irvine, the then Haney Chevrolet Service Manager, removed the original carburetor and accompanying idle speed solenoid from said Chevrolet Corvette, and installed a new carburetor without said idle speed solenoid, thereby rendering the idle speed solenoid inoperative.

4. On... August 23, 1972, Donald McDowell, on instructions given him by Douglas Irvine, rendered inoperative the transmission control spark system on said Chevrolet Corvette.

5. The transmission control spark system and the idle speed solenoid are emission control devices or elements of design within the meaning of [the Clean Air Act] and the regulations promulgated thereunder.

There remained for trial by the jury two genuine issues of fact raised by defendant's affirmative defenses:

1. Whether or not Donald McDowell, a mechanic of the defendant, and/or Douglas Irvine, defendant's service manager, were acting within the scope of their employment or agency with Haney Chevrolet, Inc., on or about August 23, 1972, when the idle speed solenoid was removed from said Chevrolet Corvette and when the transmission control spark system on said Chevrolet Corvette was rendered inoperative; and

2. Whether or not Donald McDowell and/or Douglas Irvine knowingly removed or rendered inoperative said devices or systems with the intent that they remain permanently removed or inoperative....

Body of Opinion

Judge Young

For reasons set forth it is ordered that a directed verdict be entered on the Government's civil penalty claim in favor of the plaintiff. There remains at the conclusion of all the evidence no genuine issue of fact for determination by the jury on either of the questions specified to be tried before the jury. Without weighing the credibility of the witnesses, there can be but one reasonable conclusion as to the verdict in this case; therefore, a directed verdict in favor of the plaintiff is required....

On the agency question which was specified before trial for determination by the jury, the evidence presented dictated but one conclusion: that defendant's service manager and mechanic were acting within the scope of their employment with the defendant on or about August 23, 1972, when they removed the idle speed solenoid and rendered inoperative the transmission controlled spark system on Mr. Ellis' Chevrolet Corvette. It is uncontroverted that the defendant's service manager and mechanic removed or rendered inoperative these emission control devices in the regular course of the duties in the defendant's service garage during their normal day-to-day activites and in the general furtherance of defendant's business interests. Clearly, neither Mr. Irvine nor Mr. McDowell performed any of this work on the Corvette toward any personal ends; rather, the work was done to serve the defendant's business interests. Under Florida law, an employer is liable for the improper acts of its employees or agents committed in the scope of their employment, even though they may have deviated from the employer's instructions.... Therefore, a directed verdict in favor of the United States is required on this issue.

The other question which was specified prior to trial for determination by the jury involves the issue of whether or not the defendant's service manager and mechanic knowingly removed or rendered inoperative these emission control devices or systems with the intent that they remain permanently removed or inoperative. Defendant has contended that its employees removed or rendered inoperative said devices or systems with the intent that they remain so only temporarily until a solution to the Corvette's engine problems could be found. Defendant further contended that to leave the devices engaged on the Corvette until a solution was found would present a fire hazard to the occupants of the vehicle....

The statute states that it is unlawful for a dealer "knowingly to remove or render inoperative" certain emission control devices or elements of design from a vehicle. It is well-settled that an act is done knowingly when it is done voluntarily and intentionally, and not by mistake or accident. The Court interprets that the prohibited act of "removal or rendering inoperative a device or element of design" is complete within the meaning of this statute when the dealer knowingly removes or renders inoperative the emission control devices or elements of design on a particular vehicle and voluntarily relinquishes custody and control of the vehicle, (or custody and control by an agent or employee of the dealer) with the emission control devices or elements of design removed or rendered inoperative.

While common sense dictates that the dealer or an agent or employee of the dealer may remove or render inoperative any such emission control devices or elements of designs on a vehicle for purposes of testing that vehicle while in his custody and control, the statute must be interpreted to prohibit the dealer or his agent or employee from removing or rendering inoperative any such emission control devices or elements of design and thereafter releasing such vehicle from his custody and control without first reengaging and making operative all devices or elements of design previously removed or rendered inoperative by him.

In this case it is uncontroverted that Mr. Irvine, defendant's service manager, voluntarily permitted Mr. Ellis to take his Corvette from defendant's service garage after the idle speed solenoid had been removed and the transmission controlled spark system had been rendered inoperative. Thereafter, Ellis traded in the Corvette at a dealer in St. Petersburg who in turn sold the vehicle with the solenoid still removed and the TCS system still inoperative to another private party.

There is therefore no possible construction of the evidence which could be other than that the defendant, through its employees, permitted the Corvette to leave the custody and control of the defendant with the solenoid removed and the TCS system inoperative. On the second remaining issue then this Court concludes that the plaintiff is entitled to prevail as a matter of law and there is nothing to submit to a jury. . . .

Judgment and Result

A civil penalty of $500 was imposed on Haney Chevrolet, Inc. No injunction (court order against repeat offenses, violation of which would be a crime) was imposed on Haney Chevrolet because the court thought repeat offenses were unlikely.

Questions

1. If a corporation cannot do anything for itself but must act through its agents, why was the suit brought against Haney Chevrolet, Inc., instead of the service manager, Doug Irvine, or the mechanic who actually removed the solenoid at Irvine's direction?
2. How does it reflect on the ability of U.S. car manufacturers to build effective air pollution devices in 1972 if the Chevy dealer had to remove an air pollution control device to keep the Corvette from starting on fire? (Fortunately, since that time air pollution control technology has improved.)
3. Why should Haney Chevrolet, Inc., be liable here at all if illegal acts are beyond the scope of the agent/servant's duties?
4. Was the $500 civil penalty excessive, too lenient, or about right? How much harm can removing the air pollution control device on one car do?

1990 Amendments[4]

In November 1990 President Bush signed into law the Clean Air Act of 1990, which contained the first major amendments to the Clean Air Act since 1977. Before discussing changes the 1990 Amendments make, it is important to emphasize that much of the Clean Air Act's structure—such as SIPs and primary and secondary air quality standards—remains.

Principal features of the 1990 Amendments include stricter emission limits for cars, provisions designed to slow destruction of the earth's ozone layer, and sections to control acid rain and toxic pollutants. The 1990 Act also provides for compensation to workers displaced by the Act, which is estimated to be $250 million over 5 years. The estimated costs of the 1990 Act are $20–25 billion per year. However, failure to control air pollution would also exact costs in the form of health care, days missed from work, and destruction of lakes, forests, and other property.

Stricter Vehicle Emissions. The present tailpipe emission levels are set at 0.41 grams per mile for hydrocarbons and 1.0 grams per mile for nitrogen oxide. Many, but not all, cars produced in model year 1994 would have to reduce hydrocarbons by 35 percent and nitrogen oxides by 60 percent from present levels. In the 1996 model year, all new cars would have to meet this standard. Starting in 1992 oil companies would have to offer less polluting gasolines. Also, beginning in 1998 manufacturers have to build auto pollution equipment having a life of 10 years or 100,000 miles. See Table 24.5 for a listing of pollution emissions over the past 30 years.

Controls on Ozone Depletion. Because ozone depletion only came to be recognized as a significant air pollution problem after the 1977 Clean Air Act amendments, no

[3] The authors acknowledge reliance on government documents in preparing this segment.

TABLE 24.5 National Air Pollutant Emissions: 1970 to 1997

YEAR	PM-10	PM-10, fugitive dust[1]	Sulfur dioxide	Nitrogen dioxides	Volatile organic compounds	Carbon monoxide	Lead
1970	13,190	(NA)	31,161	21,639	30,817	128,761	220,869
1975	7,803	(NA)	28,011	23,151	25,895	115,968	159,659
1980	7,287	(NA)	25,905	24,875	26,167	116,702	74,153
1984	6,220	(NA)	23,470	23,172	25,572	114,262	42,217
1985	4,695	40,889	23,230	23,488	24,227	115,644	22,890
1986	4,553	46,582	22,544	23,329	23,480	110,437	14,763
1987	4,492	38,041	22,308	22,806	23,193	108,879	7,681
1988	5,424	55,851	22,767	24,526	24,167	117,169	7,053
1989	4,590	48,650	22,907	24,057	22,383	104,447	5,468
1990	5,425	24,419	23,678	23,436	20,935	96,794	4,975
1991	5,329	24,122	23,056	23,520	21,063	97,790	4,168
1992	5,515	23,865	22,818	23,789	20,642	94,400	3,808
1993	3,680	24,196	22,476	24,046	20,830	94,526	3,911
1994	5,294	25,461	21,878	24,345	21,465	98,854	4,043
1995	4,306	22,454	19,189	23,768	20,558	89,151	3,924
1996	8,481	24,716	19,812	23,465	19,293	90,929	3,910
1997	8,428	25,153	20,369	23,582	19,214	87,451	3,915

NA Not available. [1] Sources such as agricultural tilling, construction, mining and quarrying, paved roads, unpaved roads, and wind erosion.

[In thousands of tons, except as indicated. PM-10=Particulate matter of less than ten microns. Methodologies to estimate data for 1970 to 1984 period and 1985 to present emissions differ. Beginning with 1985, the estimates are based on a modified National Acid Precipitation Assessment Program inventory]

Source: U.S. Environmental Protection Agency, *National Air Pollutant Emission Trends*, 1990-1997.

specific sections of prior federal law focused on protecting the atmosphere's ozone layer.

Various chemicals shown to be the cause of ozone depletion—specifically chlorofluorocarbons, hydrochlorofluorocarbons, and carbon tetrachloride—are phased out or banned by the 1990 Act. Chlorofluorocarbons and carbon tetrachloride are phased out through the 1990s and totally banned after the year 2000. A few regulations will require recycling and disposal of such chemicals from refrigeration and air conditioning equipment. Table 24.6 provides a listing of pollutant sources.

Acid Rain. For the first time, the 1990 Act adds to the Clean Air Act provisions to curb acid rain. Acid rain was not viewed as a serious problem when the 1977 amendments to the Clean Air Act were passed. Among the harms caused by acid rain are the destruction of lakes as habitats for aquatic life, particularly in the northeastern United States and eastern Canada, and harm to forests. Sources of acid rain have been identified as sulfur dioxide and nitrogen oxide, mainly from coal-burning power plants.

The overall objective of the 1990 Act is to halve present levels of nitrogen oxide and sulfur dioxide. The dates by which this objective would be met are several. By January 1, 1995, sulfur dioxide emissions would be cut 5 million tons annually and 10 million tons annually by the year 2000. Much of the reduction would result from tougher emission standards applied to 111 coal-burning utility plants in more than 20 states. Utilities would also have to cut nitrogen oxide by 2–4 million tons yearly within two years after 1990, and further such restrictions would take effect in 1997. These and other greenhouse emission statistics are provided in Table 24.7.

Limiting Toxic Air Pollutants. Law prior to the 1990 Act forced the U.S. Environmental Protection Agency (EPA) to protect the public from toxic air pollution

TABLE 24.6 Air Pollutant Emissions, by Pollutant and Source: 1997

SOURCE	Particulates[1]	Sulfur dioxide	Nitrogen oxides	Volatile organic compounds	Carbon monoxide	Lead
Total	**33,581**	**20,369**	**23,582**	**19,214**	**87,451**	**3,915**
Fuel combustion, stationary sources	1,101	17,259	10,724	860	4,817	496
Electric utilities	290	13,082	6,178	51	406	64
Industrial	314	3,365	3,270	217	1,110	17
Other fuel combustion	497	813	1,276	593	3,301	415
Residential	388	179	858	568	3,042	7
Industrial processes	861	1,664	804	1,527	4,779	2,251
Chemical and allied product manufacture	70	301	167	458	1,287	159
Metals processing	220	552	102	73	2,465	2,038
Petroleum and related industries	41	385	115	538	364	(NA)
Other	530	427	421	458	663	54
Solvent utilization	6	1	3	6,483	6	(NA)
Storage and transport	114	2	6	1,377	26	(NA)
Waste disposal and recycling	296	50	103	449	1,242	646
Highway vehicles	268	320	7,035	5,230	50,257	19
Light-duty gas vehicles and motorcycles	56	129	2,875	2,755	27,036	12
Light-duty trucks	40	96	1,901	1,968	18,364	7
Heavy-duty gas vehicles	9	11	326	268	3,349	-
Diesels	163	84	1,932	239	1,508	(NA)
Off highway[2]	466	1,060	4,560	2,430	16,755	503
Miscellaneous[3]	30,469	13	346	858	9,568	(NA)

[In thousands of tons, except as indicated]

- Represents zero. NA Not available. [1] Represents both PM-10 and PM-10 fugitive dust. [2] Includes emissions from farm tractors and other farm machinery, construction equipment, industrial machinery, recreational marine vessels, and small general utility engines such as lawn mowers. [3] Includes emissions such as from forest fires and other kinds of burning, various agricultural activities, fugitive dust from paved and unpaved roads, and other construction and mining activities, and natural sources.

Source: U.S. Environmental Protection Agency, *National Air Pollutant Emission Trends*, 1990-1997.

with an ample safety margin. However, since 1970 the EPA has regulated only seven toxins found in the air.

The 1990 Act expands the toxic air pollutant list to 189 and forces EPA to list more than 200 categories of hazardous pollutant sources (such as oil refineries) for which air pollution standards would be promulgated. Best control equipment available (BCEA) would have to be installed by most polluters between 1995 and 2003.

The 1990 Act creates a new agency, the Chemical Safety Board, to determine why chemical accidents occur. Also, the act mandates formal safety reviews of industrial plants and would give the public access to these reports.

Marketable Air Pollution Rights. The 1990 amendments of the Clean Air Act created a structure that allowed marketable air pollution rights. Recall from the Chapter 19 that anything that meets the three-pronged *Howey* test is legally a "security." In the *Howey* case, cultivated rows of orange trees marketed interstate were "securities." Thus it should come as no surprise that if an air polluter removes more sulfur dioxide than the Clean Air Act requires, the amount by which the polluter "exceeds" the legally

TABLE 24.7 Emissions of Greenhouse Gases, by Type and Source: 1990 to 1997

TYPE AND SOURCE	UNIT	1990	1992	1993	1994	1995	1996	1997
Carbon dioxide:								
Carbon content, total[1]	Mil. metric tons	1,355.9	1,360.6	1,393.6	1,413.8	1,428.1	1,478.8	1,500.8
Energy sources	Mil. metric tons	1,346.1	1,352.1	1,379.8	1,398.4	1,411.7	1,460.6	1,479.6
Methane:								
Gas, total [1]	Mil. metric tons	30.20	30.41	29.68	29.91	30.02	29.15	29.11
Energy sources	Mil. metric tons	10.79	10.83	10.11	10.13	10.36	9.89	9.99
Landfills	Mil. metric tons	11.11	10.89	10.82	10.75	10.66	10.54	10.38
Agricultural sources	Mil. metric tons	8.18	8.56	8.62	8.90	8.86	8.59	8.60
Nitrous oxide, total	1,000 metric tons	964	1,008	1,022	1,080	1,037	1,021	1,011
Agriculture	1,000 metric tons	646	670	670	706	650	635	642
Energy sources	1,000 metric tons	208	228	237	252	265	260	264
Industrial sources	1,000 metric tons	94	93	98	103	104	107	87
Nitrogen oxide, total [1]	Mil. metric tons	21.55	21.87	22.18	22.55	21.68	21.26	(NA)
Energy related	Mil. metric tons	20.41	20.86	21.20	21.41	20.68	20.24	(NA)
Stationary source full combustion	Mil. metric tons	9.85	9.89	10.05	9.97	9.79	9.49	(NA)
Transportation	Mil. metric tons	10.55	10.98	11.14	11.45	10.88	10.75	(NA)
Nonmethane volatile organic compounds (VOCs), total [1]	Mil. metric tons	18.92	18.68	18.85	19.46	18.59	17.23	(NA)
Energy related	Mil. metric tons	8.90	8.83	8.77	9.07	8.35	8.16	(NA)
Transportation	Mil. metric tons	8.00	7.82	7.88	8.18	7.38	7.19	(NA)
Industrial processes	Mil. metric tons	8.18	8.50	8.65	8.79	8.81	8.21	(NA)
Solid waste disposal	Mil. metric tons	0.89	0.92	0.95	0.95	0.97	0.39	(NA)
Carbon monoxide, total	Mil. metric tons	87.44	86.16	86.32	90.29	81.26	80.43	(NA)
Energy related	Mil. metric tons	71.96	74.61	74.61	76.27	69.61	68.71	(NA)
Transportation	Mil. metric tons	67.10	69.16	69.67	71.40	64.36	63.45	(NA)
Stationary source fuel combustion	Mil. metric tons	4.86	5.45	4.94	4.87	5.25	5.26	(NA)
Industrial processes	Mil. metric tons	4.33	4.12	4.22	4.18	4.18	4.19	(NA)
Chloroflurocarbons (CFCs) gases [2]	1,000 metric tons	193	143	141	104	97	63	46
Hydrofluorocarbons	1,000 metric tons	7	4	7	9	13	18	22
Hydrochloroflurocarbons (HCFCs) gases[3]	1,000 metric tons	80	84	82	93	107	119	133
Other chemicals:								
Carbon tetrachloride	1,000 metric tons	32	22	19	16	5	(NA)	(NA)
Methyl Cloroform	1,000 metric tons	158	108	93	77	46	4	(NA)
Sulfur hexafluoride	1,000 metric tons	1	1	1	1	1	1	1

[Emission estimates were mandated by Congress through Section 1605(a) of the Energy Policy Act of 1992 (Title XVI). Gases that contain carbon can be measured either in terms of the full molecular weight of the gas or just in terms of their carbon content]

NA Not available. [1] Includes minor sources not shown separately. [2] Covers principally CFC-11, CFC-12, and CFC-113. [3] Covers principally HCFC-22.

Source: U.S. Energy Information Administration, *Emissions of Greenhouse Gases in the United States*, annual.

required cleanup—called a *credit*—can be sold to another air polluter. Each credit represents one ton of sulfur dioxide. Thus, if a utility company reduces sulfur dioxide emissions by 100 tons more than it legally has to, it may sell these 100 credits to other air polluters who, for example, cannot meet their sulfur dioxide emission requirements. It is, in essence, a marketable pollution right.

Under the 1990 Amendments the marketable pollution rights concept has been thus far applied to sulfur removal only and to slightly over 100 power plants around the United States. Each power plant has a sulfur dioxide allowance. If a particular power plant fails to meet its allowance by 1995, then it must pay a fine of $2,000 for every ton of emissions over its allowed level. If a power plant sees that it will not meet its standard, it would pay for the other power plant's credits (assuming they exist), as long as they cost less than $2,000 each, the amount of the fine per ton.

SOLID WASTE: RESOURCE CONSERVATION AND RECOVERY ACT

In general, waste (or garbage) disposal in the United States is primitive. Our consumption-oriented society yields more than 154 million tons of municipal waste, not counting sewage, each year. Sewage and agriculture runoff are not considered as solid waste here. Even though technology in many areas has improved, we still commonly use a trash disposal method known for more than 100 years: **open dumping**.

Solid waste disposal was considered a state and local government concern before 1965. In 1965, Congress passed the Solid Waste Disposal Act, the first federal statute to deal with the effect of dumping on the environment. This act gave federal money to states and municipalities for waste disposal research. However, garbage was still viewed as mainly a state and municipal matter.

Congress amended the Solid Waste Disposal Act when it passed the Resource Recovery Act of 1970. This federal law recognized the economic benefits of **recycling** (recovery and reuse of resources from trash and waste). It gave federal money to urban areas with severe solid waste problems.

In the early 1970s, the federal role in solid waste was limited, consisting of several elements:

1. Construction of waste management and resource recovery demonstration projects
2. Technical and financial aid to state agencies' recycling waste management projects
3. National research and development on collection, recovery, recycling, and safe disposal of nonrecoverable waste
4. Federal guidelines (nonbinding suggestions on the proper way to collect, transport, separate, recover, and dispose of solid waste)
5. Occupational training grants

However, because solid waste disposal continued to be viewed as primarily a state and municipal matter, the federal role was limited. Then the roof fell in with several disclosures in the mid-1970s.

1. The Hudson River contained massive PCB (toxic oil) contamination.
2. Love Canal in Buffalo, New York, was filled with discarded chemicals that threatened the health of hundreds of families living nearby.
3. Kepone (a pesticide) dumped at Hopewell, Virginia, into the James River had caused serious human health damage as well as harm to fisheries in the James River and Chesapeake Bay.

These disclosures merely hinted at the secret dumping and disposal of hazardous wastes nationwide that threatened groundwater, surface water, and public health. People built houses on top of buried radioactive waste simply because they were unaware of the presence of hazardous material.

Congress enacted the Toxic Substances Control Act and the Resource Conservation and Recovery Act of 1976 RCRA) to deal with these problems. RCRA is a federal statute that deals with solid waste problems on a national basis. RCRA tries to control solid waste management practices that pose a danger to public health. It also regulates hazardous and nonhazardous solid wastes. RCRA defines solid wastes to include waste solids, sludges, liquids, and contained gases. Solid and dissolved sewage, irrigation return flows, industrial discharge covered by NPDES permits, and some radioactive wastes are not covered. RCRA defines a *hazardous waste* as one that may cause or significantly contribute to serious illness or death or that poses a substantial threat to human health or the environment if managed improperly.

Goals

RCRA has two main goals: to control management of solid waste that would endanger public health or the environment, and to encourage resource conservation and recovery. See Table 24.8 concerning solid waste.

TABLE 24.8 Generation and Recovery of Selected Materials in Municipal Solid Water: 1980 to 1997

ITEM AND MATERIAL	1980	1990	1991	1992	1993	1994	1995	1996	1997
Waste generated, total	**151.5**	**205.2**	**204.6**	**208.9**	**211.8**	**214.2**	**211.4**	**209.2**	**217.0**
Paper and paperboard	54.7	72.7	71.0	74.3	77.4	80.8	81.7	79.7	83.8
Ferrous metals	11.6	12.6	12.7	12.1	11.9	11.8	11.6	11.8	12.3
Aluminum	1.8	2.8	2.8	2.9	2.9	3.0	3.0	3.0	3.0
Other nonferrous metals	1.1	1.1	1.1	1.1	1.1	1.4	1.3	1.3	1.3
Glass	15.0	13.1	12.6	13.1	13.6	13.4	12.8	12.3	12.0
Plastics	7.9	17.1	17.7	18.4	19.0	19.3	18.9	19.8	21.5
Yard waste	27.5	35.0	35.0	35.0	33.3	31.5	29.7	27.9	27.7
Other wastes	31.9	50.7	51.7	52.1	52.5	53.1	52.4	53.5	55.3
Materials recovered, total	**14.5**	**33.6**	**37.0**	**40.6**	**43.8**	**50.8**	**55.0**	**57.4**	**60.8**
Paper and paperboard	11.9	20.2	22.5	24.5	25.5	29.5	32.7	33.2	34.9
Ferrous metals	0.4	2.6	3.1	3.4	3.9	4.0	4.1	4.4	4.7
Aluminum	0.3	1.0	1.0	1.1	1.0	1.2	1.0	1.0	1.1
Other nonferrous metals	0.5	0.7	0.7	0.7	0.7	1.0	0.8	0.8	0.8
Glass	0.8	2.6	2.6	2.9	3.0	3.1	3.1	3.2	2.9
Plastics	-	0.4	0.5	0.6	0.7	0.9	1.0	1.1	1.1
Yard waste	-	4.2	4.8	5.4	6.9	8.0	9.0	10.4	11.5
Other wastes	0.6	1.8	1.9	2.0	2.1	3.1	3.2	3.3	3.8
Percent of generation recovered, total	**9.6**	**16.4**	**18.1**	**19.4**	**20.7**	**23.7**	**26.0**	**27.4**	**28.0**
Paper and paperboard	21.8	27.8	31.7	33.0	32.9	36.5	40.0	41.6	41.7
Ferrous metals	3.4	20.4	24.1	27.7	32.8	33.9	35.5	37.2	38.4
Aluminum	16.7	35.9	35.5	38.7	35.7	37.8	34.6	34.3	35.1
Other nonferrous metals	45.5	66.4	65.5	63.4	63.1	73.3	64.3	66.7	65.4
Glass	5.3	20.0	20.3	22.0	22.1	23.3	24.5	25.8	24.3
Plastics	-	2.2	2.5	3.3	3.5	4.9	5.2	5.4	5.2
Yard waste	-	12.0	13.7	15.4	20.8	25.4	30.3	37.2	41.4
Other wastes	1.9	3.6	3.7	3.9	4.0	5.9	6.1	6.2	6.8

- Represents zero.

[In millions of tons, except as indicated. Covers post-consumer residential and commercial solid wastes which comprise the major portion of typical municipal collections. Excludes mining, agricultural and industrial processing, demolition and construction wastes, sewage sludge, and junked autos and obsolete equipment wastes. Based on material-flows estimating procedure and wet weight as generated]

Source: Franklin Associates, Ltd., Prairie Village, KS, *Characterization of Municipal Solid Waste in the United States: 1998.* Prepared for the U.S. Environmental Protection Agency.

Implementation

RCRA tries to accomplish its goals in several ways. First, the federal government gives money and know-how to state and municipal governments so they can develop programs to deal with land disposal of solid wastes. Second, it uses cradle-to-grave (from creation to disposal) regulation of hazardous wastes. Third, the act provides for resource recovery and conservation, such as removing metal beer cans from waste and reusing the metal. Fourth, through regulations the EPA establishes federal standards and a permit program for controlling hazardous wastes. States meeting these standards may run their own hazardous waste control programs. If they do not meet federal standards, the EPA runs the program.

The heart of the hazardous waste control programs is a **manifest system**, which is similar to a permit system. Any entity generating hazardous wastes must get a permit (manifest) to manage it on personal property or to ship it to an EPA-approved treatment, storage, or disposal facility. The idea of the manifest system is that a piece of paper accompanies each hazardous waste as soon as it is created and until it is disposed of. This system lets society know where the hazardous wastes are so that people will not unwittingly be building houses on them, cutting them, or doing anything else with them unknowingly.

Note that the manifest system applies only to hazardous wastes. The manifest system has caused a great deal of controversy. A former EPA official estimated that 750,000 hazardous materials are generated in the United States. There is much paperwork and expense for those generating hazardous waste (mainly the chemical industry), given the paper trail of the manifest system. On the other hand, we are talking about hazardous wastes—things that cause or significantly contribute to serious illness or death or that pose a substantial threat to human health or the environment if improperly managed.

Sanctions

RCRA has criminal and civil penalties. Civil penalties can be as much as $25,000 per day per violation. Criminal penalties include up to one year prison terms and as much as $25,000 per day fine per offense, or both. One question is whether the EPA will be given enough money to implement RCRA.

The following case shows how both corporations and responsible employees can be criminally liable under RCRA.

United States v. Johnson & Towers, Inc.

U.S. Court of Appeals (3d Cir.)
741 F.2d 662 (1984)

Background and Facts:

The criminal prosecution in this case arose from the disposal of chemicals at a plant owned by Johnson & Towers in Mount Laurel, New Jersey. In its operations the company, which repairs and overhauls large motor vehicles, uses degreasers and other industrial chemicals that contain chemicals such as methylene chloride and trichlorethylene, classified as "hazardous wastes" under the Resource Conservation and Recovery Act. During the period relevant here, the waste chemicals from cleaning operations were drained into a holding tank and, when the tank was full, pumped into a trench. The trench flowed from the plant property into Parker's Creek, a tributary of the Delaware River. Under RCRA, generators of such waste must obtain a permit for disposal from the Environmental Protection Agency. The EPA had neither issued nor received an application for a permit for Johnson & Towers' operations.

The indictment named as defendants Johnson & Towers and two of its employees, Jack Hopkins, a foreman, and Peter Angel, the service manager in the trucking department. According to the indictment, over a three-day period federal agents saw workers pump waste from the tank into the trench, and on the third day observed toxic chemicals flowing into the creek ...

The counts under RCRA charged that the defendants "did knowingly treat, store, and dispose of, and did cause to be treated, stored and disposed of hazardous wastes without having obtained a permit... in that the defendants discharged, deposited, injected, dumped, spilled, leaked and placed degreasers... into the trench. ..." The indictment alleged that both Angel and Hopkins "managed, supervised and directed a substantial portion of Johnson & Towers' operations... including those related to the treatment, storage and disposal of the hazardous wastes and pollutants" and that the chemicals were discharged by "the defendants and others at their discretion." The indictment did not otherwise detail Hopkins' and Angel's activities or responsibilities.

Johnson & Towers pled guilty to the RCRA counts. Hopkins and Angel pled not guilty, and then moved to dismiss counts 2, 3, and 4. The court concluded that the RCRA criminal provision applies only to "owners and operators," i.e., those obligated under the statute to obtain a permit. Since neither Hopkins nor Angel was an "owner" or "operator," the district court granted the motion as to the RCRA charges but held that the individuals could be liable on these three counts under 18 U.S.C.§2 for aiding and abetting. The court denied the government's motion for reconsideration, and the government appealed to this court under 18 U.S.C. §3731 (1982).

Body of Opinion

Circuit Judge Sloviter

The permit provision in section 6925, referred to in section 6928(d), requires "each person owning or operating a facility for the treatment, storage, or disposal of hazardous waste identified or listed under this subchapter to have a permit" from the EPA.

The parties offer contrary interpretations of section 6928(d)(2)(A). Defendants consider it an administrative enforcement mechanism, applying only to those who come within section 6925 and fail to comply; the government reads it as penalizing anyone who handles hazardous waste without a permit or in violation of a permit. Neither party has cited another case, nor have we found one, considering the application of this criminal provision to an individual other than an owner or operator.

...Congress enacted RCRA in 1976 as a "cradle-to-grave" regulatory scheme for toxic materials, providing "nationwide protection against the dangers of improper hazardous waste disposal."... RCRA was enacted to provide "a multifaceted approach towards solving the problems associated with the 3–4 billion tons of discarded materials generated each year, and the problems resulting from the anticipated 8% annual increase in the volume of such waste."

* * *

[4] However, our conclusion that "knowingly" applies to all elements of the offense in section 6928(d)(2)(A) does not impose on the government as difficult a burden as it fears. On this issue,... under certain regulatory statutes requiring "knowing" conduct the government need prove only knowledge of the actions taken and not of the statute forbidding them....

The principle that ignorance of the law is no defense applies whether the law be a statute or a duly promulgated and published regulation. In the context of these proposed 1960 amendments we decline to attribute to Congress the inaccurate view that that Act requires proof of knowledge of the law, as well as the facts, and that it intended to endorse that interpretation by retaining the word "knowingly."

Judgment and Result

We hold that section 6928(d)(2)(A) covers employees as well as owners and operators of the facility who knowingly treat, store, or dispose of any hazardous waste, but that the employees can be subject to criminal prosecution only if they knew or should have known that there had been no compliance with the permit requirement of section 6925.

Questions

1. Who were the defendants in the case—the corporation and certain employees responsible for handling hazardous wastes?
2. Under what positive law were the defendants charged?
3. Is it a crime to knowingly dump hazardous waste without a RCRA permit obtained from EPA? How could defendants be convicted of knowingly dumping wastes if they did not know the statute existed forbidding such dumping?
4. How could the legal ethics of positive law and natural law react to the result holding both the company and responsible employees liable for dumping the hazardous wastes?
5. Which of the business ethics noted in Chapter 1 is/are in evidence in the case?

TOXIC SUBSTANCES CONTROL ACT

The Toxic Substances Control Act (TOSCA) is a federal law passed in 1976. As an enabling act, it receives its authority from Congress for an administrative agency (the

EPA, in this case) to regulate the manufacture, use, and disposal of toxic substances. TOSCA became law so the public could learn more about chemicals' possible adverse effects on humans as well as on air, water, and natural resources.

TOSCA expressly recognizes that disposing of many human-made chemicals involves unreasonable risks to both natural resources (such as groundwater, where we get much of our drinking water) and humans. TOSCA gives the EPA power to make cradle-to-grave regulations controlling disposal of all toxic organic chemicals now found in groundwater supplies. The EPA has been slow (and is behind) in implementing the waste regulations.

Control of Toxic Chemicals

Recall that TOSCA gives EPA the power to regulate chemicals over their entire life cycle (from development through manufacture to disposal). TOSCA orders the EPA to inventory the approximately 55,000 chemicals in interstate commerce. TOSCA next requires chemical manufacturers to notify the EPA of all new chemical substances before they are made, as part of the PMN, or **pre–manufacture notice** requirement. TOSCA also lets the EPA make record-keeping, testing, and reporting requirements at all stages of toxic chemicals' life (again, the cradle-to-grave part of TOSCA).

Once the EPA has all of the information about toxic chemicals, TOSCA authorizes it to stop the manufacture of new chemicals that present an unreasonable risk to people or the environment, which is done only after the EPA studies the data submitted by industry. This authority represents great regulatory power over the chemical industry. However, the risks are great, because only *toxic* chemicals are at issue. The EPA also has the power under TOSCA to issue temporary limits on chemicals if the EPA has insufficient information to decide whether a chemical presents unreasonable risks.

TOSCA limits the EPA's regulatory power over the chemical industry in one important way: the EPA has the burden of proof to show that a new chemical presents an unreasonable risk to people. In other words, chemicals are presumed safe and nontoxic until the EPA proves otherwise. Tables 24.9 and 24.10 offer some statistics about toxic chemicals and waste.

Criticisms of TOSCA

A number of criticisms of TOSCA have come from both environmental (proregulatory) and chemical industry (antiregulatory) groups. The chemical industry complains about the red tape, cost, and possible loss of trade secrets because of TOSCA's reporting requirements. Environmental groups complain that the EPA has been slow to regulate. Since TOSCA's passage in 1976, only a few chemical classes have been regulated (including PCBs, chlorofluorocarbons, phthalate esters, chlorinated benzenes, and chloromethane).

Even the EPA has complaints about TOSCA, also based on slowness. EPA officials worry about the staff shortage, which delays putting TOSCA into effect. Also the EPA complains about industry foot-dragging in supplying information the EPA needs to study the possible toxic effects of chemicals. This problem is particularly troublesome because the burden of showing that chemicals are toxic is on the EPA. Toxins that creep into the water, the air, and the food chain (through fertilizers and insecticides, for example) pose serious a threat of long-term, perhaps irreversible damage to humans and the environment.

TABLE 24.9 Toxic Chemical Releases, by Industry: 1988 to 1996

INDUSTRY	1987 SIC[1] code	Core Chemicals[2]				Expanded Chemical List[3]	
		1988	**1994**	**1995**	**1996**	**1995**	**1996**
Total	**(X)**	**3,352,959**	**1,982,786**	**1,895,290**	**1,823,765**	**2,530,786**	**2,433,507**
Food and kindred products	20	8,378	6,014	5,120	5,121	86,467	83,303
Tobacco products	21	342	135	95	73	2,034	4,153
Textile mill products	22	35,798	16,346	15,656	15,280	18,501	17,328
Apparel and other textile products	23	1,026	1,381	1,260	1,742	1,287	1,865
Lumber and wood products	24	32,982	32,986	30,435	27,117	34,835	36,243
Furniture and fixtures	25	63,363	52,135	41,530	35,652	41,780	35,877
Paper and allied products	26	207,603	185,334	178,775	172,799	238,317	227,563
Printing and publishing	27	61,188	34,387	30,896	28,270	31,156	28,466
Chemical and allied products	28	1,047,782	537,483	539,600	513,043	844,232	785,178
Petroleum and coal products	29	72,781	46,877	42,593	43,077	64,141	68,887
Rubber and misc. plastic products	30	158,314	125,462	114,765	105,358	127,168	116,409
Leather and leather products	31	13,024	5,104	4.026	3,814	4,476	4,242
Stone, clay, glass products	32	40,539	17,359	19,053	23,264	32,324	38,740
Primary metal industries	33	629,354	433,886	455,029	496,663	524,041	564,535
Fabricated metals products	34	160,370	99,572	90,441	77,611	97,039	90,254
Industrial machinery and equip.	35	69,747	27,120	22,852	19,162	26,203	22,061
Electronic, electric equipment	36	132,719	36,672	31,457	33,753	40,456	41,765
Transportation equip.	37	208,392	128,139	114,746	105,232	121,155	111,353
Instruments and related products	38	58,085	14,328	12,955	10,359	17,859	15,350
Miscellaneous	39	32,593	15,350	13,286	9,843	13,869	10,270
Multiple codes	20-39	308,351	149,011	122,437	91,158	152,531	120,779
No codes	20-39	11,229	17,704	8,281	5,377	10,918	8,885

[**In thousands of pounds (3,352,959 represents 3,352,959,000).** Based on reports filed as required by section 313 of the Emergency Planning and Community Right-to-Know Act (EPCRA, or Title III of the Superfund Amendments and Reauthorization Act of 1986), Public Law 99-499. Owners and operators of facilities that are classified within Standard Classification Code groups 20 through 39, have 10 or more full-time employees, and that manufacture, process, or otherwise uses any listed toxic chemical in quantities greater than the established threshold in the course of a calendar year are covered and required to report]

X Not applicable. [1] Standard Industrial Classification. [2] Chemicals covered for all reporting years. [3] The Environmental Protection Agency added 286 chemicals and chemical categories to the EPCRA section list of 313 list of toxic chemicals.

Source: U.S. Environmental Protection Agency, *1996 Toxics Release Inventory.*

NUCLEAR WASTE POLICY ACT

In 1982 Congress passed the Nuclear Waste Policy Act (NWPA). It provided guidelines under which the federal government would design, construct, and operate nationally at least two high-level waste (HLW) dumps. In addressing what to do with highly toxic waste, the NWPA proposed deep underground injection of HLW.

TABLE 24.10 Toxic Releases, by State: 1988 to 1996

STATE AND OUTLYING AREAS	Core Chemicals 1988	1994	1995	1996	STATE AND OUTLYING AREAS	Core Chemicals 1988	1994	1995	1996
Total	**3,352,959**	**1,982,786**	**1,895,290**	**1,823,765**	MT	35,630	46,460	42,644	47,204
U.S. total	**3,337,537**	**1,971,577**	**1,885,211**	**1,815,062**	NE	16,936	13,735	11,171	8,881
AL	109,690	96,649	100,495	89,469	NV	2,352	3,209	3,369	3,294
AK	3,715	1,095	2,164	1,684	NH	13,866	2,395	1,940	1,750
AZ	66,236	30,775	33,875	46,258	NJ	45,018	14,025	12,399	10,645
AR	41,078	29,329	24,495	22,915	NM	30,386	17,230	17,946	18,339
CA	109,318	42,362	36,146	30,989	NY	99,656	37,902	30,361	26,028
CO	15,736	4,081	3,489	3,690	NC	132,027	80,753	72,493	67,973
CT	37,800	11,219	8,644	6,388	ND	1,195	988	1,207	773
DE	8,635	4,096	2,902	1,986	OH	202,152	116,096	122,236	115,228
DC	1	56	57	9	OK	32,895	15,344	15,995	15,216
FL	61,527	71,434	52,111	46,914	OR	21,562	18,011	18,449	24,647
GA	86,767	43,827	39,792	38,468	PA	134,852	95,110	95,914	90,529
HI	848	531	562	448	RI	7,713	6,789	3,017	2,452
ID	7,349	9,149	10,081	10,753	SC	66,070	47,640	48,112	47,374
IL	134,594	89,071	82,882	76,549	SD	2,393	2,108	1,872	1,364
IN	184,554	82,653	88,801	91,419	TN	126,484	104,915	94,684	88,191
IA	43,028	22,728	21,124	17,500	TX	318,632	199,765	205,724	187,485
KS	30,301	17,408	17,612	17,570	UT	123,836	67,175	69,144	73,876
KY	66,444	32,512	30,570	30,941	VT	1,734	632	544	294
LA	250,845	114,824	122,286	128,789	VA	112,329	43,829	40,613	40,555
ME	15,356	6,879	6,594	5,273	WA	28,273	20,770	22,336	21,890
MD	20,037	11,451	11,858	9,381	WV	39,416	20,852	19,679	17,445
MA	31,879	9,950	8,351	8,951	WI	60,707	39,397	32,875	31,566
MI	132,693	103,055	85,889	78,426	WY	16,741	880	1,144	1,356
MN	55,948	20,826	18,338	15,846	Guam	-	-	3	3
MS	59,600	42,834	39,671	39,321	Puerto Rico	12,829	9,693	8,840	7,468
MO	90,704	56,772	50,552	49,770	Virgin Island	2,593	1,516	1,236	1,232

[In thousands of pounds (3,352,959 represents 3,352,959,000). Excludes delisted chemicals, chemicals added in 1990, 1991, 1994, and 1995, and aluminum oxide, ammonia, hydrochloric acid, and sulfuric acid.

- Represents zero. Z Less than 500 pounds.

Source: U.S. Environmental Protection Agency, Office of Pollution Prevention and Toxics, *1996 Toxics Release Inventory*, annual.

Through an elaborate process, the NWPA decides which "lucky" states will receive the HLW. The Department of Energy (DOE) names "potentially acceptable sites." Then, within 90 days, DOE must tell the governors and state legislatures of these sites that they are candidates. DOE also must develop regs for HLW disposal and then apply these regs to at least five potentially suitable candidate sites.

In 1983, DOE identified nine potentially acceptable sites (one in Nevada, one in Washington state, two in Texas, two in Utah, one in Louisiana, and two in Mississippi). DOE must then recommend to the president three of the nominated sites for detailed study, but DOE must have a public hearing *before* recommending a site. The president may then approve or disapprove a site but must submit to Congress an endorsement of one site from the three sites recommended by DOE.

The presidentially approved site then becomes *the* site after 60 days unless the affected state submits notice of disapproval to Congress. If such notice is given to Congress, the site is disapproved unless, within 90 days of getting notice, Congress passes a resolution of siting approval.

Several federal agencies regulate nuclear waste disposal. DOE designs, builds, and operates federal nuclear dumps. The NRC licenses them, and the EPA has authority under other federal laws to promulgate regs to protect the general environment from off-site nuclear releases from the site. One such law is the federal Safe Drinking Water Act. Several states and an environmental group argued that the EPA should use its authority under the Safe Drinking Water Act to stop on-site nuclear contamination. *NRDC. v. U.S EPA* deals with the matter.

The National Resources Defense Council is a private environmental activist group: ***http://www.nrdc.org***

Natural Resources Defense Council v. U.S. EPA

U.S. Court of Appeals (First Cir.)
824 F. 2d 1258 (1987)

Background and Facts:

This is a petition to review the standards promulgated by the Environmental Protection Agency (EPA) for the long-term disposal of high-level radioactive waste under the Nuclear Waste Policy Act of 1982, 42 U.S.C.§§10101–10226 (1982). The states of Maine and Vermont, and the Natural Resources Defense Council, Conservation Law Foundation of New England, and Environmental Policy Institute were the original petitioners. Later Minnesota and Texas also challenged the same standards in separate proceedings. All suits have been consolidated in this circuit. A coalition of nuclear power utilities has been permitted to intervene.

Body of Opinion

Chief Judge Levin H. Campbell

The challenged standards were written by the EPA to regulate harmful releases into the environment from radioactive waste stored in repositories planned for its disposal. (The standards also regulate releases occurring while the waste is being managed prior to its disposal.)

The waste in question is derived from the fissioning of nuclear fuel in commercial nuclear power plants and in military reactors. Some of the material is first reprocessed so as to recover unfissioned uranium and plutonium. Reprocessing results in a transfer of most of the radioactivity into acidic liquids that are later converted into solid radioactive waste. Some spent nuclear fuel is not reprocessed and itself becomes a waste. Collectively this waste is called high level waste ("HLW"). It is extremely toxic and will maintain its toxicity for thousands of years.

Recognizing the need for repositories within which to dispose safely of the growing amounts of HLW, Congress in 1982 enacted the Nuclear Waste Policy Act (NWPA). The Act provides for a coordinated effort within the federal government to design, construct and operate nationally at least two HLW disposal facilities. Without foreclosing other disposal methods, Congress focused in the NWPA on the creation of repositories located deep underground. These will depend on the surrounding underground rock formations together with engineered barriers, to contain safely the radioactivity from these wastes.

The underground repositories are expected to be constructed using conventional mining techniques in geologic media such as granite, basalt (solidified lava), volcanic tuff (compacted volcanic ash) or salt. The solidified high level waste will be housed in canisters placed in boreholes drilled into the mine floor. When the repository is full, it will be backfilled and sealed.

In the NWPA, Congress prescribed a complex process for selecting the sites of the high level waste repositories. . . . Under this format, DOE in February of 1983 identified nine potentially acceptable sites (a Nevada site in tuff; a Washington site in basalt; two Texas sites in bedded salt; two Utah sites in bedded salt; one Louisiana site in a salt dome; and two Mississippi sites in salt domes).

The Act required DOE to recommend to the President three of the nominated sites for detailed characterization studies. The President may then approve or disapprove a nominated site. In December 1984 DOE tentatively identified five sites for possible detailed site characterization. Three of these sites were formally recommended for detailed site characterization studies (Yucca Mountain site in Nevada; Deaf Smith County site in Texas; and the Hanford site in Washington).

Nominated sites recommended to and approved by the President are then to be characterized by DOE. After conducting the detailed site characterization studies, DOE must make a recommendation to the President concerning the final site approval. Before DOE recommends a site it must hold public hearings, must notify any affected state or Indian tribe, and must prepare an environmental impact statement for each site to be recommended to the President. The President must then submit to Congress an endorsement of one site from the three sites characterized and recommended by DOE. . . .

The site recommended by the President becomes the approval site for the first repository after sixty days, unless the affected state or Indian tribe submits to Congress a notice of disapproval. If such notice of disapproval is received, the site is disapproved unless, during the first ninety days after receipt of the notice, Congress passes a resolution of repository siting approval. The same site approval process is prescribed for the selection of a second federal repository site.

Several federal agencies share responsibility for building, licensing and laying down standards for the HLW repositories. The Department of Energy is to design, build and operate each federally owned repository. However, the Nuclear Regulatory Commission (NRC) has responsibility to license the repositories. Under its licensure powers, the NRC regulates the construction of the repositories, licenses the receipt and possession of high level radioactive waste at the repositories, and authorizes the closure and decommissioning of repositories.

The EPA also has a major regulatory role. The Act provides that EPA,

> *pursuant to authority under other provisions of law*, shall, by rule, promulgate generally applicable standards for protection of the general environment from offsite releases from radioactive material in repositories.

The language, "pursuant to authority under other provisions of law," refers to the EPA's responsibility and authority under the Atomic Energy Act of 1954. The Reorganization Plan No. 3 of 1970 (which was the vehicle used by the executive branch to organize the newly formed Environmental Protection Agency) transferred to the EPA certain functions of the Atomic Energy Commission

> to the extent that such functions of the Commission consist of establishing generally applicable environmental standards for the protection of the general environment from radioactive material.

It is these generally applicable HLW environmental standards, recently promulgated by the EPA pursuant to the directive of the NWPA, which we are now called upon to review. DOE must follow these standards when siting, designing, constructing and operating the repositories. The NRC must likewise obey them when licensing the repositories. EPA's standards will also apply to defense-related DOE facilities (not licensed by the NRC) which store and dispose of defense-related waste. . . .

Subpart B, 40 C.F.R. §191.11–.18 (1986), entitled "Environmental Standards for Disposal," is intended to ensure long-term protection of public health and the environment from releases of radiation *after* the HLW has been stored in the chosen manner. Although this subpart was developed having in mind storage at underground repositories, the standards are said to apply also to any other disposal method that may be chosen.

Subpart B comprises four different types of environmental standards. The first type is the *general containment requirements*. These require that nuclear waste disposal systems be designed to provide a reasonable expectation, based on performance assessment, that the cumulative release of radiation to anywhere in the "accessible environment," for 10,000 years after disposal, shall not exceed certain designated levels.

The term "accessible environment" is defined as the atmosphere; land surfaces; surface waters; oceans; and all of the "lithosphere" that is beyond the "controlled area." The "lithosphere," as defined, includes the entire solid part of the earth below the surface, including any ground water contained within it. The "controlled area" is the surface and underground area (and any ground water found therein) immediately surrounding the repository "that encompasses no more than 100 square kilometers and extends horizontally no more than 5 kilometers in any direction" for the disposed waste.

These definitions taken together show that the general containment requirements limit the total, cumulative release of radiation, for 10,000 years, anywhere in the environment, *outside the controlled area*. Within the controlled area itself, the general containment requirements are inapplicable and, therefore, they place no limits on radiation release. . . .

According to the EPA, the above general containment requirements constitute the principal protection mechanism of the HLW environmental standards. If cumulative releases are within these levels, overall adverse health effects upon the general population will be low. The EPA estimates that the general containment requirements limit population risks from the disposal of these wastes to "no more than the midpoint of the range of estimated risks that future generations would have been exposed to if the uranium ore used to create the wastes had never been mined."

* * *

IV. Do EPA's Regulations Violate the Safe Drinking Water Act?

Part C of the Safe Drinking Water Act, (1982) (SDWA), indicates that the EPA has a duty to assure that underground sources of drinking water will not be endangered by any underground injection. Petitioners argue here that endangerment of such drinking water is bound to result if HLW is disposed of, underground, under standards no more stringent than the EPA's current HLW regulations. Since violations of the SDWA are inevitable, so petitioners argue, the present regulations are "not in accordance with law" and hence invalid.

To understand this argument we must first look at the SDWA, an Act which preceded the NWPA. The SDWA was enacted in 1974 to assure safe drinking water supplies, protect especially valuable aquifers, and protect drinking water from contamination by the underground injection of waste. The SDWA required the EPA to promulgate standards to protect public health, by setting either (1) maximum containment levels for pollutants in a public water supply, or (2) a treatment technique to reduce the pollutants to an acceptable level if the maximum contaminant level is not economically or technologically attainable.

We conclude that the primary disposal method being considered, underground repositories, would likely constitute an "underground injection" under the SDWA.

* * *

(2) Do the Regulations under review sanction activities that will "Endanger Drinking Water"?

Part C of the SDWA speaks of the EPA's duty "to assure that underground sources of drinking water will not be *endangered* by any underground injection." [Emphasis supplied.] Assuming, as discussed above, that the planned disposal of HLW in underground repositories amounts to "underground injection," will such injection, if carried out under the EPA's current HLW standards, endanger underground sources of drinking water? We believe the answer is "yes."

As noted, the term "endanger" is defined in the SDWA to include any injection which may result in the presence "in underground water which supplies or can reasonably by expected to supply any public water systems of any contaminant . . . if the presence of such contaminant may result in such system's not complying with any national primary drinking water regulation." 42 U.S.C. §300h (d)(2). Measured against this definition, the HLW standards permit contamination of most categories of underground water within the so-called controlled area without restriction of any type. More fundamentally, they permit water supplies *outside* the controlled area to be contaminated by radiation up to individual exposure levels that exceed the levels allowed in national primary drinking water regulations. It follows that the HLW regulations under review not only do not "assure" the non-endangerment of underground sources of drinking water, but sanction disposal facilities allowing certain levels of endangerment as that term is used in the SDWA.

Judgment and Result

The Court of Appeals, Levin H. Campbell, Chief Judge, held that (1) because the Agency did not consider the interrelationship of high level waste rules and the Safe Drinking Water Act and thus failed either to reconcile two regulatory standards or to adequately explain divergence, the Agency was arbitrary and capricious in its promulgation of individual protection requirements; (2) the Agency did not provide adequate explanation for selecting 1,000-year design criterion. Petition for review of rules granted in part; rules vacated in part and remanded.

Questions

1. In the case, does the court believe the EPA took into account the legal requirements under the Safe Drinking Water Act when it regulated nuclear waste?
2. What was the source of the nuclear waste here?
3. One legal ethic involves balancing competing claims. How would you state the competing claims in the preceding case?
4. Recall that at least one Reagan EPA official went to jail for official misconduct. Does the preceding case suggest that the EPA's environmental awareness has improved?
5. Who watches the environment if the EPA does not? Who sued EPA here?
6. In mid-1999 it looked as if the federal authorities had settled on Yucca Mountain, 100 miles northwest of Las Vegas, in Nevada, as the permanent site of the United States' nuclear waste. The cost of this storage is expected to be about $43 billion over the next century paid by taxing nuclear power. To date about $3 billion has been spent on this storage. It is estimated that the most dangerous radioactive emitters will have decayed by the year 3000, at which time the housings for this waste are projected to leak because of inherent limitations of the housing. By the year 12,010 regulators predict the radioactive dosage to farmers in a nearby valley will be 0.007 millirems per year—insignificant. The actual waste containers are expected to corrode by the year 102,010. Do you feel any safer?

COMPREHENSIVE ENVIRONMENTAL RESPONSE, COMPENSATION, AND LIABILITY ACT

The United States has estimated 25,000–50,000 abandoned hazardous waste dumps. (Professor Frank Popper of Rutgers Law School calls them "LULUs," locally unwanted land uses.) Wastes in these dumps threaten public health and water supplies. To help clean up these dumps, Congress enacted the Comprehensive Environmental Response Compensation and Liability Act of 1980 (CERCLA). Congress originally created a $1.6 billion fund, called the Superfund, made up of industrial and federal appropriations to assist the federal government in cleaning up and containing these dumps. After correcting the environmental degradation at a dump, the government bills the dump's present owners and operators as well as transporters of hazardous wastes to the dump. Such persons are known as potentially responsible parties (PRPs). Court interpretations of CERCLA hold responsible parties strictly liable, that is, liable even if they were not negligent in dumping the hazardous wastes. Hazardous waste sites in each state are listed in Table 24.11.

CERCLA itself does not address the matter of joint and several liability, but court decisions interpreting CERCLA do impose joint and several liability on those partly liable for the hazardous waste dump. Thus, if 100 persons without a permit each dump one barrel of hazardous wastes at a hazardous waste site, any one of the 100 could be held by the federal government for the entire cleanup of the site. The one who pays the full cleanup amount could then sue the other 99 dumpers for their pro rata share of the cleanup costs, assuming they could be found.

Another problem PRPs face with CERCLA is that they can be held liable for waste dumped before CERCLA was passed. In effect, CERCLA has retroactive impact. Further, CERCLA holds a wide range of persons liable for hazardous waste cleanup including the present site owner, the site owners when the waste was dumped, transporters of the waste, and the operator of the dump even if not the landowner.

TABLE 24.11 Hazardous Waste Sites on the National Priority List, by State: 1998

STATE AND OUTLYING AREAS	Total sites	Rank	Percent distribution	Federal	Nonfederal	STATE AND OUTLYING AREAS	Total sites	Rank	Percent distribution	Federal	Nonfederal
Total	**1,258**	**(X)**	**(X)**	**161**	**1,097**	Montana	9	42	0.7	-	9
United States	**1,245**	**(X)**	**100.00**	**160**	**1,085**	Nebraska	10	38	0.8	1	9
Alabama	12	32	1.0	3	9	Nevada	1	49	0.1	-	1
Alaska	7	43	0.6	6	1	New Hampshire	18	20	1.4	1	17
Arizona	10	39	0.8	3	7	New Jersey	111	1	8.9	6	105
Arkansas	11	36	0.9	-	11	New Mexico	11	34	0.9	1	10
California	96	3	7.7	23	73	New York	84	4	6.7	4	80
Colorado	17	22	1.4	3	14	North Carolina	24	17	1.9	2	22
Connecticut	14	29	1.1	1	13	North Dakota	-	50	0.0	-	-
Delaware	17	23	1.4	1	16	Ohio	36	10	2.9	5	31
District of Columbia	1	(X)	0.1	1	-	Oklahoma	12	30	1.0	1	11
Florida	53	6	4.3	6	47	Oregon	11	35	0.9	2	9
Georgia	16	25	1.3	2	14	Pennsylvania	100	2	8.0	6	94
Hawaii	4	45	0.3	3	1	Rhode Island	12	31	1.0	2	10
Idaho	9	41	0.7	2	7	South Carolina	25	16	2.0	2	23
Illinois	43	8	3.5	4	39	South Dakota	2	48	0.2	1	1
Indiana	30	13	2.4	-	30	Tennessee	15	28	1.2	4	11
Iowa	17	21	1.4	1	16	Texas	32	11	2.6	4	28
Kansas	11	37	0.9	2	9	Utah	16	24	1.3	4	12
Kentucky	16	26	1.3	1	15	Vermont	9	40	0.7	-	9
Louisiana	15	27	1.2	1	14	Virginia	27	15	2.2	9	18
Maine	12	33	1.0	3	9	Washington	47	7	3.8	14	33
Maryland	18	19	1.4	8	10	West Virginia	7	44	0.6	2	5
Massachusetts	31	12	2.5	8	23	Wisconsin	40	9	3.2	-	40
Michigan	71	5	5.7	1	70	Wyoming	3	46	0.2	1	2
Minnesota	27	14	2.2	2	25	Guam	2	(X)	(X)	1	1
Mississippi	3	47	0.2	-	3	Puerto Rico	9	(X)	(X)	-	9
Missouri	22	18	1.8	3	19	Virgin Islands	2	(X)	(X)	-	2

[Includes both proposed and final sites listed on the National Priorities List for the Superfund program as authorized by the Comprehensive Environmental Response, Compensation, and Liability Act of 1980 and the Superfund Amendments and Reauthorization of 1986]

- Represents zero. X not applicable.

Source: U.S. Environmental Protection Agency, *Supplementary Materials: National Priorities List, Proposed Rule*, December 1998.

A practical way for PRPs to cap their CERCLA liability is found under section 122 of CERCLA, which creates a site participation agreement for total cleanup liability among PRPs. Such agreements allow similarly situated PRPs to establish a contribution bar to future cleanup liability.

CERCLA generally exempts creditors of the aforementioned liable parties from cleanup liability; but what if a creditor with a mortgage (or other type of security interest) on the dump operator's property has the right to or has exercised management over the dump site operator? Do any of these events cause the creditor to lose the exemption from CERCLA liability and make it liable as an owner or operator? The *Fleet Factors* case held creditors liable when the creditor's involvement in the management process influenced a facility's treatment of hazardous waste. Following the *Fleet* case the EPA tried to "soften" its application to parties such as commercial lenders by promulgating regulations "clarifying" CERCLA's application to creditors. So far EPA's regulations have been of uncertain comfort to creditors.

The following CERCLA case indicates whether an owner of property on which hazardous waste is dumped can sue transporters and others for all of the cleanup costs.

Prisco v. A & D Carting Corp.

U.S. Court of Appeals (2nd Cir.)
168 F.3d 593 (1999)

Background and Facts:

In the spring of 1987, Thomas and Filomena Prisco, husband and wife, began an attempt to increase the value of their land by leveling a portion of it using as fill waste construction and demolition materials delivered to the site by a variety of business entities. They discovered they could also make substantial sums by permitting others to dispose of waste on their property for a fee. The efforts entangled them with two New York State law enforcement officials who said that they would operate the landfill on the State's behalf. One or both of the officers may have been engaged in an undercover operation designed to obtain information about corruption in the construction and demolition industry. The landfill operation nonetheless was soon shut down by state environmental authorities. Hazardous substances have since been leaching from the Prisco property into the surrounding wetlands.

In 1991, the Priscos filed suit in the U.S. District Court for the Southern District of New York against a host of private and public defendants, asserting causes of action under the Comprehensive Environmental Response, Compensation, and Liability Act (CERCLA) in addition to other legal claims. Sometime between then and trial Thomas Prisco died....

Filomena Prisco continued the suit in her own behalf and as administratrix of his estate.... After a simultaneous jury trial on the state claims and bench trial on the federal statutory claims, on October 1, 1997, the district court dismissed her CERCLA claims. She appeals from that judgment.

Body of Opinion

Circuit Judge Sack

CERCLA is a "broad remedial statute...enacted to ensure "that those responsible for any damage, environmental harm, or injury from chemical poisons bear the costs of their actions."... As a remedial statute, CERCLA should be construed liberally to give effect to its purposes....

CERCLA addresses in particular the costs of responding to the release or threatened release of "hazardous substances," as that term is defined by CERCLA. ... Towards that end, section 107, the quantity or concentration of the hazardous substance is not a factor.... Congress planned for the 'hazardous substance' definition to include even minimal amounts of pollution.... Rather, in order, to make out a prima facie case under §107, a plaintiff must establish five elements.... The plaintiff must prove that:

First, the defendant falls within one of the four categories of potentially responsible parties set forth in §107.... The categories include: 1) the owner and operator of...a facility, 2) any person who at the time of disposal of any hazardous substance owned or operated any facility at which such hazardous substances were disposed of, 3) any person who by contract, agreement, or otherwise arranged with a transporter for transport for disposal or treatment, of hazardous substances owned or possessed by such person, by any other party or entity, at any facility or incineration vessel owned or operated by another party or entity and containing such hazardous substances, and 4) any person who accepts or accepted any hazardous substance for transport to disposal or treatment facilities, incineration vessels or sites selected by such persons....

Second, the facility is indeed a "facility" as defined by s 101 (9) of CERCLA....

Third, "there is a release or a threatened release of hazardous substances at the facility."...

Fourth, the plaintiff incurred costs in responding to the release or threatened release ("response costs")....

And fifth, the costs incurred conform to the National Contingency Plan....

Once the plaintiff establishes these elements, the defendant is strictly liable for the presence of the hazardous substances unless it succeeds in invoking one of the statutory defenses.... It is not a defense that the particular hazardous substance attributable to a specific defendant is not linked to the plaintiff's response costs....

Although not heretofore raised in these proceedings, a serious problem meets Prisco's case at the threshold. Where a party seeking to recover response costs is itself a potentially responsible party within the meaning of §107...he or she may not bring suit for full cost recovery under §107 as Prisco has. Such a plaintiff is limited instead to an action for contribution from other potentially responsible parties under CERCLA §113.... Prisco, being the owner at all relevant times of the Prisco landfill, has the characteristics of a potentially responsible party within the meaning of § 107. Accordingly, although the issue appears to have gone unnoticed until now, it seems that Prisco's CERCLA claims should not have proceeded under §107, but, if at all, only under §113....

This raises the question whether the dismissal of Prisco's CERCLA claim therefore should be affirmed on the grounds, not argued here or below, that it was improper from its inception or the claim should be construed to be one under §113 although not pleaded.... The question need not be resolved, however. The elements of an action under §113 are the same as those under §107.... Because we find that the district court correctly determined that Prisco failed to establish the elements of a §107 claim, the same result necessarily would obtain even were we to construe the claim as one for contribution under §113....

Judgment and Result

The court of appeals affirmed the district court's dismissal of Prisco's CERCLA claim.

Questions

1. Can someone who has violated CERCLA bring a CERCLA claim? Against whom and for what?
2. Was enough evidence presented to hold others liable to Prisco for the cleanup here?
3. Who, besides the owner of property onto which hazardous substances are dumped, can be liable for cleanup costs under CERCLA?
4. What are the elements a plaintiff must establish to make a successful CERCLA claim?

Amending CERCLA

There are a number of proposals to amend CERCLA. As of this writing, none has been enacted. Among the proposed amendments are the following: (1) cap liability for transporters and generators at 10 percent of the total cleanup costs of municipal solid waste sites; (2) full repeal of the retroactive liability under CERCLA for multiparty sites; (3) add to the federal amount available for cleanup of hazardous waste sites. These are only some of the proposals. Clearly, these proposals are controversial and some violate the "polluter pays" principle, which is the heart of CERCLA.

ENDANGERED SPECIES ACT

Dr. David A. Etnier probably never expected that his swimming would popularize an obscure federal law—the Endangered Species Act. Etnier, a University of Tennessee ichthyologist (fish expert), was swimming in the Little Tennessee River (Little T) when he saw a strange fish. It turned out to be a previously unknown perch species *Percina imostoma tanasi*, now popularly called the snail darter.

The Tennessee Valley Authority (TVA), a federally owned corporation, was building a multipurpose dam (called the Tellico Dam) on the Little T. The dam was to control flooding, enhance recreation, promote industrial development, and generate power by increasing the pool size of another dam (within eyesight of the Tellico Dam) about one mile away on the Tennessee River. The Tellico Dam itself does not have any power generators.

As a result of Dr. Etnier's discovering the snail darter, an environmental group sued TVA to stop construction of the Tellico Dam. The legal basis for the environmental group's action was the Endangered Species Act of 1973. The act said that federal money may not be spent on any federal agency project that would wipe a fish, plant, or wild animal species off the face of the earth.

The act authorized the U.S. secretary of the interior to designate those species that were endangered. Once the secretary designates a species as endangered, federal funding of any federal agency project that would extinguish or threaten to extinguish such species in the foreseeable future must end. The act also imposed fines on private parties caught transporting, buying, selling, importing, or exporting endangered species.

http://

For the website to the National Audobon Society, a major private environmental protection group, go to ***http://www.audobon.org***

The act established a two-tier review process to oversee the "correctness" of the secretary of the interior's designations. The second-tier review committee has the power to exempt a project from the act even if it endangers a species' existence.

If the secretary of the interior designates a species as endangered and the review committees do not reverse this decision, the federal project stops unless either Congress or the courts reverse the secretary's decision. This happened in the snail darter's case. The U.S. Supreme Court upheld the secretary's designation of the snail darter as endangered; but then Congress passed a statute amending the Endangered Species Act by exempting the Tellico Dam from it.

Although the media played up the way the three-inch snail darter stopped the $100-million-plus Tellico Dam project, one point is obscured: At the time of the Tellico lawsuit, TVA had spent about $17 million on the dam structure itself. The remaining $85 million was sunk into planning and land acquisition costs. Some people felt that, had TVA been forced to stop the project and resell the land that it had acquired through condemnation, the appreciated value of the land would have exceeded the $17 million loss on the unused dam. TVA might have lost nothing. This is, of course, only speculation.

One last note about this case: The Tellico dam was eventually built, and the snail darter survives. Table 24.12 summarizes endangered species statistics.

TABLE 24.12 Threatened and Endangered Wildlife and Plant Species—Number: 1999

ITEM	Mammals	Birds	Reptiles	Amphibians	Fishes	Snails	Clams	Crustaceans	Insects	Arachnids	Plants
Total Listings	336	274	114	26	121	29	71	20	41	5	706
Endangered species total	**312**	**253**	**79**	**17**	**80**	**19**	**63**	**17**	**32**	**5**	**569**
United States	61	75	14	9	69	18	61	17	28	5	568
Foreign	251	178	65	8	11	1	2	-	4	-	1
Threatened species total	**24**	**21**	**35**	**9**	**41**	**10**	**8**	**3**	**9**	-	**137**
United States	8	15	21	8	41	10	8	3	9	-	135
Foreign	16	6	14	1	-	-	-	-	-	-	2

[As of **April.** Endangered species: One in danger of becoming extinct throughout all or a significant part of its natural range. Threatened species: One likely to become endangered in the foreseeable future]

- Represents zero

Source: U.S. Fish and Wildlife Service, *Endangered Species Technical Bulletin*, quarterly.

STAGES IN ENVIRONMENTAL LAW

Window Dressing

Three discernible stages in U.S. environmental law have taken place in the past 40 years. The first stage was the "window dressing" stage. This stage ran from about 1948 (in the case of the Federal Water Pollution Control Act) to the mid-1950s (in the case of federal air pollution control). In this era, Congress recognized the problems of air and water pollution and created "paper remedies"—solutions that sounded good on paper (in the form of statutes) but for various reasons did not work.

Hue and Cry

The second stage was the "hue and cry" era. It lasted roughly from 1965 (with passage of the Clean Air Act amendments) until about 1977 (with passage of the Surface Mining Control and Reclamation Act). In the hue-and-cry period, the public awoke to find air, water, and general environmental quality declining. The public saw evidence of environmentally related disease (cancer, emphysema), property damage (faster decay of buildings), and natural resource degradation (injury to lakes and trees from acid rain). People demanded laws to solve such problems. Congress responded the Clean Air Act amendments of 1965 and 1970, NEPA, the 1972 amendments to the Federal Water Pollution Control Act, the Noise Control Act of 1972, the Toxic Substances Control Act (TOSCA), and the Resource Conservation and Recovery Act of 1976 (RCRA). Because virtually all of these laws were enabling acts, they authorized federal agencies (mainly the EPA) to make regulations to deal with environmental problems. The EPA usually, although sometimes slowly, did its duty. The public and businesses soon faced thousands of new regulations.

Hard Look

The flood of federal regulations led to the third and present stage of U.S. environmental law—the "hard-look" era. In the hard-look era, businesses and individuals faced with incredible pollution control costs articulately question environmental control. They demand cost-benefit analysis for statutes and regulations to ensure that such programs are worth as much as or more than they cost. Regulated parties demand to see the data and studies (the so-called development documents) that form the basis for agency regulations. They want to question the design, execution, and technical rigor of the study.

If the basis for the regulations is open to question, why should regulated parties spend billions of dollars to comply with them? In this respect, businesses rightly point to a key legal shortcoming: Business seldom has the right to cross-examine federal agency experts who designed, executed, or drew conclusions from the study that was the factual basis for the regulations. Why should an agency expert responsible for the spending of billions be beyond question? However, agency experts' studies, data, and opinions can be questioned. They are questioned when industry and other regulated parties contact the agency and ask about the study. Agency experts (through agency lawyers) must also answer a reviewing court's questions when industry sues an agency about the regulations. The agency must answer the court's questions, usually prompted by industry, or the regulations are invalidated as arbitrary, capricious, and unreasonable or lacking substantial evidence.

Practical Effects

Changes have occurred in environmental laws as a result of the hard-look era. A loosening of regulation on less harmful pollutants and greater control on toxins have taken place. This shift is evident from the 1977 amendments to the Federal Water Pollution Control Act (or FWPCA, or Clean Water Act), which reclassified pollutants into toxins, conventional, and unconventional pollutants. Although toxins receive the BAT (best available treatment), the conventional and nonconventional pollutants meet less stringent controls. If the 1977 amendments to the FWPCA had not occurred, all water pollutants would be subject to the expensive BAT. The 1977 Clean Water Act amendments made water pollution control more practical. The 1987 Clean Water Act amendments add new sanctions to help control water pollution.

Other examples of how the hard look has affected environmental law include development of the bubble policy, emission offsets, and marketable pollution rights in air pollution control. The bubble policy views an entire factory as within a huge bubble. The total amount of air pollution let off by the whole factory is limited; but individual air pollution sources (smokestacks, for example) for the factory may discharge different pollution levels if all outlets together stay within the total pollution level for the whole factory. This practice lets industry control air pollution where it is cheapest and not control so much where it is expensive to do so. Previously, all outlets had to meet the same emission (pollution control) requirements. Current policy, however, provides flexibility and possible cost savings for business. However, policing such an arrangement is more difficult for air pollution inspectors.

One problem business faces is building new plants in areas with bad air quality (so-called nonattainment areas where the ambient air quality standards are not met). **Emission offsets** let a business move into a nonattainment area only if it reduces the amount of pollution in the area by the amount its new source will add, which is called the emission offset policy. Emission offsets can be obtained in at least two ways. If a business already has a pollution source in the nonattainment area, its pollution level can be reduced. The new source may then pollute by as much as the pollution reduction (offset) from the existing source.

Another way a business can build in a nonattainment area is by buying an existing source's rights to pollute (discharge). This practice is now allowed in Louisville, Kentucky, and a few other parts of the United States. The whole idea of offsets and marketable pollution rights is to maintain air quality while allowing economic development.

Although environmental law is far from perfect, it is more refined and developed than at any time in U.S history.

CHAPTER SUMMARY

The environmental ethic refers to the desire to conserve and use wisely limited natural resources as well as to maintain the ability of the planet earth to sustain human, plant, and animal life.

Among the institutions involved in environmental law are private environmental groups such as the National Resources Defense Council, the Environmental Defense Fund, the Sierra Club, and others. Governmental agencies concerned with environmental protection include the U.S. Environmental Protection Agency, the Department of the Interior, the Department of Defense (particularly the Army Corps of Engineers), the Department of Agriculture, the Department of Transportation, and the various states' departments of environment (sometimes called departments of natural resources).

The National Environmental Policy Act (NEPA) established the Council on Environmental Quality (CEQ) and imposed the requirement that federal agencies prepare environmental impact statements (EISs) before they take certain actions affecting the environment.

Water pollution control is largely governed by the Clean Water Act, a federal law that has been amended several times. The Clean Water Act makes it illegal to discharge a pollutant from a point source without an NPDES permit. For nonpoint sources of water pollution, the Clean Water Act relies on area-wide waste treatment programs. Civil and criminal sanctions may be brought against violators of the Clean Water Act.

The Clean Air Act tries to control air pollution by regulating stationary and mobile sources of pollution. Among the regulated air pollutants are particulates, sulfur dioxide, ozone, nitrogen oxide, and carbon monoxide. The state implementation plan (SIP) is a major ingredient in air pollution control. Primary air quality standards aim to protect public health, while secondary air quality standards try to protect welfare. In 1990 Congress amended the Clean Air Act by tightening air pollution standards for cars, adding to the protections of the earth's ozone layer. The 1990 amendments also address acid rain and toxic pollutants. The Clean Air Act has both civil and criminal sanctions.

The Resource Conservation and Recovery Act of 1976 (RCRA) uses the manifest system to control hazardous wastes. RCRA also regulates nonhazardous wastes that pose a danger to public health. RCRA has civil and criminal penalties.

Congress enacted the Toxic Substances Control Act (TOSCA) to regulate the manufacture, use, and disposal of toxic substances.

CERCLA, the Comprehensive Environmental Response Compensation and Liability Act, was passed to clean up the thousands of abandoned hazardous waste dumps. Superfund was passed to help the federal government clean up hazardous waste dumps; the government bills the dump's owners for the costs of cleaning up such dumps. Present owners, operators, and transporters of hazardous wastes to the dump are liable for cleanup of the dump.

MANAGER'S ETHICAL DILEMMA

"It's a NIMBY case," shouted Bob Johnson to his assistant. Bob looked out his factory window at the pickets in front of his plutonium processing plant. The picketers all condemned his plant's waste disposal—process water dumped into a local lake, and plutonium waste buried in a local landfill. The picketers wanted a cleanup of the waste dump and lake. Recently an EPA study revealed excessively high levels of radioactive materials in the dump and lake.

Bob's plant had provided the local population with high-paying white- and blue-collar jobs for more than 20 years. In fact, the city of Hanunder had begged Bob to locate his plant there 40 years ago. Now it was NIMBY (not in my backyard).

The EPA wanted Bob to clean up his prior waste disposal and also to build an expensive state-of-the-art containment for future plutonium waste disposal if he wanted to continue dumping locally. Bob's original plant met all treatment requirements when it was built as state-of-the-art. However, evidence mounted over the years that then state-of-the-art hazardous waste disposal would be inadequate to contain hazardous wastes over the long term (for example, because of leaks in the containment vessels); and leakage did occur, justifying renewed cleanup efforts.

Bob suddenly got what he thought was a brilliant idea. He had seen on a TV program a Chinese entrepreneur who owned a large piece of land with a deep gorge on it. For a fee, the Chinese entrepreneur would allow persons to dump any kind of waste in it. Discuss the ethical considerations of this scenario.

Discussion Questions

1. Some commentators see nations that have weak environmental protections as realizing economic benefits from pursuing such questionable policies. For example, certain Asian and Central and South American nations have allowed the export of wood from tropical forests thereby contributing to destruction of tropical rain forests. Such natural resources, which do not have a scarcity value because they have few environmental restrictions on their harvesting, provide a competitive advantage to these emerging nations with a desire for higher living standards for its inhabitants. Suppose that the World Trade Organization was considering an amendment to its trade provisions that allowed nations to bar foreign-made goods if not made under laws as protective as the nation into which they were to be imported. Would you favor or argue against such a change in international trade law? (You may want to review the Tuna/Dolphin case in Chapter 8.)
2. Many environmental statutes, such as the Clean Air and Clean Water acts, create both civil and criminal liability for violators. Should criminal sanctions be put in environmental statutes? Are environmental offenses violent? Can they cause death or widespread health problems? What should be the test for deciding whether to make an act a crime—its social offensiveness or harm?
3. A leading think tank in Washington, D.C., the Brookings Institution, revealed the results of its study of the Clean Air Act. The study concluded that air quality in the United States had improved, but this improvement was the result of switching from coal to cleaner fuels and the downturn in the nation's economy, and not the result of the Clean Air Act. The Brookings study did note that the act had reduced pollutants from new sources and new cars and trucks. However, the study concluded existing sources (old factories, cars, and trucks) of pollution are unaffected by the act. The Brookings study made several recommendations for amending the act:

   a. Shift the burden for pollution control from new sources to existing sources.

   b. Expand the "bubble" and "offset" policies.

   c. Encourage marketable discharge licenses and effluent fees.

   d. Change pollutants regulated by the national ambient air quality standards (NAAQS) from total suspended particulates (TSP) and sulfur dioxide to fine respirable particulates and acid sulfates.

   e. Give states total authority for state implementation plans (SIPs) subject only to EPA's power to reject an SIP within a reasonable time.

   Given the Brookings study and recommendations, do you think Congress did enough when it passed the 1990 Clean Air Act Amendments? Is the general direction of the Brookings recommendations to toughen, weaken, fine-tune, or do something else?
4. The Clean Air and Clean Water acts have built on each other. That is, one was passed or amended, and the other copied the ideas used. For example, the 1963 Clean Air Act was based on the 1948 Federal Water Pollution Control Act. Actually, neither was successful. Nonetheless, concepts from one law crept into the other. For example, states were given a role in enforcing the Clean Air Act. They have been given the opportunity to enforce the permit program under the Clean Water Act. Are the problems of air and water pollution similar enough to justify such copying?
5. In late 1980, Congress enacted the Comprehensive Environmental Response, Compensation, and Liability Act of 1980, popularly called the "Superfund Act." It authorized $1.6 billion to clean up abandoned hazardous waste spills and dumps. The bill also authorized the federal government to recover cleanup costs from responsible parties. What industry groups will likely sustain major financial and liability burdens because of the Superfund Act? Is it fair to impose such liability? What legal ethics discussed in Chapter 1 are involved here?
6. The EPA promulgated "Beverage Container Guidelines" (regulations). It described a system for resource conservation recommended to state and local governments. The Resource Conservation and Recovery Act of 1976 (RCRA) requires that executive agencies ensure compliance with EPA's guidelines. The guidelines require all beverage containers sold at federal facilities to be made returnable by requiring a five-cent deposit as an incentive for consumers to return empty bottles for reuse or recycling. Returnable containers need not be refillable. Cans and nonrefillable bottles may be used. Beverages in sealed containers sold on federal facilities must be

labeled returnable, and deposits must be refunded to the consumer when containers are returned. Dealers are forbidden to procure beverages in containers from distributors refusing to cooperate in the program. The United States Brewers Association, Inc., asked a U.S. court of appeals to review the EPA's refusal to repeal these guidelines. What was the result? [*United States Ass'n v. EPA*, 600 F.2d 974 (1974)]

7. "NEPA is an environmental Magna Carta." Discuss this statement.
8. Refer to the legal ethics discussed in Chapter 1. Which ethics support environmental law? Which challenge the environmental movement?
9. The state of Ohio got a state court injunction directing William Kovacs to clean up a hazardous waste disposal site. Kovacs did not obey the injunction. Ohio then went to state court and got appointment of a receiver to take possession of Kovacs's property and other assets and put the injunction into effect. The receiver took possession of Kovacs's site but had not completed his task when Kovacs filed a personal bankruptcy petition. To force part of Kovacs's postbankruptcy income to pay the receiver's tasks, Ohio went to state court to discover Kovacs's income and assets. Kovacs asked the bankruptcy court to stay (stop) Ohio's state court action. The bankruptcy court did so. Ohio then filed a claim in bankruptcy court, asking for a declaration that Kovacs's obligation under the state injunction was not a dischargeable bankruptcy debt (technically, not a "debt" or "liability on a claim"). The bankruptcy court ruled against Ohio, as did the the Sixth Circuit Court of Appeals. What result in the U.S. Supreme Court? [*Ohio v. Kovacs*, 469 U.S. 274, 105 S.Ct. 705, 83 C.Ed. 2d 649 (1985)]

Suggested Readings

Articles

BARLOW, "Why the Christian Right Must Protect the Environment: Theocentricity in the Political Workplace," 23 *Boston College Environmental Affairs Law Review* 781 (1996).

BUCKLEY, "Environmental Audit: Review and Guidelines," 7 *Environmental & Planning Law Journal* 127 (1990).

GREEN, "Control of Air Pollutant Emissions from Aircraft Engines: Local Impacts of National Concern," 5 *The Environmental Lawyer* 513 (1999).

GREEN, "Regulating Toxic Substances: A Philosophy of Science and the Law," 37 *Jurimetrics Journal of Law, Science, and Technology* 205 (1997).

GREEN, "Successors and CERCLA: The Imperfect Analogy to Product Liability and an Alternative Proposal," 87 *Northwestern University Law Review* 897 (1993).

HARE, "Reluctant Soldiers: The Criminal Liability of Corporate Officers for Negligent Violations of the Clean Water Act," 138 *University of Pennsylvania Law Review* 935 (1990).

LYNCH, "The Federal Advisory Committee Act: An Obstacle to Ecosystem Management by Federal Agencies?" 71 *Washington Law Review* 431 (1996).

MAYER, "Lessons in Law from *A Civil Action*," 16 *Journal of Legal Studies Education* 113 (1998).

POINDEXTER, "Addressing Morality in Urban Brownfield Redevelopment: Using Stakeholder Theory to Craft Legal Process," 15 *Virginia Environmental Law Journal* 37 (1995).

STEINBERG, "Can EPA Sue Other Federal Agencies?" 17 *Ecology Law Quarterly* 317 (1990).

APPENDIX

I

THE CONSTITUTION OF THE UNITED STATES OF AMERICA

We the People of the United States, in Order to form a more perfect Union, establish Justice, insure domestic Tranquility, provide for the common defence, promote the general Welfare, and secure the Blessings of Liberty to ourselves and our Posterity, do ordain and establish this Constitution for the United States of America.

ARTICLE I

Section 1

All legislative Powers herein granted shall be vested in a Congress of the United States, which shall consist of a Senate and House of Representatives.

Section 2

The House of Representatives shall be composed of Members chosen every second Year by the People of the several States, and the Electors in each State shall have the Qualifications requisite for Electors of the most numerous Branch of the State Legislature.

No Person shall be a Representative who shall not have attained to the Age of twenty five Years, and been seven Years a Citizen of the United States, and who shall not, when elected, be an Inhabitant of that State in which he shall be chosen.

Representatives and direct Taxes shall be apportioned among the several States which may be included within this Union, according to their respective Numbers, which shall be determined by adding to the whole Number of free Persons, including those bound to Service for a Term of Years, and excluding Indians not taxed, three fifths of all other Persons. The actual Enumeration shall be made within three Years after the first Meeting of the Congress of the United States, and within every subsequent Term of ten Years, in such Manner as they shall by Law direct. The Number of Representatives shall not exceed one for every thirty Thousand, but each State shall have at Least one Representative; and until such enumeration shall be made, the State of New Hampshire shall be entitled to choose three, Massachusetts eight, Rhode Island and Providence Plantations one, Connecticut five, New York six, New Jersey four, Pennsylvania eight, Delaware one, Maryland six, Virginia ten, North Carolina five, South Carolina five, and Georgia three.

When vacancies happen in the Representation from any State, the Executive Authority thereof shall issue Writs of Election to fill such vacancies.

The House of Representatives shall use their Speaker and other Officers; and shall have the sole Power of Impeachment.

Section 3

The Senate of the United States shall be composed of two Senators from each State, chosen by the Legislature thereof, for six Years; and each Senator shall have one Vote.

Immediately after they shall be assembled in Consequence of the first Election, they shall be divided as equally as may be into three Classes. The Seats of the Senators of the first Class shall be vacated at the Expiration of the second Year, of the second Class at the Expiration of the fourth Year, and of the third Class at the Expiration of the sixth Year, so that one third may be chosen every second Year; and if Vacancies happen by Resignation, or otherwise, during the Recess of the Legislature of any State, the Executive thereof may make temporary Appointments until the next Meeting of the Legislature, which shall then fill such Vacancies.

No Person shall be a Senator who shall not have attained to the Age of thirty Years, and been nine Years a Citizen of the United States, and who shall not, when elected, be an Inhabitant of that State for which he shall be chosen.

The Vice President of the United States shall be President of the Senate, but shall have no Vote, unless they be equally divided.

The Senate shall choose their other Officers, and also a President pro tempore, in the Absence of the Vice President, or when he shall exercise the Office of President of the United States.

The Senate shall have the sole Power to try all Impeachments. When sitting for that Purpose, they shall be on Oath or Affirmation. When the President of the United States is tried the Chief Justice shall preside: And no Person shall be convicted without the Concurrence of two thirds of the Members present.

Judgment in Cases of Impeachment shall not extend further than to removal from Office, and disqualification to hold and enjoy any Office of honor, Trust or Profit under the United States; but the Party convicted shall nevertheless be liable and subject to Indictment, Trial, Judgment and Punishment, according to Law.

Section 4

The Times, Places and Manner of holding Elections for Senators and Representatives, shall be prescribed in each State by the Legislature thereof; but the Congress may at any time by Law make or alter such Regulations, except as to the Places of choosing Senators.

The Congress shall assemble at least once every Year, and such Meeting shall be on the first Monday in December, unless they shall by Law appoint a different Day.

Section 5

Each House shall be the Judge of the Elections, Returns and Qualifications of its own Members, and a Majority of each shall constitute a Quorum to do Business; but a smaller Number may adjourn from day to day, and may be authorized to compel the Attendance of absent Members, in such Manner and under such Penalties as each House may provide.

Each House may determine the Rules of its Proceedings, punish its Members for disorderly Behaviour, and, with the Concurrence of two thirds, expel a Member.

Each House shall keep a Journal of its Proceedings, and from time to time publish the same, excepting such Parts as may in their Judgment require Secrecy; and the Yeas and Nays of the Members of either House on any question shall, at the Desire of one fifth of those Present, be entered on the Journal.

Neither House, during the Session of Congress, shall, without the Consent of the other, adjourn for more than three days, nor to any other Place than that in which the two Houses shall be sitting.

Section 6

The Senators and Representatives shall receive a Compensation for their Services, to be ascertained by Law, and paid out of the Treasury of the United States. They shall in all Cases, except Treason, Felony and Breach of the Peace, be privileged from Arrest during their Attendance at the Session of their respective Houses and in going to and returning from the same; and for any Speech or Debate in either House, they shall not be questioned in any other Place.

No Senator or Representative shall, during the Time for which he was elected, be appointed to any civil Office under the Authority of the United States, which shall have been created, or the Emoluments whereof shall have been increased during such time; and no Person holding any Office under the United States, shall be a Member of either House during his Continuance in Office.

Section 7

All Bills for raising Revenue shall originate in the House of Representatives; but the Senate may propose or concur with amendments as on other Bills.

Every Bill which shall have passed the House of Representatives and the Senate, shall, before it become a Law, be presented to the President of the United States; If he approve he shall sign it, but if not he shall return it, with his Objections to that House in which it shall have originated, who shall enter the Objections at large on their Journal, and proceed to reconsider it. If after such Reconsideration two thirds of that House shall agree to pass the Bill, it shall be sent, together with the Objections, to the other House, by which it shall likewise be reconsidered, and if approved by two thirds of that House, it shall become a Law. But in all such Cases the Votes of both Houses shall be determined by Yeas and Nays, and the Names of the Persons voting for and against the Bill shall be entered on the Journal of each House respectively. If any Bill shall not be returned by the President within ten Days (Sundays excepted) after it shall have been presented to him, the Same shall be a Law, in like Manner as if he had signed it, unless the Congress by their Adjournment prevent its Return, in which Case it shall not be a Law.

Every Order, Resolution, or Vote to which the Concurrence of the Senate and House of Representatives may be necessary (except on a question of Adjournment) shall be presented to the President of the United States; and before the Same shall take Effect, shall be approved by him, or being disapproved by him, shall be repassed by two thirds of the Senate and House of Representatives, according to the Rules and Limitations prescribed in the Case of a Bill.

Section 8

The Congress shall have Power to lay and collect Taxes, Duties, Imposts and Excises, to pay the Debts and provide for the common Defence and general Welfare of the United States; but all Duties, Imposts and Excises shall be uniform throughout the United States;

To borrow Money on the credit of the United States;

To regulate Commerce with foreign Nations, and among the several States, and with the Indian Tribes;

To establish an uniform Rule of Naturalization, and uniform Laws on the subject of Bankruptcies throughout the United States;

To coin Money, regulate the Value thereof, and of foreign Coin, and fix the Standard of Weights and Measures;

To provide for the Punishment of counterfeiting the Securities and current Coin of the United States;

To establish Post Offices and post Roads;

To promote the Progress of Science and useful Arts, by securing for limited Times to Authors and Inventors the exclusive Right to their respective Writings and Discoveries;

To constitute Tribunals inferior to the supreme Court;

To define and punish Piracies and Felonies committed on the high Seas, and Offences against the Law of Nations;

To declare War, grant Letters of Marque and Reprisal, and make Rules concerning Captures on Land and Water;

To raise and support Armies, but no Appropriation of Money to that Use shall be for a longer Term than two Years;

To provide and maintain a Navy;

To make Rules for the Government and Regulation of the land and naval Forces;

To provide for calling forth the Militia to execute the Laws of the Union, suppress Insurrections and repel Invasions;

To provide for organizing, arming, and disciplining the Militia, and for governing such Part of them as may be employed in the Service of the United States, reserving to the States respectively, the Appointment of the Officers, and the Authority of training the Militia according to the discipline prescribed by Congress;

To exercise exclusive Legislation in all Cases whatsoever, over such District (not exceeding ten Miles square) as may, by Cession of particular States, and the Acceptance of Congress, become the Seat of the Government of the United States, and to exercise like Authority over all Places purchased by the Consent of the Legislature of the State in which the Same shall be, for the Erection of Forts, Magazines, Arsenals, dock-Yards, and other needful Buildings;—And

To make all Laws which shall be necessary and proper for carrying into Execution the foregoing Powers, and all other Powers vested by this Constitution in the Government of the United States, or in any Department or Officer thereof.

Section 9

The Migration or Importation of such Persons as any of the States now existing shall think proper to admit, shall not be prohibited by the Congress prior to the Year one thousand eight hundred and eight, but a Tax or duty may be imposed on such Importation, not exceeding ten dollars for each Person.

The Privilege of the Writ of Habeas Corpus shall not be suspended, unless when in Cases of Rebellion or Invasion the public Safety may require it.

No Bill of Attainder or ex post facto Law shall be passed.

No Capitation, or other direct, Tax shall be laid, unless in Proportion to the Census or Enumeration herein before directed to be taken.

No Tax or Duty shall be laid on Articles exported from any State.

No Preference shall be given by any Regulation of Commerce or Revenue to the Ports of one State over those of another; nor shall Vessels bound to, or from, one State, be obliged to enter, clear or pay Duties in another.

No Money shall be drawn from the Treasury, but in Consequence of Appropriations made by Law; and a regular Statement and Account of the Receipts and Expenditures of all public Money shall be published from time to time.

No Title of Nobility shall be granted by the United States: And no Person holding any Office of Profit or Trust under them, shall, without the Consent of the Congress, accept of any present, Emolument, Office, or Title, of any kind whatever, from any King, Prince or foreign State.

Section 10

No State shall enter into any Treaty, Alliance, or Confederation; grant Letters of Marque and Reprisal; coin Money; emit Bills of Credit; make any Thing but gold and silver Coin a Tender in Payment of Debts; pass any Bill of Attainder, ex post facto Law, or Law impairing the Obligation of Contracts, or grant any Title of Nobility.

No State shall, without the Consent of the Congress, lay any Imposts or Duties on Imports or Exports, except what may be absolutely necessary for executing its inspection Laws: and the net Produce of all Duties and Imposts, laid by any State on Imports or Exports, shall be for the Use of the Treasury of the United States; and all such Laws shall be subject to the revision and Control of the Congress.

No State shall, without the Consent of Congress, lay any Duty of Tonnage, keep Troops, or Ships of War in time of Peace, enter into any Agreement or Compact with another State, or with a foreign Power, or engage in War, unless actually invaded, or in such imminent Danger as will not admit of delay.

ARTICLE II

Section 1

The executive Power shall be vested in a President of the United States of America. He shall hold his Office during the Term for four Years, and, together with the Vice President, chosen for the same Term, be elected, as follows:

Each State shall appoint, in such Manner as the Legislature thereof may direct, a Number of Electors, equal to the whole Number of Senators and Representatives to which the State may be entitled in the Congress: but no Senator or Representative, or Person holding an Office of Trust or Profit under the United States, shall be appointed an Elector.

The Electors shall meet in their respective States, and vote by Ballot for two Persons, of whom one at least shall not be an Inhabitant of the same State with themselves. And they shall make a List of all the Persons voted for, and of the Number of Votes for each; which List they shall sign and certify, and transmit sealed to the Seat of the Government of the United States, directed to the President of the Senate. The President of the Senate shall, in the Presence of the Senate and House of Representatives, open all the Certificates, and the Votes shall then be counted. The Person having the greatest Number of Votes shall be the President, if such Number be a Majority of the whole Number of Electors appointed; and if there be more than one who have such Majority, and have an equal Number of Votes, then the House of Representatives shall immediately choose by Ballot one of them for President; and if no Person have a Majority, then from the five highest on the List the said House shall in like Manner choose the President. But in choosing the President, the Votes shall be taken by States, the Representation from each State having one Vote; a quorum for this Purpose shall consist of a Member or Members from two thirds of the States, and a Majority of all the States shall be necessary to a Choice. In every Case, after the Choice of the President, the Person having the greater Number of Votes of the Electors shall be the Vice President. But if there should remain two or more who have equal Votes, the Senate shall choose from them by Ballot the Vice President.

The Congress may determine the Time of choosing the Electors, and the Day on which they shall give their Votes; which Day shall be the same throughout the United States.

No Person except a natural born Citizen, or a Citizen of the United States, at the time of the Adoption of this Constitution, shall be eligible to the Office of President; neither shall any Person be eligible to that Office who shall not have attained to the Age of thirty five Years, and been fourteen years a Resident within the United States.

In Case of the Removal of the President from Office, or of his Death, Resignation, or Inability to discharge the Powers and Duties of the said Office, the Same shall devolve on the Vice President, and the Congress may by Law provide for the Case of Removal, Death, Resignation or Inability, both of the President and Vice President, declaring what Officer shall then act as President, and such Officer shall act accordingly, until the Disability be removed, or a President shall be elected.

The President shall, at stated Times, receive for his Services, a Compensation, which shall neither be increased nor diminished during the Period for which he shall have been elected, and he shall not receive within that Period any other Emolument from the United States, or any of them.

Before he enter on the Execution of his Office, he shall take the following Oath or Affirmation:—"I do solemnly swear (or affirm) that I will faithfully execute the Office of President of the United States, and will to the best of my Ability, preserve, protect and defend the Constitution of the United States."

Section 2

The President shall be Commander in Chief of the Army and Navy of the United States, and of the Militia of the several States, when called into the actual Service of the United States; he may require the Opinion, in writing, of the principal Officer in each of the executive Departments, upon any Subject relating to the Duties of their respective Offices, and he shall have Power to grant Reprieves and Pardons for Offences against the United States, except in Cases of Impeachment.

He shall have Power, by and with the Advice and Consent of the Senate, to make Treaties, provided two thirds of the Senators present concur; and he shall nominate, and by and with the Advice and Consent of the Senate, shall appoint Ambassadors, other public Ministers and Consuls, Judges of the supreme Court, and all other Officers of the United States, whose Appointments are not herein otherwise provided for, and which shall be established by Law: but the Congress may by Law vest the Appointment of such inferior Officers, as they think proper, in the President alone, in the Courts of Law, or in the Heads of Departments.

The President shall have Power to fill up all Vacancies that may happen during the Recess of the Senate, by granting Commissions which shall expire at the End of their next Session.

Section 3

He shall from time to time give to the Congress Information of the State of the Union, and recommend to their Consideration such Measures as he shall judge necessary and expedient; he may, on extraordinary Occasions, convene both Houses, or either of them, and in Case of Disagreement between them, with Respect to the Time of Adjournment, he may adjourn them to such Time as he shall think proper; he shall receive Ambassadors and other public Ministers; he shall take Care that the Laws be faithfully executed, and shall Commission all the Officers of the United States.

Section 4

The President, Vice President and all Civil Officers of the United States shall be removed from Office on Impeachment for, and Conviction of, Treason, Bribery, or other high Crimes and Misdemeanors.

ARTICLE III

Section 1

The judicial Power of the United States, shall be vested in one supreme Court, and in such inferior Courts as the Congress may from time to time ordain and establish. The Judges, both of the supreme and inferior Courts, shall hold their Offices during good Behaviour, and shall, at stated Times, receive for their

Services, a Compensation, which shall not be diminished during their Continuance in Office.

Section 2

The judicial Power shall extend to all Cases, in Law and Equity, arising under this Constitution, the Laws of the United States, and Treaties made, or which shall be made under their Authority;—to all Cases affecting Ambassadors, other public Ministers and Consuls;—to all Cases of admiralty and maritime Jurisdiction;—to Controversies to which the United States shall be a Party;—to Controversies between two or more States;—between a State and Citizens of another State;—between Citizens of different States;—between Citizens of the same State claiming Lands under Grants of different States, and between a State, or the Citizens thereof, and foreign States, Citizens or Subjects.

In all Cases affecting Ambassadors, other public Ministers and Consuls, and those in which a State shall be a Party, the supreme Court shall have original Jurisdiction. In all the other Cases before mentioned, the supreme Court shall have appellate Jurisdiction, both as to Law and Fact, with such Exceptions, and under such Regulations as the Congress shall make.

The Trial of all Crimes, except in Cases of Impeachment, shall be by Jury; and such Trial shall be held in the State where the said Crimes shall have been committed; but when not committed within any State, the Trial shall be at such Place or Places as the Congress may by Law have directed.

Section 3

Treason against the United States, shall consist only in levying War against them, or in adhering to their Enemies, giving them Aid and Comfort. No Person shall be convicted of Treason unless on the Testimony of two Witnesses to the same overt Act, or on Confession in open Court.

The Congress shall have Power to declare the Punishment of Treason, but no Attainder of Treason shall work Corruption of Blood or Forfeiture except during the Life of the Person attainted.

ARTICLE IV

Section 1

Full Faith and Credit shall be given in each State to the public Acts, Records, and judicial Proceedings of every other State. And the Congress may by general Laws prescribe the Manner in which such Acts, Records and Proceedings shall be proved and the Effect thereof.

Section 2

The Citizens of each State shall be entitled to all Privileges and Immunities of Citizens in the several States.

A Person charged in any State with Treason, Felony, or other Crime, who shall flee from Justice, and be found in another State, shall on Demand of the executive Authority of the State from which he fled, be delivered up, to be removed to the State having Jurisdiction of the Crime.

No Person held to Service or Labour in one State, under the Laws thereof, escaping into another, shall, in Consequence of any Law or Regulation therein, be discharged from such Service or Labour, but shall be delivered up on Claim of the Party to whom such Service or Labour may be due.

Section 3

New States may be admitted by the Congress into this Union; but no new State shall be formed or erected within the Jurisdiction of any other State; nor any State be formed by the Junction of two or more States, or Parts of States, without the Consent of the Legislatures of the States concerned as well as of the Congress.

The Congress shall have Power to dispose of and make all needful Rules and Regulations respecting the Territory or other Property belonging to the United States; and nothing in this Constitution shall be so construed as to Prejudice any Claims of the United States, or of any particular State.

Section 4

The United States shall guarantee to every State in this Union a Republican Form of Government, and shall protect each of them against Invasion; and on Application of the Legislature, or of the Executive (when the Legislature cannot be convened) against domestic Violence.

ARTICLE V

The Congress, whenever two thirds of both Houses shall deem it necessary, shall propose Amendments to this Constitution, or, on the Application of the Legislatures of two thirds of the several States, shall call a Convention for proposing Amendments, which, in either Case, shall be valid to all Intents and Purposes, as Part of this Constitution, when ratified by the Legislatures of three fourths of the several States, or by Conventions in three fourths thereof, as the one or the other Mode of Ratification may be proposed by the Congress; Provided that no Amendment which may be made prior to the Year One thousand eight hundred and eight shall in any Manner affect the first and fourth Clauses in the Ninth Section of the first Article; and that no State, without its Consent, shall be deprived of its equal Suffrage in the Senate.

ARTICLE VI

All Debts contracted and Engagements entered into, before the Adoption of this Constitution, shall be as valid against the United States under this Constitution, as under the Confederation.

This Constitution, and the Laws of the United States which shall be made in Pursuance thereof; and all Treaties made, or which shall be made, under the Authority of the United States, shall be the supreme Law of the Land; and the judges in every State shall be bound thereby, any Thing in the Constitution or Laws of any State to the Contrary notwithstanding.

The Senators and Representatives before mentioned, and the Members of the several State Legislatures, and all executive and judicial Officers, both of the United States and of the several States, shall be bound by Oath or Affirmation, to support this Constitution; but no religious Test shall ever be required as a Qualification to any Office or public Trust under the United States.

ARTICLE VII

The Ratification of the Conventions of nine States, shall be sufficient for the Establishment of this Constitution between the States so ratifying the Same.

AMENDMENT I [1791]

Congress shall make no law respecting an establishment of religion, or prohibiting the free exercise thereof; or abridging the freedom of speech, or of the press; or the right of the people peaceably to assemble and to petition the Government for a redress of grievances.

AMENDMENT II [1791]

A well regulated Militia, being necessary to the security of a free State, the right of the people to keep and bear Arms, shall not be infringed.

AMENDMENT III [1791]

No Soldier shall, in time of peace be quartered in any house, without the consent of the Owner, nor in time of war, but in a manner to be prescribed by law.

AMENDMENT IV [1791]

The right of the people to be secure in their persons, houses, papers, and effects, against unreasonable searches and seizures, shall not be violated, and no Warrants shall issue, but upon probable cause, supported by Oath or affirmation, and particularly describing the place to be searched, and the persons or things to be seized.

AMENDMENT V [1791]

No person shall be held to answer for a capital, or otherwise infamous crime, unless on a presentment or indictment of a Grand Jury, except in cases arising in the land or naval forces, or in the Militia, when in actual service in time of War or public danger; nor shall any person be subject for the same offence to be twice put in jeopardy of life or limb; nor shall be compelled in any criminal case to be a witness against himself, nor be deprived of life, liberty, or property, without due process of law; nor shall private property be taken for public use, without just compensation.

AMENDMENT VI [1791]

In all criminal prosecutions, the accused shall enjoy the right to a speedy and public trial, by an impartial jury of the State and district wherein the crime shall have been committed, which district shall have been previously ascertained by law, and to be informed of the nature and cause of the accusation; to be confronted with the witnesses against him; to have compulsory process for obtaining Witnesses in his favor, and to have Assistance of Counsel for his defence.

AMENDMENT VII [1791]

In Suits at common law, where the value in controversy shall exceed twenty dollars, the right of trial by jury shall be preserved, and no fact tried by a jury, shall be otherwise reexamined in any Court of the United States, than according to the rules of the common law.

AMENDMENT VIII [1791]

Excessive bail shall not be required nor excessive fines imposed, nor cruel and unusual punishments inflicted.

AMENDMENT IX [1791]

The enumeration in the Constitution, of certain rights, shall not be construed to deny or disparage others retained by the people.

AMENDMENT X [1791]

The powers not delegated to the United States by the Constitution, nor prohibited by it to the States, are reserved to the States respectively, or to the people.

AMENDMENT XI [1798]

The Judicial power of the United States shall not be construed to extend to any suit in law or equity, commenced or prosecuted against one of the United States by Citizens of another State, or by Citizens or Subjects of any Foreign State.

AMENDMENT XII [1804]

The Electors shall meet in their respective states and vote by ballot for President and Vice-President, one of whom, at least, shall not be an inhabitant of the same state with themselves; they shall name in their ballots the person voted for as President, and in distinct ballots the person voted for as Vice-President, and they shall make distinct lists of all persons voted for as President, and of all persons voted for as Vice-President, and of the number of votes for each, which lists they shall sign and certify, and transmit sealed to the seat of the government of the United States, directed to the President of the Senate;—The President of the Senate shall, in the presence of the Senate and House of Representatives, open all the certificates and the votes shall then be counted;—The person having the greatest number of votes for President, shall be the President, if such number be a majority of the whole number of Electors appointed; and if no person have such majority, then from the persons having the highest numbers not exceeding three on the list of those voted for as President, the House of Representatives shall choose immediately, by ballot, the President. But in choosing the President, the votes shall be taken by states, the representation from each state having one vote; a quorum for this purpose shall consist of a member or members from two-thirds of the states, and a majority of all the states shall be necessary to a choice. And if the House of Representatives shall not choose a President whenever the right of choice shall devolve upon them, before the fourth day of March next following, then the Vice-President shall act as President, as in the case of the death or other constitutional disability of the President—The person having the greatest number of votes as Vice-President, shall be the Vice-President, if such number be a majority of the whole number of electors appointed, and if no person have a majority, then from the two highest numbers on the list, the Senate shall choose the Vice-President; a quorum for the purpose shall consist of two-thirds of the whole number of Senators, and a majority of the whole number shall be necessary to a choice. But no person constitutionally ineligible to the office of President shall be eligible to that of Vice-President of the United States.

AMENDMENT XIII [1865]

Section 1

Neither slavery nor involuntary servitude, except as punishment for crime whereof the party shall have been duly convicted, shall exist within the United States, or any place subject to their jurisdiction.

Section 2

Congress shall have power to enforce this article by appropriate legislation.

AMENDMENT XIV [1868]

Section 1

All persons born or naturalized in the United States and subject to the jurisdiction thereof, are citizens of the United States and of the State wherein they reside. No State shall make or enforce any law which shall abridge the privileges or immunities of citizens of the United States; nor shall any State deprive any person of life, liberty, or property, without due process of law; nor deny to any person within its jurisdiction the equal protection of the laws.

Section 2

Representatives shall be apportioned among the several States according to their respective numbers, counting the whole number of persons in each State, excluding Indians not taxed. But when the right to vote at any election for the choice of electors for President and Vice President of the United States, Representatives in Congress, the Executive and Judicial officers of a State, or the members of the Legislature thereof, is denied to any of the male inhabitants of such State, being twenty-one years of age, and citizens of the United States, or in any way abridged, except for participation in rebellion, or other crime, the basis of representation therein shall be reduced in the proportion which the number of such male citizens shall bear to the whole number of male citizens twenty-one years of age in such State.

Section 3

No person shall be a Senator or Representative in Congress, or elector of President and Vice President, or hold any office, civil or military, under the United States, or under any State, who, having previously taken an oath, as a member of Congress, or as an officer of the United States, or as a member of any State legislature, or as an executive or judicial officer of any State, to support the Constitution of the United States, shall have engaged in insurrection or rebellion against the same, or given aid or comfort to the enemies thereof. But Congress may by a vote of two-thirds of each House, remove such disability.

Section 4

The validity of the public debt of the United States, authorized by law, including debts incurred for payment of pensions and bounties for services in suppressing insurrection or rebellion, shall not be questioned. But neither the United States nor any State shall assume or pay any debt or obligation incurred in aid of insurrection or rebellion against the United State, or any claim for the loss or emancipation of any slave; but all such debts, obligations and claims shall be held illegal and void.

Section 5

The Congress shall have power to enforce, by appropriate legislation, the provisions of this article.

AMENDMENT XV [1870]

Section 1

The right of citizens of the United States to vote shall not be denied or abridged by the United States or by any State on account of race, color, or previous condition of servitude.

Section 2

The Congress shall have power to enforce this article by appropriate legislation.

AMENDMENT XVI [1913]

The Congress shall have power to lay and collect taxes on incomes, from whatever source derived, without apportionment among the several States, and without regard to any census or enumeration.

AMENDMENT XVII [1913]

The Senate of the United States shall be composed of two Senators from each State, elected by the people thereof, for six years; and each Senator shall have one vote. The electors in each State shall have the qualifications requisite for electors of the most numerous branch of the State legislatures.

When vacancies happen in the representation of any State in the Senate, the executive authority of such State shall issue writs of election to fill such vacancies: *Provided,* That the legislature of any State may empower the executive thereof to make temporary appointments until the people fill the vacancies by election as the legislature may direct.

This amendment shall not be so construed as to affect the election or term of any Senator chosen before it becomes valid as part of the Constitution.

AMENDMENT XVIII [1919]

Section 1

After one year from the ratification of this article the manufacture, sale, or transportation of intoxicating liquors within, the importation thereof into, or the exportation thereof from the United States and all territory subject to the jurisdiction thereof for beverage purposes is hereby prohibited.

Section 2

The Congress and the several States shall have concurrent power to enforce this article by appropriate legislation.

Section 3

This article shall be inoperative unless it shall have been ratified as an amendment to the Constitution by the legislatures of the several States, as provided in the Constitution, within seven years from the date of the submission hereof to the States by the Congress.

AMENDMENT XIX [1920]

The right of citizens of the United States to vote shall not be denied or abridged by the United States or by any State on account of sex.

Congress shall have power to enforce this article by appropriate legislation.

AMENDMENT XX [1933]

Section 1

The terms of the President and Vice President shall end at noon on the 20th day of January, and the terms of Senators and Representatives at noon on the 3d day of January, of the years in which such terms would have ended if this article had not been ratified; and the terms of their successors shall then begin.

Section 2

The Congress shall assemble at least once in every year, and such meeting shall begin at noon on the 3d day of January, unless they shall by law appoint a different day.

Section 3

If, at the time fixed for the beginning of the term of the President, the President elect shall have died, the Vice President elect shall become President. If the President shall not have been chosen before the time fixed for the beginning of his term, or if the President elect shall have failed to qualify, then the Vice President elect shall act as President until a President shall have qualified; and the Congress may by law provide for the case wherein neither a President elect nor a Vice President elect shall have qualified, declaring who shall then act as President, or the manner in which one who is to act shall be selected, and such person shall act accordingly until a President or Vice President shall have qualified.

Section 4

The Congress may by law provide for the case of the death of any of the persons from whom the House of Representatives may choose a President whenever the right of choice shall have devolved upon them, and for the case of death of any of the persons from whom the Senate may choose a Vice President whenever the right of choice shall have devolved upon them.

Section 5

Sections 1 and 2 shall take effect on the 15th day of October following the ratification of this article.

Section 6

This article shall be inoperative unless it shall have been ratified as an amendment to the Constitution by the legislatures of three-fourths of the several States within seven years from the date of its submission.

AMENDMENT XXI [1933]

Section 1

The eighteenth article of amendment to the Constitution of the United States is hereby repealed.

Section 2

The transportation or importation into any State, Territory, or possession of the United States for delivery or use therein of intoxicating liquors, in violation of the laws thereof, is hereby prohibited.

Section 3

This article shall be inoperative unless it shall have been ratified as an amendment to the Constitution by conventions in the several states, as provided in the Constitution, within seven years from the date of the submission hereof to the States by the Congress.

AMENDMENT XXII [1951]

Section 1

No person shall be elected to the office of the President more than twice, and no person who has held the office of President, or acted as President, for more than two years of a term to which some other person was elected President shall be elected to the office of the President more than once. But this Article shall not apply to any person holding the office of President when this Article was proposed by the Congress, and shall not prevent any person who may be holding the office of President, or acting as President, during the term within which the Article becomes operative from holding the office of President or acting as President during the remainder of such term.

Section 2

This article shall be inoperative unless it shall have been ratified as an amendment to the Constitution by the legislatures of three-fourths of the several States within seven years from the date of its submission to the States by the Congress.

AMENDMENT XXIII [1961]

Section 1

The District constituting the seat of Government of the United States shall appoint in such manner as the Congress may direct:

A number of electors of President and Vice President equal to the whole number of Senators and Representatives in Congress to which the District would be entitled if it were a State, but in no event more than the least populous State; they shall be in addition to those appointed by the States, but they shall be considered, for the purposes of the election of President and Vice President, to be electors appointed by a State; and they shall meet in the District and perform such duties as provided by the twelfth article of amendment.

Section 2

The Congress shall have power to enforce this article by appropriate legislation.

AMENDMENT XXIV [1964]

Section 1

The right of citizens of the United States to vote in any primary or other election for President or Vice President, for electors for President or Vice President, or for Senator or Representative in Congress, shall not be denied or abridged by the United States or any State by reason of failure to pay any poll tax or other tax.

Section 2

The Congress shall have power to enforce this article by appropriate legislation.

AMENDMENT XXV [1967]

Section 1

In case of the removal of the President from office or of his death or resignation, the Vice President shall become President.

Section 2

Whenever there is a vacancy in the office of the Vice President, the President shall nominate a Vice President who shall take office upon confirmation by a majority vote of both Houses of Congress.

Section 3

Whenever the President transmits to the President pro tempore of the Senate and the Speaker of the House of Representatives his written declaration that he is unable to discharge the powers and duties of his office, and until he transmits to them a written declaration to the contrary, such powers and duties shall be discharged by the Vice President as Acting President.

Section 4

Whenever the Vice President and a majority of either the principal officers of the executive departments or of such other body as Congress may by law provide, transmit to the President pro tempore of the Senate and the Speaker of the House of Representatives their written declaration that the President is unable to discharge the powers and duties of his office, the Vice President shall immediately assume the powers and duties of the office as Acting President.

Thereafter, when the President transmits to the President pro tempore of the Senate and the Speaker of the House of Representatives his written declaration that no inability exists, he shall resume the powers and duties of his office unless the Vice President and a majority of either the principal officers of the executive department or of such other body as Congress may by law provide, transmit within four days to the President pro tempore of the Senate and the Speaker of the House of Representatives their written declaration that the President is unable to discharge the powers and duties of his office. Thereupon Congress shall decide the issue, assembling within forty-eight hours for that purpose if not in session. If the Congress, within twenty-one days after receipt of the latter written declaration, or, if Congress is not in session, within twenty-one days after Congress is required to assemble, determines by two-thirds vote of both Houses that the President is unable to discharge the powers and duties of his office, the Vice President shall continue to discharge the powers and duties of his office, the Vice President shall continue to discharge the same as Acting President; otherwise, the President shall resume the powers and duties of his office.

AMENDMENT XXVI [1971]

Section 1

The right of citizens of the United States, who are eighteen years of age or older to vote shall not be denied or abridged by the United States or by any State on account of age.

Section 2

The Congress shall have power to enforce this article by appropriate legislation.

APPENDIX II

THE SHERMAN ACT (Excerpts)

SECTION 1. TRUSTS, ETC., IN RESTRAINT OF TRADE ILLEGAL; PENALTY

Every contract, combination in the form of trust or otherwise, or conspiracy, in restraint of trade or commerce among the several States, or with foreign nations, is declared to be illegal. Every person who shall make any contract or engage in any combination or conspiracy hereby declared to be illegal shall be deemed guilty of a felony, and, on conviction thereof, shall be punished by fine not exceeding one million dollars if a corporation, or, if any other person, one hundred thousand dollars or by imprisonment not exceeding three years, or by both said punishments, in the discretion of the court.

SECTION 2. MONOPOLIZING TRADE A FELONY; PENALTY

Every person who shall monopolize, or attempt to monopolize, or combine or conspire with any other person or persons, to monopolize any part of the trade or commerce among the several States, or with foreign nations, shall be deemed guilty of a felony, and, on conviction thereof, shall be punished by fine not exceeding one million dollars if a corporation, or, if any other person, one hundred thousand dollars or by imprisonment not exceeding three years, or by both said punishments, in the discretion of the court.

APPENDIX III

THE ROBINSON-PATMAN ACT (Excerpts)

SECTION 2. DISCRIMINATION IN PRICE, SERVICES, OR FACILITIES—PRICE; SELECTION OF CUSTOMERS

(a) It shall be unlawful for any person engaged in commerce, in the course of such commerce, either directly or indirectly, to discriminate in price between different purchasers of commodities of like grade and quality, where either or any of the purchases involved in such discrimination are in commerce, where such commodities are sold for use, consumption, or resale within the United States or any Territory thereof or the District of Columbia or any insular possession or other place under the jurisdiction of the United States, and where the effect of such discrimination may be substantially to lessen competition or tend to create a monopoly in any line of commerce, or to injure, destroy, or prevent competition with any person who either grants or knowingly receives the benefit of such discrimination, or with customers of either of them; *Provided,* That nothing herein contained shall prevent differentials which make only due allowance for differences in the cost of manufacture, sale, or delivery resulting from the differing methods or quantities in which such commodities are to such purchasers sold or delivered: *Provided,* however, That the Federal trade Commission may, after due investigation and hearing to all interested parties, fix and establish quantity limits, and revise the same as it finds necessary, as to particular commodities or classes of commodities, where it finds that available purchasers in greater quantities are so few as to render differentials on account thereof unjustly discriminatory or promotive of monopoly in any line of commerce; and the foregoing shall then not be construed to permit differentials based on differences in quantities greater than those so fixed and established: And *provided further,* That nothing herein contained shall prevent persons engaged in selling goods, wares, or merchandise in commerce from selecting their own customers in bona fide transactions and not in restraint of trade: And *provided further,* That nothing herein contained shall prevent price changes from time to time where in response to changing conditions affecting the market for or the marketability of the goods concerned, such as but not limited to actual or imminent deterioration of perishable goods, obsolescence of seasonal goods, distress sales under court process, or sales in good faith in discontinuance of business in the goods concerned.

BURDEN OF REBUTTING PRIMA-FACIE CASE OF DISCRIMINATION

(b) Upon proof being made, at any hearing on a complaint under this section, that there has been discrimination in price or services or facilities furnished, the burden of rebutting the prima-facie case thus made by showing justification shall be upon the person charged with a violation of this section, and unless justification shall be affirmatively shown the Commission is authorized to issue an order terminating the discrimination: *Provided,* however, That nothing herein contained shall prevent a seller rebutting the prima-facie case thus made by showing that his lower price or the furnishing of services or facilities to any purchaser or purchasers was made in good faith to meet an equally low price of a competitor, or the services or facilities furnished by a competitor.

PAYMENT OR ACCEPTANCE OF COMMISSION, BROKERAGE OR OTHER COMPENSATION

(c) It shall be unlawful for any person engaged in commerce, in the course of such commerce, to pay or grant, or to receive or accept, anything of value as a commission, brokerage, or other compensation, or any allowance or discount in lieu thereof, except for services rendered in connection with the sale or purchase of goods, wares, or merchandise, either to the other party to such transaction or to an agent, representative, or other intermediary therein where such intermediary is acting in fact for or in behalf, or is subject to the direct or indirect control, of any party to such transaction other than the person by whom such compensation is so granted or paid.

PAYMENT FOR SERVICES OR FACILITIES FOR PROCESSING OR SALE

(d) It shall be unlawful for any person engaged in commerce to pay or contract for the payment of anything of value to or for the benefit of a customer of such person in the course of such commerce as compensation or in consideration for any services or facilities furnished by or through such customer in connection with the processing, handling, sale or offering for sale of any products or commodities manufactured, sold, or offered for sale by such person, unless such payment or consideration is available on proportionally equal terms to all other customers competing in the distribution of such products or commodities.

FURNISHING SERVICES OR FACILITIES FOR PROCESSING, HANDLING, ETC.

(e) It shall be unlawful for any person to discriminate in favor of one purchaser against another purchaser or purchasers of a commodity bought for resale, with or without processing, by contracting to furnish or furnishing, or by contributing to the furnishing of, any services or facilities connected with the processing, handling, sale, or offering for sale of such commodity so purchased upon terms not accorded to all purchasers on proportionally equal terms.

KNOWINGLY INDUCING OR RECEIVING DISCRIMINATORY PRICE

(f) It shall be unlawful for any person engaged in commerce, in the course of such commerce, knowingly to induce or receive a discrimination in price which is prohibited by this section.

SECTION 3. DISCRIMINATION IN REBATES, DISCOUNTS, OR ADVERTISING SERVICE CHARGES; UNDERSELLING IN PARTICULAR LOCALITIES; PENALTIES

It shall be unlawful for any person engaged in commerce, in the course of such commerce, to be a party to, or assist in, any transaction of sale, or contract to sell, which discriminates to his knowledge against competitors of the purchaser, in that, any discount, rebate, allowance, or advertising service charge is granted to the purchaser over and above any discount, rebate, allowance, or advertising service charge available at the time of such transaction to said competitors in respect of a sale of goods of like grade, quality, and quantity; to sell, or contract to sell, goods in any part of the United States at prices lower than those exacted by said person elsewhere in the United States for the purpose of destroying competition, or eliminating a competitor in such part of the United States; or, to sell, or contract to sell, goods at unreasonably low prices for the purpose of destroying competition or eliminating a competitor.

Any person violating any of the provisions of this section shall, upon conviction thereof, be fined not more than $5,000 or imprisoned not more than one year, or both.

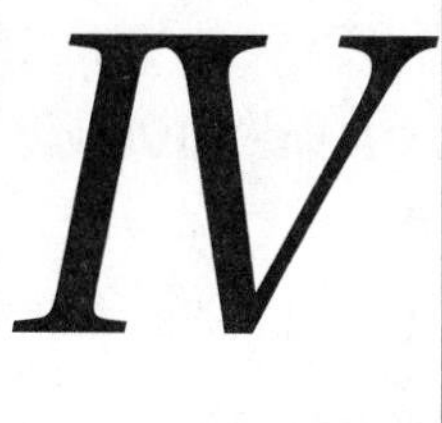

APPENDIX IV

SECTION 402A OF THE RESTATEMENT (SECOND) OF TORTS

SECTION 402A. SPECIAL LIABILITY OF SELLER OF PRODUCT FOR PHYSICAL HARM TO USER OR CONSUMER

(1) One who sells any product in a defective condition unreasonably dangerous to the user or consumer or to his property is subject to liability for physical harm thereby caused to the ultimate user or consumer, or to his property, if
 (a) the seller is engaged in the business of selling such a product, and
 (b) it is expected to and does reach the user or consumer without substantial change in the condition in which it is sold.

(2) The rule stated in Subsection (1) applies although
 (a) the seller has exercised all possible care in the preparation and sale of his product, and
 (b) the user or consumer has not bought the product from or entered into any contractual relation with the seller.

APPENDIX

V

UNIFORM COMMERCIAL CODE (Selected Provisions)

SECTION 1-103. SUPPLEMENTARY GENERAL PRINCIPLES OF LAW APPLICABLE

Unless displaced by the particular provisions of this Act, the principles of law and equity, including the law merchant and the law relative to capacity to contract, principal and agent, estoppel, fraud, misrepresentation, duress, coercion, mistake, bankruptcy, or other validating or invalidating cause shall supplement its provisions.

SECTION 1-201. GENERAL DEFINITIONS

Subject to additional definitions contained in the subsequent Articles of this Act which are applicable to specific Articles or Parts thereof, and unless the context otherwise requires, in this Act:

(1) "Action" in the sense of a judicial proceeding includes recoupment, counterclaim, set-off, suit in equity and any other proceedings in which rights are determined.

(2) "Aggrieved party" means a party entitled to resort to a remedy.

(3) "Agreement" means the bargain of the parties in fact as found in their language or by implication from other circumstances including course of dealing or usage of trade or course of performance as provided in this Act (Sections 1-205 and 2-208). Whether an agreement has legal consequences is determined by the provisions of this Act, if applicable; otherwise by the law of contracts (Section 1-103). (Compare "Contract.")

(4) "Bank" means any person engaged in the business of banking.

(5) "Bearer" means the person in possession of an instrument, document or title, or certified security payable to bearer or endorsed in blank.

(6) "Bill of lading" means a document evidencing the receipt of goods for shipment issued by a person engaged in the business of transporting or forwarding goods, and includes an airbill. "Airbill" means a document serving for air transportation as a bill of lading does for marine or rail transportation, and includes an air consignment note or air waybill.

(7) "Branch" includes a separately incorporated foreign branch of a bank.

(8) "Burden of establishing" a fact means the burden of persuading the triers of fact that the existence of the fact is more probable than its non-existence.

(9) "Buyer in ordinary course of business" means a person who in good faith and without knowledge that the sale to him is in violation of the ownership rights or security interest of a third party in the goods buys in ordinary course from a person in the business of selling goods of that kind but does not include a pawnbroker. All persons who sell minerals or the like (including oil and gas) at wellhead or minehead shall be deemed to be persons in the business of selling goods of that kind. "Buying" may be for cash or by exchange of other property or on secured or unsecured credit and includes receiving goods or documents of title under a preexisting contract for sale but does not include a transfer in bulk or as security for or in total or partial satisfaction of a money debt.

(10) "Conspicuous" means A term or clause written so that a reasonable person against whom it is to operate ought to have noticed it. A printed head in capitals (as: NONNEGOTIABLE BILL OF LADING) is conspicuous. Language in the body of a form is "conspicuous." Whether a term or clause is "conspicuous" or not is for decision by the court.

(11) "Contract" means the total legal obligation which results from the parties' agreement as affected by this Act and any other applicable rules of law. (Compare "Agreement.")

(12) "Creditor" includes a general creditor, a secured creditor, a lien creditor and any representative of creditors, including an assignee for the benefit of creditors, a trustee in bankruptcy, a receiver in equity and an executor or administrator of an insolvent debtor's or assignor's estate.

(13) "Defendant" includes a person in the position of defendant in a cross-action or counterclaim.

(14) "Delivery" with respect to instruments, documents of title, chattel paper, or certificated securities means voluntary transfer of possession.

(15) "Document of title" includes bill of lading, dock warrant, dock receipt, warehouse receipt or order for the delivery of goods, and also any other document which in the regular course of business or financing is treated as adequately evidencing that the person in possession of it is entitled to receive, hold and dispose of the document and the goods it covers. To be a document of title a document must purport to be issued by or addressed to a bailee and purport to cover goods in the bailee's possession which are either identified or are fungible portions of an identified mass.

(16) "Fault" means wrongful act, omission or breach.

(17) "Fungible" with respect to goods or securities means goods or securities of which any unit is, by nature or usage of trade, the equivalent of any other like unit. Goods which are not fungible shall be deemed fungible for the purposes of this Act to the extent that under a particular agreement or document unlike units are treated as equivalents.

(18) "Genuine" means free of forgery or counterfeiting.

(19) "Good faith" means honesty in fact in the conduct or transaction concerned.

(20) "Holder" means a person who is in possession of a document of title or an instrument or a certificated investment security drawn, issued, or endorsed to him or his orders or to bearer or in blank.

(21) "Honor" is to pay or to accept and pay, or where a credit so engages to purchase or discount a draft complying with the terms of the credit.

(22) "Insolvency proceedings" includes any assignment for the benefit of creditors or other proceedings intended to liquidate or rehabilitate the estate of the person involved.

(23) "Insolvent" means a person who either has ceased to pay his debts in the ordinary course of business or cannot pay his debts as they become due or is insolvent within the meaning of the federal bankruptcy law.

(24) "Money" means a medium of exchange authorized or adopted by a domestic or foreign government as a part of its currency.

(25) "Notice" of a fact means when a person
 (a) has actual knowledge of it; or
 (b) has received a notice or notification of it; or
 (c) from all the facts and circumstances known to him at the time in question has reason to know that it exists.

 A person "knows" or has "knowledge" of a fact when he has actual knowledge of it. "Discover" or "learn" or a word or phrase of similar import refers to knowledge rather than to reason to know. The time and circumstances under which a notice or notification may cease to be effective are not determined by this Act.

(26) A person "notifies" or "gives" a notice or notification to another by taking such steps as may be reasonably required to inform the other in ordinary course whether or not such other actually comes to know of it. A person "receives" a notice or notification when
 (a) it comes to his attention; or
 (b) it is duly delivered at the place of business through which the contract was made or at any other place held out by him as the place for receipt of such communications.

(27) Notice, knowledge or a notice of notification received by an organization is effective for particular transaction from the time when it is brought to the attention of the individual conducting that transaction, and in any event from the time when it would have been brought to his attention if the organization had exercised due diligence. An organization exercises due diligence if it maintains reasonable routines for communicating significant information to the person conducting the transaction and there is reasonable compliance with the routines. Due diligence does not require an individual acting for the organization to communicate information unless such communication is part of his regular duties or unless he has reason to know of the transaction and that the transaction would be materially affected by the information.

(28) "Organization" includes a corporation, government or government subdivision or agency, business trust, estate, trust, partnership or association, two or more persons having a joint or common interest, or any other legal or commercial entity.

(29) "Party," as distinct from "third party," means a person who has engaged in a transaction or made an agreement within this Act.

(30) "Person" includes an individual or an organization (See Section 1-102).

(31) "Presumption" or "presumed" means that the trier of fact must find the existence of the fact presumed unless and until evidence is introduced which would support a finding of its nonexistence.

(32) "Purchase" includes taking by sale, discount, negotiation, mortgage, pledge, lien, issue, or reissue, gift or any other voluntary transaction creating an interest in property.

(33) "Purchaser" means a person who takes by purchase.

(34) "Remedy" means any remedial right to which an aggrieved party is entitled with or without resort to a tribunal.

(35) "Representative" includes an agent, an officer of a corporation or association, and a trustee, executor or administrator of an estate, or any other person empowered to act for another.

(36) "Rights" includes remedies.

(37) "Security interest" means an interest in personal property or fixtures which secures payment or performance of an obligation. The retention or reservation of title by a seller of goods notwithstanding shipment or delivery to the buyer (Section 2-401) is limited in effect to a reservation of a "security interest." The term also includes any

interest of a buyer of accounts or chattel paper which is subject to Article 9. The special property interest of a buyer of goods on identification of such goods to a contract for sale under Section 2-401 is not a "security interest," but a buyer may also acquire a "security interest" by complying with Article 9. Unless a lease or consignment is intended as security, reservation of title thereunder is not a "security interest" but a consignment is in any event subject to the provisions on consignment sales (Section 2-326). Whether a lease is intended as security is to be determined by the facts of each case; however, (a) the inclusion of an option to purchase does not of itself make the lease one intended for security, and (b) an agreement that upon compliance with the terms of the lease the lessee shall become or has the option to become the owner of the property for no additional consideration or for a nominal consideration does make the lease one intended for security.

(38) "Send" in connection with any writing or notice means to deposit in the mail or deliver for transmission by any other usual means of communication with postage or cost of transmission provided for and properly addressed and in the case of an instrument to an address specified thereon or otherwise agreed, or if there be none to any address reasonable under the circumstances. The receipt of any writing or notice within the time at which it would have arrived if properly sent has the effect of a proper sending.

(39) "Signed" includes any symbol executed or adopted by a party with present intention to authenticate a writing.

(40) "Surety" includes guarantor.

(41) "Telegram" includes message transmitted by radio, teletype, cable, any mechanical method of transmission, or the like.

(42) "Term" means that portion of an agreement which relates to a particular matter.

(43) "Unauthorized" signature or indorsement means one made without actual, implied or apparent authority and includes a forgery.

(44) "Value." Except as otherwise provided with respect to negotiable instruments and bank collections (Sections 3-303, 4-208 and 4-209), a person gives "value" for rights if he acquires them

(a) in return for a binding commitment to extend credit or for the extension of immediately available credit whether or not drawn upon and whether or not a charge-back is provided for in the event of difficulties in collection; or

(b) as security for or in total or partial satisfaction of a pre-existing claim; or

(c) by accepting delivery pursuant to a pre-existing contract for purchase; or

(d) generally in return for any consideration sufficient to support a simple contract.

(45) "Warehouse receipt" means a receipt issued by a person engaged in the business of storing goods for hire.

(46) "Written" or "writing" includes printing, typewriting or any other intentional reduction to tangible form.

SECTION 1-203. OBLIGATION OF GOOD FAITH

Every contract or duty within this Act imposes an obligation of good faith in its performance or enforcement.

SECTION 1-205. COURSE OF DEALING AND USAGE OF TRADE

(1) A course of dealing is a sequence of previous conduct between the parties to a particular transaction which is fairly to be regarded as establishing a common basis of understanding for interpreting their expressions and other conduct.

(2) A usage of trade is any practice or method of dealing having such regularity of observance in a place, vocation or trade as to justify an expectation that it will be observed with respect to the transaction in question. The existence and scope of such a usage are to be proved as facts. If it is established that such a usage is embodied in a written trade code or similar writing the interpretation of the writing is for the court.

(3) A course of dealing between parties and any usage of trade in the vocation or trade in which they are engaged or of which they are or should be aware give particular meaning to and supplement or qualify terms of an agreement.

(4) The express terms of an agreement and an applicable course of dealing or usage of trade shall be construed wherever reasonable as consistent with each other; but when such construction is unreasonable express terms control both course of dealing and usage of trade and course of dealing controls usage of trade.

(5) An applicable usage of trade in the place where any part of performance is to occur shall be used in interpreting the agreement as to that part of the performance.

(6) Evidence of a relevant usage of trade offered by one party is not admissible unless and until he has given the other party such notice as the court finds sufficient to prevent unfair surprise to the latter.

SECTION 2-314. IMPLIED WARRANTY: MERCHANTABILITY; USAGE OF TRADE

(1) Unless excluded or modified (Section 2-316), a warranty that the goods shall be merchantable is implied in a contract for their sale if the seller is a merchant with respect to goods of that kind. Under this section the serving for value of food or drink to be consumed either on the premises or elsewhere is a sale.

(2) Goods to be merchantable must be at least such as
  (a) pass without objection in the trade under the contract description; and
  (b) in the case of fungible goods, are of fair average quality within the description; and
  (c) are fit for the ordinary purposes for which such goods are used; and
  (d) run, within the variations permitted by the agreement, of even kind, quality and quantity within each unit and among all units involved; and
  (e) are adequately contained, packaged, and labeled as the agreement may require; and
  (f) conform to the promises or affirmations of fact made on the container or label if any.

(3) Unless excluded or modified (Section 2-316) other implied warranties may arise from course of dealing or usage of trade.

SECTION 2-315. IMPLIED WARRANTY: FITNESS FOR PARTICULAR PURPOSE

Where the seller at the time of contracting has reason to know any particular purpose for which the goods are required and that the buyer is relying on the seller's skill of judgment to select or furnish suitable goods, there is unless excluded or modified under the next section an implied warranty that the goods shall be fit for such purpose.

SECTION 2-302. UNCONSCIONABLE CONTRACT OR CLAUSE

(1) If the court as a matter of law finds the contract or any clause of the contract to have been unconscionable at the time it was made the court may refuse to enforce the contract, or it may enforce the remainder of the contract without the unconscionable clause, or it may so limit the application of any unconscionable clause as to avoid any unconscionable result.

(2) When it is claimed or appears to the court that the contract or any clause thereof may be unconscionable the parties shall be afforded a reasonable opportunity to present evidence as to its commercial setting, purpose and effect to aid the court in making the determination.

SECTION 2-313. EXPRESS WARRANTIES BY AFFIRMATION, PROMISE, DESCRIPTION, SAMPLE

(1) Express warranties by the seller are created as follows:
  (a) Any affirmation of fact or promise made by the seller to the buyer which relates to the goods and becomes part of the basis of the bargain creates an express warranty that the goods shall conform to the affirmation or promise.
  (b) Any description of the goods which is made part of the basis of the bargain creates an express warranty that the goods shall conform to the description.
  (c) Any sample or model which is made part of the basis of the bargain creates an express warranty that the whole of the goods shall conform to the sample or model.

(2) It is not necessary to the creation of an express warranty that the seller use formal words such as "warrant" or "guarantee" or that he have a specific intention to make a warranty, but an affirmation merely of the value of the goods or a statement purporting to be merely the seller's opinion or commendation of the goods does not create a warranty.

SECTION 2-105. DEFINITIONS: "GOODS"

(1) "Goods" means all things (including specially manufactured goods) which are movable at the time of identification of the contract for sale other than the money in which the price is to be paid, investment securities (Article 8) and things in action. "Goods" also includes the unborn young of animals and growing crops and other identified things attached to realty as described in the section on goods to be severed from realty (Section 2-107).

SECTION 2-107. GOODS TO BE SEVERED FROM REALTY; RECORDING

(1) A contract for the sale of minerals or the like (including oil and gas) or a structure or its materials to be removed from realty is a contract for the sale of goods within this Article if they are to be severed by the seller but until severance a purported present sale thereof which is not effective as a transfer of an interest in land is effective only as a contract to sell.

(2) A contract for the sale apart from the land of growing crops or other things attached to realty and capable of severance without material harm thereto but not described in subsection (1) or of timber to be cut is a contract for the sale of goods within this Article whether the subject matter is to be severed by the buyer or by the seller even though it forms part of the realty at the time of contracting, and the parties can by identification effect a present sale before severance.

SECTION 2-202. SCOPE: CERTAIN SECURITY AND OTHER TRANSACTIONS EXCLUDED FROM THIS ARTICLE

Unless the context otherwise requires, this Article applies to transactions in goods: it does not apply to any transaction which, although in the form of an unconditional contract to sell or present sale, is intended to operate only as a security transaction, nor does this Article impair or repeal any statute regulating sales to consumers, farmers or other specified classes of buyers.

SECTION 2-103. DEFINITIONS AND INDEX OF DEFINITIONS

(1) In this Article unless the context otherwise requires
  (a) "Buyer" means a person who buys or contracts to buy goods.
  (b) "Good faith" in the case of a merchant means honesty in fact and the observance of reasonable commercial standards of fair dealing in the trade.
  (c) "Receipt" of goods means taking physical possession of them.
  (d) "Seller" means a person who sells or contracts to sell goods.

SECTION 2-104. DEFINITIONS: "MERCHANT"; "BETWEEN MERCHANTS"

(1) "Merchant" means a person who deals in goods of the kind or otherwise by his occupation holds himself out as having knowledge or skill peculiar to the practices or goods involved in the transaction or to whom such knowledge or skill may be attributed by his employment of an agent or broker or other intermediary who by his occupation holds himself out as having such knowledge or skill. . . .
(3) "Between merchants" means in any transaction with respect to which both parties are chargeable with the knowledge or skill of merchants.

SECTION 2-316. EXCLUSION OR MODIFICATION OF WARRANTIES

(1) Words or conduct relevant to the creation of an express warranty and words or conduct tending to negate or limit warranty shall be construed wherever reasonable as consistent with each other; but subject to the provisions of this Article on parol or extrinsic evidence (Section 2-202) negation or limitation is inoperative to the extent that such construction is unreasonable.
(2) Subject to subsection (3), to exclude or modify the implied warranty of merchantability or any part of it in the language must mention merchantability and in case of a writing must be conspicuous, and to exclude or modify any implied warranty of fitness the exclusion must be by a writing and conspicuous. Language to exclude all implied warranties of fitness is sufficient if it states, for example, that "There are no warranties which extend beyond the description on the face hereof."
(3) Notwithstanding subsection (2)
  (a) unless the circumstances indicate otherwise, all implied warranties are excluded by expressions like "as is," "with all faults," or other language which in common understanding calls the buyer's attention to the exclusion of warranties and makes plain that there is no implied warranty; and
  (b) when the buyer before entering into the contract has examined the goods or the sample or model as fully as he desired or has refused to examine the goods there is no implied warranty with regard to defects which an examination ought in the circumstances to have revealed to him; and
  (c) an implied warranty can also be excluded or modified by course of dealing or course of performance or usage of trade.
(4) Remedies for breach of warranty can be limited in accordance with the provisions of this Article on liquidation or limitation of damages and on contractual modification of remedy (Section 2-718 and 2-719).

SECTION 2-317. CUMULATION AND CONFLICT OF WARRANTIES EXPRESS OR IMPLIED

Warranties either express or implied shall be construed as consistent with each other and as cumulative, but if such construction is unreasonable the intention of the parties shall determine which warranty is dominant. In ascertaining that intention the following rules apply:
  (a) Exact or technical specifications displace an inconsistent sample or model or general language of description.
  (b) A sample from an existing bulk displaces inconsistent general language of description.
  (c) Express warranties displace inconsistent implied warranties other than an implied warranty of fitness for a particular purpose.

SECTION 2-318. THIRD-PARTY BENEFICIARIES OF WARRANTIES EXPRESS OR IMPLIED

Alternative A

A seller's warranty whether express or implied extends to any natural person who is in the family or household of his buyer or who is a guest in his home if it is reasonable to expect that such person may use, consume or be affected by the goods and who is injured in person by breach of the warranty. A seller may not exclude or limit the operation of this section.

Alternative B

A seller's warranty whether express or implied extends to any natural person who may reasonably be expected to use, consume or be affected by the goods and who is injured in person by breach of the warranty. A seller may not exclude or limit the operation of this section.

Alternative C

A seller's warranty whether express or implied, extends to any person who may reasonably be expected to use, consume or be affected by the goods and who is injured by breach of the warranty. A seller may not exclude or limit the operation of this section with respect to injury to the person of an individual to whom the warranty extends.

SECTION 2-714. BUYER'S DAMAGES FOR BREACH IN REGARD TO ACCEPTED GOODS

(1) Where the buyer has accepted goods and given notification (subsection (3) of Section 2-607) he may recover as damages for any non-conformity of tender the loss resulting in the ordinary course of events from the seller's breach as determined in any manner which is reasonable.

(2) The measure of damages for breach of warranty is the difference at the time and place of acceptance between the value of the goods accepted and the value they would have had if they had been as warranted, unless special circumstances show proximate damages of a different amount.

(3) In a proper case any incidental and consequential damages under the next section may also be recovered.

SECTION 2-715. BUYER'S INCIDENTAL AND CONSEQUENTIAL DAMAGES

(1) Incidental damages resulting from the seller's breach include expenses reasonably incurred in inspection, receipt, transportation and care and custody of goods rightfully rejected, any commercially reasonable charges, expenses or commissions in connection with effecting cover and any other reasonable expense incident to the delay or other breach.

(2) Consequential damages resulting from the seller's breach include
   (a) any loss resulting from general or particular requirements and needs of which the seller at the time of contracting had reason to know and which could not reasonably be prevented by cover or otherwise; and
   (b) injury to person or property proximately resulting from any breach of warranty.

SECTION 2-719. CONTRACTUAL MODIFICATION OR LIMITATION OF REMEDY

(1) Subject to the provisions of subsections (2) and (3) of this section and of the preceding section on liquidation and limitation of damages,
   (a) the agreement may provide for remedies in addition to or in substitution for those provided in this Article and may limit or alter the measure of damages recoverable under this Article, as by limiting the buyer's remedies to return of the goods and repayment of the price or to repair and replacement of nonconforming goods or parts; and
   (b) resort to a remedy as provided is optional unless the remedy is expressly agreed to be exclusive, in which case it is the sole remedy.

(2) Where circumstances cause an exclusive or limited remedy to fail of its essential purpose, remedy may be had as provided in this Act.

(3) Consequential damages may be limited or excluded unless the limitation or exclusion is unconscionable. Limitation of consequential damages for injury to the person in the case of consumer goods is prima facie unconscionable but limitation of damages where the loss is commercial is not.

SECTION 2-725. STATUTE OF LIMITATIONS IN CONTRACTS FOR SALE

(1) An action for breach of any contract for sale must be commenced within four years after the cause of action has accrued. By the original agreement the parties may reduce the period of limitation to not less than one year but may not extend it.

(2) A cause of action accrues when the breach occurs, regardless of the aggrieved party's lack of knowledge of the breach. A breach of warranty occurs when tender of delivery is made, except that where a warranty explicitly extends to future performance of the goods and discovery of the breach must await the time of such performance the cause of action accrues when the breach is or should have been discovered.

(3) Where an action commenced within the time limited by subsection (1) is so terminated as to leave available a remedy by another action for the same breach such other action may be commenced after the expiration of the time limited and within six months after the termination of the first action unless the termination resulted from voluntary discontinuance or from dismissal for failure or neglect to prosecute.

(4) This section does not alter the law on tolling of the statute of limitations nor does it apply to causes of action which have accrued before this Act becomes effective.

GLOSSARY

ANPRs Advance notice of proposed agency rulemakings published in the *Federal Register* warning the public that an agency will soon propose a regulation.

APA Administrative Procedure Act; law governing procedures for most federal administrative agencies.

Abatement Period Regarding OSHA it refers to a time period OSHA gives an employer to correct OSHA violations.

Abnormal Use (or Product Misuse) A product liability defense involving what its name suggests: the plaintiff's misuse of a product.

Absolute Privilege A person may make the defamatory remark maliciously or without necessity.

Abuse of Process An intentional tort where defendant uses civil or criminal legal procedures for an improper purpose.

Acceptance Offeree's manifestation of assent to the terms of an offer made to offeree; forms a contract if made while offer still "alive."

Accepted Credit Card As defined by the Truth-in-Lending Act and Regulation—a credit card a person has applied for, received, used, or authorized someone else to use.

Accountings Court orders directing the presentation of income and expense records to an authorized party.

Accredited Persons Large or sophisticated securities buyers not formally entitled to as much information about a security offering.

Act Utilitarianism Maximizing one's happiness even if it means breaking the positive law.

Actual Notice Actual contact in person, phone, or letter; actual notice to third persons with whom agent has actually dealt is required when agencies end; distinguished from constructive notice (such as notice in trade journal).

Adequacy of the Consideration The general rule that courts look at a contract to see whether each of the parties gave the other enough or a fair amount for what it got from the other party under the contract.

Adjudicate Decide at a legal hearing satisfying procedural due process requirements.

Adjudicatory Hearing Hearing before a governmental body such as a court or administrative agency

Adjustment Word used in labor law to describe a way of settling an unfair labor practice case that basically is an informal settlement.

Administrative Agency Nonjudicial, nonlegislative governmental lawmaker, such as the SEC (Securities and Exchange Commission).

Administrative Hearing A proceeding somewhat resembling a trial that is held before an administrative agency to determine whether laws enforced by the agency have been violated.

Administrative Law Statutes, regulations, rules, and case laws dealing with the general subject of administrative agencies.

Administrative Penalties Assessed by the EPA or other regulatory agency for violation of agency rules

Administrative Quasi-Judicial Agencies Nonjudicial, nonlegislative government entities with rule-making authority.

Administrative Regulations Laws made by government agencies.

Administrator A person appointed by a probate judge to administer an estate if the will names no one to be executor or if there is no will.

Admissions Against Interest Exception to the hearsay rule of evidence; if a person says or does something against his or her pecuniary or proprietary interests this evidence may be let in at trial even if the person saying or doing it cannot be cross-examined.

Advance Money paid to another for services or goods the other has not yet given.

Adverse Possession A way to acquire title to realty by openly, hostilely, and continuously holding the property for a statutory period of time.

Advisory Opinion In general, a formal opinion issued by a court on a question of law that is not embodied in a concrete case or controversy. In FTC practice, a nonbinding opinion by the Federal Trade Commission issued to parties seeking the FTC's advice on whether a particular business practice violates the laws the FTC enforces.

Affidavit A written sworn statement given before someone with the power to administer oaths (such as notary public).

Affirmative Easement A right to use someone else's land.

Agreements to Agree Not a contract; agreements in which two people decide to form a contract at some future time.

Air Quality Control Region (AQCR) The entire United States is divided into AQCRs to help control air pollution.

Allocative Efficiency The state of an economy in which resources are placed where they yield the most good (or utility).

Alternative Dispute Resolution (ADR) Any means of settling legal disputes without using courts, including conciliation, mediation, and arbitration.

Ambient Air Quality Standards The legal requirements for general air quality in the environment.

Ambulatory A will may be changed any number of times before the testator dies unless the testator has made the will as a binding contract.

Anarchy Lawless society; society where no one has the power to make rules binding all.

Annotated Footnotes further explaining something in a text; for example, a code would be annotated to cases interpreting words in the code.

Annotated Code A lengthy statute that refers to particular cases interpreting it.

Annual Percentage Rate of Interest APR One of two items a creditor must disclose to a debtor under the Truth-in-Lending Act.

Answer The document a defendant files with a court after being sued civilly, which "answers" plaintiff's complaint.

Anti-backsliding A provision that prevents reissuance of an NPDES permit with less stringent limits than the permit it replaces.

Antitrust Law Statutes enacted by Congress to prevent restraint of trade and anticompetitive behavior.

Apparent Authority An agent's authority resulting from something the principal does that leads third persons to believe the agent has authority.

Arbitrary, Capricious, and Unreasonable Test An evidentiary test used to decide whether certain agency actions are supported by enough facts.

Arbitration A way to settle disputes by staying out of court; the disputants hire a third party who makes a decision the parties agree to be bound to.

Area-Wide Waste Treatment Program Under federal water pollution control law the way to control nonpoint pollutants (such as general runoff from a field).

Asset Merger When two or more companies join together by one's buying the other's (others') assets and the buying company remains in existence while the merged (purchased) company (companies) ceases (cease) to exist.

Assumed Risk *see* Assumption of Risk.

Assumption of Risk A negligence defense also applicable in some strict liability cases and in many product liability cases. It requires that the plaintiff knowingly accept a certain risk of his or her own free will. An assumption of risk defense can be created by contract. Here, though, the needed voluntariness (because of unequal bargaining power) or knowledge (because of fine print terms) may not be present.

Attorney at Law Professional trained in the law who is admitted to practice law in one or more U.S. jurisdictions usually after passage of bar exam.

Attorney General Society's attorney.

Attorney in Fact A written agency.

Autrefois Acquit A plea in a criminal case that in effect says, "I have already been tried and acquitted for this so leave me alone because the constitution's double jeopardy clause says you should."

Autrefois Convict A plea in a criminal case that in effect says, "I have already been tried for this and convicted so leave me alone because the constitution's double jeopardy clause says you should."

Award The word describing an arbitrator's decision.

Bailment The separation of title and possession to personal, not real, property.

Bailment for the Sole Benefit of the Bailee This form of bailment benefits only the borrower.

Bailment for the Sole Benefit of the Bailor This form of bailment benefits only the owner of the bailed property.

Bait Advertising Businesses advertise goods or services at unusually low prices to attract buyers into the seller's business.

Balancing Competing Claims The idea that law is a weighing of competing claims with the heavier prevailing; Roscoe Pound's sociological school of law.

Barter A transaction that exchanges goods for other goods, rather than exchanging goods for money.

Basis of the Bargain Damages The basic type of contractual recovery. Generally, it is a value of the performance as promised minus the value of the performance as received.

Beneficiary Person(s) holding equitable or beneficial title to property in a trust.

Best Available Treatment (BAT) A type of treatment designed to clean water of its pollution. A stricter type of water pollution treatment than BPT.

Best Conventional Treatment (BCT) A type of water pollution treatment for conventional pollutants.

Best Management Practices Term in environmental law that refers to certain business field techniques that can reduce certain types of pollution (e.g., a tarp over a coal pile can reduce water pollution from rain water runoff from the coal pile).

Best Practicable Treatment Control (BPT) A type of treatment designed to clean water of its pollution. An intermediate form of water pollution treatment.

Beyond a Reasonable Doubt The test for the amount of evidence the prosecutor must prove in a criminal case to get a conviction.

Bilateral Contract A contract formed by each of two parties exchanging promises—"a promise for a promise."

Bill A proposed law that has not yet been passed by the legislature nor signed by the chief executive.

Binding Arbitration Where a third party, not a court, is selected by parties to a dispute to settle it after hearing both parties' claims and whose decision the parties agree to follow.

Blue Sky Laws State laws regulating the sale of securities.

Body Politic The society subject to particular government; the people and businesses subject to a rule.

Bona Fide Occupational Qualification (BFOQ) A defense that protects defendants from Title VII liability.

Boulwareism Term used in labor law where management studies employee demands and makes its best offer at the start of bargaining. It represents a rejection of bargaining given its initial refusal to modify its offer.

Breach of Duty The first element of a negligence case; usually, the failure to act as a reasonable person.

Breach of Warranty of Authority An agent's breaking his or her duty to third persons by believing to have and claiming to have authority to represent a principal when such authority does not exist.

Brief A set of papers containing a lawyer's argument in a lawsuit; also, a way to analyze law cases.

Bubble Policy Idea in pollution control that treats an entire facility with several discharge points as one discharge so the various discharge points in the facility can be "netted" so if one discharge point more than satisfies pollution control requirements, it can make up for outlets not meeting standards. An imaginary bubble over an entire factory allows netting for the entire facility.

Business Ethics Values used in the business community to determine proper conduct.

Business Judgment Rule A rule that holds corporate management harmless from stockholder suits for good faith errors that would injure the corporation.

Business Trust A business organized in the form of a trust; similar in many ways to a corporation.

Buyer in the Ordinary Course of Business (BIOC) Any entrusting of possession of goods to a merchant who deals in goods of that kind gives the merchant the power to transfer all rights of the entruster to a buyer.

C

C.F.R. *Code of Federal Regulations.*

Capital Surplus Account A corporate account that holdings earnings over and above expenses, representing the earnings of the shareholders.

Case Style *see* "Style of a Case"

Categorical Imperative Kant's ethical idea that we should act in the way that we would want rules to be; similar to the "Golden Rule."

Causa Mortis A gift that results when a donor thinks he or she is about to die, makes a gift based on this belief, and then actually dies because of the particular threat of death.

Cause of Action A rule of law entitling the plaintiff to recover if certain elements are proven.

Caveat Emptor Let the buyer beware.

Caveat Venditor Let the seller beware.

Cease and Desist Orders Orders from administrative agencies telling someone (such as a business) to stop doing something.

Cellar-Kefauver Amendment A federal law passed in 1950 that plugged a loophole in the Clayton Act by outlawing certain asset mergers (certain stock mergers had been forbidden 36 years earlier).

Chancellor The "judge" in a chancery (or equity) court.

Chancery Court A type of civil court where a case can start; the chancellor (judge) in such a court applies equitable principles (ideas of fairness) to decide the cases.

Charter State authorization for someone to act in a certain capacity (for instance, as a corporation).

Checkoff A term used in labor law to describe a system for collecting union dues, which involves the employer's deducting the union dues from the employee/union member's check and forwarding this amount to the union; a union security device.

Churning A situation that occurs when brokers trade a client's account excessively given the client's investment goals and sophistication.

Circuit Courts The basic trial-level courts.

Civil Disobedience The idea that people break the positive law when it violates much more important natural law.

Civil Law Law that determines rights and duties between private persons; or law of certain European countries relying mainly on codes of law instead of judicial opinions as the main source of law.

Civil Penalties Penalties obtained from federal district court involving unfair or deceptive acts or practices where a private party knowingly violates a trade regulation rule defining such acts or practices, or a private party knowingly violates a C&D order involving such acts or practices, even if the order involved some other party.

Civilization Ethic The idea that law's frustrating people's basic desires and instincts produces civilization (one of Sigmund Freud's ideas).

Clayton Act A federal antitrust law passed in 1914 that addresses several antitrust matters including interlocking directorates, race discrimination, exclusive dealing, tying contracts, requirements contracts, and mergers. The Clayton Act creates only civil, not criminal violations.

Close Corporation A corporation whose stock is held by few persons. Often "family" corporations.

Code A statute that attempts to cover all law (such as the U.S. code or a state code) or all on a particular subject (such as the Uniform Commercial Code).

Codes of Federal Regulations (CFR) A set of federal books organized so that all regulations of a particular agency are together in one (or several) books.

Commerce Clause The clause of the U.S. Constitution giving Congress power to regulate commerce among the several states (interstate commerce). The commerce clause is the main constitutional basis for the extensive congressional regulation of U.S. society that exists today. It also is an implicit check on state laws that unduly hinder or burden interstate commerce.

Commercial Paper Promissory notes (two-party instruments), drafts and checks (three-party instruments), and certificates of deposit (acknowledgment by a bank of receipt of money with a promise to repay it).

Commercial Speech Speech intended to advance the economic interests of the speaker and his or her audience. Advertising is the best example. This sort of speech now receives First Amendment protection, but not as much protection as other forms of First Amendment speech.

Common Law Law made by judges when deciding a case not governed by other kinds of law.

Common Pleas Court A low-level court with power to try both small civil and criminal cases.

Community Property During a marriage, when one spouse acquires property, half of it belongs to the other spouse even if the deed is made out specifically in the name of one spouse.

Comparable Worth Provisions Laws that apply only to public employment; they say that relevant government units should not discriminate in pay between female-dominated jobs and male-dominated jobs if those jobs have comparable overall worth to the employer.

Comparative Fault Often used as a synonym for comparative negligence. As used here, however, the term refers to a doctrine whereby the plaintiff's recovery is reduced in proportion to his percentage share of the overall fault (not just negligence) causing his injury.

Comparative Negligence A modification of contributory negligence in which the fact-finder makes some percentage allocation of fault between plaintiff and defendant, and makes the plaintiff's recovery equal the defendant's percentage share of the plaintiff's losses. Perhaps one-half of the states have instituted comparative negligence. In some states, it will apply only where the defendant is more than fifty percent at fault.

Compensatory Something (usually a law) designed to restore one person injured by another.

Compensatory Damages Money a lawbreaker must pay to a legally injured person to put him or her in the position he or she was in before legal injury occurred.

Complaint Case A type of lawsuit brought under the Wagner Act in which a claim is made by either an employer or the union that an unfair labor practice has been committed.

Concealment A type of fraud in which a defendant misrepresents by covering up or not disclosing a fact he or she has a duty to disclose.

Conciliation A situation in which the two disputants get together and work things out between themselves without having anyone else present.

Conciliation Discussions Attempts to settle informally a Title VII Civil Rights Act of 1964 case.

Concurrent Powers Those powers that both Congress and the states can exercise.

Concurrent Resolution Rules legislatures pass to govern their internal workings. Technically they bind on one outside the legislature and thus are not laws.

Condominium A way individuals can own the space between the walls of their unit. Owners have equal interest in the common areas of the entire complex.

Confusion The commingling of different owners' fungible goods, which are nearly identical in characteristics, such as commodities.

Conglomerate Merger When two (or more) companies in unrelated businesses combine with the acquiring company continuing and the acquired company ceasing to exist and becoming part of the acquiring company.

Consciously Parallel Conduct An antitrust idea in which oligopolistic competitors who compete in price and other ways knowing that competitors are doing likewise are illegally agreeing to restrain trade.

Consensual Relations An arrangement entered into by mutual consent of the parties, but do not necessarily possess all the elements of a contract.

Consent Decree A judgment, ruling, or order made by a court or an administrative agency with the consent of the parties. Generally, its terms are the result of a prior agreement between the parties settling the matter before the court or agency.

Consent Order As used in Chapter 21, a kind of consent decree in which an alleged violator of a law enforced by the Federal Trade Commission agrees to stop a certain business practice, but does not admit any violation of the law.

Consequential Damages Although this term has no good general definition, it refers to those damages, caused by the breach of a contract, that are more remote from the breach than basis of the bargain damages. They include personal injury, property damage, and indirect economic loss (e.g., lost profits) caused by the breach.

Conservative When used in modern political/social/economic contexts refers generally to someone who prefers the status quo rather than trying new approaches to deal with problems and situations; refers to someone who prefers individual or private sector solutions to social problems rather than governmental solutions.

Consideration In contract situations what one person must give up or give to the person one is contracting with to make the other's promises binding; voluntary relinquishment of a known right bargained for in exchange for another's rights.

Consignment(s) Legal arrangement where seller of goods keeps title (ownership) but transfers possession to distributor who agrees to resell them; a type of bailment (separation of title and possession of goods).

Consolidation When two companies combine to form a totally new company (neither of the joining companies survives).

Constitution Basic law of a society; society's legal framework and basic principles; social contract or compact.

Constitutional Government Government limited by law and answerable to the people ruled.

Constructive Notice Notice in a newspaper or other media; required when agencies end for third persons with whom agent has not actually dealt.

Consumer Product Article customarily produced or distributed for a consumer's use, consumption, or enjoyment in or around a residence or a school, in recreation, or otherwise.

Consumption Ethic The social value that says it is good to use up natural resources without regard to long-term social needs.

Contingent Fee A lawyer's fee that is based on a percentage of the money the lawyer wins for a client in a civil lawsuit.

Contract Agreement between competent parties enforceable in court.

Contract Bar Rule A rule of labor law that prevents holding representation election while a union-employer collective bargaining agreement is in effect.

Contract Clause A provision in Article 1, section 10 of the U.S. Constitution preventing the states from impairing the obligations of existing contracts, both private and governmental.

Contracts Contrary to Public Opinion Contracts that offer some public sense of natural law and, when courts (judges) so decide, will not be enforceable.

Contributory Negligence A negligence defense sometimes applicable in product liability cases generally. It involves the plaintiff's failure to act as a reasonably self-protective person. It is a complete defense no matter how trivial the plaintiff's fault.

Contributory Pensions Pensions paid into by both the employer and employees.

Conversion An intentional tort involving wrongful interference with the dominion and control by one person of another's personalty. The type of lawsuit one person brings against another if the other steals goods (movables) from him or her.

Corporate Enabling Act A statute that lets people form a corporation if they follow a certain procedure.

Corporate Promoter One who develops a market for corporate stock of a corporation about to be organized. One who organizes corporations and interests others in subscribing to its stock.

Corporation A legal, artificial person that is a popular business organizational form.

Corporation by Estoppel A court-created doctrine that says that if persons act like corporations even though they are unincorporated and third persons deal with these corporate pretenders, then the third persons may not later challenge the lack of corporateness.

Corporations for Profit Corporations that can divide profits among shareholders; however, they do not necessarily have to earn a profit to be so classified.

Corporations Not for Profit Corporations that cannot turn over earnings to their members.

Counterclaim A legal claim a civil defendant makes against the person suing.

Counter-offer An offer made by the offeree back to the original offeror and in response to the original offer; it ends the original offer and is an offer back to the original offeror.

County Court Low-level courts that hear disputes involving small amounts of money and other small matters.

Court of Original Jurisdiction Court where a case starts.

Court System A hierarchy of judges who hear cases and interpret law. The United States has two court systems: state and federal.

Courts of Record Courts in which a public official (usually) takes a transcript of what is said in court.

Coverage Requirement A federal requirement for employee retirement plans that discourages an employer from merely giving certain employees (often top officers only) retirement contributions but requires some spreading of employer retirement contributions to most employees.

Credit Card As defined by the Truth-in-Lending Act and Regulation Z, a single credit device used to buy something on credit.

Crime Wrong against society.

Criminal Conspiracy Agreement to commit a lawful act in an unlawful way or an unlawful act; often requires some significant step to carry out this agreement.

Criminal Law Laws designed to protect social values and which punish violators.

Criminal Procedure Steps in a criminal lawsuit; rules telling order of events in criminal lawsuit.

Criteria Documents In pollution control law, refers to scientific studies that are the basis for air or water pollution control regulations.

Cumulative Voting A way of voting corporate shares that allows minority shareholders (if the minority is large enough) to elect members of the board of directors. Shareholders may cast as many votes for director as they have shares multiplied by the number of directors to be elected;

then a shareholder may cumulate or vote all of his or her shares for one (or more) board candidates.

Curtesy A man's interest in his wife's property.

Damages Money, property, or human loss that the law permits a person to recover in the form of money from the person(s) injuring him or her.

Damnum Absque Injuria Latin for "a loss has occurred but there is no legal way to obtain recovery"; loss without a remedy.

Debt Collector Under the Fair Debt Collection Practices Act anyone other than the creditor or creditor's attorney who tries to collect debts owed to another person.

Decertification Election In labor law refers to an election at a unionized employer's plant where unionized employees vote to decide whether to continue having the union represent them.

Deeds Documents that transfer ownership to realty.

Defamation Oral or written, published untrue statement about another that holds up the person spoken about to ridicule, contempt, or scorn.

Default Judgment What the plaintiff wins in civil lawsuit because the defendant fails to answer the complaint within the required time.

Deferral States States that have met certain federal requirements entitling them to enforce the Federal Age Discrimination in Employment Act.

Defined Benefit Plans Periodic payment into the plan varies so that the benefits ultimately received will be a definite—often indexed—dollar amount.

Defined Contribution Plans Periodic payment into the plan is fixed.

Defined Pension Plans Pension plans that promise retirees a certain amount when they retire.

Defunctness A rule of labor law that says that if a union is a collective bargaining representative but it does not function actively as such, a representation election can be held even though an unexpired collective bargaining agreement exists.

Del Credere Agent An agent who sells for a principal and who guarantees to pay the principal if the buyer does not.

Delivery Delivery involves the present handing over of control to something from the donor to the donee. Delivery can be either actual (the donor's handing over a ring to the donee) or constructive (the donor's handing over something representing the item being given, such as the keys to a car when one is giving a car).

Democracy Government in which the ruled make the rules.

Demurrer A defendant's responsive pleading to plaintiff's complaint that, in effect, says plaintiff does not state a cause of action.

De Novo Trial New trials, starting from scratch; typically this happens when a case has been tried at an administrative hearing and then is appealed to a trial court.

Deontology Ethics; an examination of proper or "right" conduct, moral obligation, and duty.

Deposition A document that preserves testimony of witnesses or parties to a lawsuit; the deposition is taken before the trial.

Derivative Suit A civil lawsuit where the plaintiff sues on behalf of someone else (who is often unable to sue on its behalf, such as a corporation against its board of directors).

Deterrence Discouraging persons who did not commit crimes from community crime by punishing criminals; one of the four basic objectives of criminal law.

Devises Realty given by will.

Dictum (Dicta) Remarks a judge makes in a legal opinion that are not necessary to decide a case. (Dictum is singular; dicta, plural).

Direct Emission Standards Air pollution controls for buildings (plants, businesses, and the like) and other immovables.

Directed Verdict Where a trial judge tells the jury what its verdict will be.

Discharge In bankruptcy, the objective of going bankrupt; a discharge is a defense (usually successful) against a creditor's attempting to collect a discharged debt.

Disclaimer A term in a contract (often a contract for the sale of goods) by which one party (usually a seller) attempts to prevent the other party from recovering under a particular theory of recovery. If a disclaimer is enforced its effect is to block all recovery under that theory of recovery.

Dismissal Word used in labor law to describe a way of settling an unfair labor practice case by, in effect, "throwing the case out."

Disparate Impact Theory A Title VII theory most often used in cases involving a large number of plaintiffs. The plaintiffs must show that the employment practice they are challenging has an adverse impact on the basis of race, color, religion, sex, or national origin. The employer must show that the challenged practice is job related for the position in question and consistent with business necessity. The plaintiffs may show that the employer's legitimate business needs can be advanced by an alternative employment practice that is less discriminatory than the challenged practice.

Disparate Treatment Theory A Title VII theory most often used by a single plaintiff or a small number of plaintiffs to allege some isolated instance or instances of discrimination that cannot be proven by direct evidence.

Dissolution Selling one's assets and going out of business. In antitrust cases, breaking up a business that restrains trade into several smaller businesses.

District Attorney Society's attorney.

District Courts Courts hearing cases involving relatively small civil matters, such as a homeowner's breaking a contract with a painter, or criminal matters, such as a bank teller's embezzling $1,500.

Diversity Cases (*See* Diversity of Citizenship).

Diversity of Citizenship A type of federal court jurisdiction that exists because the lawsuit is between people from different states or people *from* a state and citizens of another country.

Divest *see* Divestiture.

Divestiture In antitrust cases forcing a firm found restraining trade to sell off part of its operations.

Docket A list of cases to be tried in a court or other tribunal.

Domestic Corporation A corporation organized under the laws of the state one is speaking about.

Domestic Relations Court Divorce court (sometimes handles juvenile delinquency matters).

Dominant Estate The property enjoying the benefit of an easement.

Donative Intent The idea that the gift giver must presently intend to make a gift, not just want to give at some unspecified future time.

Donee The person receiving a gift.

Donor The giver of the gift.

Dower A woman's interest in her husband's property.

Dual Agency Where an agent represents both parties to a contract.

Due Diligence Individuals sued must meet a standard of care regarding information in their part of the registration statement; if the individuals are experts, such as lawyers, they must meet the diligence of their professions.

Due Process A constitutional guarantee, contained in the Fifth and Fourteenth Amendments and thus applicable to both the federal government and the states, that basically requires government to provide fair procedures before it deprives a person of life, liberty, or property. Occasionally, however, due process has been given a substantive meaning and used as the basis for attacking laws regulating social and economic matters.

Duress In contract cases such illegal force or the threat of force as deprives a person of his or her free will to decide whether to enter a contract.

Duress Rule *see* Duress.

Duties When used in connection with the tort of negligence it refers to obligations people automatically have regarding others (such as the duty to be careful).

Duty of Care A principle based on common law negligence principles. The elements are negligence, breach of the standard care, proximate cause, and damages.

Duty to Indemnify Duty of a principal to pay the agent any losses the agent necessarily incurs while working on the principal's behalf.

Duty to Reimburse Duty of a principal to pay an agent for any money the agent has to spend to perform his or her duties for the principal.

EPA U.S. Environmental Protection Agency; federal agency whose main job is protecting the environment.

Easement A nonpossessory right to use someone else's realty for some purpose.

Easement Appurtenant A benefit to another piece of land, which is usually adjacent to the servient estate.

Easement in Gross A benefit to a certain person or business, such as a power line easement for a utility.

Economic Impact Statements Requirement under 1977 Amendments to the Clean Air Act that forces the EPA to decide the economic costs that will be caused by new Clean Air Act regulations.

Economic Strikes Employee strikes motivated by employee economic demands.

Economic Substantive Due Process A now-insignificant form of substantive due process that once provided the courts with the ability to strike down forms of economic regulation that interfered with freedom of contract.

Effluent Guidelines General water pollution standards for categories of industrial polluters.

Effluent Limitations Water pollution limits for particular polluters.

Election Bar Rule A rule in labor law that prevents employees from voting on whether to have a union represent them within a certain period after a previous representation election.

Eminent Domain The governmental power to condemn property. It must be for public purposes and requires just compensation.

Emission Offset Policy Term used in air pollution control law to refer to the idea that new polluters may build in nonattaimnent areas if they do not increase "net pollution" in the area (they do this by purchasing existing polluters' pollution rights, which is called the emission offset policy).

Emission Offsets Concept in pollution control that lets a polluter sell its rights to discharge in a given geographic area to someone else in that same geographic area.

Employer-Independent Contractor Relationship In this relationship, the employer does not have the right to control the means by which the independent contractor performs the work. The employer does retain the right to control the end or object of the work.

En Banc Term describing rare cases when all judges in a particular court of appeals hear a case; usually courts of appeals have several panels, each of which is made up of three or some other number of judges who decide cases; when a case is important, all judges from all panels of the particular court of appeals sit as judges in the case (this can be as many as seventeen judges).

Enabling Act A status that gives an agency authority to propose and promulgate regulations.

Enabling Statutes *See* Enabling Act.

Enumerated Powers Those congressional powers listed by Article 1, §8 or some other law making provision of the Constitution.

Environmental Assessment A preliminary report private parties (such as businesses) must fill out and turn in to a federal agency before the agency prepares its environmental impact statement.

Environmental Impact Statement (EIS) A report that a federal agency must prepare before it does anything major that affects the quality of the human environment.

Environmental Protection Agency (EPA) A federal agency that makes law by issuing regulations involving the environment.

Equal Protection The requirement that government not deny the "equal protection of the laws," which applies both to the states and the federal government.

Equitable Remedies What certain courts (called equity or chancery courts) give to an injured person (such as specific performance) when legal remedies (usually money) are inadequate.

Equitable Title A title, also called a beneficial title, to property subject to a trust.

Equity Fairness; a type of court that gives equitable remedies.

Equity Courts Courts that give equitable remedies (such as injunctions and specific performance) instead of legal remedies; also called *chancery courts*.

Estate The land and buildings on the land owned by a person.

Ethical Unity When ethics of different ethical schools agree on a particular result or solution to a problem.

Ethics Refers to the study of what is right, good, or moral conduct in a given set of circumstances; ethics involves the study of clashes of moral values.

Ex Parte A legal proceeding where only one party is present (for example, a court hearing where the defendant is present but plaintiff is absent).

Ex Post Facto Law Retroactive criminal law that works to the disadvantage of the accused.

Excited Utterance A statement sounding as if it were an offer made when one is emotionally aroused by some event, which is not legally regarded as an offer because of the speaker's excited state of mind.

Exclusive Benefit Rule A rule under the Employee Retirement Income Security Act that forbids pension assets from being used other than to fund pensions.

Exclusive Dealing Contract A business arrangement by which one business agrees to handle only one particular brand of a product as a condition to getting the seller's desirable product.

Exculpatory Clauses Contract that clauses excuse someone from liability.

Executed Contract Contract that has been performed by both parties.

Execution Legal way creditors seize debtor's property to pay debts.

Executor A person named in a will to manage and resolve an estate.

Executory Contract Formed but unperformed contract.

Exempt Property *see* Exemptions.

Exempt Securities Securities that are excused from part or all of the registration process under various federal securities laws (exemptions also exist under state securities laws).

Exempt Transactions Certain securities sales that do not have to be fully registered with the Securities and Exchange Commission.

Exemptions Laws that prevent creditors from seizing certain property of a debtor. Also, items not available to the partnership when its creditors seek execution against partnership property for partnership debts.

Experience Rating A way of deciding what a particular employer's unemployment tax liability is based on the amount of past unemployment for its workers.

Express Authority Power a principal spells out for an agent in oral or written words.

Express Contract A contract that the parties form by writing or saying their respective promises in words.

Express Warranty A contractual promise arising from a seller's actual words (or, in some cases, from conduct from which a promise can be readily inferred). As a general proposition, express warranties are made openly and voluntarily.

Extortion A felony in which a holder of public office demands property from another by threatening to misuse his or her public office unless the property is given.

F

FOIA Exemptions The several types of federal agency information that a person may not get by filing an FOIA request.

FOIA Request A request by anyone pursuant to the federal Freedom of Information Act for information a federal agency has in its possession.

FTC Act A federal law passed in 1914 that created the Federal Trade Commission and empowered it to attack unfair competition and various anticompetitive practices.

FWPCA Federal Water Pollution Control Act (also known as the Clean Water Act).

Failing Company Defense A defense available to a Clayton Act section 7 defendant; the defense allows a healthy company to merge with a failing company because such a merger is unlikely to hurt competition.

False Imprisonment A type of intentional tort where the defendant unjustifiably confines or restrains the plaintiff for an appreciable period of time.

False Light A type of invasion of privacy; an intentional tort occurring when the defendant makes the plaintiff appear other than how the plaintiff actually is.

Fault Legal idea that someone is not liable unless he/she/it broke a legal duty resulting in harm to someone else.

Federal Exemptions Federal law that prevents certain property of a debtor in bankruptcy from being taken to pay the debtor's creditors.

Federal Preemption A doctrine which makes certain state laws unconstitutional under the Supremacy Clause even though there is no direct verbal clash between state and federal law. The general idea is that congressional action preempted the states from acting within an area staked out by Congress for exclusive federal control.

Federal Question A type of federal court jurisdiction based on the lawsuits involving an interpretation of some federal law.

Federal Register A "newspaper-like" federal publication giving public notice of proposed and promulgated federal regulations, notice of agency meetings, presidential proclamations, and other agency proclamations.

***Federal Register* System** The *U.S. Government Manual, Federal Register,* and *Code of Federal Regulations.*

Federal Reporter Set of books containing cases decided by all U.S. Courts of Appeals.

Federal Supplement Set of books containing cases decided by all U.S. Federal District Courts.

Federal Supremacy The doctrine that the Constitution, laws, and treaties of the United States defeat all inconsistent state laws in case of a clash between them.

Federal Trade Commission Act An act establishing the Federal Trade Commission to focus on maintenance of economic competition and consumer protection.

Federalism Government organized so there are dual (two) sovereigns, state and federal, each with its appropriate sphere of operation.

Fee Simple Absolute A type of estate in realty; the estate in realty that confers the greatest number of rights on the holder of the estate.

Fellow Servant Doctrine A legal rule which says that if a worker is injured by a co-worker's negligence or misconduct, the injured employee may not recover from their employer.

Felony A serious crime.

Feminism When used in a legal context the idea that there should be study of the positive law to determine whether women are placed in legally subordinate positions, not given equal employment opportunities, or are legally debilitated from self-actualizing as are their male counterparts.

Fiduciaries Trustees who hold the legal title to the trust res. As such, they have the highest duty of good faith in maintaining the trust. They must avoid conflicts of interest and must account to the trust beneficiaries.

Fiduciary Duty Duty of great faithfulness and confidence to avoid conflicts of interest or any other form of "double dealing."

Fiduciary Responsibility *See* Fiduciary Duty.

Finance Charge One of two items creditors must disclose to debtors under the Truth-in-Lending Act.

Finder A person who locates lost property.

Firm Offer A written offer made by a merchant in which the merchant assures by the offer's terms that the offer will be held open for a definite time up to three months or for a reasonable time up to three months if no definite time is stated, which offer is signed by the merchant; such offers may not be revoked for the term of the offer; such offers are legalized by Article 2-205 of the UCC.

Five-to-Fifteen Year Graduated Vesting A formula for calculating vesting of employer contributions to employee retirement plans.

Fixed Fee A lawyer's fee that is definite and certain in total dollar amount and that does not depend on whether the lawyer wins or loses the lawsuit.

Fixture Property classification denoting personalty attached to realty with the intent of making the personalty permanently part of the realty; fixtures can regain their identity as personalty by the process known as severance.

Foreign Corporation A corporation organized under the laws of a state other than that one is speaking about.

Formal Complaint In connection with the Federal Trade Commission, it refers to the complaint the FTC hands to an alleged FTC Act violator. Also, in civil lawsuits, refers to complaint plaintiff files with court clerk, which is served on defendant.

Franchise A relationship in which one party (the franchisee) obtains the right to sell goods or services under a marketing plan substantially dictated by another party (the franchisor).

Franchisee The party who sells goods or services under a marketing plan substantially dictated by another party.

Franchisor The party who dictates the market plan for the franchisee.

Frank, Jerome Legal realist who said law is what trial courts and juries do in fact irrespective of what the positive law is.

Fraud An intentional tort occurring where there is misrepresentation of a material fact, knowledge of the misrepresentation by the person misrepresenting, intent to misrepresent, damages sustained by the other person, and the other person reasonably relies on this misrepresentation.

Fraudulent Conveyance Transfer of property that in some way misrepresents, such as a debtor's transfer of property to relatives pretending it is sold to them when in fact the relative intends to retransfer the property to the debtor after the creditors leave.

Freedom of Contract The idea that people can determine the course of their own lives by making their own contracts unprotected or unassisted by any government agency; this idea is most defensible if people have economic and political equality.

Freedom of Speech A constitutional principle, contained in the First Amendment and made applicable to the states through the Fourteenth Amendment, that gives a high degree of protection to "speech" in its many forms.

Front Pay Future salary until a Civil Rights Act Title VII plaintiff becomes employed in the rightful place in the workforce.

Fundamental Rights Certain rights that, when they are denied by government, are protected by requiring that the strict scrutiny test be met in order for the denial to be constitutional.

Fungible Goods Goods that are uniform in size, shape, or nature, such as commodities.

GATT General Agreement on Tariffs and Trade. A multiparty treaty among more than 100 nations, designed to lower tariff barriers between member nations.

Garnishment A legal way for a creditor to get a debtor's property held by a third person (such as a bank account).

General Agent A person who acts in many activities for the benefit of and under the control of another.

General Duty Standard An OSHA standard requiring an employer to maintain a generally safe place to work.

General Jurisdiction The power of a court to hear all types of lawsuits (for example, will cases, murder cases, breach of contract cases, and others).

General Partner A partner with unlimited personal liability in either a conventional partnership or limited partnership.

Gift A way to transfer title to property by delivery of the item, donative intent of the giver, and acceptance by the recipient.

Golden Parachutes High benefit severance contracts top management gives itself, particularly when the company becomes the target for a takeover attempt.

Government Action Activity of government involving individual rights, which is regulated by the Constitution's individual rights protections, including those found in the First, Fifth, and Fourteenth Amendments.

Government Manual A book containing names of all federal agencies and information about them.

Governmental Corporation Organization that exists for a social goal rather than a profit motive, such as the Federal Deposit Insurance Corporation.

Grand Jury Jury used in criminal law to determine if enough evidence shows probable cause that a crime has been committed and that the person arrested committed it. Grand juries issue "true bills" or "indictments" if they believe the prosecutor has established probable cause or "no true bills" if the prosecutor fails to establish probable cause.

Gratuitous Agent A person (agent) who does something for another expecting to receive no pay.

Grease Payments Amounts given to persons (often low-level government employees) to induce them to perform their jobs faster.

Greenhouse Effect Higher temperatures at the earth's surface caused by increased carbon dioxide.

Group Boycotts In antitrust law where competitors agree not to buy from or sell to certain persons; a per se Sherman Act violation.

HIDC Rule Rule that an HIDC (holder in due course) of a negotiable instrument takes it free of personal defenses (such as fraud or duress).

Hart-Scott-Rodino Antitrust Improvement Act A federal law that, among other things, requires that companies planning to merge notify the U.S. Justice Department and Federal Trade Commission before they merge to get premerger approval.

Historical School of Law The idea that positive law reflects long-standing customs.

Holder in Due Course (HIDC) Good faith purchaser of a negotiable instrument for value without notice of any defense that would prevent the HIDC from collecting on it.

Holographic Will A will in the testator's (testatrix's) handwriting and signed by the testator.

Homestead Exemption A debtor's right to keep creditors from taking all or part of the debtor's equity (ownership) in his or her principal residence.

Horizontal Division of Markets Where competitors at the same competitive level agree to divide markets to reduce competition; a per se Sherman Act violation.

Horizontal Mergers When two (or more) competing corporations combine by asset or stock purchase with the acquired company (companies) ceasing to exist and becoming part of the acquiring company, which continues to exist after the merger.

Horizontal Price Fixing Where competitors at the same competitive level agree to fix prices to reduce competition; a per se Sherman Act violation.

Hot Cargo Contracts Voluntary agreements between a union and a neutral employer by which the neutral employer agrees to put pressure on the employer with which the union has a dispute.

Hybrid Rulemakings A way to make agency regulations, which adds more procedures, such as hearings, to the notice and comment of the informal rulemaking process.

ICC The Interstate Commerce Commission; a federal administrative agency.

Illegal Contracts Contracts whose formation or performance violates some positive law.

Imminently Hazardous Consumer Product A product that presents an unreasonable risk of death, serious illness, and severe personal injury.

Implied Created by operation of law, often by inference from the relevant facts and circumstances.

Implied Authority Power an agent gets as a result of performing necessary activities to carry out the agent's express authority.

Implied Contract A contract formed when the parties' actions but not words indicate that they intend to form a contract; contract formed by conduct, not words.

Implied Powers Those powers "necessary and proper" for effectuating Congress's inherent or enumerated powers. An example would be the power to regulate intrastate matters affecting interstate commerce.

Implied Warranty A warranty arising by operation of law. Implied warranties do not depend on the consent of the party giving the warranty. They contravene "freedom of contract" principles and are usually imposed to protect the buyer.

Implied Warranty of Merchantability A warranty in Article 2 of the UCC that states that a warranty that the goods shall be merchantable is implied in a contract for their sale if the seller is a merchant with respect to goods of that kind.

In Pari Delicto Where two persons are equally culpable or guilty, in which case the law leaves them where it finds them helping neither.

***In Personam* Jurisdiction** Power of a court (or other legal authority) over a particular person.

***In Rem* Jurisdiction** Power over property ("rem" is Latin for "thing").

Incapacity When used in a legal sense it refers to the law's decision that certain people (such as minors, insane people, and drunks) cannot protect themselves so it allows them to escape (avoid) their contracts.

Incipiency Doctrine An antitrust rule that says if a merger would start to reduce competition between the merging companies and start to concentrate economic power in an industry, the merger violates section 7 of the Clayton Act.

Indemnified Repaid for a loss.

Independent Constitutional Checks Limits on congressional power, which exist outside the provision granting Congress power to act in the first place. The Bill of Rights and the Fourteenth Amendment are examples. These limits are the principal checks on congressional lawmaking power today.

Indictment The complaint in a criminal lawsuit.

Indirect Economic Loss A wide range of economic harm resulting from a product defect or negligence. Examples include lost profits and loss of business goodwill.

Industry Guides Nontechnical statements issued by the Federal Trade Commission designed to tell business what is and is not permitted by FTC regulations.

Inference of Negligence Case in which plaintiff has proven negligence unless a defendant has some defense.

Informal Complaints Used in reference to certain consumer, general public, and business complaints filed with the Federal Trade Commission about a business practice the complainant thinks violates FTC rules and regulations. Different from the formal complaint the FTC hands to an alleged FTC Act violator.

Information In criminal procedure the information serves the same purpose as the indictment (the complaint in the criminal lawsuit).

Infringe To use property without authorization, including trademarks, patents, copyrights, etc.

Injunctions Equity court orders to a person to do or not do something. A type of equitable remedy.

Injunctive Relief Enforcement device used by agencies against businesses that are violating agency rules.

Innocent Misrepresentation If someone unknowingly states something is a fact when it is not which induces someone else to enter a contract, it is called innocent misrepresentation and is a basis for the party to whom the representation is made to escape the contract in question.

Integration A term which when used in connection with employee retirement pensions means that pensions will take into account retirement accounts received from different sources (such as workers' compensation) and thereby reduce the pension coming from one source (such as from a private employer's pension plan).

Intentional Infliction of Mental Distress An intentional tort in which defendant knowingly causes plaintiff extreme mental suffering; usually accompanies physical injury although in extreme cases mental distress alone can be recoverable.

Intentional Torts Civil wrongs where the defendant has some sort of intent.

Interbrand Competition Competition between sellers of different brands of the same type product (for example competition between Ford and Chevrolet dealers).

Interest in the Partnership The right to receive profits and surplus from a partnership.

Intermediate Strict Scrutiny The sort of equal protection strict scrutiny applying to discrimination based on sex, illegitimacy, and alienage. In gender discrimination cases, it involves the requirement that the challenged law have a substantial relation to the advancement of an important governmental purpose.

Internal Morality of Law The idea Professor Lon Fuller posited of eight criteria that positive law must meet to be moral. These items are: there must be rules; rules must be promulgated; rules must be clear; rules should not be retroactive; rules should be noncontradictory; rules should not demand the impossible; rules should not change often; and officials should follow the rules.

Interpretative Regulations Rules of administrative agencies that usually take effect as soon as they are made and are not binding as law.

Interstate Commerce Clause The portion of Article I, § 8 giving Congress the power to regulate commerce "among the several states." This clause is now probably the single most important source of congressional lawmaking authority.

Interstate Commerce Commission (ICC) A federal regulatory agency that makes law by issuing regulations governing interstate commerce.

Interstitial Lawmaking Judicial lawmaking by filling gaps in statutes.

Inter Vivos Trusts that take effect during the settlor's life.

Intestate Dying without a will

Intrusion Upon Solitude or Seclusion A type of invasion of privacy; an intentional tort.

Invasion of Privacy An intentional tort where defendant does one of four things to the plaintiff (1) invades plaintiff's peace and solitude; (2) holds plaintiff up in a false light; (3) uses plaintiff's name or likeness without authorization; or (4) publicly discloses some private fact about plaintiff.

Invitations to Negotiate Statements or actions one party makes trying to induce the other party to make an offer; not an offer.

Involuntary Bankruptcy A debtor's being forced into bankruptcy by creditors, against the debtor's will.

Joint and Several Liability Liability in which a partner could be forced to pay the entire tort judgment obtained against a copartner who injured others within the scope of the partnership.

Joint Resolution A law passed by the legislature, similar in effect to a statute.

Joint Tenants Two or more persons who own equal shares in realty at the same time and have the "right of survivorship" feature.

Judgment Creditor A person who, when a lawsuit ends, is owed money as a result of the lawsuit.

Judgment Debtor A person who, when a lawsuit ends, owes money as a result of the lawsuit.

Judgment Notwithstanding the Verdict Where a trial judge, after a jury has given its verdict, gives a judgment different from what the verdict is on the grounds that no reasonable jury could have done what the jury has just done.

Judgment Proof When a person is so poor that he or she is not worth suing because a judgment against him or her could not be paid; a person with few if any assets.

Judicare A plan for providing legal assistance to members of the public much as medicare provides medical help to the public.

Judicial Review The power of courts to declare the idioms of other government bodies unconstitutional.

Jurisdiction The power of a court to decide a case.

Jurisprudence The study of different legal philosophies (ideas about what law is or is supposed to be).

Justice of the Peace Courts Low-level courts dealing with minor civil or criminal matters.

Knowing Endangerment
When one entity (person or business) knowingly places another person in imminent danger of death or serious bodily injury.

Knowing Violations Negligent release of hazardous substances that a person knows or reasonably should have known could cause personal injury or property damage.

LLC Limited liability company. A form of business organization combining the "pass-through" advantages of partnerships with respect to federal income taxation (and sometimes state income taxation, too) with the entity and limited liability aspects of the corporate form.

LLP Limited liability partnership. A form of business organization, usually of professional partnerships, that limits liability of professional malpractice to the person who commits the malpractice, not to the partnership.

Laboratory Conditions Word used in labor law to describe the neutral atmosphere that is supposed to exist when employees vote to decide whether to have a union represent them.

Laissez Faire Economy with few, if any, government restrictions on business.

Law Courts Courts that give legal remedies (such as money damages) instead of equitable remedies (such as specific performance).

Law of Large Numbers The idea that as the number of events (or numbers) increases, the likelihood of unusual things occurring increases.

Law Merchant Customs of merchants that came to be included into positive law.

Lawyers Edition Set of privately published books containing U.S. Supreme Court decisions in chronological order.

Lead Agency Words used in certain environmental law matters where several agencies are involved in a matter, but one fills out an EIS for all agencies involved.

Leasehold A temporary possessory interest in real estate; a lease.

Legal Ethic of Planning A view of law that uses decision theory to decide what the law should be.

Legal Fiction Something the law says exists or is true even though our senses tell us it does not exist; for example, the idea that corporations are people. Legal fictions are created to achieve some desirable social objective such as justice.

Legal Guardian Someone a court appoints to manage someone else's (called a "ward") affairs.

Legal Realist A person who believes law is what trial judges and juries do even though positive law may require something else.

Legal Remedies The usual recovery an injured person receives in a civil lawsuit; damages (money) is the most common legal remedy.

Legally Void A contract with serious flaws that cannot be enforced even if it is written.

Legislative Regulations Agency regulations that are legally binding; also called substantive regulations.

Legislative Veto When a legislature nullifies an agency regulation.

Liberal When used in modern political/social/economic contexts refers generally to someone who is inclined to try new approaches to dealing with situations and problems; refers to someone favoring a governmental or socialized approach to solving problems rather than private sector or individual solutions.

License The right extended to a person to enter onto another's realty for a limited time and purpose. A patron's sitting in a movie theater is a license.

Life Estate A type of estate in realty that lasts as long as the holder of the estate is alive.

Limited Liability The idea that a person's financial responsibility for something has limits, said of corporate shareholders with respect to corporate debts.

Limited Partner Partner in a limited partnership where liability is limited to a fixed amount.

Limited Partnership A partnership formed pursuant to a state statute that requires only one general partner and lets at least one other partner limit liability for limited partnership debts.

Litigants Plaintiff(s) and defendant(s) in a lawsuit.

LLC Limited liability company. A form of business organization combining the "pass-through" advantages of partnerships with respect to federal income taxation (and sometimes state income taxation, too) with the entity and limited liability aspects of the corporate form.

Loans Where creditors give a borrower money (instead of goods) to use for a period of time and charge a fee for this service.

Lockout In labor law, the employer's temporary refusal to allow employees to work by locking up the plant.

Long-Arm Statute Statutes that let a state get in personam jurisdiction over out-of-staters for certain wrongs committed within the state (usually in such incidents as auto accidents). Also, a law that allows state A's court to reach into another state B and assert personal jurisdiction over one of B's citizens based on some occurrence in state A.

Lost Property Personalty that has been unintentionally, involuntarily parted with by the owner.

M

Mailbox Rule Rule of contract law that says acceptance is effective when sent ("put in mailbox") by offeree (not when received by offeror).

Malingering False claims of injury or illness to escape work or increase damage recovery from someone.

Malpractice Negligence suits brought against professionals such as physicians, lawyers, engineers, architects, veterinarians, and accountants who have not performed their contractual duties to their clients with requisite care.

Mandamus Orders Court orders telling someone to do something (such as telling an administrative agency to do a nondiscretionary duty).

Manifest System Term used in environmental law to refer to a way to trace hazardous wastes by keeping a paper record (called a "manifest system") of them.

Marketable Pollution Rights Idea in pollution control that allows one polluter in a nonattainrnent air quality area to sell its right to emit pollutants there to someone else in the same area.

Massachusetts Trust Business organization form in the form of a trust; similar in many ways to a corporation.

Master-Servant Relationship A relationship arising when a person (the "master") employs another person (the "servant") to perform physical tasks not involving the making of contracts with third persons. The tasks are often of a menial sort, such as gardening or cleaning.

Mediation Involves using a neutral third party (called a mediator) to hear both sides of a dispute and to communicate between the disputants to get them to compromise.

Merchant As defined by UCC section 2-104, a merchant is either a party who regularly deals in goods of the kind sold (e.g., a bicycle manufacturer selling bicycles), or by occupation holds itself out as having knowledge or skill peculiar to the goods involved in the sale (e.g., a heating supply contractor installing a furnace). The UCC often imposes special rules where one or both parties to the transaction are merchants.

Merger When two companies combine in such a way that one company continues to exist after the merger.

Miller-Tydings Act A federal law passed in 1937 that allowed states to pass laws permitting resale price maintenance without violating a federal antitrust statute. Repealed in 1975.

Minors Persons below a certain age set by each state designed to protect young people from making unwise contracts and taking part in other activities society deems is unwise for them.

Mirror Image Rule of contract law that says acceptances must conform exactly to the terms of the offer or else the acceptance is ineffective to form a contract.

Misdemeanor Insignificant crime.

Mobile Sources Term used in air pollution control law to refer to autos and other vehicles that contribute to air pollution.

Model Business Corporation Act A model statute drafted by scholars and practitioners in the corporate law area that contains what they think are desirable features for corporate law.

Model Statutes Suggested laws that a legislature might pass; often suggested by some organization of scholars or practitioners.

Monarchy Government in which only one person makes the rules.

Monopolies Economy in which market segments have only one seller.

Monopolistic Competition Market in which many sellers compete but in which a particular seller has some distinctive feature to its product or service that gives a limited "monopoly" pricing ability over its competitors.

Monopoly Power The ability of a firm to raise prices above the competitive level for a sustained period of time, and to profit by doing so.

Motion for Summary Judgment A motion a party to a lawsuit makes that, in effect, says "Because no fact issues, just legal issues, are present, you decide the case without a jury trial, judge."

Motion to Dismiss A legal argument a civil defendant makes to cause the judge to "throw a plaintiff's case out of court."

Multiple-Conscience Problem A problem with the natural law theory that occurs because natural law means what each person thinks is right and yet each person's idea of "right" could differ from everyone else's, leaving one with no agreement on what is "right" even though all may agree that the "right thing" should be done.

Municipal Corporations Cities and towns that have been given charters by the state to govern a geographic area.

Municipal Courts Low-level courts dealing with minor civil or criminal matters.

Mutual Benefit Bailment A bailment in which both the bailee and bailor benefit.

National Conference of Commissioners on Uniform State Laws A group of legal scholars who draft suggested laws for states; suggested laws—called model acts—are designed to simplify, make uniform, and modernize the law.

National Environmental Policy Act (NEPA) A federal law that tells federal administrative agencies to take environmental factors into account when they decide to do major activities that affect the quality of the human environment.

Natural Law What each individual thinks is fair, right, and just.

Negative Easement An easement that prevents someone from doing something on one's land, such as stopping the building of a structure if it would block the sunlight to the dominant estate.

Negligence A type of tort (civil wrong) that holds a person liable for damages proximately caused by carelessness (conduct not living up to the standard of an ordinary, reasonable, prudent person).

Negligence Per Se In negligence law, a breach of duty based on the violation of a statute.

Negotiable Note A type of negotiable instrument; a signed writing having an unconditional promise to pay a sum certain (exact amount) of money (any country's currency) at an exact date or on demand (when asked) that has certain words (called words of negotiability) implying that the person originally issuing the note intended that person(s) other than the person originally receiving the note could legally come into possession of it.

Noerr Doctrine An antitrust idea that allows competitors to join together to petition the government without violating the antitrust laws.

Noise Emission Limits Amounts of noise the EPA lets certain products produce.

Nolo Contendere A plea of "no contest" in a criminal case that neither admits nor denies the indictment; a type of plea bargain.

Nominal Damages Symbolic damages that are a small amount of money a lawbreaker pays to a victim to show a wrong was done but the victim was not harmed.

Noncontributory Pensions Retirement plans into which only the employer pays.

Noncriteria Pollutants Air pollutants other than the five basic criteria pollutants (ozone, carbon monoxide, sulfur dioxide, particulates, and nitrogen dioxide). The criteria pollutants (plus hydrocarbons) are what the EPA focuses its attention on controlling.

Nondelegable Duties Certain duties a master or principal has that, because of various public policy reasons, the master or principal remains liable for even if someone else performs them.

Nondeterioration Standards Used in air pollution control to refer to federal standards for clean air areas that exceed air quality standards and that federal law continues to maintain.

Nondiscretionary Duty Used in connection with administrative agencies to describe agency duties that must be done and that a court will order an agency to do if it does not do them voluntarily.

Nonexempt Property A debtor's property that, according to Bankruptcy Code, may be divided among creditors to discharge debts.

Nonexistent Principal A principal that does not legally exist, such as a corporation not yet organized.

Nonlitigation Legal work not involving lawsuits.

Norms of Conduct How people act and the effect they have on positive law.

Norris-LaGuardia Act A federal labor law that, among other things, removed jurisdiction of federal courts to issue injunctions in labor disputes.

Nuisance A type of tort (civil wrong) where someone or something injures or annoys another or his or her property.

OSHA Walkaround Privilege Right of an employer and employee subject to OSHA to accompany the OSHA inspector during a plant inspection.

Obiter Dicta *See* Dicta.

Objective Intent The intent attributed to a person who appears to a reasonable third person to be making an offer to contract.

Objective Standard A test of liability based on the defendant's behavior or some other physical fact, and not on what the actor (defendant) thinks.

Objective Test Regarding contracts, a test to determine whether a contract exists based on what a reasonable third person would think the people allegedly making the contract have done.

Objective Theory of Contracts Way to determine whether a contract exists; the theory says that if a reasonable person would say that two parties appear to have made a contract, a contract exists in the eyes of the law even though the parties did not subjectively intend to form a contract.

Offensive Use of the Pass-On Theory A theory of recovering in an antitrust lawsuit where an antitrust plaintiff claims it was damaged by buying goods priced higher because of an "upstream" antitrust violation (someone the plaintiff did not buy directly from) and the plaintiff tries to recover from the "upstream" antitrust violator. This action is not allowed.

Offer A definite, communicated expression one party makes to another objectively intending to form a contract stating what the offeror will do and what the offeror expects in return from the offeree.

Offeree Person to whom an offer is made.

Offeror Person who makes an offer.

Oligarchy Government in which a small group makes the rules.

Ombudspersons Agency officials who act as inspectors of agencies to ensure that the agencies follow the law.

Open Dumping Way to get rid of solid waste by dumping it on land and not covering it.

Open Meeting Law A law forcing certain agency meetings to be open to the public. Also called "Sunshine Acts."

Operation of Law The idea that the law does something automatically when certain events occur (such as ending an agency when the agent dies).

Options Contracts whose subject matter is an offer.

Ordinances Laws passed by municipalities (cities and towns).

Organic Acts Statutes giving an administrative agency the legal right to exist.

Orphan Lands Word used in environmental law to refer to abandoned strip-mined land where no reclamation efforts have been made.

PC Professional corporation.

Paid in Capital Account Contains the total number of dollars paid into a company by stockholders for stock.

Paper Remedies Remedies that theoretically exist ("exist on the pages of the books") but which, as a practical matter, do not exist.

Parens Patriae Latin for "parent of the country"; an antitrust doctrine that gives state attorneys general the authority to enforce the Sherman Act.

Partially Disclosed Principal Agency where the identity of the agent and fact of agency are known but the principal's identity is unknown.

Partnership Two or more persons carrying on as co-owners of a business for profit. A form of business.

Partnership by Estoppel Where a person holds out another as a partner, and a third person reasonably relies on this holding out and damages result, the person holding out or permitting another to be held out as a partner is stopped from saying the person held out is not a partner.

Pass-On Defense A defense in an antitrust civil lawsuit in which the defendant says that the plaintiff may not recover its antitrust damages because the plaintiff passed on its damages to its customers. This defense is not allowed.

Pass-On Theory Antitrust theory that asserts that an antitrust defendant can claim the plaintiff (a direct buyer from an antitrust violator) passed on its antitrust damages to its customers (this defensive use of pass-on is not allowed). Also pass-on may not be used offensively by indirect buyers, one or more steps removed from antitrust violators in the production-distribution chain.

Patent A legal monopoly conferred by the government (the patentor) on the private party (patentee). The patent entitles the patentee to exclude anyone else from making, using, or selling the patented item for a period of 20 years from the date of the application.

Patent License Permission from a patent holder for another to use the patented item, usually in exchange for royalties.

***Per Se* Offenses** Certain antitrust offenses that are so obviously socially harmful that the government does not have to show any particular economic harm to prove its case (harm is presumed).

Percentage of Disability A way of paying injured employees covered by workers' compensation when a loss occurs not expressly covered in the workers' comp schedule of recoveries.

Peremptory Challenges Challenges to a prospective juror where the challenging lawyer does not have to tell why the prospective juror is excused from jury duty.

Perfected Security Interest A creditor's claim on certain property of a debtor where the claim is superior to certain other creditors' claims to the same property.

Periodic Tenancy A tenancy created by implication in the case of holdover tenants from whom the landlord accepts rent for a discrete period such as a week or month after the lease has expired.

Permanent Injunction A court order telling someone never to do something; punishment for breaking such an injunction is being jailed.

Personal Injury Usually bodily harm resulting from negligence or product defeats; includes losses attributable to pain and suffering, mental distress, inconvenience, loss of companionship and consortium, injury to reputation, lost earnings, and so on.

Personalty Moveable property such as clothing, vehicles, furniture.

Philosophical Positivism The idea that the only real thing in the world is that which can be objectively pointed to, that is, "seeing is believing." Facts and data are evidence of themselves and thus are "real." Distinguished from feelings or ideas.

Plea Bargain A deal between the prosecutor and a criminal defendant, often where a guilty defendant pleads guilty to a lesser offense to escape the cost of trial.

Pleadings The complaint and answer in a civil lawsuit.

Pocket Parts Pamphlets inserted in the back of law books (statute books and case books) to update them with recently made laws.

Point Sources Definite points from which any kind of pollutant is discharged into the nation's waters.

Police Magistrates Courts that deal with minor legal violations—traffic violations, for example—of both a civil and criminal nature.

Police Power The power to regulate for the public health, safety, morals, and welfare. All the states possess this power. For all practical purposes, Congress possesses this power also, especially under the interstate commerce clause.

Positive Law Rules laid down by political superiors on political inferiors where there are sanctions (punishments) if the law is broken.

Powers of Attorney Written agency under which one person may do future acts for another person.

Preconstruction Review Mechanism Term used in air pollution control law to refer to the review that new buildings must go through before they are built to insure they comply with air pollution standards.

Preempted Where a federal statue so completely fills or dominates an area of law that the state has no legal power to pass law in the subject matter area.

Prejudgment Attachment A creditor's obtaining a legal claim on specific property of the debtor before a lawsuit is held to determine if the debtor in fact owes the creditor anything.

Prejudgment Garnishment *See* Prejudgment Wage Garnishment.

Prejudgment Wage Garnishment A creditor's obtaining payment from a debtor by obtaining a part of the debtor's weekly wages before a court determines whether the "debtor" owes the creditor anything.

Pre-Manufacture Notice Concept in environmental law referring to requirement that chemical makers tell the EPA about new, planned chemicals before they are made.

Premerger Notification The notice two companies planning to merge must give the FTC and Justice Department before they merge.

Preponderance of the Evidence A test in civil law, which a jury uses to decide whether enough evidence exists to find for the plaintiff.

Pretreat When used in connection with water pollution, it refers to certain industrial dischargers' taking some pollutants out of their waste discharge before dumping it in the city sewer.

Prevention of Significant Deterioration Term used in air pollution control to mean essentially the same thing as nondeterioration standards (preventing areas with air quality higher than federal law requires from having a drop in air quality to general federal standards).

***Prima Facie* Case** A case strong enough to enable the plaintiff to win the suit unless contradicted by persuasive evidence from the defendant.

***Prima Facie* Evidence** Enough evidence to get a case before a jury.

Primary Activities In labor activities, they are the direct economic weapons: in the case of employees, they use strikes; in the case of employers, they use lockouts.

Primary Air Quality Standards When used in connection with air pollution, refers to air pollution control laws designed to protect public health.

Primary Line Price Discrimination Involves economic injury to competitors of the discriminating seller; for example, a large manufacturer might finance its low prices in areas where it faces strong competition by charging higher prices in areas where competition is weak.

Primary Market The sale of new or just issued securities.

Primary Rights Substantive law.

Principal-Agent Relationship Occurs when one person (the principal) employs another (the agent) to enter business relations (usually contracts) with third persons

Privilege Defense to defamation; basically says that even if defendant's statement about plaintiff is otherwise true certain policy reasons (such as absolute free expression on the floor of the legislature) make defendant's remarks not a basis for a successful defamation suit; some types of privilege are qualified and others are absolute.

Privity of Contract Contractual relationship between two parties. If A sells goods to B, who in turn sells the goods to C, both A and B, as well as B and C, are "in" privity of contract, but A and C are not.

Privity Rule Rule of sales law that requires a plaintiff buyer to have contracted directly with a defendant seller before certain legal claims (e.g., breach of warranty) can be made against the seller. This rule has been largely abandoned.

Pro Se *See* Pro Se Litigant

***Pro Se* Litigant** A party to a lawsuit who does not have a lawyer.

Probable Cause Cause to believe a crime was committed and the person arrested committed it. Also the test for a grand jury's issuing an indictment.

Probate Court Court that deals with wills and estates.

Procedural Due Process A basic requirement of procedural fairness imposed on the federal government and the states by the Fifth and Fourteenth amendments; notice and fair hearing.

Procedural Law Rules governing steps in lawsuits or legal matters.

Procedural Rules Rules establishing how the legal system, courts, etc. are to operate.

Procedural Unconscionability A form of unconscionability involving either the way contract terms are packaged (e.g., fine print), or the factors that made a party enter into a contract (e.g., "sales hype").

Producer The creator of a particular trademark in use long enough so that the public associates the mark with the producer.

Product Liability Responsibility of manufacturers and sellers for any harm to purchasers of a product or other parties resulting from defective goods.

Product Market The market in which a product exists dependent upon the substitutability of other products for that product.

Product Safety Standards A standard reasonably necessary to prevent or reduce an unreasonable risk associated with the product, used as an enforcement device by the Consumer Product Safety Commission to promote product safety.

Productive Efficiency The ability of an economy to make goods and services in a way that uses the least amount of resources.

Professional Corporation A form of business organization reserved for those in the learned professions, which often limits the liability of shareholder professionals in some way.

Profits The right to enter someone else's real estate to remove the soil or what the soil produces, such as minerals, crops, or water.

Promissory Notes A written promise to pay a sum certain in money (any country's currency) at a future certain date or on demand. It is a two-party document; that is, only two persons—a person promising to pay, called the note's "maker," and a second, called the "payee" are mentioned on the front ("face") of the note.

Property The rights one person has regarding other people with respect to something; the rights a person or people have to something.

Property Damage Economic loss to property resulting from damage caused by negligence or a defective product.

Proportionately Liable Liability of outside directors for losses dependent upon their involvement in the losses.

Proposed Order When used in connection with Federal Trade Commission law enforcement, refers to orders the FTC plans to issue in particular cases.

Proposed Rulemaking When an agency publishes a regulation in the *Federal Register,* which the agency wants to make binding as law at a future time, unless the public can convince the agency the proposed regulation is unwise.

Prosecutor Society's attorney.

Prospectus Part of a registration statement that must be given to a securities buyer before or at the sale of certain securities.

Power of Attorney Express authority, granted only in writing, to one person to enable him or her to act for another.

Proximate Cause A term used to describe the legal issue presented by the degree of proximity or closeness between breach of duty and injury required in a negligence case. In most jurisdictions, it is based on the reasonable foreseeability of the plaintiff's injury having resulted from the defendant's breach.

Public Function Doctrine A branch of state action doctrine in which a finding of state action is based on the fact that a private body performs the same functions as a governmental body. A "company town" is an example. The public function doctrine is virtually dead by now.

Public Law Law that deals with matters affecting all or a large part of society, such as the Social Security Act, OSHA, and the Clean Water Act.

Public Nuisance Conduct or the use of property in a way that annoys or interferes with public rights.

Public Policy Refers to desirable goals or conduct.

Puffing Seller's talk that is legally only opinion and not fact and therefore may not be the basis for a lawsuit based on fraud.

Punitive Used to describe laws that punish. Criminal laws are punitive.

Punitive (or Exemplary) Damages Damages imposed on a party as a sort of penalty for particularly egregious behavior. Usually, some sort of recklessness or malicious behavior is required for their imposition. Punitive damages are most common in tort cases.

Qualified Said of a foreign corporation once it establishes its corporate existence in a state other than the state of incorporation; once a foreign corporation is qualified in another state, it may do intrastate business there.

Qualified Employee Retirement Plan A retirement plan meeting certain federal requirements and which employer contributions to are tax deductible by the employer.

Qualified Privilege A right to make defamatory statements limited only by motive and manner in which the remarks are made.

Quasi in Rem *See* Quasi in Rem Jurisdiction.

Quasi in Rem Jurisdiction Power of a court or other legal authority over a person because the court has physical control over some item of the person's property.

Quasi-Contract Contract imposed by a court (judge) on a situation where there actually is no contract but the court wants to avoid unjust enrichment.

Quid Quo Pro Sexual Harassment A form of sexual harassment involving some kind of linkage, connection, or trade between the employee's submission to sex-related behavior and tangible job consequences.

Ratification Retroactive authority a principal gives someone who, without authority, purports to act for another and whose acts the purported principal fully approves when he or she learns of them.

Rational Basis Test The basic equal protection test and the test applied to economic regulation. It requires only that the challenged law have a reasonable relationship with a valid governmental purpose. It is not much of an obstacle to government regulation of the economy.

Rawls, John Twentieth-century natural law philosopher who advanced the notion of the "original position" (suppose that you were behind a veil of ignorance and did not know what your status in life or characteristics were; this is the original position and is used to justify positive laws such as affirmative action).

Real Estate Investment Trust (REIT) A trust device used to own real estate. A business organization form.

Real Estate Syndications Arise when several persons own property. The vehicle for the joint ownership could be a limited partnership, partnership, trust, or corporation.

Realty Property classification denoting realty and buildings; immovables.

Reasonable Person Standard The basic test used to determine whether a breach of duty has occurred in a negligence case. The defendant's behavior is compared to the way a hypothetical reasonable person would have behaved under the circumstances.

Recidivism In criminal law it refers to repeating criminal conduct.

Reclamation Word used in environmental law to refer to efforts to restore surface mined land to the condition it was in before it was surface mined.

Recycling Reusing something; a conservation measure.

Red-Herring Prospectus A prospectus for the sale of securities that has red printing on it and which contains insufficient information to make it an offer or a prospectus.

Redlining Where lenders on houses refuse to make loans to borrowers in declining neighborhoods.

Redress Compensation given to injured parties or consumers by a business that violated a trade regulation rule.

Reg-Neg Regulations that are negotiated. It involves the appointment of a committee by an official of the agency responsible for the rule; the committee meets, shares information relevant to drafting the proposed regulation, comes up with a report, and then submits it to the agency with authority to promulgate it.

Registered Agent A person named by corporate organizers on whom process can be served if someone wishes to sue the particular corporation.

Registers Files information with the U.S. Patent and Trademark Office concerning a trademark, which limits its use by any other entity.

Registration Statement A document that must be filed with the Securities and Exchange Commission before one can offer certain securities for public sale.

Regulation Z A regulation promulgated under the Truth-in-Lending Act.

Regulations Law made by an administrative agency.

Regulatory Flexibility Act A federal statute passed in 1980 that adds certain procedures to help small entities participate in and cope with federal agency rulemaking.

Regulatory Flexibility Agenda A list published twice per year by each federal agency telling what regulations it intends to publish in the near future.

Regulatory Occupational License A type of permit one needs to do some types of work, where the main purpose of the occupational license is to protect the public from incompetent, unethical persons.

Rehabilitation In criminal law it refers to helping criminals become socially valuable members of society. One of the four basic objectives of criminal law.

Rejection Unqualified refusal by the offeree communicated to the offeror that the offer is not satisfactory; ends an offer.

Remedy Limitation A term in a contract (often a contract for the sale of goods) by which one party (usually a seller) attempts to block the other party's (usually the buyer's) recovery of certain kinds of damages. Remedy limitations are often confused with disclaimers, but differ because they attempt to restrict a party's remedies, not the party's liability under a particular theory of recovery.

Reporters Books containing judges' opinions deciding lawsuits.

Representation Case A type of lawsuit brought under the Wagner Act in which the employer or union alleges that a particular union should or should not be the collective bargaining representative for an employer.

Representative Democracy Form of government wherein the persons ruled elect representatives who make the society's rules.

Requirements Contract In a requirements contract, the buyer agrees to purchase all its requirements of a particular commodity from the seller.

Res Property in a trust.

Res Ipsa Loquitur A way to prove a breach of duty in negligence cases where the accident would not ordinarily have occurred without someone's negligence, and the thing causing the harm is exclusively within the control of the defendant. The doctrine assists the plaintiff because it enables proof of the breach where this would not otherwise be possible yet. Latin for "the thing speaks for itself."

Res Judicata Latin for "the matter has already been decided." Said of civil cases where a lawsuit on the matter has already occurred.

Resale Price Maintenance Where a manufacturer or distributor refuses to sell goods to a retailer unless the retailer agrees to sell to the public at certain minimum price.

Rescission Most often, a contract remedy whereby the court returns the parties to their original precontractual position.

Respondeat Superior The employer (superior) must answer for the employee's (agent's or servant's) wrongs committed at work.

Respondent The alleged violator.

Restitution Returning something to someone else; a type of contract or tort remedy.

Restraint Imprisonment of a criminal; one of the four basic objectives of criminal law.

Retribution Punishment of a criminal; one of the four basic objectives of criminal law.

Retrofit Requirement Term used in environmental law to refer to the idea that when new stricter pollution control requirements take effect, existing products and polluters must "upgrade" to meet them. Failure to impose retrofit requirements in new pollution laws "grandfathers in" existing polluters.

Revenue-Raising Occupational License A law whose purpose is to raise money to pay for state government.

Reverse FOIA Case A case where someone tries to stop a federal agency from giving information in its possession over to the public because the information is covered by an FOIA exemption.

Revocation When an offeror calls back his or her offer; a way to end an offer.

Right of Survivorship The idea that the joint tenant who die before other joint tenants loses all interest in the property.

Right-to-Sue Letter A procedural requirement in Title VII Civil Rights Act of 1964 cases.

Risk Spreading The dispersion of the higher economic risks of such principles as strict liability among all the parties who benefit from such a policy.

Robinson-Patman Act Federal antitrust law passed in 1936 which prohibits certain pricing practices.

Rule Against Perpetuities A law regarding trusts that limits the length of their existence.

Rule of 45 A formula for calculating vesting of employer contributions to employee retirement plans.

Rule of Law All citizens—the president, governors, members of the Supreme Court, star athletes, and average citizens—must obey the rules.

Rule of Reason A rule of law used to interpret section I of the Sherman Antitrust law; to be a crime under section I of the Sherman Act the defendant's conduct must cause an unreasonable restraint of trade; it is not used in per se antitrust cases.

Rule Utilitarianism Maximizing one's happiness while still obeying the positive law.

Rules Law made by an administrative agency.

Sale of Goods Transaction in which the ownership of goods shifts from one party to another in exchange for equivalent consideration, usually money.

SEC Securities and Exchange Commission; a major federal administrative agency.

Savigny Legal philosopher advancing the historical school of law which emphasizes longstanding custom.

Schism A rule of labor law that says if a split in top union officials occurs a representation election can be held even though an unexpired collective bargaining agreement exists.

Scope of Employment Limit of one's job.

Search Warrant Governmental document entitling government officials to search private property for suspected legal violations or evidence of violations.

Secondary Boycotts Any combination of its purpose and effect is to coerce customers, patrons, or suppliers, through fear of loss or bodily harm, to withhold or withdraw their business from an employer the union has a dispute with.

Secondary Line Price Discrimination Price discrimination that causes economic injury to competitors of the favored buyer.

Secondary Market Old securities bought and sold daily.

Secondary Rights Remedies of primary rights (substantive law is broken).

Secondary Standards When used in connection with air pollution control, refers to air pollution control laws designed to protect public welfare (such as property and aesthetics).

Securities and Exchange Commission (SEC) a major federal administrative agency.

Self-Insuring An employer's decision not to hire an insurance company to help it administer losses.

Service Mark The equivalent of a trademark for service providers rather than actual goods.

Servient Estate Property that is subject to an easement.

Session Laws Laws published in the order they were passed by the legislature and before they are in code form.

Settlement A way plaintiff and defendant end a lawsuit by reaching an agreement without fully trying the case; a settlement can occur any time in a lawsuit before it otherwise ends.

Settlor Person who establishes a trust.

706 Agencies State or municipal civil rights agencies which have met legal requirements under section 706 of the Civil Rights Act of 1964.

Sham Transactions Matters that appear to be contracts but are not contracts and are made to cheat creditors or the taxing authorities.

Share Subscriptions What a corporate promoter sells to persons desiring to invest in stock of a corporation about to be organized.

Shareholders People who purchase corporate shares; stockholders.

Shares Pieces of a corporation offered for sale to investors.

Shelf Registration Registering securities under federal securities laws but not immediately offering them for sale.

Sherman Antitrust Act Federal antitrust law enacted in 1890 which outlaws contracts, combinations, or conspiracies in restraint of trade and monopolizing or attempts to monopolize. It makes certain acts both crimes (felonies) and civil treble damage actions.

Showing of Employee Interest Word used in federal labor law to describe when enough employees want the National Labor Relations Board to hold a representative election to decide whether a union will represent the employees.

Simple Resolution "Housekeeping" rules dealing with running only one house of Congress. Not a law.

Skip Tracing Trying to locate debtors.

Social Compact Basic legal organization of government, usually contained in a document called a "constitution."

Social Contract *See* Social Compact; meanings are identical.

Social Offers Statements offering to take part in a social event and are offers but are not legally considered offers in form due in part to the fact that courts do not want to get too involved in individuals' personal affairs and also because a remedy would be difficult to fashion.

Socialization of Risk A term used to describe the process whereby the economic risks of certain activities are effectively spread out through society, or socialized. Typically, it involves putting increased legal responsibility (often through strict liability) on the defendant, which then increases its prices to reflect the additional resulting costs. In this way, the economic burden of allowing greater plaintiff recoveries is "spread out" through society.

Sociological School of Law The idea that people's conduct shapes the law (Ehrlich's view) or that law is the result of weighing competing claims to see which is heavier (Pound's view).

Sole Proprietor One person who owns all of the assets and is solely liable for all of its liabilities. A legal form of business.

Sovereign The highest political authority in a society; the state (or government); supreme lawmaker in a society.

Special Agent Someone who acts for and under the control of another in a very limited matter (such as an agent hired to do one thing).

Special 301 A section of the 1988 Trade Act; its purpose is to develop a strategy to protect intellectual property rights and to assume market access for U.S. business.

Specific Intent Crimes Crimes in which the intent required is different from the intent to do the act that is the crime (such as "assault with intent to murder").

Specific Performance Equity court order to a person to perform a contract exactly as agreed. A kind of equitable remedy.

Spending Power Congressional power to spend for the general welfare. This power can be used to regulate by making compliance with certain behavior a condition for getting federal money.

Stakeholder Any entity or person affected by the operation of a business; includes stockholders, customers, employees, suppliers, and the community in which the business operate.

Standards of Performance Used to describe air pollution control measures for new sources (new plants, buildings, and other sources emitting air pollutants).

Standing A question of the plaintiff's proximity to the violation.

State Action The requirement that, in order for certain independent constitutional checks to apply, there must be action by a governmental body, state or federal. This doctrine generally frees private bodies from having to obey these constitutional requirements.

State Blue Book A book published by each state that explains its government regulations and includes a list of state administrative agencies.

State Exemptions Property that cannot be taken by creditors to pay a person's debts because state law does not allow (exempts) it.

State Implementation Plans (SIPs) General plans each state has to control air pollution.

State of Nature Society in a prelaw, politically unorganized situation; stage of political development before a body politic is formed.

State Right-to-Work Laws State laws that allow employees at a unionized employer to refuse to join the union or pay dues.

State Usury Laws State laws setting limits on the rate of interest creditors can charge borrowers.

Statute of Descent A statutory will the legislature has made for people who die without a will.

Statute of Frauds State laws requiring that certain contracts be in writing or evidenced by a writing.

Statute of Limitations A period of time within which a particular lawsuit must begin. If suit is not entered within this period, the plaintiff loses his or her right to sue. The applicable time period differs with the particular cause of action the plaintiff is asserting. The period may begin to run at different times depending on the cause of action in question.

Statute of Repose A time limitation for the beginning of a suit, which applies to product liability cases. It runs from the time the product is sold to the last party in the chain of distribution not buying for resale. The most common such time period is ten years.

Statutes Laws made by legislators.

Statutory Construction Judicial lawmaking by filling gaps in statutes.

Stock Dividend When a corporation issues a dividend in the form of its own stock and transfers capital from a retained earnings account to a paid-in capital account to reflect this issuance.

Stock Merger When two or more companies join together by one's buying the other's (others') shares of stock and the buying company retains existence while the merged (purchased) company (companies) ceases (cease) to exist.

Stock Proxy A shareholder's written authorization to someone else to vote the shares.

Stock Split When a corporation divides its equity into more parts.

Stockholders People who purchase corporate shares; shareholders.

Straight Bankruptcy Bankruptcy under Chapter 7 of the federal bankruptcy code; which involves the debtor's turning over nonexempt assets to a bankruptcy trustee, the trustee's selling these assets and paying off creditors to the extent that assets exist, and discharging the debtor of all dischargeable debts.

Strict Liability Tort liability without fault. That is, liability imposed irrespective of whether the defendant intended to cause harm, was reckless, or was negligent.

Strict Liability Criminal Statue A criminal statute that requires only an act but no intent to commit a crime.

Strict Scrutiny An equal protection doctrine generally requiring that governmental classifications be necessary to the advancement of a compelling governmental interest.

Strike In labor laws, employees' temporary refusal to work.

Style (of a Case) Names of plaintiff(s) and defendant(s) in a lawsuit.

Subject Matter Jurisdiction The power of a court or other legal authority to deal with the type of case in question. For example, a probate court may decide the validity of wills but may not try murder cases.

Subjective Intent What persons allegedly making a contract think they have done.

Sublet When a tenant assigns his or her lease to another tenant.

Substantial Evidence Test An evidentiary test used to decide whether certain agency actions are supported by enough facts.

Substantial Product Hazard A substantial risk of injury to the public, which may result from the failure to comply with a Consumer Product Safety Commission rule or from a product defect.

Substantive Due Process A doctrine according to which certain state or federal substantive laws might be unconstitutional because they interfere with certain protected liberties and cannot be justified by important governmental interests.

Substantive Law Laws governing our relationships with other people and things in society; different than procedural law.

Substantive Regulations Agency rules that have the effect of law; they must be made in accordance with the Administrative Procedure Act.

Substantive Rules Legal rules setting out rights, duties, and standards of behavior applying to the public at large.

Substantive Unconscionability A form of unconscionability involving the terms of the contract—specifically, the duties and burdens they impose on the parties.

Sunset Laws Laws that cause an administrative agency to end at a certain time.

Sunshine Exemptions Certain agency meetings that do not have to be open to the public under open meeting or "sunshine" laws.

Superior Agent Rule A rule holding corporate principals liable only for crimes of high-level employees.

Superior Courts State courts of general jurisdiction where major civil or criminal lawsuits usually start. These are courts of record with possible jury trials, unlike municipal, justice of the peace, domestic relations, common pleas, juvenile, and probate courts.

Supremacy Clause Article VI of the Constitution that establishes the principle of federal supremacy.

Supreme Court Reporter A set of privately published books containing U.S. Supreme Court decisions in chronological order.

Survival Statutes Statutes that keep a cause of action from dying when the person who has the cause of action dies; for example survival statutes give the dependents of a person killed in an auto accident a claim against the person who killed him or her.

Suspect Classification Governmental discrimination based on race or national origin, sex, illegitimacy, and alienage. These classifications all get some form of equal protection strict scrutiny.

Taft-Hartley Act A major federal labor law passed in 1947.

Takings Clause Part of the Fourteenth Amendment due process provision that states that private property shall not be taken for public use without just compensation.

Target Corporation A term used in corporate law to describe a corporation that persons outside the corporation wish to buy, usually by stock purchase.

Taxing Power Congressional power to lay and collect taxes. Basically used to raise revenue, this congressional power is also an important regulatory tool.

Ten-Year Vesting A formula for calculating vesting of employer contributions to employee retirement plans.

Tenancy By the Entirety A specialized form of joint tenancy; the joint tenants must be spouses.

Tenancy for Years A lease beginning and ending at a definite time covering a definite period.

Tenancy in Partnership Ownership that occurs when business partners own property together; this form of tenancy has the right of survivorship feature.

Tenant in Partnership The way partners own partnership property.

Tenants in Common The type of ownership that occurs where two or more people have title to an interest in realty.

Tender Offer An offer to company shareholders to buy their shares with an eye toward taking over the company.

Tender Offeror Someone who makes a tender offer.

Territorial Market That region of the country in which a firm can increase its price without drawing in new competitors and without losing sales to competitors outside the region.

Tertiary Line Price Discrimination Price discrimination that economic injury to competitors of the favored buyer's buyers.

Testamentary A trust that takes effect at the settler's death.

Testator The maker of a will.

Theories of Product Liability Recovery Legal rules stating the points a plaintiff must prove in order to recover damages from a seller of defective goods.

Thirty-Day Regulation Governing Mail-Order Merchandise A Federal Trade Commission regulation that protects consumers buying goods by mail.

Tied Product A product one must buy in order to be able to buy another product.

Title Property concept used to identify the owner of property.

Title Documents Pieces of paper that tell who owns certain types of property, such as vehicles and real estate.

Titles Major parts of long statutes.

Tombstone Ad A written ad for securities. The ad has black borders (usually) and is not an offer because it does not have enough information. An ad for securities designed to generate public interest in the upcoming offering that is not legally an offer.

Tort A civil wrong that is not a breach of contract.

Trade Fixtures Such items as signs and counters, which are firmly attached to the realty, and remain the tenant's personal property.

Trade Regulation Rules Federal Trade Commission regulations governing various business practices.

Transferability of Shares A characteristic of corporate stock that lets a shareholder sell or transfer the stock to someone else.

Treasury Shares A corporation's issued shares that it has purchased in the market and holds as an asset.

Treble Damages Triple damages.

Trespass A type of tort (civil wrong) in which one person unlawfully interferes with another's property or person.

Trust Legal way to hold property in which there are two titles; one legal, the other equitable.

Trustee Person(s) holding legal title to property in a trust.

Turbidity The presence of microscopic particulates in the air.

Tying Arrangement *See* Tying Contracts.

Tying Contracts In antitrust law, where a business agrees to sell desired goods or services conditioned on the buyer's agreeing to purchase another less desired good or service (this practice often violates the antitrust laws).

Tying Product A product that can be bought only if one first buys another product (called a "tied" product).

Unannotated Without footnotes explaining the text (said of codes or statutes where no footnotes exist, referring to cases interpreting or refining the code).

Unannotated Code A lengthy statute that does not refer to particular cases interpreting it.

Unauthorized Appropriation A type of invasion of privacy; an intentional tort occurring when defendant uses plaintiff's name or likeness without permission.

Unconscionability An open-ended contract doctrine under which courts refuse to enforce especially one-sided contracts or contract terms.

Underwriters Persons who buy securities expecting to resell them to dealers, who in turn resell them to the public.

Undisclosed Principal A type of agency relationship where the third person knows neither the fact that an agency exists nor that the person dealt with is an agent nor the principal's identity.

Undue Influence Where a trust relationship (although not necessarily a formal trust) exists between two people who make a contract, and the one in whom the other places trust "double-crosses" the trusting person, making the contract to the disadvantage of the trusting party. These are grounds for a court to declare the contract voidable (not enforceable).

Unenforceable Contracts Those contracts failing to meet a procedural or formal requirement, making them unenforceable.

Unfair Labor Practice A legal wrong that gives rise to a cause of action.

Uniform Guidelines on Employee Selection Procedures (UGESP) Equal Employment Opportunity Guidelines that help employers comply with federal civil rights laws.

Uniform Limited Partnership Act A model statute that permits people to form limited partnerships.

Unilateral Contract A contract formed when one party promises something in exchange for the other's act ("a promise for an act").

United States Reports A set of books containing cases in chronological order decided by the U.S. Supreme Court; the publisher is U.S. government, which is not noted for its speed in publishing these books.

Unrestricted, Unreserved Earned Surplus A requirement that puts limits on dividend declarations by directors.

U.S. Claims Court A federal court where people can sue the U.S. government.

U.S. Court of Appeals A federal, multi-judge appellate court.

U.S. Court of International Trade A federal court with the power to hear cases involving tariff matters.

Use Immunity A rule of criminal procedural law that says if the prosecutor gives a criminal suspect immunity from prosecution if the suspect gives the prosecutor information about crimes, the prosecutor will not in any way use that information to convict the person giving the information.

Utilitarian Theory of Law Bentham's view that law should produce the greatest good for the greatest number.

Valid Contract A contract that has no legal flaws.

Vertical Merger When two (or more) companies at different levels of the production and distribution cycle combine by asset or stock merger so the acquiring company remains in existence and the acquired company ceases to exist by becoming part of the acquiring company.

Vertical Price Fixing Where businesses at different levels in the distribution chain agree to price fix; a per se Sherman Act violation.

Vest To give someone property rights or the equivalent.

Vested Benefits Benefits that are someone's property and that cannot be taken away unless the person is given due process of law.

Void Of no legal effect; said of illegal contracts.

Voidable In contract matters, a contract that because of some legal flaw can be set aside by at least one of the parties to it.

Voidable Title A flawed ownership in property, which allows the holder of the property to pass "good," i.e., flawless, title to good faith purchasers for value without notice of the flaw; this flaw would let another person claim superior title to the property and take it away from the person with the voidable title.

Voir Dire The questioning of prospective jurors to see whether they are appropriate to sit on the jury in a particular case.

Voluntary Bankruptcy A debtor's entering bankruptcy of his or her own free will.

Wagner Act The National Labor Relations Act passed in 1935.

Waiting Period The period between the filing of a registration statement and the time when the sale of the securities involved can occur.

Waive To voluntarily give up a legal right, such as "waive jury trial."

Waiver-of-Defenses Clause Used with references to commercial paper referring to words that cause a person signing a note to give up certain defenses they would have had against a person later buying the note.

Ward Someone not qualified to manage his or her own affairs (a legal incompetent); also a political subdivision.

Warnings or Instructions Product safety standards requiring adequate disclosure to consumers to prevent or reduce any unreasonable risk associated with a product.

Warrant Court order, such as arrest warrant.

Warranty A contractual promise as to the nature of a thing sold.

Wheeler-Lea Act A federal law passed in 1938 that expanded coverage of the Federal Trade Commission Act to allow the FTC to stop unfair competition even if a business were not injured; Wheeler-Lea made it sufficient if a consumer were injured.

Whipsaw Strikes Strikes in which unions in a multi employer bargaining unit "play employers off against one another" by striking some but not all employers in the bargaining unit.

Will A piece of paper on which a testator indicates the persons who will take his or her property when he or she dies.

Withdrawal Words used in labor law to decide a way of settling an unfair labor practice case by, in effect, the complaining party's dropping its complaint.

Work Environment Sexual Harassment Sexually related behavior that is so severe or pervasive that it affects work performance and/or creates an intimidating, hostile, or offensive working environment.

Workers' Compensation A system of paying workers for damages resulting from job-related injuries, illness, or death; the system abandons fault as a basis for assigning liability for such work-related losses; the employer bears the cost (in the immediate sense) of such losses.

World Trade Organization The successor organization to GATT.

Writ of Execution A legal device that lets a public official take certain property of a debtor, sell it, and use the proceeds to pay off a debt owed a creditor.

Wrongful Interference with Contractual Relations An intentional tort in which a third party knows that two other persons have a contract and knowingly interferes with that contract.

INDEX

WEST'S ONLINE RESEARCH GUIDE--GLOBAL

Updates and Additions at http://www.westbuslaw.com

organizations

European Union	http://europa.eu.int/
Parliament	http://www.europarl.eu.int/sg/tree/en/default.htm
Council	http://ue.eu.int/index.htm
United Nations	http://www.un.org/
International Law Commission	http://www.un.org/law/ilc/index.htm
Commission on International Trade Law (UNCITRAL)	http://www.uncitral.org
World Intellectual Property Organization	http://www.wipo.org/
Arbitration and Mediation Center	http://arbiter.wipo.int/
World Trade Organization	http://www.wto.org/
International Organization for Standardization (ISO)	http://www.iso.ch/
International Chamber of Commerce	http://www.iccwbo.org/
International Center for Commercial Law	http://www.icclaw.com/
ABA Section on International Law	http://www.abanet.org/intlaw/home.html
International Law Association	http://www.ila-hq.org/

conventions, constitutions and treaties

International Treaties (American Society of International Law)	http://www.asil.org/resource/treaty1.htm
Multilateral Treaties (Tufts University)	http://fletcher.tufts.edu
UN Convention on Contracts for the International Sale of Goods (Pace University)	http://www.cisg.law.pace.edu/
United Nations Treaty Collection	http://untreaty.un.org
World Constitutions	http://www.urich.edu/~jpjones/confinder/const.htm

courts

European Union Court of Justice	http://curia.eu.int/en/index.htm
United Nations International Court of Justice	http://www.icj-cij.org/

news and information

Africa News	http://www.africanews.org/africa.html
BBC World Service	http://www.bbc.co.uk/worldservice/index.shtml
China Daily	http://www.chinadaily.net/cndy/cd_cate1.html
CNN World News	http://www.cnn.com/WORLD/index.html
Foreign and International Law Resources on the Internet (Cornell Law Library)	http://www.lawschool.cornell.edu/library/International_Resources/foreign.htm
ForeignWire	http://www.foreignwire.com/
International Herald Tribune	http://www.iht.com/
International Law Center (Law Journal Extra!)	http://www.ljx.com/practice/internat/
***Newsweek* International**	http://www.newsweek-int.com/
The Japan Times	http://www.japantimes.co.jp/
The World Factbook (CIA)	http://www.odci.gov/cia/publications/factbook/